Education Law

Education Law, Sixth Edition provides a comprehensive survey of the legal problems and issues confronting school leaders, teachers, and policymakers today. Court cases accompanied by explanation and analysis can help aspiring educators understand the subtlety and richness of the law. Accordingly, each of the 12 thematic chapters begins with an overview, concludes with a summary, and balances an explanation of the important principles of education law with actual court decisions to illuminate those issues most relevant for educational policy and practice.

This updated and expanded Sixth Edition includes:

- Revision of case law, education policy, and citations to reflect the most recent decisions and developments in the field.
- Cases and commentary on key topics such as constitutional rights of students in public schools, school discipline, safety, and zero tolerance policies, school choice and parental rights claims, the regulation of charter schools and home-based education, cyberbullying and the regulation of online speech, racial and sexual harassment policies, and collective bargaining, unions, and working conditions.
- eResources accessible at www.routledge.com/9780367195250 include a Glossary for students, Chapter Outlines and Abstracts for instructors, as well as Tables of Cases.

J.C. Blokhuis is Associate Professor of Social Development Studies at the University of Waterloo and a former Kluge Fellow at the Library of Congress, USA.

Jonathan Feldman is a Lecturer of Law at Cornell Law School, USA.

Michael Imber is Professor Emeritus of Educational Leadership and Policy Studies at the University of Kansas, USA.

Tyll van Geel is Earl B. Taylor Professor Emeritus at the University of Rochester, USA.

Education Law

Sixth Edition

J.C. Blokhuis
University of Waterloo

Jonathan Feldman
Cornell Law School

Michael Imber
University of Kansas

Tyll van Geel .
University of Rochester

 Routledge
Taylor & Francis Group

NEW YORK AND LONDON

Sixth edition published 2021
by Routledge
52 Vanderbilt Avenue, New York, NY 10017

and by Routledge
2 Park Square, Milton Park, Abingdon, Oxon, OX14 4RN

Routledge is an imprint of the Taylor & Francis Group, an informa business

First edition published by McGraw-Hill 1992
Fifth edition published by Routledge 2014

Library of Congress Cataloging-in-Publication Data
Names: Blokhuis, J. C., author. | Feldman, Jonathan (Attorney), author. |
Imber, Michael, author. | Van Geel, Tyll, author. | Imber, Michael.
Education law.
Title: Education law / J.C. Blokhuis, University of Waterloo, Jonathan
Feldman, Cornell Law School, Michael Imber, University of Kansas, Tyll van
Geel, University of Rochester..
Identifiers: LCCN 2020010500 (print) | LCCN 2020010501 (ebook) |
ISBN 9780367195236 (Hardback) | ISBN 9780367195250 (Paperback) |
ISBN 9780429202926 (Bbook)
Subjects: LCSH: Educational law and legislation--United States--Cases. |
School management and organization--Law and legislation--United
States--Cases.
Classification: LCC KF4119 .I46 2020 (print) | LCC KF4119 (ebook) | DDC
344.73/07--dc23
LC record available at https://lccn.loc.gov/2020010500
LC ebook record available at https://lccn.loc.gov/2020010501

ISBN: 978–0–367–19523–6 (hbk)
ISBN: 978–0–367–19525–0 (pbk)
ISBN: 978–0–429–20292–6 (ebk)

Typeset in Goudy
by Swales & Willis, Exeter, Devon, UK

Visit the eResources: www.routledge.com/9780367195250

For Tyll and Katy

Gigantes enim stabimus cuius humeris ...

Contents in Brief

Detailed Contents

Preface to the Sixth Edition

This updated and expanded edition includes cases and commentary on the First, Fourth, Fifth, and Fourteenth Amendment rights of students in public schools; on school discipline and zero tolerance policies; on school choice and parental rights claims; on voucher programs and state aid to nonpublic schools; on the regulation of charter schools and home-based education; on cyber-bullying and the regulation of online speech; on racial and sexual harassment policies; on school safety and the privacy rights of students and teachers; and on collective bargaining, unions, and working conditions for teachers and other public school employees.

All 12 chapters have been updated in light of court decisions and statutory developments over the past six years. Indeed, there is more new material in this edition than ever before. Chapter 6 is entirely new, focusing on the procedural and substantive due process rights of students in public schools under the Fifth and Fourteenth Amendments. To retain the 12-chapter format, we consolidated material on teacher employment and working conditions with material on collective bargaining and unions into Chapter 11.

J.C. Blokhuis is both the lead and coordinating author of this edition, and is primarily responsible for Chapters 1, 2, 3, 4, 5, 6, and 12. He would like to thank Renison University College at the University of Waterloo for granting a sabbatical leave to complete this project, and Cornell Law School for sharing its outstanding library and research facilities. He would also like to thank Robert Fantauzzi for his tireless research assistance, and John Tillson and Winston C. Thompson for their Pedagogies of Punishment symposia, where participants commented helpfully on drafts of Chapters 4 and 6.

Jonathan Feldman is the co-author of this edition, and is primarily responsible for Chapters 7, 8, 9, 10, and 11. He would like to thank Cornell Law School for its institutional support. In particular, he would like to thank Cornell law students Katie Nugent and Yinan Xuan and Cornell law librarian Matthew Morrison for their outstanding research assistance.

Every chapter in this edition builds on the foundational work of **Tyll van Geel** and **Michael Imber**, whose 25-year partnership began after a chance encounter at an American Educational Research Association event. For continuity and to honor Mickey upon his retirement from this project years ago, we placed his name first on the cover of the Fifth Edition.

Our collaboration with **Tyll van Geel** was *not* a product of chance. **J.C. Blokhuis** chose to pursue his doctoral studies at the University of Rochester in order to work with Tyll, who remains a role model and cherished friend. **Jonathan Feldman**, a former public interest attorney who has worked on a number of high-profile school finance, special education, and Title IX cases (including several discussed in this book) has had a long association with Tyll, who remains an inspirational colleague and dear friend. To honor his contributions to this project and to our lives and careers, we have included citations to Tyll's substantial body of legal scholarship in this edition, from *Authority to Control the School Program* (1976) to *Understanding Supreme Court Opinions* (2008) to *Homeland Security Law: A Primer* (2018), along with a number of his law review articles and commentaries. We are proud to carry on Tyll's scholarly legacy. Accordingly, we have dedicated this edition to Tyll, the giant on whose shoulders we so gratefully stand, and to Katy, the giant on whose shoulders Tyll so lovingly stands. Thank you, Tyll and Katy. We love you, too.

We are educators with expertise in law, and we have written this book specifically for educators in leadership positions and programs. As *educators*, we hope the cases and materials in this book will facilitate lively class discussions on the implications of developments in law for educational policy and practice. As *legal scholars*, we hope this book will provide school leaders and policy-makers with the kind of knowledge they need to do their jobs well. We have attempted to present the array of legal questions and problems routinely encountered by teachers and school officials in American K-12 schools, both public and private. We have not attempted to review the laws in every state, and nothing in this book should be construed as legal advice. Rather, we have focused on generally applicable principles, noting areas where the specifics may vary from one state to the next, one district to the next, and one building to the next.

As in the previous edition, we have done our best to make the material in this book accessible to legal neophytes. Each of the 12 thematic chapters begins with an overview and concludes with a summary. We have selected both landmark Supreme Court cases and significant cases from state and federal courts to illustrate important legal concepts and developments. The featured cases have been edited to focus on the issues most important for educators. Dissenting opinions and discussions of technical and procedural matters have mostly been removed, as have most internal references, citations, and footnotes.

Most importantly, we would like to thank our readers for choosing *Education Law*, Sixth Edition. The circumstances and personalities figuring in some of our featured cases will undoubtedly remind readers of situations and characters they have encountered in schools. The most rewarding class discussions often begin when students connect new material to their prior knowledge and experiences. We hope this book will continue to facilitate the kind of engaging and fruitful class discussions that educators most enjoy.

J.C. Blokhuis
Jonathan Feldman

About the Authors

J.C. Blokhuis (Ph.D., University of Rochester; J.D., University of Ottawa) is Associate Professor of Social Development Studies at the University of Waterloo and a former Kluge Fellow at the Library of Congress, USA.

Jonathan Feldman (J.D., New York University) is a Lecturer of Law at Cornell Law School, USA.

Michael Imber (Ph.D., Stanford University) is Professor Emeritus of Educational Leadership and Policy Studies at the University of Kansas, USA.

Tyll van Geel (Ed.D., Harvard University; J.D., Northwestern University) is Earl B. Taylor Professor Emeritus at the University of Rochester, USA.

1 Understanding Education Law

In liberal democratic societies, adults are generally free to conduct their affairs as they choose, provided their actions do not cause harm to others.[1] Law is the foundation for the "ordered liberty" that undergirds our way of life. It structures our interactions with others in every aspect of our personal, professional, and civic lives. It mediates conflicts between our individual preferences and the public good.[2] The development of each child's capacity to govern herself in accordance with "ordered liberty" in an American constitutional context has long been counted among the most important aims of public education in this country.[3]

"[L]aw increasingly permeates all forms of social behavior. In subtle—and at times, not-so-subtle—ways, law governs our entire existence and our every action," note sociologists.[4] Educators and school officials perform their duties within a legal landscape that constrains them from doing some things while empowering them to do others. Legislatures create local school districts and give school officials the authority to raise taxes and borrow money, to acquire property, to construct buildings, to hire and fire school employees, to purchase supplies, to prescribe the curriculum, and to discipline students.

At the same time, the law limits the exercise of all these powers in various ways. The Constitution provides limited free speech rights for students and teachers in publicly-funded schools; guarantees them procedural protections when they are disciplined; and prohibits policies that wrongfully discriminate on the basis of race, national origin, gender, disability, or religion. The courts provide for the formal resolution of disputes and processes by which students, parents, teachers, and taxpayers can seek redress for alleged infringements of their rights.

This chapter provides a general survey of the landscape of education law, introducing the **sources of law** that affect the operation of public and private schools, the structure of the federal and state **court systems**, and the **role of the courts** in making, interpreting, and applying "the complex and voluminous set of laws" that govern the education of children in the United States. To help current and future educators and administrators understand the implications of case law for their own practice and to help current and future educators and administrators engage in legal research, this chapter also outlines the elements of a **judicial opinion**, the structure of a **case brief**, and the use of **legal citations**.

Sources of Law

The landscape of education law includes federal and state constitutional provisions, federal and state statutes and regulations, countless local district and school policies, and an array of common

---

1 JOEL FEINBERG, HARM TO OTHERS: THE MORAL LIMITS OF THE CRIMINAL LAW (1984).
2 HENRY J. ABRAHAM, FREEDOM AND THE COURT: CIVIL RIGHTS AND LIBERTIES IN THE UNITED STATES (1987).
3 RANDALL R. CURREN, ARISTOTLE ON THE NECESSITY OF PUBLIC EDUCATION (2000).
4 S. VAGO, A. NELSON, V. NELSON AND S.E. BARKAN, LAW AND SOCIETY (5th ed. 2018): 3.

law principles and doctrines. While these **sources of law** generally complement one another, they occasionally conflict. To further complicate matters, rules of law originate at the federal, state, and local levels.

The Constitution

The Constitution is the supreme law of the land. It establishes the union of the states; it separates the executive, legislative, and judicial branches of the federal government; it delegates responsibilities to the federal government while reserving others to the states. Most importantly for our purposes, the Constitution outlines rights for individuals vis-à-vis the State. It recognizes and protects individual liberty interests by limiting the scope of government action. Because public schools and school districts are **creatures of the State** (emanations of government), the Constitution regulates the relationships between public school officials, teachers, and students. Though it applies to state legislation concerning private schools, the Constitution does *not* regulate the relationships between private school officials, teachers, and students.

Although it mentions neither "education" nor "schools," the Constitution has been interpreted to empower Congress to use its taxing and spending authority for educational purposes and to impose conditions on schools that receive federal funds. Constitutionally, the federal role in governing public schools and school districts is extremely limited, as the Tenth Amendment clearly stipulates that "powers not delegated to the United States by the Constitution, nor prohibited by it to the States, are reserved to the States respectively, or to the people." Because the power to create and operate public school systems has neither been delegated to Congress nor prohibited from the states, the United States does not have a centralized educational governance and policymaking structure.[5] The resulting system of state and local control complicates education law because rules, policies, and standards can vary from state to state, from district to district, and since the advent of charter schools, from one building (or part of a building) to the next.

The Constitution remains extremely relevant to education law because *all* state education laws, *all* school district policies, and *all* public school practices must be consistent with its provisions. As we shall see in the chapters that follow, important cases in education law typically involve state statutes, district policies, or administrative practices found to violate First Amendment guarantees of freedom of speech and religion, Fourth Amendment protection from unreasonable searches, or Fourteenth Amendment due process and equal protection requirements.

State Constitutions

In keeping with the Tenth Amendment, the basic power to control education is reserved to the states. However, the Constitution does not *require* the states to exercise this power, and for several decades following its adoption, they did not. Over the course of the **Common School Movement** in the nineteenth century, the people of each state adopted constitutional provisions requiring their legislatures to establish and maintain public school systems.[6]

Some state constitutions contain vague language requiring legislatures to support public education, broadly construed. For example, Article IX, Section I of the California constitution provides simply that, "A general diffusion of knowledge and intelligence being essential to the preservation of the rights and liberties of the people, the Legislature shall encourage by all suitable means the

---

5 Tyll Van Geel, Authority To Control The School Program (1976).
6 Freeman R. Butts, Public Education In The United States: From Revolution To Reform (1978); Lawrence A. Cremin, American Education: The National Experience, 1783–1876 (1980); Carl F. Kaestle, Pillars Of The Republic: Common Schools And American Society, 1780–1860 (1983).

promotion of intellectual, scientific, moral, and agricultural improvement." Other state constitutions contain provisions requiring the legislature to establish, maintain and support common schools. For example, Article XI, Section 1 of the New York constitution says "The legislature shall provide for the maintenance and support of a system of free common schools, wherein all the children of this state may be educated." Article VIII, Section 201 of the Mississippi constitution indicates that "The Legislature shall, by general law, provide for the establishment, maintenance and support of free public schools upon such conditions and limitations as the Legislature may prescribe."

Some state constitutions describe in general terms how public schools will be governed or operated. For example, Section 183 of the Kentucky constitution says "The General Assembly shall, by appropriate legislation, provide for an *efficient* system of common schools throughout the State" [emphasis added]. Article VIII, Section 2 of the Michigan constitution says

> The legislature shall maintain and support a system of free public elementary and secondary schools as defined by law. Every school district shall provide for the education of its pupils without discrimination as to religion, creed, race, color or national origin.

A number of state constitutions describe—often in lofty terms—the aims and purposes of public education. For example, Article VII, Section 1 of the Texas constitution says

> A general diffusion of knowledge being essential to the preservation of the liberties and rights of the people, it shall be the duty of the Legislature of the State to establish and make suitable provision for the support and maintenance of an efficient system of public free schools.

Article X, Section 1 of the Illinois constitution provides that, "A fundamental goal of the People of the State is the educational development of all persons to the limits of their capacities. The State shall provide for an efficient system of high quality public educational institutions and services ..."

Some state constitutions do far more, with specific provisions guaranteeing efficiency, safety, security, quality, and maximum class sizes. For example, Article IX, Section 1 of the Florida constitution provides that:

> The education of children is a fundamental value of the people of the State of Florida. It is, therefore, a paramount duty of the state to make adequate provision for the education of all children residing within its borders. Adequate provision shall be made by law for a uniform, efficient, safe, secure, and high quality system of free public schools that allows students to obtain a high quality education and for the establishment, maintenance, and operation of institutions of higher learning and other public education programs that the needs of the people may require ...

Many state constitutions also create state boards of education or state superintending agencies, and some grant these agencies independent authority. Most contain provisions mirroring the federal Constitution, prohibiting the establishment of religion, and guaranteeing the equal protection of the laws. Indeed, some state constitutions offer greater protection for individual rights than the federal Constitution. While they may provide *more*, they may not provide *less*. Under Article VI, Clause 2, known as the **supremacy clause**, state constitutions must not contradict the federal Constitution, either by permitting what it prohibits or by prohibiting what it permits.

Federal and State Statutes

Congress and state legislatures execute their powers and duties through the enactment of statutes. Federal statutes must be consistent with the Constitution, while state statutes must be consistent with both the federal Constitution and the relevant state constitution. To the extent that any state law conflicts with federal law, it is **preempted**, or "without effect."[7]

Most statutes controlling the operation of public schools are enacted by state legislatures. In every state, the laws governing education are organized by topic and published either as an education code or as a section of the general laws of the state. Although the specifics vary greatly, most state legislatures have enacted statutes that:

- require most parents to enroll their children in a public school, a private school, or an approved educational program;
- create and regulate local public school districts and local school boards;
- set the qualifications for public school teachers and administrators;
- prescribe curricular content and learning aims for public schools;
- establish minimum requirements for high school graduation;
- create and maintain school funding systems;
- establish guidelines for student discipline and employee discipline;
- outline the duties, powers, and limitations of local trustees and boards of education;
- regulate aspects of private, charter, and online school programs;
- regulate aspects of home-based education; and
- delegate educational authority to state agencies and officers.

Federal statutes are particularly influential because, unlike state laws, they apply throughout the United States. We have already noted that the Tenth Amendment prevents the federal government from controlling education. Nevertheless, Congress exercises considerable influence in this area by virtue of its power to regulate interstate commerce and its ability to impose conditions and accountability requirements on local schools and school districts receiving federal funding. For example, Congress has enacted laws of general applicability that provide protection and assistance for persons with disabilities. Schools and other employers are also prohibited from engaging in certain forms of discrimination. The two most significant federal statutes in terms of their effects on the programs of local public schools are the **Every Student Succeeds Act (ESSA)** (see Chapter 3) and the **Individuals with Disabilities Education Act (IDEA)** (see Chapter 8).

Section 1983 and Tortious Violations of Federal Law

Enacted as part of the *Civil Rights Act* of 1871,[8] the federal law known as **Section 1983** provides as follows:

> Every person who, under color of any statute, ordinance, regulation, custom or usage of any State or Territory or the District of Columbia, subjects or causes to be subjected, any citizen of the United States or other person within the jurisdiction thereof to the deprivation of any rights, privileges, or immunities secured by the Constitution and laws, shall be liable to the party injured in any action at law, suit in equity, or other proper proceeding for redress.

Section 1983 does not itself create any substantive rights; it only authorizes suits for money damages for the violation of rights that other bodies of law establish. Throughout this book, we see examples of plaintiffs who have included Section 1983 claims in their constitutional challenges

---

7 Maryland v. Louisiana, 451 U.S. 725 (1981); Murphy v. NCAA, 138 S. Ct. 1461 (2018).
8 42 U.S.C. § 1983.

and tort suits against school officials and school districts. Section 1983 also applies to violations of rights protected by federal anti-discrimination and other statutes.[9]

Section 1983 can only be used to bring suit against people whose actions are "fairly attributable" to the State. Private wrongdoers, such as parents who abuse their children,[10] or students who racially or sexually harass other students, are not subject to Section 1983 suits, even if they are receiving state benefits.[11] Public school employees acting in furtherance of their job-related duties and the educational goals of the school are generally regarded as acting "under color of state law" for the purposes of Section 1983 liability. Thus, a principal who conducts a search of students without a reasonable suspicion that a particular student has drugs (in furtherance of the goal of maintaining a safe school) may be subject to a Section 1983 suit.

In *Monell v. Department of Social Services of New York*,[12] the Supreme Court held that Section 1983 could be used to bring suit against local government bodies like school districts, and that **sovereign immunity** cannot bar such suits. However, a local government unit cannot be held liable solely because it employs a wrongdoer, as the doctrine of ***respondeat superior*** does not operate under Section 1983. Nor as a general proposition will local government units be held responsible for a failure to take affirmative steps to protect individuals from wrongdoing by other private individuals. Local government units may claim **qualified immunity** from judgments under Section 1983,[13] provided the defendant officials acted in good faith and did not violate a **clearly established** statutory or constitutional right.[14]

Damages awarded under Section 1983 are not based on the value or importance of the violated right, but on actual losses sustained by plaintiffs. Plaintiffs may also be able to obtain punitive damages against individual defendants who act with **malice**.[15] Punitive damages against a school district itself are not permitted. The Supreme Court has found that only individuals, not government entities, can act with malice.[16] In its view, punitive damages against a government entity would punish taxpayers. Even with these limitations, individuals who win Section 1983 lawsuits can sometimes receive large awards.

Federal and State Regulations

Regulations differ from both constitutions and statutes. Most regulations are created by public departments, agencies, or bureaus that in turn are created by statutes. Regulations are designed to implement the goals and fill in the details of legislation. If a statute applies to schools, any regulations associated with it will apply as well. A regulation is legally binding if it meets three requirements: (1) It must have been adopted in accordance with procedures prescribed in the governing statute; (2) its substance must be consistent with the aims and purposes of the governing statute; and (3) the governing statute itself must be constitutional.

Many of the specifics of education law are found in regulations issued by state departments of education, the US Department of Education or its predecessors, and other state and federal agencies. For example, most of the rules governing the treatment of students with disabilities under the *IDEA* are contained in regulations created by the Department of Education. States also have

---

9   Seamons v. Snow, 84 F.3d 1226 (10th Cir. 1996); Lillard v. Shelby County Bd. of Educ., 76 F.3d 716 (6th Cir. 1996); Williams v. Sch. Dist. of Bethlehem, 998 F.2d 168 (3d Cir. 1993).
10 DeShaney v. Winnebago County Dep't of Social Serv., 489 U.S. 189 (1989).
11 Mentavlos v. Anderson, 249 F.3d 301 (4th Cir. 2001), *cert. denied*, 543 U.S. 952 (2001).
12 436 U.S. 658 (1978); *see also* Owen v. Independence, 445 U.S. 622 (1980).
13 Wood v. Strickland, 420 U.S. 308 (1975); Scheuer v. Rhodes, 416 U.S. 232 (1974).
14 Harlow v. Fitzgerald, 457 U.S. 800 (1982).
15 Carey v. Piphus, 435 U.S. 247 (1978); Memphis Cmty. Sch. Dist. v. Stachura, 477 U.S. 299 (1986).
16 City of Newport v. Fact Concerts, Inc., 453 U.S. 247 (1981).

extensive sets of regulations that provide further details concerning educational programs and services for students with disabilities.

The Common Law

Constitutions are adopted by the people, statutes are enacted by legislatures, regulations are implemented by government agencies, and the common law is created by courts. Judges apply common law rules and equitable principles developed over time to resolve the disputes before them, particularly in civil suits involving schools and school officials. By contrast, in constitutional and statutory cases, judges interpret and apply the law "on the books," or as written by other authorities.

Received from England in the colonial period, the common law originally had both **civil** and **criminal** branches, as well as an **equity** or **chancery** division. Virtually all common law crimes have since been extinguished by statute in the United States. For educators in general and school officials in particular, the civil branch of the common law remains extremely important, however. This branch is divided into contracts and torts. **Contract law** establishes the conditions under which an exchange of promises creates enforceable obligations. **Tort law** deals with intentional or negligent acts causing harm (see Chapter 12). For the most part, there are only minor variations in the adjudication of contract and tort cases from one state to the next.

School Board Policies

Subject to the scope of authority delegated to them by the state legislature, school boards may issue their own rules and regulations. All such enactments must be consistent with federal and state constitutional provisions, federal and state statutes, all regulations associated with federal and state statutes, and the common law. For example, school boards must comply with state **open meeting laws** enacted pursuant to the federal *Government in the Sunshine Act* of 1976.[17] "Sunshine laws" require that the meetings of all government agencies be open to the public, with limited exceptions. Most require advance notice of the time, place, and purpose of all government agency meetings.[18] "It is essential to the maintenance of a democratic society that public business be performed in an open and public manner," declares the Rhode Island statute, "and that the citizens be advised of and aware of the performance of public officials and the deliberations and decisions that go into the making of public policy."[19]

The Courts and Education Law

Courts perform three overlapping functions of great importance to educators and school officials.[20] First, courts apply constitutional provisions, legislation, and regulations to the disputes brought before them. Second, courts rule on the constitutionality of statutes, policies, and administrative actions. Third, courts provide official interpretations of the federal Constitution and federal statutes, state constitutions and state statutes, and the common law. In performing these functions, courts must frequently deal with broad, ambiguous, or vague language in statutes, regulations, and policies. It is one thing to know, for example, that the Fourteenth Amendment requires "equal protection of the laws" for all persons, and quite another to determine whether affirmative action programs are consistent with this requirement.

---

17 5 U.S.C. § 552b.
18 Ann Taylor Schwing, Open Meeting Laws (3d ed. 2011).
19 RI Gen L § 42-46-1.
20 *See* Tyll Van Geel, The Courts And American Education Law (1987).

Differing interpretive approaches add to the complexity of court opinions, particularly in constitutional cases. **Originalists** like Supreme Court Justice Neil Gorsuch, following in the footsteps of the late Antonin Scalia, believe constitutional interpretation should be based solely on the original intent of the framers, or the plain meaning of the text at the time it was drafted. **Loose constructionists** or **organicists** like Ruth Bader Ginsburg, following in the footsteps of Oliver Wendell Holmes, Jr., Thurgood Marshall, and Louis D. Brandeis, treat the Constitution as a "living" document that evolves over time.[21] The interpretation of statutes and common law principles can be equally contentious.

Regardless of the interpretative approach employed, the decisions rendered by courts form a body of jurisprudence known as **case law**. The study of education law—or any other area of law—is primarily a study of case law because judicial opinions provide an authoritative interpretation of constitutional provisions, statutes, and the common law. We study case law to find out who prevailed in a particular legal dispute, and why. By studying the rulings of courts in particular cases, we hope to learn to conduct ourselves lawfully in similar situations.

Decisions in factually similar cases from the past are referred to as **precedents**. Precedents are extremely important in the common law tradition, reflecting a **principle of fundamental justice** that like cases should be treated alike. A critical difference in the facts may make a precedent **distinguishable** from a pending case. Whether an otherwise binding precedent can be distinguished is a recurring question in court proceedings.

Decisions made by the highest court in each state generate **mandatory precedents** for the lower courts of that state. However, such decisions are merely **persuasive precedents** for courts in other states. While a mandatory precedent from a higher court must be followed, individual courts may decline to follow their own previous rulings. Decisions by the US Supreme Court generate mandatory precedents that bind all courts in all states, but the highest court in the land is not itself bound by *stare decisis*.

Federal and State Judicial Systems

There are both federal and state courts. Both systems are organized into three levels: **trial courts**, **appellate courts**, and **supreme courts**. Federal and state courts vary in the kinds of cases they may decide but in both systems, courts at all levels are limited to dealing with cases that are brought before them. A court cannot declare that a newly enacted statute is unconstitutional unless and until someone successfully challenges its constitutionality. In most instances, constitutional challenges can only be initiated by persons whose interests have been directly affected by a statute. Such individuals are said to have **standing** to raise constitutional claims before the courts.[22]

The Federal Court System

The federal court system deals almost exclusively with cases involving the Constitution or federal statutes or regulations. Only in certain limited and exceptional circumstances will the federal courts deal with conflicts regarding the interpretation of state constitutions, state statutes, or the common law. Nevertheless, federal court decisions have played an important role in shaping education law.

There are 95 federal trial courts called **US District Courts**. Each state has at least one, and heavily populated states may have several, each with jurisdiction over a different region of the

---

21 BRUCE ACKERMAN, "THE HOLMES LECTURES: THE LIVING CONSTITUTION" (2007). Faculty Scholarship Series. Paper 116.
22 Warth v. Seldin, 422 U.S. 490 (1975); Gill v. Whitford, 138 S. Ct. 1916 (2018).

Table 1.1 Jurisdiction of Federal Circuit Courts

Circuit	Jurisdiction
1st	Maine, Massachusetts, New Hampshire, Puerto Rico, Rhode Island
2nd	Connecticut, New York, Vermont
3rd	Delaware, New Jersey, Pennsylvania, Virgin Islands
4th	Maryland, North Carolina, South Carolina, Virginia, West Virginia
5th	Louisiana, Mississippi, Texas
6th	Kentucky, Ohio, Michigan, Tennessee
7th	Illinois, Indiana, Wisconsin
8th	Arkansas, Iowa, Minnesota, Missouri, Nebraska, North Dakota, South Dakota
9th	Alaska, Arizona, California, Guam, Hawaii, Idaho, Montana, Nevada, Northern Mariana Islands, Oregon, Washington
10th	Colorado, Kansas, New Mexico, Oklahoma, Utah, Wyoming
11th	Alabama, Florida, Georgia
D.C.	Washington, D.C.
Federal	Court of Appeals for Veterans Claims, Court of Appeals for Federal Claims, and Court of Appeals for International Trade (plus administrative agency boards)

state. These courts hear evidence in order to build the factual record of cases brought before them. Their primary function, once the facts are determined, is to apply the law as found in the Constitution, federal statutes, and relevant higher court precedents.

The intermediate appellate courts in the federal system are the **US Courts of Appeals** or **Circuit Courts**. There are 13 federal circuit courts—11 with jurisdiction over a group of states, one for the District of Columbia, and one consisting of three specialized federal courts and a number of administrative agency boards. Table 1.1 indicates the jurisdiction of each circuit.

The function and procedures of both the intermediate and highest appellate courts differ greatly from trial courts. These multi-member courts conduct no trials and hear no new evidence. Their sole function is to review the records of lower courts to determine if **errors of law** have been committed. Errors of law come in many forms, including incorrect instructions to juries, wrongful applications of rules of evidence, procedural mistakes, and misinterpretations of the Constitution, relevant statutes, or other rules of law.

After considering both written and oral arguments from both sides of the case, the judges vote, reach a decision, and begin the process of opinion writing. This may entail some bargaining among the judges regarding the rationale for the decision and the relevant legal rules and principles. If an appellate court decides that an error of law has been made, it can **overrule** the trial court or it can **remand** the case for rehearing.

Decisions by a US Court of Appeal create mandatory precedents for all federal district courts within its jurisdiction. For example, a ruling by the Court of Appeals for the Second Circuit would be binding on federal district courts in Connecticut, New York, and Vermont. Elsewhere, the ruling would merely be persuasive.

The Supreme Court serves as the highest authority on the meaning of federal statutes and the Constitution. As such, it tends to hear appeals in cases that raise especially important or novel points of law and in cases that have significant and widespread consequences. When there are inconsistencies in rulings issued by the US Courts of Appeals on a particular legal question, the Supreme Court is more likely to grant *certiorari*—leave to hear an appeal—in a case involving that question. Although the Supreme Court receives more than 7000 requests for *certiorari* each year, it generally agrees to hear only 100–150 appeals.

Because the Supreme Court has nine members, it takes the agreement of five to form a **majority opinion**. Precedent is created only if at least five justices agree on the disposition of a case and the rationale for the decision. Justices who disagree with the decision may issue **dissenting opinions** but only majority opinions have the force of law. Similarly, justices agreeing with the outcome but disagreeing with the rationale may issue separate, non-binding, **concurring opinions**.

Even when there is no majority agreement on the rationale for a decision, the outcome of the case is still decided by majority vote. There may be a **plurality opinion** supported by a majority of the justices on the winning side and one or more concurring and dissenting opinions. If the Court is badly split, there may not even be a plurality opinion. Instead, the Court will issue a brief, unsigned *per curiam* decision stating the outcome of the case and the concurring and dissenting opinions. If there is no majority opinion, no precedent is created. When the Court is deadlocked on even the outcome of a case, with one judge not participating, the lower court is affirmed and no precedent is created.

State Court Systems

State courts hear cases involving state constitutional law, state statutes, and common law. Many education cases are decided in state courts because they raise no federal legal questions. For example, cases of alleged negligence by school officials are usually heard in state courts. However, cases raising both state and federal questions may also be heard in state courts.

The structure of state judiciaries mirrors the federal system: **trial courts, intermediate** or **appellate courts**, and in most states, a **high court** often (but not always) called a supreme court. As in the federal system, the opinions of intermediate or appellate courts are binding only on lower courts within their respective jurisdictions, so it is possible for different intermediate or appellate courts within the same state to reach conflicting legal conclusions. One of the roles of the high court in each state is to reconcile any such discrepancies. Its rulings are binding on all other courts within the state, but not on federal courts or the courts of other states.

Elements of a Judicial Opinion

Trial courts sometimes, intermediate courts often, and highest courts almost always conclude their proceedings with a written opinion. Judicial opinions are comprised of a set of components or elements that provide the information necessary to understand who won the case and why. A standard opinion contains the case name, an overview of the facts, a review of the procedural history of the case, a restatement of the claims and arguments of both sides, a statement of the issue(s), rulings and rationales, and the case disposition.[23]

Case Name

Almost all cases are named for the **parties** to the case. The natural or legal person who brings a suit to trial is called the **plaintiff** (or **complainant**) and the natural or legal person against whom the suit is brought is the **defendant** (or **respondent**). In trial court opinions, the name of the case is *Plaintiff v. Defendant.*

If the trial court decision is appealed, the initiator of the appeal (the loser of the previous round) is called the **petitioner** (or **appellant**) and the other party is the **respondent** (or **appellee**). In the federal system and most other courts, the name of the case is *Petitioner v. Respondent.*

---

23 T.R. van Geel, Understanding Supreme Court Opinions (6th ed. 2008).

Overview of the Facts

Judicial opinions generally recount who did what to whom, when, where, how, and why. The court describes the conflict between the parties as determined from the evidence presented at trial.

Procedural History

Judicial opinions usually include a review of earlier decisions in the case by lower courts. For example, a decision of a highest court may indicate that the trial court ruled for the petitioner and that the appellate court reversed the decision.

Summary of the Claims

The court may then summarize the claims of the parties and the arguments offered in support of these claims. For example, if the parties disagree about the correct interpretation of a statute, the court will review the impugned provisions and discuss the contentions of the parties.

Summary of the Issues

In every case, the parties disagree about the facts, the proper application of the law to the facts, or both. The resulting questions of fact and law are at issue in the case. For example, a negligence case may turn on whether a teacher was present when a student was injured (a question of fact) or whether the cause of the injury was reasonably foreseeable (a question of law).

Often courts structure their analyses by dividing complex issues into a series of smaller ones. These may be organized in a logical sequence analogous to a flow chart. For example, a court may first decide whether expressive conduct regulated under a school policy falls into a category of speech protected by the First Amendment. If the answer is yes, then it must next determine whether the school met the appropriate standard for regulating protected speech.

Rulings and Rationales

The main body of a judicial opinion includes **rulings** on questions of fact and law, along with a **rationale** (or justification) for each ruling. Rulings are also referred to as **holdings**, **findings**, or **conclusions**. A brief statement encapsulating the material facts and major conclusions of law may also be referred to as the **holding** of the case. Rulings interpreting a constitutional or statutory provision may allude to **principles**, **rules**, **standards**, or **doctrines** to guide the courts in similar situations.

Courts arrive at their rulings through deductive reasoning with the relevant facts and rules of law as premises. The deductive argument also provides the justification for the decision. Here is an illustrative syllogism:

> **Premise 1**: Arshiya was driving at 40 mph on Westmount Road.
> (This is a matter of fact.)
>
> **Premise 2**: The speed limit on Westmount Road is 30 mph, and exceeding this speed limit is the legal wrong of speeding.
> (This is a matter of law.)
>
> **Conclusion**: Arshiya has committed the legal wrong of speeding.
> (This is the ruling.)

While the facts may be straightforward, the application of the relevant legal rules, principles, or tests may not be. For example, if the law required that drivers maintain a *reasonable* speed (rather than a specific speed limit), it would be much more difficult to decide whether Arshiya had committed the legal wrong of speeding in this case.

Disposition

Having resolved the legal issues and having explained its reasoning, the court concludes with an order indicating what must be done by the parties. If the defendant wins a trial, the trial court will simply dismiss the case and perhaps order the plaintiff to pay court and legal fees. If the plaintiff wins, the trial court will fashion a remedy for the injustice the plaintiff has suffered. Depending on the type of case, the law may permit various remedies including the payment of monetary damages, the issuance of an injunction, a declaration of unconstitutionality, or other relief. An appellate court can dispose a case by affirming the trial court decision, by modifying it in some respect, by reversing it, or by **remanding** it with the outcome no longer in doubt.

Interpreting judicial opinions can be difficult. Lawyers and judges disagree about the meaning of precedents just as they disagree about the meaning of statutes and constitutional provisions. For example, the Supreme Court has found that prayer and other religious observances in public schools violates the First Amendment, but is reciting the Pledge of Allegiance, which includes the phrase, "under God," a religious observance?[24]

It is important not to confuse the holding of a court with *obiter dicta*, or judicial side comments. For example, if the judge in the speeding case above had written, "Although an emergency might justify exceeding the speed limit, there was no emergency here," it would be obiter dicta—mere speculation by the judge. It would be incorrect to conclude that drivers may exceed speed limits in emergencies based on this judicial aside.

Case Briefs

Students in law schools must read hundreds of court decisions each year. It would be impossible to make sense of thousands of pages of text without a formal method of interpretation and analysis. Hence students are usually required to write **case briefs**, "a basic legal skill that can be learned only through practice."[25] In writing case briefs, a student "summarizes the elements of a court decision into a usable document for further study and referral."[26]

The central role of case briefs in the study of law may be one of the legacies of Christopher Columbus Langdell, Dean of the Harvard Law School from 1870 to 1895. Langdell is widely credited with introducing the "case method" approach to teaching fundamental legal principles. From Harvard, the case method was eventually adopted by law schools throughout the English-speaking world, along with professional development programs from medicine to business administration.[27] Langdell believed that students should arrive at an understanding of legal principles by closely reading numerous individual cases selected by professors and compiled into casebooks like this one.

While there is no single "correct" way to write a case brief, we recommend a structure that closely corresponds to the basic features of a court decision outlined in the previous section. Here is an example, based on a decision by the US Court of Appeals for the Sixth Circuit.

---

24 *See* Freedom from Religion Foundation v. Hanover School District, 626 F.3d 1 (1st Cir. 2010).
25 Gertrude Block, Effective Legal Writing For Law Students And Lawyers (1999): 9.
26 David L. Stader, Law And Ethics In Educational Leadership (2007): 30.
27 Bruce A. Kimball, The Inception Of Modern Professional Education: C.C. Langdell, 1826–1906 (2009).

Case Name

Lowery v. Jefferson County Board of Education[28]

Overview of the Facts

The appellants were the parents of students who had been cut from their school football team. They expressed their displeasure with school officials at the next school board meeting. When they sought permission to speak at a subsequent school board meeting, they were turned down.

Procedural History

At trial, the court described the parents' claims as "frivolous" and accused them of filing the lawsuit to harass the defendants. The jury found in favor of the school board and the trial court ordered the parents to pay the district's legal fees of $87,216.49.

Summary of the Claims

The appellants claimed the school board violated their First Amendment rights by denying them a second opportunity to air their grievances. The defendants relied on Board of Education Policy 1.404, ROA 35, which required that speech not be "frivolous," "repetitive," or "harassing."

Summary of the Issues

Had the trial court made an error of law? Had the school board engaged in viewpoint suppression by denying the parents a second opportunity to speak? Did the court err in awarding legal fees?

Rulings and Rationales

Because a school board meeting is a "designated" or "limited" public forum, the school board could regulate the time, place, and manner of speech (see Chapter 4). Its policy limiting speech that was "frivolous," "repetitive," or "harassing" was narrowly tailored to maintain order. It was therefore not viewpoint suppression to deny the parents a second opportunity to air their grievances against school officials, as this was likely to be repetitive. However, as the suit was not frivolous, the trial court erred in ordering the plaintiffs to pay the defendants' legal fees.

Disposition

The Appeals Court affirmed the decision of the trial court in favor of the school board, but reversed the trial court's order that the parents pay the district's legal fees.

Legal Citations

Legal citations contain a series of numbers and abbreviations indicating where the full text of a judicial opinion has been published. Volumes of published opinions, known as **case reporters**, used to be available only in law libraries. Nowadays, the full text of federal and state court decisions, as well as federal and state statutes and regulations, can easily be found using subscription database services such as LexisNexis® and Westlaw.

28 586 F.3d 427 (6th Cir. 2009).

Case citations all follow the same basic format. A case citation for a Supreme Court decision with each of its elements identified appears below:

Brown v. Board of Education,	347	U.S.	483	(1954)
Case Name	Volume	Reporter	Page	Year

This case is found on page 483 of volume 347 in the case reporter known as *United States Reports,* abbreviated to "U.S." in case citations. It is the official government publication for Supreme Court opinions. As indicated in Table 1.2, several private case reporters also publish Supreme Court opinions. The most commonly cited of these is the *Supreme Court Reporter* (S. Ct.). For example, the *Brown* case may also be cited as 74 S. Ct. 686, indicating that the opinion may be found on page 686 of volume 74. In this book, we cite the *Supreme Court Reporter* when a *United States Reports* citation is not available.

Citations to lower federal courts give the same information as Supreme Court citations, with the specific circuit or district court indicated in parentheses before the date. Here is the case citation for the case from the US Court of Appeals for the Sixth Circuit that we briefed in the previous section, with each of its elements identified:

Lowery v. Jefferson County Board of Education, 586	F.3d	427	(6th Cir. 2009)
Case Name Volume	Reporter	Page	Circuit Year

Here is a case citation for a federal district court decision with each of its elements identified:

Bronx Household of Faith v. Board of Education, 855 F. Supp. 2d	44	(S.D.N.Y.	2012)
Case Name Volume Reporter	Page	District State	Year

Citations to lower federal court decisions may include information about the subsequent actions of higher courts. For example, in *Lowry* ex rel. *Crow v. Watson Chapel School District,* 540 F.3d 752 (8th Cir. 2008), *cert. denied,* 555 U.S. 1212 (2009), the subsequent citation indicates that the Supreme Court declined to hear an appeal. Subsequent citations may indicate that a decision was later affirmed (*aff'd*) or reversed (*rev'd*) on appeal. State case citations follow the same format, but they have their own case reporters.

Statutory citations are similar to case citations, but a section (§) number is given instead of a page number. The preferred sources for federal statutes are the *United States Code* (U.S.C.); *Statutes at Large* (Stat.); and the *United States Code Annotated* (U.S.C.A.). A statutory citation for a piece of federal legislation with each of its elements identified appears below:

20	U.S.Code §	1681	(1972)
Volume	Abbreviation	Section	Year

Table 1.2 Reporters for Federal Court Decisions

Abbreviation	Full Title	Courts Reported	Publisher
U.S.	United States Reports	Supreme Court	US government
S. Ct.	Supreme Court Reporter	Supreme Court	Thomson Reuters
F.3d	Federal Reporter, 3rd series	Circuit Courts	Thomson Reuters
F. Supp. 2d	Federal Supplement, 2nd series	District Courts	Thomson Reuters

This citation refers to section 1681 in volume 20 of the *United States Code*, published in 1972. It is not necessary to include the year in statutory citations because the volume and section numbers remain constant. Federal statutes are often better known by their popular names. For example, the above citation comes from Title IX of the Education Amendments of 1972, better known as "Title IX." Under section 1681, "No person in the United States shall, on the basis of sex, be excluded from participation in, be denied the benefits of, or be subjected to discrimination under any education program or activity receiving Federal financial assistance …"

Federal regulations are published in the *Code of Federal Regulations* (C.F.R.) and in the *Federal Register* (F.R.). Citations give the volume, abbreviation, section or page, and (sometimes) the year of publication. A citation for a federal regulation with its elements identified appears below:

83	FR	61532	(2018)
Volume	Abbreviation	Section	Year

This citation refers to regulations from the Department of Education concerning federal grants to charter school management organizations.

Complete information concerning legal citations may be found in *The Bluebook*, published by the Harvard Law Review Association every five years.[29] Expert advice is also available online at www.law.cornell.edu/citation.[30]

Summary

The law plays a part in everything that educators do in the course of their duties. Some practices are required by law, some are prohibited, and the rest are permitted. Education law comes from a variety of sources, including the US Constitution, state constitutions, federal and state statutes and regulations, the common law, and local school policies.

It falls to the courts to interpret and apply laws in the course of resolving the disputes before them. Courts also resolve inconsistencies between laws and rule on the validity of laws that might contradict higher authorities. Ultimately, case law provides an official interpretation of what the law requires, prohibits, and permits to guide educators and school officials in similar circumstances.

At both the federal and state levels, the court system consists of trial courts, courts of appeal, and a highest court. In the federal system, these are known as district courts, circuit courts of appeal, and the Supreme Court. Trial courts hear evidence, determine facts, and apply the law. Appellate courts correct errors of law at lower levels. Appellate courts in general, and the Supreme Court in particular, focus on issues of broad significance. Majority decisions by the Supreme Court are binding on all courts throughout the country.

Most written judicial opinions feature certain common elements that students can use to structure a case brief. The facts of the case are the events and actions that gave rise to the dispute before the court. The issues are the disputed questions of law or fact. The holdings of a court include a rationale for its decisions on the issues before it. A uniform system of legal citation is employed to help catalog and research case law, federal and state statutes, and federal and state regulations.

---

29 THE BLUEBOOK: A UNIFORM SYSTEM OF CITATION (20th ed. 2015).
30 PETER W. MARTIN, INTRODUCTION TO BASIC LEGAL CITATION (2017).

2 Compulsory Schooling and School Choice

In every state, custodial parents and other persons having care and control of children are required by law to enroll them in a public school or state-approved alternative. State legislation typically specifies the period of **mandatory attendance**, the age at which children must be enrolled in school, the age at which students may withdraw or be withdrawn from school, **residency** and other eligibility criteria for attendance in particular districts or schools, and the types of schools or educational programs that satisfy compulsory schooling requirements. In most states, local school officials are responsible for enforcing compulsory schooling laws. School officials may also be responsible for monitoring or evaluating local alternatives to **public schools**.

This chapter explores **compulsory schooling laws**, beginning with an overview of their history and rationale. We then consider the circumstances in which individuals or groups have sought exemptions from compulsory schooling laws. We then examine how states regulate **public schools** (including **charter schools** and **online schools**), **private schools** (including **parochial schools**), and **home-based education** programs, focusing on constitutional challenges to state aid for **parochial schools**.

Compulsory Schooling Laws: An Overview

The "Old Deluder Satan" Act of 1647, widely-regarded as one of the first compulsory schooling laws,[1] required every township of at least 50 households in the Massachusetts Bay Colony to hire a schoolmaster to teach all children within the township to read and write. The Puritans believed that individuals unable to read the Bible for themselves were vulnerable to the influence of priests, whom they regarded as agents of the devil. Moreover, every township with 100 households was required to establish a grammar school to prepare young men for divinity studies at Harvard College, founded in 1636.

During the early days of the Republic, proponents of compulsory schooling argued that democratic institutions could not survive without a well-educated citizenry. Although Thomas Jefferson drafted his Bill for the More General Diffusion of Knowledge in 1779, universal public school systems did not become a reality until the late nineteenth century. At that time, an expansive conception of the doctrine of *parens patriae* ("the State as parent") provided a primary legal basis for the enactment of compulsory schooling laws designed to serve the interests of children as future citizens, along with the public interest in maintaining republican dispositions and institutions. Then as now, compulsory schooling laws required parents to share **custody** with publicly-certified teachers for limited periods of time. By compelling all parents to send their children to school, each state ensured, at least in theory, that all children would have access to public knowledge and opportunities for social, economic, and civic participation beyond what their parents might

---

1 See *Records of the Governor and Company of the Massachusetts Bay in New England* (1853), II: 203.

provide. In the wake of the Industrial Revolution, many parents were incidentally freer to manage the competing demands of domestic life and paid employment. Moreover, compulsory schooling laws greatly facilitated the enforcement of laws restricting child labor.[2]

Although **compulsory schooling laws** vary from state to state, most have retained certain common features, including the following:

Age Requirements

Most compulsory schooling laws stipulate the ages at which children are required and not required to be enrolled in school, as well as the ages at which children are eligible and ineligible to attend school. In New York, for example, children who turn six on or before December 1 must attend from the start of classes in September of that year. Children who turn six after December 1 must begin the following September.

Students in New York may legally withdraw from school without parental consent at age 16, unless they attend school in a district that has opted to extend compulsory schooling to age 17. Students electing to withdraw must remain in school until the end of the school year in which they turn 16 or 17, as the case may be.[3] Most other states require attendance until age 17 or 18, unless the student has parental consent to drop out, obtains full-time employment, or has already graduated from high school.[4]

In most states, legislation compels schools to enroll students who are older or younger than those required to attend. In New York, schools in some districts must enroll students at age five upon parental request. As noted earlier, students in New York are not required to attend after age 16 (or 17 in some districts), but anyone who has not received a high school diploma is entitled to attend a public school within the district in which he or she resides until age 21.[5]

Duration of the School Year and School Day

Compulsory schooling laws typically stipulate the minimum length of the school day and the minimum length of the school year. These requirements may vary for public schools (including charter schools), and private schools (including parochial schools). They may also vary for online and other home-based education programs.

Acceptable Institutions and Programs

Compulsory schooling laws typically describe the kinds of programs that will satisfy compulsory schooling requirements. In all states, public and approved private schools are permissible choices.

---

2 Randall Curren & J.C. Blokhuis, *The Prima Facie Case against Homeschooling*, 25 Pub. Aff. Q. 1 (2011): 1–19 at 1.

3 N.Y. EDUC. LAW § 3205.

4 Students must remain in school until age 16 in Alaska, Arizona, Delaware, Florida, Georgia, Idaho, Iowa, Montana, New Jersey, New York, North Carolina, North Dakota, Vermont, and Wyoming. Students must remain in school until age 17 in Alabama, Arkansas, Colorado, Illinois, Maine, Minnesota, Mississippi, Missouri, Pennsylvania, South Carolina, and West Virginia. Students must remain in school until age 18 in California, Connecticut, Hawaii, Indiana, Kansas, Louisiana, Maryland, Michigan, Nebraska, Nevada, New Hampshire, New Mexico, Ohio, Oklahoma, Oregon, Rhode Island, South Dakota, Tennessee, Utah, Virginia, Washington, the District of Columbia, and Wisconsin. Students must remain in school until age 19 in Texas. In Massachusetts, local school districts set the maximum age for compulsory school attendance; see MASS. GEN. LAWS Ch. 76, § 1.

5 N.Y. EDUC. LAW § 3205.

Exemptions

Compulsory schooling laws typically outline acceptable grounds for claiming an exemption. In some states, these grounds may include living in a **remote area**, such that regular attendance at any bricks-and-mortar school would be impossible or impractical.

Enforcement

Compulsory schooling laws typically provide for the appointment of an **attendance officer** with authority to initiate criminal and civil proceedings against **truant students** and their custodial parents or guardians. While compulsory schooling laws require that children be enrolled in schools for specific periods of time, they also restrict the ability of schools to deregister truant students. In New York, for example, a student must have been absent at least 20 consecutive days before a public school may deregister the student, provided there has been no response from the student or the parent(s) or guardian(s). Deregistered students may re-enroll at any time.[6]

The common law of the late eighteenth and early nineteenth centuries afforded parents, particularly fathers, almost unlimited freedom to rear their children, along with a right to their earnings. Hence when compulsory schooling laws were enacted in the nineteenth century, some parents sought exemptions on this basis. State courts usually rejected such challenges, citing the State's compelling need to ensure an educated citizenry,[7] and in child labor cases, the State's *parens patriae* duty to protect and promote the welfare of children.[8] The following case from Indiana illustrates the approach taken by courts at the time:

STATE v. BAILEY
Supreme Court of Indiana
61 N.e. 730 (1901)

ALEXANDER DOWLING, J.

The appellee was charged upon affidavit before a justice of the peace with having neglected, omitted and refused to send his child, Vory Bailey, to school, in violation of the provisions of the compulsory education law of this State. He was convicted before the justice, and, upon an appeal from that judgment to the circuit court, the affidavit was quashed. The State appeals.

The constitutionality of the act is assailed by the appellee ... because it invades the natural right of man [sic] to govern and control his own children. ...

The natural rights of a parent to the custody and control of his [sic] infant child are subordinate to the power of the State, and may be restricted and regulated by municipal laws. One of the most impor-

tant natural duties of the parent is his [sic] obligation to educate his [sic] child, and this duty he owes not to the child only, but to the commonwealth. If he [sic] neglects to perform it, or wilfully refuses to do so, he [sic] may be coerced by law to execute such civil obligation. The welfare of the child, and the best interests of society require that the State shall exert its sovereign authority to secure to the child the opportunity to acquire an education.

Statutes making it compulsory upon the parent, guardian, or other person having the custody and control of children to send them to public or private schools for longer or shorter periods, during certain years of the life of such children, have not only been upheld as strictly within the constitutional power of the legislature, but have generally been regarded

6 N.Y. EDUC. LAW § 3205 (1-a).
7 Fogg v. Bd. of Educ., 82 A. 173 (N.H. 1912); State v. Hoyt, 146 A. 170 (N.H. 1929).
8 State v. Rodefer, 5 Ohio N.P. 337 (Ct. Com. Pl. 1907); Commonwealth v. Wormser, 67 Pa. Super. 444 (1917).

as necessary to carry out the express purposes of the Constitution itself. ...

To carry out the enlightened and comprehensive system of education enjoined by the Constitution of this State, a vast fund, dedicated exclusively to this purpose, has been set apart. Revenues to the amount of more than $2,000,000 annually are distributed among the school corporations of the State. No parent can be said to have the right to deprive his [sic] child of the advantages so provided, and to defeat the purpose of such munificent appropriations. ...

For the error of the court in sustaining the appellee's motion to quash the affidavit, the judgment is reversed.

⚖

Parents do not have a constitutional right to be totally free from state regulations concerning the education or upbringing of their children.[9] In *Prince v. Massachusetts*,[10] the Supreme Court affirmed that

> the State as *parens patriae* may restrict the parent's control by requiring school attendance, regulating or prohibiting the child's labor and in many other ways. Its authority is not nullified merely because the parent grounds his [sic] claim to control the child's course of conduct on religion or conscience.

Claims by parents that compulsory attendance laws violate their due process, equal protection, freedom of speech, freedom of assembly, or privacy rights have generally been dismissed.[11] The courts have also found that compulsory education laws requiring persons having "care and control of a child" to "cause the child to attend school regularly" are not unconstitutionally vague.[12]

Parents who fail to enroll their children in a public or an approved private school or home-based education program may face fines for statutory offenses including **truancy**. In extreme cases, they may lose custody for **educational neglect**.[13] Children who refuse to attend school may be declared persons in need of supervision or services, or placed in foster homes or juvenile facilities.[14]

A number of states actively discourage students from dropping out of high school. In Massachusetts, students wishing to leave school must attend an exit interview with school officials to discuss their reasons for leaving and to receive information "about the benefits of earning a high school diploma, the detrimental effects of leaving school, and alternative education programs and services available to the student."[15] In some cases, students who leave school may be required to attend night school.[16]

About half of all states deny driver's licenses to high school dropouts under 18 years of age, suspend or revoke the licenses of habitual truants, or both.[17] In West Virginia, district superin-

---

9 *See* JEFFREY SHULMAN, THE CONSTITUTIONAL PARENT: RIGHTS, RESPONSIBILITIES, AND THE ENFRANCHISEMENT OF THE CHILD (2014).

10 321 U.S. 158 (1944); *see also Ex parte* Crouse, 4 Whart. 9 (1839).

11 Concerned Citizens for Neighborhood Sch. v. Bd. of Educ. of Chattanooga, 379 F. Supp. 1233 (E.D. Tenn. 1974); State v. Anderson, 427 N.W.2d 316 (N.D. 1988); State v. DeLaBruere, 577 A.2d 254 (Vt. 1990); People v. Bennett, 501 N.W.2d 106 (Mich. 1993); Combs v. Homer-Center Sch. Dist., 540 F.3d 231 (3d Cir. 2008).

12 State v. White, 509 N.W.2d 434 (Wis. Ct. App. 1993); *In re* S.M., 824 A.2d 593 (Vt. 2003).

13 Matter of Jamol F., 878 N.Y.S.2d 581 (Fam. Ct. 2009); State v. Stacy S. (*In re* Laticia S.), 844 N.W.2d 841 (Neb. App. 2014); *In re* Welfare of Children of D. M. J., 2015 Minn. App. Unpub. LEXIS 1156 (Dec. 14, 2015) [*unpublished*]; *In re* Marterrio H., 2017 Tenn. App. LEXIS 236 (Ct. App. Apr. 12, 2017); M.B. v. Commonwealth, 2018 Ky. App. Unpub. LEXIS 204 (Ct. App. Apr. 13, 2018) [*unpublished*]; *In re* B.B., B.C., & B.B., 208 A.3d 244 (Vt. 2019).

14 MICH. COMP. LAWS § 380.1596; FLA. STAT. §§ 984.03, 984.151, 1003.26.

15 MASS. GEN. LAWS Ch. 76, § 1.

16 MASS. GEN. LAWS Ch. 76, § 18.

17 TEX. TRANSPORTATION CODE ANN. 521.204; WIS. STAT. 118.163; OHIO REV. CODE ANN. 4510.32; MD. TRANSPORTATION CODE ANN. §16-105; CAL. VEHICLE CODE 13202.7.

tendents must report dropouts to the Department of Motor Vehicles (DMV).[18] In Tennessee, students must remain in school and make adequate progress to maintain their driver's licenses.[19] In Kentucky, students who fail four or more courses in a semester may lose their license.[20] Statutes imposing penalties for school failure or requiring schools to share academic performance data with other state agencies may raise equal protection, due process, or privacy issues.[21]

School Choice

The State's authority to regulate parental custody in the interests of children notwithstanding, the Constitution places significant limits on compulsory schooling laws. Perhaps most importantly, the Fourteenth Amendment requires that states not unduly restrict **school choice** by requiring enrollment in public schools *only*. As the following landmark decision illustrates, parents have a **due process** right under the Fourteenth Amendment to enroll their children in approved private and parochial schools.

⚖️

PIERCE v. SOCIETY OF SISTERS
Supreme Court of the United States
268 U.S. 510 (1925)

MR. JUSTICE MCREYNOLDS delivered the opinion of the Court.

These appeals are from decrees, based upon undenied allegations, which granted preliminary orders restraining appellants from threatening or attempting to enforce the *Compulsory Education Act* adopted November 7, 1922 by the voters of Oregon. They present the same points of law; there are no controverted questions of fact. Rights said to be guaranteed by the Federal Constitution were specially set up, and appropriate prayers asked for their protection.

The challenged Act, effective September 1, 1926, requires every parent, guardian, or other person having control or charge or custody of a child between eight and sixteen years to send him [sic] "to a public school for the period of time a public school shall be held during the current year" in the district where the child resides; and failure so to do is declared a misdemeanour ...

The manifest purpose is to compel general attendance at public schools by normal children, between eight and sixteen, who have not completed the eighth grade. And without doubt enforcement of the statute would seriously impair, perhaps destroy, the profitable features of appellees' business, and greatly diminish the value of their property.

Appellee, the Society of Sisters, is an Oregon corporation, organized in 1880, with power to care for orphans, educate and instruct the youth, establish and maintain academies or schools, and acquire necessary real and personal property. It has long devoted its property and effort to the secular and religious education and care of children, and has acquired the valuable good will of many parents and guardians. It conducts interdependent primary and high schools and junior colleges, and maintains orphanages for the custody and control of children between eight and sixteen. In its primary schools many children between those ages are taught the subjects usually pursued in Oregon public schools during the first eight years.

Systematic religious instruction and moral training according to the tenets of the Roman Catholic Church are also regularly provided. All courses of study, both temporal and religious, contemplate continuity of training under appellee's charge; the primary schools are essential to the system and the most profitable. It owns valuable buildings, especially constructed and equipped for school purposes. The business is remunerative—the annual income from primary schools exceeds thirty thousand dollars—and the successful conduct of this requires longtime

18 W. VA. CODE 18-8-11.
19 TENN. CODE ANN. 49-6-3017.
20 KY. REV. STAT. ANN. § 159.051.
21 D.F. v. Codell, 127 S.W.3d 571 (Ky. 2003).

contracts with teachers and parents. The *Compulsory Education Act* of 1922 has already caused the withdrawal from its schools of children who would otherwise continue, and their income has steadily declined. The appellants, public officers, have proclaimed their purpose strictly to enforce the statute.

After setting out the above facts, the Society's bill alleges that the enactment conflicts with the right of parents to choose schools where their children will receive appropriate mental and religious training, the right of the child to influence the parents' choice of a school, the right of schools and teachers therein to engage in a useful business or profession, and is accordingly repugnant to the Constitution and void. And, further, that unless enforcement of the measure is enjoined, the corporation's business and property will suffer irreparable injury.

Appellee Hill Military Academy is a private corporation organized in 1908 under the laws of Oregon, engaged in owning, operating, and conducting for profit an elementary, college preparatory, and military training school for boys between the ages of five and twenty-one years. The elementary department is divided into eight grades, as in the public schools; the college preparatory department has four grades, similar to those of the public high schools; the courses of study conform to the requirements of the State Board of Education. Military instruction and training are also given, under the supervision of an Army officer. It owns considerable real and personal property, some useful only for school purposes. The business and incident good will are very valuable. In order to conduct its affairs, long-time contracts must be made for supplies, equipment, teachers, and pupils. Appellants, law officers of the State and County, have publicly announced that the Act of November 7, 1922, is valid, and have declared their intention to enforce it. By reason of the statute and threat of enforcement, appellee's business is being destroyed and its property depreciated; parents and guardians are refusing to make contracts for future instruction of their sons, and some are being withdrawn.

The Academy's bill states the foregoing facts and then alleges that the challenged Act contravenes the corporation's rights guaranteed by the Fourteenth Amendment, and that unless appellants are restrained from proclaiming its validity and threatening to enforce it, irreparable injury will result. The prayer is for an appropriate injunction.

No answer was interposed in either case, and after proper notices they were heard by three judges … on motions for preliminary injunctions upon the specifically alleged facts. The court ruled that the Fourteenth Amendment guaranteed appellees against the deprivation of their property without due process of law consequent upon the unlawful interference by appellants with the free choice of patrons, present and prospective. It declared the right to conduct schools was property, and that parents and guardians, as a part of their liberty, might direct the education of children by selecting reputable teachers and places. Also, that appellees' schools were not unfit or harmful to the public, and that enforcement of the challenged statute would unlawfully deprive them of patronage, and thereby destroy appellee's business and property. Finally, that the threats to enforce the Act would continue to cause irreparable injury; and the suits were not premature.

No question is raised concerning the power of the State reasonably to regulate all schools, to inspect, supervise, and examine them, their teachers and pupils; to require that all children of proper age attend some school, that teachers shall be of good moral character and patriotic disposition, that certain studies plainly essential to good citizenship must be taught, and that nothing be taught which is manifestly inimical to the public welfare.

The inevitable practical result of enforcing the Act under consideration would be destruction of appellees' primary schools, and perhaps all other private primary schools for normal children within the State of Oregon. These parties are engaged in a kind of undertaking not inherently harmful, but long regarded as useful and meritorious. Certainly there is nothing in the present records to indicate that they have failed to discharge their obligations to patrons, students, or the State. And there are no peculiar circumstances or present emergencies which demand extraordinary measures relative to primary education.

Under the doctrine of *Meyer v. Nebraska*,[22] we think it entirely plain that the Act of 1922 unreasonably interferes with the liberty of parents and guardians to direct the upbringing and education of children under their control. As often heretofore pointed out, rights guaranteed by the Constitution may not be abridged by legislation which has no reasonable relation to some purpose within the competency of the State.

22 262 U.S. 390 (1923).

The fundamental theory of liberty upon which all governments in this Union repose excludes any general power of the State to standardize its children by forcing them to accept instruction from public teachers only. The child is not the mere creature of the State; those who nurture him and direct his destiny have the right, coupled with the high duty, to recognize and prepare him [sic] for additional obligations.

Appellees are corporations, and therefore, it is said, they cannot claim for themselves the liberty which the Fourteenth Amendment guarantees. Accepted in the proper sense, this is true. … But they have business and property for which they claim protection. These are threatened with destruction through the unwarranted compulsion which appellants are exercising over present and prospective patrons of their schools. And this court has gone very far to protect against loss threatened by such action. …

Generally it is entirely true, as urged by counsel, that no person in any business has such an interest in possible customers as to enable him [sic] to restrain exercise of proper power of the State upon the ground that he [sic] will be deprived of patronage. But the injunctions here sought are not against the exercise of any proper power. Plaintiffs asked protection against arbitrary, unreasonable, and unlawful interference with their patrons, and the consequent destruction of their business and property. Their interest is clear and immediate, within the rule approved in many cases where injunctions have issued to protect business enterprises against interference with the freedom of patrons or customers.

The suits were not premature. The injury to appellees was present and very real, not a mere possibility in the remote future. If no relief had been possible prior to the effective date of the Act, the injury would have become irreparable. Prevention of impending injury by unlawful action is a well-recognized function of courts of equity. The decrees below are affirmed.

Understanding the *Pierce* decision can be challenging. In the Oregon courts, the sectarian Society of Sisters had initially invoked the **First Amendment**, but when its claims were consolidated with those of the non-sectarian Hill Military Academy, only the **Fourteenth Amendment** provided common ground. Thus *Pierce* was decided as a freedom of contract case under the **due process** provisions of the Fourteenth Amendment, rather than the more specific **free exercise** guarantees within the First Amendment. Indeed, when *Pierce* was appealed to the Supreme Court, it was still unclear whether *state* governments were bound by the First Amendment. One week *after* its decision in *Pierce*, the Supreme Court determined that the Fourteenth Amendment made the First Amendment applicable to state governments.[23]

The **Due Process Clause** prohibits state actions that "deprive any person of life, liberty, or property without due process of law." **Due process** was an elastic and sometimes abstract concept used by courts during the early part of the twentieth century to protect a variety of individual interests against improper or unjustified government intrusion. In *Pierce*, the Court protected the property interest of private schools to remain in business and the liberty interest of parents to direct the upbringing of their children. Although the Court recognized the State's need to ensure that all children receive an education, its justification for requiring public school attendance was not strong enough to overcome these interests.

Although the **Due Process Clause** is no longer used to limit government regulation of business, the right of private schools to exist and the general right of parents to choose approved private schools for their children is not likely to be challenged in the foreseeable future. In his concurring opinion in *Troxel v. Granville*,[24] Justice Souter observed that

23 Gitlow v. New York, 268 U.S. 652 (1925).
24 530 U.S. 57, 78–79 (2000) (*concurring*).

[parental] choice about a child's social companions is not essentially different from the designation of the adults who will influence the child in school. Even a State's considered judgment about the preferable political and religious character of schoolteachers is not entitled to prevail over a parent's choice of private school.

This does not mean, however, that parents may satisfy their obligation to have their children educated by enrolling them in any educational program they wish. On the contrary, the *Pierce* Court recognized that for the State to satisfy its need for an educated citizenry, some regulation of private schools was needed. The types of regulation that states impose on private schools and home-based education programs are addressed later in this chapter.

Exemptions from Compulsory Schooling Laws

Three general categories of exceptions to the requirements of compulsory schooling laws have been recognized. First, some parents and children must be excused from some of the requirements of compulsory schooling laws for **constitutional reasons**. Second, some states exempt certain **categories of children**. Third, state courts have sometimes accepted **idiosyncratic reasons** for failing to comply with compulsory education laws. Each of these categories is very limited in scope.

Constitutional Exemptions

Compulsory schooling laws have long engendered conflicts between state interests and parental preferences. Parents seeking exemptions from compulsory schooling laws generally accept that their children should learn to read and write, but are wary of other aspects of public schooling. In the following watershed case, a group of Old Order Amish and Conservative Amish Mennonite parents preferred to educate their children at home after the eighth grade. They claimed that the enforcement of compulsory schooling laws would violate their free exercise rights under the First Amendment and their due process rights under the Fourteenth Amendment. Prioritizing the interests of Amish parents over those of their children and the State, the Supreme Court granted an unprecedented constitutional exemption from compulsory schooling laws to members of Amish faith communities.

WISCONSIN v. YODER
Supreme Court of the United States
406 U.S. 205 (1972)

MR. CHIEF JUSTICE BURGER delivered the opinion of the Court.

On complaint of the school district administrator for the public schools, respondents were charged, tried, and convicted of violating the compulsory attendance law in Green County Court and were fined the sum of $5 each. Respondents defended on the ground that the application of the compulsory attendance law violated their rights under the First and Fourteenth Amendments. The trial testimony showed that respondents believed, in accordance with the tenets of Old Order Amish communities generally, that their children's attendance at high school, public or private, was contrary to the Amish religion and way of life. They believed that by sending their children to high school, they would not only expose themselves to the danger of the censure of the church community, but, as found by the county court, also endanger their own salvation and that of their children. The State stipulated that respondents' religious beliefs were sincere.

In support of their position, respondents presented as expert witnesses scholars on religion and education whose testimony is un-contradicted. They expressed their opinions on the relationship of the Amish belief concerning school attendance to the more general tenets of their religion, and described the impact that compulsory high school attendance could have on the continued survival of Amish communities as they exist in the United States today. The history of the Amish sect was given in some detail, beginning with the Swiss Anabaptists of the sixteenth century who rejected institutionalized churches and sought to return to the early, simple, Christian life, de-emphasizing material success, rejecting the competitive spirit, and seeking to insulate themselves from the modern world. As a result of their common heritage, Old Order Amish communities today are characterized by a fundamental belief that salvation requires life in a church community separate and apart from the world and worldly influence. This concept of life aloof from the world and its values is central to their faith. ...

[The] Amish objection to formal education beyond the eighth grade is firmly grounded in these central religious concepts. They object to the high school and higher education generally, because the values they teach are in marked variance with Amish values and the Amish way of life; they view secondary school education as an impermissible exposure of their children to a "worldly" influence in conflict with their beliefs. ...

The Amish do not object to elementary education through the first eight grades as a general proposition because they agree that their children must have basic skills in the "three R's" in order to read the Bible, to be good farmers and citizens, and to be able to deal with non-Amish people when necessary in the course of daily affairs. ...

I.

There is no doubt as to the power of a State, having a high responsibility for education of its citizens, to impose reasonable regulations for the control and duration of basic education. ... Providing public schools ranks at the very apex of the function of a State. Yet even this paramount responsibility was, in *Pierce*,[25] made to yield to the right of parents to provide an equivalent education in a privately operated

system. There the Court held that Oregon's statute compelling attendance in a public school from age eight to age 16 unreasonably interfered with the interest of parents in directing the rearing of their offspring, including their education in church-operated schools.

As that case suggests, the values of parental direction of the religious upbringing and education of their children in their early and formative years have a high place in our society. Thus, a State's interest in universal education, however highly we rank it, is not totally free from a balancing process when it impinges on fundamental rights and interests, such as those specifically protected by the Free Exercise Clause of the First Amendment, and the traditional interest of parents with respect to the religious upbringing of their children so long as they, in the words of *Pierce*, "prepare [them] for additional obligations."

It follows that in order for Wisconsin to compel school attendance beyond the eighth grade against a claim that such attendance interferes with the practice of a legitimate religious belief, it must appear either that the State does not deny the free exercise of religious belief by its requirement, or that there is a state interest of sufficient magnitude to over-ride the interest claiming protection under the Free Exercise Clause. ...

II.

We come then to the quality of the claims of the respondents concerning the alleged encroachment of Wisconsin's compulsory school attendance statute on their rights and the rights of their children to the free exercise of the religious beliefs they and their forebears have adhered to for almost three centuries. In evaluating those claims we must be careful to determine whether the Amish religious faith and their mode of life are, as they claim, inseparable and interdependent.

A way of life, however virtuous and admirable, may not be interposed as a barrier to reasonable state regulation of education if it is based on purely secular considerations; to have the protection of the Religion Clauses, the claims must be rooted in religious belief. Although a determination of what is a "religious" belief or practice entitled to constitutional protection may present a most delicate question, the very concept of ordered liberty precludes allowing every person to make his [*sic*] own standards on matters of conduct in which society as a whole has important interests. Thus, if the Amish asserted their claims because of their subjective evaluation and rejection of the contemporary secular values accepted by the majority, much as Thoreau rejected the social values of his time and isolated himself at Walden Pond, their claims would not rest on a religious basis. Thoreau's choice was philosophical and personal rather than religious, and such belief does not rise to the demand of Religion Clauses.

Giving no weight to such secular considerations, however, we see that the record in this case abundantly supports the claim that the traditional way of life of the Amish is not merely a matter of personal preference, but one of deep religious conviction, shared by an organized group, and intimately related to daily living. That the Old Order Amish daily life and religious practice stem from their faith is shown by the fact that it is in response to their literal interpretation of the Biblical injunction from the Epistle of Paul to the Romans, "be not conformed to this world …" This command is fundamental to the Amish faith. …

The impact of the compulsory attendance law on respondent's practice of the Amish religion is not only severe, but inescapable, for the Wisconsin law affirmatively compels them, under threat of criminal sanction, to perform acts undeniably at odds with fundamental tenets of their religious belief.

Nor is the impact of the compulsory attendance law confined to grave interference with important Amish religious tenets from a subjective point of view. It carries with it precisely the kind of objective danger to the free exercise of religion that the First Amendment was designed to prevent. As the record shows, compulsory school attendance to age 16 for Amish children carries with it a very real threat of undermining the Amish community and religious practice as they exist today; they must either abandon belief and be assimilated into society at large, or be forced to migrate to some other and more tolerant region.

In sum, the unchallenged testimony of acknowledged experts in education and religious history, almost 300 years of consistent practice, and strong evidence of a sustained faith pervading and regulating respondents' entire mode of life support the claim that enforcement of the State's requirement of compulsory formal education after the eighth grade would gravely endanger if not destroy the free exercise of respondents' religious beliefs.

III.

Neither the findings of the trial court nor the Amish claims as to the nature of their faith are challenged in this Court by the State of Wisconsin. Its position is that the State's interest in universal compulsory formal secondary education to age 16 is so great that it is paramount to the undisputed claims of respondents that their mode of preparing their youth for Amish life, after the traditional elementary education, is an essential part of their religious belief and practice. Nor does the State undertake to meet the claim that the Amish mode of life and education is inseparable from and a part of the basic tenets of their religion. …

Wisconsin concedes that under the Religion Clauses religious beliefs are absolutely free from the State's control, but it argues that "actions," even though religiously grounded, are outside the protection of the First Amendment. But our decisions have rejected the idea that religiously grounded conduct is always outside the protection of the Free Exercise Clause. It is true that activities of individuals, even when religiously based, are often subject to regulation by the States in the exercise of their undoubted power to promote the health, safety, and general welfare, or the Federal Government in the exercise of its delegated powers. But to agree that religiously grounded conduct must often be subject to the broad police power of that State is not to deny that there are areas of conduct protected by the Free Exercise Clause of the First Amendment and thus beyond the power of the State to control, even under regulations of general applicability. …

Nor can this case be disposed of on the ground that Wisconsin's requirement for school attendance to age 16 applies uniformly to all citizens of the State and does not, on its face, discriminate against religions or a particular religion, or that it is motivated by legitimate secular concerns. A regulation neutral on its face may, in its application, nonetheless offend the constitutional requirement for governmental neutrality if it unduly burdens the free exercise of religion. …

We turn, then, to the State's broader contention that its interest in its system of compulsory education is so compelling that even the established religious practices of the Amish must give way. …

The State advances two primary arguments in support of its system of compulsory education. It notes, as Thomas Jefferson pointed out early in our history, that some degree of education is necessary to prepare citizens to participate effectively and intelligently in our open political system if we are to preserve freedom and independence. Further, education prepares individuals to be self-reliant and self-sufficient participants in society. We accept these propositions.

However, the evidence adduced by the Amish in this case is persuasively to the effect that additional one or two years of formal high school for Amish children in place of their long-established program of informal vocational education would do little to serve those interests. Respondents' experts testified at trial, without challenge, that the value of all education must be assessed in terms of its capacity to prepare the child for life. It is one thing to say that compulsory education for a year or two beyond the eighth grade may be necessary when its goal is the preparation of the child for life in modern society as the majority live, but it is quite another if the goal of education be viewed as the preparation of the child for life in the separated agrarian community that is the keystone of the Amish faith.

The State attacks respondents' position as one fostering "ignorance" from which the child must be protected by the State. No one can question the State's duty to protect children from ignorance but this argument does not square with the facts disclosed in the record. Whatever their idiosyncrasies as seen by the majority, this record strongly shows that the Amish community has been a highly successful social unit within our society, even if apart from the conventional "mainstream." Its members are productive and very law-abiding members of society; they reject public welfare in any of its usual modern forms. ...

It is neither fair nor correct to suggest that the Amish are opposed to education beyond the eighth-grade level. What this record shows is that they are opposed to conventional formal education of the type provided by a certified high school because it comes at the child's crucial adolescent period of religious development. Dr. Donald Erickson, for example, testified that their system of learning-by-doing was an "ideal system" of education in terms of preparing Amish children for life as adults in the Amish community. ...

The State, however, supports its interest in providing an additional one or two years of compulsory high school education to Amish children because of the possibility that some such children will choose to leave the Amish community and that if this occurs they will be ill-equipped for life. The State argues that if Amish children leave their church they should not be in the position of making their way in the world without the education

available in the one or two additional years the State requires.

However, on this record, that argument is highly speculative. There is no specific evidence of the loss of Amish adherents by attrition, nor is there any showing that upon leaving the Amish community Amish children, with their practical agricultural training and habits of industry and self-reliance, would become burdens on society because of educational shortcomings. Indeed, this argument of the State appears to rest primarily on the State's mistaken assumption, already noted, that the Amish do not provide any education for their children beyond the eighth grade, but allows them to grow in "ignorance." To the contrary, not only do the Amish accept the necessity for formal schooling through the eighth-grade level, but continue to provide what has been characterized by the undisputed testimony of expert educators as an "ideal" vocational education for their children in the adolescent years.

There is nothing in this record to suggest that the Amish qualities of reliability, self-reliance, and dedication to work would fail to find ready markets in today's society. Absent some contrary evidence supporting the State's position, we are unwilling to assume that persons possessing such valuable vocational skills and habits are doomed to become burdens on society should they determine to leave the Amish faith, nor is there any basis in the record to warrant a finding that an additional one or two years of formal school education beyond the eighth grade would serve to eliminate any such problem that might exist.

Insofar as the State's claim rests on the view that a brief additional period of formal education is imperative to enable the Amish to participate effectively and intelligently in our democratic process, it must fall. The Amish alternative to formal secondary school education has enabled them to function effectively in their day-to-day life under self-imposed limitations on relations with the world, and to survive and prosper in contemporary society as a separate, sharply identifiable and highly self-sufficient community for more than 200 years in this country. In itself this is strong evidence that they are capable of fulfilling the social and political responsibilities of citizenship without compelled attendance beyond the eighth grade at the price of jeopardizing their free exercise of religious belief.

When Thomas Jefferson emphasized the need for education as a bulwark of a free people against tyranny, there is nothing to indicate he had in mind compulsory education through any fixed age beyond a basic education. Indeed, the Amish communities singularly parallel and reflect many of the virtues of Jefferson's ideal of the "sturdy yeoman" who would form the basis of what he considered as the ideal of the democratic society. Even their idiosyncratic separateness exemplifies the diversity we profess to admire and encourage.

The requirement for compulsory education beyond the eighth grade is a relatively recent development in our history. Less than 60 years ago, the educational requirements of almost all of the States were satisfied by the completion of the elementary grades, at least where the child was regularly and lawfully employed. The independence and successful functioning of the Amish community for a period approaching almost three centuries and more than 200 years in this country are strong evidence that there is at best a speculative gain, in terms of meeting the duties of citizenship, from an additional one or two years of compulsory formal education. Against this background it would require a more particularized showing from the State on this point to justify the severe interference with religious freedom such additional, compulsory attendance would entail. ...

IV.

Finally, the State, on authority of *Prince v. Massachusetts*,[26] argues that a decision exempting Amish children from the State's requirement fails to recognize the substantive right of the Amish child to a secondary education, and fails to give due regard to the power of the State as *parens patriae* to extend the benefit of secondary education to children regardless of the wishes of their parents. Taken at its broadest sweep, the Court's language in *Prince* might be read to give support to the State's position. However, the Court was not confronted in *Prince with* a situation comparable to that of the Amish as revealed in this record; this is shown by the Court's severe characterization of the evils that it thought the legislature could legitimately associate with child labor, even when performed in the company of an adult. The Court later took great care to confine *Prince* to a narrow scope in *Sherbert v. Verner*,[27] when it stated:

On the other hand, the Court has rejected challenges under the Free Exercise Clause to governmental regulation of certain overt acts prompted by religious beliefs or principles, for "even when the action is in accord with one's religious convictions, [it] is not totally free from legislative restrictions." The conduct or actions so regulated have invariably posed some substantial threat to public safety, peace or order.

This case, of course, is not one in which any harm to the physical or mental health of the child or to the public safety, peace, order, or welfare has been demonstrated or may be properly inferred. The record is to the contrary, and any reliance on that theory would find no support in the evidence. ...

The duty to prepare the child ... must be read to include the inculcation of moral standards, religious beliefs, and elements of good citizenship. *Pierce*, of course, recognized that where nothing more than the general interest of the parent in the nurture and education of his children is involved, it is beyond dispute that the State acts "reasonably" and constitutionally in requiring education to age 16 in some public or private school meeting the standards prescribed by the State.

However read, the Court's holding in *Pierce* stands as a charter of the rights of parents to direct the religious upbringing of their children. And, when the interests of parenthood are combined with a free exercise claim of the nature revealed by this record, more than merely a "reasonable relation to some purpose within the competency of the State" is required to sustain the validity of the State's requirement under the First Amendment.

To be sure, the power of the parent, even when linked to a free exercise claim, may be subject to limitation under *Prince* if it appears that parental decisions will jeopardize the health or safety of the child, or have a potential for significant social burdens. But in this case, the Amish have introduced persuasive evidence undermining the arguments the State has advanced to support its claims in terms of the welfare of the child and society as a whole. The record strongly indicates that accommodating the religious objections of the Amish by forgoing one, or at most two, additional years of compulsory education will not impair the physical or mental health of the child, or result in an inability to be self-supporting or to discharge the duties and responsibilities of citizenship, or in any other way materially detract from the welfare of society. ...

26 321 U.S. 158 (1944).
27 374 U.S. 398 (1963).

V.

For the reasons stated we hold … that the First and Fourteenth Amendments prevent the State from compelling respondents to cause their children to attend formal high school to age 16. …

Nothing we hold is intended to undermine the general applicability of the State's compulsory school-attendance statutes or to limit the power of the State to promulgate reasonable standards that, while not impairing the free exercise of religion, provide for continuing agricultural vocational education under parental and church guidance by the Old Order Amish or others similarly situated. The States have had a long history of amicable and effective relationships with church-sponsored schools, and there is no basis for assuming that, in this related context, reasonable standards cannot be established concerning the content of the continuing vocational education of Amish children under parental guidance, provided always that state regulations are not inconsistent with what we have said in this opinion.

⚖️

Under the First Amendment, government "shall make no law … prohibiting the free exercise" of religion. In *Yoder*, the plaintiffs sought exemption from a generally applicable law on the ground that compliance would violate their **free exercise** rights. As in other **free exercise** cases, the Court's approach involved balancing the religious interests of the plaintiffs against the state's interests in enforcing the law. First, the Court imposed on the plaintiffs the burden of proving that their claim was **religious**, not merely philosophical or moral; that their belief was **sincere**, not a ruse to avoid an onerous law; and that the law had a **severe impact** on the exercise of their religion. Only after the Amish had met their burden of proof did the Court examine whether State interests were strong enough to justify infringement of the plaintiffs' free exercise rights. Wisconsin would have prevailed if it had been able to convince the Court that enforcement of the law was necessary to the achievement of a compelling state interest, but it was unable to do so.

Despite its outcome, *Yoder* strongly affirms the basic principles of compulsory schooling laws. The Court did not exempt members of Amish communities from *all* compulsory schooling, only the last two years. It based its decision in part on the fact that the Yoder children were effectively taking part in home-based vocational education programs after the eighth grade. The Court also signaled a strong presumption in favor of compulsory schooling laws by confining its decision to members of Amish faith communities. Nevertheless, members of other faith communities throughout the country have repeatedly cited the *Yoder* decision when seeking exemptions from compulsory schooling laws. This is hardly surprising. When an exception is made for members of one religious group, members of other groups can claim similar entitlements on **equal protection** and other grounds.

Absence for Religious Observance

In *Church of God v. Amarillo Independent School District*,[28] a district court considered whether public school must excuse students who miss school to fulfill religious obligations. The case was brought on behalf of 24 students who were obliged to be absent from school for 10 to 12 days per year, including seven consecutive days to attend a religious convocation. The school district had adopted a policy imposing serious academic penalties for students missing more than two days per year for religious reasons. The students claimed this policy violated their **free exercise** rights under the First Amendment.

28 511 F. Supp. 613 (N.D. Tex. 1981), *aff'd*, 670 F.2d 46 (5th Cir. 1982).

The court began its analysis by pointing out that a law or policy will not necessarily pass constitutional muster just because it applies to members of all faith communities equally. The Free Exercise Clause may be used to challenge laws that are "fair in form, but discriminatory in operation." A facially-neutral law that burdens the practice of a specific religion will be declared unconstitutional unless the State can demonstrate a compelling reason for its enforcement. Employing the standard mode of **free exercise** analysis, the court found that the students' belief that they had to miss school was **religious**; that their belief was **sincere**; and that enforcement of the policy would have a **severe impact** because the students could not meet their religious obligations without significantly damaging their academic records.

Finally, the court turned to the question of whether the district's reasons for its attendance policy were sufficient to justify the burden its policy placed on student members of the Church of God. The district argued that "regular attendance in public school is necessary for a student's academic development" and that "accommodating the holy days of various and diverse religious groups would work an unreasonable burden on the teachers." With regard to the first argument, the court looked to the *Yoder* decision:

> The school district's interest in [the attendance policy] does not approach the magnitude of the state's interest in *Wisconsin v. Yoder*. Here we are not concerned with a religious sect that insists on keeping their children away from school. We are concerned only with the effect of a handful of absences on the Plaintiffs' academic development. This interest, standing alone, does not justify the burden placed on the free exercise of religion.

With regard to the second argument, the court noted that no teacher had ever complained about the extra work for makeup assignments engendered by the prior, more permissive attendance policy. Moreover, teachers had routinely provided and evaluated makeup work for students who missed class for sickness or sports. Thus, the court concluded that the district's attendance policy was an unconstitutional violation of the students' free exercise rights. The court implied that there was a limit on how much religiously motivated absence a school district would have to tolerate, but offered little guidance as to the magnitude of that limit.

Church of God was cited affirmatively in *Citizens for Quality Education San Diego v. Barrera*,[29] a recent case in which the plaintiffs alleged that an initiative developed by the San Diego Unified School District to address anti-Muslim bullying established "a subtle, discriminatory scheme" to favor Islam over other religions, in violation of the Establishment Clause. The district court found there was "nothing nefarious" in the District's initiative, noting that "respect for the religious observances of others is a fundamental civil virtue that government (including the public schools) can and should cultivate."

In *Employment Division, Department of Human Resources of Oregon v. Smith*,[30] a case involving employees of a drug treatment organization who were fired after using peyote for sacramental purposes, the Court took a much stricter approach to free exercise claims than in *Church of God*. The Court ruled that the Constitution is not violated by generally applicable laws that incidentally and unintentionally burden the free exercise of religion, implying that school districts and states may enforce the kind of policy struck down in *Church of God* and the compulsory schooling laws successfully challenged in *Yoder*. However, the *Smith* court held that free exercise claims are to be given greater weight when they involve "not the Free Exercise Clause alone, but the Free Exercise Clause in conjunction with other constitutional protections, such as … the right of parents, acknowledged in *Pierce v. Society of Sisters*, to direct the education of their children."

29 333 F. Supp. 3d 1003 (S.D. Cal. 2018).
30 494 U.S. 872 (1990).

In response to the *Smith* decision, Congress enacted the **Religious Freedom Restoration Act of 1993**,[31] which prohibits governments from "substantially burdening" a person's exercise of religion even if the burden results from a rule of general applicability unless the government can demonstrate the burden (1) furthers a compelling governmental interest; and (2) is the least restrictive means of furthering that interest, restoring the compelling interest test outlined in *Yoder*.

Categorical Exemptions

Compulsory schooling laws in some states continue to excuse specified **categories of children** from their requirements. Alabama excuses students with certain physical or mental conditions, students who would have to walk over two miles to public school due to a lack of public transportation, and children who are legally employed.[32] California has special rules for students who work in the entertainment industry.[33] Virginia exempts students from families opposed to schooling on religious grounds, students who have a justified fear for their safety in schools, students with contagious diseases, and unvaccinated students.[34] New Jersey and Washington exempt children with mental or physical disabilities preventing them from attending school.[35] In such cases, federal and state statutes may require the state to provide educational services even if the parents choose *not* to send the child to school (see Chapter 8).

Idiosyncratic Exemptions

In some cases, parents charged with violating compulsory schooling laws have attempted to defend themselves by objecting to conditions at local schools. However, a parent may not unilaterally withdraw a child from school to protest conditions at the school. Nor may a parent remove a child from school to compel the school to change its educational program.[36] In *In re Baum*,[37] a seventh-grade student of Blackfoot heritage wrote a report on the historic maltreatment of Native Americans. In response, her teacher wrote, "I agree with your feelings of anger. However, I have an uncle who is a Wampanoag Indian [sic] and his point of view is that the Indians [sic] got what they deserved." When the student asked her teacher about the comment, she replied that "Indians [sic] on reservations are lazy because they do not get off and get jobs." The entire exchange occurred in front of the class. The student's mother withdrew her from school and was ultimately found guilty of neglect for failing to make alternative arrangements that would satisfy compulsory schooling requirements.

Parents have occasionally prevailed when conditions in schools pose a significant health and safety risk to their children.[38] In *In re Ian D.*,[39] a boy testified that he was unable to attend school for more than 100 days because of constant abuse and ridicule from other students, noting that "his repeated pleas to school authorities for protection and assistance resulted in no meaningful action." Moved by this testimony, the court ruled in the student's favor, citing the so-called **"choice of evils" doctrine** that permits violations of criminal statutes necessitated by exigent

---

31 42 U.S.C. § 2000bb *et seq.*
32 ALA. CODE §§ 16-28-5, 16-28-6.
33 CAL. EDUC. CODE §§48410-48416.
34 VA. CODE ANN. § 22.1-254.
35 N.J. REV. STAT. § 18A:38-26; WASH. REV. CODE ANN. § 28A:225.010(c).
36 Matter of William A.A., 24 A.D.3d 1125 (N.Y. App. 2005).
37 *In re* Baum, 61 A.D.2d 123 (N.Y. App. 1978).
38 *In re* Brian H., 784 N.Y.S.2d 919 (2003); Matter of William A.A., 24 A.D.3d 1125 (N.Y. App. 2005).
39 439 N.Y.S.2d 613 (N.Y. Fam. Ct. 1981).

circumstances. The court also ordered the board of education to transfer the student to another school where he could make a fresh start.

An implicit premise in *Ian D.* seems to be that the State has an obligation to provide **safe schools**. This obligation was affirmed in New York with the enactment of the *Dignity for All Students Act* in 2012. Its purpose is "to afford all students in public schools an environment free of discrimination and harassment" of the kind endured by Ian D. and countless other students in public schools throughout the country.[40] However, the legislation creates no private right of action against schools for violating its provisions.[41]

Eligibility Criteria for Enrollment in Public Schools

Until the 1970s, most states exempted children with various disabilities from compulsory school attendance on the assumption that they could not benefit from schooling or that their presence would harm others.[42] For some children, the consequences of such policies were severe. In *In re Kevin Sampson*,[43] a 15-year-old boy was exempted from compulsory schooling laws because he suffered from neurofibromatosis, leaving his face and neck severely disfigured. As a result, he never learned to read. Today, excluding children like Kevin from school would be considered a violation of federal and state constitutional guarantees of equal protection and various federal and state statutes (see Chapter 8).

Compulsory schooling laws in many states have retained eligibility criteria relating to **age**, **vaccination status**, **custodial requirements**, and **residency requirements** for enrollment in public schools. In recent years, many states have adopted **open enrollment** policies. A few states have sought to institute **immigration status** checks.

Age

State laws establish the minimum and maximum age of children eligible to receive an education in public schools. Typically, children must be five by a specified date in order to start kindergarten, and six by a specified date in order to start first grade. Parents have challenged age requirements as a violation of state constitutional guarantees and the Equal Protection Clause without success.[44]

Vaccination Status

Most states require specified **vaccinations** prior to admission to public schools, and in many cases, to private schools. More than a century ago, in *Jacobson v. Massachusetts*,[45] the Supreme Court upheld the authority of the State to enforce compulsory vaccination laws on grounds of public safety:

> But the liberty secured by the Constitution of the United States to every person within its jurisdiction does not import an absolute right in each person to be, at all times and in all circumstances, wholly

---

40   N.Y. EDUC. LAW § 11(7).
41   C.T. v. Valley Stream Union Free Sch. Dist., 201 F. Supp. 3d 307 (E.D.N.Y. 2016); Motta v. Eldred Cent. Sch. Dist., 141 A.D.3d 819 (N.Y. App. Div. 2016); Shantz v. Union-Endicott Cent. Sch. Dist., 2019 U.S. Dist. LEXIS 11933 (N.D.N.Y. Jan 25, 2019).
42   State *ex rel.* Beattie v. Bd. of Educ. of Antigo, 172 N.W. 153 (Wis. 1919).
43   65 Misc. 2d 658 (NY Fam. Ct. 1970).
44   Zweifel v. Joint Dist., 251 N.W.2d 822 (Wis. 1977); Hammond v. Marx, 406 F. Supp. 853 (D. Me. 1975); O'Leary v. Wisecup, 364 A.2d 770 (Pa. 1976).
45   197 U.S. 11 (1905).

freed from restraint. There are manifold restraints to which every person is necessarily subject for the common good. On any other basis organized society could not exist with safety to its members. Society based on the rule that each one is a law unto himself would soon be confronted with disorder and anarchy.

Real liberty for all could not exist under the operation of a principle which recognizes the right of each individual person to use his own, whether in respect of his person or his property, regardless of the injury that may be done to others. This court has more than once recognized it as a fundamental principle that "persons and property are subjected to all kinds of restraints and burdens, in order to secure the general comfort, health, and prosperity of the State; of the perfect right of the legislature to do which no question ever was, or upon acknowledged general principles ever can be made, so far as natural persons are concerned."

"Even liberty itself, the greatest of all rights, is not unrestricted license to act according to one's own will. It is only freedom from restraint under conditions essential to the equal enjoyment of the same right by others. It is then liberty regulated by law."

Upon the principle of self-defense, of paramount necessity, a community has the right to protect itself against an epidemic of disease which threatens the safety of its members. It is to be observed that when the regulation in question was adopted, smallpox, according to the recitals in the regulation adopted by the Board of Health, was prevalent to some extent in the city of Cambridge and the disease was increasing. If such was the situation—and nothing is asserted or appears in the record to the contrary—if we are to attach any value whatever to the knowledge which, it is safe to affirm, is common to all civilized peoples touching smallpox and the methods most usually employed to eradicate that disease, it cannot be adjudged that the present regulation of the Board of Health was not necessary in order to protect the public health and secure the public safety.

If the mode adopted by the Commonwealth of Massachusetts for the protection of its local communities against smallpox proved to be distressing, inconvenient or objectionable to some—if nothing more could be reasonably affirmed of the statute in question—the answer is that it was the duty of the constituted authorities primarily to keep in view the welfare, comfort and safety of the many, and not permit the interests of the many to be subordinated to the wishes or convenience of the few.

There is, of course, a sphere within which the individual may assert the supremacy of his own will and rightfully dispute the authority of any human government, especially of any free government existing under a written constitution, to interfere with the exercise of that will. But it is equally true that in every well-ordered society charged with the duty of conserving the safety of its members the rights of the individual in respect of his liberty may at times, under the pressure of great dangers, be subjected to such restraint, to be enforced by reasonable regulations, as the safety of the general public may demand.

In *Zucht v. King*,[46] the plaintiffs argued that mandatory immunization requirements for students seeking admission to private schools violated their **free exercise** rights. However, the Supreme Court followed its earlier decision in *Jacobson*, justifying mandatory immunization on grounds of public safety.

According to the Centers for Disease Control and Prevention (CDC),[47] there were 1,243 confirmed individual cases of measles in 31 states in the first nine months of 2019—the greatest

---

46 260 U.S. 174 (1922).
47 Centers for Disease Control and Research, Measles Cases and Outbreaks. Online at www.cdc.gov/measles/cases-outbreaks.html (last accessed April 26, 2020).

outbreak in the United States since 1992.[48] The CDC attributed more than 75 percent of the cases in 2019 to outbreaks in New York, and in particular, to communities where groups of people are unvaccinated.

In light of this ongoing public health crisis, state governments have restricted or eliminated religious or conscientious exemptions from mandatory vaccination requirements for admission to public and private schools. In 2016, California amended its Health and Safety Code to require that school authorities "not unconditionally admit" any child for the first time to "any private or public elementary or secondary school, child care center, day nursery, nursery school, family day care home, or development center," or advance any child to seventh grade, unless he or she has been fully immunized against ten specific diseases and "[a]ny other disease deemed appropriate by the State Department of Public Health."[49] In *Love v. State Department of Education*,[50] four parents unsuccessfully challenged this amendment on state constitutional grounds. The highest court in California ruled that compulsory vaccination did not violate any child's interest in education. The legislative amendment promoted a compelling governmental interest in ensuring health and safety, and it was narrowly tailored to achieve that interest.

In *Flynn v. Estevez*,[51] an appellate court in Florida upheld the dismissal of a parent's suit against a Catholic diocesan school for refusing to enroll her non-immunized child. Citing the **ecclesiastical abstention doctrine** under the First Amendment, the lower court found that the mandatory vaccination statute was a neutral state law that did not violate religious freedoms, and there was no free-standing federal or state free exercise right for parents to refuse immunization as a condition of school admission.

In 2019, New York followed California's lead, repealing legislation allowing parents to opt out of immunization requirements for admission to public and private schools within the state.[52] In *V.D. v. New York*,[53] the parents of six children with disabilities unsuccessfully sought an injunction, arguing that state legislation requiring that their children be immunized conflicted with their rights under the federal **Individuals with Disabilities Education Act** (IDEA).[54] "Mandatory vaccination laws are a permissible use of state police power, and states are free to pass laws that mandate compliance with immunization requirements," noted the court. "New York's repeal … imposes an obligation on all parents that is perfectly consistent with the requirements of the IDEA."

Custodial Requirements

For children whose parents do not live together, school districts may require documentation indicating which parent has legal authority to make day-to-day decisions. In most states, unless a child is emancipated, his or her primary residence is presumed to be that of the custodial parent.[55] In *Watts v. Mannheim Township School District*,[56] a case in which a mother and father who shared custody of a child both resided in the same school district, a Pennsylvania court held that the district had a duty to provide the child with transportation to and from both residences.

---

48 Alaska, Arizona, California, Colorado, Connecticut, Florida, Georgia, Hawaii, Idaho, Illinois, Indiana, Iowa, Kentucky, Maine, Maryland, Massachusetts, Michigan, Missouri, New Mexico, Nevada, New Hampshire, New Jersey, New York, Ohio, Oklahoma, Oregon, Pennsylvania, Texas, Tennessee, Virginia, and Washington reported measles outbreaks to the CDC in the first nine months of 2019.
49 CAL HEALTH & SAF CODE §§ 120335, 120370.
50 29 Cal. App. 5th 980 (2018).
51 221 So. 3d 1241 (Fla. Dist. Ct. App. 2017).
52 N.Y. PUB. HEALTH LAW § 2164(6).
53 403 F. Supp. 3d 76 (E.D.N.Y. 2019).
54 20 U.S.C. § 1400, *et seq.*
55 State *ex rel.* Frasier v. Whaley, 234 N.W.2d 909 (Neb. 1975).
56 84 A.3d 378 (Pa. Commw. Ct. 2014).

In *Roxbury Township Board of Education v. West Milford Board of Education*,[57] the highest court in New Jersey held that where separated parents reside in different school districts, "the student's domicile is the school district of the parent or guardian with whom the student lives for the majority of the school year ... regardless of which parent has legal custody." The presumption that a child's primary residence is that of his or her custodial parent may be rebutted, for example, by establishing that the child lives with a legal guardian, in which case the child's residence is that of the guardian. In *State ex rel. Grosso v. Boardman Local School District*,[58] an Ohio appellate court found the school district had a legal duty to admit a child who lived with her aunt and uncle in the district. The child's biological parents lived in Nevada, but her aunt and uncle had been granted legal custody, and the child "lived, slept, and ate at her aunt's and uncle's home, so she was not a 'nonresident pupil'."

Residency Requirements

With the notable exception of fee-paying international students,[59] states have historically prohibited school districts from admitting non-residents. In *Martinez v. Bynum*,[60] the Supreme Court held that residency requirements do not violate the constitutional right to interstate travel. In *Paynter v. State*,[61] the New York Court of Appeals upheld residency requirements in the face of a state constitutional challenge. Plaintiffs had argued, unsuccessfully, that the residency requirements fostered *de facto* segregation by preventing students of color in a racially isolated urban district from transferring to more integrated suburban districts (see Chapter 7).

When students are allowed to transfer out of their home districts, parents or, in some circumstances, the home district may be required to pay **tuition**. Some states permit students to attend school in any district that declares itself open to students from outside its boundaries unless the racial balance in a district under a court desegregation order is adversely affected.[62] In districts not under a court desegregation order, accepting or rejecting students for transfer explicitly on the basis of race (even with the aim of fostering racial integration) is unconstitutional.[63]

The issue of **residency** is closely tied to financial responsibility, and this can be particularly contentious for children in **residential programs** (for special educational needs) or **juvenile facilities** (by order of a court). Children's services agencies and residential institutions can be designated as legal guardians.[64] Still, state laws treat different classifications of institutionalized children differently for the purposes of financial responsibility. In *Antioch Community High School District 17 v. Board of Education*,[65] a school district sought reimbursement for the educational services it had provided to a minor at a private residential alcohol and drug treatment facility within its boundaries. The highest court in Illinois held that the school district could not obtain reimbursement because the minor had been placed in the residential facility by a juvenile court for purposes unrelated to education. In 2012, the Court of Appeals of New York ruled that while state law guarantees all children with disabilities aged five to 21 in residential care facilities a free appropriate public

---

57 662 A.2d 976 (N.J. App. Div. 1995); cert. denied, 670 A.2d 1066 (1996); *see also* I.J. v. Bd. of Educ. of Hamilton, 2016 N.J. Super. Unpub. LEXIS 149 (Super. Ct. App. Div. Jan. 26, 2016) [*unpublished*].
58 2009 Ohio App. LEXIS 4277 (September 25, 2009).
59 Rodrigue Ceda Makindu v. Ill. High Sch. Ass'n, 40 N.E.3d 182 (Ill. App. 2d 2015).
60 461 U.S. 321 (1983).
61 100 N.Y.2d 434 (2003).
62 IOWA CODE § 282.18.
63 Parents Involved in Community Schools v. Seattle Sch. Dist. No. 1, 551 U.S. 701 (2007).
64 *In re* K.R., 2016 Ohio App. LEXIS 1299 (March 24, 2016); Orange Cty. Dep't of Educ. v. Cal. Dep't of Educ., 668 F.3d 1052 (9th Cir. 2011).
65 868 N.E.2d 1068 (Ill. App. 2007).

education, tuition costs are to be borne by parents or "the entity or agency placing the child in the institution."[66]

Some courts have held that a child does not satisfy residency requirements if her caregiver has power of attorney but not legal custody or guardianship.[67] In *Feaster v. Portage Public School*,[68] the Michigan Supreme Court ruled that a child who lives with an adult having power of attorney may qualify for residency in the district where the adult lives. In *Israel S. v. Board of Education of Oak Park & River Forest High School District 200*,[69] an Illinois appellate court found that the district acted beyond its powers in requiring that students prove they were residing with a legal guardian or that they were residing apart from their parents due to incapacity or hardship.

Establishing residency can be challenging for children with an incarcerated parent. In *Velazquez v. East Stroudsburg Area School District*,[70] a Pennsylvania appellate court overturned a lower court ruling denying enrollment to a student who had lived with his grandmother since his father's incarceration ten years earlier. The father had sent the district notarized letters indicating the grandmother had his full permission to act as the student's guardian.

Establishing residency can also be challenging for military families. In *A.M.S. ex rel. A.D.S. v. Board of Education of City of Margate*,[71] the plaintiff was on active duty in the US Army, with tours in South Carolina, Arizona, Washington, Iraq, New Jersey, and Germany. Following the death of his wife, whose child he had adopted, he stayed with his parents in Margate for six weeks of bereavement leave. He then returned to active duty, granting power of attorney to his parents, who sought to enroll their grandchild in a local school. The school district denied enrollment, citing its residency requirements. The highest court in New Jersey upheld a subsequent decision by the State Board finding the plaintiff resided within the district.

Establishing residency can also be especially challenging for homeless children. In 1988, Congress enacted the **McKinney-Vento Homeless Assistance Act**,[72] which requires each state to ensure that homeless children have equal access to the same free, appropriate public education as other children. New York responded by permitting the parents of homeless children to decide where they will attend school. In Georgia, homeless children must be allowed either to remain in the district in which they were enrolled prior to becoming homeless or to enroll in their present location.[73] In *Lampkin v. District of Columbia*,[74] the D.C. Circuit Court found the *McKinney Act* includes a private right of action against government officials.

Open Enrollment

School boards are required to provide an education to children residing in the district or participating in approved transfer programs. There is, however, no constitutional requirement that students be given a choice in terms of which district school they will attend.[75] The most significant constraint is that students may not be assigned to schools on the basis of race or other criteria in violation of the Equal Protection Clause or federal civil rights statutes. In *Parents Involved in*

---

66 Board of Educ. of the Garrison Union Free Sch. Dist. v. Greek Archdiocese Institute of St. Basil, 18 N.Y.3d 355 (N.Y. Ct. App. 2012).
67 Joshua C. v. Western Heights Indep. Sch. Dist. No. 1–41, 898 P.2d 1324 (Okla. Ct. App. 1995).
68 547 N.W.2d 328 (Mich. 1996).
69 N.E.2d 1264 (Ill. App. 3d 1992).
70 949 A.2d 354 (Pa. Commw. Ct. 2008).
71 976 A.2d 402 (N.J. Super. Ct. App. Div. 2009).
72 42 U.S.C. §§ 11301–11489.
73 GA. COMP. R. & REGS. 160-5-1.282(2)(b)(1)(I).
74 Lampkin v. District of Columbia, 27 F.3d 605 (D.C. Cir. 1994).
75 Palmer v. Bloomfield Hills Bd. of Educ., 417 N.W.2d 505 (Mich. Ct. App. 1987).

Community Schools v. Seattle School District No. 1,[76] the Supreme Court ruled in a plurality opinion that school districts may not use race as a criterion in assigning students to schools even if their goal is to promote "racial balance."

In recent years, many states have responded to calls for greater parental choice by implementing **open enrollment** legislation. **Open enrollment** allows students to select or transfer to a public school of their choice, rather than the public school to which they were or would be assigned based on their residence. Thirty-three states and the District of Columbia permit **intra-district** enrollments or transfers, while 43 states permit **inter-district** enrollments or transfers.[77]

Immigration Status

In 1975, Texas began withholding funds from local school districts enrolling the children of undocumented immigrants. At least one school district began charging tuition for such children in an attempt to recover lost revenue. In *Plyler v. Doe*,[78] a divided Supreme Court struck down the Texas law on the ground that denial of public funding for the children of undocumented immigrants violated the Fourteenth Amendment. The Court found the policy imposed a discriminatory burden on children brought illegally into the country through no fault of their own. The Court also found that denying such children the benefits of public education furthered no substantial state interest, noting that it could lead to "the creation and perpetuation of a subclass of illiterates within our boundaries, surely adding to the problems and costs of unemployment, welfare, and crime."

In 2012, the Hispanic Interest Coalition of Alabama challenged the constitutionality of the *Beason-Hammon Alabama Taxpayer and Citizen Protection Act*.[79] Among other things, the legislation required local school officials to verify the immigration status of children and their parents. Following *Plyler*, the Eleventh Circuit struck down these provisions,[80] finding they presented "similar obstacles to the ability of an undocumented child to obtain an education."

In the wake of the *Hispanic Interest Coalition* case, President Barack Obama issued an executive branch memorandum known as **Deferred Action for Childhood Arrivals** (DACA). The Secretary of the Department of Homeland Security followed with a DACA Memo encouraging government officials not to enforce federal immigration laws against children who came to the United States before age 16. Individuals who met the criteria in the DACA Memo qualified for "deferred action" on deportation for renewable two-year terms, with eligibility for work permits. In 2017, the Trump Administration announced plans to phase out DACA. In *Estrada v. Becker*,[81] a group of DACA recipients unsuccessfully challenged a Georgia Board of Regents policy requiring the three most selective colleges and universities in the state not to admit DACA recipients. The Eleventh Circuit found the policy was rationally related to a legitimate government interest and did not violate the Equal Protection Clause.

The Regulation of Private Schools and Home-Based Education

It often falls to the courts to assess the constitutionality of state regulation of private alternatives to public schooling. To do so requires balancing the State's interests in ensuring the education of all children against the Fourteenth Amendment right of parents to direct the upbringing of their

---

76 551 U.S. 701 (2007).
77 MICAH ANN WIXOM, POLICY SNAPSHOT: OPEN ENROLLMENT. EDUCATION COMMISSION OF THE STATES (January, 2019), Online at www.ecs.org/open-enrollment/(last accessed April 26, 2020).
78 457 U.S. 202 (1982).
79 ALA. CODE § 31-13-28.
80 Hispanic Interest Coal. v. Governor of Ala., 691 F.3d 1236 (11th Cir. 2012).
81 917 F.3d 1298 (11th Cir. 2019).

children. As the *Pierce* Court recognized, if states could not regulate private schools, they would have no way of ensuring that the goals of compulsory schooling are met. Private school students might be limited to one particular subject or skill, or they might be taught nothing at all. However, if the State's power to regulate private schools were unlimited, private schools could become indistinguishable from public schools, rendering parental choice meaningless. This argument was successfully invoked in *State v. Whisner*,[82] a case involving a parochial school subject to comprehensive regulations in Ohio.

After World War I, a number of states sought to foster majoritarian beliefs and values and the exclusive use of the English language in private and public schools. In 1923, two years before *Pierce*,[83] the Supreme Court considered a Nebraska law requiring that all instruction in private schools be in English and barring the teaching of any modern foreign language until after the eighth grade.

⚖️

MEYER v. NEBRASKA
Supreme Court of the United States
262 U.S. 390 (1923)

MR. JUSTICE MCREYNOLDS delivered the opinion of the Court.

Plaintiff in error was tried and convicted in the District Court for Hamilton County, Nebraska, under an information which charged that on May 25, 1920, while an instructor in Zion Parochial School, he unlawfully taught the subject of reading in the German language to Raymond Parpart, a child of ten years, who had not attained and successfully passed the eighth grade. ...

The Supreme Court of the State affirmed the judgment of conviction. It declared the offense charged and established was "the direct and intentional teaching of the German language as a distinct subject to a child who had not passed the eighth grade," in the parochial school maintained by Zion Evangelical Lutheran Congregation, a collection of Biblical stories being used therefore. And it held that the statute forbidding this did not conflict with the Fourteenth Amendment, but was a valid exercise of the police power. The following excerpts from the opinion sufficiently indicate the reasons advanced to support the conclusion:

The salutary purpose of the statute is clear. The legislature had seen the baneful effects of permitting foreigners, who had taken residence in this country, to rear and educate their children in the language of their native land. The result of that condition was found to be inimical to our own safety. To allow the children of foreigners, who had emigrated here, to be taught from early childhood the language of the country of their parents was to rear them with that language as their mother tongue. It was to educate them so that they must always think in that language, and, as a consequence, naturally inculcate in them the ideas and sentiments foreign to the best interests of this country. The statute, therefore, was intended not only to require that the education of all children be conducted in the English language, but that, until they had grown into that language and until it had become a part of them, they should not in the schools be taught any other language. The obvious purpose of this statute was that the English language should be and become the mother tongue of all children reared in this state. The enactment of such a statute comes reasonably within the police power of the state ...

The problem for our determination is whether the statute as construed and applied unreasonably infringes the liberty guaranteed to the plaintiff in error by the Fourteenth Amendment. "No State shall ... deprive any person of life, liberty, or property, without due process of law."

---

82 351 N.E.2d 750 (Ohio 1976).
83 268 U.S. 510 (1925).

While this Court has not attempted to define with exactness the liberty thus guaranteed, the term has received much consideration and some of the included things have been definitely stated. Without doubt, it denotes not merely freedom from bodily restraint but also the right of the individual to contract, to engage in any of the common occupations of life, to acquire useful knowledge, to marry, establish a home and bring up children, to worship God according to the dictates of his [sic] own conscience, and generally to enjoy those privileges long recognized at common law as essential to the orderly pursuit of happiness by free men [sic]. The established doctrine is that this liberty may not be interfered with, under the guise of protecting the public interest, by legislative action which is arbitrary or without reasonable relation to some purpose within the competency of the State to effect. Determination by the legislature of what constitutes proper exercise of police power is not final or conclusive but is subject to supervision by the courts.

The American people have always regarded education and acquisition of knowledge as matters of supreme importance which should be diligently promoted. The Ordinance of 1787 declares, "Religion, morality, and knowledge being necessary to good government and the happiness of mankind, schools and the means of education shall forever be encouraged." Corresponding to the right of control, it is the natural duty of the parent to give his [sic] children education suitable to their station in life; and nearly all the States, including Nebraska, enforce this obligation by compulsory laws.

Practically, education of the young is only possible in schools conducted by especially qualified persons who devote themselves thereto. The calling always has been regarded as useful and honorable, essential, indeed, to the public welfare. Mere knowledge of the German language cannot reasonably be regarded as harmful. Heretofore it has been commonly looked upon as helpful and desirable. Plaintiff in error taught this language in school as part of his occupation. His right thus to teach and the right of parents to engage him so to instruct their children, we think, are within the liberty of the Amendment.

The challenged statute forbids the teaching in school of any subject except in English; also the teaching of any other language until the pupil has attained and successfully passed the eighth grade, which is not usually accomplished before the age of twelve. The Supreme Court of the State has held that "the so-called ancient or dead languages" are

not "within the spirit or the purpose of the act." Latin, Greek, Hebrew are not proscribed; but German, French, Spanish, Italian and every other alien speech are within the ban. Evidently the legislature has attempted materially to interfere with the calling of modern language teachers, with the opportunities of pupils to acquire knowledge, and with the power of parents to control the education of their own.

It is said the purpose of the legislation was to promote civic development by inhibiting training and education of the immature in foreign tongues and ideals before they could learn English and acquire American ideals; and "that the English language should be and become the mother tongue of all children reared in this State." It is also affirmed that the foreign born population is very large, that certain communities commonly use foreign words, follow foreign leaders, move in a foreign atmosphere, and that the children are thereby hindered from becoming citizens of the most useful type and the public safety is imperiled.

That the State may do much, go very far, indeed, in order to improve the quality of its citizens, physically, mentally and morally, is clear; but the individual has certain fundamental rights which must be respected. The protection of the Constitution extends to all, to those who speak other languages as well as to those born with English on the tongue. Perhaps it would be highly advantageous if all had ready understanding of our ordinary speech, but this cannot be coerced by methods which conflict with the Constitution—a desirable end cannot be promoted by prohibited means. …

The desire of the legislature to foster a homogeneous people with American ideals prepared readily to understand current discussions of civic matters is easy to appreciate. Unfortunate experiences during the late war and aversion toward every characteristic of truculent adversaries were certainly enough to quicken that aspiration. But the means adopted, we think, exceed the limitations upon the power of the State and conflict with rights assured to plaintiff in error. The interference is plain enough and no adequate reason therefore in time of peace and domestic tranquility has been shown.

The power of the State to compel attendance at some school and to make reasonable regulations for all schools, including a requirement that they shall give instructions in English, is not questioned. Nor has challenge been made of the State's power to prescribe a curriculum for institutions which it supports. Those matters are not met within the present controversy.

Our concern is with the prohibition approved by the [Nebraska] Supreme Court. *Adams v. Tanner* pointed out that mere abuse incident to an occupation ordinarily useful is not enough to justify its abolition,[84] although regulation may be entirely proper. No emergency has arisen which renders knowledge by a child of some language other than English so clearly harmful as to justify its inhibition with the consequent infringement of rights long freely enjoyed. We are constrained to conclude that the statute as applied is arbitrary and without reasonable relation to any end within the competency of the State.

As the statute undertakes to interfere only with teaching which involves a modern language, leaving complete freedom as to other for the suggestion that the purpose was to protect the child's health by limiting his mental activities. It is well known that proficiency in a foreign language seldom comes to one not instructed at an early age, and experience shows that this is not injurious to the health, morals or understanding of the ordinary child. The judgment of the court below must be reversed and the cause remanded for further proceedings not inconsistent with this opinion. Reversed.

⚖️

In *Meyer* and a companion case from Iowa with similar facts,[85] the Supreme Court recognized the right of states to impose curricular requirements on private schools designed to foster the physical, mental, moral, and civic development of their students. At the same time, it recognized the right of parents to direct the upbringing of their children. Notably, Justice Oliver Wendell Holmes dissented in both cases, finding the statutory bans in Nebraska and Iowa on instructing schoolchildren in the German language to be "lawful and proper."[86]

In *Farrington v. Tokushige*,[87] the Court subsequently rejected a Hawaii law regulating the private academies that children attended in addition to public school. The law prohibited attendance at these schools until after the second grade, limited attendance to six hours a week, and thoroughly regulated their curricula. Taken together, the *Pierce*, *Meyer*, and *Tokushige* trilogy makes it clear that states may only prohibit curricular offerings in private schools that are clearly "inimical to the public welfare." The power of the State to require private schools to teach certain subjects and topics is generally accepted. However, states may not prohibit the teaching of *additional* subjects, even though these may reduce the amount of time available to teach required subjects.

Today, most states prescribe a core curriculum of subjects for private and parochial schools. Some states add particular topics such as "patriotism" or "good citizenship."[88] No state prohibits private schools from teaching any particular topics, and it remains an open question what topics, if any, might be so clearly "inimical to the public welfare" that they could be prohibited. Do parents have a constitutional right to send their children to private schools teaching anarchism or fascism? Given the great weight placed by modern courts on parental rights, the answer might well be that they do. Indeed, in *Runyan v. McCrary*,[89] the Supreme Court noted in **dicta** that "parents have a First Amendment right to send their children to educational institutions that promote the belief that racial segregation is desirable, and … children have an equal right to attend such institutions."

---

84 244 U.S. 590 (1917).
85 Bartels v. Iowa, 262 U.S. 404 (1923).
86 See Justin Driver, The Schoolhouse Gate: Public Education, the Supreme Court, and the Battle for the American Mind (2018).
87 273 U.S. 284 (1927).
88 See Randall Curren and Charles Dorn, Patriotic Education In A Global Age (2018); Michael Rebell, Flunking Democracy: Schools, Courts, And Civic Participation (2018); see also Michael Hand, Book review: Randall Curren and Charles Dorn, Patriotic Education in a Global Age, 16(1) Theory and Research in Education 132–33 (2018); Jonathan Feldman, Book Review: Michael Rebell, Flunking Democracy: Schools, Courts, and Civic Participation, 17(2) Theory and Research in Education 234–35 (2019).
89 427 U.S. 160 (1976).

There have been numerous challenges to state regulations applicable to private and parochial schools. These generally fall into three categories: (1) alleged violations of the constitutional rights of students; (2) alleged violations of the constitutional rights of parents; and (3) alleged violations of the constitutional rights of private school officials and the schools themselves. These are not mutually-exclusive categories, and plaintiffs often invoke all three types when challenging state regulations applicable to private schools.

Patriotic Exercises

In *Circle School v. Pappert*,[90] a Pennsylvania statute required all public, private, and parochial schools to display the US flag in every classroom and to provide for the recitation of the Pledge of Allegiance or national anthem each day. Students could opt out of the Pledge or anthem on religious or personal grounds. In such cases, school officials were required to notify parents or guardians that their child had opted out. Students successfully challenged the parental notification requirement on First Amendment grounds. The Third Circuit affirmed there was no convincing government interest at stake in requiring parental notification when students in private schools exercised their right not to speak. The court also found the statute violated the First Amendment right of private schools to "free expressive association."

In *Frazier v. Winn*,[91] a case involving public school students, the Eleventh Circuit upheld a Florida statute requiring parental consent for students to decline to recite the Pledge. In the court's view, students had limited free speech rights under the First Amendment and could choose for themselves whether or not to stand for the Pledge. Allowing parents to decide whether their children would actually recite the Pledge was consistent with their due process rights under the Fourteenth Amendment.

Standardized Testing

In *Ohio Association of Independent Schools v. Goff*,[92] the Sixth Circuit rejected a Fourteenth Amendment challenge to the state's mandatory program of proficiency testing in five subject areas in private schools. Parents argued that the testing forced private schools to align their curricula with public schools, depriving them of their due process right to direct, by choice of school, the education of their children. Other courts have upheld prior state review of private school programs, the investigation of private schools by local school boards, and mandatory reporting requirements for private school enrollment and attendance data.[93]

Teacher Qualifications

The *Pierce* opinion suggested that those who provide instruction in private schools must be qualified teachers. Although most states place no specific requirements on private school teachers or require only that they be "qualified" or hold a bachelor's degree, a minority of states insist that private school teachers hold certification. This requirement has proved controversial, especially

---

90 270 F. Supp. 2d 616 (E.D. Pa. 2003), *aff'd*, Circle Sch. v. Pappert, 381 F.3d 172 (3d Cir. 2004).

91 535 F.3d 1279 (11th Cir. 2008); *see also* LaShan Arceneaux v. Klein Independent School District, 2018 U.S. Dist. LEXIS 85431 (S.D. Tex. May 22, 2018), *dismissed in part, motion denied in part*, 2018 U.S. Dist. LEXIS 122018 (S.D. Tex., July 20, 2018), *later proceeding at* 2019 U.S. Dist. LEXIS 52004 (S.D. Tex., Mar. 27, 2019).

92 92 F.3d 419 (6th Cir. 1996).

93 Murphy v. Arkansas, 852 F.2d 1039 (8th Cir. 1988); Johnson v. Charles City Cmty. Sch. Bd. of Educ., 368 N.W.2d 74 (Iowa 1985); Blount v. Dep. of Educ. & Cultural Serv., 551 A.2d 1377 (Me. 1988); New Life Baptist Church Acad. v. East Longmeadow, 885 F.2d 940 (1st Cir. 1989); Fellowship Baptist Church v. Benton, 815 F.2d 486 (8th Cir. 1987); State v. De LaBruere, 577 A.2d 254 (Vt. 1990).

for parochial schools.[94] In *Sheridan Road Baptist Church v. Department of Education*,[95] a parochial school unsuccessfully challenged Michigan's certification requirements for its teachers. In order to obtain certification, prospective teachers had to obtain a bachelor's degree from an "approved" university in Michigan or elsewhere, with specified credits in education, liberal arts, and the subjects they wished to teach. Adopting the standard **free exercise** analysis, the court found the infringement on free exercise rights was minimal and that it was outweighed by the state's interest.

Background Checks

To better protect children enrolled in private schools from harm at the hands of private school employees, many states require private schools to conduct criminal background checks and sex offender registry checks of all prospective employees in order to maintain their status as approved alternatives to public schools under their compulsory schooling laws. In Illinois, private schools will not receive "Non-Public School Recognition Status" unless they require all applicants to authorize a fingerprint-based criminal history records check prior to employment.[96] Maryland requires its Department of Education to revoke the approved status of any private school that knowingly employs a person convicted of child sexual abuse.[97] Louisiana prohibits public and private schools from employing any person in any capacity who has been convicted of a crime involving children or who has pleaded no contest when charged with such an offense.[98] Pennsylvania requires criminal background checks for "all current and prospective employees of public and private schools ... including, but not limited to, teachers, substitutes, janitors, cafeteria workers, independent contractors and their employees,"[99] but not for independent contractors who have no direct contact with students.[100]

Federal Regulation of Private Schools

Because private schools are not state agencies, they are not generally bound by the Constitution. Thus, for example, private schools may require their students to engage in prayer or to attend worship services. Nevertheless, several federal statutes prohibit racial and other forms of discrimination in private school **admissions** and **employment practices**. A statute known as **Section 1981** prohibits racial discrimination in the formation of contracts.[101] On this basis, in *Runyon v. McCrary*,[102] the Supreme Court ruled private schools may not deny admission on the basis of race.[103] In 2006, the Ninth Circuit ruled that the longstanding practice of a private school in Hawaii of giving preference in admissions to students of Native Hawaiian ancestry did not violate Section 1981,[104] but a subsequent Supreme Court ruling suggests the Ninth Circuit's interpretation of Section 1981 might not be correct.[105] Private schools that engage in **racial discrimination**

---

94 *See* State v. Melin, 428 N.W.2d 227 (N.D. 1988).
95 396 N.W.2d 373 (Mich. 1988).
96 105 ILL. COMP. STAT. 5/2-3.25o.
97 MD. CODE ANN., EDUC. § 2-206.1.
98 LA REV. STAT. ANN. § 17:15(A)(1).
99 24 PA. STAT. ANN. § 1-111.
100 United Union of Roofers, Waterproofers & Allied Workers, Local Union No. 37 v. N. Allegheny Sch. Dist., 167 A.3d 303 (Pa. Commw. Ct. 2017).
101 42 U.S.C. § 1994.
102 427 U.S. 160 (1976).
103 *See also* Patterson v. McLean Credit Union, 491 U.S. 164 (1989); Brown v. Dade Christian Sch., Inc., 556 F.2d 310 (5th Cir. 1977).
104 Doe v. Kamehameha Schs./Bernice Pauahi Bishop Estate, 470 F. 3d 827 (9th Cir. 2006) (*en banc*).
105 Parents Involved in Community Schools v. Seattle Sch. District No. 1, 551 U.S. 701 (2007).

in any of their policies or practices may lose their tax-exempt status even if the discrimination is based on religious belief.[106]

In addition, if a private school receives federal money, it is subject to **Title VI** of the *Civil Rights Act of 1964*, which prohibits discrimination on the basis of race by programs receiving federal funds (see Chapter 7).[107] According to the broad definition of "program" adopted by Congress, a private school with a federally-assisted lunch program would be required to comply with Title VI in all its endeavors, not just its lunch program.[108] Failure to do so could mean the loss of all federal funds. In *Goodman v. Archbishop Curley High School*,[109] a district court in Maryland refused to dismiss Title IX claims by a librarian who was terminated after reporting an inappropriate sexual relationship between a student and a teacher at an all-boys Catholic school. The librarian claimed school officials knew about the sexual abuse and wished to avoid negative publicity, and that they retaliated against her by terminating her for not reporting suspected abuse promptly.

Similarly, private schools receiving federal money are prohibited from discriminating on the basis of gender by Title IX.[110] Parochial schools are exempt from Title IX, but not Title VI, to the extent that the law conflicts with the tenets of their sponsoring faith group (see Chapter 7).[111] Private schools that participate in the National School Lunch Program must comply with non-discrimination requirements of the Department of Agriculture.[112] In some states, anti-discrimination statutes applicable to private schools may be more stringent than federal requirements.

Private schools receiving federal funds are prohibited from discriminating against "otherwise qualified" students with disabilities by the *Rehabilitation Act of 1973*.[113] They "may not, on the basis of handicap, exclude a qualified handicapped person from the program if the person can, with minor adjustments, be provided an appropriate education …" (see Chapter 8).[114] The qualification "with minor adjustments" means that unlike public schools, private schools may refuse to serve students with disabilities if they are not equipped to provide them with an appropriate education.

The *Americans with Disabilities Act* (ADA)[115] requires private schools, whether they receive federal funds or not, to make "reasonable modifications" in their practices and policies, and to provide "auxiliary aids and services" for persons with disabilities, unless such modifications would "fundamentally alter" the nature of the services offered or result in an "undue burden."[116] The law also requires schools to remove structural, architectural, and communication barriers in existing facilities and transportation barriers in existing vehicles if removal is "readily achievable" (see Chapter 8).

Schools under the control of religious organizations are exempt from the provisions of ADA dealing with discrimination against **students** with disabilities,[117] but not from provisions dealing with discrimination against **employees** with disabilities.[118] However, the Supreme Court has carved out a **ministerial exception** to these rules. In *Hosanna-Tabor Evangelical Lutheran*

---

106 Bob Jones Univ. v. United States, 461 U.S. 574 (1983).
107 42 U.S.C. § 2000(d); Guardians Ass'n v. Civil Serv. Comm'n, 463 U.S. 582 (1983); Flanagan v. President of Georgetown Coll., 417 F. Supp. 377 (D.D.C. 1976).
108 20 U.S.C. § 1687.
109 195 F. Supp. 3d 767 (D. Md. 2016).
110 20 U.S.C. § 1681.
111 34 C.F.R. § 106.12.
112 7 C.F.R. § 15.1.
113 29 U.S.C. § 794.
114 34 C.F.R. § 104.39; Hunt v. St. Peter Sch., 963 F. Supp. 843 (W.D. Mo. 1997).
115 42 U.S.C. § 12101–12213.
116 Thomas v. Davidson Acad., 846 F. Supp. 611 (M.D. Tenn. 1994).
117 28 C.F.R. § 36.104.
118 42 U.S.C. § 12112.

Church & School v. EEOC,[119] the Court barred an *ADA* lawsuit against a parochial school by an employee with disabilities on the ground that she was not a teacher but a "commissioned minister." The Court found it would violate the First Amendment to foist an unwanted minister on a faith community.

In *Fratello v. Archdiocese of New York*,[120] the Third Circuit affirmed that a dismissed parochial school principal's employment discrimination claims were barred by the ministerial exception. The court found the principal qualified as a minister because she had held herself out as a spiritual leader at the school. However, in *Biel v. St. James High School*,[121] the Ninth Circuit denied a ministerial exception to claims under the *ADA* by a fifth-grade teacher dismissed from a Catholic school after being diagnosed with breast cancer. The court found the *Hosanna-Tabor* decision

> could not be read to exempt from federal employment law all those who intermingle religious and secular duties but who do not preach their employers' beliefs, teach their faith, carry out their mission, and guide their religious organization on its way.

Most federal laws protecting students in private schools apply to employees as well. In addition, Title VII of the **Civil Rights Act of 1964** forbids employment discrimination in private schools on the basis of gender, race, color, religion, or national origin (see Chapter 10).[122] Title VII's prohibition of discrimination based on religion does not, however, apply to parochial schools. One section of the law specifically permits religious organizations to employ people of a particular faith.[123] A different section also permits hiring on the basis of religion by schools, colleges, and universities owned, supported, or controlled by a particular religious organization, or if the curriculum of the school is directed toward the "propagation" of their faith.[124] Based on these exceptions, one court permitted a Catholic school to dismiss a non-Catholic, previously divorced teacher because her marriage to a Catholic violated church doctrine.[125]

However, Title VII's prohibitions of discrimination based on race, gender, and national origin do apply to parochial schools,[126] except to their hiring of ministers.[127] In addition to Title VII, private schools may be subject to certain state civil rights and labor relations laws.[128] The *National Labor Relations Act*, however, does not apply to private schools.[129] Catholic institutions have challenged one of the mandates in the *Affordable Care Act* requiring religious hospitals, schools, and charities to include copay-free birth control in their employer-provided health insurance coverage.[130]

---

119 132 S. Ct. 694 (2012).
120 863 F.3d 190 (2d Cir. 2017).
121 911 F.3d 603 (9th Cir. 2018), *reh'g denied*, 2019 U.S. App. LEXIS 18884 (9th Cir., June 25, 2019).
122 42 U.S.C. § 2000(e).
123 42 U.S.C. § 2000e–1.
124 42 U.S.C. § 2000e–2(e)(2).
125 Little v. Wuerl, 929 F.2d 944 (3d Cir. 1991).
126 Whitney v. Greater N.Y. Corp. of Seventh-Day Adventists, 401 F. Supp. 1363 (S.D.N.Y. 1975); EEOC v. Pacific Press Publ'g Ass'n, 676 F.2d 1272 (9th Cir. 1982).
127 EEOC v. Southwestern Baptist Theological Seminary, 651 F.2d 277 (5th Cir. 1981): McClure v. Salvation Army, 460 F.2d 553 (5th Cir. 1972).
128 Dayton Christian Sch. v. Ohio Civil Rights Comm'n, 766 F.2d 932 (6th Cir. 1985), *rev'd on other grounds*, 477 U.S. 619 (1986); Catholic High Sch. Ass'n of Archdiocese v. Culvert, 573 F. Supp. 1550 (S.D.N.Y.1983), *rev'd*, 753 F.2d 1161 (2d Cir. 1985).
129 N.L.R.B. v. Catholic Bishop of Chicago, 440 U.S. 490 (1979).
130 124 STAT. 119, PUBLIC LAW 111–148.

State Regulation of Home-Based Education

In *Pierce*,[131] the Supreme Court made it clear that parents may contract with private schools for the education of their children, but it did not specifically address **home-based education**. Until the 1990s, most states either prohibited homeschooling or were silent on its legality, and homeschooling parents were routinely prosecuted. In *State v. Edgington*,[132] a New Mexico court upheld a ban on homeschooling to help ensure that children were brought into contact with people in addition to their parents. In the court's view, they should be exposed "to at least one [additional] set of attitudes, values, morals, lifestyles and intellectual abilities." Parents claiming that their religious beliefs *required* them to teach their children at home usually lost in court.[133] In a few cases, parents succeeded in convincing a court that, in some circumstances, homeschooling was a constitutional right subject to reasonable state regulation.

Most states now permit **home-based education**, with some treating it as a type of private or non-public schooling. By permitting home-based education with little or no regulation or oversight, compulsory schooling laws have lost much of their vigor in many states.[134] Prosecutions of parents for engaging in home-based education are now rare.

In New York and Pennsylvania, public school administrators are charged with enforcing some or all of the statutory restrictions on home-based education programs.[135] Pennsylvania requires district superintendents to ensure that home-schooled students receive an "appropriate education." The statute requires home-schooling parents to submit documentation to prove that their child is receiving instruction and making sustained progress in a specified set of subjects.[136] In *Combs v. Homer Center School District*,[137] homeschooling parents claimed the Act impermissibly impinged on their free exercise rights. The district court rejected the challenge, finding the Act did not place a "substantial burden" on the parents' ability to educate their children as their religion required. In some states, the burden of proof is on homeschooling parents to show they are meeting the requirements of state law, but in others the state bears the burden of showing that a home-based program is inadequate.[138]

According to the Home School Legal Defense Association, an organization that has successfully challenged compulsory schooling laws in a number of states, regulatory frameworks for home-based education fall into the following four categories:[139]

> **No Notice** [to State officials is required] in Alaska, Connecticut, Idaho, Illinois, Indiana, Iowa, Michigan, Missouri, New Jersey, Oklahoma, and Texas
> **Low Regulation** in Alabama, Arizona, California, Delaware, Georgia, Kansas, Kentucky, Mississippi, Montana, Nebraska, Nevada, Utah, Wisconsin, and Wyoming

131 268 U.S. 510 (1925).
132 663 P.2d 374 (N.M. Ct. App. 1983).
133 Burrow v. State, 669 S.W.2d 441 (Ark. 1984); *In re* S.M., 824 A.2d 593 (Vt. 2003); Svoboda v. Andrisek, 514 N.E.2d 1140 (Ohio Ct. App. 1986); North Dakota v. Anderson, 427 N.W.2d 316 (N.D. 1988); Blount v. Department of Educational and Cultural Svcs., 551 A.2d 1377 (Me. 1988); North Dakota v. Toman, 436 N.W.2d 10 (N.D. 1989); Van Inwagen v. Sanstead, 440 N.W.2d 513 (N.D. 1989); Floyd v. Smith, 820 F. Supp. 350 (E.D. Tenn. 1993); Combs et al. v. Norwin Sch. Dist. et al., 540 F.3d 231 (3d Cir. 2008).
134 *See* JAMES G. DWYER AND SHAWN F. PETERS, HOMESCHOOLING: THE HISTORY AND PHILOSOPHY OF A CONTROVERSIAL PRACTICE (2019).
135 Blackwelder v. Safnauer, 689 F. Supp. 106 (N.D.N.Y. 1988), *aff'd*, 866 F.2d 548 (2d Cir. 1989).
136 24 P.S. § 13-1327.1(e).
137 468 F. Supp. 2d 738 (W.D. Pa. 2006).
138 State v. Moorhead, 308 N.W.2d 60 (Iowa 1981); Scoma v. Chicago Bd. of Educ., 391 F. Supp. 452 (N.D. Ill. 1974); State v. Vaughn, 207 A.2d 537 (N.J. 1965).
139 *See* Homeschool Laws in Your State, HOME SCHOOL LEGAL DEFENSE ASSOCIATION, https://hslda.org/content/laws/ (last accessed April 26, 2020).

Moderate Regulation in Colorado, Florida, Hawaii, Louisiana, Maine, Maryland, Minnesota, New Hampshire, North Carolina, North Dakota, Oregon, South Carolina, South Dakota, Tennessee, Virginia, Washington, and West Virginia

High Regulation in Massachusetts, New York, Pennsylvania, Rhode Island, and Vermont.

Using statutory language compiled by the US Department of Education, we can compare the **reporting requirements, curricular requirements, teacher qualification requirements, eligibility for state assessments,** and **access to public schools** for home-based education in **Michigan** (a "No Notice" state) and **Pennsylvania** (a "High Regulation" state).[140]

Reporting Requirements

Michigan

- The annual reporting of a home school to the Michigan Department of Education is not required unless the student has special needs and is requesting special education services from the local public school or intermediate school district.
- A home school may operate as a **nonpublic school**, but under this option the home school must be in compliance with approved nonpublic school regulations.[141]

Pennsylvania

- Parents may refer to the Pennsylvania *Religious Freedom Protection Act* (RFPA), which allows for homeschooling if parents substantiate a substantial burden on the free exercise of their religious beliefs.[142]
- An affidavit and accompanying attachments, submitted to the superintendent of the student's district of residence, is required to commence a home education program. The initial year, the supervisor may begin a home education program at any time by submitting the documentation; however, the documentation is due by August 1 on subsequent years of a home education program.[143]
- A home education program is **not** considered a **nonpublic school** in Pennsylvania.[144]

Curricular Requirements

Michigan

- Home schooling satisfies the compulsory attendance law if "the child is being educated at the child's home by his or her parent or legal guardian in an organized educational program in the subject areas of reading, spelling, mathematics, science, history, civics, literature, writing, and English grammar."[145]

---

140 U.S. DEPARTMENT OF EDUCATION, State Regulation of Private and Home Schools. Online at www2.ed.gov/about/inits/ed/non-public-education/regulation-map/index.html (last accessed April 26, 2020).
141 MCL §380.1561(3)(a) and 4.
142 P.L. §1701, Act 214.
143 24 P.S. §13-1327.1 (b).
144 P.S. §13-1327.1 (b).
145 MCL §380.1561(3)(f).

Pennsylvania

- The school district of residence shall, at the request of the supervisor, lend to the home education program copies of the school district's planned courses, textbooks, and other curricular materials appropriate to the student's age and grade level.[146]
- Mandatory courses and days or hours of instruction are defined for the elementary level (grades K-6) and the secondary level (grades 7–12).[147] Graduation requirements are defined.[148]
- Portfolios must include a written evaluation of the student's educational progress. This may be provided by a Pennsylvania certified teacher with two years of teaching experience at the level at which they are evaluating, a licensed clinical or school psychologist or a non-public teacher or administrator who has at least two years of teaching experience within the last ten years at the level they are evaluating.[149] A portfolio must be submitted to the superintendent's office of the student's district of residence by the end of the school year to account for all homeschooling up to age 17.[150]

Teacher Qualifications

Michigan

- Parents or guardians that register their home schools must have **a minimum of a bachelor's degree** to be qualified to teach their children. Families whose religious beliefs preclude the teacher certification requirements are exempt.

Pennsylvania

- Home education programs are conducted, in compliance with the state's laws and regulations, by a parent, guardian, or any such person who has legal custody of a child or children.[151]
- The parent or guardian or such person having legal custody of the child or children, who must have **a high school diploma or its equivalent**, is designated as the "supervisor" and is responsible for the provision of instruction.[152]

State Assessments

Michigan

- Homeschool students may participate in state assessments. Any student may contact the resident school district and take the test administered at that school district.[153] A homeschool student's assessment scores will be reported individually to the student.

---

146 24 P.S.§13-1327.1 (f).
147 24 P.S. §13 1327.1 (c).
148 24 P.S. §13 1327.1 (d).
149 24 P.S. §13-1327.1 (e)(2).
150 24 P.S. §13-1327.1 (h), 22 Pa Code §11.13.
151 24 P.S. §13-1327.1 (b).
152 22 Pa Code § 4.72, 24 P.S. §13-1327.1 (a).
153 MCL §§380.1279g and 388.1704b.

Pennsylvania

- Homeschooled students in grades three, five, or eight must take, and report in their portfolio, the results of the statewide tests (PSSA) or another nationally normed standardized achievement test, as approved by the state department of education, in reading/language arts and mathematics.[154]

Access to Public Schools

Michigan

- Homeschool students may enroll in "nonessential elective courses," such as band, drama, art, physical education, music, computer, and Advanced Placement courses at the resident public school.[155] Permission for participation in interscholastic activities is at the discretion of the local public school district.

Pennsylvania

- Homeschooled students may be allowed to attend curricular classes in the student's district of residence's schools. These services are provided at the discretion of the district; parents must consult the district's policy on this matter.[156]
- Homeschooled students have the same access to participate in extracurricular activities (such as, but not limited to, clubs, musical ensembles, athletics and theatrical productions) of the public school district where they reside as do students who are enrolled in the school. All eligibility criteria, try-out criteria, policies, rules, and regulations are applicable.[157]

State Aid for Online Charter Schools

Online education programs have proliferated in recent years. **State virtual schools** are among the largest providers of online education programs in the country, with 429 full-time virtual schools enrolling 295,518 students, and 296 blended schools enrolling 116,716 students in 34 states in 2017.[158] As the name implies, **state virtual schools** are created and funded by states to provide online courses and services to school districts.[159]

Virtual schools may be operated by for-profit **education management organizations** (EMOs) or by non-profit **charter management organizations** (CMOs). Arizona, California, Massachusetts, Michigan, and Wisconsin are among the states that allow for-profit EMOs to manage charter schools, including **online charter schools**. Virtual schools operated by for-profit EMOs were three times as large as other virtual schools, enrolling 61.8 percent of all virtual school students in 2017. About half of all **virtual schools** are **online charter schools**, accounting for 75.7 percent of **online education** enrollment.[160]

Online charter schools typically rely on certified teachers working remotely with large numbers of students, along with parents working within the home to provide ongoing tutorial support. Thus

154 24 P.S. §13-1327.1 (e)(1).
155 MCL §388.1766b; see Snyder v. Charlotte Pub. Sch. Dist., 365 N.W.2d 151 (Mich. 1984).
156 22 Pa. Code §11.41.
157 24 P.S. §13-1327.1(f.1).
158 G. Miron, C. Shank & C. Davidson, *Full-Time Virtual and Blended Schools: Enrollment, Student Characteristics, and Performance.* Boulder, CO: National Education Policy Center, 2018. Retrieved from http://nepc.colorado.edu/publication/virtual-schools-annual-2018 (last accessed April 26, 2020).
159 Digital Learning Collaborative, "State Virtual Schools." Online at www.digitallearningcollab.com/state-virtual-schools (last accessed April 26, 2020).
160 G. Miron, C. Shank & C. Davidson, *Full-Time Virtual and Blended Schools: Enrollment, Student Characteristics, and Performance.* Boulder, CO: National Education Policy Center, 2018. Retrieved from http://nepc.colorado.edu/publication/virtual-schools-annual-2018 (last accessed April 26, 2020).

online charter schools differ from other forms of home-based education. Most are publicly-funded and to some extent publicly-regulated, though their educational benefits relative to traditional public schools are disputed.[161] According to a National Education Policy Center report,[162] **state virtual schools** performed far better based on school performance ratings (53.8 percent acceptable) than **online charter schools** (20.7 percent), while graduation rates of 50.7 percent fell far short of the national average of 83 percent.

Pennsylvania permits **online charter schools**,[163] provided they comply with the requirements of its Charter School Law.[164] In authorizing charter schools, the legislature sought to allow parents and teachers to establish and maintain schools funded by, but operated independently from, existing school districts.[165] But because local school districts must pay fees for each student enrolled in charter schools, including online schools, disputes over enrollment levels and costs have been especially common in Pennsylvania.

In *Pennsylvania School Boards Association v. Zogby*,[166] the plaintiffs unsuccessfully challenged the legality of cyber schools after a number of school districts declined to pay fees levied by an education management organization. In *Foreman v. Chester-Upland School District*,[167] the Commonwealth Court of Pennsylvania held that a school district could not limit enrollment in charter schools, finding this was a matter for the charter school boards to decide.[168] In *Richard Allen Preparatory School v. School District of Philadelphia*,[169] the court affirmed that the defendant school district lacked authority to deny funding for students beyond its caps, citing state legislation specifically prohibiting financially distressed districts from imposing caps on charter school enrollments.[170] In the following long-running case, the highest court in Pennsylvania ultimately held that a public school did not have a duty to provide funding for students below its own minimum age for kindergarten who were enrolled in kindergarten programs in a cyber charter school.

⚖️

SLIPPERY ROCK AREA SCHOOL DISTRICT v. PENNSYLVANIA CYBER CHARTER SCHOOL
Supreme Court of Pennsylvania
31 A.3d 657 (2011)

MADAME JUSTICE ORIE MELVIN—

We granted review to determine whether a public school district is obligated to fund a kindergarten program offered by a cyber charter school for a four-year-old student when the district has exercised its discretion not to offer such a program in its public schools. For the reasons that follow, we conclude that the school district is not required to fund the program. Accordingly, we reverse the order of the Commonwealth Court.

---

161 J. Anderson, 'Students of Online Schools Are Lagging.' *New York Times* (January 6, 2012), online at www.nytimes.com/2012/01/06/education/students-of-virtual-schools-are-lagging-in-proficiency.html?_r=1&emc=eta1; Saul, S. (2011, Dec. 12). 'Profits and Questions at Online Charter Schools,' *New York Times*. Available online at www.nytimes.com/2011/12/13/education/online-schools-score-better-on-wall-street-than-in-classrooms.html?_r=1&emc=eta1 (last accessed April 26, 2020).

162 G, Miron, C. Shank & C. Davidson, *Full-Time Virtual and Blended Schools: Enrollment, Student Characteristics, and Performance*. Boulder, CO: National Education Policy Center (2018). Retrieved from http://nepc.colorado.edu/publication/virtual-schools-annual-2018 (last accessed April 26, 2020).

163 24 PA. STAT. ANN. § 17-1722-A(a).

164 24 PA. STAT. ANN. § 17-1717-A; 24 PA. STAT. ANN. § 17-1725-A.

165 24 PA. STAT. ANN. § 17-1702-A.

166 802 A.2d 6 (Pa. Commw. Ct. 2002).

167 941 A.2d 108 (Pa. Commw. Ct. 2008).

168 24 Pa. Stat. Ann. § 1723-A(d).

169 123 A.3d 1101 (Pa. Commw. Ct. 2015).

170 24 Pa. Stat. Ann. § 1723-A(d).

The Charter School Law ("CSL") provides for the funding of charter schools by requiring a school district to pay the charter school for each student residing in the district who attends the charter school. If a school district fails to make the payment, the CSL authorizes the Secretary of Education to deduct the appropriate amount from the state's payments to the district.

On October 25, 2006, the Secretary notified Appellant, Slippery Rock Area School District that funds had been deducted from the district's state subsidy and were made payable to Appellee, Pennsylvania Cyber Charter School ("Cyber School"). The Secretary deducted funds because Slippery Rock failed to pay Cyber School for numerous students residing in the district who were attending Cyber School. Pursuant to section 17-1725-A(a)(6) of the CSL, the Secretary advised Slippery Rock that it had thirty days in which to contest the deductions.

By letter dated November 21, 2006, Slippery Rock notified the Department that the deduction was "inaccurate." Slippery Rock objected to the withholding of $1,716.63 for a four-year-old female student enrolled in Cyber School's kindergarten program. Slippery Rock asserted that the deduction for this student was "contrary to law" because the Public School Code of 1949 requires the district "to educate every person, residing in the district, between the ages of six and twenty-one years." ...

Slippery Rock argued that it was not obligated to pay for the education of a student who could not, because of her age, enroll in the district. Slippery Rock maintained that Cyber School must abide by the district's admission policy in order to receive payment. Since there were no disputed factual issues, the hearing officer certified the case to the Secretary for disposition.

By opinion and order dated January 8, 2008, the Secretary granted Cyber School's motion and dismissed Slippery Rock's objection. The Secretary observed that section 5–503 of the PSC gives school districts the discretion to establish and maintain kindergarten programs. The Secretary reasoned that the mere fact that school districts have the discretion to establish a kindergarten does not prohibit a cyber charter school from implementing a similar program. ...

Recognizing that the CSL grants the board of trustees of a cyber charter school the authority to set polices relating to the operation of the school, including the curriculum, the Secretary found that Cyber School can establish a kindergarten program for four-year-old students. The Secretary concluded, "Slippery Rock cannot deny payment to [Cyber School] simply because Slippery Rock does not have a four-year-old kindergarten program."

Consequently, the Secretary granted Cyber School's motion to dismiss Slippery Rock's objection. Slippery Rock filed a petition for review with the Commonwealth Court.

In a unanimous *en banc* opinion, the Commonwealth Court affirmed the order of the Secretary. ... Slippery Rock filed a petition for allowance of appeal with this Court, which we granted limited to the following issue:

Whether, pursuant to the Public School Code and the Charter School Law, a school district that has exercised its discretion not to provide a kindergarten program to four-year-old students within its district is nevertheless obligated to fund a kindergarten program provided by a cyber charter school for a four-year-old student residing within that same district? ...

The issue before this Court is one of statutory construction and is a pure question of law. Questions of law are subject to a de novo standard of review, and the scope of review is plenary.

Our inquiry is guided by the principles set forth in the *Statutory Construction Act*, including the primary maxim that the object of statutory construction is to ascertain and effectuate legislative intent. The best indication of legislative intent is the plain language of the statute. ...

The relationship between a local school district and a charter school is set forth in the PSC, which subsumes the CSL. The parties argue that there is tension between the PSC and the CSL in that a school district could be required to fund educational programs at a cyber charter school when the school district has elected not to provide similar services in the public schools. Before we can reach the ultimate issue of funding, we must first determine whether Cyber School has the authority to set the enrollment age for its kindergarten program. Cyber School claims that it is vested with such authority under the provisions in the CSL that delineate the procedures for establishing a cyber charter school. Therefore, we begin our analysis with a review of those statutory provisions. ...

A review of the statutory framework indicates that cyber charter schools have the ability to set the "grade or age levels served by the school," while the school and its board of trustees have the authority to implement and enforce the specified policy. Consequently, we find that Cyber School has the authority to set its enrollment age at four years and zero months for admission into its kindergarten program.

We recognize, however, that the General Assembly has not granted Cyber School unfettered authority under section 17-1719-A. We observe that section 17-1719-A(3) is necessitated by the very nature of charter schools. In our view, this section derives from the fact that a charter school may offer a limited curriculum, electing—under the clear language of the CSL—to serve only particular grade levels.

Stated differently, a charter school may operate exclusively as an elementary school, a middle school, a high school, or a combination thereof. Thus, the statutory provision requiring a cyber charter school to set forth in its application the "age or grades" to be served stems, at least in part, from the fact that a cyber charter school need not offer a complete education to its students. Section 17-1719-A addresses the issue by requiring the school to identify its intended scope in the charter application. As such, while the CSL grants Cyber School the authority to set the "ages or grades" to be served, this authority is limited and cannot be viewed as the "expansive" grant of power urged by Cyber School.

It is undisputed that a school district has the discretionary authority to establish a kindergarten program and the concomitant ability to set the admission age. Under section 5–503 of the PSC, "The board of school directors may establish and maintain kindergartens for children between the ages of four and six years." ... When kindergarten is provided, the board of school directors shall establish the district's minimum entry age to kindergarten. The minimum entry age to kindergarten may not be less than 4 years, no months, before the first day of the school term.

The regulation is clear and unambiguous: when kindergarten is provided, it is the province of the board of school directors to set the minimum entry age for the entire district. ... Cyber charter schools are, under the express terms of the CSL, bound by the Chapter 11 regulations. Since the regulation is clear on its face, we find the "modified reading" advanced by the Secretary and adopted by the Commonwealth Court to be in error. There is no justification for reading "board of school directors" to include the board of trustees at the cyber charter school. Such an interpretation runs counter to the express language of the regulation. In finding that it is necessary to include the board of trustees of the cyber charter school to avoid an "absurd" result, the Secretary disregarded the plain meaning of the regulation under the pretext of pursuing the spirit of the CSL. Since there is no ambiguity in the language, we cannot condone such an interpretation. ...

Thus, a plain reading of the applicable statutes and regulations reveals that the General Assembly granted both Cyber School and Slippery Rock the ability to set the enrollment age for a kindergarten program. It is not immediately apparent, however, where the authority of one of these entities ends and the other begins. Thus, it is evident that the General Assembly created a gap when it failed to articulate whether it is a cyber charter school's or a school district's policy that prevails in the event of a conflict regarding funding. When faced with such a conflict, we hold that the cyber charter school is bound by the policy of the school district in which the student resides. Our holding is guided by the recognition that the district's funding obligation is inextricably linked to its duty to provide a public education. ...

When faced with a recalcitrant school district, the CSL authorizes the Secretary to "deduct the amount, as documented by the charter school, from any and all State payments made to the district after receipt of documentation from the charter school." Thus, the CSL does not address the funding obligation of a school district in instances where the admissions policy of the cyber charter school does not mimic that of the school district.

In the absence of statutory guidance, we return to the Chapter 11 regulations of the Pennsylvania Administrative Code. Section 11.11, "Entitlement of resident children to attend public schools," provides in pertinent part, "A school aged child is entitled to attend the public schools of the child's district of residence." The regulation further specifies that a child's district of residence is the district in which the child's parents or guardian reside. Section 11.12 defines "school age" as follows:

School age is the period of a child's life from the earliest admission age to a school district's kindergarten program until graduation from high school or the end of the school term in which a student reaches the age of 21 years, whichever occurs first.

Thus, a child is entitled to enroll in the public schools of their district of residence only when the child meets the school district's minimum entrance age to kindergarten. Before such time, the district bears no obligation to educate the child and, by extension, bears no obligation to fund educational programs for the child.

In the instant case, the earliest a child may enroll in Slippery Rock's kindergarten program is the age of five. Since a four-year-old resident of the Slippery Rock School District may not attend the public schools, the district does not have to pay for the child's admission to Cyber School. Accordingly, while a cyber charter school may set its own entrance age for kindergarten, the school district does not have the commensurate obligation to pay where the cyber charter school's policy does not align with that of the school district.

To hold that Slippery Rock is obligated to fund educational opportunities for students not yet eligible to attend the district's public schools would allow those students who enroll in Cyber School to receive greater benefits than a similarly-situated student who chooses to attend the public school. Additionally, forcing Slippery Rock to pay for the education of a student who could not, because of her age, enroll in the district would override the district's admissions policy. There is nothing in the PSC or the CSL that compels or sanctions such a result. ... Thus, while Cyber School may offer educational programs to students who are too young to attend classes in the Slippery Rock School District, Cyber School is precluded from billing the district for those same students. ... The order of the Commonwealth Court is reversed.

State Aid for Private Schools

Despite the legal disputes examined earlier in this chapter, states are not always hostile to private schools. In fact, many states wish to encourage private school attendance for political or philosophical reasons—or to save money. While charter school fees are paid by school districts, private school fees are not. However, governmental aid to private schools can take many forms, and many of these forms are controversial because the vast majority of private schools are **parochial** or **sectarian**. The basic question examined in this section is whether various forms of state aid to **parochial schools** violate the **Establishment Clause** of the First Amendment.

In the early days of the United States, financial aid to private schools was quite common and was widely regarded as a practical way to foster an educated citizenry. State support of parochial schools was not seen as a violation of the US Constitution because under the First Amendment, "Congress"—that is, the federal government—"shall make no law respecting an establishment of religion." As noted earlier, it was not until 1925 that the Supreme Court applied Fourteenth Amendment restrictions to state governments.[171] In 1940, the Establishment Clause became applicable to the states.[172]

Nevertheless, by the late nineteenth century, state aid to religious schools had become controversial. Some states continued to assist parochial schools by offering free transportation or textbooks to their students, while others rejected these measures and passed laws discouraging private school attendance. A proposed federal constitutional amendment prohibiting the use of any state tax money to aid parochial schools was considered in 1876 but ultimately failed.

In many states, the most valuable and politically and legally contentious form of state aid to parochial schools was an **exemption from property tax**. By 1918, 14 state constitutions required the legislature to grant property tax exemptions and 19 others authorized them. In many of the latter group of states, exemptions were repeatedly granted and rescinded. In *Walz v. Tax Commission*,[173] the Supreme Court upheld property tax exemptions for private religious, educational, and charitable institutions in New York.

In *Everson v. Board of Education*,[174] the Supreme Court considered the constitutionality of a state-financed transportation program for students enrolled in parochial schools. In deciding the

171 Gitlow v. New York, 268 U.S. 652 (1925).
172 Cantwell v. Connecticut, 310 U.S. 296 (1940).
173 397 U.S. 664 (1970).
174 330 U.S. 1 (1947).

case, the Court for the first time employed Thomas Jefferson's metaphor that the First Amendment erected "a wall of separation between Church and State." This meant that governments could not pass laws that aided one religion, aided all religions, or preferred one religion over another. In this case, however, the Court concluded that the transportation program did not constitute "aid" to parochial schools; it was "a general program to help parents get their children, regardless of their religion, safely and expeditiously to and from accredited schools." The Court noted that the transportation program was on the "verge" of what the Establishment Clause would allow.

In *McCollum v. Board of Education*,[175] the Court found a program enabling an interfaith group to offer religious instruction to students on public school premises unconstitutional. The classes were taught by members of the clergy at no expense to the schools, and were attended for 30–45 minutes per week by students whose parents had signed consent forms. Students who did not attend were required to pursue their studies elsewhere in the building. Relying on the "no aid" principle in its *Everson* decision the previous year, the Court found the program provided "sectarian groups an invaluable aid."

In *Zorach v. Clauson*,[176] the Court found no constitutional violation in a program that allowed public school students to receive religious instruction in private centers during school hours. Attendance was taken on behalf of the public school in these centers, and students attended with parental consent. To reach its conclusion, the Court abandoned the strict separation doctrine used in *Everson* and *McCollum*. The First Amendment, said the Court, did not require "that in every and all respects there shall be a separation of Church and State." What was prohibited was "concert, or union or dependency one on the other." The **release-time** arrangement was merely an accommodation of the public school schedule to a program of outside religious instruction.

In *Board of Education v. Allen*,[177] the Court upheld a program of lending secular textbooks to students enrolled in parochial schools. In this case, the Court invoked yet another standard for analyzing challenges to programs of state aid to parochial schools. It found the program had **neither the purpose nor the primary effect** of aiding religion.

In *Lemon v. Kurtzman*,[178] a case involving state subsidies for teachers employed in parochial schools, the Court employed a framework for analyzing alleged violations of the Establishment Clause that has since become the standard. Combining elements of the doctrines used in *Zorach* and *Allen*, the three-part **Lemon test** holds that a government policy or practice violates the Establishment Clause if (a) its **purpose** is to endorse or disapprove of religion; (b) its **primary effect** is to aid or inhibit religion; or (c) it creates **excessive entanglement** between Church and State. In the next chapter, we review the use of the *Lemon* test as applied to the programs and practices of public schools.

The application of the *Lemon* test to programs of government aid to **parochial schools** has resulted in a number of inconsistent decisions. The Supreme Court has found the following forms of aid to parochial schools to be **permissible**:

- Supply of state-prepared standardized tests and scoring services;[179]
- Provision of speech, hearing, and psychological services whether offered at the parochial school or a neutral place;[180]

---

175 333 U.S. 203 (1948).
176 343 U.S. 306 (1952).
177 392 U.S. 236 (1968).
178 403 U.S. 602 (1971).
179 Wolman v. Walter, 433 U.S. 229 (1977).
180 Wolman v. Walter, 433 U.S. 229 (1977).

- Provision of diagnostic speech, hearing, and psychological services in parochial schools;[181]
- Cash reimbursement for costs associated with state-mandated testing and reporting requirements in connection with tests prepared by the state, but scored by parochial school personnel;[182]
- State income tax deductions, available to both public and private school parents for expenses incurred for tuition, textbooks, and transportation to school;[183]
- Federal grants for care and prevention services regarding teenage pregnancy provided by religious and nonreligious organizations.[184]

However, the Supreme Court has found the following forms of aid to parochial schools to be **impermissible**:

- Subsidizing teacher salaries;[185]
- Subsidizing secular courses;[186]
- Loan of instructional materials and equipment other than textbooks such as maps and audiovisual equipment;[187]
- Subsidizing transportation for field trips;[188]
- Grants for maintenance of school facilities;[189]
- Per-student funding to maintain enrollment and other records;[190]
- Provision of remedial and accelerated instructional services, guidance, counseling, testing, and speech and hearing services on the premises of a parochial school;[191]
- Provision of remedial and enrichment courses on parochial school grounds during the school day;[192]
- Provision of community education programs on parochial school grounds during non-school hours;[193]
- Partial tuition credits for parents with children in private schools.[194]

In *Aguilar v. Felton*,[195] the Supreme Court considered whether it was permissible under the Establishment Clause for a public school district to provide Title I services in parochial schools. The district used federal funds to send teachers to religious schools to provide federally mandated, supplementary remedial education to qualifying students. Steps were taken to ensure that the publicly paid teachers would not be involved in religious activities and that the classrooms in which they worked would be free of religious adornment. The Court, relying primarily on the entanglement prong of the Establishment Clause, found the program impermissible nonetheless. Twelve years later, in the wake of large increases in public funds to transport parochial school students off

---

181 Wolman v. Walter, 433 U.S. 229 (1977).
182 Committee for Pub. Educ. & Religious Liberty v. Regan, 444 U.S. 646 (1980).
183 Mueller v. Allen, 463 U.S. 388 (1983).
184 Bowen v. Kendrick, 487 U.S. 589 (1988).
185 Lemon v. Kurtzman, 403 U.S. 602 (1971).
186 Lemon v. Kurtzman, 403 U.S. 602 (1971).
187 Wolman v. Walter, 433 U.S. 229 (1977).
188 Grand Rapids Sch. Dist. v. Ball, 473 U.S. 373 (1985).
189 Committee for Pub. Educ. & Religious Liberty v. Nyquist, 413 U.S. 756 (1973).
190 Wolman v. Walter, 433 U.S. 229 (1977).
191 Meek v. Pittenger, 421 U.S. 349 (1975).
192 Grand Rapids Sch. Dist. v. Ball, 473 U.S. 373 (1985).
193 Grand Rapids Sch. Dist. v. Ball, 473 U.S. 373 (1985).
194 Committee for Pub. Educ. & Religious Liberty v. Nyquist, 413 U.S. 756 (1973).
195 473 U.S. 402 (1985).

campus to receive Title I services and significant public and government sentiment against the *Aguilar* decision, the Supreme Court reached the opposite conclusion in *Agostini v. Felton*.[196]

While it was unusual at the time for the Supreme Court to overrule a recent decision, *Agostini* is consistent with the Court's approach to most Establishment Clause cases. The **neutrality doctrine** has refined but not replaced the ***Lemon* test**. Under this doctrine, it is permissible for a religious organization such as a parochial school to receive assistance from a governmental program as long as the program is religiously neutral. This means the assistance must be available to all on the basis of non-religious criteria. Most often this requirement will be satisfied if individuals receive benefits that they may, at their discretion, transfer to either religious or secular organizations. Thus, in the ensuing decades, the Court has:

- Authorized payment of public funds to a visually impaired person for vocational services even when the recipient used the funds to pay his tuition at a Christian college to prepare himself for a career as a pastor, missionary, or youth director;[197]
- Upheld a system of federal grants for public and nonpublic organizations, including religious organizations, for counseling services and research concerning premarital adolescent sexual relations and pregnancy;[198]
- Held that although a school district may limit the use of its property to school activities, once a district makes its facilities available for after-hour use for social, civic, and recreational purposes, it may not deny the use of those facilities to a religious group solely because of the religious message of the group;[199]
- Concluded that, under the *Individuals with Disabilities Education Act*, providing a publicly funded sign-language interpreter to a deaf student attending a religious school did not violate the Establishment Clause;[200] and
- Prohibited a state from redrawing school district boundaries to create a religiously homogeneous school district.[201]

In 2000, the **neutrality doctrine** was accepted by the four Supreme Court justices who wrote the plurality opinion in *Mitchell v. Helms*.[202] The Court upheld a state aid program that purchased and then loaned computers, books, and other educational materials and teaching aids to public and private schools, including parochial schools, on the ground that aid provided to a broad range of groups or persons without regard to religion is **permissible**. "If the religious, irreligious, and areligious are all alike eligible for governmental aid, no one would conclude that any indoctrination that any particular recipient conducts has been done at the behest of the government," wrote the Court.

In *Zorach v. Clauson*,[203] the Supreme Court declared that the Establishment Clause prohibited "concert, or union or dependency" of religious organizations and the State, but such partnerships became commonplace with the establishment of the White House Office of Faith-Based and Neighborhood Partnerships under President George W. Bush in 2001. This executive office allows faith-based organizations to apply for federal funding for social services, including educational programs and services. In *Hein v. Freedom from Religion Foundation*,[204] the constitutionality

---

196 521 U.S. 203 (1997).
197 Witters v. Wash. Dep't of Servs. for the Blind, 474 U.S. 481 (1986).
198 Bowen v. Kendrick, 487 U.S. 589 (1988).
199 Lamb's Chapel v. Center Moriches Union Free Sch. Dist., 508 U.S. 384 (1993).
200 Zobrest v. Catalina Foothills Sch. Dist., 509 U.S. 1 (1993).
201 Bd. of Educ. of Kiryas Joel Village Sch. Dist. v. Grumet, 512 U.S. 687 (1994).
202 530 U.S. 793 (2000).
203 343 U.S. 306 (1952).
204 551 U.S. 587 (2007).

of this program was challenged. The Supreme Court held that taxpayers did not have standing to challenge the constitutionality of funding decisions made by the executive branch.

Voucher Programs

Voucher programs have proliferated in recent years, particularly in the wake of the appointment of Betsy DeVos as Secretary of Education in 2017. But the idea of giving parents government-funded vouchers to pay tuition at schools of their own choosing is not new.[205] In 1955, influential free-market economist Milton Friedman argued in favor of using vouchers to pay for tuition at the private or public school of a parent's choice, claiming competition would lead to better schools and better educational outcomes for all.[206]

In *Zelman v. Simmons-Harris*,[207] the Supreme Court applied the **neutrality doctrine** and held that a voucher program in Cleveland did not violate the Establishment Clause, even though parents were permitted to use the vouchers at parochial schools. Government checks were distributed to parents in Cleveland according to financial need, with families with incomes below 200 percent of the poverty line eligible to receive 90 percent of private school tuition. Parents choosing private schools simply endorsed their checks over to the school. Any private school, including parochial schools, could accept program students so long as they were located within the district boundaries, met statewide standards, and agreed not to discriminate on the basis of race, religion, or ethnic background. Of the 56 private schools participating in the voucher program, 46 were parochial schools. "We believe that the program challenged here is a program of true private choice, consistent with *Mueller*, *Witters*, and *Zobrest*, and thus constitutional," wrote the Court:

> As was true in those cases, the Ohio program is neutral in all respects toward religion. It is part of a general and multifaceted undertaking by the State of Ohio to provide educational opportunities to the children of a failed school district. It confers educational assistance directly to a broad class of individuals defined without reference to religion, *i.e.*, any parent of a school-age child who resides in gram permits the participation of all schools within the district, religious or nonreligious. Adjacent public schools also may participate and have a financial incentive to do so. Program benefits are available to participating families on neutral terms, with no reference to religion. The only preference stated anywhere in the program is a preference for low-income families, who receive greater assistance and are given priority for admission at participating schools …

> In sum, the Ohio program is entirely neutral with respect to religion. It provides benefits directly to a wide spectrum of individuals, defined only by financial need and residence in a particular school district. It permits such individuals to exercise genuine choice among options public and private, secular and religious. The program is therefore a program of true private choice. In keeping with an unbroken line of decisions rejecting challenges to similar programs, we hold that the program does not offend the Establishment Clause.

In the wake of the *Zelman* decision, however, some state courts ruled that their state constitutions prohibited vouchers as governmental aid to parochial schools. In *Bush v. Holmes*,[208] the Florida Supreme Court ruled that a voucher program violated a state constitutional requirement

---

205   *See* Sigal R. Ben-Porath and Michael C. Johanek, Making Up Our Mind: What School Choice Is Really About (2019).

206   Milton Friedman, *The Role of Government in Education, in* Economics And The Public Interest, 123–44 (Robert A. Solo, ed. 1955).

207   536 U.S. 639 (2002).

208   919 So. 2d 392 (Fla. 2006).

that education be provided through a "uniform" system of "public schools." In *Cain v. Horne*,[209] the Arizona Supreme Court ruled that a voucher program permitting students with disabilities to attend private schools violated its state constitution. "The voucher programs appear to be a well-intentioned effort to assist two distinct student populations with special needs. But we are bound by our constitution," wrote the court. "There may well be ways of providing aid to these student populations without violating the constitution. But [it] does not permit appropriations of public money to private and sectarian schools ..."

"Neo-Vouchers"

Voucher programs have moved beyond government checks or certificates to more elaborate mechanisms described by some critics as "neo-vouchers". These include **personal use education tax credit** programs, **donation tax credit** programs, and **education savings accounts (ESAs)**.

Personal use tax credit programs provide tax credits to individuals for costs incurred in the education of their children, including tuition fees at private and parochial schools. Donation tax credit programs provide tax credits to individuals or corporations who donate to non-profit organizations offering scholarships to students in private and parochial schools. ESAs are perhaps the most complex of neo-voucher mechanisms. They allow parents who withdraw their children from public schools to receive a deposit of public funds into special savings accounts from which funds can be disbursed for private school tuition, fees, and incidental expenses.

According to a 2019 National Education Policy Center report,[210]

> Neo-vouchers currently exist in 19 states, while traditional vouchers are available in at least 15 states plus the District of Columbia. Five states have education savings accounts like Arizona's that cover not only tuition but other educational expenses such as those related to home schooling; five provide individual tax credits for private school expenses; and four offer individual tax deductions.

In 2016, in *Schwartz v. Lopez*,[211] the Nevada Supreme Court found the State improperly directed funds appropriated for K-12 public education to ESAs, in violation of state constitutional mandates. Two years later, in *Espinoza v. Montana Department of Revenue*,[212] the Montana Supreme Court found the state's dollar-for-dollar tax credit program for donations of up to $150 to organizations offering tuition scholarships for students in private schools violated the state constitution. The Supreme Court granted **certiorari** in the case in June, 2019 while allowing the Cato Institute and other conservative groups to file **amicus curiae** briefs.[213] Its decision in *Espinoza* will be featured in the next edition of this book.

Summary

In all 50 states, custodial parents and others having care and control of children are required to enroll them in public schools (including charter schools), or a state-approved alternative (including an approved private or parochial school, virtual school, or home-based education program). Compulsory schooling laws are justified by the independent welfare and developmental interests

209 202 P.3d 1178 (Ariz. 2009) (*en banc*).
210 National Education Policy Center (2019, Feb. 21). "Has the Tide Turned Against Vouchers?" Online at https://nepc. colorado.edu/publication/newsletter-vouchers-022119 (last accessed April 26, 2020).
211 382 P.3d 886 (Nev. 2016).
212 435 P.3d 603 (Mont. 2018).
213 Espinoza v. Mont. Dep't of Revenue, 2019 U.S. LEXIS 4405 (U.S., June 28, 2019).

of children and by the need for an educated citizenry to sustain republican traditions and institutions. Parents have a constitutional right to direct the upbringing of their children, but there is no constitutional right to be entirely free of governmental regulation in the interests of children.

The Constitution requires that children from Amish families be excused from attending school after the eighth grade, but this exemption from compulsory schooling laws has very limited application to children in other faith communities. Some states excuse legally employed children, emancipated minors, and children who live far from any brick-and-mortar schools. Although children with disabilities were sometimes categorically exempted from compulsory schooling laws in the past, federal and state laws now require that all children with disabilities receive a free, appropriate public education.

State laws include requirements for enrollment in public schools. Minimum and maximum age requirements, vaccination requirements, and residency requirements have all survived constitutional challenge. However, many states now have open enrollment policies permitting parents to choose any school they wish within and sometimes beyond their local district.

Although parents have a constitutional right to choose public or private schooling for their children, the State retains the power to regulate private schools and home-based education to ensure the goals of compulsory schooling laws are met. The State may require the teaching of particular subjects or topics but cannot forbid the teaching of additional topics. States may also regulate the minimum duration of the private school day and year, require reporting of enrollment and achievement data, impose standardized testing requirements, and set qualifications for teachers in private schools and home-based education programs. The State may not impose regulations designed to make private schools indistinguishable from public schools. Federal law prohibits racial discrimination in private school admissions and employment practices.

All states now permit home-based education. A handful of states impose fairly extensive requirements designed to ensure that children in home-based education programs receive an adequate education. Elsewhere, the regulation of home-based education tends to be lax. Many states now permit publicly-funded charter schools, including online charter schools, though there is considerable variation in terms of how virtual schools are administered.

Many forms of government aid to parochial schools have been found to violate the Establishment Clause. However, transportation programs, the lending of secular textbooks, assistance with the costs of state-mandated testing, the provision of legally mandated services to students with disabilities, tax breaks for parents, and property tax exemptions for parochial schools themselves are constitutionally permissible. Some voucher programs are permissible under the Establishment Clause, even if they include parochial schools. However, some state constitutions prohibit voucher programs which divert funds appropriated for public education to parents or to parochial schools.

3 Regulating the Public School Curriculum

Public schooling is an important mechanism for shaping the cultural, political, ideological, and religious landscape of choice for future adults. To control the public school curriculum is to decide what millions of American children will come to know, value, and believe. Hence debate over public schooling in general and the public school curriculum in particular has long been acrimonious.[1] In the previous chapter, we focused on **compulsory schooling laws** and the regulation of **private** and **parochial schools**, **virtual schools**, and **home-based education**. In this chapter, we examine the authority of the federal government, state governments, and local school boards to regulate what is taught in **public schools**.[2]

The independent welfare and developmental interests of children safeguarded by the State as *parens patriae* have long been held to include access to public knowledge, diverse formative influences, and opportunities beyond what parents are willing or able to provide.[3] Because parents have a constitutional right to direct the education or upbringing of their children, the courts have often been called upon to balance the competing interests of children, their parents, and the State.[4] Based on the Constitution and a number of federal and state statutes, parents, students, and school personnel have challenged **prayers** and other **religious observances** in public schools, the teaching of **evolution and creationism**, the recitation of the **Pledge of Allegiance**, **sex education**, **standardized testing**, and a wide array of policies and programs. In this chapter, we explore these and other curricular disputes.

Authority to Regulate the Public School Curriculum

Federal Authority

Under the **Tenth Amendment** (see Chapter 1), education is an area of jurisdiction reserved to the states. Thus states have historically been responsible for shaping the public school curriculum. However, the federal government has constrained state and local authority through civil rights statutes (including the *Individuals with Disabilities Education Act*) and through funding programs with programmatic requirements attached (such as the *Every Student Succeeds Act*). As we shall see in this chapter, the **judicialization of education**,[5] particularly though constitutional

1 See Justin Driver, The Schoolhouse Gate: Public Education, The Supreme Court, And The Battle For The American Mind (2018); See also Jonathan Zimmerman and Emily Robertson, The Case For Contention: Teaching Controversial Issues In American Schools (2017).
2 See Tyll van Geel, Authority To Control The School Program (1976).
3 See J.C. Blokhuis, *Whose Custody Is It, Anyway? Homeschooling from a Parens Patriae Perspective*, 8(2) Theory and Research in Education 199–222 (2010); see also J.C. Blokhuis, *Student Rights and the Special Characteristics of the School Environment in American Jurisprudence*, 49(1) Journal of Philosophy of Education 65–85 (2015).
4 See Jeffrey Shulman, The Constitutional Parent: Rights, Responsibilities, And The Enfranchisement Of The Child (2014).
5 See J.C. Blokhuis and R. Curren, *Judicialization in Education*, in Oxford Research Encyclopedia of Education [forthcoming 2021].

challenges and Section 1983 suits filed in the federal courts, has yielded dramatic changes to the curriculum of public schools over the past half century.

State Authority

As we saw in the previous chapter, the primary mechanisms of curricular control include state laws and regulations requiring schools to teach specified courses and topics, to classify students by age and grade, and to set minimum course and credit requirements for graduation.

Extra-Legal Influences

Beyond formal governance structures and the courts, there are many extra-legal influences on the public school curriculum (including textbook publishers, teacher unions and professional associations, parental rights organizations, education management organizations, and an array of special interest groups). Teachers and school officials tend to exercise considerable control over their own classrooms and schools. This control may be viewed as delegated either explicitly by the school board or implicitly (by the failure of state and local authorities to intervene). The following programs have affected the public school curriculum in many states.

Textbook Adoption Programs

Departments of Education in Alabama, California, Florida, Idaho, Mississippi, New Mexico, North Carolina, Oklahoma, Oregon, South Carolina, Tennessee, Texas, Utah, Virginia, and West Virginia have the power to approve textbooks and materials for use in public schools. The market share of the largest states in this group can result in textbooks aligned with criteria specific to those states. Other states are "open territory," meaning they allow individual schools or districts to adopt textbooks and supplementary materials (including study guides, websites, and teacher editions).[6]

Standardized Testing Programs

In recent years, all states have implemented accountability programs based on standardized testing. These programs have significantly increased the degree of state control over both the allocation of curricular time and the content of courses. Though not required to do so by law, many districts base their curricular offerings on the content of standardized tests. In states with minimum competency testing programs, teachers typically devote significant instructional time "teaching to the test."

Sex Education Programs

State laws requiring or authorizing local school districts to offer a particular course usually leave it to local school boards to develop their own syllabi and to choose their own instructional methods. **Sex education** is a major exception. A number of states mandate sex education while specifying topics or instructional approaches that may and may not be used. Some states require that **abstinence** be taught as the best way to avoid pregnancy and sexually transmitted diseases.[7] For

---

6 See *Current Textbook Adoption Schedule* (July, 2019), PUBLISHERS.ORG. Online at https://publishers.org/our-markets/prek-12-learning/instructional-materials-adoption (last accessed October 14, 2019).

7 LA. REV. STAT. ANN. 17:281; MISS. CODE ANN. § 37–13–171; N.J. STAT. § 18A:35–4.20; R.I. GEN. LAWS § 16–22–18; MO. REV. STAT. § 170.015.

example, Arizona permits instruction on acquired immune deficiency syndrome (AIDS), allowing school districts to develop their own course of study for each grade while at the same time requiring that instruction "be appropriate to the grade level in which it is offered, be medically accurate, promote abstinence, discourage drug abuse, and dispel myths regarding transmission of the human immunodeficiency virus."[8] Alabama requires that any sex education program in public schools

> shall, as a minimum, include and emphasize the following:
>
> (1) Abstinence from sexual intercourse is the only completely effective protection against unwanted pregnancy, sexually transmitted diseases, and acquired immune deficiency syndrome (AIDS) when transmitted sexually.
> (2) Abstinence from sexual intercourse outside of lawful marriage is the expected social standard for unmarried school-age persons.[9]

Moreover, despite widespread acceptance of marriage and other LGBTQ rights by society at large and by the Supreme Court,[10] South Carolina prohibits courses discussing "alternate sexual lifestyles from heterosexual relationships, including, but not limited to, homosexual relationships except in the context of instruction concerning sexually transmitted diseases."[11] Louisiana stipulates that "No sex education course offered in the public schools of the state shall utilize any sexually explicit materials depicting male or female homosexual activity."[12] Missouri prohibits providers of abortion services from offering, sponsoring, or furnishing "any course materials or instruction relating to human sexuality or sexually transmitted diseases."[13] Idaho requires both parental and community involvement in the development of sex education programs.[14] Most states allow parents to opt their children out of sex education classes.[15]

In 2019, the following provisions in the Texas Education Code came into effect:[16]

> Any course materials and instruction relating to human sexuality, sexually transmitted diseases, or human immunodeficiency virus or acquired immune deficiency syndrome shall be selected by the board of trustees with the advice of the local school health advisory council and must:
>
> (1) present abstinence from sexual activity as the preferred choice of behavior in relationship to all sexual activity for unmarried persons of school age;
> (2) devote more attention to abstinence from sexual activity than to any other behavior;
> (3) emphasize that abstinence from sexual activity, if used consistently and correctly, is the only method that is 100 percent effective in preventing pregnancy, sexually transmitted diseases, infection with human immunodeficiency virus or acquired immune deficiency syndrome, and the emotional trauma associated with adolescent sexual activity;

8   ARIZ. REV. STAT. § 15–716.
9   CODE OF ALA. § 16–40A-2.
10 Obergefell v. Hodges, 135 S. Ct. 2584 (2015).
11 S.C. CODE ANN. § 59–32–30.
12 LA. REV. STAT § 17:281.
13 MO. REV. STAT § 170.015.
14 IDAHO CODE § 33–1610.
15 See, e.g., CODE OF ALA. § 16–40A-2; TEX. EDUC. CODE § 28.004.
16 TEX. EDUC. CODE § 28.004.

(4) direct adolescents to a standard of behavior in which abstinence from sexual activity before marriage is the most effective way to prevent pregnancy, sexually transmitted diseases, and infection with human immunodeficiency virus or acquired immune deficiency syndrome; and

(5) teach contraception and condom use in terms of human use reality rates instead of theoretical laboratory rates, if instruction on contraception and condoms is included in curriculum content.

English Language Instruction Programs

Arizona requires that all children in its public schools "be taught English by being taught in English." The state limits sheltered English immersion courses for English language learners to "a temporary transition period not normally intended to exceed one year."[17]

Art, Music, and Physical Education Programs

Most people now take it for granted that public schools offer music, art, and physical education classes, but this was not always so. In a mostly older body of case law, plaintiffs argued that local school boards lacked the authority to implement courses and programs beyond reading, writing, and arithmetic. School boards prevailed in almost all these cases.[18]

Commercial Programs

In *Dawson v. East Side Union High School District*,[19] a California appellate court upheld the authority of a local school board to contract with a **private firm** offering video equipment in exchange for ten minutes of current events programming featuring **commercial messages**.[20] The court found that *Channel One News* served valid educational purposes and noted that individual students could opt out if they wished. The contract would have been approved even in the absence of an opt-out provision because the statutory authority of local school boards to offer or require courses of their own choosing was well-settled.[21]

In *Wallace v. Knox County Board of Education*,[22] a parent unsuccessfully challenged the board's use of *Channel One News* on constitutional grounds. The Sixth Circuit held there was no Establishment Clause violation because no religion was involved; there was no Equal Protection violation because students could opt out of viewing the program. *Channel One News* was discontinued in 2018.[23]

Programs by Popular Demand

With claims supported by state statutes, parents may compel schools to offer particular courses or programs. Some states require school districts to maintain kindergartens or to provide foreign language instruction when petitioned by a specified number of parents or students. In Massachusetts,

17 ARIZ. REV. STAT. § 15–752.
18 *See, e.g.*, State *ex rel.* Andrews v. Webber, 8 N.E. 708 (Ind. 1886); Alexander v. Phillips, 254 P. 1056 (Ariz. 1927).
19 Dawson v. E. Side Union High Sch. Dist., 28 Cal. App. 4th 998 (1994).
20 *See* J.C. Blokhuis, *Channel One: When Private Interests and the Public Interest Collide*, 45(2) AMERICAN EDUCATIONAL RESEARCH JOURNAL 343–363 (2008); *see also* H. Brighouse, *Channel One, the anti-commercial principle, and the discontinuous ethos*, 9 EDUCATIONAL POLICY 528–549 (2005).
21 *See* New Jersey Educ. Ass'n v. Trenton Bd. of Educ., 91 N.J.A.R.ld (EDU) 481 (1992); State v. Whittle Communications, 402 S.E.2d 556 (N.C. 1991); *rehearing denied*, 404 S.E.2d 878 (N.C. 1991).
22 1993 U.S. App. LEXIS 20477 (6th Cir. Aug. 10, 1993) [*unpublished*].
23 National Education Policy Center, *The Demise of Channel One News* (August 2, 2018); online at https://nepc.colorado.edu/publication/newsletter-channel-one-080218 (last accessed October 29, 2019).

30 students or five percent of students enrolled in a high school, whichever is less, may demand that a course be taught.[24]

Constitutional Objections to Religious Observances in Public Schools

Although some parents may still oppose the teaching of art, music, or physical education in public schools, most seem content either to accept the public school curriculum or to opt for a **private school** or **home-based education** program. There have been very few constitutional challenges to the teaching of core subjects in public schools in the last century. This does not mean that states may implement any programs or courses they wish without fear of parental complaint. When public schools address value-laden issues on which there is public disagreement, some parents are sure to object.[25] If an objection can be framed in constitutional terms, litigation often results.

Since the Civil Rights Era, the most common constitutional objections to public school programs have involved claims that the **"wall of separation"** between church and state has been breached. Yet until the 1960s, there did not seem to be much of a wall at all. Bible readings, organized prayers, and a variety of other religious observances and ceremonies were common features of public school programs in every state. Many Catholics found the Protestant ethos in public schools offensive, prompting the establishment of a parallel system of private Catholic schools.[26]

In 1962, in *Engel v. Vitale*,[27] the Supreme Court held that the daily recital of a non-denominational prayer composed by the New York Board of Regents violated the Establishment Clause. The following year, the Court found Bible readings in public schools violated the Establishment clause in the following watershed case.

⚖️

SCHOOL DISTRICT OF ABINGTON TOWNSHIP v. SCHEMPP
Supreme Court of the United States
374 U.S. 203 (1963)

MR. JUSTICE CLARK delivered the opinion of the Court.

Once again we are called upon to consider the scope of the provision of the First Amendment to the United States Constitution which declares that "Congress shall make no law respecting an establishment of religion, or prohibiting the free exercise thereof ..." These companion cases present the issues in the context of state action requiring that schools begin each day with readings from the Bible. While raising the basic questions under slightly different factual situations, the cases permit joint treatment. In light of the history of the First Amendment and of our cases interpreting and applying its

requirements, we hold that the practices at issue and the laws requiring them are unconstitutional under the Establishment Clause, as applied to the States through the Fourteenth Amendment. ...

No. 142

The Commonwealth of Pennsylvania by law requires that

At least ten verses from the Holy Bible shall be read, without comment, at the opening of each public school on each school day. Any child shall be excused from such Bible reading, or attending

---

24 MASS. ANN. LAWS Ch. 71, § 13.
25 See M. Hand, *What should we teach as controversial? A defense of the epistemic criterion*, 58(2) EDUCATIONAL THEORY 213–228 (2008).
26 *See* SIGAL R. BEN-PORATH AND MICHAEL C. JOHANEK, MAKING UP OUR MIND: WHAT SCHOOL CHOICE IS REALLY ABOUT (2019).
27 370 U.S. 421 (1962).

such Bible reading, upon the written request of his parent or guardian.

The Schempp family, husband and wife and two of their three children, brought suit to enjoin enforcement of the statute, contending that their rights under the Fourteenth Amendment to the Constitution of the United States are, have been, and will continue to be violated unless this statute be declared unconstitutional as violative of these provisions of the First Amendment. They sought to enjoin the appellant school district, wherein the Schempp children attend school, and its officers and the Superintendent of Public Instruction of the Commonwealth from continuing to conduct such readings and recitation of the Lord's Prayer in the public schools of the district pursuant to the statute. A three-judge statutory District Court for the Eastern District of Pennsylvania held that the statute is violative of the Establishment Clause of the First Amendment as applied to the States by the Due Process Clause of the Fourteenth Amendment and directed that appropriate injunctive relief issue. ...

The appellees Edward Lewis Schempp, his wife Sidney, and their children, Roger and Donna, are of the Unitarian faith and are members of the Unitarian Church in Germantown, Philadelphia, Pennsylvania, where they ... regularly attend religious services ... The ... children attend the Abington Senior High School, which is a public school operated by appellant district.

On each school day at the Abington Senior High School between 8:15 and 8:30 a.m., while the pupils are attending their home rooms or advisory sections, opening exercises are conducted pursuant to the statute. The exercises are broadcast into each room in the school building through an intercommunications system and are conducted under the supervision of a teacher by students attending the school's radio and television workshop. Selected students from this course gather each morning in their school's workshop studio for the exercises, which include readings by one of the students of 10 verses of the Holy Bible, broadcast to each room in the building. This is followed by the recitation of the Lord's Prayer, likewise over the intercommunications system, but also by the students in the various classrooms, who are asked to stand and join in repeating the prayer in unison. The exercises are closed with the flag salute and such pertinent announcements as are of interest to the students. Participation in the opening exercises,

as directed by the statute, is voluntary. The student reading the verses from the Bible may select the passages and read from any version he chooses, although the only copies furnished by the school are the King James Version, copies of which were circulated to each teacher by the school district. During the period in which the exercises have been conducted the King James, the Douay and the Revised Standard versions of the Bible have been used, as well as the Jewish Holy Scriptures. There are no prefatory statements, no questions asked or solicited, no comments or explanations made and no interpretations given at or during the exercises. The students and parents are advised that the student may absent himself [sic] from the classroom or, should he [sic] elect to remain, not participate in the exercises.

At the first trial Edward Schempp and the children testified as to specific religious doctrines purveyed by a literal reading of the Bible "which were contrary to the religious beliefs which they held and to their familial teaching." The children testified that all of the doctrines to which they referred were read to them at various times as part of the exercises. Edward Schempp testified at the second trial that he had considered having Roger and Donna excused from attendance at the exercises but decided against it for several reasons, including his belief that the children's relationships with their teachers and classmates would be adversely affected ...

The trial court, in striking down the practices and the statute requiring them, made specific findings of fact that the children's attendance at Abington Senior High School is compulsory and that the practice of reading 10 verses from the Bible is also compelled by law. ...

III.

Almost a hundred years ago in *Minor v. Board of Education of Cincinnati*,[28] Judge Alphonso Taft, father of the revered Chief Justice, in an unpublished opinion stated the ideal of our people as to religious freedom as one of absolute equality before the law, of all religious opinions and sects ... The government is neutral, and, while protecting all, it prefers none, and it disparages none. Before examining this "neutral" position in which the Establishment and Free Exercise Clauses of the First Amendment place our Government it is well that we discuss the reach of the Amendment under the cases of this Court.

---

28 23 Ohio St. 211 (1872).

First, this Court has decisively settled that the First Amendment's mandate that "Congress shall make no law respecting an establishment of religion, or prohibiting the free exercise thereof" has been made wholly applicable to the States by the Fourteenth Amendment ... Second, this Court has rejected unequivocally the contention that the Establishment Clause forbids only governmental preference of one religion over another. Almost 20 years ago in *Everson*,[29] the Court said that "[n]either a state nor the Federal Government can set up a church. Neither can pass laws which aid one religion, aid all religions, or prefer one religion over another." ...

The same conclusion has been firmly maintained ever since that time ... [I]n *Everson*, this Court ... held that the Amendment

requires the state to be neutral in its relations with groups of religious believers and non-believers; it does not require the state to be their adversary. State power is no more to be used so as to handicap religions than it is to favor them. ...

Finally, in *Engel v. Vitale*,[30] only last year, these principles were so universally recognized that the Court, without the citation of a single case and over the sole dissent of Mr. Justice Stewart, reaffirmed them. The Court found the 22-word prayer used in "New York's program of daily classroom invocation of God's blessings as prescribed in the Regent's prayer ... [to be] a religious activity." It held that "it is no part of the business of government to compose official prayers for any group of the American people to recite as a part of a religious program carried on by government." In discussing the reach of the Establishment and Free Exercise Clauses of the First Amendment the Court said:

Although these two clauses may in certain instances overlap, they forbid two quite different kinds of governmental encroachment upon religious freedom. The Establishment Clause, unlike the Free Exercise Clause, does not depend upon any showing of direct governmental compulsion and is violated by the enactment of laws which establish an official religion whether those laws operate directly to coerce non-observing individuals or not. This is not to say, of course, that laws officially prescribing a particular form of religious worship do not involve coercion

of such individuals. When the power, prestige and financial support of government is placed behind a particular religious belief, the indirect coercive pressure upon religious minorities to conform to the prevailing officially approved religion is plain.

And in further elaboration the Court found that the "first and most immediate purpose [of the Establishment Clause] rested on the belief that a union of government and religion tends to destroy government and to degrade religion." When government, the Court said, allies itself with one particular form of religion, the inevitable result is that it incurs "the hatred, disrespect and even contempt of those who hold contrary beliefs." ...

V.

The wholesome "neutrality" of which this Court's cases speak thus stems from a recognition of the teachings of history that powerful sects or groups might bring about a fusion of governmental and religious functions or a concert or dependency of one upon the other to the end that official support of the State or Federal Government would be placed behind the tenets of one or of all orthodoxies. This the Establishment Clause prohibits. And a further reason for neutrality is found in the Free Exercise Clause, which recognizes the value of religious training, teaching and observance and, more particularly, the right of every person to freely choose his own course with reference thereto, free of any compulsion from the state. This the Free Exercise Clause guarantees. Thus, as we have seen, the two clauses may overlap.

As we have indicated, the Establishment Clause has been directly considered by this Court eight times in the past score of years and, with only one Justice dissenting on the point, it has consistently held that the clause withdrew all legislative power respecting religious belief or the expression thereof. The test may be stated as follows: what are the purpose and the primary effect of the enactment? If either is the advancement or inhibition of religion then the enactment exceeds the scope of legislative power as circumscribed by the Constitution. That is to say that to withstand the strictures of the Establishment Clause there must be a secular legislative purpose and a primary effect that neither advances nor inhibits religion.

29 330 U.S. 1 (1947).
30 370 U.S. 421 (1962).

The Free Exercise Clause, likewise considered many times here, withdraws from legislative power, state and federal, the exertion of any restraint on the free exercise of religion. Its purpose is to secure religious liberty in the individual by prohibiting any invasions thereof by civil authority. Hence it is necessary in a free exercise case for one to show the coercive effect of the enactment as it operates against him in the practice of his religion. The distinction between the two clauses is apparent—a violation of the Free Exercise Clause is predicated on coercion while the Establishment Clause violation need not be so attended.

Applying the Establishment Clause principles to the cases at bar we find that the States are requiring the selection and reading at the opening of the school day of verses from the Holy Bible and the recitation of the Lord's Prayer by the students in unison … The trial court in No. 142 has found that such an opening exercise is a religious ceremony and was intended by the State to be so. We agree with the trial court's finding as to the religious character of the exercises. Given that finding, the exercises and the law requiring them are in violation of the Establishment Clause. …

The conclusion follows that in both cases the laws require religious exercises and such exercises are being conducted in direct violation of the rights of the appellees and petitioners. Nor are these required exercises mitigated by the fact that individual students may absent themselves upon parental request, for that fact furnishes no defense to a claim of unconstitutionality under the Establishment Clause. Further, it is no defense to urge that the religious practices here may be relatively minor encroachments on the First Amendment. The breach of neutrality that is today a trickling stream may all too soon become a raging torrent and, in the words of Madison, "it is proper to take alarm at the first experiment on our liberties."

It is insisted that unless these religious exercises are permitted a "religion of secularism" is established in the schools. We agree of course that the State may not establish a "religion of secularism" in the sense of affirmatively opposing or showing hostility to religion, thus "preferring those who believe in no religion over those who do believe." We do not agree, however, that this decision in any sense has that effect. In addition, it might well be said that one's education is not complete without a study of comparative religion or the history of religion and its relationship to the advancement of civilization. It certainly may be said that the Bible is worthy of study for its literary and historic qualities. Nothing we have said here indicates that such study of the Bible or of religion, when presented objectively as part of a secular program of education, may not be effected consistently with the First Amendment.

But the exercises here do not fall into those categories. They are religious exercises, required by the States in violation of the command of the First Amendment that the Government maintain strict neutrality, neither aiding nor opposing religion.

Finally, we cannot accept that the concept of neutrality, which does not permit a State to require a religious exercise even with the consent of the majority of those affected, collides with the majority's right to free exercise of religion. While the Free Exercise Clause clearly prohibits the use of state action to deny the rights of free exercise to anyone, it has never meant that a majority could use the machinery of the State to practice its beliefs. …

The place of religion in our society is an exalted one, achieved through a long tradition of reliance on the home, the church and the inviolable citadel of the individual heart and mind. We have come to recognize through bitter experience that it is not within the power of government to invade that citadel, whether its purpose or effect be to aid or oppose, to advance or retard. In the relationship between man [sic] and religion, the State is firmly committed to a position of neutrality. … Applying that rule to the facts of these cases, we affirm the judgment in No. 142. …

⚖

The **Establishment Clause** prohibits governmental practices which advance or inhibit religion in general, or which privilege one religion over another. In *Schempp*, government-sponsored prayers and Bible readings, even if arguably non-denominational, were found to have both the **purpose** and **primary effect** of advancing religion, the first two prongs of the ***Lemon* test**. Even though participation was voluntary, the Court recognized that religious exercises in public schools signal government approval. The Court also rejected the argument that removing organized prayer from school was an expression of hostility toward religion and the argument that it established a "religion of secularism." Nothing prevented students from praying voluntarily before or after school or even silently during the school day.

Since the 1960s, federal courts have relied on the analyses in *Schempp* and *Vitale* while deploying the **Lemon test** to decide cases involving the Establishment Clause. In *Lynch v. Donnelly*,[31] the Court ruled that the inclusion of a crèche in a municipal Christmas display did not violate the Establishment Clause, finding "insufficient evidence to establish that the inclusion of the crèche is a purposeful or surreptitious effort to express some kind of subtle governmental advocacy of a particular religi[on]." In her concurring opinion in that case, Justice Sandra Day O'Connor added what is sometimes referred to as an "**endorsement test**" to *Lemon* by refining its second prong: "Endorsement sends a message to non-adherents that they are outsiders, not full members of the political community, and an accompanying message to adherents that they are insiders, favored members of the political community. Disapproval sends the opposite message."[32] Five years later, in *County of Allegheny v. American Civil Liberties Union*,[33] the Supreme Court adopted this **enhanced Lemon test** in determining whether a crèche in the Allegheny County Courthouse and an 18-foot menorah in Pittsburgh's city hall violated the Establishment Clause. Justice O'Connor, in a concurring opinion, found that the crèche had the unconstitutional effect of conveying a government endorsement of Christianity, while the menorah, displayed alongside other religious symbols, conveyed a message of pluralism and freedom of belief. Hence a menorah in one public setting was constitutional, while a nativity scene in another public setting was unconstitutional.

The uncertainty generated by the *Lynch* and *Allegheny* decisions was reflected in subsequent decisions in the federal courts. In *Breen v. Runkel*,[34] a district court in Michigan rejected the argument that academic freedom protects a teacher's right to pray and read the Bible in class. In *Washegesic v. Bloomingdale Public School*,[35] the same district court found that the posting of a two-foot by three-foot picture of Jesus at a busy intersection in the school's hallways violated the Establishment Clause. In *Jager v. Douglas County School District*,[36] the Eleventh Circuit prohibited coaches from leading their teams with prayers before athletic events. In the following landmark case, a divided Supreme Court resolved these disagreements.

⚖️

LEE v. WEISMAN
Supreme Court of the United States
505 U.S. 577 (1992)

JUSTICE KENNEDY delivered the opinion of the Court.

School principals in the public school system of the city of Providence, Rhode Island, are permitted to invite members of the clergy to offer invocation and benediction prayers as part of the formal graduation ceremonies for middle schools and for high schools. The question before us is whether including clerical members who offer prayers as part of the official school graduation ceremony is consistent with the Religion Clauses of the First Amendment, provisions the Fourteenth Amendment makes applicable with full force to the States and their school districts.

31 465 U.S. 668 (1984).
32 465 U.S. 668 (1984).
33 492 U.S. 573 (1989).
34 614 F. Supp. 355 (W.D. Mich. 1985).
35 813 F. Supp. 559 (W.D. Mich. 1993), *aff'd*, 33 F.3d 679 (6th Cir. 1994).
36 862 F.2d 824 (11th Cir. 1989).

A

Deborah Weisman graduated from Nathan Bishop Middle School, a public school in Providence, at a formal ceremony in June 1989. She was about 14 years old. For many years it has been the policy of the Providence School Committee and the Superintendent of Schools to permit principals to invite members of the clergy to give invocations and benedictions at middle school and high school graduations. Many, but not all, of the principals elected to include prayers as part of the graduation ceremonies. Acting for himself and his daughter, Deborah's father, Daniel Weisman, objected to any prayers at Deborah's middle school graduation, but to no avail. The school principal, petitioner Robert E. Lee, invited a rabbi to deliver prayers at the graduation exercises for Deborah's class. Rabbi Leslie Gutterman, of the Temple Beth El in Providence, accepted. ...

II

These dominant facts mark and control the confines of our decision: State officials direct the performance of a formal religious exercise at promotional and graduation ceremonies for secondary schools. Even for those students who object to the religious exercise, their attendance and participation in the state-sponsored religious activity are in a fair and real sense obligatory, though the school district does not require attendance as a condition for receipt of the diploma. ...

The principle that government may accommodate the free exercise of religion does not supersede the fundamental limitations imposed by the Establishment Clause. It is beyond dispute that, at a minimum, the Constitution guarantees that government may not coerce anyone to support or participate in religion or its exercise, or otherwise act in a way which "establishes a [state] religion or religious faith, or tends to do so." ... The State's involvement in the school prayers challenged today violates these central principles.

That involvement is as troubling as it is undenied. A school official, the principal, decided that an invocation and a benediction should be given; this is a choice attributable to the State, and from a constitutional perspective it is as if a state statute decreed that the prayers must occur. The principal chose the religious participant, here a rabbi, and that choice is also attributable to the State. The reason for the choice of a rabbi is not disclosed by the record, but the potential for divisiveness over the choice of a

particular member of the clergy to conduct the ceremony is apparent.

Divisiveness, of course, can attend any state decision respecting religions, and neither its existence nor its potential necessarily invalidates the State's attempts to accommodate religion in all cases. The potential for divisiveness is of particular relevance here though, because it centers around an overt religious exercise in a secondary school environment where ... subtle coercive pressures exist and where the student had no real alternative which would have allowed her to avoid the fact or appearance of participation.

[The] State's role did not end with the decision to include a prayer and with the choice of a clergyman. Principal Lee provided Rabbi Gutterman with a copy of the "Guidelines for Civic Occasions," and advised him that his prayers should be nonsectarian. Through these means the principal directed and controlled the content of the prayers. Even if the only sanction for ignoring the instructions were that the rabbi would not be invited back, we think no religious representative who valued his or her continued reputation and effectiveness in the community would incur the State's displeasure in this regard. It is a cornerstone principle of our Establishment Clause jurisprudence that "it is no part of the business of government to compose official prayers for any group of the American people to recite as a part of a religious program carried on by government," and that is what the school officials attempted to do.

Petitioners argue, and we find nothing in the case to refute it, that the directions for the content of the prayers were a good-faith attempt by the school to ensure that the sectarianism which is so often the flashpoint for religious animosity be removed from the graduation ceremony. The concern is understandable, as a prayer which uses ideas or images identified with a particular religion may foster a different sort of sectarian rivalry than an invocation or benediction in terms more neutral. The school's explanation, however, does not resolve the dilemma caused by its participation. The question is not the good faith of the school in attempting to make the prayer acceptable to most persons, but the legitimacy of its undertaking that enterprise at all when the object is to produce a prayer to be used in a formal religious exercise which students, for all practical purposes, are obliged to attend. ...

The lessons of the First Amendment are as urgent in the modern world as in the eighteenth century when it was written. One timeless lesson is that if citizens are subjected to state-sponsored religious exercises, the State disavows its own duty to guard and respect that sphere of inviolable conscience and belief which is the mark of a free people. To compromise that principle today would be to deny our own tradition and forfeit our standing to urge others to secure the protections of that tradition for themselves.

As we have observed before, there are heightened concerns with protecting freedom of conscience from subtle coercive pressure in the elementary and secondary public schools. ... Our decisions in *Engel v. Vitale* and *School Dist. of Abington* recognize, among other things, that prayer exercises in public schools carry a particular risk of indirect coercion. The concern may not be limited to the context of schools, but it is most pronounced there. What to most believers may seem nothing more than a reasonable request that the nonbeliever respect their religious practices, in a school context may appear to the nonbeliever or dissenter to be an attempt to employ the machinery of the State to enforce a religious orthodoxy.

We need not look beyond the circumstances of this case to see the phenomenon at work. The undeniable fact is that the school district's supervision and control of a high school graduation ceremony places public pressure, as well as peer pressure, on attending students to stand as a group or, at least, maintain respectful silence during the invocation and benediction. This pressure, though subtle and indirect, can be as real as any overt compulsion. Of course, in our culture standing or remaining silent can signify adherence to a view or simple respect for the views of others. And no doubt some persons who have no desire to join a prayer have little objection to standing as a sign of respect for those who do. But for the dissenter of high school age, who has a reasonable perception that she is being forced by the State to pray in a manner her conscience will not allow, the injury is no less real. There can be no doubt that for many, if not most, of the students at the graduation, the act of standing or remaining silent was an expression of participation in the rabbi's prayer. That was the very point of the religious exercise. It is of little comfort to a dissenter, then, to be told that for her the act of standing or remaining in silence signifies mere respect, rather than participation. What matters is that, given our social conventions, a reasonable dissenter in this milieu could believe that the group exercise signified her own participation or approval of it.

Finding no violation under these circumstances would place objectors in the dilemma of participating, with all that implies, or protesting. We do not address whether that choice is acceptable if the affected citizens are mature adults, but we think the State may not, consistent with the Establishment Clause, place primary and secondary school children in this position. ... To recognize that the choice imposed by the State constitutes an unacceptable constraint only acknowledges that the government may no more use social pressure to enforce orthodoxy than it may use more direct means. ...

There was a stipulation in the District Court that attendance at graduation and promotional ceremonies is voluntary. Petitioners and the United States, as amicus, made this a center point of the case, arguing that the option of not attending the graduation excuses any inducement or coercion in the ceremony itself. The argument lacks all persuasion. Law reaches past formalism. And to say a teenage student has a real choice not to attend her high school graduation is formalistic in the extreme. True, Deborah could elect not to attend commencement without renouncing her diploma; but we shall not allow the case to turn on this point. Everyone knows that in our society and in our culture high school graduation is one of life's most significant occasions. A school rule which excuses attendance is beside the point. Attendance may not be required by official decree, yet it is apparent that a student is not free to absent herself from the graduation exercise in any real sense of the term "voluntary," for absence would require forfeiture of those intangible benefits which have motivated the student through youth and all her high school years. Graduation is a time for family and those closest to the student to celebrate success and express mutual wishes of gratitude and respect, all to the end of impressing upon the young person the role that it is his or her right and duty to assume in the community and all of its diverse parts. ...

The Government's argument gives insufficient recognition to the real conflict of conscience faced by the young student. The essence of the Government's position is that with regard to a civic, social occasion of this importance it is the objector, not the majority, who must take unilateral and private action to avoid compromising religious scruples, hereby electing to miss the graduation exercise. This turns conventional First Amendment analysis on its head.

It is a tenet of the First Amendment that the State cannot require one of its citizens to forfeit his or her rights and benefits as the price of resisting conformance to state-sponsored religious practice. To say that a student must remain apart from the ceremony at the opening invocation and closing benediction is to risk compelling conformity in an environment analogous to the classroom setting, where we have said the risk of compulsion is especially high. Just as in *Engel v. Vitale* and *School Dist. of Abington v. Schempp*, where we found that provisions within the challenged legislation permitting a student to be voluntarily excused from attendance or participation in the daily prayers did not shield those practices from invalidation, the fact that attendance at the graduation ceremonies is voluntary in a legal sense does not save the religious exercise. …

The sole question presented is whether a religious exercise may be conducted at a graduation ceremony in circumstances where, as we have found, young graduates who object are induced to conform. No holding by this Court suggests that a school can persuade or compel a student to participate in a religious exercise. That is being done here, and it is forbidden by the Establishment Clause of the First Amendment.

For the reasons we have stated, the judgment of the Court of Appeals is affirmed.

In *Lee*, the Supreme Court added a "**coercion analysis**," observing that "state-sponsored and state-directed religious exercise[s]" create "subtle coercive pressures" for participation and conformity of belief.[37] And in *Lynch v. Donnelly*,[38] as noted earlier, the Supreme Court added an "**endorsement test**" to determine whether religious symbols and exercises in public contexts distinguished "favored insiders" from "disfavored outsiders."[39] Both the Fifth and Sixth Circuits subsequently barred local school boards from opening their public meetings with prayers in opinions emphasizing the presence of students at such meetings.

In the wake of *Lee*, some school districts sought ways to include prayers at school-sponsored public events without running afoul of the Establishment Clause. These efforts sought to take advantage of the fact that students themselves have limited First Amendment rights (see Chapter 4). If a prayer could be considered the private speech of a student rather than "school-sponsored" speech, it might survive an Establishment Clause challenge. In *Santa Fe Independent School District v. Doe*,[40] a case involving the selection of students to deliver an invocation of their own choosing at football games, the Supreme Court rejected this theory. In its view, the invocations were authorized by a government policy, and their primary purpose was to preserve the past practice of opening football games with a prayer. In *Cole v. Oroville Union High School District*,[41] a student elected to give an invocation and a co-valedictorian wanted to deliver, respectively, a sectarian prayer and a Christian talk. The principal of the school denied both students permission to present the material they had prepared. The students claimed their free speech rights had been violated, but the Ninth Circuit found the circumstances were similar to those in *Santa Fe*. If the principal had permitted the students to speak, the school would have violated the Establishment Clause.

Recitation of the Pledge of Allegiance

In the following illustrative case, the First Circuit applied the **enhanced *Lemon* Test** in a First Amendment challenge to a New Hampshire law requiring public schools to set aside part of the school day for students wishing to participate in a teacher-led recitation of the Pledge of Allegiance.[42] The plaintiffs argued that because the Pledge contains the phrase "under God," it constituted a religious exercise akin to a prayer.

---

37 505 U.S. 577 (1992).
38 Doe v. Tangipahoa Parish Sch. Bd., 473 F.3d 188 (5th Cir. 2006); Coles v. Cleveland Bd. of Educ., 171 F.3d 369 (6th Cir. 1999).
39 465 U.S. 668 (1984).
40 530 U.S. 290 (2000).
41 228 F. 3d 1092 (9th Cir. 2000); *see also* Lassonde v. Pleasanton Unified Sch. Dist., 320 F.3d 979 (9th Cir. 2003).
42 New Hampshire School Patriot Act, N.H. Rev. Stat. Ann. § 194:15-c.

⚖️

FREEDOM FROM RELIGION FOUNDATION v. HANOVER SCHOOL DISTRICT

US Court of Appeals for the First Circuit
626 F.3d 1 (2010)

SANDRA L. LYNCH, Chief Judge

The question presented is whether the New Hampshire *School Patriot Act*, which requires that the state's public schools authorize a period during the school day for students to voluntarily participate in the recitation of the Pledge of Allegiance, violates the First Amendment to the Constitution of the United States. ...

A. The Pledge Does Not Violate the Establishment Clause

Under the Establishment Clause, "Congress shall make no law respecting an establishment of religion." Although applicable originally only against the federal government, the Establishment Clause was incorporated to apply to the states by the Fourteenth Amendment.

In determining whether a law runs afoul of this prohibition, the Supreme Court has articulated three interrelated analytical approaches: the three-prong analysis set forth in *Lemon v. Kurtzman*;[43] the "endorsement" analysis, first articulated by Justice O'Connor in her concurrence in *Lynch v. Donnelly* and applied by a majority of the Court in *County of Allegheny v. ACLU*;[44] and the "coercion" analysis of *Lee v. Weisman*.[45] Before applying the three approaches to the case before us, we first address a few general matters.

FFRF's argument is that the School Districts' Pledge practices pursuant to the New Hampshire Act are religious for purposes of the First Amendment because the Pledge itself is a religious exercise in that it uses the phrase "under God." FFRF argues that despite the voluntary nature of any student participation in the Pledge, the result is nonetheless the establishment by the state of religion.

As to the first part of the argument, we begin with the unremarkable proposition that the phrase "under God" has some religious content. In our view, mere repetition of the phrase in secular ceremonies does not by itself deplete the phrase of all religious content. A belief in God is a religious belief. That the phrase has some religious content is demonstrated by the fact that those who are religious, as well as those who are not, could reasonably be offended by the claim that it does not.

That the phrase "under God" has some religious content, however, is not determinative of the New Hampshire Act's constitutionality. This is in part because the Constitution does not "require complete separation of church and state." The fact of some religious content is also not dispositive because there are different degrees of religious and non-religious meaning. The Supreme Court has upheld a wide variety of governmental actions that have some religious content. The Pledge and the phrase "under God" are not themselves prayers, nor are they readings from or recitations of a sacred text of a religion. That fact does not itself dispose of the constitutional question either. There are many religiously infused practices that do not rise to the level of prayer that are clearly prohibited by the Establishment Clause. ...

Special considerations are involved when a claim involves public school students. In the Establishment Clause context, public schools are different, in part because the students are not adults, and in part because a purpose of a public school is to inculcate values and learning. "Recognizing the potential dangers of school-endorsed religious practice," the Supreme Court has "shown particular 'vigilan[ce]' in monitoring compliance with the Establishment Clause in elementary and secondary schools.'" For example, while the Court has upheld a state legislature's practice of opening each day with a prayer led by a chaplain paid with state funds, it has repeatedly found that prayers, invocations, and other overtly religious activities in public schools violate the Establishment Clause. The question is where along this spectrum of cases falls the voluntary, teacher-led recitation of the Pledge, including the phrase "under

---

43 403 U.S. 602 (1971).
44 465 U.S. 668 (1984); 492 U.S. 573 (1989).
45 505 U.S. 577 (1992).

God," by pupils in New Hampshire's public schools. We turn to the Court's different analytical measures for Establishment Clause claims.

1. The Three-Factored Lemon Analysis

Under the *Lemon* analysis, a court must consider three factors: "First, the statute must have a secular legislative purpose; second, its principal or primary effect must be one that neither advances nor inhibits religion; finally, the statute must not foster 'an excessive government entanglement with religion.'" As FFRF does not allege entanglement, the third prong is not at issue here.

FFRF concedes that the New Hampshire Act has a secular purpose—the promotion of patriotism—but insists that this does not end the inquiry. FFRF argues that Congress had an impermissible religious purpose when it added the words "under God" to the text of the Pledge in 1954, and that this fact must be considered in our analysis. Even if so, the argument does not go to the first factor. We look at the purpose of New Hampshire when it enacted the statute in 2002, in the aftermath of the tragedy of September 11, 2001. Because FFRF has stipulated that New Hampshire had a secular purpose, its claim of impermissible governmental purpose clearly fails on the first prong of Lemon.

FFRF argues, under the second factor, that the principal or primary effect of the New Hampshire Act is the advancement of religion. The Pledge's affirmation that ours is a "nation, under God" is not a mere reference to the fact that many Americans believe in a deity, nor to the undeniable historical significance of religion in the founding of our nation. …

In looking at the effect of the state's creation of a daily period for the voluntary recitation of the Pledge, we must consider the text as a whole and must take account of context and circumstances. It takes more than the presence of words with religious content to have the effect of advancing religion, let alone to do so as a primary effect. As to context, there is no claim that a student is required to advance a belief in theism (or monotheism), nor is there any claim that a student is even encouraged by the faculty to say the Pledge if the student chooses not to do so.

By design, the recitation of the Pledge in New Hampshire public schools is meant to further "the policy of teaching our country's history to the elementary and secondary pupils of this state." … As the Court has observed, "the Pledge of Allegiance evolved as a common public acknowledgment of the ideals that our flag symbolizes. Its recitation is a patriotic exercise designed to foster national unity and pride in those principles." In reciting the Pledge, students promise fidelity to our flag and our nation, not to any particular God, faith, or church. The New Hampshire School Patriot Act's primary effect is not the advancement of religion, but the advancement of patriotism through a pledge to the flag as a symbol of the nation.

2. The Endorsement Analysis

Under the related endorsement analysis, courts must consider whether the challenged governmental action has the purpose or effect of endorsing, favoring, or promoting religion. … At the heart of FFRF's claim is its argument that those students who choose not to recite the Pledge for reasons of non-belief in God are quite visibly differentiated from other students who stand and participate. The result, FFRF argues, is that the recitation of the Pledge makes the Doe children outsiders to their peer group on the grounds of their religion.

FFRF's premise is that children who choose not to recite the Pledge become outsiders based on their beliefs about religion. That premise is flawed. Under the New Hampshire Act, both the choice to engage in the recitation of the Pledge and the choice not to do so are entirely voluntary. The reasons pupils choose not to participate are not themselves obvious. There are a wide variety of reasons why students may choose not to recite the Pledge, including many reasons that do not rest on either religious or anti-religious belief. These include political disagreement with reciting the Pledge, a desire to be different, a view of our country's history or the significance of the flag that differs from that contained in the Pledge, and no reason at all. Even students who agree with the Pledge may choose not to recite the Pledge. Thus, the Doe children are not religiously differentiated from their peers merely by virtue of their non-participation in the Pledge. …

Adopting the view of the objective observer fully aware of the relevant circumstances, we conclude there has been no endorsement of religion. The state legislature passed the New Hampshire Act in the aftermath of September 11, 2001 with the intent of fostering patriotism … and that is the statute's effect. Taken in the context of the words of the whole Pledge, the phrase "under God" does not convey a message of endorsement.

The importance of context in the endorsement inquiry is made clear by two cases in which the Supreme Court has addressed the display of crèches at Christmas. In the first case, *Lynch*, the Court concluded that although a crèche displayed by the city was itself religious, the fact that it was located in a broader holiday display clarified to the reasonable observer that the city was, as part of the holiday, simply acknowledging religion with the crèche and not endorsing it. By contrast, the Court in County of Allegheny concluded that a display of a crèche in a county courthouse with an angel bearing a banner proclaiming "*Gloria in Excelsis Deo*," with no surrounding secular objects to change the message conveyed, was an unconstitutional endorsement of religion. Along this spectrum, the two-word phrase "under God" in the thirty-one words of the Pledge is much closer to the crèche at issue in *Lynch*. The phrase is surrounded by words that modify its significance—not by changing its meaning, but rather by providing clarity to the message conveyed and its purpose. ... Here, the words "under God" appear in a pledge to a flag—itself a secular exercise, accompanied by no other religious language or symbolism. We reject FFRF's claim of unconstitutional endorsement.

3. *The Coercion Analysis*

Relying heavily on Lee, FFRF finally argues that the recitation of the Pledge in public school classrooms unconstitutionally coerces the Doe children to "recite a purely religious ideology."

Lee invalidated a public school's practice of inviting members of the clergy to give a nonsectarian prayer at its graduation ceremonies. Although attendance at the ceremonies and participation during the prayer were voluntary, the Court found that there was indirect pressure on attending students to stand or maintain respectful silence during the prayer, and that because silence during prayer signifies participation, this practice was unconstitutional. Lee held that "the Constitution guarantees that government may not coerce anyone to support or participate in religion or its exercise."

Coercion need not be direct to violate the Establishment Clause, but rather can take the form of "subtle coercive pressure" that interferes with an individual's "real choice" about whether to participate in the activity at issue. In public schools, this danger of impermissible, indirect coercion is most pronounced because of the "young impressionable

children whose school attendance is statutorily compelled." As *Lee* stated, "prayer exercises in public schools carry a particular risk of indirect coercion. The concern may not be limited to the context of schools, but it is most pronounced there." FFRF contends that the Pledge, while not a prayer, is more problematic than the prayer at issue in *Lee*. It argues that the students in this case are younger and more impressionable; that they are led by teachers whom they respect as authorities, rather than by a member of the clergy whom they do not know; that those who participate are encouraged to verbalize the words, rather than merely listen; that the Pledge occurs every day, rather than once or twice in their school career; that a refusal to participate in the recitation of the Pledge is more obvious than refusing to listen to a prayer; and that unlike at a graduation ceremony, the students do not have their parents next to them to support them in their non-participation. These concerns do not make the New Hampshire Act unconstitutional.

At least two factors distinguish *Lee* from this case. First, like other courts that have reviewed the Pledge, we think it relevant that the religious content of the phrase "under God" is couched in a non-religious text. This fact is not dispositive, but it is significant. It removes the case from the direct scope of *Lee*, where the Court explained: "These dominant facts mark and control the confines of our decision: State officials direct the performance of a formal religious exercise ..." Recitation of the Pledge is not a formal religious exercise. Second, the logic of *Lee* does not apply directly to the case before us. The *Lee* finding of unconstitutional coercion can be read to result from a three-step analysis involving two premises and a conclusion. The Court found that students were being coerced into silence during the saying of the prayer; that silence was, in the eyes of the community, functionally identical to participation in the prayer; and that therefore, students were being functionally coerced into participation in the prayer in violation of the Constitution.

A key premise is different here. While in *Lee*, "the act of standing or remaining silent was an expression of participation in the rabbi's prayer," silence by students is not an expression of participation in the Pledge. Rather, a student who remains silent during the saying of the Pledge engages in overt non-participation ... [which] is not itself an expression of either religious or non-religious belief. FFRF's claim of unconstitutional coercion under *Lee* fails.

B. The Pledge Does Not Violate the Free Exercise Clause

Under the Free Exercise Clause, the government may not

(1) compel affirmation of religious beliefs; (2) punish the expression of religious doctrines it believes to be false; (3) impose special disabilities on the basis of religious views or religious status; or (4) lend its power to one side or the other in controversies over religious authorities or dogma.

The First Amendment's prohibition on laws "prohibiting the free exercise" of religion is incorporated against the states by the Fourteenth Amendment. FFRF contends that the recitation of the Pledge in the Doe children's classrooms violates their ability to freely believe in atheism or agnosticism, and places an unconstitutional burden on the Doe parents' free exercise right to instill their religious values in their children. This claim is foreclosed by *Parker*.[46]

In *Parker*, we explained that "[p]ublic schools are not obliged to shield individual students from ideas which potentially are religiously offensive, particularly when the school imposes no requirement that the student agree with or affirm those ideas, or even participate in discussions about them." Because the Doe children allege mere exposure to the religious content of the Pledge, they cannot state a claim under the Free Exercise Clause, nor can their parents, as "the mere fact that a child is exposed on occasion in public school to a concept offensive to a parent's religious belief does not inhibit the parent from instructing the child differently."

C. The Pledge Does Not Violate the Equal Protection Clause

Under the Equal Protection Clause of the Fourteenth Amendment, the Constitution "guarantees that those who are similarly situated will be treated alike." Invoking the Equal Protection Clause, FFRF contends that the School Districts have a duty to show equal respect for the Does' atheist and agnostic beliefs, that they are in breach of this duty by leading students in affirming that God exists, and that they created a social environment that perpetuates prejudice against atheists and agnostics. However, the New Hampshire Act does "not require different treatment of any class of people because of their religious beliefs," nor does it "give preferential treatment to any particular religion." Rather, as the district court found,

it applies equally to those who believe in God, those who do not, and those who do not have a belief either way, giving adherents of all persuasions the right to participate or not participate in reciting the pledge, for any or no reason.

Therefore, FFRF's equal protection claim fails. …

We hold that the New Hampshire School Patriot Act and the voluntary, teacher-led recitation of the Pledge by the state's public school students do not violate the Constitution. …

The Ninth Circuit reached the same conclusion in a similar case, *Newdow v. Rio Linda Union School District*.[47] Two years later, in *Ahlquist v. City of Cranston*,[48] a federal district court in Rhode Island found two large Christian prayer murals on either side of the stage in a public school auditorium violated the Establishment Clause and ordered their removal. Four years later, in *Freedom from Religion Foundation v. New Kensington Arnold School District*,[49] the Third Circuit upheld the constitutional claims of a parent concerning a six-foot stone monument inscribed with the Ten Commandments that had been installed near the entrance of the gymnasium at the high school her daughter wished to attend.

46 Parker v. Hurley, 514 F.3d 87 (1st Cir. 2008).
47 597 F.3d 1007 (9th Cir. 2010).
48 Ahlquist v. City of Cranston, 840 F. Supp. 2d 507 (D.R.I. 2012).
49 832 F.3d 469 (3d Cir. 2016).

Prayers at School Board Meetings

In *Marsh v. Chambers*,[50] a case involving a constitutional challenge to the employment of a chaplain to deliver prayers at the opening of each legislative session in Nebraska, the Supreme Court enunciated a **legislative prayer exception** to the Establishment Clause. In 2014, a divided Supreme Court upheld this exception in *Town of Greece v. Galloway*,[51] a case involving an Establishment Clause challenge to a town board's practice of opening its meetings with prayers by Christian ministers. Four years later, in the following illustrative case, the Ninth Circuit declined to extend the legislative prayer exception to school boards and enjoined the respondent board from including prayers at meetings attended by students.

⚖️

FREEDOM FROM RELIGION FOUNDATION v. CHINO VALLEY UNIFIED SCHOOL DISTRICT BOARD OF EDUCATION
US Court of Appeals for the Ninth Circuit
896 F.3d 1132 (2018)

PER CURIAM:

The Establishment Clause serves intertwined purposes, pertaining to individual freedom and the democratic nature of our system of government. The Clause protects "the individual's freedom to believe, to worship, and to express himself in accordance with the dictates of his own conscience." It likewise ensures that the government in no way acts to make belief—whether theistic or nontheistic, religious or nonreligious—relevant to an individual's membership or standing in our political community. The Establishment Clause, grounded in experiences of persecution, affirms the fundamental truth that no matter what an individual's religious beliefs, he has a valued place in the political community. These principles are central to our analysis in the context of public schools. Because children and adolescents are just beginning to develop their own belief systems, and because they absorb the lessons of adults as to what beliefs are appropriate or right, we are especially attentive to Establishment Clause concerns raised by religious exercise in the public school setting. This case implicates just such concerns. ...

I. Background

The Board is the governing body for the school district and accordingly oversees all district schools. The Board holds roughly eighteen public meetings

per year. These meetings for some period of years included a public prayer, until enjoined by the district court. In October 2013, the Board adopted an official policy regarding the prayer practice, permitting an invocation at each Board meeting and providing a means for the Board to select the prayer-giver. The Board's policy and practice of prayer are at issue in this appeal.

A. Board Meetings

The Board meetings share a familiar structure. After a roll call and opportunity for public comment on closed-session items, the first portion of the meeting is closed to the public. During this time, the Board's five adult, non-student members make decisions on student discipline, including suspension and expulsion, student readmission, negotiations with the employee labor union, and hiring, firing, and discipline of district personnel.

The open portion of the meetings begins with a report by the Board president on the preceding closed session. Next, a member of the school community—sometimes, a student—recites the Pledge of Allegiance, and the Junior Reserve Officers' Training Corps presents the colors. Then, there is an opening prayer, usually led by a member of the clergy. On occasion, a Board member or member of the audience leads the prayer instead. A "student

50 463 U.S. 783 (1983).
51 572 U.S. 565 (2014).

showcase"—presentations by classes or student groups from the district—often follows the opening prayer. At times, the Board also sets aside time for "student recognition," to highlight the academic and extracurricular accomplishments of students in the district. ...

Both the student showcase and the student recognition components of the meeting center on the accomplishments of students of all ages—from elementary school to high school—who are in attendance. Musical or dance performances by elementary school students are common. For example, at one meeting second-graders sang folk songs; another meeting featured the elementary school's advanced band students. Sometimes, the "student showcase" is academic. Elementary and high school students make presentations to the Board on their studies in innovative classes. ...

The Board's student representative is also an active participant in the meetings. She is president of the Student Advisory Council and sits on the Board to represent student interests. The student representative votes with the Board in the open session, though her vote is recorded separately. During the period for comment at meetings, she discusses issues of importance to the student community. The Board meetings are open to any member of the public. They are also broadcast on local television.

B. *The Board's Prayer Policy and Practice*

The Board has included prayer as part of its meetings at least since 2010. In September 2013, the Foundation sent the Board a letter requesting that it "refrain from scheduling prayers as part of future school board meetings." One month later, the Board adopted a policy regarding invocations at board meetings. The prayer policy provides for prayer delivery "by an eligible member of the clergy or a religious leader in the boundaries of" the district. Should the selected member of the clergy not appear, the Board president can solicit a volunteer from the Board or audience.

The Board selects clergy for each meeting pursuant to a list of eligible local religious leaders and chaplains kept by the superintendent's designee. ... Invited clergy have typically given the prayers. However, Board members gave the opening prayer at least four times after the adoption of the policy. The president of the California School Employees Association and the district's director of secondary curriculum also provided opening prayers on different occasions. At least twice, community members gave prayers.

C. *Expression of Religious Beliefs at Board Meetings*

Historically—including after the adoption of the prayer policy, and during the pendency of the litigation now before us—Board members' invocation of Christian beliefs, Bible readings, and further prayer were a regular feature of Board meetings. Board members stressed that they viewed such religious engagement as central to the mission and life of the school community. In a meeting in February 2014, following adoption of the prayer policy, Board member Andrew Cruz stated, "I think there are very few districts of that powerfulness of having a board such as ourselves having a goal. And that one goal is under God, Jesus Christ." At another meeting, then-Board president James Na "urged everyone who does not know Jesus Christ to go and find Him." Na informed the assembled audience in May 2014, "God appointed us to be here—whether you to be teachers, or our staff members, or our principals, or our directors, assistant superintendents ..." At another meeting, he instructed the teachers and the assembled audience: "anything you desire, depend on God." Cruz publicly thanked a school principal "for placing God before herself and praying for every classroom on Saturday."

During Board meetings from 2013 to 2015, Na and Cruz regularly endorsed prayer, read Bible verses, and reaffirmed their Christian beliefs. A third member of the five-member Board that approved the prayer policy, Charles Dickie, gave the invocation at the Board meetings at least three times and was identified by Na as a future "neighbor ... in heaven," after Na discussed Dickie's missionary work in Africa at a Board meeting. No Board member sought to halt any of the religious comments.

The religious discussion at Board meetings included specific comments on the opening prayers given by outside clergy. At a June 2013 meeting, Cruz stated that the pastor who had given the opening invocation "was right, in his prayers, that I need [to] first look up to Jesus Christ for serving our students." At another meeting following the adoption of the prayer policy, Na thanked the Christian pastor who gave an opening prayer "for your serving the Lord Jesus Christ and serving all of our students because we do need your prayers [on a] daily basis."

Na and Cruz's explicit linkages of the work of the Board, teachers, and the school community to Christianity, and their endorsement of prayer by the faculty, were frequent. Minutes from one meeting state that Cruz "praised personnel for putting God first." On another occasion, Cruz described "one voice united in prayer at Chino," and read Romans 15:6—"so that with one mind and one voice you may glorify the God and Father of our Lord Jesus Christ"—to the Board-meeting audience. ... The record contains at least fourteen instances in which Cruz read Bible verses to the assembled district community during the period set aside for Board-member comment. ...

III. The Establishment Clause Claim

... The Board's prayer policy and practice violate the Establishment Clause. The invocations to start the open portions of Board meetings are not within the legislative-prayer tradition that allows certain types of prayer to open legislative sessions. This is not the sort of solemnizing and unifying prayer, directed at lawmakers themselves and conducted before an audience of mature adults free from coercive pressures to participate, that the legislative-prayer tradition contemplates. Instead, these prayers typically take place before groups of schoolchildren whose attendance is not truly voluntary and whose relationship to school district officials, including the Board, is not one of full parity.

Because prayer at the Chino Valley Board meeting falls outside the legislative-prayer tradition, we apply the three-pronged test first articulated in *Lemon v. Kurtzman* for determining whether a governmental policy or action is an impermissible establishment of religion. ...

A. *The Legislative Prayer Tradition*

The Board members argue that the Board's prayer practice falls within the legislative-prayer tradition ... Under the *Marsh-Greece* framework,[52] "prayer practice [that] fits within the tradition long followed in Congress and the state legislatures" is not subject to typical Establishment Clause analysis because such practice "was accepted by the Framers and has withstood the critical scrutiny of time and political change." Accordingly, the Supreme Court has found prayer at the start of state legislative sessions and town board meetings commensurate with that tradition and not in violation of the Establishment Clause.

Marsh and *Town of Greece* together identify certain characteristics of setting and content that mark legislative prayer. The prayer occurs "at the opening of legislative sessions," in order to "lend gravity to the occasion" and "invite[] lawmakers to reflect upon shared ideals and common ends before they embark on the fractious business of governing." The audience consists of "mature adults" who during the prayer are "free to enter and leave with little comment and for any number of reasons." The Court has distinguished the atmosphere in which legislative prayer occurs from that of a school function in which district personnel "retain a high degree of control over" the event. The legislative prayer itself is a "symbolic expression," not a time "to proselytize or advance any one, or to disparage any other, faith or belief."

Three other circuits have previously evaluated whether prayer during the meeting of a public school board falls within the *Marsh-Greece* legislative-prayer tradition.[53] The Third and Sixth Circuits both have held legislative-prayer analysis inapplicable to prayer practices at school-board meetings. While the Fifth Circuit more recently held that a school board's prayer practice constituted legislative prayer consistent with the terms of the *Marsh-Greece* exception,[54] it distinguished *Indian River* and *Coles* on the ground that, in both those cases, a student representative sat on the school board. The Fifth Circuit too, then, has suggested that where a student is a board member, prayer at board meetings may present constitutional difficulties. Here, there is a student representative at every meeting.

In evaluating whether the identified historical tradition of legislative prayer does indeed encompass a particular prayer practice, we must undertake a "fact-sensitive" inquiry, in which we take into account "the setting in which the prayer arises and the audience to whom it is directed," the content of the prayer, and "the backdrop of historical practice." This approach is consistent with the analysis undertaken by each of the three circuits that have previously addressed prayer at school-board meetings.

Upon undertaking this analysis, we find that the practice of prayer at Chino Valley Board meetings does not "fit[] within the tradition long followed in Congress and the state legislatures." The audience and timing of the prayers, as well as the religious

52 Marsh v. Chambers, 463 U.S. 783 (1983); Town of Greece v. Galloway, 572 U.S. 565 (2014).
53 Doe v. Indian River Sch. Dist., 653 F.3d 256 (3d Cir. 2011), *cert. denied*, 565 U.S. 1157 (2012); Coles *ex rel.* Coles v. Cleveland Bd. of Educ., 171 F.3d 369 (6th Cir. 1999).
54 Am. Humanist Ass'n v. McCarty, 851 F.3d 521 (5th Cir. 2017), *cert. denied*, 138 S. Ct. 470 (2017).

preaching at the Board meetings, diverge from the legislative-prayer tradition; and the history of the legislative-prayer tradition is inapplicable to a public school board. We therefore conclude that the *Marsh-Greece* exception does not control or govern our analysis.

B. *No Legislative Prayer Exception*

The setting of legislative prayers—"at the opening of legislative sessions," where the audience comprises "mature adults" who are "free to enter and leave with little comment and for any number of reasons"—only dimly resembles that of Chino Valley Board meetings. The Board's meetings are not solely a venue for policymaking, they are also a site of academic and extracurricular activity and an adjudicative forum for student discipline. Consequently, many members of the audience—and active participants in the meetings—are children and adolescents whose attendance is not truly voluntary and whose relationship with the Board is unequal. Unlike a session of Congress or a state legislature, or a meeting of a town board, the Chino Valley Board meetings function as extensions of the educational experience of the district's public schools. The presence of large numbers of children and adolescents, in a setting under the control of public-school authorities, is inconsonant with the legislative-prayer tradition.

Both *Marsh* and *Town of Greece* emphasize that the audience for the prayers at issue consisted of adults—"adult citizens, firm in their own beliefs," who consequently could "tolerate and perhaps appreciate" legislative prayer. As *Town of Greece* explained, "[a]dults often encounter"—and, our law presumes, are well-equipped to handle—"speech they find disagreeable." For adults, legislative prayer does not pose an insurmountable constitutional problem, because adults "presumably are not readily susceptible to religious indoctrination or peer pressure."

We have always, though, been careful to distinguish the special Establishment Clause difficulty posed by requiring children and adolescents to make this choice—particularly in a school setting. *Lee* makes clear that we draw this distinction because we recognize that minors' beliefs and actions are often more vulnerable to outside influence. *Marsh* contrasted the adult plaintiff's relative lack of vulnerability to potential coercion with children's susceptibility to indoctrination and peer pressure. Even for older adolescents, "our history is replete with laws and judicial recognition that children can-

not be viewed simply as miniature adults." We recognize, in a variety of legal contexts, children's and adolescents' greater susceptibility to peer pressure and other pressures to conform to social norms and adult expectations.

The audience for the prayers at issue in this case differs markedly from that at the legislative sessions in *Marsh* and *Town of Greece* in that many of the attendees at Chino Valley Board meetings are adolescents and children—some as young as second grade. The presence of these children is integral to the meeting: they perform for the Board, assembled audience, and television viewers; they receive awards; and one among their number sits on the Board and participates in the Board's deliberative process. This audience, unlike the audience in the legislative-prayer cases, therefore implicates the concerns with mimicry and coercive pressure that have led us to "be[] particularly vigilant in monitoring compliance with the Establishment Clause." Government-sponsored prayer in this context therefore poses a greater Establishment Clause problem than prayer at the legislative sessions in *Marsh* and *Town of Greece*.

The prayer audience at Chino Valley Board meetings differs from that at legislative sessions not only in age but also in its relationship with the policy-making body. The nature of the Board's mandate, and the Board's relationship to the population whom it serves, are dissimilar from the function of Congress, a state legislature, or a town board and the relationships of those bodies to their constituents.

Unlike legislative entities for which legislative prayer is constitutionally permissible, school districts—and by extension, school boards—exercise control and authority over the student population. California law provides: "Every school district shall be *under the control* of a board of school trustees or a board of education." The school board's power extends to "initiat[ing] and carry[ing] on any program [or] activity" or "otherwise act[ing] in any manner which is not in conflict with or inconsistent with" law or "the purposes for which school districts are established."

In California, any "employee of a school district"—that is, a person employed by the Board— may exercise over students "the amount of physical control reasonably necessary ... to maintain proper and appropriate conditions conducive to learning." Beyond direct physical control, the school district also holds a more subtle power over the students' academic and professional futures, which manifests itself in the program at Board meetings. For example, the Board's power to suspend and expel students is a power to determine students' continued membership in the district community. The Board also waives high school graduation requirements in specific cases, and bestows recognition on particular district students. The student board member's authority is subject to the continued goodwill of the Board: under Board bylaws, the Board delegates authority to the student, and any authority the student has is "an exercise in student responsibilities." Unlike the legislative sessions in *Marsh* and *Town of Greece*, where constituents may replace legislators and need not fear their exercise of comprehensive control, students do not enjoy such autonomy.

Moreover, legislators and constituents hold equal status as adult members of the political community, which means that in the ordinary course of events constituents may feel free to exit or voice dissent in response to a prayer at a legislative session. Minors in the school district essentially lack those options. For student attendees, then, the school-board meetings in which the prayer occurs, and the relationship between students and the Board, lack the democratic hallmarks present in legislative sessions and in constituents' relationship with the legislature.

Further, academic and social pressures make students' presence at the Board meetings not meaningfully voluntary. Children attend the Chino Valley Board meetings pursuant to academic or extracurricular obligations. The student representative on the Board, for instance, attends pursuant to her duty to "provide continuing input for board deliberations." Student presentations at meetings—such as presentations by sixth-grade students reading chapters from their autobiographies—expand on in-class educational activities.

Neither *Marsh* nor *Town of Greece* implicated the audience's access to, and experience of, a public-school education. A requirement that a child choose whether to participate in a religious exercise or to dissent in order to participate in a complete educational experience, on par with that of her peers, implicates graver Establishment Clause considerations than the prayers at public meetings found to be within the *Marsh-Greece* tradition. In sum, the nature of the audience at the Chino Valley Board meetings, and the nature of its relationship with the governmental entity making policy, are very different from those within the *Marsh-Greece* legislative-prayer tradition.

Beyond the factors specific to the Chino Valley Board meetings, prayer at school-board meetings cannot be understood as part of the historical tradition of legislative prayer identified in *Marsh* and *Town of Greece*. The history of public schools in the United States, and their intersection with the Establishment Clause, does not support the application of the *Marsh-Greece* exception to the practices of public school boards, including school-board prayer. *Marsh-Greece* analysis applies to "a practice that was accepted by the Framers" and that, consequently, was historically understood as consonant with the Establishment Clause.

At the time of the Framing, however, "free public education was virtually non-existent." The Bill of Rights had not yet been incorporated, nor had its instrument of incorporation even been adopted. The Framers consequently could not have viewed the Establishment Clause as relevant to local schools' and school boards' actions. ... We follow the same approach here and decline to apply the *Marsh-Greece* historical framework for legislative prayer to an institution essentially unknown to the Framers—a public school board. We can make no inference as to whether the Framers would have approved of prayer at school-board meetings in any context, much less in the factual circumstances at issue here, given the lack of free universal public education in the late 1700s.

C. *The Lemon [Test]*

Instead of the legislative-prayer analysis, we apply the three-pronged Establishment Clause test articulated in *Lemon v. Kurtzman*.[55] The Chino Valley Board's prayer policy and practice fails the *Lemon* test and is therefore unconstitutional.

The *Lemon* test remains the dominant mode of Establishment Clause analysis. Under that test, a governmental practice "[f]irst ... must have a secular legislative purpose; second, its principal or primary effect must be one that neither advances nor inhibits religion; finally ... [it] must not foster 'an excessive entanglement with religion.'"

Our *Lemon* analysis is sequential. That is, if the action fails the first prong of *Lemon*, we need not analyze prongs two and three. We find that the Board's prayer policy and practice lacks a secular legislative purpose and therefore, under *Lemon*, violates the Establishment Clause.

---

55 403 U.S. 602 (1971).

The requirement of neutrality among religions, and "between religion and nonreligion," is at the heart of our Establishment Clause. Accordingly, government action violates the first prong of *Lemon* when the government's predominant purpose is to advance or favor religion. A secular purpose for the action may not be "merely secondary to a religious objective," and it must "be genuine, not a sham." We evaluate purpose from the standpoint of an observer cognizant "of the traditional external signs that show up in the text, legislative history, and implementation of the statute, or comparable official act." As such an observer, we possess a "reasonable memor[y]," cognizant of the "context in which [the] policy arose."

The Board's prayer policy provides two purported secular purposes: "solemnization" of the Board meetings, and "acknowledg[ing] and express[ing] the Board of Education's respect for the diversity of religious denominations and faiths represented and practiced" among the district's residents. Of these two purposes, the Board proffers the solemnization rationale as the key motivator. The first paragraph of the prayer policy states that it exists "in order to solemnize proceedings of the Board of Education." Only at the very end, in stating that the policy "is not intended … to affiliate the Board of Education with, nor express the Board of Education's preference for, any faith or religious denomination," does the policy express the second goal of acknowledging religious diversity. Nevertheless, we examine both, with sensitivity to the interplay among expressed purposes.

In evaluating purpose, we regularly take into account the statements of governmental officials involved in a policy's enactment. As we examine the Board's proffered purposes for the policy in the context of litigation, we must keep in mind that, shortly after the adoption of the policy, a Board member publicly, at a Board meeting, described the Board's goal as the furtherance of Christianity. An elected official's public statements directly contradicting the purposes that a policy or bill expresses on its face call into question those expressed purposes.

In light of the history of Christian prayer at Board meetings, endorsed by Board members, the prayer policy's provision for a solemnizing invocation does not constitute a permissible secular purpose. In *Santa Fe Independent School District v. Doe*,[56] the Supreme Court found that the school district's purported secular purposes for the student-led invocation at the start of high-school football games—solemnization

and free expression—did not pass muster under *Lemon*'s first prong. In its evaluation, the Court looked in part to the means-end fit between the policy's expressed purposes and its "approval of only one specific kind of message, an 'invocation.'" Because other messages that were not invocations could equally well serve the expressed purposes, the policy's restriction of the message to an invocation made those expressed purposes suspect.

Here, too, Chino Valley's choice to restrict the opening message to an invocation belies the expressed purposes of the policy. There is no secular reason to limit the solemnization to prayers or, relatedly, to have a presupposition in the policy that the solemnizers will be religious leaders. Rather, these aspects of the policy point to a religious purpose.

Next, the Board's second expressed purpose of demonstrating respect for religious diversity also fails the secularity test for multiple reasons. First, the means-end fit is off in that the policy does not capture all the religious diversity in Chino Valley. The policy limits invited prayer-givers to religious leaders with established religious communities within the district's boundaries. However, there are people of minority faiths living within the borders of the Chino Valley Unified School District whose faith lacks a sufficient critical mass to sustain an established community within the district's borders. For instance, roughly two percent of California's population is Buddhist, two percent is Jewish, one percent is Mormon, one percent is Orthodox Christian, and one percent belongs to religions besides Buddhism, Christianity, Islam, Hinduism, or Judaism. But, there are no religious communities from these traditions on the Board's list of eligible congregations. Far from highlighting the full range of religious diversity and beliefs, the invocation policy reinforces the dominance of particular religious traditions.

Second, the purpose of respecting religious diversity, to the extent that it does not encompass *non*-religious belief systems and their diversity, is itself constitutionally suspect. Atheists and agnostics comprise four percent and five percent of the California population, respectively. Neither the purpose of respecting religious diversity nor the means of doing so via prayer acknowledges or respects the beliefs of nonreligious citizens in the district. Hence, Chino Valley's failure to acknowledge nonreligious beliefs undermines the validity of the second putative secular purpose for its prayer policy.

---

56 530 U.S. 290 (2000).

While the lack of a secular purpose is sufficient to find the Board's policy and practice unconstitutional, the prayers in this appeal also fail the second and third prongs of the *Lemon* test. Under the second prong, the principal or primary effect of the prayers at the Board meetings cannot be said to "neither advance[] nor inhibit[] religion." Instead, the prayers frequently advanced religion in general and Christianity in particular. Under the third prong, the Board's policy and practice fostered an "excessive government entanglement" with religion. There are many ways besides prayer both to acknowledge the community's religious diversity and to solemnize the Board meetings. Readings about the import of religious diversity, the pluralistic nature of our society, or leaders from various religious (and explicitly nonreligious) traditions could provide for serious reflection, without conveying an explicitly religious message or performing a religious activity during the Board meeting. Hence, the means-end fit here is skewed in the same way that it was in *Santa Fe*: an invocation is not necessary to accomplish these purposes.

In sum, the existence of equally available secular means of accomplishing the Board's stated purposes, coupled with the history of Christian prayer, demonstrates that the prayer policy's purpose is predominantly religious in violation of the Establishment Clause. ... The policy and practice of prayer at Chino Valley Board meetings violates the Establishment Clause. The scope of injunctive relief is appropriate, because it merely prohibits governmental action that violates the Constitution and does not infringe upon constitutional rights. Affirmed.

Moments of Silence

In *Wallace v. Jaffree*,[57] the Supreme Court concluded that an Alabama law authorizing public schools to incorporate "moments of silence for meditation or voluntary prayer" into the school day was unconstitutional because it lacked a secular purpose. Other federal courts found formally organized moments of silence unconstitutional on the ground that their purpose was to encourage prayer.[58] In *Brown v. Gilmore*,[59] the Fourth Circuit upheld a Virginia statute requiring schools to establish a "minute of silence" allowing each student to "meditate, pray, or engage in any other silent activity which does not interfere with, distract, or impede other pupils in the like exercise of individual choice." Despite the reference to prayer in the statute, the court concluded the statute was religiously neutral and that it served a secular purpose insofar as it fostered "the liberties secured by the Constitution." In *Croft v. Governor of Texas*,[60] a district court upheld a Texas statute requiring schools to "provide for the observance of one minute of silence" during which "each student may, as the student chooses, reflect, pray, meditate, or engage in any other silent activity that is not likely to interfere with or distract another student."

In *Doe v. Indian River School District*,[61] the Third Circuit applied the **enhanced *Lemon* test** to find that moments of silence at school board meetings regularly attended by parents and students violated the Establishment Clause. According to the Court, student attendance at board meetings was akin to student participation in sporting events (as in *Santa Fe Independent School District v. Doe*)[62] and graduation ceremonies (as in *Lee v. Weisman*).[63]

57 472 U.S. 38 (1985).
58 Doe v. Sch. Bd. of Ouachita Parish, 274 F.3d 289 (5th Cir. 2001); May v. Cooperman, 780 F.2d 240 (3d Cir. 1985); *app. dismissed*, 484 U.S. 72 (1987); Walter v. W. Va. Bd. of Educ., 610 F. Supp. 1169 (S.D. W. Va. 1985); *but see* Gaines v. Anderson, 421 F. Supp. 337 (D. Mass. 1976).
59 258 F.3d 265 (4th Cir. 2001).
60 530 F. Supp. 2d 825 (N.D. Tex. 2008).
61 653 F.3d 256 (3d Cir. 2011).
62 530 U.S. 290 (2000).
63 505 U.S. 577 (1992).

The Study of Religious Materials

In *Schempp*, the Supreme Court described Bible study as permissible "when presented objectively as part of a secular program of education." If religious materials are merely used as examples of a type of literature or as part of a study of secular history, world cultures, or comparative religion, then the Constitution is not violated.[64] The courts have consistently found Bible study programs involving teachers and materials selected by private religious groups to be unconstitutional.[65] Instructors for courses involving the study of religious materials may not be hired on the basis of their religious beliefs, and religious tenets must not be advanced through such courses. In the following illustrative case, the Fourth Circuit upheld an Establishment Clause challenge to a long-running 'Bible in Schools' program in West Virginia.

⚖️

DEAL v. MERCER COUNTY BOARD OF EDUCATION
US Court of Appeals for the Fourth Circuit
911 F.3d 183 (2018), *cert. denied*, 2019 U.S. LEXIS 5658 (2019)

DIANA GRIBBON MOTZ, Circuit Judge:

The "Bible in the Schools" (BITS) program is a Bible instruction course that has been taught in Mercer County Schools for nearly 80 years. The program offers 30 minutes of weekly Bible instruction for elementary school students and 45 minutes for middle school students "as a part of the regular school day." Participation is ostensibly voluntary, since parents must return a permission slip to allow their children to attend. In practice, nearly all students participate.

Since 1986, the County itself has administered the BITS program and designed its curriculum for use by specially employed BITS teachers. The curriculum includes lessons covering the story of Moses, the Crucifixion, and the Ten Commandments. Notwithstanding the County's administrative role, the program is privately funded by Bluefield Bible Study Fund, Inc., a 501(c)(3) organization.

Appellants Elizabeth Deal and her daughter, Jessica, live in Mercer County. When Jessica entered first grade at Memorial Primary School, her mother received a permission slip to allow Jessica to participate in BITS. Deal, who identifies as agnostic, sought to teach her daughter about "multiple religions" to allow Jessica to "make her own religious choices." Because Deal believed that the school's weekly Bible lessons were incompatible with these goals, she withheld her permission. When the Bible program began

later that year, a school official separated Jessica from her classmates and placed her "in a coatroom area" in the back of the classroom during the Bible class. After Deal protested to the principal, school officials relocated Jessica, usually to another classroom, the library, or a computer lab. The County never offered any alternative instruction to Jessica during the BITS program.

Jessica alleges that she faced harassment from other students because she did not participate in BITS. For example, one student told Jessica that she and her mother were going to hell. Their experiences left appellants feeling marginalized and excluded in the community, ultimately prompting Deal to enroll Jessica in a neighboring school district for the fourth grade, where she has remained since. Deal alleges that "[t]he [BITS] program and the treatment [Jessica] received … were a major reason for her removal."

Shortly after relocating Jessica, appellants filed this action alleging that the BITS program violates the Establishment Clause and seeking injunctive relief and nominal damages. The County moved to dismiss for lack of standing and failure to state a claim. During the briefing period, the County notified the district court that the Board of Education had suspended BITS for at least a year to "review" the program's curriculum.

---

64 Herdahl v. Pontotoc County Sch. Dist., 933 F. Supp.582 (N.D. Miss. 1996); Hall v. Bd. of Sch. Comm'rs of Conecuh County, 656 F.2d 999 (5th Cir. Unit B Sept. 1981), *modified*, 707 F.2d 464 (11th Cir. 1983); Doe v. Human, 725 F. Supp. 1499 (W.D. Ark. 1989), and 725 F. Supp. 1503 (W.D. Ark. 1989), *aff'd*, 923 F.2d 857 (8th Cir. 1990); Crockett v. Sorenson, 568 F. Supp. 1422 (W.D. Va. 1983); Wiley v. Franklin, 474 F. Supp. 525 (E.D. Tenn. 1979).

65 Doe v. Porter, 370 F.3d 558 (6th Cir. 2004).

Counsel for the County later suggested at oral argument before the district court that the suspended version of the program would not return, but news reports, which Mercer County itself submitted, quoted Superintendent Akers as saying that the County was "fighting" to retain BITS. After oral argument and supplemental briefing, the district court granted the County's motion to dismiss, reasoning that appellants lacked standing to sue and that, as a result of the program's suspension, their case was no longer ripe. This appeal followed. ...

A.

... Appellants allege three separate injuries, one already sustained and two ongoing. First, they assert that while Jessica attended school in Mercer County, they suffered direct, unwelcome contact with the BITS program. Second, they allege that they continue to avoid the BITS program by sending Jessica to a neighboring school district, expending resources to do so. Finally, appellants assert that they suffer from ongoing feelings of marginalization and exclusion.

The County concedes, as it must, that each of these allegations state cognizable injuries. But notwithstanding the ongoing nature of two of appellants' asserted injuries, the County argues that these harms are not sufficiently imminent to permit a court to grant injunctive relief.

This framing of the issue fundamentally misapprehends appellants' claims. Appellants seek relief not just for past injuries or from some speculative future injury, which would implicate the imminence requirement. Rather, appellants also claim to suffer from two actual, ongoing injuries: (1) near-daily avoidance of contact with an alleged state-sponsored religious exercise, and (2) enduring feelings of marginalization and exclusion resulting therefrom. ...

B.

The County further contends, and the district court held, that since Jessica no longer attends a Mercer County school, appellants also lack standing because an injunction would not meaningfully redress their injuries.

To satisfy the redressability element of standing, a plaintiff "must show that 'it is likely, as opposed to merely speculative, that the injury will be redressed by a favorable decision.'" The burden imposed by this requirement is not onerous. Plaintiffs "need not show that a favorable decision will relieve [their]

every injury." Rather, plaintiffs "need only show that they personally would benefit in a tangible way from the court's intervention."

In fact, an injunction would redress both of the ongoing, independent injuries that appellants allege here. If the district court were to enjoin the County from offering the BITS program to students in the future, Deal would no longer feel compelled to send Jessica to a neighboring school district to avoid what Deal views as state-sponsored religious instruction.

Moreover, an injunction would also alleviate appellants' ongoing feelings of marginalization. We have explained that

[f]eelings of marginalization and exclusion are cognizable forms of injury, particularly in the Establishment Clause context, because one of the core objectives of modern Establishment Clause jurisprudence has been to prevent the State from sending a message to non-adherents of a particular religion "that they are outsiders, not full members of the political community."

An injunction would eliminate the source of that message and thereby redress appellants' alleged injuries.

Resisting this result, the County maintains that appellants' avoidance-based injuries are not redressable because Deal did not avow in the complaint that she would re-enroll her daughter in a Mercer County school if the district court were to issue an injunction. But appellants' feelings of marginalization constitute an independently actionable injury. And in any event, our standing jurisprudence does not require such formalism. Rather, "[t]he removal of even one obstacle to the exercise of one's rights, even if other barriers remain, is sufficient to show redressability." Applied here, the "opportunity" to return Jessica to her home district, in addition to alleviating appellants' ongoing feelings of marginalization, is surely a "tangible benefit" sufficient to confer standing.

III.

In addition to concluding that appellants lacked standing to seek injunctive relief, the district court held that appellants' claims were not ripe. The court reasoned that, in view of the BITS program's suspension, the court could not "evaluate the content of future BITS classes because they do not exist." In so holding, the district court seems to have concluded that because BITS was unlikely to return in its current form, a challenge to it was moot. Where, as here, the parties do not dispute the relevant jurisdictional facts, we review a district court's dismissal based on ripeness and mootness *de novo*. ...

The district court erred in treating the temporary suspension of the BITS program as raising ripeness concerns. Appellants challenge only the BITS program as it existed at the time the suit was filed. To be sure, any challenge brought now to a future version of BITS would face ripeness concerns. This is so because the Establishment Clause requires us to undertake a fact-intensive inquiry that may prove impossible until the precise contours of a redesigned Bible instruction course are known. But that is not this case. The County cannot, as it evidently seeks to do here, reframe this case as an unripe challenge to some future iteration of BITS in order to avoid the demanding requirements of demonstrating mootness.

B.

In reaching its contrary conclusion on ripeness, the district court implicitly determined that appellants' challenge to the suspended BITS program was also moot. Unlike standing, which "is determined at the commencement of a lawsuit[,] ... subsequent events can moot" an otherwise validly raised claim. A case becomes moot "when the issues presented are no longer 'live' or the parties lack a legally cognizable interest in the outcome." ...

[A] party asserting mootness bears a "heavy burden of persuading" the court that "subsequent events [make] it absolutely clear that the allegedly wrongful behavior could not reasonably be expected to recur." In its written submission to this court, the County did not even attempt to meet this standard, persisting instead in its dogged attempt to reframe the issue as one of ripeness. When pressed at oral argument, the County reversed course and suggested that appellants' claims are both moot (as to the suspended program) and not ripe (as to any future reimplementation of a new program). Even assuming this argument is not forfeited, it is meritless.

The County has consistently described the BITS program as "suspend[ed]," rather than eliminated outright. Indeed, the County has characterized the suspension as part of a regular review process, a dubious suggestion in view of the program's uninterrupted, decades-long history.

Moreover, we have held a defendant does not meet its burden of demonstrating mootness when it retains authority to "reassess" the challenged policy "at any time." Here, news reports submitted to the district court by the County itself emphasized that the County was "still vigorously contesting" this suit and "fighting" to retain the BITS program. Rather than enhancing the County's case, these press reports reveal the precise problem with relying on a party's voluntary cessation of unconstitutional activity to establish mootness. Indeed, we have routinely found such evidence insufficient. Nor do we find compelling the fact that BITS teachers received a notice from the Mercer County Board of Education that their employment might be terminated. To the extent this has persuasive value, it is undercut by Superintendent Akers' description of the notices as a "precautionary measure" driven solely by this litigation and the school district's "mandatory timelines" for informing teachers of their ongoing employment status. Such equivocal evidence cannot save the County's mootness claim.

In sum, the County has not carried its burden of showing that subsequent events make it "absolutely clear" that the suspended version of the BITS program will not return in identical or materially indistinguishable form. Appellants' current claims are therefore not moot. Of course, this does not prevent the district court from addressing mootness in the future if presented with that issue.

IV

Appellants have adequately pled ongoing injuries that, if proven, are redressable by an injunction. Moreover, subsequent events have not rendered appellants' present claims moot or not ripe. Accordingly, the judgment of the district court is reversed and remanded.

The following year, the Fourth Circuit considered whether statements about Islam presented in a high school world history class violated the Establishment Clause. The appellant student contended that school officials had endorsed Islam over Christianity and had coerced her into professing a belief in Islam.

⚖

WOOD v. ARNOLD
US Court of Appeals for the Fourth Circuit
915 F.3D 308 (2019), *cert. denied*, 2019 U.S. LEXIS 6431 (2019)

BARBARA MILANO KEENAN, Circuit Judge

During the 2014–2015 school year, Wood was an eleventh-grade student at La Plata High School, a public high school in Charles County, Maryland. Arnold was La Plata's principal, and Morris was employed as one of the school's vice-principals.

As an eleventh-grade student, Wood was required to take a world history course, which was part of the school's social studies curriculum. The year-long course covered time periods from the year "1500 to the [p]resent." Among the topics covered in the course were the Renaissance and Reformation, the Enlightenment period, the Industrial Revolution, and World Wars I and II. The topics were divided into separate units, with each unit generally being taught over a period of between ten and twenty days. The smallest unit of the world history course, encompassing five days, was entitled "The Muslim World." The unit was "designed to explore, among other things, formation of Middle Eastern empires including the basic concepts of the Islamic faith and how it along with politics, culture, economics, and geography contributed to the development of those empires."

As part of the "Muslim World" unit, Wood's teacher presented the students with a PowerPoint slide entitled "Islam Today," which contrasted "peaceful Islam" with "radical fundamental Islam." The slide contained the statement that "Most Muslim's [sic] faith is stronger than the average Christian" (the comparative faith statement). The school's content specialist, Jack Tuttle, testified that use of the comparative faith statement was inappropriate, and that he would have advised a teacher who was considering teaching this statement "[n]ot to do that."

Wood also was required to complete a worksheet summarizing the lesson on Islam. The worksheet addressed topics such as the growth and expansion of Islam, the "beliefs and practices" of Islam, and the links between Islam, Judaism, and Christianity. Part of the worksheet required the students to "fill in the blanks" to complete certain information comprising the "Five Pillars" of Islam. Included in that

assignment was the statement: "There is no god but Allah and Muhammad is the messenger of Allah," a portion of a declaration known as the *shahada* …

Wood's father … asserted to the defendants that Islam should not be taught in the public school and demanded that his daughter be given alternative assignments. … Wood later sued the defendants, alleging that they violated the Establishment Clause by "impermissibly endors[ing] and advanc[ing] the Islamic religion." …

A.

Wood contends that through the comparative faith statement, "Most Muslim's [sic] faith is stronger than the average Christian," the defendants endorsed a view of Islam over Christianity in violation of the Establishment Clause. Wood also argues that the assignment requiring students to write a portion of the *shahada* impermissibly advanced the Islamic religion and compelled Wood to "den[y] the very existence of her God." According to Wood, the challenged materials lacked any secular purpose and had the "effect of promoting and endorsing Islam." We disagree with Wood's argument.

The Establishment Clause provides that "Congress shall make no law respecting an establishment of religion, or prohibiting the free exercise thereof." In evaluating an Establishment Clause claim, we apply the three-prong test set forth in *Lemon v. Kurtzman*.[66] Under this test, to withstand First Amendment scrutiny, "government conduct (1) must be driven in part by a secular purpose; (2) must have a primary effect that neither advances nor inhibits religion; and (3) must not excessively entangle church and State." The government violates the Establishment Clause if the challenged action fails any one of the *Lemon* factors.

Before applying the *Lemon* test, we must determine the proper scope of our inquiry, namely, whether we should examine the challenged materials in isolation or in the broader context of the world history curriculum. Wood asserts that we must analyze each statement on its own, apart from the

---

66 403 U.S. 602 (1971).

subject matter of the class. We disagree with Wood's contention.

The Supreme Court has emphasized that for purposes of an Establishment Clause analysis, context is crucial. To "[f]ocus exclusively on the religious component of any activity would inevitably lead to [the activity's] invalidation under the Establishment Clause." Thus, when determining the purpose or primary effect of challenged religious content, courts, including this Circuit, consistently have examined the entire context surrounding the challenged practice, rather than only reviewing the contested portion.

Indeed, common sense dictates a context-driven approach. Viewing the challenged statements in isolation would violate the analysis mandated by the Supreme Court in *Lemon*. As we have stated, *Lemon* first requires us to consider whether teaching the challenged materials had some secular purpose. Such a determination can only be made by considering the academic framework in which those materials were presented. And in requiring us to determine whether the primary effect of the challenged materials was to advance or inhibit religion, *Lemon* necessarily requires consideration of the contextual setting in which those materials were used ... Thus, any attempt on our part to strip statements from their context invariably would lead to confusion and misinterpretation when applying the *Lemon* test.

Manifestly, if courts were to find an Establishment Clause violation every time that a student or parent thought that a single statement by a teacher either advanced or disapproved of a religion, instruction in our public schools "would be reduced to the lowest common denominator." Such a focus on isolated statements effectively would transform each student, parent, and by extension, the courts, into *de facto* "curriculum review committee[s]," monitoring every sentence for a constitutional violation. School authorities, not the courts, are charged with the responsibility of deciding what speech is appropriate in the classroom. Although schools are not "immune from the sweep of the First Amendment," academic freedom is itself a concern of that amendment. Such academic freedom would not long survive in an environment in which courts micromanage school curricula and parse singular statements made by teachers. Because the challenged materials were presented as part of Wood's world history curriculum, it is in that context that we examine them.

The first prong of the *Lemon* test asks whether the government's conduct has an "adequate secu-

lar object." This directive requires an "inquiry into the subjective intentions of the government." This part of the *Lemon* test imposes a "fairly low hurdle," requiring the government to show that it had a "plausible secular purpose" for its action. Notably, the government's purpose need not be "exclusively secular." Rather, it is only "[w]hen the government acts with the ostensible and predominant purpose of advancing religion" that it violates the Establishment Clause's "touchstone" principle of religious neutrality. So long as the proffered secular purpose is "genuine, not a sham, and not merely secondary to a religious objective," that purpose will satisfy *Lemon*'s first prong.

The Supreme Court has recognized the secular value of studying religion on a comparative basis. In this case, the comparative faith statement was part of an academic unit in which students studied Middle Eastern empires and the role of Islam. The unit did not focus exclusively on Islam's core principles, but explored "among other things, formation of Middle Eastern empires including the basic concepts of the Islamic faith and how it along with politics, culture, economics, and geography contributed to the development of those empires." Nothing in the record indicates that the comparative faith statement was made with a subjective purpose of advancing Islam over Christianity, or for any other predominately religious purpose. Nor does the record show that the proffered secular purpose of teaching about Muslim empires in the context of world history was pretextual. Thus, on its face, the comparative faith statement was introduced for a genuine secular purpose.

Similarly, the *shahada* assignment was a tool designed to assess the students' understanding of the lesson on Islam. In total, the worksheet included 17 questions with 27 blank entries to be completed by the students on the history of Islam, "beliefs and practices" of Muslims, and links between Islam, Judaism, and Christianity. The students were not required to memorize the *shahada*, to recite it, or even to write the complete statement of faith. Instead, the worksheet included a variety of factual information related to Islam and merely asked the students to demonstrate their understanding of the material by completing the partial sentences. This is precisely the sort of academic exercise that the Supreme Court has indicated would not run afoul of the Establishment Clause. Because the school had a predominately secular purpose in teaching world history, we conclude that both the comparative faith statement and the *shahada* assignment satisfy the first prong of *Lemon*.

To meet the second prong of *Lemon*, the challenged government action "must have a primary effect that neither advances nor inhibits religion." This requirement sets an objective standard, which "measure[s] whether the principal effect of government action is to suggest government preference for a particular religious view or for religion in general." We have "refine[d]" this analysis by incorporating the Supreme Court's "endorsement test," which asks whether a reasonable, informed observer would conclude that government, by its action, has endorsed a particular religion or religion generally. Thus, in this Circuit, the primary effect prong asks whether, "irrespective of government's actual purpose," a reasonable, informed observer would understand that "the practice under review in fact conveys a message of endorsement or disapproval" of a religion. ...

The use of both the comparative faith statement and the *shahada* assignment in Wood's world history class involved no more than having the class read, discuss, and think about Islam. The comparative faith statement appeared on a slide under the heading "Peaceful Islam v. Radical Fundamental Islam." The slide itself did not advocate any belief system but instead focused on the development of Islamic fundamentalism as a political force. And the *shahada* assignment appeared on the student worksheet under the heading "Beliefs and Practices: The Five Pillars." Thus, the assignment asked the students to identify the tenets of Islam, but did not suggest that a student should adopt those beliefs as her own.

This is not a case in which students were being asked to participate in a daily religious exercise, or a case in which Islamic beliefs were posted on a classroom wall without explanation. Rather, the challenged materials were "integrated into the school curriculum" and were directly relevant to the secular lessons being taught. These types of educational materials, which identify the views of a particular religion, do not amount to an endorsement of religion. A reasonable observer, aware of the world history curriculum being taught, would not view the challenged materials as communicating a message of endorsement.

Additionally, we note that the challenged materials constituted only a very small part of the school's world history curriculum. As we have explained, we must view the effect of the challenged materials within the context in which they were used. Wood does not argue that the world history class itself advanced any religion. Indeed, she readily admits that it is permissible to teach "how the Islamic faith contributed to the development of politics, culture, and geography." As a matter of common sense, an objective observer would not perceive a singular statement such as the comparative faith statement, or a lone question about a religion's core principle on a fill-in-the-blank assignment, as an endorsement or disapproval of religion. Therefore, we conclude that the primary effect of both the comparative faith statement and the *shahada* assignment was to teach comparative religion, not to endorse any religious belief. Accordingly, the use of the challenged materials satisfies *Lemon*'s second prong.

The final prong of the *Lemon* test asks whether the government's action created "an excessive entanglement between government and religion," which "is a question of kind and degree." Excessive entanglement "typically" involves "the government's 'invasive monitoring' of certain activities in order to prevent religious speech," or the funding of religious schools or instruction. Excessive entanglement may also be shown when the government's entanglement has "the effect of advancing or inhibiting religion."

We need not dwell long on the entanglement prong. As already discussed, neither the comparative faith statement nor the *shahada* assignment advanced or inhibited any religion. And there is no evidence in the record that these materials were obtained from a religious institution or benefited any such institution. Finally, there is no evidence that use of the challenged materials resulted in "invasive monitoring" of activities to prevent or advance religious speech. Under the world history curriculum, it appears that lessons on the Muslim world constituted, at most, five days of a year-long course. Thus, we conclude that neither the comparative faith statement nor the *shahada* assignment resulted in an excessive entanglement with religion. Because the challenged materials satisfy all three prongs of the *Lemon* test, we hold that the district court properly granted summary judgment to the defendants on Wood's Establishment Clause claim. ... For these reasons, we affirm the district court's judgment.

Released Time

In the following illustrative case, the Fourth Circuit held that a **released time** policy allowing students to earn credits for off-campus religious courses taught by private instructors in South Carolina did not violate the Establishment Clause.[67]

⚖️

MOSS v. SPARTANBURG COUNTY SCHOOL DISTRICT SEVEN
US Court of Appeals for the Fourth Circuit
683 F.3d 599 (2012), *cert. denied*, 568 U.S. 1011 (2012)

PAUL V. NIEMEYER, Circuit Judge

In 2007, South Carolina's Spartanburg County School District Seven adopted a policy allowing public school students to receive two academic credits for off-campus religious instruction offered by private educators. The parents of two students at Spartanburg High School commenced this action against the School District, alleging that the policy impermissibly endorses religion and entangles church and State, in violation of the Establishment Clause of the First Amendment. ...

Since at least 1992, a number of school districts in South Carolina have allowed students to be released for part of the school day in order to receive off-campus religious instruction. Initially, the students who availed themselves of this opportunity did not receive grades or academic credit, which made enrollment difficult for some students. In 2006, the South Carolina General Assembly found that "the absence of an ability to award [academic credit] ha[d] essentially eliminated the school districts' ability to accommodate parents' and students' desires to participate in released time programs," and it responded by enacting the *Released Time Credit Act*.[68] ...

Early in 2007, a private, unaccredited religious education organization, Spartanburg County Bible Education in School Time ("Spartanburg Bible School"), approached a number of South Carolina school districts, including Spartanburg County School District Seven, requesting that they allow students to participate in a released time religious course—a two-semester Christian worldview class—

for academic credit. In discussions with School District Seven, the school officials conveyed their preference that administrators receive grades under the released time program as transfer credits from accredited private schools, rather than from unaccredited education providers, such as Spartanburg Bible School. This arrangement would be consistent with the School District's practice of receiving grades awarded by a private school, including grades for religious courses, when a private school student transfers into public school. The officials explained that by receiving released time grades through a private school "transfer transcript," the School District could obviate the need for school officials to become involved in assessing the "quality" of religious released-time courses.

Following the School District's preference, Spartanburg Bible School entered into an arrangement with Oakbrook Preparatory School, an accredited private Christian school, by which Spartanburg Bible School could submit its grades through Oakbrook to Spartanburg High School. Under the arrangement, Oakbrook agreed to review and monitor Spartanburg Bible School's curriculum, its teacher qualifications, and educational objectives, and to award course credit and grades given by the Bible School before transferring them to Spartanburg High School. In carrying out the arrangement, Oakbrook reviewed syllabi, spoke with instructors, suggested minor curricular adjustments, and satisfied itself that the Spartanburg Bible School course was academically rigorous.

---

67 See B. Bindewald, *The Good, the Bad, and the Ugly of Released Time for Religious Education: Reflections on the Program's 100th Anniversary*, 65(1) JOURNAL OF PHILOSOPHY AND HISTORY OF EDUCATION 81–94 (2015); *see also* B. Bindewald, *Evangelical Released Time for Religious Education in South Carolina: A Normative Case Study*, 13(1) THEORY AND RESEARCH IN EDUCATION 105–120 (2015).
68 S.C. Code Ann. § 59-39-112(A).

After Spartanburg Bible School began its instruction under the arrangement with Oakbrook and Spartanburg High School, Spartanburg High School never actively or directly engaged in promoting the Spartanburg Bible School course or any other released time course. The Spartanburg Bible School course was not listed in the Spartanburg High School course catalog, and the Bible School was not permitted to advertise itself in Spartanburg High School classrooms. While the Bible School did provide Spartanburg High School guidance counselors with flyers, the counselors were authorized to discuss Spartanburg Bible School or the flyers with parents and students only after they expressed an interest in learning about the program. Spartanburg High School did, however, allow Spartanburg Bible School to staff an informational table at its annual registration open house for parents and students, as it did for other outside organizations, such as military and college recruiters.

Over a period of three years, 20 Spartanburg High School students, out of the roughly 1,500 students in the school each year, elected to participate in the released time course at Spartanburg Bible School. ...

Establishment Clause

The Mosses concede that off-campus released time initiatives are generally constitutional, as allowed by *Zorach v. Clauson* [and] *Smith v. Smith*.[69] They contend, however, that the School District's released time program in this case is different from that approved in *Zorach* because it provides academic credit for released time coursework, whereas such credit was not part of the off-campus educational program approved in *Zorach*. As they assert, "this giving of academic credit is the centerpiece of this case." They argue that awarding academic credit advances religion more than does traditional released time. It alters the legal relationship between public school and student for religious reasons by giving a grade. It rewards a student for religious participation. It tells the world that the school approves of the student's mastery of religious precepts that have been taught ... [Spartanburg Bible School] students are not just getting an excused absence to pursue religious instruction; their religious life is being promoted and approved.

The School District contends that its released time policy is constitutional under the holdings of *Zorach* and *Smith*,[70] and the fact that the School District gives credit for the released time course is, it argues, no different than the widely accepted practice of giving course credit to students who transfer from private religious schools to public schools. The School District argues that its policy "simply makes it possible to accommodate parents' and students' wish for released time education."

The First Amendment states that "Congress shall make no law respecting an establishment of religion," and the Supreme Court has applied this principle against the states through the Fourteenth Amendment. To pass muster under the Establishment Clause, government conduct (1) must be driven in part by a secular purpose; (2) must have a primary effect that neither advances nor inhibits religion; and (3) must not excessively entangle church and State. ...

In the context of these principles, the Supreme Court has made clear that public schools have broad, but not unlimited, discretion to release students from their secular lessons so as to accommodate their desires to engage in religious instruction. The Court first addressed released time religious education in *Illinois* ex rel. *McCollum v. Board of Education*,[71] where it held unconstitutional an Illinois program that released students from secular coursework to receive religious lessons delivered by privately employed religious teachers on public school grounds. In explaining its conclusion, the Court emphasized that "the state's tax-supported public school buildings [were] used for the dissemination of religious doctrines" in the context of compulsory public education.

A few years later, however, the Court considered and upheld a released time program that allowed students to pursue off-campus religious instruction at no cost to the public school system. The *Zorach* Court readily distinguished the program before it from the one it had struck down in *McCollum*, explaining that New York City's public schools "do no more than accommodate their schedules to a program of outside religious instruction." Because the school system displayed "no partiality to any one [religious] group" and because the lessons were conducted off-campus, the Court concluded that the New York City program "follows the best of our traditions" by "respect[ing]

69 343 U.S. 306 (1952); 523 F.2d 121 (4th Cir. 1975).
70 Zorach v. Clauson, 343 U.S. 306 (1952); Smith v. Smith, 523 F.2d 121 (4th Cir. 1975).
71 333 U.S. 203 (1948).

the religious nature of our people and accommo-dat[ing] the public service to their spiritual needs."

We have since concluded that *Zorach* remains good law and held that an off-campus released time program satisfies all three requirements of the Lemon test. In *Smith*, we examined a Harrisonburg, Virginia program permitting public school students to attend religious courses held at trailers and churches in close proximity to public schools and applied the holding of *Zorach* in light of the post-*Zorach* frame-work set forth by the Supreme Court in *Lemon*. We determined (1) that the purpose of the program was secular in that "the schools aim[ed] only to accom-modate the wishes of the students' parents"; (2) that the program resulted in no more entanglement than did the program at issue in *Zorach*; and (3) that the primary effect of the program was not the imper-missible advancement or endorsement of religion, because the policy "is a largely passive and admin-istratively wise response to a plenitude of parental assertions of the right to direct the upbringing and education of children under their control."

The distinctions between the released time pro-gram before the Court in *McCollum*, on the one hand, and the programs at issue in *Zorach* and *Smith*, on the other, guide the proper disposition of this case. In *McCollum*, the public school brought reli-gious instructors into the school to conduct classes in the school's classrooms, while students normally occupying those classrooms for secular courses went elsewhere, and the School District's superinten-dent approved and supervised each of the religious instructors brought into the school. In invalidating the program, the Court noted that the State used "the State's tax-supported public school buildings" to "disseminat[e] religious doctrines" and employed "the state's compulsory public school machinery" to provide religious education to the students there.

By contrast, in *Zorach* and *Smith*, the public school permitted students to leave school grounds to receive religious instruction off campus and agreed to receive reports of the students' attendance at those classes. Under these circumstances, the Supreme Court and this court concluded that the public schools did "no more than accommodate their schedules to a pro-gram of outside religious instruction." Indeed, the Court suggested that if public schools were not per-mitted to accommodate the religious desires of stu-dents and parents in this fashion, the result would be an unconstitutionally hostile environment toward religion. Here, the School District's released time policy takes place off campus and expressly prohib-its any use of public staff or funds for its execution. The circumstances before us are therefore far more similar to those in *Zorach* and *Smith* than those in *McCollum*.

The fact that a public school accepts credits for released time courses does not alter the analy-sis under any one of *Lemon*'s three prongs in view of the neutral administrative manner adopted by the School District for accepting those credits. The School District employed a model in which primary responsibility for evaluating released time courses lay with accredited private schools, not the public schools. Thus, under this model, an unaccredited entity, such as Spartanburg Bible School, could offer a released time course and assign grades to participat-ing students for transfer to the public school system if it received a stamp of approval from an accredited private school. In this manner, the released time grades are handled much like the grades of a student who wishes to transfer from an accredited private school into a public school within the School Dis-trict; the public school accepts the grades without individually assessing the quality or subject matter of the course, trusting the private school accreditation process to ensure adequate academic standards. This model has enabled the School District to accommo-date the desires of parents and students to participate in private religious education in Spartanburg County while avoiding the potential perils inherent in any governmental assessment of the "quality" of religious instruction. ...

Also important to our conclusion is the govern-ing principle that private religious education is an integral part of the American school system. Indeed, States are constitutionally obligated to allow chil-dren and parents to choose whether to fulfill their compulsory education obligations by attending a secular public school or a religious private school. It would be strange and unfair to penalize such students when they attempt to transfer into the public school system by refusing to honor the grades they earned in their religious courses, potentially preventing them from graduating on schedule with their public school peers. Far from establishing a state religion, the acceptance of transfer credits (including religious credits) by public schools sensibly accommodates the "genuine choice among options public and private, secular and religious."[72]

Apart from the central issue of academic credit, the plaintiffs also contend that the School District

---

72 Zelman v. Simmons-Harris, 536 U.S. 639 (2002).

otherwise became excessively entangled with the Spartanburg Bible School. In particular, they claim that the School District not only accommodated, but actively promoted, the Spartanburg Bible School course by allowing it to bring informational flyers to the guidance counselor's office; to host a table at the annual student registration fair; and to visit homerooms so as to solicit student participation. These arguments are unpersuasive in light of the record. School District officials carefully maintained a neutral relationship with the Spartanburg Bible School, neither encouraging nor discouraging student participation in the Bible School's course. ...

We see no evidence that the program has had the effect of establishing religion or that it has entangled the School District in religion. As was the General Assembly and School District's purpose, the program properly accommodates religion without establishing it, in accordance with the First Amendment. Affirmed.

Religious Holidays and Music

Celebrating religious holidays can present legal and political problems for public schools. When does a holiday pageant become too much like a religious service? This question was addressed by the Eight Circuit in *Florey v. Sioux Falls School District 49–5*.[73] The case involved a school district that had adopted policies concerning the observance of religious holidays that had both a secular and religious basis, including a rule that "music, art, literature and drama having a religious theme or basis" may be included in the school curriculum only if "presented in a prudent and objective manner and as a traditional part of the cultural and religious heritage of the particular holiday." The Eighth Circuit rejected the claims of students that the inclusion of music and other material with a religious theme or heritage in a school holiday pageant violated the Establishment Clause. Applying the *Lemon* test, the Eighth Circuit found the primary effect of the policy was educational, not religious. "We view the thrust of these rules to be the advancement of the students' knowledge of society's cultural and religious heritage," wrote the court, "as well as the provision of an opportunity for students to perform a full range of music, poetry and drama that is likely to be of interest to the students and their audience."

The court in *Florey* acknowledged that its decision would not resolve "for all times, places or circumstances the question of when Christmas carols, or other music or drama having religious themes" could be performed by students in public schools without offending the First Amendment. New challenges were quick to materialize. In *Doe v. Duncanville Independent School District*,[74] the Fifth Circuit approved the use of a piece entitled, "The Lord Bless You and Keep You" by a high school choir, finding that "repeated singing of a particular religious song [does not amount] to an endorsement of religion." In *Bauchman v. West High School*,[75] a Jewish member of a student choir alleged that the teacher selected two explicitly religious songs for the choir to perform at the school's graduation. Citing *Florey*, the Tenth Circuit observed that the First Amendment did not forbid all mention of religion in public schools. Applying the *Lemon* test, the court found the two songs had been selected for secular purposes, including the promotion of friendship and goodwill.

These cases indicate that the use of religious music is generally permissible as long as it is part of a secular program of music instruction and performance.[76] This principle was affirmed by a district court in Indiana in *Freedom from Religion Foundation v. Concord Community School District*.[77] In that case, an elaborate annual "Christmas Spectacular" that had been challenged on First Amend-

73 619 F.2d 1311 (8th Cir. 1980).
74 Doe v. Duncanville Indep. Sch. Dist., 70 F.3d 402 (5th Cir. 1995).
75 Bauchman v. W. High Sch., 132 F.3d 542 (10th Cir. 1997).
76 *See* Brian A. Whitaker, *Religious Music in the Public Schools: A Guide for School Districts*, BYU Educ. & L. J. 339 (2003).
77 207 F. Supp. 3d 862 (N.D. Ind. 2016).

ment grounds was modified by school officials to include Kwanzaa and Chanukah songs and performances alongside a depiction of the birth of Jesus. The court found the modified Christmas Spectacular furthered secular purposes, noting that the nativity scene "[made] the show both musically and visually pleasing and engaging. It also presumably involved a degree of stagecraft and lighting design, thus providing outlets for students in those areas, too."

The Establishment Clause and the Curriculum

Parents have claimed that public schools violate the Establishment Clause with curricular content that promotes or inhibits religious beliefs. Parents have also sought exemptions from unwanted topics and subjects based on free exercise claims under the First Amendment or the right to direct the upbringing of their children under the Fourteenth Amendment.[78]

Evolution and Creationism

In *Epperson v. Arkansas*,[79] the Supreme Court considered the constitutionality of an Arkansas statute prohibiting public school teachers from teaching "the theory or doctrine that mankind [sic] ascended or descended from a lower order of animals." The case was brought by a biology teacher after her school district adopted a textbook containing a chapter on evolution. The Court pointed out that the state's authority over the public school curriculum is limited by the Establishment Clause.

> [T]here can be no doubt that Arkansas has sought to prevent its teachers from discussing the theory of evolution because it is contrary to the belief of some that the Book of Genesis must be the exclusive source of doctrine as to the origin of man [sic],

wrote the Court. "No suggestion has been made that Arkansas' law may be justified by considerations of state policy other than the religious views of some of its citizens." Having found no secular purpose, the Court resolved the teacher's dilemma by finding the law unconstitutional.

Because legislatures could not bar the teaching of evolution in the wake of *Epperson*, fundamentalist groups attempted to use judicial means to eliminate it. In *Wright v. Houston Independent School District*,[80] the plaintiffs claimed that public schools established the religion of secularism by teaching evolution uncritically and without reference to the biblical account of creation. "In the case at bar, the offending material is peripheral to the matter of religion," wrote the court. "Teachers of science in the public schools should not be expected to avoid the discussion of every scientific issue on which some religion claims expertise."

Unsuccessful efforts to eliminate evolution from the public school curriculum prompted demands for "balanced treatment." Opponents of evolution wanted state legislatures to require the teaching of creationism as an alternative to the theory of evolution. If evolution were taught, then scientific creationism would also have to be taught. However, as the Supreme Court explained in finding "balanced treatment" laws unconstitutional in *Edwards v. Aguillard*,[81] their purpose was "to advance the religious viewpoint that a supernatural being created humankind" and thus to promote religion:

> [T]he purpose of the *Creationism Act* was to restructure the science curriculum to conform with a particular religious viewpoint. Out of many possible science subjects taught in the public schools, the legislature

78 See Benjamin Justice and Colin Macleod, *Have A Little Faith: Religion, Democracy, And The American Public School* (2016).
79 393 U.S. 97 (1968); *see also* Scopes v. State, 53 A.L.R. 821 (Tenn. 1927).
80 366 F. Supp. 1208 (S.D. Tex. 1972), *aff'd*, 486 F.2d 137 (5th Cir. 1973).
81 482 U.S. 578 (1987); *see also* McLean v. Ark. Bd. of Educ., 529 F. Supp. 1255 (E.D. Ark. 1982).

chose to affect the teaching of the one scientific theory that historically has been opposed by certain religious sects. As in *Epperson*, the legislature passed the Act to give preference to those religious groups which have as one of their tenets the creation of humankind by a divine creator ... Because the primary purpose of the *Creationism Act* is to advance a particular religious belief, the Act endorses religion in violation of the First Amendment.

Disappointed with the outcome of *Edwards*, a school board in Louisiana adopted a policy that required its teachers to read the following "disclaimer" every time evolution was mentioned in one of its classrooms:

> It is hereby recognized by the Tangipahoa Board of Education that the lesson to be presented, regarding the origin of life and matter, is known as the Scientific Theory of Evolution and should be presented to inform students of the scientific concept and is not intended to influence or dissuade the Biblical version of Creation or any other concept.

> It is further recognized by the Board of Education that it is the basic right and privilege of each student to form his/her own opinion or maintain beliefs taught by parents on this very important matter of the origin of life and matter. Students are urged to exercise critical thinking and gather all information possible and closely examine each alternative toward forming an opinion.

In *Freiler v. Tangipahoa Parish Board of Education*,[82] the Fifth Circuit found the disclaimer violated the Establishment Clause. The policy had the purpose and effect, not as the board claimed of promoting critical thinking, but of protecting and maintaining religious belief. After *Freiler*, a Georgia school district with the stated purpose of promoting critical thinking required that its science textbooks bear the following sticker:

> This textbook contains material on evolution. Evolution is a theory, not a fact, regarding the origin of living things. This material should be approached with an open mind, studied carefully, and critically considered.

In *Selman v. Cobb County School District*,[83] a district court in Georgia found the sticker unconstitutional for endorsing the view of Christian fundamentalists that evolution was a "problematic" theory. It misled students by using the term *theory* in the colloquial sense of "a questionable opinion or hunch," and it targeted only evolution as a topic to be approached with an open mind. Thus, the court concluded "that an informed, reasonable observer would interpret the Sticker to convey a message of endorsement of religion."

Intelligent Design

In *Kitzmiller v. Dover Area School District*,[84] a district court in Pennsylvania undertook a particularly thorough review of a school district policy on the teaching of evolution, garnering national attention. The case involved the following disclaimer to be read by teachers:

> The Pennsylvania Academic Standards require students to learn about Darwin's Theory of Evolution and eventually to take a standardized test of which evolution is a part. Because Darwin's Theory is a theory, it continues to be tested as new evidence is discovered. The Theory is not a fact. Gaps in the

---

82 185 F.3d 337 (5th Cir. 1999).
83 390 F. Supp. 2d 1286 (N.D. Ga. 2005).
84 400 F. Supp. 2d 707 (M.D. Pa. 2005).

Theory exist for which there is no evidence. A theory is defined as a well-tested explanation that unifies a broad range of observations.

Intelligent Design is an explanation of the origin of life that differs from Darwin's view. The reference book, *Of Pandas and People*, is available for students who might be interested in gaining an understanding of what Intelligent Design actually involves.

With respect to any theory, students are encouraged to keep an open mind. The school leaves the discussion of the Origins of Life to individual students and their families ...

After a trial that lasted about a month, the court concluded that the disclaimer violated the Establishment Clause. The court viewed intelligent design as a form of creationism, repackaged as part of a strategic response to the exclusion of creationism from the public school curriculum. The court noted that evolution was the only scientific theory that the board had chosen to challenge, that intelligent design was inherently religious, and that the disclaimer policy promoted religion.[85]

In *C.F. v. Capistrano Unified School District*,[86] a student claimed his First Amendment rights were violated by a teacher whose comments in an AP history course conveyed hostility toward religion. Applying the *Lemon* test, the Ninth Circuit found no secular purpose in the teacher's insistence that creationism was "superstitious nonsense." However, the Ninth Circuit affirmed that the teacher was entitled to qualified immunity. "At some point a teacher's comments on religion might cross the line and rise to the level of unconstitutional hostility," concluded the court.

But without any cases illuminating the [line] between permissible and impermissible discussion of religion in a college level history class, we cannot conclude that a reasonable teacher standing in Corbett's shoes would have been on notice that his actions might be unconstitutional.

Magic, Witchcraft, and the Supernatural

In *Kunselman v. Western Reserve Local School District Board of Education*,[87] students unsuccessfully challenged the district's use of a "Blue Devil" mascot under the Establishment Clause. The Fifth Circuit held that the mascot symbolized athletics, concluding that no reasonable person would regard it as advancing or inhibiting religion. In *Guyer v. School Board of Alachua County*,[88] a parent unsuccessfully challenged a Halloween display including images of witches, cauldrons and brooms, claiming the school board violated the Establishment Clause by promoting Wicca. The court held there was no danger that the community would think the school board was endorsing a particular religion with its Halloween decorations. In *Fleischfresser v. Directors of School District 200*,[89] parents unsuccessfully challenged the inclusion of books on "wizards, sorcerers, giants, and unspecified creatures with supernatural powers" in the district's supplemental reading program, arguing that the series "indoctrinates children in values directly opposed to their Christian beliefs by teaching tricks, despair, deceit, parental disrespect and by denigrating Christian symbols and holidays" in violation of the Establishment Clause. The Seventh Circuit held that the reading series did not violate the Establishment Clause because its purpose was not exclusively religious and its primary effect was not to endorse religion.

85 *See* ADAM LAATS AND HARVEY SIEGEL, TEACHING EVOLUTION IN A CREATION NATION (2016).
86 654 F.3d 975 (9th Cir. 2011).
87 70 F.3d 931 (6th Cir. 1995).
88 634 So.2d 806 (Fla. Ct. App. 1994).
89 15 F.3d 680 (7th Cir. 1994).

The issues may become more complex when students are asked to participate in ceremonies or rituals with religious elements. In *Brown v. Woodland Joint Unified School District*,[90] parents unsuccessfully claimed that a classroom activity in which children pretended to be witches violated the Establishment Clause. The Ninth Circuit applied the *Lemon* test and concluded that the classroom activity was not an endorsement of witchcraft. In *Altman v. Bedford Central School District*,[91] a district court ruled that the school district violated the Establishment Clause by asking students to construct an altar-like structure and participate in a ceremony that promoted the religion of Gaia. The Second Circuit overturned the decision, noting that the Earth Day ceremony was intended to promote respect for the environment. In *Sedlock v. Baird*,[92] parents unsuccessfully argued that a public school yoga program violated the Establishment Clause. "For many in this country, the practice of yoga is an entirely secular experience undertaken for reasons such as increasing physical flexibility, decreasing pain, and reducing stress," noted the court. "For others, the practice of yoga is a religious ritual, undertaken for spiritual purposes." Applying the *Lemon* test, the court found the yoga program had a secular purpose and that it did not advance or inhibit religion or excessively entangle the school district in religion.

The Free Exercise Clause and the Curriculum

Not all objections to school programs are based solely on the Establishment Clause. In *Mozert v. Hawkins County Board of Education*,[93] parents objected to a school program designed to promote critical thinking, tolerance, and moral development. They claimed that books which exposed their children to ideas and values contrary to their religious beliefs violated their Free Exercise rights under the First Amendment and wanted the school to provide their children with an alternative program consistent with their faith. The Sixth Circuit found the plaintiffs had not shown that the school's programs and materials placed a burden on their religious practices or beliefs.[94] Exposure to contrary views is not the same as requiring or compelling religious beliefs:

> Although it is not clear that the plaintiffs object to all critical reading, Mrs. Frost did testify that she did not want her children to make critical judgments and exercise choices in areas where the Bible provides the answer. There is no evidence that any child in the Hawkins County schools was required to make such judgments. It was a goal of the school system to encourage this exercise, but nowhere was it shown that it was required. When asked to comment on a reading assignment, a student would be free to give the Biblical interpretation of the material or to interpret it from a different value base. The only conduct compelled by the defendants was reading and discussing the material in the Holt series, and hearing other students' interpretations of those materials. This is the exposure to which the plaintiffs objected. What is absent from this case is the critical element of compulsion to affirm or deny a religious belief or to engage or refrain from engaging in a practice forbidden or required in the exercise of a plaintiff's religion.

In the following illustrative case, the First Circuit declined to grant parents an exemption under the Free Exercise Clause from public school programs designed to encourage respect and other civic values.

90 27 F.3d 1373 (9th Cir. 1994).
91 245 F.3d 49 (2d Cir. 2001).
92 235 Cal. App. 4th 874 (2015).
93 827 F.2d 1058 (6th Cir. 1987).
94 *See* Tyll van Geel, *Mozert v. Hawkins County Public Schools, the Supreme Court, and Mr. Breyer: A Comment*, 21 J.L. & EDUC. 445 (1992).

⚖️

PARKER v. HURLEY
US Court of Appeals for the First Circuit
514 F.3D 87 (2008)

SANDRA L. LYNCH, Circuit Judge.

Two sets of parents, whose religious beliefs are offended by gay marriage and homosexuality, sued the Lexington, Massachusetts school district in which their young children are enrolled. They assert that they must be given prior notice by the school and the opportunity to exempt their young children from exposure to books they find religiously repugnant. Plaintiffs assert violations of their own and their children's rights under the Free Exercise Clause and their substantive parental and privacy due process rights under the U.S. Constitution.

The Parkers object to their child being presented in kindergarten and first grade with two books that portray diverse families, including families in which both parents are of the same gender. The Wirthlins object to a second-grade teacher's reading to their son's class a book that depicts and celebrates a gay marriage. The parents do not challenge the use of these books as part of a nondiscrimination curriculum in the public schools, but challenge the school district's refusal to provide them with prior notice and to allow for exemption from such instruction. They ask for relief until their children are in seventh grade. ...

The U.S. District Court dismissed plaintiffs' complaint for failure to state a federal constitutional claim upon which relief could be granted. Plaintiffs appeal. ...

B. The Parkers

David and Tonia Parker's sons, Jacob and Joshua Parker, and Joseph and Robin Wirthlin's son, Joseph Robert Wirthlin, Jr., are students at Estabrook Elementary School in Lexington, Massachusetts. Both families assert that they are devout Judeo-Christians and that a core belief of their religion is that homosexual behavior and gay marriage are immoral and violate God's law.

In January 2005, when Jacob Parker ("Jacob") was in kindergarten, he brought home a "Diversity Book Bag." This included a picture book, *Who's in a Family?*, which depicted different families, including single-parent families, an extended family, interracial families, animal families, a family without children, and—to the concern of the Parkers—a family

with two dads and a family with two moms. The book concludes by answering the question, "Who's in a family?": "The people who love you the most!" The book says nothing about marriage.

The Parkers were concerned that this book was part of an effort by the public schools "to indoctrinate young children into the concept that homosexuality and homosexual relationships or marriage are moral and acceptable behavior." Such an effort, they feared, would require their sons to affirm a belief inconsistent with their religion. On January 21, 2005, they met with Estabrook's principal, Joni Jay ("Jay"), to request that Jacob not be exposed to any further discussions of homosexuality. Principal Jay disagreed that the school had any obligation under section 32A to notify parents in advance of such class discussions. In March 2005, the Parkers repeated their request that "no teacher or adult expose [Jacob] to any materials or discussions featuring sexual orientation, same-sex unions, or homosexuality without notification to the Parkers and the right to 'opt out,'" this time including in their communication the then-Superintendent of Lexington's schools, William Hurley ("Hurley"), and two other district-wide administrators. Id. P 34. This request was met with the same response. A further meeting to discuss these issues was held at Estabrook on April 27, 2005, which resulted in Mr. Parker's arrest when he refused to leave the school until his demands were met.

As the 2005–2006 school year began, Paul Ash ("Ash"), the current Superintendent, released a public statement explaining the school district's position that it would not provide parental notification for "discussions, activities, or materials that simply reference same-gender parents or that otherwise recognize the existence of differences in sexual orientation." When Jacob entered first grade that fall, his classroom's book collection included Who's in a Family? as well as Molly's Family, a picture book about a girl who is at first made to feel embarrassed by a classmate because she has both a mommy and a mama but then learns that families can come in many different varieties. In December 2005, the Parkers repeated their request for advance notice, which Superintendent Ash again denied.

C. The Wirthlins

We turn to the other plaintiff family. In March 2006, an Estabrook teacher read aloud King and King to her second grade class, which included Joseph Robert Wirthlin, Jr. ("Joey"). This picture book tells the story of a prince, ordered by his mother to get married, who first rejects several princesses only to fall in love with another prince. A wedding scene between the two princes is depicted. The last page of the book shows the two princes kissing, but with a red heart superimposed over their mouths. There is no allegation in the complaint that the teacher further discussed the book with the class. That evening, Joey told his parents about the book; his parents described him as "agitated" and remembered him calling the book "so silly." Eventually the Wirthlins were able to secure a meeting with the teacher and Jay on April 6, 2006, to object to what they considered to be indoctrination of their son about gay marriage in contravention of their religious beliefs. Jay reiterated the school district's position that no prior notice or exemption would be given.

D. Procedural History

On April 27, 2006, the Parkers and the Wirthlins filed suit on behalf of themselves and their children in federal district court against Hurley, Ash, Jay, and Joey Wirthlin's teacher, as well as the town of Lexington, the members of its school board, and other school district administrators.

The complaint alleges that the public schools are systematically indoctrinating the Parkers' and the Wirthlins' young children contrary to the parents' religious beliefs and that the defendants held "a specific intention to denigrate the [families'] sincere and deeply-held faith." They claim, under 42 U.S.C. § 1983, violations of their and their children's First Amendment right to the free exercise of religion and of their Fourteenth Amendment due process right to parental autonomy in the upbringing of their children, as well as of their concomitant state rights. ...

The plaintiffs argue that their ability to influence their young children toward their family religious views has been undercut in several respects. First, they believe their children are too young to be introduced to the topic of gay marriage. They also point to the important influence teachers have on this age group. They fear their own inability as parents to counter the school's approval of gay marriage, particularly if parents are given no notice that such

curricular materials are in use. As for the children, the parents fear that they are "essentially" required "to affirm a belief inconsistent with and prohibited by their religion." The parents assert it is ironic, and unconstitutional under the Free Exercise Clause, for a public school system to show such intolerance towards their own religious beliefs in the name of tolerance. ...

[W]e approach the parents' claims as the [Supreme] Court did in Yoder.[95] In that case, the Court did not analyze separately the due process and free exercise interests of the parent-plaintiffs, but rather considered the two claims interdependently, given that those two sets of interests inform one another. ... While we accept as true plaintiffs' assertion that their sincerely held religious beliefs were deeply offended, we find that they have not described a constitutional burden on their rights, or on those of their children.

In Yoder, the Court found unconstitutional Wisconsin's application of its compulsory school attendance law to Amish parents who believed that any education beyond eighth grade undermined their entire, religiously focused way of life. The heart of the Yoder opinion is a lengthy consideration of "the interrelationship of belief with [the Amish] mode of life, the vital role that belief and daily conduct play in the continued survival of Old Order Amish communities and their religious organization," and how as a result compulsory high school education would "substantially interfer[e] with the religious development of the Amish child and his integration into the way of life of the Amish faith community." The Court thus found Wisconsin's compulsory attendance law to be flatly incompatible with the plaintiffs' free exercise rights and parental liberty interests, which it considered in tandem. That is, compulsory attendance at any school—whether public, private, or home-based—prevented these Amish parents from making fundamental decisions regarding their children's religious upbringing and effectively overrode their ability to pass their religion on to their children, as their faith required. Further, the parents in Yoder were able to demonstrate that their alternative informal vocational training of their older children still met the state's professed interest behind its compulsory attendance requirement.

To the extent that Yoder embodies judicial protection for social and religious "sub-groups from the public cultivation of liberal tolerance," plaintiffs are correct to rely on it. But there are substantial dif-

95 Wisconsin v. Yoder, 406 U.S. 205 (1972).

ferences between the plaintiffs' claims in *Yoder* and the claims raised in this case. One ground of distinction is that the plaintiffs have chosen to place their children in public schools and do not live, as the Amish do, in a largely separate culture. There are others. While plaintiffs do invoke *Yoder's* language that the state is threatening their very "way of life," they use this language to refer to the centrality of these beliefs to their faith, in contrast to its use in *Yoder* to refer to a distinct community and lifestyle. Exposure to the materials in dispute here will not automatically and irreversibly prevent the parents from raising Jacob and Joey in the religious belief that gay marriage is immoral. Nor is there a criminal statute involved, or any other punishment imposed on the parents if they choose to educate their children in other ways. They retain options, unlike the parents in *Yoder*. Tellingly, *Yoder* emphasized that its holding was essentially *sui generis*, as few sects could make a similar showing of a unique and demanding religious way of life that is fundamentally incompatible with any schooling system. Plaintiffs' case is not *Yoder*. …

We turn afresh to plaintiffs' complementary due process and free exercise claims. Plaintiffs' opening premise is that their rights of parental control are fundamental rights. They rely on a Supreme Court decision recognizing a substantive due process right of parents "to make decisions concerning the care, custody, and control of their children." … Plaintiffs argue their request for notice and exemption is simply a logical extension of their parental rights under *Meyer* and *Pierce*,[96] as reinforced by their free exercise rights. … Plaintiffs say … they are not attempting to control the school's power to prescribe a curriculum. The plaintiffs accept that the school system "has a legitimate secular interest in seeking to eradicate bias against same-gender couples and to ensure the safety of all public school students." They assert that they have an equally sincere interest in the accommodation of their own religious beliefs and of the diversity represented by their contrary views. Plaintiffs specifically disclaim any intent to seek control of the school's curriculum or to impose their will on others. They do not seek to change the choice of books available to others but only to require notice of the books and an exemption, and even then only up to the seventh grade. Nonetheless, we have found no federal case under the Due Process Clause which has permitted parents to demand an exemption for

their children from exposure to certain books used in public schools.

The due process right of parental autonomy might be considered a subset of a broader substantive due process right of familial privacy. … We turn then to whether the combination of substantive due process and free exercise interests give the parents a cause of action.

The First Amendment's prohibition on laws "respecting an establishment of religion, or prohibiting the free exercise thereof" applies to the states through the Fourteenth Amendment. In Smith, the Supreme Court noted that the "free exercise of religion means, first and foremost, the right to believe and profess whatever religious doctrine one desires." As a result, the government may not, for example, (1) compel affirmation of religious beliefs; (2) punish the expression of religious doctrines it believes to be false; (3) impose special disabilities on the basis of religious views or religious status; or (4) lend its power to one side or the other in controversies over religious authorities or dogma.

The Free Exercise Clause, importantly, is not a general protection of religion or religious belief. It has a more limited reach of protecting the free exercise of religion. …

Preliminarily, we mark the distinction between the alleged burden on the parents' free exercise rights and the alleged burden on their children's. The right of parents "to direct the religious upbringing of their children" is distinct from (although related to) any right their children might have regarding the content of their school curriculum. This is not a new distinction. In *Prince v. Massachusetts*,[97] the Court explained that

two claimed liberties are at stake. One is the parent's, to bring up the child in the way [the parent desires], which for appellant means to teach him the tenets and the practices of their faith. The other freedom is the child's, to observe these [tenets and practices].

We start with the parents' claim.

Generally, the fundamental parental control/free exercise claims regarding public schools have fallen into several types of situations: claims that failure to provide benefits given to public school students violates free exercise rights, claims that plaintiffs should not be subjected to compulsory education, demands for removal of offensive material from the curric-

96 Meyer v. Nebraska, 262 U.S. 390 (1923); Pierce v. Society of Sisters, 268 U.S. 510 (1925).
97 321 U.S. 158 (1944).

ulum, and, as here, claims that there is a constitutional right to exemption from religiously offensive material.

In two cases in which plaintiffs did not raise a related parental rights due process claim, federal courts have rejected free exercise claims seeking exemptions from the schools' assignment of particular books. In *Fleischfresser*,[98] the parents sought to prevent the use of the Impressions Reading Series as a supplemental reading program for an elementary school. The parents complained that the series fostered a belief in the existence of superior beings and indoctrinated their children in values such as despair, deceit, and parental disrespect, values different from their Christian beliefs. The Seventh Circuit held that any burden on free exercise rights was, at most, minimal. The parents were not precluded from meeting their religious obligation to instruct their children, nor were the parents or children compelled to do anything or refrain from doing anything of a religious nature. Thus, no coercion existed.

In *Mozert v. Hawkins County Board of Education*,[99] which is more factually similar to this case, the Sixth Circuit rejected a broader claim for an exemption from a school district's use of an entire series of texts. The parents in that case asserted that the books in question taught values contrary to their religious beliefs and that, as a result, the school violated the parents' religious beliefs by allowing their children to read the books and violated their children's religious beliefs by requiring the children to read them. The court, however, found that exposure to ideas through the required reading of books did not constitute a constitutionally significant burden on the plaintiffs' free exercise of religion. In so holding, the court emphasized that "the evil prohibited by the Free Exercise Clause" is "governmental compulsion either to do or refrain from doing an act forbidden or required by one's religion, or to affirm or disavow a belief forbidden or required by one's religion," and reading or even discussing the books did not compel such action or affirmation.

In the present case, the plaintiffs claim that the exposure of their children, at these young ages and in this setting, to ways of life contrary to the parents' religious beliefs violates their ability to direct the religious upbringing of their children. We try to identify the categories of harms alleged. The parents do not allege coercion in the form of a direct

interference with their religious beliefs, nor of compulsion in the form of punishment for their beliefs, as in *Yoder*. Nor do they allege the denial of benefits. Further, plaintiffs do not allege that the mere listening to a book being read violated any religious duty on the part of the child. There is no claim that as a condition of attendance at the public schools, the defendants have forced plaintiffs—either the parents or the children—to violate their religious beliefs. In sum there is no claim of direct coercion.

The heart of the plaintiffs' free exercise claim is a claim of "indoctrination": that the state has put pressure on their children to endorse an affirmative view of gay marriage and has thus undercut the parents' efforts to inculcate their children with their own opposing religious views. The Supreme Court, we believe, has never utilized an indoctrination test under the Free Exercise Clause, much less in the public school context. The closest it has come is *Barnette*,[100] a free speech case that implicated free exercise interests and which Smith included in its hybrid case discussion. In *Barnette*, the Court held that the state could not coerce acquiescence through compelled statements of belief, such as the mandatory recital of the pledge of allegiance in public schools. It did not hold that the state could not attempt to inculcate values by instruction, and in fact carefully distinguished the two approaches. We do not address whether or not an indoctrination theory under the Free Exercise Clause is sound. Plaintiffs' pleadings do not establish a viable case of indoctrination, even assuming that extreme indoctrination can be a form of coercion.

First, as to the parents' free exercise rights, the mere fact that a child is exposed on occasion in public school to a concept offensive to a parent's religious belief does not inhibit the parent from instructing the child differently. A parent whose "child is exposed to sensitive topics or information [at school] remains free to discuss these matters and to place them in the family's moral or religious context, or to supplement the information with more appropriate materials." The parents here did in fact have notice, if not prior notice, of the books and of the school's overall intent to promote toleration of same-sex marriage, and they retained their ability to discuss the material and subject matter with their children. Our outcome does not turn, however, on whether the parents had notice.

---

98   Fleischfresser v. Dirs. of Sch. Dist. 200, 15 F.3d 680 (7th Cir. 1994).
99   827 F.2d 1058 (6th Cir. 1987).
100 West Virginia State Board of Education v. Barnette, 319 U.S. 624 (1943).

Turning to the children's free exercise rights, we cannot see how Jacob's free exercise right was burdened at all: two books were made available to him, but he was never required to read them or have them read to him. Further, these books do not endorse gay marriage or homosexuality, or even address these topics explicitly, but merely describe how other children might come from families that look different from one's own. There is no free exercise right to be free from any reference in public elementary schools to the existence of families in which the parents are of different gender combinations.

Joey has a more significant claim, both because he was required to sit through a classroom reading of King and King and because that book affirmatively endorses homosexuality and gay marriage. It is a fair inference that the reading of King and King was precisely intended to influence the listening children toward tolerance of gay marriage. That was the point of why that book was chosen and used. Even assuming there is a continuum along which an intent to influence could become an attempt to indoctrinate, however, this case is firmly on the influence-toward-tolerance end. There is no evidence of systemic indoctrination. There is no allegation that Joey was asked to affirm gay marriage. Requiring a student to read a particular book is generally not coercive of free exercise rights.

Public schools are not obliged to shield individual students from ideas which potentially are religiously offensive, particularly when the school imposes no requirement that the student agree with or affirm those ideas, or even participate in discussions about them. The reading of King and King was not instruction in religion or religious beliefs.

On the facts, there is no viable claim of "indoctrination" here. Without suggesting that such showings would suffice to establish a claim of indoctrination, we note the plaintiffs' children were not forced to read the books on pain of suspension. Nor were they subject to a constant stream of like materials. There is no allegation here of a formalized curriculum requiring students to read many books affirming gay marriage. The reading by a teacher of one book, or even three, and even if to a young and impressionable child, does not constitute "indoctrination."

Because plaintiffs do not allege facts that give rise to claims of constitutional magnitude, the district court did not err in granting defendants' motion to dismiss the claims under the U.S. Constitution.

III.

Public schools often walk a tightrope between the many competing constitutional demands made by parents, students, teachers, and the schools' other constituents. The balance the school struck here does not offend the Free Exercise or Due Process Clauses of the U.S. Constitution. We do not suggest that the school's choice of books for young students has not deeply offended the plaintiffs' sincerely held religious beliefs. If the school system has been insufficiently sensitive to such religious beliefs, the plaintiffs may seek recourse to the normal political processes for change in the town and state. They are not entitled to a federal judicial remedy under the U.S. Constitution. ... Affirmed.

Sexuality and Gender Identity

As noted earlier, sex education is a curricular matter over which the federal and state governments exercise considerable control. It has also been a frequent target of parental objection on religious grounds. In *Cornwell v. State Board of Education*,[101] parents argued that a program of "family life and sex education" violated the Establishment Clause. The court disagreed:

> ... [T]he purpose and primary effect here is not to establish any particular religious dogma or precept, and the [program] does not directly or substantially involve the state in religious exercises or in the favoring of religion or any particular religion.

While the *Cornwell* plaintiffs wanted to eliminate sex education from the school program, other parents have sought only to exempt their children. In *Valent v. New Jersey State Board of Educa-*

101 314 F. Supp. 340 (D. Md. 1969), *aff'd*, 428 F.2d 471 (4th Cir. 1970).

tion,[102] the court rejected the argument that sex education violated the plaintiffs' free exercise rights. In *Brown v. Hot, Sexy & Safer Productions*,[103] parents unsuccessfully challenged an AIDS awareness program that included frank and graphic discussions of sex, emphasizing "safe sex" over abstinence. The parents claimed the program violated both their free exercise rights and their right to control the upbringing of their children. The First Circuit found the program constitutional. "If all parents had a fundamental constitutional right to dictate individually what the schools teach their children," wrote the court, "the schools would be forced to create a curriculum for each student whose parents had genuine moral disagreements with the school's choice of subject matter."

The Free Speech Clause and the Curriculum

Although the religion clauses have been the primary basis for constitutional challenges to school programs, the **Free Speech Clause** has also been used in an atypical way. Rather than asserting a right to express their own ideas, plaintiffs claim either **a right not to speak** or **a right to know**.[104]

A Right Not to Speak

In *Pierce*, the Supreme Court affirmed the power of the State to ensure that "studies plainly essential to good citizenship … be taught, and … nothing … manifestly inimical to the public welfare." In *Minersville School District v. Gobitis*,[105] the Court in 1940 upheld a requirement that students salute the flag and recite the Pledge of Allegiance on this basis. Three years later, the Court reconsidered the same issue in the following watershed case.

WEST VIRGINIA STATE BOARD OF EDUCATION v. BARNETTE
Supreme Court of the United States
319 U.S. 624 (1943)

MR. JUSTICE JACKSON delivered the opinion of the Court.

Following the decision by this Court on June 3, 1940, in *Minersville School District v. Gobitis*,[106] the West Virginia legislature amended its statutes to require all schools therein to conduct courses of instruction in history, civics, and in the Constitutions of the United States and of the State "for the purpose of teaching, fostering and perpetuating the ideals, principles and spirit of Americanism, and increasing the knowledge of the organization and machinery of the government." Appellant Board of Education was directed, with advice of the State Superintendent of Schools, to "prescribe the courses of study covering these subjects" for public schools. The Act made it the duty of private, parochial and denominational schools to prescribe courses of study "similar to those required for the public schools."

The Board of Education on January 9, 1942, adopted a resolution containing recitals taken largely from the Court's *Gobitis* opinion and ordering that the salute to the flag become "a regular part of the program of activities in the public schools," that all teachers and pupils "shall be required to participate in the salute honoring the Nation represented by the Flag; provided, however, that refusal to salute the Flag be regarded as an act of insubordination, and shall be dealt with accordingly."

---

102 274 A.2d 832 (N.J. Sup. Ct. Ch. Div. 1971); *see also* Leebaert v. Harrington, 193 F. Supp. 2d 491 (D. Conn. 2002).
103 68 F.3d 525 (1st Cir. 1995).
104 *See* Tyll van Geel, *Citizenship Education and the Free Exercise of Religion*, 34(1) Akron L. Rev 293–382 (2000).
105 310 U.S. 586 (1940).
106 310 U.S. 586 (1940).

The resolution originally required the "commonly accepted salute to the Flag" which it defined. Objections to the salute as "being too much like Hitler's" were raised by the Parent and Teachers Association, the Boy and Girl Scouts, the Red Cross, and the Federation of Women's Clubs. Some modification appears to have been made in deference to these objections, but no concession was made to Jehovah's Witnesses. What is now required is the "stiff-arm" salute, the saluter to keep the right hand raised with palm turned up while the following is repeated: "I pledge allegiance to the Flag of the United States of America and to the Republic for which it stands; one Nation, indivisible, with liberty and justice for all."

Failure to conform is "insubordination" dealt with by expulsion. Readmission is denied by statute until compliance. Meanwhile the expelled child is "unlawfully absent" and may be proceeded against as a delinquent. His parents or guardians are liable to prosecution, and if convicted are subject to fine not exceeding $50 and jail term not exceeding thirty days.

Appellees, citizens of the United States and of West Virginia, brought suit in the United States District Court for themselves and others similarly situated asking its injunction to restrain enforcement of these laws and regulations against Jehovah's Witnesses. The Witnesses are an unincorporated body teaching that the obligation imposed by law of God is superior to that of laws enacted by temporal government. Their religious beliefs include a literal version of Exodus, Chapter 20, verses 4 and 5, which says:

Thou shalt not make unto thee any graven image, or any likeness of anything that is in heaven above, or that is in the earth beneath, or that is in the water under the earth; thou shalt not bow down thyself to them nor serve them.

They consider that the flag is an "image" within this command. For this reason, they refuse to salute it.

Children of this faith have been expelled from school and are threatened with exclusion for no other cause. Officials threaten to send them to reformatories maintained for criminally inclined juveniles. Parents of such children have been prosecuted and are threatened with prosecutions for causing delinquency. ...

This case calls upon us to reconsider a precedent decision, as the Court throughout its history often has been required to do. Before turning to the *Gobitis*

case, however, it is desirable to notice certain characteristics by which this controversy is distinguished.

The freedom asserted by these appellees does not bring them into collision with rights asserted by any other individual. It is such conflicts which most frequently require intervention of the State to determine where the rights of one end and those of another begin. But the refusal of these persons to participate in the ceremony does not interfere with or deny rights of others to do so. Nor is there any question in this case that their behavior is peaceable and orderly. The sole conflict is between authority and rights of the individual. The State asserts power to condition access to public education on making a prescribed sign and profession and at the same time to coerce attendance by punishing both parent and child. The latter stand on a right of self-determination in matters that touch individual opinion and personal attitude.

As the present Chief Justice said in dissent in the *Gobitis* case, the State may "require teaching by instruction and study of all in our history and in the structure and organization of our government, including the guaranties of civil liberty, which tend to inspire patriotism and love of country." Here, however, we are dealing with a compulsion of students to declare a belief. They are not merely made acquainted with the flag salute so that they may be informed as to what it is or even what it means. The issue here is whether this slow and easily neglected route to aroused loyalties constitutionally may be short-cut by substituting a compulsory salute and slogan. This issue is not prejudiced by the Court's previous holding that where a State, without compelling attendance, extends college facilities to pupils who voluntarily enroll, it may prescribe military training as part of the course without offense to the Constitution. It was held that those who take advantage of its opportunities may not on ground of conscience refuse compliance with such conditions. In the present case attendance is not optional. That case is also to be distinguished from the present one because, independently of college privileges or requirements, the State has power to raise militia and impose the duties of service therein upon its citizens.

There is no doubt that, in connection with the pledges, the flag salute is a form of utterance. Symbolism is a primitive but effective way of communicating ideas. The use of an emblem or flag to symbolize some system, idea, institution, or personality, is a short cut from mind to mind. Causes and nations, political parties, lodges and ecclesiastical groups seek to knit the loyalty of their followings to a flag or banner, a color or design. The State announces rank, function, and authority through crowns and maces, uniforms and black robes; the church speaks through the Cross, the Crucifix, the altar and shrine, and clerical raiment. Symbols of State often convey political ideas just as religious symbols come to convey theological ones. Associated with many of these symbols are appropriate gestures of acceptance or respect: a salute, a bowed or bared head, a bended knee. A person gets from a symbol the meaning he puts into it, and what is one man's [sic] comfort and inspiration is another's jest and scorn.

Over a decade ago Chief Justice Hughes led this Court in holding that the display of a red flag as a symbol of opposition by peaceful and legal means to organized government was protected by the free speech guaranties of the Constitution. Here it is the State that employs a flag as a symbol of adherence to government as presently organized. It requires the individual to communicate by word and sign his [sic] acceptance of the political ideas it thus bespeaks. Objection to this form of communication when coerced is an old one, well known to the framers of the Bill of Rights.

It is also to be noted that the compulsory flag salute and pledge requires affirmation of a belief and an attitude of mind. It is not clear whether the regulation contemplates that pupils forego any contrary convictions of their own and become unwilling converts to the prescribed ceremony or whether it will be acceptable if they simulate assent by words without belief and by a gesture barren of meaning. It is now a commonplace that censorship or suppression of expression of opinion is tolerated by our Constitution only when the expression presents a clear and present danger of action of a kind the State is empowered to prevent and punish. It would seem that involuntary affirmation could be commanded only on even more immediate and urgent grounds than silence. But here the power of compulsion is invoked without any allegation that remaining passive during a flag salute ritual creates a clear and present danger that would justify an effort even to muffle expression. To sustain the compulsory flag salute we are required to say that a Bill of Rights which guards the individual's right to speak his own mind, left it open to public authorities to compel him to utter what is not in his mind.

Whether the First Amendment to the Constitution will permit officials to order observance of ritual of this nature does not depend upon whether as a voluntary exercise we would think it to be good, bad or merely innocuous. Any credo of nationalism is likely to include what some disapprove or to omit what others think essential, and to give off different overtones as it takes on different accents or interpretations. If official power exists to coerce acceptance of any patriotic creed, what it shall contain cannot be decided by courts, but must be largely discretionary with the ordaining authority, whose power to prescribe would no doubt include power to amend. Hence validity of the asserted power to force an American citizen publicly to profess any statement of belief or to engage in any ceremony of assent to one, presents questions of power that must be considered independently of any idea we may have as to the utility of the ceremony in question.

Nor does the issue as we see it turn on one's possession of particular religious views or the sincerity with which they are held. While religion supplies appellees' motive for enduring the discomforts of making the issue in this case, many citizens who do not share these religious views hold such a compulsory rite to infringe constitutional liberty of the individual. It is not necessary to inquire whether non-conformist beliefs will exempt from the duty to salute unless we first find power to make the salute a legal duty.

The *Gobitis* decision, however, assumed, as did the argument in that case and in this, that power exists in the State to impose the flag salute discipline upon school children in general. The Court only examined and rejected a claim based on religious beliefs of immunity from an unquestioned general rule. The question which underlies the flag salute controversy is whether such a ceremony so touching matters of opinion and political attitude may be imposed upon the individual by official authority under powers committed to any political organization under our Constitution. We examine rather than assume existence of this power and, against this broader definition of issues in this case, reexamine specific grounds assigned for the *Gobitis* decision.

1.   It was said that the flag-salute controversy confronted the Court with "the problem which Lincoln cast in memorable dilemma: 'Must a government of necessity be too strong for the liberties of its people, or too weak to maintain its own existence?'" and that the answer must be in favor of strength.

     We think these issues may be examined free of pressure or restraint growing out of such considerations. It may be doubted whether Mr. Lincoln would have thought that the strength of government to maintain itself would be impressively vindicated by our confirming power of the State to expel a handful of children from school. Such over-simplification, so handy in political debate, often lacks the precision necessary to postulates of judicial reasoning. If validly applied to this problem, the utterance cited would resolve every issue of power in favor of those in authority and would require us to override every liberty thought to weaken or delay execution of their policies.

Government of limited power need not be anemic government. Assurance that rights are secure tends to diminish fear and jealousy of strong government, and by making us feel safe to live under it makes for its better support. Without promise of a limiting Bill of Rights it is doubtful if our Constitution could have mustered enough strength to enable its ratification. To enforce those rights today is not to choose weak government over strong government. It is only to adhere as a means of strength to individual freedom of mind in preference to officially disciplined uniformity for which history indicates a disappointing and disastrous end.

The subject now before us exemplifies this principle. Free public education, if faithful to the ideal of secular instruction and political neutrality, will not be partisan or enemy of any class, creed, party, or faction. If it is to impose any ideological discipline, however, each party or denomination must seek to control, or failing that, to weaken the influence of the educational system. Observance of the limitations of the Constitution will not weaken government in the field appropriate for its exercise.

2. It was also considered in the *Gobitis* case that functions of educational officers in States, counties and school districts were such that to interfere with their authority "would in effect make us the school board for the country."

The Fourteenth Amendment, as now applied to the States, protects the citizen against the State itself and all of its creatures—Boards of Education not excepted. These have, of course, important, delicate, and highly discretionary functions, but none that they may not perform within the limits of the Bill of Rights. That they are educating the young for citizenship is reason for scrupulous protection of Constitutional freedoms of the individual, if we are not to strangle the free mind at its source and teach youth to discount important principles of our government as mere platitudes.

Such Boards are numerous and their territorial jurisdiction often small. But small and local authority may feel less sense of responsibility to the Constitution, and agencies of publicity may be less vigilant in calling it to account. The action of Congress in making flag observance voluntary and respecting the conscience of the objector in a matter so vital as raising the Army contrasts sharply with these local regulations in matters relatively trivial to the welfare of the nation. There are village tyrants as well as village Hampdens, but none who acts under color of law is beyond reach of the Constitution.

3. The *Gobitis* opinion reasoned that this is a field "where courts possess no marked and certainly no controlling competence," that it is committed to the legislatures as well as the courts to guard cherished liberties and that it is constitutionally appropriate to "fight out the wise use of legislative authority in the forum of public opinion and before legislative assemblies rather than to transfer such a contest to the judicial arena," since all the "effective means of inducing political changes are left free."

The very purpose of a Bill of Rights was to withdraw certain subjects from the vicissitudes of political controversy, to place them beyond the reach of majorities and officials and to establish them as legal principles to be applied by the courts. One's right to life, liberty, and property, to free speech, a free press, freedom of worship and assembly, and other fundamental rights may not be submitted to vote; they depend on the outcome of no elections.

In weighing arguments of the parties it is important to distinguish between the due process clause of the Fourteenth Amendment as an instrument for transmitting the principles of the First Amendment and those cases in which it is applied for its own sake. The test of legislation which collides with the Fourteenth Amendment, because it also collides with the principles of the First, is much more definite than the test when only the Fourteenth is involved. Much of the vagueness of the due process clause disappears when the specific prohibitions of the First become its standard. The right of a State to regulate, for example, a public utility may well include, so far as the due process test is concerned, power to impose all of the restrictions which a legislature may have a "rational basis" for adopting. But freedoms of speech and of press, of assembly, and of worship may not be infringed on such slender grounds. They are susceptible of restriction only to prevent grave and immediate danger to interests which the State may lawfully protect. It is important to note that while it is the Fourteenth Amendment which bears directly upon the State it is the more specific limiting principles of the First Amendment that finally govern this case.

Nor does our duty to apply the Bill of Rights to assertions of official authority depend upon our possession of marked competence in the field where the invasion of rights occurs. True, the task of translating the majestic generalities of the Bill of Rights, conceived as part of the pattern of liberal government in the eighteenth century, into concrete restraints on officials dealing with the problems of the twentieth century, is one to disturb self-confidence. These principles grew in soil which also produced a philosophy that the individual was the center of society, that his liberty was attainable through mere absence of governmental restraints, and that government should be entrusted with few controls and only the mildest supervision over men's [sic] affairs. We must transplant these rights to a soil in which the laissez-faire concept or principle of non-interference has withered at least as to economic affairs, and social advancements are increasingly sought through closer integration of society and through expanded and strengthened governmental controls. These changed conditions often deprive precedents of reliability and cast us more than we would choose upon our own judgment. But we act in these matters not by authority of our competence but by force of our commissions. We cannot, because of modest estimates of our competence in such specialties as public education, withhold the judgment that history authenticates as the function of this Court when liberty is infringed.

4. Lastly, and this is the very heart of the *Gobitis* opinion, it reasons that "National unity is the basis of national security," that the authorities have "the right to select appropriate means for its attainment," and hence reaches the conclusion that such compulsory measures toward "national unity" are constitutional. Upon the verity of this assumption depends our answer in this case.

National unity as an end which officials may foster by persuasion and example is not in question. The problem is whether under our Constitution compulsion as here employed is a permissible means for its achievement.

Struggles to coerce uniformity of sentiment in support of some end thought essential to their time and country have been waged by many good as well as by evil men. Nationalism is a relatively recent phenomenon but at other times and places the ends have been racial or territorial security, support of a dynasty or regime, and particular plans for saving souls. As first and moderate methods to attain unity have failed, those bent on its accomplishment must resort to an ever-increasing severity. As governmental pressure toward unity becomes greater, so strife becomes more bitter as to whose unity it shall be. Probably no deeper division of our people could proceed from any provocation than from finding it necessary to choose what doctrine and whose program public educational officials shall compel youth to unite in embracing. Ultimate futility of such attempts to compel coherence is the lesson of every such effort from the Roman drive to stamp out Christianity as a disturber of its pagan unity, the Inquisition, as a means to religious and dynastic unity, the Siberian exiles as a means to Russian unity, down to the fast failing efforts of our present totalitarian enemies. Those who begin coercive elimination of dissent soon find themselves exterminating dissenters. Compulsory unification of opinion achieves only the unanimity of the graveyard.

It seems trite but necessary to say that the First Amendment to our Constitution was designed to avoid these ends by avoiding these beginnings. There is no mysticism in the American concept of the State or of the nature or origin of its authority. We set up government by consent of the governed, and the Bill of Rights denies those in power any legal opportunity to coerce that consent. Authority here is to be controlled by public opinion, not public opinion by authority.

The case is made difficult not because the principles of its decision are obscure but because the flag involved is our own. Nevertheless, we apply the limitations of the Constitution with no fear that freedom to be intellectually and spiritually diverse or even contrary will disintegrate the social organization. To believe that patriotism will not flourish if patriotic ceremonies are voluntary and spontaneous instead of a compulsory routine is to make an unflattering estimate of the appeal of our institutions to free minds. We can have intellectual individualism and the rich cultural diversities that we owe to exceptional minds only at the price of occasional eccentricity and abnormal attitudes. When they are so harmless to others or to the State as those we deal with here, the price is not too great. But freedom to differ is not limited to things that do not matter much. That would be a mere shadow of freedom. The test of its substance is the right to differ as to things that touch the heart of the existing order.

If there is any fixed star in our constitutional constellation, it is that no official, high or petty, can prescribe what shall be orthodox in politics, nationalism, religion, or other mat-

ters of opinion or force citizens to confess by word or act their faith therein. If there are any circumstances which permit an exception, they do not now occur to us. We think the action of the local authorities in compelling the flag salute and pledge transcends constitutional limitations on their power and invades the sphere of intellect and spirit which it is the purpose of the First Amendment to our Constitution to reserve from all official control.

The decision of this Court in *Minersville School District v. Gobitis* and the holdings of those few *per curiam* decisions which preceded and foreshadowed it are overruled, and the judgment enjoining enforcement of the West Virginia Regulation is Affirmed.

Since *Barnette*, schools have been prohibited from insisting that students participate in flag salutes or other patriotic ceremonies. Students may not be forced to stand during the ceremony or to leave the room if they choose not to participate.[107] In *Circle School v. Pappert*,[108] the Third Circuit affirmed a lower court ruling that a statute requiring schools to notify parents if their child refused to participate in the flag salute violated the free speech rights of students. Whether it is permissible to include a flag salute in a school's daily program—as many schools do and as some states require—has long been controversial.[109] However, as discussed earlier in this chapter, both the First Circuit and the Ninth Circuit have ruled that reciting the Pledge of Allegiance in schools has the inculcation of patriotism as its secular purpose. Hence the voluntary, teacher-led recitation of the Pledge by public school students does not violate the Constitution.[110]

Community Service Requirements

The right not to speak has had little effect on the program of schools, apart from these exemptions from reciting the Pledge. In *Steirer v. Bethlehem Area School District*,[111] the Third Circuit rejected a student's claim that a school's program of compulsory community service required her to embrace and express a belief in the value of altruism. Community service requirements have also prevailed against claims that they violate the right of parents to direct the upbringing of their children and against claims that they violate the Thirteenth Amendment, which prohibits involuntary servitude.[112]

---

107 Lipp v. Morris, 579 F.2d 834 (3d Cir. 1978); Goetz v. Ansell, 477 F.2d 636 (2d Cir. 1973); Banks v. Bd. of Pub. Instruction of Dade County, 450 F.2d 1103 (5th Cir. 1971).
108 Circle Sch. v. Phillips, 270 F. Supp. 2d 616 (E.D. Pa. 2003), *aff'd*, Circle Sch. v. Pappert, 381 F.3d 172 (3d Cir. 2004).
109 See Randall Curren and Charles Dorn, Patriotic Education In A Global Age (2018).
110 Newdow v. Rio Linda Union Sch. Dist., 597 F.3d 1007 (9th Cir. Cal. 2010); Freedom from Religion Foundation v. Hanover Sch. Dist., 626 F.3d 1 (1st Cir. 2010).
111 Steirer v. Bethlehem Area Sch. Dist., 987 F.2d 989 (3d Cir. 1993).
112 Herndon v. Chapel Hill-Carrboro, 89 F.3d 174 (4th Cir. 1996); Immediato v. Rye Neck Sch. Dist., 73 F.3d 454 (2d Cir. 1996).

The Right to Know

In 1981, the Supreme Court addressed the censorship of library books in *Board of Education v. Pico*.[113] The case was brought by a group of students who claimed that their free speech rights were violated when the school board, at the urging of a politically conservative lobbying organization, removed nine books from the school library. *Pico* produced no majority opinion. Although five of the nine justices agreed that the Constitution placed some limits on a school board's authority to remove books, they could not agree on an appropriate test for determining those limitations.[114] The plurality opinion sought to balance the authority of the school board to attempt to prepare students for adult citizenship by inculcating them with democratic values with the students' right to receive ideas. The right to receive ideas, said the opinion, "follows ineluctably from the *sender's* First Amendment right to send them."

In *American Civil Liberties Union of Florida v. Miami-Dade County School Board*,[115] officials removed a travel book about Cuba from the school library following a complaint from a parent that the book did not accurately portray life under the Castro regime. Applying the approach of the plurality opinion in *Pico*, the district court barred removal of the books, citing the constitutional rights of students to access them.

In *Counts v. Cedarville School District*,[116] parents successfully challenged a policy requiring students to obtain parental permission before checking out *Harry Potter* books from their school library. The school board had restricted access to the books because they dealt with witchcraft and the occult. The district court held it was not properly within the board's power to prevent students from reading about witchcraft, noting that the parental permission policy violated students' First Amendment rights.

Access to the Internet

The **Children's Internet Protection Act** (CIPA)[117] permits schools to receive federal financial assistance in obtaining Internet access if they agree to use filtering software that blocks all access to legally obscene material and child pornography. In *United States v. American Library Association*,[118] the Supreme Court ruled that placing such conditions on the availability of federal funds was not a violation of free speech rights.

Federal Regulation of Public School Programs and Policies

A variety of federal statutes regulate the programs and policies of public schools. These laws generally operate by attaching conditions to federal funding. In Chapter 6, we discuss federal laws designed to ensure race and gender equity in public schools. In Chapter 7, we discuss federal laws recognizing the special educational rights of children with disabilities and English-language learners. In Chapter 4, we discuss the **Equal Access Act**,[119] a federal law designed to promote the recognition of student rights of free speech and association in schools. In Chapter 12, we discuss the **Family Education Rights and Privacy Act** (FERPA),[120] which regulates the maintenance

---

113 457 U.S. 853 (1981).
114 *See* Tyll van Geel, *The Search for Constitutional Limits on Governmental Authority to Inculcate Youth*, 62(2) TEXAS L. REV. 197–297 (1983).
115 439 F. Supp.1242 (S.D. Fla. 2006).
116 295 F. Supp. 2d 996 (W.D. Ark. 2003).
117 47 U.S.C. § 247.
118 539 U.S. 194 (2003).
119 20 U.S.C. § 4071.
120 20 U.S.C. § 1232g.

of student records. Three additional federal statutes regulate the programs and policies of public schools: the **Hatch Amendment**, the **Copyright Act**, and the **Every Student Succeeds Act**.

The Hatch Amendment

The **Protection of Pupil Rights Amendment** (PPRA),[121] also known as the **Hatch Amendment**, has two main provisions.[122] The first requires that all instructional materials used by schools in connection with research or experimentation be available for parental inspection. The second requires schools to obtain written parental consent before minor students are required to participate in surveys, analyses, or evaluations which may reveal information about political affiliations; mental and psychological problems; sexual behavior and attitudes; illegal, anti-social, self-incriminating and demeaning behavior; religious practices, affiliations, or beliefs; or income; or which may elicit critical appraisals of other individuals with whom students have close family relationships or legally privileged relationships (including lawyers, physicians, and ministers). Failure to comply with the *Hatch Amendment* could result in the loss of federal funds.

The Copyright Act

The **Copyright Act of 1976**,[123] as subsequently amended,[124] regulates the duplication of material for use in classrooms. A copyright owner enjoys a set of intellectual property rights, including an exclusive right to reproduce the work, to sell copies, and to perform or display the work. Thus, the excessive duplication of copyrighted materials without permission can violate the law. The circumstances under which duplication is permitted are known as "fair use."[125]

The *Copyright Act* states that "the fair use of a copyrighted work … for purposes such as criticism, comment, news reporting, teaching (including multiple copies for classroom use, scholarship, or research) is not an infringement of copyright." But the "fair use" exception for teaching is not unlimited. In an era in which teachers can download and distribute copyrighted material in seconds, the Ninth Circuit's interpretation of "fair use" in the following illustrative case remains critically important for public school districts seeking to avoid liability under the *Copyright Act*.

⚖️

MARCUS v. ROWLEY AND SAN DIEGO UNIFIED SCHOOL DISTRICT
US Court of Appeals for the Ninth Circuit
695 F.2d 1171 (1983)

MARIANA R. PFAELZER, District Judge:

This is an appeal from a dismissal on the merits of a suit for copyright infringement brought by a public school teacher who is the owner of a registered copyright to a booklet on cake decorating. The defendant, also a public school teacher, incorporated a substantial portion of the copyrighted work into a booklet which she prepared for use in her classes.

121 20 U.S.C. § 1232h.
122 *See* U.S. Department Of Education, PPRA For Parents. Online at www2.ed.gov/policy/gen/guid/fpco/ppra/parents.html (last accessed November 5, 2019).
123 17 U.S.C. §§ 101–810.
124 Copyright Renewal Act, 106 Stat. 264 (1992); No Electronic Theft Act, 111 Stat. 2678 (1997); Digital Millennium Copyright Act, 112 Stat. 2860 (1998); Copyright Term Extension Act, 112 Stat. 2827 (1998); Family Entertainment and Copyright Act, 119 Stat. 218 (2005).
125 *See* Stanford University Libraries, Copyright And Fair Use. Online at https://fairuse.stanford.edu (last accessed November 5, 2019).

Both parties moved the district court for summary judgment. The district court denied both motions and dismissed the action on the merits on the ground that defendant's copying of plaintiff's material constituted fair use. We reverse.

I. Factual Background

From September 1972 to June 1974, plaintiff, Eloise Toby Marcus was employed by the defendant, San Diego Unified School District ("District") as a teacher of home economics. Plaintiff resigned from the District's employ in 1974 and taught adult education classes intermittently from 1975 to 1980. Shortly after leaving her teaching position with the District, she wrote a booklet entitled "Cake Decorating Made Easy". Plaintiff's booklet consisted of thirty-five pages of which twenty-nine were her original creation. The remaining six pages consisted of material incorporated with the permission of the authors of the materials for which the authors were given appropriate credit.

Plaintiff properly registered the copyright for "Cake Decorating Made Easy" with the Register of Copyrights, and one hundred and twenty-five copies of the booklet were published in the spring of 1975. All of the copies of plaintiff's booklet contained a designation of copyright as evidenced by an encircled "c" followed by "1975 Eloise Marcus." This designation appeared on the table of contents page, the first page, and the page following the cover-title sheet.

Plaintiff sold all but six of the copies of her booklet for $2.00 each to the students in the adult education cake decorating classes which she taught. Plaintiff's profit was $1.00 on the sale of each booklet. Copies of plaintiff's booklet were never distributed to or sold by a bookstore or other outlet. Plaintiff never authorized anyone to copy or reproduce her booklet or any part of it.

Defendant, Shirley Rowley ("Rowley"), teaches food service career classes in the District. In the spring of 1975, she enrolled in one of plaintiff's cake decorating classes and purchased a copy of plaintiff's book. During the following summer, Rowley prepared a booklet entitled "Cake Decorating Learning Activity Package" ("LAP") for use in her food service career classes. The LAP consisted of twenty-four pages and was designed to be used by students who wished to study an optional section of her course devoted to cake decorating. Defendant had fifteen copies of the LAP made and put them in a file so that they would be available to her students. She

used the LAP during the 1975, 1976 and 1977 school years. The trial court found that sixty of Rowley's two hundred and twenty-five students elected to study cake decorating. The trial court further found that neither Rowley nor the District derived any profit from the LAP.

Rowley admits copying eleven of the twenty-four pages in her LAP from plaintiff's booklet. The eleven pages copied consisted of the supply list, icing recipes, three sheets dealing with color flow and mixing colors, four pages showing how to make and use a decorating bag, and two pages explaining how to make flowers and sugar molds. Four additional pages in defendant's LAP also appear in plaintiff's booklet, but these pages primarily contain information collected by and used with the permission of the Consumer Service Department of the American Institute of Baking. Twenty pages of plaintiff's booklet were not included in Rowley's LAP. Rowley did not give plaintiff credit for the eleven pages she copied, nor did she acknowledge plaintiff as the owner of a copyright with respect to those pages.

Plaintiff learned of Rowley's LAP in the summer of 1977 when a student in plaintiff's adult education class refused to purchase plaintiff's book. The student's son had obtained a copy of the LAP from Rowley's class. After examining Rowley's booklet, the student accused plaintiff of plagiarizing Rowley's work. Following these events, plaintiff made a claim of infringement against Rowley and the District. Both denied infringement and the plaintiff filed suit.

The parties filed cross-motions for summary judgment. The trial court denied both motions for summary judgment and dismissed the case on the merits. The ground for dismissal was that the defendant's copying of the plaintiff's material for nonprofit educational purposes constituted fair use. ...

III. The Doctrine of Fair Use

Fair use is most often defined as the "privilege in others than the owner of a copyright to use the copyrighted material in a reasonable manner without his consent, notwithstanding the monopoly granted to the owner ..." This doctrine was judicially created to "avoid rigid application" of the copyright laws when that application would defeat the law's original purpose which was the fostering of creativity. Because the doctrine was developed with a view to the introduction of flexibility and equity into the copyright laws, it has evolved in such a manner as to elude precise definition. It is clear, however, that "assuming the applicable criteria are met, fair use can extend to the reproduction of copyrighted material for purposes of classroom teaching." Thus, a later House Report listed, among examples of fair use, the "reproduction by a teacher or student of a small part of a work to illustrate a lesson ..."

A. The Purpose and Character of the Use

The first factor to be considered in determining the applicability of the doctrine of fair use is the purpose and character of the use, and specifically whether the use is of a commercial nature or is for a nonprofit educational purpose. It is uncontroverted that Rowley's use of the LAP was for a nonprofit educational purpose and that the LAP was distributed to students at no charge. These facts necessarily weigh in Rowley's favor. Nevertheless, a finding of a nonprofit educational purpose does not automatically compel a finding of fair use. ...

In this case, both plaintiff's and defendant's booklets were prepared for the purpose of teaching cake decorating, a fact which weighs against a finding of fair use. Because fair use presupposes that the defendant has acted fairly and in good faith, the propriety of the defendant's conduct should also be weighed in analyzing the purpose and character of the use.

Here, there was no attempt by defendant to secure plaintiff's permission to copy the contents of her booklet or to credit plaintiff for the use of her material even though Rowley's copying was for the most part verbatim. Rowley's conduct in this respect weighs against a finding of fair use.

B. The Nature of the Copyrighted Work

The second factor to be weighed is the nature of the copyrighted work ... [A]nalysis of this factor requires consideration of whether the work is "informational" or "creative." ... Here, plaintiff's booklet involved both informational and creative aspects. Some pages in her booklet undoubtedly contained information available in other cake decorating books or in recipe books. Other parts of her booklet contained creative hints she derived from her own experiences or ideas; certainly the manner in which plaintiff assembled her book represented a creative expression. Thus, on balance, it does not appear that analysis of this factor

is of any real assistance in reaching a conclusion as to applicability of fair use.

C. The Amount and Substantiality of the Portion Used

The third factor to be considered is the amount and substantiality of the portion used in relation to the copyrighted work as a whole. Any conclusion with respect to this factor requires analysis of both the quantity and quality of the alleged infringement.

With respect to this factor, this court has long maintained the view that wholesale copying of copyrighted material precludes application of the fair use doctrine. Other courts are in accord with this principle, and two courts have specifically addressed the issue in relation to copying for educational purposes.

Wihtol v. Crow involved alleged infringement by the defendant, a school teacher and church choir director, of a hymn entitled "My God and I".[126] The defendant Crow incorporated plaintiff's original piano and solo voice composition into an arrangement for his choirs. He made forty-eight copies of his arrangement and had the piece performed on two occasions: once by the high school choir at the school chapel, and once in church on Sunday. The music was identified as "arranged [by] Nelson E. Crow", but no reference was made to plaintiff as the original composer. The Eighth Circuit affirmed the trial court's finding that Crow had infringed plaintiff's copyright and in addressing the issue of whether Crow's copying constituted fair use, the court stated that

whatever may be the breadth of the doctrine of 'fair use', it is not conceivable to us that the copying of all, or substantially all, of a copyrighted song can be held to be a 'fair use' merely because the infringer had no intent to infringe.

The court in *Encyclopaedia Britannica Educational Corp. v. Crooks* also considered the issue of fair use in the educational context.[127] In that case, three corporations which produced educational motion picture films sued the Board of Cooperative Educational Services of Erie County ("BOCES") for videotaping several of plaintiffs' copyrighted films without permission. BOCES distributed the copied films to

126 309 F.2d 777 (8th Cir. 1962).
127 447 F. Supp. 243 (W.D.N.Y. 1978).

schools for delayed student viewing. Defendants' fair use defense was rejected on the ground that although defendants were involved in non-commercial copying to promote science and education, the taping of entire copyrighted films was too excessive for the fair use defense to apply.

In this case, almost 50 percent of defendant's LAP was a verbatim copy of plaintiff's booklet and that 50 percent contained virtually all of the substance of defendant's book. Defendant copied the explanations of how to make the decorating bag, how to mix colors, and how to make various decorations as well as the icing recipes. In fact, the only substantive pages of plaintiff's booklet which defendant did not put into her booklet were hints on how to ice a cake and an explanation of how to make leaves. Defendant argues that it was fair to copy plaintiff's booklet because the booklet contained only facts which were in the public domain. Even if it were true that plaintiff's book contained only facts, this argument fails because defendant engaged in virtually verbatim copying. Defendant's LAP could have been a photocopy of plaintiff's booklet but for the fact that defendant retyped plaintiff's material. This case presents a clear example of both substantial quantitative and qualitative copying.

D. The Effect of the Use Upon the Potential Market for or Value of the Copyrighted Work

The final factor to be considered with respect to the fair use defense is the effect which the allegedly infringing use had on the potential market for or value of the copyrighted work. The 1967 House Report points out that this factor is often seen as the most important criterion of fair use, but also warned that it "must almost always be judged in conjunction with the other three criteria." The Report explains that "a use which supplants any part of the normal market for a copyrighted work would ordinarily be considered an infringement." Here, despite the fact that at least one of plaintiff's students refused to purchase her booklet as a result of defendant's copying, the trial court found that it was unable to conclude that the defendant's copying had any effect on the market for the plaintiff's booklet. ...

Thus, despite the trial court's finding, we conclude that the factors analyzed weigh decisively in favor of the conclusion of no fair use. This conclusion is in harmony with the Congressional guidelines which, as a final point, also merit consideration with respect to the issue of fair use in an educational context.

IV. The Congressional Guidelines

The question of how much copying for classroom use is permissible was of such major concern to Congress that, although it did not include a section on the subject in the revised Act, it approved a set of guidelines with respect to it. The guidelines represent the Congressional Committees' view of what constitutes fair use under the traditional judicial doctrine developed in the case law. The guidelines were designed to give teachers direction as to the extent of permissible copying and to eliminate some of the doubt which had previously existed in this area of the copyright laws. The guidelines were intended to represent minimum standards of fair use. Thus, while they are not controlling on the court, they are instructive on the issue of fair use in the context of this case.

The guidelines relating to multiple copies for classroom use indicate that such copying is permissible if three tests are met. First, the copying must meet the test of "brevity" and "spontaneity." "Brevity" is defined, for prose, as "either a complete article, story or essay of less than 2,500 words, or an excerpt from any prose work of not more than 1,000 words or ... 10 percent of the work, whichever is less ..." Rowley's copying would not be permissible under either of these tests.

The guidelines also provide a separate definition of "brevity" for "special works." "Special works" are works "which often combine language with illustrations and which are intended sometimes for children and at other times for a more general audience." Plaintiff's booklet arguably would fall into this category. The guidelines provide that, notwithstanding the guidelines for prose, "'special works' may not be reproduced in their entirety; however, an excerpt comprising not more than two of the published pages of such special work and containing not more than 10 percent of the words found in the text thereof, may be reproduced." Rowley's copying would not be permissible under this test.

Under the guidelines, "spontaneity" requires that

the copying is at the instance and inspiration of the individual teacher, and ... the inspiration and decision to use the work and the moment of its use for maximum teaching effectiveness are so close in time that it would be unreasonable to expect a timely reply to a request for permission.

Defendant compiled her LAP during the summer of 1975 and first used it in her classes during the 1975–1976 school year. She also used the LAP for the following two school years. Rowley's copying would not meet this requirement either.

The second test under the guidelines is that of "cumulative effect". This test requires that the copied material be for only one course in the school. This aspect of the test would probably be met on these facts. The test also limits the number of pieces which may be copied from the same author and the number of times a teacher may make multiple copies for one course during one term. These latter two tests also appear to be met. The facts indicate that defendant copied only one piece of plaintiff's work. Defendant's conduct,

therefore, would satisfy the second test under the guidelines.

The third test requires that each copy include a notice of copyright. As stated, defendant's LAP did not acknowledge plaintiff's authorship or copyright and therefore would not meet this test.

In conclusion, it appears that Rowley's copying would not qualify as fair use under the guidelines. ... The order of the district court is reversed, summary judgment is entered for the plaintiff, and the case is remanded for a determination of damages pursuant to the provisions of the *Copyright Act*. Reversed and remanded.

The Every Student Succeeds Act

The *Every Student Succeeds Act* (ESSA), signed into law by President Obama in December, 2015, is the most recent reauthorization of the *Elementary and Secondary Education Act* (ESEA) of 1965.

ESSA replaced the 2001 reauthorization of the *ESEA*, **No Child Left Behind** (NCLB). NCLB represented a kind of high water mark in terms of federal control of the public school program in this country, with federal education appropriations jumping from $42.1 billion in 2001 to $56.2 billion in 2002 following its enactment.[128] NCLB combined a grant program (Title I) for schools with high concentrations of students in poverty with new assessment, accountability, and reform mechanisms affecting many aspects of school operations. Both the grant program and the accountability components of NCLB were designed to promote improvement in high-poverty schools with a view to bringing all students to a state-specified level of proficiency by 2014. Schools that failed to make Adequate Yearly Progress (AYP) for five consecutive years could be taken over by the state or "restructured" as charter schools with a new staff complement. With school districts across the country struggling to meet their NCLB targets by the 2014 deadline, the Obama Administration granted waivers to 33 states in 2012. In exchange for these waivers, the states had to adopt their own accountability mechanisms, much as they had done before NCLB.

ESSA has retained some key NCLB provisions, including the standardized testing of students in public schools each year from the third to the eighth grades, the disaggregation of student achievement data by demographic group (including economically disadvantaged students, students from major ethnic and racial groups, children with disabilities, and English language learners); and by subgroup (for male and female students, students whose parents are migrant workers, homeless students, students in foster care, and students whose parents are in the military). *ESSA* contains modified NCLB accountability mechanisms for low-performing schools and its focus on narrowing achievement gaps.[129] Still, *ESSA* marks a retreat of sorts for the federal government, as it restores the establishment of standards and accountability mechanisms to state governments, much as the

---

128 *See* Patrick McGuinn, *From ESEA to NCLB, in* The Every Child Succeeds Act: What It Means For Schools, Systems, And States (F.M. Hess and M. Eden, eds., 2017), 13–28 at p. 25.

129 *See* Charles Barone, *What ESSA Says: Continuities and Departures, in* The Every Child Succeeds Act: What It Means For Schools, Systems, And States (F.M. Hess and M. Eden, eds., 2017) 59–73 at p. 67.

NCLB waivers did in 2014. Charles Barone, director of policy at Education Reform Now (ERN), makes the following observations in this regard:[130]

> *ESSA* closely resembles the waiver accountability system, though with a few twists. States must identify the bottom 5 percent of all schools in the state for interventions that will be conducted by school districts with state approval. High schools with graduation rates less than 67 percent must also be identified and sanctioned.
>
> Instead of "focus schools," *ESSA* requires states to identify a third category of schools, designated as "targeted support schools," in which any subgroup of students is consistently underperforming, as determined by the state. This provision has a slightly stronger tie to subgroup accountability than its analogue under waivers. *ESSA* requires states to notify the local educational agencies overseeing targeted schools and ensure that those schools are informed of their status. It's then up to staff in that school to come up with an intervention plan to improve outcomes for lagging subgroups. Additional targeted support is required in schools in which the underperforming subgroup tests in the bottom 5 percent.

Title I, the federal program for the support of disadvantaged students under *ESSA*, was funded at $15 billion in 2016.[131] As with past iterations of the *ESEA*, Title I funding is designed to prepare all students for success in college and in future careers. Under *ESSA*, schools are required to offer all students college and career counseling in addition to advanced placement (AP) courses.

Summary

While the State needs very good reasons to regulate the programs of private schools, it can impose almost any curricular requirement on public schools unless there are very good reasons *not* to do so. In practice, most states have chosen to delegate some of their curricular authority to local school boards. Since 1965, the federal government has been heavily involved in regulating public school programs, mostly through funding mechanisms with conditions attached. Decisions concerning standards, accountability, graduation requirements, mandated subjects, course content, instructional methods, and textbooks are made through complex processes that often involve multiple levels of government and a range of stakeholder groups.

Constitutional challenges to public school programs and policies are usually based on the First Amendment. Plaintiffs have successfully relied on the **Establishment Clause** to challenge organized prayers and religious observances in classrooms, at graduation ceremonies, and at school board meetings. Applying the **enhanced *Lemon* test**, including both a **coercion analysis** and an **endorsement analysis**, the courts have prohibited on-campus programs lacking a secular purpose, having the advancement or inhibition of religion as their primary purpose or effect, or entailing excessive entanglement between organized religion and the State. Plaintiffs claiming that the curriculum of public schools establishes secularism or secular humanism have not been successful.

On-campus Bible study programs have been found unconstitutional while off-campus "released time" programs have been found constitutional. Holiday music and pageants, as well as secular programs of study aimed at exposing students to diverse religious traditions and perspectives have been found constitutional. However, parents do not have a **free exercise** right to exempt their children from public school programs and materials which expose them to ideas at odds with their particular faith commitments, including programs promoting equity, respect for diversity, sexual-

---

130 *Id.*, 70.
131 *Id.*, 59.

ity and gender identity, and the theory of evolution. Neither parents nor school staff members may modify the public school curriculum to suit their individual beliefs and preferences.

Plaintiffs have successfully claimed a **right not to speak** under the First Amendment, allowing students to opt out of the recitation of the Pledge of Allegiance and other patriotic observances. Some plaintiffs have successfully claimed a **right to know** in cases involving either restrictions on access to or the removal of books and materials from from public school libraries.

Federal legislation with important implications for what is taught in public schools includes the *Copyright Act*. Under this legislation, "fair use" does not allow teachers to make unlimited use of copyrighted material in their classrooms.

The *ESSA* of 2015 is the most recent reauthorization of the ***Elementary and Secondary Education Act*** (ESEA) of 1965, replacing the ***No Child Left Behind Act*** (NCLB) of 2001. *ESSA* has restored responsibility for standards and accountability mechanisms to the states while retaining some key *NCLB* provisions, including the standardized testing of students in public schools each year from the third to the eighth grades and the disaggregation of student achievement data by demographic group (including economically disadvantaged students, students from major ethnic and racial groups, children with disabilities, and English language learners). Like previous reauthorizations of the *ESEA*, *ESSA* includes federal funding for the improvement of low-performing schools and the narrowing of achievement gaps with a view to improving student outcomes across demographic groups.

4 The First Amendment Rights of Students

In the American constitutional context, adults are presumed to be capable of making decisions for themselves without causing harm to others or the common good. They are presumed to have an interest in **self-governance**, the essence of individual liberty. Limiting governmental constraints on the exercise of individual liberties is a primary function of the Bill of Rights in general and of the First Amendment in particular. Competent adults are both at liberty and subject to law.

The situation for children is quite different.[1] As **legal minors**, children are neither fully at liberty nor fully subject to law. They are instead subject to the **custodial authority** of their parents or legal guardians, parental delegates, and other persons standing in the place of parents (*in loco parentis*). Custody generally refers to care and control, but it is also the common law mechanism by which adults exercise legal authority to make decisions for minor children. This distinction is based on **legal status**, not age, so it does not violate the Equal Protection Clause:

> Children are not a suspect class under the Equal Protection Clause, and a statutory classification of minor children with permanent legal disabilities due to diminished capacity is not a suspect classification ... The controlling principle is that the State as *parens patriae* of children may legislate for their protection, care, and custody.[2]

The "State as parent" has a duty to safeguard the welfare and developmental interests of every child within its territorial jurisdiction. As we saw in Chapter 2, compulsory schooling laws requiring parents to enroll their children in state-approved educational programs were predicated on the broad authority of the State to regulate custody, essentially requiring parents to share custody with state-approved teachers for periods of time. In American jurisprudence,

> The parents, as natural guardians, are responsible to the State for the child's well-being. The natural rights of a parent to the custody and control of his or her infant child are subject to the power of the State and may be restricted and regulated by appropriate legislative or judicial action.[3]

In both public and private schools, teachers and school officials are legally responsible for the care and control of the students in their charge. The common law duties of care of teachers and school officials are discussed in greater detail in Chapter 12. More importantly, public and private schools are custodial environments in the sense that teachers and school officials exercise custodial authority as parental delegates (in the case of private schools) or as parental delegates and agents of the State (in public schools).

---

1 J.C. Blokhuis, *Student Rights and the Special Characteristics of the School Environment in American Jurisprudence*, 49(1) Journal of Philosophy of Education 65–85 (2015).
2 628 Am Jur 2d Constitutional Law §897.
3 59 Am Jur 2d Parent and Child §18.

The Constitution does not apply to relationships between private actors, so it does not apply to parental decisions within families. Nor does it apply to private schools, where teachers and school officials continue to regulate student speech and student conduct as parental delegates (*in loco parentis*). Public schools, however, are **state agencies**. Thus the Constitution applies to decisions made by school officials inside the school gates, even though it does not apply to the decisions made by parents outside the school gates.[4]

Students in public schools are routinely told by teachers and other school officials—**agents of the State**—to be quiet, to turn off their phones, and to refrain from criticizing authorities, praying, proselytizing, using vulgar language, and many other things. In other contexts, agents of the State could not require such things of adults—or punish them for non-compliance—without violating the Constitution. But because most K-12 students are legal minors subject to custody, they do not have all the liberty rights and constitutional protections afforded to adults: "Because of the State's custodial and tutorial authority over [them], public school students are subject to greater degree of control and administrative supervision than is permitted over a free adult."[5]

In this chapter, we examine how the legal status of children and the custodial nature of school authority have limited the free speech rights available to students in public schools under the First Amendment. In Chapters 5 and 6, we examine how these "special characteristics of the school environment" have limited the Fourth, Fifth, and Fourteenth Amendment rights of students in public schools.

Freedom of Speech: An Overview

"Speech on matters of public concern … is at the heart of the First Amendment's protection," wrote Chief Justice Roberts in *Snyder v. Phelps*.[6] "The First Amendment reflects a profound national commitment to the principle that debate on public issues should be uninhibited, robust, and wide-open … because speech concerning public affairs is more than self-expression; it is the essence of self-government." Accordingly, "speech on public issues occupies the highest rung of the hierarchy of First Amendment values, and is entitled to special protection."

Courts typically extend broad-based, vigorous protection to most forms of speech and expression. Of course, no rights are absolute. Some forms of speech are so damaging that to protect them would do more harm than good. "Falsely shouting fire in a theatre and causing a panic" is a frequently cited example from Oliver Wendell Holmes, Jr. a century ago to illustrate why speech that is both false and likely to incite violence or panic does *not* receive First Amendment protection.[7] The courts have since produced an extensive body of free speech decisions involving a complex set of definitions, tests, and rules.

What Counts as "Speech"?

Because the First Amendment specifically refers to *speech*, at issue in many cases is whether some sort of expressive conduct qualifies. In *Citizens United v. Federal Communications Commission*,[8] the Supreme Court in 2010 recognized campaign spending by corporations and labor unions as a form of speech protected under the First Amendment.

---

4 Blokhuis, supra note 1 at 72.
5 67B Am Jur 2d Schools §284.
6 562 U.S. 443 (2011).
7 Schenk v. United States, 249 U.S. 47 (1919).
8 558 U.S. 310 (2010).

Is sleeping in a park a form of speech? In *Clark v. Community for Creative Non-Violence*,[9] a case involving people who slept in a park to draw attention to homelessness, the Supreme Court said it was. Is displaying the flag with a peace symbol attached a form of speech? Is dousing the flag in kerosene and setting it alight a form of speech? In both *Spence v. Washington* and *Texas v. Johnson*, the Supreme Court said yes.[10] "In deciding whether particular conduct possesses sufficient communicative elements to bring the First Amendment into play," wrote the Court in *Johnson*, quoting from its earlier decision in *Spence*, "we have asked whether '[a]n intent to convey a particularized message was present, and [whether] the likelihood was great that the message would be understood by those who viewed it.'"[11] These two questions remain the test for determining if a specific expressive act counts as "speech" for First Amendment purposes.

Hair Length

Is the length of a student's hair a form of speech? Like flag burning and peace symbols and wearing black armbands, many young people wore their hair long as a form of protest during the Vietnam War era.[12] "The federal courts have spent a great deal of time discussing the subject of hair," wrote the district court judge in *Bishop v. Colaw* in 1971, citing eight cases in which school districts had not been found to violate free speech rights with hair length regulations,[13] and eight cases in which the federal courts reached the opposite conclusion.[14] Finding that a student's hair length was not "symbolic conduct" akin to wearing black armbands to protest American military involvement in Vietnam, the *Bishop* court allowed the school district to enforce its hair length policies.[15]

Cases challenging such policies on First Amendment grounds often failed during the Vietnam War era because many courts would not consider hair length a form of speech.[16] In *Olff v. East Side Union High School District*,[17] a 15-year-old was denied enrolment because his long hair violated the school's policy that "a boy's hair shall not fall below the eyes in front and shall not cover the ears, and it shall not extend below the collar in back." In *New Rider v. Board of Education*,[18] three seventh-grade Pawnee students were indefinitely suspended for violating a similar school policy. The Supreme Court denied *certiorari* in both cases, despite vigorous dissents from Justices Douglas (joined by Justice Marshall in *New Rider*):

> This Court has consistently, over my dissents, refused to review lower court decisions passing on the constitutionality of school hair-length regulations, whether such regulations have been upheld or struck down, and regardless of the grounds on which the lower courts have reached their conclusions. I have

---

9 468 U.S. 288 (1984).
10 418 U.S. 405 (1974); 491 U.S. 397 (1989).
11 Texas v. Johnson, 491 U.S. 397 (1989).
12 Bishop v. Colaw, 450 F.2d 1069 (8th Cir. 1971); Gfell v. Rickelman, 441 F.2d 444 (6th Cir. 1971).
13 Stevenson v. Wheeler County Board of Education, 306 F. Supp. 97 (S.D. Ga. 1969); Farrell v. Smith, 310 F. Supp. 732 (D. Me. 1970); Giangreco v. Center School District, Civil Action 17661-3 (W.D. Mo. 1969); Brownlee v. Bradley County, 311 F. Supp. 1360 (E.D. Tenn. 1970); Schwartz v. Galveston Independent School District, 309 F. Supp. 1034 (S.D. Texas 1970); Davis v. Firment, 408 F.2d 1085 (5th Cir. 1969); Leonard v. School Committee of Attleboro, 349 Mass. 704, 212 N.E. 2d 468 (1965); Crews v. Cloncs, 303 F. Supp. 1370 (S.D. Ind. 1969).
14 Richards v. Thurston, 304 F. Supp. 449 (D. Mass. 1969); Zachry v. Brown, 299 F. Supp. 1360 (N.D. Ala. F. Supp. 1316 (D. Colo. 1969); Calbillo v. 1967); Brick v. Board of Education, 305 San Jacinto Junior College, 305 F. Supp. 857 (S.D. Texas 1969); Westley v. Rossi, 305 F. Supp. 706 (D. Minn. 1969); Sims v. Colfax Community School District, 307 F. Supp. 485 (S.D. Iowa 1970); Crossen v. Fatsi, 309 F. Supp. 114 (D. Conn. 1970); Reichenberg v. Nelson, 310 F. Supp. 248 (D. Neb. 1970).
15 445 F.2d 932 (9th Cir. 1971).
16 Jackson v. Dorrier, 424 F.2d 213 (6th Cir. 1970); *but see* Bishop v. Colaw, 450 F.2d 1069 (8th Cir. 1971).
17 445 F.2d 932 (9th Cir. 1971).
18 414 U.S. 1097 (1973).

noted the deep division among the Circuits on this issue, and have thought that it is an issue of particular personal interest to many and of considerable constitutional importance. Petitioners were not wearing their hair in a desired style simply because it was the fashionable or accepted style, or because they somehow felt the need to register an inchoate discontent with the general malaise they might have perceived in our society. They were in fact attempting to broadcast a clear and specific message to their fellow students and others—their pride in being.

Native American students have invoked free speech in conjunction with other constitutional rights to bar enforcement of hair length policies. In *Alabama & Coushatta Tribes of Texas v. Big Sandy Independent School District*,[19] the plaintiffs argued that long hair was a form of speech and that it was an aspect of their religion and culture. The school district was unable to prove that the hair regulation was necessary to maintain order in the school. In a more recent case, the Fifth Circuit found that a district policy requiring a Native American pre-kindergarten student to wear his long hair "in a bun on top of his head or in a braid tucked into his shirt" violated his free speech rights, though the case was ultimately decided under the *Texas Religious Freedom Restoration Act (TRFRA)*.[20]

In recent years, hair length policies have been challenged successfully under the Fourteenth Amendment or state or federal civil rights legislation rather than the First Amendment. For example, in *Hayden v. Greensburg Community School Corporation*,[21] a student successfully challenged a policy requiring male basketball players to keep their hair short. The Seventh Circuit found that because the policy did not apply to female basketball players, it deprived Hayden of equal protection by discriminating against him on the basis of sex.

Clothing and Accessories

As with hair length, most courts have not considered clothing or accessories to be forms of speech for First Amendment purposes. In *Olesen v. Board of Education*,[22] a federal court upheld a policy banning "gang regalia", including the wearing of earrings by male students. Darryl Oleson claimed he wore a single earring to "express his individuality and ... be attractive to the young women in his school." He unsuccessfully argued the policy violated his free speech and equal protection rights. Eight years later, in *Bivens v. Albuquerque Public Schools*, the Tenth Circuit upheld a policy banning saggy pants as a "gang regalia." The student claimed he wore saggy pants to express his link with African-American urban youth culture. He unsuccessfully argued the policy violated his free speech rights.[23]

In *Dreaming Bear v. Fleming*,[24] a federal court denied a Lakota student's free speech challenge to a school policy requiring him to wear a cap and gown over his traditional clothing at his school convocation. Another federal court denied a Cherokee student's free speech challenge to a school policy preventing her from attaching an eagle feather to her graduation cap in *Griffith v. Caney Valley Public Schools*.[25] In *Bar-Navon v. Brevard County School Board*,[26] a student suspended for

---

19 817 F. Supp. 1319 (E.D. Tex. 1993), *remanded*, 20 F.3d 469 (5th Cir. 1994).
20 A.A. v. Needville Indep. Sch. Dist., 611 F.3d 248 (5th Cir. 2010).
21 743 F.3d 569 (7th Cir. 2014).
22 Olesen v. Bd. of Educ. of Sch. Dist. No. 228, 676 F. Supp. 820 (N.D. Ill. 1987).
23 Bivens v. Albuquerque Pub. Schs., 899 F. Supp. 556 (D.N.M. 1995).
24 714 F. Supp. 2d 972 (D.S.D. 2010).
25 157 F. Supp. 3d 1159 (N.D. Okla. 2016).
26 290 Fed. Appx. 273 (11th Cir. 2008).

wearing jewelry in her tongue, nasal septum, lip, navel, and chest as a way of expressing her individuality unsuccessfully raised free speech claims against the school district. The Eleventh Circuit upheld the policy against body piercings on the ground that school officials had a duty to maintain a safe and hygienic learning environment.

Logos and Messages

In *Palmer v. Waxahachie Independent School District*,[27] a student challenged a school dress code prohibiting all clothing bearing messages (including one with the slogan "free speech"). The dress code allowed logos of curricular clubs and organizations and school athletic teams, along with logos smaller than two inches by two inches. Palmer argued that the exemption for small logos and school-sponsored team logos meant the dress code was not content neutral. The Fifth Circuit upheld the dress code, finding it content neutral and declaring that the school district was "in no way attempting to suppress any student's expression through its dress code."

In *Zamecnik v. Indian Prairie School District #204*,[28] a student claimed school officials violated his free speech rights by barring him from wearing a t-shirt with the slogan "Be Happy, Not Gay" at school. The Seventh Circuit found in favor of the student:

> As one would expect in a high school of more than 4,000 students, there had been incidents of harassment of homosexual students. But we thought it speculative that allowing the plaintiff to wear a T-shirt that said "Be Happy, Not Gay" would have even a slight tendency to provoke such incidents, or for that matter to poison the educational atmosphere. Speculation that it might is … too thin a reed on which to hang a prohibition of the exercise of a student's free speech.

School Uniforms

In recent years, a number of states have permitted schools to institute mandatory school uniform policies to help reduce "gang regalia" and promote school safety.[29] Initially, mandatory uniform policies easily withstood constitutional scrutiny. In *Canady v. Bossier Parish School Board*,[30] the Fifth Circuit found school uniforms raised free speech issues because the clothing choices of students had "communicative content" relating to their heritage, religious beliefs, and political views. Nonetheless, the Court upheld the policy. In *Jacobs v. Clark County School District*,[31] students argued that a mandatory school uniform policy violated their free speech rights. The Ninth Circuit found that the school uniform policy was a valid and neutral law of general applicability that did not implicate the First Amendment at all. But a decade later, in *Frudden v. Pilling*,[32] the Ninth Circuit found that a policy requiring students to wear a uniform featuring a stylized gopher (the school mascot) and the motto "Tomorrow's Leaders" violated their First Amendment rights.[33]

---

27 579 F.3d 502 (5th Cir. 2009).
28 636 F.3d 874 (7th Cir. 2011).
29 *See, e.g.*, CDCR 5-B2408 (District of Columbia, 2019); ORC Ann. 3313.665 (Ohio, 2019); C.R.S. 22-32-109.1 (Colorado, 2018); Utah Code Ann. § 53G-7-802 (Utah, 2018).
30 Canady v. Bossier Parish Sch. Bd., 240 F.3d 437 (5th Cir. 2001); *see also* Littlefield v. Forney Indep. Sch. Dist., 268 F.3d 275 (5th Cir. 2001).
31 526 F.3d 419 (9th Cir. 2008).
32 877 F.3d 821 (9th Cir. 2017).
33 See, generally, Galen Sherwin, *Five Things Public Schools Can and Can't Do When It Comes to Dress Codes*, ACLU.ORG (30 May, 2017); online at www.aclu.org/blog/womens-rights/womens-rights-education/5-things-public-schools-can-and-cant-do-when-it-comes (last accessed April 26, 2020).

Independent Student Speech

Until the Civil Rights era, children in the United States were regarded as having only the *custodial* interests associated with minority status, not the *liberty* interests associated with majority status. Students were expected to obey their teachers in much the same way they were expected to obey their parents, because teachers in both private and public schools stood *in loco parentis*:

> One of the most sacred duties of parents, is to train up and qualify their children, for becoming useful and virtuous members of society; this duty cannot be effectually performed without the ability to command obedience, to control stubbornness, to quicken diligence, and to reform bad habits,

wrote a North Carolina court in 1837. "The teacher is the substitute of the parent ... and in the exercise of these delegated duties, is invested with his [*sic*] power."[34] Apart from the Supreme Court ruling in *West Virginia v. Barnette*,[35] which prohibited school officials from requiring that students salute the flag (see Chapter 3), there were no *constitutional* limits on the authority of public school officials to make rules concerning student expression and conduct and to discipline students accordingly.

The situation changed dramatically in the 1960s, when the Supreme Court issued three decisions extending constitutional protection to minors in custodial contexts. Writing for the Court in *Kent v. United States*,[36] Justice Abe Fortas concluded that a minor charged with an offense received "neither the protections accorded to adults nor the solicitous care and regenerative treatment postulated for children" under the *parens patriae* doctrine. The following year, he applied the due process protections of the Fourteenth Amendment to juvenile court proceedings in *In re Gault*.[37] Two years later, at the height of the tumultuous Vietnam Era, he ascribed limited First Amendment rights to students in public schools in the following landmark decision:

TINKER v. DES MOINES INDEPENDENT SCHOOL DISTRICT
Supreme Court of the United States
393 U.S. 503 (1969)

MR. JUSTICE FORTAS delivered the opinion of the Court.

Petitioner John F. Tinker, 15 years old, and petitioner Christopher Eckhardt, 16 years old, attended high schools in Des Moines, Iowa. Petitioner Mary Beth Tinker, John's sister, was a 13-year-old student in junior high school.

In December 1965, a group of adults and students in Des Moines held a meeting at the Eckhardt home. The group determined to publicize their objections to the hostilities in Vietnam and their support for a truce by wearing black armbands during the holi-day season and by fasting on December 16 and New Year's Eve. Petitioners and their parents had previously engaged in similar activities, and they decided to participate in the program.

The principals of the Des Moines schools became aware of the plan to wear armbands. On December 14, 1965, they met and adopted a policy that any student wearing an armband to school would be asked to remove it, and if he refused he would be suspended until he returned without the armband. Petitioners were aware of the regulation that the school authorities adopted.

---

34   State v. Pendergrass, 19 N.C. 365 (1837).
35   319 U.S. 624 (1943).
36   383 U.S. 541 (1966).
37   387 U.S. 1 (1967).

On December 16, Mary Beth and Christopher wore black armbands to their schools. John Tinker wore his armband the next day. They were all sent home and suspended from school until they would come back without their armbands. They did not return to school until after the planned period for wearing armbands had expired—that is, until after New Year's Day.

This complaint was filed in the United States District Court by petitioners, through their fathers, under § 1983 of Title 42 of the United States Code. It prayed for an injunction restraining the respondent school officials and the respondent members of the board of directors of the school district from disciplining the petitioners, and it sought nominal damages. After an evidentiary hearing the District Court dismissed the complaint. It upheld the constitutionality of the school authorities' action on the ground that it was reasonable in order to prevent disturbance of school discipline. The court referred to but expressly declined to follow the Fifth Circuit's holding in a similar case that the wearing of symbols like the armbands cannot be prohibited unless it "materially and substantially interferes with the requirements of appropriate discipline in the operation of the school."

I.

The District Court recognized that the wearing of an armband for the purpose of expressing certain views is the type of symbolic act that is within the Free Speech Clause of the First Amendment. As we shall discuss, the wearing of armbands in the circumstances of this case was entirely divorced from actually or potentially disruptive conduct by those participating in it. It was closely akin to "pure speech" which, we have repeatedly held, is entitled to comprehensive protection under the First Amendment.

First Amendment rights, applied in light of the special characteristics of the school environment, are available to teachers and students. It can hardly be argued that either students or teachers shed their constitutional rights to freedom of speech or expression at the schoolhouse gate. This has been the unmistakable holding of this Court for almost 50 years. In *Meyer v. Nebraska*,[38] and *Bartels v. Iowa*,[39] this Court, in opinions by Mr. Justice McReynolds, held that the Due Process Clause of the Fourteenth Amendment prevents States from forbidding the teaching of a foreign language to young students. Statutes to this effect, the Court held, unconstitutionally interfere with the liberty of teacher, student, and parent.

In *West Virginia v. Barnette*,[40] this Court held that under the First Amendment, the student in public school may not be compelled to salute the flag. Speaking through Mr. Justice Jackson, the Court said: The Fourteenth Amendment, as now applied to the States, protects the citizen against the State itself and all of its creatures—Boards of Education not excepted. These have, of course, important, delicate, and highly discretionary functions, but none that they may not perform within the limits of the Bill of Rights. That they are educating the young for citizenship is reason for scrupulous protection of Constitutional freedoms of the individual, if we are not to strangle the free mind at its source and teach youth to discount important principles of our government as mere platitudes.

On the other hand, the Court has repeatedly emphasized the need for affirming the comprehensive authority of the States and of school officials, consistent with fundamental constitutional safeguards, to prescribe and control conduct in the schools. Our problem lies in the area where students in the exercise of First Amendment rights collide with the rules of the school authorities.

II.

The problem posed by the present case does not relate to regulation of the length of skirts or the type of clothing, to hairstyle, or deportment. It does not concern aggressive, disruptive action or even group demonstrations. Our problem involves direct, primary First Amendment rights akin to "pure speech."

The school officials banned and sought to punish petitioners for a silent, passive expression of opinion, unaccompanied by any disorder or disturbance on the part of petitioners. There is here no evidence whatever of petitioners' interference, actual or nascent, with the schools' work or of collision with the rights of other students to be secure and to be let alone. Accordingly, this case does not concern speech or action that intrudes upon the work of the schools or the rights of other students.

38 262 U.S. 390 (1923).
39 262 U.S. 404 (1923).
40 319 U.S. 624 (1943).

Only a few of the 18,000 students in the school system wore the black armbands. Only five students were suspended for wearing them. There is no indication that the work of the schools or any class was disrupted. Outside the classrooms, a few students made hostile remarks to the children wearing armbands, but there were no threats or acts of violence on school premises.

The District Court concluded that the action of the school authorities was reasonable because it was based upon their fear of a disturbance from the wearing of the armbands. But, in our system, undifferentiated fear or apprehension of disturbance is not enough to overcome the right to freedom of expression. Any departure from absolute regimentation may cause trouble. Any variation from the majority's opinion may inspire fear. Any word spoken, in class, in the lunchroom, or on the campus, that deviates from the views of another person may start an argument or cause a disturbance. But our Constitution says we must take this risk, and our history says that it is this sort of hazardous freedom—this kind of openness—that is the basis of our national strength and of the independence and vigor of Americans who grow up and live in this relatively permissive, often disputatious, society.

In order for the State in the person of school officials to justify prohibition of a particular expression of opinion, it must be able to show that its action was caused by something more than a mere desire to avoid the discomfort and unpleasantness that always accompany an unpopular viewpoint. Certainly where there is no finding and no showing that engaging in the forbidden conduct would "materially and substantially interfere with the requirements of appropriate discipline in the operation of the school," the prohibition cannot be sustained.

In the present case, the District Court made no such finding, and our independent examination of the record fails to yield evidence that the school authorities had reason to anticipate that the wearing of the armbands would substantially interfere with the work of the school or impinge upon the rights of other students. Even an official memorandum prepared after the suspension that listed the reasons for the ban on wearing the armbands made no reference to the anticipation of such disruption.

On the contrary, the action of the school authorities appears to have been based upon an urgent wish to avoid the controversy which might result from the expression, even by the silent symbol of armbands, of opposition to this Nation's part in the conflagration in Vietnam. It is revealing, in this respect, that the meeting at which the school principals decided to issue the contested regulation was called in response to a student's statement to the journalism teacher in one of the schools that he wanted to write an article on Vietnam and have it published in the school paper. (The student was dissuaded.)

It is also relevant that the school authorities did not purport to prohibit the wearing of all symbols of political or controversial significance. The record shows that students in some of the schools wore buttons relating to national political campaigns, and some even wore the Iron Cross, traditionally a symbol of Nazism. The order prohibiting the wearing of armbands did not extend to these. Instead, a particular symbol—black armbands worn to exhibit opposition to this Nation's involvement in Vietnam—was singled out for prohibition. Clearly, the prohibition of expression of one particular opinion, at least without evidence that it is necessary to avoid material and substantial interference with schoolwork or discipline, is not constitutionally permissible.

In our system, state-operated schools may not be enclaves of totalitarianism. School officials do not possess absolute authority over their students. Students in school as well as out of school are "persons" under our Constitution. They are possessed of fundamental rights which the State must respect, just as they themselves must respect their obligations to the State. In our system, students may not be regarded as closed-circuit recipients of only that which the State chooses to communicate. They may not be confined to the expression of those sentiments that are officially approved. In the absence of a specific showing of constitutionally valid reasons to regulate their speech, students are entitled to freedom of expression of their views. As Judge Gewin, speaking for the Fifth Circuit, said, school officials cannot suppress "expressions of feelings with which they do not wish to contend."

In *Meyer v. Nebraska*,[41] Mr. Justice McReynolds expressed this Nation's repudiation of the principle that a State might so conduct its schools as to "foster a homogeneous people." He said:

In order to submerge the individual and develop ideal citizens, Sparta assembled the males at seven into barracks and entrusted their subsequent edu-

41 262 U.S. 390 (1923).

cation and training to official guardians. Although such measures have been deliberately approved by men of great genius, their ideas touching the relation between individual and State were wholly different from those upon which our institutions rest; and it hardly will be affirmed that any legislature could impose such restrictions upon the people of a State without doing violence to both letter and spirit of the Constitution.

This principle has been repeated by this Court on numerous occasions during the intervening years. In *Keyishian v. Board of Regents*,[42] Mr. Justice Brennan, speaking for the Court, said:

The vigilant protection of constitutional freedoms is nowhere more vital than in the community of American schools … The classroom is peculiarly the "marketplace of ideas." The Nation's future depends upon leaders trained through wide exposure to that robust exchange of ideas which discovers truth out of a multitude of tongues, [rather] than through any kind of authoritative selection.

The principle of these cases is not confined to the supervised and ordained discussion which takes place in the classroom. The principal use to which the schools are dedicated is to accommodate students during prescribed hours for the purpose of certain types of activities. Among those activities is personal intercommunication among the students. This is not only an inevitable part of the process of attending school; it is also an important part of the educational process. A student's rights, therefore, do not embrace merely the classroom hours. When he is in the cafeteria, or on the playing field, or on the campus during the authorized hours, he may express his opinions, even on controversial subjects like the conflict in Vietnam, if he does so without "materially and substantially interfer[ing] with the requirements of appropriate discipline in the operation of the school" and without colliding with the rights of others. But conduct by the student, in class or out of it, which for any reason—whether it stems from time, place, or type of behavior—materially disrupts classwork or involves substantial disorder or invasion of the rights of others is, of course, not immunized by the constitutional guarantee of freedom of speech.

Under our Constitution, free speech is not a right that is given only to be so circumscribed that it exists in principle but not in fact. Freedom of expression would not truly exist if the right could be exercised only in an area that a benevolent government has provided as a safe haven for crackpots. The Constitution says that Congress (and the States) may not abridge the right to free speech. This provision means what it says. We properly read it to permit reasonable regulation of speech-connected activities in carefully restricted circumstances. But we do not confine the permissible exercise of First Amendment rights to a telephone booth or the four corners of a pamphlet, or to supervised and ordained discussion in a school classroom.

If a regulation were adopted by school officials forbidding discussion of the Vietnam conflict, or the expression by any student of opposition to it anywhere on school property except as part of a prescribed classroom exercise, it would be obvious that the regulation would violate the constitutional rights of students, at least if it could not be justified by a showing that the students' activities would materially and substantially disrupt the work and discipline of the school. In the circumstances of the present case, the prohibition of the silent, passive "witness of the armbands," as one of the children called it, is no less offensive to the Constitution's guarantees.

As we have discussed, the record does not demonstrate any facts which might reasonably have led school authorities to forecast substantial disruption of or material interference with school activities, and no disturbances or disorders on the school premises in fact occurred. These petitioners merely went about their ordained rounds in school. Their deviation consisted only in wearing on their sleeve a band of black cloth, not more than two inches wide. They wore it to exhibit their disapproval of the Vietnam hostilities and their advocacy of a truce, to make their views known, and, by their example, to influence others to adopt them. They neither interrupted school activities nor sought to intrude in the school affairs or the lives of others. They caused discussion outside of the classrooms, but no interference with work and no disorder. In the circumstances, our Constitution does not permit officials of the State to deny their form of expression … We reverse and remand for further proceedings consistent with this opinion.

42 385 U.S. 589 (1967).

In *Tinker*, the Supreme Court recognized that "First Amendment rights, applied in light of the special characteristics of the school environment, are available to teachers and students." Public school officials cannot pick and choose the substantive messages they will allow, lest "state-operated schools … [become] enclaves of totalitarianism." Public school officials could nevertheless prohibit independent student speech if it was **materially and substantially disruptive** to the legitimate educational mission of the school. This became the basic rule regarding the regulation by school officials of all manner of student speech, regardless of how and where the speech occurred. As we have seen in the hair length and clothing cases discussed earlier in this chapter, the lower courts were inconsistent in defining "speech" and in applying the material and substantial disruption test.

Justice Fortas did not explicitly define the "special characteristics of the school environment" in *Tinker*. Instead, he cited a canonical statement by Curtis C. Shears in the *American Bar Association Journal*: "The basic right of a juvenile is not to liberty but to custody. He has the right to have someone take care of him, and if his parents do not afford him this custodial privilege, the law must do so."[43] Like many law school graduates trying to come to terms with the ascription of constitutional rights to minors in custodial contexts in *Kent*, *Gault*, and *Tinker*, Hillary Rodham cautioned at the time that, "Asserting that children are entitled to rights and enumerating their needs does not clarify the difficult issues surrounding [their] legal status."[44]

The Supreme Court began retreating from *Kent*, *Gault*, and *Tinker* almost immediately. Over the next two and a half decades, *in loco parentis* regained significance as the Court limited the scope of the constitutional rights for students enunciated in *Tinker*. In 1995, Justice Antonin Scalia specifically defined the "special characteristics of the school environment" in terms of the "custodial and tutelary" relationship between public school officials and students in *Vernonia School District 47j v. Acton*.[45] That case involved a seventh-grader challenging a school policy mandating random drug testing of all interscholastic athletes (see Chapter 5). "[T]he legitimacy of certain privacy expectations vis-à-vis the State may depend on the individual's legal relationship with the State," Justice Scalia wrote. "Central, in our view, to the present case is the fact that the subjects of the Policy are (1) children, who (2) have been committed to the temporary custody of the State as schoolmaster."

Since then, the Supreme Court has further limited the sweep of *Tinker* by identifying a number of circumstances in which the **material and substantial disruption** rule does not apply. First, it ruled that in cases involving **school-sponsored speech**, such as an assembly or student newspaper, the regulatory authority that school officials enjoy is greater than in cases involving **independent student speech**. Second, following a line of reasoning first applied in lower court decisions, the Supreme Court added **new categories of student speech** to those which do not enjoy the protection of the First Amendment in public schools.

School-Sponsored Student Speech

In this section, we consider student speech that is part of the curriculum or otherwise sponsored or endorsed by school officials. As the following landmark decision from the Supreme Court shows, school officials have much greater leeway to regulate speech in these circumstances.

---

43 C.C. Shears, Legal Problems Peculiar to Children's Courts, 48 AMERICAN BAR ASSOCIATION JOURNAL 48 (1962); Blokhuis, supra note 1 at 67.

44 H. Rodham, Children under the Law, 43(4) HARVARD EDUCATIONAL REVIEW 487 (1973); Blokhuis, supra note 1 at 78.

45 515 U.S. 646 (1995).

⚖️

HAZELWOOD SCHOOL DISTRICT v. KUHLMEIER
Supreme Court of the United States
484 U.S. 260 (1988)

JUSTICE WHITE delivered the opinion of the Court.

This case concerns the extent to which educators may exercise editorial control over the contents of a high school newspaper produced as part of the school's journalism curriculum.

I.

Petitioners are the Hazelwood School District in St. Louis County, Missouri; various school officials; Robert Eugene Reynolds, the principal of Hazelwood East High School; and Howard Emerson, a teacher in the school district. Respondents are three former Hazelwood East students who were staff members of *Spectrum*, the school newspaper. They contend that school officials violated their First Amendment rights by deleting two pages of articles from the May 13, 1983, issue of *Spectrum*.

Spectrum was written and edited by the Journalism II class at Hazelwood East. The newspaper was published every three weeks or so during the 1982–1983 school year. More than 4,500 copies of the newspaper were distributed during that year to students, school personnel, and members of the community.

The Board of Education allocated funds from its annual budget for the printing of *Spectrum*. These funds were supplemented by proceeds from sales of the newspaper. The printing expenses during the 1982–1983 school year totaled $4,668.50; revenue from sales was $1,166.84. The other costs associated with the newspaper—such as supplies, textbooks, and a portion of the journalism teacher's salary—were born[e] entirely by the Board.

The Journalism II course was taught by Robert Stergos for most of the 1982–1983 academic year. Stergos left Hazelwood East to take a job in private industry on April 29, 1983, when the May 13 edition of Spectrum was nearing completion, and petitioner Emerson took his place as newspaper adviser for the remaining weeks of the term.

The practice at Hazelwood East during the spring 1983 semester was for the journalism teacher to submit page proofs of each *Spectrum* issue to Principal Reynolds for his review prior to publication. On May 10, Emerson delivered the proofs of the May 13 edition to Reynolds, who objected to two of the articles scheduled to appear in that edition. One of the stories described three Hazelwood East students' experiences with pregnancy; the other discussed the impact of divorce on students at the school.

Reynolds was concerned that, although the pregnancy story used false names "to keep the identity of these girls a secret," the pregnant students still might be identifiable from the text. He also believed that the article's references to sexual activity and birth control were inappropriate for some of the younger students at the school. In addition, Reynolds was concerned that a student identified by name in the divorce story had complained that her father "wasn't spending enough time with my mom, my sister and I" prior to the divorce, "was always out of town on business or out late playing cards with the guys," and "always argued about everything" with her mother. Reynolds believed that the student's parents should have been given an opportunity to respond to these remarks or to consent to their publication. He was unaware that Emerson had deleted the student's name from the final version of the article.

Reynolds believed that there was no time to make the necessary changes in the stories before the scheduled press run and that the newspaper would not appear before the end of the school year if printing were delayed to any significant extent. He concluded that his only options under the circumstances were to publish a four-page newspaper instead of the planned six-page newspaper, eliminating the two pages on which the offending stories appeared, or to publish no newspaper at all. Accordingly, he directed Emerson to withhold from publication the two pages containing the stories on pregnancy and divorce. He informed his superiors of the decision, and they concurred.

Respondents subsequently commenced this action in the United States District Court for the Eastern District of Missouri seeking a declaration that their First Amendment rights had been violated, injunctive relief, and monetary damages. After a bench trial, the District Court denied an injunction, holding that no First Amendment violation had occurred. ...

The Court of Appeals for the Eighth Circuit reversed. … [It] found "no evidence in the record that the principal could have reasonably forecast that the censored articles or any materials in the censored articles would have materially disrupted classwork or given rise to substantial disorder in the school." School officials were entitled to censor the articles on the ground that they invaded the rights of others, according to the court, only if publication of the articles could have resulted in tort liability to the school. The court concluded that no tort action for libel or invasion of privacy could have been maintained against the school by the subjects of the two articles or by their families. Accordingly, the court held that school officials had violated respondents' First Amendment rights by deleting the two pages of the newspaper. We granted *certiorari*, and we now reverse.

II.

Students in the public schools do not "shed their constitutional rights to freedom of speech or expression at the schoolhouse gate." They cannot be punished merely for expressing their personal views on the school premises—whether "in the cafeteria, or on the playing field, or on the campus during the authorized hours,"—unless school authorities have reason to believe that such expression will "substantially interfere with the work of the school or impinge upon the rights of other students." We have nonetheless recognized that the First Amendment rights of students in the public schools "are not automatically co-extensive with the rights of adults in other settings," and must be "applied in light of the special characteristics of the school environment." A school need not tolerate student speech that is inconsistent with its "basic educational mission," even though the government could not censor similar speech outside the school. …

B.

The question whether the First Amendment requires a school to tolerate particular student speech—the question that we addressed in *Tinker*—is different from the question whether the First Amendment requires a school affirmatively to promote particular student speech.[46] The former question addresses educators' ability to silence a student's personal expres-

sion that happens to occur on the school premises. The latter question concerns educators' authority over school-sponsored publications, theatrical productions, and other expressive activities that students, parents, and members of the public might reasonably perceive to bear the imprimatur of the school. These activities may fairly be characterized as part of the school curriculum, whether or not they occur in a traditional classroom setting, so long as they are supervised by faculty members and designed to impart particular knowledge or skills to student participants and audiences.

Educators are entitled to exercise greater control over this second form of student expression to assure that participants learn whatever lessons the activity is designed to teach, that readers or listeners are not exposed to material that may be inappropriate for their level of maturity, and that the views of the individual speaker are not erroneously attributed to the school. Hence, a school may in its capacity as publisher of a school newspaper or producer of a school play "disassociate itself," not only from speech that would "substantially interfere with [its] work … or impinge upon the rights of other students," but also from speech that is, for example, ungrammatical, poorly written, inadequately researched, biased or prejudiced, vulgar or profane, or unsuitable for immature audiences.

A school must be able to set high standards for the student speech that is disseminated under its auspices—standards that may be higher than those demanded by some newspaper publishers or theatrical producers in the "real" world—and may refuse to disseminate student speech that does not meet those standards. In addition, a school must be able to take into account the emotional maturity of the intended audience in determining whether to disseminate student speech on potentially sensitive topics, which might range from the existence of Santa Claus in an elementary school setting to the particulars of teenage sexual activity in a high school setting. A school must also retain the authority to refuse to sponsor student speech that might reasonably be perceived to advocate drug or alcohol use, irresponsible sex, or conduct otherwise inconsistent with "the shared values of a civilized social order," or to associate the school with any position other than neutrality on matters of political controversy. Otherwise, the schools would be unduly constrained from fulfilling their role as "a principal instrument in awakening

---

46 393 US 503 (1969).

the child to cultural values, in preparing him for later professional training, and in helping him to adjust normally to his environment."

Accordingly, we conclude that the standard articulated in *Tinker* for determining when a school may punish student expression need not also be the standard for determining when a school may refuse to lend its name and resources to the dissemination of student expression. Instead, we hold that educators do not offend the First Amendment by exercising editorial control over the style and content of student speech in school-sponsored expressive activities so long as their actions are reasonably related to legitimate pedagogical concerns.

This standard is consistent with our oft-expressed view that the education of the Nation's youth is primarily the responsibility of parents, teachers, and state and local school officials, and not of federal judges. It is only when the decision to censor a school-sponsored publication, theatrical production, or other vehicle of student expression has no valid educational purpose that the First Amendment is so "directly and sharply implicate[d]," as to require judicial intervention to protect students' constitutional rights.

III.

We also conclude that Principal Reynolds acted reasonably in requiring the deletion from the May 13 issue of *Spectrum* of the pregnancy article, the divorce article, and the remaining articles that were to appear on the same pages of the newspaper. The initial paragraph of the pregnancy article declared that "[a]ll names have been changed to keep the identity of these girls a secret." The principal concluded that the students' anonymity was not adequately protected, however, given the other identifying information in the article and the small number of pregnant students at the school. Indeed, a teacher at the school credibly testified that she could positively identify at least one of the girls and possibly all three. It is likely that many students at Hazelwood East would have been at least as successful in identifying the girls. Reynolds therefore could reasonably have feared that the article violated whatever pledge of anonymity had been given to the pregnant students. In addition, he could reasonably have been concerned that the article was not sufficiently sensitive to the privacy interests of the students' boyfriends and parents, who were discussed in the article but who were given no opportunity to consent to its publication or to offer a response. The article did not contain graphic accounts of sexual activity. The girls did comment in the article, however, concerning their sexual histories and their use or non-use of birth control. It was not unreasonable for the principal to have concluded that such frank talk was inappropriate in a school-sponsored publication distributed to 14-year-old freshmen and presumably taken home to be read by students' even younger brothers and sisters.

The student who was quoted by name in the version of the divorce article seen by Principal Reynolds made comments sharply critical of her father. The principal could reasonably have concluded that an individual publicly identified as an inattentive parent—indeed, as one who chose "playing cards with the guys" over home and family—was entitled to an opportunity to defend himself as a matter of journalistic fairness. These concerns were shared by both of Spectrum's faculty advisers for the 1982–1983 school year, who testified that they would not have allowed the article to be printed without deletion of the student's name.

Principal Reynolds testified credibly at trial that, at the time that he reviewed the proofs of the May 13 issue during an extended telephone conversation with Emerson, he believed that there was no time to make any changes in the articles, and that the newspaper had to be printed immediately or not at all. It is true that Reynolds did not verify whether the necessary modifications could still have been made in the articles, and that Emerson did not volunteer the information that printing could be delayed until the changes were made. We nonetheless agree with the District Court that the decision to excise the two pages containing the problematic articles was reasonable given the particular circumstances of this case. These circumstances included the very recent replacement of Stergos by Emerson, who may not have been entirely familiar with *Spectrum* editorial and production procedures, and the pressure felt by Reynolds to make an immediate decision so that students would not be deprived of the newspaper altogether.

In sum, we cannot reject as unreasonable Principal Reynolds' conclusion that neither the pregnancy article nor the divorce article was suitable for publication in *Spectrum*. Reynolds could reasonably have concluded that the students who had written and edited these articles had not sufficiently mastered those portions of the Journalism II curriculum that pertained to the treatment of controversial issues and personal attacks, the need to protect the privacy of individuals whose most intimate concerns are to be revealed in the newspaper, and "the legal, moral, and ethical restrictions imposed upon journalists within [a] school community" that includes adolescent subjects and readers. Finally, we conclude that the principal's decision to delete two pages of Spectrum, rather than to delete only the offending articles or to require that they be modified, was reasonable under the circumstances as he understood them. Accordingly, no violation of First Amendment rights occurred. The judgment of the Court of Appeals for the Eighth Circuit is therefore REVERSED.

In 2013, the Second Circuit affirmed that *Hazelwood* remains the governing standard in school-sponsored speech cases. In *A.C. v. Taconic Hills School District*,[47] school officials prohibited an eighth-grade student from concluding her graduation speech with a blessing. School officials had regularly engaged in prior review of graduation speeches in the past. Because (a) reasonable observers would regard a graduation speech as school-sponsored and (b) the blessing would constitute purely religious speech, the school could impose content-based restrictions without violating the First Amendment.

Determining whether student speech is school-sponsored is not always so easy. In *Bannon v. School District of Palm Beach County*,[48] students were invited to paint murals on plywood panels temporarily erected around a construction project. When school officials required that some religious themes be painted over, students raised First Amendment claims. The Eleventh Circuit affirmed that expressive activities were curricular if they were (a) supervised by faculty members and (b) designed to impart particular knowledge or skills to student participants. The court found the removal of religious themes to be a reasonable, content-based restriction rationally related to the legitimate pedagogical concern that religious debates should be avoided in public school contexts.

In *Corder v. Lewis Palmer School District No. 38*,[49] the Tenth Circuit permitted school officials to discipline a student who had inserted a religious message into her approved graduation speech. School officials in such cases may be obligated by the Establishment Clause to prohibit prayers and blessings to avoid the appearance of endorsing religion.[50] Yet in so doing, school officials walk a thin legal line. They must not engage in viewpoint discrimination by limiting religious perspectives if they have allowed non-religious perspectives on the same topics.[51] In *Nurre v. Whitehead*,[52] the Ninth Circuit affirmed that school officials had imposed reasonable content restrictions when they prevented a student ensemble from performing a religious song at a graduation ceremony.

Prior Review

May school officials insist on reviewing convocation or campaign speeches or photos or editorials prior to their delivery or publication? In what circumstances? Under what criteria? The Supreme Court has not considered these questions, and the federal circuit courts have given differing answers.

47 510 Fed. Appx. 3 (2d Cir. 2013) [*unpublished*]; *cert. denied*, 571 U.S. 828 (2013).
48 Bannon v. Sch. Dist. of Palm Beach County, 387 F.3d 1208 (11th Cir. 2004).
49 Corder v. Lewis Palmer School Dist. No. 38, 566 F.3d 1219 (10th Cir. 2009), *cert. denied*, 55 U.S. 1048 (2009).
50 Cole v. Oroville Union High Sch. Dist., 228 F.3d 1092 (9th Cir. 2000).
51 Griffith v. Butte School Dist. No. 1, 2010 Mont. 246, 244 P.3d 321 (Mont. 2010).
52 580 F.3d 1087 (9th Cir. 2009), *cert. denied*, 559 U.S. 1025 (2010).

In *Eisner v. Stamford Board of Education*,[53] the Second Circuit affirmed that the standards for determining whether student-produced material may be distributed cannot be vague or overbroad (see Chapter 6). There must be clear notice to students of when prior approval is required and from whom. Reviews must be completed within a clear and short period of time, with the understanding that distribution may proceed if there is no response within the time period. Finally, students must be made aware of an appeals process. Based on these criteria, a federal district court struck down a school's prior review system because it lacked clear standards, including a specific time period for review.[54] In *Muller v. Jefferson Lighthouse School*,[55] the Seventh Circuit applied a somewhat different set of criteria in striking down a system of prior review found to be "*per se* unreasonable."

In *Burch v. Barker*,[56] the Ninth Circuit specifically rejected *Eisner* and prohibited the school from enforcing *any* system of prior review. That case involved students punished for distributing an unofficial newspaper. School officials argued that prior review and censorship were needed "for the safe operation of the school, to avoid distractions, hurt feelings and career damage to the faculty, to further parental and community expectations and to avoid potential school liability." However, the court found there had been no disruption relating to the distribution of this or any other publication at the school and no one believed its contents reflected the view of the school administration. Thus, concluded the court, the prior-review rule was based on exactly the sort of "undifferentiated fear or apprehension of disturbance" that the *Tinker* court rejected as a justification for limitations on student speech.

In response to *Hazelwood*, a number of states introduced "Student Publications" laws giving editorial control of student newspapers to students and relieving school districts from liability for what students publish.[57] Where these laws exist, school officials may not engage in prior review or censorship of school newspapers; they may only advise students of possible legal, moral, or journalistic problems with their work. In 2019, a federal court in Kansas allowed a lawsuit to proceed against a school district for stopping students from taking pictures for a student newspaper and speaking out for gun control during a nationwide walkout following the mass shooting in Parkland, Florida.[58]

Categories of Unprotected Speech

There are some categories of speech that do not receive First Amendment protection inside or outside of schools. These include **obscenity, fighting words, threats**, and **defamation of private citizens**.

Legally, **obscenity** is graphic expression that meets three conditions: (a) the average person applying contemporary community standards would find that, taken as a whole, it appeals to prurient interests; (b) it depicts or describes in a patently offensive way sexual conduct as defined in state law; and (c) taken as a whole, it lacks serious literary, artistic, political, or scientific value.[59]

---

53 440 F.2d 803 (2d Cir. 1971).

54 M.B. *ex rel.* Martin v. Liverpool Cent. Sch. Dist., 487 F. Supp. 2d 117 (N.D. 2007); *see also* Westfield High Sch. L.I.F.E. Club v. City of Westfield, 249 F. Supp.2d 98 (D. Mass. 2003).

55 Muller v. Jefferson Lighthouse Sch., 98 F.3d 1530 (7th Cir. 1996); *see also* Sullivan v. Houston Indep. Sch. Dist., 475 F.2d 1071 (5th Cir. 1973).

56 861 F.2d 1149 (9th Cir. 1988); *see also* Fujishima v. Bd. of Educ., 460 F.2d 1355 (7th Cir. 1972).

57 KAN. STAT. ANN. §§ 72.1504-72.1506.

58 M.C. *ex rel.* Chudley v. Shawnee Mission Unified Sch. Dist. No. 512, 2019 U.S. Dist. LEXIS 12,984 (D. Kan. January 28, 2019).

59 Miller v. California, 413 U.S. 15 (1973).

Fighting words are those which by their very utterance inflict injury or tend to incite an immediate breach of the peace.[60]

A **threat** is a statement that a reasonable speaker would expect to be interpreted as a serious expression of intent to harm.[61]

Defamation is a complex concept that for present purposes may be defined as a false statement that diminishes a person's reputation (see Chapter 12).

Because these categories of speech are not protected by the First Amendment, public school officials may prohibit them and punish students who engage in them. In 2002, for example, the Eighth Circuit upheld the expulsion of a student who had written a letter threatening to rape and murder his former girlfriend.[62] As discussed more fully later in this chapter, the courts have also permitted school officials to suspend students for **threats** sent via text or social media.

The categories of speech that receive *limited* First Amendment protection include **commercial speech**, **offensive** or **indecent speech**, and **defamation of public figures**. To receive any protection, **commercial speech**—advertisements—must not be about an illegal activity and must not be misleading. For commercial speech that meets these criteria, government may still impose regulations if (a) its interest in regulating is substantial; (b) the regulation directly advances that interest; and (c) the regulation is narrowly tailored to achieve the objective.[63]

Unprotected Categories of Student Speech

School officials may prohibit **obscenity**, **fighting words**, **threats**, and **defamation of private figures** because these categories of speech receive no First Amendment protection. In addition, there are several categories of student speech or expression that some courts have excluded from First Amendment protection in public schools, including speech that is **offensive**, **lewd**, or **vulgar**. The law regarding **offensive speech**—speech dealing with excrement or sexual activity in a vulgar or indecent way—is not completely settled, but regulation appears permissible when such speech (delivered in a television or radio broadcast, for example) would be accessible to children.[64]

The Supreme Court has also recognized that speech that falls outside the legal definition of obscenity may nonetheless be **obscene-as-to-minors**, and have allowed schools officials to prohibit such speech.[65] In order to be classified as obscene-as-to-minors, material must (1) appeal to the prurient interest of minors; (2) violate prevailing standards in the adult community of suitability for minors; and (3) lack any serious artistic, literary, political, or scientific value for minors.[66]

Offensive, Lewd, or Vulgar Speech

In the following landmark opinion, the Supreme Court ruled that school officials may prohibit school-sponsored student speech that is "indecent, lewd, and offensive to modesty and decency."

---

60 Chaplinsky v. New Hampshire, 315 U.S. 568 (1942).
61 Lovell v. Poway Unified Sch. Dist., 90 F.3d 367 (9th Cir. 1996).
62 Doe *ex rel.* Doe v. Pulaski County Special Sch. Dist., 306 F.3d 616 (8th Cir. 2002); *compare* J.S. *ex rel.* H.S. v. Bethlehem Area Sch. Dist., 807 A.2d 847 (Pa. 2002).
63 Bd. of Trustees of State Univ. of N.Y. v. Fox, 492 U.S. 469 (1989); Cent. Hudson Gas & Elec. Corp. v. Pub. Serv. Comm'n., 447 U.S. 557 (1980); Liquormart, Inc. v. Rhode Island, 517 U.S. 484 (1996).
64 FCC v. Pacifica Found., 438 U.S. 726 (1978); FCC v. Fox Television, 556 U.S. 502 (2009).
65 Ginsberg v. New York, 390 U.S. 629 (1968).
66 *See* Bystrom v. Fridley High School, 822 F.2d 747 (8th Cir. 1987).

⚖️

BETHEL SCHOOL DISTRICT v. FRASER
Supreme Court of the United States
478 U.S. 675 (1986)

CHIEF JUSTICE BURGER delivered the opinion of the Court.

We granted *certiorari* to decide whether the First Amendment prevents a school district from disciplining a high school student for giving a lewd speech at a school assembly.

A

On April 26, 1983, respondent Matthew N. Fraser, a student at Bethel High School in Pierce County, Washington, delivered a speech nominating a fellow student for student elective office. Approximately 600 high school students, many of whom were 14-year-olds, attended the assembly. Students were required to attend the assembly or to report to the study hall. The assembly was part of a school-sponsored educational program in self-government. Students who elected not to attend the assembly were required to report to study hall. During the entire speech, Fraser referred to his candidate in terms of an elaborate, graphic, and explicit sexual metaphor.

Two of Fraser's teachers, with whom he discussed the contents of his speech in advance, informed him that the speech was "inappropriate and that he probably should not deliver it," and that his delivery of the speech might have "severe consequences."

During Fraser's delivery of the speech, a school counselor observed the reaction of students to the speech. Some students hooted and yelled; some by gestures graphically simulated the sexual activities pointedly alluded to in respondent's speech. Other students appeared to be bewildered and embarrassed by the speech. One teacher reported that on the day following the speech, she found it necessary to forgo a portion of the scheduled class lesson in order to discuss the speech with the class.

A Bethel High School disciplinary rule prohibiting the use of obscene language in the school provides: "Conduct which materially and substantially interferes with the educational process is prohibited, including the use of obscene, profane language or gestures."

The morning after the assembly, the Assistant Principal called Fraser into her office and notified him that the school considered his speech to have been a violation of this rule. Fraser was presented with copies of five letters submitted by teachers, describing his conduct at the assembly; he was given a chance to explain his conduct, and he admitted to having given the speech described and that he deliberately used sexual innuendo in the speech. Fraser was then informed that he would be suspended for three days, and that his name would be removed from the list of candidates for graduation speaker at the school's commencement exercises.

Fraser sought review of this disciplinary action through the School District's grievance procedures. The hearing officer determined that the speech given by respondent was "indecent, lewd, and offensive to the modesty and decency of many of the students and faculty in attendance at the assembly." The examiner determined that the speech fell within the ordinary meaning of "obscene," as used in the disruptive-conduct rule, and affirmed the discipline in its entirety. Fraser served two days of his suspension, and was allowed to return to school on the third day.

B

Respondent, by his father as guardian ad litem, then brought this action in the United States District Court for the Western District of Washington. Respondent alleged a violation of his First Amendment right to freedom of speech and sought both injunctive relief and monetary damages under 42 U. S. C. § 1983. The District Court awarded respondent $278 in damages, $12,750 in litigation costs and attorney's fees, and enjoined the School District from preventing respondent from speaking at the commencement ceremonies. Respondent, who had been elected graduation speaker by a write-in vote of his classmates, delivered a speech at the commencement ceremonies on June 8, 1983.

The Court of Appeals for the Ninth Circuit affirmed the judgment of the District Court holding that respondent's speech was indistinguishable from the protest armband in *Tinker*.[67] The court explicitly rejected the School District's argument that the speech, unlike the passive conduct of wearing a

---

67 393 U.S. 503 (1969).

black armband, had a disruptive effect on the educational process. The Court of Appeals also rejected the School District's argument that it had an interest in protecting an essentially captive audience of minors from lewd and indecent language in a setting sponsored by the school, reasoning that the School District's "unbridled discretion" to determine what discourse is "decent" would "increase the risk of cementing white, middle-class standards for determining what is acceptable and proper speech and behavior in our public schools." Finally, the Court of Appeals rejected the School District's argument that, incident to its responsibility for the school curriculum, it had the power to control the language used to express ideas during a school-sponsored activity. We granted *certiorari*. We reverse.

II

This Court acknowledged in *Tinker* that students do not "shed their constitutional rights to freedom of speech or expression at the schoolhouse gate." The Court of Appeals read that case as precluding any discipline of Fraser for indecent speech and lewd conduct in the school assembly. That court appears to have proceeded on the theory that the use of lewd and obscene speech in order to make what the speaker considered to be a point in a nominating speech for a fellow student was essentially the same as the wearing of an armband in *Tinker* as a form of protest or the expression of a political position.

The marked distinction between the political "message" of the armbands in *Tinker* and the sexual content of respondent's speech in this case seems to have been given little weight by the Court of Appeals. In upholding the students' right to engage in a non-disruptive, passive expression of a political viewpoint in *Tinker*, this Court was careful to note that the case did "not concern speech or action that intrudes upon the work of the schools or the rights of other students."

It is against this background that we turn to consider the level of First Amendment protection accorded to Fraser's utterances and actions before an official high school assembly attended by 600 students.

III

The role and purpose of the American public school system were well described by two historians, who stated:

[Public] education must prepare pupils for citizenship in the Republic ... It must inculcate the habits and manners of civility as values in themselves conducive to happiness and as indispensable to the practice of self-government in the community and the nation.

In *Ambach v. Norwick*,[68] we echoed the essence of this statement of the objectives of public education as the "[inculcation of] fundamental values necessary to the maintenance of a democratic political system."

These fundamental values of "habits and manners of civility" essential to a democratic society must, of course, include tolerance of divergent political and religious views, even when the views expressed may be unpopular. But these "fundamental values" must also take into account consideration of the sensibilities of others, and, in the case of a school, the sensibilities of fellow students. The undoubted freedom to advocate unpopular and controversial views in schools and classrooms must be balanced against the society's countervailing interest in teaching students the boundaries of socially appropriate behavior. Even the most heated political discourse in a democratic society requires consideration for the personal sensibilities of the other participants and audiences. ...

Surely it is a highly appropriate function of public school education to prohibit the use of vulgar and offensive terms in public discourse. Indeed, the "fundamental values necessary to the maintenance of a democratic political system" disfavor the use of terms of debate highly offensive or highly threatening to others. Nothing in the Constitution prohibits the states from insisting that certain modes of expression are inappropriate and subject to sanctions. The inculcation of these values is truly the "work of the schools." The determination of what manner of speech in the classroom or in school assembly is inappropriate properly rests with the school board.

The process of educating our youth for citizenship in public schools is not confined to books, the curriculum, and the civics class; schools must teach by example the shared values of a civilized social order. Consciously or otherwise, teachers—and indeed the older students—demonstrate the appropriate form of civil discourse and political expression by their conduct and deportment in and out of class. Inescapably, like parents, they are role models. The schools, as instruments of the state, may determine that the

68   441 U.S. 68 (1979).

essential lessons of civil, mature conduct cannot be conveyed in a school that tolerates lewd, indecent, or offensive speech and conduct such as that indulged in by this confused boy.

The pervasive sexual innuendo in Fraser's speech was plainly offensive to both teachers and students—indeed to any mature person. By glorifying male sexuality, and in its verbal content, the speech was acutely insulting to teenage [female] students. The speech could well be seriously damaging to its less mature audience, many of whom were only 14 years old and on the threshold of awareness of human sexuality. Some students were reported as bewildered by the speech and the reaction of mimicry it provoked.

This Court's First Amendment jurisprudence has acknowledged limitations on the otherwise absolute interest of the speaker in reaching an unlimited audience where the speech is sexually explicit and the audience may include children. In *Ginsberg v. New York*,[69] this Court upheld a New York statute banning the sale of sexually oriented material to minors, even though the material in question was entitled to First Amendment protection with respect to adults. …

We hold that petitioner School District acted entirely within its permissible authority in imposing sanctions upon Fraser in response to his offensively lewd and indecent speech. Unlike the sanctions imposed on the students wearing armbands in *Tinker*, the penalties imposed in this case were unrelated to any political viewpoint. The First Amendment does not prevent the school officials from determining that to permit a vulgar and lewd speech such as respondent's would undermine the school's basic educational mission. A high school assembly or classroom is no place for a sexually explicit monologue directed towards an unsuspecting audience of teenage students. Accordingly, it was perfectly appropriate for the school to disassociate itself to make the point to the pupils that vulgar speech and lewd conduct is wholly inconsistent with the "fundamental values" of public school education. … The judgment of the Court of Appeals for the Ninth Circuit is REVERSED.

The courts have given school officials considerable leeway to regulate **lewd, vulgar, profane, or plainly offensive** speech, even if it does not meet the legal definition of obscene-as-to-minors.[70] In *Pyle v. South Hadley School Committee*,[71] the First Circuit allowed school officials to ban t-shirts with the messages, "Coed Naked Band; Do It To The Rhythm," and "See Dick Drink. See Dick Drive. See Dick Die. Don't Be a Dick." More recently, the Third Circuit upheld the First Amendment claims of middle school students who had worn bracelets associated with a national breast cancer awareness campaign bearing the slogans, "I ♥ Boobies! (Keep a Breast)" and "check y♥ur self!! (Keep a Breast)" at school. The court explained:[72]

> We agree with the District Court that neither *Fraser* nor *Tinker* can sustain the bracelet ban. The scope of a school's authority to restrict lewd, vulgar, profane, or plainly offensive speech under *Fraser* is a novel question left open by the Supreme Court, and one which we must now resolve. We hold that *Fraser*, as modified by the Supreme Court's later reasoning in *Morse v. Frederick*,[73] sets up the following framework:
>
> (1) plainly lewd speech, which offends for the same reasons obscenity offends, may be categorically restricted regardless of whether it comments on political or social issues,
> (2) speech that does not rise to the level of plainly lewd but that a reasonable observer could interpret as lewd may be categorically restricted as long as it cannot plausibly be interpreted as commenting on political or social issues, and

69 390 U.S. 629 (1968).
70 Chandler v. McMinnville Sch. Dist., 978 F.2d 524 (9th Cir. 1992); *see also* Doninger v. Niehoff, 527 F.3d 41 (2d Cir. 2008), *cert. denied*, 565 U.S. 976 (2011).
71 861 F. Supp. 157 (D. Ma. 1994), *modified*, 55 F.3d 20 (1st Cir. 1995).
72 B.H. v. Easton Area School Dist., 725 F.3d 293 (3rd Cir. 2013), *cert. denied*, 572 U.S. 1002 (2014).
73 551 U.S. 393 (2007).

(3) speech that does not rise to the level of plainly lewd and that could plausibly be interpreted as commenting on political or social issues may not be categorically restricted.

Because the bracelets here are not plainly lewd and because they comment on a social issue, they may not be categorically banned under *Fraser*. The School District has also failed to show that the bracelets threatened to substantially disrupt the school under *Tinker*.

More recently, in *B.L. v. Mahanoy Area School District*,[74] a case reminiscent of *Cohen v. California*,[75] a district court granted an injunction barring school officials from removing a student from the cheerleading squad for writing "fuck school fuck softball fuck cheer fuck everything" in a "selfie" posted on Snapchat from an off-campus location. The court found the student's words were protected by the First Amendment.

Threats

Threats are not protected by the First Amendment inside or outside of schools. A threat is a statement that a reasonable person would interpret as a serious expression of intent to harm. The person making the threat does not actually have to harbor intent to harm. The speaker need not communicate the threat directly to the person being threatened. Perhaps not surprisingly, the courts have sometimes had difficulty in deciding what constitutes a threat.

In *LaVine v. Blaine School District*,[76] a principal expelled a student who showed his teacher a poem he had written about death, suicide, and murder. The Ninth Circuit upheld the suspension, noting that the principal had considered the student's disciplinary history, family situation, recent break-up and subsequent stalking of his former girlfriend, and a school shooting in a nearby city. In *Porter v. Ascension Parish School*,[77] a student drew a picture at home depicting his high school soaked in gasoline, two students with guns, and a third student throwing a brick at the principal while using racial and homophobic epithets and the F-word. Two years later, the student's younger brother showed the picture to his school bus driver, who confiscated it and gave it to the principal. The Fifth Circuit found it constituted a threat and upheld both the older brother's expulsion and the younger brother's suspension. In *Boim v. Fulton County School District*,[78] a teacher confiscated a student's private notebook in which she had described her daydream of shooting a teacher. The Eleventh Circuit upheld her suspension. In *Ponce v. Socorro Independent School District*,[79] a student described an imaginary Nazi plan to commit an attack on his high school in his diary. The Fifth Circuit upheld his suspension.

In *McNeil v. Sherwood School District 88J*,[80] the Ninth Circuit upheld the expulsion of a high school student who had created a "hit list" in his personal journal naming 22 students and a former school employee and stating "All These People *Must* Die." The journal was discovered by the student's mother, who reported it to her therapist, who in turn alerted the police and the school.

74 376 F. Supp. 3d 429 (M.D. Pa. 2019).
75 403 U.S. 15 (1971).
76 257 F.3d 981 (9th Cir. 2001), *cert. denied*, 536 US 959 (2002).
77 301 F. Supp. 2d 576 (M.D. La. 2004), *aff'd*, 393 F.3d 608 (2004), *cert. denied*, 544 U.S. 1062 (2005).
78 494 F.3d 978 (11th Cir. 2007); *see also* Finkle v. Bd. of Educ. of Syosset Cent. Sch. Dist., 386 F. Supp. 2d 119 (E.D.N.Y. 2005), *aff'd*, 180 Fed. Appx. 232 (2006), *cert. denied*, 549 U.S. 1179 (2007).
79 508 F.3d 765 (5th Cir. 2007); *see also* Johnson, v. Brighton Area School Dist., 2008 U.S. Dist. LEXIS 72023 (W.D. Pa. 2008); *cf.* Murakowski v. University of Delaware, 575 F. Supp.2d 571 (D. Del. 2008).
80 918 F.3d 700 (9th Cir. 2019).

In these and other cases, the courts have permitted the punishment of students for depictions of violence that did not fit the legal definition of a "threat."[81]

Conversely, in *Norris v. Cape Elizabeth School District*,[82] a district court in Maine granted a preliminary injunction to bar school officials from suspending a student who had posted a note in a school bathroom reading, "THERE'S RAPIST IN OUR SCHOOL, AND YOU KNOW WHO IT IS." The court rejected claims by school officials that the note was defamatory and constituted a threat of harm or violence, finding the student's claim that she had been punished for engaging in core political speech on "the prevalence of sexual violence and the danger of inaction by those in positions of power" was likely to succeed under *Tinker*.

In a recent case involving a **cyberattack on school officials**, the Fifth Circuit deployed the **material and substantial disruption** standard from *Tinker* to uphold the suspension of a student who had posted an "incredibly profane and vulgar rap recording" on YouTube and Facebook making allegations of sexual misconduct against two coaches and threatening to shoot them in the face.

> Primarily at issue is whether, consistent with the requirements of the First Amendment, off-campus speech directed intentionally at the school community and reasonably understood by school officials to be threatening, harassing, and intimidating to a teacher satisfies the almost 50-year-old standard for restricting student speech, based on a reasonable forecast of a substantial disruption,

wrote the Court in *Bell v. Itawamba County School Board*.[83] "Because that standard is satisfied in this instance, the summary judgment is affirmed."

Advocating Illegal Drug Use

In 2007, the Supreme Court created a new category of unprotected speech. Finding that student speech **advocating illegal drug use** falls outside the scope of the First Amendment, the **material and substantial disruption** standard enunciated in *Tinker* would not apply.

MORSE v. FREDERICK
Supreme Court of the United States
551 U.S. 393 (2007)

CHIEF JUSTICE ROBERTS delivered the opinion of the Court.

I.

On January 24, 2002, the Olympic Torch Relay passed through Juneau, Alaska, on its way to the winter games in Salt Lake City, Utah. The torchbearers were to proceed along a street in front of Juneau-Douglas High School (JDHS) while school was in session. Petitioner Deborah Morse, the school principal, decided to permit staff and students to participate in the Torch Relay as an approved social event or class trip. Students were allowed to leave

81 Doe *ex rel.* Doe v. Pulaski County Special Sch. Dist., 263 F.3d 833 (8th Cir. 2001); Doe *ex rel.* Doe v. Pulaski County Special Sch. Dist., 306 F.3d 616 (8th Cir. 2002); J.S. v. Bethlehem Area Sch. Dist., 807 A.2d 847 (Pa. 2002); S.G. *ex rel.* A.G. v. Sayreville Bd. of Educ., 333 F.3d 417 (3d Cir. 2003), *cert. denied*, 540 U.S. 1104 (2004).
82 2019 U.S. Dist. LEXIS 184099 (D. Me. Oct. 24, 2019).
83 799 F.3d 379 (5th Cir. 2015).

class to observe the relay from either side of the street. Teachers and administrative officials monitored the students' actions.

Respondent Joseph Frederick, a JDHS senior, was late to school that day. When he arrived, he joined his friends (all but one of whom were JDHS students) across the street from the school to watch the event. Not all the students waited patiently. Some became rambunctious, throwing plastic cola bottles and snowballs and scuffling with their classmates. As the torchbearers and camera crews passed by, Frederick and his friends unfurled a 14-foot banner bearing the phrase: "BONG HiTS 4 JESUS." The large banner was easily readable by the students on the other side of the street.

Principal Morse immediately crossed the street and demanded that the banner be taken down. Everyone but Frederick complied. Morse confiscated the banner and told Frederick to report to her office, where she suspended him for ten days. Morse later explained that she told Frederick to take the banner down because she thought it encouraged illegal drug use, in violation of established school policy. Juneau School Board Policy No. 5520 states: "The Board specifically prohibits any assembly or public expression that … advocates the use of substances that are illegal to minors …" In addition, Juneau School Board Policy No. 5850 subjects "[p]upils who participate in approved social events and class trips" to the same student conduct rules that apply during the regular school program.

Frederick administratively appealed his suspension, but the Juneau School District Superintendent upheld it, limiting it to time served (eight days). In a memorandum setting forth his reasons, the superintendent determined that Frederick had displayed his banner "in the midst of his fellow students, during school hours, at a school-sanctioned activity." He further explained that Frederick "was not disciplined because the principal of the school 'disagreed' with his message, but because his speech appeared to advocate the use of illegal drugs."

The superintendent continued:

The common-sense understanding of the phrase "bong hits" is that it is a reference to a means of smoking marijuana. Given [Frederick's] inability or unwillingness to express any other credible meaning for the phrase, I can only agree with the principal and countless others who saw the banner as advocating the use of illegal drugs. [Frederick's] speech was not political. He was not advocating the legalization of marijuana or promoting a religious belief. He was displaying a fairly silly message promoting illegal drug usage in the midst of a school activity, for the benefit of television cameras covering the Torch Relay. [Frederick's] speech was potentially disruptive to the event and clearly disruptive of and inconsistent with the school's educational mission to educate students about the dangers of illegal drugs and to discourage their use.

Relying on our decision in *Fraser*,[84] the superintendent concluded that the principal's actions were permissible because Frederick's banner was "speech or action that intrudes upon the work of the schools." The Juneau School District Board of Education upheld the suspension.

Frederick then filed suit under 42 U.S.C. §1983 alleging that the school board and Morse had violated his First Amendment rights. He sought declaratory and injunctive relief, unspecified compensatory damages, punitive damages, and attorney's fees. The District Court granted summary judgment for the school board and Morse, ruling that they were entitled to qualified immunity and that they had not infringed Frederick's First Amendment rights. …

The Ninth Circuit reversed. Deciding that Frederick acted during a "school-authorized activit[y]," and "proceed[ing] on the basis that the banner expressed a positive sentiment about marijuana use," the court nonetheless found a violation of Frederick's First Amendment rights because the school punished Frederick without demonstrating that his speech gave rise to a "risk of substantial disruption." The court further concluded that Frederick's right to display his banner was so "clearly established" that a reasonable principal in Morse's position would have understood that her actions were unconstitutional, and that Morse was therefore not entitled to qualified immunity.

We granted *certiorari* on two questions: whether Frederick had a First Amendment right to wield his banner, and, if so, whether that right was so clearly established that the principal may be held liable for damages. We resolve the first question against Frederick, and therefore have no occasion to reach the second.

---

84 Bethel School District v. Fraser, 478 U.S. 675 (1986).

II.

At the outset, we reject Frederick's argument that this is not a school-speech case—as has every other authority to address the question. The event occurred during normal school hours. It was sanctioned by Principal Morse "as an approved social event or class trip," and the school district's rules expressly provide that pupils in "approved social events and class trips are subject to district rules for student conduct." Teachers and administrators were interspersed among the students and charged with supervising them. The high school band and cheerleaders performed. Frederick, standing among other JDHS students across the street from the school, directed his banner toward the school, making it plainly visible to most students. Under these circumstances, we agree with the superintendent that Frederick cannot "stand in the midst of his fellow students, during school hours, at a school-sanctioned activity and claim he is not at school." There is some uncertainty at the outer boundaries as to when courts should apply school-speech precedents.

III.

The message on Frederick's banner is cryptic. It is no doubt offensive to some, perhaps amusing to others. To still others, it probably means nothing at all. Frederick himself claimed "that the words were just nonsense meant to attract television cameras." But Principal Morse thought the banner would be interpreted by those viewing it as promoting illegal drug use, and that interpretation is plainly a reasonable one.

As Morse later explained in a declaration, when she saw the sign, she thought that "the reference to a 'bong hit' would be widely understood by high school students and others as referring to smoking marijuana." She further believed that "display of the banner would be construed by students, District personnel, parents and others witnessing the display of the banner, as advocating or promoting illegal drug use"—in violation of school policy.

We agree with Morse. At least two interpretations of the words on the banner demonstrate that the sign advocated the use of illegal drugs. First, the phrase could be interpreted as an imperative: "[Take] bong hits …"—a message equivalent, as Morse explained in her declaration, to "smoke marijuana" or "use an illegal drug." Alternatively, the phrase

could be viewed as celebrating drug use—"bong hits [are a good thing]," or "[we take] bong hits"—and we discern no meaningful distinction between celebrating illegal drug use in the midst of fellow students and outright advocacy or promotion.

The pro-drug interpretation of the banner gains further plausibility given the paucity of alternative meanings the banner might bear. The best Frederick can come up with is that the banner is "meaningless and funny." The dissent similarly refers to the sign's message as "curious," "ambiguous," "nonsense," "ridiculous," "obscure," "silly," "quixotic," and "stupid." Gibberish is surely a possible interpretation of the words on the banner, but it is not the only one, and dismissing the banner as meaningless ignores its undeniable reference to illegal drugs.

The dissent mentions Frederick's "credible and uncontradicted explanation for the message—he just wanted to get on television." But that is a description of Frederick's motive for displaying the banner; it is not an interpretation of what the banner says. The way Frederick was going to fulfill his ambition of appearing on television was by unfurling a pro-drug banner at a school event, in the presence of teachers and fellow students.

Elsewhere in its opinion, the dissent emphasizes the importance of political speech and the need to foster "national debate about a serious issue," as if to suggest that the banner is political speech. But not even Frederick argues that the banner conveys any sort of political or religious message. Contrary to the dissent's suggestion, this is plainly not a case about political debate over the criminalization of drug use or possession.

IV.

The question thus becomes whether a principal may, consistent with the First Amendment, restrict student speech at a school event, when that speech is reasonably viewed as promoting illegal drug use. We hold that she may.

In *Tinker*,[85] this Court made clear that "First Amendment rights, applied in light of the special characteristics of the school environment, are available to teachers and students." *Tinker* involved a group of high school students who decided to wear black armbands to protest the Vietnam War. School officials learned of the plan and then adopted a policy prohibiting students from wearing armbands.

85 393 U.S. 503 (1969).

When several students nonetheless wore armbands to school, they were suspended. The students sued, claiming that their First Amendment rights had been violated, and this Court agreed.

Tinker held that student expression may not be suppressed unless school officials reasonably conclude that it will "materially and substantially disrupt the work and discipline of the school." The essential facts of *Tinker* are quite stark, implicating concerns at the heart of the First Amendment. The students sought to engage in political speech, using the armbands to express their "disapproval of the Vietnam hostilities and their advocacy of a truce, to make their views known, and, by their example, to influence others to adopt them." Political speech, of course, is "at the core of what the First Amendment is designed to protect." The only interest the Court discerned underlying the school's actions was the "mere desire to avoid the discomfort and unpleasantness that always accompany an unpopular viewpoint," or "an urgent wish to avoid the controversy which might result from the expression." That interest was not enough to justify banning "a silent, passive expression of opinion, unaccompanied by any disorder or disturbance."

This Court's next student speech case was *Fraser*.[86] ... [We] distill from *Fraser* two basic principles. First, *Fraser*'s holding demonstrates that "the constitutional rights of students in public school are not automatically coextensive with the rights of adults in other settings." Had Fraser delivered the same speech in a public forum outside the school context, it would have been protected. In school, however, Fraser's First Amendment rights were circumscribed "in light of the special characteristics of the school environment." Second, *Fraser* established that the mode of analysis set forth in *Tinker* is not absolute. Whatever approach *Fraser* employed, it certainly did not conduct the "substantial disruption" analysis prescribed by *Tinker*.

Our most recent student speech case, [Hazelwood],[87] concerned "expressive activities that students, parents, and members of the public might reasonably perceive to bear the imprimatur of the school." ... [Hazelwood] does not control this case because no one would reasonably believe that Frederick's banner bore the school's imprimatur. The case is nevertheless instructive ... [Hazelwood] acknowledged that schools may regulate some speech "even

though the government could not censor similar speech outside the school." And, like *Fraser*, it confirms that the rule of *Tinker* is not the only basis for restricting student speech.

Drawing on the principles applied in our student speech cases, we have held in the Fourth Amendment context that "while children assuredly do not 'shed their constitutional rights ... at the schoolhouse gate,' ... the nature of those rights is what is appropriate for children in school." ... Even more to the point, these cases also recognize that deterring drug use by schoolchildren is an "important—indeed, perhaps compelling" interest. Drug abuse can cause severe and permanent damage to the health and well-being of young people:

School years are the time when the physical, psychological, and addictive effects of drugs are most severe. Maturing nervous systems are more critically impaired by intoxicants than mature ones are; childhood losses in learning are lifelong and profound; children grow chemically dependent more quickly than adults, and their record of recovery is depressingly poor. And of course the effects of a drug-infested school are visited not just upon the users, but upon the entire student body and faculty, as the educational process is disrupted.

Just five years ago, we wrote: "The drug abuse problem among our Nation's youth has hardly abated since *Vernonia* was decided in 1995.[88] In fact, evidence suggests that it has only grown worse."

The problem remains serious today. About half of American 12th graders have used an illicit drug, as have more than a third of 10th graders and about one-fifth of 8th graders. Nearly one in four 12th graders has used an illicit drug in the past month. Some 25 percent of high schoolers say that they have been offered, sold, or given an illegal drug on school property within the past year.

Congress has declared that part of a school's job is educating students about the dangers of illegal drug use. It has provided billions of dollars to support state and local drug-prevention programs, and required that schools receiving federal funds under the *Safe and Drug-Free Schools and Communities Act* of 1994 certify that their drug prevention programs

86 478 U.S. 675 (1986).
87 484 U.S. 260 (1988).
88 515 U.S. 646 (1995).

"convey a clear and consistent message that … the illegal use of drugs [is] wrong and harmful." Thousands of school boards throughout the country—including JDHS—have adopted policies aimed at effectuating this message. … Student speech celebrating illegal drug use at a school event, in the presence of school administrators and teachers, thus poses a particular challenge for school officials working to protect those entrusted to their care from the dangers of drug abuse.

The "special characteristics of the school environment," and the governmental interest in stopping student drug abuse—reflected in the policies of Congress and myriad school boards, including JDHS—allow schools to restrict student expression that they reasonably regard as promoting illegal drug use. *Tinker* warned that schools may not prohibit student speech because of "undifferentiated fear or apprehension of disturbance" or "a mere desire to avoid the discomfort and unpleasantness that always accompany an unpopular viewpoint." The danger here is far more serious and palpable. The particular concern to prevent student drug abuse at issue here, embodied in established school policy, extends well beyond an abstract desire to avoid controversy.

Petitioners urge us to adopt the broader rule that Frederick's speech is proscribable because it is plainly "offensive" as that term is used in *Fraser*. We think this stretches *Fraser* too far; that case should not be read to encompass any speech that could fit under some definition of "offensive." After all, much political and religious speech might be perceived as offensive to some. The concern here is not that Frederick's speech was offensive, but that it was reasonably viewed as promoting illegal drug use. …

School principals have a difficult job, and a vitally important one. When Frederick suddenly and unexpectedly unfurled his banner, Morse had to decide to act—or not act—on the spot. It was reasonable for her to conclude that the banner promoted illegal drug use—in violation of established school policy—and that failing to act would send a powerful message to the students in her charge, including Frederick, about how serious the school was about the dangers of illegal drug use. The First Amendment does not require schools to tolerate at school events student expression that contributes to those dangers.

The judgment of the United States Court of Appeals for the Ninth Circuit is reversed, and the case is remanded for further proceedings consistent with this opinion.

Joseph Frederick was 18 when he unfurled his "BONG HiTS 4 JESUS" banner on a city sidewalk. Any other adult in Juneau was at liberty to hoist the same banner on the same sidewalk, yet Principal Morse could suspend Frederick for doing so without violating the First Amendment because Frederick was cast as (a) a *pupil* (b) **promoting illegal drug use** (c) at a **school-sponsored event**. As an adult, however, Frederick had standing to sue his school principal under 42 U.S.C. §1983. It was probably not the most appropriate case for the Chief Justice to affirm the "custodial and tutelary" relationship between public school officials and students.[89] Justice Clarence Thomas opined in a footnote that "the fact that Frederick was 18 and not a minor under Alaska law is inconsequential."

Further Regulatory Considerations

The degree of First Amendment protection may depend on the location or **forum** in which speech or expressive conduct occurs.

Forums of Speech

A **traditional public forum** is a place such as a public street or park that has customarily been open to the public for purposes of assembly, demonstrations, speeches, and other expressive activities.

89 J.C. Blokhuis, *Student Rights and the Special Characteristics of the School Environment in American Jurisprudence*, 49(1) JOURNAL OF PHILOSOPHY OF EDUCATION 65–85 (2015), 73.

Speech in traditional public forums may be regulated only if the regulations are necessary to achieve a compelling state interest and narrowly drawn to achieve that end. Viewpoint and speaker-based suppression are prohibited, though reasonable regulations concerning the time, place, and manner of speech are permissible.

A **designated public forum** is a place which has been made available to the public by explicit policy or longstanding practice. A school auditorium during non-school hours may qualify as a designated public forum if it has been made available to outside groups for meetings or events. If so, then the same rules apply as if it were a traditional public forum.

A **limited public forum** is a place which has been made available to the public for specific purposes. In such cases, the government may enforce reasonable, viewpoint-neutral regulations. For example, a school district may disallow the use of an auditorium for political campaign rallies. A school board meeting is a limited public forum (see Chapter 3).

A **non-public forum** is a place neither traditionally nor by designation open to the public for expressive activities. A school auditorium that has never been rented to outside groups may qualify as a non-public forum. Regulation of access to the non-public forum for speech activities need only be reasonable and viewpoint-neutral.[90]

Content

Regulation of speech based solely on the **viewpoint** that is being expressed is strictly prohibited by the First Amendment. As the Supreme Court has stated, "If there is a bedrock principle underlying the First Amendment, it is that the government may not prohibit the expression of an idea simply because society finds the idea offensive or disagreeable."[91]

Regulation of speech based on **subject matter** is generally also impermissible unless the suppression occurs in a limited public forum or a non-public forum. Regulation based on subject matter in a traditional public forum or designated public forum must satisfy the strict scrutiny test: The regulation must be necessary to serve a compelling governmental interest.

Regulation of speech based on the identity of the **speaker** is usually viewed by courts as equivalent to viewpoint suppression and is thus prohibited. In some cases, however, courts apply the rules of subject-matter regulation to speaker-based regulation.

Desire to avoid predicted **adverse effects** is a common rationale for regulation of speech. Schools often wish to prohibit speech that they fear might cause students to engage in dangerous or illegal behaviors like fighting or drug use. When government seeks to block speech because of its predicted adverse effects, it bears the burden of showing that the speech was likely to incite "imminent lawless action."[92] An older version of this test allowed for the prohibition of speech that created a **clear and present danger** of an evil the government was entitled to prevent.[93]

Time, Place, Manner

Finally, government may seek to regulate the **time**, the **place**, or the **manner** of speech. For example, the use of a loudspeaker truck may be limited to certain hours and the loudness of the sound emitted may be limited to a certain decibel level. Content-neutral regulations like these are per-

---

90 Perry Educ. Ass'n v. Perry Local Educators Ass'n, 460 U.S. 37 (1983); Ark. Educ. Television Comm'n v. Forbes, 523 U.S. 666 (1998); Cornelius v. NAACP Legal Def. & Educ. Fund, Inc., 473 U.S. 788 (1985); Lamb's Chapel v. Center Moriches Union Free Sch. Dist., 508 U.S. 384 (1993).
91 Texas v. Johnson, 491 U.S. 397 (1989).
92 Brandenburg v. Ohio, 395 U.S. 444 (1969).
93 Schenck v. United States, 249 U.S. 47 (1919).

missible if they further an important or substantial governmental interest and if the restriction of speech is no greater than necessary to further that interest.[94]

The *Tinker* Court viewed the school as a microcosm of a democratic society, with students enjoying limited First Amendment rights, though not free speech rights coextensive with those of adults in other contexts. At a time when university campuses across the country were riven with anti–Vietnam War protests, the *Tinker* Court recognized that school officials had a legitimate interest in maintaining an orderly environment. The *Tinker* test says that school officials may prohibit student speech that causes, or is reasonably likely to cause, **material and substantial disruption**.

Material and Substantial Disruption

The most important implication of this test is that school officials may not punish or prohibit speech merely because of a disagreement with the ideas expressed. Nor may they act to suppress or punish speech because of a generalized fear of disruption. However, among lower court decisions that have relied on *Tinker*, the term "disruption" has come to include not just the physical or noisy interruption of school operations, but also, for example, distraction, psychological stress of various kinds, the interruption of administrative routines, and even parental pressure brought to bear on school officials.

Tinker also authorizes schools to enforce reasonable regulations limiting the **time, place**, and **manner** of student expression even in traditional public forums as long as the regulations are necessary for the school to perform its educational function. Time, place, and manner regulations are designed not to impede the expression of ideas but only to ensure an orderly and efficient use of facilities. Examples include allowing distribution of student-written literature before or after school but not during school hours (**time**), permitting students to post notices on some bulletin boards but not others (**place**), and allowing student-initiated speech during lunchtime but prohibiting the use of amplification devices (**manner**).

To be constitutionally permissible, such regulations must meet four criteria: (a) the regulation must be **content-neutral** (i.e., not based on the subject matter or content of the speech); (b) the regulation must serve **a significant governmental purpose** such as safety; (c) the regulation must be **narrowly tailored** (i.e., not substantially broader than necessary to achieve its purpose); and (d) the regulation must leave ample **alternative means to reach the target audience**.[95]

In 2009, the Sixth Circuit affirmed a school rule preventing a 14-year-old student from distributing anti-abortion leaflets in the school hallways between classes while allowing him to distribute them during lunch hours from a table in the cafeteria.[96] Because the hallways constituted non-public forums, the school district was entitled to impose time, place, and manner restrictions so long as they were viewpoint neutral and reasonable.

In *K.A. v. Pocono Mountain School District*,[97] the Third Circuit affirmed a district court ruling in favor of a fifth-grade student who had been prohibited from distributing invitations to a Christmas party before the start of her class. The court affirmed that a forum analysis was not necessary because the invitations did not fall within any of the **categories of unprotected student speech** (as in *Fraser*) and was not **school-sponsored speech** (as in *Hazelwood*). Significantly, the court held the *Tinker* test should apply in school-based free speech cases, regardless of the age of the stu-

---

94 United States v. O'Brien, 391 U.S. 367 (1968).
95 Ward v. Rock Against Racism, 491 U.S. 781 (1989), *aff'd in part, rev'd in part*, 848 F. 2d 367 (1988); Clark v. Cmty for Creative Non-Violence, 468 U.S. 288 (1984).
96 M.A.L. v. Kinsland, 543 F.3d 841 (6th Cir. 2008); *see also* Morgan v. Plano Independent Sch. Dist., 589 F.3d 740 (5th Cir. 2009), *cert. denied*, 561 U.S. 1025 (2010).
97 710 F.3d 99 (3d Cir. 2013).

dents concerned. "Because K.A.'s speech did not fall within any of the categories that obviate the material risk of substantial disruption test, the District Court correctly chose not to employ forum analysis," concluded the court. "The fact that K.A. was only in the fifth-grade and the invitation originated from her church does not mandate a different approach."

Problematic Varieties of Independent Student Speech

"Sexting"

In *B.H. v. Easton Area School District*,[98] school officials sought to prevent students from wearing "I ♥ boobies! (KEEP A BREAST)" bracelets as part of a national breast cancer awareness campaign. The Third Circuit found the bracelets could not be banned without violating the First Amendment rights because they were not plainly lewd and could reasonably be interpreted as political speech. School officials had been concerned that allowing the bracelets would require them to permit "other messages that were sexually oriented." In response, the court acknowledged that school officials have an extremely difficult job. "Besides the teaching function, school administrators must deal with students distracted by cell phones in class and poverty at home, parental under- and over-involvement, bullying and **sexting** …"

In response to the widespread problem of "sexting" by students, many states added provisions to their education laws specifically proscribing sexually explicit text messages. New Jersey's provisions are illustrative:[99]

§ 18A:35–4.32. Findings, declarations relative to "sexting"

The Legislature finds and declares that:

a. The teenage practice of "sexting," sending a sexually explicit text message, is a nationwide issue for students, parents, school administrators, and law enforcement officials.
b. What many teens do not realize is that, by law, a sexual image of any person under the age of 18 is child pornography. Prosecutors in several states have charged teenagers who have engaged in this behavior with criminal offenses, including distribution of child pornography.
c. Pursuant to a law which became effective in April, 2012, the New Jersey Legislature provided for a diversionary program for juveniles who are criminally charged for "sexting" or posting sexual images and permits them to participate in a remedial education or counseling program as an alternative to criminal prosecution.
d. Beyond the legal consequences of this behavior, however, sexting also has significant non-legal consequences including, but not limited to, the effect on relationships, loss of educational and employment opportunities, and being barred or removed from school programs and extracurricular activities.
e. Because of the unique characteristics of cyberspace and the Internet, a single sext has the potential to cause long-term and possibly unforeseen consequences, and result in severe embarrassment, ridicule, cyberbullying, and lasting mental and emotional trauma.
f. It is imperative that students understand at a young age the severity of sending sexually explicit text messages and the impact that these actions have on the students themselves, their victims, and the community and that they receive instruction on how and why to refrain from this very dangerous behavior.

---

98 B.H. *ex rel.* Hawk v. Easton Area School District, 725 F.3d 293 (3d Cir. 2013), *cert. denied,* 572 U.S. 1002 (2014).
99 N.J. Stat. § 18A:35–4.32.

As noted by the New Jersey legislature, the substantial body of criminal law that prohibits the distribution and possession of **child pornography** has been augmented with new statutes criminalizing "**sexting**." A Florida statute prohibits the use of the computer or other electronic device to transmit to another a photograph which depicts nudity, meaning

> the showing of the human male or female genitals, pubic area, or buttocks with less than a fully opaque covering; or the showing of the female breast with less than a fully opaque covering of any portion thereof below the top of the nipple; or the depiction of covered male genitals in a discernibly turgid state.[100]

While the constitutionality of these newer criminal laws has not been tested in court, the authority of school officials to discipline students for "**sexting**" under state education laws seems clear. There is not much doubt regarding the constitutionality of state statutes prohibiting the transmission of depictions of sexually explicit conduct involving children.[101]

Religious Speech

Religious speech receives vigorous First Amendment protection, so religious speech by students can present serious problems for public school officials. Students who wish to discuss their religious views among themselves during their free time have a right to do so. But what about students who wish to publicize and promote their religious views among their schoolmates? Does freedom of speech protect the right to proselytize at school? Does the Establishment Clause require the school to prohibit this form of speech? Do other students have a right to be protected from being proselytized at school?

In *Thompson v. Waynesboro Area School District*,[102] a federal court found in favor of students who had been prohibited from distributing religious literature in their school's hallways. School officials argued that they had a duty to protect other students from receiving religious literature, and that they had to avoid the appearance of endorsing any religious viewpoint. However, the court concluded on the basis of testimony by the school's principal that "the restrictions … were at least to some extent content based." School officials had permitted the distribution of other types of literature written by outside groups and the time, place, and manner of distribution had been non-disruptive.

Other courts have issued rulings similar to *Thompson*.[103] In *Morgan v. Swanson*,[104] school officials blocked elementary school students from including religious messages in the goodie bags they planned to exchange in class at a winter party. The students were told they could hand them out on a public sidewalk. The Fifth Circuit ruled that the prohibition violated the free speech rights of the students, rejecting the claim that elementary school students are not covered by *Tinker*. In *Adler v. Duval County School Board*,[105] the Eleventh Circuit ruled that the delivery of a religious graduation speech by a student did not violate the Establishment Clause because it was independent, not school-sponsored speech. This ruling implies that religious speech by students can only be

---

100 Fla Stat. §§847.0141 and 847.001; *see also* 13 V.S.A. §2802(b).
101 La. R.S. 14:81.1.1; R.I. Gen. Laws § 11-9-1.4.
102 673 F. Supp. 1379 (M.D. Pa. 1987).
103 Slotterback v. Interboro Sch. Dist., 766 F. Supp. 280 (E.D. Pa. 1991); Rivera v. E. Otero Sch. Dist., R-1, 721 F. Supp. 1189 (D. Colo. 1989); Nelson v. Moline Sch. Dist. No. 40, 725 F. Supp. 965 (C.D. Ill. 1989).
104 Morgan v. Swanson, 627 F.3d 170 (5th Cir. 2010) and 659 F.3d 359 (5th Cir. 2011); *see also* M.B. *ex rel.* Martin v. Liverpool Cent. Sch. Dist., 487 F. Supp. 2d 117 (N.D. 2007).
105 250 F.3d 1330 (11th Cir. 2001).

regulated in accordance with the *Tinker* test. If the school had had a significant role in selecting the graduation speaker or in deciding what was said, a religious graduation speech would likely violate the Establishment Clause.[106]

Political Speech

The courts have generally been willing to protect the **political speech** rights of students, including a right to make statements about government policy, government officials, and even public school administrators. Thus, at least two cases have found against schools that prohibited students from wearing t-shirts calling former president George W. Bush an "international terrorist."[107] The schools involved in these cases were unable to show that the t-shirts were or were likely to become materially and substantially disruptive to the need for discipline and order within the school. However, the same did not hold true in the case of a student given a 10-day suspension for writing "Free A-Train" on the back of his hands in support of a recently-expelled gang leader accused of shooting a police officer.[108] There was evidence that the gang's support of A-Train had led to numerous phone calls from anxious parents, interruptions in class, the intimidation of other students, and even a "near riot" when officials sought to deal with two students who wore t-shirts bearing the slogan. The courts have also allowed school officials to ban t-shirts with messages promoting violence and vigilantism.[109]

School officials often feel obliged to suppress speech or expression that is offensive to a segment of the student body or that undermines attempts by the school to promote tolerance and respect for diversity. As we have seen, school officials may prohibit students from wearing or displaying the Confederate flag if this would cause material and substantial disruption.[110] However, in *Castorina* ex rel. *Rewt v. Madison County School Board*,[111] school officials did not prevail in their attempt to ban Confederate flag shirts because there was no showing of disruption and the school had permitted other students to wear clothing venerating Malcolm X. In *Madrid v. Anthony*,[112] the court upheld the prohibition of t-shirts that read, "We are Not Criminals" and "Border Patrol"— representing opposite sides in an ongoing immigration debate.

In *Harper v. Poway Unified School District*,[113] a student was required to spend a day in a conference room doing homework after he refused to remove a t-shirt declaring homosexuality to be contrary to God's will. The Ninth Circuit rejected the student's claim that his free speech rights had been violated, reasoning that school officials may prohibit

---

106 Cole v. Oroville Union High Sch. Dist., 228 F.3d 1092 (9th Cir. 2000), *cert. denied*, 532 U.S. 905 (2001).
107 Guiles v. Marineau, 461 F.3d 320 (2d Cir. 2006), *cert denied*, 551 U.S. 1162 (2007); Barber v. Dearborn Pub. Sch., 286 F. Supp. 2d 847 (E.D. Mich. 2003).
108 Brown *ex rel.* Brown v. Cabell County Bd. of Educ., 714 F. Supp. 2d 587 (S.D. W. Va. 2010); *see also* Kuhr v. Millard Public Sch. Dist., 2012 U.S. Dist. LEXIS 56189 (D. Neb. 2012).
109 Miller v. Penn Manor School District, 588 F.Supp.2d 606 (E.D. Pa. 2008).
110 Scott v. Sch. Bd. of Alachua County, 324 F.3d 1246 (11th Cir. 2003), *cert. denied*, 540 U.S. 824 (2003); Denno v. Sch. Bd. of Volusia County Florida, 218 F.3d 1267 (11th Cir. 2000), *cert. denied*, 531 U.S. 958 (2000), *reh'g denied*, 235 F. 3d 1347 (2000); West v. Derby Unified Sch. Dist. No. 260, 206 F.3d 1358 (10th Cir. 2000), *cert. denied*, 531 U.S. 825 (2000); Melton v. Young, 465 F.2d 1332 (6th Cir. 1972).
111 246 F.3d 536 (6th Cir. 2001); *see also* Defoe *ex rel.* Defoe v. Spiva, 625 F.3d 324 (6th Cir.2010), *reh'g denied*, 674 F.3d 505 (6th Cir. Tenn. 2011), *cert. denied*, 132 S. Ct. 399 (2011); B.W.A. v. Farmington R-7 School Dist., 554 F.3d 734 (8th Cir. 2009); A.M. *ex rel.* McAllum v. Cash, 585 F.3d 214 (5th Cir. 2009); Barr v. Lafon, 538 F.3d 554 (6th Cir. 2008), *reh'g denied*, 553 F.3d 463 (6th Cir. 2009), *cert. denied*, 130 S. Ct. 63 (2009).
112 510 F. Supp. 2d 425 (S.D. Tex. 2007).
113 445 F.3d 1166 (9th Cir. 2006), *cert. granted but vacated as moot*, 549 U.S. 1262 (2007); *see also* Governor Wentworth Reg. Sch. Dist. v. Hendrickson, 421 F. Supp. 2d 410 (D.N.H. 2006); Bar-Navon v. Sch. Bd. of Brevard County, 2007 U.S. Dist. LEXIS 82044 (M.D. Fla. 2007), *aff'd*, 290 Fed. Appx. 273 (2008).

Speech that attacks high school students who are members of minority groups that have historically been oppressed, subjected to verbal and physical abuse, and made to feel inferior, serves to injure and intimidate them, as well as to damage their sense of security and interfere with their opportunity to learn.

The court noted that disagreements may justify social or political debate "but they do not justify students in high schools assaulting their fellow students with demeaning statements."

In contrast, other courts have allowed students to display slogans attacking the beliefs and practices of other students including, in one case, a t-shirt that read "INTOLERANT Jesus said … I am the way, the truth and the life. John 14:6" and "Homosexuality is a sin! Islam is a lie! Abortion is murder! Some issues are just black and white!" The court found an insufficient basis to anticipate that there would be disruption.[114] A federal district court said students must be permitted to sport slogans in support of gay rights and held that any "disruptions" that occurred "were indistinguishable from the typical background noise of high school."[115] The Seventh Circuit later affirmed that a student could not be punished or prevented from wearing a t-shirt with the slogan, "Be Happy, Not Gay."[116]

Issues such as abortion may involve both **political speech** and **religious speech** by students in public school contexts. In the following case, the Tenth Circuit affirmed that students' First Amendment rights were not violated when school officials stopped them from distributing rubber fetus dolls to protest abortion and "put God back into the schools" due to the **material and substantial disruption** that actually ensued.

⚖️

TAYLOR v. ROSWELL INDEPENDENT SCHOOL DISTRICT
US Court of Appeals for the Tenth Circuit
713 F.3d 25 (2013)

SCOTT MILNE MATHESON, JR., Circuit Judge

The plaintiffs are, or at all relevant times were, high school students from Roswell, New Mexico, who belong to a religious group called "Relentless" ("Plaintiffs"). They sued Roswell Independent School District and Superintendent Michael Gottlieb in his official capacity (collectively "the District") seeking declaratory and injunctive relief. Their complaint alleged that school officials violated their First and Fourteenth Amendment rights by preventing them from distributing 2,500 rubber fetus dolls to other students. It also challenged the District's policies requiring preapproval before distributing any non-school-sponsored material on school grounds. A magistrate judge granted summary judgment for the District on all claims, and Plaintiffs appealed. Exercising jurisdiction under 28 U.S.C. § 1291, we affirm the dismissal of Plaintiffs' free speech, free exercise, and equal protection claims. We also affirm dismissal of Plaintiffs' facial challenge to Roswell District's preapproval policies. We note that the public school setting is important to our analysis.

I. Background

A. Factual History

The five plaintiffs in this case are, or at all relevant times were, students of two high schools, Roswell

---

114 Nixon v. Northern Local Sch. Dist. Bd. of Educ., 383 F. Supp. 2d 965 (S.D. Ohio, E.D. 2005); *see also* Chambers v. Babbit, 145 F. Supp. 1068 (D. Minn. 2001).

115 Gillman v. School Bd. for Holmes Cnty., Fl., 567 F. Supp.2d 1359 (N.D. Fla. 2008).

116 Nuxoll *ex rel.* Nuxoll v. Indian Prairie Sch. Dist., 523 F.3d 668 (7th Cir. 2008), *aff'd*, 636 F.3d 874 (2011); Zamecnik v. Indian Prairie Sch. Dist. No. 204, 710 F. Supp.2d 711 (N.D. Ill. 2010).

and Goddard High. They belong to a religious youth group called Relentless, which is affiliated with a local church called Church on the Move. Relentless is not affiliated with any school. Relentless members testified in depositions that they routinely engaged in religious expression at school. For example, they often spoke to other students, in groups and one-on-one, about their religious beliefs and anti-abortion views; and they regularly prayed, silently and aloud, while on school grounds, including during class. Plaintiffs were never disciplined or asked to stop these activities.

In late 2009, Plaintiffs and other Relentless members began an outreach campaign to express kindness and charity to fellow students and teachers, and to "put God back into the schools." Each week they distributed different items at both schools. A pastor from Church on the Move, Tim Aguilar, led the students in organizing and planning these events and was present on school grounds for the distributions. Relentless initially gave 220 McDonald's chicken salad sandwiches (donated by a church member) to the faculty at both high schools. In ensuing weeks, they distributed to students and faculty hot chocolate, candy canes with religious messages, and "affirmation rocks" with scriptural references painted on one side.

When these distributions began, Roswell District had two policies concerning distribution of non-school related materials on campus. Policy 7110 required advance permission from the District before distribution in any quantity of promotional items or advertisements on campus. A separate, long-standing but unwritten policy required students to obtain permission before on-campus distribution of non-school-sponsored literature. These policies are described in more detail later in this section. The Relentless students did not seek permission before distributing the previously mentioned items. They were not disciplined, reprimanded, or asked to stop. There is no evidence these distributions caused disruption.

1. The Rubber Fetus Doll Distributions

On January 29, 2010, Pastor Aguilar and the Relentless students planned to distribute 2,500 small rubber dolls, one to every student at both schools. Each two-inch doll was designed to be a realistic representation of a human fetus. A card attached to each doll explained that it represented the actual size and weight of a "12-week old baby," that is, a fetus at 12 weeks of gestation. One side of the card encour-

aged students to visit or call the Chaves County Pregnancy Resource Center, a clinic affiliated with Church on the Move. The other side featured a Relentless logo and [a] scriptural passage. ...

At Goddard High, Pastor Aguilar and eight or nine Relentless students set up tables in the lobby and began the distribution about 7:30 a.m. They approached every student entering the school and offered a doll. The entrances were not blocked, and the Relentless members allowed those who declined to take a doll to continue on their way. Assistant Principal Brian Luck arrived and noticed the distribution. He went to his office and radioed other administrators to ask whether the students had approval for the distribution. Assistant Principal Michelle Edgett responded that the students did not have approval and told Mr. Luck he should "probably" take possession of the dolls. On his way back to the lobby, Mr. Luck saw several students throwing what looked like small rubber balls at the wall. The "balls" turned out to be dismembered heads of the rubber fetus dolls. Several female students stopped him to complain. Relentless members were not among those dismembering or throwing the dolls.

Mr. Luck approached the Relentless students and said, "It's time to shut this down ... Some people are getting offended." He took the remaining dolls and told the students they would be returned at the end of the day. At this point, the Relentless group had distributed more than 300 dolls at Goddard High.

Later that morning, a Goddard High administrator called the principal of Roswell High, Ruben Bolaños, to ask if a similar distribution was underway at Roswell High. Principal Bolaños was not on campus, so he telephoned a campus security officer and instructed him to investigate and to confiscate the dolls "[i]f it's a disruption to the educational process." Two campus security guards at Roswell High investigated and eventually determined the dolls should be confiscated.

Both schools experienced doll-related disruptions that day. Many students pulled the dolls apart, tearing the heads off and using them as rubber balls or sticking them on pencil tops. Others threw dolls and doll parts at the "popcorn" ceilings so they became stuck. Dolls were used to plug toilets. Several students covered the dolls in hand sanitizer and lit them on fire. One or more male students removed the dolls' heads, inverted the bodies to make them resemble penises, and hung them on the outside of their pants' zippers.

Teachers at both schools complained that students' preoccupation with the dolls disrupted classroom instruction. While teachers were trying to instruct, students threw dolls and doll heads across classrooms, at one another, and into wastebaskets. Some teachers said the disruptions took eight to 10 minutes each class period, and others said their teaching plans were derailed entirely. An honors freshman English class canceled a scheduled test because students had become engaged in name calling and insults over the topic of abortion. A Roswell security officer described the day as "a disaster" because of the dolls. ...

3. *Roswell District Policies Regarding On-Campus Distributions*

... At the time of the rubber doll distribution, the District had a long-standing, unwritten policy of requiring students to obtain approval before distributing non-school-sponsored material on school grounds. In May 2010, the District formalized this unwritten policy when it promulgated Policy 5195, captioned "Distribution of Non School Sponsored Literature." This policy requires that students obtain approval from the school administration before distributing more than 10 copies of "any non-school sponsored literature." **Section 2** of the policy provides that approval may be withheld if the school district administration "reasonably determines" that the distribution:

a. Would cause a substantial disruption or a material interference with the normal operation of the school or school activities.
b. Is potentially offensive to a substantial portion of the school community due to the depiction or description of sexual conduct, violence, morbidity or the use of language which is profane or obscene and which is inappropriate for the school environment as judged by the standards of the school community.
c. Is libelous or which violates the rights of privacy of any person.
d. Is false or misleading or misrepresents facts.
e. Is demeaning to any race, religion, sex, or ethnic group.
f. Encourages violation of local, state or federal laws.

Sections 1 and **3** of the policy describe certain procedural safeguards. The District must approve or deny a distribution request within five school days. This time may be extended only with written approval of Superintendent Gottlieb. The District must provide a written explanation of the reasons for any denial. Students whose requests are denied have a right to two appeals. The first appeal is made directly to Superintendent Gottlieb, with a final appeal to the Board of Education. If a student appeals to the Board, it must provide a hearing within 10 school days and render its decision at its next regular meeting. ...

B. *Procedural History*

Plaintiffs' Second Amended Complaint sought injunctive relief and alleged three counts. Count I included two First Amendment speech claims. First, Plaintiffs brought a facial challenge against the District's preapproval policies for non-school-sponsored material, alleging the policies are unconstitutional prior restraints and are unconstitutionally vague. Second, they challenged the policies as applied to Plaintiffs, claiming that the District's refusal to allow them to distribute the fetus dolls violated their free speech rights. Count II alleged violation of Plaintiffs' free exercise rights. ...

II. Discussion

Plaintiffs claim that when the schools prevented them from distributing the rubber fetus dolls, their constitutional rights to free speech, free exercise of religion, and equal protection were violated. They also claim that the speech violation was the product of school policies that are unconstitutional on their face as prior restraints and for reasons of vagueness and overbreadth. As we explain below, Plaintiffs' free speech challenges fail because school officials reasonably forecasted that the distribution would cause substantial disruption and because the distribution did cause substantial disruption. Plaintiffs' free exercise and equal protection claims fail because the decision to stop the distribution was not based on religion, and Plaintiffs failed to show they were treated differently from similarly situated students.

Plaintiffs' facial challenge to the school policy also fails. The policy is not unconstitutional under the prior restraint doctrine because it constrains official discretion and contains adequate procedural safeguards–and because it applies to the school environment where greater deference is given to school officials. It is not void for vagueness because students of ordinary intelligence can understand its meaning and it neither authorizes nor encourages arbitrary or discriminatory enforcement. ...

In First Amendment cases, we are obligated "to make an independent examination of the whole record in order to make sure that the judgment does not constitute a forbidden intrusion on the field of free expression." We first consider the free speech challenge to the District's refusal to allow the rubber fetus distribution. ...

The magistrate judge analyzed Plaintiffs' free speech claim under two standards developed in *Tinker* and *Hazelwood* and held that the District was entitled to summary judgment under both standards. We affirm under the *Tinker* standard. *Hazelwood* is inapplicable because the expression at issue here is [independent] student speech and not school-sponsored speech.[117]

Two important questions are not at issue. First, this case does not turn on whether the content of Plaintiffs' message warrants First Amendment protection—there is no question that it does. The record shows Plaintiffs meant to convey a religious and political message when they distributed the rubber dolls, and the Constitution requires they be permitted to express these views at school in some form. For example, the District almost certainly may not prevent Plaintiffs from sharing their religious views in non-disruptive small group discussions with other students who wish to participate; nor can the District exercise editorial control over the content of Plaintiffs' private expression or decide whether to approve Plaintiffs' distribution of materials on the basis of their viewpoint. Insofar as the District has acknowledged that Plaintiffs' many other religiously-themed distributions at both schools did not disrupt the school environment, it correctly allowed those distributions to continue.

Second, the parties do not contest that the District was allowed, under *Tinker* and *Fraser*, to confiscate already-distributed rubber dolls from any students who threw them, used them to harm school property, or displayed them as props for lewd or obscene expressions of their own.

What is contested is whether the District violated Plaintiffs' free speech rights when it stopped their on-campus distribution of large quantities of the rubber fetus dolls. The answer depends on whether school officials reasonably forecasted that this particular form of expression (i.e., mass distribution of hundreds or thousands of three-dimensional rubber dolls to public high school students during the school day) would create a substantial disruption to school discipline.

In the following discussion, we determine that Plaintiffs' claims involve private—that is, non-school-sponsored—student speech and therefore fall under the Tinker standard. Applying *Tinker*, we hold that the District did not violate Plaintiffs' free speech rights because it reasonably forecasted that distribution of the rubber dolls would lead to a substantial disruption.

1. The *Tinker* Standard Applies to Plaintiffs' Distribution

Restrictions on student speech in public schools are analyzed under one of two standards. Tinker governs private student speech; Hazelwood governs school-sponsored speech. Private student expression that is unconnected to any school-sponsored activity is subject to the more stringent *Tinker* standard. In *Tinker*, the plaintiffs were punished for wearing black armbands at school to express their disagreement with U.S. involvement in the Vietnam War. The Supreme Court held that the school could not restrict this speech unless the school reasonably forecasted that the speech would cause substantial disruption to the school environment.

In contrast, the Supreme Court has explained that student speech is analyzed under the *Hazelwood* standard when "students, parents, and members of the public might reasonably perceive [the speech] to bear the imprimatur of the school." At issue in *Hazelwood* was a school's decision to censor the content of a high school newspaper published as part of the school's journalism program. Schools "do not offend the First Amendment by exercising editorial control over the style and content of student speech in school-sponsored expressive activities," provided the restrictions "are reasonably related to legitimate pedagogical concerns."

In the present case, "[n]o one would reasonably believe" the distribution of rubber fetuses "bore the school's imprimatur." As in *Tinker*, Plaintiffs were expressing their private views, and their expression was not part of any school-sponsored program. The *Tinker* standard therefore applies.

2. *The District's Actions Did Not Violate Plaintiffs' Free Speech Rights*

a. Further Background on the **Tinker** *Standard*

Under *Tinker*, a public school may not restrict private student expression unless the school reasonably forecasts it "would materially and substantially inter-

---

117 393 U.S. 503 (1969); 484 U.S. 260 (1988).

fere with the requirements of appropriate discipline in operation of the school," or "impinge upon the rights of other students."

A disruption need not actually materialize. School officials may act to prevent problems as long as the situation "might reasonably [lead] authorities to forecast" substantial disruption or interference with the rights of others. This forecast must be reasonable. Officials may not restrict speech based on "undifferentiated fear or apprehension of disturbance" or a "mere desire to avoid the discomfort and unpleasantness that always accompany an unpopular viewpoint."

For a school's forecast to be reasonable, courts generally require that it be based on a "concrete threat" of substantial disruption. *Tinker* rejected the idea that a "silent, passive" expression that merely provokes discussion in the hallway constitutes such a threat, particularly if that expression is political. The Second and Third Circuits have reinforced this notion, overturning schools' bans on t-shirts criticizing George W. Bush ...

b. *Tinker Applied to the Fetus Doll Distribution*

Plaintiffs' distribution conveyed a political and religious message and would likely merit First Amendment protection outside the school context. Inside the school walls, however, we must consider whether the expression was, or was reasonably forecast to be, disruptive. Unlike in Tinker, the expression here was neither silent nor passive. It involved proactive contact with large numbers of other students. The items

being distributed remained on school grounds in the hands of students throughout the school day. The sheer number of items also created strong potential for substantial disruption.

Furthermore, these fetus dolls were made of rubber—a material that could easily be, and was, pulled apart, bounced against walls, and stuck to ceilings. The dolls' small size made them tempting projectiles and toilet-clogging devices. This scenario carries more potential for disruption than the passive, silent act of wearing a t-shirt or a black armband. And that potential quickly came to fruition. The record is replete with reports of doll-related disruptions throughout the day on January 29, 2010, including substantial disruptions to classroom instruction, damage to school property (the ceilings and plumbing), and risks to student safety (the fire-starting and doll-throwing).

Plaintiffs note that most disruptions occurred only because of wrongful behavior of third parties and that no Plaintiffs participated in these activities. They argue that preventing their speech because of bad acts of others amounts to banning leafleting because of litterbugs. This argument might be effective outside the school context, but it ignores the "special characteristics of the school environment," where the government has a compelling interest in protecting the educational mission of the school and ensuring student safety. ...

In short, there is ample undisputed evidence that the District had permissible reasons for stopping the distribution. Plaintiffs' free speech rights were therefore not violated.

Hate Speech

Cases that appear to involve **hate speech** pose difficult legal problems. Student speech that casts members of marginalized groups in a negative light, no matter how invidious, is nonetheless **political speech**. Many examples of hate speech (such as the t-shirts described in previous sections) express some sort of political or religious sentiment but in a manner designed to provoke, attack, or offend. Hate speech that falls into the unprotected categories of **threats** or **fighting words** may be banned, but **independent student speech** that is political or religious may only be regulated if it meets the material and substantial disruption standard in *Tinker*.

In *R.A.V. v. City of St. Paul*,[118] the Supreme Court ruled that cities and states may not suppress speech that gives offense to members of marginalized groups merely because of disagreement with the hateful viewpoint being expressed. *Tinker* also prohibits the regulation of student speech

118 505 U.S. 377 (1992).

merely because of disagreement with the viewpoint expressed but permits regulation of speech that is materially and substantially disruptive or invasive of the rights of others. The latter standard has not been extensively explored in case law but presumably it permits, at a minimum, suppressing and punishing speech that constitutes an **invasion of privacy** or **defamation** of another member of the school community (see Chapter 12).

As a practical matter, hate speech within the context of a diverse school environment will often meet the **material and substantial disruption** test. In addition, there are federal statutes that require schools to prevent student-on-student **racial or sexual harassment** (see Chapter 7).

Drafting regulations that prohibit hate speech without being unconstitutionally vague or over-broad can be challenging. A rule is impermissibly vague if people "of common intelligence must necessarily guess at its meaning and differ as to its application."[119] An example would be a school rule against "speaking in an irritating manner." A rule is impermissibly overbroad if its effect is to prohibit not only speech that the government is permitted to regulate but also speech that is pro-tected by the First Amendment.[120] An example would be a school rule against speech that makes another person "feel uncomfortable." While this rule could be applied (permissibly) to prohibit lewd talk, threats, and slander, it could also be used (impermissibly) to suppress dissenting opin-ions on sensitive topics like abortion.

The Third Circuit found that the phrase "ill will" in a school's anti-racial harassment policy was overbroad and probably vague as well in *Sypniewski v. Warren Hills Regional Board of* Education.[121] In *Saxe v. State College Area School District*,[122] the Third Circuit found similar problems with a school's anti-harassment policy that prohibited "verbal … conduct … which offends, denigrates or belittles an individual because of … actual or perceived race, religion, color, national origin, gen-der, sexual orientation, disability, or other personal characteristics." Citing *Fraser, Hazelwood*, and *Tinker*, the court found that the policy would impermissibly allow the school to prohibit student speech that was not lewd, school-sponsored, or disruptive and to engage in viewpoint discrimina-tion. The court noted that school rules whose effect is to prohibit only speech defined by federal law as racial harassment (see Chapter 7) may be permissible.

Heckler's Veto

What if a speaker's views are so unpopular that the audience threatens violence? Is the speech then considered **fighting words**? Has it inspired **imminent lawless action**? Can the speaker therefore be punished? If so, then a hostile audience may negate the right to speak freely. This seems to have occurred in *Dariano v. Morgan Hill Unified School District*,[123] a case in which students claimed their First Amendment rights had been violated when school officials asked them to remove t-shirts bearing images of the American flag, turn them inside out, or go home. School officials claimed they feared the t-shirts would incite race-related violence during a Cinco de Mayo celebration. The Ninth Circuit found in favor of the school district. In *Holloman v. Harland*,[124] the Eleventh Circuit found in favor of a student who had raised his fist during the flag salute. "It is unques-tionably easy for a principal to preclude the outburst by preventing the student from [engaging in expressive conduct]," wrote the court. "To do so, however, is to sacrifice freedom upon the altar of order, and allow the scope of our liberty to be dictated by the inclinations of the unlawful mob."

---

119 Connally v. General Constr. Co., 269 U.S. 385 (1926).
120 Gooding v. Wilson, 405 U.S. 518 (1972).
121 307 F.3d 243 (3d Cir. 2002); *but see* West v. Derby Unified Sch. Dist. No. 260, 206 F.3d 1358 (10th Cir. 2000), *cert. denied*, 531 U.S. 825 (2000).
122 Saxe v. State College Area Sch. Dist., 240 F.3d 200 (3d Cir. 2001).
123 767 F.3d 764 (9th Cir. 2014).
124 Holloman v. Harland, 370 F.3d 1252 (11th Cir. 2004).

Some expressive acts also have the potential to be psychologically disruptive to an unreceptive audience. This was part of the *Harper* court's rationale for allowing the school to suppress anti-gay sentiments, and it is part of the reason that **threats** and **fighting words** may be prohibited. In formulating the **material and substantial disruption** standard in *Tinker*, the Supreme Court was primarily concerned with physical disruptions. But as in *Harper*, some courts have broadened the notion to include the potential to produce psychological stress in other students.

In *Trachtman v. Anker*,[125] the court permitted school officials to ban the distribution of a questionnaire eliciting "rather personal and frank information about [other] students' sexual attitudes, preferences, knowledge and experience." School officials had instituted the rule because they feared that students asked to complete the questionnaire might be harmed psychologically, even though no one was forced to do so and students were alerted to the subject matter of the questionnaire. The danger of the *Trachtman* court's reasoning is that like the **heckler's veto**, it has the potential to abrogate *Tinker* by allowing school officials to ban speech that other students might find upsetting.

Bullying and Cyberbullying

Bullying, whether it occurs directly on the school premises or indirectly through social media or the Internet—sometimes called **cyberbullying**—can implicate several bodies of law: state statutory law specifically addressing bullying (see Chapter 5); federal anti-discrimination laws that prohibit various forms of harassment (see Chapter 7); the ***Americans with Disabilities Act (ADA)***, ***Rehabilitation Act***, and ***Individuals with Disabilities Education Act (IDEA)*** (see Chapter 8); criminal law; tort law (see Chapter 12); and the First Amendment.

States have focused considerable attention on **bullying** in recent years because of its pervasiveness and harmfulness. However, different states have defined "bullying" in different ways. A federal report states that

> Researchers have traditionally defined bullying as a repeated pattern of aggressive behavior that involves an imbalance of power and that purposefully inflicts harm on the bullying victim. Bullying assumes a variety of forms including direct physical or verbal actions that cause physical or emotional distress, or indirect acts of social aggression that are used to damage a victim's personal relationships or social standing.[126]

Studies indicate that students who are bullied show increased anxiety levels and psychosomatic symptoms and experience higher rates of eating disorders and aggressive-impulsive behavior problems, poor self-esteem, depression, and suicidal ideations. Such students have also been shown to demonstrate lower academic achievement and school connectedness, as well as higher rates of truancy and disciplinary problems.[127]

Bullying in school contexts may fall into one of the following four categories:

Category A

Bullying that takes the form of **physical violence** raises no First Amendment issues because hitting, punching, or spitting or urinating on another student are not speech.

---

125 563 F.2d 512 (2d Cir. 1977).
126 U.S. Department of Education, Office of Planning, Evaluation and Policy Development, Policy and Program Studies Service, Analysis of State Bullying Laws and Policies, Washington, D.C. 2011, p. 1.
127 *Id.*, p. 3.

Category B

Bullying that takes the form of an excluded category of speech in school contexts (including **threats, fighting words**, or **lewd or vulgar language**), may be controlled without violating the First Amendment.

Bullying that meets the definition of **harassment** (see Chapters 7 and 8) is not protected by the First Amendment and must be stopped. Bullying that constitutes tortious conduct, including **defamation** and **intentional infliction of mental distress** (see Chapter 12) could likely be stopped and punished without violating the First Amendment. *Tinker* arguably stands for the rule that speech that "invades the rights of others" may be restricted by school officials without giving rise to successful First Amendment challenges.

Category C

This category includes the kinds of speech activities that frequently occur on school premises outside of class time which could not be controlled without violating the First Amendment absent **material and substantial disruption**. Examples of these would include one-off arguments, trash-talk, insults, rude gestures, and gossip.

Category D

This category includes speech that is persistently or repeatedly directed at specific people and is designed to make them feel bad about themselves.

If the bullying falls into Categories A or B, it may be controlled. If it falls into Category C, the First Amendment would stand in the way of control. If the bullying falls into Category D, it must be controlled. Here is one formal definition of Category D bullying based on California law:[128]

> **Bullying** means any severe or pervasive physical or verbal act or conduct, including communications made in writing or by means of an electronic act, and including one or more acts committed by a pupil or group of pupils as defined … directed toward one or more pupils that has or can be reasonably predicted to have the effect of one or more of the following:
>
> - Placing a reasonable student or group of students in fear of harm to their person or property.
> - Causing a reasonable student or group of students to experience a substantially detrimental effect on their physical or mental health.
> - Causing a reasonable student or group of students to experience substantial interference with their academic performance.
> - Causing a reasonable student or group of students to experience substantial interference with their ability to participate in or benefit from the services, activities, or privileges provided by a school.

Note that this provision does not require proof that the speaker(s) intended to have the listed effects, and it focuses on the "reasonable student," not on the effects of the speech of the actual victim (who might be an especially sensitive person). Activities that could be covered by this definition include spreading rumors or lies about another student, repeatedly ridiculing or mocking or taunting or insulting another student or invading the privacy of another student.

---

128 Cal. Ed. Code § 48900(r).

The question is whether a state law or school policy like this could withstand a First Amendment challenge. The approach most likely to be taken by the courts in deciding this question is to use the **material and substantial disruption** test from *Tinker*. This is precisely the approach the Fourth Circuit took in the following paradigmatic **cyberbullying** case.

⚖️

KOWALSKI v. BERKELEY COUNTY SCHOOLS
United States Court of Appeals for the Fourth Circuit
652 F.3d 565 (2011), *cert. denied*, 565 U.S. 1173 (2012)

PAUL V. NIEMEYER, Circuit Judge

When Kara Kowalski was a senior at Musselman High School in Berkeley County, West Virginia, school administrators suspended her from school for five days for creating and posting to a MySpace.com webpage called "S.A.S.H.," which Kowalski claims stood for "Students Against Sluts Herpes" and which was largely dedicated to ridiculing a fellow student. Kowalski commenced this action, under 42 U.S.C. § 1983, against the Berkeley County School District and five of its officers, contending that in disciplining her, the defendants violated her free speech and due process rights under the First and Fourteenth Amendments. She alleges, among other things, that the School District was not justified in regulating her speech because it did not occur during a "school-related activity," but rather was "private out-of-school speech."

The district court entered summary judgment in favor of the defendants, concluding that they were authorized to punish Kowalski because her webpage was "created for the purpose of inviting others to indulge in disruptive and hateful conduct," which caused an "in-school disruption."

Reviewing the summary judgment record *de novo*, we conclude that in the circumstances of this case, the School District's imposition of sanctions was permissible. Kowalski used the Internet to orchestrate a targeted attack on a classmate, and did so in a manner that was sufficiently connected to the school environment as to implicate the School District's recognized authority to discipline speech which "materially and substantially interfere[es] with the requirements of appropriate discipline in the operation of the school and collid[es] with the rights of others." Accordingly, we affirm.

I

On December 1, 2005, Kara Kowalski, who was then a 12th grade student at Musselman High School in the Berkeley County School District, returned home

from school and, using her home computer, created a discussion group webpage on MySpace.com with the heading "S.A.S.H." Under the webpage's title, she posted the statement, "No No Herpes, We don't want no herpes." Kowalski claimed in her deposition that "S.A.S.H." was an acronym for "Students Against Sluts Herpes," but a classmate, Ray Parsons, stated that it was an acronym for "Students Against Shay's Herpes," referring to another Musselman High School Student, Shay N., who was the main subject of discussion on the webpage.

After creating the group, Kowalski invited approximately 100 people on her MySpace "friends" list to join the group. MySpace discussion groups allow registered users to post and respond to text, comments, and photographs in an interactive fashion. Approximately two dozen Musselman High School students responded and ultimately joined the group. Kowalski later explained that she had hoped that the group would "make other students actively aware of STDs," which were a "hot topic" at her school. Ray Parsons responded to the MySpace invitation at 3:40 p.m. and was the first to join the group, doing so from a school computer during an after-hours class at Musselman High School. Parsons uploaded a photograph of himself and a friend holding their noses while displaying a sign that read, "Shay Has Herpes," referring to Shay N. The record of the webpage shows that Kowalski promptly responded, stating, "Ray you are soo funny!=)" It shows that shortly thereafter, she posted another response to the photograph, stating that it was "the best picture [I]'ve seen on myspace so far! ! ! !" Several other students posted similar replies. Parsons also uploaded to the "S.A.S.H." webpage two additional photographs of Shay N., which he edited. In the first, he had drawn red dots on Shay N.'s face to simulate herpes and added a sign near her pelvic region, that read, "Warning: Enter at your own risk." In the second photograph, he captioned Shay N.'s face with a sign that read, "portrait of a whore." ...

The next morning, Shay N.'s parents, together with Shay, went to Musselman High School and filed a harassment complaint with Vice Principal Becky Harden regarding the discussion group, and they provided Harden with a printout of the "S.A.S.H." webpage. Shay thereafter left the school with her parents, as she did not want to attend classes that day, feeling uncomfortable about sitting in class with students who had posted comments about her on the MySpace webpage. ...

School administrators concluded that Kowalski had created a "hate website," in violation of the school policy against "harassment, bullying, and intimidation." For punishment, they suspended Kowalski from school for 10 days and issued her a 90-day "social suspension," which prevented her from attending school events in which she was not a direct participant. Kowalski was also prevented from crowning the next "Queen of Charm" in that year's Charm Review, having been elected "Queen" herself the previous year. In addition, she was not allowed to participate on the cheerleading squad for the remainder of the year. After Kowalski's father asked school administrators to reduce or revoke the suspension, Assistant Superintendent Rick Deuell reduced Kowalski's out-of-school suspension to 5 days, but retained the 90-day social suspension.

Kowalski claims that, as a result of her punishment, she became socially isolated from her peers and received cold treatment from teachers and administrators. She stated that she became depressed and began taking prescription medication for her depression. Kowalski acknowledged that at the beginning of each school year, including her senior year, she had received a Student Handbook which included the School District's Harassment, Bullying, and Intimidation Policy, as well as the Student Code of Conduct. The Harassment, Bullying, and Intimidation Policy prohibited

any form of ... sexual ... harassment ... or any bullying or intimidation by any student ... during any school-related activity or during any education-sponsored event, whether in a building or other property owned, use[d] or operated by the Berkeley Board of Education. ...

In granting summary judgment to the defendants, in addition to ruling against Kowalski on

her free speech claim, the district court denied Kowalski's due process claim, concluding (1) that Kowalski was on notice that she could be punished for her off-campus behavior and (2) that she was provided with an opportunity to be heard prior to her suspension ... We review the district court's rulings *de novo*.

II

Kowalski contends first that the school administrators violated her free speech rights under the First Amendment by punishing her for speech that occurred outside the school. She argues that because this case involved "off-campus, non-school related speech," school administrators had no power to discipline her. As she asserts, "The [Supreme] Court has been consistently careful to limit intrusions on students' rights to conduct taking place on school property, at school functions, or while engaged in school-sponsored or school-sanctioned activity." She maintains that

no Supreme Court case addressing student speech has held that a school may punish students for speech away from school—indeed every Supreme Court case addressing student speech has taken pains to emphasize that, were the speech in question to occur away from school, it would be protected.

The Berkeley County School District and its administrators contend that school officials "may regulate off-campus behavior insofar as the off-campus behavior creates a foreseeable risk of reaching school property and causing a substantial disruption to the work and discipline of the school," citing *Doninger v. Niehoff*.[129] Relying on *Doninger*, the defendants note that Kowalski created a webpage that singled out Shay N. for harassment, bullying and intimidation; that it was foreseeable that the off-campus conduct would reach the school; and that it was foreseeable that the off-campus conduct would "create a substantial disruption in the school." The question thus presented is whether Kowalski's activity fell within the outer boundaries of the high school's legitimate interest in maintaining

129 527 F.3d 41 (2d Cir. 2008).

order in the school and protecting the well-being and educational rights of its students.

The First Amendment prohibits Congress and, through the Fourteenth Amendment, the States from "abridging the freedom of speech." It is a "bedrock principle" of the First Amendment that "the government may not prohibit the expression of an idea simply because society finds the idea itself offensive or disagreeable." While students retain significant First Amendment rights in the school context, their rights are not coextensive with those of adults. Because of the "special characteristics of the school environment," school administrators have some latitude in regulating student speech to further educational objectives. ...

Although the Supreme Court has not dealt specifically with a factual circumstance where student speech targeted classmates for verbal abuse, in *Tinker* it recognized the need for regulation of speech that interfered with the school's work and discipline, describing interference as speech that "disrupts classwork," creates "substantial disorder," or "collid[es] with" or "inva[des]" "the rights of others."[130] ...

The *Tinker* Court referred to this amplified statement of its test later in its opinion in shorthand when it concluded that the regulation of armbands "would violate the constitutional rights of students, at least if it could not be justified by a showing that the students' activities would materially and substantially disrupt the work and discipline of the school." Because, in *Tinker*, the students' wearing of the armbands "neither interrupted school activities nor sought to intrude in the school affairs or the lives of others," there was "no interference with work and no disorder" to justify regulation of the speech. Thus, the language of *Tinker* supports the conclusion that public schools have a "compelling interest" in regulating speech that interferes with or disrupts the work and discipline of the school, including discipline for student harassment and bullying. ...

Just as schools have a responsibility to provide a safe environment for students free from messages advocating illegal drug use, schools have a duty to protect their students from harassment and bullying in the school environment. ... Far from being a situation where school authorities "suppress speech on political and social issues based on disagreement with the viewpoint expressed," school administrators must be able to prevent and punish harassment and bullying in order to provide a safe school environment conducive to learning.

We are confident that Kowalski's speech caused the interference and disruption described in *Tinker* as being immune from First Amendment protection. The "S.A.S.H." webpage functioned as a platform for Kowalski and her friends to direct verbal attacks towards classmate Shay N. ... This is not the conduct and speech that our educational system is required to tolerate, as schools attempt to educate students about "habits and manners of civility" or the "fundamental values necessary to the maintenance of a democratic political system."

While Kowalski does not seriously dispute the harassing character of the speech on the "S.A.S.H." webpage, she argues mainly that her conduct took place at home after school and that the forum she created was therefore subject to the full protection of the First Amendment. This argument, however, raises the metaphysical question of where her speech occurred when she used the Internet as the medium. Kowalski indeed pushed her computer's keys in her home, but she knew that the electronic response would be, as it in fact was, published beyond her home and could reasonably be expected to reach the school or impact the school environment. She also knew that the dialogue would and did take place among Musselman High School students whom she invited to join the "S.A.S.H." group and that the fallout from her conduct and the speech within the group would be felt in the school itself. Indeed, the group's name was "Students Against Sluts Herpes" and a vast majority of its members were Musselman students. As one commentator on the webpage observed, "wait til sees the page lol." Moreover, as Kowalski could anticipate, Shay N. and her parents took the attack as having been made in the school context, as they went to the high school to lodge their complaint.

There is surely a limit to the scope of a high school's interest in the order, safety, and well-being of its students when the speech at issue originates outside the schoolhouse gate. But we need not fully define that limit here, as we are satisfied that the nexus of Kowalski's speech to Musselman High School's pedagogical interests was sufficiently strong to justify the action taken by school officials in carrying out their role as the trustees of the student body's well-being.

Of course, had Kowalski created the "S.A.S.H." group during school hours, using a school-provided

130 393 U.S. 503 (1969).

computer and Internet connection, this case would be more clear-cut, as the question of where speech that was transmitted by the Internet "occurred" would not come into play. To be sure, a court could determine that speech originating outside of the schoolhouse gate but directed at persons in school and received by and acted on by them was in fact in-school speech. In that case, because it was determined to be in-school speech, its regulation would be permissible not only under *Tinker* but also, as vulgar and lewd in-school speech, under *Fraser*.

We need not resolve, however, whether this was in-school speech and therefore whether *Fraser* could apply because the School District was authorized by *Tinker* to discipline Kowalski, regardless of where her speech originated, because the speech was materially and substantially disruptive in that it "interfer[ed] … with the schools' work [and] colli[ded] with the rights of other students to be secure and to be let alone." Given the targeted, defamatory nature of Kowalski's speech, aimed at a fellow classmate, it created "actual or nascent" substantial disorder and disruption in the school.

First, the creation of the "S.A.S.H." group forced Shay N. to miss school in order to avoid further abuse. Moreover, had the school not intervened, the potential for continuing and more serious harassment of Shay N. as well as other students was real. Experience suggests that unpunished misbehavior can have a snowballing effect, in some cases resulting in "copycat" efforts by other students or in retaliation for the initial harassment. Other courts have similarly concluded that school administrators' authority to regulate student speech extends, in the appropriate circumstances, to speech that does not originate at the school itself, so long as the speech eventually makes its way to the school in a meaningful way. …

Thus, even though Kowalski was not physically at the school when she operated her computer to create the webpage and form the "S.A.S.H." MySpace group and to post comments there, other circuits have applied Tinker to such circumstances. To be sure, it was foreseeable in this case that Kowalski's conduct would reach the school via computers, smartphones, and other electronic devices, given that most of the "S.A.S.H." group's members and the target of the group's harassment were Musselman High School students. Indeed, the "S.A.S.H." webpage did make its way into the school and was accessed first by Musselman student Ray Parsons at 3:40 p.m., from a school computer during an after-hours class. Furthermore, as we have noted, it created a reasonably foreseeable substantial disruption there. At bottom, we conclude that the school was authorized to discipline Kowalski because her speech interfered with the work and discipline of the school. …

V

Kowalski's role in the "S.A.S.H." webpage, which was used to ridicule and demean a fellow student, was particularly mean-spirited and hateful. The webpage called on classmates, in a pack, to target Shay N., knowing that it would be hurtful and damaging to her ability to sit with other students in class at Musselman High School and have a suitable learning experience. While each student in the "S.A.S.H." group might later attempt to minimize his or her role, at bottom, the conduct was indisputably harassing and bullying, in violation of Musselman High School's regulations prohibiting such conduct.

Kowalski asserts that the protections of free speech and due process somehow insulate her activities from school discipline because her activity was not sufficiently school-related to be subject to school discipline. Yet, every aspect of the webpage's design and implementation was school-related. Kowalski designed the website for "students," perhaps even against Shay N.; she sent it to students inviting them to join; and those who joined were mostly students, with Kowalski encouraging the commentary. The victim understood the attack as school-related, filing her complaint with school authorities. Ray Parsons, who provided the vulgar and lewd—indeed, defamatory—photographs understood that the object of the attack was Shay N., and he participated from a school computer during class, to the cheering of Kowalski and her fellow classmates, whom she invited to the affair.

Rather than respond constructively to the school's efforts to bring order and provide a lesson following the incident, Kowalski has rejected those efforts and sued school authorities for damages and other relief. Regretfully, she yet fails to see that such harassment and bullying is inappropriate and hurtful and that it must be taken seriously by school administrators in order to preserve an appropriate pedagogical environment. Indeed, school administrators are becoming increasingly alarmed by the phenomenon, and the events in this case are but one example of such bullying and school administrators' efforts to contain it. Suffice it to hold here that, where such speech has a sufficient nexus with the school, the Constitution is not written to hinder school administrators' good faith efforts to address the problem. The judgment of the district court is AFFIRMED.

Student Speech Targeting School Officials

Protests

Protests against school policies or personnel may fall into the category of **political speech**. Courts generally give students broad latitude to criticize the policies and practices of their schools as well as teachers and school officials. In *Depinto* v. *Bayonne Board of Education*,[131] fifth-grade students wore buttons with a photograph of a Hitler Youth group to protest their school's mandatory uniform policy. A federal court found students had a First Amendment right to wear the buttons, rejecting claims by school officials that the image was **lewd, vulgar, indecent, or plainly offensive**, that the image could be viewed as **school-sponsored speech**, that the image was likely to cause **material and substantial disruption**, and that *Tinker* should be interpreted differently for elementary school students. As noted earlier, the federal circuit courts had disagreed on whether elementary school students are entitled to the same First Amendment protections as high school students.[132]

In *Seamons* v. *Snow*,[133] a student-athlete, after having been tied naked to his locker by his teammates, reported his hazing to the football coach. The coach then gathered the team together and accused the student of betraying the team. When the student-athlete refused to apologize, the coach cut him from the team. The Tenth Circuit affirmed that the student-athlete's complaint was not disruptive, and hence protected speech under the First Amendment.

Protests against school policies or personnel can sometimes be materially and substantially disruptive to the school and its programs. In *Lowery* v. *Euverard*,[134] three football players circulated a petition expressing hatred of their coach and a desire not to play for him. When the school found out about the petition, the three players were cut from the team. The Sixth Circuit agreed with school officials that damage to team cohesion and morale met the material and substantial disruption test under *Tinker*. In *Pinard* v. *Clatskanie School District*,[135] members of a basketball team signed a petition demanding the resignation of a coach who had been verbally abusive. The players then refused to play, forcing the school to use junior varsity players. The protesting players were permanently suspended from the team. The Ninth Circuit affirmed that while the petition itself was protected speech, the students' refusal to play the game was disruptive, so the suspension was upheld. In *Wildman* v. *Marshalltown School District*,[136] the Eighth Circuit upheld the dismissal of a student-athlete for "suborning insubordination" after she had circulated a letter calling on her teammates to "stand up for what we believe in."

Insults

In a 1976 case, a federal court upheld the suspension of a student who shouted, "There's Stear … He's a prick" at a teacher in a local shopping mall because, in the view of the court, these were "fighting words."[137] But students have prevailed in more recent cases involving similar off-campus speech directed at teachers or other students. In *Klein* v. *Smith*,[138] the court protected a student from suspension for giving his teacher the finger in a restaurant because it did not constitute "fighting words" and "any possible connection to … the proper and orderly operation of the

---

131 514 F. Supp. 2d 633 (N.J. 2007).
132 M.A.L. v. Kinsland, 543 F.3d 841 (6th Cir. 2008); *see also* Morgan v. Plano Independent Sch. Dist., 589 F.3d 740 (5th Cir. 2009), *cert. denied*, 130 S. Ct. 3503 (2010).
133 84 F.3d 1226 (10th Cir. 1996).
134 497 F.3d 584 (6th Cir. 2007), *cert. denied*, 555 U.S. 825 (2008).
135 467 F.3d 755 (9th Cir. 2006).
136 Wildman v. Marshalltown Sch. Dist., 249 F.3d 768 (8th Cir. 2001).
137 Fenton v. Stear, 423 F. Supp. 767 (W.D. Pa. 1976).
138 635 F. Supp. 1440 (D. Me. 1986).

school's activities [was] … far too attenuated to support discipline against Klein for violating the rule prohibiting vulgar or discourteous conduct toward a teacher."

Of course, the Internet and social media now allow speech activities initiated off-campus to find their way onto the campus easily via on-campus computers and personal electronic devices. Given that *Tinker* may apply to cyberbullying and other off-campus speech activities, the question before the courts becomes whether the speech is reasonably likely to cause (or has in fact caused) **material and substantial disruption**.

The courts have not hesitated to conclude that the disruption standard in *Tinker* is satisfied when online speech depicts violence against individual students or school officials, or when online speech includes **threats**. In *Wisniewski v. Board of Education*,[139] a student was suspended for creating an icon for his instant message account depicting one of his teachers being shot in the head with a caption beneath reading, "Kill Mr. VanderMolen." The Second Circuit upheld the suspension, finding that the icon's off-campus display "pose[d] a reasonably fore-seeable risk that [it] would come to the attention of school authorities and … materially and substantially disrupt the work and discipline of the school." As noted earlier, the Fifth Circuit recently deployed the **material and substantial disruption** standard from *Tinker* in *Bell v. Itawamba County School Board*,[140] upholding the suspension of a student who had posted an "incredibly profane and vulgar rap recording" on YouTube and Facebook making allegations of sexual misconduct against two coaches and threatening to shoot them in the face, among other things. And in *McKinney v. Huntsville School District*,[141] a federal court upheld the suspension and subsequent expulsion of a student who had posted a photo of himself on Instagram wearing a trench coat and holding an AR-15 rifle—the same weapon used in the Parkland shooting in Florida ten days earlier.

Cyberattacks

In *Doninger v. Niehoff*,[142] a student was barred from running for office after she referred to school officials as "douchebags" in a blog post. The student argued it was clearly established that off-campus speech could not be the subject of school discipline. The Second Circuit disagreed:

> It is … incorrect to urge, as Doninger does, that Supreme Court precedent necessarily insulates students from discipline for speech-related activity occurring away from school property, no matter its relation to school affairs or its likelihood of having effects—even substantial and disruptive effects—in school.

> This Court's 1979 decision in *Thomas* similarly fails to establish that off-campus speech may never properly be disciplined. In *Thomas*, public school students were punished for publishing and distributing to their peers a lewd, satirical newspaper. The production, publication, and distribution of the paper occurred almost entirely off campus, although some copies eventually found their way to school grounds and drew the attention of school officials. This Court concluded that because the students' activities were deliberately designed to take place away from school, such that "any activity within the school itself was *de minimis*," the school, in punishing them, had "ventured out of the school yard and into the general community," and the punishment imposed could not "withstand the proscription of the First Amendment."

139 494 F.3d 34 (2d Cir. 2007), *cert. denied*, 552 U.S. 1296 (2008).
140 799 F.3d 379 (5th Cir. 2015).
141 350 F. Supp. 3d 757 (W.D. Ark. 2018).
142 Doninger v. Niehoff, 527 U.S. 41 (2d Cir. 2008), *cert. denied*, 565 U.S. 976 (2011); Wisniewksi v. Board of Education, 494 F.3d 34 (2d Cir. 2007), *cert. denied*, 552 U.S. 1296 (2008); Bell v. Itawmba Cty. Sch. Bd., 2012 U.S. Dist. LEXIS 34839 (N.D. E.D. Miss., 2010).

The *Thomas* Court noted, however, that it could "envision a case in which a group of students incites substantial disruption within the school from some remote locale," suggesting that such behavior, simply not present in the case before it, might appropriately be disciplined. Judge Newman, moreover, concurring in the result in *Thomas*, explicitly noted that "[s]chool authorities ought to be accorded some latitude to regulate student activity that affects matters of legitimate concern to the school community, and territoriality is not necessarily a useful concept in determining the limit of their authority."

Other courts have been far more reluctant to permit discipline of students for cyberattacks against school officials, provided they do not involve **true threats**.

$$\overset{\triangle}{\underset{\triangle}{\mid}}$$

J.S. v. BLUE MOUNTAIN SCHOOL DISTRICT
US Court of Appeals for the Third Circuit
650 F.3d 915 (2011) (*en banc*), *cert. denied*, 565 U.S. 1156 (2012)

MICHAEL A. CHAGARES, Circuit Judge
 … This case arose when the School District suspended J.S. for creating, on a weekend and on her home computer, a MySpace profile (the "profile") making fun of her middle school principal, James McGonigle. The profile contained adult language and sexually explicit content. J.S. and her parents sued the School District under 42 U.S.C. § 1983 and state law, alleging that the suspension violated J.S.'s First Amendment free speech rights, that the School District's policies were unconstitutionally overbroad and vague, that the School District violated the Snyders' Fourteenth Amendment substantive process rights to raise their child, and that the School District acted outside of its authority in punishing J.S. for out-of-school speech.

Because J.S. was suspended from school for speech that indisputably caused no substantial disruption in school and that could not reasonably have led school officials to forecast substantial disruption in school, the School District's actions violated J.S.'s First Amendment free speech rights. We will accordingly reverse and remand that aspect of the District Court's judgment. …

I.

J.S. was an Honor Roll eighth grade student who had never been disciplined in school until December 2006 and February 2007, when she was twice disciplined for dress code violations by McGonigle. On Sunday, March 18, 2007, J.S. and her friend K.L., another eighth grade student at Blue Mountain Middle School, created a fake profile of McGonigle, which they posted on MySpace, a social networking website. The profile was created at J.S.'s home, on a computer belonging to J.S.'s parents.

The profile did not identify McGonigle by name, school, or location, though it did contain his official photograph from the School District's website. The profile was presented as a self-portrayal of a bisexual Alabama middle school principal named "M-Hoe." The profile contained crude content and vulgar language, ranging from nonsense and juvenile humor to profanity and shameful personal attacks aimed at the principal and his family. For instance, the profile lists M-Hoe's general interests as: "detention, being a tight ass, riding the fraintrain, spending time with my child (who looks like a gorilla), baseball, my golden pen, fucking in my office, hitting on students and their parents." In addition, the profile stated in the "About me" section:

HELLO CHILDREN[.] yes. it's your oh so wonderful, hairy, expressionless, sex addict, fagass, put on this world with a small dick PRINCIPAL[.] I have come to myspace so i can pervert the minds of other principal's [sic] to be just like me. I know, I know, you're all thrilled[.] Another reason I came to myspace is because—I am keeping an eye on you students (who[m] I care for so much)[.] For those who want to be my friend, and aren't in my school[,] I love children, sex (any kind), dogs, long walks on the beach, tv, being a dick head, and last but not least my darling wife who looks like a man (who satisfies my needs) MY FRAINTRAIN …

Though disturbing, the record indicates that the profile was so outrageous that no one took its content seriously. J.S. testified that she intended the profile to be a joke between herself and her friends. At her deposition, she testified that she created the profile because she thought it was "comical" insofar as it was so "outrageous."

Initially, the profile could be viewed in full by anyone who knew the URL (or address) or who otherwise found the profile by searching MySpace for a term it contained. The following day, however, J.S. made the profile "private" after several students approached her at school, generally to say that they thought the profile was funny. By making the profile "private," J.S. limited access to the profile to people whom she and K.L. invited to be a MySpace "friend." J.S. and K.L. granted "friend" status to about twenty-two School District students.

The School District's computers block access to MySpace, so no Blue Mountain student was ever able to view the profile from school. McGonigle first learned about the profile on Tuesday, March 20, 2007, from a student who was in his office to discuss an unrelated incident. ...

McGonigle ultimately decided that the creation of the profile was a Level Four Infraction under the Disciplinary Code of Blue Mountain Middle School, Student-Parent Handbook, as a false accusation about a staff member of the school and a "copyright" violation of the computer use policy, for using McGonigle's photograph. At his deposition, however, McGonigle admitted that he believed the students "weren't accusing me. They were pretending they were me." ...

McGonigle met with J.S. and her mother Terry Snyder and showed Mrs. Snyder the profile. He told the children's parents that J.S. and K.L. would receive ten days out-of-school suspension, which also prohibited attendance at school dances. McGonigle also threatened legal action. J.S. and her mother both apologized to McGonigle, and J.S. subsequently wrote a letter of apology to McGonigle and his wife.

McGonigle next contacted MySpace, provided the URL for the profile and requested its removal, which was done. McGonigle also contacted Superintendent Romberger to inform her of his decision regarding J.S. and K.L.'s punishment. Although Romberger could have overruled McGonigle's decision, she agreed with the punishment. On Friday, March 23, 2007, McGonigle sent J.S.'s parents a disciplinary notice, which stated that J.S. had been suspended for ten days. The following week, Romb-erger declined Mrs. Snyder's request to overrule the suspension. ...

The School District asserted that the profile disrupted school in the following ways. There were general "rumblings" in the school regarding the profile. More specifically, on Tuesday, March 20, McGonigle was approached by two teachers who informed him that students were discussing the profile in class. Randy Nunemacher, a Middle School math teacher, experienced a disruption in his class when six or seven students were talking and discussing the profile; Nunemacher had to tell the students to stop talking three times, and raised his voice on the third occasion. The exchange lasted about five or six minutes. Nunemacher also testified that he heard two students talking about the profile in his class on another day, but they stopped when he told them to get back to work. Nunemacher admitted that the talking in class was not a unique incident and that he had to tell his students to stop talking about various topics about once a week. Another teacher, Angela Werner, testified that she was approached by a group of eighth grade girls at the end of her Skills for Adolescents course to report the profile. Werner said this did not disrupt her class because the girls spoke with her during the portion of the class when students were permitted to work independently.

The School District also alleged disruption to Counselor Frain's job activities. Frain canceled a small number of student counseling appointments to supervise student testing on the morning that McGonigle met with J.S., K.L., and their parents. Counselor Guers was originally scheduled to supervise the student testing, but was asked by McGonigle to sit in on the meetings, so Frain filled in for Guers. This substitution lasted about twenty-five to thirty minutes. There is no evidence that Frain was unable to reschedule the canceled student appointments, and the students who were to meet with her remained in their regular classes. ...

J.S. and her parents filed this action against the School District, Superintendent Romberger, and Principal McGonigle. By way of stipulation, on January 7, 2008, all claims against Romberger and McGonigle were dismissed, and only the School District remained as a defendant. After discovery, both parties moved for summary judgment.

After analyzing the above facts, the District Court granted the School District's summary judgment motion on all claims, though specifically acknowledging that *Tinker* does not govern this case because no "substantial and material disruption" occurred. ...

Applying a variation of the *Fraser* and *Morse* standard,[143] the District Court held that

as vulgar, lewd, and potentially illegal speech that had an effect on campus, we find that the school did not violate the plaintiff's rights in punishing her for it even though it arguably did not cause a substantial disruption of the school.

The Court asserted that the facts of this case established a connection between off-campus action and on-campus effect. ... Ultimately, the District Court held that although J.S.'s profile did not cause a "substantial and material" disruption under *Tinker*, the School District's punishment was constitutionally permissible because the profile was "vulgar and offensive" under *Fraser* and J.S.'s off-campus conduct had an "effect" at the school. In a footnote, the District Court also noted that "the protections provided under *Tinker* do not apply to speech that invades the rights of others." ...

III.

Although the precise issue before this Court is one of first impression, the Supreme Court and this Court have analyzed the extent to which school officials can regulate student speech in several thorough opinions that compel the conclusion that the School District violated J.S.'s First Amendment free speech rights when it suspended her for speech that caused no substantial disruption in school and that could not reasonably have led school officials to forecast substantial disruption in school.

A.

We begin our analysis by recognizing the "comprehensive authority" of teachers and other public school officials. ... The authority of public school officials is not boundless, however. The First Amendment unquestionably protects the free speech rights of students in public school. ... The exercise of First Amendment rights in school, however, has to be

"applied in light of the special characteristics of the school environment," and thus the constitutional rights of students in public schools "are not automatically coextensive with the rights of adults in other settings." Since *Tinker*, courts have struggled to strike a balance between safeguarding students' First Amendment rights and protecting the authority of school administrators to maintain an appropriate learning environment.

The Supreme Court established a basic framework for assessing student free speech claims in *Tinker*, and we will assume, without deciding, that *Tinker* applies to J.S.'s speech in this case. The Court in *Tinker* held that "to justify prohibition of a particular expression of opinion," school officials must demonstrate that "the forbidden conduct would materially and substantially interfere with the requirements of appropriate discipline in the operation of the school." This burden cannot be met if school officials are driven by "a mere desire to avoid the discomfort and unpleasantness that always accompany an unpopular viewpoint." Moreover, "*Tinker* requires a specific and significant fear of disruption, not just some remote apprehension of disturbance." Although *Tinker* dealt with political speech, the opinion has never been confined to such speech.

As this Court has emphasized, with then-Judge Alito writing for the majority, *Tinker* sets the general rule for regulating school speech, and that rule is subject to several narrow exceptions. The first exception is set out in *Fraser*, which we interpreted to permit school officials to regulate "'lewd,' 'vulgar,' 'indecent,' and 'plainly offensive' speech in school." The second exception to *Tinker* is articulated in *Hazelwood*, which allows school officials to "regulate school-sponsored speech (that is, speech that a reasonable observer would view as the school's own speech) on the basis of any legitimate pedagogical concern."

The Supreme Court recently articulated a third exception to *Tinker*'s general rule in *Morse*. Although, prior to this case, we have not had an opportunity to analyze the scope of the *Morse* exception, the Supreme Court itself emphasized the narrow reach of its decision. In *Morse*, a school punished a student for unfurling, at a school-sponsored event, a large banner containing a message that could reasonably be interpreted as promoting illegal drug use. ...

143 478 U.S. 675 (1986); 551 U.S. 393 (2007).

B.

… [T]he School District now argues that it was justified in punishing J.S. under *Tinker* because of "facts which might reasonably have led school authorities to forecast substantial disruption of or material interference with school activities …" Although the burden is on school authorities to meet *Tinker's* requirements to abridge student First Amendment rights, the School District need not prove with absolute certainty that substantial disruption will occur.

The facts in this case do not support the conclusion that a forecast of substantial disruption was reasonable. …

J.S. created the profile as a joke, and she took steps to make it "private" so that access was limited to her and her friends. Although the profile contained McGonigle's picture from the school's website, the profile did not identify him by name, school, or location. Moreover, the profile, though indisputably vulgar, was so juvenile and nonsensical that no reasonable person could take its content seriously, and the record clearly demonstrates that no one did. Also, the School District's computers block access to MySpace, so no Blue Mountain student was ever able to view the profile from school. And, the only printout of the profile that was ever brought to school was one that was brought at McGonigle's express request. Thus, beyond general rumblings, a few minutes of talking in class, and some officials rearranging their schedules to assist McGonigle in dealing with the profile, no disruptions occurred. …

As the Supreme Court has admonished, an "undifferentiated fear or apprehension of disturbance is not enough to overcome the right to freedom of expression." If *Tinker's* black armbands—an ostentatious reminder of the highly emotional and controversial subject of the Vietnam war—could not "reasonably have led school authorities to forecast substantial disruption of or material interference with school activities," neither can J.S.'s profile, despite the unfortunate humiliation it caused for McGonigle.

Courts must determine when an "undifferentiated fear or apprehension of disturbance" transforms into a reasonable forecast that a substantial disruption or material interference will occur. … The School District [contends] that the profile was accusatory and aroused suspicions among the school community about McGonigle's character because of the profile's

references to his engaging in sexual misconduct. As explained above, however, this contention is simply not supported by the record. The profile was so outrageous that no one could have taken it seriously, and no one did. Thus, it was clearly not reasonably foreseeable that J.S.'s speech would create a substantial disruption or material interference in school, and this case is therefore distinguishable from the student speech at issue in *Doninger*, *Lowery*, and *LaVine*.[144]

Moreover, unlike the students in *Doninger*, *Lowery*, and *LaVine*, J.S. did not even intend for the speech to reach the school—in fact, she took specific steps to make the profile "private" so that only her friends could access it. The fact that her friends happen to be Blue Mountain Middle School students is not surprising, and does not mean that J.S.'s speech targeted the school. Finally, any suggestion that, absent McGonigle's actions, a substantial disruption would have occurred, is directly undermined by the record. If anything, McGonigle's response to the profile exacerbated rather than contained the disruption in the school.

The facts simply do not support the conclusion that the School District could have reasonably forecasted a substantial disruption of or material interference with the school as a result of J.S.'s profile. Under *Tinker*, therefore, the School District violated J.S.'s First Amendment free speech rights when it suspended her for creating the profile.

C.

Because *Tinker* does not justify the School District's suspension of J.S., the only way for the punishment to pass constitutional muster is if we accept the School District's argument—and the District Court's holding—that J.S.'s speech can be prohibited under the *Fraser* exception to *Tinker*. The School District argues that although J.S.'s speech occurred off campus, it was justified in disciplining her because it was "lewd, vulgar, and offensive [and] had an effect on the school and the educational mission of the District." The School District's argument fails at the outset because *Fraser* does not apply to off-campus speech. …

Thus, under the Supreme Court's precedent, the *Fraser* exception to *Tinker* does not apply here. In other words, *Fraser's* "lewdness" standard cannot be extended to justify a school's punishment of J.S. for

---

144 Doninger v. Niehoff, 642 F.3d 334 (2d Cir. 2011); Lowery v. Euverard, 497 F.3d 584 (6th Cir. 2007); LaVine v. Blaine Sch. Dist., 257 F.3d 981 (9th Cir. 2001).

use of profane language outside the school, during non-school hours. ...

The School District points out that "a hard copy or printout of the profile actually came into the school." However, the fact that McGonigle caused a copy of the profile to be brought to school does not transform J.S.'s off-campus speech into school speech. The flaws of a contrary rule can be illustrated by extrapolating from the facts of *Fraser* itself. As discussed above, the Supreme Court emphasized that Fraser's speech would have been protected had he delivered it outside the school. Presumably, this protection would not be lifted if a school official or Fraser's fellow classmate overheard the off-campus speech, recorded it, and played it to the school principal. Similarly here, the fact that another student printed J.S.'s profile and brought it to school at the express request of McGonigle does not turn J.S.'s off-campus speech into on-campus speech.

Under these circumstances, to apply the *Fraser* standard to justify the School District's punishment of J.S.'s speech would be to adopt a rule that allows school officials to punish any speech by a student that takes place anywhere, at any time, as long as it is about the school or a school official, is brought to the attention of a school official, and is deemed "offensive" by the prevailing authority. Under this standard, two students can be punished for using a vulgar remark to speak about their teacher at a private party, if another student overhears the remark, reports it to the school authorities, and the school authorities find the remark "offensive." There is no principled way to distinguish this hypothetical from the facts of the instant case. Accordingly, we conclude that the *Fraser* decision did not give the School District the authority to punish J.S. for her off-campus speech.

Neither the Supreme Court nor this Court has ever allowed schools to punish students for off-campus speech that is not school-sponsored or at a school-sponsored event and that caused no substantial disruption at school. We follow the logic and letter of these cases and reverse the District Court's grant of summary judgment in favor of the School District and denial of J.S.'s motion for summary judgment on her free speech claim. An opposite holding would significantly broaden school districts' authority over student speech and would vest school officials with dangerously overbroad censorship discretion. We will remand to the District Court to determine appropriate relief on this claim.

In a dissenting opinion joined by five additional judges, Judge Fisher cautioned that

The majority embraces a notion that student hostile and offensive online speech directed at school officials will not reach the school. But with near-constant student access to social networking sites on and off campus, when offensive and malicious speech is directed at school officials and disseminated online to the student body, it is reasonable to anticipate an impact on the classroom environment. I fear that our Court has adopted a rule that will prove untenable ...

I respectfully dissent from the decision that the suspension of J.S. for making false and malicious accusations against her principal in the form of lewd and offensive speech violated her First Amendment rights.

In student free speech cases, courts must grapple with the issue of promoting freedom of expression while maintaining a conducive learning environment. I believe the majority has unwisely tipped the balance struck by *Tinker, Fraser, [Hazelwood]*, and *Morse*, thereby jeopardizing schools' ability to maintain an orderly learning environment while protecting teachers and school officials against harmful attacks.

In *Layshock v. Hermitage School District*,[145] a companion case to *J.S. v. Blue Mountain*, the Third Circuit again ruled against the school district. In *Layshock*, school officials suspended a student,

---

145 Layshock v. Hermitage School Dist., 650 F.3d 205 (3rd Cir. 2011) *(en banc), cert denied*, 565 U.S. 1156 (2012); *See also* J.C. *ex rel.* R.C. v. Beverly Hills Unified Sch. Dist., 711 F. Supp. 2d (C.D. Cal. 2010); Requa v. Kent School Dist. No. 415, 492 F. Supp. 2d 1272 (W.D. Wash. 2007).

placed him in an alternate education program, and prevented him from participating in graduation ceremonies for creating a fake online profile of his school principal in which he described him as a drunk and a steroid user with a "small dick." The Third Circuit rejected the district's argument the student's speech was vulgar and lewd under *Fraser*, holding that *Fraser* could not apply to out of school speech and "the use of the district's website" to access the profile (not to create it) does not constitute entering the school. School officials conceded that the fake profile did not cause disruption under *Tinker*.

Freedom of Association and Use of School Facilities

By forming associations and speaking as a group, individuals can amplify their voices. Although freedom of association is not explicitly guaranteed by the First Amendment, the Supreme Court has recognized it as a corollary of free speech. Accordingly, in *Healy v. James*,[146] the Supreme Court ruled that public colleges may not deny official recognition to student political organizations or bar them from campus except by application of the *Tinker* test.

Freedom of association cases at the high school level generally follow *Healy* in prohibiting schools from banning student groups because they embrace disfavored ideas. For example, in *Dixon v. Beresh*,[147] a federal court found in favor of students whose Young Socialists organization had been denied recognition. School officials in that case had acted under a school board policy forbidding recognition of any group "advocating controversial ideas." The court reasoned that there was no legitimate forecast of "material and substantial disruption as required by *Tinker*."

Dixon is consistent with the general **free speech doctrine** prohibiting school officials from engaging in **viewpoint discrimination** in regulating student speech. Recall that viewpoint discrimination is impermissible in all forums of speech, including **limited public forums** (see Section 4.5). In *East High School Prism Club v. Seidel*,[148] students obtained an injunction prohibiting the school from denying recognition to a club that "sought to serve as a prism through which historical and current events, institutions, and culture could be viewed in terms of the impact, experience and contributions of gays and lesbians." Similarly, the Third Circuit found that impermissible viewpoint discrimination had occurred when a Bible club was denied permission to meet in an "activity period" that served as a **limited public forum**.[149]

In *Christian Legal Society v. Martinez*,[150] the Supreme Court considered whether schools may deny the use of their facilities to groups that discriminate on the basis of race, gender, religion, or sexual orientation. Recognition as an official student organization would give the Christian Legal Society (CLS) access to school funding and facilities including the school's email system. To obtain recognition, an organization had to "allow any student to participate, become a member, or seek leadership positions in the organization, regardless of [her] status or beliefs." But the CLS required its members to attest in writing to certain religious doctrines, including the belief that sexual activity should occur only in the context of marriage between a man and a woman. CLS filed a suit claiming that denial of recognition violated its free speech rights. In deciding the case, the Court relied on the **limited public forum** framework (see **Section 4.5**). The Supreme Court found that the school's "all-comers" policy was reasonably related to a number of the objectives of

---

146 408 U.S. 169 (1972).
147 361 F. Supp. 253 (E.D. Mich. 1973).
148 95 F. Supp. 2d 1239 (C.D. Utah 2000); *see also* Gay Lib v. Univ. of Mo., 558 F.2d 848 (8th Cir. 1977); Gay Student Serv. v. Tex. A&M Univ., 737 F.2d 1317 (5th Cir. 1984).
149 Donovan v. Punxsutawney Area Sch. Bd., 336 F.3d 211 (3d Cir. 2003).
150 561 U.S. 661 (2010).

its limited forum. The Court also concluded that the policy was viewpoint neutral. "It is, after all, hard to imagine a more viewpoint-neutral policy than one requiring all student groups to accept all comers."

The Equal Access Act

The federal **Equal Access Act** (EAA)[151] complements the freedom-of-association rights granted to students by the First Amendment. The EAA states in part:

> It shall be unlawful for any public secondary school which receives Federal financial assistance and which has a limited open forum to deny equal access or a fair opportunity to, or discriminate against, any students who wish to conduct a meeting within that limited open forum on the basis of the religious, political, philosophical, or other content of the speech at such meetings.

Schools are not required by the Act to grant recognition to non-curricular clubs. A school might legitimately decide not to recognize any student group for administrative ease or to reserve its resources for school-sponsored purposes.[152] But if a school provides an opportunity for even one non-curricular student group to use school premises during non-instructional time, a limited open forum requiring non-discriminatory access in accordance with EAA has been created.[153] The statute further specifies that:

> Schools shall be deemed to offer a fair opportunity to students who wish to conduct a meeting within its limited open forum if such school uniformly provides that—
>
> (1) the meeting is voluntary and student-initiated;
> (2) there is no sponsorship of the meeting by the school, the government, or its agents or employees;
> (3) employees or agents of the school or government are present at religious meetings only in a non-participatory capacity;
> (4) the meeting does not materially and substantially interfere with the orderly conduct of educational activities within the school; and
> (5) non-school persons may not direct, conduct, control, or regularly attend activities of student groups.

In Board of Education of the *Westside Community Schools v. Mergens*,[154] the Supreme Court defined "non-curricular related student group" to mean:

> any student group that does not directly relate to the body of courses offered by the school. In our view, a student group directly relates to a school's curriculum if the subject matter of the group is actually taught, or will soon be taught, in a regularly offered course; if the subject matter of the group concerns the body of courses as a whole; if participation in the group is required for a particular course; or if participation in the group results in academic credit. We think this limited definition of groups that directly relate to the curriculum is a commonsense interpretation of the Act that is consistent with Congress' intent to provide a low threshold for triggering the Act's requirements.

---

151 20 U.S.C. § 4071.
152 Student Coalition for Peace v. Lower Merion Sch. Dist. Bd. of Sch. Dirs., 776 F.2d 431 (3d Cir. 1985).
153 High Gay/Straight Alliance v. Bd. of Educ. of Salt Lake City Sch. Dist., 81 F. Supp. 2d 1166 (D. Utah 1999).
154 496 U.S. 226 (1990).

For example, a French club would directly relate to the curriculum if a school taught French in a regularly offered course or planned to teach the subject in the near future. A school's student government would generally relate directly to the curriculum to the extent that it addresses concerns, solicits opinions, and formulates proposals pertaining to the body of courses offered by the school. If participation in a school's band or orchestra were required for the band or orchestra classes, or resulted in academic credit, then those groups would also directly relate to the curriculum. The existence of such groups at a school would not trigger the Act's obligations.

On the other hand, unless a school could show that groups such as a chess club, a stamp collecting club, or a community service club fell within our description of groups that directly relate to the curriculum, such groups would be "non-curriculum related student groups" for purposes of the Act. The existence of such groups would create a "limited open forum" under the Act and would prohibit the school from denying equal access to any other student group on the basis of the content of that group's speech. Whether a specific student group is a "non-curriculum related student group" will therefore depend on a particular school's curriculum, but such determinations would be subject to factual findings well within the competence of trial courts to make.

Based on this definition, the Court ruled that denial of recognition to a student-initiated "Christian Club" by a school that recognized a variety of other non-curriculum related student groups violated the EAA. The Court also rejected the contention that the Act itself violates the Establishment Clause. Other courts have relied on *Mergens* in ruling that a drama club is non-curricular even if the school has a course devoted to the study, but not performance of plays[155] and that a Key Club (student service organization) was non-curricular.[156] In general, for a club to be curricular, there must be a significant connection to a school course, not just a tangential connection or overlap.[157]

EAA only applies when non-curricular clubs are given access to school facilities during "non-instructional time," but the distinction between instructional and non-instructional time is not always obvious. Two circuit courts have issued conflicting rulings. The Third Circuit ruled that a school's "activity period" when students were free to go to club meetings, study hall, or student government meetings, take make-up tests, or attend tutoring was non-instructional time. The fact that the activity period fell within the school day when attendance was mandatory did not make the period instructional time.[158] The Ninth Circuit ruled that a time called "student/staff time" was instructional time because student attendance in the school was required despite the fact that no formal classroom instruction took place except on a voluntary basis.[159] In a different case, the Ninth Circuit held that a lunch period was non-instructional time since no instruction took place during this time and students were not required to remain on campus.[160]

The *EAA* prohibits a school making access to its facilities contingent upon an organization protected by the Act changing its name, refraining from talking about sex or controversial topics, or modifying its membership rules.[161] Qualifying clubs must also be given the same access to equipment, services, and financial support as other clubs.[162]

---

155 Boyd County High Sch. GSA v. Bd. of Educ. of Boyd County, 258 F. Supp. 2d 667, 690–91 (E.D. Ky. 2003), *cert denied*, 555 U.S. 1171 (2009).
156 Pope v. East Brunswick Bd. of Educ., 12 F.3d 1244 (3d Cir. 1993).
157 Colin *ex rel.* Colin v. Orange Unified Sch. Dist., 83 F. Supp. 2d 1135 (C.D. Cal. 2000).
158 Donovan v. Punxsutawney Area Sch. Bd., 336 F.3d 211 (3d Cir. 2003).
159 Prince v. Jacoby, 303 F.3d 1074 (9th Cir. 2002), *cert denied*, 540 U.S. 813 (2003).
160 Ceniceros v. Board of Trustees, 106 F.3d 878, 880 (9th Cir. 1997).
161 Colin *ex rel.* Colin v. Orange Unified Sch. Dist., 83 F. Supp. 2d 1135 (C.D. Cal. 2000).
162 Prince v. Jacoby, 303 F.3d 1074 (9th Cir. 2002), cert denied 540 U.S. 813 (2003).

The EAA does permit schools to exclude a club if its presence would materially and substantially disrupt the school. But one court made clear that exclusion is only justified if the club itself behaves disruptively. When segments of a Kentucky community threw a school district into turmoil over the possible recognition of a gay-student club, the court ruled that this community-generated disruption did not justify non-recognition of the club.[163] Put another way, student groups cannot lose their rights under EAA as a result of a **heckler's veto**.

Use of School Facilities by Outside Groups

Community organizations, camps, scouting groups, and religious organizations often wish to meet in public schools, to distribute materials on campus or through internal mail systems, and otherwise take advantage of school facilities. As with student groups, some of the most difficult issues arise with regard to outside groups that wish to use school facilities for religious purposes. Does permitting an outside group to use its facilities for prayer or worship violate the Establishment Clause? Does the denial of permission constitute a violation of the religious group's free speech or free exercise rights?

In *Lamb's Chapel v. Center Moriches Union Free School District*,[164] a New York state law had authorized local school boards to permit the use of school property for ten specific purposes. The list included social, civic, recreational, and entertainment but not religious purposes. The Center Moriches district denied permission to a local evangelical organization, Lamb's Chapel, to show a six-part film series advocating that "Christian family values [be] instilled at an early stage," finding the series "church related." The Supreme Court unanimously ruled against the school district. In its view, the district need not have permitted any after-hours use of its property. However, once the district voluntarily made its facilities available for use by outside groups after hours, it could not enforce rules designed to exclude expression of specific points of view:

> That all religions and all uses for religious purposes are treated alike under [the rule] does not answer the critical question of whether it discriminates on the basis of viewpoint to permit school property to be used for the presentation of all views about family issues and child-rearing except those dealing with the subject matter from a religious viewpoint. There is no suggestion [that] a lecture or film about child-rearing and family values would not be a use for social or civic purposes otherwise permitted by [the] Rule. That subject matter is not one that the District has placed off-limits to any and all speakers. Nor is there any indication … that the application to exhibit the particular film involved here was or would have been denied for any reason other than the fact that the presentation would have been from a religious perspective. In our view denial on that basis was plainly invalid … "although a speaker may be excluded from a nonpublic forum if he wishes to address a topic not encompassed within the purpose of the forum … or if he is not a member of the class of speakers for whose special benefit the forum was created" … the government violates the First Amendment when it denies access to a speaker solely to suppress the point of view he espouses on an otherwise includible subject.

The Court further concluded that to permit Lamb's Chapel to use the facilities would not violate the Establishment Clause because it would have neither the purpose nor primary effect of advancing or inhibiting religion and would not foster excessive entanglement with religion.

In *Good News Club v. Milford Central School*,[165] the Supreme Court again ordered a school district to make its facilities available to a private Christian organization to hold weekly after-school

163 Boyd County High Sch. GSA v. Bd. of Educ. of Boyd County, 258 F. Supp. 2d 667 (E.D. Ky. 2003).
164 508 U.S. 384 (1993).
165 533 U.S. 98 (2001).

meetings for elementary school students at which the students sang religious songs, received Bible lessons, memorized scripture, and were instructed in Christian religious doctrine. The only difference between the activities in Lamb's Chapel and in this case, according to the Court, was that the Good News Club chose to teach Christian moral lessons through live storytelling and prayer, whereas in Lamb's Chapel, Christian moral lessons were taught through film. There was no violation of the Establishment Clause because, in the Court's view, students could attend only with parental permission. Central to the decision in *Good News Club* was the majority's conclusion that "the club's activities do not constitute mere religious worship, divorced from any teaching of moral values."

This issue has spawned a long running legal struggle between the organization called Bronx Household of Faith and the New York City Board of Education. School No. 10 prohibited Bronx Household from holding Sunday worship services in its auditorium. This led first to a round of litigation based on the free speech clause of First Amendment and Good News Club—litigation that culminated in a decision by the Second Circuit upholding the ban because it did not constitute viewpoint discrimination, but only banned a type of activity—the conduct of worship services.[166] The majority defined worship services as "a collective activity characteristically done according to an order prescribed by and under the auspices of an organized religion, typically but not necessarily conducted by an ordained official of the religion."

Bronx Household continued to seek access to the auditorium and went back to court again seeking an injunction, but this time based on the free exercise clause of the First Amendment.[167] A federal district court issued a temporary restraining order in favor of Bronx Household. The court characterized the ban as one that banned an activity because the activity was undertaken for religious reasons, i.e., the ban on the activity was not neutral. Accordingly, the court said the ban could only withstand the free exercise challenge if it was narrowly tailored to serve a compelling state purpose. The court went on to conclude that the defendants' efforts to avoid violating the Establishment Clause was not a compelling state interest insofar as it was only seeking to block religious services during non-school hours. Finally, in 2014, the Second Circuit found that the federal district court's decision had been "erroneous." The Court concluded that the school board's regulations were constitutional in light of its wish to avoid the liability associated with violating the Establishment Clause.[168]

Schools districts sometimes wish to raise money by selling access to school resources and facilities to outside groups for communicative purposes. Examples include selling advertisements in school publications or on school buildings and commemorative tiles and bricks to be erected on school walls or grounds. If a school carries out a program like this in a manner that creates a designated public forum (that is, it opens the forum for indiscriminate use by the general public or some segment of the public), then it may not decide to exclude a particular message based on its content. Such programs usually create only a limited public forum, allowing the school district to regulate based on content (but not on viewpoint).[169]

School districts may also maintain non-public forums in which all speech is school-sponsored. In school-*sponsored* forums, the school is permitted to limit access to designated speakers and to maintain control of content as long as its actions are based on legitimate pedagogical concerns.

---

166 Bronx Household of Faith v. Bd. of Educ. of City of New York 650 F.3d 30 (2d Cir. 2011), *cert. denied*, 565 U.S. 1087 (2011).

167 Bronx Household of Faith v. Bd. of Educ. of City of New York, 2012 U.S. Dist. LEXIS 2338 (S.D. N.Y. 2012).

168 Bronx Household of Faith v. Bd. of Educ. of City of New York, 750 F.3d 184 (2d Cir. 2014), *cert. denied*, 575 U.S. 946 (2015).

169 *See* Hills v. Scottsdale Unified Sch. Dist. No. 48, 329 F.3d 1044 (9th Cir. 2003), *cert. denied*, 540 U.S. 1149 (2004); Seidman v. Paradise Valley Unified Sch. Dist. No. 69, 327 F. Supp. 2d 1098 (Ariz. D. 2004); DiLoreto v. Downey Unified Sch. Dist. Bd. of Educ., 196 F.3d 958 (9th Cir. 1999), *cert. denied*, 529 U.S. 1067 (2000).

The school would, for example, be permitted (and also required by the Establishment Clause) to ban any speech that promotes or denigrates religion. Thus in *Busch v. Marple Newtown School District*,[170] the Third Circuit upheld a decision by school officials to stop a parent from reading from the Bible during a classroom session in which parents had been invited to read from their favorite books. Speech is school-sponsored only if a reasonable observer would view it as emanating from the school. One court rejected the claim that messages composed by parents on bricks they purchased for permanent placement on school grounds was school-sponsored speech. Another court reached the same conclusion regarding pamphlets placed in student mailboxes pursuant to a school policy that gave access to the mailboxes to outside groups.[171]

In *Planned Parenthood v. Clark County School District*,[172] the Ninth Circuit upheld a school policy denying Planned Parenthood the opportunity to purchase advertising in school publications, finding the exclusion of birth control products and information to be viewpoint neutral. In 2008, the Fourth Circuit rejected a claim that a district had turned its website and e-mail systems into public forums by including information from third parties and links to third party web pages. The court found the links to other websites were selected by the district to support its own messages. The district had "disclaimed" the contents of the linked website, emphasizing that only its own content should be taken as its "speech."[173] More recently, the Fourth Circuit affirmed that statements concerning Islamic beliefs made in the context of a world history class by a teacher (not an outside group) did not violate the Establishment Clause because the material was introduced to teach comparative religion and not to endorse any religious belief.[174]

Summary

Freedom of speech is a bedrock principle in American jurisprudence. But no rights are absolute. Over time, courts have developed an extensive set of doctrines that explicate the scope of governmental power to regulate speech. In general, governments may regulate speech only when necessary to achieve a compelling state purpose, and regulations of speech must be no more extensive than necessary to achieve that purpose.

Students have a constitutional right to freedom of speech and expression, but the First Amendment rights of students in public schools are not coextensive with those of adults in other contexts. They are limited because of the "special characteristics of the school environment" in American jurisprudence, which takes into account the legal status of most students as minors and the **custodial and tutelary** nature of the authority of public school officials as both parental delegates and agents of the State.

There are certain categories of speech including **obscenity, threats, fighting words**, and **defamation of private citizens** that receive no constitutional protection. Governments and their agencies, including schools, may prohibit or regulate these categories of speech as much as they wish. There are additional categories of speech including **lewd, vulgar**, and **obscene-as-to-minors** speech that receive no First Amendment protection in public schools. The Supreme Court has added speech **advocating illegal drug use** to this list.

School officials may regulate speech occurring as part of their curriculum or in any situation in which student speech appears to be school-sponsored. In these situations, regulation is per-

---

170 Busch v. Marple Newtown Sch. Dist., 567 F.3d 89 (3d Cir. 2009), *cert. denied*, 558 U.S. 1158 (2010).
171 Rusk v. Clearview Local Schs., 379 F.3d 418 (6th Cir. 2004); Demmon v. Loudon County Pub. Schs., 342 F. Supp. 2d 474 (E.D. Va. 2004).
172 Planned Parenthood v. Clark County Sch. Dist., 941 F.2d 817 (9th Cir. 1991) (*en banc*).
173 Page v. Lexington County Sch. Dist. One, 531 F.3d 275 (4th Cir. 2008).
174 Wood v. Charles County Public Schools, 915 F.3d 308 (4th Cir. 2019).

missible as long as it is **reasonably related to legitimate educational concerns**. However, even in school-sponsored situations, prohibition of student speech because of a disagreement with the viewpoint being expressed is constitutionally dubious.

Student speech or expression that does not fall into one of the unprotected categories and is not school-sponsored generally receives the highest level of legal protection. In *Tinker*, the Supreme Court ruled that independent student speech may only be prohibited if it is **materially and substantially disruptive** or if it **invades the rights of others**. Accordingly, efforts on the part of states and local school officials to control peer **bullying** and **cyberbullying** will usually be upheld by the courts. Reasonable regulation of the **time, place, and manner** of speech designed to accommodate competing demands for facilities is permitted, but regulation of independent student speech based on its **content or viewpoint** is rarely justified.

The free speech principles discussed in this chapter can be extremely complex. As we have seen, some student speech can be tasteless, obnoxious, hurtful, and without any apparent social or artistic value. On such occasions, school officials should bear in mind that a central educational purpose of public schools is to prepare future adult citizens to be self-governing in accordance with reason and reasonable laws, capable of exercising their liberty rights—including their First Amendment rights—in a manner that does not cause **harm to others**. This can best be accomplished by letting students exercise free speech rights at school in accordance with their evolving capacities, consistent with the **custodial and tutelary** nature of school authority in American jurisprudence.

5 The Fourth Amendment Rights of Students

In Chapter 4, we observed that children are **legal minors** and that public school officials exercise **custodial and tutelary** authority. These "special characteristics of the school environment" have limited the constitutional rights of students in American jurisprudence. Public school officials may regulate student conduct, including expressive conduct, without violating the First Amendment, if it is necessary to promote legitimate educational goals, to protect persons or property, or to prevent disruption.

Public and private school officials are legally responsible for the **care and control** of the students in their charge. At common law, they must protect their students from harm, and they must prevent their students from causing harm. For public school officials, **school shootings** and persistent public concern over **school safety** has led to crackdowns on violence, crime, weapons, gang activity, drugs, and bullying in recent years. **Safe School Acts** in many states empower school officials to investigate these kinds of misbehavior while imposing penalties should they fail to do so adequately. For example, in many states school administrators may face liability for **negligent indifference** if they fail to report criminal activity on school property to law enforcement officials.

Some state constitutions have made **safe schools** a right for all students.[1] Recognizing that school safety has psychological dimensions, the *Every Student Succeeds Act* (ESSA) includes resources for school districts to enhance trust and respect, to address traumatic stress and other student mental health and behavioral issues, and to promote overall student success.[2]

Because public school officials are agents of the State, they "face the daunting task of evaluating potential threats of violence and keeping their students safe without impinging on their constitutional rights."[3] Many of the most difficult questions in education law concern the conflict between the constitutional rights of students and the common law and statutory duties of public school officials to maintain safe and orderly school environments.

Students in many public schools across the country are now expected to pass through metal detectors at the schoolhouse gate; to accept surveillance cameras in common areas; to submit to searches of their lockers, their bags, their vehicles, and their persons; to consent to mouth swabbing and urinalysis; and to respond to questions from school officials investigating misconduct. In other contexts, agents of the State could not require such things of adults—or punish them for non-compliance—without violating the Constitution. But again, because most K-12 students are **legal minors**, they do not have—and cannot claim—all the liberty rights and constitutional protections afforded to adults in other contexts. In American jurisprudence, "Because of the State's custodial and tutorial authority over [them], public

1 Philip Leon M. v. Greenbrier County Bd. of Educ., 484 S.E.2d 909 (W. Va. 1996).
2 National Association of School Psychologists, *ESSA School Safety for Decision-Makers* (2019) online at www.nasponline. org/research-and-policy/current-law-and-policy-priorities/policy-priorities/the-every-student-succeeds-act/essa-implementation-resources/essa-school-safety-for-decision-makers (last accessed April 10, 2019).
3 Wynar v. Douglas County Sch. Dist., 728 F.3d 1062 (9th Cir. 2013).

school students are subject to greater degree of control and administrative supervision than is permitted over a free adult."[4]

In this chapter, we outline the limited **Fourth Amendment** rights of public school students when school officials undertake **searches** or **seizures** of their persons or belongings in the course of investigating misconduct. In Chapter 6, we outline the **due process** rights of public students when school officials adjudicate guilt and assign penalties and punishments.

The Fourth Amendment: An Overview

The Fourth Amendment provides that individuals are "to be secure in their persons, houses, papers, and effects, against **unreasonable searches and seizures**." In *Katz v. United States*,[5] another important Civil Rights Era decision, the Supreme Court held that the Fourth Amendment protects the **privacy** of individuals, along with their **persons** and their **property**.

Search Warrants

In criminal contexts, the Fourth Amendment requires that **search warrants** be issued by a judge or magistrate based on **probable cause**. Search warrants must be supported by an **oath** or affirmation, and must describe in detail the places to be searched, the items to be seized, and the individuals to be arrested.

The Supreme Court has identified some exceptions to the Fourth Amendment requirements for search warrants. In *Terry v. Ohio*,[6] two men convicted of carrying concealed weapons challenged the constitutionality of the pat-down search conducted by a police officer who had observed them engaging in suspicious behavior. The Supreme Court concluded that members of the public may be patted down for weapons and drugs if police officers reasonably believe they may be armed or dangerous. Justice William O. Douglas dissented, protesting that **probable cause** was the appropriate Fourth Amendment standard. Routine **"stop-and-frisk"** searches and vehicular searches at traffic stops have become highly controversial in New York and other major cities due to their association with **racial profiling**.[7]

In addition, search warrants are not required in **exigent circumstances**, when evidence is in **plain view**, or when a search is conducted with valid **consent**.

Exigent Circumstances

In *Armijo v. Peterson*,[8] a high school student was detained by police during a warrantless search of his home. School officials had received a tip from two female students that members of rival gangs were planning to bring guns to school, call in a bomb threat, and open fire on students. A parent alerted school officials that "a student named Chris" would call in the bomb threat. An anonymous caller subsequently made two bomb threats, prompting a lockdown and evacuation of the school. Chris Armijo was released after a search of his phones revealed he had not called in the bomb threats. The Tenth Circuit appellate held that **exigent circumstances** justified the warrantless entry of his home and his detention while his phones were searched.

---

4 67B Am Jur 2d Schools §284.
5 389 U.S. 347 (1967).
6 392 U.S. 1 (1968).
7 *See, e.g.,* Phillip Atiba Goff, *On Stop-and-Frisk, We Can't Celebrate Just Yet,* New York Times (January 7, 2018); online at www.nytimes.com/2018/01/07/opinion/stop-and-frisk-celebrate.html (last accessed April 27, 2020).
8 601 F.3d 1065 (10th Cir. 2010), *cert. denied,* 562 U.S. 1224 (2011).

Plain View

In *Ziegler v. Martin County School District*,[9] a group of high school students challenged the constitutionality of their detention by a **school resource officer** and subsequent Breathalyzer testing at the entrance to their school prom. The school resource officer had found empty champagne bottles and cups on their "party bus." The Eleventh Circuit affirmed that the search of the bus did not violate the students' Fourth Amendment rights because the driver had given **valid consent** to the search, the bottles and cups were in **plain view**, and the driver confirmed they belonged to the students.

Valid Consent

If someone **consents** to a search, the Fourth Amendment imposes no constraints, whether the search is conducted by police officers or school officials. However, **waivers** of constitutional rights are never presumed by the courts. For this reason, the Supreme Court found mandatory dues payments to public sector unions by non-members without their **affirmative consent** to be unconstitutional in *Janus v. AFSCME*.[10] "By agreeing to pay," wrote the Court, "non-members are waiving their First Amendment rights, and such a waiver cannot be presumed" (see Chapter 11).

Waivers

Waivers of constitutional rights are valid only when **knowingly and intelligently** given. As the Supreme Court put it in *Johnson v. Zerbst*,[11] "The determination of whether there has been an intelligent waiver … must depend, in each case, upon the particular facts and circumstances surrounding that case, including the background, experience, and conduct of the accused." There is, moreover, a strong presumption that a person would not knowingly waive a constitutional right when doing so would reveal evidence of wrongdoing.

In *Tarter v. Raybuck*,[12] the Sixth Circuit considered whether a student had consented to a search by school officials who observed him smoking and exchanging money for plastic bags of a substance they believed to be marijuana. School officials first asked Tarter to remove his jacket and searched his outer clothing. When they asked Tarter to remove his pants, he refused. The Sixth Circuit found Tarter had not **knowingly and intelligently** waived his Fourth Amendment rights: "That he may have acquiesced in the initial search does not necessarily demonstrate the relinquishment of his rights to challenge his initial search," wrote the Court. "In fact, David Tarter's testimony was that he only submitted to the search because he was afraid. Furthermore, there is no indication he even was aware that he might have had a constitutional right to object to a search."

Accordingly, a student who empties his or her pockets after being ordered to do so has not consented to the search. Nor would consent be valid if school officials took an intimidating or coercive approach. In *Cummerlander v. Patriot Preparatory Academy Inc.*,[13] a federal court ruled against officials at a charter school who had coerced a student into providing a urine sample by threatening to expel him. School officials were denied qualified immunity because they ought to have known their approach was unconstitutional. The court also noted that a policy authorizing

9 831 F.3d 1309 (11th Cir. 2016).
10 139 S. Ct. 2448 (2018).
11 304 U.S. 458 (1938).
12 742 F.2d 977 (6th Cir. 1984).
13 86 F. Supp. 3d 808 (S.D. Ohio, 2015).

drug tests under threat of expulsion—based on rumors, no less—fell "far short" of Fourth Amendment standards.

Parental Consent

For searches involving young children, **parental consent** must likewise be **knowingly and intelligently** given. In *Dubbs v. Head Start, Inc.*,[14] nurses conducted genital exams on students based on assurances that parental consent forms had been signed. The Tenth Circuit found the exams were searches for Fourth Amendment purposes because they constituted intrusive activity by a representative of the federal Head Start program. However, parents had *not* signed any forms giving explicit consent to genital exams, and it was not reasonable for those involved to believe otherwise. In *G.E.C. v. North Kansas City School District No. 74*,[15] a federal court denied a motion to dismiss a school nurse who had used her personal cell phone to take pictures of a first-grade student's vaginal area. She then uploaded the pictures to her personal email account, then forwarded them to the school principal. The court found that because the nurse had failed to obtain parental consent and had acted under color of state law, she violated the student's Fourth Amendment rights.

Searches by Public School Officials

There is another exception to Fourth Amendment requirements for search warrants that is particularly relevant for the purposes of this chapter: Although other significant limitations still apply, public school officials do not require **warrants** to conduct searches in the course of investigating student misconduct. In *Webb v. McCullough*,[16] for example, the Sixth Circuit found that the search of a student's hotel room by a school official during a school trip exceeded neither the Fourth Amendment limits on his authority (as a state agent) nor the common law limits on his authority (*in loco parentis*). In *Thompson v. Carthage School District*,[17] the Eight Circuit held that school officials did not violate the Fourth Amendment when they conducted pat-down searches of students suspected of carrying dangerous weapons on school property.

When school officials have reason to believe a student has committed a **criminal act** or violated a **school rule**, they may investigate. When the safety of other students or school personnel is at stake, school officials may have a **common law duty of care** to investigate and mitigate any risk of harm (see Chapter 12). As noted earlier, school officials in many states also have a **statutory duty** to report any criminal activity on school property to local law enforcement agencies.

The investigation of misconduct can take many forms, including **surveillance, interviews**, and **searches**. School officials routinely search students' persons, including their clothing, backpacks, purses, and bags. They sometimes search personal electronic devices, vehicles, and lockers. In public schools, these kinds of searches can implicate the Fourth Amendment rights of students. Under what circumstances are searches undertaken by public school officials **reasonable** for Fourth Amendment purposes? After many years of conflicting lower court decisions, the Supreme Court addressed this question in the following seminal case.

---

14 336 F.3d 1194 (10th Cir. 2003), *cert. denied*, 540 U.S. 1179 (2004).
15 2018 U.S. Dist. LEXIS 103634 (W.D. Mo. June 21, 2018).
16 828 F.2d 1151 (6th Cir. 1987).
17 87 F.3d 979 (8th Cir. 1996); *see also* Salyer v. Hollidaysburg Area Sch. Dist., 2018 U.S. Dist. LEXIS 124191 (W.D. Pa. July 25, 2018).

NEW JERSEY v. T.L.O.
Supreme Court of the United States
469 U.S. 325 (1985)

JUSTICE WHITE delivered the opinion of the Court.

We granted *certiorari* in this case to examine the appropriateness of the exclusionary rule as a remedy for searches carried out in violation of the Fourth Amendment by public school authorities. Our consideration of the proper application of the Fourth Amendment to the public schools, however, has led us to conclude that the search that gave rise to the case now before us did not violate the Fourth Amendment. Accordingly, we here address only the questions of the proper standard for assessing the legality of searches conducted by public school officials and the application of that standard to the facts of this case.

I

On March 7, 1980, a teacher at Piscataway High School in Middlesex County, N. J., discovered two girls smoking in a lavatory. One of the two girls was the respondent T.L.O., who at that time was a 14-year-old high school freshman. Because smoking in the lavatory was a violation of a school rule, the teacher took the two girls to the Principal's office, where they met with Assistant Vice Principal Theodore Choplick. In response to questioning by Mr. Choplick, T.L.O.'s companion admitted that she had violated the rule. T.L.O., however, denied that she had been smoking in the lavatory and claimed that she did not smoke at all.

Mr. Choplick asked T.L.O. to come into his private office and demanded to see her purse. Opening the purse, he found a pack of cigarettes, which he removed from the purse and held before T.L.O. as he accused her of having lied to him. As he reached into the purse for the cigarettes, Mr. Choplick also noticed a package of cigarette rolling papers. In his experience, possession of rolling papers by high school students was closely associated with the use of marihuana. Suspecting that a closer examination of the purse might yield further evidence of drug use, Mr. Choplick proceeded to search the purse thoroughly. The search revealed a small amount of marihuana, a pipe, a number of empty plastic bags, a substantial quantity of money in one-dollar bills, an index card that appeared to be a list of students who owed T.L.O. money, and two letters that implicated T.L.O. in marihuana dealing.

Mr. Choplick notified T.L.O.'s mother and the police, and turned the evidence of drug dealing over to the police. At the request of the police, T.L.O.'s mother took her daughter to police headquarters, where T.L.O. confessed that she had been selling marihuana at the high school. On the basis of the confession and the evidence seized by Mr. Choplick, the State brought delinquency charges against T.L.O. in the Juvenile and Domestic Relations Court of Middlesex County. Contending that Mr. Choplick's search of her purse violated the Fourth Amendment, T.L.O. moved to suppress the evidence found in her purse as well as her confession, which, she argued, was tainted by the allegedly unlawful search. The Juvenile Court denied the motion to suppress. Although the court concluded that the Fourth Amendment did apply to searches carried out by school officials, it held that

a school official may properly conduct a search of a student's person if the official has a reasonable suspicion that a crime has been or is in the process of being committed, or reasonable cause to believe that the search is necessary to maintain school discipline or enforce school policies.

Applying this standard, the court concluded that the search conducted by Mr. Choplick was a reasonable one. The initial decision to open the purse was justified by Mr. Choplick's well-founded suspicion that T.L.O. had violated the rule forbidding smoking in the lavatory. Once the purse was open, evidence of marihuana violations was in plain view, and Mr. Choplick was entitled to conduct a thorough search to determine the nature and extent of T.L.O.'s drug-related activities. Having denied the motion to suppress, the court on March 23, 1981, found T. L. O. to be a delinquent and on January 8, 1982, sentenced her to a year's probation. ...

The New Jersey Supreme Court agreed with the lower courts that the Fourth Amendment applies to searches conducted by school officials. The court also rejected the State of New Jersey's argument that the exclusionary rule should not be employed to prevent the use in juvenile proceedings of evidence unlawfully seized by school officials. Declining to consider whether applying the rule to the fruits of searches by school officials would have any deterrent value, the court held simply that the precedents of this Court establish that "if an official search violates constitutional rights, the evidence is not admissible in criminal proceedings."

With respect to the question of the legality of the search before it, the court agreed with the Juvenile Court that a warrantless search by a school official does not violate the Fourth Amendment so long as the official "has reasonable grounds to believe that a student possesses evidence of illegal activity or activity that would interfere with school discipline and order." However, the court, with two justices dissenting, sharply disagreed with the Juvenile Court's conclusion that the search of the purse was reasonable. According to the majority, the contents of T.L.O.'s purse had no bearing on the accusation against T.L.O., for possession of cigarettes (as opposed to smoking them in the lavatory) did not violate school rules, and a mere desire for evidence that would impeach T.L.O.'s claim that she did not smoke cigarettes could not justify the search.

Moreover, even if a reasonable suspicion that T.L.O. had cigarettes in her purse would justify a search, Mr. Choplick had no such suspicion, as no one had furnished him with any specific information that there were cigarettes in the purse. Finally, leaving aside the question whether Mr. Choplick was justified in opening the purse, the court held that the evidence of drug use that he saw inside did not justify the extensive "rummaging" through T.L.O.'s papers and effects that followed. ...

II

In determining whether the search at issue in this case violated the Fourth Amendment, we are faced initially with the question whether that Amendment's prohibition on unreasonable searches and seizures applies to searches conducted by public school officials. We hold that it does.

It is now beyond dispute that "the Federal Constitution, by virtue of the Fourteenth Amendment, prohibits unreasonable searches and seizures by state officers." Equally indisputable is the proposition that the Fourteenth Amendment protects the rights of students against encroachment by public school officials[.] ...

[T]he State of New Jersey has argued that the history of the Fourth Amendment indicates that the Amendment was intended to regulate only searches and seizures carried out by law enforcement officers; accordingly, although public school officials are concededly state agents for purposes of the Fourteenth Amendment, the Fourth Amendment creates no rights enforceable against them.

It may well be true that the evil toward which the Fourth Amendment was primarily directed was the resurrection of the pre-Revolutionary practice of using general warrants or "writs of assistance" to authorize searches for contraband by officers of the Crown. But this Court has never limited the Amendment's prohibition on unreasonable searches and seizures to operations conducted by the police. Rather, the Court has long spoken of the Fourth Amendment's strictures as restraints imposed upon "governmental action"—that is, "upon the activities of sovereign authority." Accordingly, we have held the Fourth Amendment applicable to the activities of civil as well as criminal authorities[.] ...

Notwithstanding the general applicability of the Fourth Amendment to the activities of civil authorities, a few courts have concluded that school officials are exempt from the dictates of the Fourth Amendment by virtue of the special nature of their authority over schoolchildren. Teachers and school administrators, it is said, act *in loco parentis* in their dealings with students: their authority is that of the parent, not the State, and is therefore not subject to the limits of the Fourth Amendment.

Such reasoning is in tension with contemporary reality and the teachings of this Court. We have held school officials subject to the commands of the First Amendment, and the Due Process Clause of the Fourteenth Amendment. If school authorities are state actors for purposes of the constitutional guarantees of freedom of expression and due process, it is difficult to understand why they should be deemed to be exercising parental rather than public authority when conducting searches of their students. More generally, the Court has recognized that "the concept of parental delegation" as a source of school authority is not entirely "consonant with compulsory education laws." Today's public school officials do not merely exercise authority voluntarily conferred on them by individual parents; rather, they act in furtherance of publicly mandated educational and disciplinary policies. In carrying out searches and other disciplinary functions pursuant to such policies, school officials act as representatives of the State, not merely as surrogates for the parents, and they cannot claim the parents' immunity from the strictures of the Fourth Amendment.

III

To hold that the Fourth Amendment applies to searches conducted by school authorities is only to begin the inquiry into the standards governing such searches. Although the underlying command of the Fourth Amendment is always that searches and seizures be reasonable, what is reasonable depends on the context within which a search takes place. The determination of the standard of reasonableness governing any specific class of searches requires "balancing the need to search against the invasion which the search entails." On one side of the balance are arrayed the individual's legitimate expectations of privacy and personal security; on the other, the government's need for effective methods to deal with breaches of public order.

We have recognized that even a limited search of the person is a substantial invasion of privacy. We have also recognized that searches of closed items of personal luggage are intrusions on protected privacy interests, for "the Fourth Amendment provides protection to the owner of every container that conceals its contents from plain view." A search of a child's person or of a closed purse or other bag carried on her person, no less than a similar search carried out on an adult, is undoubtedly a severe violation of subjective expectations of privacy.

Of course, the Fourth Amendment does not protect subjective expectations of privacy that are unreasonable or otherwise "illegitimate." ... The State of New Jersey has argued that because of the pervasive supervision to which children in the schools are necessarily subject, a child has virtually no legitimate expectation of privacy in articles of personal property "unnecessarily" carried into a school. This argument has two factual premises: (1) the fundamental incompatibility of expectations of privacy with the maintenance of a sound educational environment; and (2) the minimal interest of the child in bringing any items of personal property into the school. Both premises are severely flawed.

Although this Court may take notice of the difficulty of maintaining discipline in the public schools today, the situation is not so dire that students in the schools may claim no legitimate expectations of privacy. We have recently recognized that the need to maintain order in a prison is such that prisoners retain no legitimate expectations of privacy in their cells, but it goes almost without saying that "[the] prisoner and the schoolchild stand in wholly different circumstances, separated by the harsh facts of criminal conviction and incarceration." We are not yet ready to hold that the schools and the prisons need be equated for purposes of the Fourth Amendment.

Nor does the State's suggestion that children have no legitimate need to bring personal property into the schools seem well anchored in reality. Students at a minimum must bring to school not only the supplies needed for their studies, but also keys, money, and the necessaries of personal hygiene and grooming. In addition, students may carry on their persons or in purses or wallets such non-disruptive yet highly personal items as photographs, letters, and diaries. Finally, students may have perfectly legitimate reasons to carry with them articles of property needed in connection with extracurricular or recreational activities. In short, schoolchildren may find it necessary to carry with them a variety of legitimate, non-contraband items, and there is no reason to conclude that they have necessarily waived all rights to privacy in such items merely by bringing them onto school grounds.

Against the child's interest in privacy must be set the substantial interest of teachers and administrators in maintaining discipline in the classroom and on school grounds. Maintaining order in the classroom has never been easy, but in recent years, school disorder has often taken particularly ugly forms: drug use and violent crime in the schools have become major social problems. ...

How, then, should we strike the balance between the schoolchild's legitimate expectations of privacy and the school's equally legitimate need to maintain an environment in which learning can take place? It is evident that the school setting requires some easing of the restrictions to which searches by public authorities are ordinarily subject. The warrant requirement, in particular, is unsuited to the school environment: requiring a teacher to obtain a warrant before searching a child suspected of an infraction of school rules (or of the criminal law) would unduly interfere with the maintenance of the swift and informal disciplinary procedures needed in the schools. ...

The school setting also requires some modification of the level of suspicion of illicit activity needed to justify a search. Ordinarily, a search—even one that may permissibly be carried out without a warrant—must be based upon "probable cause" to believe that a violation of the law has occurred. However, "probable cause" is not an irreducible requirement of a valid search. The fundamental command of the Fourth Amendment is that searches and seizures be reasonable, and although "both the concept of probable cause and the requirement of a warrant bear on the reasonableness of a search, ... in certain limited circumstances neither is required." ...

We join the majority of courts that have examined this issue in concluding that the accommodation of the privacy interests of schoolchildren with the substantial need of teachers and administrators for freedom to maintain order in the schools does not require strict adherence to the requirement that searches be based on probable cause to believe that the subject of the search has violated or is violating the law. Rather, the legality of a search of a student should depend simply on the reasonableness, under all the circumstances, of the search.

Determining the reasonableness of any search involves a twofold inquiry: first, one must consider "whether the ... action was justified at its inception;" second, one must determine whether the search as actually conducted "was reasonably related in scope to the circumstances which justified the interference in the first place." Under ordinary circumstances, a search of a student by a teacher or other school official will be "justified at its inception" when there are reasonable grounds for suspecting that the search will turn up evidence that the student has violated or is violating either the law or the rules of the school. Such a search will be permissible in its scope when the measures adopted are reasonably related to the objectives of the search and not excessively intrusive in light of the age and sex of the student and the nature of the infraction.

This standard will, we trust, neither unduly burden the efforts of school authorities to maintain order in their schools nor authorize unrestrained intrusions upon the privacy of schoolchildren. By focusing attention on the question of reasonableness, the standard will spare teachers and school administrators the necessity of schooling themselves in the niceties of probable cause and permit them to regulate their conduct according to the dictates of reason and common sense. At the same time, the reasonableness standard should ensure that the interests of students will be invaded no more than is necessary to achieve the legitimate end of preserving order in the schools.

IV

There remains the question of the legality of the search in this case. We recognize that the "reasonable grounds" standard applied by the New Jersey Supreme Court in its consideration of this question is not substantially different from the standard that we have adopted today. Nonetheless, we believe that the New Jersey court's application of that standard to strike down the search of T.L.O.'s purse reflects a somewhat crabbed notion of reasonableness. Our review of the facts surrounding the search leads us to conclude that the search was in no sense unreasonable for Fourth Amendment purposes.

The incident that gave rise to this case actually involved two separate searches, with the first—the search for cigarettes—providing the suspicion that gave rise to the second—the search for marihuana. Although it is the fruits of the second search that are at issue here, the validity of the search for marihuana must depend on the reasonableness of the initial search for cigarettes, as there would have been no reason to suspect that T.L.O. possessed marihuana had the first search not taken place. Accordingly, it is to the search for cigarettes that we first turn our attention.

The New Jersey Supreme Court pointed to two grounds for its holding that the search for cigarettes was unreasonable. First, the court observed that possession of cigarettes was not in itself illegal or a violation of school rules. Because the contents of T.L.O.'s purse would therefore have "no direct bearing on the infraction" of which she was accused (smoking in a lavatory where smoking was prohibited), there was no reason to search her purse. Second, even assuming that a search of T.L.O.'s purse might under some circumstances be reasonable in light of the accusation made against T.L.O., the New Jersey court concluded that Mr. Choplick in this particular case had no reasonable grounds to suspect that T.L.O. had cigarettes in her purse. At best, according to the court, Mr. Choplick had "a good hunch."

Both these conclusions are implausible. T.L.O. had been accused of smoking, and had denied the accusation in the strongest possible terms when she stated that she did not smoke at all. Surely it cannot be said that under these circumstances, T.L.O.'s possession of cigarettes would be irrelevant to the charges against her or to her response to those charges. T.L.O.'s possession of cigarettes, once it was discovered, would both corroborate the report that she had been smoking and undermine the credibility of her defense to the charge of smoking. To be sure, the discovery of the cigarettes would not prove that T.L.O. had been smoking in the lavatory; nor would it, strictly speaking, necessarily be inconsistent with her claim that she did not smoke at all. But it is universally recognized that evidence, to be relevant to an inquiry, need not conclusively prove the ultimate fact in issue, but only have "any tendency to make the existence of any fact that is of consequence to the determination of the action more probable or less probable than it would be without the evidence." The relevance of T.L.O.'s possession of cigarettes to the question whether she had been smoking and to the credibility of her denial that she smoked supplied the necessary "nexus" between the item searched for and the infraction under investigation. Thus, if Mr. Choplick in fact had a reasonable suspicion that T.L.O. had cigarettes in her purse, the search was justified despite the fact that the cigarettes, if found, would constitute "mere evidence" of a violation.

Of course, the New Jersey Supreme Court also held that Mr. Choplick had no reasonable suspicion that the purse would contain cigarettes. This conclusion is puzzling. A teacher had reported that T.L.O. was smoking in the lavatory. Certainly this report gave Mr. Choplick reason to suspect that T.L.O. was carrying cigarettes with her; and if she did have cigarettes, her purse was the obvious place in which to find them. Mr. Choplick's suspicion that there were cigarettes in the purse was not an "inchoate and unparticularized suspicion or 'hunch',"; rather, it was the sort of "common-sense [conclusion] about human behavior" upon which "practical people"—including government officials—are entitled to rely. Of course, even if the teacher's report were true, T.L.O. might not have had a pack of cigarettes with her; she might have borrowed a cigarette from someone else or have been sharing a cigarette with another student. But the requirement of reasonable suspicion is not a requirement of absolute certainty: "sufficient probability, not certainty, is the touchstone of reasonableness under the Fourth Amendment ..." Accordingly, it cannot be said that Mr. Choplick acted

unreasonably when he examined T.L.O.'s purse to see if it contained cigarettes.

Our conclusion that Mr. Choplick's decision to open T.L.O.'s purse was reasonable brings us to the question of the further search for marihuana once the pack of cigarettes was located. The suspicion upon which the search for marihuana was founded was provided when Mr. Choplick observed a package of rolling papers in the purse as he removed the pack of cigarettes. Although T.L.O. does not dispute the reasonableness of Mr. Choplick's belief that the rolling papers indicated the presence of marihuana, she does contend that the scope of the search Mr. Choplick conducted exceeded permissible bounds when he seized and read certain letters that implicated T.L.O. in drug dealing. This argument, too, is unpersuasive. The discovery of the rolling papers concededly gave rise to a reasonable suspicion that T.L.O. was carrying marihuana as well as cigarettes in her purse. This suspicion justified further exploration of T.L.O.'s purse, which turned up more evidence of drug-related activities: a pipe, a number of plastic bags of the type commonly used to store marihuana, a small quantity of marihuana, and a fairly substantial amount of money. Under these circumstances, it was not unreasonable to extend the search to a separate zippered compartment of the purse; and when a search of that compartment revealed an index card containing a list of "people who owe me money" as well as two letters, the inference that T.L.O. was involved in marihuana trafficking was substantial enough to justify Mr. Choplick in examining the letters to determine whether they contained any further evidence. In short, we cannot conclude that the search for marihuana was unreasonable in any respect.

Because the search resulting in the discovery of the evidence of marihuana dealing by T.L.O. was reasonable, the New Jersey Supreme Court's decision to exclude that evidence from T.L.O.'s juvenile delinquency proceedings on Fourth Amendment grounds was erroneous. Accordingly, the judgment of the Supreme Court of New Jersey is reversed.

Declining to view school officials as analogous to either parents or police officers for Fourth Amendment purposes, the Supreme Court held that they must have **reasonable grounds** to believe that a search of a *specific* student will produce relevant evidence that the student has violated a *specific* school rule or law. The Supreme Court also placed limits on the **nature** and **scope** of a search undertaken by school officials.

Reasonable Grounds

Although it is impossible to state a precise definition of **reasonable grounds**, courts are unlikely to accept a vague suspicion unsupported by evidence of a specific act of wrongdoing. Thus, in *Matter of Pima County Juvenile Action*,[18] a student was seen near bleachers where students were known to have engaged in drug use. The principal had no personal knowledge of the student's conduct, had received no prior reports of any drug use by the student, and no other reason to suspect the student had drugs in his pockets. Thus the court concluded that the principal did not have reasonable grounds to search the student. In a similar case, however, a search of two boys found without passes in a bathroom known as a haven for the use and sale of drugs was upheld.[19]

In *Commonwealth v. Smith*,[20] the Massachusetts Court of Appeals upheld the search of a student who violated an order not to return to school without his parent, bypassed a metal detector, and was found in an unauthorized area. In *Rhodes v. Guarricino*,[21] a district court found a school official was justified in searching a student's hotel room on a field trip after smelling marijuana in the hallway. In *Rinker v. Sipler*,[22] another district court upheld a search based on the observation that the student "looked stoned." In another case, New York's highest court held that it was permissible for a school official to feel the outside of a book bag after it made a metallic clanging noise. Having felt the outline of a gun, it was reasonable for school officials to search the bag.[23]

In *Cales v. Howell Public Schools*,[24] a security guard caught a student ducking behind cars in the school parking lot. The student also gave a false name when questioned. In finding the search in this case illegal, the court wrote:

> [We do] not read *T.L.O.* so broadly as to allow a school administrator the right to search a student because that student acts in such a way so as to create a reasonable suspicion that the student has violated *some* rule or law.

However, in *Anders v. Fort Wayne Community Schools*,[25] the search of a student's car was justified at its inception because the student was out of class without a pass, there was a history of students smoking in the parking lot, and the student had lied about going to his car to retrieve an assignment.

Informants

Sometimes statements by an informant can give rise to the reasonable suspicion necessary to justify a search. Often the issue depends on the trustworthiness of the informant in the circumstances.[26] One court declared that information supplied by a student informant may be the basis for a search "[a]bsent information that a particular student informant may be untrustworthy."[27]

---

18 733 P.2d 316 (Ariz. Ct. App. 1987).
19 *In re* Bobby B., 218 Cal. Rptr. 253 (Cal. Ct. App. 1985).
20 889 N.E.2d 439 (Mass. App. Ct. 2008).
21 54 F. Supp. 2d 186 (S.D.N.Y. 1999).
22 264 F. Supp. 2d 181 (M.D. Pa. 2003).
23 *In re* Gregory, 82 N.Y.2d 588 (N.Y. 1993).
24 635 F. Supp. 454 (E.D. Mich. 1985); *see also* State v. Pablo R. 137 P.3d 1198 (N.M. App. 2006).
25 124 F. Supp. 2d 618 (N.D. Ind. 2000).
26 New Mexico v. Michael G., 748 P.2d 17 (N.M. Ct. App. 1987).
27 In the Interest of S.C. v. State, 583 So. 2d 188 (Miss. 1991).

In another case, an informant who had established a good working relationship with the school staff by working as an office aide was deemed reliable.[28] In another case, a school's failure to check whether student informants were trustworthy—the informants were in fact students who had a possible motive to falsely accuse the searched student of carrying drugs—led the court to conclude that the search (which turned up no drugs) was illegal.[29]

May school officials conduct a search based on an anonymous tip? This was addressed in *In re Juvenile 2006–406*.[30] On two separate occasions, a teacher reported to the vice principal information that students, whom the teacher did not name, had reported that another student possessed drug paraphernalia. The court concluded the search was reasonable at its inception because, while the vice principal did not know the tipsters, he did know the teacher.

Individualized Suspicion

School officials must have reasonable grounds to suspect a specific individual or individuals prior to engaging in a search. Although the Supreme Court said nothing in *T.L.O.* about sweep searches, a number of courts have declared them impermissible.[31] There are a number of exceptions to this rule, however, including the **random drug testing** of students and the use of **metal detectors** and **sniffer dogs** (both discussed later). In addition, some courts have upheld sweep searches when school officials believe that a student may be carrying a weapon. The necessity of keeping the school free of weapons was found to justify these searches even in the absence of **individualized suspicion**.[32]

Drug Testing

Courts will permit **drug testing** of particular students if the **individualized suspicion** requirement of *T.L.O.* is met. In *Hedges v. Musco*,[33] the Third Circuit found that a school had the authority to insist on a blood test and urinalysis for a student who "seemed uncharacteristically talkative and outgoing. In addition, her face was flushed; her eyes were glassy and red; and her pupils were dilated." However, in *Willis v. Anderson*,[34] a student suspended for fighting challenged school officials who had advised him that his refusal to submit to a drug test would lead to his expulsion. The Seventh Circuit found there was not enough of a connection between fighting and drug use to provide a basis for the individualized suspicion needed to justify urinalysis.

In the following significant case, the Supreme Court held that **random drug testing** may be justified in situations where drug use is especially prevalent or dangerous, the purpose of the testing is to assist rather than to punish the students, the testing system is reliable and the results confidential, and in situations such as competitive sports where continued drug use carries more than the usual dangers.

---

28 Phaneuf v. Cipriano, 330 F. Supp. 2d 74 (D. Conn. 2004).
29 Fewless *ex rel.* Fewless v. Bd. of Educ. of Wayland, 208 F. Supp. 2d 806 (W.D. Mich. 2002); *see also In re* Doe, 91 P.3d 485 (Hawaii 2004).
30 931 A.2d 1229 (N.H. 2007).
31 Burnham v. West, 681 F. Supp. 1160 (E.D. Va. 1987); Bellnier v. Lund, 438 F. Supp. 47 (N.D.N.Y. 1977); Kuehn v. Renton Sch. Dist. No. 403, 694 P.2d 1078 (Wash. 1985); Horton v. Goose Creek Indep. Sch. Dist., 690 F.2d 470 (5th Cir. 1982); *but see* DesRoches v. Caprio, 156 F.3d 571 (4th Cir. 1998).
32 Thompson v. Carthage Sch. Dist., 87 F.3d 979 (8th Cir. 1996); *In re* Alexander B., 270 Cal. Rptr. 342 (Cal. Ct. App. 1990).
33 204 F.3d 109 (3d Cir. 2000).
34 158 F.3d 415 (7th Cir. 1998), *cert. denied*, 526 U.S. 1019 (1999).

⚖️

VERNONIA SCHOOL DISTRICT 47J v. ACTON
Supreme Court of the United States
515 U.S. 646 (1995)

JUSTICE SCALIA delivered the opinion of the Court.

The Student Athlete Drug Policy adopted by School District 47J in the town of Vernonia, Oregon, authorizes random urinalysis drug testing of students who participate in the District's school athletics programs. We granted *certiorari* to decide whether this violates the Fourth and Fourteenth Amendments to the United States Constitution.

I

A

Petitioner Vernonia School District 47J (District) operates one high school and three grade schools in the logging community of Vernonia, Oregon. As elsewhere in small-town America, school sports play a prominent role in the town's life, and student athletes are admired in their schools and in the community.

Drugs had not been a major problem in Vernonia schools. In the mid-to-late 1980's, however, teachers and administrators observed a sharp increase in drug use. Students began to speak out about their attraction to the drug culture, and to boast that there was nothing the school could do about it. Along with more drugs came more disciplinary problems. Between 1988 and 1989 the number of disciplinary referrals in Vernonia schools rose to more than twice the number reported in the early 1980's, and several students were suspended. Students became increasingly rude during class; outbursts of profane language became common.

Not only were student athletes included among the drug users but, as the District Court found, athletes were the leaders of the drug culture. This caused the District's administrators particular concern, since drug use increases the risk of sports-related injury. ...

Initially, the District responded to the drug problem by offering special classes, speakers, and presentations designed to deter drug use. It even brought in a specially trained dog to detect drugs, but the drug problem persisted. ... At that point, District officials began considering a drug-testing program. They held a parent "input night" to discuss the proposed Student Athlete Drug Policy (Policy), and the parents in attendance gave their unanimous approval. The school board approved the Policy for implementation in the fall of 1989. Its expressed purpose is to prevent student athletes from using drugs, to protect their health and safety, and to provide drug users with assistance programs.

B

The Policy applies to all students participating in interscholastic athletics. Students wishing to play sports must sign a form consenting to the testing and must obtain the written consent of their parents. Athletes are tested at the beginning of the season for their sport. In addition, once each week of the season the names of the athletes are placed in a "pool" from which a student, with the supervision of two adults, blindly draws the names of 10 percent of the athletes for random testing. Those selected are notified and tested that same day, if possible.

The student to be tested completes a specimen control form which bears an assigned number. Prescription medications that the student is taking must be identified by providing a copy of the prescription or a doctor's authorization. The student then enters an empty locker room accompanied by an adult monitor of the same sex. Each boy selected produces a sample at a urinal, remaining fully clothed with his back to the monitor, who stands approximately 12 to 15 feet behind the student. Monitors may (though do not always) watch the student while he produces the sample, and they listen for normal sounds of urination. Girls produce samples in an enclosed bathroom stall, so that they can be heard but not observed. After the sample is produced, it is given to the monitor, who checks it for temperature and tampering and then transfers it to a vial.

The samples are sent to an independent laboratory, which routinely tests them for amphetamines, cocaine, and marijuana. Other drugs, such as LSD, may be screened at the request of the District, but the identity of a particular student does not determine which drugs will be tested. The laboratory's procedures are 99.94 percent accurate. The District follows strict procedures regarding the chain of custody and access to test results. The laboratory does not know the identity of the students whose samples it tests.

It is authorized to mail written test reports only to the superintendent and to provide test results to District personnel by telephone only after the requesting official recites a code confirming his authority. Only the superintendent, principals, vice-principals, and athletic directors have access to test results, and the results are not kept for more than one year.

If a sample tests positive, a second test is administered as soon as possible to confirm the result. If the second test is negative, no further action is taken. If the second test is positive, the athlete's parents are notified, and the school principal convenes a meeting with the student and his parents, at which the student is given the option of (1) participating for six weeks in an assistance program that includes weekly urinalysis, or (2) suffering suspension from athletics for the remainder of the current season and the next athletic season. The student is then retested prior to the start of the next athletic season for which he or she is eligible. The Policy states that a second offense results in automatic imposition of option (2); a third offense in suspension for the remainder of the current season and the next two athletic seasons.

C

In the fall of 1991, respondent James Acton, then a seventh grader, signed up to play football at one of the District's grade schools. He was denied participation, however, because he and his parents refused to sign the testing consent forms. The Actons filed suit, seeking declaratory and injunctive relief from enforcement of the Policy on the grounds that it violated the Fourth and Fourteenth Amendments[.] ... We granted *certiorari*.

II

The Fourth Amendment to the United States Constitution provides that the Federal Government shall not violate "the right of the people to be secure in their persons, houses, papers, and effects, against unreasonable searches and seizures ..." We have held that the Fourteenth Amendment extends this constitutional guarantee to searches and seizures by state officers, including public school officials[.] ...

We have found ... "special needs" to exist in the public school context. There, the warrant requirement "would unduly interfere with the maintenance of the swift and informal disciplinary procedures [that

are] needed," and "strict adherence to the requirement that searches be based on probable cause" would undercut "the substantial need of teachers and administrators for freedom to maintain order in the schools." The school search we approved in *T.L.O.*,[35] while not based on probable cause, *was* based on individualized *suspicion* of wrongdoing. ...

III

The first factor to be considered is the nature of the privacy interest upon which the search here at issue intrudes. The Fourth Amendment does not protect all subjective expectations of privacy, but only those that society recognizes as "legitimate." What expectations are legitimate varies, of course, with context, depending, for example, upon whether the individual asserting the privacy interest is at home, at work, in a car, or in a public park. In addition, the legitimacy of certain privacy expectations vis-à-vis the State may depend upon the individual's legal relationship with the State. ... Central, in our view, to the present case is the fact that the subjects of the Policy are (1) children, who (2) have been committed to the temporary custody of the State as schoolmaster.

Traditionally at common law, and still today, unemancipated minors lack some of the most fundamental rights of self-determination—including even the right of liberty in its narrow sense, i.e., the right to come and go at will. They are subject, even as to their physical freedom, to the control of their parents or guardians. When parents place minor children in private schools for their education, the teachers and administrators of those schools stand in loco parentis over the children entrusted to them. In fact, the tutor or schoolmaster is the very prototype of that status. As Blackstone describes it, a parent

may ... delegate part of his parental authority, during his life, to the tutor or schoolmaster of his child; who is then in *loco parentis*, and has such a portion of the power of the parent committed to his charge, *viz.* that of restraint and correction, as may be necessary to answer the purposes for which he is employed.

In *T.L.O.*, we rejected the notion that public schools, like private schools, exercise only parental power over their students, which of course is not subject to constitutional constraints. Such a view of things, we said, "is not entirely 'consonant with

35 New Jersey v. T.L.O., 469 U.S. 325 (1985).

compulsory education laws,'" and is inconsistent with our prior decisions treating school officials as state actors for purposes of the Due Process and Free Speech Clauses. But while denying that the State's power over schoolchildren is formally no more than the delegated power of their parents, *T.L.O.* did not deny, but indeed emphasized, that the nature of that power is custodial and tutelary, permitting a degree of supervision and control that could not be exercised over free adults.

"[A] proper educational environment requires close supervision of schoolchildren, as well as the enforcement of rules against conduct that would be perfectly permissible if undertaken by an adult." While we do not, of course, suggest that public schools as a general matter have such a degree of control over children as to give rise to a constitutional "duty to protect," we have acknowledged that for many purposes "school authorities act *in loco parentis*," with the power and indeed the duty to "inculcate the habits and manners of civility." Thus, while children assuredly do not "shed their constitutional rights … at the schoolhouse gate," the nature of those rights is what is appropriate for children in school.

Fourth Amendment rights, no less than First and Fourteenth Amendment rights, are different in public schools than elsewhere; the "reasonableness" inquiry cannot disregard the schools' custodial and tutelary responsibility for children. …

Legitimate privacy expectations are even less with regard to student athletes. School sports are not for the bashful. They require "suiting up" before each practice or event, and showering and changing afterwards. Public school locker rooms, the usual sites for these activities, are not notable for the privacy they afford. The locker rooms in Vernonia are typical: No individual dressing rooms are provided; shower heads are lined up along a wall, unseparated by any sort of partition or curtain; not even all the toilet stalls have doors. As the United States Court of Appeals for the Seventh Circuit has noted, there is "an element of 'communal undress' inherent in athletic participation."

There is an additional respect in which school athletes have a reduced expectation of privacy. By choosing to "go out for the team," they voluntarily subject themselves to a degree of regulation even higher than that imposed on students generally. …

It is a mistake, however, to think that the phrase "compelling state interest," in the Fourth Amendment context, describes a fixed, minimum quantum of governmental concern, so that one can dispose of a case by answering in isolation the question: Is there a compelling state interest here? Rather, the phrase describes an interest that appears important enough to justify the particular search at hand, in light of other factors that show the search to be relatively intrusive upon a genuine expectation of privacy. Whether that relatively high degree of government concern is necessary in this case or not, we think it is met.

That the nature of the concern is important—indeed, perhaps compelling—can hardly be doubted. Deterring drug use by our Nation's schoolchildren is at least as important as enhancing efficient enforcement of the Nation's laws against … drug use … School years are the time when the physical, psychological, and addictive effects of drugs are most severe … And of course the effects of a drug-infested school are visited not just upon the users, but upon the entire student body and faculty, as the educational process is disrupted.

In the present case, moreover, the necessity for the State to act is magnified by the fact that this evil is being visited not just upon individuals at large, but upon children for whom it has undertaken a special responsibility of care and direction. Finally, it must not be lost sight of that this program is directed more narrowly to drug use by school athletes, where the risk of immediate physical harm to the drug user or those with whom he is playing his sport is particularly high. Apart from psychological effects, which include impairment of judgment, slow reaction time, and a lessening of the perception of pain, the particular drugs screened by the District's Policy have been demonstrated to pose substantial physical risks to athletes. …

As to the efficacy of this means for addressing the problem: It seems to us self-evident that a drug problem largely fueled by the "role model" effect of athletes' drug use, and of particular danger to athletes, is effectively addressed by making sure that athletes do not use drugs. Respondents argue that a "less intrusive means to the same end" was available, namely, "drug testing on suspicion of drug use." We have repeatedly refused to declare that only the "least intrusive" search practicable can be reasonable under the Fourth Amendment. …

Taking into account all the factors we have considered above—the decreased expectation of privacy, the relative unobtrusiveness of the search, and the severity of the need met by the search—we conclude Vernonia's Policy is reasonable and hence constitutional.

In the wake of the *Vernonia* decision, some school districts initiated drug testing for all students engaged in extracurricular activities, including choir and debate teams. The Supreme Court addressed the constitutionality of generalized drug testing policies in the following significant case.

⚖️

BOARD OF EDUCATION v. EARLS
Supreme Court of the United States
536 U.S. 822 (2002)

JUSTICE THOMAS delivered the opinion of the Court.

I.

The city of Tecumseh, Oklahoma, is a rural community located approximately 40 miles southeast of Oklahoma City. The School District administers all Tecumseh public schools. In the fall of 1998, the School District adopted the Student Activities Drug Testing Policy (Policy), which requires all middle and high school students to consent to drug testing in order to participate in any extracurricular activity. In practice, the Policy has been applied only to competitive extracurricular activities sanctioned by the Oklahoma Secondary Schools Activities Association, such as the Academic Team, Future Farmers of America, Future Homemakers of America, band, choir, pom-pom, cheerleading, and athletics. Under the Policy, students are required to take a drug test before participating in an extracurricular activity, must submit to random drug testing while participating in that activity, and must agree to be tested at any time upon reasonable suspicion. The urinalysis tests are designed to detect only the use of illegal drugs, including amphetamines, marijuana, cocaine, opiates, and barbiturates, not medical conditions or the presence of authorized prescription medications.

At the time of their suit, both respondents attended Tecumseh High School. Respondent Lindsay Earls was a member of the show choir, the marching band, the Academic Team, and the National Honor Society. Respondent Daniel James sought to participate in the Academic Team. They alleged that the Policy violates the Fourth Amendment as incorporated by the Fourteenth Amendment and requested injunctive and declarative relief. They also argued that the School District

failed to identify a special need for testing students who participate in extracurricular activities, and that the "Drug Testing Policy neither addresses a proven problem nor promises to bring any benefit to students or the school."

Applying the principles articulated in *Vernonia School Dist. 47J v. Acton,*[36] in which we upheld the suspicionless drug testing of school athletes, the United States District Court for the Western District of Oklahoma rejected respondents' claim that the Policy was unconstitutional and granted summary judgment to the School District ... The United States Court of Appeals for the Tenth Circuit reversed, holding that the Policy violated the Fourth Amendment. We granted *certiorari* and now reverse.

II.

The Fourth Amendment to the United States Constitution protects "the right of the people to be secure in their persons, houses, papers, and effects, against unreasonable searches and seizures." Searches by public school officials, such as the collection of urine samples, implicate Fourth Amendment interests. We must therefore review the School District's Policy for "reasonableness," which is the touchstone of the constitutionality of a governmental search.

In the criminal context, reasonableness usually requires a showing of probable cause. The probable cause standard, however, "is peculiarly related to criminal investigations" and may be unsuited to determining the reasonableness of administrative searches where the "Government seeks to prevent the development of hazardous conditions." The Court has also held that a warrant and finding of probable cause are unnecessary in the public school context because such requirements "would unduly interfere with the maintenance of the swift and informal disciplinary procedures [that are] needed."

36 515 U.S. 646 (1995).

Given that the School District's Policy is not in any way related to the conduct of criminal investigations, respondents do not contend that the School District requires probable cause before testing students for drug use. Respondents instead argue that drug testing must be based at least on some level of individualized suspicion. It is true that we generally determine the reasonableness of a search by balancing the nature of the intrusion on the individual's privacy against the promotion of legitimate governmental interests. But we have long held that "the Fourth Amendment imposes no irreducible requirement of [individualized] suspicion."

"In certain limited circumstances, the Government's need to discover such latent or hidden conditions, or to prevent their development, is sufficiently compelling to justify the intrusion on privacy entailed by conducting such searches without any measure of individualized suspicion." Therefore, in the context of safety and administrative regulations, a search unsupported by probable cause may be reasonable "when 'special needs, beyond the normal need for law enforcement, make the warrant and probable-cause requirement impracticable.'"

Significantly, this Court has previously held that "special needs" inhere in the public school context. While schoolchildren do not shed their constitutional rights when they enter the schoolhouse, "Fourth Amendment rights ... are different in public schools than elsewhere; the 'reasonableness' inquiry cannot disregard the schools' custodial and tutelary responsibility for children." In particular, a finding of individualized suspicion may not be necessary when a school conducts drug testing.

In Vernonia,[37] this Court held that the suspicionless drug testing of athletes was constitutional. The Court, however, did not simply authorize all school drug testing, but rather conducted a fact-specific balancing of the intrusion on the children's Fourth Amendment rights against the promotion of legitimate governmental interests. Applying the principles of Vernonia to the somewhat different facts of this case, we conclude that Tecumseh's Policy is also constitutional.

A.

We first consider the nature of the privacy interest allegedly compromised by the drug testing. As in Vernonia, the context of the public school environment serves as the backdrop for the analysis of the

privacy interest at stake and the reasonableness of the drug testing policy in general.

A student's privacy interest is limited in a public school environment where the State is responsible for maintaining discipline, health, and safety. Schoolchildren are routinely required to submit to physical examinations and vaccinations against disease. Securing order in the school environment sometimes requires that students be subjected to greater controls than those appropriate for adults.

Respondents argue that because children participating in nonathletic extracurricular activities are not subject to regular physicals and communal undress, they have a stronger expectation of privacy than the athletes tested in Vernonia. This distinction, however, was not essential to our decision in Vernonia, which depended primarily upon the school's custodial responsibility and authority.

In any event, students who participate in competitive extracurricular activities voluntarily subject themselves to many of the same intrusions on their privacy as do athletes. Some of these clubs and activities require occasional off-campus travel and communal undress. All of them have their own rules and requirements for participating students that do not apply to the student body as a whole. For example, each of the competitive extracurricular activities governed by the Policy must abide by the rules of the Oklahoma Secondary Schools Activities Association, and a faculty sponsor monitors the students for compliance with the various rules dictated by the clubs and activities. This regulation of extracurricular activities further diminishes the expectation of privacy among schoolchildren. We therefore conclude that the students affected by this Policy have a limited expectation of privacy.

B.

Next, we consider the character of the intrusion imposed by the Policy. Urination is "an excretory function traditionally shielded by great privacy." But the "degree of intrusion" on one's privacy caused by collecting a urine sample "depends upon the manner in which production of the urine sample is monitored." Under the Policy, a faculty monitor waits outside the closed restroom stall for the student to produce a sample and must "listen for the normal sounds of urination in order to guard against tampered specimens and to insure an accurate chain of custody." The monitor then pours the sample into

37 Vernonia School District 47J v. Acton, 515 U.S. 646 (1995).

two bottles that are sealed and placed into a mailing pouch along with a consent form signed by the student. This procedure is virtually identical to that reviewed in *Vernonia*, except that it additionally protects privacy by allowing male students to produce their samples behind a closed stall. Given that we considered the method of collection in *Vernonia* a "negligible" intrusion, the method here is even less problematic.

In addition, the Policy clearly requires that the test results be kept in confidential files separate from a student's other educational records and released to school personnel only on a "need to know" basis. Respondents nonetheless contend that the intrusion on students' privacy is significant because the Policy fails to protect effectively against the disclosure of confidential information and, specifically, that the school "has been careless in protecting that information: for example, the Choir teacher looked at students' prescription drug lists and left them where other students could see them." But the choir teacher is someone with a "need to know," because during off-campus trips she needs to know what medications are taken by her students. Even before the Policy was enacted the choir teacher had access to this information. In any event, there is no allegation that any other student did see such information. This one example of alleged carelessness hardly increases the character of the intrusion. Moreover, the test results are not turned over to any law enforcement authority. Nor do the test results here lead to the imposition of discipline or have any academic consequences.

Rather, the only consequence of a failed drug test is to limit the student's privilege of participating in extracurricular activities. Indeed, a student may test positive for drugs twice and still be allowed to participate in extracurricular activities. After the first positive test, the school contacts the student's parent or guardian for a meeting. The student may continue to participate in the activity if within five days of the meeting the student shows proof of receiving drug counseling and submits to a second drug test in two weeks. For the second positive test, the student is suspended from participation in all extracurricular activities for 14 days, must complete four hours of substance abuse counseling, and must submit to monthly drug tests. Only after a third positive test will the student be suspended from participating in any extracurricular activity for the remainder of the school year, or 88 school days, whichever is longer.

Given the minimally intrusive nature of the sample collection and the limited uses to which the test results are put, we conclude that the invasion of students' privacy is not significant.

C.

Finally, this Court must consider the nature and immediacy of the government's concerns and the efficacy of the Policy in meeting them. This Court has already articulated in detail the importance of the governmental concern in preventing drug use by schoolchildren. The drug abuse problem among our Nation's youth has hardly abated since *Vernonia* ... In fact, evidence suggests that it has only grown worse. As in *Vernonia*, "the necessity for the State to act is magnified by the fact that this evil is being visited not just upon individuals at large, but upon children for whom it has undertaken a special responsibility of care and direction." The health and safety risks identified in *Vernonia* apply with equal force to Tecumseh's children. Indeed, the nationwide drug epidemic makes the war against drugs a pressing concern in every school.

Additionally, the School District in this case has presented specific evidence of drug use at Tecumseh schools. Teachers testified that they had seen students who appeared to be under the influence of drugs and that they had heard students speaking openly about using drugs. A drug dog found marijuana cigarettes near the school parking lot. Police officers once found drugs or drug paraphernalia in a car driven by a Future Farmers of America member. And the school board president reported that people in the community were calling the board to discuss the "drug situation." We decline to second-guess the finding of the District Court that "viewing the evidence as a whole, it cannot be reasonably disputed that the [School District] was faced with a 'drug problem' when it adopted the Policy."

Respondents consider the proffered evidence insufficient and argue that there is no "real and immediate interest" to justify a policy of drug testing non-athletes. We have recognized, however, that "[a] demonstrated problem of drug abuse ... [is] not in all cases necessary to the validity of a testing regime," but that some showing does "shore up an assertion of special need for a suspicionless general search program." The School District has provided sufficient evidence to shore up the need for its drug testing program.

Furthermore, this Court has not required a particularized or pervasive drug problem before allowing the government to conduct suspicionless drug testing. For instance, the Court upheld the drug testing of customs officials on a purely preventive basis, without any documented history of drug use by such officials. In response to the lack of evidence relating to drug use, the Court noted generally that "drug abuse is one of the most serious problems confronting our society today," and that programs to prevent and detect drug use among customs officials could not be deemed unreasonable. Likewise, the need to prevent and deter the substantial harm of childhood drug use provides the necessary immediacy for a school testing policy. Indeed, it would make little sense to require a school district to wait for a substantial portion of its students to begin using drugs before it was allowed to institute a drug testing program designed to deter drug use.

Given the nationwide epidemic of drug use, and the evidence of increased drug use in Tecumseh schools, it was entirely reasonable for the School District to enact this particular drug testing policy. We reject the Court of Appeals' novel test that

any district seeking to impose a random suspicionless drug testing policy as a condition to participation in a school activity must demonstrate that there is some identifiable drug abuse problem among a sufficient number of those subject to the testing, such that testing that group of students will actually redress its drug problem.

Among other problems, it would be difficult to administer such a test. As we cannot articulate a threshold level of drug use that would suffice to justify a drug testing program for schoolchildren, we refuse to fashion what would in effect be a constitutional quantum of drug use necessary to show a "drug problem."

Respondents also argue that the testing of non-athletes does not implicate any safety concerns, and that safety is a "crucial factor" in applying the special needs framework. They contend that there must be "surpassing safety interests" in order to override the usual protections of the Fourth Amendment. Respondents are correct that safety factors into the special needs analysis, but the safety interest furthered by drug testing is undoubtedly substantial for all children, athletes and non-athletes alike. We know all too well that drug use carries a variety of health risks for children, including death from overdose.

We also reject respondents' argument that drug testing must presumptively be based upon an individualized reasonable suspicion of wrongdoing because

such a testing regime would be less intrusive. In this context, the Fourth Amendment does not require a finding of individualized suspicion, and we decline to impose such a requirement on schools attempting to prevent and detect drug use by students. Moreover, we question whether testing based on individualized suspicion in fact would be less intrusive. Such a regime would place an additional burden on public school teachers who are already tasked with the difficult job of maintaining order and discipline. A program of individualized suspicion might unfairly target members of unpopular groups. The fear of lawsuits resulting from such targeted searches may chill enforcement of the program, rendering it ineffective in combating drug use. In any case, this Court has repeatedly stated that reasonableness under the Fourth Amendment does not require employing the least intrusive means, because "the logic of such elaborate less-restrictive-alternative arguments could raise insuperable barriers to the exercise of virtually all search-and-seizure powers."

Finally, we find that testing students who participate in extracurricular activities is a reasonably effective means of addressing the School District's legitimate concerns in preventing, deterring, and detecting drug use. While in *Vernonia* there might have been a closer fit between the testing of athletes and the trial court's finding that the drug problem was "fueled by the 'role model' effect of athletes' drug use," such a finding was not essential to the holding. *Vernonia* did not require the school to test the group of students most likely to use drugs, but rather considered the constitutionality of the program in the context of the public school's custodial responsibilities. Evaluating the Policy in this context, we conclude that the drug testing of Tecumseh students who participate in extracurricular activities effectively serves the School District's interest in protecting the safety and health of its students.

III.

Within the limits of the Fourth Amendment, local school boards must assess the desirability of drug testing schoolchildren. In upholding the constitutionality of the Policy, we express no opinion as to its wisdom. Rather, we hold only that Tecumseh's Policy is a reasonable means of furthering the School District's important interest in preventing and deterring drug use among its schoolchildren. Accordingly, we reverse the judgment of the Court of Appeals.

In *Miller v. Wilkes*,[38] a case decided after *Vernonia* and before *Earls*, a student barred from extra-curricular activities for refusing to participate in a random drug testing program at her school claimed the program violated her Fourth Amendment rights. The Eight Circuit found in favor of the school district, noting that school officials had "an important and immediate interest in discouraging drug and alcohol use by its students, and the random testing policy served to promote that interest."

Random, suspicionless drug and alcohol testing programs like those upheld in *Vernonia* and *Earls* may be impermissible under some state constitutions. They may also raise pedagogical concerns. Four dissenting judges in *Earls* noted that these kinds of school policies send a message that conflicts with their educational mission:

> In regulating an athletic program or endeavoring to combat an exploding drug epidemic, a school's custodial obligations may permit searches that would otherwise unacceptably abridge students' rights. When custodial duties are not ascendant, however, schools' tutelary obligations to their students require them to "teach by example" by avoiding ... measures that diminish constitutional protections.

The specific design of random drug testing programs is likely to be subject to scrutiny, especially with regard to student privacy concerns. In *Weber v. Oakridge School District 76*,[39] the Oregon Court of Appeals found a policy requiring students to reveal all the prescription drugs they were taking—even if the prescription was one that could not affect their drug test results—was a privacy violation under the state constitution. The court concluded that if the policy allowed a student to prove that a positive test was caused by lawfully prescribed medications, it would pass constitutional muster. In *Doe v. Little Rock School District*,[40] students successfully challenged a district policy allowing for sweep searches of randomly selected classrooms for weapons and drugs. Students were required to leave their bags and purses and all their belongings, including the contents of their pockets, on their desks and wait in the hall while school officials searched their belongings. The Eight Circuit found that generalized concerns about weapons and drugs were not sufficient to justify school officials' "substantial intrusions upon the students' privacy interests."

In *Joy v. Penn-Harris-Madison School Corporation*,[41] a policy requiring all students involved in extracurricular activities and all students who drove to school to be tested for drugs, alcohol, and nicotine was challenged. School officials argued that young drivers, like young athletes, were more likely to cause injuries and accidents while intoxicated. The Seventh Circuit upheld the drug testing policy for students engaging in extracurricular activities, but concluded that random testing of student drivers for nicotine was unconstitutional. School officials had not identified any serious risks associated with driving while using tobacco.

Metal Detectors and Sniffer Dogs

Heightened concern over the dangers posed by student possession of weapons and use of drugs has led some schools to implement programs of relatively nonintrusive searches without the **individualized suspicion** required by *T.L.O.* Requiring students to walk through **metal detectors** are searches for Fourth Amendment purposes. But the courts have found such searches to be reasonable, given the need to achieve a safe school, the nondiscriminatory nature of the searches, and the minimal infringement of the students' privacy.[42]

38 172 F.3d 574 (8th Cir. 1999).
39 56 P.3d 504 (Or. Ct. App. 2002).
40 380 F.3d 349 (8th Cir. 2004).
41 212 F.3d 1052 (7th Cir. 2000).
42 *In re* S.S., 680 A.2d 1172 (Pa. Super. Ct. 1996); *In re* F.B., 658 A.2d 1378 (Pa. Super. Ct. 1995); New York v. Dukes, 580 N.Y.S.2d 850 (N.Y. Crim. Ct. 1992); Illinois v. Pruitt, 662 N.E.2d 450 (Ill. App. Ct. 1996).

The courts have also upheld searches for weapons or drugs in the absence of **individualized suspicion**. In *Thompson v. Carthage School District*,[43] school officials found crack cocaine in a student's coat pocket in the course of a search of all male students in grades six through 12 for knives. The search was prompted by a report from a bus driver of newly-slashed seats that morning. The student challenged his expulsion on the ground that the school officials who found crack cocaine in his coat pocket lacked "individualized, particularized suspicion" that he was carrying a weapon or other contraband and argued that the evidence gained should have been excluded on this basis. The Eight Circuit held (a) that the exclusionary rule could not be applied to prevent school officials from disciplining students based upon the "fruits of a search" conducted on school grounds and (b) that a generalized and minimally-invasive search for dangerous weapons was reasonable in the circumstances and thus consistent with the Fourth Amendment.

The Supreme Court has said that the use of **sniffer dogs** to search luggage at airports is not a search for Fourth Amendment purposes.[44] It has affirmed that the Fourth Amendment protects *people*, not *places*.[45] In public schools, where students have a reduced expectation of privacy when using common areas, including their desks, their lockers, and the school parking lot, **sniffer dogs** may be used to search vehicles and lockers and desks and backpacks for drugs and weapons, but *not* students themselves.

In the following case, the Eighth Circuit affirmed that a **sniffer dog** search of backpacks and belongings left in a classroom during a routine drug sweep did not constitute an unreasonable search or seizure under the Fourth Amendment.

⚖️

BURLISON v. SPRINGFIELD PUBLIC SCHOOLS
US Court of Appeals for the Eighth Circuit
708 F.3d 1034 (2013)

DIANA E. MURPHY, Circuit Judge.

Mellony and Douglas Burlison brought this action on behalf of their son C.M. under 42 U.S.C. § 1983 and the Missouri Constitution, alleging that Springfield Public Schools (the district), superintendent Norm Ridder, principal Ron Snodgrass, and sheriff James Arnott violated C.M.'s constitutional rights by briefly separating him from his backpack during a drug dog exercise in his high school classroom. The district court granted summary judgment to the district, its officials, and the sheriff after concluding that the policies used during the drug dog visit "appear[ed] to be reasonable and not in any way a deprivation of a federal right." The Burlisons appeal, and we affirm.

I.

C.M. was a freshman at the district's Central High School during the 2009 to 2010 school year. In April 2010 two deputies from the Greene County sheriff's department arrived at the school with two drug dogs to conduct a brief survey of randomly selected areas in the building. …

On the day of the drug detection activity, C.M. was informed that his science classroom had been chosen to be sniffed by a drug dog. The dog was held by a deputy sheriff thirty to fifty feet from C.M.'s classroom while a school police officer instructed the students and teacher to leave the room. All backpacks, purses, and other personal items were to be left behind. C.M. left his backpack and books in the room and went into the hallway where he could no longer see his belongings. He alleges that his backpack was fully zipped when he left the room.

Once the room was cleared of students, a deputy sheriff took the drug dog into C.M.'s classroom. Video footage shows that the deputy sheriff and drug dog left the classroom after approximately five

43 87 F.3d 979 (8th Cir. 1996).
44 United States v. Place, 462 U.S. 696 (1983).
45 Segura v. United States, 468 U.S. 796 (1984).

minutes. During that time the drug dog did not alert to anything. Although district personnel and the deputy sheriff who handled the drug dog testified that no student possessions were searched in this classroom, C.M. stated that after he went back inside he "felt like the pockets [of his backpack] had been unzipped and stuff." ...

The drug dog visit to C.M.'s high school was done in accordance with Board of Education policy JFG and school police services's standard operating procedure 3.4.1. Policy JFG was enacted to "balance each student's right to privacy" with "the need to maintain an appropriate learning environment." It permits student property to be "screened in conjunction with law enforcement by using animals trained to locate and/or detect weapons and prohibited drugs."

The school police services's procedure allows drug dogs to be used at the district's secondary school buildings "to protect the safety and health of the [d]istrict's faculty, staff and students." It permits dogs to sniff student lockers, desks, backpacks, and similar items when they are not in the possession of students. The procedure states that "once a drug detection dog has completed sniffing an area, the dog handler and drug detection dog will retire from the area." The director of school police services has further clarified that a student's possessions will only be searched if a drug dog has twice alerted on the same property.

District personnel created procedures for drug detection surveys like the April 2010 visit to C.M.'s classroom in order to address a known drug problem in the district. C.M. testified that he knew a lot of high school students were using drugs. District records show that the number of drug incidents in the district from 2000 to 2011 ranged from 89 to 205 per year. A school police officer from C.M.'s high school testified that he "frequently received reports from students, parents, and teachers about the use of illegal and prescription drugs in the school." He handled drug related incidents on average three or more times per week, leading him to believe that "there was and is a drug problem" at the high school. ...

II.

[...] The Fourth Amendment protects the "right of the people to be secure in their persons, houses, papers, and effects, against unreasonable searches seizures." The Fourteenth Amendment extends this constitutional guarantee to searches and seizures by state officers, including public school officials. A seizure of property under the Fourth Amendment

occurs when there is "some meaningful interference with an individual's possessory interests in that property." Not "every governmental interference with a person's property constitutes a seizure of that property under the Constitution." ...

The Fourth Amendment demands that seizure of property be reasonable, but "what is reasonable depends on the context." A student's privacy interest "is limited in a public school environment where the State is responsible for maintaining discipline, health, and safety." Students do retain Fourth Amendment rights at school, but those rights "are different in public schools than elsewhere." That is because schools have a "legitimate need to maintain an environment in which learning can take place." Thus, a reasonableness inquiry must consider schools' "custodial and tutelary responsibility for children" and the fact that students have a "lesser expectation of privacy than members of the population generally."

To determine whether a school's actions violated the Fourth Amendment, the Supreme Court has "conducted a fact-specific balancing of the intrusion on the children's Fourth Amendment rights against the promotion of legitimate governmental interests." In considering the constitutionality of a school policy requiring suspicionless drug testing of students who participate in extracurricular activities, the Supreme Court considered "the nature of the privacy interest allegedly compromised," "the character of the intrusion imposed," and "the nature and immediacy of the government's concerns and the efficacy of the Policy in meeting them.". In *Earls*, the Court concluded that the school's policy was "a reasonable means of furthering ... important interest[s] in preventing and deterring drug use among its schoolchildren."

Assuming that C.M.'s belongings were seized in this case when the school police officer directed that they be left in the classroom for approximately five minutes while the drug dog survey occurred, we conclude that the seizure was part of a reasonable procedure to maintain the safety and security of students at the school. Since C.M. is a high school student, he has a "lesser expectation of privacy" than the general public. He was only separated from his belongings for a short period of time while the deputy sheriff safely and efficiently completed the drug dog walkabout. Requiring students to be separated from their property during such a reasonable procedure avoids potential embarrassment to students, ensures that students are not targeted by dogs, and decreases the possibility of dangerous interactions between dogs and children.

C.M.'s freedoms were not unreasonably curtailed by his brief separation from his possessions because he normally would not have been able to access or move his backpack during class time without permission. In Little Rock, we concluded that a school's search policy was unconstitutional where it required all students to leave their belongings in a classroom and allowed school personnel to search each student's property. We noted that a drug dog procedure like the one completed in C.M.'s school in April 2010 would not raise the same type of constitutional issues. That is because such a drug dog survey is "minimally intrusive, and provide[s] an effective means for adducing the requisite degree of individualized suspicion to conduct further, more intrusive searches."

The drug dog procedure at C.M.'s school was the type of minimally intrusive activity which we referenced in Little Rock. C.M. was separated from his backpack only for a short period of time and school personnel were only to search a student's belongings if a drug dog alerted twice on the same property.

The district and its officials have shown an immediate need for a drug dog procedure because there is substantial evidence showing there was a drug problem in district buildings. The Supreme Court has repeatedly emphasized the strong government interest in preventing drug use by students. Drug problems in schools are "serious in terms of size, the kinds of drugs being used, and the consequences of that use both for our children and the rest of us." That is because "drug use carries a variety of health risks for children, including death from overdose." C.M. testified that he knew students at his school who used drugs and a school police officer stated that he believed there "was and is a drug problem" at C.M.'s high school. The district also provided records substantiating the number of drug incidents from 2000 to 2011. According to those records the district had 154 drug related incidents during C.M.'s freshman year. The procedures used by district personnel and the deputy sheriff at C.M.'s school in April 2010 reasonably addressed concerns over drug usage in school in a manner that was minimally intrusive to students and their belongings.

We conclude that the brief separation of C.M. and his belongings was reasonable and did not deprive him of a constitutionally protected right. … For these reasons, we affirm the judgment of the district court.

Strip Searches

The requirement of **individualized suspicion** is enforced with the greatest vigor in connection with **strip searches**. The more intrusive the search, the more likely it is that the courts will insist that school officials have good reasons to suspect the student.[46] The Sixth Circuit allowed a strip search based on a tip from an informant only after the court had satisfied itself that the school official had questioned the informant to make sure the tip was not motivated by malice.[47] In finding a strip search impermissible the Second Circuit wrote, "[A]cceptance of one student's accusatory statement to initiate a highly intrusive search of other students—with no meaningful inquiry or corroboration—concerns us."[48]

The point of the search must be to uncover relevant evidence that would help to establish that a student did in fact violate a specific school rule or law. In *T.L.O.*, the search began with a view to showing a student had smoked a cigarette in the girls' lavatory. In the course of that search, evidence of drug dealing came into **plain view**. This justified continuing the search, in effect a second search, for additional relevant evidence of drug use or drug dealing.

Even if a search is **justified at its inception**, *T.L.O.* places limits on the scope of the search. A school search must not be excessive in light of the age and sex of the student searched and, most importantly, the nature of the infraction suspected. Under 42 U.S.C.S. § 1983, school

---

46 Cornfield v. Consol. High Sch. Dist. No. 230, 991 F.2d 1316 (7th Cir. 1993); Kennedy v. Dexter Consol. Sch., 955 P.2d 693 (N.M. Ct. App. 1998).
47 Williams v. Ellington, 936 F.2d 881 (6th Cir. 1991).
48 Phaneuf v. Fraikin, 448 F.3d 591 (2d Cir. 2006).

officials may be personally sued for actual and even punitive damages for violations of students' Fourth Amendment rights. The danger of losing such a suit is particularly high with regard to strip searches because the scope of these searches often cannot be justified under the criteria established in *T.L.O.* and subsequent lower court decisions. Moreover, the harm caused by unjustified strip searches can be significant.[49]

In *T.J. v. State*,[50] a school official in Florida had reasonable grounds to believe a student was carrying a knife. He opened the student's purse and, not seeing the knife, proceeded to also open a small zippered pocket inside the purse that had no bulge in it. He felt inside the pocket, found no knife but felt a plastic bag, which he could feel contained no knife. Nevertheless, he removed the bag, which contained rock cocaine. The court ruled that the scope of this search exceeded the *T.L.O.* guidelines:

> While school safety may readily justify a basic search for weapons, the student's interest in privacy should preclude a scavenger hunt after the basic search has produced no weapons … These drugs were discovered during a search extended by simple curiosity rather than suspicion.

In *West Virginia* ex rel. *Galford v. Mark Anthony B.*,[51] the Supreme Court of West Virginia held that a strip search of a student suspected of stealing $100 was excessive in light of the nature of the crime being investigated. Even though the money was found in the student's underwear, the court said that the student's "suspected conduct did not pose the type of immediate danger to others that might conceivably necessitate and justify a warrantless strip search."

In *Jenkins v. Talladega City Board of Education*,[52] the Eleventh Circuit found strip searches of two eight-year-olds to find the $7 they had allegedly stolen unreasonable. "*T.L.O.* forbids school officials from undertaking the most intrusive of searches where the infraction is relatively minor and presents no threat of imminent danger," wrote the court. In *Carlson* ex rel. *Stuczynksi v. Bremen High School*,[53] two female students alleged to have stolen $60 were required to strip naked and shake out their gym clothes. The district court found this to be unreasonable.

The courts will permit highly intrusive searches in **exigent circumstances** and when steps are taken to make sure the search is no more embarrassing than necessary. In general, intrusive searches for drugs or weapons are more likely to pass constitutional muster than searches for missing money or goods. A federal district court upheld a highly intrusive search of a student who, when he was questioned about the possession of marijuana, appeared stoned and smelled of marijuana. The strip search was undertaken only after a search of the student's pockets, shoes, and socks did not yield drugs. The court found the search permissible in scope because the plaintiff was not nude during the search, no women were present, his genitals were not examined and he was not "touched inappropriately." The assistant principal only ran his hands around the interior of the boxer shorts to make sure nothing was hidden inside, but the student was not asked to remove them.[54] Another court ruled in favor of school officials who strip searched a 16-year-old who appeared to have an unusual bulge in the crotch and whose name had been associated several times with drug dealing and use.[55]

---

49 Bell v. Marseilles Elementary Sch., 160 F. Supp. 2d 883 (N.D. Ill. 2001); Kennedy v. Dexter Consol. Sch., 10 P.3d 115 (N.M. 2000); *compare* Thomas ex rel. Thomas v. Roberts, 261 F.3d 1160 (11th Cir. 2001), *cert. granted, vacated*, 536 U.S. 953 (2002), *on remand*, 232 F.3d 950 (2003).
50 538 So. 2d 1320 (Fla. Dist. Ct. App. 1989).
51 433 S.E. 2d 41 (W.Va. 1993).
52 95 F.3d 1036 (11th Cir. 1996).
53 423 F. Supp. 2d 823 (N.D. Ill. 2006).
54 Rinker v. Sipler, 264 F. Supp. 2d 181 (M.D. Pa. 2003).
55 Cornfield v. Consol. High Sch. Dist. No. 230, 991 F.2d 1316 (7th Cir. 1993).

In the following significant case, the Supreme Court found school officials who conducted a strip search of a 13-year-old student in the hope of finding ibuprofen or naproxen tablets violated her Fourth Amendment rights.

⚖️

SAFFORD UNIFIED SCHOOL DISTRICT #1 v. REDDING
Supreme Court of the United States
557 U.S. 364 (2009)

JUSTICE SOUTER delivered the opinion of the Court.

The issue here is whether a 13-year-old student's Fourth Amendment right was violated when she was subjected to a search of her bra and underpants by school officials acting on reasonable suspicion that she had brought forbidden prescription and over-the-counter drugs to school. Because there were no reasons to suspect the drugs presented a danger or were concealed in her underwear, we hold that the search did violate the Constitution, but because there is reason to question the clarity with which the right was established, the official who ordered the unconstitutional search is entitled to qualified immunity from liability.

I

The events immediately prior to the search in question began in 13-year-old Savana Redding's math class at Safford Middle School one October day in 2003. The assistant principal of the school, Kerry Wilson, came into the room and asked Savana to go to his office. There, he showed her a day planner, unzipped and open flat on his desk, in which there were several knives, lighters, a permanent marker, and a cigarette. Wilson asked Savana whether the planner was hers; she said it was, but that a few days before she had lent it to her friend, Marissa Glines. Savana stated that none of the items in the planner belonged to her.

Wilson then showed Savana four white prescription-strength ibuprofen 400-mg pills, and one over-the-counter blue naproxen 200-mg pill, all used for pain and inflammation but banned under school rules without advance permission. He asked Savana if she knew anything about the pills. Savana answered that she did not. Wilson then told Savana that he had received a report that she was giving these pills to fellow students; Savana denied it and

agreed to let Wilson search her belongings. Helen Romero, an administrative assistant, came into the office, and together with Wilson they searched Savana's backpack, finding nothing.

At that point, Wilson instructed Romero to take Savana to the school nurse's office to search her clothes for pills. Romero and the nurse, Peggy Schwallier, asked Savana to remove her jacket, socks, and shoes, leaving her in stretch pants and a T-shirt (both without pockets), which she was then asked to remove. Finally, Savana was told to pull her bra out and to the side and shake it, and to pull out the elastic on her underpants, thus exposing her breasts and pelvic area to some degree. No pills were found.

Savana's mother filed suit against Safford Unified School District #1, Wilson, Romero, and Schwallier for conducting a strip search in violation of Savana's Fourth Amendment rights. ...

II

The Fourth Amendment "right of the people to be secure in their persons ... against unreasonable searches and seizures" generally requires a law enforcement officer to have probable cause for conducting a search.

Probable cause exists where "the facts and circumstances within [an officer's] knowledge and of which [he] had reasonably trustworthy information [are] sufficient in themselves to warrant a man of reasonable caution in the belief that" an offense has been or is being committed, and that evidence bearing on that offense will be found in the place to be searched.

In T.L.O.,[56] we recognized that the school setting "requires some modification of the level of suspicion of illicit activity needed to justify a search,"

---

56 New Jersey v. T.L.O., 469 U.S. 325 (1985).

and held that for searches by school officials "a careful balancing of governmental and private interests suggests that the public interest is best served by a Fourth Amendment standard of reasonableness that stops short of probable cause." We have thus applied a standard of reasonable suspicion to determine the legality of a school administrator's search of a student, and have held that a school search "will be permissible in its scope when the measures adopted are reasonably related to the objectives of the search and not excessively intrusive in light of the age and sex of the student and the nature of the infraction."

A number of our cases on probable cause have an implicit bearing on the reliable knowledge element of reasonable suspicion, as we have attempted to flesh out the knowledge component by looking to the degree to which known facts imply prohibited conduct, the specificity of the information received, and the reliability of its source. At the end of the day, however, we have realized that these factors cannot rigidly control, and we have come back to saying that the standards are "fluid concepts that take their substantive content from the particular contexts" in which they are being assessed. Perhaps the best that can be said generally about the required knowledge component of probable cause for a law enforcement officer's evidence search is that it raises a "fair probability" or a "substantial chance" of discovering evidence of criminal activity. The lesser standard for school searches could as readily be described as a moderate chance of finding evidence of wrongdoing.

III

A

In this case, the school's policies strictly prohibit the nonmedical use, possession, or sale of any drug on school grounds, including "[a]ny prescription or over-the-counter drug, except those for which permission to use in school has been granted pursuant to Board policy." A week before Savana was searched, another student, Jordan Romero … told the principal and Assistant Principal Wilson that "certain students were bringing drugs and weapons on campus," and that he had been sick after taking some pills that "he got from a classmate." On the morning of October 8, the same boy handed Wilson a white pill that he said Marissa Glines had given him. He told Wilson that students were planning to take the pills at lunch.

Wilson learned from Peggy Schwallier, the school nurse, that the pill was Ibuprofen 400mg, available only by prescription. Wilson then called Marissa out of class. Outside the classroom, Marissa's teacher handed Wilson the day planner, found within Marissa's reach, containing various contraband items. Wilson escorted Marissa back to his office.

In the presence of Helen Romero, Wilson requested Marissa to turn out her pockets and open her wallet. Marissa produced a blue pill, several white ones, and a razor blade. Wilson asked where the blue pill came from, and Marissa answered, "I guess it slipped in when she gave me the IBU 400s." When Wilson asked whom she meant, Marissa replied, "Savana Redding." Wilson then enquired about the day planner and its contents; Marissa denied knowing anything about them. Wilson did not ask Marissa any follow-up questions to determine whether there was any likelihood that Savana presently had pills[,] neither asking when Marissa received the pills from Savana nor where Savana might be hiding them.

Schwallier did not immediately recognize the blue pill, but information provided through a poison control hotline indicated that the pill was a 200-mg dose of an anti–inflammatory drug, generically called naproxen, available over the counter. At Wilson's direction, Marissa was then subjected to a search of her bra and underpants by Romero and Schwallier, as Savana was later on. The search revealed no additional pills.

It was at this juncture that Wilson called Savana into his office and showed her the day planner. Their conversation established that Savana and Marissa were on friendly terms: while she denied knowledge of the contraband, Savana admitted that the day planner was hers and that she had lent it to Marissa. Wilson had other reports of their friendship from staff members, who had identified Savana and Marissa as part of an unusually rowdy group at the school's opening dance in August, during which alcohol and cigarettes were found in the girls' bathroom. Wilson had reason to connect the girls with this contraband, for Wilson knew that Jordan Romero had told the principal that before the dance, he had been at a party at Savana's house where alcohol was served. Marissa's statement that the pills came from Savana was thus sufficiently plausible to warrant suspicion that Savana was involved in pill distribution.

This suspicion of Wilson's was enough to justify a search of Savana's backpack and outer clothing. If a student is reasonably suspected of giving out contraband pills, she is reasonably suspected of carrying them on her person and in the carryall that has become an item of student uniform in most places today. If Wilson's reasonable suspicion of pill distribution was not understood to support searches of outer clothes and backpack, it would not justify any search worth making. And the look into Savana's bag, in her presence and in the relative privacy of Wilson's office, was not excessively intrusive, any more than Romero's subsequent search of her outer clothing.

B

Here it is that the parties part company, with Savana's claim that extending the search at Wilson's behest to the point of making her pull out her underwear was constitutionally unreasonable. The exact label for this final step in the intrusion is not important, though strip search is a fair way to speak of it. Romero and Schwallier directed Savana to remove her clothes down to her underwear, and then "pull out" her bra and the elastic band on her underpants. Although Romero and Schwallier stated that they did not see anything when Savana followed their instructions, we would not define strip search and its Fourth Amendment consequences in a way that would guarantee litigation about who was looking and how much was seen. The very fact of Savana's pulling her underwear away from her body in the presence of the two officials who were able to see her necessarily exposed her breasts and pelvic area to some degree, and both subjective and reasonable societal expectations of personal privacy support the treatment of such a search as categorically distinct, requiring distinct elements of justification on the part of school authorities for going beyond a search of outer clothing and belongings.

Savana's subjective expectation of privacy against such a search is inherent in her account of it as embarrassing, frightening, and humiliating. The reasonableness of her expectation (required by the Fourth Amendment standard) is indicated by the consistent experiences of other young people similarly searched, whose adolescent vulnerability intensifies the patent intrusiveness of the exposure. ... The common reaction of these adolescents simply registers the obviously different meaning of a search exposing the body from the experience of nakedness or near undress in other school circumstances. Changing for gym is getting ready for play; exposing for a search is responding to an accusation reserved for suspected wrongdoers and fairly understood as so degrading that a number of communities have decided that strip searches in schools are never reasonable and have banned them no matter what the facts may be[.]

The indignity of the search does not, of course, outlaw it, but it does implicate the rule of reasonableness as stated in *T.L.O.*, that "the search as actually conducted [be] reasonably related in scope to the circumstances which justified the interference in the first place." The scope will be permissible, that is, when it is "not excessively intrusive in light of the age and sex of the student and the nature of the infraction."

Here, the content of the suspicion failed to match the degree of intrusion. Wilson knew beforehand that the pills were prescription-strength ibuprofen and over-the-counter naproxen, common pain relievers equivalent to two Advil, or one Aleve. He must have been aware of the nature and limited threat of the specific drugs he was searching for, and while just about anything can be taken in quantities that will do real harm, Wilson had no reason to suspect that large amounts of the drugs were being passed around, or that individual students were receiving great numbers of pills.

Nor could Wilson have suspected that Savana was hiding common painkillers in her underwear. Petitioners suggest, as a truth universally acknowledged, that "students ... hid[e] contraband in or under their clothing," and cite a smattering of cases of students with contraband in their underwear. But when the categorically extreme intrusiveness of a search down to the body of an adolescent requires some justification in suspected facts, general background possibilities fall short; a reasonable search that extensive calls for suspicion that it will pay off. But non-dangerous school contraband does not raise the specter of stashes in intimate places, and there is no evidence in the record of any general practice among Safford Middle School students of hiding that sort of thing in underwear; neither Jordan nor Marissa suggested to Wilson that Savana was doing that, and the preceding search of Marissa that Wilson ordered yielded nothing. Wilson never even determined when Marissa had received the pills from Savana; if it had been a few days before, that would weigh heavily against any reasonable conclusion that Savana presently had the pills on her person, much less in her underwear.

In sum, what was missing from the suspected facts that pointed to Savana was any indication of danger to the students from the power of the drugs or their quantity, and any reason to suppose that Savana was carrying pills in her underwear. We think that the combination of these deficiencies was fatal to finding the search reasonable.

In so holding, we mean to cast no ill reflection on the assistant principal, for the record raises no doubt that his motive throughout was to eliminate drugs from his school and protect students from what Jordan Romero had gone through. Parents are known to overreact to protect their children from danger, and a school official with responsibility for safety may tend to do the same. The difference is that the Fourth Amendment places limits on the official, even with the high degree of deference that courts must pay to the educator's professional judgment.

We do mean, though, to make it clear that the T.L.O. concern to limit a school search to reasonable scope requires the support of reasonable suspicion of danger or of resort to underwear for hiding evidence of wrongdoing before a search can reasonably make the quantum leap from outer clothes and backpacks to exposure of intimate parts. The meaning of such a search, and the degradation its subject may reasonably feel, place a search that intrusive in a category of its own demanding its own specific suspicions.

The strip search of Savana Redding by school officials looking for Ibuprofen tablets violated her constitutional rights. The school official who directed the search was not entitled to qualified immunity because the relevant constitutional principles were clearly established at the time. In other words, the school official ought to have known that a strip search was unreasonable (and thus unconstitutional) in the circumstances.

In *Knisley v. Pike County Joint Vocational School District*,[57] students in a nursing class were strip searched after another student reported the theft of a credit card. The Sixth Circuit affirmed that school officials who had conducted a strip search of students several years earlier were not entitled to qualified immunity, noting that the Supreme Court in *Safford* had affirmed its earlier decision in *Beard v. Whitmore Lake School District*.[58] In that case, students in a co-ed physical education class were strip searched after another student reported the theft of several hundred dollars from her purse. When students objected to the search, school officials told them to "shut up."

Given the constitutional problems associated with strip searches in public schools, some states have categorically prohibited them.[59] One might be forgiven for thinking this would put an end to the matter. However, in *D.H. v. Clayton County School District*,[60] the Eleventh Circuit denied qualified immunity to a school official who forced a seventh-grade student to strip naked in front of his peers. The search was justified at its inception, as the school official had reasonable grounds to believe it would yield marijuana. But the school official violated the student's Fourth Amendment rights because he ought to have known that compelling him to strip in front of his peers was intrusive and embarrassing. In 2018, in *Littell v. Houston Independent School District*,[61] the Fifth Circuit likewise denied qualified immunity to school officials who undertook a mass strip search of sixth-grade students after $50 went missing in a choir class.

Surveillance Cameras

Surveillance cameras are now ubiquitous. Their use by public school officials to monitor students in entranceways, hallways, and other common areas does *not* constitute a search for Fourth Amendment purposes. This was not always clear. In *Stern v. New Haven Community School*,[62] a case from 1981, a high school student was suspended after school officials observed him—through a two-way

57 604 F.3d 977 (6th Cir. 2010), *cert. denied*, 562 U.S. 962 (2010).
58 244 Fed. Appx. 607 (6th Cir. 2007), *cert. denied*, 572 U.S. 1048 (2014).
59 § 167.166 MO. REV. STAT.
60 830 F.3d 1306 (11th Cir. 2016).
61 894 F.3d 616 (5th Cir. 2018).
62 Stern v. New Haven Cmty. Sch., 529 F. Supp. 31 (E.D. Mich. 1981).

mirror—buying marijuana in a bathroom. The court found school officials had not violated the student's Fourth Amendment rights with their surveillance of the bathroom. Their duty to maintain order and discipline outweighed the privacy interests of students, even in non-public areas.

In the following illustrative case, the Sixth Circuit affirmed that students in public schools have a clearly established right under the Fourth Amendment *not* to be subject to surveillance in areas where they have a reasonable expectation of privacy, including bathrooms and locker rooms.

⚖️

BRANNUM v. OVERTON COUNTY SCHOOL BOARD
US Court of Appeals for the Sixth Circuit
516 F.3d 489 (2008)

JAMES L. RYAN, Circuit Judge.

Thirty-four Tennessee middle school students sued various officials of the Overton County, Tennessee, public school system under 42 U.S.C. § 1983 and others, alleging that the defendant school authorities violated the students' constitutional right to privacy by installing and operating video surveillance equipment in the boys' and girls' locker rooms in Livingston Middle School (LMS), and by viewing and retaining the recorded images.

The defendant Overton County school board members, the director of schools, the LMS principal, and the assistant principal, moved for summary judgment claiming qualified immunity. The district court denied their motions and they now appeal.

We conclude that the district court correctly denied summary judgment to the school officials, who are not entitled to claim the defense of qualified immunity, and incorrectly denied summary judgment to the defendant board members and the Director of Schools, who are immune.

I.

In an effort to improve security at LMS, the Overton County School Board approved the installation of video surveillance equipment throughout the school building. The school board engaged the education technology firm, Edutech, Inc., to install cameras and monitoring equipment. The board ordered the Director of Schools, William Needham, to oversee the project. Needham delegated his authority for the installation of the monitoring equipment to the LMS Principal, Melinda Beaty, who delegated her authority to the Assistant Principal, Robert Jolley. None of the defendants promulgated any guidelines, written or otherwise, determining the number, location, or operation of the surveillance cameras.

After several meetings, Assistant Principal Jolley and an Edutech representative decided to install the cameras throughout the school in areas facing the exterior doors, in hallways leading to exterior doors, and in the boys' and girls' locker rooms. The cameras were installed and were operational by July 2002. The images captured by the cameras were transmitted to a computer terminal in Jolley's office where they were displayed and were stored on the computer's hard drive. Jolley testified that, in September 2002, he discovered that the locker room cameras were videotaping areas in which students routinely dressed for athletic activities. He said that he immediately notified Principal Beaty of the situation and suggested that the placement of the cameras be changed. But, the cameras were not removed nor were their locations changed for the remainder of the fall semester.

In addition to Jolley receiving the images on his computer, they were also accessible via remote internet connection. Any person with access to the software username, password, and Internet Protocol (IP) address could access the stored images. Neither Jolley nor anyone else had ever changed the system password or username from its default setting. The record indicates that the system was accessed ninety-eight different times between July 12, 2002, and January 10, 2003, including through internet service providers located in Rock Hill, South Carolina; Clarksville, Tennessee; and Gainsboro, Tennessee.

During a girls' basketball game at LMS on January 9, 2003, visiting team members from Allons Elementary School noticed the camera in the girls' locker room and brought this to the attention of their coach, Kathy Carr. Carr questioned Principal Beaty, who assured Carr that the camera was not activated. In fact, the camera was activated and had recorded images of the Allons team members in their undergarments when they changed their clothes. After the game, Carr reported the camera incident to the Allons school principal, who contacted Defendant Needham later that evening. Needham immediately accessed the security system from his home and viewed the recorded images. The following morning, January 10, Needham, Beaty, and two other officials viewed the images in Needham's office by remote access. Needham later stated that in his opinion, the videotapes of the 10- to 14-year old girls contained "nothing more than images of a few bras and panties." School employees removed the locker room cameras later that day.

From July 2002 to January 2003, when the cameras were operational, a number of children from Overton County Schools and schools from the surrounding counties used the LMS locker rooms for athletic events and were videotape recorded while changing their clothes.

II.

The plaintiffs insist at the outset that this court lacks jurisdiction to hear the defendants' appeal because denial of summary judgment on the ground of qualified immunity does not constitute a "final decision" under 28 U.S.C. § 1291. It is true that as a general rule, a denial of summary judgment is not an appealable final judgment, but there are exceptions, and this case presents one of them. The law is well-settled that an order denying a defendant public official a right to assert a defense of qualified immunity is the procedural equivalent of an appealable final judgment.

Qualified immunity is not a mere defense to liability; it is a rule of law that the defendant public official is immune to suit and any obligation to defend it. If a public official is unable to appeal the denial of qualified immunity immediately, he would be forced to endure the cost, expense, and inconvenience of defending an action to which he may be immune. To require him to delay his appeal challenging the trial court's rejection of his qualified immunity defense until the underlying liability issue is determined, would defeat one of the very purposes for which the doctrine exists. Thus, we have jurisdiction to consider an interlocutory appeal from the denial of qualified immunity, but only to the extent the appeal turns on an issue of law.

For purposes of this appeal, the appellants have conceded the plaintiffs' version of the facts and raise only the issue of the students' right to privacy from videotaping under the Fourth Amendment. For these reasons, we are satisfied that the order rejecting the defendants' claim of qualified immunity is a final judgment and that we have jurisdiction to entertain the defendants' appeal. We proceed, now, to the substantive issue.

III.

Congress enacted 42 U.S.C. § 1983 to permit an injured person to recover in federal court against defendants who violate a plaintiff's federal statutory or constitutional rights while acting under color of state law. There is no dispute in this case that the defendant school officials were acting under color of state law when they authorized the installation and operation of the security cameras at LMS. However, public officials are entitled to be dismissed from a lawsuit on qualified immunity grounds if they can show that they did not violate any of the plaintiff's federal statutory or constitutional rights that were "clearly established" at the time of the alleged misconduct and of which the defendants could reasonably be expected to have been aware.

On appeal of a district court's order denying summary judgment on qualified immunity grounds, we consider all the relevant facts in the light most favorable to the plaintiffs and review de novo the district court's determination on the legal question of the availability of qualified immunity. The approach we take in determining whether the defendants are entitled to claim the legal defense of qualified immunity is to decide whether a constitutional right of the students was violated and whether the constitutional right violated was clearly established and one of which the defendants can reasonably be expected to have been aware.

A.

The students argue that their constitutionally protected right to privacy encompasses the right not to be videotaped while dressing and undressing in school athletic locker rooms—a place specifically designated by the school authorities for such intimate, personal activity. The plaintiffs also argue that the basis of their privacy right resides in the Due Process Clause of the Fourteenth Amendment as well as in the Fourth Amendment as made applicable to the states through incorporation into the Fourteenth Amendment. We conclude that the privacy right involved here is one protected by the Fourth Amendment's guarantee against unreasonable searches, and that in this case, the defendants violated the students' rights under the amendment.

Before explaining our Fourth Amendment analysis, we think it might be useful to explain why we do not assess the students' privacy claims under the Due Process Clause of the Fourteenth Amendment. This court has held that the constitutional right to privacy, which includes the right to shield one's body from exposure to viewing by the opposite sex, derives from the Fourth Amendment, rather than the Due Process Clause. We are aware that some circuits have found that the same privacy right is located in the Due Process Clause. However, since the Fourth Amendment approach is the precedent in this circuit, and the Supreme Court seems to prefer it, we will follow our precedent.

B.

The Fourth Amendment to the United States Constitution provides that the federal government shall not violate "[t]he right of the people to be secure in their persons, houses, papers, and effects, against unreasonable searches and seizures ..." The Supreme Court has held that the Fourth Amendment applies in the public school context to protect students from unconstitutional searches conducted by school officials. Neither the Supreme Court nor this court has ever addressed the applicability of video surveillance to the Fourth Amendment's proscription against unreasonable searches. However, the Supreme Court has applied the amendment's guarantees to practices that were not in existence at the time the amendment was enacted and has instructed that in such cases, the ultimate measure of the constitutionality of such searches is one of "reasonableness." Some other courts that have considered the constitutional implications of video surveillance have held that such practices are subject to the strictures of the Fourth Amendment.

This court has considered the constitutional implications of surveillance policies in the context of prison security. In Kent,[63] there was the question whether a policy allowing female prison guards to observe male inmates in the shower and in various states of undress violated the prisoner-appellant's privacy right under the Fourth Amendment. We noted that "[n]either the Supreme Court nor the Sixth Circuit has ever expressly recognized that the fourth amendment 'right to privacy' encompasses the right to shield one's naked body from view by members of the opposite sex." We concluded, however:

Perhaps it is merely an abundance of common experience that leads inexorably to the conclusion that there must be a fundamental constitutional right to be free from forced exposure of one's person to strangers of the opposite sex when not reasonably necessary for some legitimate, overriding reason, for the obverse would be repugnant to notions of human decency and personal integrity.

Before Kent, we had not articulated the Fourth Amendment's protection as extending to the "right to shield one's naked body from view by members of the opposite sex." But, since Kent, we have recognized this privacy right. We recognize, of course, that this is not a case of "naked bodies" being viewed by the surveillance cameras, but rather underwear clad teen and pre-teen boys and girls. However, the difference is one of degree, rather than of kind.

Our conclusion, mentioned earlier, that the method of surveillance involved in this case–video cameras–is governed by the Fourth Amendment, is informed by the Supreme Court's reasoning in Vernonia and T.L.O., in which the Court addressed the constitutional prerequisites of valid school searches. The standards for testing the constitutionality of searches in the public school setting depend, to considerable extent, on the context. As the Court pointedly observed in Vernonia,[64] the students' "Fourth Amendment rights ... are different in public schools than elsewhere; the 'reasonableness' inquiry cannot disregard the schools' custodial and tutelary responsibility for children."

In T.L.O.,[65] the Court offered a framework for analyzing this issue that we think is helpful in this case: First, we consider whether the state action—the installation of the cameras—"was justified at its inception"; and second, whether the search—here the videotaped surveillance—"as actually conducted 'was reasonably related in scope to the circumstances which justified the [surveillance/search] in the first place.'"

A student search is justified in its inception when there are reasonable grounds for suspecting that the search will garner evidence that a student has violated or is violating the law or the rules of the school, or is in imminent danger of injury on school premises. In this case, the policy of setting up video surveillance equipment throughout the school was instituted for the sake of increasing security, which

63 Kent v. Johnson, 821 F.2d 1220 (6th Cir. 1987).
64 Vernonia Sch. Dist. 47J v. Acton, 515 U.S. 646 (1995).
65 New Jersey v. T.L.O., 469 U.S. 325 (1985).

is an appropriate and common sense purpose and not one subject to our judicial veto. However, the scope and manner in which the video surveillance was conducted is subject to Fourth Amendment limitations, and therefore, appropriate for our inquiry.

A search—and there can be no dispute that videotaping students in a school locker room is a search under the Fourth Amendment—is "permissible in its scope when the measures adopted are reasonably related to the objectives of the search and not excessively intrusive in light of the age and sex of the student and the nature of the infraction." It is a matter of balancing the scope and the manner in which the search is conducted in light of the students' reasonable expectations of privacy, the nature of the intrusion, and the severity of the school officials' need in enacting such policies, including particularly, any history of injurious behavior that could reasonably suggest the need for the challenged intrusion.

To meet the requirements imposed by the Constitution, the method chosen by the defendants to improve school building security in this case need not have been the only method available or even the one this court might have chosen; it is necessary, however, that the method chosen was, in the circumstances, justifiably intrusive in light of the purpose of the policy being carried out.

The Fourth Amendment does not protect all expectations of privacy; only those that society recognizes as reasonable and legitimate. The Supreme Court has acknowledged that generally, students have a less robust expectation of privacy than is afforded the general population. Indeed, this expectation may be even less for student athletes in locker rooms, which the Court has previously observed are places "not notable for the privacy they afford." This does not mean, however, that a student's expectation of privacy in his or her school locker room is nonexistent. In fact, we have stated before that even in locker rooms, students retain "a significant privacy interest in their unclothed bodies."

Unlike the situation in Vernonia, where the students and their parents were well aware that participation in school sports was conditioned on the students submitting to the drug testing policies, neither the students nor their parents in this case were aware of the video surveillance in the locker rooms, to say nothing of the videotaping. Further, while the Court in Vernonia pointed out the lower level of privacy typically associated with school locker rooms, we are satisfied that students using the LMS locker rooms could reasonably expect that no one, especially the school administrators, would videotape them, without their knowledge, in various states of undress while they changed their clothes for an athletic activity.

C.

Video surveillance is inherently intrusive. As one authority has put it, a video camera "sees all, and forgets nothing." In Vernonia, the Supreme Court addressed the intrusiveness of a procedure employed for obtaining urine samples from students in order to conduct drug screening. The male students produced urine samples at a urinal along a wall while a male monitor watched from a distance. The female students produced samples in individual enclosed stalls while a female monitor stood outside. Neither the males nor the females were forced to remove their clothing before the monitors or expose themselves to the monitors. The Court determined that the procedural precautions directed at ensuring the privacy of the students were significant, which helped to ensure that the policy was minimally invasive in practice.

In Beard,[66] we considered the constitutionality of a strip search conducted by the school officials when a student reported that she was missing some money. The male and female students were separated and taken to different places in the school. The female students, while in full view of the others and the school officials, were required to lift up their shirts and pull down their pants without removing their undergarments. The males, on the other hand, were forced to remove their outer clothing and pull down their undergarments for inspection by the school official. We found that the character and scope of this search was unreasonably intrusive upon the students' privacy.

In this case, the scope of the search consisted of the video recording and image storage of the children while changing their clothes. In Vernonia, procedural safeguards were put into place to protect the students' privacy, but in this case, the school officials wholly failed to institute any policies designed to protect the privacy of the students and did not even advise the students or their parents that students were being videotaped. Likewise, as the female students in Beard were inspected while in their undergarments, the students here were also observed in their undergarments while they were in the school locker rooms. We believe that the scope of the secret surveillance in this case, like the strip search in Beard, significantly invaded the students' reasonable expectations of privacy.

---

66 Beard v. Whitmore Lake Sch. Dist., 402 F.3d 598 (6th Cir. 2005).

D.

In determining whether a search is excessive in its scope, "the nature and immediacy of the governmental concern" that prompted the search is considered. Of course, a valid purpose does not necessarily validate the means employed to achieve it. In order to satisfy the constitutional requirements, the means employed must be congruent to the end sought.

In *Vernonia* and *T.L.O.*, the governmental concern was in preventing the trafficking and possession of illegal drugs on school property. In *T.L.O.*, the search was conducted because of a suspicion that the girls were in possession of contraband, and the scope of the search consisted of inspecting a student's purse. In *Vernonia*, the drug testing was prompted by the concern that student athletes were involved in drug use and the search was limited to students voluntarily participating in scholastic sports who were required to produce urine samples in circumstances designed to ensure the student athlete's privacy. In this case, the defendants were prompted to install video surveillance cameras by a concern that school safety measures should be enhanced.

It is indisputable that the operation of the video cameras intruded upon the students' privacy; the question is whether, given the purpose for which the cameras were operating, the intrusion was reasonable. One measure of reasonableness is the congruence or incongruence of the policy to be served (student safety), and the means adopted to serve it.

Surveillance of school hallways and other areas in which students mingle in the normal course of student life is one thing; camera surveillance of students dressing and undressing in the locker room—a place specifically set aside to offer privacy—is quite another. The two do not stand on equal footing.

Stated differently, the surveillance methodology employed, in particular the installation and operation of the cameras in the locker rooms, in order to be reasonable in its scope, must be congruent to the need for such a search in order to serve the policy goal of school safety and security. There is nothing whatsoever in this record to indicate that the defendants entertained any concerns about student safety or security in the locker rooms that would reasonably justify the installation of the cameras to record all the activities there. The defendants do not claim that any misconduct occurred in these areas in the past or that the plan to install the surveillance equipment in the school locker rooms was adopted because of any reasonable suspicion of wrongful activity or injurious behavior in the future. Indeed, the record suggests that the school board members and Director Needham were not even aware that cameras were positioned to monitor activities in the locker rooms.

While at a hypothetical level there might exist a heightened concern for student safety in the "privacy" of student locker rooms, that does not render any and all means of detection and deterrence reasonable. As the commonly understood expectation for privacy increases, the range and nature of permissible government intrusion decreases.

Given the universal understanding among middle school age children in this country that a school locker room is a place of heightened privacy, we believe placing cameras in such a way so as to view the children dressing and undressing in a locker room is incongruent to any demonstrated necessity, and wholly disproportionate to the claimed policy goal of assuring increased school security, especially when there is no history of any threat to security in the locker rooms.

We are satisfied that both the students' expectation of privacy and the character of the intrusion are greater in this case than those at issue in *Vernonia* and *T.L.O.* We conclude that the locker room videotaping was a search, unreasonable in its scope, and violated the students' Fourth Amendment privacy rights.

IV.

Our conclusion that the students' constitutional rights were violated does not end the inquiry, however. Under the qualified immunity doctrine, public officials cannot be held liable for violating a person's constitutional rights unless the right was clearly established at the time of the alleged improper conduct. The underlying principle here is that a person's right to recover damages for a public official's misconduct violating the person's constitutional protection, does not stand on the same footing as a person's right to recover damages for injuries caused by a non-governmental tortfeasor. The policy of the law is that governmental administrative officials are sometimes "given a pass" for violating a citizen's constitutional rights because, if it were otherwise, government officials would be undesirably inhibited in exercising the broad discretion given them to carry out their duties wisely, effectively, and without fear of personal liability if they make a mistake that injures someone.

The "pass" does not extend, however, to violating a constitutional right that is "clearly established" and of which the violator is, or ought to have been, aware ...

Some personal liberties are so fundamental to human dignity as to need no specific explication in our Constitution in order to ensure their protection against government invasion. Surreptitiously videotaping the plaintiffs in various states of undress is plainly among them. Stated differently, and more specifically, a person of ordinary common sense, to say nothing of professional school administrators, would know without need for specific instruction from a federal court, that teenagers have an inherent personal dignity, a sense of decency and self-respect, and a sensitivity about their bodily privacy that are at the core of their personal liberty and that are grossly offended by their being surreptitiously videotaped while changing their clothes in a school locker room. These notions of personal privacy are "clearly established" in that they inhere in all of us, particularly middle school teenagers, and are inherent in the privacy component of the Fourth Amendment's proscription against unreasonable searches. But even if that were not self-evident, the cases we have discussed, supra,

would lead a reasonable school administrator to conclude that the students' constitutionally protected privacy right not to be surreptitiously videotaped while changing their clothes is judicially clearly established.

We therefore conclude that the plaintiffs have adequately alleged a Fourth Amendment violation of their constitutional right to privacy because the students had a reasonable expectation of privacy and the invasion of the students' privacy in this case was not justified by the school's need to assure security. We further conclude that this constitutional violation is actionable because this particular right was clearly established at the time of the videotaping, such that a reasonable person who knew or ought to have known of the videotaping would be aware that what he or she was doing violated the Fourth Amendment. Therefore, the school officials directly involved in the decision to install the cameras and responsible for determining their locations, that is, defendants Beaty and Jolley, are not entitled to qualified immunity. ...

Seizures by Public School Officials

The **unreasonable seizure** of the person or property of a student by public school officials is prohibited by the Fourth Amendment. In evaluating a claim that school officials unreasonably detained a student in the course of an investigation, courts employ a framework similar to the one formulated by the Supreme Court in *T.L.O.* A seizure is constitutionally permissible if it is (a) **justified at its inception** and (b) **justified in its scope**.

Holding Students for Questioning

In *Edwards v. Rees*,[67] the Tenth Circuit used this approach and upheld the 20-minute detention of a student for questioning in the course of an investigation into an anonymous bomb threat. The court found the detention was justified at its inception because other students had implicated the student, and the detention was justified in its length given the seriousness of the threat. In *Shuman v. Penn Manor School District*,[68] school officials held a student accused of sexual misconduct in a conference room for almost four hours. During this time, the student did homework. He was allowed to eat lunch in the cafeteria and get a drink of water. The court agreed that the student had been detained, as a reasonable person in his position would believe he was not free to leave. The Third Circuit held that the serious nature of the allegation, the need to investigate it, and the accommodations afforded the student all supported a finding of reasonableness in the circumstances.

In *Milligan v. City of Slidell*,[69] school officials removed a student from class to question him about rumors of a fight taking place after school. The Fifth Circuit found the school's interest

67 883 F.2d 882 (10th Cir. 1989).
68 422 F.3d 141 (3d Cir. 2005).
69 226 F.3d 652 (5th Cir. 2000).

in preventing violence took priority over the student's privacy interests in the circumstances, noting that "Students at school ... have a significantly lesser expectation of privacy in regard to the temporary 'seizure' of their persons than does the general population." In *Wyatt v. Fletcher*,[70] the Fifth Circuit likewise denied the Fourth Amendment claims of a student whose coaches had taken her into a locker room, locked the door, and allegedly yelled at her about an affair with an older woman. In granting the coaches qualified immunity, the court found "there is simply no clearly established constitutional right—and *Wyatt* cites none—that protects students from being privately questioned, even forcefully, even in a locked locker room."

In *Wallace v. Batavia School District 101*,[71] a school official briefly grasped a student's elbow to expedite her departure from a classroom in the course of a loud shouting match. The Seventh Circuit found no violation of the Fourth Amendment in the circumstances, noting that the school official had acted reasonably to maintain order and discipline in the classroom. In *Wofford v. Evans*,[72] classmates accused a student of bringing a gun to school. The student was held for questioning by school officials and the police. The Fourth Circuit found it was reasonable for school officials to detain the student until they had confirmed there was no gun on school property.

Restraint and Seclusion

In *C.N. v. Willmar Public Schools, Independent School District No. 347*,[73] the Eight Circuit affirmed that a special education teacher did not violate the Fourth Amendment rights of a student whose individualized education plan (IEP) allowed for the use of restraints and seclusion. In *Crochran v. Columbus City Schools*,[74] a student with autism and ADHD fell and damaged his teeth after school officials had placed him in a Velcro body sock. The Sixth Circuit found that while the use of a body sock constituted a seizure, its therapeutic use was not unreasonable in the circumstances.

In *Couture v. Board of Education of the Albuquerque Public Schools*,[75] a student who had been repeatedly placed in a timeout room by his teachers, the principal, and the school psychologist claimed the "timeouts" were seizures contrary to the Fourth Amendment. The Tenth Circuit found the student's behavior often posed a threat to the emotional, psychological, and physical safety of the students and teachers and that the timeouts were expressly prescribed by the student's IEP. Thus there was no Fourth Amendment violation, and school officials were entitled to qualified immunity. In *Ebonie S. and Pueblo School District 60*,[76] the Tenth Circuit similarly affirmed that providing a student with special needs with a desk that restricted her movements did not constitute a seizure under the Fourth Amendment, as "the desk did not infringe on the fundamental right to be free from bodily restraint."

Although establishing an unlawful seizure might pose hurdles for students with disabilities, such students might also be able to challenge restraints or seclusion as violations of the *Americans with Disabilities Act (ADA)* or Section 504 (see Chapter 8).[77]

---

70 718 F.3d 496 (5th Cir. 2015).
71 68 F.3d 1010 (7th Cir. 1995).
72 390 F.3d 318 (4th Cir. 2004).
73 591 F.3d 624 (8th Cir. 2010).
74 748 Fed. Appx. 682 (6th Cir. 2018) [*unpublished*].
75 535 F.3d 1243 (10th Cir. 2008).
76 695 F.3d 1051 (10th Cir. 2012).
77 *See* United States Department of Education, Office for Civil Rights, Dear Colleague Letter: Restraint and Seclusion of Students with Disabilities (December 28, 2016); Online at www2.ed.gov/about/offices/list/ocr/letters/colleague-201612-504-restraint-seclusion-ps.pdf (last accessed April 27, 2020).

Personal Electronic Devices

Students of all ages bring personal electronic devices with them to school, including web-enabled media players and smart phones. Their ubiquity has given rise to a number of problems for school officials, from classroom distractions to cyberbullying and "sexting" (see Chapter 4).

A number of states have authorized or required school districts to develop policies governing the possession and use of personal electronic devices by students on school property.[78] Some school policies may require, for example, that phones be turned off during school hours. Others permit their use, provided students do not disrupt the educational process, compromise academic integrity, violate school rules, or invade the privacy of others. Penalties typically include **confiscation** of the devices for varying periods of time. The confiscation of a personal electronic device by public school officials in accordance with school policies is unlikely to constitute an **unreasonable seizure** under the Fourth Amendment. But constitutional problems may arise if school officials engage in a search of confiscated devices without meeting the reasonable suspicion requirements of *T.L.O.*, particularly if school rules do not contemplate this.

In *Busso and Centano v. Elizabethtown Independent School District*,[79] a federal court allowed a series of claims to proceed against school officials who had confiscated students' smart phones. It was not their *seizure* but their subsequent *search* of the devices that violated the Fourth Amendment, as there was nothing in the school policies authorizing this. Legal problems for the school district were compounded when a school official found nude photographs of students on the phones he had illegally searched and later uploaded them to the Internet.

In the following illustrative case, a student was barred from attending his out-of-district school for behavioral infractions including sending text messages in class. He argued that school officials violated his Fourth Amendment rights by searching his confiscated phone. School officials argued they had reasonable grounds to read the student's text messages. The Sixth Circuit disagreed.

G.C. v. OWENSBORO PUBLIC SCHOOLS
U.S. Court of Appeals for the Sixth Circuit
711 F.3d 623 (2013)

KAREN NELSON MOORE, Circuit Judge.

Plaintiff-Appellant G.C. began attending school in the Owensboro Public School District as an out-of-district student in 2005. In September 2009, G.C. was caught sending text messages in class. School officials confiscated his cell phone and read the text messages. Because this was the last in a series of disciplinary infractions, Superintendent Dr. Larry Vick revoked G.C.'s out-of-district status, barring him from attending Owensboro High School. G.C. filed suit, raising both federal and state-law claims[.] ...

The defendants moved for summary judgment, which the district court granted. G.C. appeals the district court's resolution of three of his claims: (1) his due-process claim, in which he argues that he was

denied a hearing prior to expulsion as required by Kentucky statute; (2) his Fourth Amendment claim based on the September 2009 search, in which he contends that school officials violated his constitutional rights when they read text messages on his phone without the requisite reasonable suspicion[.] ...

For the reasons stated below, we REVERSE the district court's grant of summary judgment on G.C.'s due process claim and on G.C.'s Fourth Amendment claim based on the September 2009 search. ...

I. Background

From 2005 to 2008, G.C. enrolled as an out-of-district student in the Owensboro Public School

78 *See, e.g.*, KRS 158.165.
79 2018 U.S. Dist. LEXIS 70813 (W.D. Ky. Apr. 27, 2018).

District. Owensboro Public School District has a reciprocal agreement with Daviess County Public School District, the district where G.C.'s parents reside, that allows a limited number of students to enroll in the district where they do not reside. ...

During his freshman year at Owensboro High School, G.C. began to have disciplinary problems. Shortly thereafter, he communicated with school officials that he used drugs and was disposed to anger and depression. The relevant incidents and discussions are as follows. On September 12, 2007, the first incident in the record, G.C. was given a warning for using profanity in class. In February 2008, G.C. visited Smith's office and expressed to Smith "that he was very upset about an argument he had with his girlfriend, that he didn't want to live anymore, and that he had a plan to take his life." In this same meeting, G.C. told Smith "that he felt a lot of pressure because of football and school and that he smoked marijuana to ease the pressure." As a result of this interaction, Smith met with G.C.'s parents and suggested that he be evaluated for mental health issues. G.C.'s parents took him to a treatment facility that day.

On November 12, 2008, G.C. was given a warning for excessive tardies, and on November 17, 2008, G.C. was disciplined for fighting and arguing in the boys' locker room. On March 5, 2009, G.C. walked out of a meeting with Summer Bell, the prevention coordinator at the high school, and left the building without permission. G.C. made a phone call to his father and was located in the parking lot at his car, where there were tobacco products in plain view. G.C. then went to Smith's office, and Smith avers that G.C. "indicated he was worried about the same things we had discussed before when he had told me he was suicidal." She states that she "was very concerned about [G.C.'s] well-being because he had indicated he was thinking about suicide again. I, therefore, checked [G.C.'s] cell phone to see if there was any indication he was thinking about suicide." The record also indicates that G.C. visited a treatment center that day, and the counselor recommended that he be admitted for one to two weeks.

On March 9, 2009, school officials convened a hearing with G.C. and his parents regarding the March 5 incident, at which both G.C. and school officials gave testimony. G.C. was placed on probation and assigned four days of in-school suspension. On April 8, 2009, G.C. was suspended after yelling and hitting a locker. At the end of the 2008–2009 academic year, Burnette recommended that Vick revoke G.C.'s authorization to attend Owensboro High School. Vick did not follow this recommen-

dation, and on June 15, 2009, he met with G.C.'s parents to discuss "what was expected of [G.C.] to be permitted to continue attending the [Owensboro Public School District] as an out-of-district student." According to Vick, he described the expectations as follows:

At this meeting, I explained to [G.C.'s] parents that they had three options regarding their son's education. First, I told them they could send [G.C.] to the [Daviess County Public School District] since they resided in that school district with their son. I told them their second option was to actually move into the [Owensboro Public School District] and that, upon so doing, [G.C.] would be entitled to all the rights of a resident student. Finally, I told them that despite ... Burnette's recommendation, I would allow [G.C.] to continue to attend school in the [Owensboro Public School District] as a nonresident student for the 2009–2010 school year on the condition and understanding that, if he had any further disciplinary infraction, this privilege would be immediately revoked and he would be required to return to his home school district.

On August 6, 2009, G.C.'s parents registered G.C. to attend Owensboro High School for the 2009–2010 academic year. Unlike in years past, however, they filled out an in-district registration form and listed G.C.'s physical address as that of his grandparents, who lived in the Owensboro Public School District. On the same form, they stated that G.C. lived with his parents, who maintained their residence in the Daviess County School District.

On September 2, 2009, G.C. violated the school cell-phone policy when he was seen texting in class. G.C.'s teacher confiscated the phone, which was brought to Brown, who then read four text messages on the phone. Brown stated that she looked at the messages "to see if there was an issue with which I could help him so that he would not do something harmful to himself or someone else." Brown explained that she had these worries because she

was aware of previous angry outbursts from [G.C.] and that [he] had admitted to drug use in the past. I also knew [he] drove a fast car and had once talked about suicide to [Smith]. ... I was concerned how [he] would further react to his phone being taken away and that he might hurt himself or someone else.

After this incident, Burnette recommended to Vick that G.C.'s out-of-district privilege be revoked, and this time Vick agreed. G.C.'s parents were contacted and told that they could appeal the decision if desired. On October 15, 2009, Vick, Burnette, and other school officials met with G.C.'s parents and their attorney. Vick explained that G.C. "had violated the condition of his out-of-district privilege to attend Owensboro High School by texting in class." Despite the revocation, Vick avers that G.C. continued to have the right to attend high school in Daviess County.

On October 21, 2009, G.C. filed an action for declaratory and injunctive relief, as well as compensatory and punitive damages, in the U.S. District Court for the Western District of Kentucky. G.C. alleged violations of his First, Fourth, and Fifth Amendment rights as well as violations of the Kentucky Constitution. ...

IV. Fourth Amendment Claim

G.C. ... maintains that the September 2009 search was not supported by a reasonable suspicion that would justify school officials reading his text messages. The defendants respond that reasonable suspicion existed to search his phone in September 2009 given his documented drug abuse and suicidal thoughts, particularly under the lower standard applied to searches in a school setting. They argue that the searches were limited and "aimed at uncovering any evidence of illegal activity" or any indication that G.C. might hurt himself.

The Supreme Court has implemented a relaxed standard for searches in the school setting:

[T]he legality of a search of a student should depend simply on the reasonableness, under all the circumstances, of the search. Determining the reasonableness of any search involves a twofold inquiry: first, one must consider whether the action was justified at its inception; second, one must determine whether the search as actually conducted was reasonably related in scope to the circumstances which justified the interference in the first place.

Because this court has yet to address how the T.L.O. inquiry applies to the search of a student's cell phone,[80] the parties point to two district court cases that have addressed this issue. In J.W. v. DeSoto County School District,[81] the case relied upon by the defendants and cited by the district court, a fac-

ulty member observed a student using his cell phone in class, took the cell phone from the student, and "opened the phone to review the personal pictures stored on it and taken by [the student] while at his home." The district court found the faculty member's actions reasonable, explaining that "[i]n assessing the reasonableness of the defendants' actions under T.L.O., a crucial factor is that [the student] was caught using his cell phone at school." The court further reasoned that "[u]pon witnessing a student improperly using a cell phone at school, it strikes this court as being reasonable for a school official to seek to determine to what end the student was improperly using that phone." Such broad language, however, does not comport with our precedent.

A search is justified at its inception if there is reasonable suspicion that a search will uncover evidence of further wrongdoing or of injury to the student or another. Not all infractions involving cell phones will present such indications. Moreover, even assuming that a search of the phone were justified, the scope of the search must be tailored to the nature of the infraction and must be related to the objectives of the search. Under our two-part test, using a cell phone on school grounds does not automatically trigger an essentially unlimited right enabling a school official to search any content stored on the phone that is not related either substantively or temporally to the infraction. Because the crux of the T.L.O. standard is reasonableness, as evaluated by the circumstances of each case, we decline to adopt the broad standard set forth by DeSoto and the district court.

G.C. directs the panel to Klump v. Nazareth Area School District,[82] a case in which a student was seen using his cell phone, followed by two school officials accessing the student's text messages and voice mail; searching the student's contacts list; using the phone to call other students; and having an online conversation with the student's brother. The court initially determined that the school officials were "justified in seizing the cell phone, as [the student] had violated the school's policy prohibiting use or display of cell phones during school hours." The court found that the school officials were not, however, justified in calling other students, as "[t]hey had no reason to suspect at the outset that such a search would reveal that [the student] himself was violating another school policy." The court further discussed the text messages read by the school officials, concluding that although the school

80 New Jersey v. T.L.O., 469 U.S. 325 (1985).
81 2010 U.S. Dist. LEXIS 116328 (N.D. Miss. Nov. 1, 2010).
82 425 F. Supp. 2d 622 (E.D. Pa. 2006).

officials ultimately found evidence of drug activity on the phone, for the purposes of a Fourth Amendment claim, the court must consider only that which the officials knew at the inception of the search:

the school officials did not see the allegedly drug-related text message until after they initiated the search of [the] cell phone. Accordingly ... there was no justification for the school officials to search [the] phone for evidence of drug activity.

We conclude that the fact-based approach taken in *Klump* more accurately reflects our court's standard than the blanket rule set forth in *DeSoto*.

G.C.'s objection to the September 2009 search centers on the first step of the *T.L.O.* inquiry— whether the search was justified at its inception. G.C. argues that the school officials had no reasonable grounds to suspect that a search of his phone would result in evidence of any improper activity. The defendants counter that the search was justified because of G.C.'s documented drug abuse and suicidal thoughts. Therefore, they argue, the school officials had reason to believe that they would find evidence of unlawful activity on G.C.'s cell phone or an indication that he was intending to harm himself or others.

We disagree, though, that general background knowledge of drug abuse or depressive tendencies, without more, enables a school official to search a student's cell phone when a search would otherwise be unwarranted. The defendants do not argue, and there is no evidence in the record to support the conclusion, that the school officials had any specific reason at the inception of the September 2009 search to believe that G.C. then was engaging in any unlawful activity or that he was contemplating injuring himself or another student. Rather, the evidence in the record demonstrates that G.C. was sitting in class when his teacher caught him sending two text messages on his phone. When his phone was confiscated by his teacher pursuant to school policy, G.C. became upset. The defendants have failed to demonstrate how anything in this sequence of events indicated to them that a search of the phone would reveal evidence of criminal activity, impending contravention of additional school rules, or potential harm to anyone in the school. On these facts, the defendants did not have a reasonable suspicion to justify the search at its inception. ...

We therefore REVERSE the district court's grant of summary judgment as to G.C.'s Fourth Amendment claim based on the September 2009 search. ...

The Sixth Circuit affirmed that school officials' knowledge of G.C.'s prior drug use and suicidal ideations did not give rise to a reasonable suspicion justifying a search of his confiscated phone, as G.C. had not been engaged in any criminal activity or violation of school rules (other than using his phone in class). In *J.W. v. Desoto County School District*,[83] one of the cases criticized by the Sixth Circuit in G.C., a district court found school officials did not violate a student's Fourth Amendment rights by confiscating and searching the cell phone he had been caught using in class, in violation of a **zero tolerance policy**. The phone contained images depicting gang-related activity, and the student was accordingly expelled as a threat to school safety. "Public actors step upon a very slippery slope when students are expelled on this basis, particularly if the school district's opinions in this regard are based largely on subjective impressions of a student's private activities off school grounds," wrote the court. "The slope is even [more slippery] when, as here, the school district only obtained the evidence of those activities by conducting a search which, while not unconstitutional, does tread into a constitutionally sensitive area."

It seems clear that law enforcement authorities may search cell phones without a warrant. In *State v. Patino*,[84] the Rhode Island Supreme Court found the defendant did not have a reasonable expectation of privacy, and hence no standing to challenge the warrantless search and seizure of his girlfriend's phone on Fourth Amendment grounds. The Supreme Court denied *certiorari* in that case.

---

83 2010 U.S. Dist. LEXIS 116328 (N.D. Miss. Nov. 1, 2010).
84 State v. Patino, 93 A.3d 40 (R.I. 2014), *cert. denied*, 135 S. Ct. 947 (2015), *aff'd*, 188 A.3d 646 (R.I. 2018), *cert. denied*, 139 S. Ct. 490 (2018).

The Eleventh Circuit subsequently distinguished the circumstances in G.C. from those in its unpublished opinion in *Jackson v. McCurry*.[85] In that case, a parent aggressively confronted school officials after they had searched his daughter's phone. The court found school officials had not violated the Fourth Amendment, as they had acted on corroborated allegations that his daughter had made fun of another student in text messages, in violation of a school rule against bullying. School officials found no incriminating messages, returned the phone, and no disciplinary action was taken against the student. School officials could bar the parent from school property and board meetings without violating his constitutional rights because his behavior constituted a threat to the safety of faculty and students.

School Resource Officers

When **criminal investigations** extend into schools, police officers must follow the same constitutional guidelines as at other times. As we have seen, however, public school officials are subject to more lenient Fourth Amendment standards in light of the custodial and tutelary nature of the school environment.

The distinction between a **police investigation** and a **school investigation** depends primarily on whether a search or seizure is conducted by **police officers** or **school officials**. This distinction is not always clear, particularly for **school resource officers** (SROs). The Department of Justice defines SROs as "sworn law enforcement officers responsible for safety and crime prevention in schools. A local police department, sheriff's agency, or school system typically employs SROs who work closely with school administrators in an effort to create a safer environment."[86] SROs are now a fixture in public schools across the country.[87] The following case illustrates how SROs can blur distinctions between public school officials and police officers.

⚖️

A.M. *ex rel.* F.M. v. HOLMES
US Court of Appeals for the Tenth Circuit
830 F.3d 1123 (2016), *cert. denied*, 137 S. Ct. 2151 (2017)

JEROME HOLMES, Circuit Judge.

Plaintiff-Appellant A.M. filed this action under 42 U.S.C. § 1983 on behalf of her minor child, F.M., against two employees of the Albuquerque Public Schools—specifically, Cleveland Middle School ("CMS") Principal Susan LaBarge and Assistant Principal Ann Holmes—and against Officer Arthur Acosta of the Albuquerque Police Department ("APD"). A.M. brought several claims stemming from two school-related events: (1) the May, 2011 arrest of F.M. for allegedly disrupting his physical-

education class, and (2) the November 2011 search of F.M. for contraband. …

I. Background

A. May 2011 Arrest of F.M.

On May 19, 2011, CMS physical-education teacher Margaret Mines Hornbeck placed a call on her school-issued radio to request assistance with a student. Officer Acosta, the school resource officer,

85 2019 U.S. App. LEXIS 7237 (11th Cir. 2019).

86 Office of Community-Oriented Policing Services (COPS), "What Is a School Resource Officer?" Washington, DC: US Department of Justice. Online at https://cops.usdoj.gov/supportingsafeschools (last accessed April 17, 2019).

87 *See, e.g.,* Rachael Pesta, *Labeling and the Differential Impact of School Discipline on Negative Life Outcomes: Assessing Ethno-Racial Variation in the School-to-Prison Pipeline*, 64(11) Crime & Delinquency 1489–1512 (2018); Joseph B. Ryan et al., *The Growing Concerns Regarding School Resource Officers*, 53(3) Intervention in School and Clinic 188–192 (2018); Christina Pigott, Ami Stearns and David Khey, *School Resource Officers and the School to Prison Pipeline: Discovering Trends of Expulsions in Public Schools*, 43(1) American Journal of Criminal Justice 120–138 (2018).

responded to the call. As he approached the designated classroom, he saw a student—later identified as F.M., who was then thirteen years old and in the seventh grade—sitting on the hallway floor adjacent to the classroom while Ms. Mines-Hornbeck stood in the hallway near the classroom door. Other students were peering through the doorway.

Ms. Mines-Hornbeck explained that F.M. had generated several fake burps, which made the other students laugh and hampered class proceedings. After F.M. ignored her requests to stop making those noises, Ms. Mines-Hornbeck ordered him to sit in the hallway. F.M. nominally complied, but once he was situated in the hallway, he leaned into the classroom entranceway and continued to burp and laugh. This obliged Ms. Mines-Hornbeck to "hav[e] to deal with [F.M.] repeatedly" and rendered her unable to continue teaching the class.

Ms. Mines-Hornbeck told Officer Acosta that she "need[ed] [F.M.] removed from [t]here" because she could not control F.M. At some point during Ms. Mines-Hornbeck's conversation with Officer Acosta, F.M. interjected, saying, "That didn't happen. No, that's not true." Nonetheless, based on what he had observed, Officer Acosta asked F.M. to come with him. F.M. cooperated; he accompanied Officer Acosta to CMS's administrative office and waited in a chair while Officer Acosta retrieved a computer from his patrol car.

Officer Acosta then informed F.M. that, "[b]ecause of the disruptions [he] saw," he would be arresting F.M. for interfering with the educational process ... a petty misdemeanor offense. Once again, F.M. stated that he had done nothing wrong. However, Officer Acosta did not "go into great detail with [F.M.]," which is to say that he did not invite further discussion of F.M.'s version of events. Aware that he possessed complete discretion concerning whether to arrest F.M. or issue a citation, Officer Acosta believed that he had a legitimate basis to arrest (i.e., probable cause) based on (1) Ms. Mines-Hornbeck's statement that F.M.'s (fake) burping and other specified misconduct prevented her from controlling her class, and (2) his observation that, when he responded to Ms. Mines-Hornbeck's call, "there was no more teaching going on," because Ms. Mines-Hornbeck was monitoring F.M. in the hallway. Officer Acosta thus drafted the necessary incident report, leaving F.M. outside the administrative office. He did not place F.M. in handcuffs at that point because F.M. posed no flight risk and "was not combative."

When Officer Acosta advised Ms. LaBarge of his plan to arrest F.M., Ms. LaBarge prepared a disciplinary referral slip that denoted "Police or Outside Agency" action and imposed a one-day suspension to be served May 20, 2011. She gave Officer Acosta "the duplicate ... Parent/Student copy" of the referral slip. Meanwhile, pursuant to school policy, Ms. LaBarge's administrative assistant attempted to notify A.M. She called the two telephone numbers listed in F.M.'s enrollment records, but to no avail: the first number had been disconnected, and the second number lacked a functioning voicemail account.

After completing his paperwork, Officer Acosta said to F.M., "Let's go to the car." F.M. responded, "Okay," and walked to Officer Acosta's patrol car without incident. Although he had not "laid a finger on [F.M.] ... up to th[at] point," Officer Acosta told F.M. when they reached the vehicle that he would be performing a pat-down search "per APD policy." F.M. indicated that he had no weapons or contraband on his person, and Officer Acosta found neither during the pat-down search. At that point, Officer Acosta handcuffed F.M., placed him in the patrol car, and drove him to the juvenile detention center. ...

F.M. served his suspension and did not return to CMS for the remainder of the 2010–2011 school year. Not surprisingly, the story of his arrest garnered some publicity. A.M. "spoke publicly" about the incident and "provided interviews to local news media." According to Officer Acosta, news coverage of F.M.'s arrest "was on the airways quite a bit," much to the chagrin of school administrators.

B. November 2011 In-School Search of F.M.

A.M. re-enrolled F.M. at CMS for the 2011–2012 school year. F.M. was attending school on November 8, 2011, the date of the second event prompting this litigation. That morning, a CMS student approached a teacher to report having witnessed a potential drug transaction on campus. The student recounted having seen approximately five other students carrying small baggies containing what appeared to be marijuana; these individuals seemed to be exchanging money for drugs. ...

Ms. Holmes was notified of the student's report and "contacted [Officer Acosta] on the school radio ... in regards to [the] suspicious situation." Officer Acosta then retrieved the school's security-camera footage to see if it might assist school administrators' efforts to identify the students of interest. During their review of the footage corresponding to the time and place described by the reporting student, Ms. Holmes and Ms. LaBarge recognized the five students involved in the suspicious transaction—including, as relevant here, F.M. These students were summoned to the administrative office while school representatives endeavored to contact the students' parents to inform them that their children would be searched in connection with a suspected drug transaction. The only student for whom a parent could not be reached was F.M.

All of the students were searched in a conference room next to Ms. LaBarge's office. Several adults were present: Ms. LaBarge, Ms. Holmes, Officer Acosta, a male teacher, and APD Officer Kiel Higgins. The first four searches and interviews were audio-recorded. According to Officer Acosta, these four students were asked to remove their shoes and empty their pockets. Two students stated that they had seen marijuana, "but [they] stopped short of saying who had it in their possession." Another student reported seeing F.M. with money. No drugs were found on any of the first four students.

As for F.M., one of the adults videotaped his search and interview using Officer Higgins's lapel camera. F.M. emptied his pockets and produced $200 in cash, including a $100 bill. Ms. Holmes asked F.M. if he had anything he was not supposed to have, and F.M. answered that he had a marijuana-leaf belt buckle. A search of F.M.'s backpack produced, among other items, a red bandana and a belt buckle displaying an image of a marijuana leaf. Both items violated CMS's prohibition of "bandanas," "gang-related" clothing, and apparel displaying "inappropriate messages or symbols."

F.M. was wearing "numerous layers of clothing," including a long-sleeved athletic shirt, a short-sleeved shirt layered over the first shirt, a pair of jeans, two pairs of athletic shorts, and boxer-shorts underwear. When prompted, he took off his shoes. F.M. also complied with a request to remove his jeans and place them on a table after demonstrating that he was wearing shorts underneath. At the school administrators' behest, the male teacher inspected F.M.'s waistband. He flipped down the waistband of the first pair of athletic shorts to reveal the second pair. The teacher left undisturbed the waistbands of F.M.'s other pair of athletic shorts and his boxer shorts. F.M. then removed one pair of athletic shorts and his short-sleeved shirt, which left him wearing a long-sleeved shirt, a pair of athletic shorts, and boxer-shorts underwear. Shortly thereafter, F.M. donned the rest of his clothing. The search of F.M.'s person, his removed clothing, and his backpack yielded no marijuana.

While F.M. was in the office, the school received a return phone call from A.M. Ms. LaBarge communicated with A.M., describing the events and the items recovered in the search of F.M. During the conversation, A.M. confirmed that F.M. had left home carrying $200 that morning. Ms. LaBarge elected "not [to] discipline F.M. for the suspected drug transaction due to his mother's corroboration of" why he possessed $200 in cash. However, Ms. LaBarge imposed a three-day in-school suspension, marking "Dress Code Violation," "General Disruptive Conduct," and "Gang-Related Activity—red bandana" on the associated referral form.

Later that day, Ms. LaBarge met with A.M. to explain the search and suspension. She subsequently stated that A.M. "stormed out" after "refus[ing] to listen" and saying "her attorney would contact [the school]." F.M. did not return to CMS. …

2. Unlawful-Arrest Claim

We now address whether the district court erred in granting qualified immunity to Officer Acosta on A.M.'s claim that he arrested F.M. without probable cause in violation of the Fourth Amendment. For the reasons discussed herein, we conclude (as the district court did) that Officer Acosta is entitled to qualified immunity. …

Officer Acosta alleges that he based his decision to arrest on two factors: (1) Ms. Mines Hornbeck's statement that F.M.'s (fake) burping and other specified misconduct prevented her from controlling her class, and (2) his observation that, when he responded to Ms. Mines-Hornbeck's call, "there was no more teaching going on," because Ms. Mines-Hornbeck was monitoring F.M. in the hallway. In sum, Officer Acosta asserts that F.M.'s behavior constituted an obvious and willful interference with the educational process—as described by the statute—and that his (Officer Acosta's) recognition of the interference supplied him with the requisite probable cause to arrest F.M. …

B. Clearly-Established-Law Analysis

A.M. insists that Officer Acosta's arrest of F.M. for his burping and other horseplay in Ms. Mines-Hornbeck's classroom violated clearly established law because F.M.'s conduct patently did not rise to the level of seriousness envisioned [by the statute]. In this regard, A.M. reasons, "At worst, F.M. was being a class-clown and engaged in behavior that would have subjected generations of school boys to an after-school detention, writing lines, or a call to his parents." …

We believe the text of N.M. Stat. Ann. § 30-20-13(D) manifests the New Mexico legislature's intent to prohibit a wide swath of conduct that interferes with the educational process. The statute renders unlawful, *inter alia*, the commission of "any act which would ... interfere with" or "disrupt" school functioning and, thereby, "interfere with the educational process." ... The ordinary meaning of these statutory terms would seemingly encompass F.M.'s conduct because F.M.'s burping, laughing, and leaning into the classroom stopped the flow of student educational activities, thereby injecting disorder into the learning environment, which worked at cross-purposes with Ms. Mines Hornbeck's planned teaching tasks.

More to the point, we cannot conclude that the plain terms of subsection (D) would have given a reasonable law-enforcement officer in Officer Acosta's shoes fair warning that if he arrested F.M. for engaging in his classroom misconduct he (i.e., the officer) would be violating F.M.'s Fourth Amendment right to be free from an arrest lacking in probable cause. Though A.M. suggests that the New Mexico legislature only sought to criminalize more serious conduct, there is no such limiting language in subsection (D)'s plain terms, and we decline to read such a limitation into the statute. And A.M. offers no statutory analysis to bolster her conclusory assertion to this effect. ...

1. Unreasonable-Search Claim

A.M. first contends with respect to Ms. Holmes that "the district court erred in finding that F.M.'s Fourth Amendment rights were not clearly established" under extant case law as of November 8, 2011 (the date of the in-school search). ... We conclude that the court correctly granted qualified immunity to Ms. Holmes on the unreasonable-search claim because, on A.M.'s version of the facts (insofar as they are borne out by the record), the search of F.M. was supported by reasonable suspicion. Thus, we rest our affirmance regarding this claim on our specific conclusion that A.M. has failed to carry her burden of demonstrating that Ms. Holmes committed a Fourth Amendment violation. ...

[The Supreme] Court has expressly recognized "that the school setting 'requires some modification of the level of suspicion of illicit activity needed to justify a search,'"—*viz.*, in-school searches do not require a predicate finding of probable cause. ...

As the [Supreme] Court has explained more recently, "[t]he lesser standard for school searches could as readily be described as a moderate chance of finding evidence of wrongdoing." We have understood these holdings to mean that a school search "need only be [1] 'justified at its inception' and [2] 'reasonably related in scope to the circumstances which justified the interference in the first place.'"

a. Justified at Inception

T.L.O. makes clear that ordinarily

a search of a student by a ... school official will be 'justified at its inception' when there are reasonable grounds for suspecting that the search will turn up evidence that the student has violated or is violating either the law or the rules of the school.[88]

The official need not possess absolute certainty that a search will produce such evidence; rather, "sufficient probability ... is the touchstone of reasonableness" in the school-search context.

A.M. asserts that the search of F.M. was not justified at its inception due to "the absence of any particularized evidence pointing to possession of drugs on the person of F.M." We disagree.

In fact, the record clearly bespeaks Ms. Holmes's awareness of a considerable quantum of particularized evidence when she initiated the challenged search. A student anonymously reported seeing F.M. participating in a suspected drug transaction on school grounds. It would have been reasonable for Ms. Holmes to take this report seriously, given CMS's apparently ongoing problem of student drug-trafficking. In this regard, Officer Acosta confirmed not only that CMS had "a lot of issues with drugs," but also that he had made several in-school arrests related to marijuana.

Acting on the student report, Ms. Holmes perused security-camera footage depicting the time and location provided by the reporting student. Ms. Holmes's review bolstered the student's "tip": she saw F.M. standing in a closed circle of students—apparently holding a roll of money and passing something to other students in the cohort. In light of her observations, she summoned the students depicted in the video to the administrative office.

Interviewing and searching F.M.'s four identified peers revealed the following: two students said they had seen someone with marijuana at school that day; another student said F.M. was carrying cash; and at least three students said that the "circle" incident involved marijuana. Guided by the relaxed standard of *T.L.O.*, we are satisfied that this information suggested a reasonable probability that marijuana (or evidence of other illegal-drug possession or distribution) might be found by searching the fifth student involved ... *T.L.O.* only requires "reasonable grounds" for believing that a search will unearth evidence of wrongdoing, and in this case the fore-

---

88 New Jersey v. T.L.O., 469 U.S. 325 (1985).

going evidence, taken together, rendered sufficiently reasonable the expectation that evidence of rule violations might be found in a search of F.M. ...

Again, given all of these factors, we conclude that the record demonstrates articulable and particularized indicia of a sufficient probability of wrongdoing by F.M. This plainly satisfies the *T.L.O.* Court's controlling formulation of the school-search rubric; consequently, we conclude that the search of F.M. was justified at its inception.

b. *Reasonable in Scope*

Once the search of F.M. began, it could remain constitutionally sound only insofar as it was "permissible in its scope" by using measures "reasonably related to the objectives of the search and not excessively intrusive" under the totality of the circumstances. We conclude that it was.

To begin, it is settled under *Safford* that a search of a student which is justified at its inception is also justified as to outer clothing and a backpack.[89] Pursuant to *Safford*, "[i]f a student is reasonably suspected of giving out contraband [items], [he] is reasonably suspected of carrying them on [his] person and in the carryall that has become an item of student uniform in most places today"—that is, the backpack. *Safford* suggests that this is true as a matter of logic: "if '[a school administrator's] reasonable suspicion of [contraband] distribution were not understood to support searches of outer clothes and backpack, it would not justify any search worth making.'"

Here, A.M. argues that the search of F.M. transcended outer clothing and effects; she claims it ventured into the realm of an unjustified strip search. Before asking F.M. to remove any clothing, Ms. Holmes obtained certain clues from his pockets and backpack suggesting the possibility of a drug transaction. Namely, she found $200 in cash—an arguably unusual amount of money for a middle-school student to carry, and certainly a relevant factor in a drug-related investigation. Ms. Holmes also found a belt bearing the image of a marijuana leaf, which at least reasonably indicated F.M.'s interest in, or affiliation with the use of, marijuana. Finally, Ms. Holmes found a bandana, which we have considered "gang-related clothing" in describing evidence obtained in searches. These foregoing items provided support to continue the search of F.M.

Though for purposes of qualified immunity we ordinarily do accept the facts that a plaintiff like A.M. alleges, we do so only insofar as those facts have a basis in the record—as relevant here, only insofar as A.M.'s account of the search does not patently conflict with the record's video footage. The video demonstrates that F.M. was first asked to remove his shoes and his jeans, leaving him in a short-sleeved shirt, a long-sleeved shirt, two pairs of athletic shorts, and boxer-shorts underwear. He then flipped down the waistband of his outer pair of athletic shorts, but he left undisturbed the waistbands of his other pair of athletic shorts and his boxer shorts. Finally, he removed his outer pair of athletic shorts and his outer (short-sleeved) shirt so that when the search concluded, he was still wearing a long-sleeved shirt, a pair of athletic shorts, and underwear. Soon afterward, he got dressed as he had been prior to the search.

Based on this sequence of events, we believe A.M. stretches the term "strip search" beyond recognition in her attempt to apply it here. The video unequivocally shows that F.M. was only prompted to remove outer clothing and that he was wearing additional layers of non-intimate street clothing underneath the removed items. Thus, because the scope of the search at all times remained reasonable, the search satisfied the strictures of the Fourth Amendment. ...

Unlike the student in *Safford*, in this case F.M. was at all times covered by at least one pair of pants (athletic shorts), one shirt, and underwear. The search of F.M. can therefore only be fairly characterized as implicating outerwear, even though it involved more than one layer of clothing. Mindful that the reporting student claimed to have seen baggies of marijuana, we conclude that asking F.M. to remove more than one external article of clothing was consistent with the objective of detecting small items. In light of the foregoing, we are satisfied that the search of F.M. was not excessively intrusive in its scope; rather, we hold that it was thoroughly reasonable in that regard.

In sum, we conclude that Ms. Holmes's search of F.M. was supported by reasonable suspicion as required by the Supreme Court's holding in *T.L.O.* The search was both justified at its inception and reasonable in scope. Accordingly, A.M. has failed to demonstrate any Fourth Amendment violation premised on an unreasonable search by Ms. Holmes.

We therefore affirm the district court's grant of qualified immunity to Ms. Holmes on this claim. ...

89 Safford Unified School District No. 1 v. Redding, 557 U.S. 364 (2009).

In dissent, Justice Neil Gorsuch (subsequently appointed to the Supreme Court) wryly observed,

> If a seventh grader starts trading fake burps for laughs in gym class, what's a teacher to do? Order extra laps? Detention? A trip to the principal's office? Maybe. But then again, maybe that's too old school. Maybe today you call a police officer. And maybe today the officer decides that, instead of just escorting the now compliant thirteen-year-old to the principal's office, an arrest would be a better idea. So out come the handcuffs and off goes the child to juvenile detention. My colleagues suggest the law permits exactly this option and they offer ninety-four pages explaining why they think that's so. Respectfully, I remain unpersuaded.

Unreasonable or Excessive Force

The **use of force** by public school officials is constrained by the potential for liability in civil suits for a number of **intentional torts** including **assault, battery, false imprisonment**, and **intentional infliction of mental suffering** (see Chapter 12). School officials have nonetheless resorted to the use of force to prevent students from harming themselves or others, from damaging school property, or from disrupting the educational process. In this section, we consider **constitutional limits** on the use of force by school officials in such circumstances.

As we have seen, the **Fourth Amendment** offers limited rights to students in public schools to be free from the **unreasonable search or seizure** of their persons and their property. Invasions of privacy, unreasonable detention, and the use of **unreasonable or excessive force** by public school officials may violate the Fourth Amendment in addition to the **due process** right of students to be secure in their persons and effects—usually phrased in terms of **bodily integrity** and **personal liberty** (see Chapter 6).

Examples of the use of force by school officials include detaining a student after class, escorting a student to the principal's office, stopping a fight by pulling students apart, knocking a weapon from a student's hand, or even shooting an armed student in self-defense.[90] But when is the use of force **unreasonable or excessive**, such that it violates the Fourth Amendment rights of students? The following case is illustrative.

⚖️

P.B. v. KOCH
US Court of Appeals for the Ninth Circuit
96 F.3d 1298 (1996)

BETTY B. FLETCHER, Circuit Judge:

Defendant Alfred Koch, the principal of Preston High School, a public high school in Preston, Idaho, appeals from the district court's denial of his motion for summary judgment on the grounds of qualified immunity. Three students, N.B., L.G., and D.D., sued Koch for use of excessive force. N.B. claims that Koch slapped him in the face and grabbed his neck. L.G. claims that Koch grabbed him by the neck and punched him in the chest. D.D. claims that Koch grabbed him by the neck and threw him head first into the lockers. Koch does not dispute that he used force against the students,

although he disputes portions of the plaintiffs' accounts of the incidents. Koch moved for qualified immunity, contending that his conduct did not violate clearly established constitutional rights. The district court denied the motion, concluding that students have a clearly established liberty interest in freedom from arbitrary corporal punishment. Koch appeals.

We affirm. The students had by 1990 a clearly established constitutional right to be free from the force allegedly used by Koch. No reasonable principal in 1990 could have thought it lawful to engage in the conduct plaintiffs allege.

---

90 Penley v. Eslinger, 605 F.3d 843 (11th Cir. 2010).

N.B.

On September 14, 1990, N.B., a 15-year-old sophomore, was with several friends in the Preston High school parking lot after a school football game. He was talking with a friend about Preston's quarterback, whom they agreed always wanted to have his own way. N.B. then said something like "Yeah, Heil Hitler," referring to the quarterback.

Koch walked by and heard the words "Heil Hitler." He assumed they were directed at him. Without giving N.B. a chance to explain, Koch admits that he "hit [N.B.] with the back hand and then the front hand" across the mouth. Koch grabbed N.B.'s neck and squeezed, causing bruises which turned purple and lasted for a couple of days. N.B. went to the emergency room and was given Advil and an ice pack. He was hoarse for several days. N.B. reported the incident to the police, who investigated and charged Koch with assault and battery. Koch pled guilty and was placed on three months' probation.

L.G.

At the time of the incident, January 1991, L.G. was a freshman at Soda Springs High School and played on the freshman basketball team. His team had just played the Preston team at Preston. He was sitting in the bleachers watching the varsity game. During halftime, the drill team began a special service for their recently deceased drill teacher. L.G. testifies that he was unaware of the special program being performed. Koch approached L.G. and his seatmates and asked them to be quiet. L.G. did not hear him. L.G. testifies that Koch "grabbed me by the arm and pulled me outside and punched me around, and he punched me in the chest." Koch again "grabbed [him] by the neck and pulled [him] out again." The incident has affected L.G. emotionally because he has trouble trusting people.

Although Koch disputes the details of the incident, he does admit that he used physical force which he guesses he did not have to use.

D.D.

On March 27, 1991, Koch saw D.D. wearing his hat in the school corridor and asked him to remove it. D.D. did so, but put his hat back on after passing Koch. Koch snatched the hat off D.D.'s head. According to D.D.:

Mr. Koch had his hands around my neck. And when he grabbed me ... he was jerking me around and I was trying to get him to let go of my neck, and he told me to come with him and so he was turning me around. [As] we got by the lockers, he was just yelling, he was blowing his stack. And he threw me headfirst into the lockers, and my head had hit into the lockers and I fell to my knees when my head hit into the lockers. And he grabbed me by the back of my neck again and lifted me up ... He yanked me into his office and ... he hit me in the chest with the back of his hand.

According to Koch, he did not push or shove D.D.; D.D. "stumbled and fell to the ground." The police investigated the incident but did not file charges against Koch. On April 17, 1991, the School Board heard evidence regarding these incidents. The Board voted to place Koch on probation for one year.

In 1991, N.B., L.G. and D.D., through their mothers, filed suit against Koch in the district of Idaho seeking declaratory and injunctive relief and damages pursuant to 42 U.S.C. § 1983. They also sued as defendants Superintendent Bowler and members of the School Board, claiming that Koch had assaulted and battered many students before and that had these defendants adequately disciplined Koch in the past, the incidents would not have occurred. ...

III

Government officials enjoy qualified immunity from civil damages unless their conduct violates "clearly established constitutional rights of which a reasonable person would have known." Determining whether a public official is entitled to qualified immunity "requires a two-part inquiry: (1) Was the law governing the state official's conduct clearly established? (2) Under that law could a reasonable state official believe his conduct was lawful?" ...

Although children sent to public school are lawfully confined to the classroom, arbitrary corporal punishment represents an invasion of personal security to which their parents do not consent when entrusting the educational mission to the State.

In reliance on *Ingraham* and other Supreme Court decisions,[91] the Third, Fourth, Sixth, Eighth, and Tenth Circuits had each held prior to 1990 that excessive corporal punishment can violate a student's substantive due process rights. There is no reason to doubt that the Ninth Circuit would have

91 Ingraham v. Wright, 430 U.S. 651 (1977).

followed these cases in 1990–1991 to conclude that physical attacks on a student by a principal in the manner alleged here violate the Constitution. Moreover, although the Ninth Circuit had not explicitly addressed a student's right to be free from arbitrary corporal punishment or other excessive force, established due process principles prohibiting arbitrary, irrational, and malicious state action clearly indicated that excessive force by a principal against a student violated the student's constitutional rights. The Fourteenth Amendment protects against the government's interference with "an individual's bodily integrity."

The Ninth Circuit has set forth factors to consider in determining whether substantive due process has been violated:

In determining whether substantive due process rights have been violated, we will look to such factors as the need for the governmental action in question, the relationship between the need and the action, the extent of harm inflicted, and whether the action was taken in good faith or for the purpose of causing harm.

In the instant case, there was no need to use force against the three students. Accordingly, the force Koch allegedly used—slapping, punching, and choking the students—bears no reasonable relation to the need. Because there was no need for force, one can reasonably infer that Koch took these actions not in good faith but for the purpose of causing harm. In this context, the deliberate and intentional harm allegedly inflicted—causing pain, bruising, and emotional injury—is significant.

Whether we describe the "right" as the right to bodily integrity, the right to be free from "unjustified intrusions on personal security," the right to be free from excessive force, or the right to be free from arbitrary and excessive corporal punishment, it is clear that a principal, who physically assaulted his students in the manner Koch allegedly did, has violated their clearly established constitutional rights. Accordingly, we conclude that Koch's alleged use of excessive force in 1990 to 1991 violated plaintiffs' clearly established rights.

B.

For essentially the same reasons, Koch could not have reasonably believed his alleged conduct to be lawful. In light of the Supreme Court's holding that students are protected from unjustified intrusions on personal security and out-of-circuit cases holding that arbitrary corporal punishment is unconstitutional, no reasonable principal could think it constitutional to intentionally punch, slap, grab, and slam students into lockers. Moreover, excessive force against a prisoner or suspect was clearly unconstitutional at the time. No reasonable school official could think a student not entitled to equivalent protection from attacks on his bodily integrity.

All government officials are on notice that it is unlawful to use excessive force against citizens. Although reasonable minds can differ over the appropriateness and the amount of corporal punishment under certain circumstances, reasonable minds cannot differ over the appropriateness of Koch's alleged conduct. Koch's use of force does not satisfy a standard of "objective legal reasonableness." The district court properly denied Koch's motion for summary judgment on the grounds of qualified immunity. … The plaintiffs had by 1990 a clearly established constitutional right to be free from the force allegedly used by Koch. AFFIRMED.

Shoving, Grabbing, and Dragging

In *Wallace v. Batavia School District 101*,[92] the Seventh Circuit concluded that a school official did not violate the Fourth Amendment when he grabbed a student by the wrist and elbow to stop an escalating argument. In *Campbell v. McAlister*,[93] the Fifth Circuit found a school resource officer did not use excessive force when he allegedly "slammed [the student] to the floor" and "dragged [him] along the ground to the principal's office." In *Fernández-Salicrup v. Figueroa-Sancha*,[94] the

92 68 F.3d 1010 (7th Cir. 1995).
93 162 F.3d 94 (5th Cir. 1998) [*unpublished*], *cert. denied*, 526 U.S. 1018 (1999).
94 790 F.3d 312 (1st Cir. 2015).

First Circuit found that a police officer did not use excessive force in violation of the Fourth Amendment when he shoved and pulled at a student's arm as she tried to evade arrest from inside the schoolhouse gate. The student had been among a crowd of students throwing eggs, rocks, and tree branches at officers guarding a public housing project across the street from their school to protest a visit by the governor of Puerto Rico.

Handcuffs and Restraints

In *Gray v. Bostic*,[95] the Eleventh Circuit concluded that a school resource officer who handcuffed a nine-year-old student "to impress upon her the serious nature of committing crimes that can lead to arrest, detention or incarceration" used excessive force. There was no potential threat to anyone's safety, and the student was not engaging in any disruptive behavior. "Bostic's conduct in handcuffing Gray, a compliant, nine-year-old girl for the sole purpose of punishing her was an obvious violation of Gray's Fourth Amendment rights," wrote the court.

In the following illustrative case involving a school official who taped a student to a tree, the Ninth Circuit affirmed that the use of **excessive force** is actionable as a Fourth Amendment violation.

⚖️

DOE v. STATE OF HAWAII DEPARTMENT OF EDUCATION
US Court of Appeals for the Ninth Circuit
334 F.3d 906 (2003)

MARY M. SCHROEDER, Chief Judge:

This is a 42 U.S.C. § 1983 case against an elementary school vice principal who taped a second grade student's head to a tree for disciplinary purposes. The district court correctly denied the vice principal's motion for summary judgment on the basis of qualified immunity. Indeed, our decision in *P.B. v. Koch* compelled that result.[96] We publish this opinion to clarify the issue that we left open in *Koch* regarding whether claims of excessive force by a school official generally should be decided under the Constitution's Fourth Amendment or under the Due Process Clause.

We now hold that Doe is entitled to proceed under the Fourth Amendment, in light of the Supreme Court's direction to analyze § 1983 claims under more specific constitutional provisions, when applicable, rather than generalized notions of due process.

The facts are not complicated. In February 1998, Plaintiff John Doe was a second-grader at Pukalani Elementary School. Doe's teacher sent him to the defendant, Vice Principal David Keala, to be disciplined for fighting, but Doe then refused to stand still

against a wall for his time-out punishment. Keala followed through on his threat to take Doe outside and tape him to a nearby tree if he did not stand still. The vice principal used masking tape to tape Doe's head to the tree. The record is unclear as to whether Doe's face was pressed against the bark. The tape remained for about five minutes until a fifth-grade girl told Keala that she did not think he should be doing that. He instructed the girl to remove the tape, which she did.

In January 2000, Doe filed this action in the district court. The complaint alleged both state and federal claims. Keala moved for summary judgment, arguing, among other things, that he was entitled to qualified immunity. Keala appeals the district court's order denying qualified immunity on the § 1983 claim. We ... affirm.

Analysis

A public official is not entitled to qualified immunity if his conduct violates "clearly established constitutional rights of which a reasonable person would have known." The Supreme Court's decision in *Saucier v. Katz* dictates our qualified immunity analysis.[97] We

95 458 F.3d 1295 (11th Cir. 2006).
96 96 F.3d 1298 (9th Cir. 1996).
97 533 U.S. 194 (2001).

must first determine whether the defendant's alleged conduct constituted a constitutional violation. If so, the defendant is entitled to qualified immunity only if the constitutional right that he allegedly violated was not clearly established.

A. *Constitutional Violation*

Doe argues that Keala's conduct in taping his head to the tree violated his rights under both the Fourth and Fourteenth Amendments. In *Koch*, we declined to resolve whether a student's claim of excessive force by a school official is more appropriately brought under the Fourth Amendment, rather than under substantive due process standards inherent in the Fourteenth Amendment. We suggested in a footnote that we might agree with the Seventh Circuit's decision that the Fourth Amendment analysis generally applies in the school context. We do so now.

In *Graham v. Connor*,[98] the Supreme Court directed courts to analyze claims of excessive force under a more specific constitutional provision, if one applies, rather than the general notion of substantive due process. The Court concluded that in most cases, the appropriate constitutional provision will be either the Fourth Amendment's protection against unreasonable seizures or the Eighth Amendment's ban on cruel and unusual punishments. The *Graham* rule is grounded in the notion that the specific constitutional provisions provide more guidance to judicial decision makers than the more open-ended concept of substantive due process. Although Graham dealt with the criminal context, we have recognized the movement away from substantive due process and toward the Fourth Amendment outside the criminal context as well.

It is clear that the Fourth Amendment applies in the school environment. Additionally, the Fifth, Seventh, and Tenth Circuits have all recognized that the Fourth Amendment governs a teacher's seizure of a student. We agree that Doe's Fourth Amendment right to be free from an unreasonable seizure "extends to seizures by or at the direction of school officials." We hold that Doe's claim is appropriately brought under the Fourth Amendment, not the Due Process Clause.

Keala argues that the Fourth Amendment should not apply because this case does not involve a law enforcement official acting in an investigatory capacity. The Fourth Amendment applies, however, to government conduct motivated by "investigatory or administrative purposes." Keala was a school administrator performing an administrative function by disciplining Doe and maintaining order in the school. His conduct is therefore within the scope of the Fourth Amendment.

We recognize that it may be possible for a school official to use excessive force against a student without seizing or searching the student, and that the Fourth Amendment would not apply to such conduct. We therefore do not foreclose the possibility that under some circumstances, a student's excessive force claim against a school official might be more appropriately analyzed under the Due Process Clause of the Fourteenth Amendment than under the Fourth Amendment.

Having concluded that Doe's claim should proceed under the Fourth Amendment, we turn to whether Doe can establish that Keala's conduct constituted an unreasonable seizure. Viewing the facts and evidence in Doe's favor as the nonmoving party, we hold that there is sufficient evidence to find a Fourth Amendment violation.

Doe has alleged a seizure here in the constitutional sense. Such a seizure occurs when there is a restraint on liberty to the degree that a reasonable person would not feel free to leave. Being held to a tree with tape for five minutes was such a restraint on Doe's liberty, and constituted a seizure within the meaning of the Fourth Amendment's prohibition against unreasonable search and seizure.

A seizure violates the Fourth Amendment if it is objectively unreasonable under the circumstances. In applying the Fourth Amendment in the school context, the reasonableness of the seizure must be considered in light of the educational objectives Keala was trying to achieve. In *T.L.O.*,[99] the Supreme Court considered the reasonableness of a search in a school. The court stressed that the search must be reasonably related to its purpose, and must not be "excessively intrusive in light of the age and sex of the student and the nature of the infraction."

At the time that Keala taped him to the tree, Doe's only offense had been "horsing around" and refusing to stand still. There is no indication that Doe was fighting or that he posed a danger to other students. Doe was eight years old. Taping his head to a tree for five minutes was so intrusive that a fifth grader observed it was inappropriate. There is sufficient evidence for a fact finder to conclude that

98 490 U.S. 386 (1989).
99 New Jersey v. T.L.O., 469 U.S. 325 (1985).

Keala's conduct was objectively unreasonable in violation of the Fourth Amendment.

B. *Clearly Established Right*

We now address an alleged violation of a student's right to be free of excessive physical punishment or restraint. We observed in Koch that the right of a student to be free from excessive force at the hands of teachers employed by the state was clearly established as early as 1990. There need not be a case dealing with these particular facts to find Keala's conduct unreasonable. Indeed, it is difficult to imagine this situation recurring with any frequency. The district court therefore properly concluded that Doe's right to be free from excessive forcible restraint was clearly established in 1998, when the events giving rise to this case occurred.

The order of the district court denying qualified immunity is AFFIRMED. The case is REMANDED for further proceedings on Plaintiff's Fourth Amendment claim.

Fatal Force

In *Penley v. Eslinger*,[100] the Eleventh Circuit concluded that a police officer who fatally shot a 15-year-old student in a school bathroom had not used excessive force in violation of his Fourth Amendment rights. The court found the officer had probable cause to believe the student posed a serious threat to the lives of officers and others, as he had earlier taken hostages, refused to drop his weapon, and was pointing the gun at the officer at the moment he was shot. In *Cole v. Carson*,[101] police officers intercepted and shot an armed 17-year-old student two miles from his high school. The Fifth Circuit noted that under the Fourth Amendment, the officers could not use deadly force in the absence of an immediate threat. The case was remanded to determine whether the officers reasonably perceived an imminent threat in the circumstances.

Pepper Spray and Tasers

In *J.W. v. Birmingham Board of Education*,[102] students argued that school officials had violated their Fourth Amendment rights by failing to offer any decontamination assistance after pepper spraying them. The Eleventh Circuit concluded that school officials were entitled to qualified immunity because the constitutionality of the use of **pepper spray** was not clearly established. The Second Circuit came to a similar conclusion in a recent decision on the use of a **taser** to subdue a deaf student.

MUSCETTE v. GIONFRIDDO
US Court of Appeals for the Second Circuit
910 F.3d 65 (2018)

DENNIS JACOBS, Circuit Judge:

Defendant-Appellant Paul Gionfriddo, a police officer in the town of West Hartford, appeals from the denial of his motion for qualified immunity in the United States District Court for the District of Connecticut. A.M. alleges that his Fourth Amendment right to be free from excessive force was violated when he was tased by Officer Gionfriddo following an incident at his school, the American School for the Deaf, in West Hartford, Connecticut. Officer Gionfriddo argues that he reasonably believed that the use of the taser was necessary to

100 605 F.3d 843 (11th Cir. 2010).
101 905 F.3d 334 (5th Cir. 2018).
102 904 F.3d 1248 (11th Cir. 2018).

subdue A.M., because A.M. ignored his instructions, even after he warned A.M. that he would use the taser if his instructions were ignored.

A.M.—who is deaf and communicates primarily in American Sign Language ("ASL")—disputes that he received the instructions and warnings. Officer Gionfriddo responds that it was reasonable for him to believe that his verbal instructions and warnings were translated to A.M. by the faculty members, because he observed them signing to A.M. when he gave the instructions and warnings.

Officer Gionfriddo moved for summary judgment on the ground of qualified immunity. The district court denied the motion, ruling that questions of fact precluded a ruling on qualified immunity. We reverse.

Background

The following facts are undisputed, unless otherwise noted. The plaintiffs, Audley and Judith Muschette, are the parents of A.M., a 12-year-old boy who is profoundly deaf and communicates primarily in ASL. On April 30, 2013, A.M. got into a confrontation over a takeout food order with a teacher at his school. A.M. became angry, ran from the dorm, and entered a nearby, fenced-off construction area.

The teacher, Christopher Hammond, followed. When Hammond approached, A.M. picked up a stick and hit Hammond. A.M. also threw rocks at Hammond, hitting him at least once. A.M. picked up a large rock in the construction area, Hammond and the other faculty who were gathered at the scene left the construction area, leaving A.M. sitting alone and holding the rock.

The Dean, Ron Davis, called 911 and reported a student was "out of control" and "making the situation dangerous". Officer Gionfriddo went to the school, and was soon joined by a second officer, Christopher Lyth. Dean Davis advised Officer Gionfriddo that A.M. had gotten into a disagreement with Hammond, and had been throwing things at staff members.

After the briefing, Officers Gionfriddo and Lyth approached the construction area with Hammond and Dean Davis, where A.M. remained sitting with a large rock in his hands. Dean Davis, Officer Gionfriddo, and Officer Lyth positioned themselves behind A.M., while Hammond stood approximately 15 feet in front of A.M., facing A.M., Dean Davis, and the officers. Officer Gionfriddo gave verbal instructions to put down the rock. Dean Davis translated the instructions into ASL, and Hammond, who

was facing A.M., signed in A.M.'s direction. When A.M. did not let go of the rock, Officer Gionfriddo verbally warned A.M. that he would use the taser if A.M. did not put down the rock, and Davis again translated this message to Hammond, who signed toward A.M.

When A.M. again appeared to ignore the warning, Officer Gionfriddo tased A.M., and Officer Lyth unsuccessfully attempted to get A.M. into handcuffs. After Officer Gionfriddo deployed the taser a second time, Officer Lyth was able to secure the handcuffs.

A.M. does not dispute that Officer Gionfriddo gave verbal instructions and warnings, or that Davis and Hammond were signing when those instructions and warnings were given. But he denies that he actually received and understood any of those instructions or warnings, or even knew that police officers were at the school until he was tased. A.M. argues that Officer Gionfriddo's belief that his instructions and warnings were being translated and understood by A.M. was unreasonable, and therefore that Officer Gionfriddo's use of the taser was unreasonable.

Officer Gionfriddo moved for summary judgment on the ground of qualified immunity. The district court denied the motion, finding that "Gionfriddo's entitlement to immunity depends on factual disputes that will hinge on credibility determinations, which must be made by the jury." This appeal followed.

Discussion

… "Qualified immunity protects officials from liability for civil damages as long as their conduct does not violate clearly established statutory or constitutional rights of which a reasonable person would have known." When a defendant invokes qualified immunity, courts consider whether the plaintiff has shown "(1) that the [defendant] violated a statutory or constitutional right, and (2) that the right was 'clearly established' at the time of the challenged conduct."

Officer Gionfriddo does not argue on appeal that the plaintiff has failed to allege a constitutional violation (of the Fourth Amendment right to be free from excessive force), and we therefore decline to address whether there was such a violation. Instead, Officer Gionfriddo argues that he is entitled to qualified immunity because his use of force in this case did not violate any clearly established right or, alternatively, that it was objectively reasonable for him to believe that his conduct was lawful.

The primary factual dispute identified by the district court is whether Officer Gionfriddo's instructions and warnings were successfully conveyed to

A.M. Officer Gionfriddo alleges that Hammond translated his verbal warnings to A.M. and that the warnings were understood by A.M. A.M. disputes this account. He argues that he was not disobeying the officer or resisting arrest, because the officer's instructions and warnings were not conveyed to him in ASL, and that the use of a taser under those circumstances was excessive.

It is clearly established that officers may not use a taser against a compliant or non-threatening suspect. Under A.M.'s theory of the case, this clearly established right was violated. A.M. alleges that his failure to comply with the instructions was not a choice to be non-compliant and threatening, but rather the result of his ignorance that any instructions were given. Therefore, the right A.M. argues was infringed—the right to be free from a taser when one is compliant with an officer's instructions and non-threatening—was clearly established.

However, Officer Gionfriddo is entitled to qualified immunity because it was objectively reasonable for him to believe that, given the undisputed facts, his conduct complied with this clearly established law.

To determine whether the relevant law was clearly established, we consider the specificity with which a right is defined, the existence of Supreme Court or Court of Appeals case law on the subject, and the understanding of a reasonable officer in light of pre-existing law.

An officer is entitled to qualified immunity if "any reasonable officer, out of the wide range of reasonable people who enforce the laws in this country, could have determined that the challenged action was lawful." "[O]ur inquiry [on qualified immunity] is not whether the officer should have acted as he did. Nor is it whether a singular, hypothetical entity exemplifying the 'reasonable officer' … would have acted in the same way."

Given the undisputed facts of this case, we cannot say that no reasonable officer, situated as Officer Gionfriddo was, would have used a taser to secure A.M.

On arrival at the American School for the Deaf, Officer Gionfriddo was faced with a 12-year-old boy who had fled his dorm and hunkered down in a restricted construction area, holding a large rock. Officer Gionfriddo had been informed that A.M. had thrown a folding chair at a staff member, struck Hammond with a stick, and hurled rocks at Hammond and other staff members. Officer Gionfriddo

therefore had a reasonable basis to believe that A.M. posed a threat to himself or the other staff members and that there was a risk of further flight over the terrain of a construction site. Moreover, Officer Gionfriddo had a reasonable basis to believe that his instructions and warnings were being conveyed to A.M. and that A.M. was ignoring them. When Officer Gionfriddo approached A.M. in the construction area, he gave verbal instructions to A.M. to put down the rock. Officer Gionfriddo observed Davis signing to Hammond, who in turn signed "very animated[ly and] very purposeful[ly]" to A.M.

The intermediary signers were a teacher and a dean at a school for the deaf, who could be counted upon to communicate with a deaf student. When A.M. did not comply, Officer Gionfriddo verbally warned A.M. that he would use the taser if A.M. did not put down the rock, and Officer Gionfriddo again observed Davis signing to Hammond, who signed to A.M. It was only then—when it appeared to Officer Gionfriddo that A.M. was ignoring his instructions—that Officer Gionfriddo deployed the taser. Officer Gionfriddo deployed the taser a second time to allow Officer Lyth to secure handcuffs on A.M.

A.M. makes no argument that is particular to the second deployment. He argues that the second deployment was even more unreasonable, but he makes the same arguments as to both. He does not argue that the second taser use was unreasonable even if the first was reasonable. A.M. disputes whether he received Officer Gionfriddo's instructions, but "our focus is not on [A.M.'s] motivations but instead on the sequence of events from the perspective of a reasonable officer at the scene."

Under these circumstances, we cannot say that no reasonable officer would have believed that the use of the taser to subdue A.M. was lawful. We have repeatedly concluded in summary orders that it is not unreasonable for an officer to use a taser in analogous circumstances. A.M. argues that it was unreasonable for Officer Gionfriddo to believe that Hammond was conveying his instructions and warnings to A.M., because Officer Gionfriddo admitted that A.M.'s head was down and that he could not tell if A.M.'s eyes were open. But Officer Gionfriddo actually testified that he "saw A.M. shaking his head with his head down" after Hammond signed to him.

In any event, one may be looking up even if one's head is down. And Officer Gionfriddo had a reasonable basis for presuming that his warnings were being conveyed to A.M.: he observed Hammond signing to A.M. after he gave verbal warnings (which supports an inference that Hammond believed that A.M.

was seeing him), and Hammond gave no indication that he believed his communication to A.M. was unsuccessful.

A.M. also argues that Officer Gionfriddo's reliance on Hammond to accurately convey his instructions and warnings was unreasonable because Hammond was the victim of A.M.'s stick-hitting and rock-throwing. But a reasonable officer could believe that Hammond would fulfill his responsibility as a teacher (and a translator) to accurately convey serious warnings from a police officer, even if he had

been the object of a student's tantrum. A reasonable officer need not assume that Hammond wished to harm a student in his charge, and would act on that wish by purposefully mistranslating Officer Gionfriddo's warnings. Moreover, Dean Davis, who was translating the warnings to Hammond, never indicated to Officer Gionfriddo that Hammond's translation was inaccurate.

Accordingly, because it was objectively reasonable for Officer Gionfriddo to believe that his conduct was lawful, he is entitled to qualified immunity.

Qualified Immunity Update

It is important to note that courts may find particular uses of force to be **excessive** or **unreasonable** while at the same time shielding school officials from liability with a finding of **qualified immunity** (as in the preceding case and others in this section). In the preceding case, it should also be noted that although Officer Gionfriddo was granted qualified immunity, the case still proceeded against other defendants.

Until 2009, the courts were required to undertake the approach adopted by the Eleventh Circuit in *J.W. v. Birmingham Board of Education* and by the Second Circuit in *Muscette v. Gionfriddo* in resolving qualified immunity claims by school officials. Under this two-step approach, based on the Supreme Court decision in *Saucier v. Katz*,[103] courts had to assess the facts in a manner most favorable to the plaintiff and decide whether the defendant's actions violated a constitutional right. They then had to consider whether the right was clearly established. In *Pearson v. Callahan*,[104] the Supreme Court overruled *Saucier*, holding that the two-step approach "should not be regarded as mandatory in all cases." Courts may now address directly whether a right was clearly established, rather than first determining whether a violation occurred as alleged by the plaintiff.[105]

Summary

Many of the cases featured in this chapter illustrate the tensions between the Fourth Amendment rights of students (to be free from unreasonable searches and seizures) and the common law and statutory duties of public school officials (to maintain safe and orderly learning environments). Federal and state statutes have made school safety a priority and have imposed enhanced duties on public school officials to investigate instances of drug use or trafficking, criminal activity, bullying and harassment, gang-related activity, and possession of weapons, among other things.

In light of the special characteristics of the school environment, the Fourth Amendment rights of students are not coextensive with those of adults in other contexts. Students may generally be subject to searches and seizures by public school officials without the need for a warrant or probable cause. To pass constitutional muster, school officials must have reasonable grounds to undertake a search. The scope of the search must be reasonable in the circumstances, including the age and maturity of the student and the nature of the infraction. Consent to a search must be

---

103 533 U.S. 194 (2001).
104 555 U.S. 223 (2009).
105 Gallardo v. Hanford Joint Union Sch. Dist., 2014 U.S. Dist. LEXIS 26142 (E.D. Cal. Feb. 26, 2014).

knowingly and intelligently given. The surveillance of students in common areas of the school is not considered a search for Fourth Amendment purposes, though students do have a right to privacy in non-public areas including locker rooms and bathrooms.

Sweep searches for drugs and weapons without individualized suspicion are generally permissible in light of the duty of school officials to comply with statutory mandates. Random drug testing is permissible to reduce the risks associated with participation in many extracurricular activities while impaired. The use of sniffer dogs for such purposes is permissible for bags and possessions, but not for searching students themselves. Strip searches are rarely justifiable under the Fourth Amendment in the absence of exigent circumstances, and are prohibited by statute in a number of states.

Seizures by public school officials include the detention of students for questioning and the confiscation of their personal property. As with searches, seizures undertaken by public school officials must be justified at inception and reasonable in scope in the circumstances. Interfering with the bodily integrity or personal liberty of a student by means of a search or seizure may violate the Fourth Amendment, particularly if the force used is excessive in the circumstances. However, even deadly force can be justified in exigent circumstances, particularly where a student poses a serious risk of imminent harm to others.

In order to be found liable in a Section 1983 suit for constitutional or statutory rights violations, the rights must have been clearly established at the time of the infraction. Otherwise, public school officials may be granted qualified immunity.

6 The Due Process Rights of Students

Historically, school officials executed delegated parental authority with few—if any—formal rules. Students were expected to behave, and it was left to teachers and school officials to maintain order, investigate misconduct, and punish students as they saw fit. Parents have long been presumed to act in the best interests of their children as they exercise day-to-day care and control. Acting *in loco parentis*, school officials exercised similarly broad discretionary authority over the minor children in their temporary **charge** or **custody**, making and enforcing codes of conduct with few constitutional constraints until the Civil Rights Era.[1]

In the 1960s the Supreme Court issued a trilogy of decisions extending limited constitutional rights to minors in custodial contexts, including students in public schools.[2] In *Kent v. United States*,[3] the Court recognized that the exercise of unchecked discretionary authority could have serious disadvantages:

> There is evidence, in fact, that there may be grounds for concern that the child [in custodial contexts] receives the worst of both worlds: [getting] neither the [constitutional] protections accorded to adults nor the solicitous care and regenerative treatment postulated for children.

In *In re Gault*,[4] Justice Fortas noted, "Departures from established principles of due process have frequently resulted not in enlightened procedure, but in arbitrariness." And as we saw in Chapter 4, the Court in *Tinker* ascribed limited First Amendment rights to students in public schools to engage in non-disruptive speech and expressive conduct.[5]

In Chapter 5, we considered the Fourth Amendment rights of students when public school officials engage **in searches and seizures**. In this chapter, we consider the **procedural** and **substantive due process** rights of students under the **Fifth** and **Fourteenth Amendment** in the custodial and tutelary context of public schools. The authority of public school officials to **enforce rules**, to **adjudicate guilt**, and **impose penalties and punishments** is similar in some respects to that exercised by officials in the **criminal justice system**. In the "special characteristics of the school environment," however, public school officials are subject to more relaxed constitutional constraints.

Natural Justice: An Overview

The exercise of disciplinary authority without **formal rules** raises **due process** concerns associated with principles of **natural justice** such as **fairness** and **impartiality**. Among other things, **fairness**

---

1 West Virginia State Board of Education v. Barnette, 319 U.S. 624 (1943).
2 Kent v. United States, 383 U.S. 541 (1966); In re Gault, 387 U.S. 1 (1967); Tinker v. Des Moines Independent Community School District, 393 U.S. 503 (1969).
3 383 U.S. 541 (1966).
4 387 U.S. 1 (1967).
5 393 U.S. 503 (1969).

requires that people be notified in advance of what constitutes acceptable behavior and what does not, so that they may conduct themselves accordingly. People may be punished only for violating rules adopted prior to the commission of those acts. Formal rules include school codes of conduct distributed to students and parents, as well as district policies, and state and federal statutes and regulations. Codification helps to reduce **bias**, **differential treatment**, and **caprice** in the enforcement of school rules.

In the wake of the *Kent*, *Gault*, and *Tinker* decisions, the courts initially struck a compromise on the **due process** rights of students in public schools. On the one hand, school officials could discipline students for fighting and vandalism, even without formal rules in place, because students could reasonably be presumed to know that such behaviors were wrong.[6] On the other hand, school officials could not discipline students for breaking informal or unwritten rules if they could not reasonably be presumed to know that such behaviors were wrong. Today, public school districts routinely publish codes of conduct to comply with state and federal law, to facilitate enforcement, and to avoid costly litigation. But even formal rules may violate due process principles associated with **natural justice**, including the requirement that rules be **clear** and **narrowly tailored**.

Unconstitutional Vagueness

Under the due process provisions of the Fifth and Fourteenth Amendments, a rule is **unconstitutionally vague** if persons "of common intelligence must necessarily guess at its meaning and differ as to its application."[7] School rules need not be as precisely crafted as criminal laws, but the courts insist that they give students a reasonable opportunity to know and understand what they may and may not do. In *Soglin v. Kauffman*,[8] for example, a rule prohibiting "misconduct" was found to be unconstitutionally vague. In *Galveston Independent School District v. Boothe*,[9] rules prohibiting "inappropriate actions" and "unacceptable behaviors" were found to be **unconstitutionally vague**. In the following illustrative case, the Fourth Circuit ruled that a group of students had standing to challenge two South Carolina statutes on this basis.

⚖️

KENNY v. WILSON
US Court of Appeals for the Fourth Circuit
885 F.3d 280 (2018)

ALBERT DIAZ, Circuit Judge:

In this case, a group of former and current South Carolina students and a nonprofit organization filed suit under 42 U.S.C. § 1983 challenging S.C. Code Ann. § 16-17-420 (the "Disturbing Schools Law") and S.C. Code Ann. § 16-17-530 (the "Disorderly Conduct Law") as unconstitutionally vague. The district court dismissed the complaint for lack of standing. ...

I.

Before turning to the merits, we set out the relevant statutes. We then describe the plaintiffs involved,

---

6 Richards v. Thurston, 424 F.2d 1281 (1st Cir. 1970); Shanley v. Northeast Indep. Sch. Dist., Bexar County, 462 F.2d 960 (5th Cir. 1972).
7 Connally v. Gen. Constr., 269 U.S. 385 (1926).
8 418 F.2d 163 (7th Cir. 1969).
9 590 S.W.2d 553 (Tex. Ct. App. 1979).

the allegations of the complaint, and the basis for the district court's decision.

A.

The *Disturbing Schools Law*, which all plaintiffs challenge, states:

(A) It shall be unlawful:

   (1) for any person willfully or unnecessarily (a) to interfere with or to disturb in any way or in any place the students or teachers of any school or college in this State, (b) to loiter about such school or college premises or (c) to act in an obnoxious manner thereon; or

   (2) for any person to (a) enter upon any such school or college premises or (b) loiter around the premises, except on business, without the permission of the principal or president in charge.

The *Disorderly Conduct Law*, which two plaintiffs (D.S. and S.P.) challenge on behalf of a class of elementary and secondary public school students, states:

Any person who shall (a) be found on any highway or at any public place or public gathering in a grossly intoxicated condition or otherwise conducting himself in a disorderly or boisterous manner, (b) use obscene or profane language on any highway or at any public place or gathering or in hearing distance of any schoolhouse or church … shall be deemed guilty of a misdemeanor and upon conviction shall be fined not more than one hundred dollars or be imprisoned for not more than thirty days.

B.

Plaintiffs include four individuals and one organization—minors D.S. and S.P., Niya Kenny, Taurean Nesmith, and Girls Rock Charleston. D.S. and S.P. represent the proposed class of elementary and secondary public school students in South Carolina. Girls Rock is suing on behalf of its members and itself. D.S. and S.P. are high school students. D.S. (who is black and has learning disabilities) was charged with violating the *Disturbing Schools Law* "after becoming involved in a physical altercation which she did not initiate and in which she was the only person who sustained an injury, a lump on her head." S.P. (who is white and suffers from mood and

conduct disabilities) was charged with violating the *Disorderly Conduct Law* after she cursed at a student who had been teasing her and refused to leave the library with the principal as instructed.

Kenny and Nesmith are young adults who were previously arrested and charged with violating the Disturbing Schools Law when they expressed concerns about police conduct. When Kenny (who is black) was in high school, she saw a school resource officer pull a female student from her desk, drag her on the floor, and handcuff her. Kenny "attempted to document the incident and called out for someone to do something to stop the violent treatment of her classmate." In response, Kenny was arrested and charged with violating the *Disturbing Schools Law*. The experience left Kenny scared and humiliated, and she withdrew from high school. She later obtained her G.E.D. Nesmith (who is also black) attends Benedict College. He alleges that a campus police officer arrested him on suspicion of violating both statutes after he complained that the officer was engaged in racial profiling and questioned the officer's request that he produce identification.

Girls Rock is a nonprofit organization that "provides mentorship, music and arts education, and leadership development to young people in Charleston, South Carolina." Girls Rock "operates an afterschool program serving at-risk youth" and is "guided by core principles that include challenging criminalization." The complaint describes two members of Girls Rock—K.B. and D.D. K.B. is Latina and was charged with violating the *Disturbing Schools Law* at age thirteen after she arrived late to gym class and loudly protested when she was asked to leave and go to the "tardy sweep" room. K.B. was sentenced to probation and referred to Girls Rock. When K.B. returned to school, she was placed in a program called "Twilight," through which "she was provided no more than three hours of computer-based education per day." The Twilight program "did not provide access to the courses necessary to obtain a high school diploma." D.D. is black and was charged with violating the *Disturbing Schools Law* at her Charleston middle school after she was sent out of class for talking and then proceeded to speak with another student in the hallway. She too was placed on probation and ordered to participate in the Twilight program.

C.

The plaintiffs' complaint outlines two § 1983 claims. First, all plaintiffs challenge the *Disturbing Schools Law* as unconstitutionally vague on its face and, second, D.S. and S.P. also challenge the *Disorderly Conduct Law* as unconstitutionally vague as applied to elementary and secondary public school students in South Carolina. Both claims allege (in sum and substance) that the statutes violate plaintiffs' right to due process under the Fourteenth Amendment because they fail to provide sufficient notice of prohibited conduct and encourage arbitrary and discriminatory enforcement. Plaintiffs claim that both statutes criminalize behavior that is indistinguishable from typical juvenile behavior, which schools address on a daily basis without resorting to the criminal justice system. For example, students, including some as young as seven, have been charged under the statutes for cursing, refusing to follow directions, or getting in a physical altercation that doesn't result in any injuries. The complaint further alleges that some students are arrested and charged simply for expressing concerns about police conduct.

According to plaintiffs, criminal charges under the two statutes are among the leading reasons young people enter the juvenile justice system in South Carolina. Between 2010 and 2016, over 9,500 young people throughout the state were referred to the Department of Juvenile Justice under the *Disturbing Schools Law*, a statistic that excludes those students seventeen and older who are charged and prosecuted as adults. Plaintiffs also allege that students arrested for violating the statutes are less likely to graduate and more likely to feel stigmatized and afraid, making it difficult to engage in the classroom. When a student's behavior is characterized as "criminal," the school is likely to impose a harsher punishment, diminishing the student's educational opportunities through expulsion, suspension, or placement in alternative settings that do not offer coursework necessary to graduate.

Plaintiffs claim that the statutes are enforced in a discriminatory manner, leaving racial minorities and students with disabilities especially vulnerable. In 2014–2015 black students in South Carolina were nearly four times as likely to be charged under the *Disturbing Schools Law* compared to their white classmates. In Charleston County, a charge under the Disturbing Schools Law was the number one reason young people entered the juvenile justice system and black students were more than six times as likely to be charged for the offense compared to white students. Plaintiffs allege that such racial disparities in discipline cannot be explained by differences in behavior among students of different races.

The individual plaintiffs and members of Girls Rock—all of whom have previously been charged under one of the two statutes—fear future arrest if, while on or around the grounds of a school, their actions are interpreted to fall under any of the broad terms of the statutes. Additionally, Girls Rock alleges that, as an organization, it is "substantially burdened in its mission by the continued practice of charging students" under the *Disturbing Schools* Law. Girls Rock volunteers attend hearings with its members and present testimony on their behalf. These hearings divert time and resources away from "developing programming and providing direct services to young people and attending to administrative business necessary to sustain the operations of the organization, such as writing grant proposals and conducting fundraising activities."

Plaintiffs seek: (1) a declaratory judgment that the statutes violate their right to due process under the Fourteenth Amendment; (2) a preliminary and permanent injunction enjoining defendants from enforcing the laws; and (3) an order enjoining defendants from considering or retaining any of plaintiffs' records relating to the *Disturbing Schools* or *Disorderly Conduct* charges filed against them. ...

A.

Consistent with the *Babbitt* standard for alleging injury,[10] plaintiffs S.P., D.S., and Nesmith say that they are students who fear that their actions will be interpreted to come within the broad terms of the statutes. They attend school without knowing which of their actions could lead to a criminal conviction, which deprives them of notice of prohibited conduct and "may authorize and even encourage arbitrary and discriminatory enforcement" in violation of their right to due process. Additionally, attending school inevitably involves expressive conduct and these three plaintiffs allege that the statutes restrict their ability "to engage with school," "speak out against abuses," or "participate in conversations about policing," and therefore limit their right to free speech under the First Amendment.

Turning to the second part of the *Babbitt* standard, there is a credible threat of future enforcement so long as the threat is not "imaginary or wholly speculative," "chimerical," or "wholly conjectural." Threat of prosecution is especially credible when defendants have not "disavowed enforcement" if plaintiffs engage in similar conduct in the future. Furthermore,

10 Babbitt v. UFW Nat'l Union, 442 U.S. 289 (1979).

there is a presumption that a "non-moribund statute that facially restricts expressive activity by the class to which the plaintiff belongs presents such a credible threat."

We find that S.P. and D.S. face a credible threat of future arrest or prosecution under the *Disturbing Schools Law* and *Disorderly Conduct Law*, and that Nesmith faces a credible threat of arrest or prosecution under the *Disturbing Schools Law* because these three plaintiffs regularly attend schools where they allege there may be future encounters with school resource officers or other law enforcement; they have been prosecuted under the laws in the past; and the defendants have not disavowed enforcement if plaintiffs engage in similar conduct in the future. Further, plaintiffs allege that black students and students with disabilities are more likely to be criminally charged with violating the statutes. S.P. is disabled, Nesmith is black, and D.S. is both disabled and black. Thus, the threat of enforcement is particularly credible with respect to these three plaintiffs.

Moreover, the presumption of a credible threat applies. Plaintiffs plausibly allege that the two statutes are regularly enforced against students like S.P., D.S., and Nesmith; they restrict students' expressive activity, including anything perceived as "disturbing," "obnoxious," "disorderly," or "boisterous"; and they tend to chill students' engagement in the classroom as well as their ability to speak out against police and participate in conversations about policing. As a result, we may presume that, as students in South Carolina, S.P., D.S., and Nesmith face a credible threat of prosecution.

B.

The district court concluded that there was no credible threat of prosecution because plaintiffs' future injuries are just as speculative and hypothetical as the alleged future injury in *City of Los Angeles v. Lyons*.[11] We disagree. In *Lyons*, the plaintiff sought to enjoin the Los Angeles Police Department's use of chokeholds when an officer faces no threat of deadly force. The plaintiff had previously been handcuffed and choked by a police officer during the course of a traffic stop, but the court held that "[a]bsent a sufficient likelihood that he will again be wronged in a similar way, *Lyons* is no more entitled to an injunction than any other citizen of Los Angeles."

However, *Lyons* did not involve a pre-enforcement challenge to a statute or any allegation of a chilling effect on the plaintiffs exercise of his First Amendment rights. The plaintiff there was seeking injunctive relief based on the conduct of a single police officer during a single traffic stop. In fact, the Court in *Lyons* explained that there would have been an actual controversy if Lyons had "allege[d] that he would have another encounter with the police" and "that the City ordered or authorized police officers to act in such manner." That is precisely what plaintiffs allege here—specifically, that there will be future encounters with officers at school and that the statutes in question authorize defendants to violate their rights to due process and free speech. Relatedly, unlike *Lyons*, D.S., S.P., and Nesmith allege they will be subject to arrest or prosecution for engaging in activity protected by the Constitution. The defendants say that the plaintiffs cannot satisfy the *Babbitt* test because the South Carolina courts have provided limiting constructions that clarify the reach of the statutes. Again, we do not agree.

Sarratt was an appeal from a criminal conviction.[12] The question was whether Sarratt, who had yelled profanities at his mother in a municipal parking lot, had violated the *Disorderly Conduct Law*. The South Carolina Court of Appeals accepted the lower court's determination that profane language alone can't constitute a violation of the Disorderly Conduct Law in light of the First Amendment and "must be accompanied by fighting words or other behavior such as gross intoxication." The court then found that Sarratt had used fighting words because he yelled loudly and directed vulgarities at his mother, and it therefore upheld his conviction. *Sarratt* clarifies that profane language alone cannot constitute a violation of the law, but it says nothing at all about how to interpret other vague phrases in the Disorderly Conduct Law like "conducting [oneself] in a disorderly or boisterous manner" or even what conduct must accompany profane language for there to be a criminal conviction. Thus, it remains plausible that the *Disorderly Conduct Law* is vague, particularly as applied to elementary and secondary students (who are in many ways disorderly or boisterous by nature).

In re Amir is also not dispositive as to whether the *Disturbing Schools Law*, as interpreted by the state court,[13] infringes on plaintiffs' rights to due process and free expression. There, the plaintiff

11 461 U.S. 95 (1983).
12 City of Landrum v. Sarratt, 572 S.E.2d 476 (S.C. Ct. App. 2002).
13 In re Amir X.S., 639 S.E.2d 144 (S.C. 2006).

challenged the *Disturbing Schools Law* as unconstitutionally vague and overbroad in violation of the First Amendment. The Supreme Court of South Carolina did not reach the merits of the vagueness challenge, holding instead that the statute was not overly broad because it draws "the very same constitutional line drawn by *Tinker* and its progeny."

Tinker held that a school district could not punish students for wearing black armbands to school in protest of the Vietnam War because there was no "material interference" with school activities. The *Tinker* Court explained that

conduct by the student, in class or out of it, which for any reason—whether it stems from time, place, or type of behavior—materially disrupts classwork or involves substantial disorder or invasion of the rights of others is, of course, not immunized by the constitutional guarantee of freedom of speech.

As for *Tinker*'s progeny, the primary case discussed in *In re Amir*, [which] involved a city ordinance prohibiting a person, while on grounds adjacent to a building in which a school is in session, from willfully making a noise or diversion that disturbs the peace or good order of the school session. The Court there held the ordinance was a reasonable time, place, manner regulation and thus not overbroad. It also held that "[a]lthough the question is close," the ordinance was not impermissibly vague because it forbids "willful activity at fixed times—when school is in session—and at a sufficiently fixed place—'adjacent' to the school."

Unlike the school regulation in *Tinker* or the city ordinance in [*Amir*], the *Disturbing Schools Law* is a criminal law that applies to all people who in "any way or in any place" willfully or unnecessarily disturb students or teachers of any school or college. We note also that both *In re Amir* and *Tinker* are cases addressing overbreadth challenges; neither

consider the separate question of whether a statute's prohibitions are unconstitutionally vague and allow for arbitrary or discriminatory enforcement. In short, we do not think these cases foreclose the plaintiffs' claims here.

Finally, defendants say that plaintiffs fail to allege an intent to engage in a specific course of conduct proscribed by the statutes. But it is precisely because the statutes are so vague that plaintiffs can't be more specific. Plaintiffs allege that they can be criminally prosecuted for just about any minor perceived infraction and that they can't predict the type of conduct that will lead to an arrest. In any event, plaintiffs don't need to allege a specific intent to violate the statutes for purposes of standing. In *Babbitt*, for example, a farmworkers' union and others sought declaratory judgment that Arizona's farm labor statute was unconstitutional, and requested an injunction against its enforcement. In particular, the union claimed that the statute's provision limiting union publicity directed at consumers of agricultural products "unconstitutionally penalize[d] inaccuracies inadvertently uttered in the course of consumer appeals." The Court there held that the union's challenge "plainly pose[d] an actual case or controversy" because even though the union did "not plan to propagate untruths" as prohibited by the statute, the union nevertheless contended "that erroneous statement is inevitable in free debate." (internal quotation marks omitted). In other words, it was enough that the union alleged an intent to engage in conduct that would inevitably—albeit incidentally—violate the statute. Likewise, plaintiffs here contend that behavior perceived as "obnoxious" or "boisterous" is inevitable on school grounds.

For the reasons given, we conclude that S.P., D.S., and Nesmith's allegations are sufficient to establish an injury in fact. We therefore vacate the district court's judgment and remand for further proceedings consistent with this opinion.

Unconstitutional Overbreadth

A rule is **unconstitutionally overbroad** if it infringes on the First Amendment rights of students by prohibiting more than necessary to achieve its purposes. The problem arises most often in connection with the regulation of speech or expressive conduct.[14] For example, a student punished for distributing religious literature in violation of a school rule banning the distribution of *any* literature could object that the rule is overbroad.

14 Bd. of Airport Comm'rs of Los Angeles v. Jews for Jesus, Inc., 482 U.S. 569 (1987); Broadrick v. Oklahoma, 413 U.S. 601 (1973).

In *Stephenson v. Davenport Community School District*,[15] the Eighth Circuit found a school rule prohibiting "Gang related activities such as display of 'colors,' symbols, signals, signs, etc." to be unconstitutionally vague and overbroad, leaving students unclear about what was not allowed and giving school officials too much discretion. The court noted that students could have been punished for wearing cross earrings or baseball caps or for leaving their shoelaces untied. In the following illustrative case, the Seventh Circuit distinguished the speech-related activities associated with the impugned rule in *Stephenson* from the conduct associated with a rule prohibiting "gang-like activity".

⚖️

FULLER v. DECATUR PUBLIC SCHOOL BOARD
US Court of Appeals for the Seventh Circuit
251 F.3d 662 (2001)

TERENCE T. EVANS, Circuit Judge

On September 17, 1999, a violent fight broke out in the bleachers at a high school football game in Decatur, Illinois, leaving spectators scrambling to escape the melee. The students involved in the fight were members of rival street gangs—the Vice Lords and the Gangster Disciples. As so often happens these days, a bystander caught the fight on videotape. It showed participants punching and kicking each other without concern for the safety of others in the stands. Six students who attended three different high schools in the Decatur Public School District were expelled from school for 2 years for their roles in the fight. The fight and the expulsions received considerable media attention as well as the attention of the Reverend Jesse Jackson and Illinois Governor George Ryan. When the dust settled, the original 2-year expulsions were reduced to expulsions for the remainder of the school year with the students being given the opportunity to attend an alternative high school. ...

[S]ome of the students, by their parents, brought this action pursuant to 42 U.S.C. § 1983, alleging that their constitutional rights were violated because one of the three school disciplinary rules they were found to have violated was void for vagueness. At trial, the district court ruled for the School District, denying the students' request for declaratory relief. The students appeal.

The students expelled were Roosevelt Fuller and Errol Bond, who attended Stephen Decatur High School; Gregory Howell and Shawn Honorable, who were students at Eisenhower High School; and Terence Jarrett and Courtney Carson, who were

students at MacArthur High School. The fight in which the students were involved began on one end of the bleachers and traveled all the way to the other end. Fans were jumping over the railing, trying to get onto the track which surrounds the football field, to escape the fight. The principal at MacArthur said he had never seen a fight as bad as this one in his 27 years in education. ...

In this court the students seek a ruling that the prohibition against "gang-like activity" is facially unconstitutional because it lacks clear definitions of what the prohibited conduct is. Because the expulsions were based at least in part on this rule, the students ... contend that their due process rights were denied. Because the period of expulsion has ended, the students recognize that any remedy is necessarily limited, but they seek an order sending the case back to the district court for a determination whether expungement of the disciplinary records is an appropriate remedy. ...

If the students' constitutional rights were violated, expungement might very well be an appropriate equitable remedy. The problem for the students, however, is convincing us that their rights were, in fact, violated. Rule 10, in place when the trouble started, prohibits students from engaging in "gang-like activities." It provides:

As used herein, the phrase "gang-like activity" shall mean any conduct engaged in by a student 1) on behalf of any gang, 2) to perpetuate the existence of any gang, 3) to effect the common purpose and design of any gang and 4) or to represent a gang affiliation, loyalty or membership in any

15 110 F.3d 1303 (8th Cir. 1997).

way while on school grounds or while attending a school function. These activities include recruiting students for membership in any gang and threatening or intimidating other students or employees to commit acts or omissions against his/her will in furtherance of the common purpose and design of any gang.

A violation of the rule is grounds for suspension or expulsion from school.

The students argue that the phrase "gang-like activity" is unconstitutionally vague on its face. They point out that provisions penalizing "gang" involvement, without clear definitions of prohibited conduct, have been held unconstitutional by other courts.

Whatever is true of other rules, Rule 10 is not devoid of standards. It delineates specific activities which are covered by the rule: recruiting students for membership in a gang, threatening or intimidating other students to commit acts or omissions against their will in furtherance of the purpose of the gang. It is different from the rule in *Stephenson*, which is directed at gang-related activities such as "display of 'colors', symbols, signals, signs, etc."—activities more likely to implicate First Amendment rights. Similarly, the rule in another case the students cite, *West v. Derby Unified School District No. 260*,[16] goes primarily to speech-related activities. On the other hand, in our case, the rule on its face and certainly as applied to these students prohibits threatening and intimidating actions taken in the name of a gang. With that in mind, we turn to the students' constitutional challenge.

A rule, regulation, or law can be facially unconstitutional under two different theories. First, laws that inhibit the exercise of First Amendment rights can be invalidated under the overbreadth doctrine. The students do not proceed under this theory. Rather, they rely on the second, which is that even if a law does not reach a substantial amount of constitutionally protected conduct, it can be found to be impermissibly void if it fails to define the offense with sufficient definiteness that ordinary people can understand what conduct is prohibited and it fails to establish standards to permit enforcement in a non-arbitrary, non-discriminatory manner. A facial challenge in the latter situation is limited. In *Village*

of Hoffman Estates v. Flipside, Hoffman Estates, Inc.,[17] the Court said:

A law that does not reach constitutionally protected conduct and therefore satisfies the overbreadth test may nevertheless be challenged on its face as unduly vague, in violation of due process. To succeed, however, the complainant must demonstrate that the law is impermissibly vague in all of its applications.

Furthermore, the nature of the law affects the analysis. An enactment imposing criminal sanctions demands more definiteness than one which regulates economic behavior, Hoffman Estates, or as is relevant in our case, one which regulates the conduct of students in the school setting. In *Bethel v. Fraser*,[18] the Supreme Court said:

Given the school's need to be able to impose disciplinary sanctions for a wide range of unanticipated conduct disruptive of the educational process, the school disciplinary rules need not be as detailed as a criminal code which imposes criminal sanctions.

Recently, in *City of Chicago v. Morales*,[19] the Supreme Court considered a facial challenge to a Chicago ordinance. The ordinance prohibited criminal street gang members from loitering with one another or other persons in any public place. Justice Stevens, joined by Justices Souter and Ginsburg, recognized that the ordinance did not have a sufficiently substantial impact on conduct protected by the First Amendment to subject it to a facial overbreadth challenge. Rather, the ordinance was characterized as a criminal law which contained no *mens rea* requirement and which infringed on the constitutionally protected right to liberty. ...

For a number of reasons, we conclude that no facial challenge can be made to Rule 10. It is doubtful whether Rule 10 proscribes behavior which is protected under any constitutional provision. It is questionable whether it involves free speech rights. In addition, gang membership seems not to implicate the right of association. ... Not only does Rule 10 have very little to do with the Constitution, it also is not a criminal law but merely a school disciplinary rule. In order to prevail, the students here need

16 206 F.3d 1358 (10th Cir. 2000).
17 455 U.S. 489 (1982).
18 478 U.S. 675 (1986).
19 527 U.S. 41 (1999).

to show that the rule is unconstitutional in all its applications, which would include its application to them—in other words, that it is unconstitutional as applied. When the rule does not reach a "substantial amount of constitutionally protected conduct," we must uphold a facial challenge "only if the enactment is impermissibly vague in all of its applications. A plaintiff who engages in some conduct that is clearly proscribed cannot complain of the vagueness of the law as applied to the conduct of others."

Is the rule unconstitutional as applied to these students? The phrase the students contend is vague is "gang-like activity." The rule goes on to say that "gang-like activity" is conduct engaged in "on behalf of any gang," "to perpetuate the existence of any gang," "to effect the common purpose" of a gang, or "to represent a gang affiliation, loyalty or membership ..." Fighting in support of one's gang falls under more than one of these definitions. Ironically, in *Morales* the problem with the anti-loitering ordinance was that "loitering" was defined as remaining "in any one place with no apparent purpose." It was the phrase "no apparent purpose" that was found to

be overly vague, not the phrase "a criminal street gang member" which was also found in the ordinance. ...

It is hard to see why police officers might be given discretion to determine who might be a gang member in the context of a criminal law, but school officials cannot determine, in the context of school discipline, what gang-like activity is, especially when what is at issue is a violent fight between rival members of well-known street gangs ... That any persons charged with keeping the peace—*e.g.*, police officers or school officials—have an obligation to break up a violent fight in the stands at a high school football game cannot be disputed. Then later, when a careful investigation reveals that the fight was between well-known rival street gangs, it is reasonable for school officials to see the fight as "gang-like activity." In fact, the students do not say that the fight was not gang-related.

As applied in this case, the school disciplinary rule, even before it was changed, was sufficiently definite to withstand this constitutional challenge. The decision of the district court is affirmed.

Due Process: An Overview

In criminal cases, the adjudication of guilt is guided by additional principles of **natural justice**, including a **presumption of innocence** and a burden of proof on the state to establish guilt **beyond a reasonable doubt**. Whatever the accusation, the defendant has the right to a **fair and impartial trial**. Extensive procedural safeguards and rules of evidence maximize the likelihood of a just verdict while respecting basic human rights and dignity. These same principles apply to disciplinary actions in public schools. Both the Constitution and state statutes impose **procedural** and **substantive due process** requirements designed to ensure fairness and minimize error. States are free to grant accused students *more* procedural safeguards than the Constitution requires, but never fewer.

Procedural Due Process

Both the **Fifth Amendment** and the **Fourteenth Amendment** include clauses stating that no person shall "be deprived of life, liberty, or property, without due process of law." Although the concept of due process has never been fully defined, it embodies a principle of **even-handedness**. In its procedural sense, due process includes a **right to be heard**. At the minimum, it requires that individuals not be punished or deprived of their rights by the State without first being given a chance to tell their side of the story. Another important due process principle is **proportionality**. The greater the contemplated deprivation of life, liberty, or property, the more extensive the procedures must be to guard against an unjust verdict. And if a person is found guilty, there are limits on permissible punishments, no matter the crime. The Eighth Amendment prohibits "**cruel and unusual punishments**," among other things.

Substantive Due Process

As we observed in Chapter 5, the Fourth Amendment provides limited rights to students in public schools to be free from the unreasonable search or seizure of their persons and their property. **Invasions of privacy, unreasonable detention**, and the use of unreasonable or **excessive force** by public school officials may also violate the **substantive due process rights** of students under the Fourteenth Amendment, which outlaws arbitrary deprivations of **life, liberty, or property**.

These interests are sometimes phrased in terms of **bodily integrity** and **personal security**. In *Bolling v. Sharpe*,[20] an important desegregation case preceding *Brown v. Board of Education*,[21] the Supreme Court interpreted the term **"liberty"** in the Due Process Clause of the Fourteenth Amendment broadly: "[Liberty] is not confined to mere freedom from bodily restraint. [It] extends to the full range of conduct which the individual is free to pursue, and it cannot be restricted except for a proper governmental objective." Two decades later, in *Ingraham v. Wright*,[22] the Supreme Court affirmed that students in public schools have substantive due process rights under the Fourteenth Amendment "to be free from, and to obtain judicial relief for, unjustified intrusions on personal security."

The Fifth Amendment: An Overview

The **Fifth Amendment** includes **a right against self-incrimination**, widely understood as **a right not to testify** ("to plead the Fifth"), **a right to counsel**, and **a right to remain silent**, which many will recognize from the *Miranda* warnings depicted in movies and police dramas. In *Miranda v. Arizona*,[23] an important Civil Rights Era decision, the Supreme Court found that the Fifth Amendment requires police officers to remind individuals of their constitutional rights when they are taken into custody and questioned.

In the absence of police involvement, however, students do not have the right to remain silent. Public school officials are not required to provide *Miranda* warnings in the course of investigating student misconduct.[24] In *S.E. v. Grant County Board of Education*,[25] a case involving a student who had coaxed an Adderall tablet from a classmate with disabilities, the Sixth Circuit affirmed that an assistant principal who questioned a student while the school resource officer was on sick leave was not required to advise the student of her *Miranda* rights.

The Exclusionary Rule

In criminal cases, the judge-made **exclusionary rule** requires the suppression of evidence seized in violation of constitutional guidelines.[26] In *Thompson v. Carthage School District*,[27] a case involving alleged Fourth Amendment violations by school officials who found crack cocaine in the plaintiff student's coat pocket in the course of a search for weapons, the Eighth Circuit ruled **the exclusionary rule** does not apply in school disciplinary hearings. Barry C. Feld has criticized this approach, noting that "Because school personnel are less well-versed in Fourth Amendment doctrine than police officers and also enjoy qualified immunity for reasonable, good-faith mistakes, they have

---

20 347 U.S. 497 (1954).
21 347 U.S. 483 (1954).
22 430 U.S. 651 (1977).
23 384 U.S. 436 (1966).
24 Boynton v. Casey, 543 F. Supp. 995 (D. Me. 1982).
25 544 F.3d 633 (6th Cir. 2008), *cert. denied*, 556 U.S. 1208 (2009).
26 Mapp v. Ohio, 367 U.S. 643 (1961).
27 87 F.3d 979 (8th Cir. 1996).

scant motivation to learn or respect limits without some systemic impetus for constitutional con-formity."[28] Some lower courts have held that the exclusionary rule should apply.[29]

Double Jeopardy

The **Double Jeopardy Clause** of the Fifth Amendment provides that no person shall be "subject for the same offense to be twice put in jeopardy of life or limb." Students have argued that because public schools and courts are agencies of the State, they should not be subject to both school discipline and criminal or juvenile court proceedings. However, the courts have rejected the argu-ment that being punished at school precludes being punished again in court for the same offense (and *vice versa*).[30] In *Borovac v. Churchill County School District*,[31] discussed later in this chapter, a district court found "no legally cognizable claim for double jeopardy in the student discipline context." In its view, subsequently upheld by the Ninth Circuit, "the double jeopardy clause of the Fifth Amendment protects only against the imposition of multiple criminal punishments for the same offense."

However, as noted earlier, the Supreme Court extended a number of **procedural due process** rights to minors in custodial contexts in a trilogy of watershed opinions in the 1960s. In *Kent v. United States*,[32] a 16-year-old was taken into police custody on charges of rape and robbery. He was questioned repeatedly for 24 hours and confessed to some of the charges. The Juvenile Court of the District of Columbia waived its jurisdiction in his case without a hearing or investigation, allowing the U.S. District Court to try Kent as an adult. The Supreme Court overturned Kent's conviction and remanded the case, holding that the Juvenile Court had violated his due process rights in waiving its jurisdiction. Writing for the majority, Justice Fortas observed:

> The theory of the District's *Juvenile Court Act*, like that of other jurisdictions, is rooted in social welfare philosophy rather than in the *corpus juris*. Its proceedings are designated as civil rather than criminal. The Juvenile Court is theoretically engaged in determining the needs of the child and of society rather than adjudicating criminal conduct. The objectives are to provide measures of guidance and rehabili-tation for the child and protection for society, not to fix criminal responsibility, guilt and punishment. The State is *parens patriae* rather than prosecuting attorney and judge. But the admonition to function in a "parental" relationship is not an invitation to procedural arbitrariness.

> Because the State is supposed to proceed in respect of the child as *parens patriae* and not as adversary, courts have relied on the premise that the proceedings are "civil" in nature and not criminal, and have asserted that the child cannot complain of the deprivation of important rights available in criminal cases. It has been asserted that he [*sic*] can claim only the fundamental due process right to fair treat-ment. For example, it has been held that he [*sic*] is not entitled to bail; to indictment by grand jury; to a speedy and public trial; to trial by jury; to immunity against self-incrimination; to confrontation of his accusers; and in some jurisdictions … he [*sic*] is not entitled to counsel.

> studies and critiques in recent years raise serious questions as to whether actual performance measures well enough against theoretical purpose to make tolerable the immunity of the process from the reach of

---

28 Barry C. Feld, T.L.O *and Redding's Unanswered (Misanswered) Fourth Amendment Questions: Few Rights and Fewer Remedies*, 80 Miss. L.J. 847, 882 (2011).
29 *See* Jones v. Latexo Independent School District, 499 F.Supp. 223 (E.D. Texas 1980).
30 Matter of C.M.J., 915 P.2d 62 (Kan. 1996); Clements v. Bd. of Trustees of Sheridan County Sch. Dist., 585 P.2d 197 (Wyo. 1978).
31 2012 U.S. Dist. LEXIS 9693 (D. Nev. Jan. 27, 2012) (*internal quotations omitted; emphasis added*), *aff'd*, 621 Fed. Appx. 479 (9th Cir. 2015).
32 383 U.S. 541 (1966).

constitutional guaranties applicable to adults. There is much evidence that some juvenile courts, including that of the District of Columbia, lack the personnel, facilities and techniques to perform adequately as representatives of the State in a *parens patriae* capacity, at least with respect to children charged with law violation. There is evidence, in fact, that there may be grounds for concern that the child receives the worst of both worlds: that he [*sic*] gets neither the protections accorded to adults nor the solicitous care and regenerative treatment postulated for children.

The Supreme Court stopped short of extending to juvenile court proceedings "the constitutional guaranties which would be applicable to adults charged with the serious offenses for which Kent was tried." It would take that step the following year in *In re Gault*,[33] a case involving a 15-year-old taken into custody after a neighbor alleged he had made a lewd phone call. The juvenile court declared him a **delinquent** and sent him to an industrial school until he turned 21. Writing for a majority on the Court, Justice Fortas systematically reviewed the **procedural due process** rights of adults under the **Fifth Amendment**, including the right to receive **notice of charges**, the right to **counsel**, the right to **confront one's accuser**, the right against **self-incrimination**, and the right to **cross-examine witnesses**.

⚖

In re GAULT
Supreme Court of the United States
387 U.S. 1 (1967)

MR. JUSTICE FORTAS delivered the opinion of the Court.

This is an appeal under 28 U. S. C. § 1257 (2) from a judgment of the Supreme Court of Arizona affirming the dismissal of a petition for a writ of *habeas corpus*. The petition sought the release of Gerald Francis Gault, appellants' 15-year-old son, who had been committed as a juvenile delinquent to the State Industrial School by the Juvenile Court of Gila County, Arizona. The Supreme Court of Arizona … held that Arizona's Juvenile Code is to be read as "impliedly" implementing the "due process concept." It then proceeded to identify and describe "the particular elements which constitute due process in a juvenile hearing." It concluded that the proceedings ending in commitment of Gerald Gault did not offend those requirements. We do not agree, and we reverse.

We begin with a statement of the facts. … A boy is charged with misconduct. The boy is committed to an institution where he may be restrained of liberty for years. It is of no constitutional consequence—and of limited practical meaning—that the institution to which he is committed is called an Industrial School. The fact of the matter is that, however euphemistic the title, a "receiving home" or an "industrial school" for juveniles is an institution of confinement in which the child is incarcerated for a greater or lesser time. His world becomes "a building with white-washed walls, regimented routine and institutional hours …" Instead of mother and father and sisters and brothers and friends and classmates, his world is peopled by guards, custodians, state employees, and "delinquents" confined with him for anything from waywardness to rape and homicide.

In view of this, it would be extraordinary if our Constitution did not require the procedural regularity and the exercise of care implied in the phrase "due process." Under our Constitution, the condition of being a boy does not justify a kangaroo court. The traditional ideas of Juvenile Court procedure, indeed, contemplated that time would be available and care would be used to establish precisely what the juvenile did and why he did it—was it a prank of adolescence or a brutal act threatening serious consequences to himself or society unless corrected? Under traditional notions, one would assume that in a case like that of Gerald Gault, where the juvenile appears to have a home, a working mother and father, and an older brother, the Juvenile Judge would have made

33 387 U.S. 1 (1967).

a careful inquiry and judgment as to the possibility that the boy could be disciplined and dealt with at home, despite his previous transgressions. ...

The essential difference between Gerald's case and a normal criminal case is that safeguards available to adults were discarded in Gerald's case. The summary procedure as well as the long commitment was possible because Gerald was 15 years of age instead of over 18. If Gerald had been over 18, he would not have been subject to Juvenile Court proceedings. For the particular offense immediately involved, the maximum punishment would have been a fine of $5 to $50, or imprisonment in jail for not more than two months. Instead, he was committed to custody for a maximum of six years.

If he had been over 18 and had committed an offense to which such a sentence might apply, he would have been entitled to substantial rights under the Constitution of the United States as well as under Arizona's laws and constitution. The United States Constitution would guarantee him rights and protections with respect to arrest, search and seizure, and pretrial interrogation. It would assure him of specific notice of the charges and adequate time to decide his course of action and to prepare his defense. He would be entitled to clear advice that he could be represented by counsel, and, at least if a felony were involved, the State would be required to provide counsel if his parents were unable to afford it. If the court acted on the basis of his confession, careful procedures would be required to assure its voluntariness. If the case went to trial, confrontation and opportunity for cross-examination would be guaranteed. So wide a gulf between the State's treatment of the adult and of the child requires a bridge sturdier than mere verbiage, and reasons more persuasive than cliché can provide. ...

In *Kent v. United States*,[34] we stated that the Juvenile Court Judge's exercise of the power of the state as *parens patriae* was not unlimited. We said that "the admonition to function in a 'parental' relationship is not an invitation to procedural arbitrariness." With respect to the waiver by the Juvenile Court to the adult court of jurisdiction over an offense committed by a youth, we said that "there is no place in our system of law for reaching a result of such tremendous consequences without ceremony—without hearing, without effective assistance of counsel, without a statement of reasons." We announced with respect to such waiver proceedings that while

We do not mean ... to indicate that the hearing to be held must conform with all of the requirements of a criminal trial or even of the usual administrative hearing; but we do hold that the hearing must measure up to the essentials of due process and fair treatment.

We reiterate this view, here in connection with a juvenile court adjudication of "delinquency," as a requirement which is part of the Due Process Clause of the Fourteenth Amendment of our Constitution. We now turn to the specific issues which are presented to us in the present case.

III. Notice of Charges

Appellants allege that the Arizona Juvenile Code is unconstitutional or alternatively that the proceedings before the Juvenile Court were constitutionally defective because of failure to provide adequate notice of the hearings. No notice was given to Gerald's parents when he was taken into custody on Monday, June 8. On that night, when Mrs. Gault went to the Detention Home, she was orally informed that there would be a hearing the next afternoon and was told the reason why Gerald was in custody. The only written notice Gerald's parents received at any time was a note on plain paper from Officer Flagg delivered on Thursday or Friday, June 11 or 12, to the effect that the judge had set Monday, June 15, "for further Hearings on Gerald's delinquency."

A "petition" was filed with the court on June 9 by Officer Flagg, reciting only that he was informed and believed that "said minor is a delinquent minor and that it is necessary that some order be made by the Honorable Court for said minor's welfare." The applicable Arizona statute provides for a petition to be filed in Juvenile Court, alleging in general terms that the child is "neglected, dependent or delinquent." The statute explicitly states that such a general allegation is sufficient, "without alleging the facts." There is no requirement that the petition be served and it was not served upon, given to, or shown to Gerald or his parents. ...

We cannot agree with the court's conclusion that adequate notice was given in this case. Notice, to comply with due process requirements, must be given sufficiently in advance of scheduled court proceedings so that reasonable opportunity to prepare

---

34 383 U.S. 541 (1966).

will be afforded, and it must "set forth the alleged misconduct with particularity." It is obvious, as we have discussed above, that no purpose of shielding the child from the public stigma of knowledge of his having been taken into custody and scheduled for hearing is served by the procedure approved by the court below. The "initial hearing" in the present case was a hearing on the merits. Notice at that time is not timely; and even if there were a conceivable purpose served by the deferral proposed by the court below, it would have to yield to the requirements that the child and his parents or guardian be notified, in writing, of the specific charge or factual allegations to be considered at the hearing, and that such written notice be given at the earliest practicable time, and in any event sufficiently in advance of the hearing to permit preparation.

Due process of law requires notice of the sort we have described—that is, notice which would be deemed constitutionally adequate in a civil or criminal proceeding. It does not allow a hearing to be held in which a youth's freedom and his parents' right to his custody are at stake without giving them timely notice, in advance of the hearing, of the specific issues that they must meet. Nor, in the circumstances of this case, can it reasonably be said that the requirement of notice was waived.

IV. Right to Counsel

Appellants charge that the Juvenile Court proceedings were fatally defective because the court did not advise Gerald or his parents of their right to counsel, and proceeded with the hearing, the adjudication of delinquency and the order of commitment in the absence of counsel for the child and his parents or an express waiver of the right thereto.

The Supreme Court of Arizona … argued that "The parent and the probation officer may be relied upon to protect the infant's interests." Accordingly, it rejected the proposition that "due process requires that an infant have a right to counsel." …

We do not agree. Probation officers, in the Arizona scheme, are also arresting officers. They initiate proceedings and file petitions which they verify, as here, alleging the delinquency of the child; and they testify, as here, against the child. And here the probation officer was also superintendent of the Detention Home. The probation officer cannot act as counsel for the child. His role in the adjudicatory hearing, by statute and in fact, is as arresting officer and witness against the child. Nor can the judge represent the child. There is no material difference in

this respect between adult and juvenile proceedings of the sort here involved. In adult proceedings, this contention has been foreclosed by decisions of this Court.

A proceeding where the issue is whether the child will be found to be "delinquent" and subjected to the loss of his liberty for years is comparable in seriousness to a felony prosecution. The juvenile needs the assistance of counsel to cope with problems of law, to make skilled inquiry into the facts, to insist upon regularity of the proceedings, and to ascertain whether he has a defense and to prepare and submit it. The child "requires the guiding hand of counsel at every step in the proceedings against him." Just as in *Kent v. United States*, we indicated our agreement with the United States Court of Appeals for the District of Columbia Circuit that the assistance of counsel is essential for purposes of waiver proceedings, so we hold now that it is equally essential for the determination of delinquency, carrying with it the awesome prospect of incarceration in a state institution until the juvenile reaches the age of 21. …

We conclude that the Due Process Clause of the Fourteenth Amendment requires that in respect of proceedings to determine delinquency which may result in commitment to an institution in which the juvenile's freedom is curtailed, the child and his parents must be notified of the child's right to be represented by counsel retained by them, or if they are unable to afford counsel, that counsel will be appointed to represent the child. …

V. Confrontation, Self-incrimination, Cross-examination

Appellants urge that the writ of *habeas corpus* should have been granted because of the denial of the rights of confrontation and cross-examination in the Juvenile Court hearings, and because the privilege against self-incrimination was not observed. The Juvenile Court Judge testified at the *habeas corpus* hearing that he had proceeded on the basis of Gerald's admissions at the two hearings. Appellants attack this on the ground that the admissions were obtained in disregard of the privilege against self-incrimination. If the confession is disregarded, appellants argue that the delinquency conclusion, since it was fundamentally based on a finding that Gerald had made lewd remarks during the phone call to Mrs. Cook, is fatally defective for failure to accord the rights of confrontation and cross-examination which the Due Process Clause of the Fourteenth

Amendment of the Federal Constitution guarantees in state proceedings generally.

Our first question, then, is whether Gerald's admission was improperly obtained and relied on as the basis of decision, in conflict with the Federal Constitution. For this purpose, it is necessary briefly to recall the relevant facts.

Mrs. Cook, the complainant, and the recipient of the alleged telephone call, was not called as a witness. Gerald's mother asked the Juvenile Court Judge why Mrs. Cook was not present and the judge replied that "she didn't have to be present." So far as appears, Mrs. Cook was spoken to only once, by Officer Flagg, and this was by telephone. The judge did not speak with her on any occasion. Gerald had been questioned by the probation officer after having been taken into custody. The exact circumstances of this questioning do not appear but any admissions Gerald may have made at this time do not appear in the record. Gerald was also questioned by the Juvenile Court Judge at each of the two hearings. The judge testified in the habeas corpus proceeding that Gerald admitted making "some of the lewd statements ... [but not] any of the more serious lewd statements." There was conflict and uncertainty among the witnesses at the habeas corpus proceeding—the Juvenile Court Judge, Mr. and Mrs. Gault, and the probation officer—as to what Gerald did or did not admit. We shall assume that Gerald made admissions of the sort described by the Juvenile Court Judge, as quoted above. Neither Gerald nor his parents were advised that he did not have to testify or make a statement, or that an incriminating statement might result in his commitment as a "delinquent."

The Arizona Supreme Court rejected appellants' contention that Gerald had a right to be advised that he need not incriminate himself. It said: "We think the necessary flexibility for individualized treatment will be enhanced by a rule which does not require the judge to advise the infant of a privilege against self-incrimination."

In reviewing this conclusion of Arizona's Supreme Court, we emphasize again that we are here concerned only with a proceeding to determine whether a minor is a "delinquent" and which may result in commitment to a state institution. Specifically, the question is whether, in such a proceeding, an admission by the juvenile may be used against him in the absence of clear and unequivocal

evidence that the admission was made with knowledge that he was not obliged to speak and would not be penalized for remaining silent. In light of *Miranda v. Arizona*,[35] we must also consider whether, if the privilege against self-incrimination is available, it can effectively be waived unless counsel is present or the right to counsel has been waived. ... It would indeed be surprising if the privilege against self-incrimination were available to hardened criminals but not to children. The language of the Fifth Amendment, applicable to the States by operation of the Fourteenth Amendment, is unequivocal and without exception. And the scope of the privilege is comprehensive. ...

Against the application to juveniles of the right to silence, it is argued that juvenile proceedings are "civil" and not "criminal," and therefore the privilege should not apply. It is true that the statement of the privilege in the Fifth Amendment, which is applicable to the States by reason of the Fourteenth Amendment, is that no person "shall be compelled in any criminal case to be a witness against himself." However, it is also clear that the availability of the privilege does not turn upon the type of proceeding in which its protection is invoked, but upon the nature of the statement or admission and the exposure which it invites. The privilege may, for example, be claimed in a civil or administrative proceeding, if the statement is or may be inculpatory.

It would be entirely unrealistic to carve out of the Fifth Amendment all statements by juveniles on the ground that these cannot lead to "criminal" involvement. In the first place, juvenile proceedings to determine "delinquency," which may lead to commitment to a state institution, must be regarded as "criminal" for purposes of the privilege against self-incrimination. To hold otherwise would be to disregard substance because of the feeble enticement of the "civil" label-of-convenience which has been attached to juvenile proceedings. Indeed, in over half of the States, there is not even assurance that the juvenile will be kept in separate institutions, apart from adult "criminals." In those States juveniles may be placed in or transferred to adult penal institutions after having been found "delinquent" by a juvenile court. For this purpose, at least, commitment is a deprivation of liberty. It is incarceration against one's will, whether it is called "criminal" or "civil." And our Constitution

---

35 384 U.S. 436 (1966).

guarantees that no person shall be "compelled" to be a witness against himself when he is threatened with deprivation of his liberty—a command which this Court has broadly applied and generously implemented in accordance with the teaching of the history of the privilege and its great office in mankind's battle for freedom. ...

We conclude that the constitutional privilege against self-incrimination is applicable in the case of juveniles as it is with respect to adults. We appreciate that special problems may arise with respect to waiver of the privilege by or on behalf of children, and that there may well be some differences in technique—but not in principle—depending upon the age of the child and the presence and competence of parents. The participation of counsel will, of course, assist the police, Juvenile Courts and appellate tribunals in administering the privilege. If counsel was not present for some permissible reason when an admission was obtained, the greatest care must be taken to assure that the admission was voluntary, in the sense not only that it was not coerced or suggested, but also that it was not the product of ignorance of rights or of adolescent fantasy, fright or despair.

The "confession" of Gerald Gault was first obtained by Officer Flagg, out of the presence of Gerald's parents, without counsel and without advising him of his right to silence, as far as appears. The judgment of the Juvenile Court was stated by the judge to be based on Gerald's admissions in court. Neither "admission" was reduced to writing, and, to say the least, the process by which the "admissions" were obtained and received must be characterized as lacking the certainty and order which are required of proceedings of such formidable consequences. Apart from the "admissions," there was nothing upon which a judgment or finding might be based. There was no sworn testimony. Mrs. Cook, the complainant, was not present. The Arizona Supreme Court held that "sworn testimony must be required of all witnesses including police officers, probation officers and others who are part of or officially related to the juvenile court structure." We hold that this is not enough. No reason is suggested or appears for a different rule in respect of sworn testimony in juvenile courts than in adult tribunals. Absent a valid confession adequate to support the determination of the Juvenile Court, confrontation and sworn testimony by witnesses available for cross-examination were essential for a finding of "delinquency" and an order committing Gerald to a state institution for a maximum of six years. ...

As we said in *Kent*, with respect to waiver proceedings, "there is no place in our system of law for reaching a result of such tremendous consequences without ceremony ..." We now hold that, absent a valid confession, a determination of delinquency and an order of commitment to a state institution cannot be sustained in the absence of sworn testimony subjected to the opportunity for cross-examination in accordance with our law and constitutional requirements. ... For the reasons stated, the judgment of the Supreme Court of Arizona is reversed and the cause remanded for further proceedings not inconsistent with this opinion. It is so ordered.

The Fourteenth Amendment: An Overview

The Due Process Clause of the Fourteenth Amendment prohibits the State from depriving "any person of **life, liberty, or property** without due process of law." In the wake of *Kent*, *Gault*, and *Tinker*,[36] most federal courts applied the **Due Process Clause** to students in public schools, but there was considerable disagreement on how much process was required in particular circumstances. Six years after *Tinker*, the Supreme Court recognized that students in public schools could not be deprived of their **property interest** in receiving a public education without **due process**. Its decision in the following watershed case remains the **due process** touchstone when suspension or expulsion is contemplated as a punishment for student misconduct in public schools.[37]

---

36 393 U.S. 503 (1969).
37 See Lisa L. Swem, Goss v. Lopez *to today: The Evolution of Student Discipline NSBA COSA School Law Seminar* (March 24, 2017). Online at https://cdn-Files.Nsba.Org/S3fs-Public/08.%20goss%20v.%20lopez%20to%20today%20paper. Pdf (last accessed May 18, 2019).

GOSS v. LOPEZ
Supreme Court of the United States
419 U.S. 565 (1975)

MR. JUSTICE WHITE delivered the opinion of the Court.

This appeal by various administrators of the Columbus, Ohio, Public School System (CPSS) challenges the judgment of a three-judge federal court, declaring that appellees—various high school students in the CPSS—were denied due process of law contrary to the command of the Fourteenth Amendment in that they were temporarily suspended from their high schools without a hearing either prior to suspension or within a reasonable time thereafter, and enjoining the administrators to remove all references to such suspensions from the students' records.

I.

Ohio law, Rev. Code Ann. § 3313.64 (1972), provides for free education to all children between the ages of six and 21. Section 3313.66 of the Code empowers the principal of an Ohio public school to suspend a pupil for misconduct for up to 10 days or to expel him [sic]. In either case, he [sic] must notify the student's parents within 24 hours and state the reasons for his [sic] action. A pupil who is expelled, or his [sic] parents, may appeal the decision to the Board of Education and in connection therewith shall be permitted to be heard at the board meeting. The Board may reinstate the pupil following the hearing. No similar procedure is provided in § 3313.66 or any other provision of state law for a suspended student. Aside from a regulation tracking the statute, at the time of the imposition of the suspensions in this case the CPSS itself had not issued any written procedure applicable to suspensions. Nor, so far as the record reflects, had any of the individual high schools involved in this case. Each, however, had formally or informally described the conduct for which suspension could be imposed.

The nine named appellees, each of whom alleged that he or she had been suspended from public high school in Columbus for up to 10 days without a hearing pursuant to § 3313.66, filed an action under 42 U.S.C. § 1983 against the Columbus Board of Education and various administrators of the CPSS. The complaint sought a declaration that § 3313.66 was unconstitutional in that it permitted public school administrators to deprive plaintiffs of their rights to an education without a hearing of any kind, in violation of the procedural due process component of the Fourteenth Amendment. It also sought to enjoin the public school officials from issuing future suspensions pursuant to § 3313.66 and to require them to remove references to the past suspensions from the records of the students in question.

The proof below established that the suspensions arose out of a period of widespread student unrest in the CPSS during February and March 1971. Six of the named plaintiffs, Rudolph Sutton, Tyrone Washington, Susan Cooper, Deborah Fox, Clarence Byars, and Bruce Harris, were students at the Marion-Franklin High School and were each suspended for 10 days on account of disruptive or disobedient conduct committed in the presence of the school administrator who ordered the suspension. ...

Two named plaintiffs, Dwight Lopez and Betty Crome, were students at the Central High School and McGuffey Junior High School, respectively. The former was suspended in connection with a disturbance in the lunchroom which involved some physical damage to school property. Lopez testified that at least 75 other students were suspended from his school on the same day. He also testified below that he was not a party to the destructive conduct but was instead an innocent bystander. Because no one from the school testified with regard to this incident, there is no evidence in the record indicating the official basis for concluding otherwise. Lopez never had a hearing.

Betty Crome was present at a demonstration at a high school other than the one she was attending. There she was arrested together with others, taken to the police station, and released without being formally charged. Before she went to school on the following day, she was notified that she had been suspended for a 10-day period. Because no one from the school testified with respect to this incident, the record does not disclose how the McGuffey Junior High School principal went about making the decision to suspend Crome, nor does it disclose on what information the decision was based. It is clear from the record that no hearing was ever held. ...

On the basis of this evidence, the three-judge court declared that plaintiffs were denied due process of law because they were "suspended without hearing prior to suspension or within a reasonable time thereafter," and that Ohio Rev. Code Ann. § 3313.66 (1972) and regulations issued pursuant thereto were unconstitutional in permitting such suspensions. It was ordered that all references to plaintiffs' suspensions be removed from school files. ... The defendant school administrators have appealed the three-judge court's decision. Because the order below granted plaintiffs' request for an injunction—ordering defendants to expunge their records—this Court has jurisdiction of the appeal pursuant to 28 U.S.C. § 1253. We affirm.

II.

At the outset, appellants contend that because there is no constitutional right to an education at public expense, the Due Process Clause does not protect against expulsions from the public school system. This position misconceives the nature of the issue and is refuted by prior decisions. The Fourteenth Amendment forbids the State to deprive any person of life, liberty, or property without due process of law. Protected interests in property are normally "not created by the Constitution. Rather, they are created and their dimensions are defined" by an independent source such as state statutes or rules entitling the citizen to certain benefits. Here, on the basis of state law, appellees plainly had legitimate claims of entitlement to a public education. Ohio Rev. Code Ann. §§ 3313.48 and 3313.64 (1972 and Supp. 1973) direct local authorities to provide a free education to all residents between five and 21 years of age, and a compulsory-attendance law requires attendance for a school year of not less than 32 weeks. It is true that § 3313.66 of the Code permits school principals to suspend students for up to 10 days; but suspensions may not be imposed without any grounds whatsoever. All of the schools had their own rules specifying the grounds for expulsion or suspension. Having chosen to extend the right to an education to people of appellees' class generally, Ohio may not withdraw that right on grounds of misconduct, absent fundamentally fair procedures to determine whether the misconduct has occurred. ...

The authority possessed by the State to prescribe and enforce standards of conduct in its schools although concededly very broad, must be exercised consistently with constitutional safeguards. Among other things, the State is constrained to recognize a student's legitimate entitlement to a public education as a property interest which is protected by the Due Process Clause and which may not be taken away for misconduct without adherence to the minimum procedures required by that Clause. The Due Process Clause also forbids arbitrary deprivations of liberty. "Where a person's good name, reputation, honor, or integrity is at stake because of what the government is doing to him," the minimal requirements of the Clause must be satisfied. School authorities here suspended appellees from school for periods of up to 10 days based on charges of misconduct. If sustained and recorded, those charges could seriously damage the students' standing with their fellow pupils and their teachers as well as interfere with later opportunities for higher education and employment. It is apparent that the claimed right of the State to determine unilaterally and without process whether that misconduct has occurred immediately collides with the requirements of the Constitution.

Appellants proceed to argue that even if there is a right to a public education protected by the Due Process Clause generally, the Clause comes into play only when the State subjects a student to a "severe detriment or grievous loss." The loss of 10 days, it is said, is neither severe nor grievous and the Due Process Clause is therefore of no relevance. Appellants' argument is again refuted by our prior decisions; for in determining "whether due process requirements apply in the first place, we must look not to the 'weight' but to the nature of the interest at stake." Appellees were excluded from school only temporarily, it is true, but the length and consequent severity of a deprivation, while another factor to weigh in determining the appropriate form of hearing, "is not decisive of the basic right" to a hearing of some kind. The Court's view has been that as long as a property deprivation is not *de minimis*, its gravity is irrelevant to the question whether account must be taken of the Due Process Clause. A 10-day suspension from school is not *de minimis* in our view and may not be imposed in complete disregard of the Due Process Clause.

A short suspension is, of course, a far milder deprivation than expulsion. But, "education is perhaps the most important function of state and local governments," and the total exclusion from the educational process for more than a trivial period, and certainly if the suspension is for 10 days, is a serious event in the life of the suspended child. Neither the property interest in educational benefits temporarily denied nor the liberty interest in reputation, which is also implicated, is so insubstantial that suspension may constitutionally be imposed by any procedure the school chooses, no matter how arbitrary.

III.

"Once it is determined that due process applies, the question remains what process is due." We turn to that question, fully realizing as our cases regularly do that the interpretation and application of the Due Process Clause are intensely practical matters and that "[t]he every nature of due process negates any concept of inflexible procedures universally applicable to every imaginable situation." ... There are certain bench marks to guide us, however. *Mullane v. Central Hanover Trust Co.*,[38] a case often invoked by later opinions, said that

[m]any controversies have raged about the cryptic and abstract words of the Due Process Clause but there can be no doubt that at a minimum they require that deprivation of life, liberty or property by adjudication be preceded by notice and opportunity for hearing appropriate to the nature of the case.

"The fundamental requisite of due process of law is the opportunity to be heard," a right that "has little reality or worth unless one is informed that the matter is pending and can choose for himself [*sic*] whether to ... contest." At the very minimum, therefore, students facing suspension and the consequent interference with a protected property interest must be given some kind of notice and afforded some kind of hearing. "Parties whose rights are to be affected are entitled to be heard; and in order that they may enjoy that right they must first be notified."

It also appears from our cases that the timing and content of the notice and the nature of the hearing will depend on appropriate accommodation of the competing interests involved. The student's interest is to avoid unfair or mistaken exclusion from the educational process, with all of its unfortunate consequences. The Due Process Clause will not shield him from suspensions properly imposed, but it disserves both his interest and the interest of the State if his suspension is in fact unwarranted. The concern would be mostly academic if the disciplinary process were a totally accurate, unerring process, never mistaken and never unfair. Unfortunately, that is not the case, and no one suggests that it is. Disciplinarians, although proceeding in utmost good faith, frequently act on the reports and advice of others; and the controlling facts and the nature of the conduct under challenge are often disputed. The risk of error is not at all trivial, and it should be guarded against

if that may be done without prohibitive cost or interference with the educational process.

The difficulty is that our schools are vast and complex. Some modicum of discipline and order is essential if the educational function is to be performed. Events calling for discipline are frequent occurrences and sometimes require immediate, effective action. Suspension is considered not only to be a necessary tool to maintain order but a valuable educational device. The prospect of imposing elaborate hearing requirements in every suspension case is viewed with great concern, and many school authorities may well prefer the untrammeled power to act unilaterally, unhampered by rules about notice and hearing. But it would be a strange disciplinary system in an educational institution if no communication was sought by the disciplinarian with the student in an effort to inform him of his dereliction and to let him tell his side of the story in order to make sure that an injustice is not done. ...

We do not believe that school authorities must be totally free from notice and hearing requirements if their schools are to operate with acceptable efficiency. Students facing temporary suspension have interests qualifying for protection of the Due Process Clause, and due process requires, in connection with a suspension of 10 days or less, that the student be given oral or written notice of the charges against him and, if he denies them, an explanation of the evidence the authorities have and an opportunity to present his side of the story. The Clause requires at least these rudimentary precautions against unfair or mistaken findings of misconduct and arbitrary exclusion from school.

There need be no delay between the time "notice" is given and the time of the hearing. In the great majority of cases the disciplinarian may informally discuss the alleged misconduct with the student minutes after it has occurred. We hold only that, in being given an opportunity to explain his version of the facts at this discussion, the student first be told what he is accused of doing and what the basis of the accusation is ... Since the hearing may occur almost immediately following the misconduct, it follows that as a general rule notice and hearing should precede removal of the student from school. We agree with the District Court, however, that there are recurring situations in which prior notice and hearing cannot be insisted upon. Students whose presence poses a continuing danger to persons or property or an ongoing threat of disrupting the academic process may be immediately removed from

38 339 U.S. 306 (1950).

school. In such cases, the necessary notice and rudimentary hearing should follow as soon as practicable, as the District Court indicated.

In holding as we do, we do not believe that we have imposed procedures on school disciplinarians which are inappropriate in a classroom setting. Instead we have imposed requirements which are, if anything, less than a fair-minded school principal would impose upon himself [sic] in order to avoid unfair suspensions. …

We stop short of construing the Due Process Clause to require, countrywide, that hearings in connection with short suspensions must afford the student the opportunity to secure counsel, to confront and cross-examine witnesses supporting the charge, or to call his own witnesses to verify his version of the incident. Brief disciplinary suspensions are almost countless. To impose in each such case even truncated trial-type procedures might well overwhelm administrative facilities in many places and, by diverting resources, cost more than it would save in educational effectiveness. Moreover, further formalizing the suspension process and escalating its formality and adversary nature may not only make it too costly as a regular disciplinary tool but also destroy its effectiveness as part of the teaching process.

On the other hand, requiring effective notice and informal hearing permitting the student to give his version of the events will provide a meaningful hedge against erroneous action. At least the disciplinarian will be alerted to the existence of disputes about facts and arguments about cause and effect. He may then determine himself to summon the accuser, permit cross-examination, and allow the student to present his own witnesses. In more difficult cases, he may permit counsel. In any event, his discretion will be more informed and we think the risk of error substantially reduced. Requiring that there be at least an informal give-and-take between student and disciplinarian, preferably prior to the suspension, will add little to the fact-finding function where the disciplinarian himself has witnessed the conduct forming the basis for the charge. But things are not always as they seem to be, and the student will at least have the opportunity to characterize his [sic] conduct and put it in what he [sic] deems the proper context.

We should also make it clear that we have addressed ourselves solely to the short suspension, not exceeding 10 days. Longer suspensions or expulsions for the remainder of the school term, or permanently, may require more formal procedures. Nor do we put aside the possibility that in unusual situations, although involving only a short suspension, something more than the rudimentary procedures will be required.

IV.

The District Court found each of the suspensions involved here to have occurred without a hearing, either before or after the suspension, and that each suspension was therefore invalid and the statute unconstitutional insofar as it permits such suspensions without notice or hearing. Accordingly, the judgment is affirmed.

⚖

Goss resolved the major questions concerning the application of the **Fourteenth Amendment** in public schools: Because all states had made public school attendance a statutory right, students had a corresponding property interest in receiving an education. Any non-trivial deprivation of this interest would require **due process**. Because deprivation of even one day of schooling is "a serious event in the life of the suspended child," it is not trivial. Hence suspensions of any length required due process. Except under emergency circumstances, a **hearing** should precede a student's exclusion from school. For short-term suspensions, defined by the court as ten days or less, due process requires **notice of the charges** and of **the case against the student**, followed by an **opportunity to be heard** and to **refute the charges**. The ruling in *Goss* accommodated both the student's right to fair treatment and the school's need to act quickly and without undue expenditure of resources.

Hearing Not Required

Although *Goss* provided a framework for applying due process in disciplinary cases in public schools, the lower courts were left to determine when hearings were *not* required. Most courts do not require hearings for punishments other than exclusion from school, either because these types of punishments are not considered deprivations of liberty or property, or because they are considered trivial. For example, in *Couture v. Board of Education of the Albuquerque Public Schools*,[39] the Tenth Circuit ruled that temporarily placing a student with disabilities in a "timeout" area did not trigger a due process hearing:

> Moreover, the assumption that the timeouts were a deprivation of M.C.'s right of education under these circumstances is questionable. At M.C.'s age and given his severe emotional and behavioral difficulties, teaching him self-control was among the most important components of his educational program. As shown by the prescription of timeouts in his IEP, these sessions were not an interruption of his education; they were part of his education. Even assuming that the timeouts were ineffective, or even counterproductive, they cannot be treated as equivalent to denying him the education to which he is legally entitled.

> Further, a teacher's ability to manage his or her classroom would be inappropriately undermined by a hearing requirement prior to placing the student in timeout … This is an undue administrative burden we will not impose unless the timeouts rise to the level of the functional equivalent of a lengthy in-school suspension.

Although students have a statutory right to receive a public education, they have no property right to any of its particular components. Thus, courts have said that denying a student a place on an extracurricular sports team, a role in a play, a place in the band, or admission to the academic honor society or an advanced placement course does not require a hearing.[40] In *Vetrano v. Miller Place Union Free School District*,[41] a district court ruled that a student who was not allowed to continue performing in a variety show after deviating from the approved script was not deprived of a property interest. Participating in an extra-curricular activity was not "something for which students have a constitutionally protected interest meriting due process protections," wrote the court. In *Harrington v. Jamesville Dewitt Central School District*,[42] a student who had been given two days of after-school detention for plagiarism alleged the detentions deprived him of his right to an education in violation of the due process clause. "Here," wrote the court, the student "was not suspended from school or denied an education when the district imposed detention on him for his alleged plagiarism—he was punished by having to spend *more* time at school." Other courts have denied the due process claims of students whose grades were reduced for academic (as opposed to disciplinary) reasons,[43] or who were prohibited from attending graduation ceremonies.[44]

Confessions

Some courts have been willing to regard the admission of guilt by a student as either as a waiver of the right to a hearing or as demonstrating no practical need for one.[45] However, there may be

---

39 535 F.3d 1243 (10th Cir. 2008).
40 Seamons v. Snow, 84 F.3d 1226 (10th Cir. 1996); Mazevski v. Horseheads Cent. Sch. Dist., 950 F. Supp. 69 (W.D.N.Y. 1997); Hebert v. Ventetuolo, 638 F.2d 5 (1st Cir. 1981); Bernstein v. Menard, 557 F. Supp. 90 (E.D. Va. 1982), *appeal dismissed*, 728 F.2d 252 (4th Cir. 1984); *but see* Duffley v. N.H. Interscholastic Athletic Ass'n, 446 A.2d 462 (N.H. 1982).
41 369 F. Supp. 3d 462 (E.D.N.Y. 2019).
42 2017 U.S. Dist. LEXIS 54930 (N.D.N.Y. Apr. 11, 2017).
43 Campbell v. Bd. of Educ. of New Milford, 475 A.2d 289 (Conn. 1984).
44 Swany v. San Ramon Valley Unified Sch. Dist., 720 F. Supp. 764 (N.D. Cal. 1989); Fowler v. Williamson, 448 F. Supp. 497 (W.D.N.C. 1978); Dolinger v. Driver, 498 S.E.2d 252 (Ga. 1998).
45 Keough v. Tate County Bd. of Educ., 748 F.2d 1077 (5th Cir. 1984); Coffman v. Kuehler, 409 F. Supp. 546 (N.D. Tex. 1976).

prudential reasons for holding a hearing even when a student confesses. In the following illustrative case, subsequently affirmed by the Ninth Circuit, school officials initially imposed a two-day suspension on a student who admitted to hazing and sexually harassing a teammate on the school wrestling team. A disciplinary panel was convened for a hearing only after local media questioned the leniency of the punishment.

⚖️

BOROVAC v. CHURCHILL COUNTY SCHOOL DISTRICT
US District Court for the District of Nevada
2013 U.S. Dist. LEXIS 92823 (D. Nev. 2013), *aff'd*, 621 Fed. Appx. 479 (9th Cir. 2015)

LARRY R. HICKS, United States District Judge.

On December 3, 2010, Borovac, then a senior within CCSD and a member of his school's wrestling team, severely hazed and sexually harassed a fellow student and teammate while on an overnight wrestling trip. On December 10, 2010, Borovac was interviewed by defendant Lords, the school principal, about the incident and admitted to these transgressions. Thereafter, Borovac was disciplined by Lords, serving two (2) Saturday detentions and being banned from all overnight trips with the wrestling team.

On December 21, 2010, defendant Lords again interviewed Borovac concerning alleged photos of the incident and for further clarification of all surrounding facts, including Borovac's direct involvement. On December 22, 2010, school was dismissed for winter break. On January 10, 2011, the day before school resumed, Lords contacted Borovac's parents and informed them that commencing January 11, 2011, Borovac was suspended from school for ten (10) days. Correspondence was sent confirming the suspension and setting a formal expulsion hearing for January 24, 2011. At the formal disciplinary hearing, defendant Lords presented the charges against Borovac, who was represented by counsel, and testified as to Borovac's confession. The disciplinary panel ultimately suspended Borovac for the remainder of the school year, but permitted him to finish his education through CCSD's distance education program, which he did, earning a diploma at the same time as his fellow classmates.

On May 10, 2011, Borovac filed a complaint against defendants alleging five causes of action: (1) Due Process violation; (2) breach of contract; (3) negligent hiring, training, and supervision; (4) intentional infliction of emotional distress; and (5) injunctive and declaratory relief. …

A. Due Process for Ten (10) Day Suspension

In his complaint, Borovac alleges that he received no notice of the possibility of further discipline after his initial interview and discipline by defendant Lords on December 10, 2010. As such, Borovac contends that his subsequent suspension was in violation of his procedural due process rights.

Nevada law provides that a student shall not be suspended from school or expelled from the school district until the student has been given notice and an opportunity to be heard. However, constitutional due process for school suspensions does not require a formal hearing. For any suspension up to ten (10) days, due process requires only that a student "be given oral or written notice of the charges against him and, if he denies them, an explanation of the evidence the authorities have and an opportunity to present his side of the story." This can be accomplished by an "'informal give-and-take' between the student and the administrative body dismissing him that would, at least, give the student 'the opportunity to characterize his conduct and put it in what he deems the proper context.'"

The court has reviewed the documents and pleadings on file in this matter and finds that defendants satisfied all procedural due process requirements prior to suspending Borovac for ten days. Although Borovac was not notified that he could face additional discipline up to and including a ten-day suspension after he had already served two Saturday detentions, due process under *Goss* does not require such notification of possible discipline. Nor does due process require that all discipline up to and including a ten-day suspension be meted out at the same time. Rather, due process under *Goss* simply requires an opportunity for the student to respond to the charges against him before discipline is meted out. Only if a student denies the charges against him, does due process require additional safeguards before he is suspended.

Here, the undisputed evidence in this action establishes that Borovac knew the charges against him for severely hazing and sexually harassing another student and that he discussed the incident with defendant Lords. He was further given a full opportunity to tell his side of the story, twice, and describe in detail his initiation and participation in the incident. Further, at no time did he deny his part in the incident. Based on the record before the court, the court finds that Borovac was provided the requisite procedural due process prior to being suspended for ten days. Accordingly, the court shall grant defendants' motion as to this issue.

B. Substantive Due Process

In his complaint, Borovac also alleges that his substantive due process rights were violated because his suspension was not rationally related to his underlying conduct, but was instead a response to increased media attention about the incident and public backlash at administrators.

A suspension is not rationally related to an offense if it is "patently unreasonable or disproportionate to the offense." The evidence in this action establishes that Borovac's suspension was rationally related to his offense. Regardless of the school board's additional concerns about media attention arising from the incident or the school board's desire to "send a message," the modest punishment of a single semester suspension imposed against Borovac—

during which he was allowed to take distance learning classes and earn his diploma at the same time as his peers—is neither patently unreasonable or disproportionate to his offense.

Borovac engaged in actions which included severe hazing, degradation, and sexual harassment of a fellow student. His actions included taping the victim to a table, including taping the victim's mouth and eyes shut; pulling down the victim's shorts and exposing his genitalia; spanking the victim with a spatula; placing the victim outside of the room and into a hotel hallway while still taped to the table; throwing condoms on the victim; taking pictures of the victim throughout the entire incident; and urinating on the victim while the victim was in the shower. A one-semester suspension from campus for this vile, admitted conduct is not patently unreasonable or disproportionate.

Additionally, the court recognizes that the recommendation to the board from defendant Lords to the school board was for expulsion. Yet, the board opted for the much less severe sanction of a single semester suspension with distance learning education. This fact alone significantly diminishes Borovac's claim that he was improperly disciplined because of other considerations including the school board wanting to "send a message." Therefore, the court finds that Borovac's one-semester suspension was rationally related to his offense. Accordingly, the court shall grant defendants' motion as to this issue ... IT IS SO ORDERED.

Post-Suspension Hearings

In *Goss*, the Supreme Court noted that, "Students whose presence poses a continuing danger to persons or property or an ongoing threat of disrupting the academic process may be immediately removed from school," and that in such cases, the notice and rudimentary hearing requirements of due process should follow "as soon as practicable." This exception has been applied with increasing frequency since the passage of the federal **Gun-Free Schools Act of 1994**,[46] which requires school officials to expel or suspend for at least one year any student who brings a firearm onto school property. Most states have modified their own statutes to comply with this federal mandate and have banned weapons of all kinds from school property.[47]

In *Williams v. Cambridge Board of Education*,[48] two students with prior criminal records were accused by three classmates of planning to shoot up their school three days after the Columbine tragedy. School officials initiated "emergency removal" proceedings against the students, who were placed in a juvenile facility. The students unsuccessfully challenged their removal from

---

46 20 U.S.C. § 7151.
47 *See, e.g.*, W. VA. CODE § 18A–5–1a.
48 370 F.3d 630 (6th Cir. 2004).

school on due process grounds. Law enforcement officials in the case had probable grounds to take the students into custody, and their emergency removal and detention was not a school suspension requiring notice or a hearing. In other cases involving weapons and threats of violence, it has been deemed procedurally sufficient for school officials to advise students of the reasons for their immediate suspension. In *Brian A. v. Stroudsburg Area School District*,[49] a tenth-grade student who left a note reading, "There's a Bomb in this School bang bang!! [*sic*]" on a table in his art class unsuccessfully challenged his suspension and subsequent expulsion on due process grounds. The student, who had previously been involved with bombing a shed at a school in another state, contended he had written the note as a joke and forgotten to throw it away. In *Clodfelter v. Alexander County Board of Education*,[50] a student challenged his ten-day suspension on due process grounds after school officials found drug paraphernalia and a knife while searching his vehicle for the jacket that he and another student had been fighting over. The court found the student had been given adequate notice of the reasons for his suspension prior to his arrest on charges of possession of a knife, theft, possession of drug paraphernalia, and possession of marijuana. In *C.Y. v. Lakeview Public Schools*,[51] the due process claims of a ninth-grade student were denied after she was suspended and subsequently expelled for bringing a steak knife to school and threatening to stab a fellow student. The student had tweeted, "stab stab stab. Going to stab stab stab you today to see your insides, ya ya ya [*sic*]." The Sixth Circuit found the student had received adequate notice of the reasons for her initial ten-day suspension.

Many states have gone further, requiring that students be excluded from school if they compromise school safety in specific ways. In Massachusetts, for example, school officials are required to suspend students they deem a **threat** to other students and staff.[52] California requires suspensions for the **use of force**, for **possession of a controlled substance**, for **theft**, for **obscenity**, and for **intimidating witnesses** in a school disciplinary hearing, among other things.[53] And as noted earlier, many states require school districts to adopt comparable policies to address **bullying, gang-related activity, harassment, intimidation**, and **threats of violence**.[54]

Due process challenges to the suspension of students for violating school rules based on statutory mandates like these have generally been unsuccessful. In *S.G. v. Sayreville Board of Education*,[55] a kindergarten student was suspended for saying "I'm going to shoot you" while playing "cops and robbers" at recess. The Third Circuit affirmed qualified immunity for school officials, finding the prohibition of speech threatening violence and the use of firearms was related to reasonable pedagogical concerns and denying the student's free speech, due process, and equal protection claims.

Thus, in *Jahn v. Farnsworth*,[56] the Sixth Circuit affirmed that due process did not require school officials to show a student video evidence of his theft of a laptop before suspending him for ten days and recommending he be suspended for the remainder of the school year in a subsequent hearing. After being sent home, the 17-year-old committed suicide by driving into an abutment. His father unsuccessfully sued the school district for wrongful death.[57] In *McKinley v. Lott*,[58] a student unsuccessfully challenged his arrest and detention in a juvenile facility after he admitted

49 141 F. Supp. 2d 502 (M.D. Pa. 2001).
50 2016 U.S. Dist. LEXIS 175014 (W.D.N.C. Dec. 19, 2016).
51 557 Fed. Appx. 426 (6th Cir. 2014) [*unpublished*].
52 Doe v. Superintendent of Sch. of Worcester, 653 N.E.2d 1088 (Mass. 1995).
53 CAL. EDUC. CODE § 48900.
54 CONN. GEN. STAT. § 10–222d; OR. REV. STAT. § 339.356; TENN.CODE ANN. § 49–6-1016; 14 DEL. C. § 4112D; N.J. STAT. § 18A:37–15; IOWA CODE § 280.28; S.C. CODE ANN. § 59–63–140; S.C. CODE ANN. § 59–63–140; R.I. GEN. LAWS § 16–21–26; A.C.A. § 6–18–514; W. VA. CODE § 18–2C-3.
55 333 F.3d 417 (3d Cir. 2003).
56 617 Fed. Appx. 453 (6th Cir. 2015) [*unpublished*].
57 Estate of Jahn v. Farnsworth, 2017 Mich. App. LEXIS 855 (Mich. Ct. App. May 23, 2017).
58 2005 U.S. Dist. LEXIS 26866 (E.D. Tenn. Oct. 27, 2005).

to smoking marijuana on school property, in violation of a zero tolerance policy and criminal laws. In *Sandusky v. Smith*,[59] a student was assigned to an alternative school for bringing alcohol, which she had dyed green and placed in mouthwash bottles, on a school trip. The court denied her substantive due process claims, because assignment to an alternative school does not deprive a student of her property interest in receiving a public education. And in the following illustrative case, a student who used instant messaging to make threats about committing a school shooting unsuccessfully challenged his suspension and subsequent expulsion on procedural and substantive due process grounds.

⚖️

WYNAR v. DOUGLAS COUNTY SCHOOL DISTRICT
US Court of Appeals for the Ninth Circuit
728 F.3d 1062 (2013)

M. MARGARET MCKEOWN, Circuit Judge

With the advent of the Internet and in the wake of school shootings at Columbine, Santee, Newtown and many others, school administrators face the daunting task of evaluating potential threats of violence and keeping their students safe without impinging on their constitutional rights. It is a feat like tightrope balancing, where an error in judgment can lead to a tragic result. Courts have long dealt with the tension between students' First Amendment rights and "the special characteristics of the school environment." But the challenge for administrators is made all the more difficult because, outside of the official school environment, students are instant messaging, texting, emailing ... and otherwise communicating electronically, sometimes about subjects that threaten the safety of the school environment. At the same time, school officials must take care not to overreact and to take into account the creative juices and often startling writings of the students.

In this case, Landon Wynar, a student at Douglas High School, engaged in a string of increasingly violent and threatening instant messages sent from home to his friends bragging about his weapons, threatening to shoot specific classmates, intimating that he would "take out" other people at a school shooting on a specific date, and invoking the image of the Virginia Tech massacre. His friends were alarmed and notified school authorities, who temporarily expelled Landon based in large part on these instant messages.

We affirm the district court's grant of summary judgment to the school district. The messages presented a real risk of significant disruption to school activities and interfered with the rights of other students. Under the circumstances, the school district did not violate Landon's rights to freedom of expression or due process. ...

II. Procedural Due Process Claim

Under Nevada law, Landon had a property interest in his public education and was therefore entitled to due process before he could be suspended. Landon received adequate due process before both his 10-day suspension and his 90-day expulsion.

A. 10-Day Suspension

The Supreme Court explained in *Goss* that

due process requires, in connection with a suspension of 10 days or less, that the student be given oral or written notice of the charges against him and, if he denies them, an explanation of the evidence the authorities have and an opportunity to present his side of the story.

Landon does not argue that Douglas County did not comply with these requirements. Instead, he complains that the county did not comply with its own regulatory procedures for suspension and that it did not notify Landon's parents before meeting with him at the juvenile detention center.

Before suspending Landon for 10 days, the school administrators who met with him at the

59 2012 U.S. Dist. LEXIS 142225 (W.D. Ky. Oct. 2, 2012).

detention center told him that they had evidence that he had made threats on MySpace and that they wanted to get his side of the story, but Landon asserts that they did not follow exactly the school district's administrative regulations requiring that he be told of the "specific rules, policies, or procedures that are alleged to have been violated" and that, if the evidence supported the allegations, the consequences could include suspension. As the district court noted, "defendants' purported failure to comply with their own administrative procedure does not, itself, constitute a violation of constitutional due process."

The notice Landon received was constitutionally adequate. Neither the Constitution nor the school district's policies require parental notification prior to imposing a 10-day suspension or prior to meeting with a student.

B. 90-Day Expulsion

Although the Constitution does not require that a school give a student "the opportunity to secure counsel, to confront and cross-examine witnesses supporting the charge, [and] to call his own witnesses to verify his version of the incident" before a short suspension, suspensions longer than 10 days or "expulsions for the remainder of the school term, or permanently, may require more formal process." Neither the Supreme Court nor our own circuit has mandated specific procedures for a suspension of 90 days. "Due process is flexible and calls for such procedural protections as the particular situation demands."

In determining whether Landon received adequate due process, we consider Landon's interest in his education at Douglas High School; "the risk of an erroneous deprivation of such interest through the procedures used, and the probable value, if any, of additional or substitute procedural safeguards;" and Douglas County's interest, including the not-insignificant burdens that the additional safeguards would entail. We note that, "administrative proceedings need not cleave to strict state evidentiary rules."

Before his expulsion, Landon received written notice of the charges and a list of possible witnesses. He was given "the right to be represented by an advocate of [his] choosing, including counsel," to present evidence and to call and cross-examine witnesses. Landon argues his due process rights were violated because he was not provided with evidence in advance of the hearing and because no witness testified to any disruption and hence he could not cross-examine on that point.

The additional procedures conceived by Landon were not constitutionally required. To begin, Landon had the key evidence—he acknowledged writing the messages and he had access to them through his MySpace account. As to witnesses on disruption, this is a question of the weight of the evidence, not a due process violation. In any event, *Tinker* does not require actual disruption before a school can impose discipline.

III. Due Process Notice Claim

Landon's notice argument—that his expulsion violated due process because he could not have known that he could be expelled for writing the MySpace messages is without legal support. "Given the school's need to be able to impose disciplinary sanctions for a wide range of unanticipated conduct disruptive of the educational process, the school disciplinary rules need not be as detailed as a criminal code which imposes criminal sanctions."

Apart from common sense, the school's student handbook, which is distributed at the beginning of each year, gave adequate warning to Landon that he could face sanctions for his alarming statements about shooting classmates. The handbook reproduced verbatim the portion of § 392.4655 that the school board found Landon to have violated. In addition, the handbook stated in a separate section that behavior that was "intimidating, harassing, threatening, or disruptive" was subject to disciplinary action. Landon was also on notice that he could face discipline even for certain off-campus actions. Unlike the portion of § 392.4655 dealing with fights, the portion dealing with threats does not contain a geographic limitation. ...

Landon's argument that he could not be expelled because he did not intend to harm or intimidate anyone is equally unpersuasive. Douglas County's correspondence with Landon's parents and the board minutes stated that Landon was being charged with a violation of board policy and an administrative statute without an intent requirement ... In any event, the school was not acting in the role of a government prosecutor enforcing a criminal statute. Douglas County was not required to prove Landon's subjective intent in writing the messages before expelling him. AFFIRMED.

In both *Crawford v. Deer Creek Public School* and *Heyne v. Metro Nashville Public Schools*,[60] the courts found that a school's failure to comply with its own procedural rules does not in itself constitute a Due Process Clause violation.

Proportionality

It is important to remember that due process requirements are not directly related to the seriousness of a student's *misconduct*. Rather, they are determined by the nature and weight of the contemplated *punishment*. As noted earlier, any punishment entailing the deprivation of a public school student's liberty or property interests creates a need for due process. The greater the weight of the contemplated deprivation, the more due process is required. Using a series of short-term suspensions for the same offense is not a permissible way to avoid the more extensive due process required for a long-term suspension.[61]

The courts generally judge the weight of a suspension by its duration, not by the severity of its impact. In *Lamb v. Panhandle Community Unit School District No. 2*,[62] a student was suspended for the last three days of the school year. As a result, he missed final examinations, failed three courses, and could not graduate. The student claimed that he should have been afforded extensive due process because of the great effect the punishment had on his life. The court disagreed, finding that a suspension of three days was short-term regardless of what happened over the course of those three days.[63]

Burden of Proof

Exclusion from school for more than ten days requires **formal notice** of specific charges, the penalty contemplated, and the time and place of the hearing. A notice letter that is misleading or confusing regarding the proposed penalty, particularly when expulsion is involved, may violate due process.[64] The hearing should be conducted by an impartial tribunal, and is often the school board itself.[65] The accused student should have the opportunity to present evidence and refute adverse evidence.[66] A finding of guilt must be based on **substantial evidence** with the district bearing the **burden of proof**. Less demanding than the "beyond a reasonable doubt" standard used in criminal proceedings, **substantial evidence** requires a showing that guilt is more likely than innocence or, as one court put it, "such relevant proof as adequate to support a conclusion of ultimate fact."[67]

The courts have taken inconsistent positions on a number of procedural due process matters when long-term suspension is contemplated, including whether students are entitled to a list of witnesses prior to the hearing,[68] whether anonymous affidavits are permitted,[69] whether students

---

60 228 F. Supp. 3d 1262 (W.D. Okla. 2017) and 655 F.3d 556 (6th Cir. 2011); *see also* Brown v. University of Kansas, 599 F.App'x 833 (10th Cir. 2015).

61 *See* Patrick v. Success Acad. Charter Schs., Inc., 354 F. Supp. 3d 185 (E.D.N.Y. 2018).

62 826 F.2d 526 (7th Cir. 1987).

63 *See also* Keough v. Tate County Bd. of Educ., 748 F.2d 1077 (5th Cir. 1984).

64 Brown v. Bd. of Educ. of Rochester City Sch. Dist., No. 04-CV-6596L, 2005 WL 17838 (W.D.N.Y. Jan. 4, 2005).

65 Sullivan v. Houston Indep. Sch. Dist., 475 F.2d 1071 (5th Cir. 1973), *cert. denied*, 414 U.S. 1032 (1973); *see also* Heyne v. Metro. Nashville Pub. Sch., 655 F.3d 556 (6th Cir. 2011).

66 Dixon v. Ala. State Bd. of Educ., 294 F.2d 150 (5th Cir. 1961).

67 Mandell v. Bd. of Educ., 662 N.Y.S.2d 598 (N.Y. App. Div. 1997); Washington v. Smith, 618 N.E.2d 561 (Ill. App. Ct. 1993).

68 Keough v. Tate County Bd. of Educ., 748 F.2d 1077 (5th Cir. 1984); *followed in* Thoele v. Hamlin, 747 Fed. Appx. 242 (5th Cir. 2019) [*unpublished*]; S.K. v. Anoka-Hennepin Indep. Sch. Dist. No. 11, 399 F. Supp. 2d 963 (D. Minn. 2005); Porter v. Ascension Parish Sch. Bd., 301 F. Supp. 2d 576 (M.D. La. 2004); Robinson v. St. Tammany Parish Pub. Sch., 983 F. Supp. 2d 835 (E.D. La. 2013).

69 Newsome v. Batavia Local Sch. Dist., 842 F.2d 920 (6th Cir. 1988); *followed in* E.K. v. Stamford Bd. of Educ., 557 F. Supp. 2d 272 (D. Conn. 2008); Pomeroy v. Ashburnham Westminster Reg'l Sch. Dist., 410 F. Supp. 2d 7 (D. Mass. 2006); C.Y. v. Lakeview Pub. Schs, 2013 U.S. Dist. LEXIS 66658 (E.D. Mich. 2013).

have a right to cross-examine adverse witnesses,[70] and whether students are entitled to a recording or transcript of the hearing.[71] Given these and other uncertainties, public school officials should provide extensive procedural due process whenever long-term exclusion is contemplated. They should endeavor to apply standardized disciplinary procedures to avoid the appearance of prejudice, to minimize the potential for litigation, and most importantly, to prevent unjust punishments.

The Imposition of Punishment

The **imposition of punishment** is the last phase of student discipline and is in some respects analogous to **sentencing** in the criminal justice system. Severe punishments have the potential to adversely affect students' life prospects, whereas lenient punishments may fail to instruct students as to the severity of their infractions or to deter further wrongdoing. The appropriateness of punishment in particular cases has generated more litigation than other aspects of student discipline.[72] As we have seen, students have challenged the wording of school rules. They have claimed that evidence of their wrongdoing was gathered unlawfully, and that due process protections were not scrupulously observed. Federal and state constitutions and statutes as well as the common law all bear on the authority of school officials to punish students. Lawsuits directly challenging the authority of school officials to impose a particular punishment in response to a particular offense—or to impose any punishments at all—have become more common. And in recent decades, parents have claimed that school disciplinary decisions and curricular offerings violate a substantive due process right to direct the education or upbringing of their children.

Corporal Punishment

State common law and criminal statutes generally prohibit the use of force by one person against another with certain exceptions, including **self-defense** and **defense of others**. Parents and persons standing *in loco parentis* may invoke a **privilege** to use **reasonable force** against the children in their charge for disciplinary purposes.[73] Whether a particular use of force qualifies as "reasonable" depends on the circumstances, including the purposes for which it was used; the age, sex, and level of maturity of the student; the extent of the harm inflicted; and whether it was unnecessarily degrading. The privilege is lost if the force is **excessive**. The privilege can only be invoked to shield a parent or person standing *in loco parentis* from civil or criminal liability. School officials risk losing their licensure—and their jobs—where professional codes of conduct or district policies have categorically prohibited the use of force in general or the use of corporal punishment in particular.

In *Ingraham v. Wright*,[74] a student claimed school officials violated his Eighth Amendment right to be free from cruel and unusual punishment after they paddled him twenty times with a wooden paddle two feet in length, three to four inches wide and one-half inch thick. The Supreme Court

---

70 Bogle-Assegai v. Bloomfield Bd. of Educ., 467 F. Supp. 2d 236 (D. Conn. 2006); B.S. *ex rel.* Schneider v. Bd. of Sch. Trustees, 255 F. Supp. 2d 891 (N.D. Ind. 2003).

71 Jaksa v. Regents of Univ. of Mich., 597 F. Supp. 1245 (E.D. Mich. 1984), *aff'd*, 787 F.2d 590 (6th Cir. 1988).

72 *See* Campbell F. Scribner and Bryan R. Warnick, Discipline, Punishment, And The Moral Community Of Schools (2021).

73 *See* Cynthia Godsoe, *Redefining Parental Rights: The Case of Corporal Punishment*, (October 23, 2018). Brooklyn Law School, Legal Studies Paper No. 575. Available at SSRN: https://ssrn.com/abstract=3271873 (last accessed April 27, 2020).

74 430 U.S. 651 (1977).

rejected this claim, finding that the **Eighth Amendment** applied only in criminal proceedings. In any event, said the Court:

> Public school teachers and administrators are privileged at common law to inflict only such corporal punishment as is reasonably necessary for the proper education of the child; any punishment going beyond the privilege may result in both civil and criminal liability. As long as the schools are open to the public scrutiny, there is no reason to believe that the common-law constraints will not effectively remedy and deter excesses such as those alleged in this case.

The Supreme Court concluded that **procedural due process** under the Fourteenth Amendment did not include notice of charges or a hearing prior to the imposition of corporal punishment in public schools. However, the **substantive due process** protections under the Fourteenth Amendment did apply to students in public schools.

Recall that under the complex concept of **substantive due process**, the State must have adequate justification before depriving individuals of their **life, liberty, or property** interests. Thus students may seek redress for corporal punishment by school officials by claiming that their substantive due process rights under the Fourteenth Amendment have been violated. As the Fifth Circuit explained in *Woodard v. Los Fresnos Independent School District*,[75] "Corporal punishment is a deprivation of substantive due process when it is arbitrary, capricious, or wholly unrelated to the legitimate state goal of maintaining an atmosphere conducive to learning." Such claims are not always successful. In *Serafin v. School of Excellence in Education*,[76] an 18-year-old student who was paddled for leaving the campus of her charter school unsuccessfully claimed her substantive due process rights had been violated. "This Court has already decided that Texas affords adequate remedies for excessive corporal punishment claims such as this," concluded the Fifth Circuit. "Because there are adequate local remedies, Serafin's substantive due process claims must fail as a matter of law."

The State-Created Danger Doctrine

In *DeShaney v. Winnebago County Department of Social Services*,[77] a four-year-old boy was severely injured by his father after the Department of Social Services failed to act on repeated reports of abuse.[78] The Supreme Court held that the State is responsible for protecting individuals from harm by private actors only when (1) they are in the physical custody of the State; or (2) when the State itself created the risk of harm. In the wake of the *DeShaney* decision, the courts held that the "physical custody" requirement is met only in cases in which the State exercises exclusive custodial authority, a "special relationship" applicable to children in juvenile institutions and foster care. Compulsory schooling laws require that parents share custodial authority with school officials for limited periods of time while retaining primary custodial authority.

Thus in *Doe v. Covington County School District*,[79] the Fifth Circuit denied the claims of a nine-year-old student who was sexually assaulted after school officials allowed a complete stranger posing as her father (and other family members) to take her out of school during the school day on multiple occasions. Because the student did not have a "special relationship" with the school,

---

75 Woodard v. Los Fresnos Indep. Sch. Dist., 732 F.2d 1243 (5th Cir. 1984).
76 252 Fed. Appx. 684 (5th Cir. 2007), *cert. denied*, 554 U.S. 922 (2008).
77 489 U.S. 189 (1989); *see also* Town of Castle Rock v. Gonzales, 545 U.S. 748 (2005).
78 *See* LYNN CURRY, THE DESHANEY CASE: CHILD ABUSE, FAMILY RIGHTS, AND THE DILEMMA OF STATE INTERVENTION (2007).
79 675 F.3d 849 (2012).

the court found the district had no constitutional duty to protect her from harm at the hands of a private actor. "Public schools do not take students into custody and hold them there against their will in the same way that a state takes prisoners, involuntarily committed mental health patients, and foster children into its custody," wrote the court. "Without a special relationship, a public school has no constitutional duty to ensure that its students are safe from private violence."

The Due Process Clause does not protect individuals from unjustified deprivations of their liberty and property interests by private actors, but what happens when the State is complicit in harmful actions by private actors? The courts have created the **state-created danger doctrine** to address such situations.[80] To successfully invoke this doctrine in a **substantive due process** claim under the Fourteenth Amendment, plaintiffs must establish that:[81]

(1) the harm ultimately caused was **foreseeable and fairly direct**;
(2) a State agent acted with a degree of culpability that **shocks the conscience**;
(3) a relationship between the State and the plaintiff existed such that the plaintiff was a **foreseeable victim**; and
(4) a State agent affirmatively used his or her authority in a way that **created a danger** to the plaintiff or that rendered the plaintiff **more vulnerable** to danger.

In *Stahl v. East Porter County School Corporation*,[82] the Seventh Circuit denied the state-created danger claims of a student who was bullied by her classmates, finding that school officials had not "instigated, created, or increased the bullying" and that the responses of school officials did not sufficiently "shock the conscience." In *Morrow v. Balaski*,[83] the Third Circuit likewise denied the claims of a bullied student, finding that school officials had not created or enhanced the danger to the student by allowing a suspended bully to return to school following her suspension. However, in the following illustrative case with factual similarities to *Doe v. Covington County School District*,[84] the plaintiffs easily met the "conscience-shocking" standard.

⚖️

L.R. v. SCHOOL DISTRICT OF PHILADELPHIA
US Court of Appeals for the Third Circuit
836 F.3d 235 (2016)

JULIO M. FUENTES, Circuit Judge

Teachers not only educate our children, but also provide them with sources of care and comfort outside the home. Recognizing that the threat of civil liability might discourage teachers and other public servants from taking on such significant roles, courts have developed a doctrine of qualified immunity that, in many instances, shields them from civil lawsuits. But there are exceptions and this is one of those cases. In January 2013, a teacher in the Philadelphia School District allowed a kindergarten student to leave his classroom with an adult who failed to identify herself. The adult sexually assaulted the child later that day. In the early hours of the next morning, a sanitation worker found the child in a playground after hearing her cries. The child's parent sued the teacher, who claims he is immune from suit.

We hold that the parent's allegations sufficiently state a constitutional violation of the young child's clearly established right to be free from exposure

---

80 *See* Erwin Chemerinsky, *The State-Created Danger Doctrine*, 23 Touro Law Review 1–26 (2007).
81 *Citing* Bright v. Westmoreland County, 443 F.3d 276 (3d Cir. 2006).
82 799 F.3d 793 (7th Cir. 2015).
83 719 F.3d 160 (3d Cir. 2013).
84 675 F.3d 849 (2012).

by her teacher to an obvious danger. In short, we conclude that it is shocking to the conscience that a kindergarten teacher would allow a child in his care to leave his classroom with a complete stranger. Accordingly, we will affirm the District Court's denial of qualified immunity. ...

A. Factual Background

Because this case comes to us on a motion to dismiss, the allegations are taken from the complaint and are assumed true for purposes of this appeal. On an ordinary school day in January 2013, Christina Regusters entered W.C. Bryant Elementary School in Philadelphia, Pennsylvania, where Jane was enrolled as a kindergarten student. Regusters proceeded directly to Jane's classroom, where she encountered Defendant Reginald Littlejohn, Jane's teacher. Per Philadelphia School District policy, Littlejohn asked Regusters to produce identification and verification that Jane had permission to leave school. Regusters failed to do so. Despite this failure, Littlejohn allowed Jane to leave his classroom with Regusters. Later that day, Regusters sexually assaulted Jane off school premises, causing her significant physical and emotional injuries.

B. Procedural Background

Jane's parent and natural guardian, L.R., filed this civil rights lawsuit under 42 U.S.C. § 1983 against Reginald Littlejohn in his individual capacity, the School District of Philadelphia, and the School Reform Commission of the School District of Philadelphia (collectively, the "Defendants"). L.R. alleges that Littlejohn deprived Jane of her Fourteenth Amendment rights under a state-created danger theory. Specifically, L.R. alleges that by releasing her daughter to an unidentified adult, Littlejohn created the danger that resulted in Jane's physical and emotional harm. Defendants moved to dismiss under the Federal Rules of Civil Procedure, arguing that the complaint does not allege a constitutional violation and, even if it did, Littlejohn is entitled to qualified immunity.

The District Court denied Defendants' motion. It explained that, "ordinary common sense and experience dictate that there is an inherent risk of harm in releasing a five-year-old [child] to an adult stranger who has failed to produce identification and authorization for release despite being asked to do so." For the reasons that follow, we will affirm.

III. Discussion

The primary purpose of qualified immunity is to shield public officials "from undue interference with their duties and from potentially disabling threats of liability." This immunity can be overcome, however, when public officials violate clearly established constitutional rights of which a reasonable person would have been aware. In the words of the Supreme Court, qualified immunity protects "all but the plainly incompetent or those who knowingly violate the law."

To resolve a claim of qualified immunity, courts engage in a two-pronged inquiry: (1) whether the plaintiff sufficiently alleged the violation of a constitutional right, and (2) whether the right was "clearly established" at the time of the official's conduct. "[W]hether a particular complaint sufficiently alleges a clearly established violation of law cannot be decided in isolation from the facts pleaded." Thus the sufficiency of L.R.'s pleading is both "inextricably intertwined with" and "directly implicated by" Littlejohn's qualified immunity defense.

A. Substantive Due Process Claim under the State-Created Danger Theory

The threshold question in any § 1983 lawsuit is whether the plaintiff has sufficiently alleged a deprivation of a constitutional right. L.R.'s claim invokes the substantive component of the Due Process Clause of the Fourteenth Amendment, which "protects individual liberty against certain government actions regardless of the fairness of the procedures used to implement them." ...

Affirmative Use of Authority Creating or Increasing Danger

We begin with the fourth element, as it is typically the most contested. This element asks whether the state's conduct created or increased the risk of danger to the plaintiff. As we noted in *Bright*,[85] "[i]t is misuse of state authority, rather than a failure to use it, that can violate the Due Process Clause."

This element is often contested because of the inherent difficulty in drawing a line between an affirmative act and a failure to act. Often times there is no clear line to draw; virtually any action may be characterized as a failure to take some alternative action. For example, Defendants attempt to reframe Littlejohn's alleged actions as inactions, or failures. They argue

---

85 Bright v. Westmoreland County, 43 F.3d 276 (3d Cir. 2006).

that Littlejohn's failure to follow School District policy, failure to obtain proper identification from Regusters, and failure to obtain verification from Regusters that Jane had been permitted to leave school are not affirmative acts. This strategy is unavailing.

Rather than approach this inquiry as a choice between an act and an omission, we find it useful to first evaluate the setting or the "status quo" of the environment before the alleged act or omission occurred, and then to ask whether the state actor's exercise of authority resulted in a departure from that status quo. This approach, which is not a new rule or concept but rather a way to think about how to determine whether this element has been satisfied, helps to clarify whether the state actor's conduct "created a danger" or "rendered the citizen more vulnerable to danger than had the state not acted at all."

The setting here is a typical kindergarten classroom. Children in this setting are closely supervised by their teacher. Their freedom of movement is restricted. Indeed, they are not likely to use the bathroom without permission, much less wander unattended from the classroom. In the classroom, the teacher acts as the gatekeeper for very young children who are unable to make reasoned decisions about when and with whom to leave the classroom. Viewed in this light, Jane was safe in her classroom unless and until her teacher, Littlejohn, permitted her to leave. ...

Littlejohn's actions resulted in a drastic change to the classroom status quo, not a maintenance of a situation that was already dangerous. And unlike in Morrow,[86] the presence or absence of a school policy is largely irrelevant to L.R.'s claim. Littlejohn's actions in asking Regusters for proper identification and verification, and then permitting Jane to leave with Regusters despite her failure to produce either, amounted to an affirmative misuse of his authority as Jane's teacher and "gatekeeper."

Defendants contend that there is no constitutional right to have a school official intervene to prevent an unauthorized person from removing a child from school. But this was not just a failure to intervene. Under the facts as pled, Littlejohn had the authority to release Jane from his classroom and used it. By allowing Jane to leave his classroom with an unidentified adult, Littlejohn "created or increased the risk [of harm] itself."

We find clear parallels between this case and our seminal state-created danger case, Kneipp v. Tedder.[87]

There, police officers stopped a couple walking home from a tavern, released the husband first to relieve the babysitter, and then left the visibly intoxicated wife to walk home alone in the cold. Police later discovered the wife unconscious at the bottom of an embankment near her home. She suffered permanent brain damage as a result of her exposure to the cold. We concluded that the officers created a dangerous situation or at least made the intoxicated woman more vulnerable to danger. This was because the officers chose to displace the caretaker of someone who was clearly unable to care for herself. Having taken on responsibility for the woman's wellbeing, the officers thereafter abandoned it and, in so doing, subjected a vulnerable individual to an obvious risk of harm—walking home alone in the cold while highly intoxicated.

The dynamic of a kindergarten classroom is similar. The state is responsible for the safety of very young children unable to care for themselves. Indeed, it is a responsibility the state undertakes when young children are left in its care. When Littlejohn surrendered that responsibility by releasing Jane to an unidentified adult, thereby terminating her access to the school's care, he affirmatively misused his authority just as culpably as the officers in Kneipp misused theirs. ...

Foreseeable and Fairly Direct Harm

Next, we ask whether "the harm ultimately caused was a foreseeable and a fairly direct result of the state's actions." L.R. alleges that Littlejohn "w[as] aware that releasing pupils to unidentified and otherwise unverified adults would result in harm to those pupils, including but not limited to sexual assault." Defendants counter that the complaint is devoid of any facts that support the inference that Littlejohn could have known of Regusters' intent to harm Jane. That is not the appropriate inquiry. Rather, the plaintiff must only "allege an awareness on the part of the state actors that rises to the level of actual knowledge or an awareness of risk that is sufficiently concrete to put the actors on notice of the harm." We think the risk of harm in releasing a five-year-old child to a complete stranger was obvious. ...

Here, it was foreseeable that releasing a young child to a stranger could result in harm to the child. This inherent risk is not only a matter of experience as a teacher in charge of a kindergarten classroom,

86 Morrow v. Balaski, 719 F.3d 160 (3d Cir. 2013) (en banc).
87 95 F.3d 1199 (3d Cir. 1996).

but, as in *Kneipp*, it is also a matter of common sense. Regardless of which of the many apparent risks of harm—whether kidnapping, child pornography, human trafficking, sexual assault or some other violation—came to pass, Littlejohn knew, or should have known, about the risk of his actions. We also conclude that the harm ultimately caused to Jane was a fairly direct result of Littlejohn's conduct. …

Conscience-Shocking Conduct

We next consider whether Littlejohn's actions "shock the conscience." The Supreme Court has emphasized that the "touchstone of due process" is protection against arbitrary government action. Government action is "arbitrary in the constitutional sense" when it is "so egregious, so outrageous, that it may fairly be said to shock the contemporary conscience." The level of culpability required for behavior to shock the conscience largely depends on the context in which the action takes place. In a "hyper-pressurized environment," such as a high-speed police chase, intent to harm is required. But in situations "where deliberation is possible and officials have the time to make 'unhurried judgments,'" deliberate indifference is sufficient." On the facts as pled, the appropriate culpability standard here is deliberate indifference, since there is nothing to indicate that Littlejohn faced circumstances requiring him to make a quick decision. We have defined deliberate indifference as requiring a "conscious disregard of a substantial risk of serious harm." That is, "deliberate indifference might exist without actual knowledge of a risk of harm when the risk is so obvious that it should be known."

As we have already explained, the risk of harm in releasing a five-year-old child to an unidentified, unverified adult is "so obvious" as to rise to the level of deliberate indifference. The fact that there was a school policy in place prohibiting the release of pre-kindergarten through eighth grade students to an adult without proper documentation tends to show that school officials were aware that releasing a young child to a stranger is inherently dangerous. What is more, whether or not that policy existed, the fact that Littlejohn asked Regusters for her identification illustrates that Littlejohn himself was indeed aware of the risk of harm in releasing Jane to a stranger, even if he was unaware of Regusters' specific criminal intent. That he still allowed Jane to leave despite Regusters' failure to produce iden-

tification or verification, we think, rises to conscience-shocking behavior.

To support their contention that Littlejohn's conduct could not shock the conscience, Defendants direct us to *Doe* ex rel. *Magee v. Covington County School District*,[88] a Fifth Circuit case with some factual similarity to this case. In *Doe*, school employees on six separate occasions allowed a nine-year-old student to be checked out from school by a man claiming to be her father but who bore no relationship to her and was not listed on her check-out form. On each occasion, the man sexually assaulted the young student and then returned her to school. The Fifth Circuit concluded that, even assuming it recognized a state-created danger theory (to date it has not officially adopted this doctrine), the allegations failed because the complaint did "not allege that the school knew about an immediate danger to [the student's] safety." By contrast, we are comfortable concluding that Littlejohn's conduct in releasing Jane to an adult who failed to identify herself demonstrated a "conscious disregard of a substantial risk of serious harm."

Foreseeable Victim

The "foreseeable victim" element requires that some sort of relationship exist between the state actor and the plaintiff such that the plaintiff was a foreseeable victim of the state actor's conduct. This element is satisfied easily here. Jane was a member of the discrete class of kindergarten children for whose benefit the School District's release policy had been instituted. In this sense, Jane was a foreseeable victim of Littlejohn's actions. For these reasons, we conclude that L.R. has sufficiently alleged all the elements of a state-created danger claim.

B. Whether the Right Was Clearly Established

Having concluded that L.R. has sufficiently alleged a violation of her daughter's substantive due process rights, we next ask whether the right was clearly established at the time of Littlejohn's actions. We conclude it was. …

In light of the specific allegations in the complaint, however, the right at issue here is an individual's right to not be removed from a safe environment and placed into one in which it is clear that harm is likely to occur, particularly when the individual may, due to youth or other factors, be especially vulnerable to the risk of harm. Framed in this way, and surveying both

88 675 F.3d 849 (5th Cir. 2012) (*en banc*).

our case law and that of our sister circuits, we conclude that this right was clearly established at the time of Littlejohn's actions. Although there is no case that directly mirrors the facts here, as in *Estate of Lagano*,[89] there are sufficiently analogous cases that should have placed a reasonable official in Littlejohn's position on notice that his actions were unlawful.

Our decision in *Kneipp* is key. There, the officers' decision to separate an intoxicated woman from her caretaker at the time, her husband, and the subsequent abandoning of the woman in her vulnerable state, led us to conclude that the officers could be liable for creating or enhancing the danger to which the woman was exposed. Similarly, in *Rivas v. City of Passaic*,[90] we held that emergency medical technicians who told police officers that a man in the midst of a seizure had assaulted them, but failed to tell them about the man's medical condition, could have created or enhanced the danger that ultimately led to his death. We explained that, at the time of the defendants' actions, it was clearly established that "state actors may not abandon a private citizen in a dangerous situation, provided that the state actors are aware of the risk of serious harm and are partly responsible for creating the opportunity for that harm to happen."

Other circuits have come to similar conclusions under analogous circumstances. For example, in *White v. Rochford*,[91] the Seventh Circuit held that police officers who "abandon children and leave them in health-endangering situations after having arrested their custodian and thereby deprived them of adult protection" violate the children's "right to be free from unjustified intrusions upon physical and emotional well-being." There, officers arrested the children's uncle for drag racing, then left the children with the immobilized car on a major highway on a cold evening. The concurring judge explained that arresting the uncle removed the children's only protection against danger, and by not providing any alternative protection, the officers unnecessarily exposed the children to obvious hazards. As the Seventh Circuit later articulated in *Bowers v. DeVito*,[92]

[i]f the state puts a [person] in a position of danger from private persons and then fails to protect him, it will not be heard to say that its role was merely passive; it is as much an active tortfeasor as if it had thrown him into a snake pit.

Similarly, in *Wood v. Ostrander*,[93] the Ninth Circuit held that a police officer who left a female passenger stranded late at night in a high-crime area after arresting the driver violated her constitutional right to personal security. The court explained that "the inherent danger facing a woman left alone at night in an unsafe area is a matter of common sense."

This notion is not limited to circumstances in which police officers abandon private citizens in dangerous situations. In *Currier v. Doran*,[94] the Tenth Circuit held that the plaintiff sufficiently pled a state-created danger claim when state social workers failed to investigate numerous allegations of child abuse and recommended that the children's abusive father assume legal custody. In denying qualified immunity, the court concluded that a reasonable state official at the time would have known that "reckless, conscience shocking conduct that altered the status quo and placed a child at substantial risk of serious, immediate, and proximate harm was unconstitutional." The Tenth Circuit had previously held that the parents of a special education student who committed suicide established a state-created danger claim when school officials sent the student home after he was acting up in school, despite knowing that he was having suicidal thoughts, he had access to firearms in his house, and his parents were not home. Against this backdrop, we conclude that the state of the law in 2013 was sufficiently clear to put Littlejohn on notice that permitting a kindergarten student to leave his classroom with an unidentified adult could lead to a deprivation of that student's substantive due process rights.

IV. *Conclusion*

State-created danger cases often involve unsettling facts and this case is no different. Even so, our resolution of the legal issues is straightforward. Exposing a young child to an obvious danger is the quintessential example of when qualified immunity should not shield a public official from suit. Accordingly, the order of the District Court is affirmed.

89 Estate of Lagano v. Bergen County Prosecutor's Office, 769 F.3d 850 (3d Cir. 2014).
90 365 F.3d 181 (3d Cir. 2004).
91 592 F.2d 381 (7th Cir. 1979).
92 686 F.2d 616 (7th Cir. 1982).
93 879 F.2d 583 (9th Cir. 1989).
94 242 F.3d 905 (10th Cir. 2001).

Unreasonable or Excessive Force

In *Hall v. Tawney*,[95] the Fourth Circuit found that whether or not school officials may be held liable for **unreasonable or excessive force** in violation of a student's substantive due process rights depends on the severity of the injury caused by the punishment, the proportionality of the punishment to the need for it, and whether the punishment was motivated by **malice or sadism** and was **shocking to the conscience**. Other circuits have adopted similar tests for addressing claims that the use of force by school officials violates the substantive due process rights of students,[96] including the four guiding questions developed by the Third Circuit:[97]

(1) Was there a **pedagogical justification** for the use of force?
(2) Was the force utilized **excessive** to meet the **legitimate objective** in this situation?
(3) Was the force applied in **a good-faith effort** to maintain or restore discipline or **maliciously and sadistically** for the very purpose of causing harm?
(4) Was there a **serious injury**?

The question, according to the Sixth Circuit in the following illustrative case, is

> whether the force applied caused injury so **severe**, was so **disproportionate** to the need presented, and was so inspired by **malice or sadism** rather than a merely careless or unwise excess of zeal that it amounted to a **brutal and inhumane abuse of official power** literally **shocking the conscience**.

⚖️

GOHL v. LIVONIA PUBLIC SCHOOL DISTRICT
US Court of Appeals for the Sixth Circuit
836 F.3d 672 (2016), *cert. denied*, 138 S.Ct. 56 (2017)

JEFFREY S. SUTTON, Circuit Judge

Sharon Turbiak, a twelve-year special education veteran, taught a preschool class that required sensitivity to mentally and physically disabled children. The allegations contained in this lawsuit, filed by the mother of one of her students, suggest she had considerable trouble on that score, as do the school district's actions in firing her. The question at hand is whether her conduct also violated the United States Constitution, two federal statutes (the *Americans with Disabilities Act* and the *Rehabilitation Act*), and Michigan law. Because Gohl did not provide sufficient evidence from which a reasonable jury could find in her favor, as the district court concluded in a thorough 39-page opinion granting summary judgment to the defendants, we affirm.

I.

J.G. was born with hydrocephalus, a disorder that causes an unsafe buildup of fluid in the brain. He underwent numerous surgeries to correct or ameliorate the condition. At age three, his mother, Lauren Gohl, enrolled him in the morning session of the Moderate Cognitive Impairment Program at Webster Elementary School, which offered educational and therapeutic services for students like him. His teacher was Sharon Turbiak, a long-time special education teacher. During the school year, Turbiak faced several complaints about her teaching (and her relationship with her colleagues) and one complaint about her teaching of J.G.

In October 2011, a special-needs specialist approached the principal at Webster, Shellie Moore, and passed along some concerns from other

95 Hall v. Tawney, 621 F.2d 607 (4th Cir. 1980).
96 *See* Webb v. McCullough, 828 F.2d 1151 (6th Cir. 1987); Domingo v. Kowalski, 810 F.3d 403, 411 (6th Cir. 2016).
97 *See* Gohl v. Livonia Pub. Sch. Sch. Dist., 836 F.3d 672 (6th Cir. 2016).

staff members about Turbiak's classroom behavior. Moore looked into the issue and over the next few days catalogued concerns about Turbiak. According to Moore, an occupational therapist reported that Turbiak's class was "a very uncomfortable place to work" and that some on Turbiak's team thought she was overly "harsh with [the] children, holding their faces or chins tightly and yelling in their faces."

A speech pathologist thought that Turbiak "used too much force by pushing on children's shoulders," and that the "lower functioning children in the classroom were frustrating to Ms. Turbiak and … were most vulnerable to possible rough treatment." A paraprofessional called Moore in tears, worrying that Turbiak's bad behavior was "escalating." An occupational therapist said that Turbiak was "gruff and abrupt"; that Turbiak once force-fed a gagging and crying student; and that Turbiak "picked up [children] from the floor by one arm and that there was the potential to dislocate a small shoulder." Not one of these incidents, the parties agree, involved J.G.

On the advice of Cynthia DeMan, the Director of Personnel for Livonia Public Schools, Moore met with Turbiak to discuss her teaching. During the meeting, Turbiak admitted that she was "feeling unappreciated at Webster" and that she was "stressed out because of the level of disability of her students and the reduction of support." Turbiak also explained that she was not as "touchy feely" as her co-workers, had high expectations for her students, and "wanted them to make gains while in her classroom." The next morning, even though Moore told Turbiak not to question the members of her team, Turbiak called a meeting to find out who had complained to the administration. This did not help matters. Members of Turbiak's team went to Moore again, telling her about the meeting and adding that they feared retaliation.

The next day, November 2, 2011, Turbiak and her union representative met with DeMan. The meeting focused on Turbiak's strained relations with her colleagues rather than on mistreatment of students. DeMan sent Turbiak home for a few days and followed up with a consultation letter, which explained, at heart, that, if Turbiak was not more professional with staff and students, she would be subject to disciplinary action. The letter urged Turbiak to follow "best practices" and to avoid "laps[ing] into inappropriate behaviors with either staff or students." But the letter did not specifically accuse Turbiak of abusing students.

The meeting helped. For four months, no one reported any mistreatment of students by Turbiak or complained about friction between her and other employees. The peace ended on March 5, 2012, when a social worker, Diane Sloboda, saw Turbiak "grab [J.G.] by the top of his head and jerk it back quite aggressively. She also yelled 'You need to listen' very close to his face." Sloboda told Principal Moore about the incident. Moore called the central office and was instructed to send Turbiak over that afternoon. Turbiak and her union representative met with DeMan and Dorothy Chomicz, a director of human resources. Turbiak denied any "grab[bing]" or "yell[ing]." She said she was using a special education technique called "redirecting" to focus and hold J.G.'s attention after he threw a ring-stacking toy.

Consistent with this technique, she said she put her hand on the back of J.G.'s head "to keep [it] from bouncing around,"—a problem for J.G.—and "[s]poke directly" to him. Chomicz, trained as a special education teacher and familiar with this technique, thought this sounded reasonable and sent Turbiak back to her classroom.

Later in March, one of Turbiak's paraprofessionals, Nancy Respondek, was accused of spanking a student (not J.G.), after which the school investigated the incident and whether Turbiak was behaving "in accordance with [the] guidelines" set forth in DeMan's November consultation letter. After the investigation, the district placed Turbiak and Respondek on administrative leave. Gohl filed this lawsuit on J.G.'s behalf, alleging that Livonia Public Schools, Turbiak, Respondek, Moore, and other members of the school system violated J.G.'s rights under federal and state law. The district court granted summary judgment for the defendants on Gohl's federal claims and declined to exercise supplemental jurisdiction over the state law claims.

II.

On appeal, Gohl claims the district court should have allowed four sets of her claims to go to a jury: (1) the substantive due process claim against Turbiak; (2) the *Americans with Disabilities Act* and *Rehabilitation Act* claims against Livonia Public Schools; (3) the equal protection claims against all defendants; and (4) all of the claims involving municipal liability for Livonia Public Schools.

Our standard of review is not new. We construe the record in Gohl's favor. To fend off summary judgment, Gohl must present evidence that would permit a reasonable jury to find in J.G.'s favor.

(1) **Substantive due process claim**. Gohl maintains that Turbiak violated J.G.'s right to be "free from excessive force under the [Fourteenth] Amendment." She premises the argument on two types of alleged abuse: the March 5 head-grabbing incident and exposure to a psychologically abusive teacher. We address each one separately.

The Due Process Clause of the Fourteenth Amendment protects individuals from the arbitrary actions of government employees, but "only the most egregious official conduct can be said to be arbitrary in the constitutional sense." The question is

whether the force applied caused injury so severe, was so disproportionate to the need presented, and was so inspired by malice or sadism rather than a merely careless or unwise excess of zeal that it amounted to a brutal and inhumane abuse of official power literally shocking the conscience.

Physical abuse. We recently applied the "shocks the conscience" test to allegations just like Gohl's. In *Domingo*,[98] the parents of disabled students challenged a similar use of physical force—a special education teacher's use of the redirection technique that Turbiak used on March 5 with J.G. In rejecting the parents' claim, we adopted the Third Circuit's "useful, though not necessarily exhaustive" analysis of the "shocks the conscience" standard in public schools, asking four guiding questions: (1) "Was there a pedagogical justification for the use of force?" (2) "Was the force utilized excessive to meet the legitimate objective in this situation?" (3) "Was the force applied in a good-faith effort to maintain or restore discipline or maliciously and sadistically for the very purpose of causing harm?" And (4) "Was there a serious injury?" Just as these factors precluded relief as a matter of law in *Domingo*, they preclude relief here.

As to the first consideration—pedagogical justification—Turbiak had one. Unrebutted testimony reflects that Turbiak used an established special education technique, "redirection," to make J.G. pick up a ring-stacking toy he had knocked off a table. Turbiak said so in her meeting with DeMan and Chomicz immediately after the incident. She said so again in her deposition. And Gohl offers no

evidence to refute the claim. Requiring a child to clean up a mess he made not only fits with a common-sense understanding of what teachers typically do, but it also fits with the demands of J.G.'s Individualized Education Program—as provided under the *Individuals with Disabilities Education Act*.[99] Whatever one thinks about the timing or manner in which Turbiak used this technique here, no one can credibly deny that Turbiak had a pedagogical purpose in using it.

As to the second factor—excessiveness—we agree with Gohl that a reasonable jury could conclude that Turbiak used more force than needed. Turbiak's action bothered Sloboda, the only adult witness, enough for Sloboda to report it to the principal. Turbiak denies that she "grabbed" or "yelled," but in a she-said/she-said dispute at summary judgment, our standard of review settles the issue. We view the evidence in the light most favorable to Gohl and thus must accept Sloboda's version of events.

Even then, nothing about that account helps Gohl demonstrate that Turbiak wasn't making "a good-faith effort to maintain or restore discipline"— the third factor. This record does not permit a jury to find that Turbiak was acting "maliciously and sadistically for the very purpose of causing harm." She used an established technique to achieve a legitimate pedagogical goal, and, according to Turbiak's unrebutted testimony, she achieved it. J.G. "willingly picked up the ring stackers" after being redirected.

The last question is whether there was a "serious injury." There was not. Sloboda said she saw Turbiak "letting [J.G.'s] head go. [J.G.] did not appear to be in distress. He gave no scream or cry. When his head returned back down he did not indicate that he was in any—in pain or in discomfort." Nor did any physical injury ever show up. True, in *Domingo* we refused to endorse a "bright-line rule" requiring evidence of physical, rather than psychological, injury. To that end, Gohl, in her deposition testimony, implied that J.G. was psychologically harmed by the head-grabbing incident. But Gohl testified that J.G.'s psychological symptoms began only after he left school for the summer, and there is no evidence in the record suggesting that Turbiak's actions would have caused psychological symptoms with such a delayed onset.

---

98 Domingo v. Kowalski, 810 F.3d 403, 411 (6th Cir. 2016).
99 20 U.S.C. § 1400.

That leaves just one of the four factors favoring Gohl. No doubt this is not a counting exercise, and at any rate the list of factors is not exhaustive. All of this makes comparisons to similar cases helpful—perhaps most helpful. Domingo awarded summary judgment to a special education teacher accused of acts ranging from too-forceful "redirection" of her students to gagging a student and binding him to a gurney. Judge Boggs dissented in part, arguing that the binding and gagging incident presented a genuine issue for a jury. But he agreed—the court was unanimous on this point— that under the circumstances "grabbing [a] student's face, squeezing his or her cheeks, and pointing the student's face" could not have shocked the conscience.

The head-grabbing incident here mirrors the head-grabbing incident in *Domingo* and involves far less illegitimate force than the act of binding a student to a gurney and gagging him. What was true in *Domingo* is true here. While Turbiak's "educational and disciplinary methods ... may have been inappropriate" and "insensitive," they are not "unconstitutional."

The March 5 head-grabbing also is less severe than the incident in *Lillard v. Shelby County Board of Education*,[100] where we affirmed summary judgment in favor of a teacher who slapped a student without a legitimate pedagogical goal. That episode didn't shock the conscience as a matter of law. Neither did this one.

Webb v. McCullough does not lead to a contrary conclusion.[101] In the midst of a class trip to Hawaii, a student locked herself in a hotel bathroom after being told she'd be sent home for drinking, breaking curfew, and having a boy in her room. Her angry chaperone burst through the bathroom door, which struck the student and knocked her to the floor, after which he "grabbed [her] from the floor, threw her against the wall, and slapped her." Because "the record d[id] not demonstrate that the alleged blows ... were in any way disciplinary," those acts were malicious in a way that forceful "redirecting" surely is not. The district court correctly rejected this claim.

Psychological abuse. Gohl also insists that J.G. was psychologically injured by Turbiak's bullying of other students, even if not by the March 5 incident directed at J.G. We disagree for two reasons. First, Gohl has not presented enough evidence for a reasonable jury to conclude that J.G. was injured at all. The only expert authority in support of Gohl's psychological injury theory is the report from Dr. Sharon Hall, which says that behavior like Turbiak's "may" cause students to be psychologically harmed. R. 206-12 at 27-28. But that expert, who is not a psychologist, never examined J.G. And that expert never opined that the possibility of psychological injury ("may" cause an injury) became a reality here (did cause an injury). The only evidence of any effect on J.G. is Gohl's testimony that, starting in the summer after J.G. left Webster Elementary, J.G. began to exhibit "anxiety, opening and closing anything and everything, having things done a certain way or panic, panic ... And still, to this day, he grabs my face to get my attention ... [I]t's a daily thing." That evidence does not suffice for a reasonable jury to find a psychological injury at all, much less a serious injury traceable to Turbiak.

Second, the novelty of Gohl's theory of injury means that she cannot overcome Turbiak's qualified immunity. Government employees are generally shielded from civil liability unless their conduct violates a clearly established constitutional right such that a reasonable official would have known that his conduct was unlawful. The Fourteenth Amendment's right to be free from excessive force may include, we have said, protection from physical force that causes only psychological injury. But we have never said that purely psychological bullying can suffice to shock the conscience. And we certainly have not said so with clarity that "place[s] the ... constitutional question beyond debate." That necessarily means that the right Gohl asserts is not clearly established, making Turbiak eligible for qualified immunity. ...

The appropriate standard of review in this case permits the conclusion that Turbiak was not a good teacher—indeed a poor one. And it explains why the school district fired her. But it does not permit us to draw inferences and conclusions that the record and the law cannot support and inferences that even the plaintiff does not ask us to draw. For these reasons, we affirm.

100 76 F.3d 716 (6th Cir. 1996).
101 828 F.2d 1151 (6th Cir. 1987).

Corporal punishment in schools has been banned in 32 states (plus the District of Columbia).[102] It is permitted in private schools in every state except New Jersey and Iowa. Corporal punishment remains legal in public schools in 19 states,[103] but actively practiced in 15 (as all the school districts in the other four states have banned it).[104] As with Sharon Turbiak in *Gohl*,[105] teachers and other school officials who employ corporal punishment in violation of local district policies may face dismissal, even if their actions are not found to violate the substantive due process rights of students. They may also face civil or even criminal liability for excessive physical punishment resulting in harm. In deciding whether a particular instance of corporal punishment is improper, the courts consider whether local district regulations concerning corporal punishment were followed.[106]

Zero Tolerance Policies

Historically, state legislatures delegated to local school boards, usually in broad and general terms, the authority to maintain discipline and order in the schools.[107] Local school boards remain primarily responsible for the formulation of codes of conduct for students, and local school officials remain primarily responsible for investigating misconduct and imposing punishments. But federal and state statutes have played a significant role in shaping the disciplinary landscape of public schools in recent decades. **Safe School Acts**, for example, empower school officials to investigate criminal activity on school property while at the same time imposing liability for **negligent indifference** should the officials fail to report any such activity to law enforcement. In *Cuesta v. School Board of Miami-Dade County*,[108] the plaintiff was one of nine students involved in producing and distributing a pamphlet containing racist attacks and depictions of violence against the principal, who reported the matter to the police. The plaintiff alleged that both her arrest and a subsequent strip search by police were unconstitutional. The Eleventh Circuit found school officials could not be held liable for the actions of law enforcement officers acting on reports of criminal behavior filed in accordance with state law.

High profile school shootings, including those at Columbine High School in Littleton, Colorado in 1999; Sandy Hook Elementary School in Newtown, Connecticut in 2012; Margery Stoneman Douglas High School in Parkland, Florida, Santa Fe High School in Santa Fe, New Mexico in 2018, and Saugus High School in Santa Clarita, California in 2019 have led to repeated crackdowns on **violence** and **threats of violence, weapons, gang activity, drugs, tobacco and alcohol**, and **bullying** in schools. **Zero tolerance policies** and enhanced criminal penalties in a number of states have tended to limit the discretion of school officials to assess guilt and assign punishments in such cases because long-term suspension or expulsion is required.

Many students suspended or expelled from public schools for violating zero tolerance policies have challenged the constitutionality of their punishments, arguing that their procedural due

---

102 Alaska, California, Connecticut, Delaware, District of Columbia, Hawaii, Illinois, Iowa, Maine, Maryland, Massachusetts, Michigan, Minnesota, Montana, Nebraska, Nevada, New Hampshire, New Jersey, New Mexico, New York, North Carolina, North Dakota, Ohio, Oregon, Pennsylvania, Rhode Island, South Dakota, Utah, Vermont, Virginia, Washington, West Virginia, and Wisconsin.

103 Alabama, Arkansas, Florida, Georgia, Idaho, Indiana, Kansas, Kentucky, Louisiana, Mississippi, Missouri, Oklahoma, South Carolina, Tennessee, and Texas.

104 Arizona, Colorado, North Carolina, and Wyoming.

105 836 F.3d 672 (6th Cir. 2016), *cert. denied*, 138 S. Ct. 56 (2017).

106 P.B. v. Koch, 96 F.3d 1298 (9th Cir. 1996); Thompson v. Iberville Parish Sch. Bd., 372 So. 2d 642 (La. Ct. App. 1979); B.L. v. Dep't of Health & Rehabilitative Serv., 545 So. 2d 289 (Fla. Dist. Ct. App. 1989); People v. Wehmeyer, 509 N.E.2d 605 (Ill. App. Ct. 1987); Rolando v. Sch. Dir. of Dist. No. 125, County of LaSalle, 358 N.E.2d 945 (Ill. App. Ct. 1976); Calway v. Williamson, 36 A.2d 377 (Conn. 1944).

107 *See, e.g.*, N.Y. EDUC. CODE § 3214.3-a.

108 285 F.3d 962 (11th Cir. 2002).

process rights under the Fifth Amendment or their **substantive due process** rights under the Fourteenth Amendment were violated. As we saw earlier in this chapter in a series of cases including *Wynar v. Douglas County School District*,[109] these kinds of challenges are rarely successful, particularly when students are punished for threatening or engaging in school violence.

In order to succeed in a substantive due process challenge to a mandatory punishment under a zero tolerance policy, students must demonstrate (a) that their punishment constituted a **deprivation of a liberty or property interest**; and (b) that their punishment bore **no rational relationship to the offense** or the **educational mission of the school**. Thus, in *Vann v. Stewart*,[110] a tenth-grade student unsuccessfully challenged his one-year suspension on due process grounds for bringing a pocket knife to school and threatening a former girlfriend with it. Wrote the court:

> [We] cannot conclude that the punishment imposed by school officials in this case bore no rational relationship to plaintiff's offense. State authorities have expressed a legitimate interest in maintaining "safe and secure learning environments." In an effort to comply with state law adopted pursuant to that interest, local officials adopted a zero tolerance policy that includes a one-year suspension for violations. [The student] admits that he possessed a pocketknife in violation of the local policy and that he was aware he could receive a one-year suspension.

In *Bundick v. Bay City Independent School District*,[111] a student unsuccessfully challenged his suspension and subsequent expulsion on substantive due process grounds after a machete was found in a toolbox in his truck. He claimed, among other things, that he was unreasonably denied a right to participate in extracurricular activities and his class graduation. "Despite his suspension and subsequent expulsion, Bundick's education continued. In fact, he completed his studies by the end of the school year, earned sufficient credits to graduate and received his diploma," wrote the court. "Accordingly, Bundick cannot complain of being deprived of [his property interest in receiving] a basic education."

In *Price v. New York City Board of Education*,[112] students claimed that a school rule banning the possession (as opposed to the *use*) of cell phones on school property was unreasonable, but the court concluded that the rule had a rational basis related to the educational mission of the school: "Any enforcement system focusing on use, rather than possession, requires teachers … to observe and enforce the ban and become involved in confronting students and punishment decisions, in detriment of their pedagogical mission."

Suspensions or expulsions **under zero tolerance policies** may be vulnerable to substantive due process challenges if the language of the policy is unclear or if the policy is applied in an arbitrary manner.[113] But again, successful challenges are rare. In *James P. v. Lemahieu*,[114] a student found to be inebriated at a school luau successfully challenged his suspension under a zero tolerance policy that prohibited the *possession* of alcohol: "Robert was guilty of being intoxicated at a school function, which is not covered by the statute unless 'possession' is interpreted to include 'present in the body'," wrote the court. "This is an unlikely interpretation, especially since the context of the provision prohibits the possession of other tangible items, such as knives and weapons—items which cannot be consumed." In *Colvin v. Lowndes County, Mississippi School District*,[115] a district court overturned the one-year suspension of a sixth-grade student with a disability for possession

---

109 728 F.3d 1062 (9th Cir. 2013).
110 445 F. Supp. 2d 882 (E.D. Tenn. 2006).
111 140 F. Supp. 2d 735 (S.D. Tex. 2001).
112 837 N.Y.S. 2d 507 (Sup. 2007); *aff'd* 855 N.Y.S.2d 530 (N.Y. 1st A.D. 2008).
113 *See* Seal v. Morgan, 229 F.3d 567 (6th Cir. 2000); J.M. v. Webster County Bd. of Educ., 534 S.E.2d 50 (W. Va. 2000).
114 84 F. Supp. 2d 1113 (D. Haw. 2000).
115 114 F. Supp. 2d 504 (N.D. Miss. 2000).

of a small knife. The court found that rigid adherence to the zero tolerance policy without con-sideration of the individual circumstances of the case was arbitrary, in violation of the student's substantive due process rights. "Individualized punishment by reference to all relevant facts and circumstances regarding the offense and the offender is a hallmark of our criminal justice system," wrote the court.

Zero tolerance policies trace their origins to the "War on Drugs" launched by the Nixon Administration in 1971. In the 1980s, the George H.W. Bush Administration funded a national anti-drug media campaign aimed specifically at young people and, by 1989, school districts in California and New York had implemented policies mandating automatic expulsion for any student found in possession of drugs on school property. In the 1990s, zero tolerance policies were adopted by school districts nationwide, applying to possession and use of drugs, along with tobacco and alcohol. As previously noted, after the Clinton Administration passed the **Gun-Free Schools Act of 1994**, students found in possession of firearms and other weapons on school property were subject to mandatory expulsion. By the end of the 1990s, 94 percent of all schools had implemented zero tolerance policies for weapons and firearms, 87 percent for alcohol, and 79 percent for tobacco.[116] Many states authorized school districts to employ police officers and other specialized security personnel to assist with maintaining order and discipline. The authorizing statutes vary significantly from state to state as to the circumstances and con-ditions under which **School Resource Officers** (SROs) may be employed, their legal status, the extent of their law enforcement authority, and whether they may carry weapons.[117] In 2014, 46 percent of high schools, 42 percent of middle schools, and 18 percent of elementary schools nationwide reported having at least one law enforcement officer on site, with higher rates in urban schools.[118]

Zero tolerance policies have two related characteristics that have made them the subject of withering criticism by legal scholars. First, zero tolerance policies require students to be punished even when they did not knowingly or intentionally bring drugs or weapons or other contraband onto school property. Second, zero tolerance policies do not allow school officials to exercise discretion to modify statutory punishments in light of the circumstances, including the age, disci-plinary history, and intent of the student.

Yet mandatory suspensions and expulsions under zero tolerance policies have been routinely upheld by the courts, despite reservations occasionally expressed by some members of the judiciary. In *Safford Unified School District No. 1 v. Redding*,[119] the Supreme Court case involving a middle school student who was subjected to a strip search by school officials looking for Ibuprofen tablets pursuant to a zero tolerance policy, Justice Clarence Thomas lamented the resulting decline in the exercise of discretionary *in loco parentis* authority:

> For example, one community questioned a school policy that resulted in "an 11-year-old [being] arrested, handcuffed and taken to jail for bringing a plastic butter knife to school." In another, "[a]t least one school board member was outraged" when 14 elementary-school students were suspended for "imitating drug activity" after they combined Kool-Aid and sugar in plastic bags. Individuals within yet another

---

116 David M. Pedersen, *Zero-Tolerance Policies*, in School Violence: From Discipline To Due Process 48 (James C. Hanks ed., 2004); *see also* Catherine Y. Kim, Daniel J. Losen & Damon T. Hewitt, The School-To-Prison Pipe-line: Structuring Legal Reform 79 (2010).

117 *See* 24 P.S. § 7–778; NEV. REV. STAT. ANN. § 280.287; TEX. EDUC. CODE § 37.081; O.C.G.A. § 20–8-5.

118 A. Karteron, *Arrested Development: Rethinking Fourth Amendment Standards for Seizures and Uses of Force in Schools*, 18 Nev. L.J. 863 at 872 (2018), *citing* E. Blad & A. Harwin, *Black Students More Likely to Be Arrested at School*, Education Week (Jan. 24, 2017). Online at www.edweek.org/ew/articles/2017/01/25/black-students-more-likely-to-be-arrested. html (last accessed April 27, 2020).

119 557 U.S. 364 (2009).

school district protested a "zero-tolerance" policy toward weapons that had become "so rigid that it force[d] schools to expel any student who belongs to a military organization, a drum-and-bugle corps or any other legitimate extracurricular group and is simply transporting what amounts to harmless props."

"Students have challenged zero tolerance as a violation of due process, but even in [extreme] cases ..., lower courts consistently conclude that the Constitution provides no meaningful check on these policies," notes legal scholar Derek W. Black. "[They] have been so consistently emphatic in their position that scholars and advocates have all but conceded the constitutionality of zero tolerance."[120] The following illustrative case from the Sixth Circuit remains both a touchstone and a cautionary tale—a rare example of a successful substantive due process challenge by a student who unwittingly violated a zero tolerance policy.

⚖️

SEAL v. MORGAN
US Court of Appeals for the Sixth Circuit
229 F.3d 567 (2000)[121]

RONALD LEE GILMAN, Circuit Judge.

In this action brought pursuant to 42 U.S.C. § 1983, Dustin Wayne Seal seeks monetary damages to compensate him for the Knox County Board of Education's 1996 decision to expel him from high school after a friend's knife was found in the glove compartment of Seal's car. Seal, who denied any knowledge of the knife's presence in the car while it was on school property, argues that the Board's action was irrational and violated his right to due process of law. ...

I. Factual Background

In the fall of 1996, Seal was a junior at Powell High School in Knox County, Tennessee. On October 30, 1996, a friend of Seal's named Ray Pritchert, who was also a student at Powell High, became embroiled in an out-of-school dispute with another Powell High student who had begun dating Pritchert's ex-girlfriend. As a result, Pritchert started carrying around a hunting knife. The knife had a three-and-one-half inch blade and bore the inscription "Ray loves Jennie" (apparently Pritchert's ex-girlfriend). Seal knew that Pritchert had the knife, because Pritchert showed it to him that day. The next night, Seal went to pick up

his girlfriend at her house, accompanied by Pritchert and another friend, David Richardson. Seal was driving his mother's car, because his own was not working. Pritchert, still carrying the knife, placed it on the floorboard of the car behind the driver's seat where Seal was sitting. When they arrived at the girlfriend's house, Seal went in to get her. Richardson, still in the car, placed the knife in the car's glove compartment. Whether Seal actually saw the knife when it was on the car's floorboard, or at any other point when the knife was in his mother's car, is not entirely clear from the record. It is, however, uncontroverted that Seal knew that Pritchert had been carrying a knife around, and that Pritchert had the knife on his person when he was in the car on October 31, 1996.

The following night was Friday, November 1, 1996. Seal, again driving his mother's car, drove his girlfriend and Pritchert to Powell High. All three were members of the Powell High band, and the Powell High football team had a game scheduled that night. The three had worn their band uniforms, but were informed after entering the school that they would not be required to wear their uniforms that night. They then returned to the car, which Seal had parked in the Powell High parking lot, so that they could put on the clothes they had planned to wear after

120 Derek W. Black, *The Constitutional Limit of Zero Tolerance in Schools*, 99 MINN. L. REV. 823 at 825, 826 (2015), *citing* Eric Blumenson & Eva S. Nilsen, *One Strike and You're Out? Constitutional Constraints on Zero Tolerance in Public Education*, 81 WASH. U. L.Q. 65, 108 (2003) and Aaron Sussman, *Learning in Lockdown: School Police, Race, and the Limits of Law*, 59 UCLA L. REV. 788, 831–835 (2012); *see also* DEREK W. BLACK, ENDING ZERO TOLERANCE: THE CRISIS OF ABSOLUTE SCHOOL DISCIPLINE (2016).

121 *Rehearing* en banc *denied*, 2000 U.S. App. LEXIS 34067 (6th Cir. 2000).

changing out of their band uniforms. After changing, Seal and Pritchert went back into the school building. There, the band director, Gregory Roach, pulled Pritchert aside and asked him if he and Seal had been drinking. Pritchert said that they had not. Roach let Seal and Pritchert enter the band room, because he did not smell alcohol on Pritchert's breath.

About fifteen minutes later, Roach summoned Seal and Pritchert to his office. There they were joined by Charles Mashburn, the vice-principal of Powell High. Mashburn announced that four students had reported seeing the two of them drinking alcohol. Although Mashburn searched both Seal's and Pritchert's coats and instrument cases, he found no evidence to suggest that either student had been drinking or possessed alcoholic beverages. Mashburn then announced that he needed to search Seal's car for a flask, because one of the assistant band directors said he saw either Seal or Pritchert with a flask, with both students chewing gum and checking the other's breath. Seal consented to the search. Mashburn did not find a flask. He did, however, find two cigarettes in a crumpled pack in the back of the car, a bottle of amoxicillin pills (an antibiotic for which Seal had a prescription) in the console, and Pritchert's knife in the glove compartment.

Mashburn subsequently had Seal accompany him to his office, where he directed Seal to write out a statement about what had just occurred. Seal asked Mashburn what he should write in the statement, and Mashburn replied that Seal should explain why the knife was in the glove compartment. Seal's entire statement reads as follows:

Went to Roach's office because he thought or had been told that we had a flask and had been drinking, so we went and Mr. Mashburn searched the car. He found a knife and 2 cigs. The knife was there because Ray's ex-girlfriend's boyfriend had been following us around with a few of his friends so we were a little uneasy.

Mashburn then prepared a form Notice of Disciplinary Hearing for Long-Term Suspension From School, charging Seal with possession of a knife, possession of tobacco, and possession of "pills." On November 6, 1996, Powell High's principal, Vicki Dunaway, conducted a disciplinary hearing. After hearing from both Seal and Mashburn, she suspended Seal pending expulsion for possession of a knife. It does not appear from the record that she took any action against Seal for his possession of the two cigarettes or the antibiotic pills. Seal appealed, and on November 14, 1996, Jimmie Thacker, Jr., the

Board of Education's disciplinary hearing authority, conducted an appeal hearing.

Seal attended this hearing, as did his parents, his girlfriend, Principal Dunaway, and David Richardson (the student who had placed the knife in the glove compartment of the car belonging to Seal's mother). At the hearing, Seal testified that he knew that Pritchert had had the knife on his person on October 31, 1996, at a time when Seal was driving Pritchert around in his mother's car, but that he had no idea that the knife was in his car on November 1, or at any other time when the car was on school property. Richardson testified that Seal had not been in his mother's car when Richardson put Pritchert's knife in the glove compartment, and that as far as Richardson could tell, Seal did not know that the knife was there. Seal's girlfriend also testified that as far as she knew, Seal did not know the knife was in the glove compartment of his mother's car.

On November 18, 1996, Thacker notified Seal's mother by letter that he had decided to uphold Principal Dunaway's decision to suspend Seal pending expulsion by the Board. In pertinent part, the letter read as follows:

Testimony and written statements presented during the hearing place the knife in the glove compartment of the car your son was driving and which he parked on the campus of Powell High School. Possession of a weapon on school property is a violation of Knox County Policy JCCC; therefore, I am upholding the principal's decision to suspend Dustin pending expulsion by the board of education.

The next day, Seal's mother telephoned school authorities to indicate that she and Seal wanted to appeal Thacker's decision to the Board. On November 22, 1996, Thacker notified Seal's mother by certified mail that the Board would consider the appeal of Seal's discipline for "possession of a weapon on school campus" at its next meeting.

The Board heard Seal's appeal on December 4, 1996. Seal was represented by counsel, who forcefully argued that Seal had no idea that the knife was in his mother's car either on November 1, 1996, or at any other time that the car was on school property. Board member Sam Anderson responded:

My concern was because the … in our record it shows possession of a knife, possession of tobacco, possession of pills. You know, it doesn't just signify a weapon. And … you know … and either [sic] of the three are justification …

Anderson then asked Seal whether he had ever seen the knife in his car. Seal said that he had not. He admitted that he knew that Pritchert had the knife the day before November 1, 1996—off school property—but insisted that he thought Pritchert had simply taken it with him, and that it had not been left in his mother's car. Anderson then explained that

the problem I see is that we always have to be consistent in sending a clear message to students. Two or three years ago we were dealing with guns, guns, guns. Now, it's down to knives, knives, knives and I don't want to send a confusing message. Justin [sic], you are responsible for what's in your car and that's where I'm torn but I would have to say that you have to be held responsible as a driver for what's in your car. And that's a problem that you're going to have to deal with.

At another Board member's suggestion, the Board then voted unanimously to rule on the appeal based on the record from the hearings conducted before Principal Dunaway and Disciplinary Hearing Authority Thacker. Anderson then made a motion to uphold Thacker's recommendation to expel Seal, which was approved unanimously. The entire transcript of the Board's proceedings as it relates to Seal spans three pages. In contrast, the transcript of the hearing conducted by Thacker is over fifty pages long.

In pertinent part, the Knox County Board of Education policy pursuant to which Seal was expelled provides that students may not "possess, handle, transmit, use or attempt to use any dangerous weapon [including knives] in school buildings or on school grounds at any time" and that students who are found to have violated the policy "shall be subject to suspension and/or expulsion of not less than one ... year." The policy also provides that the Superintendent "shall have the authority to modify this suspension requirement on a case-by-case basis," although Superintendent Morgan has argued that it is "not clear" whether he has the power to modify a suspension or expulsion once it has been finally approved by the Board.

Generally, Tennessee law delegates to its local boards of education broad authority to formulate rules for student conduct and to prescribe appropriate remedies for the violation of those rules. Before the 1996–1997 school year, however, the Tennessee legislature directed each of its local school boards to develop and adopt, and to file annually with the state commissioner of education, written policies and procedures that would "impose swift, certain and severe disciplinary sanctions on any student" who, among other things, "brings a ... dangerous weapon" onto school property, or "possesses a dangerous weapon" on school property. Specifically, the legislature encouraged "each local and county board of education ... to include within such policies and procedures a zero tolerance policy toward any student who engages in such misconduct." ...

III. Analysis

A. The Board

There is no abstract federal constitutional right to process for process's sake. Rather, the Fourteenth Amendment provides that one may not be deprived of life, liberty, or property without due process of law. State law determines what constitutes "property" for due process purposes. It is undisputed that Seal enjoyed a property interest in his public high school education under Tennessee law. Tennessee not only provides its citizens with the right to a free public education, but [also] requires them to attend school through the age of eighteen.

Due process has two components. The first, procedural due process (often summarized as "notice and an opportunity to be heard") is a right to a fair procedure or set of procedures before one can be deprived of property by the state. Even when it is clear that one is entitled to due process, "the question remains what process is due." The answer to the question of what process is due "depends on appropriate accommodation of the competing interests involved." In the context of disciplining public school students, the student's interest is "to avoid unfair or mistaken exclusion from the educational process, with all of its unfortunate consequences." Schools, of course, have an unquestionably powerful interest in maintaining the safety of their campuses and preserving their ability to pursue their educational mission.

The district court rejected Seal's claim that he was denied procedural due process, concluding that he had received all of the process that he was due. Even though Seal, in his brief on appeal, asserts that he was "owed both the substantive and procedural components of the due process law and was denied such," he does not really argue that the Board used unfair procedures before expelling him. Rather, his complaint is with the substantive result—the ultimate decision to expel him. His argument is thus one of substantive due process, the other component of due process. In essence, Seal argues that the Board's ultimate decision was irrational in light of the facts uncovered by the procedures afforded him.

The Due Process Clause provides "heightened protection against government interference with certain fundamental rights and liberty interests." Government actions that burden the exercise of those fundamental rights or liberty interests are subject to strict scrutiny, and will be upheld only when they are narrowly tailored to a compelling governmental interest. The list of fundamental rights and liberty interests … is short, and the Supreme Court has expressed very little interest in expanding it. In fact, the Supreme Court has held explicitly that the right to attend public school is not a fundamental right for the purposes of due process analysis.

The Supreme Court has also recognized the uniquely destructive potential of overextending substantive due process protection. Indeed, the Court has specifically cautioned that, "judicial interposition in the operation of the public school system of the Nation raises problems requiring care and restraint," and that, "by and large, public education in our nation is committed to the control of state and local authorities."

Government actions that do not affect fundamental rights or liberty interests and do not involve suspect classifications will be upheld if it they are rationally related to a legitimate state interest. In the context of school discipline, a substantive due process claim will succeed only in the "rare case" when there is "no 'rational relationship between the punishment and the offense.'"

That said, suspending or expelling a student for weapons possession, even if the student did not knowingly possess any weapon, would not be rationally related to any legitimate state interest. No student can use a weapon to injure another person, to disrupt school operations, or, for that matter, any other purpose if the student is totally unaware of its presence. Indeed, the entire concept of possession—in the sense of possession for which the state can legitimately prescribe and mete out punishment—ordinarily implies knowing or conscious possession.

We would have thought this principle so obvious that it would go without saying. The Board, however, devotes a great deal of the discussion in its briefs to arguing that "*scienter*" is not required by its "Zero Tolerance Policy," and that the criminal law requirement that possession of a forbidden object be knowing or conscious possession is a "technicality" that should not be "transported into school suspension cases." Frankly, we find it difficult to understand how one can argue that the requirement of conscious possession is a "technicality."

We asked counsel at oral argument whether the Board was seriously arguing that it could expel a student for unconsciously possessing a dangerous weapon, posing a hypothetical example involving a high school valedictorian who has a knife planted in his backpack without his knowledge by a vindictive student. The question was whether the valedictorian would still be subject to mandatory expulsion under the Board's Zero Tolerance Policy, even if the school administrators and the Board members uniformly believed the valedictorian's explanation that the knife had been planted.

Counsel for the Board answered yes. After all, counsel argued, the Board's policy requires "Zero Tolerance," and the policy does not explicitly say that the student must know he is carrying a weapon. Only after the Board's counsel sensed—correctly—that this answer was very difficult to accept did counsel backtrack, suggesting that perhaps an exception could be made for our unfortunate hypothetical valedictorian. We find it impossible to take this suggestion seriously, however, and not simply because counsel had just finished arguing the opposite. The suggestion is totally inconsistent with the Board's position in this case, which is that the Zero Tolerance Policy uniformly requires expulsion whenever its terms are violated. …

The Board is, of course, correct when it observes that this is not a criminal case, and that its decision to expel Seal is not vulnerable to a substantive due process attack unless it is irrational. We believe, however, that the Board's Zero Tolerance Policy would surely be irrational if it subjects to punishment students who did not knowingly or consciously possess a weapon. The hypothetical case involving the planted knife is but one illustration of why.

Another example would be a student who surreptitiously spikes the punch bowl at a school dance with grain alcohol, with several students, none of whom having any reason to know that alcohol has been added to the punch, taking a drink. Suppose that the school has a code of conduct that mandates suspension or expulsion for any student who possesses or consumes alcohol on school property, but does not specifically provide that the alcohol must be knowingly possessed or consumed. Under the Board's reasoning, the student who spiked the punch bowl would of course be subject to suspension or expulsion, but so would any of the students who innocently drank from the punch bowl, even if the school board was completely convinced that the students had no idea that alcohol had been added to the punch. Suspending the students who drank from the punch bowl, not realizing that alcohol had been added, would not rationally advance the school's legitimate interest in preventing underage students from drinking alcohol on school premises any more than suspending a handful of students chosen at random from the school's directory.

A student who knowingly possesses a weapon and is caught with it can, of course, be lying when he or she claims not to have known of its existence. Simply because a student may lie about what he knew, however, does not mean that it is unnecessary to address the question of what he knew before meting out punishment. The Board, for its part, freely concedes that "the record does not reflect what the Board did or did not consider with respect to [Seal's] knowledge," but argues that "in the absence of findings of fact [by the Board], it ought not be concluded that the Board failed to consider [Seal's] knowledge."

Well, why not? The Board's attorney has insisted that Seal's knowledge was completely irrelevant, and that the Board's Zero Tolerance Policy required Seal's expulsion regardless of whether he knew the knife was in his car. At the Board meeting during which the Board voted to expel Seal, Board Member Sam Anderson, who as far as can be determined from the record is the only person having anything to do with the decision to expel Seal who even considered the question of what Seal did or did not know, suggested that it would send a "confusing message" to do anything besides expel Seal, regardless of whether Seal had any idea that the knife was in his car. Then again, he also apparently thought that Seal could have been expelled just as easily for having a prescription antibiotic in his car.

In the case before us, we must remember that it was the Board, not Seal, that moved for summary judgment. As the non-moving party, Seal was entitled to have all reasonable inferences drawn in his favor. The absence of any evidence about what the Board concluded regarding Seal's knowledge is exactly why the Board is not entitled to summary judgment. …

Similarly, the record provides no clue as to how the Board viewed Seal's written statement to Vice-Principal Mashburn on the night in question. Was it a confession … or was it an after-the-fact deduction (as Seal insists) by Seal about how and when the knife must have gotten into the glove compartment. The dissent apparently concludes that the Board could rationally have decided that the statement was a confession, even though there is absolutely no indication in the record that this is what the Board actually decided.

We also find ourselves unable to take much comfort in the Board's frequent reminders in its brief and at oral argument that it afforded Seal a number of hearings, expending a significant amount of time in the process, before expelling him. Indeed, one could just as easily view this case as a challenge to the Board's procedures, the obvious defect in which is that they make no attempt to separate out students who knowingly possessed a weapon on school property from those who did not. Based on the evidence of record, it appears that nothing that Seal could have said at any of those hearings would have made one bit of difference. Because there was no dispute that the knife was in Seal's car when on school property, the Board insists that it was required under its Zero Tolerance Policy to expel Seal, whether or not he had any idea that the knife was in his car. We are prepared to take the Board at its word.

A school board can, of course, disbelieve the student's explanation and conclude that the student knowingly violated school policies. If that occurs, due process would be satisfied as long as the procedures afforded the student were constitutionally adequate and the conclusion was rational. The Board argues that the district court "erred by substituting its own view of the facts for that of the Hearing Officer and the Board of Education." Again, this begs the question—which nothing in the record answers—of what the views of the hearing officer and the Board were. Did the Board expel him because it disbelieved Seal's explanation, did it expel him despite believing his explanation completely, or did it expel him without deciding the issue, in the belief that Seal's knowledge was simply irrelevant to the decision? Of these possibilities, the first one would have been permissible if rationally supported by the record, but the other two would not have been.

It may be correct, as the Board argues, that as a matter of "state law, case law or its own rules," the Board is not required to make formal findings of fact in expulsion cases. As a matter of federal constitutional law, however, the Board may not expel students from school arbitrarily or irrationally. To accept the Board's argument would be to allow it to effectively insulate itself even from rational basis review, as long as the decision the Board reached might have been rational. What is at issue in the present case, however, is not whether the Board could have made a decision that would have been rationally related to a legitimate state purpose, but whether it actually did so.

The fact that we must defer to the Board's rational decisions in school discipline cases does not mean that we must, or should, rationalize away its irrational decisions. And when it is not clear that the Board's decision was rational, because it is impossible to conscientiously determine from the record what the

Board's actual decision was, then the Board, as well as other school boards with similar "Zero Tolerance" policies, should not be entitled to summary judgment in civil rights actions arising from their decisions to impose long-term suspensions and expulsions.

On the basis of the record presented, a reasonable trier of fact could conclude that Seal was expelled for a reason that would have to be considered irrational. We therefore conclude that the district court correctly denied the Board's motion for summary judgment.

The district court, however, did more than deny the Board's motion for summary judgment. By ordering that the case "proceed to trial by jury ... only to determine the amount of damages to be awarded" to Seal, the district court effectively entered summary judgment against the Board on the issue of liability. It did this even though Seal had not moved for summary judgment.

In appropriate circumstances, we acknowledge that a district court may enter summary judgment against the moving party in the absence of a cross-motion. In the present case, however, we do not believe that this disposition was appropriate.

As noted above, one cannot determine conclusively from the record in its present state why Seal was expelled. We do not believe that a reasonable fact-finder would be compelled to find that the Board expelled him for an irrational reason, i.e., without making any determination of whether Seal consciously possessed the knife, or despite believing Seal's explanation that he did not. The Board might conceivably be able to show that it expelled Seal for a reason that would have to be accepted as rational. Accordingly, we will affirm the judgment of the district court to the extent that it denied the Board's motion for summary judgment, reverse the judgment of the district court to the extent that it entered summary judgment against the Board on the issue of liability, and remand the case for further proceedings. ...

B. Superintendent Morgan

The doctrine of qualified immunity generally shields government officials from civil liability for performing discretionary functions "insofar as their conduct does not violate clearly established statutory or constitutional rights of which a reasonable person would have known." In determining whether an official is entitled to qualified immunity, "the contours of the right must be sufficiently clear that a reasonable official would understand that what he is doing violates that right."

As an abstract matter, the right of public school students not to be expelled arbitrarily or irrationally has been clearly established since at least the Supreme Court's decision in *Goss v. Lopez*,[122] which held that long-term suspensions and expulsions must comport with minimal standards of due process. More concretely, however, we do not believe that the contours of that right were sufficiently clear to put a reasonable school superintendent on notice in 1996 that a school disciplinary policy's lack of a conscious-possession requirement could produce irrational expulsions and thus violate the legal rights of students expelled under the policy. For this reason, we will reverse the judgment of the district court to the extent that it denied Superintendent Morgan's motion for summary judgment, and remand with instructions to enter summary judgment in his favor.

For the future, however, we expect that our opinion today will clarify the contours of a student's right not to be expelled for truly unknowing or unconscious possession of a forbidden object. Because we have concluded that Superintendent Morgan was entitled to summary judgment on the basis of qualified immunity, we need not and do not address the question—which Superintendent Morgan's counsel conceded at oral argument was "not clear"—of whether he had the authority to disturb the decision to expel Seal once it was finally made by the Board.

IV. Conclusion

We would not for a minute minimize the Board's obligation to maintain the safety of its campuses, and its right to mete out appropriate discipline (including expulsion) to students who commit serious violations of its rules. But we cannot accept the Board's argument that because safety is important, and because it is often difficult to determine a student's state of mind, that it need not make any attempt to ascertain whether a student accused of carrying a weapon knew that he was in possession of the weapon before expelling him.

The decision to expel a student from school is a weighty one, carrying with it serious consequences for the student. We understand full well that the decision not to expel a potentially dangerous student

---

122 419 U.S. 565 (1975).

also carries very serious potential consequences for other students and teachers. Nevertheless, the Board may not absolve itself of its obligation, legal and moral, to determine whether students intentionally committed the acts for which their expulsions are sought by hiding behind a Zero Tolerance Policy that purports to make the students' knowledge a non-issue. We are also not impressed by the Board's argument that if it did not apply its Zero Tolerance Policy ruthlessly, and without regard for whether students accused of possessing a forbidden object knowingly possessed the object, this would send an inconsistent message to its students. Consistency is not a substitute for rationality.

⚖

Because of the criminal charges filed against him, Dustin Seal wasn't able to find a job after his expulsion from school. "He wanted to be an attorney," said his father, "but he couldn't even work at McDonald's."[123] Seal subsequently agreed to a $30,000 settlement with the school district. Though the criminal charges were eventually dropped, he was not allowed to return to school. He worked various odd jobs, including laying flooring and installing cable. "I'd rather have just finished school, graduated with my class and went [sic] to college," he said.[124] Dennis Seal filed suit against the school district for wrongful death after his son's suicide at age 22, six months after the settlement.[125]

Subsequent substantive due process challenges to mandatory punishments under zero tolerance policies have mostly been unsuccessful.

- In *Ratner v. Loudoun County Public Schools*,[126] a 13-year-old student challenged his long-term suspension on due process grounds. The circumstances of his case closely mirrored one of the hypotheticals offered by the Sixth Circuit in *Seal* the previous year. A schoolmate brought a knife to school and told Ratner she had contemplated killing herself the night before. Concerned for her safety, Ratner took the knife and put it in his locker. But the zero tolerance policy in effect at his school required that he be suspended for possessing a weapon, regardless of his well-meaning intentions. "However harsh the result in this case, the federal courts are not properly called upon to judge the wisdom of a zero tolerance policy of the sort alleged to be in place at Blue Ridge Middle School or of its application to Ratner," concluded the Fourth Circuit.

- In *Simonian v. Fowler Unified School District*,[127] a student was suspended for three months in accordance with a zero tolerance policy after "a pinhead-sized leaf of marijuana found stuck to a piece of rubber lining on the bottom of the front console glove compartment" of his father's car, which he had taken to school. The student was unaware of the speck of marijuana, a quantity that was neither discernible nor useful, and which would not have given rise to possession charges under criminal statutes.

- In *Morgan v. Snider High School*,[128] a student was expelled for giving a classmate who had smoked marijuana and who was subsequently found to be in possession of marijuana seeds a ride to school, in violation of a zero tolerance policy. "It is not the role of the Court to question what the Plaintiffs see as a lack of compassion, or to second-guess the disciplinary

---

123 *Quoted in* W. Joiner, *One strike and you're out of school—Youthful suicides, financial ruin, families torn apart for minor infractions: How post-Columbine hysteria is wrecking lives*, SALON.COM. Online at www.salon.com/2004/02/02/zero_tolerance_2/ (last accessed June 9, 2019).

124 *Quoted in* Associated Press, *School pays expelled student $30,000 in zero tolerance case*, DAILY BEACON (August 27, 2011). Online at www.utdailybeacon.com/news/school-pays-expelled-student-30-000-in-zero-tolerance-case/article_303d6fd8-9ac0-5bbe-8603-7dd438a3c87a.html (last accessed April 27, 2020).

125 See JACQUELINE A. STEFKOVICH, BEST INTERESTS OF THE STUDENT: APPLYING ETHICAL CONSTRUCTS TO LEGAL CASES IN EDUCATION (2006).

126 16 Fed. Appx. 140 (4th Cir. 2001) [*unpublished*], *cert. denied*, 534 U.S. 1114 (2002).

127 2008 U.S. Dist. LEXIS 12915 (E.D. Cal. Feb. 19, 2008).

128 2007 U.S. Dist. LEXIS 79103 (N.D. Ind. Oct. 23, 2007).

decision of the school's administrators," wrote the court. "At most, the Plaintiffs established that the Defendants have zero tolerance towards, and will seek the expulsion of, anyone introducing … narcotics onto school property, an attitude that is hardly 'without reasonable justification,' or that 'shocks the conscience.'"

- In *Piekosz-Murphy v. Board of Education of Community High School District No. 230*,[129] a student was expelled from the National Honor Society for briefly attending a party where alcohol was present, in violation of a zero tolerance policy. The student left the event upon discovering there was alcohol, and did not imbibe. "N.M. admitted that he knew that alcohol was being consumed at the party. N.M. had the option of self-reporting the party to school officials because it was a first-time offense," wrote the court. "Under these circumstances, the school's discipline of N.M. does not 'shock the conscience.'" The court then added, "[T]he Supreme Court has emphasized that '[i]t is not the role of the federal courts to set aside decisions of school administrators which the court may view as lacking a basis in wisdom or compassion.'"[130]
- In *Langley v. Monroe County School District*,[131] a student was sent to an alternative school after school officials found half a can of beer her mother had left in a cup holder the night before. The school board upheld the punishment, even though the student was completely unaware of the beer can when she took her mother's car to school. "Under the school district's zero tolerance policy," wrote the court, "her knowledge was wholly irrelevant." The student's due process claims failed because being sent to an alternative school did not deprive her of a public education. The former honor roll student subsequently withdrew from high school and later obtained a GED.
- In *Brett N. v. Community Unit School District No. 303*,[132] a student suspended for five days for violating a zero tolerance policy on fighting unsuccessfully challenged his punishment on the ground that he had been defending himself in an unprovoked attack. The court upheld the policy, which stipulated that "Any action a student takes to inflict physical contact may be considered fighting—including, but not limited to, self-defense."
- In *Cuff v. Valley Central School District*,[133] a ten-year-old student was suspended for six days for a number of drawings depicting violence, in violation of a zero tolerance policy, including a drawing of an astronaut expressing a desire to blow up his school. "The record now before us demonstrates that it was reasonably foreseeable that the astronaut drawing could create a substantial disruption at the school," concluded the Second Circuit. "Whether B.C. intended his 'wish' as a joke or never intended to carry out the threat is irrelevant. Nor does it matter that B.C. lacked the capacity to carry out the threat expressed in the drawing."

In *Hinterlong v. Arlington Independent School District*,[134] a case remarkably similar to *Seal*, a student was placed in an alternative school after a few drops of a liquid that smelled like alcohol were found in his car by school officials acting on an anonymous tip. Hinterlong insisted he had no knowledge of the presence of the liquid in his car and argued it had been planted there. The Texas Court of Appeals denied his due process claims, despite agreeing with the Sixth Circuit in *Seal* on zero tolerance policies:

> School districts' zero tolerance policies, as a whole, have promoted consistency over rationality. Arguments can be made that appeals, processes, and procedures provided to a student after application of a zero tolerance policy are worthless because each appeal, process, or procedure simply affirms zero tolerance; that is, such procedural due process is meaningless because no one within the process can

129 858 F. Supp. 2d 952 (N.D. Ill. 2012).
130 *Citing* Wood v. Strickland, 420 U.S. 308 (1975).
131 264 Fed. Appx. 366 (5th Cir. 2008) [*unpublished*].
132 2009 U.S. Dist. LEXIS 12444 (N.D. Ill. Feb. 18, 2009).
133 677 F.3d 109 (2d Cir. 2012).
134 2010 Tex. App. LEXIS 1010 (Tex. Ct. App. 2010).

circumvent the policy. Moreover, strict adherence to zero tolerance policies without consideration of the student's *mens rea* would appear to run afoul of substantive due process notions.

But here, the facts before the trial court demonstrated that Hinterlong suffered no deprivation of procedural due process or substantive due process because there was a way for Hinterlong to obtain consideration of his *mens rea*, to present evidence that he lacked knowledge of the Ozarka water bottle and its contents, and to thereby circumvent continued application of the zero tolerance policy.

As noted above, Hinterlong received hearings before the vice principal, the principal, the administrative appeal panel, and the superintendent. The superintendent, Dr. Mac Bernd, testified that he informed Hinterlong that he would overturn the decision of the administrative appeal panel, thereby returning Hinterlong to Arlington Martin High School, if Hinterlong would provide one or more pieces of specified evidence, including an analysis of the substance in question showing that it was not alcohol, polygraph results from Hinterlong showing that he did not have prior knowledge of the bottle or of its contents, or testimony from an independent witness substantiating the allegation that the bottle was "planted" in Hinterlong's vehicle. Hinterlong, his mother, and Dr. Bernd all testified that Hinterlong did not supply any of the specified items of evidence that would have allowed Dr. Bernd to overturn the decision of the administrative appeal panel. The record thus demonstrates that no evidence was presented by Hinterlong to escape application of the zero tolerance policy.

Matthew Hinterlong lost his appeal because he was neither willing nor able to prove his innocence, as school officials required.[135] He was sent to an alternative school for one term, graduated at the end of the following term, and went on to university. "He went through a lot, and it was a pretty traumatic experience for him," said his attorney, Mike Barragan. "It ruined his senior year in high school, and it caused a lot of embarrassment for him."[136]

In the wake of the *Hinterlong* case, Texas joined a handful of states in passing legislation requiring public school officials to consider **extenuating circumstances, intent**, and the **disciplinary histories** of students accused of violating zero tolerance policies.[137] As noted by legal scholar Rebecca Morton, North Carolina followed suit in 2011 with legislation allowing school officials "to consider student intent, disciplinary and academic history, benefits of alternatives to suspension, and other mitigating or aggravating factors."[138] Colorado allowed school officials to consider the particular circumstances behind zero tolerance violations in 2012,[139] while Massachusetts limited the circumstances in which expulsion may be imposed and allowed school officials to substitute suspensions at their discretion.[140]

Because school officials are now required or permitted to exercise discretion and take account of individual circumstances when students violate zero tolerance policies in Texas, North Carolina, and Colorado, the policies may no longer qualify as *zero* tolerance. The Massachusetts approach, on the other hand, may have returned zero tolerance policies to their original purpose—to help keep guns and violence out of schools.[141]

135 J. Gorman, *Student Loses Zero-Tolerance Booze Battle*, COURTHOUSE NEWS SERVICE (February 22, 2010). Online at www.courthousenews.com/student-loses-zero-tolerance-booze-battle/ (last accessed June 16, 2019).

136 *Quoted in* T. Shurley, *Martin High grad will keep fighting zero-tolerance-policy case despite latest setback*, FORT WORTH STAR-TELEGRAM (February 25, 2010). Online at www.star-telegram.com/living/family/moms/article3825008.html (last accessed June 16, 2019).

137 TEX. EDUC. CODE ANN. § 37.001(a)(4); *see* Rebecca Morton, *Returning Decision to School Discipline Decisions: An Analysis of Recent, Anti-Zero Tolerance Legislation*, 91 WASH. U. L. REV. 757 (2014) at FN36.

138 N.C. GEN. STAT. ANN. §§ 115C-390.1, 390.2; Morton, *id.* at 756–7.

139 COLO. REV. STAT. § 22-33-106 (1.2); Morton, *id.* at 767.

140 MASS. GEN. LAWS ch. 71, §§ 37H-37H1/2; Ibid. at 769.

141 *See* Kim Fries & Todd A. DeMitchell, *Commentary, Zero Tolerance and the Paradox of Fairness: Viewpoints from the Classroom*, 36 J.L. & EDUC. 211 (2007).

Thus, in *J.R. v. Penns Manor Area School District*,[142] a Pennsylvania case involving a 12-year-old who was suspended and subsequently expelled for taking part in a conversation on "who[m] they would shoot if they were to do a school shooting." The court dismissed the student's due process claims, observing that, "As a result of the horrific instances of school violence occurring on school grounds in recent years, school administrators have been increasingly more aggressive in adopting zero tolerance policies when it comes to students who threaten violence."

Academic Penalties

Academic penalties for **unexcused absences** have been challenged with mixed results. Some courts have said that schools have the authority to lower grades for non-attendance; others have disagreed.[143] In *Slocum v. Holton Board of Education*,[144] the policy of lowering grades when a student failed to make up missed days by attending study sessions was found not to be arbitrary. Ten years later, a US District Court in California imposed a fine of $500 per day on a school district found in contempt for failing to modify an attendance policy that included lower grades for non-attendance.[145]

Cases challenging academic penalties for **misbehavior** have also produced mixed results. In *Smith v. School City of Hobart*,[146] the court rejected on due process grounds a school's policy of lowering grades for nonacademic misconduct. "Reducing grades unrelated to academic conduct results in a skewed and inaccurate reflection of a student's academic performance," wrote the court. But in a case in which a student was expelled for the term for violating a school's drug policy and stripped of all credit earned, the court found that punishment not to be unconstitutionally excessive.[147] In *Katzman v. Cumberland Valley School District*,[148] a school suspended a student for five days, expelled her from the cheerleading squad and National Honor Society, excluded her from all school activities, and reduced her grades by ten points for the entire term because she ordered a glass of wine while on a field trip. The court concluded that the lowering of grades was an "illegal application of the Board's discretion." But in *South Gibson School Board v. Sollman*,[149] the court upheld a zero tolerance policy that required that the student be expelled and lose all credit for the semester, even credit already earned, when drug-sniffing dogs found a small amount of marijuana in his truck.

Parental Rights Claims

In the Progressive Era, the **life, liberty, and property** interests protected by the Due Process Clause included **freedom of contract**.[150] The Fourteenth Amendment was used to protect employers and even to undermine legislative reforms in the interests of workers in a number of cases. In *Lochner v. New York*,[151] for example, the Supreme Court struck down legislation limiting working hours for

---

142 2019 U.S. Dist. LEXIS 162 (W.D. Pa. Jan. 2, 2019).
143 Campbell v. Bd. of Educ., 475 A.2d 289 (Conn. 1984); Bitting v. Lee, 564 N.Y.S.2d 791 (N.Y. App. Div. 1990) (*ruling for school*); Gutierrez v. Sch. Dist., 585 P.2d 935 (Colo. Ct. App. 1978) (*ruling for student*).
144 429 N.W. 2d 607 (Mich. Ct. App. 1988).
145 Citizens for Lawful & Effective Attendance Policies v. Sequoia Union High Sch. Dist., 1998 U.S. Dist. LEXIS 8485 (N.D. Cal. June 4, 1998).
146 811 F. Supp. 391 (N.D. Ind. 1993); *see also* Hamer v. Bd. of Educ., 383 N.E.2d 231 (Ill. Ct. App. 1978).
147 Fisher v. Burkburnett Independent Sch. Dist., 419 F. Supp. 1200 (N.D. Tex. 1976); *see also* New Braunfels Indep. Sch. Dist. v. Armke, 658 S.W.2d 330 (Tex. Ct. App. 1983).
148 479 A.2d 671 (Pa. Commw. Ct. 1984).
149 768 N.E.2d 437 (Ind. 2002).
150 *See* Tyll van Geel, *The Prisoner's Dilemma and Education Policy*, 3 Notre Dame J.L. Ethics & Pub. Pol'y 301 (1988).
151 198 U.S. 45 (1905).

bakers based on freedom of contract principles. In *Pierce v. Society of Sisters*,[152] freedom of contract was the basis on which the Court struck down pending legislation that would have put private schools out of business by requiring all parents in Oregon to enroll their children in public schools. In *Meyer v. Nebraska*, the Court held that substantive due process protected "the teacher's right to teach and the right of parents to engage the teacher." **Freedom of contract** was counted among Fourteenth Amendment liberties, including

> the right of the individual to contract, to engage in any of the common occupations of life, to acquire useful knowledge, to marry, establish a home and bring up children, to worship God according to the dictates of his own conscience, and generally to enjoy those privileges long recognized at common law as essential to the orderly pursuit of happiness by free men [*sic*].

The Court repudiated its *Lochner* line of decisions in 1937,[153] but parents continued to assert a right to direct the upbringing of their children based on *Pierce* and *Meyer*. In *Prince v. Massachusetts*,[154] the Court declared, "It is cardinal with us that the custody, care and nurture of the child reside first in the parents, whose primary function and freedom include preparation for obligations the state can neither supply nor hinder." And in *Wisconsin v. Yoder*,[155] the Court found that, "However read, the Court's holding in *Pierce* stands as a charter of the rights of parents to direct the religious upbringing of their children."

Reviewing these and other precedents in *Troxel v. Granville*,[156] Justice Sandra Day O'Connor concluded that "it cannot now be doubted that the Due Process Clause of the Fourteenth Amendment protects the fundamental right of parents to make decisions concerning the care, custody, and control of their children." In dissent, Justice Antonin Scalia pointed out that

> Only three holdings of this Court rest in whole or in part upon a substantive constitutional right of parents to direct the upbringing of their children—two of them from an era rich in substantive due process holdings that have since been repudiated,

citing *Meyer*, *Pierce*, and *Yoder*. In his view, "the theory of unenumerated parental rights underlying these three cases [had] small claim to *stare decisis* protection."

Troxel marked the beginning of a more recent wave of substantive due process claims that public school officials violate "the fundamental right of parents to make decisions concerning the care, custody, and control of their children" in the course or making curricular and disciplinary decisions. As we have seen in previous chapters, such parental rights claims are often added to laundry lists of alleged constitutional violations in Section 1983 suits. For example, in *Parker v. Hurley*,[157] the First Circuit declined to grant religious parents offended by homosexuality an exemption from public school programs designed to encourage respect and diversity (see Chapter 3). The parents unsuccessfully raised a number of constitutional claims in their Section 1983 suit, including a right to direct how public schools teach their children. In *J.S. v. Blue Mountain School District*,[158] the parents of a student suspended for making fun of her school principal in a

---

152   268 U.S. 510 (1925).
153   West Coast Hotel v. Parrish, 300 U.S. 379 (1937).
154   321 U.S. 158 (1944).
155   406 U.S. 205 (1972).
156   530 U.S. 57 (2000).
157   514 F.3D 87 (2008).
158   650 F.3d 915 (3d Cir. 2011) (*en banc*), *cert. denied*, 565 U.S. 1156 (2012); *see also* CLM v. Sherwood Sch. Dist. 88J, 2016 U.S. Dist. LEXIS 186750 (D. Or. Dec. 30, 2016).

vulgar MySpace profile unsuccessfully claimed the district violated their "fundamental right to direct the upbringing of their child by regulating her out-of-school conduct," among other things (see Chapter 4).

In *Parents for Privacy v. Dallas School District No. 2*,[159] parents objecting to a policy allowing transgender students to use school facilities corresponding to their gender identity unsuccessfully claimed that the Fourteenth Amendment gave them the exclusive right "to instill moral standards and values in their children, and to direct their education and upbringing" which, in their view, included "a right to determine whether and when their minor children endure the risk of being exposed to members of the opposite sex in intimate, vulnerable settings like restrooms, locker rooms and showers."

In *T.L. v. Sherwood Charter School*,[160] parents barred from campus brought a long list of alleged federal statutory and constitutional violations, including an unsuccessful claim that their substantive due process right to direct the upbringing of their children included a right to access their child's charter school. "[N]o court has extended a parent's fundamental liberty interest in the care of his or her children to a parental right to physically access a child's school," noted the district court, finding that the parents in this case had "no substantive due process right to access school property, regardless of the purpose of [their] intended visit." The court found that because parents have no constitutional right to be on school property, no due process protections are required when school officials prohibit parental access.

The Equal Protection Clause

Equal protection claims may be filed in Section 1983 suits when school officials discriminate on the basis of race, religion, gender, or national origin when punishing students.[161] Federal statutes also prohibit racial or gender discrimination in student discipline (see Chapter 7) and place significant limitations on the punishment of students with disabilities (see Chapter 8). Students singled out for more severe punishment than other wrongdoers for reasons *other* than race, religion, gender, or national origin sometimes raise equal protection claims, but school officials will prevail as long as there is a rational basis for the differential treatment.[162] For example, courts are likely to uphold a more severe punishment for a ringleader or repeat offender.[163]

Summary

Students have challenged school punishments on procedural and substantive due process grounds, mostly without success. As long as punishments are reasonable in light of the student's infraction and the purpose for which they are given, as long as punishments are not so severe as to shock the conscience, and as long as punishments are not applied in a discriminatory manner, the courts have tended to defer to school officials or to grant them qualified immunity. Still, the Fifth and Fourteenth Amendments, state statutes, and district policies place important limitations on the authority of public school officials to maintain discipline in ways that implicate the life, liberty, or property interests of students. School officials who ignore these due process limitations place their schools at risk of litigation and their jobs in jeopardy.

---

159 326 F. Supp. 3d 1075 (D. Or. 2018).
160 2014 U.S. Dist. LEXIS 28818 (D. Or. Mar. 6, 2014).
161 Hawkins v. Coleman, 376 F. Supp. 1330 (N.D. Tex. 1974).
162 Smith v. Severn, 129 F.3d 419 (7th Cir. 1997); Bryant v. Ind. Sch. Dist. No. I-38, 334 F.3d 928 (10th Cir. 2003).
163 See Reed v. Vermilion Local Sch. Dist., 614 N.E.2d 1101 (Ohio Ct. App. 1992).

7 The Equal Protection Rights of Students

This is the first of three chapters dealing with **equity in education**. In this chapter, we address **equality of educational opportunity** for members of historically disadvantaged groups based on race, gender, national origin, sexual orientation, and first language. We address the equal protection rights of students, along with **affirmative action policies**, classification by age and ability, remedies for *de jure* and *de facto* segregation and other forms of **race-based discrimination**. We also address federal anti-discrimination statutes including **Title IX, Title VI**, and **Title VII**, along with the rights of **English Language Learners** (ELLs) under the *Equal Educational Opportunities Act* (*EEOA*).

For more than 60 years, the search for equality of educational opportunity has been the subject of more influential litigation than any other educational issue. Even after all this time, however, the meanings of terms like **equity** and **equal opportunity** have not been fully clarified. Does equity mean providing the same education to everyone or does it mean providing all students with an education tailored to their particular characteristics and needs? Does equity require spending the same amount on each student or more on some than others or should equity be viewed in terms of outcomes? Should everyone be given whatever education is necessary to reach a certain level of achievement? Issues like these play a central role in the cases and principles discussed in all three chapters.

The Equal Protection Clause and Race-Based Discrimination

African-American plaintiffs successfully challenged the notion that states are free to provide whatever education they choose to whomever they wish in *Brown v. Board of Education*.[1] The legal foundation of the *Brown* decision in particular and of the quest for equality of opportunity in education in general is the **Equal Protection Clause** of the Fourteenth Amendment. Under this provision, no state shall "deny to any person within its jurisdiction the **equal protection of the laws**." Over the years, the Supreme Court has repeatedly been called upon to define and interpret these simple-sounding words.[2]

In rough terms, to deny **equal protection of the laws** is to treat an individual or group differently from others without sufficient reason. The Fourteenth Amendment permits the classification and differential treatment of individuals if an adequate justification is provided, but otherwise prohibits discrimination. Because the law tends to be categorical, state agencies categorize individuals in myriad ways. For example, as we have seen, state laws categorize persons under the age of 18 as **legal minors** for many purposes. Federal and state laws distinguish US citizens from non-citizens,[3] felons from non-felons,[4] and persons with limited vision from persons with

---

1 347 U.S. 483 (1954).
2 *See* Tyll van Geel, *Racial Discrimination from Little Rock to Harvard*, 49 U. Cin. L. Rev. 49 (1980).
3 *See* Tyll van Geel, Homeland Security Law: A Primer (2019).
4 *See* Michelle Alexander, The New Jim Crow: Mass Incarceration In The Age Of Colorblindness, 2e (2020).

20/20 vision. Clearly, there may be adequate justification for differential treatment based on a criminal conviction (allowing felons to be incarcerated), a physical difference (allowing persons with limited vision to be denied driver's licenses), or age (allowing children to be subject to the substituted decision-making authority of their parents and legal guardians). As previously noted, in American jurisprudence, "Children are not a **suspect class** under the Equal Protection Clause, and a statutory classification of minor children with permanent legal disabilities due to diminished capacity is not a **suspect classification**."[5]

Other bases of classification such as race, religion, or gender may not be adequate to legitimate differential treatment. How do courts determine if a particular classification is suspect? A typical equal protection case begins with an individual or group alleging that they have been denied a benefit or suffered a burden unfairly. In many cases, the criteria used by governments to allocate benefits and burdens are overt. This was the case before *Brown*, when students were classified by race and assigned to public schools based solely and explicitly on that basis. Sometimes, however, the classification criteria used by governments are not overt. This may occur when, for example, a school board uses a "freedom of choice" or an "open-enrollment" policy as a pretext to maintain segregated schools.[6] In cases like these, the Supreme Court has placed the burden of establishing the actual basis of the differential treatment on the plaintiffs. For example, when race-based discrimination is claimed but not acknowledged, the plaintiffs must prove that government policies were in fact driven by considerations of race.

Once differential treatment has been established, who bears the burden of proving whether it is justified? According to the Supreme Court, the answer depends in part on the type of classification. When race is the criterion, the government bears the burden of proof, and it must provide an extremely strong justification for its law or policy. In imposing this heavy burden of proof, courts employ **strict scrutiny**. Under this test, a law or policy is presumed unconstitutional unless the government can show that it is **necessary to achieve a compelling state interest** and that the law or policy is **narrowly tailored** to achieve its ends (i.e., a race-based classification is used to the least extent possible). In other words, laws or policies subject to strict scrutiny will be declared unconstitutional unless they are found essential to the attainment of a legitimate and extremely important goal.

As we show later in this chapter and in subsequent chapters, courts do not impose the ultimate burden of persuasion on the government in *all* equal protection cases. Nor do they always require such a strong justification for differential treatment. Courts do impose this heavy burden on the government in race-based discrimination cases because of the pervasiveness of racism in American history. Accordingly, when a court sees a policy formulated on the basis of race, it suspects that race-based discrimination may again be occurring and it wants strong and convincing assurances from the government that this is not the case. Strict scrutiny promotes the goal of equal protection by imposing a burden that the government is rarely able to meet.

Strict scrutiny is also used in cases involving **fundamental rights**, but these are generally not applicable to equal educational opportunity claims in the federal courts.[7]

The Equal Protection Clause: A History

The Fourteenth Amendment was adopted in 1868, in the aftermath of the Civil War, to protect the legal and political rights of newly-emancipated African-Americans. Eleven years later, in *Strauder v. West Virginia*,[8] the Supreme Court invoked the Amendment for the first time to strike

5 628 Am Jur 2d Constitutional Law §897.
6 Green v. County Sch. Bd. of New Kent County, 391 U.S. 430 (1968).
7 San Antonio Indep. Sch. Dist. v. Rodriguez, 411 U.S. 1 (1973).
8 100 U.S. 303 (1879).

down a law barring African-Americans from serving on juries. The case was easy because the law was clearly and overtly discriminatory. As the Court said, the Fourteenth Amendment protected African-Americans from "legal discriminations, implying inferiority in civil society, lessening the security of their enjoyment of rights which others enjoy, and discriminations which are steps toward reducing them to the condition of a subject race."

In 1886, the Court for the first time recognized the existence of race-based discrimination in the application of a facially neutral law. In *Yick Wo v. Hopkins*,[9] all white applicants who sought waivers from a law prohibiting the operation of laundries in wooden buildings received them, while none of the 200 Asian applicants did. The Court found that when a law is administered "with an evil eye and an unequal hand" to favor members of one race over another, it is unconstitutional.

> The discrimination is admitted. No reason for it is shown, and the conclusion cannot be resisted, that no reason for it exists except hostility to the race and nationality to which the petitioners belong, and which in the eye of the law is not justified.

Ten years later, in *Plessy v. Ferguson*,[10] the Court upheld a Louisiana statute requiring "separate but equal" accommodations on trains. The Court rejected the claim that the Louisiana statute had a stigmatizing effect on African-Americans and found the race-based segregation to be constitutionally permissible. The *Plessy* Court did not employ the strict scrutiny test because it had not yet been developed for use in any kind of case. Rather, the Court placed the burden of proof on the plaintiff to show that the law lacked adequate justification. In his famous dissenting opinion, Justice John Marshall Harlan paved the way for *Plessy*'s eventual demise:

> The white race deems itself to be the dominant race in this country ... But in view of the Constitution, in the eye of the law, there is in this country no superior, dominant, ruling class of citizens. There is no caste here. Our Constitution is color-blind, and neither knows nor tolerates classes among citizens. In respect of civil rights, all citizens are equal before the law ... It is therefore to be regretted that this high tribunal, the final expositor of the fundamental law of the land, has reached the conclusion that it is competent for a State to regulate the enjoyment by citizens of their civil rights solely upon the basis of race ... In my opinion, the judgment this day rendered will, in time, prove to be quite as pernicious as the decision made ... in the *Dred Scott* case.

In 1938, the Court took its first step toward adopting the strict scrutiny test. In *United States v. Carolene Products Co.*,[11] the Court said that the usual presumption that laws and policies are constitutional may be weakened in cases where the impugned legislation (a) concerns matters specifically addressed by the Bill of Rights; (b) affects the right to vote or to disseminate information or interferes with political organizations; or (c) is aimed at "religious or racial minorities." The Court specifically noted that there might be a need for "a correspondingly more searching judicial inquiry" when "prejudice against discrete and insular minorities curtails the normal political processes ordinarily to be relied upon to protect" them. With these *dicta*, the Court signaled that it would use something like strict scrutiny to deal with legislation designed to disadvantage members of marginalized groups.

Another 1938 case directly involved race-based discrimination in education. In *Missouri ex rel. Gaines v. Canada*,[12] the plaintiff challenged a policy of the University of Missouri Law

9 118 U.S. 356 (1886).
10 163 U.S. 537 (1896).
11 304 U.S. 144 (1938).
12 305 U.S. 337 (1938).

School denying admission to African-American students. Missouri had no separate law school for African-Americans, so it offered to pay the plaintiff's tuition at an out-of-state school. The Court declared that Missouri's policy violated the Equal Protection Clause even under the "separate but equal" doctrine. For the first time, the Supreme Court ordered an all-white law school to admit an African-American student.[13] Two years earlier, the Maryland Court of Appeals had issued the first integration order as a remedy for a similar Equal Protection Clause violation in *Pearson v. Murray*.[14]

These cases provided the basis for a sustained assault, led by the National Association for the Advancement of Colored People (NAACP), on segregated higher education systems in a number of states. In *Sweatt v. Painter*,[15] the Supreme Court agreed that the white and African-American law schools in Texas were unequal in intangible ways, including the reputation of the faculty, the experience of the administration, the position and influence of alumni. As in *Gaines* and *Murray* 12 years earlier, the Supreme Court ordered an all-white law school to admit an African-American student.

In *McLaurin v. Oklahoma State Regents*,[16] decided the same year as *Sweatt*, the African-American plaintiff was segregated from the white students at the University of Oklahoma. He was assigned to a desk in an anteroom, restricted to the mezzanine of the library, and required to eat at a separate table in the cafeteria. The Court rejected these arrangements, describing McLaurin as

> handicapped in his pursuit of effective graduate instruction. Such restrictions impair and inhibit his ability to study, to engage in discussion and exchange views with other students, and, in general, to learn his profession … The removal of the state restrictions will not necessarily abate individual and group predilections, prejudices and choices. But at the very least, the state will not be depriving appellant of the opportunity to secure acceptance by his fellow students on his own merits.

None of these cases directly overturned the doctrine of "separate but equal," but they were steps toward its elimination. Nor did these cases embrace the use of the strict scrutiny test.

The Supreme Court had in fact applied strict scrutiny in *Korematsu v. United States*,[17] a 1944 case challenging the exclusion of all persons of Japanese ancestry from much of the West Coast following the attack on Pearl Harbor. "[A]ll legal restrictions which curtail the civil rights of a single racial group are immediately suspect," wrote the Court. "That is not to say all such restrictions are unconstitutional. It is to say that courts must subject them to the most rigid scrutiny." The Court concluded that the exclusion order was justified by national security concerns, making *Korematsu* one of the rare racial discrimination cases in which a government policy passed the strict scrutiny test. In *Trump v. Hawaii*,[18] Chief Justice Roberts noted that "*Korematsu* was gravely wrong the day it was decided, has been overruled in the court of history, and—to be clear—has no place in law under the Constitution."

No comparable evolution was occurring in the Court's application of the Equal Protection Clause to cases *not* involving race-based discrimination. In *Goesaert v. Cleary*,[19] the plaintiff challenged a Michigan law denying bartending licenses to women other than the wives or daughters of bar owners. The Court found the policy reasonable, ostensibly because bar owners could be relied upon to "protect" their wives and daughters from what would otherwise be a "morally hazardous" environment for any other female bartender:

---

13 Goodwin Liu, *State Courts and Constitutional Structure*, 128 YALE L.J. 1304, 1354 (2019).
14 169 Md. 478 (1936).
15 339 U.S. 629 (1950).
16 339 U.S. 637 (1950).
17 323 U.S. 214 (1944).
18 138 S. Ct. 2392 (2018).
19 335 U.S. 464 (1948).

While Michigan may deny to all women opportunities for bartending, Michigan cannot play favorites among women without rhyme or reason. The Constitution in enjoining the equal protection of the laws upon States precludes irrational discrimination as between persons or groups of persons in the incidence of a law … Since bartending by women may, in the allowable legislative judgment, give rise to moral and social problems against which it may devise preventive measures, the legislature need not go to the full length of prohibition if it believes that as to a defined group of females other factors are operating which either eliminate or reduce the moral and social problems otherwise calling for prohibition. Michigan evidently believes that the oversight assured through ownership of a bar by a barmaid's husband or father minimizes hazards that may confront a barmaid without such protecting oversight.

The dissenting justices would have none of it:

The statute arbitrarily discriminates between male and female owners of liquor establishments. A male owner, although he himself is always absent from his bar, may employ his wife and daughter as barmaids. A female owner may neither work as a barmaid herself nor employ her daughter in that position, even if a man is always present in the establishment to keep order. This inevitable result of the classification belies the assumption that the statute was motivated by a legislative solicitude for the moral and physical well-being of women who, but for the law, would be employed as barmaids. Since there could be no other conceivable justification for such discrimination against women owners of liquor establishments, the statute should be held invalid as a denial of equal protection.

In contrast to **strict scrutiny**, the Court in *Goesaert* used a **rational basis** test. This test places the burden of proof on the plaintiff to show (a) that the impugned law or policy does not serve a legitimate purpose, or (b) that the classification is not connected in any reasonable way to a legitimate goal. In most equal protection cases not involving race-based discrimination, the rational basis test applies, and the plaintiff must refute the presumption of constitutionality. This presumption can be overcome only by showing that the legislature was pursuing illegitimate purposes in creating the impugned law or policy, or that its method of achieving a legitimate purpose was irrational or unreasonable. This can rarely be accomplished.

In sum, when *Brown v. Board of Education* reached the Supreme Court in 1954, jurisprudence on the Equal Protection Clause had three dimensions. First, in higher education cases involving race-based segregation, the "separate but equal" doctrine was being enforced in a way that was forcing some all-white institutions to integrate. Second, in other race-based discrimination cases, the Court was moving toward the use of the strict scrutiny test. Third, in cases involving discrimination on grounds *other* than race, the Court was bending over backward to uphold laws using the rational basis test.

Race-Based Segregation

Encouraged by the success of its challenges to government-enforced segregation in public higher education, the NAACP turned its attention to elementary and secondary schools. The original plan was to deploy the strategy used successfully in the graduate and law school cases. Suits would be brought in various parts of the country designed to demonstrate that separate public schools were in fact unequal. Then, in midstream, the NAACP decided to attack the "separate but equal" doctrine directly. Thus, the argument made to the Supreme Court in *Brown v. Board of Education* and its companion case, *Bolling v. Sharpe*,[20] was that *Plessy* should be overruled.

20 347 U.S. 497 (1954).

⚖️

BROWN v. BOARD OF EDUCATION (BROWN I)
Supreme Court of the United States
347 U.S. 483 (1954)

MR. CHIEF JUSTICE WARREN delivered the opinion of the Court.

These cases come to us from the States of Kansas, South Carolina, Virginia, and Delaware. They are premised on different facts and different local conditions, but a common legal question justifies their consideration together in this consolidated opinion. In each of the cases, minors of the [African-American] race, through their legal representatives, seek the aid of the courts in obtaining admission to the public schools of their community on a non-segregated basis. In each instance, they had been denied admission to schools attended by white children under laws requiring or permitting segregation according to race. This segregation was alleged to deprive the plaintiffs of the equal protection of the laws under the Fourteenth Amendment. In each of the cases other than the Delaware case, a three-judge federal district court denied relief to the plaintiffs on the so-called "separate but equal" doctrine announced by this Court in *Plessy v. Ferguson*.[21] Under that doctrine, equality of treatment is accorded when the races are provided substantially equal facilities, even though these facilities be separate. In the Delaware case, the Supreme Court of Delaware adhered to that doctrine, but ordered that the plaintiffs be admitted to the white schools because of their superiority to the [African-American] schools.

The plaintiffs contend that segregated public schools are not "equal" and cannot be made "equal," and that hence they are deprived of the equal protection of the laws. Because of the obvious importance of the question presented, the Court took jurisdiction. Argument was heard in the 1952 Term, and re-argument was heard this Term on certain questions propounded by the Court.

Re-argument was largely devoted to the circumstances surrounding the adoption of the Fourteenth Amendment in 1868. It covered exhaustively consideration of the Amendment in Congress, ratification by the states, then existing practices in racial segregation, and the views of proponents and opponents of the Amendment. This discussion and our own investigation convince us that, although these sources cast some light, it is not enough to resolve the problem with which we are faced. At best, they are inconclusive. The most avid proponents of the post-War Amendments undoubtedly intended them to remove all legal distinctions among "all persons born or naturalized in the United States." Their opponents, just as certainly, were antagonistic to both the letter and the spirit of the Amendments and wished them to have the most limited effect. What others in Congress and the state legislatures had in mind cannot be determined with any degree of certainty.

An additional reason for the inconclusive nature of the Amendment's history, with respect to segregated schools, is the status of public education at that time. In the South, the movement toward free common schools, supported by general taxation, had not yet taken hold. Education of white children was largely in the hands of private groups. Education of [African-Americans] was almost nonexistent, and practically all [members] of the race were illiterate. In fact, any education of [African-Americans] was forbidden by law in some states. Today, in contrast, many [African-Americans] have achieved outstanding success in the arts and sciences as well as in the business and professional world. It is true that public school education at the time of the Amendment had advanced further in the North, but the effect of the Amendment on Northern States was generally ignored in the congressional debates. Even in the North, the conditions of public education did not approximate those existing today. The curriculum was usually rudimentary; ungraded schools were common in rural areas; the school term was but three months a year in many states; and compulsory school attendance was virtually unknown. As a consequence, it is not surprising that there should be so little in the history of the Fourteenth Amendment relating to its intended effect on public education.

In the first cases in this Court construing the Fourteenth Amendment, decided shortly after its adoption, the Court interpreted it as proscribing all state-imposed discriminations against [African-Americans]. The doctrine of "separate but

---

21 163 U.S. 537 (1896).

equal" did not make its appearance in this Court until 1896 in the case of *Plessy v. Ferguson*,[22] involving not education but transportation. American courts have since labored with the doctrine for over half a century … In *Sweatt v. Painter*,[23] the Court expressly reserved decision on the question whether *Plessy v. Ferguson* should be held inapplicable to public education.

In the instant cases, that question is directly presented. Here, unlike *Sweatt v. Painter*, there are findings below that the [African-American] and white schools involved have been equalized, or are being equalized, with respect to buildings, curricula, qualifications and salaries of teachers, and other "tangible" factors. Our decision, therefore, cannot turn on merely a comparison of these tangible factors in the [African-American] and white schools involved in each of the cases. We must look instead to the effect of segregation itself on public education.

In approaching this problem, we cannot turn the clock back to 1868 when the Amendment was adopted, or even to 1896 when *Plessy v. Ferguson* was written. We must consider public education in the light of its full development and its present place in American life throughout the Nation. Only in this way can it be determined if segregation in public schools deprives these plaintiffs of the equal protection of the laws.

Today, education is perhaps the most important function of state and local governments. Compulsory school attendance laws and the great expenditures for education both demonstrate our recognition of the importance of education to our democratic society. It is required in the performance of our most basic public responsibilities, even service in the armed forces. It is the very foundation of good citizenship. Today it is a principal instrument in awakening the child to cultural values, in preparing him [sic] for later professional training, and in helping him [sic] to adjust normally to his [sic] environment. In these days, it is doubtful that any child may reasonably be expected to succeed in life if he [sic] is denied the opportunity of an education. Such an opportunity, where the state has undertaken to provide it, is a right which must be made available to all on equal terms.

We come then to the question presented: Does segregation of children in public schools solely on the basis of race, even though the physical facilities and other "tangible" factors may be equal, deprive the children of the minority group of equal educational opportunities? We believe that it does.

In *Sweatt v. Painter*, in finding that a segregated law school for [African-Americans] could not provide them equal educational opportunities, this Court relied in large part on "those qualities which are incapable of objective measurement but which make for greatness in a law school." In *McLaurin v. Oklahoma State Regents*, the Court,[24] in requiring that [an African-American] admitted to a white graduate school be treated like all other students, again resorted to intangible considerations: "… his ability to study, to engage in discussions and exchange views with other students, and, in general, to learn his profession." Such considerations apply with added force to children in grade and high schools. To separate them from others of similar age and qualifications solely because of their race generates a feeling of inferiority as to their status in the community that may affect their hearts and minds in a way unlikely ever to be undone. The effect of this separation on their educational opportunities was well stated by a finding in the Kansas case by a court which nevertheless felt compelled to rule against the [African-American] plaintiffs:

Segregation of white and [African-American] children in public schools has a detrimental effect upon the [African-American] children. The impact is greater when it has the sanction of the law; for the policy of separating the races is usually interpreted as denoting the inferiority of the [African-American] group. A sense of inferiority affects the motivation of a child to learn. Segregation with the sanction of law, therefore, has a tendency to [retard] the educational and mental development of [African-American] children and to deprive them of some of the benefits they would receive in [an] integrated school system.

Whatever may have been the extent of psychological knowledge at the time of *Plessy v. Ferguson*, this finding is amply supported by modern authority. Any language in *Plessy v. Ferguson* contrary to this finding is rejected.

We conclude that in the field of public education the doctrine of "separate but equal" has no place.

22 163 U.S. 537 (1896).
23 339 U.S. 629 (1950).
24 339 U.S. 637 (1950).

Separate educational facilities are inherently unequal. Therefore, we hold that the plaintiffs and others similarly situated for whom the actions have been brought are, by reason of the segregation complained of, deprived of the equal protection of the laws guaranteed by the Fourteenth Amendment. This disposition makes unnecessary any discussion whether such segregation also violates the Due Process Clause of the Fourteenth Amendment.

Because these are class actions, because of the wide applicability of this decision, and because of the great variety of local conditions, the formulation of decrees in these cases presents problems of considerable complexity. On re-argument, the consideration of appropriate relief was necessarily subordinated to the primary question—the constitutionality of segregation in public education. We have now announced that such segregation is a denial of the equal protection of the laws. In order that we may have the full assistance of the parties in formulating decrees, the cases will be restored to the docket, and the parties are requested to present further argument on Questions 4 and 5 previously propounded by the Court for the re-argument this Term. The Attorney General of the United States is again invited to participate. The Attorneys General of the states requiring or permitting segregation in public education will also be permitted to appear as *amici curiae* ...

De Jure *Segregation*

De jure segregation occurs by law. By contrast, **de facto segregation** occurs for other reasons. *Brown I* (the first in a series of *Brown* decisions) rejected only *de jure* segregation in public schools. Although the decision did not refer explicitly to the strict scrutiny test, the *Bolling* decision issued at the same time did: "[C]lassifications based solely upon race must be scrutinized with particular care, since they are contrary to our traditions and hence constitutionally suspect." The *Bolling* decision indicated that *de jure* segregation would be unconstitutional even if the Equal Protection Clause did not exist. "Segregation in public education," wrote the Court, "constitutes an arbitrary deprivation of ... liberty in violation of the Due Process Clause." Even if the physical facilities and other resources were similar, segregation in and of itself had deeply harmful effects on African-American students. *De jure* segregation was essentially an expression of white supremacy. Such offensive policies violated deeply held views of equality.

The Supreme Court's reasoning in the school segregation cases would later be deployed to bar *de jure* segregation in public places of all kinds.[25] Still, questions concerning the scope of these rulings remained unsettled: Did *Brown I* and *Bolling* prohibit only segregation brought about overtly, or would segregation accomplished covertly also be found unconstitutional? Would the Court reject only *de jure* discrimination or would it also strike down statutes and policies that had as an unintended discriminatory impact on people of color? It took a long time, many cases, and much confusion for answers to these questions to emerge.

Today, the Equal Protection Clause prohibits both overt and covert discrimination. All intentional government discrimination, whether overt or covert, is *de jure* discrimination, and *de jure* discrimination is unconstitutional. The Equal Protection Clause does not prohibit policies that have an unintended discriminatory impact. Unintended discrimination is *de facto*, and *de facto* discrimination is not unconstitutional.[26]

Segregation that arises entirely as a result of private, non-government decisions or as a result of social conditions outside the government's control has been found by the Supreme Court not to violate the Equal Protection Clause. This explains why so many schools remain racially segregated

25 Gayle v. Browder, 352 U.S. 903 (1956); Holmes v. Atlanta, 350 U.S. 879 (1955); Mayor of Baltimore v. Dawson, 350 U.S. 877 (1955).
26 Keyes v. Sch. Dist. No. 1, Denver, 413 U.S. 189 (1973); Washington v. Davis, 426 U.S. 229 (1976).

more than six decades after *Brown*: Students tend to be assigned to schools in their neighborhoods, and many neighborhoods are segregated for reasons other than intentional government action.

Intent to Discriminate

Proving intent to discriminate is the key to success in many race-based discrimination cases. Legislative or administrative awareness of the discriminatory consequences of a policy is not enough to prove intent to discriminate. A policy will not be found intentionally discriminatory if adopted *in spite of* a discriminatory impact, but a policy will be found intentionally discriminatory if adopted *because* of a discriminatory impact.[27]

To be successful, plaintiffs are not required to prove directly that the government tried to subject them to inferior treatment. If overt intentions cannot be established, intent to discriminate may be inferred from a pattern of actions whose only foreseeable consequences were segregative or otherwise discriminatory. The adoption of a law or policy that a rational decision-maker should have known would have a discriminatory effect is evidence of intent to discriminate. When foreseeability is combined with other corroborating evidence, intent to discriminate may be inferred.

Among the kinds of evidence that may help to prove intent to discriminate are the historical background and specific series of events leading to a policy decision, departures from normal policymaking procedures, contemporaneous statements by policymakers, minutes of meetings and reports, and statements of officials at trial.[28] The effort to prove intentional segregation can be bolstered by two presumptions: (a) where it has been shown that a district engaged in intentional segregation affecting a substantial portion of its schools, a finding that the entire district is intentionally discriminatory is warranted absent a showing that the district is divided into clearly unrelated units; and (b) even if the district is subdivided into unrelated units, proof of intentional discrimination in one unit is evidence of an intent to discriminate in others.[29] A persistent pattern of activity with a segregative impact by a school board may also lead to a finding of intent to discriminate.

Plaintiffs need not prove that the intent to discriminate was accompanied by a desire to harm. People may discriminate based on benevolent or paternalistic motives. Rather, all that needs to be established is that "but for" the consideration of race, the decision would have been different.[30] The question has been formulated this way: "[S]uppose the adverse effects of the challenged governmental decision fell on whites instead of African-Americans ... Would the decision have been different? If the answer is yes, then the decision was made with discriminatory intent." This has been called the "reversing of groups test": Would government have made the same decision if the races of those affected had been reversed?[31] If not, the court will find the policy unconstitutional unless it can survive strict scrutiny.

In *Diaz v. San Jose Unified School District*,[32] the plaintiffs alleged that the school board had intentionally discriminated against Latinx students by creating and maintaining segregated schools. Courts view segregation by ethnicity the same way as segregation by race. The school board in *Diaz* admitted that it had "maintained ethnically imbalanced schools" and even that it had "omitted courses of action that would have reduced the imbalance," but it claimed that the segregation resulted from adherence to a "neighborhood school" policy and was thus *de facto*. Finding that

---

27 Personnel Adm'r of Massachusetts v. Feeney, 442 U.S. 256 (1979).
28 Arlington Heights v. Metro. Hous. Dev. Corp., 429 U.S. 252 (1977).
29 Keyes v. Sch. Dist. No. 1, Denver, 413 U.S. 189 (1973).
30 Arlington Heights v. Metro. Hous. Dev. Corp., 429 U.S. 252 (1977).
31 David A. Strauss, *Discriminatory Intent and the Taming of Brown*, 56 U. CHI. L. REV. 935, 957 (1989).
32 733 F.2d 660 (9th Cir. 1984).

the board had intentionally segregated the district, the court noted that over a period of years, the board had made decisions concerning the creation and modification of attendance areas, the building of new schools, faculty assignments, and the provision of transportation. In virtually every instance, the board had chosen the "more segregative alternative," even when the other alternative would have been cheaper or more efficient. Furthermore, the board continued to make segregative decisions even after it was ordered by the state to reduce the level of segregation in its schools and despite its full knowledge that its policies were having exactly the opposite effect. Thus, the segregation was found to be *de jure* and therefore unconstitutional.

In cases like *Diaz*, the strict scrutiny test is often deployed implicitly. Proof of intent to discriminate is also evident when the government has no adequate justification for its actions. The government cannot meet its burden of proof under strict scrutiny because the reason for its policy was to separate students by race. If it had a compelling reason for its policies, the government would have articulated it in the first place. School districts with no history of *de jure* segregation need not take affirmative steps to change policies that create *de facto* segregation. But school districts that have been found to be *de jure* segregated do have an affirmative obligation to disestablish their dual systems, undo the effects of segregation, and prevent an increase in segregation.[33] Failure to take these positive steps is itself proof of intent to discriminate.

De Facto Segregation

Although only *de jure* segregation violates the Equal Protection Clause, some state constitutions may prohibit even *de facto* segregation. In *Paynter v. State of New York*,[34] the highest court of New York was presented with a pattern of imbalance typical of many urban areas throughout the United States. In the Rochester school system, over 80 percent of students were non-white, and 90 percent were poor. In the suburbs surrounding Rochester, 91 percent of students were white, and only 16 percent were poor. The academic performance rates appeared to reflect the effects of this *de facto* segregation, as 84 percent of suburban high school seniors graduated on time, compared with only 27 percent of their city counterparts.

The plaintiffs claimed that the state's "fault lies in practices and policies that have resulted in high concentrations of racial minorities and poverty in the [Rochester] school district, leading to abysmal student performance." Plaintiffs argued that in schools marked by high concentrations of students living in poverty and racial isolation, it was impossible to provide an education that met state constitutional requirements. The court acknowledged that research did establish a correlation between concentrations of poverty and racial isolation, and poor educational performance. Nevertheless, the court concluded that it could not rule for plaintiffs: Allowing students "to attend schools outside their districts at no additional cost [would] diminish local control and participation, as the residents of more attractive districts would end up having to provide for students from other districts."

The court also implied that the state constitution only spoke to school funding inequities, as opposed to inequities imposed by *de facto* segregation. Yet the plaintiffs had argued that access to middle-class peers, as found in integrated schools, was itself an educational "input," not unlike inputs commonly associated with educational funding, such as access to preschool and smaller class sizes (see Chapter 9). This view of educational inputs has received some support.[35]

---

33 Columbus Bd. of Educ. v. Penick, 443 U.S. 449 (1979); Dayton Bd. of Educ. v. Brinkman, 443 U.S. 526 (1979).

34 290 A.D.2d 95 (NY Sup Ct 2001), *aff'd*, 797 N.E.2d 1225 (NY Ct App. 2003).

35 Paynter v. State of New York, 797 N.E.2d at 1247 n. 7 (Smith, J., dissenting); *see* Derek W. Black, *Middle Income Peers as Educational Resources and the Constitutional Right to Equal Access*, 53 Boston College L. Rev. 1 (2012).

In *Sheff v. O'Neill*,[36] the Connecticut Supreme Court found that its state constitution prohibited *de facto* segregation. Although statewide the school population was 25.7 percent minority, the schools of Hartford were 92.4 percent minority. In the suburbs surrounding Hartford, only seven of 21 districts had minority school populations greater than ten percent. The court noted that the state had an "affirmative constitutional obligation to provide all public school children with substantially equal educational opportunity" and that "[e]xtreme racial and ethnic isolation … deprives schoolchildren of a substantially equal educational opportunity … whether the segregation results from intentional conduct or from unorchestrated demographic factors." Thus, the court declared that the school districting system in the state was unconstitutional.

Unlike the New York constitution, the Connecticut constitution contains an explicit anti-segregation clause. It is one of only three state constitutions to contain such a clause, the others being New Jersey and Hawaii. This may help to explain the different outcomes in *Paynter* and *Sheff*. The decision in *Sheff* also seems consistent with the psychological evidence discussed in the original *Brown* decision. Surely the effects of segregation on students of color are harmful whether they result from school districting practices, district assignment policies, or "white flight".

In *Cruz-Guzman v. State*,[37] a recent case resembling *Paynter* and *Sheff*, the plaintiffs alleged that public schools in Minneapolis and Saint Paul were

> "disproportionately comprised of students of color and students living in poverty, as compared with a number of neighboring and surrounding schools and districts." These segregated and "hyper-segregated" schools have significantly worse academic outcomes in comparison with neighboring schools and suburban school districts in measures such as graduation rates; pass rates for state-mandated Basic Standards Tests; and proficiency rates in math, science, and reading. [Plaintiffs] describe these racially and socioeconomically segregated schools as "separate and unequal" from "neighboring and surrounding whiter and more affluent suburban schools" and detail the extensive harms of racial and socioeconomic segregation.

The plaintiffs further alleged that the state had contributed to both school segregation and disparate educational outcomes through

> boundary decisions for school districts and school attendance areas; the formation of segregated charter schools and the decision to exempt charter schools from desegregation plans; the use of federal and state desegregation funds for other purposes; the failure to implement effective desegregation remedies; and the inequitable allocation of resources.

The Court of Appeals refused to dismiss the suit, in part because education is a **fundamental right** under the Minnesota constitution. Thus in Minnesota and in New Jersey, where a similar suit has been filed,[38] the courts will hear of the harms imposed by *de facto* school segregation.

Remedying De Jure Segregation

After declaring that *de jure* segregation violated the Equal Protection Clause in *Brown I*, the Supreme Court had to face the practical question of what remedy to order. Clearly, it was too much to expect that states with dual education systems and long histories of white supremacy would comply with Supreme Court rulings mandating desegregation. A year after *Brown I*, the Court issued the following opinion:

---

36 678 A.2d 1267 (Conn. 1996).
37 916 N.W.2d 1 (Minn. 2018).
38 See https://images.law.com/contrib/content/uploads/documents/292/segregation.pdf (last accessed April 18, 2020).

⚖️
BROWN v. BOARD OF EDUCATION (BROWN II)
Supreme Court of the United States
349 U.S. 294 (1955)

MR. CHIEF JUSTICE WARREN delivered the opinion of the Court.

These cases were decided on May 17, 1954. The opinions of that date, declaring the fundamental principle that racial discrimination in public education is unconstitutional, are incorporated herein by reference. All provisions of federal, state, or local law requiring or permitting such discrimination must yield to this principle. There remains for consideration the manner in which relief is to be accorded.

Because these cases arose under different local conditions and their disposition will involve a variety of local problems, we requested further argument on the question of relief. In view of the nationwide importance of the decision, we invited the Attorney General of the United States and the Attorneys General of all states requiring or permitting racial discrimination in public education to present their views on that question. ...

Full implementation of these constitutional principles may require solution of varied local school problems. School authorities have the primary responsibility for elucidating, assessing, and solving these problems; courts will have to consider whether the action of school authorities constitutes good faith implementation of the governing constitutional principles. Because of their proximity to local conditions and the possible need for further hearings, the courts which originally heard these cases can best perform this judicial appraisal. Accordingly, we believe it appropriate to remand the cases to those courts.

In fashioning and effectuating the decrees, the courts will be guided by equitable principles. Traditionally, equity has been characterized by a practical flexibility in shaping its remedies and by a facility for adjusting and reconciling public and private needs. These cases call for the exercise of these traditional attributes of equity power. At stake is the personal interest of the plaintiffs in admission to public schools as soon as practicable on a non-discriminatory basis. To effectuate this interest may call for elimination of a variety of obstacles in making the transition to school systems operated in accordance with the constitutional principles set forth in our May 17, 1954 decision. Courts of equity may properly take into account the public interest in the elimination of such obstacles in a systematic and effective manner. But it should go without saying that the vitality of these constitutional principles cannot be allowed to yield simply because of disagreement with them.

While giving weight to these public and private considerations, the courts will require that the defendants make a prompt and reasonable start toward full compliance with our May 17, 1954 ruling. Once such a start has been made, the courts may find that additional time is necessary to carry out the ruling in an effective manner. The burden rests upon the defendants to establish that such time is necessary in the public interest and is consistent with good faith compliance at the earliest practicable date. To that end, the courts may consider problems related to administration, arising from the physical condition of the school plant, the school transportation system, personnel, revision of school districts and attendance areas into compact units to achieve a system of determining admission to the public schools on a non-racial basis, and revision of local laws and regulations which may be necessary in solving the foregoing problems. They will also consider the adequacy of any plans the defendants may propose to meet these problems and to effectuate a transition to a racially non-discriminatory school system. During this period of transition, the courts will retain jurisdiction of these cases.

The judgments below, except that in the Delaware case, are accordingly reversed and the cases are remanded to the District Courts to take such proceedings and enter such orders and decrees consistent with this opinion as are necessary and proper to admit to public schools on a racially nondiscriminatory basis with all deliberate speed the parties to these cases. The judgment in the Delaware case—ordering the immediate admission of the plaintiffs to schools previously attended only by white children—is affirmed. ...

⚖️

In hindsight, the vague, open-ended remedy announced in *Brown II* seems overly timid, especially when compared to the broad philosophical vision of *Brown I*. Essentially, *Brown II* reasserts the ruling that *de jure* segregation is illegal and orders local authorities to make a "good faith" effort to "carry out the ruling" at the "earliest practicable date," and "with all deliberate speed." Lower federal courts were charged with supervising the desegregation effort, but warned that in doing so they were to pay attention to "varied local school problems" and the importance of "reconciling public and private needs." Perhaps the Court believed that the lower federal courts could formulate specific remedies that would take into account both constitutional requirements and local social conditions. Perhaps it was further hoped that acknowledging the need for a transition period would eventually foster peaceful compliance with the Constitution.

The ensuing years brought very little movement toward desegregation and little further involvement by the Court itself. In the decade following *Brown*, the Supreme Court issued only three additional opinions dealing with the most blatant cases.[39]

The *Brown* decision—and the resistance it engendered—did much to galvanize an active and vocal civil rights movement. In turn, the work of this movement led to the adoption of the most sweeping civil rights legislation since Reconstruction, the **Civil Rights Act of 1964**.[40] This law, among other things, prohibited race-based discrimination in programs receiving federal assistance and barred discrimination in employment on the basis of race, gender, and religion. Based on this law, a vigorous federal effort began to dismantle segregated school systems. For the first time, opponents of *de jure* segregation had a potent practical weapon: States refusing to desegregate faced a total cutoff of federal education funds.

Emboldened by the passage of this new *Civil Rights Act*, the Supreme Court decided that it had waited long enough for the states to comply with *Brown*. In *Green v. County School Board of New Kent County*,[41] the Court invalidated a "freedom of choice" attendance plan allowing each student the choice of attending either a formerly African-American or a formerly white school within the district. In practice, virtually all students continued to attend the same schools. Although neutral on its face, the plan served to perpetuate the segregated school system. What the Court now wanted was a student attendance plan that would integrate the schools. "The burden on the school board today," wrote Justice Brennan, "is to come forward with a plan that promises realistically to work now."

The Court underscored its more aggressive stance a year later in a *per curiam* opinion in which it said that the *Brown II* era "of all deliberate speed" was over.[42] All schools that had ever been segregated by law were now on notice that only desegregation plans that worked well and quickly would be acceptable. These decisions, however forceful, still left lower federal courts, state legislatures, and school boards with important unanswered questions: Exactly what kind of desegregation plans should and could be ordered by the lower courts? What remedies were available to accomplish the mandate of *Brown*? The answers to these questions were provided in a series of Supreme Court opinions that spanned several decades.

Swann v. Charlotte-Mecklenburg Board of Education[43] involved a large, formerly segregated southern school district. In 1969, after several years of operating under a district court-approved desegregation plan, more than 50 percent of African-American students continued to attend schools that were more than 99 percent African-American. Responding to the mandate of the *Green* case,

---

39 Cooper v. Aaron, 358 U.S. 1 (1958); Goss v. Bd. of Educ. of Knoxville, 373 U.S. 683 (1963); Griffin v. Sch. Bd. of Prince Edward County, 377 U.S. 218 (1964).
40 42 U.S.C. § 2000(d) *et seq.*
41 391 U.S. 430 (1968).
42 Alexander v. Holmes County Bd. of Educ., 396 U.S. 19 (1969).
43 402 U.S. 1 (1971).

the district court imposed a new and more aggressive approach to desegregation. The plan grouped urban African-American schools with suburban white schools within the district into attendance zones, with some busing of students in both directions. The school district challenged the district court's power to impose such a plan.

In upholding the plan, the Supreme Court declared: (a) that the district court could adopt as a target for individual schools a racial balance similar to the district as a whole, as long as the target did not function as a rigid quota; (b) that it is not necessarily illegal as a result of segregated living patterns for a school district under a desegregation order to maintain some single-race schools, but the school district bears the "burden of showing that such school assignments are genuinely non-discriminatory"; (c) that the grouping of schools and gerrymandering of school attendance zones is permissible as a remedy for intentional segregation; (d) that the mandatory busing of students is a permissible remedy as long as the time or distance of travel is not "so great as to either risk the health of the children or significantly impinge on the educational process"; and (e) that once the district had achieved full compliance with a desegregation order, it would be declared "unitary", and no further remedies would be authorized. Even if a formerly de jure segregated school district becomes de facto segregated, "[n]either school authorities nor district courts, are constitutionally required to make year-by-year adjustment to the racial composition of student bodies once the affirmative duty to desegregate has been accomplished and racial discrimination through official action is eliminated from the system."

In several cases following *Swann*, the Supreme Court developed doctrines that made it easier for plaintiffs to prove both that school authorities had engaged in de jure segregation and that their wrongful policies affected the entire school district, not just a portion of it. A practical consequence of these doctrines was to make it easier for the courts to order district-wide busing.[44]

The remedies approved in *Swann* were potentially effective methods of desegregation in school districts with diverse student populations. For example, Charlotte-Mecklenburg's student body was about 70 percent white and 30 percent African-American. However, no amount of redrawing of school attendance areas and busing could result in diverse student populations in predominantly African-American school districts unless predominantly white school districts were combined with predominantly African-American districts in a *Swann*-like plan.

In *Milliken v. Bradley* (Milliken I),[45] the district court attempted to impose just such an inter-district remedy. Like many large urban areas, Detroit had a mostly African-American city school district surrounded by a number of mostly white suburban districts. The city school district had been found to be de jure segregated but the surrounding districts had not. Nevertheless, the district court reasoned that a desegregation plan involving only the city district could not succeed, as only about one third of the city students were white. Any plan that aggressively distributed white students throughout the district would hasten "white flight." The district court accordingly sought to include suburban districts in its desegregation plan to achieve the constitutional mandate of desegregation.

In rejecting the district court's plan, however, the Supreme Court declared (in a 5–4 decision) that before a district court may impose a cross-district remedy,

> it must first be shown that there has been a constitutional violation within one district that produces a significant segregative effect in another district. Specifically, it must be shown that racially discriminatory acts of the state or local school districts, or of a single school district have been a substantial cause of

44   Keyes v. Sch. Dist. No. 1, Denver, 413 U.S. 189 (1973); Columbus Bd. of Educ. v. Penick, 443 U.S. 449 (1979); Dayton Bd. of Educ. v. Brinkman, 443 U.S. 526 (1979); United States v. Scotland Neck Bd. of Educ., 407 U.S. 484 (1972).
45   418 U.S. 717 (1974).

inter-district segregation. Thus an inter-district remedy might be in order where the racially discriminatory acts of one or more school districts caused racial segregation in an adjacent district, or where district lines have been deliberately drawn on the basis of race. In such circumstances an inter-district remedy would be appropriate to eliminate the inter-district segregation directly caused by the constitutional violation. Conversely, without an inter-district violation and inter-district effect, there is no constitutional wrong calling for an inter-district remedy.

Because there had been no such showing in Detroit, the district court could not impose a cross-district plan. The desegregation plan could only seek to create racial balance in individual schools similar to the racial makeup of Detroit alone—not the Detroit metro area. Justice Thurgood Marshall (who as a lawyer had argued for the plaintiffs in *Brown*) dissented, observing that

> [T]he result of a Detroit-only decree … would be to increase the flight of whites from the city … In the short run, it may seem to be the easier course to allow our great metropolitan areas to be divided up each into two cities—one white, the other black—but it is a course, I predict, our people will ultimately regret.

This observation proved prescient, as by 1990 metropolitan Detroit had the highest residential segregation in the nation, and its school systems were the second most segregated (trailing only Chicago).

If cross-district remedies are not permitted, what may district courts do to remedy *de jure* segregation in school districts like Detroit? In its next consideration of *Milliken v. Bradley* (Milliken II),[46] the district court fashioned a series of remedies designed to assure, not that integration would actually be achieved, but that the African-American students of Detroit would at least not suffer educationally from the vestiges of *de jure* segregation. The major components of the plan were a "remedial reading and communications skills program," "an in-service training program for teachers and administrators to train [them] to cope with the desegregation process" and to ensure future equitable treatment of all students, a non-biased testing program, and a "counseling and career guidance" program.

This time, the Supreme Court approved the district court's plan, finding it "essential to mandate educational components where they are needed to remedy effects of past segregation, to assure a successful desegregative effort and to minimize the possibility of re-segregation." Even though the original constitutional violation consisted of assigning students to schools based on race, the remedy need not be limited to non-discriminatory reassignment, but could include programs designed to ameliorate the harms of segregation.

In *Missouri v. Jenkins*,[47] the Supreme Court further clarified the limits of a district court's power to include such "educational components" in a desegregation remedy. In that case, the district court ordered a costly plan that included upgrading and modifying substandard facilities in Kansas City to create a system of magnet schools. In order to make it possible for the school district to pay for the plan, the court mandated a property tax increase to a higher level than state law allowed. The Supreme Court found that the lower court had overstepped its authority in directly raising taxes; however, the district court was allowed to achieve the same result by ordering the local government to raise taxes beyond the state statutory limit. The Supreme Court said that this approach better served to protect the integrity of local institutions and placed the responsibility for the remedy on those who created the problem.

46 433 U.S. 267 (1977).
47 495 U.S. 33 (1990) and 515 U.S. 70 (1995).

The magnet school-based desegregation plan was approved in *Jenkins*, as in previous cases, even though race-based quotas were employed in admitting students to schools.[48] However, in its final consideration of *Jenkins*,[49] the Court held that the district court could not continue to order salary increases for instructional personnel and extensive remedial education programs simply because "student achievement levels were still at or below the national norms at many grade levels." The ordered salary increase was simply "too far removed from an acceptable implementation of a permissible means to remedy previous legally mandated segregation."

Based on the Supreme Court's pronouncements in *Jenkins* and related cases,[50] the lower federal courts authorized a variety of techniques for ending race-based segregation, including busing, redrawn attendance zones, faculty integration, magnet schools and magnet programs within schools, student transfer programs, and school district consolidations.

Desegregation is an elusive goal in many large metropolitan areas where, after decades of white flight, a large majority of students of color continue to attend racially isolated inner-city schools. *De facto* segregation persists, as does resistance to desegregation in some places. When can it be said that a school district has fully complied with a desegregation order? When, if ever, should the courts permit a school district to operate without judicial supervision?

The Supreme Court first addressed these issues in *Pasadena City Board of Education v. Spangler*.[51] The school district sought relief from a court-ordered plan requiring it to rearrange attendance zones each year so that there would be no school where students of color were in the majority. The Supreme Court found in favor of the school district, holding that the district court had exceeded its authority in requiring annual attendance zone adjustments. "Having once implemented a racially neutral attendance pattern in order to remedy the board's perceived constitutional violations," noted the Court, "the district court had fully performed its function of providing the appropriate remedy for previous racially discriminatory patterns."

Despite *Pasadena*, it was unclear whether a school district could be declared a unitary district when all the effects of prior segregation had been eliminated. The Supreme Court addressed this question in *Board of Education of Oklahoma City Schools v. Dowell*,[52] noting that judicial supervision of a local school district was intended only as a temporary measure to ensure compliance with a desegregation order. It ruled that a formerly segregated school district should be considered unitary if "the board had complied in good faith with a desegregation decree" for a significant period of time and if "the vestiges of past discrimination had been eliminated to the extent practicable." In making the latter determination, a court should look "not only at student assignments, but to every facet of school operations—faculty, staff, transportation, extracurricular activities and facilities." In other words, once the effects of *de jure* segregation have been eliminated, a district must be considered unitary even in the face of persisting *de facto* segregation. The district courts may not require school districts to rearrange attendance zones and bus students in perpetuity when integration is stymied by demographic changes.

In *Freeman v. Pitts*,[53] the Supreme Court authorized district courts to partially withdraw from control of a school district when a particular aspect of a desegregation order had been met. If,

---

48 Davis v. E. Baton Rouge Parish Sch. Bd., 721 F.2d 1425 (5th Cir. 1983); Morgan v. Kerrigan, 530 F.2d 401 (1st Cir. 1976).
49 515 U.S. 70 (1995).
50 See Keyes v. Sch. Dist. No. 1, Denver, 413 U.S. 189 (1973); Columbus Bd. of Educ. v. Penick, 443 U.S. 449 (1979); Dayton Bd. of Educ. v. Brinkman, 443 U.S. 526 (1979); United States v. Scotland Neck Bd. of Educ., 407 U.S. 484 (1972).
51 427 U.S. 424 (1976).
52 498 U.S. 237 (1991).
53 503 U.S. 467 (1992).

for example, all traces of segregation have been eliminated from student assignment procedures, the court could cease its oversight of that aspect of the district's operations while continuing to monitor other aspects of a mandated desegregation plan. The school district would, in effect, be declared unitary one piece at a time.

Judicial supervision of school districts can continue for decades. For example, more than 40 years had elapsed since the original *Brown* decision when the courts stopped supervising student assignment plans in Topeka, Kansas.[54] The courts continued to supervise the Charlotte-Mecklenburg district for 30 years before declaring it unitary in 2001.[55] Many other school systems were declared unitary after lengthy periods of supervision, including those of Boston, Atlanta, and Houston.[56]

More than six decades after *Brown*, overt *de jure* segregation in education has largely been eradicated, but many related problems in educational law and policy remain. Most large urban school districts now enroll a student population overwhelmingly comprised of students of color, a significant percentage of whom are poor. Although the racial and socio-economic homogeneity of such districts is usually considered *de facto*, debate continues on whether it should be viewed as *de jure*. Some question whether this type of *de facto* segregation violates Title VI of the Civil Rights of 1964 (see Chapter 7). Perhaps states as a matter of sound educational policy ought to take aggressive steps to address the issue, but it is unclear what those steps might be. **Charter schools** and **voucher plans** have been instituted in a number of urban areas (see Chapter 2). Voluntary urban-suburban student exchange programs have been introduced in others.[57] Efforts to reform state school finance systems through litigation represent a third approach (see Chapter 9).

Other Forms of Race-Based Discrimination

De jure segregation is not the only form of race-based discrimination prohibited by the Equal Protection Clause. Students may claim racial discrimination in **standardized testing**, tracking and ability grouping, disciplinary policies, or other areas of school policy and practice. Even in-class student grouping policies can violate the Equal Protection Clause. In *Billings v. Madison Metropolitan School District*,[58] a teacher deliberately assigned an African-American student to a group of four students that included another African-American student because, as she explained in court, "I think in my education training sometimes we were told African-American students need a buddy, and sometimes it works well if they have someone else working with them because they view things in a global manner." The Seventh Circuit found the strict scrutiny test could not be met because the grouping rested on a stereotypical view of African-American students.

As noted earlier, plaintiffs in Equal Protection Clause cases must prove that school officials acted with intent to discriminate. It is not enough that a school policy or practice happens to have a disproportionate effect on a particular group. For example, standardized tests to assign students to ability groups may have the effect of disproportionately assigning students of color to the lowest track. Such testing would be unconstitutional if done *because of*, rather than *in spite of*, its disproportionate effect.[59] Thus, a federal court refused to block the use of a non-culturally biased

---

54 Brown v. Unified Sch. Dist. Non. 501, 56 F. Supp. 2d 1212 (D. Kan. 1999).

55 Belk v. Charlotte-Mecklenburg Bd. of Educ., 269 F.3d 305 (4th Cir. 2001).

56 Coalition to Save Our Children v. Bd. of Educ., 90 F.3d 752 (3d Cir. 1996); Morgan v. Nucci, 831 F.2d 313 (1st Cir. 1987); Calhoun v. Cook, 522 F.2d 717 (5th Cir. 1975); Ross v. Houston Indep. Sch. Dist., 699 F.2d 218 (5th Cir. 1983).

57 *See* Jennifer Jellison Holme and Kara S. Finnigan, Striving In Common: A Regional Equity Framework For Urban Schools (2018).

58 259 F.3d 807 (7th Cir. 2001).

59 Larry P. v. Riles, 793 F.2d 969 (9th Cir. 1984).

minimum competency exam even though a higher percentage of African-American students than white students had failed the test. The exam's purpose was to ensure that all students had a certain level of knowledge and skill before receiving a diploma.[60]

Student "tracking systems" within classrooms have also generally withstood legal challenges. Some tracking systems have the effect of isolating a disproportionate number of African-American students in lower track classes. When such tracking systems are motivated by pedagogical concerns rather than racial animus, they are invariably found to be constitutional. For example, in *United States v. Jefferson County School District*,[61] a formerly segregated district seeking to be declared "unitary" had instituted an ability-grouping system that was racially imbalanced. In evaluating that tracking system, the district court explained:

> At the classroom level, the student assignment analysis is usually less stringent than at the school level: With respect to student assignment among classrooms, schools are not required to adopt an allocation scheme that guarantees balanced racial ratios. In general, the only rule is that classroom assignment decisions not be motivated by discriminatory intent. For example, schools may allocate students based on ability even if ability-grouping practices … have the *effect* of creating racial imbalances within classrooms, as long as the assignment method is not based on the present results of past segregation or will remedy such results through better educational opportunities. Courts are very deferential to school districts in determining whether ability-grouping practices meet that standard.

Applying this deferential standard, the court found the school district's tracking system was not racially discriminatory or unconstitutional. Thus the court ruled that the district had achieved unitary status.

In *Young v. Montgomery County Board of Education*,[62] the school district had adopted a "majority to minority" transfer program allowing students to transfer out of their regular attendance area if this would move the racial balance of the student's new school closer to that of the district as a whole. Fearful that coaches in predominantly white schools would use the transfer provision to recruit African-American athletes, the district adopted a rule requiring transferring high school students to sit out a year before becoming eligible to play. African-American students forced to choose between not transferring and sitting out claimed that the rule violated the Equal Protection Clause, but the court disagreed. Although the burden of the policy might fall disproportionately on African-Americans, the court concluded that this result was not intentional. The policy had been adopted at the request of African-American school board members in order to prevent illegal and exploitative recruiting of African-American athletes and help the predominantly African-American schools retain student leaders and the positive effects of successful athletic teams.

Discriminatory intent can be inferred, of course, when students of color are treated differently from their similarly-situated white peers. In the following case, although the Fifth Circuit agreed that school officials had treated a student differently on numerous occasions and in various ways, the court affirmed the district court's rejection of her Equal Protection claim. This case illustrates the difficulty plaintiffs encounter in proving discriminatory intent.

---

60 Debra P. v. Turlington, 564 F. Supp. 177 (M.D. Fla. 1983), *aff'd*, 730 F.2d 1405 (11th Cir. 1984).
61 63 F. Supp. 3d 1346, 1351 (N.D. Fla. 2014) (*citations omitted*).
62 922 F. Supp. 544 (M.D. Ala. 1996).

⚖️ FENNELL v. MARION INDEPENDENT SCHOOL DISTRICT

US Court of Appeals for the Fifth Circuit
804 F.3d 398 (2015)

CAROLYN DINEEN KING, Circuit Judge

Plaintiffs—Appellants Lawanda Fennell-Kinney and Kyana Fennell, on behalf of Kyrianna Adams Fennell and Kavin Johnson, brought claims under Title VI of the *Civil Rights Act of 1964* and 42 U.S.C. § 1983 against Marion Independent School District and two of its employees, Glenn Davis and Cynthia Manley. The district court granted Defendants—Appellees' motion for summary judgment as to all claims, and Plaintiffs appeal.

I. Factual and Procedural Background

Lawanda Fennell-Kinney is the mother of sisters Kyana Fennell, Kyrianna Adams Fennell (Kyra), and Kavin Johnson, who were ages 18, 15, and 13, respectively, when this action was filed in 2012. Plaintiffs, who are African-American, claimed that Marion Independent School District (Marion ISD) and two Marion ISD employees, Glenn Davis and Cynthia Manley, discriminated against them on the basis of race and created a racially hostile educational environment. Plaintiffs' claims stem from a series of incidents that took place while Kyana, Kyra, and Kavin were enrolled in Marion ISD, a predominately Caucasian school district. We recount the relevant incidents below, organized by the nature of the harassment involved.

A. Incidents Involving Nooses

In February 2012, Fennell-Kinney drove to the Marion High School parking lot to retrieve a car seat from Kyana's car. Next to the car, Fennell-Kinney found a noose and a printed note, which stated [redacted].

Fennell-Kinney immediately reported this incident to the Marion High School assistant principal, and Kyana told the assistant principal her suspicions that one of her classmates may have been involved. The assistant principal told Fennell-Kinney that he would review the parking lot surveillance tapes. He subsequently reported the incident to Officer Haverstock, a police officer for the City of Marion who patrolled the school. ...

This was not the first incident involving a noose at the high school. The previous year, Doug Giles, another African-American student, found a noose made out of a shoelace in his locker. Giles reported the incident to Defendant Davis, who then addressed the boys' athletic class, telling them that such actions were unacceptable and would not be tolerated. When no one admitted his involvement in the incident, Davis ordered the students to run laps as punishment. Davis also informed the interim superintendent of Marion ISD about the incident.

C. Incidents Involving Defendants Davis and Manley

In early 2011, Kyana had a hairstyle with streaks of burgundy in her hair. Defendant Davis, the Athletic Director, admonished Kyana for the hairstyle. Davis told Kyana, "I know how much you people spend on your ethnic hair styles" and asked Kyana "why [she] wanted to bring attention to [her]self." Davis noted that the Marion ISD student dress code and the athletics policy manual prohibited students from having their hair in non-naturally occurring colors, including burgundy. Kyana was aware of and had signed this policy. Davis informed Kyana that she would have to change her hair color before she could continue playing sports. Kyana eventually recolored her hair. Davis, another coach, and the assistant principal had all admonished other students, including Caucasian and Hispanic students, that the students' hair coloring violated school policies. Davis and the other coach had also told the students that they would need to cut or re-dye their non-naturally occurring hair before they could participate in school athletic activities.

On April 17, 2012, the Marion girls' varsity softball team, coached by Defendant Manley, had an away game in Luling, Texas. Kyra was the starting shortstop on the team. Earlier that day, Kyra left school, with permission, after a heated argument with several other students. Kyra went to lunch with Kyana and family friends. Kyana returned to school, but Kyra remained with the family friends for the rest of the afternoon. Since Kyra was off campus with family friends, she was absent when Manley took roll in Kyra's last period athletics course. After taking roll, the members of the softball team in the class boarded the team bus, and the bus left for the away game. Kyra returned to campus prior to the scheduled departure time for the bus, but the bus was already leaving. The driver of the car Kyra was riding in waved and honked at the bus to get Manley's attention, but Manley did not see Kyra in the vehicle and continued driving. Kyra followed the bus to the Luling game. When she arrived, Manley told Kyra she could not start but could play later in the game. Thereafter, Fennell-Kinney arrived at the game to take Kyra home. Manley informed Fennell-Kinney and Kyra that Kyra would be benched for the next game if she left the game early. After a verbal confrontation between Fennell-Kinney and Manley, Fennell-Kinney and Kyra left.

Two days later, after hearing that two other students had stated that Kyana, who had a child, was a bad parent, Kyana confronted the students at the softball field. During the verbal altercation, one of the students asked Kyana "[w]hat are you going to do, kick my ass?" to which Kyana responded, "[y]es, if you want me to." Several students reported the incident to Manley, who intervened after the verbal altercation had ended. She told the students to leave each other alone and to go home. Kyana then drove away. After Kyana left, the other students involved in the altercation expressed to Manley that they were afraid of Kyana. Manley instructed the students that they could file a police report regarding the incident. Manley had never previously advised any of her players to report an incident to the police. The students ultimately filed charges against Kyana, which were later dismissed. Davis wrote an incident report to the interim superintendent and to the Marion ISD School Board regarding the altercation. Davis concluded, based on Manley's account, that Kyana bullied the other two students.

D. Other Incidents of Harassment

Plaintiffs were also harassed in other ways. In 2008, Kyra received a text message from a Caucasian classmate that showed an animation of KKK members chasing President Obama. Kyra and the classmate had a physical altercation, and both students received three-day suspensions following the incident. In 2010, one of Kyra's teachers told Kyra's class that "all black people [are] on welfare." Kyra confronted the teacher about the statement, after which the teacher threatened to send her to the office if she

"didn't pipe down." Kyra did not report the incident to anyone else at the school.

During the 2011–2012 school year, the girls' final school year in Marion ISD, the harassment continued. Kyana attended a basketball game with a friend, who joked that two other girls were "bad influences" for cheating. Ashley Smith, a Caucasian teacher who coached Kyana on the basketball team, overheard the conversation and told Kyana: "You're the bad influence. You're the one who had a kid at 17." Smith was suspended from coaching for one game and given an official reprimand from the school's athletic director. A letter regarding the incident was also placed in Smith's file. The incident prompted Fennell-Kinney to file a grievance with the school administrators. Following the incident, Kyana was also harassed by her peers at school for getting Smith into trouble.

Kavin tried out for the cheerleading squad, which prompted her peers to say that "Black girls [aren't] pretty enough to be cheerleaders." In addition, several girls recorded her tryouts on their cell phones, spreading the video around the school with the title: "Little boy tries out for cheerleading." Although Fennell-Kinney reported to the cheer sponsor (a teacher) that some of the girls had recorded Kavin's tryout, it does not appear that any of the other comments were reported to anyone at Marion ISD. Kavin was also involved in an altercation in which a Caucasian male student spat in her face and told her to "go back where you came from." Kavin reported the incident to the principal, who talked to the student about the incident.

Kyra complained to the assistant principal regarding Facebook posts from several of her classmates calling her a [redacted]. The classmates also complained to the assistant principal about Kyra's posts. The assistant principal told Kyra that he could not punish any of the girls for this conduct because it occurred outside of school.

E. Marion ISD Policies and Response to Complaints

During the time period relevant to the lawsuit, Marion ISD had in place policies prohibiting harassment, bullying, and racial discrimination. These policies are contained in the District Employee Handbook and in the Student Handbook. Marion ISD also required its employees to attend in-service training at the beginning of each school year; that training addressed issues of bullying, discrimination, and harassment prevention and reporting. ...

As a result of the above incidents, Fennell-Kinney filed a Level Three grievance before the Marion ISD Board of Trustees (Board), which was presented to the Board on May 30, 2012. The district granted some of the remedies requested by Plaintiffs and denied others. Marion ISD also required its employees to attend additional training on its discrimination, harassment, and bullying policies after the noose was found in the parking lot. The training was facilitated by the Department of Justice (DOJ) and provided by an outside organization, which was not affiliated with the district. Students were also required to attend a special assembly led by the same organization on the same topics. The district, however, refused to sign a resolution provided by the DOJ regarding the school's policies. Fennell-Kinney ultimately withdrew Kavin and Kyra from Marion ISD in the spring of 2012 and enrolled the sisters in another school district. ...

IV. Equal Protection Claims under § 1983

Plaintiffs also argue that summary judgment was improper for their equal protection claims, brought under § 1983, against Marion ISD and against Defendants Manley and Davis in their individual capacities. "Section 1983 provides a cause of action against any person who deprives an individual of federally guaranteed rights 'under color' of state law." ... One such federal right is conferred by the Equal Protection Clause, which prohibits a state from "deny[ing] to any person within its jurisdiction the equal protection of the laws." Accordingly,

[t]o state a claim of racial discrimination under the Equal Protection Clause and section 1983, the plaintiff "must allege and prove that [(1) he or she] received treatment different from that received by similarly situated individuals and that [(2)] the unequal treatment stemmed from a discriminatory intent."

To establish discriminatory intent, a plaintiff must show "that the decision maker singled out a particular group for disparate treatment and selected his course of action at least in part for the purpose of causing its adverse effect on an identifiable group."

As an initial matter, Defendants do not assert qualified immunity on appeal, and thus have waived this defense. We therefore address whether Plaintiffs have raised a genuine dispute as to each claim.

A. Marion ISD

Plaintiffs advance two primary theories in support of their equal protection claim against Marion ISD: (1) a theory premised on alleged discriminatory customs or policies and (2) a theory premised on an alleged failure to train. With respect to both theories, "a municipality cannot be held liable under § 1983 on a *respondeat superior* theory." Accordingly, "isolated unconstitutional actions by municipal employees will almost never trigger liability," but rather "the unconstitutional conduct must be directly attributable to the municipality through some sort of official action or imprimatur." The policymaker is liable if an official policy itself is unconstitutional or the policy was adopted "with 'deliberate indifference' to its known or obvious consequences." ...

Here, the record shows that the grievances at issue were not presented to the Board until May 2012, after all the incidents described above occurred. Although the record indicates that some of the incidents were reported to Marion ISD administrators and the interim superintendent, those individuals have not been delegated policymaking authority under Texas law. Thus, even assuming the alleged customs, policies, and failures to train existed among Marion ISD employees, "[t]here is no evidence that the Board knew of this behavior or condoned it."

In particular, while the Board may have known about three of the incidents prior to the May 2012 Board meeting, those alone are not sufficient to show the board had knowledge of any discriminatory custom. Moreover, the Board had previously implemented official policies prohibiting racial discrimination, bullying, and harassment. And after the parking lot noose incident, Marion ISD instituted additional anti-discrimination and anti-harassment training facilitated by the DOJ and provided by an unaffiliated organization. The district court therefore did not err in granting summary judgment as to the claim against Marion ISD under § 1983.

B. Cynthia Manley

Plaintiffs argue that the district court erred in granting summary judgment on their equal protection claim against Defendant Manley. On appeal, Plaintiffs rely on two incidents to support this claim: (1) the April 2012 Luling bus incident and (2) the April 2012 softball field altercation.

As to the Luling bus incident, Plaintiffs have failed to show that Kyra was treated differently than similarly situated peers. Kyra signed out of school on the day of the away game and missed her remaining classes that school day. While Kyra arrived on campus prior to the scheduled departure time, there is no dispute that Kyra was not present during the team's roll call. Moreover, there is no evidence in the record suggesting that Manley had ever encountered a situation in which a student signed out for lunch on a game day and failed to return in time for the team's roll call. Nor is there any evidence that she had failed to punish a student in such a situation. Plaintiffs have thus failed to show the treatment of any *similarly situated* peers, let alone that Kyra was treated differently.

Plaintiffs also point to the softball field altercation several days later between Kyana and two other students. Although there is a genuine dispute as to whether the altercation was merely verbal or involved physical contact, there is no dispute that Manley did not personally observe the incident. There is also no dispute that Manley did not impose any punishment on any of the three girls, but rather told all of the participants to leave each other alone and go home. While the evidence does suggest disparate treatment because Manley suggested that only the two students, and not Kyana, file a police report, these students were not similarly situated. The undisputed evidence shows that only those two students expressed to Manley that they were afraid of Kyana, stating that they feared that Kyana or her family would "come after them"; Kyana expressed no such concerns. Although Manley admitted to never having previously advised students to file a police report, she also testified that she had not previously had any students fight or threaten each other. Nor is there any evidence suggesting that Manley would not have given the same instructions to Kyana had she reported that she feared the other two students.

Furthermore, there is no evidence in the record suggesting that Manley acted on the basis of race in either incident … [I]n fact, Kyra herself stated that Manley's actions relating to the Luling bus incident had nothing to do with race. Thus, there is no evidence that Manley "singled out" Plaintiffs "for disparate treatment … in part for the purpose of causing [an] adverse effect on an identifiable group." The district court therefore properly granted summary judgment on the claim against Manley.

C. Glenn Davis

Plaintiffs next argue that the district court erred in granting summary judgment on their equal protection claim against Defendant Davis. On appeal, Plaintiffs rely on two incidents to support their claim against Davis: (1) the January 2011 hairstyle inci-

dent involving Kyana and (2) the April 2012 softball field altercation.

Viewed in the light most favorable to Plaintiffs, Davis made a racially offensive comment to Kyana by stating that he "know[s] how much *you people* spend on your *ethnic* hair styles." Such a comment is clearly indicative of racial animus. However, the racially offensive comment alone is insufficient to support an equal protection claim under § 1983; the comment must also be coupled with "harassment or some other conduct that deprives the victim of established rights" to constitute an equal protection violation. Here, the evidence of Davis's racial motivation was not coupled with any disparate treatment. The incident culminated in Davis informing Kyana that she would have to change her hair color before she could continue to participate in school athletic activities. There is no dispute that Kyana's hair color was in violation of the athletic policy, and there is undisputed evidence that Marion ISD officials consistently reprimanded students of all races who violated the hair color policies, requiring those students to change their hair color. Accordingly, despite Davis's racially offensive comment, there is no evidence suggesting that Kyana "received treatment different from that received by similarly situated individuals."

Furthermore, Plaintiffs have waived any claim against Davis premised on the April 2012 softball field altercation involving Kyana. The Second Amended Complaint clearly alleges that the relevant incident underlying this claim was Davis's failure to override Manley's punishment *arising from the softball bus incident involving Kyra*, not the softball field altercation involving Kyana. Although the Second Amended Complaint alleges facts relating to Manley's handling of the softball field altercation, it includes no allegations against Davis relating to his investigation and report on the altercation. This court has made clear that "[a] claim which is not raised in the complaint but, rather, is raised only in response to a motion for summary judgment is not properly before the court." Because Plaintiffs have failed to show a genuine dispute that Davis treated Plaintiffs differently from similarly situated individuals on the only incident properly raised in the complaint, we conclude that the district court correctly granted summary judgment on the claim against Davis.

V. Conclusion

For the foregoing reasons, we AFFIRM the judgment of the district court.

Despite the court's recognition that some behavior by staff was inappropriate and even offensive, the court declined to find it illegal. Nevertheless, as this case demonstrates, teachers and other school officials can potentially violate the Equal Protection Clause if they deliberately treat students differently based on race.

Affirmative Action and Voluntary Integration

Race must be taken into consideration when fashioning remedies for proven *de jure* segregation. But because *de facto* segregation is not illegal, the question of whether race may be taken into consideration when a school board voluntarily seeks to *integrate* its schools raises a very different issue. In looking to the law governing higher education, may a school employ different admissions standards for students of color in order to increase the diversity of its student body? Two Supreme Court decisions from 2003 concerning **affirmative action** in public universities provide a framework for answering this question.[63]

In *Grutter v. Bollinger*,[64] the Supreme Court issued a five-justice majority opinion and four dissenting opinions. Collectively, the dissenting opinions vigorously disagreed with virtually every significant finding of the majority. The case involved a challenge to an affirmative action admission policy at the University of Michigan Law School. Michigan's highly ranked law school annually admitted approximately ten percent of its 3,500 applicants. In selecting among the applicants, the school relied heavily on undergraduate GPA and Law School Admission Test scores but also considered personal statements, letters of recommendation, and essays in which applicants described how they would contribute to the life and diversity of the law school.

Various forms of diversity were sought, in particular "the inclusion of students from groups which have been historically discriminated against, like African-Americans, Hispanics and Native Americans, who without this commitment might not be represented in [the school's] student body in meaningful numbers." Certain minority groups (e.g., Asian-Americans) were not covered by the policy because the law school believed members of those groups were being admitted in significant numbers without special consideration. (In 2019, a district court similarly rejected claims that Harvard University had intentionally discriminated against Asian-Americans in its admissions policies.)[65]

Although the admissions staff was not directed to admit a particular percentage of minority students, the staff did pay close attention to race. Analysis by an expert witness showed that membership in the targeted minority groups was in fact an extremely strong factor but not the predominant factor in acceptance. Thirty-five percent of the minority applicants were admitted; if race had not been considered, only ten percent would have been admitted, the same percentage as majority applicants. If race had not been considered, the entering classes would have been four percent minority instead of over 14 percent.

In considering the Equal Protection claims of a white applicant denied admission under these policies, the Court employed the strict scrutiny test. Strict scrutiny would not be satisfied, said the Court, if the goal of the admission system were to reduce the historic deficit of traditionally disfavored minorities in a professional school, to remedy societal discrimination, or to increase the number of minority attorneys. However, based on the law school's insistence that diversity was essential to its educational mission, the Court found that the goal of achieving a diverse student body could provide the compelling state interest necessary to satisfy strict scrutiny.

Nevertheless, said the Court, in seeking this goal, the school could not employ a quota, could use race as only one element among others in realizing a diverse student body, could not unduly harm the members of any racial or ethnic group, and could only employ a selection process that

---

63 Gratz v. Bollinger, 539 U.S. 244 (2003); Grutter v. Bollinger, 539 U.S. 306 (2003).
64 539 U.S. 306 (2003).
65 Students for Fair Admissions, Inc. v. President & Fellows of Harvard Coll., 397 F. Supp. 3d 126 (D. Mass. 2019).

was "narrowly tailored" to meet the goal. Applying these principles, the Court concluded that the law school's policies did in fact serve the compelling state interest in creating a diverse student body and that they were narrowly tailored to meet that goal.

Narrow tailoring, said the Court, did not require exhaustion of every conceivable race-neutral alternative that might achieve a diverse student body. In any event, the law school did sufficiently consider race-neutral alternatives such as a lottery or simply lowering admission standards, but it had valid reasons for rejecting these alternatives. Nor, said the Court, did the policies amount to a quota system. The school engaged in a

> highly individualized, holistic review of each applicant's file, giving serious consideration to all the ways an applicant might contribute to a diverse educational environment. Race operated only as a plus factor in the context of individualized consideration of each and every applicant.

The school also gave substantial weight to diversity factors besides race:

> Because the Law School considers "all pertinent elements of diversity," it can (and does) select nonminority applicants who have greater potential to enhance student body diversity over underrepresented minority applicants ... The Law School frequently accepts nonminority applicants with grades and test scores lower than underrepresented minority applicants (and other nonminority applicants) who are rejected.

The Court concluded its decision with a stipulation that race-conscious policies be limited in time: "[R]acial classifications, however compelling their goals, are potentially so dangerous that they may be employed no more broadly than the interest demands ... We expect that 25 years from now, the use of racial preferences will no longer be necessary ..." The majority did not explain why it expected that the conditions justifying affirmative action in 2003 would not be present in 2028.

In *Gratz v. Bollinger*,[66] the Supreme Court *rejected* the undergraduate admission system at the University of Michigan. Admission decisions from among more than 13,000 applicants were based on a point system, with points being awarded for, among other things, GPA, test scores, special talents, alumni relationship, in-state residency, leadership, and race. Applicants automatically received 20 points, one-fifth of the points needed to guarantee admission, for membership in an underrepresented racial or ethnic minority group.

Employing the principles announced in *Grutter*, the Court in *Gratz* concluded that, unlike the law school policy, the undergraduate system was "not narrowly tailored to achieve the interest in educational diversity." It did not provide the kind of individualized consideration that was the hallmark of the admission process in *Grutter*. The automatic assignment of 20 points had the

> effect of making "the factor of race ... decisive" for virtually every minimally qualified underrepresented minority applicant ... By comparison a non-minority student with artistic talent that rivaled that of Picasso would receive at most five points. Neither the minority nor non-minority student received truly individualized consideration to determine how they would benefit the university. And the fact that providing individualized consideration to thousands of applications would create "administrative challenges" does not render constitutional an otherwise problematic system.

In *Fisher v. University of Texas*,[67] the plaintiffs challenged the two-tiered admissions policy at the University of Texas. Under this policy, approximately 75 percent of students were admitted under the "Top Ten Percent Law" (TTPL), which guaranteed admission to all graduates of Texas public

66 52 539 U.S. 244 (2003).
67 570 U.S. 297 (2013).

high schools finishing in the top ten percent of their class. Although facially neutral regarding race, this admissions policy led to increased enrollment of students of color from urban high schools. Seeking an even higher increase, however, the university also admitted some students who did not fall within TTPL, and in this admission tier the university considered race as one factor among many. The plaintiffs in *Fisher* argued that the success of TTPL, a facially neutral policy, rendered the use of race in the other admission tier unnecessary and unconstitutional. The district court rejected this position, and said that adopting such a position would create a "Catch-22" for universities: if they successfully employed race-neutral policies, they would be "rewarded" by being prohibited from ever using race-conscious admissions policies. The Fifth Circuit held that the applicant could challenge only whether the university's decision to reintroduce race as a factor in admissions was made in good faith. The Supreme Court found this to be at odds with its decision in *Grutter*, as it had not held that good faith could trump impermissible considerations of race. In deferring to the university's good faith in its use of racial classifications, the Fifth Circuit had improperly applied strict scrutiny.

The Supreme Court sent the case back to the Fifth Circuit, instructing it to employ strict scrutiny when reviewing the policy. The Fifth Circuit did so, and returned the same result—upholding the constitutionality of the university's admissions policy.

In 2016, when the Supreme Court again heard the case, it affirmed the decision of the Fifth Circuit and largely upheld the principles it had established in *Grutter* and *Gratz*. The Court noted with approval that "[t]he University did adopt an approach similar to the one in *Grutter*" for the second, "race-conscious" admissions tier. Under that tier, the Court found, "although admissions officers can consider race as a positive feature of a minority student's application, there is no dispute that race is but a 'factor of a factor of a factor' in the holistic-review calculus."[68] Because the university had engaged in a holistic, rather than quota-driven admissions process, its approach was constitutional under *Grutter*. At the same time, however, the Court cautioned that "asserting an interest in the educational benefits of diversity writ large is insufficient. A university's goals cannot be elusory or amorphous—they must be sufficiently measurable to permit judicial scrutiny of the policies adopted to reach them." In finding that the university's diversity goals met this test, the Court credited a comprehensive report the university had produced over the course of a full year.

Together, *Grutter*, *Gratz*, and *Fisher* allow for affirmative action admissions policies under certain circumstances, which could have important consequences for student assignment, transfer, and admission plans designed to promote cultural diversity and integration in K-12 public schools. However, school districts are prohibited from promoting racial diversity in their schools by "classify[ing] every student on the basis of race and … assigning each of them to schools based on that classification," as the following case illustrates:

⚖️

PARENTS INVOLVED IN COMMUNITY SCHOOLS v. SEATTLE SCHOOL DISTRICT NO. 1
Supreme Court of the United States
551 U.S. 701 (2007)

CHIEF JUSTICE ROBERTS announced the judgment of the Court …[69]

The school districts in these cases voluntarily adopted student assignment plans that rely upon race to determine which public schools certain children may attend. The Seattle school district classifies children as white or nonwhite; the Jefferson County school district as black or "other." In Seat-

---

68 Fisher v. Univ. of Texas at Austin, 136 S. Ct. 2198 (2016).
69 The judgment and some parts of the opinion are a majority opinion; Parts III-B and IV are a plurality opinion.

tle, this racial classification is used to allocate slots in oversubscribed high schools. In Jefferson County, it is used to make certain elementary school assignments and to rule on transfer requests. In each case, the school district relies upon an individual student's race in assigning that student to a particular school, so that the racial balance at the school falls within a predetermined range based on the racial composition of the school district as a whole. Parents of students denied assignment to particular schools under these plans solely because of their race brought suit, contending that allocating children to different public schools on the basis of race violated the Fourteenth Amendment guarantee of equal protection. The Courts of Appeals below upheld the plans. We granted *certiorari*, and now reverse.

I

Both cases present the same underlying legal question—whether a public school that had not operated legally segregated schools or has been found to be unitary may choose to classify students by race and rely upon that classification in making school assignments. Although we examine the plans under the same legal framework, the specifics of the two plans, and the circumstances surrounding their adoption, are in some respects quite different.

A

Seattle School District No. 1 operates 10 regular public high schools. In 1998, it adopted the plan at issue in this case for assigning students to these schools. The plan allows incoming ninth graders to choose from among any of the district's high schools, ranking however many schools they wish in order of preference.

Some schools are more popular than others. If too many students list the same school as their first choice, the district employs a series of "tiebreakers" to determine who will fill the open slots at the oversubscribed school. The first tiebreaker selects for admission students who have a sibling currently enrolled in the chosen school. The next tiebreaker depends upon the racial composition of the particular school and the race of the individual student. In the district's public schools approximately 41 percent of enrolled students are white; the remaining 59 percent, comprising all other racial groups, are classified by Seattle for assignment purposes as nonwhite. If an oversubscribed school is not within 10 percentage points of the district's overall white/

nonwhite racial balance, it is what the district calls "integration positive," and the district employs a tiebreaker that selects for assignment students whose race "will serve to bring the school into balance." If it is still necessary to select students for the school after using the racial tiebreaker, the next tiebreaker is the geographic proximity of the school to the student's residence.

Seattle has never operated segregated schools—legally separate schools for students of different races—nor has it ever been subject to court-ordered desegregation. It nonetheless employs the racial tiebreaker in an attempt to address the effects of racially identifiable housing patterns on school assignments. Most white students live in the northern part of Seattle, most students of other racial backgrounds in the southern part ...

For the 2000–2001 school year, five of these schools were oversubscribed—Ballard, Nathan Hale, Roosevelt, Garfield, and Franklin—so much so that 82 percent of incoming ninth graders ranked one of these schools as their first choice. Three of the oversubscribed schools were "integration positive" because the school's white enrollment the previous school year was greater than 51 percent—Ballard, Nathan Hale, and Roosevelt. Thus, more nonwhite students (107, 27, and 82, respectively) who selected one of these three schools as a top choice received placement at the school than would have been the case had race not been considered, and proximity been the next tiebreaker. Franklin was "integration positive" because its nonwhite enrollment the previous school year was greater than 69 percent; 89 more white students were assigned to Franklin by operation of the racial tiebreaker in the 2000–2001 school year than otherwise would have been. Garfield was the only oversubscribed school whose composition during the 1999–2000 school year was within the racial guidelines, although in previous years Garfield's enrollment had been predominantly nonwhite, and the racial tiebreaker had been used to give preference to white students ...

B

Jefferson County Public Schools operates the public school system in metropolitan Louisville, Kentucky. In 1973 a federal court found that Jefferson County had maintained a segregated school system and in 1975 the District Court entered a desegregation decree. Jefferson County operated under this decree until 2000, when the District Court dissolved the decree after finding that the district had achieved unitary status by eliminating "[t]o the greatest extent practicable" the vestiges of its prior policy of segregation. In 2001, after the decree had been dissolved, Jefferson County adopted the voluntary student assignment plan at issue in this case. Approximately 34 percent of the district's 97,000 students are black; most of the remaining 66 percent are white. The plan requires all non-magnet schools to maintain a minimum black enrollment of 15 percent, and a maximum black enrollment of 50 percent.

At the elementary school level, based on his or her address, each student is designated a "resides" school to which students within a specific geographic area are assigned; elementary resides schools are "grouped into clusters in order to facilitate integration." The district assigns students to non-magnet schools in one of two ways: Parents of kindergartners, first-graders, and students new to the district may submit an application indicating a first and second choice among the schools within their cluster; students who do not submit such an application are assigned within the cluster by the district. "Decisions to assign students to schools within each cluster are based on available space within the schools and the racial guidelines in the District's current student assignment plan." If a school has reached the "extremes of the racial guidelines," a student whose race would contribute to the school's racial imbalance will not be assigned there. After assignment, students at all grade levels are permitted to apply to transfer between non-magnet schools in the district. Transfers may be requested for any number of reasons, and may be denied because of lack of available space or on the basis of the racial guidelines.

III

A

It is well established that when the government distributes burdens or benefits on the basis of individual racial classifications, that action is reviewed under strict scrutiny. As the Court recently reaffirmed, "'racial classifications are simply too pernicious to permit any but the most exact connection between justification and classification.'" In order to satisfy this searching standard of review, the school districts must demonstrate that the use of individual racial classifications in the assignment plans here under review is "narrowly tailored" to achieve a "com-

pelling" government interest. Without attempting in these cases to set forth all the interests a school district might assert, it suffices to note that our prior cases, in evaluating the use of racial classifications in the school context, have recognized two interests that qualify as compelling. The first is the compelling interest of remedying the effects of past intentional discrimination. Yet the Seattle public schools have not shown that they were ever segregated by law, and were not subject to court-ordered desegregation decrees. The Jefferson County public schools were previously segregated by law and were subject to a desegregation decree entered in 1975. In 2000, the District Court that entered that decree dissolved it, finding that Jefferson County had "eliminated the vestiges associated with the former policy of segregation and its pernicious effects," and thus had achieved "unitary" status ... Jefferson County accordingly does not rely upon an interest in remedying the effects of past intentional discrimination in defending its present use of race in assigning students.

Nor could it. We have emphasized that the harm being remedied by mandatory desegregation plans is the harm that is traceable to segregation, and that "the Constitution is not violated by racial imbalance in the schools, without more." ... Once Jefferson County achieved unitary status, it had remedied the constitutional wrong that allowed race-based assignments. Any continued use of race must be justified on some other basis.

The second government interest we have recognized as compelling for purposes of strict scrutiny is the interest in diversity in higher education upheld in *Grutter*.[70] The specific interest found compelling in *Grutter* was student body diversity "in the context of higher education." The diversity interest was not focused on race alone but encompassed "all factors that may contribute to student body diversity." We described the various types of diversity that the law school sought:

[The law school's] policy makes clear there are many possible bases for diversity admissions, and provides examples of admittees who have lived or traveled widely abroad, are fluent in several languages, have overcome personal adversity and family hardship, have exceptional records of extensive community service, and have had successful careers in other fields.

70 539 U.S. 306 (2003).

The Court quoted the articulation of diversity from Justice Powell's opinion in *Regents of the University of California v. Bakke*,[71] noting that "it is not an interest in simple ethnic diversity, in which a specified percentage of the student body is in effect guaranteed to be members of selected ethnic groups, that can justify the use of race." Instead, what was upheld in *Grutter* was consideration of "a far broader array of qualifications and characteristics of which racial or ethnic origin is but a single though important element."

The entire gist of the analysis in *Grutter* was that the admissions program at issue there focused on each applicant as an individual, and not simply as a member of a particular racial group. The classification of applicants by race upheld in *Grutter* was only as part of a "highly individualized, holistic review," As the Court explained, "[t]he importance of this individualized consideration in the context of a race-conscious admissions program is paramount." The point of the narrow tailoring analysis in which the *Grutter* Court engaged was to ensure that the use of racial classifications was indeed part of a broader assessment of diversity, and not simply an effort to achieve racial balance, which the Court explained would be "patently unconstitutional."

In the present cases, by contrast, race is not considered as part of a broader effort to achieve "exposure to widely diverse people, cultures, ideas, and viewpoints," race, for some students, is determinative standing alone. The districts argue that other factors, such as student preferences, affect assignment decisions under their plans, but under each plan when race comes into play, it is decisive by itself. It is not simply one factor weighed with others in reaching a decision, as in *Grutter*; it is the factor. Like the University of Michigan undergraduate plan struck down in *Gratz*,[72] the plans here "do not provide for a meaningful individualized review of applicants" but instead rely on racial classifications in a "non-individualized, mechanical" way.

Even when it comes to race, the plans here employ only a limited notion of diversity, viewing race exclusively in white/nonwhite terms in Seattle and black/"other" terms in Jefferson County ... The Seattle "Board Statement Reaffirming Diversity Rationale" speaks of the "inherent educational value" in "[p]roviding students the opportunity to attend schools with diverse student enrollment". But under the Seattle plan, a school with 50 percent Asian-American students and 50 percent white students but no African-American, Native-American, or Latino students would qualify as balanced, while a school with 30 percent Asian-American, 25 percent African-American, 25 percent Latino, and 20 percent white students would not. It is hard to understand how a plan that could allow these results can be viewed as being concerned with achieving enrollment that is "broadly diverse" ...

In upholding the admissions plan in *Grutter* ... this Court relied upon considerations unique to institutions of higher education, noting that in light of "the expansive freedoms of speech and thought associated with the university environment, universities occupy a special niche in our constitutional tradition." The Court explained that "[c]ontext matters" in applying strict scrutiny, and repeatedly noted that it was addressing the use of race "in the context of higher education." The Court in *Grutter* expressly articulated key limitations on its holding—defining a specific type of broad-based diversity and noting the unique context of higher education—but these limitations were largely disregarded by the lower courts in extending *Grutter* to uphold race-based assignments in elementary and secondary schools. The present cases are not governed by *Grutter*.

B

[This part of the opinion is a plurality, not majority, opinion.]

Perhaps recognizing that reliance on *Grutter* cannot sustain their plans, both school districts assert additional interests, distinct from the interest upheld in *Grutter*, to justify their race-based assignments ... Seattle contends that its use of race helps to reduce racial concentration in schools and to ensure that racially concentrated housing patterns do not prevent nonwhite students from having access to the most desirable schools. Jefferson County has articulated a similar goal, phrasing its interest in terms of educating its students "in a racially integrated environment." Each school district argues that educational and broader socialization benefits flow from a racially diverse learning environment, and each contends that because the diversity they seek is racial diversity—not the broader diversity at issue in *Grutter*—it makes sense to promote that interest directly by relying on race alone.

71 438 U.S. 265 (1978).
72 539 U.S. 244 (2003).

The parties ... dispute whether racial diversity in schools in fact has a marked impact on test scores and other objective yardsticks or achieves intangible socialization benefits. The debate is not one we need to resolve, however, because it is clear that the racial classifications employed by the districts are not narrowly tailored to the goal of achieving the educational and social benefits asserted to flow from racial diversity. In design and operation, the plans are directed only to racial balance, pure and simple, an objective this Court has repeatedly condemned as illegitimate.

The plans are tied to each district's specific racial demographics, rather than to any pedagogic concept of the level of diversity needed to obtain the asserted educational benefits. In Seattle, the district seeks white enrollment of between 31 and 51 percent (within 10 percent of "the district white average" of 41 percent), and nonwhite enrollment of between 49 and 69 percent (within 10 percent of "the district minority average" of 59 percent). In Jefferson County, by contrast, the district seeks black enrollment of no less than 15 or more than 50 percent, a range designed to be "equally above and below Black student enrollment system-wide," based on the objective of achieving at "all schools ... an African-American enrollment equivalent to the average district-wide African-American enrollment" of 34 percent. In Seattle, then, the benefits of racial diversity require enrollment of at least 31 percent white students; in Jefferson County, at least 50 percent. There must be at least 15 percent nonwhite students under Jefferson County's plan; in Seattle, more than three times that figure. This comparison makes clear that the racial demographics in each district—whatever they happen to be—drive the required "diversity" numbers. The plans here are not tailored to achieving a degree of diversity necessary to realize the asserted educational benefits; instead the plans are tailored, in the words of Seattle's Manager of Enrollment Planning, Technical Support, and Demographics, to "the goal established by the school board of attaining a level of diversity within the schools that approximates the district's overall demographics."

The districts offer no evidence that the level of racial diversity necessary to achieve the asserted educational benefits happens to coincide with the racial demographics of the respective school districts ... Seattle's expert said it was important to have "sufficient numbers so as to avoid students feeling any kind of specter of exceptionality." The district did not attempt to defend the proposition that anything outside its range posed the "specter of exceptionality." ...

Similarly, Jefferson County's expert referred to the importance of having "at least 20 percent" minority group representation for the group "to be visible enough to make a difference," and noted that "small isolated minority groups in a school are not likely to have a strong effect on the overall school." The Jefferson County plan, however, is based on a goal of replicating at each school "an African-American enrollment equivalent to the average district-wide African-American enrollment." ...

In fact, in each case the extreme measure of relying on race in assignments is unnecessary to achieve the stated goals, even as defined by the districts ... When the actual racial breakdown is considered, enrolling students without regard to their race yields a substantially diverse student body under any definition of diversity.

In Grutter, the number of minority students the school sought to admit was an undefined "meaningful number" necessary to achieve a genuinely diverse student body. Although the matter was the subject of disagreement on the Court, the majority concluded that the law school did not count back from its applicant pool to arrive at the "meaningful number" it regarded as necessary to diversify its student body. Here the racial balance the districts seek is a defined range set solely by reference to the demographics of the respective school districts. This working backward to achieve a particular type of racial balance, rather than working forward from some demonstration of the level of diversity that provides the purported benefits, is a fatal flaw under our existing precedent. We have many times over reaffirmed that "[r]acial balance is not to be achieved for its own sake." ... Grutter itself reiterated that "outright racial balancing" is "patently unconstitutional."

Accepting racial balancing as a compelling state interest would justify the imposition of racial proportionality throughout American society, contrary to our repeated recognition that "[a]t the heart of the Constitution's guarantee of equal protection lies the simple command that the Government must treat citizens as individuals, not as simply components of a racial, religious, sexual or national class." Allowing racial balancing as a compelling end in itself would "effectively assure[e] that race will always be relevant in American life, and that the 'ultimate goal' of 'eliminating entirely from governmental decision making such irrelevant factors as a human being's race' will never be achieved". An interest "linked to nothing other than proportional representation of various races … would support indefinite use of racial classifications, employed first to obtain the appropriate mixture of racial views and then to ensure that the [program] continues to reflect that mixture." …

However closely related race-based assignments may be to achieving racial balance, that itself cannot be the goal, whether labeled "racial diversity" or anything else. To the extent the objective is sufficient diversity so that students see fellow students as individuals rather than solely as members of a racial group, using means that treat students solely as members of a racial group is fundamentally at cross-purposes with that end. …

C

The districts have … failed to show that they considered methods other than explicit racial classifications to achieve their stated goals. Narrow tailoring requires "serious, good faith consideration of workable race-neutral alternatives," and yet in Seattle several alternative assignment plans—many of which would not have used express racial classifications—were rejected with little or no consideration. Jefferson County has failed to present any evidence that it considered alternatives, even though the district already claims that its goals are achieved primarily through means other than the racial classifications.

* * *

In *Brown v. Board of Education*,[73] we held that segregation deprived black children of equal educational opportunities regardless of whether school facilities and other tangible factors were equal, because government classification and separation on grounds of race themselves denoted inferiority. It was not the inequality of the facilities but the fact of legally separating children on the basis of race on which the Court relied to find a constitutional violation in 1954. The next Term, we accordingly stated that "full compliance" with Brown required school districts "to achieve a system of determining admission to the public schools on a non-racial basis."

The parties … debate which side is more faithful to the heritage of *Brown*, but the position of the plaintiffs in Brown was spelled out in their brief and could not have been clearer: "[T]he Fourteenth Amendment prevents states from according differential treatment to American children on the basis of their color or race." What do the racial classifications at issue here do, if not accord differential treatment on the basis of race? As counsel who appeared before this Court for the plaintiffs in *Brown* put it:

We have one fundamental contention which we will seek to develop in the course of this argument, and that contention is that no State has any authority under the equal-protection clause of the Fourteenth Amendment to use race as a factor in affording educational opportunities among its citizens.

There is no ambiguity in that statement. And it was that position that prevailed in this Court, which emphasized in its remedial opinion that what was "[a]t stake is the personal interest of the plaintiffs in admission to public schools as soon as practicable on a non-discriminatory basis," and what was required was "determining admission to the public schools on a non-racial basis." What do the racial classifications do in these cases, if not determine admission to a public school on a racial basis? Before *Brown*, schoolchildren were told where they could and could not go to school based on the color of their skin. The school districts in these cases have not carried the heavy burden of demonstrating that we should allow this once again—even for very different reasons. For schools that never segregated on the basis of race, such as Seattle, or that have removed the vestiges of past segregation, such as Jefferson County, the way "to achieve a system of determining admission to the public schools on a non-racial basis," is to stop assigning students on a racial basis. The way to stop discrimination on the basis of race is to stop discriminating on the basis of race. The judgments of the Courts of Appeals for the Sixth and Ninth Circuits are reversed, and the cases are remanded for further proceedings.

Like *Grutter, Parents Involved* was an extremely contentious case. Chief Justice Roberts' opinion announcing the 5–4 decision contained key sections that do not set precedent because they received support from only a plurality of the Court. The case also produced two concurring and

---

73 347 U.S. 483 (1954).

two dissenting opinions that disagreed on many aspects of the decision. If the dissenting judges had prevailed, school districts would have been permitted to employ race as an explicit factor in student assignment with the goal of promoting racial balance and diversity within their schools.

Justice Kennedy's concurring opinion established a middle ground:

> This Nation has a moral and ethical obligation to fulfill its historic commitment to creating an integrated society that ensures equal opportunity for all of its children. A compelling interest exists in avoiding racial isolation, an interest that a school district, in its discretion and expertise, may choose to pursue. Likewise, a district may consider it a compelling interest to achieve a diverse student population. Race may be one component of that diversity, but other demographic factors, plus special talents and needs, should also be considered. Thus when individual students are assigned to schools, districts must use a multi-factor individualized decision process. What the government is not permitted to do, absent a showing of necessity not made here, is to classify every student on the basis of race and to assign each of them to schools based on that classification.

Justice Kennedy also suggested that school districts may seek to promote diversity in their student bodies by means other than race-based assignment including:

> strategic site selection of new schools; drawing attendance zones with general recognition of the demographics of neighborhoods; allocating resources for special programs; recruiting students and faculty in a targeted fashion; and tracking enrollments, performance, and other statistics by race. These mechanisms are race conscious but do not lead to different treatment based on a classification that tells each student he or she is to be defined by race, so it is unlikely any of them would demand strict scrutiny to be found permissible.

Together, the views of Justice Kennedy and the dissenting justices provide five votes for the proposition that school districts can still adopt policies that promote diversity in their student bodies. Such districts have at least two options. One is to employ a "multi-factor individualized process" for assigning students to schools in which race is one, but not the dominant, factor. The other is to adopt "mechanisms [that] are race conscious but do not lead to different treatment based on a classification that tells each student he or she is to be defined by race." As one commentator has observed, because "Justice Kennedy's controlling opinion did not rule out the use of race-conscious desegregation policies ... the Court's decision in *Parents Involved* is not nearly as damaging as many feared."[74] For example, in *Doe* ex rel. *Doe v. Lower Merion School District*,[75] racial diversity was considered in a redistricting plan, but the plan was "facially race neutral, assigning students to schools based only on the geographical areas in which they live." The Third Circuit upheld the constitutionality of the plan under *Parents Involved*, finding that such indirect consideration of race was permissible under its guidelines.

Gender Discrimination

As we saw in the *Goesaert* bartending case, **rational basis** was the traditional test for adjudicating cases of alleged sex discrimination. However, in *Frontiero v. Richardson*,[76] a plurality opinion at the Supreme Court found that classifications based upon sex, like those based on race, were

---

74 Jim Hilbert, *School Desegregation 2.0: What Is Required to Finally Integrate America's Public Schools*, 16 Nw. J. Hum Rts. 92, 118 (2018).
75 665 F.3d 524 (3d Cir. 2011).
76 411 U.S. 677 (1973).

"inherently suspect and must therefore be subjected to close judicial scrutiny." Three years later, the Court retreated, adopting a mid-level test known as **substantial relation**.

To trigger the use of the **substantial relation** test, a plaintiff must first establish the existence of either overt gender discrimination (e.g., when a law or policy explicitly treats males and females differently) or covert gender discrimination (e.g., silent preferential treatment of men or women). Once this has been accomplished, the burden of proof shifts to the government to establish that its policy serves a purpose that is both legitimate and important and that treating males and females differently is substantially related to that purpose.[77] The law or policy will be declared unconstitutional if the government fails to meet its burden.

Courts will employ this mid-level test to evaluate equal protection challenges to gender-based school policies or practices, from single-sex schools to sports teams. In *Vorchheimer v. School District of Philadelphia*,[78] a female teenager sought admission to all-male Central High School. Philadelphia also had an all-female high school of equal quality and prestige, as well as a number of coed high schools. The plaintiff's reasons for seeking admission to Central were outlined by the court as follows:

> As to Girls High, she commented, "I just didn't like the impression it gave me. I didn't think I would be able to go there for three years and not be harmed in any way by it." As to Central she said, "I liked the atmosphere and also what I heard about it, about its academic excellence." She was somewhat dissatisfied with her education at George Washington High School because of her belief that the standard which the teachers set for the students was not high enough.

Nevertheless, the court, relying on the middle-level test, rejected the constitutional challenge and upheld the sex-segregated school:

> The gravamen of the plaintiff's case is her desire to attend a specific school based on its particular appeal to her. She believes that the choice should not be denied her because of an educational policy with which she does not agree.

> We are not unsympathetic with her desire to have an expanded freedom of choice, but its costs should not be overlooked. If she were to prevail, then all public single-sex schools would have to be abolished. The absence of these schools would stifle the ability of the local school board to continue with a respected educational methodology. It follows too that those students and parents who prefer an education in a public, single-sex school would be denied their freedom of choice. The existence of private schools is no more an answer to those people than it is to the plaintiff.

The dissenting judge argued that Philadelphia had failed to meet its burden of proof under the middle-level test:

> Some showing must be made that a single-sex academic high school policy advances the Board's objectives in a manner consistent with the requirements of the Equal Protection Clause …

> The Board, as the district court emphasized, did not present sufficient evidence that coeducation has an adverse effect upon a student's academic achievement. Indeed, the Board could not seriously assert that argument in view of its policy of assigning the vast majority of its students to coeducational schools. Presumably any detrimental impact on a student's scholastic achievement attributable to coeducation

---

77 Craig v. Boren, 429 U.S. 190 (1976).
78 532 F.2d 880 (3d Cir. 1976), *aff'd* [by an equally divided Court], 430 U.S. 703 (1977).

would be as evident in Philadelphia's coeducational comprehensive schools which offer college preparatory courses as the Board suggests it would be in its exclusively academic high schools. Thus, the Board's
single-sex policy reflects a choice among educational techniques but not necessarily one substantially
related to its stated educational objectives. One of those objectives, in fact, is to provide "educational
options to students and their parents." ... The implementation of the Board's policy excluding females
from Central actually precludes achievement of this objective because there is no option of a coeducational academic senior high school.

Litigation since *Vorchheimer* suggests that the dissenting judge's position may have been correct.
After the Pennsylvania Court of Common Pleas found the single-sex policy violated the Equal
Protection Clause in a class action in 1983, Central High School began admitting female students
that year.[79]

In *Mississippi University for Women v. Hogan*,[80] a male plaintiff objected to the female-only
admissions policy at a state nursing school. The state defended its policy by noting that it offered
coeducational nursing programs at other public universities and arguing that the single-sex program served the important purpose of compensating for past discrimination against women. However, the Supreme Court found the state's position deficient on both criteria of the middle-level
test: The single-sex admission policy served no important government purpose and was not even
substantially related to the purpose proposed by the state. On the contrary, said the Court, rather
than compensating for discrimination, the admissions policy perpetuated the stereotyped and gen-
dered view of the nursing profession.

In *United States v. Virginia*,[81] the Supreme Court considered the constitutionality of the categorical exclusion of women from the Virginia Military Institute (VMI). Again employing the
middle-level test, the Court placed the burden on the state to come up with an "exceedingly
persuasive justification." The state argued that the admission of women would "destroy" the VMI
program, thus denying both men and women the opportunity to benefit from it. But the Court
disagreed:

> The notion that admission of women would downgrade VMI's stature, destroy the adversative system
> and, with it, even the school, is a judgment hardly proved, a prediction hardly different from other
> "self-fulfilling prophecies" once routinely used to deny rights or opportunities.

The Court noted that the same sorts of arguments had been made to deny women access to law
and medical schools.

In *Garrett v. Board of Education*,[82] a case that raised a variety of legal and educational issues,
a federal district court issued an injunction prohibiting the opening of single-gender elementary
schools in Detroit. These "Academies" were to "offer special programs including a class entitled 'Rites of Passage,' an Afrocentric (Pluralistic) curriculum, futuristic lessons in preparation
for twenty-first century careers, an emphasis on male responsibility, mentors, Saturday classes,
individualized counseling, extended classroom hours, and student uniform." Although the court
agreed that addressing "the crisis facing African-American males manifested by high homicide,
unemployment and drop-out rates" was an important government purpose, it nevertheless found
that the proposed "Academies" failed to meet the requirements of the middle-level test: "While

79 Newberg v. Bd. of Pub. Educ., 26 Pa. D. & C. 3d 682 (Pa. C.P. Aug. 30, 1983).
80 458 U.S. 718 (1982).
81 518 U.S. 515 (1996).
82 775 F. Supp. 1004 (E.D. Mich. 1991).

these statistics underscore a compelling need, they fall short of demonstrating that excluding girls is substantially related to the achievement of the Board's objectives." The court noted that the proposed program ignored what the school board itself admitted was an "equally urgent and unique crisis" facing urban girls. The court also concluded that the single-sex academies violated Title IX as it was then interpreted by the Department of Education.

Today, single-sex schools may be permissible under both Title IX and the Equal Protection Clause provided certain conditions are satisfied. In a recent case, a federal court upheld an optional single-sex program while evincing little sympathy for its opponents:

> No legal authority supports the conclusion that optional single-sex programs in public schools are *ipso facto* injurious to the schools' students. Unlike the separation of public school students by race, the separation of students by sex does not give rise to a finding of constitutional injury as a matter of law.[83]

The most common gender discrimination cases in K-12 public schools involve sex segregation in sports and student organizations. Female plaintiffs have their strongest chance of winning a case under the Equal Protection Clause when they have been totally excluded from playing a sport because there is no female team. In *Force v. Pierce R-VI School District*,[84] a district court employing the mid-level test ruled in favor of a female plaintiff who wished to try out for her junior high football team. Noting that even the smallest and frailest male students were allowed to try out for the team, the court rejected the school's contention that excluding female students from doing so was substantially related to the goal of ensuring the safety of the players.

When a comparable female team is available, a female plaintiff's chance of winning the right to try out for the male team is diminished if the sport involves contact.[85] In cases involving noncontact sports, plaintiffs have a good chance of winning, especially if a female team is not available.[86] The legal situation is somewhat less clear when male students seek to participate in noncontact female sports. When there is no male team available, male plaintiffs have met with mixed results.[87] Some courts have been persuaded that female teams are important for ensuring female students a fair opportunity to participate in sports. One court rejected both the constitutional and statutory arguments of a male student seeking to play on a female field hockey team.[88]

In *Communities for Equity v. Michigan High School*,[89] the plaintiffs brought an equal protection challenge to the Michigan High School Athletic Association's (MHSAA) policy of scheduling five female sports tournaments—basketball, volleyball, soccer, swimming and diving, and tennis—in the spring while scheduling the counterpart male sports tournaments in the fall, the more customary season for these sports. The court agreed with the plaintiffs that as a consequence of this schedule, the female students suffered disadvantages including decreased ability to be nationally ranked and recruited, exclusion from the excitement of "March Madness," and being forced to play on frozen or snow-covered fields for certain sports.

83 A.N.A. *ex rel.* S.F.A. v. Breckinridge Cty. Bd. of Educ., 833 F. Supp. 2d 673, 678 (W.D. Ky. 2011).
84 570 F. Supp. 1020 (W.D. Mo. 1983).
85 O'Connor v. Bd. of Educ. of Sch. Dist. 23, 545 F. Supp. 376 (N.D. Ill. 1982), and 449 U.S. 1301 (1980).
86 Brenden v. Indep. Sch. Dist. 742, 477 F.2d 1292 (8th Cir. 1973); Gilpin v. Kansas State High Sch. Activities Ass'n, 377 F. Supp. 1233 (D. Kan. 1973).
87 Clark v. Arizona Interscholastic Ass'n, 695 F.2d 1126 (9th Cir. 1982); Petrie v. Illinois High Sch. Ass'n, 394 N.E.2d 855 (Ill. App. Ct. 1979); *but see* Gomes v. Rhode Island Interscholastic League, 469 F. Supp. 659 (D.R.I.), *vacated as moot*, 604 F.2d 733 (1st Cir. 1979).
88 Williams v. Sch. Dist. of Bethlehem, 998 F.2d 168 (3d Cir. 1993).
89 377 F.3d 504 (6th Cir. 2004).

Federal Anti-Discrimination Statutes

Several federal statutes supplement the Equal Protection Clause by prohibiting various forms of discrimination. This section considers two of these statutes as they pertain to the treatment of students by schools: **Title VI** of the *Civil Rights Act of 1964*, which deals with race and ethnicity, and **Title IX** of the *Education Amendments of 1972*, which deals with gender discrimination.

Title VI (Section 601) of the *Civil Rights Act of 1964*[90] provides: "No person in the United States shall, on the grounds of race, color, or national origin, be excluded from participation in, be denied the benefits of, or be subjected to discrimination under any program or activity receiving Federal financial assistance." The Department of Education regulations implementing Title VI state that a school district may not provide different or separate treatment or services or segregate on the grounds of race, color, or national origin.[91] A school district that violates this law faces the loss of all its federal funds. Title VI applies to everything a school does even if only one program or activity receives federal funds. Thus, for example, if a school receives federal support only for its lunch program, it must nonetheless comply with Title VI in all of its activities.

Title VI supplements the Equal Protection Clause in three ways. First, although the Equal Protection Clause can be enforced only through a suit brought by parents or students directly affected by discrimination, Title VI can be enforced by the Attorney General of the United States,[92] by any federal department or agency that awards federal funds to school districts,[93] or through litigation brought by an individual.[94] Courts may use Title VI to award compensatory but not punitive damages to individual victims of discrimination by school districts.[95]

Second, unlike the Equal Protection Clause, proof of intent to discriminate may not be necessary under Title VI. If a federal agency has promulgated regulations implementing Title VI, and the regulations interpret Title VI to prohibit policies having a discriminatory impact, then proof of a discriminatory impact alone will be sufficient to prove a Title VI violation.[96] Thus, unintentional discrimination may sometimes be remedied through Title VI. But the remedy must be one sought by the Department of Education because the Supreme Court has ruled that private individuals may not sue to enforce disparate-impact regulations under Title VI.[97] That a policy has a discriminatory impact may not necessarily mean that Title VI has been violated, provided the policy has a legitimate justification. For example, a school might defend the use of a standardized test that one race fails at a higher rate than another by showing that the test is reliable and valid and that there is no less discriminatory instrument available.[98]

Third, unlike the Equal Protection Clause, Title VI applies to **private schools** that receive federal funds.

Title IX of the *Education Amendments of 1972*[99] closely parallels Title VI: "No person in the United States shall, on the basis of sex, be excluded from participation in, be denied the benefits of, or be subjected to discrimination under any education program or activity receiving Federal financial assistance." Federal law makes it clear that Title IX applies to everything a school does,

90 42 U.S.C. § 2000d.
91 34 C.F.R. § 1003 (b).
92 42 U.S.C. § 2000c-6.
93 42 U.S.C. § 2000d-1.
94 Alexander v. Choate, 469 U.S. 287 (1985); Guardians Ass'n v. Civil Serv. Comm., 463 U.S. 582 (1983).
95 Zeno v. Pine Plains Cent. Sch. Dist., 702 F. 3d 655 (2d Cir. 2012); Barnes v. Gorman, 536 U.S. 181 (2002).
96 Guardians Ass'n v. Civil Serv. Comm'n., 463 U.S. 582 (1983).
97 Alexander v. Sandoval, 532 U.S. 275 (2001).
98 See Bd. of Educ. of Sch. Dist. of New York. v. Harris, 444 U.S. 130 (1979); *see also* Elston v. Talladega County Bd. of Ed., 997 F.2d 1394 (11th Cir. 1993); Larry P. v. Riles, 495 F. Supp. 926 (N.D. Cal. 1979), *aff'd in part*, 793 F.2d 969 (9th Cir. 1984).
99 20 U.S.C. §§ 1681–1686.

even if only one activity or program receives federal funds.[100] Thus, a school's athletic program is subject to Title IX regulations even if the school's only federal funds are for special education. Like Title VI, Title IX permits lawsuits by both federal agencies and individuals and applies to any private or public school that receives federal funds.[101]

Student victims of gender discrimination may use Title IX to seek a court order ending the discrimination. Student victims of intentional gender discrimination may also be awarded monetary damages from the offending school district but not from individual perpetrators of discrimination.[102] Victims of gender discrimination may also use another federal law, Section 1983 (see Chapter 1), to seek monetary damages from individual perpetrators of discrimination.[103] The courts are split on the issue of whether Title IX prohibits unintentional gender discrimination.[104] One court ruled that Title IX prohibited a state from using a seemingly gender-neutral examination to award college scholarships because it had a discriminatory impact on female candidates.[105] Although the Supreme Court has not ruled on this issue, if its interpretation of Title VI were applied to Title IX, some unintentional gender discrimination could be prohibited.[106]

In *Jackson v. Birmingham Board of Education*,[107] the Supreme Court ruled that "indirect victims" of gender discrimination are protected from retaliation when they report violations of Title IX. In that case, the coach of a girls' basketball team complained to the school board about unequal funding. The school district failed to remedy the problem and dismissed the coach. If the coach could prove he was dismissed because he complained of sex discrimination, that would violate Title IX: "Reporting incidents of discrimination is integral to Title IX enforcement and would be discouraged if retaliation against those who report went unpunished. Indeed, if retaliation were not prohibited, Title IX's enforcement scheme would unravel."[108]

The extensive regulations issued to enforce Title IX prohibit the following:

- Admission tests that disproportionately affect male or female students, unless they can be validated as reliable predictors of educational ability and as the least prejudicial means of prediction.[109]
- Codes of student conduct that treat male and female students differently.[110]
- Counseling materials that discriminate on the basis of gender, for example, by encouraging different courses or occupations for male or female students.[111]
- Rules concerning marriage or pregnancy that treat male and female students differently.[112]

With some exceptions, Title IX regulations also prohibit sex-segregated programs and refusing to allow participation in a program on the basis of gender. Exceptions include contact sports and ability grouping in physical education classes, sex education classes, and choruses based on vocal

---

100 20 U.S.C. § 1687.
101 Cannon v. Univ. of Chicago, 441 U.S. 677 (1979).
102 Franklin v. Gwinnett County Pub. Schs., 503 U.S. 60 (1992).
103 Fitzgerald v. Barnstable Sch. Comm., 555 U.S. 246 (2009).
104 Cannon v. Univ. of Chicago, 648 F.2d 1104 (7th Cir. 1981); NAACP v. Medical Ctr. Inc., 657 F.2d 1322 (3d Cir. 1981).
105 Sharif v. New York State Educ. Dep't, 709 F. Supp. 345 (S.D.N.Y. 1989).
106 Guardians Ass'n v. Civil Serv. Comm'n, 463 U.S. 582 (1983).
107 544 U.S. 167 (2005).
108 *See* Atkinson v. LaFayette Coll., 460 F.3d 447 (3d Cir. 2006).
109 34 C.F.R. § 106.21(b)(2).
110 34 C.F.R. § 106.31(b)(4).
111 34 C.F.R. § 106.36.
112 34 C.F.R. § 106.40.

range. As noted earlier, a district court relied partly on Title IX regulations to prohibit the opening of all-male "Academies" in Detroit in 1991.[113]

But more recent changes in Title IX regulations permit sex-segregated classes and extra-curricular activities and even single-sex schools under certain specified conditions. To be permissible, single-sex programs must be undertaken to improve educational achievement, meet identified educational needs, and be voluntary. "Substantially equal" single-sex programs must be offered to students of the excluded gender, and substantially equal coeducational programs must also be provided. The school district must periodically evaluate the single-sex program to be sure it is based on genuine educational justifications and not on "overly broad generalizations about the different talents, capacities, or preferences or either sex and that any single-sex classes or extracurricular activities are substantially related to the achievement of the important objectives for the classes or extracurricular activities."[114] Even if a single-sex program is permissible under Title IX, it might still run afoul of the Equal Protection Clause.

In the case of a single-sex charter school, Title IX imposes no requirement that a substantially equal school be provided. Nevertheless, in *Reach Academy for Boys & Girls, Inc. v. Delaware Department of Education*,[115] a district court, relying in part on Title IX and in part on state law, enjoined Delaware from closing its only all-female charter school, citing the inequality that resulted when the state's all-male charter school remained open.

Non-Binary and Transgender Students

Increasingly, over the past few years, Title IX has been invoked by non-binary and transgender students to challenge discriminatory school policies. Such policies often focus on school bathrooms and locker rooms, and decree that only students who are biologically male or female may use the respective male or female facilities. In defense of such policies, school districts have argued that the legislative history of Title IX was concerned with expanding educational opportunities for girls and women, with no mention of non-binary or transgender people.

Nevertheless, the plain language of Title IX prohibits discrimination "on the basis of sex," and a number of transgender plaintiffs have successfully argued that Title IX therefore protects them from discrimination. In refusing to dismiss a transgender student's claim that he should not be barred from using the boys' bathroom at school, a federal district court aptly summarized recent developments:

> The Sixth and Seventh Circuits have … held that excluding boys and girls who are transgender from the restrooms that align with their gender identity may subject them to discrimination on the basis of sex under Title IX, the Equal Protection Clause, or both.[116]

A number of district courts have reached the same conclusion.[117]

In *A.H. v. Minersville Area School District*,[118] a district court in Pennsylvania denied the school district's motion to dismiss a transgender student's Title IX and Equal Protection Clause claims based on a bathroom policy "dictating that children must use the bathroom corresponding to the

113 Garrett v. Bd. of Educ. of Sch. Dist. of City of Detroit, 775 F. Supp. 1004 (E.D. Mich. 1991).
114 34 C.F.R. §106.34.
115 8 F. Supp. 3d 574 (D. Del. 2014).
116 *Citing* Whitaker v. Kenosha Unified School Dist. No. 1 Board of Education, 858 F.3d 1034 (7th Cir. 2017); Dodds v. United States Dep't of Educ., 845 F.3d 217 (6th Cir. 2016).
117 Evancho v. Pine–Richland Sch. Dist., 237 F. Supp. 3d 267 (W.D. Pa. 2017); Bd. of Educ. of the Highland Local Sch. Dist. v. U.S. Dep't of Educ., 208 F. Supp. 3d 850 (S.D. Ohio 2016).
118 290 F. Supp. 3d 321 (M.D. Pa. 2017).

sex listed on the student's birth certificate." In *M.A.B. v. Board of Education of Talbot County*,[119] a district court in Maryland denied a strikingly similar motion to dismiss a transgender student's Title IX and Equal Protection claims stemming from a school policy of barring him from using the boys' locker room.

In *Grimm v. Gloucester County School Board*, a transgender male student argued that his school's bathroom policy violated Title IX and the Equal Protection Clause. Grimm and his mother notified school officials of his male gender identity at the beginning of his sophomore year so that he could socially transition in all aspects of his life, including his time at school. With permission from school officials, Grimm used the boys' restroom for almost two months without incident. But the school district changed its policy in 2014 after receiving complaints from other parents.[120]

Grimm continues to be litigated in the federal courts.[121] It reached the United States Supreme Court in 2017, after the Fourth Circuit, relying on a Guidance from the Department of Education issued during the Obama administration, found for the plaintiff. The Supreme Court agreed to hear the case, but subsequently canceled when the Trump administration changed course on transgender rights and rescinded the Guidance.[122] The Supreme Court sent the case back to the Fourth Circuit, ordering it to reconsider the issue in light of the new federal guidelines.[123]

Athletics

The following Title IX regulation has had a profound effect on schools:[124]

a.   *General.* No person shall, on the basis of sex, be excluded from participation in, be denied the benefits of, be treated differently from another person or otherwise be discriminated against in any interscholastic, intercollegiate, club or intramural athletics offered by a recipient, and no recipient shall provide any such athletics separately on such basis.

b.   *Separate teams.* Notwithstanding the requirements of paragraph (a) of this section, a recipient may operate or sponsor separate teams for members of each sex where selection for such teams is based upon competitive skill or the activity involved is a contact sport. However, where a recipient operates or sponsors a team in a particular sport for members of one sex but operates or sponsors no such team for members of the other sex, and athletic opportunities for members of that sex have previously been limited, members of the excluded sex must be allowed to try-out for the team offered unless the sport involved is a contact sport. For the purposes of this part, contact sports include boxing, wrestling, rugby, ice hockey, football, basketball and other sports the purpose or major activity of which involves bodily contact.

c.   *Equal opportunity.* A recipient which operates or sponsors interscholastic, intercollegiate, club or intramural athletics shall provide equal athletic opportunity for members of both sexes. In determining whether equal opportunities are available the Director will consider, among other factors:

---

119 286 F. Supp. 3d 704 (D. Md. 2018).
120 *See* G.G. v. Gloucester County School Board; Online at www.aclu.org/cases/gg-v-gloucester-county-school-board (updated May 6, 2019, last accessed April 18, 2020).
121 302 F. Supp. 3d 730 (E.D. Va. 2018).
122 *See* Sandra Battle & T.E. Wheeler, *Dear Colleague Letter*, OFF. FOR CIV. RTS., U.S. DEP'T EDUC. & U.S. DEP'T JUSTICE 1 (Feb. 22, 2017), www2.ed.gov/about/offices/list/ocr/letters/colleague-201702-title-ix.docx (last accessed April 18, 2020).
123 Gloucester Cty. Sch. Bd. v. G. G. *ex rel.* Grimm, 137 S. Ct. 1239 (2017).
124 Section 106.41.

(1)   Whether the selection of sports and levels of competition effectively accommodate the interests and abilities of members of both sexes;
(2)   The provision of equipment and supplies;
(3)   Scheduling of games and practice time;
(4)   Travel and *per diem* allowance;
(5)   Opportunity to receive coaching and academic tutoring;
(6)   Assignment and compensation of coaches and tutors;
(7)   Provision of locker rooms, practice and competitive facilities;
(8)   Provision of medical and training facilities and services;
(9)   Provision of housing and dining facilities and services;
(10) Publicity.

Unequal aggregate expenditures for members of each sex or unequal expenditures for male and female teams if a recipient operates or sponsors separate teams will not constitute non-compliance with this section, but the Assistant Secretary may consider the failure to provide necessary funds for teams for one sex in assessing equality of opportunity for members of each sex.

These regulations have created some confusion. They allow sex-segregated teams in the following circumstances: contact sports, regardless of whether there is a team available for the excluded sex; noncontact sports, selected on a competitive basis when there is a team available for each sex; and noncontact sports, selected on a competitive basis when only one team is available provided that athletic opportunities for the excluded sex have not previously been limited, such as by inferior funding or facilities.

Thus, the regulations seem to permit separation when some of the constitutional decisions discussed earlier would not. For example, as in the *Force* case, female students have sometimes employed the Equal Protection Clause to gain the right to try out for male teams, even in contact sports. At least in those jurisdictions where these decisions have occurred, the conflicting federal regulations may not be implemented because the Constitution takes precedence over all other laws and regulations.

A "Policy Interpretation" issued by the Department of Education states that a school sponsoring an intercollegiate athletic program school may meet the requirement of "equal athletic opportunity for members of both sexes" in any of three ways:

(1) the percent of male and female athletes is substantially proportionate to the percent of male and female students enrolled at the school; or (2) the school has a history and continuing practice of expanding participation opportunities for the underrepresented sex; or (3) the school is fully and effectively accommodating the interests and abilities of the underrepresented sex.[125]

Although most of the Title IX sports litigation has focused on higher education,[126] several courts have applied these principles to elementary and secondary schools. As one court has explained,

---

125 *See generally* A POLICY INTERPRETATION: TITLE IX AND INTERCOLLEGIATE ATHLETICS, 44 Fed. Reg. 71413, 71414 (Dec. 11, 1979); online at www2.ed.gov/about/offices/list/ocr/docs/t9interp.html (last accessed April 18, 2020); CLARIFICATION OF INTERCOLLEGIATE ATHLETICS POLICY GUIDANCE: THE THREE-PART TEST, U.S. DEP'T OF EDUC. (Jan. 16, 1996); online at www2.ed.gov/about/offices/list/ocr/docs/clarific.html#two (last accessed April 18, 2020); Valerie M. Bonnette and Lamar Daniel, TITLE IX ATHLETICS INVESTIGATOR'S MANUAL, OFF. FOR CIV. RTS., U.S. DEP'T OF EDUC. (1990); online at https://files.eric.ed.gov/fulltext/ED400763.pdf; see also Cohen v. Brown University, 991 F.2d 888 (1st Cir. 1993) and 101 F.3d 155 (1st Cir. 1996).
126 *See* Elaine Chamberlain, Hannah Cornett, and Adam Yohanan, *Athletics & Title IX of the 1972 Education Amendments*, 19 GEO. J. GENDER & L. 231, 232 (2018).

once a school has decided to offer extracurricular sporting activities, "it is axiomatic … that … it may not discriminate against participation in such activities on the basis of race, religion, gender, or any other impermissible classification."[127] Moreover, several federal courts have found Title IX violations where high school athletic programs subjected girls' teams to unequal opportunities, in areas such as the scheduling of games, lighting for night games, bathroom facilities, scoreboards, batting cages, and availability of bleacher seats.[128]

In addition to federal law, some states have constitutional provisions, statutes, and regulations that also prohibit various forms of discrimination. State law may, and in some states does, impose stricter antidiscrimination requirements than federal law. For example, state law may ensure greater opportunities for female students to try out for male teams than federal law.[129]

Racial and Sexual Harassment

Racial and sexual harassment were first recognized as legally impermissible forms of discrimination in the context of employment law. The implementing regulations of Title VII of the *Civil Rights Act of 1964* provide that an employee may not be subjected to a racially or sexually hostile, intimidating, or offensive work environment. In addition to hostile-environment harassment, the regulations also recognize another form of sexual harassment known as "quid pro quo." In **quid pro quo harassment**, an employee is asked to exchange sex for job benefits (see Chapter 10).

Department of Education guidelines state that quid pro quo harassment occurs when

> a school employee explicitly or implicitly conditions a student's participation in an education program or activity or bases an educational decision on the student's submission to unwelcome sexual advances, requests sexual favors, or other verbal, nonverbal, or physical conduct of a sexual nature …

Thus, for example, in *Does v. Covington County School Board of Education*,[130] a district court ruled that quid pro quo sexual harassment had occurred when a teacher allowed a third-grade student to copy answers from his desk while he sexually touched the student.

Students may turn to the courts for redress for racial or sexual intimidation and improper sexual advances at school. Courts in recent decades have become increasingly sympathetic to the contention that students have a right not to be subjected to racial or sexual harassment by school employees or even by other students. Both hostile-environment racial or sexual harassment and quid pro quo sexual harassment against students are recognized as legal wrongs.

Students may seek redress for racial or sexual harassment under a number of different laws. The Equal Protection Clause applies only when the offender is a school official, not a fellow student,[131] and only when the victims can show that the offender intentionally discriminated on the basis of race or gender. In *Nabozny v. Podlesny*,[132] a male student identifying as gay won an Equal Protection suit against school officials who had a policy of protecting female students from sexual harassment, but who for years had refused to protect male students identifying as gay from physical assault. The plaintiff was taunted, urinated upon, and even kicked so forcefully that he sustained internal injuries, but despite repeated appeals to school officials for help, nothing was done. The

---

127 Hadley v. Rush Henrietta Cent. Sch. Dist., 409 F. Supp. 2d 164 (W.D.N.Y. 2006).
128 *See, e.g.*, Daniels v. School Bd. of Brevard Co, Florida, 985 F. Supp. 1458 (M.D. Fl. 1997); McCormick v. Mamaroneck School Dist., 370 F.3d 275 (2d Cir. 2004).
129 Darrin v. Gould, 540 P.2d 882 (Wash. 1975) (*en banc*).
130 969 F. Supp. 1264 (M.D. Ala. 1997).
131 DeShaney v. Winnebago County Dep't of Social Serv., 489 U.S. 189 (1989).
132 Nabozny v. Podlesny, 92 F.3d 446 (7th Cir. 1996); *see also* Murrell v. Sch. Dist. No.1, 186 F.3d 1238 (10th Cir. 1999).

peer harassment itself was not an Equal Protection Clause violation, but the school's discriminatory protection policy was.

The Due Process Clause also may be used to object to sexual harassment when there has been a significant violation of bodily integrity, but only when the offender is a school official. Thus, in *Doe v. Claiborne County*,[133] a student successfully brought a due process suit against a teacher who had statutorily raped her on numerous occasions. Where there has been threatened or actual bodily harm or violation (e.g., sexual assault), the racial or sexual harassment may constitute assault or battery under state civil and criminal law (see Chapter 12). Some states have statutes that provide protection from harassment based on gender, race, and a variety of other factors.[134]

In most cases, the most effective protection for students against racial or sexual harassment at school is found in federal statutes. In recent years, the Department of Education (ED) and the courts have come to view the racial harassment of a student as a violation of Title VI and the sexual harassment of a student as a violation of Title IX. The idea is that students who experience racial or sexual harassment are being denied the benefits of their school's program on the basis of race or gender, making harassment a form of discrimination.

According to ED guidelines, racial[135] or sexual[136] harassment occurs when because of race or gender a student experiences conduct

> by an employee, by another student, or by a third party that is sufficiently severe, persistent, or pervasive to limit a student's ability to participate in or benefit from an education program or activity, or to create a hostile or abusive educational environment.

The guidelines provide a list of factors to be used in determining whether racial or sexual harassment has occurred including the type, frequency, and duration of the conduct; the number of individuals involved; and whether the victim suffered falling grades or psychological distress. In *Monteiro v. Tempe Union High School District*, the Ninth Circuit agreed with the plaintiffs that slurs written in graffiti around the school constituted racial harassment.[137]

Because there has been more litigation over sexual harassment than racial harassment in schools, the law regarding sexual harassment is far more developed. The ED guidelines state that "[s]exually harassing conduct … can include unwelcome sexual advances, requests for sexual favors, and other verbal and nonverbal, or physical conduct of a sexual nature." The more severe the conduct, the less it need be persistent to constitute a violation: "Indeed, a single or isolated incident of sexual harassment may, if sufficiently severe, create a hostile environment." However, Title IX does not prohibit nonsexual touching or other nonsexual conduct. "For example, a high school athletic coach hugging a student who made a goal or a kindergarten teacher's consoling hug for a child with a skinned knee will not be considered sexual harassment." Similarly, "[a] kiss on the cheek by a first grader does not constitute sexual harassment." Nor is harassment or bullying based on animosity or bad blood covered by Title IX. One court ruled that threats, acts of intimidation, and name calling directed by male members of a gang toward a female student and her brother were not actionable under Title IX because they were based on "personal animus rather than gender."[138] But, "[a] teacher's repeatedly hugging and putting his or her arms around students under inappropriate circumstances could create a hostile environment." Thus, a school employee

133 Doe v. Claiborne County, 103 F.3d 495 (6th Cir. 1996).
134 MCLS § 37.2102; CAL. EDUC. CODE § 231.5; OR. REV. STAT § 342.700; TEX. EDUC. CODE § 37.083; REV. CODE WASH. (ARCW) § 28A.640.020.
135 59 Fed. Reg. 11447.
136 62 Fed. Reg. 12033.
137 Monteiro v. Tempe Union High School Dist., 158 F.3d 1022 (9th Cir. 1998).
138 Burwell v. Pekin Cmty. High Sch. Dist. 303, 213 F. Supp. 2d 917 (C.D. Ill. 2002).

who on several occasions touched a student's breast, buttocks, and thigh and made sexual comments to her was found to have committed wrongful sexual harassment.[139]

In general, sexual conduct directed at a student by an adult school employee constitutes harassment even if the student does not object or appears to welcome the conduct. ED guidelines state that the younger the student, the less likely the student will be deemed to have the legal capacity to consent to sexual conduct. The Seventh Circuit ruled that a 13-year-old plaintiff did not need to establish in a Title IX suit that she did not welcome the sexual advances of a teacher.[140] For older high school students, ED guidelines create a rebuttable presumption that a sexual relationship with an adult school employee is not consensual. The Supreme Court has stated that sex between a student and a school employee usually constitutes sexual harassment even if the student consents.[141]

Sexual conduct by one student toward another may constitute harassment if the conduct is unwelcome and persistent or severe. In *Davis v. Monroe County Board of Education*,[142] the Eleventh Circuit concluded that a student had been subjected to hostile-environment harassment after another student persistently touched her, brushed up against her, and made sexual comments to her. The Supreme Court has indicated that in general a single act of student-on-student harassment will not be considered sufficient to constitute a Title IX violation:

> Although, in theory, a single instance of sufficiently severe one-on-one peer harassment could be said to have such an effect, we think it unlikely that Congress would have thought such behavior sufficient to rise to this level in light of the inevitability of student misconduct and the amount of litigation that would be invited by entertaining claims of official indifference to a single instance of one-on-one peer harassment.[143]

One court ruled that a forced act of anal sex and a request for oral sex by one male student of another was not sufficiently severe and pervasive to constitute sexual harassment.[144] Even if severe and persistent, not all student-on-student harassment is sexual. In one case, a high school football player's upper-class teammates subjected him to sadistic treatment, including binding his genitals with adhesive tape. The student reported the incident to school authorities who punished the wrongdoers and forced the team to forfeit a scheduled play-off game. The victim was then subjected to nonsexual hostile acts by team members who blamed him for the forfeiture. The court ruled that the hostile environment subsequent to the initial incident was not covered by Title IX.[145] Similarly, in an elementary school case, a district court ruled that a boy's pushing and teasing, and grabbing of a girl's leg, and one incident of inappropriate touching was "nothing more than the sort of mean-spirited teasing that troublesome little boys inflict from time to time on little girls who seem vulnerable."[146]

Even if offensive behavior is sexual, Title IX is not violated unless the behavior is sufficiently severe to deny the victim access to or the benefit of an educational program. In one case a boy

---

139 Seneway v. Canon McMillan Sch. Dist., 969 F. Supp. 325 (W.D. Pa. 1997); *see also* Oona R.-S. v. Santa Rosa City Sch., 890 F. Supp. 1452 (N.D. Cal. 1995), aff'd, 143 F.3d 473 (9th Cir. 1997).
140 Mary M. v. N. Lawrence Cmty. Sch. Corp., 131 F. 3d 1220 (7th Cir. 1997).
141 Gebser v. Lago Vista Indep. Sch. Dist., 503 U.S. 60 (1998).
142 Davis v. Monroe County Bd. of Educ., 74 F.3d 1186 (11th Cir. 1996), *vacated*, 91 F.3d 1418, *aff'd*, 120 F.3d 1390 (11th Cir. 1997) (*en banc*), *rev'd*, 526 U.S. 629 (1999); *see also* Rowinsky v. Bryan Indep. Sch. Dist., 80 F.3d 1006 (5th Cir. 1996).
143 Davis v. Monroe County Bd. of Educ., 526 U.S. 629 (1999).
144 Wilson v. Beaumont Indep. Sch. Dist., 144 F. Supp. 2d 690 (E.D. Tex. 2001).
145 Seamons v. Snow, 84 F.3d 1226 (10th Cir. 1996).
146 Manfredi v. Mount Vernon Bd. of Educ., 94 F. Supp. 2d 447 (S.D.N.Y. 2000).

harassed a kindergarten girl by jumping on her back, leaning against her while holding his crotch, unzipping and lowering his pants, and kissing, groping, and inappropriately touching her. But despite the fact she was under psychological counseling, since neither the girl's attendance nor her grades suffered, the court ruled she had not been denied educational opportunities.[147] The Eleventh Circuit found no denial of access in a case in which second-grade girls were chased on the playground, jumped on, rubbed against, had their breasts touched, and were subjected to efforts to look up their skirts and spoken with about sexual acts.[148]

The Department of Education has stated that Title IX does not protect students from harassment based on their sexual orientation.[149] A number of cases have found, however, that Title IX does protect students from harassment based on their perceived lack of conformity to stereotypical gender behaviors.[150] For example, when a middle school girl was called "bitch," "dyke," "freak," "lesbian," and "gothic" by her female peers, a federal court found a link to gender-based discrimination under Title IX and refused to dismiss the case.[151] In another case involving a male student subjected to epithets such as "faggot," "queer bait," and "homo" over several years, the insults were not based on a perception of stereotypical gender behaviors, but were instead retaliation for his alleged bullying of other students. The Eighth Circuit held that the epithets were not sufficiently gender-related to fall within Title IX.[152] As a practical matter, it may be difficult to determine whether a student is being harassed because of sexual orientation or gender variance.

In any case, Title IX clearly protects students from same-sex sexual harassment. In *P.W. v. Fairport Central School District*,[153] a middle school student alleged that school officials were deliberately indifferent after other male students had repeatedly grabbed his buttocks and genitals, taunted him with lewd gestures, and made unwelcome sexual advances. Based on these serious allegations, a district court allowed his Title IX claim to proceed.

Both Title IX and the Equal Protection Clause prohibit a school district from providing greater protection from harassment to female students identifying as lesbian than to male students identifying as gay. Some state statutes may protect students from harassment based on actual or perceived sexual orientation.[154]

When racial or sexual harassment occurs at school, who may be held responsible and what sort of compensation may be awarded? Because Title VI and Title IX only apply to "programs … receiving federal financial assistance," neither individuals who commit racial or sexual harassment nor their supervisors may be sued directly under these laws.[155] Employees who racially or sexually harass students in violation of Title VI or IX (or the Equal Protection Clause)[156] may be sued under Section 1983 if certain conditions are met (see Chapter 1).[157] Peer harassers may not be sued directly under Section 1983.

---

147 Gabrielle M. v. Park Forest-Chicago Heights, Illinois. Sch. Dist. 163, 315 F.3d 817 (7th Cir. 2003).

148 Hawkins v. Sarasota County Sch. Bd., 322 F.3d 1279 (11th Cir. 2003).

149 Revised Sexual Harassment Guidance: Harassment of Students by School Employees, Other Students, or Third Parties, 66 FR 5512-01 (2001).

150 Theno v. Tonganoxie Unified School Dist. No. 464, 394 F. Supp. 2d 1299 (D. Kan. 2005); Montgomery v. Indep. Sch. Dist. No. 709, 109 F. Supp. 2d 1081 (D. Minn. 2000); Ray v. Antioch Unified Sch. Dist., 107 F. Supp. 2d 1165 (N.D. Cal. 2000).

151 Riccio v. New Haven Bd. of Educ., 467 F. Supp. 2d 219, 222 (D. Conn. 2006).

152 Wolfe v. Fayetteville, Arkansas School Dist., 648 F.3d 860 (8th Cir. 2011).

153 927 F. Supp. 2d 76 (W.D.N.Y. 2013).

154 L.W. v. Toms River Reg'l Schs. Bd. of Educ., 915 A.2d 535 (N.J. 2007).

155 Smith v. Metro. Sch. Dist. of Perry Twp., 128 F.3d 1014 (7th Cir. 1997).

156 Murrell v. Sch. Dist. No. 1, 186 F.3d 1238 (10th Cir. 1999).

157 Oona R.-S. v. Santa Rosa City Sch., 890 F. Supp. 1452 (N.D. Cal. 1995), *aff'd*, 143 F.3d 473 (9th Cir. 1997); *but see* Does v. Covington County Sch. Bd. of Educ., 930 F. Supp. 554 (M.D. Ala. 1996), and 969 F. Supp. 1264 (M.D. Ala. 1997).

Resolving a deep split among the circuit courts in 2009, the Supreme Court in *Fitzgerald v. Barnstable School Community* concluded that, "Title IX was not meant to be an exclusive mechanism for addressing gender discrimination in schools, or a substitute for Section 1983 suits as a means of enforcing constitutional rights."[158] Plaintiffs alleging unconstitutional gender discrimination in schools were encouraged to file Section 1983 suits based on the Equal Protection Clause.

In *Franklin v. Gwinnett County Public Schools*,[159] the Supreme Court held that victims of gender discrimination under Title IX, including sexual harassment, may sue their school district for money damages. The same holds true for victims of racial harassment under Title VI. However, as noted earlier, damages under Title VI are limited to compensation; punitive damages may not be awarded.[160]

Two Supreme Court decisions address the conditions under which a school may be held liable for the harassment of a student by a district employee or another student. In *Gebser v. Lago Vista Independent School District*,[161] the Supreme Court ruled that a school district cannot be held responsible for sexual harassment of a student by an employee "unless an official who at a minimum has authority to address the alleged discrimination and to institute corrective measures on the [school's] behalf has actual knowledge of discrimination in the [school's] programs and fails adequately to respond." The Court further noted that "the response must amount to **deliberate indifference** to discrimination."

In *Gebser*, the Court noted that the student-victim had not reported her sexual intimacy with the teacher to the school principal. The only warning signs came from complaints from other parents regarding sexually suggestive comments by the teacher in class. When school officials did finally learn of the sexual relationship, the teacher was fired and lost his teaching license. Thus, the facts did not prove that school officials had actual knowledge of the discrimination and failed to respond.

In *Davis v. Monroe County Board of Education*,[162] the Supreme Court ruled that a school district can be held liable for student-on-student sexual harassment when four conditions are met. First, the plaintiff must establish that the peer sexual harassment was so severe, pervasive, and objectively offensive that it undermined and distracted the plaintiff's educational experience to the point that the plaintiff was denied equal access to the school's resources and opportunities. Second, the harassment must occur in a context over which the district has substantial control, during school hours and on school grounds. Third, the school district must have actual knowledge of the harassment. Fourth, there must be proof that the school district was deliberately indifferent to the known acts of peer sexual harassment.

A school district's obligation is to respond in a manner that is not clearly unreasonable. A total failure to respond or a response that exhibits differential enforcement of school rules—for example, protecting girls but not boys or whites but not African-Americans from harassment—are two examples of unreasonable responses. Following *Gebser* and *Davis*, there has been considerable litigation over the concepts of **actual knowledge** and **deliberate indifference**, as employed in the decisions (see Chapter 12).[163]

Sexual harassment that occurs through cyberattacks can also violate Title IX. In *Feminist Majority Foundation v. Hurley*,[164] a student-run organization at a university was blamed for the

158 555 U.S. 246 (2009).
159 503 U.S. 60 (1992).
160 Zeno v. Pine Plains Cent. Sch. Dist., 702 F. 3d 655 (2d Cir. 2012); Barnes v. Gorman, 536 U.S. 181 (2002).
161 524 U.S. 274 (1998).
162 526 U.S. 629 (1999).
163 Vance v. Spencer County Pub. Sch. Dist., 231 F.3d 253 (6th Cir. 2000).
164 911 F.3d 674, 683 (4th Cir. 2018).

suspension of the school's rugby team. The rugby suspension triggered over 700 vitriolic and threatening posts on social media. Although members of the group reported to the administration that they felt unsafe and requested action, the administration "asserted that nothing could be done, that is, the University had 'no recourse for such cyber bullying.'" The Fourth Circuit refused to dismiss the plaintiffs' claims under Title IX:

> [I]n assessing whether [the administration] … had sufficient control over the harassers and the context of the harassment, we cannot conclude that [the university] could turn a blind eye to the sexual harassment that pervaded and disrupted its campus solely because the offending conduct took place through cyberspace.

To satisfy their moral and legal duty to their students and minimize their risk of legal liability, schools should adopt, publish, and abide by formal anti-discrimination and anti-harassment policies. Title IX guidelines from the Department of Education state that schools are required "to adopt and publish grievance procedures providing for prompt and equitable resolution of sex discrimination complaints, including complaints of sexual harassment and to disseminate a policy against sex discrimination."[165] Title VI guidelines specify that once a [school] has notice of a racially hostile environment, "the [school] has a legal duty to take reasonable steps to eliminate it … In evaluating a [school's] response to a racially hostile environment, [ED] will examine disciplinary policies, grievance policies, and any applicable anti-harassment policies."[166]

English Language Learners

Educators and policymakers must deal with a variety of interrelated issues to meet their educational and legal obligations to children who are non-English proficient or limited English proficient, now more commonly referred to as **English Language Learners** (ELLs). Some of the issues are phrased in the language of equity, discrimination, and civil rights. Is it equitable to provide all children with an education in the primary language of the country in which they live? Conversely, is it equitable to teach students in a language they cannot understand? Do public schools have a moral or legal responsibility to provide special English proficiency programs for ELL students?

A second group of issues is pedagogical. What is the most effective way to help ELL students become English proficient? Should English as a second language (ESL) programs be used? Under this approach, students spend most of their day in regular classes but are pulled out to receive intensive instruction in English. Or might an immersion program work best? Under one version of immersion, a bilingual teacher instructs in English but is capable of understanding students who ask questions in their first language. The curriculum is organized in a way that does not presume the students are English proficient. Or is bilingual education the best method? Under this arrangement, students are enrolled in subject matter classes taught in their first language and are provided with special instruction to learn English.

Bilingual education itself comes in several versions. Transitional bilingual programs employ subject matter instruction in the student's first language only until the student is capable of learning in all-English classes. Bilingual-bicultural maintenance programs continue instruction in the student's first language even after the attainment of English proficiency. Such programs aim to help the students develop fluency in both languages.

---

165 62 C.F.R. § 12040 (2012); see also United States Department of Education, Office for Civil Rights, "Dear Colleague" Letter on Title IX (April 4, 2011).
166 Racial Incidents and Harassment Against Students at Educational Institutions; Investigative Guidance, 59 FR 11448–01 (1994).

Finally, there are social and political questions: Is it in students' best interest to maintain proficiency in their first language or does this tend to limit their prospects later in life? Should decisions like this be made by families, students themselves, or society as a whole? Do bilingual programs foster language divisions within the United States that can lead to political instability? Is the effort to promote English an expression of cultural and racial bias? Will we as a nation be better off if our citizens are multilingual? Should major policy decisions, such as how best to educate ELL children, be centralized or left to the states or local school districts?

Given the range and complexity and lack of consensus on these issues, it is not surprising that federal law and policy have been tumultuous and inconsistent. The first federal effort to address the civil rights of ELL students was based on Title VI of the *Civil Rights Act of 1964*.[167] In 1970, six years after the law was passed, the Office for Civil Rights (OCR) issued a memorandum interpreting Title VI's prohibition against discrimination on the basis of "national origin":

> [W]here inability to speak and understand the English language excludes national origin-minority group children from effective participation in the educational program offered by a school district, the district must take affirmative steps to rectify the language deficiency in order to open its instructional program to these students.[168]

OCR's interpretation did not require intent to discriminate as a necessary element of a Title VI violation; rather, a violation would be found wherever a school's language policy had the effect of excluding ELL students from effective participation in its program. Districts in violation of Title VI could lose all their federal funds.

In 1974, OCR's interpretation of Title VI was tested in the courts. In *Lau v. Nichols*,[169] ELL students from China who were not receiving any special assistance to learn English were enrolled in all-English subject matter classes. The plaintiffs claimed that lack of special language assistance was both a form of racial discrimination in violation of the Equal Protection Clause and Title VI. The students lost in the lower courts on both claims. The Ninth Circuit wrote that "[e]very student brings to the starting line of his educational career different advantages and disadvantages caused in part by social, economic and cultural background, created and continued completely apart from any contribution by the school system." It simply was not the school district's fault if ELL students were not prepared, and no legal obligation required the schools to overcome the students' language barriers.

In reviewing the Ninth Circuit's decision, the Supreme Court did not address the students' constitutional claims. It did, however, find in the students' favor, relying solely on Title VI as interpreted by the OCR. "There is no equality of treatment," wrote the Court, "merely by providing students with the same facilities, textbooks, teachers, and curriculum; for students who do not understand English are effectively foreclosed from any meaningful education." To require a child to have already acquired basic English skills before participating in the educational program, said the Court, is to make a mockery of public education. Following the logic of the OCR interpretation, the Court said it was not necessary to show any invidious motivation on the part of the school to establish a Title VI violation. As for the remedy, the Court wrote, "Teaching English to the students of Chinese ancestry who do not speak the language is one choice. Giving instructions to this group in Chinese is another. There may be others."[170]

---

167   42 U.S.C. § 2000(d).
168   Office for Civil Rights, Identification of Discrimination of Denial of Services on the Basis of National Origin, 35 Fed. Reg. 11,595 (May 25, 1970).
169   483 F.2d 791 (9th Cir. 1973), *rev'd*, 414 U.S. 563 (1974).
170   Lau v. Nichols, 414 U.S. 563 (1974).

In 1974, the same year that *Lau* was decided, Congress adopted the *EEOA*, which provided in part:[171]

> [N]o State shall deny equal educational opportunity to an individual on account of his or her race, color, sex, or national origin, by … the failure by an educational agency to take appropriate action to overcome language barriers that impede equal participation by its students in its instructional programs.

The US Attorney General or students adversely affected by a school's language policy were empowered to file civil actions for denial of equal educational opportunity whether the school intended to discriminate or not.

In sum, both *EEOA* and Title VI require schools to provide ELL students with instruction designed to help them overcome language barriers impeding their equal participation in the school program. Title VI prohibits intentional (*de jure*) discrimination against ELL students, but does not prohibit unintentional (*de facto*) discrimination unless the federal government has issued regulations extending Title VI to unintentional discrimination.[172]

The Department of Justice has in fact issued a policy guidance document interpreting Title VI to prohibit discriminatory impact (unintentional discrimination) based on national origin (including limited English proficiency), thus requiring recipients of federal aid (including schools) "to take reasonable steps to ensure meaningful access to the information and services they provide." The policy guidance lists factors to be considered in determining whether the steps taken are reasonable: Number or proportion of limited-English proficient individuals, their frequency of contact with the program, the nature and importance of the program, and the resources available.[173] Even though Title VI has been interpreted by the federal government to extend to unintentional discrimination, individual plaintiffs may not sue to seek enforcement based on this interpretation. Enforcement must be left to a federal or perhaps a state agency.[174]

In *Castaneda v. Pickard*,[175] a case involving Mexican-American children and their parents alleging that their school district had unlawfully discriminated against them by failing to implement a bilingual education program that would help them overcome linguistic barriers and facility equal educational opportunity, the Fifth Circuit outlined the generally accepted tests for determining whether a school is meeting its obligations to ELLs under *EEOA*.[176] Among other issues, the teachers employed in the district's bilingual education program had very limited command of Spanish. The Fifth Circuit employed a three-part test for determining whether a school is meeting its obligations under *EEOA*:

1. The school must adopt a program "informed by an educational theory recognized as sound by some experts in the field or, at least, deemed a legitimate experimental strategy."
2. The actual programs and practices of the school must be "reasonably calculated to implement effectively the educational theory adopted by the school."
3. The school must be able to show that language barriers are being overcome.

---

171 20 U.S.C. § 1703(f).
172 Alexander v. Sandoval, 532 U.S. 275 (2001); Guardians Ass'n v. Civil Serv. Comm., 463 U.S. 582 (1983).
173 Civil Rights Div., Dep't of Justice, Enforcement of Title VI of the Civil Rights Act of 1964: National Origin Discrimination Against Persons with Limited English Proficiency (LEP Guidance) 65 Fed. Reg. 50123 (August 16, 2000).
174 Alexander v. Sandoval, 532 U.S. 275 (2001).
175 648 F.2d 989 (5th Cir. 1981).
176 *See also* Serna v. Portales Mun. Sch., 499 F.2d 1147 (10th Cir. 1974); Rios v. Read, 480 F. Supp. 14 (E.D.N.Y. 1978); Gomez v. Ill. State Bd. of Educ., 811 F.2d 1030 (7th Cir. 1987); Flores v. Arizona, 48 F. Supp. 2d 937 (D. Ariz., 1999), and 172 F. Supp. 2d 1225 (2000).

Other courts have employed the *Castaneda* tests in deciding cases alleging violations of *EEOA*.[177] In *Issa v. School District of Lancaster*,[178] the Third Circuit relied on these tests in ruling for a group of refugee students from war-torn countries whose education, even in their first language, had been severely curtailed. In the school to which they were assigned, they had

> one 80-minute ESL course per day. Otherwise, [the plaintiffs] … take all their content courses—science, math, social studies—with [the school's] general population under the accelerated model. In those content classes, ELLs aren't sheltered from each other by their English proficiency or from native English speakers like they are at the International School,

where the plaintiffs sought to transfer. The court found that the "plaintiffs were rushed through their high school without any meaningful regard to their ability to overcome their language barriers, to speak English, or to understand the classes they took."[179] The Third Circuit upheld an injunction requiring the district to transfer the students to the International School.

The Supreme Court itself has relied upon the *Castaneda* tests in examining the *EEOA*. In *Horne v. Flores*,[180] the lower courts found that Arizona had failed to provide adequate funding for ELL programs statewide, in violation of the *EEOA*. The Supreme Court reversed on procedural grounds, but nevertheless made an important observation regarding the *EEOA*, noting that *EEOA* compliance should be assessed largely without scrutinizing the funding made available for ELL programs. A school district or state can satisfy the *EEOA* by showing that it has developed appropriate ELL measures, whether or not it has provided increased funding for such measures.

Castaneda interpreted federal law to allow states and local school districts to decide whether to offer bilingual education or to employ some other method of assisting ELL students. The federal grant program that assists states and localities in educating ELL students—the **English Language Acquisition, Language Enhancement, and Academic Achievement Act**—also takes this position, stipulating that the law shall not be interpreted "to require a State or a local educational agency to establish, continue, or eliminate any particular type of instructional program for limited English proficient children."[181]

In recent years, there has been a trend at both the federal and state level away from advocating or offering bilingual education. Several states have formally abolished it. In 1998, for example, California voters amended the state education code to require that "all children in California public schools shall be taught English by being taught in English. In particular, this shall require that all children be placed in English language classrooms."[182] California generally prohibited school districts from using bilingual education except for children who obtained a waiver.[183] In a new referendum in 2016, however, California voters rejected this "English-only" approach, allowing school districts greater flexibility to pursue bilingual education programs.[184]

Two other issues concerning language proficiency have also been litigated. In *Martin Luther King Jr. Elementary School Children v. Michigan Board of Education*,[185] a federal district court extended

---

177 Gomez v. Ill. State Bd. of Educ., 811 F.2d 1030 (7th Cir. 1987); Teresa P. v. Berkeley Unified Sch. Dist., 724 F. Supp. 698 (N.D. Cal. 1989).

178 847 F.3d 121, 128 (3d Cir. 2017).

179 Antoine on behalf of I.A. v. Sch. Bd. of Collier Cty., 301 F. Supp. 3d 1195, 1202 (M.D. Fla. 2018).

180 557 U.S. 433 (2009).

181 20 U.S.C. § 6845 (referring to 20 U.S.C. § 6811).

182 CAL. EDUC. CODE § 305; *see* California Teachers Ass'n v. State Bd. of Educ., 271 F.3d 1141 (9th Cir. 2001); Valeria G. v. Wilson, 12 F. Supp. 2d 1007 (N.D. Cal. 1998); *see also* ARIZ. REV. STAT. ANN. § 15–751 *et seq.*

183 McLaughlin v. State Bd. of Educ., 89 Cal. Rptr. 2d 295 (Cal. Ct. App. 1999).

184 See https://edsource.org/2017/a-new-era-for-bilingual-education-explaining-californias-proposition-58/574852 (last accessed April 18, 2020).

185 451 F. Supp. 1324 (E.D. Mich. 1978).

the reasoning of *Lau* to require schools to take special steps to address the needs of speakers of African-American Vernacular English. In *Jose P. v. Ambach*,[186] another federal court found that failure to provide bilingual education to ELL students with disabilities may violate the *Rehabilitation Act of 1973* (see Chapter 8).

Classification by Age and Ability

When parents claim that a five-year-old should be permitted to start the first grade or that a precocious 12-year-old ought to be able to skip a grade, they are objecting to age grouping. Similarly, parents may object to their child's placement in a particular ability group or academic track. Parents raising these objections usually argue that exclusion from the desired program violates their child's right to a generally available educational benefit and therefore to the "equal protection of the laws." School officials respond that age and ability grouping is an educationally sound practice that improves the efficiency of the school and helps to ensure, by and large, that children and program are appropriately matched.

Because differential treatment based on age and ability do not trigger the use of the more stringent tests, courts employ the **rational basis test** to resolve these disputes. Under this test, the plaintiffs must prove either that the age or ability grouping criteria do not serve any legitimate purpose or that the classification is wholly unrelated to its alleged purpose. Despite some evidence that ability grouping in particular is educationally ineffective and even counterproductive, plaintiffs do not usually win these suits. Age and ability grouping are longstanding practices intended to serve legitimate purposes, and despite the contrary evidence, courts do not consider it unreasonable for school officials to believe that these purposes relate to the criteria of classification.[187] The major exception is when tracking is used to create racially segregated programs within schools.[188]

As discussed above, parents have the greatest chance of prevailing in a suit attacking ability grouping where the district is under court order to desegregate and the grouping has the effect of perpetuating racial segregation.[189] Similarly, parents may be successful if they can prove that tests and other procedures used to assign students to programs have a discriminatory impact on racial minorities and that the procedures were chosen *because* of this impact rather than *in spite of* it.[190]

State law and regulations may also provide a basis for objecting to a student's educational placement or program on equity grounds. For example, many states have laws mandating enriched educational services for gifted students. On the basis of one of these laws, parents in Pennsylvania were successful in establishing that their local school district had an obligation to provide their gifted child with an enrichment program, including advanced instruction in reading and math. The court made clear that the district's obligation was not to maximize the student's achievement nor to become a "Harvard or a Princeton to all who have IQ's over 130," but the district did have an obligation "to bring their talents to as complete fruition as our facilities allow."[191] However,

---

186 669 F.2d 865 (2nd Cir. 1982).
187 Sandlin v. Johnson, 643 F.2d 1027 (4th Cir. 1981); Hammond v. Marx, 406 F. Supp. 853 (D. Me. 1975).
188 McNeal v. Tate County Sch. Dist., 508 F.2d 1017 (5th Cir. 1975); Morales v. Shannon, 516 F.2d 411 (5th Cir. 1975); Moses v. Wash. Parish Sch. Bd., 330 F. Supp. 1340 (E.D. La. 1971), *aff'd*, 456 F.2d 1285 (5th Cir. 1972) (*per curiam*); Hobson v. Hansen, 269 F. Supp. 401 (D.D.C. 1967), *aff'd sub nom*, Smuck v. Hobson, 408 F.2d 175 (D.C. Cir. 1969) (*en banc*).
189 McNeal v. Tate County Sch. Dist., 508 F.2d 1017 (5th Cir. 1975); Bester v. Tuscaloosa City Bd. of Educ., 722 F.2d 1514 (11th Cir. 1984); United States v. Jefferson Cty. Sch. Dist., 63 F. Supp. 3d 1346 (N.D. Fla. 2014).
190 Larry P. v. Riles, 793 F.2d 969 (9th Cir. 1984).
191 Centennial Sch. Dist. v. Dep't of Educ., 539 A. 2d 785 (Pa. 1988).

courts have rejected claims that gifted children have a constitutional or statutory right to start school at a younger age than state statutes prescribe.[192]

Summary

The Equal Protection Clause of the Fourteenth Amendment to the Constitution prohibits the government from treating individuals or groups differently without adequate justification. This prohibition has been the basis of numerous lawsuits attacking segregation and other forms of discrimination in public schools. The Supreme Court has fashioned three separate tests for deciding equal protection cases:

1. **Strict scrutiny**. When the government concedes or a plaintiff successfully demonstrates that the criterion of classification and differential treatment is race or ethnicity, courts employ the **strict scrutiny** test. This test requires that the government justify its policy of differential treatment by showing that it is necessary to the accomplishment of a compelling state purpose. Except regarding certain affirmative action policies, this requirement is rarely met.
2. **Substantial relation**. When it is admitted or demonstrated by a plaintiff that the government is classifying on the basis of gender, courts employ the **substantial relation** or **mid-level** test. This test, although not nearly as stringent as strict scrutiny, still places the burden for justifying the policy of differential treatment on the government. Gender-based classifications will be upheld only if the government can demonstrate that they are substantially related to the achievement of an important government purpose.
3. **Rational basis**. Classifications based on characteristics other than race, ethnicity, or gender (with several minor exceptions not usually relevant to education cases) are evaluated using the least stringent test. **Rational basis** places the burden on the plaintiff to show that differential treatment by the government is wholly unrelated to any legitimate state goal. Under this test, classifications that in any way foster or promote any legitimate goal of the government will be upheld.

As a practical matter, the Equal Protection Clause prohibits any policy or practice that intentionally segregates students on the basis of race or ethnicity or intentionally provides members of a racial or ethnic minority group with an inferior education. A policy or practice will be viewed as intentionally segregative or otherwise discriminatory if it purposely seeks to separate or otherwise disadvantage members of a minority group. Thus, any conscious decision by an educational policymaker or practitioner to separate students by race will not pass constitutional muster. Actions may also be viewed as discriminatory if a rational decision-maker should have realized that the actions would disadvantage or segregate members of a minority group. However, policies that have an accidental or unforeseeable disadvantageous effect on members of particular racial or ethnic groups do not violate the Equal Protection Clause.

Beginning in 1954 with *Brown v. Board of Education*, many school districts have been found liable for intentional racial segregation and discrimination. Federal courts are authorized to order a variety of remedies for *de jure* segregation, including redrawing of attendance areas, busing, magnet schools, and remedial educational programs. Courts may not, however, transfer students into or out of districts that have not been found *de jure* segregated in order to desegregate adjacent districts. Many formerly segregated districts have fully complied with court-ordered desegregation and been declared unitary, while others continue to be supervised by the courts.

---

192 Zweifel v. Joint Dist. No. 1, 251 N.W. 2d 822 (Wis. 1977).

School districts that have not been found liable for intentional racial discrimination and those that have been declared unitary are prohibited from assigning students to schools strictly on the basis of race in order to promote integration and diversity. However, school districts still retain some authority to voluntarily address *de facto* segregation. Under some state constitutions, school districts may have a duty to address *de facto* segregation.

The Equal Protection Clause also prohibits educational practices that disfavor male or female students, unless there is very strong justification. Most programs that intentionally separate the sexes are prohibited. The major exception is athletics, but the law governing gender equality in athletics is not fully settled.

In addition to the Equal Protection Clause, Title VI of the *Civil Rights Act of 1964* and Title IX of the *Education Amendments of 1972* prohibit discrimination in education on the basis of race and gender, respectively. These statutes supplement the Constitution in a number of ways, most importantly by providing remedies for discrimination not available under the Equal Protection Clause. Title VI and Title IX also provide a great deal of specificity concerning prohibited discriminatory practices. Title IX requires equity in school athletic programs. The statutes also define racial and sexual harassment as impermissible forms of discrimination and require that schools adopt and enforce a program designed to prevent racial and sexual harassment of students by school employees or fellow students. Failure to do so may leave the school and, in some cases, individual educators vulnerable to lawsuits for monetary damages.

Legal issues aside, schools should avoid policies of classification based on race, ethnicity, or gender without strong justification. Except in extraordinary circumstances, sound educational practice dictates treating students of color the same as white students and female students the same as male students. The rights of transgender students must be honored, as well. Thus, to avoid violating the Equal Protection Clause and anti-discrimination statutes with regard to race and gender, school officials should exercise sound educational judgment and common sense.

The law regarding the treatment of English Language Learners is not nearly as extensive. However, Title VI of the *Civil Rights Act of 1964* and the *Equal Educational Opportunity Act of 1974* both require schools to take "appropriate action" to ensure that ELL students are not functionally excluded from meaningful participation in their programs. Appropriate action may include any locally chosen program that is supported by recognized educational theory and is effective in assisting ELL students in learning English. Some states have prohibited bilingual education.

Age grouping and most forms of ability grouping and tracking, although not mandated by considerations of equity, generally survive challenges based on the Equal Protection Clause. The major exception is when grouping or tracking leads to increased racial segregation in a district under court order to desegregate.

8 Students with Disabilities

In Chapter 7, we saw that the **Equal Protection Clause** prohibits most race- and gender-based classifications in public schools. Classification based on other characteristics may be justified if it is rationally related to legitimate government goals. In this chapter, we consider various types of disabilities that may sometimes justify differential educational treatment. Unlike race and gender, disabilities may in some cases require a special educational program.

School officials are not free to provide whatever education they choose to students with disabilities. Both the Constitution and extensive federal legislation and regulations require equality of educational opportunity, or, at a minimum, an adequate program of education. In fact, federal mandates may require that a more extensive program be offered for students with disabilities.

All this can get very complex: How should the educational entitlement for students with disabilities be defined? May students with disabilities who demonstrate significant behavioral challenges be excluded from school? What role should private schools play in the education of students with disabilities? In this chapter, we address these and other questions.

The Education of Students with Disabilities: A History

In 1970, there were about eight million children with disabilities in the United States. Three million of these children were not receiving an appropriate education and another million were wholly excluded from public education. Exclusion of children with disabilities was legally possible because many states exempted their parents from compulsory schooling laws. State courts generally upheld policies of excluding children with disabilities from the public schools, sometimes on the ground that their presence would have a detrimental effect on other students.[1]

In the early 1970s, the exclusion of children with disabilities from public schools gave rise to a number of federal lawsuits, most notably *PARC v. Pennsylvania* and *Mills v. Board of Education*.[2] Although the cases differed somewhat, the major findings were similar: (a) Children were excluded from the public schools because they had disabilities; (b) the effect of this policy was wholly to deprive these children of access to a publicly funded education; (c) the government's purpose in excluding them was to save money; (d) excluding children with disabilities from school was not rationally related to the goal of saving money (or to any other legitimate state goal) because uneducated people (with or without disabilities) were likely to become a much greater financial burden on the State; and therefore (e) exclusion of children with disabilities from public schools violated the Equal Protection Clause.

The rulings in *PARC* and *Mills* included both substantive and procedural requirements. Children with disabilities were to be admitted to public schools and provided with appropriate educational services in accordance with their individual needs. Schools had to follow certain procedures

---

1 State *ex rel.* Beattie v. Bd. of Educ. of Antigo, 172 N.W. 153 (Wis. 1919).
2 334 F. Supp. 1257 (E.D. Pa. 1971) and 343 F. Supp. 279 (E.D. Pa. 1972); 348 F. Supp. 866 (D.D.C. 1972).

when they classified students with disabilities, decided on their appropriate educational place-ments, reclassified them, or changed their placements. *PARC* and *Mills* were part of a nationwide campaign that included both lawsuits and legislative efforts to secure better educational services for children with disabilities. This campaign resulted in four major federal statutes designed to ensure equitable treatment for children with disabilities:

- The *Rehabilitation Act* of 1973 **[Section 504]**[3]
- The *Americans with Disabilities Act* of 1990 **[ADA]**[4]
- The *Individuals with Disabilities Education Act* **[IDEA]**[5]
- The *Every Student Succeeds Act* **[ESSA]**.[6]

Together with related state laws and extensive federal and state regulations, these statutes provide the legal framework for the education of students with disabilities. The constitutional rights of children with disabilities have not been fully explored by the courts, perhaps because these statutes have generally satisfied parental expectations for special educational services at public expense.[7]

Although the *IDEA* is the most well-known of the federal statutes regulating the education of students with disabilities, Section 504 and the *ADA* are significant as well. Both the *IDEA* and Section 504 are funding programs, with requirements that extend only to entities that accept federal funds under the Act. Under the *ADA*, however, the requirements imposed upon states and school districts are not linked to the receipt of federal funding.[8]

As we discuss in the next section, the scope of Section 504 and the *ADA* is in some ways broader than that of the *IDEA*. Section 504 and the *ADA* extend protection to students who are not covered by the *IDEA*, impose obligations in situations that the *IDEA* does not address, and prevent forms of disability-based discrimination beyond the scope of the *IDEA*. Nevertheless, both as a matter of law and as a practical matter, the *IDEA* is by far the most influential statute in affording rights to children with disabilities.

Many cases fall neatly under the *IDEA* or the *ADA* (which, in turn, often parallels Section 504). Increasingly, however, these statutes intersect or overlap, which leads both to more meaningful rights for students with disabilities and more complexity in deciphering the legal issues.

The *Rehabilitation Act* and *The Americans with Disabilities Act*

The heart of the *Rehabilitation Act* is **Section 504,** which provides as follows:

> No otherwise qualified individual with [disabilities] … shall solely by reason of her or his [disability], be excluded from the participation in, be denied the benefits of, or be subjected to discrimination under any program or activity receiving Federal financial assistance …[9]

3 29 U.S.C. §§ 701–796.
4 42 U.S.C. §§ 12101–12213.
5 20 U.S.C. §§ 1400–1485 [In 2004, the name was officially changed to the *Individuals with Disabilities Education Improvement Act* (*IDEIA*), but it is still commonly referred to as *IDEA*.].
6 20 U.S.C. §§ 6311–6322 [The *Every Student Succeeds Act* of 2015 was a reauthorization of the *No Child Left Behind Act* of 2001, a reauthorization of the *Elementary and Secondary Education Act* of 1965, as amended through P.L. 115–224, July 31, 2018.].
7 *But see* City of Cleburne v. Cleburne Living Center, 473 U.S. 432 (1985).
8 *See, e.g.,* Ash v. Maryland Transit Admin., 2019 U.S. Dist. LEXIS 39849 (D. Md. Mar. 12, 2019), *citing* United States v. Georgia, 546 U.S. 151 (2006).
9 29 U.S.C. § 701–796 [Except as otherwise noted, the discussion of RHA is based on the statutes and RHA regulations, Volume 34 C.F.R.].

The Act applies to all public and private schools that receive federal financial assistance and protects not just students with disabilities but *any person* "who (i) has a physical or mental impairment which substantially limits one or more of such person's major life activities, (ii) has a record of such an impairment, or (iii) is regarded as having such an impairment."

Thus, **Section 504**, unlike the *IDEA*, regulates a school's relationship not only with qualifying students but also with qualifying teachers and other employees (see Chapter 10). Under certain circumstances, even qualifying parents may be covered. For example, the Second Circuit has ruled that Section 504 requires a school to provide a sign-language interpreter at district expense to deaf parents at school-initiated events related to their children's education (though not for extra-curricular activities).[10]

Section 504 defines "**major life activities**" to include "caring for one's self, performing manual tasks, seeing, hearing, eating, sleeping, walking, standing, lifting, bending, speaking, breathing, learning, reading, concentrating, thinking, communicating and working." Thus, unlike the *IDEA*, which only covers students who currently need special education, Section 504 protects children with a wide range of "impairments," those with a history of life-limiting impairments, and even those who are regarded as having such impairments. For example, students with epilepsy or certain allergies or **attention deficit hyperactivity disorder** (ADHD) are covered by Section 504 even though some of them may not qualify for special education under the *IDEA*.

Like Section 504, the *ADA* covers all persons with physical or mental impairments that substantially limit **major life activities**, those with a record of such impairments, and those who are regarded as having such impairments.[11] The basic mandate of the *ADA* is that "no qualified individual with a disability shall, by reason of such disability, be excluded from participation in or be denied the benefits of services, programs or activities of a public entity, or be subjected to discrimination by any such entity." The term "qualified individual with a disability" means an individual with a disability who, with or without "reasonable modifications" to rules, policies, or practices; the removal of architectural and communication barriers; or the provision of auxiliary aids and services, meets the essential eligibility requirements for the receipt of services or participation in the program.

Whereas Section 504 regulates only entities that receive federal financial assistance, the *ADA* applies to all "**public entities**" and "**places of public accommodation**." This includes any public or private business or agency providing goods or services to the public, including virtually all public and private schools except private religious schools, which are explicitly excluded. When the two laws both apply, the requirements of the *ADA* are very often the same as Section 504.

Among the five main titles of the *ADA*, Titles II and III are directly relevant to the treatment of students. Title II protects individuals with disabilities from discrimination in the provision of services by public agencies such as schools. Title II requires that public schools be made accessible to individuals with disabilities such as by modification or removal of "architectural, communication or transportation barriers" or the "provision of auxiliary aids and services." Title III prohibits discrimination by private entities that do business with the public. Non-religious private schools are included in Title III, but, as noted above, religious private schools are specifically *excluded*.

Eligibility

Students seeking to convince a court that they should be afforded the protection of Section 504 or the *ADA* must demonstrate that they have a "mental or physical impairment" that "substantially

---

10 Rothschild v. Grottenthaler, 907 F.2d 286 (2d Cir. 1990).
11 42 U.S.C. §§ 12101–12213. [Except as otherwise noted, the discussion of *ADA* is based on the statutes and *ADA* regulations, Volumes 28, 29, 34, & 36 C.F.R.].

limits" a "major life activity" or that they have a history of or are regarded as having such an impairment. According to the Second Circuit, the impairment does not have to relate to the activity "in which the defendants are engaged." Thus, a student with chronic fatigue syndrome that did not impair her ability to learn still qualified for protection under the ADA and Section 504 at school because her condition "substantially limited her in the major life activities of walking, exerting herself, and attending classes …"[12]

The ADA excludes individuals whose presence "poses a direct threat to the health or safety of others." The term "direct threat" is defined as "a significant risk to the health or safety of others that cannot be eliminated by a modification of policies, practices, or procedures or by the provision of auxiliary aids or services." Thus, although students with contagious diseases might meet eligibility criteria, they would be excluded from coverage if they pose a direct threat to the health of other students.[13]

Prior to 2008, the Supreme Court interpreted ADA eligibility narrowly (which also affected Section 504 eligibility). First, the Court ruled that if a physical or mental impairment could be "mitigated" through the use of medical interventions (e.g., medication, eyeglasses, hearing aids), the impairment in its mitigated state would not qualify as a disability under the ADA.[14] The Court also held that a "substantial limitation" in performing major life activities meant a severe restriction, and that the impairment in question had to be "permanent or long term."[15]

The ADA Amendments Act

The **ADA Amendments Act** of 2008 (ADAAA) explicitly rejected the Supreme Court cases limiting the coverage of the ADA, and by extension, section 504.[16] The ADAAA stipulates that the definition of disability "shall be construed in favor of broad coverage of individuals," and proclaims the congressional intent "that the primary object of attention in cases brought under the ADA should be whether entities covered under the ADA have complied with their obligations," rather than focusing intently on eligibility.

In overturning the Supreme Court's ADA interpretation, Congress provided that "[a]n impairment that is episodic or in remission is a disability if it would substantially limit a major life activity when active," and the determination whether an impairment substantially limits a major life activity is to be made "without regard to the ameliorative effects of mitigating measures," except for ordinary eyeglasses or contact lenses. The ADAAA lists medication, hearing aids, cochlear implants, mobility devices, and assistive technology, as examples of the measures that can no longer be considered when assessing eligibility under the ADA and Section 504.

Of particular relevance to students, the list of **major life activities** under the ADAAA has been expanded to include reading, concentrating, thinking, and communicating, as well as hearing, speaking, and learning. The term "major life activities" now also includes operation of major bodily functions, such as "functions of the immune system, normal cell growth, digestive, bowel, bladder, neurological, brain, respiratory, circulatory, endocrine, and reproductive functions." In addition, the regulations issued pursuant to the ADAAA set forth a number of psychological conditions which will almost always trigger eligibility under the ADA and Section 504; such

---

12 Weixel v. Bd. of Educ. of City of New York, 287 F.3d 138 (2d Cir. 2002).
13 Sch. Bd. of Nassau County v. Arline, 480 U.S. 273 (1987).
14 Sutton v. United Air Lines, Inc., 527 U.S. 471 (1999), *superseded by statute*, ADA Amendments Act of 2008, Pub. L. No. 110–325, 122 Stat. 3553 (2008).
15 Toyota Motor Mfg., Ky., Inc. v. Williams, 534 U.S. 184, 197 (2002), *superseded by statute*, ADA Amendments Act of 2008, Pub. L. No. 110-325, 122 Stat. 3553 (2008).
16 *ADA Amendments Act of 2008*, Pub. L. No. 110-325, 122 Stat. 3553 (2008).

conditions include bipolar disorder, post-traumatic stress disorder (PTSD), obsessive compulsive disorder (OCD), major depressive disorder, and schizophrenia.[17]

Overall, the *ADAAA* and accompanying regulations have greatly expanded eligibility for elementary and secondary students under the ADA and Section 504.[18] In *Franchi v. New Hampton School*,[19] for example, a student claimed that she had been expelled from a private boarding school because of her eating disorder, in violation of the *ADA*. The school argued that her eating disorder did not render her eligible under the *ADA*, but the federal district court refused to dismiss the *ADA* claim. Citing the *ADAAA*, the court said that the school's view of *ADA* eligibility was "too stringent" in light of the congressional intent to expand eligibility. In *Cain v. Esthetique*,[20] officials at a vocational school discharged a student because they believed she was hallucinating. A federal court refused to dismiss the student's Section 504 claim, citing the more generous definition of a perceived disability under the *ADAAA*.

Section 504 protects "otherwise qualified individuals with [disabilities]." The issue of what constitutes an "**otherwise qualified**" individual was recently addressed in *Nardella v. Leyden High School District 212*.[21] In that case, school officials attempted to meet the needs of a teenager with "high-functioning autism" by placing him in a private educational program. The private program subsequently dismissed the student "for making rude comments to peers and staff, engaging in provocative and unproductive behaviors, and being verbally aggressive to staff and peers." The federal court held that, because the student's behaviors did not allow him to meet the program's minimal requirements, he was not "otherwise qualified" to participate in the program under Section 504.

Purposeful Discrimination

Both Section 504 and the *ADA* prohibit both **purposeful discrimination** and also actions having the unintentional effect of discriminating against those covered by the laws. Plaintiffs claiming purposeful discrimination under Section 504 bear the initial burden of establishing that

a.   they are a person with a disability under the law;
b.   they are otherwise qualified and can participate in the program with or without reasonable accommodation;
c.   they have been or are being excluded from participation in, or being denied the benefits of, or being subjected to discrimination under the program solely by reason of their disability; and
d.   the relevant program or activity is receiving federal financial assistance.[22]

Once the plaintiff has met this burden of proof, the burden then shifts to the defendant to show either (a) that the plaintiff was not otherwise qualified, or (b) that the defendant based its actions on reasons other than the plaintiff's disability. If the defendant meets this burden of proof, the plaintiff can still win by showing that the defendant acted based on discriminatory reasons or on

---

17 29 C.F.R. §1630.2.
18 Mark C. Weber, *A New Look at Section 504 and the ADA in Special Education Cases*, 16 Tex. J. C.L. & C.R. 1 (2010).
19 656 F.Supp.2d 252 (D.N.H. 2009).
20 Cain v. Esthetique, 182 F. Supp. 3d 54 (S.D.N.Y. 2016), *aff'd sub nom.* Cain v. Atelier Esthetique Inst. of Esthetics Inc., 733 F. App'x 8 (2d Cir. 2018).
21 2016 U.S. Dist. LEXIS 81379 (N.D. Ill. June 22, 2016); 2017 U.S. Dist. LEXIS 69355 (N.D. Ill. May 5, 2017).
22 Campbell v. Bd. of Educ. of Centerline Sch. Dist., 58 Fed. Appx. 162 (6th Cir. 2003); Johnson v. Thompson, 971 F.2d 1487 (10th Cir. 1992); Pushkin v. Regents of the Univ. of Colorado, 658 F.2d 1372 (10th Cir. 1981); *compare* Doe v. New York Univ., 666 F.2d 761 (2d Cir. 1981).

misconceptions or unfounded factual conclusions, or that the reasons articulated for the rejection encompass unjustified consideration of the disability itself. Some circuits have ruled that the plaintiff must also establish that the defendant's actions showed bad faith or gross misjudgment.[23] In other circuits, this is not required.[24] The following case is illustrative:

⚖️

CTL v. ASHLAND SCHOOL DISTRICT
US Court of Appeals for the Seventh Circuit
743 F.3d 524 (2014)

DIANE S. SYKES, Circuit Judge

A diabetic student and his parents sued his former public-school district for discriminating against him on the basis of his disability. The district court granted summary judgment in favor of the school district, and we affirm. None of the evidence or allegations demonstrate either intentional discrimination or a failure by the school district to reasonably accommodate his diabetes.

I. Background

Charlie Lindman is a child with Type 1 diabetes. He manages his condition with an insulin pump, a personal diabetes manager, and a continuous glucose monitor. The insulin pump delivers a steady dose of insulin and can also deliver a larger dose (bolus) on demand through the personal diabetes manager. The glucose monitor tracks Charlie's blood-glucose level and sets off an alarm if it goes above or below certain thresholds. The glucose monitor is not perfectly accurate, so a blood-glucose test is often required. If Charlie's blood-glucose level is high, he is given insulin via the personal diabetes manager, and if low, he is given a snack.

Before Charlie entered kindergarten, his parents, Eric and Nichole Lindman, worked with the Ashland School District to develop a plan (called a 504 plan) to accommodate Charlie's disability and enable him to attend public school. Charlie's 504 plan incorporated his doctor's orders for how insulin doses and snacks were to be administered at school. Another portion of Charlie's 504 plan required his school to train three adult staff members as "Trained Diabetes Personnel." These staff members had to be trained to

administer insulin using Charlie's insulin pump, to monitor and respond to the alarms from his glucose monitor, and to respond to hyper/hypoglycemia, among other things. The plan also required that all staff members who would interact with Charlie be given general training about diabetes and how to respond to certain situations.

Prior to Charlie's first day in kindergarten, the school hired Barb Vincent, a licensed nurse, to perform Charlie's diabetes care. The school also provided two separate training sessions: one general session that almost all staff who would interact with Charlie attended, and a second session specific to Charlie's equipment that the majority of those same staff attended.

The Lindmans were mostly satisfied with the school throughout their son's kindergarten year, except that they believed Vincent was the school's only staff member who had the proper training to be qualified as Trained Diabetes Personnel. Nichole communicated with the school many times about the matter, but never received a satisfactory response.

The following school year, the situation deteriorated. After the school hired Pam Webber as the school-nurse supervisor, disputes arose between Webber, the Lindmans, and Vincent over how to manage Charlie's condition. Vincent would occasionally deviate from the insulin dosage recommended by the personal diabetes manager. She communicated these decisions to the Lindmans, who approved of her exercising judgment on a case-by-case basis. Webber, on the other hand, believed that Wisconsin law required strict adherence to doctors' orders and did not allow school nurses to follow parents' instructions. Webber contacted

23 Monahan v. Nebraska, 687 F.2d 1164, 1171 (8th Cir. 1982); Sellers by Sellers v. School Bd. of City of Manassas, Va., 141 F.3d 524, 529 (4th Cir. 1998).
24 Andrew M. v. Delaware County Office of Mental Health and Mental Retardation, 490 F.3d 337 (3d Cir. 2007); Garcia v. S.U.N.Y. Health Sciences Center of Brooklyn, 280 F.3d 98, 115 (2d Cir. 2001).

Rachel Gallagher, a school-nurse consultant for the Wisconsin Department of Public Instruction, who agreed with Webber's interpretation of Wisconsin law. Gallagher also suggested that Webber contact Charlie's medical team for clarification on whether the school was permitted to modify insulin doses as the Lindmans desired, but it's unclear whether Webber actually did so.

In the fall of that school year, the Lindmans filed a complaint with the Department of Education's Office of Civil Rights, arguing that the school was violating the 504 plan by failing to have three Trained Diabetes Personnel and refusing to allow Vincent to adjust insulin doses on a case-by-case basis. They also accused Webber of obstinacy and failing to communicate with them about Charlie's treatment.

Vincent also found Webber frustrating to work with. When Vincent prodded her to learn more about the personalized care required by Charlie, Webber responded: "I'm an R.N., I can figure it out." On one school day, Vincent handed off care of Charlie to Webber. Prior to leaving, Vincent warned Webber that Charlie was trending high. When she returned, Vincent discovered that Webber had given Charlie a fruit roll-up during gym, setting off the alarm on his glucose monitor and requiring Vincent to administer an extra dose of insulin. Vincent rebuked Webber for this. Webber responded that Vincent had no right to question her treatment and from then on refused to talk to her.

Shortly thereafter, Vincent was reprimanded by the school administration for being rude in her interactions with coworkers. The school cited three separate examples, all stemming from her treatment of diabetic children. She disputed the claims and tried to explain her actions in a letter, but she was told that she needed to be more diplomatic or might be discharged. After reaching an impasse in her attempts to address the complaints, Vincent decided to resign.

After Vincent's resignation on November 5, a nurse assigned to the third through fifth grades was transferred and took over Charlie's care until the school hired two more nurses on January 18. During this time, the Lindmans grew increasingly frustrated with the school's communication and continued refusal to adjust his treatment on a case-by-case basis. Around January 25 the Lindmans decided, with the approval of their doctor, to send Charlie to school with edible fast-acting glucose to allow him to self-treat if he was feeling low. Webber again felt that this violated Charlie's 504 plan, so

the nurses requested a doctor's order, but due to a mix-up, the school did not immediately receive the doctor's orders.

On January 29 the school entered into a mediation agreement with the Lindmans to resolve the complaint they had filed with the Department of Education's Office of Civil Rights. The agreement required the school to conduct training for Webber and two other nurses by February 28. It also more generally required the school to follow the 504 plan.

On February 11 the school followed up with the Lindmans and Charlie's doctor about the fast-acting glucose. The next day Charlie's doctor faxed an order (at 4:12 p.m., after the school day ended) that permitted Charlie to eat "15 grams of carbohydrates that he [would] have with him" in the event of a low-sensor alarm from his glucose monitor. Prior to the receipt of the order, the school had a Valentine's Day party. Webber had taken Charlie's fast-acting glucose away from him and told him that a nurse would have to sit with him all day if he kept it. The Lindmans may have been confused over which happened first because they claim it was taken away in violation of Charlie's doctor's orders.

The following Monday, February 15, was a holiday. Charlie attended school on the 16th, but his parents called him in sick on the 17th and 18th. Also on the 18th, the Lindmans met with the school nurses and confronted them with Webber's actions on the 12th and 27 additional alleged violations of the 504 plan that Nichole had charted between January 25 and February 12. The meeting was unsuccessful, and the Lindmans removed Charlie from the school that very day.

The Lindmans placed Charlie in a private Catholic school with no nurses or medically trained staff and no formal plan for diabetes care for him. The Lindmans then filed a lawsuit on Charlie's behalf alleging disability discrimination in violation of section 504 of the *Rehabilitation Act* of 1973, and section 202 of the *Americans with Disabilities Act* of 1990, requesting both an injunction against the school and damages for the cost of private school. The district court granted summary judgment in favor of the school, and the Lindmans appealed.

II. Discussion

… Ashland agrees that Charlie is a qualified individual with a disability, so the only dispute is whether the school discriminated against Charlie. To prove disability discrimination, a plaintiff must show that

"(1) the defendant intentionally acted on the basis of the disability, (2) the defendant refused to provide a reasonable modification, or (3) the defendant's rule disproportionally impacts disabled people." Accommodations are "only … required when necessary to avoid discrimination on the basis of a disability." The Lindmans allege both intentional discrimination and a failure to accommodate Charlie, though they lean more heavily on the latter theory …

The Lindmans allege that they withdrew Charlie because they felt he was unsafe, and in certain circumstances a school's failure to provide a reasonably safe environment could effectively deny a disabled student the benefit of a public education. Parents do not need to wait until their child has been harmed to prove that the environment was unsafe. Ashland's actions in this case, however, do not come anywhere near this line.

The Lindmans first fault Ashland for failing to provide three Trained Diabetes Personnel as required by Charlie's 504 plan. They maintain, as they have ever since Charlie started kindergarten, that the school only had one, Barb Vincent. The district court found—and the school district argues on appeal—that the training session specific to Charlie's devices qualified all who attended the session as Trained Diabetes Personnel, fulfilling the plan requirement. However, Vincent declared that she was the only staff member who was fully qualified as Trained Diabetes Personnel and pointed to the fact that she was not allowed to take a lunch as evidence that the school had the same understanding. On one occasion when Vincent was out, the Lindmans were required to come pick Charlie up. Also, the agreement that resolved the Lindmans' complaint with the Department of Education required the school to train three staff members on Charlie's devices, implying that there weren't three Trained Diabetes Personnel prior to that time.

Reviewing this evidence in the light most favorable to the Lindmans, we are unable to draw the same conclusion the district court did. But even assuming that Vincent was the school's only staff member who qualified, the 504 plan merely requires that "[e]ither a school nurse or [Trained Diabetes Personnel] … be present at all times during school hours," and only once was that requirement not met. For this reason the school district's failure to train two additional staff members as Trained Diabetes Personnel (assuming that's a correct interpretation of the facts) was at most a minor violation of the 504 plan and in no way made Charlie unsafe or denied him the benefit of a public education …

Finally, the Lindmans accuse the school of intentional discrimination. Their theory is that Ashland purposefully frustrated the Lindmans in order to drive them out of the school so that Ashland would no longer have to deal with Charlie's disability. The evidence of such an orchestrated scheme is sparse. The Lindmans point to two comments by Ashland's Director of Pupil Services describing Charlie's mom as the "Lindman storm" and "hurricane Nicky." They also argue that the events surrounding Vincent's resignation demonstrate the school's unwillingness to listen to concerns regarding Charlie's diabetic care, even though Vincent was reprimanded for interactions with coworkers that were unrelated to Charlie. The rest of their argument reduces to little more than complaints about Webber's personality—specifically, her "rigid interpretation" of Charlie's doctor's orders and "callous and indifferent" attitude. A reasonable fact finder might agree with the Lindmans that Webber and other school staff were difficult to work with, communicated poorly, and took too rigid a view of Charlie's 504 plan and diabetic care in general. Still, none of this is enough for a jury to conclude that the school intentionally discriminated against Charlie. Affirmed.

Harassment and Section 504

Failure of school officials to protect a child with a disability from harassment also constitutes discrimination under Section 504, and may be a violation of the *IDEA* as well.[25] The courts may view harassment of students protected by Section 504 as analogous to racial or sexual harassment (see Chapter 7) and schools officials who are "deliberately indifferent" to such harassment may be

---

25 T.K. v. New York City Dept. of Educ., 779 F.Supp.2d 289 (E.D.N.Y. 2011); D. E. Ferster, *Deliberately Different: Bullying as a Denial of a Free Appropriate Public Education Under the Individuals with Disabilities Education Act*, 43 Ga. L. Rev. 191 (2008).

vulnerable to lawsuits for damages under the federal law known as Section 1983 (see Chapter 1).[26] In *Long v. Murray County School District*,[27] a case involving "severe disability discrimination," including name-calling and physical assaults, the Eleventh Circuit found the school had not been **deliberately indifferent**. School officials had investigated each incident and had made a good-faith effort to adopt and implement an anti-bullying policy.

Discrimination and the ADA

The ADA defines discrimination broadly to include:

- Using eligibility criteria that screen out individuals with disabilities from goods, services, facilities, privileges, advantages, and accommodations.
- Failing to make reasonable modifications in policies and practices to assure that individuals with disabilities are afforded goods, services, facilities, privileges, advantages, and accommodations. However, modifications and adjustments are not required if they would fundamentally alter the goods, services, facilities, privileges, advantages, or accommodations provided. Also, the removal of architectural or communication barriers is required only if removal is "readily achievable."
- Failing to provide auxiliary aids and services to assure that individuals with disabilities are not excluded from goods, services, facilities, privileges, advantages, and accommodations.

At the heart of Section 504 and the ADA is the requirement that people with disabilities not be treated differently solely by reason of their disability. Regulations prohibit imposing a surcharge on students with disabilities for attending after-school programs or a surcharge on parents with disabilities for the cost of making school functions accessible. Thus, for example, parents who are deaf or hard-of-hearing must not be charged for sign language interpretation at school functions. A school may not treat a student differently because the student is associated with someone with a known disability. By way of illustration, a child may not be excluded from a sports team because a sibling is HIV-positive.

Unintentional Discrimination

A number of students with disabilities have attempted to rely on Section 504 and the ADA in objecting to school policies having unintended discriminatory effects. The courts have usually found that eligibility requirements for school sports programs do not violate the law if they serve a valid purpose and apply equally to students with or without disabilities. Both the Sixth and Eighth Circuits have upheld rules setting a maximum age for participation in interscholastic sports, for example. The rules had the effect of excluding some students who were in school beyond the usual graduation age because of a disability. In *Sandison v. Michigan High School Athletic Association*,[28] the Sixth Circuit held that absent their disabilities, the plaintiffs would still have failed to satisfy the age requirement. In *Pottgen v. Missouri State High School Athletic Association*,[29] the Eighth Circuit

---

26 S.S. v. Eastern Kentucky Univ., 532 F.3d 445 (6th Cir. 2008); K.M. v. Hyde Park Cent. Sch. Dist., 381 F. Supp. 2d 343 (S.D. N.Y. 2005).
27 522 Fed. Appx. 576 (11th Cir. 2013).
28 64 F.3d 1026 (6th Cir. 1995).
29 40 F.3d 926 (8th Cir. 1994), *rev'd on other grounds*, 103 F.3d 720 (8th Cir. 1997); *see also* Mahan v. Agee, 652 P.2d 765 (Okla. 1982).

held that age was an essential eligibility requirement designed to promote safety for all participants. Waiving the age requirement would not be a "reasonable accommodation," but rather a "fundamental alteration" of the sports program.

More recently, in *K.L. v. Missouri State High School Activities Association*,[30] a para-athlete who had lost a leg to Bockenheimer's Syndrome argued that Section 504 required modification of the scoring system for track and field events in which she competed against teams from other schools without para-athletes. A federal court denied the claim, holding that such modifications would fundamentally alter the nature of the track and field program.

Several other courts have ruled that Section 504 and the ADA require that the application of age-eligibility requirements to students with disabilities be made on an individual basis. In one case, the plaintiff was a 19-year-old student with Down Syndrome who had spent four years in middle school. For three years, he was a member of the high school swim team, but he was deemed ineligible when he turned 19. Based on Section 504 and the ADA, the student asked for and obtained an order from the court granting him a waiver of the age rule. The court said that exclusion of the plaintiff because of his age amounted to an exclusion based on disability since it was because of his disability that he was in school at 19.[31]

On a related issue, the Sixth Circuit concluded that the ADA was not violated by a rule that prohibited students from participating in athletics after more than nine semesters of enrollment. The student with a disability in this suit had been enrolled in school for more than the permitted number of semesters but had been academically ineligible for part of the time as a result of his disability. The court found that a waiver of the rule was not required by the ADA because it would fundamentally alter interscholastic sports. Furthermore, reasoned the court, alteration of the rule was undesirable from a policy standpoint because it would encourage **redshirting**—the practice of delaying academic advancement for the sake of athletics.[32] Two years later, the Seventh Circuit reached the opposite conclusion in *Washington v. Indiana High School Athletic Association*.[33] In that case, a Catholic high school student with a learning disability argued that the athletic association's refusal to grant a waiver of its eight-semester rule violated his ADA rights. The Seventh Circuit found that the student was a qualified individual under the ADA and that waiving the eight-semester rule would be reasonable accommodation in his case.

Reasonable Accommodations

Section 504 and the ADA require modifications to school programs and other "**reasonable accommodations**" as necessary so that students with disabilities are not denied the benefits they would otherwise receive because of their disability.[34] ADA regulations require that schools

> shall make reasonable modifications in policies, practices, or procedures when the modifications are necessary to avoid discrimination on the basis of disability, unless the [school] can demonstrate that making the modifications would fundamentally alter the nature of the service, program, or activity.[35]

30 178 F. Supp. 3d 792 (E.D. Mo. 2016).
31 Denin v. Conn. Interscholastic Athletic Conference, 913 F. Supp. 663 (D. Conn. 1996), *vacated as moot*, 94 F.3d 96 (2d Cir. 1996); Univ. Interscholastic League v. Buchanan, 848 S.W.2d 298 (Tex. App. 1993); Johnson v. Florida High Sch. Athletic Ass'n, 899 F. Supp. 579 (M.D. Fla. 1995), *vacated as moot*, 102 F.3d 1172 (11th Cir. 1997).
32 McPherson v. Mich. High Sch. Athletic Ass'n, 119 F.3d 453 (6th Cir. 1997) (*en banc*).
33 181 F.3d 840 (7th Cir. 1999), *cert. denied*, 528 U.S. 1046 (1999).
34 Alexander v. Choate, 469 U.S. 287 (1985).
35 28 C.F.R. § 35.130(b)(7).

Section 504 regulations require that public elementary and secondary schools provide a program that is designed to meet "individual educational needs of [disabled] persons as adequately as the needs of non-[disabled] persons are met."[36]

In *Brookhart v. Illinois State Board of Education*,[37] the Seventh Circuit considered the legality under Section 504 of requiring students with disabilities to pass a minimum competency test (MCT) in order to graduate from high school:

> Plaintiffs in this case have no grounds on which to argue that the contents of the M.C.T. are discriminatory solely because students [with disabilities] who are incapable of attaining a level of minimum competency will fail the test. Altering the content of the M.C.T. to accommodate an individual's inability to learn the tested material because of his [disability] would be a "substantial modification," as well as a "perversion" of the diploma requirement. A student who is unable to learn because of his [disability] is surely not an individual who is qualified in spite of his [disability]. Thus denial of a diploma because of inability to pass the M.C.T. is not discrimination under the RHA.

> However, an otherwise qualified student who is unable to disclose the degree of learning he actually possesses because of the test format or environment would be the object of discrimination solely on the basis of his [disability]. It is apparent … that "to discover a blind person's knowledge, a test must be given orally or in braille." … [Section 504] requires administrative modification to minimize the effects of plaintiffs' [disabilities] on … examinations.

Brookhart illustrates well the meaning of "otherwise qualified" and of "reasonable accommodation." To exempt students with disabilities from the requirement of demonstrating the requisite level of knowledge before being awarded a diploma would negate the essential educational purpose of minimum competency testing. Conversely, to deny a student with a disability the opportunity to *demonstrate* the requisite knowledge in a modified format—for example, by giving written or signed rather than oral test instructions to deaf students—would be to discriminate on the basis of disability.[38]

In *Bercovitch v. Baldwin School, Inc.*,[39] a private school sought to expel a severely disruptive sixth-grade student diagnosed with ADHD. The student's parents argued that except for the behaviors arising out of his disability, he was "otherwise qualified" to participate in the school's educational program and that the reasonable accommodation principle required extensive modification of the school's code of conduct. The First Circuit disagreed on both counts. First, the student was not otherwise qualified because he could not meet the school's behavioral requirements even with reasonable accommodations. Second, the requested modification of the code of conduct amounted to a "significant alteration of a fundamental requirement of the school." The ADA did not require "a school to suspend its normal codes of conduct in order to tolerate disruptive and disrespectful conduct when that behavior impaired the educational experience of other students and significantly taxed the resources of the faculty and other students." In the *Nardella* case described earlier,[40] the court found that difficult behaviors may prevent students from meeting the "otherwise qualified" and "reasonable accommodation" tests in the context of private educational programs.

---

36 34 C.F.R. § 104.33.
37 697 F.2d 179 (7th Cir. 1983).
38 *See also* Rene *ex rel.* Rene v. Reed, 751 N.E.2d 736 (Ind. 2001).
39 133 F.3d 141 (1st Cir. 1998).
40 2016 U.S. Dist. LEXIS 81379 (N.D. Ill. June 22, 2016); 2017 U.S. Dist. LEXIS 69355 (N.D. Ill. May 5, 2017).

Accessibility

Both Section 504 and the *ADA* require that school facilities be accessible to students and their parents; however, schools need not make every part of a facility accessible as long as their programs and activities when viewed in their entirety are readily accessible. Also, alterations that would fundamentally alter a program or activity or result in an undue financial and administrative burden need not be undertaken. The regulations implementing the *ADA* list the types of alterations that should be made, including installing ramps, reconfiguring toilet facilities, and providing a reasonable number of wheelchair spaces dispersed throughout seating areas.

Educational Program

The educational program requirements of Section 504 overlap to some degree with those of *IDEA*, but there are important distinctions. In contrast with the *IDEA*, where a detailed individualized educational program (IEP) must provide a "roadmap" for all services provided, the Section 504 statute and regulations are silent as to whether the services provided must be committed to writing, let alone what specific items must be included. It is common practice; however, for school districts to set forth the services in a written "Section 504 Plan," and federal guidance from the US Department of Education, Office for Civil Rights (OCR) supports this practice. In such plans, qualifying students must be provided with services and accommodations designed to meet their needs as adequately as the programs provided to non-disabled students. Both academic and non-academic activities are subject to this equivalency requirement.

Like the *IDEA*, Section 504 requires that students with disabilities be thoroughly evaluated and periodically re-evaluated; that they be educated to the maximum extent possible with non-disabled peers; and that (as a best practice, rather than a legal requirement) parents be involved in the development of specialized educational programs for their children. Often, though not always, for students who qualify under the *IDEA*, compliance with the *IDEA* will satisfy the educational requirements of Section 504. However, because the *IDEA* provides more extensive protections, the Second Circuit has said that the converse is not generally true—that is, compliance with Section 504 will not necessarily satisfy the requirements of the *IDEA*.[41]

Section 504 prohibits discrimination against students with disabilities in the provision of services and materials and requires that school facilities be made accessible to those students. It also mandates modifications in classrooms; "reasonable accommodations" in courses (including teaching techniques, exam procedures); and the provision of auxiliary aids and devices. The Third Circuit has concluded that there is little difference between the affirmative obligations of *IDEA* and Section 504's prohibition against discrimination. Both laws, the court reasoned, require that students with disabilities be provided with a free appropriate public education (FAPE).[42]

However, inasmuch as Section 504 is an "equal access" statute, as opposed to a "substantive benefits" statute like *IDEA*, the meaning of FAPE under Section 504 might differ substantially from its meaning under *IDEA*. There is some authority for defining FAPE under Section 504 as affording a "commensurate opportunity" for education—that is, affording the same opportunities as afforded to non-disabled students.[43] Other authorities view FAPE under Section 504 merely as

---

41 Muller v. Committee on Special Educ., 145 F.3d 95, 105 n. 9 (2d Cir. 1998).

42 Ridgewood Bd. of Educ. v. N.E., 172 F.3d 238 (3d Cir. 1999); P.P. *ex rel.* Michael P. v. W. Chester Area Sch. Dist., 585 F.3d 727 (3d Cir. 2009).

43 Mark H. v. Lemahieu, 513 F.3d 922, 933 (9th Cir. 2008); K.M. *ex rel.* Bright v. Tustin Unified Sch. Dist., 725 F.3d 1088 (9th Cir. 2013); *see* Mark C. Weber, *A New Look at Section 504 and the ADA in Special Education Cases*, 16 Tex. J. C.L. & C.R. 1 (2010).

the right to receive reasonable accommodations.[44] Under either standard, however, the meaning of FAPE would appear to differ from the *IDEA* entitlement, which (as explained later in this chapter) is framed in terms of receiving meaningful educational benefits.

Enforcement

School districts are required to establish and publicize grievance procedures to deal with alleged violations of Section 504. Individuals may also file a grievance against a school district with the OCR within 180 days of an allegedly discriminatory action (although the OCR can waive this deadline if one demonstrates "good cause" for the delay). The OCR will investigate the allegation, and if a violation is found, the district must correct the violation. Although, in theory, a recalcitrant district risks loss of all federal funds, in practice, the vast majority of OCR complaints result in settlements.

To address violations of Section 504 or the *ADA*, individuals can also sue for compensatory monetary damages,[45] but not for punitive damages.[46] A successful complainant can also be awarded attorney's fees under either law. Finally, the *ADA* prohibits retaliation, interference, coercion, or intimidation against individuals claiming rights under the law, assisting in investigating violations, or testifying in *ADA* proceedings.

The *Individuals with Disabilities Education Act*

In 1975, two years after passage of Section 504, Congress enacted the first version of the *IDEA*.[47] Congress aimed to provide more detailed protections to students with disabilities, along with some funding for these new mandates. The *IDEA* is a grant program providing money to states that choose to participate—all states do—to help support the education of students with disabilities. To be eligible for federal funds under the *IDEA*, a state must develop a plan for providing all children with disabilities a "free, appropriate public education which emphasizes special education and related services designed to meet their unique needs." The state plan must include a system for allocating funding to local school districts. In turn, each local school district must submit an application to the state indicating how it will comply with the *IDEA* requirements.

The *IDEA* mandates that all students with disabilities receive a free, appropriate public education (FAPE). FAPE means "special education and related services that are provided at public expense, under public supervision and direction without charge and are provided in conformity with the child's individual education program (IEP)." The FAPE requirement covers students in public schools (including charter schools) and students who have been suspended or expelled. An exception exists, however, if parents choose to enroll a child with a disability in a religious or other private school.[48] In addition to mandating a FAPE, the *IDEA* requires school districts to include parents in educational decisions and to afford access to educational records regarding their children.

44 R.K. v. Bd. of Educ. of Scott County, 755 F. Supp. 2d 800 (E.D. Ky. 2010).
45 Pandazides v. Virginia Bd. of Educ., 13 F.3d 823 (4th Cir. 1994).
46 Barnes v. Gorman, 536 U.S. 181 (2002).
47 20 U.S.C. §§ 1400–1485 [Unless otherwise noted, discussion is based on the statute and *IDEA* regulations, Volume 34 C.F.R.].
48 34 C.F.R. § 300.137 (a).

Eligibility

The *IDEA* mandates services for children ages three to 21[49] who are determined to be within one or more of 13 specified categories of disability and who, "by reason thereof," need special education and related services. Categories include autism, deafness, deaf-blindness, hearing impairment, intellectual disabilities, multiple disabilities, orthopedic impairments, other health impairments, serious emotional disturbance, specific learning disabilities, speech or language impairments, traumatic brain injury, and visual impairment. The law provides extended definitions of specific learning disability, intellectual disability, other health impairments, autism, and traumatic brain injury. States have a certain amount of latitude in applying these definitions in accordance with their own statutes and regulations, so *IDEA* eligibility criteria may vary from state to state.[50] The *IDEA* also permits school districts to provide students aged three to nine who are experiencing physical, cognitive, communicative, social, emotional, or adaptive developmental delays with special education and related services.

Over the years, *IDEA* eligibility definitions at the federal level have been revised. In 2010, under "Rosa's Law," the term "mental retardation," increasingly viewed as having pejorative connotations, was replaced by the term "intellectual disability" in many federal laws, including the *IDEA*. Another recent development entails changes to the definition of "specific learning disabilities." School districts are now permitted to determine if a student has a specific learning disability by employing either a discrepancy model (comparing academic achievement to intellectual potential in specified basic-skill areas) or by a newer model based on the student's research-based response to intervention (RTI). A child shall not be identified as disabled "if the determinant factor … is lack of appropriate instruction in reading or math, or limited English proficiency."

In order to be eligible for services under the *IDEA*, a student must both fall within one of the specified categories of disability and be in need of special education and related services for that reason ("by reason thereof"). If the disability does not adversely impact the student's educational performance, the student is not eligible for services under the *IDEA*. But what does it mean for a student's educational performance to be adversely impacted? In *Mr. I. v. Maine School Administrative District No. 25*,[51] the First Circuit ruled that a student with autism who excelled academically was eligible for services under the *IDEA* because her disability adversely affected her communication and social interaction and caused her to self-mutilate in school. However, the Fifth Circuit ruled that a student with Attention Deficit Hyperactivity Disorder was not covered because the student obtained passing grades and success on standardized tests without special educational services.[52] When a student's academic performance in relation to classroom peers is "average," yet the student's disabilities prevent him from performing at his or her expected level, is *IDEA* eligibility satisfied? In *Corchado v. Rochester City School District*,[53] a federal district court said yes, pointing to evidence that the student had "regular uncontrolled seizures which affect his alertness in class."

Eligibility for special education might be viewed as a "double-edged sword" for African-American and other students of color. Historically, such students were sometimes placed in special

---

49   From birth to age three, children with disabilities are covered by Part C of *IDEA*, 20 U.S.C. § 1431.
50   *See, e.g.*, J.D. *ex rel.* J.D. v. Pawlet Sch. Dist., 224 F.3d 60 (2d Cir. 2000); M.N. v. Katonah-Lewisboro Sch. Dist., 2016 U.S. Dist. LEXIS 124892 (S.D.N.Y. 2016).
51   480 F.3d 1 (1st Cir. 2007).
52   Alvin Ind. Sch. Dist. v. A.D. *ex rel.* Patricia F., 503 F.3d 378 (5th Cir. 2007); *see also* M.N. v. Katonah-Lewisboro Sch. Dist., 2016 U.S. Dist. LEXIS 124892 (S.D.N.Y. 2016).
53   Corchado v. Rochester City School District, 86 F. Supp. 2d 168 (W.D.N.Y. 2000); *see also* Elida Local Sch. Dist. Bd. of Educ. v. Erickson, 252 F. Supp. 2d 476, 478 (N.D. Ohio 2003).

education, not to help them, but to segregate them.[54] Cognizant of this history, when Congress reauthorized the *IDEA* in 2004, it required states to have "policies and procedures designed to prevent the inappropriate over-identification or disproportionate representation by race and ethnicity of children with disabilities."[55]

Despite this admonition, when a high-achieving student of color alleged that she had been inappropriately placed in special education, one court held that she had no standing to challenge her misclassification. Although she had consistently expressed concerns that she did not belong in special education, the court found (in a Catch-22) that, because she did not actually qualify for special education, she could not invoke the *IDEA*'s dispute resolution provisions.[56]

Yet, for students of color who truly need special education services and are therefore entitled to a free appropriate public education, several commentators have argued that eligibility should not be unduly restricted. Rather, such students should be found eligible, but the services and placements provided should receive extra scrutiny to ensure they are truly appropriate and not overly restrictive.[57]

Identification, Evaluation, and Classification

Under the *IDEA*'s "child find" requirement, states and local school districts must locate, identify, and evaluate children with disabilities, even those who have never been enrolled in a public school. A school district that fails to live up to this child find requirement, for example, by over-looking "clear signs of disability" in one of its students, may be compelled later to provide compensatory services.[58] If possible, the evaluation should be completed early enough that an IEP can be in place by the beginning of the school year. If a child with a possible or apparent disability is applying for initial admission to a public school, the child—with parental consent—will usually be placed in the regular public school program until the evaluation is complete.

Before a student is evaluated, written notice explaining the proposed evaluation and the reasons for it must be given to the parents. The notice must be in the parents' native language or, if the parents do not have a written language, it must be communicated orally. If the parents refuse consent for the evaluation, the parents may agree to enter into mediation with the district or the district may request an impartial hearing to seek authorization to proceed with the evaluation. Either the district or the parents may request a review of the hearing officer's decision by the state's education agency and ultimately by a court. Similar procedures apply if parents initiate a request for an evaluation but the school district refuses. The district must provide the parents with written notice of its decision not to evaluate. Parents may then request mediation or a hearing, or avail themselves of the other dispute resolution procedures described later in this section.

Parents must also be given a copy of the procedural safeguards of the *IDEA*, including the right to be informed of and to request a hearing if they disagree with the referral or with the results of the evaluation, the IEP, or the placement. Parents also have a right to receive notice of these

---

54 Rebecca Vallas, *The Disproportionality Problem: The Overrepresentation of Black Students in Special Education and Recommendations for Reform*, 17 Va. J. Soc. Pol. L. 181, 192–96 (2009).

55 20 U.S.C. section 1412(a)(24).

56 S.H. *ex rel.* Durrell v. Lower Merion Sch. Dist., 729 F.3d 248 (3d Cir. 2013).

57 *See* Wendy F. Hensel, *Sharing the Short Bus: Eligibility and Identity under the IDEA*, 58 Hastings L.J. 1147, 1198–1201 (2007); *see also* Jonathan Feldman, *Racial Perspectives on Eligibility for Special Education: For Students of Color Who Are Struggling, Is Special Education a Potential Evil or a Potential Good?*, 20 American University Journal Of Gender, Social Policy & The Law 183 (2011).

58 Bd. of Educ. of Fayette County, Kentucky. v. L.M., 478 F.3d 307 (6th Cir. 2007); *but see* Mr. P v. W. Hartford Bd. of Educ., 885 F.3d 735 (2d Cir. 2018), *cert. denied*, 139 S. Ct. 322 (2018).

procedural safeguards once a year and in conjunction with any disciplinary action taken against the child and to examine "all records relating to" the child.

The evaluation must be in

> in the child's native language or other mode of communication and in the form most likely to yield accurate information on what the child knows and can do academically, developmentally, and functionally, unless it is clearly not feasible to so provide or administer.

The evaluation must be free of racial or cultural bias, conducted by a multidisciplinary team, and designed to assess a wide range of skills. Only validated tests tailored to assess specific areas of educational need may be used. Neither a general IQ test nor any "single procedure is to be the sole criterion for determining an appropriate educational program."

Overall, the evaluation must be designed to assess the child's strengths and weaknesses. At the conclusion of the evaluation, "a team of qualified professionals and the parent of the child" are to determine if the child has disabilities. Re-evaluation of any child found to have disabilities must take place at least every three years, or more frequently if requested by the child's parents. Parents also have a right to obtain an independent educational evaluation. The school district must reimburse the parents for the independent evaluation if an impartial hearing finds the district's evaluation was inappropriate. Regulations further specify that "A parent is entitled to only one independent educational evaluation at public expense each time the [school] conducts an evaluation with which the parent disagrees."

Despite all the procedures and safeguards, schools and parents may disagree as to whether a child is eligible for services under the IDEA. In *Yankton School District v. Schramm*,[59] a high school student with cerebral palsy had been classified as having disabilities and eligible for IDEA services. Her last IEP, written for her ninth-grade year, specified only "adaptive physical education." The rest of her program consisted of participation in regular course work with non-disabled peers. Because the student was succeeding in all her regular course work and no additional physical education was required for graduation, school officials reasoned that she no longer needed special education under the IDEA. The Eighth Circuit disagreed, observing that adaptive physical education was not the only service the student had been receiving because of her disability. The school had also provided her with shortened writing assignments, assistance in traveling from class to class, and a variety of other accommodations. Thus the school district's own actions indicated a need for special education within the meaning of the IDEA. In *D.R. v. Antelope Valley Union High School District*,[60] however, a federal court explicitly rejected the Eighth Circuit's approach, holding that a high-achieving student with an orthopedic impairment who had received accommodations did not qualify under the IDEA.

Individualized Educational Program (IEP)

Once it has been determined that a student qualifies for services under the IDEA, an IEP must be developed. The process used to develop the IEP must consist of one or more meetings attended by the child's teacher, other public school officials, the child's parents, and, where appropriate, the child. The district must take all necessary steps to ensure that the parents are able to attend the IEP meetings and understand the evaluation results, the proposed IEP, and anything else discussed at the meetings. If the student has been evaluated for the first time, a member of the evaluation team

59 93 F.3d 1369 (8th Cir. 1996).
60 D.R. *ex rel.* Courtney R. v. Antelope Valley Union High Sch. Dist., 746 F. Supp. 2d 1132 (C.D. Cal. 2010).

or someone else familiar with the procedures and results of the evaluation must also be present. If a public school has placed or proposes to place a child in a private school or program, a representative of the private school or program should also attend. In developing the IEP, the team must consider any special circumstances that may be affecting the child's educational performance such as behavioral problems or limited English proficiency. The IEP must be reviewed by the same process at least once a year and early enough so that the new IEP can be in force at the beginning of the next school year. The review should specifically address any lack of expected progress. Between annual reviews, the IEP may be modified if the parents and school officials agree.

If parents are dissatisfied with the outcome of the IEP process, they may seek review from an impartial hearing officer. Then, depending upon whether a state has designated a state agency to hear appeals, parents must appeal to this agency before proceeding to court. Failure of a school to provide parents with a meaningful opportunity to participate in the formulation of a student's IEP or to follow the other procedural requirements of IEP formulation may persuade a court to reject the IEP.[61] However, only procedural violations that have a substantive impact on FAPE are actionable. Moreover, parents who have been properly included in the process are unlikely to succeed with a claim that they did not understand what they had agreed to.[62] If parents ultimately refuse to consent to the initial delivery of services, after reasonable efforts have been made to obtain consent, the district may not seek authorization via the impartial hearing, and the district is relieved of its obligations to provide a free appropriate public education.

An IEP is a written statement that includes the child's present level of educational performance; annual goals; the special education and related services to be provided; any assistive technology to be provided; the extent to which the student will participate in the school's general program with non-disabled students; the dates for initiation and duration of services; criteria, procedures, and schedules for evaluating whether the objectives are being achieved; and a plan for informing the parents of the child's progress. IDEA regulations define special education as "specially designed instruction" to meet the unique needs of a child with a disability, including adapting "content, methodology or delivery of instruction."

Special education students must be afforded the same access to the general curriculum offered to non-disabled students, as well as extracurricular activities and non-academic activities and services, such as lunch and recess as appropriate. Related services may include transportation, special equipment such as hearing aids and computers, and a variety of other forms of assistance necessary to make it possible for the child to benefit from special education. The IEP may also include behavioral interventions if necessary, and beginning no later than age 16, transition services. **Behavioral interventions** are programs designed to deal with conduct that impedes the child's learning or that of others. **Transition services** are programs designed to ease movement from school to post-school activities including work, higher education, and vocational training.

"Free Appropriate Public Education" (FAPE)

An IEP must meet the basic IDEA requirement of providing a "free, appropriate public education." The program must be consistent with a myriad of applicable federal and state regulations that implement and supplement the IDEA. Yet, even with all these requirements and guidelines, the issue of what constitutes an appropriate education for a particular child is often difficult to resolve. Not surprisingly, given the realities of educational budgets, the imprecision of instructional methodologies, and the strong emotions involved, the program requested by parents sometimes does

---

61 Indep. Sch. Dist. No. 283 v. S.D., 88 F.3d 556 (8th Cir. 1996).
62 Blackmon *ex rel.* Blackmon v. Springfield R-XII Sch. Dist., 198 F.3d 648 (8th Cir. 1999).

not coincide with the one offered by the school. In these instances, *IDEA* and the implementing regulations do not always provide a clear solution. Courts may be called upon to resolve the issue of whether a particular program or service is required under the *IDEA* or whether a child's overall program of special education satisfies the law.

The Supreme Court provided an initial framework for deciding these issues in *Board of Education of Hendrick Hudson Central School District v. Rowley.*[63] The case involved a deaf student provisionally assigned to a regular kindergarten class to determine what supplemental services she might require. A sign language interpreter was provided for a two-week period. Amy Rowley was provided with an FM hearing aid and successfully completed her kindergarten year. The Rowleys subsequently requested a sign language interpreter on an ongoing basis and claimed their daughter had been denied a "free appropriate public education" by the district when this request was denied. Overruling the lower courts, the Supreme Court found a sign language interpreter was not required under the *IDEA*:

> Neither the District Court nor the Court of Appeals found that petitioners had failed to comply with the procedures of the Act, and the findings of neither court would support a conclusion that Amy's educational program failed to comply with the substantive requirements of the Act. On the contrary, the District Court, found that the "evidence firmly establishes that Amy is receiving an 'adequate' education, since she performs better than the average child in her class and is advancing easily from grade to grade." In light of this finding, and of the fact that Amy was receiving personalized instruction and related services calculated by the Furnace Woods school administrators to meet her educational needs, the lower courts should not have concluded that the Act requires the provision of a sign-language interpreter.

On the question of what constitutes an "appropriate" education under the *IDEA*, *Rowley* made it clear that students with disabilities are not entitled to maximize their potential. Rather, they must be provided with "some educational benefit." Like state courts in school finance cases (see Chapter 9), the Supreme Court rejected an "equality standard" in favor of an "adequacy standard."[64]

Some federal circuit courts interpreted this mandate as requiring a "meaningful benefit," whereas others set the bar lower. In particular, the Tenth Circuit held that the standard was met as long as the benefit was "merely ... more than *de minimus*." The Supreme Court rejected that approach in the following significant case:

⚖️

ENDREW F. v. DOUGLAS COUNTY SCHOOL DISTRICT
Supreme Court of the United States
137 S.Ct. 988 (2017)

CHIEF JUSTICE ROBERTS delivered the opinion of the Court.

Thirty-five years ago, this Court held that the *Individuals with Disabilities Education Act* establishes a substantive right to a "free appropriate public education" for certain children with disabilities [in *Rowley*]. We declined, however, to endorse any one standard for determining "when [students with disabilities] are receiving sufficient educational benefits to satisfy the requirements of the Act." That "more difficult problem" is before us today. ...

---

63 458 U.S. 176 (1982).
64 Samuel Bagenstos, *Educational Equality for Children with Disabilities: The 2016 Term Cases*, in American Constitution Society Supreme Court Review 2016-2017, 17–48 (S.D. Schwinn, ed., 2017).

Petitioner Endrew F. was diagnosed with autism at age two. Autism is a neurodevelopmental disorder generally marked by impaired social and communicative skills, "engagement in repetitive activities and stereotyped movements, resistance to environmental change or change in daily routines, and unusual responses to sensory experiences." A child with autism qualifies as a "[c]hild with a disability" under the *IDEA*, and Colorado (where Endrew resides) accepts *IDEA* funding. Endrew is therefore entitled to the benefits of the Act, including a FAPE provided by the State.

Endrew attended school in respondent Douglas County School District from preschool through fourth grade. Each year, his IEP Team drafted an IEP addressed to his educational and functional needs. By Endrew's fourth grade year, however, his parents had become dissatisfied with his progress. Although Endrew displayed a number of strengths ... he still "exhibited multiple behaviors that inhibited his ability to access learning in the classroom." Endrew would scream in class, climb over furniture and other students, and occasionally run away from school. He was afflicted by severe fears of commonplace things like flies, spills, and public restrooms. As Endrew's parents saw it, his academic and functional progress had essentially stalled: Endrew's IEPs largely carried over the same basic goals and objectives from one year to the next, indicating that he was failing to make meaningful progress toward his aims. His parents believed that only a thorough overhaul of the school district's approach to Endrew's behavioral problems could reverse the trend. But in April 2010, the school district presented Endrew's parents with a proposed fifth grade IEP that was, in their view, pretty much the same as his past ones. So his parents removed Endrew from public school and enrolled him at Firefly Autism House, a private school that specializes in educating children with autism.

Endrew did much better at Firefly. The school developed a "behavioral intervention plan" that identified Endrew's most problematic behaviors and set out particular strategies for addressing them. Firefly also added heft to Endrew's academic goals. Within months, Endrew's behavior improved significantly, permitting him to make a degree of academic progress that had eluded him in public school.

In November 2010, some six months after Endrew started classes at Firefly, his parents again met with representatives of the Douglas County School District. The district presented a new IEP. Endrew's parents considered the IEP no more adequate than the one proposed in April, and rejected it. They were particularly concerned that the stated plan for addressing Endrew's behavior did not differ meaningfully from the plan in his fourth grade IEP, despite the fact that his experience at Firefly suggested that he would benefit from a different approach.

In February 2012, Endrew's parents filed a complaint with the Colorado Department of Education seeking reimbursement for Endrew's tuition at Firefly. To qualify for such relief, they were required to show that the school district had not provided Endrew a FAPE in a timely manner prior to his enrollment at the private school. Endrew's parents contended that the final IEP proposed by the school district was not "reasonably calculated to enable [Endrew] to receive educational benefits" and that Endrew had therefore been denied a FAPE. An Administrative Law Judge (ALJ) disagreed and denied relief.

Endrew's parents sought review in Federal District Court. Giving "due weight" to the decision of the ALJ, the District Court affirmed. The court acknowledged that Endrew's performance under past IEPs "did not reveal immense educational growth." But it concluded that annual modifications to Endrew's IEP objectives were "sufficient to show a pattern of, at the least, minimal progress." Because Endrew's previous IEPs had enabled him to make this sort of progress, the court reasoned, his latest, similar IEP was reasonably calculated to do the same thing. In the court's view, that was all *Rowley* demanded.

The Tenth Circuit affirmed. The Court of Appeals recited language from *Rowley* stating that the instruction and services furnished to children with disabilities must be calculated to confer "*some* educational benefit." The court noted that it had long interpreted this language to mean that a child's IEP is adequate as long as it is calculated to confer an "educational benefit [that is] merely ... more than *de minimis*." Applying this standard, the Tenth Circuit held that Endrew's IEP had been "reasonably calculated to enable [him] to make *some* progress." Accordingly, he had not been denied a FAPE. We granted *certiorari* ...

While *Rowley* declined to articulate an overarching standard to evaluate the adequacy of the education provided under the Act, the decision and the statutory language point to a general approach: To meet its substantive obligation under the *IDEA*, a school must offer an IEP reasonably calculated to enable a child to make progress appropriate in light of the child's circumstances. The "reasonably calculated" qualification reflects a recognition that crafting an appropriate program of education requires a prospective judgment by school officials. The Act contemplates that this fact-intensive exercise will be informed not only by the expertise of school officials, but also by the input of the child's parents or guardians. Any review of an IEP must appreciate that the question is whether the IEP is *reasonable*, not whether the court regards it as ideal.

The IEP must aim to enable the child to make progress. After all, the essential function of an IEP is to set out a plan for pursuing academic and functional advancement ... A substantive standard not focused on student progress would do little to remedy the pervasive and tragic academic stagnation that prompted Congress to act.

That the progress contemplated by the IEP must be appropriate in light of the child's circumstances should come as no surprise. A focus on the particular child is at the core of the *IDEA*. The instruction offered must be *"specially* designed" to meet a child's *"unique* needs" through an "[i]ndividualized education program." An IEP is not a form document. It is constructed only after careful consideration of the child's present levels of achievement, disability, and potential for growth ...

One of the components of a FAPE is "special education," defined as "specially designed instruction ... to meet the unique needs of a child with a disability." In determining what it means to "meet the unique needs" of a child with a disability, the provisions governing the IEP development process are a natural source of guidance: It is through the IEP that "[t]he 'free appropriate public education' required by the Act is tailored to the unique needs of" a particular child.

The IEP provisions reflect *Rowley*'s expectation that, for most children, a FAPE will involve integration in the regular classroom and individualized special education calculated to achieve advancement from grade to grade. Every IEP begins by describing a child's present level of achievement, including explaining "how the child's disability affects the child's involvement and progress in the general education curriculum." It then sets out "a statement of measurable annual goals ... designed to ... enable the child to be involved in and make progress in the general education curriculum," along with a description of specialized instruction and services that the child will receive. The instruction and services must likewise be provided with an eye toward "progress in the general education curriculum." Similar IEP requirements have been in place since the time the States began accepting funding under the *IDEA*.

The school district protests that these provisions impose only procedural requirements—a checklist of items the IEP must address—not a substantive standard enforceable in court. But the procedures are there for a reason, and their focus provides insight into what it means, for purposes of the FAPE definition, to "meet the unique needs" of a child with a disability. When a child is fully integrated in the regular classroom, as the Act prefers, what that typically means is providing a level of instruction reasonably calculated to permit advancement through the general curriculum.

Rowley had no need to provide concrete guidance with respect to a child who is not fully integrated in the regular classroom and not able to achieve on grade level. That case concerned a young girl who was progressing smoothly through the regular curriculum. If that is not a reasonable prospect for a child, his IEP need not aim for grade-level advancement. But his educational program must be appropriatcly ambitious in light of his circumstances, just as advancement from grade to grade is appropriately ambitious for most children in the regular classroom. The goals may differ, but every child should have the chance to meet challenging objectives.

Of course this describes a general standard, not a formula. But whatever else can be said about it, this standard is markedly more demanding than the "merely more than *de minimis*" test applied by the Tenth Circuit. It cannot be the case that the Act typically aims for grade-level advancement for children with disabilities who can be educated in the regular classroom, but is satisfied with barely more than *de minimis* progress for those who cannot.

When all is said and done, a student offered an educational program providing "merely more than *de minimis*" progress from year to year can hardly be said to have been offered an education at all. For children with disabilities, receiving instruction that aims so low would be tantamount to "sitting idly ... awaiting the time when they were old enough to 'drop out.'" The *IDEA* demands more. It requires an educational program reasonably calculated to enable a child to make progress appropriate in light of the child's circumstances.

Endrew's parents argue that the Act goes even further. In their view, a FAPE is "an education that aims to provide a child with a disability opportunities to achieve academic success, attain self-sufficiency, and contribute to society that are substantially equal to the opportunities afforded children without disabilities."

This standard is strikingly similar to the one the lower courts adopted in *Rowley*, and it is virtually identical to the formulation advanced by Justice

Blackmun in his separate writing in that case. But the majority rejected any such standard in clear terms. Mindful that Congress (despite several intervening amendments to the *IDEA*) has not materially changed the statutory definition of a FAPE since *Rowley* was decided, we decline to interpret the FAPE provision in a manner so plainly at odds with the Court's analysis in that case.

We will not attempt to elaborate on what "appropriate" progress will look like from case to case. It is in the nature of the Act and the standard we adopt to resist such an effort: The adequacy of a given IEP turns on the unique circumstances of the child for whom it was created. This absence of a bright-line rule, however, should not be mistaken for "an invitation to the courts to substitute their own notions of sound educational policy for those of the school authorities which they review."

At the same time, deference is based on the application of expertise and the exercise of judgment by school authorities. The Act vests these officials with responsibility for decisions of critical importance to the life of a disabled child. The nature of the IEP process, from the initial consultation through state administrative proceedings, ensures that parents and school representatives will fully air their respective opinions on the degree of progress a child's IEP should pursue. By the time any dispute reaches court, school authorities will have had a complete opportunity to bring their expertise and judgment to bear on areas of disagreement. A reviewing court may fairly expect those authorities to be able to offer a cogent and responsive explanation for their decisions that shows the IEP is reasonably calculated to enable the child to make progress appropriate in light of his circumstances.

The judgment of the United States Court of Appeals for the Tenth Circuit is vacated, and the case is remanded for further proceedings consistent with this opinion.

In *Endrew F.*, the Supreme Court held that educational programs for students with disabilities must be "appropriately ambitious," and that schools must "focus on student progress." The Court rejected the Tenth Circuit's "merely more than *de minimus*" standard, holding instead that "every child should have the chance to meet challenging objectives." Although the focus remains on adequacy rather than equality of educational opportunity, *Endrew F.* establishes a more robust adequacy requirement than *Rowley*.[65] Moreover, *Endrew F.* establishes the "floor" for determining what constitutes an appropriate education for a student with disabilities. State statutes and regulations may prescribe a higher standard. In such cases, both federal and state courts will hold school districts to the higher standard.[66]

Defining appropriate education in terms of benefit raises the question of whether there are children with disabilities for whom no appropriate education is possible. If so, does the *IDEA* permit schools to decline to provide special education services? The First Circuit considered these issues in *Timothy W. v. Rochester School District*.[67] A lower court had ruled that Timothy, a student with significant and multiple disabilities, was not eligible for services under the *IDEA* because he could not benefit from special education. Experts testified that despite the significance of his disabilities, Timothy might benefit from certain types of stimulation, therapy, and training and that under the *IDEA*, the district was required to provide these services. Finding in favor of Timothy, the First Circuit stated its conclusions as follows:

---

65 Samuel Bagenstos, *Educational Equality for Children with Disabilities: The 2016 Term Cases*, in American Constitution Society Supreme Court Review 2016–2017, 17–48 (S.D. Schwinn, ed., 2017).

66 Burke County Bd. of Educ. v. Denton, 895 F.2d 973 (4th Cir. 1990); Bd. of Educ. of E. Windsor Reg'l Sch. Dist. v. Diamond, 808 F.2d 987 (3rd Cir. 1986); David D. v. Dartmouth Sch. Comm., 775 F.2d 411 (1st Cir. 1985); *compare* O'Toole v. Olathe Dist. Sch. Unified Sch. Dist. No. 233, 144 F.3d 692 (10th Cir. 1998); *see also* Johnson v. Indep. Sch. Dist. No. 4, 921 F.2d 1022 (10th Cir. 1990).

67 875 F.2d 954 (1st Cir. 1989).

The statutory language of the Act [IDEA], its legislative history, and the case law construing it, mandate that all children [with disabilities], regardless of the severity of their [disability], are entitled to a public education. The district court erred in requiring a benefit/eligibility test as a prerequisite to implicating the Act. School districts cannot avoid the provisions of the Act by returning to the practices that were widespread prior to the Act's passage, and which indeed were the impetus for the Act's passage, of unilaterally excluding certain children [with disabilities] from a public education on the ground that they are uneducable.

The law explicitly recognizes that education for [students with significant disabilities] is to be broadly defined, to include not only traditional academic skills, but also basic functional life skills, and that educational methodologies in these areas are not static, but are constantly evolving and improving. It is the school district's responsibility to avail itself of these new approaches in providing an education program geared to each child's individual needs. The only question for the school district to determine in conjunction with the child's parents, is what constitutes an appropriate individualized education program (IEP) for the child [with a disability]. We emphasize that the phrase "appropriate individualized education program" cannot be interpreted, as the school district has done, to mean "no educational program."

Thus, the *IDEA* does not recognize the existence of children who have disabilities too significant to benefit from some form of education, broadly defined.[68]

Finally, even if a student with disabilities is receiving educational services that are potentially beneficial, the FAPE requirement might not be met if the school fails to protect the student from harmful mistreatment by other students. In one case, a student who had been classified as having a perceptual impairment was subjected to peer harassment and bullying so persistent and severe that the student became depressed and attempted suicide. The school reclassified the student as emotionally disturbed and modified his IEP but was unable to protect him from continued bullying and harassment. When the school district refused the student's parents' request to place the student in a school in a neighboring district, the parents unilaterally transferred the student. The Third Circuit affirmed the hearing officer's finding that the first school had failed in its duty to provide an appropriate education. The district was ordered to pay the out-of-district tuition, related costs, and attorneys' fees.[69]

Intersection of the ADA and the IDEA

The *ADA* and the *IDEA* intersect in complex and often significant ways. The overlap arises in both procedural and substantive contexts. On the procedural front, the *IDEA* requires the exhaustion of administrative remedies. This means that before they can go to court, the parties to an *IDEA* dispute must undertake a lengthy dispute resolution process. Until recently, most federal courts held that these same burdensome procedures applied to school-based claims under the *ADA*, as well. This interpretation imposed hurdles for parents and students who wished to assert *ADA* claims in the school context. The Supreme Court addressed this procedural conundrum in the following significant case.

---

68 *But see* Connecticut Coal. for Justice in Educ., Inc. v. Rell, 176 A.3d 28 (Conn. 2018).
69 Shore Reg'l High Board Sch. Bd. of Educ. v. P.S., 381 F.3d 194 (3d Cir. 2004); *see also* M.L. v. Federal Way Sch. Dist., 394 F.3d 634 (9th Cir. 2005).

⚖️

FRY v. NAPOLEON COMMUNITY SCHOOLS
Supreme Court of the United States
137 S.Ct. 743 (2017)

JUSTICE KAGAN delivered the opinion of the Court.

The *Individuals with Disabilities Education Act* (*IDEA* or Act) ensures that children with disabilities receive needed special education services. One of its provisions, § 1415(*l*), addresses the Act's relationship with other laws protecting those children. Section 1415(*l*) makes clear that nothing in the *IDEA* "restrict[s] or limit[s] the rights [or] remedies" that other federal laws, including antidiscrimination statutes, confer on children with disabilities. At the same time, the section states that if a suit brought under such a law "seek[s] relief that is also available under" the *IDEA*, the plaintiff must first exhaust the *IDEA*'s administrative procedures. In this case, we consider the scope of that exhaustion requirement. We hold that exhaustion is not necessary when the gravamen of the plaintiff's suit is something other than the denial of the *IDEA*'s core guarantee—what the Act calls a "free appropriate public education."

Under the *IDEA*, an "individualized education program," called an IEP for short, serves as the "primary vehicle" for providing each child with the promised FAPE. Crafted by a child's "IEP Team"—a group of school officials, teachers, and parents—the IEP spells out a personalized plan to meet all of the child's "educational needs." Most notably, the IEP documents the child's current "levels of academic achievement," specifies "measurable annual goals" for how she can "make progress in the general education curriculum," and lists the "special education and related services" to be provided so that she can "advance appropriately toward [those] goals."

Because parents and school representatives sometimes cannot agree on such issues, the *IDEA* establishes formal procedures for resolving disputes. To begin, a dissatisfied parent may file a complaint as to any matter concerning the provision of a FAPE with the local or state educational agency (as state law provides). That pleading generally triggers a "[p]reliminary meeting" involving the contending parties; at their option, the parties may instead (or also) pursue a full-fledged mediation process. Assuming their impasse continues, the matter proceeds to a "due process hearing" before an impartial hearing officer. Any decision of the officer granting substantive relief must be "based on a determination of whether the child received a [FAPE]." If the hearing is initially conducted at the local level, the ruling is appealable to the state agency. Finally, a parent unhappy with the outcome of the administrative process may seek judicial review by filing a civil action in state or federal court.

Important as the *IDEA* is for children with disabilities, it is not the only federal statute protecting their interests. Of particular relevance to this case are two antidiscrimination laws—Title II of the *Americans with Disabilities Act* (*ADA*) and § 504 of the *Rehabilitation Act*—which cover both adults and children with disabilities, in both public schools and other settings. Title II forbids any "public entity" from discriminating based on disability; Section 504 applies the same prohibition to any federally funded "program or activity." A regulation implementing Title II requires a public entity to make "reasonable modifications" to its "policies, practices, or procedures" when necessary to avoid such discrimination. In similar vein, courts have interpreted § 504 as demanding certain "reasonable" modifications to existing practices in order to "accommodate" persons with disabilities. And both statutes authorize individuals to seek redress for violations of their substantive guarantees by bringing suits for injunctive relief or money damages. …

Petitioner E.F. is a child with a severe form of cerebral palsy, which "significantly limits her motor skills and mobility." When E.F. was five years old, her parents—petitioners Stacy and Brent Fry—obtained a trained service dog for her, as recommended by her pediatrician. The dog, a goldendoodle named Wonder, "help[s E.F.] to live as independently as possible" by assisting her with various life activities. In particular, Wonder aids E.F. by "retrieving dropped items, helping her balance when she uses her walker, opening and closing doors, turning on and off lights, helping her take off her coat, [and] helping her transfer to and from the toilet."

But when the Frys sought permission for Wonder to join E.F. in kindergarten, officials at Ezra Eby Elementary School refused the request. Under E.F.'s existing IEP, a human aide provided E.F. with one-on-one support throughout the day; that two-legged assistance, the school officials thought, rendered Wonder superfluous. In the words of one administrator, Wonder should be barred from Ezra Eby because all of E.F.'s "physical and academic needs [were] being met through the services/programs/accommodations" that the school had already agreed to. Later that year, the school officials briefly allowed Wonder to accompany E.F. to school on a trial basis; but even then, "the dog was required to remain in the back of the room during classes, and was forbidden from assisting [E.F.] with many tasks he had been specifically trained to do." And when the trial period concluded, the administrators again informed the Frys that Wonder was not welcome. As a result, the Frys removed E.F. from Ezra Eby and began homeschooling her.

In addition, the Frys filed a complaint with the U.S. Department of Education's Office for Civil Rights (OCR), charging that Ezra Eby's exclusion of E.F.'s service animal violated her rights under Title II of the ADA and § 504 of the *Rehabilitation Act*. Following an investigation, OCR agreed. The office explained in its decision letter that a school's obligations under those statutes go beyond providing educational services: A school could offer a FAPE to a child with a disability but still run afoul of the laws' ban on discrimination. And here, OCR found, Ezra Eby had indeed violated that ban, even if its use of a human aide satisfied the FAPE standard. OCR analogized the school's conduct to "requir[ing] a student who uses a wheelchair to be carried" by an aide or "requir[ing] a blind student to be led [around by a] teacher" instead of permitting him to use a guide dog or cane. Regardless whether those—or Ezra Eby's—policies denied a FAPE, they violated Title II and § 504 by discriminating against children with disabilities.

In response to OCR's decision, school officials at last agreed that E.F. could come to school with Wonder. But after meeting with Ezra Eby's principal, the Frys became concerned that the school administration "would resent [E.F.] and make her return to school difficult." Accordingly, the Frys found a different public school, in a different district, where administrators and teachers enthusiastically received both E.F. and Wonder.

The Frys then filed this suit in federal court against the local and regional school districts in which Ezra Eby is located, along with the school's principal (collectively, the school districts). The complaint alleged that the school districts violated Title II of the ADA and § 504 of the *Rehabilitation Act* by "denying [E.F.] equal access" to Ezra Eby and its programs, "refus[ing] to reasonably accommodate" E.F.'s use of a service animal, and otherwise "discriminat[ing] against

[E.F.] as a person with disabilities." According to the complaint, E.F. suffered harm as a result of that discrimination, including "emotional distress and pain, embarrassment, [and] mental anguish." In their prayer for relief, the Frys sought a declaration that the school districts had violated Title II and § 504, along with money damages to compensate for E.F.'s injuries.

The District Court granted the school districts' motion to dismiss the suit, holding that § 1415(*l*) required the Frys to first exhaust the *IDEA*'s administrative procedures. A divided panel of the Court of Appeals for the Sixth Circuit affirmed on the same ground. In that court's view, § 1415(*l*) applies if "the injuries [alleged in a suit] relate to the specific substantive protections of the *IDEA*." And that means, the court continued, that exhaustion is necessary whenever "the genesis and the manifestations" of the complained-of harms were "educational" in nature. On that understanding of § 1415(*l*), the Sixth Circuit held, the Frys' suit could not proceed: Because the harms to E.F. were generally "educational"— most notably, the court reasoned, because "Wonder's absence hurt her sense of independence and social confidence at school"—the Frys had to exhaust the *IDEA*'s procedures. …

We granted *certiorari* to address confusion in the courts of appeals as to the scope of § 1415(*l*)'s exhaustion requirement. We now vacate the Sixth Circuit's decision.

[Our] inquiry immediately reveals the primacy of a FAPE in the statutory scheme. In its first section, the *IDEA* declares as its first purpose "to ensure that all children with disabilities have available to them a free appropriate public education." That principal purpose then becomes the Act's principal command: A State receiving federal funding under the *IDEA* must make such an education "available to all children with disabilities." The guarantee of a FAPE to those children gives rise to the bulk of the statute's more specific provisions. For example, the IEP—"the centerpiece of the statute's education delivery system"—serves as the "vehicle" or "means" of providing a FAPE. And finally, as all the above suggests, the FAPE requirement provides the yardstick for measuring the adequacy of the education that a school offers to a child with a disability: Under that standard, this Court has held, a child is entitled to "meaningful" access to education based on her individual needs.

The *IDEA*'s administrative procedures test whether a school has met that obligation—and so center on the Act's FAPE requirement. As noted earlier, any decision by a hearing officer on a request for substantive relief "shall" be "based on a determination of whether the child received a free appropriate public education." Or said in Latin: In the *IDEA*'s administrative process, a FAPE denial is the *sine qua non*. Suppose that a parent's complaint protests a school's failure to provide some accommodation for a child with a disability. If that accommodation is needed to fulfill the *IDEA*'s FAPE requirement, the hearing officer must order relief. But if it is not, he cannot—even though the dispute is between a child with a disability and the school she attends. There might be good reasons, unrelated to a FAPE, for the school to make the requested accommodation. Indeed, another federal law (like the *ADA* or *Rehabilitation Act*) might *require* the accommodation on one of those alternative grounds. But still, the hearing officer cannot provide the requested relief. His role, under the *IDEA*, is to enforce the child's "substantive right" to a FAPE. And that is all.

For that reason, § 1415(*l*)'s exhaustion rule hinges on whether a lawsuit seeks relief for the denial of a free appropriate public education. If a lawsuit charges such a denial, the plaintiff cannot escape § 1415(*l*) merely by bringing her suit under a statute other than the *IDEA* ... Rather, that plaintiff must first submit her case to an *IDEA* hearing officer, experienced in addressing exactly the issues she raises. But if, in a suit brought under a different statute, the remedy sought is not for the denial of a FAPE, then exhaustion of the *IDEA*'s procedures is not required. After all, the plaintiff could not get any relief from those procedures: A hearing officer, as just explained, would have to send her away empty-handed. And that is true even when the suit arises directly from a school's treatment of a child with a disability—and so could be said to relate in some way to her education. A school's conduct toward such a child—say, some refusal to make an accommodation—might injure her in ways unrelated to a FAPE, which are addressed in statutes other than the *IDEA*. A complaint seeking redress for those other harms, independent of any FAPE denial, is not subject to § 1415(*l*)'s exhaustion rule because, once again, the only "relief" the *IDEA* makes "available" is relief for the denial of a FAPE ...

Still, an important question remains: How is a court to tell when a plaintiff "seeks" relief for the denial of a FAPE and when she does not? Here, too, the parties have found some common ground: By looking, they both say, to the "substance" of, rather than the labels used in, the plaintiff's complaint. And here, too, we agree with that view: What matters is the crux—or, in legal-speak, the gravamen—of the plaintiff's complaint, setting aside any attempts at artful pleading.

That inquiry makes central the plaintiff's own claims, as § 1415(*l*) explicitly requires. The statutory language asks whether a lawsuit in fact "seeks" relief available under the *IDEA*—not, as a stricter exhaustion statute might, whether the suit "could have sought" relief available under the *IDEA* (or, what is much the same, whether any remedies "are" available under that law). In effect, § 1415(*l*) treats the plaintiff as "the master of the claim": She identifies its remedial basis—and is subject to exhaustion or not based on that choice. A court deciding whether § 1415(*l*) applies must therefore examine whether a plaintiff's complaint—the principal instrument by which she describes her case—seeks relief for the denial of an appropriate education.

But that examination should consider substance, not surface. The use (or non-use) of particular labels and terms is not what matters. The inquiry, for example, does not ride on whether a complaint includes ... FAPE" or "IEP." After all, § 1415(*l*)'s premise is that the plaintiff is suing under a statute *other than* the *IDEA*, like the *Rehabilitation Act*; in such a suit, the plaintiff might see no need to use the *IDEA*'s distinctive language—even if she is in essence contesting the adequacy of a special education program. And still more critically, a "magic words" approach would make § 1415(*l*)'s exhaustion rule too easy to bypass. ... Section 1415(*l*) is not merely a pleading hurdle. It requires exhaustion when the gravamen of a complaint seeks redress for a school's failure to provide a FAPE, even if not phrased or framed in precisely that way.

In addressing whether a complaint fits that description, a court should attend to the diverse means and ends of the statutes covering persons with disabilities—the *IDEA* on the one hand, the *ADA* and *Rehabilitation Act* (most notably) on the other. The *IDEA*, of course, protects only "children" (well, really, adolescents too) and concerns only their schooling. And as earlier noted, the statute's goal is to provide each child with meaningful access to education by offering individualized instruction and related services appropriate to her "unique needs." By contrast, Title II of the *ADA* and § 504 of the *Rehabilitation Act* cover people with disabilities of all ages, and do so both inside and outside schools. And those statutes aim to root out disability-based discrimination, enabling each covered person (sometimes by means of reasonable accommodations) to participate equally to all others in public facilities and federally funded programs. In short, the *IDEA* guarantees individually tailored educational services, while Title II and § 504 promise non-discriminatory access to public institutions. That is not to deny some overlap in coverage: The same conduct might violate all three statutes ... But still, the statutory differences just discussed mean that a complaint brought under Title II and § 504 might instead seek relief for simple discrimination, irrespective of the *IDEA*'s FAPE obligation.

One clue to whether the gravamen of a complaint against a school concerns the denial of a FAPE, or instead addresses disability-based discrimination, can come from asking a pair of hypothetical questions. First, could the plaintiff have brought essentially the same claim if the alleged conduct had occurred at a public facility that was *not* a school— say, a public theater or library? And second, could an *adult* at the school—say, an employee or visitor— have pressed essentially the same grievance? When the answer to those questions is yes, a complaint that does not expressly allege the denial of a FAPE is also unlikely to be truly about that subject; after all, in those other situations there is no FAPE obligation and yet the same basic suit could go forward. But when the answer is no, then the complaint probably does concern a FAPE, even if it does not explicitly say so; for the FAPE requirement is all that explains why only a child in the school setting (not an adult in that setting or a child in some other) has a viable claim.

Take two contrasting examples. Suppose first that a [wheelchair user] sues his school for discrimination under Title II (again, without mentioning the denial of a FAPE) because the building lacks access ramps. In some sense, that architectural feature has educational consequences, and a different lawsuit might have alleged that it violates the *IDEA*: After all, if the child cannot get inside the school, he cannot receive instruction there; and if he must be carried inside, he may not achieve the sense of independence conducive to academic (or later to real-world) success. But is the denial of a FAPE really the gravamen of the plaintiff's Title II complaint? Consider that the child could file the same basic complaint if a municipal library or theater had no ramps. And similarly, an employee or visitor could bring a mostly identical complaint against the school. That the claim can stay the same in those alternative scenarios suggests that its essence is equality of access to public facilities, not adequacy of special education. And so § 1415(*l*) does not require exhaustion.

But suppose next that a student with a learning disability sues his school under Title II for failing to provide remedial tutoring in mathematics. That suit, too, might be cast as one for disability-based discrimination, grounded on the school's refusal to make a reasonable accommodation; the complaint might make no reference at all to a FAPE or an IEP. But can anyone imagine the student making the same claim against a public theater or library? Or, similarly, imagine an adult visitor or employee suing the school to obtain a math tutorial? The difficulty of transplanting the complaint to those other contexts suggests that its essence—even though not its wording—is the provision of a FAPE, thus bringing § 1415(*l*) into play.

A further sign that the gravamen of a suit is the denial of a FAPE can emerge from the history of the proceedings. In particular, a court may consider that a plaintiff has previously invoked the *IDEA*'s formal procedures to handle the dispute—thus starting to exhaust the Act's remedies before switching midstream. Recall that a parent dissatisfied with her child's education initiates those administrative procedures by filing a complaint, which triggers a preliminary meeting (or possibly mediation) and then a due process hearing. A plaintiff's initial choice to pursue that process may suggest that she is indeed seeking relief for the denial of a FAPE—with the shift to judicial proceedings prior to full exhaustion reflecting only strategic calculations about how to maximize the prospects of such a remedy. Whether that is so depends on the facts; a court may conclude, for example, that the move to a courtroom came from a late-acquired awareness that the school had fulfilled its FAPE obligation and that the grievance involves something else entirely. But prior pursuit of the *IDEA*'s administrative remedies will often provide strong evidence that the substance of a plaintiff's claim concerns the denial of a FAPE, even if the complaint never explicitly uses that term. ...

The Frys' complaint alleges only disability-based discrimination, without making any reference to the adequacy of the special education services E.F.'s school provided. The school districts' "refusal to allow Wonder to act as a service dog," the complaint states, "discriminated against [E.F.] as a person with disabilities ... by denying her equal access" to public facilities. The complaint contains no allegation about the denial of a FAPE or about any deficiency in E.F.'s IEP. More, it does not accuse the school even in general terms of refusing to provide the educational instruction and services that E.F. needs. As the Frys explained in this Court: The school districts "have said all along that because they gave [E.F.] a one-on-one [human] aide, that all of her … educational needs were satisfied. And we have not challenged that, and it would be difficult for us to challenge that." The Frys instead maintained, just as OCR had earlier found, that the school districts infringed E.F.'s right to equal access—even if their actions complied in full with the *IDEA*'s requirements.

And nothing in the nature of the Frys' suit suggests any implicit focus on the adequacy of E.F.'s education. Consider, as suggested above, that the Frys could have filed essentially the same complaint if a public library or theater had refused admittance to Wonder. Or similarly, consider that an adult visitor to the school could have leveled much the same charges if prevented from entering with his service dog. In each case, the plaintiff would challenge a public facility's policy of precluding service dogs … as violating Title II's and § 504's equal access requirements. The suit would have nothing to do with the provision of educational services. From all that we know now, that is exactly the kind of action the Frys have brought.

But we do not foreclose the possibility that the history of these proceedings might suggest something different. As earlier discussed, a plaintiff's initial pursuit of the *IDEA*'s administrative remedies can serve as evidence that the gravamen of her later suit is the denial of a FAPE, even though that does not appear on the face of her complaint. The Frys may or may not have sought those remedies before filing this case: None of the parties here have addressed that issue, and the record is cloudy as to the relevant facts. Accordingly, on remand, the court below should establish whether (or to what extent) the Frys invoked the *IDEA*'s dispute resolution process before bringing this suit. And if the Frys started down that road, the court should decide whether their actions reveal that the gravamen of their complaint is indeed the denial of a FAPE, thus necessitating further exhaustion.

With these instructions and for the reasons stated, we vacate the judgment of the Court of Appeals and remand the case for further proceedings consistent with this opinion.

Under *Fry*, if the "gravamen" of a complaint does not address "FAPE issues," a plaintiff can go directly to court on her *ADA* claim and bypass the *IDEA*'s time-consuming dispute resolution procedures. This should help students like Ehlena Fry, who sought to bring her service dog to school. In *Alboniga v. School Board of Broward County*,[70] another service dog case, a federal district court likewise held that the plaintiff could bypass the *IDEA*'s dispute resolution procedures. The court observed that the plaintiff's request that school officials take the dog outside to urinate during the day did not unduly burden the school, and was therefore a reasonable accommodation under the *ADA*. Other cases involving service dogs have yielded similar rulings.[71]

In addition to intersecting in the procedural context, the *ADA* and the *IDEA* often overlap in terms of substantive rights. For example, in a recent Ninth Circuit case, students who were hard-of-hearing were denied real-time transcriptions of class discussions by their schools. However, because the students already received a meaningful educational program, they could not argue that they had been denied FAPE under the *IDEA*. Instead, they argued that they were entitled to transcription services under the *ADA*. The Ninth Circuit agreed, citing the *ADA*'s mandate that people with disabilities be afforded equal access and effective communication.[72]

Because the Supreme Court in *Fry* made it easier to bring *ADA* claims in court, it is foreseeable that more such cases will be filed, allowing students with disabilities to assert their rights under the *ADA* and the *IDEA*. In light of the Ninth Circuit case, students who are deaf or hard of hearing might well be among the beneficiaries. Indeed, one commentator has suggested that the plaintiffs

70 87 F. Supp. 3d 1319 (S.D. Fla. 2015).
71 United States v. Gates-Chili Cent. Sch. Dist., 198 F. Supp. 3d 228 (W.D.N.Y. 2016); Alejandro v. Palm Beach State Coll., 843 F. Supp. 2d 1263 (S.D. Fla. 2011); *but see* A.R. v. Sch. Admin. Unit #23, 2017 U.S. Dist. LEXIS 169466 (D.N.H. Oct. 12, 2017).
72 K.M. *ex rel.* Bright v. Tustin Unified Sch. Dist., 725 F.3d 1088 (9th Cir. 2013).

in *Rowley* might have prevailed had the *ADA* been in place when they brought their case. "[A] student in Amy Rowley's position could argue today that the *ADA* requires her school to use a sign-language interpreter so she can have the same opportunity as her non-disabled classmates to hear the words spoken in the classroom." Thus, relying on the *ADA* could potentially "flip the result in *Rowley*."[73]

Related Services

It is permissible for school officials to choose a less costly program promising greater benefits, provided the less costly program meets the *Endrew F.* standard.[74] However, districts may be required to provide costly services such as residential placement or a full-time specialized tutor if the services are necessary to provide FAPE.[75] In *Cedar Rapids Community School District v. Garret F.*,[76] the Supreme Court held that a school must provide full-time "one-on-one nursing services" to a student with quadriplegia because without these services, the student could not attend school. The main issue in the *Garret F.* case was whether the requested nursing service was a related service within the meaning of the *IDEA*, which defines related services to include:[77]

> transportation and such developmental, corrective, and other supportive services as are required to assist a child with a disability to benefit from special education, and includes speech-language pathology and audiology services, interpreting services, psychological services, physical and occupational therapy, recreation, including therapeutic recreation, early identification and assessment of disabilities in children, counseling services, including rehabilitation counseling, orientation and mobility services, and medical services for diagnostic or evaluation purposes. Related services also include school health services and school nurse services, social work services in schools, and parent counseling and training.

"Related services" is a very broad concept encompassing almost anything necessary to make it possible for a child to benefit from special education. Related services may include assistive technology devices and services. The regulations define an **assistive technology device** as a piece of equipment or product used "to increase, maintain, or improve functional capabilities of [children] with disabilities" (such as an iPad), but not medical devices that are surgically implanted. An **assistive technology service** is a service that assists a child in the selection, acquisition, or use of an assistive technology, such as training a child with a disability in the use of a computer.

The Supreme Court provided the framework for deciding cases like *Garret F.* in *Irving Independent School District v. Tatro*.[78] The issue was whether a school was required to provide a student with clean intermittent catheterization (CIC), "a procedure involving the insertion of a catheter into the urethra to drain the bladder." In order to decide the case, the Court offered three guidelines for determining whether a school is obligated to provide "services that relate to both the health and education needs of students [with disabilities]." First, such services must be provided only to children who require special education. Second, services must be provided only if they are necessary to permit the child to benefit from special education. Thus, "if a particular medication or treatment may be administered to a child [with a disability] other than during the school day, a school is not required to provide nursing services to administer it." Third, services must be provided only

73 Samuel Bagenstos, *Educational Equality for Children with Disabilities: The 2016 Term Cases*, in AMERICAN CONSTITUTION SOCIETY SUPREME COURT REVIEW 2016-2017, 17–48 (S.D. Schwinn, ed., 2017).
74 Cf. Clevenger v. Oak Ridge Sch. Bd., 744 F.2d 514 (6th Cir. 1984).
75 Johnson v. Indep. Sch. Dist. No. 4, 921 F.2d 1022 (10th Cir. 1990).
76 526 U.S. 66 (1999).
77 34 C.F.R. 300.34.
78 468 U.S. 883 (1984).

if they may be performed by a nurse or other qualified person but are not required if they must be performed by a doctor. Even services that require a doctor's prescription or order must be provided if the doctor's actual presence is not necessary and the other guidelines are met. Applying these guidelines to *Tatro*, the Court determined that the school was obligated to provide CIC. The student required special education, could not attend school without the service, and CIC could be performed by a nurse or trained layperson.

The same reasoning led to the conclusion that the very expensive nursing services requested in *Garret F.* were also required by *IDEA*. That Garret needed continuous monitoring and frequent interventions by a person with a significant level of medical training and skill did not release the district from its obligation to provide the services necessary to allow Garret to benefit from education. However, as noted above, supportive medical services that require a doctor's presence, because they are beyond the capabilities of a trained nurse, need not be provided.[79] *IDEA* regulations do require that medical services for diagnosis and evaluation be provided even though they require a licensed physician if the services are necessary "to determine a child's medically related disability that results in the child's need for special education …."

In *Butler v. Evans*,[80] the Seventh Circuit ruled that parents were not entitled to reimbursement for the time their daughter stayed in a psychiatric hospital where she received medication, psychotherapy, and educational services. The child, Niki, had been diagnosed as suffering from a "mental disorder needing long-term education, structural, locked residential protective placement." The court concluded that Niki's situation was different from Garret F.'s:

> Niki's hospitalization was not an attempt to give her meaningful access to public education or to address her special educational needs within her regular school environment. This is not a case in which the disabled student needed medical assistance to remain in a regular school; Niki was committed to a psychiatric hospital. Niki might have continued to receive school assignments and some tutoring while hospitalized, but education was not the purpose of her hospitalization. Unlike in-school nursing in [*Garret F.*], Niki's inpatient medical care was necessary in itself and was not a special accommodation made necessary only to allow her to attend school or receive education.

Like any related service, transportation must be provided only if and to the extent that it is necessary to permit a child with a disability to benefit from education.[81] In one case, a deaf child capable of using the same transportation services as hearing children was denied publicly supported transportation to a private school.[82] However, in another case, transportation was a required related service for a child who needed suctioning of his tracheostomy tube and repositioning of his wheelchair during transit.[83] Another court required the district to transport a student with a disability between the public school where she received some special education services and her parochial school and ruled that the requirement did not violate the Establishment Clause.[84] In *D.C. v. Ramirez*,[85] a court required a school district to provide a student who used a wheelchair with transportation between the door of his apartment and the school bus. The court reasoned that, without such assistance, the student would be "unable to receive the education and related services guaranteed by the *IDEA* and prescribed in his IEP."

79 Detsel v. Bd. of Educ., 637 F. Supp. 1022 (N.D.N.Y. 1986), *aff'd*, 820 F.2d 587 (2d Cir. 1987) (*per curiam*).
80 225 F.3d 887 (7th Cir. 2000); *see also* Munir v. Pottsville Area Sch. Dist., 723 F.3d 423, 430 (3d Cir. 2013).
81 *See* Hurry v. Jones, 734 F.2d 879 (1st Cir. 1984); Alamo Heights Indep. Sch. Dist. v. State Bd. of Educ., 70 F.2d 1153 (5th Cir. 1986).
82 McNair v. Oak Hills Local Sch. Dist., 872 F.2d 153 (6th Cir. 1989).
83 Macomb County Intermediate Sch. Dist. v. Joshua S., 715 F. Supp. 824 (E.D. Mich. 1989).
84 Felter v. Cape Girardeau Pub. Sch. Dist., 810 F. Supp. 1062 (E.D. Mo. 1993).
85 377 F.Supp.2d 63, 70 (D.D.C. 2005).

Transition Services and Positive Behavioral Supports

In 1990, the *IDEA* was amended to reflect the need for IEPs to include **transition services**. Under *IDEA*, as one court has explained,

> Transition services are aimed at preparing students (soon to leave school) for employment, postsecondary education, vocational training, continuing and adult education, adult services, independent living, or community participation. Toward this end, Congress expects schools to develop a coordinated set of activities for each student, based upon the student's needs and taking into account the student's preferences and interests.[86]

In a case in which the transition services listed on an IEP contained generic, "boilerplate" language, a federal district court found that the IEP denied FAPE because it was "not sufficiently tailored to meet [the student's] individual needs."[87] As noted above, the *IDEA* also requires that IEPs contain positive behavioral interventions for students whose behavior is interfering with learning. Failure to include such measures on the IEP will also amount to a denial of FAPE.[88]

"Least Restrictive Environment"

IDEA demands that the FAPE offered to a child with a disability meet the requirement of "**least restrictive environment**" (LRE), also known as **inclusion**: "[T]o the maximum extent appropriate" the child must be educated with children who do not have disabilities, and special classes and schools and residential placements should be used only "when the nature or severity of the [disability] is such that education in regular classes with the use of supplementary aids and services cannot be achieved satisfactorily." The child must also receive any supplementary aids and services that are necessary for the child's participation in non-academic activities and must be placed "as close as possible" to home.

In order to meet these requirements, school districts must maintain a continuum of possible alternative placements including general education classrooms, special classes, resource rooms, special schools, home instruction, and residential placements. The *IDEA* requires that the IEP include an "explanation of the extent, if any, to which the child will not participate with non-disabled students in the regular class …" Some schools have adopted a policy of **inclusion** or **full inclusion**, meaning that all or most children with disabilities are educated in regular education classrooms all or most of the time. However, the *IDEA* does not mandate full inclusion and in fact requires special placement if the regular classroom cannot provide an appropriate education.

Disputes between parents and schools over the issue of LRE are common. Sometimes, the school advocates special placement, while parents favor education in the regular classroom, and sometimes the positions are reversed. The LRE requirement creates a presumption in favor of the regular classroom. The presumption can be rebutted by a showing that education in the regular classroom offers no meaningful educational benefit for a particular student or that a given student's behavior would prevent other students from learning. More controversial are cases in which both approaches offer educational benefit but one approach offers significantly greater benefits, or when one approach offers greater benefit but at significantly greater cost. Another common problem is how to balance the potentially greater academic benefits of out-of-class placement with the potentially greater social benefits of mainstreaming. These issues are addressed in the following illustrative case:

---

86 Yankton School Dist. v. Schramm, 900 F. Supp. 1182, 1192 (D.S.D. 1995), *aff'd*, 93 F.3d 1369 (8th Cir. 1996).
87 East Penn School Dist. v. Scott B. *ex rel.* Ronald B., 213 F.3d 628 (3d Cir. 2000).
88 R.K. v. New York City Dept. of Educ., 2011 U.S. Dist. LEXIS 32248 (E.D.N.Y. Jan. 21, 2011).

⚖️

P. *ex rel.* MR. AND MRS. P. v. NEWINGTON BOARD OF EDUCATION

US Court of Appeals for the Second Circuit

546 F.3d 111 (2008)

ROBERT A. KATZMANN, Circuit Judge

This case calls upon us to adopt a standard by which courts in this circuit should assess whether a disabled child has been placed in the "least restrictive environment," as required by the *Individuals with Disabilities Education Act (IDEA)*. The plaintiff, P., suing by and through his parents, is a child with Down Syndrome attending public school in the Town of Newington, Connecticut. He contends that the 2005–2006 Individualized Education Plan (IEP) devised for him at his elementary school did not include enough regular-classroom time, and therefore did not place him in the least restrictive environment as mandated by the *IDEA*. P. challenged the IEP before an administrative hearing officer, who held that the school complied with the statute. P. appealed that decision to the United States District Court for the District of Connecticut, which affirmed, granting summary judgment to the defendant Newington Board of Education. Today, we affirm the decision of the district court and join several of our sister circuits in holding that determining whether a student has been placed in the "least restrictive environment" requires a flexible, fact-specific analysis, considering whether, with the aid of appropriate supplemental aids and services, education in the regular classroom may be achieved, and, if not, whether the school has included the student in regular classes, programs, and activities to the maximum extent appropriate. Applying that analysis to the case before us, we affirm the decisions of the hearing officer and district court that the defendant fulfilled its obligations under the *IDEA*. ...

II. Factual Background

A. *The Development of P.'s 2004–2005 and 2005–2006 IEPs*

P. suffers from Down Syndrome, hearing impairment, and other significant health problems that have required several serious procedures, including surgery to repair a hole in his heart and multiple bowel operations, as a result of which he is not toilet trained. At the time relevant to this litigation, he was a student at the Anna Reynolds Elementary School in Newington, Connecticut. Among the assigned staff at the school working with P. have been the special-education teacher, two paraprofessionals, a speech pathologist, a physical therapist, and an occupational therapist. In the spring of 2004, when P. was eight, the school district's behavioral consultant, Greg Smith, informed his parents that it was becoming increasingly difficult to keep P. in a regular classroom, as the gap in ability between P. and his peers was growing and would grow larger. Moreover, at various times, P. had exhibited some behavior problems, including kicking, grabbing, and pulling hair. P.'s mother strongly disagreed with Smith's assessment and wanted her son to remain in a regular classroom with his non-disabled peers as much as possible.

On May 28, 2004, the group assigned to formulate P.'s IEP, the "Performance and Planning Team" (PPT), met to discuss plans for the 2004–2005 school year. At that meeting, P.'s parents stated that they wanted their son to be in a regular classroom at least 80 percent of the time during the upcoming school year. Instead, the IEP provided that P. be in the classroom for 60 percent of the school day, with "pull-out" services for occupational and speech therapy in separate classrooms, and the plan did not include any measures to deal with P.'s burgeoning behavior problems. In order to facilitate increased inclusion in the regular classroom, P.'s parents asked that a consultant specializing in such matters be hired, and in accordance with their request, the Board retained Dr. Kathleen Whitbread to evaluate P.

Dr. Whitbread completed her evaluation on December 13, 2004. In the report, based on two hours of observation of P. at home and 4.5 hours of observation of him in the classroom, Dr. Whitbread described P.'s behavior problems as "moderately serious" and opined that the PPT had done "a commendable job of ensuring that [P.] spends the majority of the day with non-disabled peers." Nevertheless, she recommended that P.'s instruction be more closely connected to the general education curriculum. Dr. Whitbread also recommended consultation with a teacher of the hearing impaired and a program of literacy instruction.

According to the testimony of his second-grade teacher, Ms. Mazur, P.'s behavior improved during 2004–2005. He was only removed from the regular classroom three times due to behavior problems that caused or risked physical harm to another person, though timeouts were used. Ms. Mazur also explained that, although she frequently co-taught classes with the special-education teacher, Nancy Wilcock, to integrate P. into regular lessons, in at least some circumstances, "[P.] will need individualized instruction to make sure that he … is receiving the best instruction without distraction."

The PPT next met with Dr. Whitbread to discuss her findings and the CCMC evaluation on February 11, 2005. At the meeting, the PPT accepted her recommendations for an ATE and literary instruction. Although Dr. Whitbread stated at the meeting that P. would benefit from additional regular-classroom time, she also contended that some of his literacy instruction might need to take place outside the classroom. The PPT did not, however, reach any conclusions and decided to reconvene in April.

Prior to the April meeting, Dr. Whitbread and Ms. Wilcock, the special-education teacher who had been working with P. for three years, exchanged e-mails regarding appropriate next steps. In one of these e-mails, Dr. Whitbread stated:

Time out of the classroom is a concern of [P.'s] parents and it is important to them that [P.] be fully included. Their goal is 100% of the time in a gen. ed. class. I have shared with them that I feel some pullout time is beneficial. To me, a reasonable goal over the next year would be to increase his time in the general ed. environment from the current 60 or 65% to about 80%. I would not recommend that this be done suddenly. I realize this is going to be a difficult discussion since there are differences in opinion about what is best for [P.]. My hope is that we can have a productive conversation, with the understanding that compromise may be necessary.

This email is consistent with Dr. Whitbread's later testimony before the hearing officer in this case, during which she confirmed that she "recommended working up to 80 percent … that in [her] experience it's not productive to go in and say right now you must do this." But Dr. Whitbread also clarified her definition of "gradual": "I would have liked to see that happen over a month, two months, maybe three months, but certainly not years."

The PPT next convened on April 15, 2005, with Dr. Whitbread again in attendance. At the meeting, the special-education teacher, Ms. Wilcock, noted that P.'s behavior had improved, but that his attention span was limited. P.'s parents again emphasized their preference that their son's regular-classroom time increase from 60 percent to 80 percent in the upcoming year. Although the PPT scheduled another meeting in June to discuss the question, it indicated that at least some of P.'s speech-therapy sessions would occur in the regular classroom, and that all parties agreed that he would undergo some physical therapy instead of regular physical education (although he would still participate in some regular physical education). Dr. Whitbread again stated her recommendation that the team "gradually increase to 80 percent inclusion for [P.]."

The PPT next met on June 3, 2005. Notes from the meeting indicate that an FBA for P. had begun two weeks prior, and that all parties agreed that the school would hire a mutually agreeable behavioral specialist. With respect to the percentage of time P. would spend in the classroom, however, the parties were unable to reach a consensus, and P.'s parents lodged their disagreement with the plan in writing. Dr. Whitbread later testified that the PPT engaged in a "very long tedious process" while attempting to determine the appropriate amount of classroom time. Ultimately, the IEP provided that P.'s regular-classroom time would increase from 60 percent to 74 percent, with participation in "all regular class[es]," except when he needed to be educated separately to "increase his focus/attention" or when he needed to be removed from the regular classroom "due to fatigue … or behavior which indicates [a] need for a break from the group." The IEP also mandated the following supplemental assistance for P.: daily check of P.'s hearing aids in the health room, adult assistance in all activities in the regular classroom, assistive computer programs, extra time and directions on assignments, routines and schedules in pictures instead of words, preferential seating, and a clear work area. The IEP also provided for weekly consultation between the regular and special education teachers.

On June 9, 2005, P.'s parents requested an administrative hearing to challenge both the 2004–2005 and 2005–2006 IEPs, primarily on the ground that P. was not sufficiently integrated into the regular classroom.

Meanwhile, the PPT met again prior to the beginning of the school year, on August 18, 2005. At that meeting, the parties agreed to the hiring of a mutually agreeable behavioral and inclusion consultant, Dr. Ann Majure. Also, by that time, the school had hired a hearing-impairment consultant and another consultant to assist with implementing assistive-technology recommendations.

During a meeting on April 7, 2006, the PPT mandated that P. be placed in a regular classroom for 80 percent or more of the school day, pursuant in part to the recommendation of Dr. Majure. At oral argument in this case, the parties noted that since that time P. has been included in the regular classroom at least 80 percent of the time.

B. Litigation before the Hearing Officer and the District Court

Pursuant to P.'s parents' request, hearing officer Mary Elizabeth Oppenheim held a hearing on P.'s parents' challenge to his 2004–2005 and 2005–2006 IEPs. She heard testimony from P.'s parents, Dr. Whitbread, Ms. Wilcock, and several other teachers and special-education professionals. After exhaustively reviewing the record, and noting that the Board bore the burden of proof in proving the IEPs' compliance with the *IDEA*, the hearing officer held in a thirty-five page opinion that the 2004–2005 IEP did not comply with *IDEA*, but that the 2005–2006 IEP did. The 2004–2005 IEP was deficient because too much of the division between regular and special classroom time was left to the discretion of school authorities and because P.'s behavioral issues were not appropriately addressed. As a "compensatory education" remedy for the deficiencies of the 2004–2005 IEP, the hearing officer required that the Board retain an inclusion consultant with "considerable experience in placing children with mental retardation in regular classes," and held that Dr. Majure, whom the school had already hired, could fill that role appropriately. The Board does not appeal the hearing officer's findings with respect to the 2004–2005 IEP.

The hearing officer found, however, that the 2005–2006 IEP complied with the requirements of the *IDEA*. Emphasizing Dr. Whitbread's statements that she thought P.'s regular-classroom time should increase gradually to 80 percent and that P. required some special-education services outside of the classroom, the hearing officer found that the PPT gave sufficient consideration to including P. in the classroom to the maximum extent appropriate. The hearing officer also took note of the extensive efforts the school had made on P.'s behalf, including the numerous supplemental aids, services, and additional teachers employed to assist P. throughout the

day, the mutually agreed-upon behavioral consultant hired in 2005, and that the school had modified the curriculum to meet P.'s needs. Moreover, it was clear that P. was included with non-disabled students for around 73 percent of the time in 2005–2006, and "participate[d] in all specials, lunch, [and] recess."

P. subsequently appealed to the United States District Court for the District of Connecticut the ruling that the 2005–2006 IEP was sufficient and the sufficiency of the remedy awarded for the deficiencies in the 2004–2005 IEP. Both parties cross-moved for summary judgment, and the district court issued an opinion affirming the hearing officer's decision and awarding P. partial attorneys' fees and costs …

III. Discussion …

B. Fashioning a Test for Assessing Placement in the "Least Restrictive Environment"

We have not yet explicitly stated a test for whether an IEP places a student in the least restrictive environment. We conclude today that the two-pronged approach adopted by the Third, Fifth, Ninth, Tenth, and Eleventh Circuits provides appropriate guidance to the district courts without "too intrusive an inquiry into the educational policy choices that Congress deliberately left to state and local school officials." Pursuant to that test, a court should consider, first, "whether education in the regular classroom, with the use of supplemental aids and services, can be achieved satisfactorily for a given child," and, if not, then "whether the school has mainstreamed the child to the maximum extent appropriate." We today explicitly endorse that two-pronged test, as elucidated and augmented by Judge Becker for the Third Circuit in *Oberti*.[89]

In sum, in determining whether a child with disabilities can be educated satisfactorily in a regular class with supplemental aids and services (the first prong of the two-part mainstreaming test we adopt today), the court should consider several factors, including: (1) whether the school district has made reasonable efforts to accommodate the child in a regular classroom; (2) the educational benefits available to the child in a regular class, with appropriate supplementary aids and services, as compared to the benefits provided in a special education class; and (3) the possible negative effects of the inclusion of the child on the education of the other students in the class. If, after considering these factors, the court

89 Oberti v. Board of Educ., 995 F.2d 1204, 1215 (3d Cir. 1993).

determines that the school district was justified in removing the child from the regular classroom and providing education in a segregated, special education class, the court must consider the second prong of the mainstreaming test—whether the school has included the child in school programs with nondisabled children to the maximum extent appropriate …

C. The Oberti Analysis Applied to This Case

We now turn to whether the Board's actions with respect to the 2005–2006 IEP pass muster under the test we have adopted, which both the district court and hearing officer referenced and applied. Our review is against the backdrop of the ultimate conclusion of the IEP, which resolved that P. would be in the regular classroom 74 percent of the time, and Dr. Whitbread's statements that P.'s regular-classroom time should be gradually ramped up to 80 percent. The first prong of the test asks whether a student can be satisfactorily educated in the regular classroom with the benefit of supplemental aids and services. As noted, we also consider whether the school made reasonable efforts to accommodate the student, the benefits and drawbacks to the student of full-time integration into the regular classroom, and the possible negative impact on other students of the disabled student's presence. Although, in light of the improvements in P.'s behavior, there did not appear to be a significant negative impact on other students arising from his inclusion in the regular classroom, we see no error in the district court's conclusions that P. could not be educated in the regular class room full-time and that the school had made significant efforts to integrate P. to the maximum extent possible. The school utilized a variety of supplemental aids, including several additional professionals, and modified the curriculum appropriately. Moreover, the hearing officer permissibly relied on the testimony of Dr. Whitbread that P. required pull-out services for reading, math, and speech therapy. We therefore agree with this district court's conclusion that "the evidence produced during the administrative proceeding demonstrates that education in the regular classroom, with the use of supplemental aids and services, could not be achieved satisfactorily for the 2005–2006 school year."

Turning to the second prong of the test, we must assess "whether the school has included the child in school programs with nondisabled children to the maximum extent appropriate." Continuing to keep in mind that the IEP mandated 74 percent inclusion in the regular classroom, as opposed to P.'s parents'

proposed 80 percent—a difference of approximately 2–3 hours per week—we find no error in the district court's conclusion that, given P.'s need for some specialized instruction outside the regular classroom, he was mainstreamed to the maximum extent appropriate.

P. argues that this Court should adopt a presumption that a student should be placed in a regular classroom 80 percent of the time and contends that the district court erred by failing to apply such a presumption. P. bases this argument on a class-action settlement in which the Connecticut State Department of Education agreed that it would be a "desired outcome[]" for disabled students to spend 80 percent of the school day with non-disabled students. Recognizing that Connecticut school authorities may have found this percentage figure useful, we conclude that mandating such a percentage in every case would be inconsistent with the *IDEA*'s directive that schools take an individualized approach to each student. We do not think that 80 percent is presumptively adequate or that less than 80 percent is presumptively inadequate. Children with disabilities must be educated with their non-disabled peers "[t]o the maximum extent appropriate." As the word "appropriate" suggests, the objective of providing an education tailored to each student's particular needs does not admit of statistical generalizations. While including students in the regular classroom as much as is practicable is undoubtedly a central goal of the *IDEA*, schools must attempt to achieve that goal in light of the equally important objective of providing an education appropriately tailored to each student's particular needs.

We recognize and appreciate P.'s parents' dedicated advocacy on his behalf. But the evidence before the hearing officer and the records of the several PPT meetings devoted to developing P.'s 2005–2006 IEP demonstrate that the school fulfilled its duty under the *IDEA* to craft a tailored educational plan that included P. in regular classes to the maximum extent appropriate. We therefore affirm the district court's conclusion that the school's actions were sufficient under the two-pronged test and that the 2005–2006 IEP placed P. in the "least restrictive environment" under the *IDEA*.

D. The Remedy for Deficiencies in the 2004-2005 IEP

P. also argues on appeal that the compensatory-education remedy mandated by the hearing officer for deficiencies in the 2004–2005 IEP was insufficient.

Those deficiencies, which the Board did not contest in the district court, were that the school district had not properly addressed P.'s behavioral problems and had failed to give sufficient consideration to mainstreaming the student for more than 60 percent of the time. In response to the inadequacies of that IEP, the hearing officer ordered that the school hire a professional consultant on issues of inclusion, and that that consultant participate in the completion of an FBA. P. argues that the remedy was illusory because the school had already hired an inclusion consultant, Dr. Majure.

We affirm the remedy awarded by the hearing officer. The *IDEA* allows a hearing officer to fashion an appropriate remedy, and we have held compensatory education is an available option under the Act to make up for denial of a free and appropriate public education. The remedy's mandates in this case-that an inclusion consultant be retained for a year, requiring the school to keep Dr. Majure on for at least that long, and completion of an FBA-appropriately addressed the problems with the IEP, especially when considered in light of the fact that P. is now included in at least 80 percent of regular-classroom activities, in part due to Dr. Majure's recommendations. We therefore see no infirmity in the hearing officer's chosen remedy.

Conclusion

The judgment of the district court granting summary judgment to the Board is AFFIRMED.

Newington explains the Second Circuit's interpretation of the least restrictive environment (**LRE**) requirement. The Third, Fifth, Tenth and Eleventh Circuits have adopted related approaches to dealing with LRE disputes.[90] However, as noted in *Newington*, other courts have offered different interpretations. In *Woods v. Northport Public School*,[91] the Sixth Circuit explained its approach:

> We consider three factors in determining whether a disabled child may be removed from the general education environment: (1) whether the disabled student would benefit from inclusion [in] general education, (2) whether such benefits would be outweighed by benefits that are not provided in an inclusive setting, and (3) whether the disabled child disrupts the general education setting ... Despite the *IDEA*'s least restrictive environment provision, Congress has recognized that regular classrooms simply will not be a suitable setting for the education of many children [with disabilities].

Similarly, the Fourth Circuit has stated that mainstreaming is not required when there are no educational benefits to be realized from placement in a general class, any marginal benefits from placement in a general class would be significantly outweighed by the benefits of a more restrictive placement, or the student would be too disruptive in the general class. The court noted that under *IDEA*, social benefits are subordinate to academic achievement.[92]

In *B.E.L. v. Hawaii Department of Education*,[93] the Ninth Circuit employed a balancing test encompassing four factors:

1. The educational benefits available in a general education classroom with supplementary aids and services as compared to the benefits available in a more restrictive environment.

---

90 Oberti v. Bd. of Educ. of Clementon Sch. Dist., 995 F.2d 1204 (3d Cir. 1993); Daniel R.R. v. State Bd. of Educ., 874 F.2d 1036 (5th Cir.1989); L.B. v. Nebo Sch. Dist., 379 F.3d 966 (10th Cir. 2004); Greer v. Rome City Sch. Dist., 950 F.2d 688 (11th Cir. 1991); *opinion withdrawn and remanded on other grounds*, 956 F.2d 1025 (11th Cir. 1992).

91 487 F. App'x 968 (6th Cir. 2012).

92 Hartmann v. Loudoun County Bd. of Educ., 118 F.3d 996 (4th Cir. 1997); *see also* Hanson *ex rel.* Hanson v. Smith, 212 F. Supp. 2d 474, 489 (D. Md. 2002).

93 711 F. App'x 426, 427 (9th Cir. 2018).

2. The non-academic benefits of the general classroom compared to the more restrictive environment.
3. The effect of the presence of the student with a disability on the teacher and other students in the general classroom.
4. The cost of placement in the general education classroom (which may be either higher or lower than the more restrictive placement).

In two separate cases, the Seventh Circuit has ruled in favor of school districts when they placed disruptive students in settings other than the regular classroom.[94]

Residential Placements

Among the most controversial placement decisions are those involving a residential facility. A residential placement is both the most restrictive and usually the most expensive option. Nevertheless, *IDEA* regulations specify that if

> placement in a … residential program is necessary to provide special education and related services to a child with a disability, the program, including nonmedical care and room and board, must be at no cost to the parents of the child.[95]

In cases involving children with emotional disturbances, the courts consider whether a residential placement is necessary to meet their educational needs, whether the facility is a hospital or an accredited educational facility, whether the program provided is prescribed by physicians or educators, the intensity of the program, and the cost as compared to non-residential educational programs.[96] Even when a major goal of residential placement is training in basic life skills, such as using a fork, getting dressed, and using the toilet, courts have required schools to pay for the placement unless an appropriate education could be provided in a non-residential setting.[97] In *Kruelle v. New Castle County School District*,[98] the Third Circuit held that if a residential placement is "part and parcel of … specially designed instruction … to meet the unique needs of a child [with a disability]," the school must pay for it.

In *Richardson Independent School District v. Michael Z.*,[99] the Fifth Circuit explicitly rejected this approach and adopted a different standard:

> In order for a residential placement to be appropriate under *IDEA*, the placement must be 1) essential in order for the disabled child to receive a meaningful educational benefit, and 2) primarily oriented toward enabling the child to obtain an education.

> Unlike *Kruelle*, this test does not make the reimbursement determination contingent on a court's ability to conduct the arguably impossible task of segregating a child's medical, social, emotional, and educational problems. The first prong of our test requires a court to find that the placement is *essential* for the child to receive a meaningful educational benefit. In other words, if a child is able to receive an educational benefit without the residential placement, even if the placement is helpful to a child's education, the school is not required to pay for it under *IDEA*.

94 Bd. of Educ. of Twp. High Sch. Dist., 211 v. Ross, 486 F.3d 267 (7th Cir. 2007); Sch. Dist. of Wisconsin Dells v. Z.S., 295 F.3d 671 (7th Cir. 2002).
95 See Drew P. v. Clarke County Sch. Dist., 877 F.2d 927 (11th Cir. 1989); 34 C.F.R. § 300.104.
96 Taylor v. Honig, 910 F.2d 627 (9th Cir. 1990); Clovis Unified Sch. Dist. v. California Office of Admin. Hearings, 903 F.2d 635 (9th Cir. 1990).
97 Abrahamson v. Hershman, 701 F.2d 233 (1st Cir.1983); Battle v. Pennsylvania, 629 F.2d 269 (3d Cir. 1980).
98 Kruelle v. New Castle County Sch. Dist., 642 F.2d 687 (3d Cir. 1981).
99 Richardson Indep. Sch. Dist. v. Michael Z, 580 F.3d 286, 299–300 (5th Cir. 2009).

The Sixth Circuit has said that cost may be considered only when comparing two options that both meet the FAPE standard, but not if a particular program or service is necessary to assure the child a free, appropriate education. Thus, in *Clevenger v. Oak Ridge School Board*,[100] the court approved a residential placement that cost $88,000 per year. However, *IDEA* does not require that states or local school districts pay for residential placements undertaken for wholly non-educational purposes.[101] Public school districts are responsible for monitoring and re-evaluating students with disabilities placed in residential facilities.

Students with Disabilities and Private Schools

If a private school student qualifies for services under *IDEA*, the public school district may at its option either make the appropriate special education available at public school or, if permitted by state law, pay for the services in the private school.[102] Recall, however, that private school students are explicitly exempted from FAPE guarantees under federal law. States may deem a home school an *IDEA*-qualifying private school.[103]

If a school district makes a FAPE available to a child with a disability in a public school, but the child's parents elect to place the child in a private school, the district does not have to pay the child's tuition or for the special costs associated with the child's disability.[104] If, however, a private facility is necessary in order to provide an appropriate education, the district must pay the cost of the child's education. If parents place their child with a disability in private school because they do not believe the public school's proposed placement is appropriate, and the parents' position is ultimately upheld by a hearing officer or court, the public school must reimburse the parents for the private school tuition and related costs such as transportation.[105] Public school districts are responsible for monitoring and re-evaluating students with disabilities placed in private schools.

Do parents in effect waive their right to reimbursement when they unilaterally place their child in a private school either prior to giving the district an opportunity to address their concerns with the public school's program or prior to even enrolling their child in the public school? In 2009, the Supreme Court answered this question, resolving a split in the courts. In *Forest Grove School Dist. v. T.A*,[106] a high school student experienced difficulty with focusing in class and completing assignments. In spite of a private evaluation diagnosing T.A. with ADHD, the public school maintained that he was not eligible for special education. In response, the parents placed him in a private academy that focused on special needs and sought reimbursement from the public school. An impartial hearing officer found that T.A. was eligible under *IDEA*, and the Ninth Circuit concluded that he was entitled to tuition reimbursement.

The Supreme Court

> conclude[d] that *IDEA* authorizes reimbursement for the cost of private special-education services when a school district fails to provide a FAPE and the private-school placement is appropriate, regardless of whether the child previously received special education or related services through the public school.

100 Clevenger v. Oak Ridge Sch. Bd., 744 F.2d 514 (6th Cir. 1984).
101 Parks v. Pavkovic, 753 F.2d 1397 (7th Cir. 1985) (*dicta*); Abrahamson v. Hershman, 701 F.2d 223 (1st Cir. 1983) (*dictum*).
102 KDM *ex rel.* WJM v. Reedsport Sch. Dist., 196 F.3d 1046 (9th Cir. 1999), *reh'g denied*, 210 F.3d 1098 (9th Cir. 2000); Jasa v. Millard Pub. Sch. Dist. No. 17, 206 F.3d 813 (8th Cir. 2000).
103 Hooks v. Clark County Sch. Dist., 228 F.3d 1036 (9th Cir. 2000).
104 Cefalu v. E. Baton Rouge Parish Sch. Bd., 117 F.3d 231 (5th Cir. 1997).
105 Burlington Sch. Comm. of Burlington v. Dep't of Educ. of Massachusetts, 471 U.S. 359 (1985); *see also* Florence County Sch. Dist. Four v. Carter, 510 U.S. 7 (1993).
106 557 U.S. 230 (2009).

The Court rejected the contention that this ruling would cause "parents to immediately enroll their children in private school without first endeavoring to cooperate with the school district," noting that, to secure reimbursement, parents would still have to establish "both that the public placement violated *IDEA* and the private school placement was proper under the Act." In *Dallas Independent School District v. Woody*,[107] the Fifth Circuit upheld reimbursement for a private school placement, explaining that the parent "was not ineligible for reimbursement merely because she first placed her daughter in a private school and then requested the local public school district pay for the tuition."

The Supreme Court has held that the provision of an ASL interpreter to a deaf student attending a parochial school does not violate the Establishment Clause.[108] Likewise, it is likely permissible for public schools to provide any related service specified by a parochial school student's IEP.[109] Nevertheless, it is doubtful whether it would be permissible for a public school district to pay a child's religious school tuition, even if the school was specially equipped to provide the child with an appropriate education.

Change of Placement

The question of what constitutes a "change of placement" for a student with a disability has been considered by a number of courts and several different definitions have been introduced. The Second Circuit said that a change in placement occurs when there is a change in the "general educational program in which the child is enrolled, rather than mere variations in the program itself." Thus, in *Concerned Parents v. New York City Board of Education*,[110] the Second Circuit found there was no change of placement when, after one school closed, the student was transferred to a similar but less innovative program. The Sixth Circuit said a change of placement occurs when a modified educational program "is not comparable to the plan set forth in the original IEP."[111] The Third Circuit said the question "has to be whether the decision is likely to affect in some significant way the child's learning experience." Thus, the court said a change in how the child was transported to school was not a change in placement.[112]

No matter how it is defined, the *IDEA* requires parental notification before a **change of placement** can occur. Parents who object to a proposed change of placement may agree to mediation or demand an impartial hearing and invoke the **stay-put** requirement. The stay-put requirement is designed to maintain the status quo during the impartial hearing and any subsequent appeals. Unless both the school and the parents agree, students must be left in their present educational placement even if one party believes that it is not an "appropriate" placement. Whether the present placement is appropriate is often the subject of the dispute. If either party wants to temporarily change the present placement before the appeals process is over, that party must go to court to effect the change.[113] The public school district must bear the cost of funding the present placement pending the outcome of the appeal process even if the present placement is in a private setting.[114]

If a student is in a school or program because of an IEP, an agreement between the parents and the school, or a court order, it is considered the student's **present placement**. However, in the

---

107 865 F.3d 303, 316 (5th Cir. 2017).
108 Zobrest v. Catalina Foothills Sch. Dist., 509 U.S. 1 (1993).
109 Agostini v. Felton, 521 U.S. 203 (1997).
110 629 F.2d 751 (2d Cir. 1980); *see also* K.L.A. v. Windham Se. Supervisory Union, 371 F. App'x 151 (2d Cir. 2010).
111 Tilton v. Jefferson County Bd. of Educ., 705 F.2d 800 (6th Cir.1983).
112 DeLeon v. Susquehanna Cmty. Sch. Dist., 747 F.2d 149 (3d Cir. 1984); *see also* Weil v. Bd. of Elementary & Secondary Educ., 931 F.2d 1069 (5th Cir. 1991).
113 Doe v. Brookline Sch. Comm., 722 F.2d 910 (1st Cir. 1983).
114 Saleh v. District of Columbia, 660 F. Supp. 212 (D.D.C. 1987).

midst of a dispute with school officials, some parents will unilaterally move their child to a private school. The question then arises whether the private school placement is the present placement pending final resolution of the dispute. The court may conclude that a parent was justified in moving the child if, for example, school officials delayed unduly in making an IEP proposal.[115] Also, if it is later determined that the public school placement was not appropriate, the parents are entitled to reimbursement for the cost of the private school.[116] To be eligible for reimbursement, parents must notify the district in a timely manner of the private school placement and their reason for moving the child.

If a student with an IEP moves from one state to another, must the new state implement the IEP? In 2004, Congress amended *IDEA* to require that the new district provide such students "services comparable to those described in the previously held IEP," until the new district has had the opportunity to conduct its own evaluations.[117] In *Pardini v. Allegheny Intermediate Unit*[118] the Third Circuit ruled that the stay-put requirement of Part B of the *IDEA* was applicable to a child in transition from Part C (services for children with disabilities ages birth to three years) to Part B (ages three to 21). The court ruled that the school district had to provide the child with a continuation of the services she had been receiving until the dispute over her initial IEP was resolved.[119]

Discipline of Students with Disabilities

Discipline of children with a disability raises many issues, including whether various forms of discipline constitute a "change of placement," whether a child may be excluded from school for disciplinary reasons, what procedures must be followed in disciplining a child with a disability, where the child is to "stay-put" pending disciplinary proceedings, and whether exceptions to the usual requirements may be made if a disruptive child is a threat to others. Central to all these questions is the principle that children with disabilities are not to be excluded from receiving special education for disciplinary reasons. All children with disabilities must receive a FAPE "including children with disabilities who have been suspended or expelled from school."

The rules concerning the discipline of students with disabilities apply both to students with IEPs and to children not yet declared eligible for special education if the school district "had knowledge … that the child was a child with a disability before the behavior that precipitated the disciplinary action occurred." A school district is deemed to have such knowledge if a parent has expressed concern in writing to supervisory or administrative personnel of the district, or to the child's teacher, that the child needs special education; or the parent has requested an evaluation; or the teacher of the child or other district personnel have expressed specific concerns about a pattern of behavior possibly indicative of disability directly to the director of special education or other supervisory personnel. A district will not be deemed to have knowledge of disability if the parent of the child has not allowed an evaluation of the child for possible disability, or has refused services after an evaluation, or the child has been evaluated and it was determined that the child was not a child with a disability. If the district is not deemed to have knowledge, yet the child is in fact disabled, the child may be subjected to disciplinary measures applied to children without disabilities who engaged in comparable behaviors. If an initial request for an evaluation is made during this time, the evaluation must be conducted in an expedited manner (meanwhile the child

---

115 Cochran v. District of Columbia, 660 F. Supp. 314 (D.D.C. 1987).
116 Bd. of Educ. of Montgomery Cty v. Brett Y., 1998 U.S. App. LEXIS 13702 (4th Cir. 1998).
117 J.F. v. Byram Twp. Bd. of Educ., 629 F. App'x 235, 238 (3d Cir. 2015).
118 420 F.3d 181 (3d Cir. 2005).
119 *But see* D.P. *ex rel.* E.P. v. Sch. Bd. of Broward Cty., 483 F.3d 725, 730 (11th Cir. 2007).

remains in the placement determined by school officials); if the child is then determined to be disabled, the rights afforded by *IDEA* will now fully apply.

For children who already have an IEP or whom the district knows to have disabilities, disciplinary measures may be employed only to the extent that the same measures are employed with children without disabilities. Any lawful form of discipline that is not a change of placement may be used. These may include verbal reprimands, denial of privileges, and detentions of reasonable duration. Whether corporal punishment of children with disabilities may be employed in places where it is otherwise allowed is an unresolved issue. It is also permissible to relocate a misbehaving child with a disability to what the law calls an "**interim alternative educational setting**" (IAES), presumably including a more restrictive placement or in-school suspension for ten days or less or to suspend the student for ten days or less without employing change of placement procedures.

Removal of a child with a disability from the child's current educational placement is deemed a **change of placement** if the removal is for more than ten consecutive school days or the

> removals … constitute a pattern—because (i) the removals total more than 10 days in a school year; (ii) the child's behavior is substantially similar to the previous incidents that resulted in the removals; and (iii) because of additional factors such as the length of each removal, the total amount of time the child has been removed, and the proximity of the removals to one another.

If a school district wishes to discipline a child with a disability in a manner that would constitute a change of placement, the IEP team must first undertake an inquiry to determine if the student's problematic behavior was a "**manifestation of the disability**." The IEP team's findings are subject to review by an impartial hearing officer at parental request. If the problematic behavior was a manifestation of the disability, the school must perform a **functional behavioral assessment** and develop a **behavioral intervention plan** as part of the student's IEP. Further disciplinary procedures involving relocation or exclusion from school require standard change of placement procedures including parental notification, IEP team deliberations, and possibly an impartial hearing and court review.

If a child with a disability brings a weapon to school or possesses or sells illegal drugs at school, the IEP team may place the student in an IAES for up to 45 days during the manifestation determination and change of placement procedures. School officials may also report any crime committed by a child with a disability to the police. An impartial hearing officer can also place a student with a disability in an IAES if the school convinces the hearing officer that it is dangerous for the student to remain in the present placement. The IAES must permit the child to continue to participate in the general curriculum and to receive the services specified in the IEP. The school must perform a functional behavioral assessment and develop a behavioral intervention plan within ten days of the IAES placement.

If problematic behavior is found not to be a manifestation of a student's disability, the student may be subjected to the same disciplinary procedures, including long-term suspension, as non-disabled students. However, students with disabilities must always continue to receive a FAPE. This means that school districts must provide home tutors or other alternative arrangements that offer a meaningful opportunity for educational benefit to students with disabilities excluded from school for any reason. In-school suspensions must also provide a meaningful opportunity to benefit.

Dispute Resolution

Where a school district and a student invoking the *IDEA* fail to agree on eligibility or the special education services required, the law provides for detailed procedures, including litigation, to help resolve the dispute. But who can utilize these procedures? Interestingly, the Supreme Court has ruled that, in addition to the rights flowing to students themselves, the *IDEA* affords parents independent rights. This means that parents of students with disabilities can invoke the law's procedural protections, and can proceed *pro se* (without the assistance of an attorney), even if the case ultimately reaches federal court.[120]

Any substantive or procedural dispute between parents and school over any aspect of the *IDEA* is subject to mediation if both sides agree to **mediation**. Mediation must be confidential, at no cost to the parents, and conducted by a knowledgeable individual chosen from a state-maintained list. If mediation is not desired or fails to produce an agreement, either side can request a hearing before an impartial hearing officer. Prior to the hearing, the district must convene a **resolution session** with the parents and others designated in the law in an attempt to reach agreement. If the resolution session does not culminate in an agreement, the impartial hearing commences. The law does not specify the level of expertise that the hearing officer must possess, but "impartial" means that the hearing officer must not be a regular employee of the district or directly involved in the care of the child. Parents may demand a hearing to insist that their child be evaluated; to protest the process or outcome of an evaluation or IEP meeting; to challenge the adequacy of special education, related services, or other aspects of the program provided; to object to changes of placement or disciplinary actions; or to claim that their procedural rights as parents have been violated.

A school district may also initiate a hearing if the district believes that parents are preventing a child with a disability from receiving an appropriate education except that a school district may not initiate a hearing to contest parental refusal of an initial placement in special education. Either parents or school district may appeal an adverse decision by a hearing officer to a designated state agency (if the state has opted to include such an agency in its administrative structure) and ultimately to a court. Courts will generally not consider complaints that have not exhausted the administrative hearing process. Violation of the procedural requirements of *IDEA* does not automatically mean that a child has been denied a FAPE. Only procedural inadequacies which result in the loss of educational opportunity are sufficient to constitute a violation of *IDEA*. An error such as missing a deadline or failure to include someone on the IEP team may in one case amount to a violation of *IDEA* and in another case, because of the circumstances, be viewed as harmless.[121]

The Supreme Court has ruled that, in *IDEA* impartial hearings, the party "seeking relief" bears the burden of proof. Parents requesting a hearing to challenge their child's IEP would bear the burden of showing that the school's program is not appropriate.[122] However, some states have adopted legislation placing the burden of proof on the school district except in cases when parents want the district to pay for placement in a private school.[123] The situation changes when a case is appealed to a court. In *Rowley*, the Supreme Court warned that the federal courts lack expertise in the area of special education and therefore ought to give due weight to the decision of the experts. Courts have interpreted this comment to mean that the burden of proof is borne by the party who seeks to challenge an impartial hearing officer's ruling,[124] but a minority of courts have held that the school district must bear the burden of proof, or, in placement disputes, that the party proposing the more restrictive environment bear the burden.[125]

---

120 Winkelman v. Parma City School District, 550 U.S. 516 (2007).
121 R.B. *ex rel.* F.B. v. Napa Valley Unified Sch. Dist., 496 F.3d 932 (9th Cir. 2007); W.G. v. Bd. of Trustees of Target Range Sch. Dist. No. 23, 960 F.2d 1479 (9th Cir. 1992).
122 Schaffer v. Weast, 546 U.S. 49 (2005).
123 N.Y. EDUC. LAW § 4404 (1)(c); MINN. STAT. ANN. § 125A.091.
124 Walczak v. Fla. Union Free Sch. Dist., 142 F.3d 119 (2d Cir. 1998); Fort Zumwalt Sch. Dist. v. Clynes, 119 F.3d 607 (8th Cir. 1997); Clyde K. v. Puyallup Sch. Dist., 35 F.3d 1396 (9th Cir. 1994); Roland M. v. Concord Sch. Comm., 910 F.2d 983 (1st Cir. 1990); Kerkam v. McKenzie, 862 F.2d 884 (D.C. Cir. 1988); Spielberg v. Henrico County Pub. Sch., 853 F.2d 256 (4th Cir. 1988).
125 Oberti v. Bd. of Educ. of Clementon Sch. Dist., 995 F.2d 1204 (3d Cir. 1993); Lascari v. Bd. of Educ. of Ramapo Indian Hills, 560 A.2d 1180 (N.J. 1989).

If parents prevail at an administrative hearing, the school district must take whatever action the hearing officer or state agency prescribes. Parents who prevail in a court case may be granted declaratory and injunctive relief—judicial orders to do what the law requires. Courts may also order remedial action such as an extended school year as a remedy for a school's failure to provide an appropriate education to a child with a disability.[126]

In addition, parents may be reimbursed for expenses incurred in providing the necessary special education or related service.[127] Parents who successfully sue a school district in court for violation of the *IDEA* may be awarded reimbursement of their attorneys' fees, but not if the parents represent themselves,[128] and not if the victory stems from an out-of-court settlement which has not been signed by a judge or impartial hearing officer.[129] Fees for the services of expert witnesses are not available in *IDEA* cases,[130] but they are in Section 504 cases.[131] Compensatory and punitive damages are not available under *IDEA*;[132] and most courts have concluded that Section 1983 cannot be used to recover damages for violations of *IDEA*.[133] The Second Circuit does allow for such damages, but only when there has been a complete denial of an administrative remedy, such as a failure to hold an impartial hearing.[134]

The *Every Student Succeeds Act* and Students with Disabilities

As we saw in Chapter 3, the *ESSA* significantly relaxed the *No Child Left Behind* Act (*NCLB*) standards requiring federal accountability for student outcomes. Under the *ESSA*, states are allowed to develop and submit their own benchmarks for such outcomes. This decentralization of authority has had major consequences for students with disabilities. For example, the *NCLB* required that special education teachers be "highly qualified," and the *IDEA* was amended to track that requirement. Under *ESSA*, however, that requirement was purged from both laws.

Although the states now have primary responsibility for advancing accountability, a few federal requirements remain. For example, if a state wishes to use an alternate assessment for students with significant cognitive disabilities, the *ESSA* sets a cap of one percent. Note that this cap is measured against all students in the state, not just students with disabilities. In other words, no more than one percent of all students tested can be offered an alternate assessment (which logically would allow roughly ten percent of students with disabilities to take such tests, depending on the classification rate in a given state).

---

126 Jefferson County Bd. of Educ. v. Breen, 853 F.2d 853 (11th Cir. 1988); Miener v. Missouri, 800 F.2d 749 (8th Cir. 1986); *but see* Alexopulos v. San Francisco Unified Sch. Dist., 817 F.2d 551 (9th Cir. 1987).

127 Hurry v. Jones, 734 F.2d 879 (1st Cir. 1984); Burr v. Ambach, 863 F.2d 1071 (2d Cir. 1988).

128 Woodside v. The Sch. Dist. of Philadelphia Bd. of Educ., 248 F.3d 129 (3d Cir. 2001); Doe v. Bd. of Educ. of Baltimore County, 165 F.3d 260 (4th Cir. 1998).

129 Buckhannon Bd. & Care Home, Inc. v. W.Va. Dep't of Health & Human Res. 532 U.S. 598 (2001); Smith v. Fitchburg Pub. Schs., 401 F.3d 16 (1st Cir. 2005); A.R. *ex rel.* R.V. v. New York City Dept. of Educ. 407 F.3d 65 (2d Cir. 2005).

130 Arlington Central Sch. Dist. Bd. of Educ. v. Murphy, 548 U.S. 291 (2006).

131 L.T. *ex rel.* B.T. v. Mansfield Twp. Sch. Dist., 2009 U.S. Dist. LEXIS 21737 (D.N.J. Mar. 17, 2009).

132 Ortega v. Bibb County Sch. Dist., 397 F.3d 1321 (11th Cir. 2005).

133 A.W. v. Jersey City Pub. Sch., 486 F.3d 791 (3d Cir. 2007), *abrogating* W.B. v. Matula, 67 F.3d 484 (3d Cir. 1995); *see also* Padilla v. Sch. Dist. No. 1, 233 F.3d 1268 (10th Cir. 2000); Sellers v. Sch. Bd. of Manassas, 141 F.3d 524 (4th Cir. 1998).

134 Polera v. Board of Education of the Newburgh Enlarged City Sch. Dist., 288 F.3d 478 (2d Cir. 2002); Streck v. Board of Educ. of East Greenbush Sch. Dist., 280 Fed. Appx. 66 (2d Cir. 2008); *see also* A. *ex rel.* A. v. Hartford Bd. of Educ., 976 F. Supp. 2d 164 (D. Conn. 2013).

Summary

This chapter considered an array of disabilities requiring educational supports and services exceeding what most students typically receive. In all cases, differential treatment of students in public schools must meet the requirements of the **Equal Protection Clause**. It must at minimum be rationally related to a legitimate state goal. Undoubtedly, classifications based on a student's disability status do meet this requirement.

In addition, federal statutes and, arguably, the Equal Protection Clause as well, require that students with disabilities receive an education from which they may reasonably be expected to benefit. The education of students with disabilities is regulated by four statutes: the *Rehabilitation Act* of 1973 (Section 504), the *Americans with Disabilities Act* (ADA), the *Individuals with Disabilities Education Act* (IDEA), and to a lesser extent by the *Every Student Succeeds Act* (ESSA). The first two laws prohibit discrimination on the basis of disability, while the IDEA makes federal money available to states and districts that follow certain guidelines. The ESSA emphasizes achievement goals for students with disabilities, although it allows states substantial leeway in setting those goals.

The purpose of these laws is to provide children with disabilities a **free appropriate public education** (FAPE) designed to meet their individual educational needs. School districts must seek out children with disabilities within their jurisdiction; provide each with a non-discriminatory, multidisciplinary evaluation of strengths and weaknesses; develop in accordance with each student's evaluation an **individualized educational program** (IEP) consisting of special education and related services; and provide services in the **least restrictive environment** (LRE). Students with disabilities must be educated in a manner designed to meet measurable goals. Throughout the process, there must be parental participation and the observance of certain procedural safeguards.

9 Public School Funding

The federal government, state governments, county and other intermediate units of government, municipal governments, and local school boards all contribute to the funding of public education. Money is collected through a variety of mechanisms including federal and state income taxes, state lotteries, sales and property taxes, and bonds. Money is in turn distributed from higher levels of government to local school boards in various ways including **categorical grants** (money given for a specific program or purpose), **block grants** (money that may be utilized for any of a number of specified purposes), **general state aid** (money that can be used for any legal purpose), state reimbursement for local expenditures, direct state provision of services, and transfers from municipal governments to local school boards. Local school boards themselves, in accordance with state law, must implement their own taxing authority. In addition, they must establish management systems for handling the money they have raised or received from other units of government. A system this complex and involving large amounts of public funds invariably raises many legal issues. These issues can be divided into two categories:

1. **Pure finance issues** concern taxation and the utilization of funds for education generally. Litigation in this category has dealt with property tax assessments and exemptions; procedures for imposing a tax or adopting a budget; disposition of assets and liabilities when school district boundaries are altered or dissolved; school accounting procedures; administration of school funds; insurance, sale, and disposition of school property; the issuance and sale of bonds; limits on indebtedness; and procedures for bidding on contracts.
2. **Educational equity and adequacy** concern constitutional and statutory mandates for (a) the provision of services; and (b) equality of opportunity. Litigation in this category has challenged inter-district and intra-district disparities in per pupil expenditures; fees charged for tuition, books, and extracurricular activities; the authority of local school boards to spend money for particular purposes; and the overall quality of education provided in a school, school district, or state.

This chapter focuses on finance issues of direct relevance to educational policy and practice. Most fall into the category of educational equity and adequacy, but some of the cases presented also touch on questions of pure finance. We begin with an overview of school finance principles.

School Funding: A Legal Perspective

The starting point for understanding the legal framework of educational finance is that there is no federal constitutional right to an education. The Constitution imposes no obligation on the federal government or state governments to operate a system of public education or to assist parents in financing private education. Thus, any governmental effort to establish a system of public schools is, from the federal perspective, voluntary. However, once government does undertake to provide a system of public schools, its effort must conform to constitutional requirements.

As we noted in Chapter 1, the federal government possesses only those powers delegated to it under the Constitution. There is no express delegation of authority, and hence no *duty* for Congress to provide funding for public education. May it spend money on schools? Historically, this has been a matter of controversy.

Though Congress has provided some assistance to education since the Northwest Ordinance of 1787, its constitutional authority to do so was not firmly established until 1936. In *United States v. Butler*,[1] the Supreme Court decided that Article I, Section 8, the General Welfare Clause, gave Congress the power to tax and spend for activities not specifically mentioned in the Constitution. Thus, the General Welfare Clause justifies the many federal grant programs Congress has authorized for elementary and secondary schools. In total, these grants amount to about eight percent of the funds expended for K–12 education.[2] As discussed in previous chapters, Congress exercises considerable influence over local schools through the conditions and accountability mechanisms attached to federal funds.

The most extensive of the federal grant programs in terms of both the funds provided and the requirements attached are the **Individuals with Disabilities Education Act** (see Chapter 8) and the **Every Student Succeeds Act** (ESSA) (see Chapter 3). The ESSA affects educational funding in several ways. First, it allocates federal funds to the districts and schools with the highest rates of poverty. Second, it continues the "maintenance of effort" requirement found in earlier iterations of the federal law. Under this provision, to receive their full allotment of federal monies, school districts cannot reduce their non-federal expenditures by more than ten percent from the previous year. This requirement aims to ensure that federal funding supplements, rather than supplants, local spending on education.[3]

Where do state governments obtain the authority to tax and spend for educational purposes? The answer begins with the **Tenth Amendment** to the Constitution: "The powers not delegated to the United States by the Constitution, nor prohibited by it to the States, are reserved to the States respectively, or to the people." Because power over education is not specifically delegated to the federal government, education is one of the powers reserved to the states. Thus, states have inherent power to tax and spend for education, if they so choose. As we observed in Chapter 1, the people of all states, through their state constitutions, have in turn required their legislatures to exercise this power.[4]

Although some state constitutions make brief mention of local school districts, most leave it entirely to the legislature to decide whether the state will provide funds for education directly to parents, operate schools itself, or delegate this authority to local school boards. In any case, all states except Hawaii have chosen to create local school districts as the primary mechanism for fulfilling their educational duties. Having chosen this option, state legislatures must then determine how local school districts are to be funded. For historical and political reasons, most states have a multi-faceted finance system involving the following features:

1. A statewide system of taxation, usually including sales and income taxes, for general revenue, some of which is used to fund schools. Some states also have specialized mechanisms for raising money for education (including lotteries).

2. A plan for the distribution of state funds to local school districts. These plans may include general financial aid distributed through formulas adopted by the legislature, grant and categorical aid programs, and reimbursement for the provision of state-mandated services.

---

1 297 U.S. 1 (1936).
2 This figure includes federal spending for such programs as Head Start and the federal free-and-reduced lunch program. See www2.ed.gov/about/overview/fed/role.html (last visited February 22, 2019).
3 See 20 USCA § 6321 and 20 USCA § 7901.
4 Tyll Van Geel, Authority To Control The School Program (1976).

3. Delegation to local government units, such as city councils, of the authority and duty to tax for education with the money raised to be turned over to local school boards.
4. Delegation to local school boards of the authority to tax and spend on behalf of their local schools, usually through local property taxes.
5. Delegation of the authority to local school boards to borrow money, typically by issuing bonds, for construction projects.

Any authority local school boards enjoy to levy taxes for their schools is delegated by the state legislature. Any taxation by a local board must be based on expressly granted or implied authority and must conform to that authority.[5] In addition to the authority to tax, school boards may have a duty to tax for certain educational purposes. This duty can and must be exercised even against the wishes of the taxpayers.[6] Each state also has a detailed set of statutory requirements controlling the raising, management, allocation, and expenditure of money by local boards.

In recent years, a number of new developments have shaped state and local school finance systems. First, cash-strapped school districts are now engaging in a wide range of commercial activities to supplement declining property tax revenues.[7] Examples include exclusive marketing agreements with soft drink and food service companies, the sale of "naming rights" for sports fields and other facilities, and even the sale of advertising space on school buses.[8] Initially, the authority of school districts to engage in these kinds of activities was disputed in a number of states.[9] Second, particularly in more affluent districts, parents have sometimes established **private educational foundations** to offset program cuts caused by a shortfall in public funds.[10] Such private expenditures are generally legal, as long as the parents do not seek to impose conditions upon districts in exchange for the private monies.

In the 44 states that permit them, along with the District of Columbia, state and local governments must provide some funding for **charter schools**. Legal disputes have arisen regarding the allocation of funds to charter schools. Because charter schools are often viewed as competing with traditional public schools for scarce dollars, and because charter schools sometimes have significant capacity to raise private funds, charter schools often receive *lower* per pupil funding and *lower* funding for capital expenditures than do traditional public schools.[11] In New Jersey, several charter school students challenged inequitable funding for charter schools on equal protection grounds, but the courts rejected this challenge, citing the need to ensure adequate funding for traditional public schools.[12] The argument that charter schools unfairly *deprive* traditional schools of funding has also been raised. In *Araujo v. Bryant*,[13] a group of parents in Mississippi unsuccessfully challenged funding mechanisms for charter schools under their state constitution.

---

5   Manges v. Freer Indep. Sch. Dist., 653 S.W.2d 553 (Tex. App. 1983), *rev'd on other grounds*, 677 S.W.2d 488 (Tex. 1984).
6   State v. L. H. Freeman et al., Bd. of Comm'rs of Elk County, 58 P.959 (Kan. 1899).
7   ALEX MOLNAR, GIVING KIDS THE BUSINESS: THE COMMERCIALIZATION OF AMERICA'S SCHOOLS (2018).
8   J.C. Blokhuis, *Channel One: When Private Interests and the Public Interest Collide*, 45(2) AMERICAN EDUCATIONAL RESEARCH JOURNAL 343–363 (2008); C. Newsome, *Pay attention: A survey and analysis of the legal battle over the integration of forced television advertising into the public school curriculum*, 24(1) RUTGERS LAW JOURNAL 281–320 (1992).
9   North Carolina v. Whittle Communications, 402 S.E.2d 556 (N.C. 1991); New Jersey Education Association et al. v. Trenton Board of Education and Whittle Communications, 92 N.J.A.R.2d (EDU) 484 (1992); Dawson v. East Side Union High School District, 28 Cal. App. 4th 998 (1994).
10 Linda Saslow, *From Educators, Caution on Parent Fund-Raisers and Foundations*, NEW YORK TIMES (New York edition), March 1, 2009, at LI5.
11 Jeanette M. Curtis, *A Fighting Chance: Inequities in Charter School Funding and Strategies for Achieving Equal Access to Public School Funds*, 55 How. L.J. 1057 (2012).
12 J.D. *ex rel.* Scipio-Derrick v. Davy, 2 A.3d 387 (N.J. Super. Ct. App. Div. 2010).
13 283 So. 3d 73 (Miss. 2019).

In sum, public school funding operates in conjunction with a complex school governance system comprising 50 separate state systems of education. With the exception of Hawaii, these systems rely on local school districts with significant authority to raise and spend money. State legislatures supplement these local funds through general aid allocated on the basis of complex formulas. Local school districts also receive federal financial assistance, mostly in the form of categorical aid and block grants. This complex system has resulted in significant inter-state and, in most states, inter-district disparities in per pupil funding. Federal financial assistance does nothing to equalize per pupil funding from state to state. In most states, inter-district disparities result from heavy reliance on money raised by local school districts through property taxes. Further disparities have arisen regarding funding for charter schools vis-à-vis traditional public schools. State aid generally has only a modest equalizing effect on per pupil expenditures.

The Constitution and School Funding

In contrast with the many nations in which education funding is centralized, the American system of federalism leads to a largely decentralized system for funding education. The Constitution does not require the states to adopt the same educational policies. Nor does it require the federal government to counteract the often significant inter-state inequalities in the funding of education. The Equal Protection Clause is not concerned with inter-state inequalities or with anything the federal government does. Rather, the clause addresses only state action and intra-state inequalities (see Chapter 7). Hence, unless Congress decides to address inter-state inequalities or the states themselves voluntarily seek to adopt uniform educational finance policies, inter-state differences in per pupil expenditures will remain.

By virtue of Article VI of the Constitution (the "**Supremacy Clause**"), state law and policy may not contradict federal law. Thus, in *Lawrence County v. Lead-Deadwood School District No. 40–1*,[14] the Supreme Court invalidated a state law directing local school boards to allocate certain federal funds according to state guidelines. The federal law granting the funds to local districts indicated that Congress intended them to be utilized at the discretion of the local board. Therefore, the state's attempt to control the funds was unconstitutional.

The most significant federal constitutional provisions affecting school finance are the First and Fourteenth Amendments. The implications of the First Amendment's religion clauses for state financing of education are discussed in Chapter 2. The Fourteenth Amendment's Equal Protection Clause prohibits intentional racial discrimination in taxation or the allocation of funds. Even under the old separate-but-equal standard, providing unequal educational services on the basis of race was unconstitutional (see Chapter 7).

What about state systems of finance that result in inter-district inequalities in the amount of money spent per pupil? Is it consistent with the Equal Protection Clause that the amount of money spent by a state on a child's education depends on the school district in which the child happens to live?

In *San Antonio Independent School District v. Rodriguez*,[15] the Supreme Court considered this issue. The plaintiffs first sought to show that inter-district inequalities in per pupil spending were a direct result of state law and policy. Texas, like most states, had created local school districts with the authority to raise taxes for their own schools. The primary revenue-raising mechanism delegated to the districts was the property tax. Different school districts had within their borders widely varying amounts of property wealth per pupil. With a given tax rate, districts that were

---

14 469 U.S. 256 (1985).
15 411 U.S. 1 (1973).

rich in terms of per-pupil property value were able to raise more money than districts that were poor. Property-poor districts could attempt to match the money raised by property-rich districts by adopting much higher tax rates, but this was politically and economically impractical in most places. Thus, given that neither state nor federal aid compensated for differences in local property tax revenues, poor districts had significantly less to spend per pupil than wealthy districts.

Realizing that their chances of winning would be greatly enhanced if the Court employed **strict scrutiny** (see Chapter 7) in evaluating their claim, the plaintiffs argued that wealth-based discrimination, like race-based discrimination, ought to trigger the use of the strict scrutiny test. In support of this claim, they cited a body of cases that dealt with very different forms of wealth discrimination and argued that most of those disadvantaged by the system were members of minority groups. The plaintiffs then argued that education is a "fundamental interest" and that when public policy discriminates regarding a fundamental interest, the strict scrutiny test ought to be used. Though not expressly mentioned in the Constitution, education is a fundamental right, they argued, because of its social importance and because a good education is necessary to the effective exercise of other constitutional rights such as freedom of speech.

The plaintiffs then argued that the school finance system in Texas could not survive strict scrutiny. The plaintiffs rejected the state's claim that its finance system was necessary to achieve a compelling state interest, namely the provision of an effective, locally controlled, system of education. They argued that the state's funding plan did not minimize administrative difficulties, did not maintain effective or meaningful local control, and did not foster an equitable distribution of educational services. In sum, they claimed, the system did not serve any purpose other than "to make wealth the basis for determining the allocation of education dollars." Neither did the state's funding plan assure all students a minimum education "unless one defines that minimum as simply the lowest level of expenditure in the State."

To be permissible under the **Equal Protection Clause**, argued the plaintiffs, a state system of educational finance had to meet a standard known as "fiscal neutrality." Fiscal neutrality requires that the quality of education in a school district as measured by per pupil expenditures may not be a function of the district's wealth but only of the total wealth of the state. The plaintiffs went on to suggest three possible finance systems that satisfied fiscal neutrality while preserving local control of education. First, the state could take over the raising of money for education and distribute equal amounts per pupil to the local districts. Local districts would then have the discretion of using this money according to their educational priorities. Second, local district boundaries could be changed to ensure that each school district had the same property wealth per pupil.

Existing boundaries could be maintained, but the state could guarantee through a revised state aid formula that a given property tax rate would yield a specific amount of money regardless of a district's property values. This kind of system is known as **power equalization**. If a district raises less money per pupil than guaranteed by the aid formula, the state provides the balance. Districts would still be free to choose different tax rates, and there still would be inter-district inequalities in the amount of money spent per pupil; however, these differences would be determined not by inter-district differences in property wealth but only by the differences in the importance different districts placed on education.

Finally, the plaintiffs' argument rested on the premise that differences in spending resulted in meaningful disparities in services, program quality, and, ultimately, educational achievement. In their brief, they urged the Court not to restrict application of the Equal Protection Clause to instances of complete denial of educational services but to apply it to *relative* deprivations as well (emphasis added):

> To be sure, a complete denial of all educational opportunity is more compelling than a relative denial. But in view of the magnitude of the differences in the capacity of state-created school districts in Texas

to raise education dollars, and in light of the vast disparities in educational expenditures between districts, plaintiffs have surely been injured in a comparable way. A complete denial of all educational opportunity is not necessary to demonstrate an unconstitutional deprivation … *Can the State of Texas open its doors to the poor, compel their attendance … and then effectively deprive them of an equal educational opportunity because of their economic status?*

As the following excerpt shows, the Supreme Court answered the plaintiffs' question in the affirmative: *Relative* deprivations of education, at least those arising from the educational finance system in Texas, did not violate the Equal Protection Clause.

⚖️

SAN ANTONIO INDEPENDENT SCHOOL DISTRICT v. RODRIGUEZ
Supreme Court of the United States
411 U.S. I (1973)

MR. JUSTICE POWELL delivered the opinion of the Court.

I.

… We must decide, first, whether the Texas system of financing public education operates to the disadvantage of some suspect class or impinges upon a fundamental right explicitly or implicitly protected by the Constitution, thereby requiring strict judicial scrutiny. If so, the judgment of the District Court should be affirmed. If not, the Texas scheme must still be examined to determine whether it rationally furthers some legitimate, articulated state purpose and therefore does not constitute an invidious discrimination in violation of the Equal Protection Clause of the Fourteenth Amendment. …

II.

A.

The wealth discrimination discovered by the District Court in this case, and by several other courts that have recently struck down school-financing laws in other States, is quite unlike any of the forms of wealth discrimination heretofore reviewed by this Court. … The individuals, or groups of individuals, who constituted the class discriminated against in our prior cases shared two distinguishing characteristics: because of their impecunity they were completely unable to pay for some desired benefit, and as a consequence, they sustained an absolute deprivation of a meaningful opportunity to enjoy that benefit. …

Even a cursory examination, however, demonstrates that neither of the two distinguishing characteristics of wealth classifications can be found here. First, in support of their charge that the system discriminates against the "poor," appellees have made no effort to demonstrate that it operates to the peculiar disadvantage of any class fairly definable as indigent, or as composed of persons whose incomes are beneath any designated poverty level. Indeed, there is reason to believe that the poorest families are not necessarily clustered in the poorest property districts. A recent and exhaustive study of school districts in Connecticut concluded that… the poor were clustered around commercial and industrial areas—those same areas that provide the most attractive sources of property tax income for school districts. Whether a similar pattern would be discovered in Texas is not known, but there is no basis on the record in this case for assuming that the poorest people—defined by reference to any level of absolute impecunity—are concentrated in the poorest districts.

Second, neither appellees nor the District Court addressed the fact that, unlike each of the foregoing cases, lack of personal resources has not occasioned an absolute deprivation of the desired benefit. The argument here is not that the children in districts having relatively low assessable property values are receiving no public education; rather, it is that they are receiving a poorer quality education than that available to children in districts having more assessable wealth. Apart from the unsettled and disputed question whether the quality of education may be determined by the amount of money expended for it, a sufficient answer to appellees' argument is that, at least where wealth is involved, the Equal Protection Clause does not require absolute equality or precisely equal advantages.

Nor, indeed, in view of the infinite variables affecting the educational process, can any system assure equal quality of education except in the most relative sense. Texas asserts that the Minimum Foundation Program provides an "adequate" education for all children in the State. By providing 12 years of free public-school education, and by assuring teachers, books, transportation, and operating funds, the Texas Legislature has endeavored to "guarantee, for the welfare of the state as a whole, that all people shall have at least an adequate program of education. This is what is meant by 'A Minimum Foundation Program of Education.'" The State repeatedly asserted in its briefs in this Court that it has fulfilled this desire and that it now assures "every child in every school district an adequate education." No proof was offered at trial persuasively discrediting or refuting the State's assertion.

For these two reasons—the absence of any evidence that the financing system discriminates against any definable category of "poor" people or that it results in the absolute deprivation of education—the disadvantaged class is not susceptible of identification in traditional terms …

This brings us, then, to the third way in which the classification scheme might be defined—district wealth discrimination. Since the only correlation indicated by the evidence is between district property wealth and expenditures, it may be argued that discrimination might be found without regard to the individual income characteristics of district residents. Assuming a perfect correlation between district property wealth and expenditures from top to bottom, the disadvantaged class might be viewed as encompassing every child in every district except the district that has the most assessable wealth and spends the most on education. …

However described, it is clear that appellees' suit asks this Court to extend its most exacting scrutiny to review a system that allegedly discriminates against a large, diverse, and amorphous class, unified only by the common factor of residence in districts that happen to have less taxable wealth than other districts. The system of alleged discrimination and the class it defines have none of the traditional indicia of suspectness: the class is not saddled with such disabilities, or subjected to such a history of purposeful unequal treatment, or relegated to such a position of political powerlessness as to command extraordinary protection from the majoritarian political process.

We thus conclude that the Texas system does not operate to the peculiar disadvantage of any suspect class. But in recognition of the fact that this Court has never heretofore held that wealth discrimination alone provides an adequate basis for invoking strict scrutiny, appellees have not relied solely on this contention. They also assert that the State's system impermissibly interferes with the exercise of a "fundamental" right and that accordingly the prior decisions of this Court require the application of the strict standard of judicial review. It is this question—whether education is a fundamental right, in the sense that it is among the rights and liberties protected by the Constitution—which has so consumed the attention of courts and commentators in recent years.

B.

… Nothing this Court holds today in any way detracts from our historic dedication to public education. We are in complete agreement with the conclusion of the three-judge panel below that "the grave significance of education both to the individual and to our society" cannot be doubted. But the importance of a service performed by the State does not determine whether it must be regarded as fundamental for purposes of examination under the Equal Protection Clause …

It is not the province of this Court to create substantive constitutional rights in the name of guaranteeing equal protection of the laws. Thus, the key to discovering whether education is "fundamental" is not to be found in comparisons of the relative societal significance of education as opposed to subsistence or housing. Nor is it to be found by weighing whether education is as important as the right to travel. Rather, the answer lies in assessing whether there is a right to education explicitly or implicitly guaranteed by the Constitution.

Education, of course, is not among the rights afforded explicit protection under our Federal Constitution. Nor do we find any basis for saying it is implicitly so protected. As we have said, the undisputed importance of education will not alone cause this Court to depart from the usual standard for reviewing a State's social and economic legislation. It is appellees' contention, however, that education is distinguishable from other services and benefits provided by the State because it bears a peculiarly close relationship to other rights and liberties accorded protection under the Constitution. Specifically, they insist that education is itself a fundamental personal right because it is essential to the effective exercise of First Amendment freedoms and to intelligent utilization of the right to vote. In asserting a nexus between speech and education, appellees urge that the right to speak is meaningless unless the speaker is capable of articulating his thoughts intelligently and persuasively. The "marketplace of ideas" is an empty forum for those lacking basic communicative tools. Likewise, they argue that the corollary right to receive information becomes little more than a hollow privilege when the recipient has not been taught to read, assimilate, and utilize available knowledge.

A similar line of reasoning is pursued with respect to the right to vote. Exercise of the franchise, it is contended, cannot be divorced from the educational foundation of the voter. The electoral process, if reality is to conform to the democratic ideal, depends on an informed electorate: a voter cannot cast his ballot intelligently unless his reading skills and thought processes have been adequately developed.

We need not dispute any of these propositions. The Court has long afforded zealous protection against unjustifiable governmental interference with the individual's rights to speak and to vote. Yet we have never presumed to possess either the ability or the authority to guarantee to the citizenry the most effective speech or the most informed electoral choice. That these may be desirable goals of a system of freedom of expression and of a representative form of government is not to be doubted. These are indeed goals to be pursued by a people whose thoughts and beliefs are freed from governmental interference. But they are not values to be implemented by judicial intrusion into otherwise legitimate state activities.

Even if it were conceded that some identifiable quantum of education is a constitutionally protected prerequisite to the meaningful exercise of either right, we have no indication that the present levels of educational expenditure in Texas provide an education that falls short. Whatever merit appellees' argument might have if a State's financing system occasioned an absolute denial of educational opportunities to any of its children, that argument provides no basis for finding an interference with fundamental rights where only relative differences in spending levels are involved and where—as is true in the present case—no charge fairly could be made that the system fails to provide each child with an opportunity to acquire the basic minimal skills necessary for the enjoyment of the rights of speech and of full participation in the political process.

Furthermore, the logical limitations on appellees' nexus theory are difficult to perceive. How, for instance, is education to be distinguished from the significant personal interests in the basics of decent food and shelter? Empirical examination might well buttress an assumption that the ill-fed, ill-clothed, and ill-housed are among the most ineffective participants in the political process, and that they derive the least enjoyment from the benefits of the First Amendment ...

Every step leading to the establishment of the system Texas utilizes today—including the decisions permitting localities to tax and expend locally, and creating and continuously expanding state aid—was implemented in an effort to extend public education and to improve its quality. Of course, every reform that benefits some more than others may be criticized for what it fails to accomplish. But we think it plain that, in substance, the thrust of the Texas system is affirmative and reformatory and, therefore, should be scrutinized under judicial principles sensitive to the nature of the State's efforts and to the rights reserved to the States under the Constitution ...

C.

We need not rest our decision, however, solely on the inappropriateness of the strict scrutiny test. A century of Supreme Court adjudication under the Equal Protection Clause affirmatively supports the application of the traditional standard of review, which requires only that the State's system be shown to bear some rational relationship to legitimate state purposes. This case represents far more than a challenge to the manner in which Texas provides for the education of its children. We have here nothing less than a direct attack on the way in which Texas has chosen to raise and disburse state and local tax revenues. We are asked to condemn the State's judgment in conferring on political subdivisions the power to tax local property to supply revenues for local interests. In so doing, appellees would have the Court intrude in an area in which it has traditionally deferred to state legislatures. This Court has often admonished against such interferences with the State's fiscal policies under the Equal Protection Clause ...

In such a complex arena in which no perfect alternatives exist, the Court does well not to impose too rigorous a standard of scrutiny lest all local fiscal schemes become subjects of criticism under the Equal Protection Clause.

In addition to matters of fiscal policy, this case also involves the most persistent and difficult questions of educational policy, another area in which this Court's lack of specialized knowledge and experience counsels against premature interference with the informed judgments made at the state and local levels. Education, perhaps even more than welfare assistance, presents a myriad of "intractable economic, social, and even philosophical problems." ... Indeed, one of the major sources of controversy concerns the extent to which there is a demonstrable correlation between educational expenditures and the quality of education—an assumed correlation underlying virtually every legal conclusion drawn by the District Court in this case. Related to the questioned relationship between cost and quality is the equally unsettled controversy as to the proper goals of a system of public education. And the question regarding the most effective relationship between state boards of education and local school boards, in terms of their respective responsibilities and degrees of control, is now undergoing searching re-examination ...

The foregoing considerations buttress our conclusion that Texas' system of public school finance is an inappropriate candidate for strict judicial scrutiny. These same considerations are relevant to the determination whether that system, with its conceded imperfections, nevertheless bears some rational relationship to a legitimate state purpose. It is to this question that we next turn our attention. ...

III.

Because of differences in expenditure levels occasioned by disparities in property tax income, appellees claim that children in less affluent districts have been made the subject of invidious discrimination. The District Court found that the State had failed even "to establish a reasonable basis" for a system that results in different levels of per-pupil expenditure. We disagree.

In its reliance on state as well as local resources, the Texas system is comparable to the systems employed in virtually every other State ... While assuring a basic education for every child in the State, it permits and encourages a large measure of participation in and control of each district's schools at the local level ... No area of social concern stands to profit more from a multiplicity of viewpoints and from a diversity of approaches than does public education.

Appellees do not question the propriety of Texas' dedication to local control of education. To the contrary, they attack the school-financing system precisely because, in their view, it does not provide the same level of local control and fiscal flexibility in all districts. Appellees suggest that local control could be preserved and promoted under other financing systems that resulted in more equality in educational expenditures. While it is no doubt true that reliance on local property taxation for school revenues provides less freedom of choice with respect to expenditures for some districts than for others, the existence of "some inequality" in the manner in which the State's rationale is achieved is not alone a sufficient basis for striking down the entire system. ...

Nor must the financing system fail because, as appellees suggest, other methods of satisfying the State's interest, which occasion "less drastic" disparities in expenditures, might be conceived. Only where state action impinges on the exercise of fundamental constitutional rights or liberties must it be found to have chosen the least restrictive alternative. It is also well to remember that even those districts that have reduced ability to make free decisions with respect to how much they spend on education still retain under the present system a large measure of authority as to how available funds will be allocated. They further enjoy the power to make numerous other decisions with respect to the operation of the schools. The people of Texas may be justified in believing that other systems of school financing, which place more of the financial responsibility in the hands of the State, will result in a comparable lessening of desired local autonomy. That is, they may believe that along with increased control of the purse strings at the state level will go increased control over local policies.

Appellees further urge that the Texas system is unconstitutionally arbitrary because it allows the availability of local taxable resources to turn on "happenstance." They see no justification for a system that allows, as they contend, the quality of education to fluctuate on the basis of the fortuitous positioning of the boundary lines of political subdivisions and the location of valuable commercial and industrial property. But any scheme of local taxation—indeed the very existence of identifiable local government units—requires the establishment of jurisdictional boundaries that are inevitably arbitrary. It is equally inevitable that some localities are going to be blessed with more taxable assets than others. Nor is local wealth a static quantity. Changes in the level of taxable wealth within any district may result from any number of events, some of which local residents can and do influence. For instance, commercial and industrial enterprises may be encouraged to locate within a district by various actions—public and private.

Moreover, if local taxation for local expenditures were an unconstitutional method of providing for education then it might be an equally impermissible means of providing other necessary services customarily financed largely from local property taxes, including local police and fire protection, public health and hospitals, and public utility facilities of various kinds ...

In sum, to the extent that the Texas system of school financing results in unequal expenditures between children who happen to reside in different districts, we cannot say that such disparities are the product of a system that is so irrational as to be invidiously discriminatory ...

IV.

[A] cautionary postscript seems appropriate. It cannot be questioned that the constitutional judgment reached by the District Court and approved by our dissenting Brothers today would occasion in Texas and elsewhere an unprecedented upheaval in public education. Some commentators have concluded that, whatever the contours of the alternative financing programs that might be devised and approved, the result could not avoid being a beneficial one. But just as there is nothing simple about the constitutional issues involved in these cases, there is nothing simple or certain about predicting the consequences of massive change in the financing and control of public education ...

The complexity of these problems is demonstrated by the lack of consensus with respect to whether it may be said with any assurance that the poor, the racial minorities, or the children in overburdened core-city school districts would be benefited by abrogation of traditional modes of financing education.

Unless there is to be a substantial increase in state expenditures on education across the board—an event the likelihood of which is open to considerable question—these groups stand to realize gains in terms of increased per-pupil expenditures only if they reside in districts that presently spend at relatively low levels, i.e., in those districts that would benefit from the redistribution of existing resources. Yet, recent studies have indicated that the poorest families are not invariably clustered in the most impecunious school districts. Nor does it now appear that there is any more than a random chance that racial minorities are concentrated in property-poor districts. Additionally, several research projects have concluded that any financing alternative designed to achieve a greater equality of expenditures is likely to lead to higher taxation and lower educational expenditures in the major urban centers, a result that would exacerbate rather than ameliorate existing conditions in those areas.

These practical considerations, of course, play no role in the adjudication of the constitutional issues presented here. But they serve to highlight the wisdom of the traditional limitations on this Court's function ... We hardly need add that this Court's action today is not to be viewed as placing its judicial imprimatur on the status quo. The need is apparent for reform in tax systems which may well have relied too long and too heavily on the local property tax. And certainly innovative thinking as to public education, its methods, and its funding is necessary to assure both a higher level of quality and greater uniformity of opportunity. These matters merit the continued attention of the scholars who already have contributed much by their challenges. But the ultimate solutions must come from the lawmakers and from the democratic pressures of those who elect them. Reversed.

As a practical matter, the *Rodriguez* decision ended the first wave of educational finance reform litigation. Reformers had hoped to use the federal courts to eliminate the significant disparities in per pupil funding that existed in almost every state. But, after *Rodriguez*, litigation to force states to more equitably redesign their educational finance systems could only be pursued in state courts.

The next Supreme Court case concerning educational finance, *Plyler v. Doe*,[16] dealt with a Texas law that totally excluded undocumented immigrant children from obtaining a free public education. Although undocumented immigrant status is not a suspect classification, the Court found that total denial of education to this group of children violated the Equal Protection Clause.

---

16 457 U.S. 202 (1982).

However, the relationship of this decision to *Rodriguez* is a bit confusing. Although the *Rodriguez* Court suggested that an absolute denial of education would probably require the use of the strict scrutiny test, in *Plyler*, the Court said even an absolute denial did not call for strict scrutiny. Instead, the Court used a sort of middle-level test similar to the one used in gender discrimination cases. Nevertheless, even when applying a lower level of judicial scrutiny, the absolute deprivation of education could not be upheld.

The Court's next school finance decision involved a challenge to a Mississippi policy of distributing income from state-owned land only to school districts where the land was located. While the funding inequalities upheld in *Rodriguez* were a "necessary" adjunct of allowing meaningful local control over school funding, *Papasan v. Allain* raised a problem of "a state decision to divide state resources unequally among school districts."[17] The Court remanded the case to the lower courts to address the question of whether the state's policy of using income from these lands only in part of the state violated the Equal Protection Clause. Adding to our uncertainty about constitutional doctrine in this area, the Court in *Papasan* announced that neither *Rodriguez* nor *Plyler* "definitively settled the questions whether a minimally adequate education was a fundamental right" and whether a statute alleged to discriminatorily infringe that right should be accorded heightened equal protection review.

Two years later, in *Kadrmas v. Dickinson Public Schools*,[18] the Supreme Court considered the issue of whether a state scheme that permitted older "non-reorganized" school districts but not "reorganized" districts to charge a busing fee violated the Equal Protection Clause. Plaintiffs argued that the fee had the potential to result in a complete deprivation of education for children whose families were too poor to pay. Plaintiffs urged the Court to apply strict scrutiny or, at minimum, the "heightened" scrutiny used in *Plyler*. However, the Court saw the case as different from *Plyler*:

> Unlike the children in that case, Sarita Kadrmas has not been penalized by the government—for illegal conduct by her parents. On the contrary, Sarita was denied access to the school bus only because her parents would not agree to pay the same user fee charged to all other families that took advantage of the service. Nor do we see any reason to suppose that this user fee will "promot[e] the creation and perpetuation of a subclass of illiterates within our boundaries, surely adding to the problems and costs of unemployment, welfare, and crime."

Nor did the Court view the busing fee as amounting to a complete denial of education for any child. Paying the fee was not a prerequisite for attending school because children were free to come to school by means other than riding the school bus. It did not matter that for children living far from school, the school bus was the only practical alternative available. Having concluded that "the statute challenged in this case discriminates against no suspect class and interferes with no fundamental right," the Court applied the rational relation test to the claim that the busing fee was unconstitutional:

> Applying the appropriate test—under which a statute is upheld if it bears a rational relation to a legitimate government objective—we think it is quite clear that a State's decision to allow local school boards the option of charging patrons a user fee for bus service is constitutionally permissible. The Constitution does not require that such service be provided at all, and it is difficult to imagine why choosing to offer the service should entail a constitutional obligation to offer it for free. No one denies that encouraging local school districts to provide school bus service is a legitimate state purpose or that

---

17 478 U.S. 265 (1986).
18 487 U.S. 450 (1988).

such encouragement would be undermined by a rule requiring that general revenues be used to subsidize an optional service that will benefit a minority of the district's families. It is manifestly rational for the State to refrain from undermining its legitimate objective with such a rule.

The Court went on to consider the related claim that the statute violated the Equal Protection Clause because it permitted user fees for a bus service only in non-reorganized school districts. Employing the **rational basis** test, the Court concluded that the appellants had failed to demonstrate that the challenged statute was arbitrary and irrational. The Court accepted the state's justification for the statute, that it was designed to encourage school district reorganization:

> … [I]t is evident that the legislature could conceivably have believed that such a policy would serve the legitimate purpose of fulfilling the reasonable expectations of those residing in districts with free busing arrangements imposed by reorganization plans. Because this purpose could have no application to non-reorganized districts, the legislature could just as rationally conclude that those districts should have the option of imposing user fees on those who take advantage of the service they are offered.

In *Gary B. v. Snyder*,[19] students claimed the deplorable condition of public schools in Detroit deprived them of access to foundational literacy, in violation of their due process and equal protection rights under the Fourteenth Amendment and their "fundamental right" to a basic education. This bold legal theory was rejected by the district court. In a controversial and promptly vacated decision, the Sixth Circuit reinstated the students' fundamental right claim:[20]

> The recognition of a fundamental right is no small matter. This is particularly true when the right in question is something that the state must affirmatively provide. But just as this Court should not supplant the state's policy judgments with its own, neither can we shrink from our obligation to recognize a right when it is foundational to our system of self-governance. … Plaintiffs have a fundamental right to a basic minimum education, meaning one that can provide them with a foundational level of literacy.

After *Rodriguez*, *Plyler*, *Kadrmas*, and *Gary B.*, federal constitutional doctrine concerning the status of education may be summarized as follows: Education is not a fundamental right under the US Constitution. Neither inter-state nor intra-state inequalities in educational opportunities (unless based on intentional racial or gender discrimination) nor policies that create economic obstacles for children wishing to exercise their legal right to attend school violate the Equal Protection Clause. However, any state scheme intentionally resulting in a total denial of education to a defined group of children is likely unconstitutional.[21]

State Constitutions and School Finance

Following the failure of the plaintiffs in *Rodriguez*, reformers seeking judicial mandates for more equitable educational finance systems turned to state courts. There have been dozens of judicial proceedings involving the appellate courts of most states.[22] In many states, educational finance-reform

19 313 F. Supp. 3d 852 (E.D. Mich. 2018).
20 Gary B. v. Whitmer, 2020 U.S. App. LEXIS 13110 (6th Cir. Apr. 23, 2020); vacated, 2020 U.S. App. LEXIS 15989 (6th Cir. 2020).
21 *See* Craig v. Selma City Sch. Bd., 801 F. Supp. 585 (S.D. Ala. 1992).
22 For a regularly updated list of such decisions in each state, see NAT'L EDUC. ACCESS NETWORK, www.school-funding.info (last visited February 6, 2019).

litigation has resulted in major judicial decisions. Some of the cases have dragged on for decades. In about half the states, plaintiffs have succeeded in convincing the court to order the state legislature to change the educational finance system, but implementation and enforcement of these court orders has often proved challenging. In some states, reformers have won some cases and lost others. In some of the states where litigation failed, reformers, in some instances with judicial support, later convinced the legislature to change the system of educational finance even in the absence of a court order.

As of 2020, Hawaii, Mississippi, Nevada, and Utah are the only states never to have had a court decision addressing school finance equity under their state constitutions. Delaware is the most recent state to join the fray. In *Delawareans for Educational Opportunity v. Carney*,[23] the court refused to dismiss claims that the state's educational finance system had failed to meet the needs of "disadvantaged students."

Arguments challenging state systems of educational finance have taken a number of different forms. The main issue in a New Hampshire case was taxpayer equity. The state constitution permitted the legislature to "impose and levy proportional and reasonable assessments, rates, and taxes …" The state's main mechanism for funding education was a locally imposed property tax, and the tax rates in various school districts around the state varied significantly. The state's highest court found the taxing mechanism unconstitutional because it unreasonably placed a differential burden on taxpayers to carry out the responsibility of providing education throughout the state. Wrote the court,

> There is nothing fair or just about taxing a home or other real estate in one town at four times the rate that similar property is taxed in another town to fulfill the same purpose of meeting the State's educational duty.[24]

A number of other cases have similarly raised constitutional challenges to differing levels of taxation as part of a broad assault on a state educational finance system. A Kansas case challenged the state's system of locally set property tax rates on the basis of the "uniform laws" clause of the state constitution.[25] An early New York case unsuccessfully advanced a principle known as **municipal overburden**. Plaintiffs argued that the state finance system was inequitable to the students and taxpayers of urban areas because it did not account for the need for urban taxpayers to support a greater variety of public services, the need for urban schools to educate a disproportionate number of high-cost students, the higher costs in urban areas for educational goods and services, and the loss of revenues under attendance-based state aid formulas in urban areas because of high rates of student absenteeism.[26] Although the New York courts rejected this argument, concerns about municipal overburden were afforded credence by New Jersey courts.[27]

The earliest cases in the first wave of school finance litigation, including *Rodriguez*, relied on the Equal Protection clause. The second wave of cases were based on state equal protection clauses. The third wave of cases have relied primarily on education articles in state constitutions, equal protection clauses in state constitutions, or on both. The third wave's goals are to ensure not

23 199 A.3d 109 (Del. Ch. 2018).
24 Claremont Sch. Dist. v. Governor, 703 A.2d 1353 (N.H. 1997).
25 Mock v. Kansas, Case No. 91-CV-1009 (Shawnee County Dist. Ct., Kan. 1991).
26 Levittown Union Free Sch. Dist. v. Nyquist, 439 N.E.2d 359 (N.Y. 1982); *but see* Campaign for Fiscal Equity v. State, 655 N.E.2d 661 (N.Y. 1995), 801 N.E.2d 326 (N.Y. 2003) and 861 N.E.2d 50 (N.Y. 2006).
27 Abbott v. Burke, 575 A.2d 359 (N.J. 1990).

only equity in state finance systems but also adequacy by increasing the level of funding available to some or all of the school districts in the state.

Educational Equity

Second wave cases often parallel *Rodriguez* in arguing that under the state equal protection clause, it is unconstitutional for a state to maintain a funding system that provides higher per pupil funding in some districts. Such cases may also claim that the state equal protection clause prohibits a system that provides an "adequate" education to some children and an "inadequate" education to others.[28]

Plaintiffs fail in these cases (and also in adequacy cases) if the court rules (a) that decisions about how and at what level to fund education are solely a legislative matter, not subject to court review; (b) that for a court to address questions of education funding would violate the principle of separation of powers between the branches of state government; (c) that state education articles are so vague and ambiguous (requiring, for example, that the legislature provide for a "thorough and efficient" system of education) that no court can claim to determine specifically how they are to be applied; or (d) that the issue of educational adequacy is **non-justiciable**—that is, incapable of resolution by a court.[29]

Plaintiffs succeed in these cases if the court finds that education is a fundamental right under the state constitution, thereby requiring the use of strict scrutiny. However, a number of state courts have declined to view education as a fundamental right under the state constitution. The Georgia Supreme Court agreed with plaintiffs that education was "vital," but no more vital than police and fire protection, water, and public health services. None of these goods or services is a fundamental right that must be provided equally to all state residents. Applying the rational basis test, the court echoed *Rodriguez* in finding that the state's funding system, despite significant disparities in per pupil funding across districts, was rationally related to the legitimate purpose of promoting local control of education.[30]

However, even if education is not a fundamental state right, a state finance system may still violate the state equal protection clause if the funding disparities between rich and poor districts are completely irrational: "Even without deciding whether the right to a public education is fundamental," wrote the Arkansas Supreme Court, "we can find no constitutional basis for the present system, as it has no rational bearing on the educational needs of the districts."[31]

In one of the earliest educational finance reform cases, *Serrano v. Priest*, the California Supreme Court ruled that the state's children have a fundamental right to an education and that the state legislature had a duty to provide an equitable system of funding. A pre-*Rodriguez* decision later superseded by legislation,[32] *Serrano* is a link between the first and second waves of educational finance-reform litigation because it was based on both the federal and state Equal Protection Clauses.

---

28 *See* Jonathan Feldman, *Separation of Powers and Judicial Review of Positive Rights Claims: The Role of State Courts in an Era of Positive Government*, 24 Rutgers Law Journal 1057 (1993).

29 Coalition for Educ. Equity v. Heineman, 731 N.W.2d 164 (Neb. 2007); Comm. for Educ. Rights v. Edgar, 672 N.E.2d 1178 (Ill. 1996); City of Pawtucket v. Sundlun, 662 A.2d 40 (R.I. 1995); Oklahoma Education Association v. State *ex rel.* Oklahoma Legislature, 158 P.3d 1058 (Okla. 2007).

30 McDaniel v. Thomas, 285 S.E.2d 156 (Ga. 1981); *see also* Lujan v. Colo. State Bd. of Educ., 649 P.2d 1005 (Colo. 1982); Bd. of Educ. of Cincinnati v. Walter, 390 N.E.2d 813 (Ohio 1979).

31 Dupree v. Alma Sch. Dist. No. 30, 651 S.W.2d 90 (Ark. 1983).

32 Crawford v. Huntington Beach Union High Sch. Dist., 98 Cal. App. 4th 1275, 121 Cal. Rptr. 2d 96 (2002).

SERRANO v. PRIEST (SERRANO I)
Supreme Court of California
487 P.2d 1241 (1971)

RAYMOND L. SULLIVAN, Justice.

Plaintiffs, Los Angeles County public school children and their parents, filed a complaint that set forth two central causes of action. First, the plaintiffs alleged that California's system of finance relied heavily on local property taxes resulting in substantial disparities in the amount of money spent per pupil among the districts of the state. Districts with smaller tax bases were not able to spend as much money per pupil as districts with larger assessed valuations. These disparities, claimed the plaintiffs, meant that children attending the property-poorer districts received a substantially inferior education in violation of the equal protection clauses of both the U.S. and California constitutions. Second, the plaintiffs alleged that as a result of this financing scheme they were required to pay a higher tax rate than taxpayers in many other districts in order to obtain for their children a similar or inferior education.

The defendants demurred claiming that none of the claims stated facts sufficient to constitute a cause of action. The trial court sustained the demurrer and dismissed the complaint; the plaintiffs appealed. On appeal the California Supreme Court assumed the facts alleged by the plaintiffs were correct for purposes of deciding whether the facts as alleged were legally sufficient to establish a violation of the two equal protection clauses. The court observed that the plaintiffs had alleged that the finance system of the state, with its heavy reliance on the local property tax, resulted in differences in the amount of money spent per pupil and that these differences were not equalized by the state aid flowing to the districts. The state aid consisted of both a "flat grant" and "equalization aid" provided in inverse proportion to the property wealth of the district. Another separate program provided "supplemental aid" to subsidize particularly poor school districts that were willing to make an extra local tax effort. These three sources of state aid did mitigate the disparities among the districts, yet the plaintiffs alleged vast disparities in the money available still persisted among the districts. The range in expenditures went from $577.49 to $1,231.72 per pupil.

III.

[W]e now take up the chief contention underlying plaintiffs' complaint, namely that the California public school financing scheme violates the equal protection clause of the Fourteenth Amendment to the United States Constitution.

As recent decisions of this court have pointed out, the United States Supreme Court has employed a two-level test for measuring legislative classifications against the equal protection clause. "In the area of economic regulation, the high court has exercised restraint, investing legislation with a presumption of constitutionality and requiring merely that distinctions drawn by a challenged statute bear some rational relationship to a conceivable legitimate state purpose."

On the other hand, in cases involving "suspect classifications" or touching on "fundamental interests," the court has adopted an attitude of active and critical analysis, subjecting the classification to strict scrutiny. Under the strict standard applied in such cases, the state bears the burden of establishing not only that it has a compelling interest which justifies the law but that the distinctions drawn by the law are necessary to further its purpose.

A. Wealth as a Suspect Classification

In recent years, the United States Supreme Court has demonstrated a marked antipathy toward legislative classifications which discriminate on the basis of certain "suspect" personal characteristics. One factor which has repeatedly come under the close scrutiny of the high court is wealth. "Lines drawn on the basis of wealth or property, like those of race are traditionally disfavored." ...

Plaintiffs contend that the school financing system classifies on the basis of wealth. We find this proposition irrefutable ... [O]ver half of all educational revenue is raised locally by levying taxes on real property in the individual school districts. Above the foundation program minimum ($355 per elementary student and $488 per high school student), the wealth of a school district, as measured by its assessed valuation, is the major determinant of educational expenditures. Although the amount of money raised locally is also a function of the rate at which the residents of a district are willing to tax themselves, as a practical matter districts with small tax bases simply cannot levy taxes at a rate sufficient to produce the revenue that more affluent districts reap with minimal tax efforts. For example, Baldwin Park citizens, who paid a school tax of $5.48 per $100 of assessed valuation in 1968–1969, were able to spend less than half as much on education as Beverly Hills residents, who were taxed only $2.38 per $100 …

[D]efendants suggest that the wealth of a school district does not necessarily reflect the wealth of the families who live there. The simple answer to this argument is that plaintiffs have alleged that there is a correlation between a district's per pupil assessed valuation and the wealth of its residents and we treat these material facts as admitted by the demurrers.

More basically, however, we reject defendants' underlying thesis that classification by wealth is constitutional so long as the wealth is that of the district, not the individual. We think that discrimination on the basis of district wealth is equally invalid. The commercial and industrial property which augments a district's tax base is distributed unevenly throughout the state. To allot more educational dollars to the children of one district than to those of another merely because of the fortuitous presence of such property is to make the quality of a child's education dependent upon the location of private commercial and industrial establishments. Surely, this is to rely on the most irrelevant of factors as the basis for educational financing …

B. Education as a Fundamental Interest

But plaintiffs' equal protection attack on the fiscal system has an additional dimension. They assert that the system not only draws lines on the basis of wealth but that it "touches upon," indeed has a direct and significant impact upon, a "fundamental interest," namely education. It is urged that these two grounds, particularly in combination, establish a demonstrable denial of equal protection of the laws. To this phase of the argument we now turn our attention.

Until the present time, wealth classifications have been invalidated only in conjunction with a limited number of fundamental interests—rights of defendants in criminal cases.

Plaintiffs' contention—that education is a fundamental interest which may not be conditioned on wealth—is not supported by any direct authority.

We, therefore, begin by examining the indispensable role which education plays in the modern industrial state. This role, we believe, has two significant aspects: first, education is a major determinant of an individual's chances for economic and social success in our competitive society; second, education is a unique influence on a child's development as a citizen and his participation in political and community life. "[T]he pivotal position of education to success in American society and its essential role in opening up to the individual the central experiences of our culture lend it an importance that is undeniable." Thus, education is the lifeline of both the individual and society.

The fundamental importance of education has been recognized in other contexts by the United States Supreme Court and by this court. These decisions—while not legally controlling on the exact issue before us—are persuasive in their accurate factual description of the significance of learning …

It is illuminating to compare in importance the right to an education with the rights of defendants in criminal cases and the right to vote—two "fundamental interests" which the Supreme Court has already protected against discrimination based on wealth. Although an individual's interest in his freedom is unique, we think that from a larger perspective, education may have far greater social significance than a free transcript or a court-appointed lawyer.

[E]ducation not only affects directly a vastly greater number of persons than the criminal law, but it affects them in ways which—to the state—have an enormous and much more varied significance. Aside from reducing the crime rate (the inverse relation is strong), education also supports each and every other value of a democratic society—participation, communication, and social mobility, to name but a few.

The analogy between education and voting is much more direct: both are crucial to participation in, and the functioning of, a democracy. Voting has been regarded as a fundamental right because it is "preservative of other basic civil and political rights …"

We are convinced that the distinctive and priceless function of education in our society warrants, indeed compels, our treating it as a "fundamental interest."

First, education is essential in maintaining what several commentators have termed "free enterprise democracy." …

Second, education is universally relevant. "Not every person finds it necessary to call upon the fire department or even the police in an entire lifetime.

Relatively few are on welfare. Every person, however, benefits from education ..."

Third, public education continues over a lengthy period of life—between 10 and 13 years. Few other government services have such sustained, intensive contact with the recipient.

Fourth, education is unmatched in the extent to which it molds the personality of the youth of society. While police and fire protection, garbage collection and street lights are essentially neutral in their effect on the individual psyche, public education actively attempts to shape a child's personal development in a manner chosen not by the child or his parents but by the state.

Finally, education is so important that the state has made it compulsory—not only in the requirement of attendance but also by assignment to a particular district and school. Although a child of wealthy parents has the opportunity to attend a private school, this freedom is seldom available to the indigent. In this context, it has been suggested that "a child of the poor assigned willy-nilly to an inferior state school takes on the complexion of a prisoner, complete with a minimum sentence of 12 years."

C. The Financing System Is Not Necessary to Accomplish a Compelling State Interest

We now reach the final step in the application of the "strict scrutiny" equal protection standard—the determination of whether the California school financing system, as presently structured, is necessary to achieve a compelling state interest.

The state interest which defendants advance in support of the current fiscal scheme is California's policy "to strengthen and encourage local responsibility for control of public education." We treat separately the two possible aspects of this goal: first, the granting to local districts of effective decision-making power over the administration of their schools; and second, the promotion of local fiscal control over the amount of money to be spent on education.

The individual district may well be in the best position to decide whom to hire, how to schedule

its educational offerings, and a host of other matters which are either of significant local impact or of such a detailed nature as to require decentralized determination. But even assuming arguendo that local administrative control may be a compelling state interest, the present financial system cannot be considered necessary to further this interest. No matter how the state decides to finance its system of public education, it can still leave this decision-making power in the hands of local districts.

The other asserted policy interest is that of a local district to choose how much it wishes to spend on the education of its children. ...

We need not decide whether such decentralized financial decision-making is a compelling state interest, since under the present financing system, such fiscal freewill is a cruel illusion for the poor school districts. We cannot agree that Baldwin Park residents care less about education than those in Beverly Hills solely because Baldwin Park spends less than $600 per child while Beverly Hills spends over $1,200. As defendants themselves recognize, perhaps the most accurate reflection of a community's commitment to education is the rate at which its citizens are willing to tax themselves to support their schools. Yet by that standard, Baldwin Park should be deemed far more devoted to learning than Beverly Hills, for Baldwin Park citizens levied a school tax of well over $5 per $100 of assessed valuation, while residents of Beverly Hills paid only slightly more than $2.

In summary, so long as the assessed valuation within a district's boundaries is a major determinant of how much it can spend for its schools, only a district with a large tax base will be truly able to decide how much it really cares about education. The poor district cannot freely choose to tax itself into an excellence which its tax rolls cannot provide. Far from being necessary to promote local fiscal choice, the present financing system actually deprives the less wealthy districts of that option ...

The judgment is reversed and the cause remanded to the trial court with directions to overrule the demurrers and to allow defendants a reasonable time within which to answer.

The California court's finding in *Serrano* that education is a fundamental right under the federal Equal Protection Clause was effectively overruled by *Rodriguez*. However, the ruling based on the California constitution still stands.[33] Recall that state high courts have the final say regarding the meaning of their state constitution.

33 Serrano v. Priest (Serrano II), 557 P.2d 929 (Cal. 1976).

Sixteen years after *Rodriguez*, the Texas Supreme Court considered a challenge to the state's educational finance system based on the state constitution in *Edgewood Independent School District v. Kirby*.[34] Like the *Serrano* court, the *Kirby* court invalidated the state's educational finance system because wealthy school districts could raise more money with the same tax rate than poorer ones. However, unlike *Serrano*, which was based on the state equal protection clause, the Texas case was based on the education article of the Texas constitution. The Texas state constitution says that in order to promote a "general diffusion of knowledge," the legislature should make "suitable provision" for an "efficient" system of education.[35] In finding the Texas system unconstitutional under this provision, the Texas Supreme Court said that the framers of the state constitution did not "intend a system with such vast disparities as now exist … The present system … provides not for a diffusion of knowledge that is general, but for one that is limited and unbalanced." Thus, said the court, "districts must have substantially equal access to similar revenues per pupil at similar levels of tax effort." That is, a given tax rate in a property-poor district should yield about the same revenues per pupil as would that tax rate in a property-rich district.

Educational Adequacy

There appears to be no pattern to the outcome of third wave school finance cases based on the wording of the education article within the relevant state constitution or the specifics of the state finance system. Given that no state's current system of finance is perfectly equitable and that any educational system can be viewed as inadequate in some ways, it would appear that some courts are more willing than others to improve educational finance systems. Some state courts have simply said that funding inequities do not prove that the state's educational system is inadequate.[36]

In *Citizens for Strong Schools, Inc. v. Florida State Board of Education*,[37] Florida's highest court strongly expressed its preference for judicial restraint in educational policymaking, noting that the petitioners had "failed to present the courts with any manageable standard by which to avoid judicial intrusion into the powers of the Legislature." In adopting a circumscribed role for judicial review of school finance systems, the Florida court relied on Pennsylvania cases. Ironically, however, Pennsylvania's highest court recently disavowed its earlier "hands-off" approach. In justifying its change of heart, the Pennsylvania Supreme Court explained:

> To the extent that our prior cases have suggested, if murkily, that a court cannot devise a judicially discoverable and manageable standard for Education Clause compliance that does not entail making a policy determination inappropriate for judicial discretion, or that we may only deploy a rubber stamp in a hollow mockery of judicial review, we underscore that we are not bound to follow precedent when it cannot bear scrutiny, either on its own terms or in light of subsequent developments.[38]

Indeed, some state courts have been willing to tackle the issue of what constitutes an adequate education. The West Virginia Supreme Court interpreted its constitution's call for a "thorough and efficient" system of education as requiring every school to develop "the minds, bodies and social morality of its charges to prepare them for useful and happy occupations, recreation and

34 777 S.W.2d 391 (Tex. 1989).
35 §1, Article 7, Texas Constitution.
36 R.E.F.I.T. v. Cuomo, 655 N.E.2d 647 (N.Y. 1995); Gould v. Orr, 506 N.W.2d 349 (Neb. 1993); McDaniel v. Thomas, 285 S.E.2d 156 (Ga. 1981).
37 262 So. 3d 127 (Fla. 2019).
38 William Penn Sch. Dist. v. Pa. Dep't of Educ., 170 A.3d 414, 457 (Pa. 2017).

citizenship, and to do so economically." The court expanded its ruling by listing the subjects and skills all children should receive, including arithmetic, social ethics, and recreation.[39]

In striking down its state finance plan, the Supreme Court of Washington took a different approach to defining a constitutionally adequate education. It suggested several ways for determining whether the educational program of the state met the state constitution's requirement for "ample provision." Ample provision could be measured in terms of the state board of education accreditation standards, or the adequacy of programs could be determined in terms of the "statewide aggregate per pupil deployment of certified and classified staff and non-salary related costs for the maintenance and operation of a school program for the normal range of student." In other words, adequacy is defined as something close to the average level of educational services that school districts have chosen to provide. This measure was termed the "collective wisdom" criterion.[40]

A Kansas court reasoned that the state constitutional requirement that the legislature provide a "suitable" system of education requires an equitable distribution of education funds. The mandate is not for equitable treatment of school districts as such as by a system of power equalization, but to offer each Kansas child an "equal educational opportunity." This does not mean the same amount of money needs to be spent on each child's education, but rather that any disparity in educational funding be justified by a "rational educational explanation." Though it did not question the adequacy of the system, the court noted that if current levels of funding were reduced, the system might become inadequate. Thus, the Kansas court found that both equity and adequacy are necessary conditions of a "suitable" system of education.[41] In *McCleary v. State*,[42] the Supreme Court of Washington reaffirmed its approach to interpreting the education clause of its state constitution, retaining jurisdiction to ensure the state legislature would fully fund a recently-enacted school finance program. The court subsequently concluded that the legislature had adequately funded the program and dismissed the case.[43]

In the following excerpt from a very long opinion, the New Jersey Supreme Court provided a detailed analysis of the meaning of the state constitutional mandate to provide for "a thorough and efficient system of free public schools." By linking the state's constitutional obligation to fund poor urban districts to the spending patterns of wealthier districts, the court attempted to address both equity and adequacy.

⚖

ABBOTT v. BURKE
NEW JERSEY SUPREME COURT
575 A.2d 359 (1990)

The opinion of the Court was delivered by ROBERT N. WILENTZ, C.J.

We again face the question of the constitutionality of our school system. We are asked in this case to rule that the *Public School Education Act of 1975*

(the Act) violates our Constitution's thorough and efficient clause.[44]

We find that under the present system the evidence compels but one conclusion: the poorer the district and the greater its need, the less the money

---

39 Pauley v. Kelley, 255 S.E.2d 859 (W. Va. 1979).
40 Seattle Sch. Dist. No. 1 v. State, 585 P.2d 71 (Wash. 1978) (*en banc*).
41 Mock v. Kansas, Consolidated Case No. 91-CV-1009 (Shawnee County Dist. Ct., Kan. 1991); *see also* Montoy v. State, No. 99-C-1738 (Shawnee County Dist. Ct., Kan. December 2, 2003).
42 McCleary v. State, 269 P.3d 227 (Wash. 2012).
43 2015 Wash. LEXIS 548 (Apr. 30, 2015).
44 N.J. Const. of 1947 art. VIII, § 4, para. 1 ("The Legislature shall provide for the maintenance and support of a thorough and efficient system of free public schools for the instruction of all the children in the State between the ages of five and eighteen years.").

available, and the worse the education. That system is neither thorough nor efficient. We hold the Act unconstitutional as applied to poorer urban school districts. Education has failed there, for both the students and the State. We hold that the Act must be amended to assure funding of education in poorer urban districts at the level of property-rich districts; that such funding cannot be allowed to depend on the ability of local school districts to tax; that such funding must be guaranteed and mandated by the State; and that the level of funding must also be adequate to provide for the special educational needs of these poorer urban districts in order to redress their extreme disadvantages.

We note the convincing proofs in this record that funding alone will not achieve the constitutional mandate of an equal education in these poorer urban districts; that without educational reform, the money may accomplish nothing; and that in these districts, substantial, far-reaching change in education is absolutely essential to success. The proofs compellingly demonstrate that the traditional and prevailing educational programs in these poorer urban schools were not designed to meet and are not sufficiently addressing the pervasive array of problems that inhibit the education of poorer urban children. Unless a new approach is taken, these schools—even if adequately funded—will not provide a thorough and efficient education.

We reject the argument, however, that funding should not be supplied because it may be mismanaged and wasted. Money can make a difference if effectively used; it can provide the students with an equal educational opportunity, a chance to succeed. They are entitled to that chance, constitutionally entitled. They have the right to the same educational opportunity that money buys for others.

On this record we find a constitutional deficiency only in the poorer urban districts, and our remedy is limited to those districts. We leave unaffected the disparity in substantive education and funding found in other districts throughout the state, although that disparity too may someday become a matter of constitutional dimension. We do so without implying in any way that such disparity is not important when considered as a matter of policy. Our decision deals not with optimum educational policy but with constitutional compliance …

The Constitutional Provision

In order to pass on plaintiffs' contention, we must once again, in the context of this case, define the scope and content of the constitutional provision. That definition is critical to our determination of a remedy. While precision in such definition is desirable, certain considerations suggest caution against constitutional absolutism in this area. First, what a thorough and efficient education consists of is a continually changing concept. As the Legislature stated:

Because the sufficiency of education is a growing and evolving concept, the definition of a thorough and efficient system of education and the delineation of all the factors necessary to be included therein, depend upon the economic, historical, social and cultural context in which that education is delivered. The Legislature must, nevertheless, make explicit provision for the design of State and local systems by which such education is delivered, and should, therefore, explicitly provide after 4 years from the effective date of this act for a major and comprehensive evaluation of both the State and local systems, and the sufficiency of education provided thereby …

We observed in *Robinson* that

[t]his statement reveals a perceptive recognition on the part of the Legislature of the constantly evolving nature of the concept being considered. It manifests an awareness that what seems sufficient today may be proved inadequate tomorrow, and even more importantly that only in the light of experience can one ever come to know whether a particular program is achieving the desired end.[45]

Second, whatever the content of a thorough and efficient education may be, the question of what must be done to achieve it is debatable, as this case well illustrates. Third, embedded in the constitutional provision itself, at least in its construction thus far by this Court, are various objectives and permissible outcomes—equality, uniformity, diversity, and disparity—that may require, if they are to be allowed, a continued general definition of the constitutional mandate.

Finally, any definition of the constitutional obligation must operate in an area where confrontation between the branches of government is not only

---

45 Robinson v. Cahill, 69 N.J. 449, 355 A.2d 129 (1976).

a distinct possibility but has been an unfortunate reality. That potential confrontation concerns one of the most important functions of government-education—and involves substantial public funds, implicates the taxing power, and is potentially of a continuing nature. The Legislature's role in education is fundamental and primary; this Court's function is limited strictly to constitutional review. The definition of the constitutional provision by this Court, therefore, must allow the fullest scope to the exercise of the Legislature's legitimate power. ...

[In agreeing to hear this case,] we reiterated the constitutional mandate as it had developed through Robinson. But we added a new element of considerable relevance to this case. We said, in effect, that the requirement of a thorough and efficient education to provide "that educational opportunity which is needed in the contemporary setting to equip a child for his role as a citizen and as a competitor in the labor market," meant that poorer disadvantaged students must be given a chance to be able to compete with relatively advantaged students. The Act and its system of education have failed in that respect, and it is that failure that we address in this case. ...

[W]e reject the State's claim that in these poorer urban districts a thorough and efficient education has been or will be achieved. The extent of failure is so deep, its causes so embedded in the present system, as to persuade us that there is no likelihood of achieving a decent education tomorrow, in the reasonable future, or ever. The State's argument is strong on paper: districts can raise all the money they want, districts must raise all the money they need to provide a thorough and efficient education, and if that fails, the State must pay the way, and the Commissioner must monitor all of this and correct any deficiencies. But for ten years and more there has been no thorough and efficient education in these districts. The factors that lead to this failure are described later, but the simplest is that these districts are just too poor to raise the money they theoretically are empowered to. We can keep the present system and its promise for the future for other districts without sacrificing these poorer urban districts to perpetual failure. They can, and as we view it, constitutionally they must, be treated differently. Judicial deference can go just so far. ...

D. The Quality of Education in the Poorer Urban Districts

The primary basis for our decision is the constitutional failure of education in poorer urban districts. The record demonstrates beyond debate that a thorough and efficient education does not exist there. Our conclusion that the constitutional mandate has not been satisfied is based both on the absolute level of education in those districts and the comparison with education in affluent suburban districts.

Plaintiffs' proofs of the significantly inferior quality of education in poorer urban districts are persuasive. While exceptions exist, at the extremes—and its strength is limited to the extremes—the comparison between the education offered to students in poorer urban districts with that offered in the richer districts is impressive. The characteristics of a substantive education are most difficult to prove; short of intensive examination of education in progress, at the school, in the classroom, proofs are necessarily circumstantial. The State did not insist that the only true measure of substantive education was on-the-scene observation, but rather that even accepting plaintiffs' evidence at face value, it fell short. The State's objections were of various kinds: it noted that the comparisons were largely limited to the extremes, the richest against the poorest, the very best against the very worst; evidence was lacking in most cases that would warrant a reliable comparative conclusion. Furthermore, the State claims that the adequacy of the education that was being afforded in poorer districts was not acknowledged. The State's basic objection is that the various circumstantial measures, such as course offerings, experience and education of the staff, and pupil/staff ratio cannot be considered reliable indicators of the quality of education. ...

[T]he level of education offered to students in some of the poorer urban districts is tragically inadequate. Many opportunities offered to students in richer suburban districts are denied to them. For instance, exposure to computers is necessary to acquire skills to compete in the workplace. In South Orange/Maplewood school district, kindergarteners are introduced to computers; children learn word processing in elementary school; middle school students are offered beginning computer programming; and high school students are offered advanced courses in several programming languages or project-oriented independent studies. Each South Orange/Maplewood school has a computer lab.

By contrast, many poorer urban districts cannot offer such variety of computer science courses. While Princeton has one computer per eight children, East Orange has one computer per forty-three children, and Camden has one computer per fifty-eight children. Camden can offer formal computer instruction to only 3.4 percent of its students. In many poorer urban districts, computers are purchased with federal or state categorical funds for use in remedial education programs. Paterson offers no computer education other than computer-assisted basic skills programs. Further, many of these districts do not have sufficient space to accommodate computer labs. In Jersey City, computer classes are being taught in storage closets.

Science education is deficient in some poorer urban districts. Princeton has seven laboratories in its high school, each with built-in equipment. South Brunswick elementary and middle schools stress hands-on, investigative science programs. However, many poorer urban districts offer science classes in labs built in the 1920s and 1930s, where sinks do not work, equipment such as microscopes is not available, supplies for chemistry or biology classes are insufficient, and hands-on investigative techniques cannot be taught. In Jersey City and Irvington, middle school science classes are taught without provision for laboratory experience. In East Orange middle schools, teachers wheel a science cart into a three-foot-by-six-foot science area for instruction. The area contains a sink, but no water, gas, or electrical lines. …

Physical education programs in some poorer urban districts are deficient. While many richer suburban school districts have flourishing gymnastics, swimming, basketball, baseball, soccer, lacrosse, field hockey, tennis, and golf teams, with fields, courts, pools, lockers, showers, and gymnasiums, some poorer urban districts cannot offer students such activities. In East Orange High School there are no such sports facilities; the track team practices in the second floor hallway. All of Irvington's elementary schools have no outdoor play space; some of the playgrounds had been converted to faculty parking lots. In a middle school in Paterson, fifth- and sixth-graders play basketball in a room with such a low ceiling that the net is placed at the level appropriate for third-graders.

Many poorer urban districts operate schools that, due to their age and lack of maintenance, are crumbling. These facilities do not provide an environment in which children can learn; indeed, the safety of children in these schools is threatened. For example, in 1986 in Paterson a gymnasium floor collapsed … In an elementary school in Paterson, the children eat lunch in a small area in the boiler room area of the basement; remedial classes are taught in a former bathroom. In one Irvington

school, children attend music classes in a storage room and remedial classes in converted closets. At another school in Irvington a coal bin was converted into a classroom. In one elementary school in East Orange, there is no cafeteria, and the children eat lunch in shifts in the first floor corridor. In one school in Jersey City, built in 1900, the library is a converted cloakroom; the nurse's office has no bathroom or waiting room; the lighting is inadequate; the bathrooms have no hot water (only the custodial office and nurse's office have hot water); there is water damage inside the building because of cracks in the facade; and the heating system is inadequate.

In contrast, most schools in richer suburban districts are newer, cleaner, and safer. They provide an environment conducive to learning. They have sufficient space to accommodate the children's needs now and in the future. While it is possible that the richest of educations can be conferred in the rudest of surroundings, the record in this case demonstrates that deficient facilities are conducive to a deficient education.

Thorough and efficient means more than teaching the skills needed to compete in the labor market, as critically important as that may be. It means being able to fulfill one's role as a citizen, a role that encompasses far more than merely registering to vote. It means the ability to participate fully in society, in the life of one's community, the ability to appreciate music, art, and literature, and the ability to share all of that with friends. As plaintiffs point out in so many ways, and tellingly, if these courses are not integral to a thorough and efficient education, why do the richer districts invariably offer them? The disparity is dramatic. Alongside these basic-skills districts are school systems offering the broadest range of courses, instruction in numerous languages, sophisticated mathematics, arts, and sciences at a high level, fully equipped laboratories, hands-on computer experience, everything parents seriously concerned for their children's future would want, and everything a child needs. In these richer districts, most of which have some disadvantaged students, one will also find the kind of special attention and educational help so badly needed in poorer urban districts that offer only basic-skills training. If absolute equality were the constitutional mandate, and "basic skills" sufficient to achieve that mandate, there would be little short of a revolution in the suburban districts when parents learned that basic skills is what their children were entitled to, limited to, and no more. …

E. The Quality of Students' Needs in the Poorer Urban Districts

This record shows that the educational needs of students in poorer urban districts vastly exceed those of others, especially those from richer districts. The difference is monumental, no matter how it is measured. Those needs go beyond educational needs; they include food, clothing and shelter, and extend to lack of close family and community ties and support, and lack of helpful role models. They include the needs that arise from a life led in an environment of violence, poverty, and despair. Urban youth are often isolated from the mainstream of society. Education forms only a small part of their home life, sometimes no part of their school life, and the dropout is almost the norm. There are exceptions, fortunately, but substantial numbers of urban students fit this pattern. The goal is to motivate them, to wipe out their disadvantages as much as a school district can, and to give them an educational opportunity that will enable them to use their innate ability. ...

We realize our remedy here may fail to achieve the constitutional object; that no amount of money may be able to erase the impact of the socioeconomic factors that define and cause these pupils' disadvantages. We realize that perhaps nothing short of substantial social and economic change affecting housing, employment, child care, taxation, welfare will make the difference for these students; and that this kind of change is far beyond the power or responsibility of school districts. We have concluded, however, that even if not a cure, money will help, and that these students are constitutionally entitled to that help.

If the claim is that additional funding will not enable the poorer urban districts to satisfy the thorough and efficient test, the constitutional answer is that they are entitled to pass or fail with at least the same amount of money as their competitors.

If the claim is that these students simply cannot make it, the constitutional answer is, give them a chance. The Constitution does not tell them that since more money will not help, we will give them less; that because their needs cannot be fully met, they will not be met at all. It does not tell them they will get the minimum, because that is all they can benefit from. Like other states, we undoubtedly have some "uneducable" students, but in New Jersey there is no such thing as an uneducable district, not under our Constitution.

All of the money that supports education is public money, local money no less than state money. It is authorized and controlled, in terms of source, amount, distribution, and use, by the State. The students of Newark and Trenton are no less citizens than their friends in Millburn and Princeton. They are entitled to be treated equally, to begin at the same starting line. Today the disadvantaged are doubly mistreated: first, by the accident of their environment and, second, by the disadvantage added by an inadequate education. The State has compounded the wrong and must right it. ...

Disparity of funding is relevant to our constitutional conclusion. That conclusion is based not only on our finding of a substantive lack in the quality of education in these poorer urban districts but also on the significant disparity of spending between them and the richer districts. That disparity strongly supports and is a necessary element of our conclusion that the education provided these students from poorer urban districts will not enable them to compete with their suburban colleagues or to function effectively as citizens in the same society. ...

Findings

From this record we find that certain poorer urban districts do not provide a thorough and efficient education to their students. The Constitution is being violated. These students in poorer urban districts have not been able to participate fully as citizens and workers in our society. They have not been able to achieve any level of equality in that society with their peers from the affluent suburban districts. We find the constitutional failure clear, severe, extensive, and of long duration. We cannot find on this record, however, that there is any constitutional violation in the other districts.

We find that in order to provide a thorough and efficient education in these poorer urban districts, the State must assure that their educational expenditures per pupil are substantially equivalent to those of the more affluent suburban districts, and that, in addition, their special disadvantages must be addressed. ...

Remedy

The Act must be amended, or new legislation passed, so as to assure that poorer urban districts' educational funding is substantially equal to that of property-rich districts. "Assure" means that such funding cannot depend on the budgeting and taxing decisions of local school boards. Funding must be certain, every year. The level of funding must also be adequate to provide for the special educational needs of these poorer urban districts and address their extreme disadvantages. ... The total additional cost of such a system in the 1989–1990 school year would have been approximately $440 million. ...

We decline to rule on plaintiffs' state equal protection claim. The core of their argument is that wealth-based disparity is causing educational disparity. They contend, in effect, that what they consider the fundamental right of education is affected by the property wealth of the school district, that the system in reality consists of a classification of students that determines their level of education by a characteristic not only irrational but suspect, the property wealth of the districts they live in, and that there is no compelling State interest to justify the classification. We referred in Robinson I to the monumental governmental upheaval that would result if the equal protection doctrine were held applicable to the financing of education and similarly applied to all governmental services. We need not deal with those implications, for the remedy afforded in this opinion, although not based on equal protection, substantially mitigates plaintiffs' equal protection claim. ...

Conclusion

This case has a special context that brings the constitutional obligation into sharp focus as it applies to the urban poor. While we necessarily deal with our system of education statewide, the issue put to us by the plaintiffs is the education of those children who live in poverty. Their cities have deteriorated and their lives are often bleak. They live in a culture where schools, studying, and homework are secondary. Their test scores, their dropout rate, their attendance at college, all indicate a severe failure of education. While education is largely absent from their lives, we get some idea of what is present from the crime rate, disease rate, drug addiction rate, teenage pregnancy rate, and the unemployment rate. Without an effective education they are likely to remain enveloped in this environment. Their overall needs are not limited to education, but that need is overwhelming.

Clearly, we are failing to solve this problem. It is the problem of bringing this important and increasingly isolated class into the life of America, for this is not just a New Jersey problem. There is progress, and there are some successes in education, but the central truth is that the poor remain plunged in poverty and severe educational deprivation. The devastation of the urban poor is more significant in New Jersey than in most states both because of our demographics and the structure of our society. Our large black and [H]ispanic population is more concentrated in poor urban areas and will remain isolated from the rest of society unless this educational deficiency in poorer urban districts is addressed.

While the constitutional measure of the educational deficiency is its impact on the lives of these students, we are also aware of its potential impact on the entire state and its economy—not only on its social and cultural fabric, but on its material well-being, on its jobs, industry, and business. Economists and business leaders say that our state's economic well-being is dependent on more skilled workers, technically proficient workers, literate and well-educated citizens. And they point to the urban poor as an integral part of our future economic strength. In short, they urge the state to go about the business of substantially improving the education of the very subjects of this litigation, the students in poorer urban districts. So it is not just that their future depends on the State, the state's future depends on them. That part of the constitutional standard requiring an education that will enable the urban poor to compete in the marketplace, to take their fair share of leadership and professional positions, assumes a new significance. ...

After all the analyses are completed, we are still left with these students and their lives. They are not being educated. Our Constitution says they must be. Included in our perspective are the stories of success. They show that the urban poor are capable, that given sufficient attention in an adequately financed system using the best knowledge and techniques available, a thorough and efficient education is achievable.

This record proves what all suspect: that if the children of poorer districts went to school today in richer ones, educationally they would be a lot better off. Everything in this record confirms what we know: they need that advantage much more than the other children. And what everyone knows is that—as children—the only reason they do not get that advantage is that they were born in a poor district. For while we have underlined the impact of the constitutional deficiency on our state, its impact on these children is far more important. They face, through no fault of their own, a life of poverty and isolation that most of us cannot begin to understand or appreciate.

We reverse the Board's decision. The Act is unconstitutional as applied to poorer urban districts.

Because of the court's urgent insistence on addressing urban inequalities, the *New York Times* editorial board described *Abbott v. Burke* as "the most important equal education ruling since *Brown v. Board of Education*."[46] The New Jersey Supreme Court required parity in educational spending between poor urban districts and affluent suburban districts in a ruling that remained in effect for nearly 20 years.

In 2008, however, the state legislature enacted a new funding formula. Instead of striving for parity, this formula attempted to determine the actual cost of funding a "thorough and efficient" education in the poorer urban districts, including affording extra "weights" in the formula to account for the greater needs of urban students. This new formula, called the **School Funding Reform Act** (*SFRA*), was found to be constitutional in 2009. The New Jersey Supreme Court said that

> The political branches of government … are entitled to take reasoned steps, even if the outcome cannot be assured, to address the pressing social, economic, and educational challenges confronting our state. They should not be locked in a constitutional straitjacket. *SFRA* deserves the chance to prove in practice that, as designed, it satisfies the requirements of our constitution.[47]

In 2011, however, the court found that the state legislature had failed to fully fund the *SFRA*, and it ordered the state to do so.[48] And in 2017, in an unpublished opinion, the court denied the state's motion for relief from this mandate.[49]

Under the New Jersey court's approach to adequacy, the educational offerings in the wealthy suburban districts are viewed as the benchmark for adequate provision of educational services, and the funding for poor urban districts should be set high enough to enable these districts to provide a similar level of services. In the seminal case of *Rose v. Council for Better Education*,[50] the Supreme Court of Kentucky found that "not only do the so-called poorer districts provide inadequate education to fulfill the needs of the students but the more affluent districts' efforts are inadequate as well, as judged by accepted national standards." In that case, the court declared the entire state funding system unconstitutional, and ordered the Kentucky legislature to devise and fund a system of education that would be both equitable and adequate. The Kentucky legislature responded by significantly changing the way education is funded in Kentucky and instituting reforms designed to improve student outcomes.[51]

In *Rose*, the Kentucky Supreme Court defined an adequate education as including reading, math, and science; "sufficient knowledge of economic, social and political systems to enable the student to make informed choices"; "sufficient understanding of governmental processes to enable the student to understand the issues that affect his or her community, state and nation"; and "sufficient levels of academic or vocational skills to … compete favorably … in the job market."

At least six states have been influenced by the Kentucky court's definition.[52] As noted earlier, a Kansas court reasoned that a "suitable" system of education requires both an adequate and

---

46 *A Visionary School Plan in Maryland*, NY Times (April 30, 2002); Online at www.nytimes.com/2002/04/30/opinion/a-visionary-school-plan-in-maryland.html (last accessed January 16, 2020).

47 Abbott v. Burke, 971 A.2d 989 (N.J. 2009).

48 Abbott v. Burke, 20 A.3d 1018 (N.J. 2011).

49 Education Law Center, History of *Abbott v. Burke*. Online at https://edlawcenter.org/litigation/abbott-v-burke/abbott-history.html (last accessed January 16, 2020).

50 Rose v. Council for Better Education, Inc., 790 S.W.2d 186 (Ky. 1989).

51 The legislative response is described in detail in Michael A. Rebell, *The Right to Comprehensive Educational Opportunity*, 47 Harv. Civ. Rights Civ. Lib. L. Rev 84–85 (2012).

52 Courts in Massachusetts, New Hampshire, and Kansas explicitly relied upon this definition, and the definition also played a role in court decisions in Alabama, North Carolina, and South Carolina. *See* Opinion of the Justices, 624 So.2d 107 (Ala. 1993); McDuffy v. Sec'y, 615 N.E.2d 516, 554 (Mass. 1993); Claremont Sch. Dist. v. Governor, 703 A.2d 1353, 1359 (N.H. 1997); Gannon v. State, 420 P.3d 477 (Kan. 2018); Leandro v. State, 488 S.E.2d 249 (N.C. 1997); Abbeville Cnty. Sch. Dist. v. State, 515 S.E.2d 535 (S.C. 1999).

equitable distribution of educational funds, adopting the Kentucky definition and requiring the state legislature to provide school districts with "reasonably equal access to substantially similar educational opportunity through similar tax effort." As of 2018, it had not yet satisfied these dual mandates.[53] By contrast, Connecticut's highest court has recently absolved the state legislature of any constitutional obligation to address the "special disadvantages" experienced by the state's poorer urban districts.[54]

In *Hoke County Board of Education v. North Carolina*,[55] the student plaintiffs claimed they were being denied the opportunity to a constitutionally mandated "sound basic education." North Carolina's highest court based its analysis on this definition of an adequate education:

> "an education that does not serve the purpose of preparing students to participate and compete in the society in which they live and work is devoid of substance and is constitutionally inadequate." [A] sound basic education … provides students with at least: (1) sufficient knowledge of fundamental mathematics and physical science to enable the student to function in a complex and rapidly changing society; (2) sufficient fundamental knowledge of geography, history, and basic economic and political systems to enable the student to make informed choices with regard to issues that affect the student personally or affect the student's community, state, and nation; (3) sufficient academic and vocational skills to enable the student to successfully engage in post-secondary education or vocational training; and (4) sufficient academic and vocational skills to enable the student to compete on an equal basis with others in formal education or gainful employment in contemporary society.

In applying this definition, the court considered both *outputs* (student outcomes) and *inputs* (expenditures and resources). The court found that with regard to at-risk students, the state had failed to provide "an equal opportunity to obtain a sound basic education." To correct the problem, the state was ordered to ensure

> (1) that every classroom be staffed with a competent, certified, well-trained teacher; (2) that every school be led by a well-trained competent principal; and (3) that every school be provided, in the most cost-effective manner, the resources necessary to support the effective instructional program within that school so that the educational needs of all children, including at-risk children, to have the equal opportunity to obtain a sound basic education, can be met.

Regarding outputs, the court concluded that

> … over the past decade, an inordinate number of Hoke County students have consistently failed to match the academic performance of their statewide public school counterparts and that such failure, measured by their performance while attending Hoke County schools, their dropout rates, their graduation rates, their need for remedial help, their inability to compete in the job markets, and their inability to compete in collegiate ranks, constitute a clear showing that they have failed to obtain [an adequate education].

By contrast, as noted above, the highest court in Connecticut in 2018 rejected the notion that the constitutional adequacy of educational funding could be determined by student outcomes. Wrote the court:[56]

53 Gannon v. State, 402 P.3d 513 (Kan. 2017) and 420 P.3d 477 (Kan. 2018).
54 Connecticut Coalition for Justice in Education Funding v. Rell, 176 A.3d 28 (Conn, 2018).
55 599 S.E.2d 365 (N.C. 2004).
56 *See* Connecticut Coalition for Justice in Education Funding v. Rell, 176 A.3d 28 (Conn, 2018).

If the court determines that educational *inputs* are minimally adequate to enable a student who takes advantage of them to perform the basic functions of an adult, it necessarily follows that poor outcomes must be caused by disadvantaging factors for which the court has no authority to order a remedy.

In *Campaign for Fiscal Equity* (*CFE*) *v. State*,[57] the highest court of New York equated a sound basic education with "the basic literacy, calculating, and verbal skills necessary to enable children to eventually function productively as civic participants capable of voting and serving on a jury."[58] In finding that the state had not met this standard with regard to New York City, the court examined a variety of inputs including teacher qualifications and class size, and several measures of school outputs including dropout rates and test scores. In 2017, the court expanded the definition of inputs to include after-school and summer programs, and it expanded the definition of outcomes to include preparation for city and state college admission requirements.[59]

Legislatures in states where courts view educational adequacy in terms of inputs face the daunting task of calculating the cost. A variety of methods have been suggested for accomplishing this task, some based on an analysis of expenditures in districts judged to be adequate or exemplary and others relying on the opinions of experts. Wyoming, Kansas, Ohio, and Maryland are among the states that have undertaken these efforts, with varying results. States where courts view adequacy in terms of outputs, such as North Carolina and, to some degree, New York, face an even more daunting task because, although funds can be targeted for demonstrably effective programs, there is not necessarily a one-to-one correspondence between inputs provided and the outcomes realized. From 1997–2008, after ruling for the plaintiffs, the New Hampshire Supreme Court was involved in an ongoing process of monitoring whether the educational assessment and accountability system adopted by the legislature "ensure[s]" delivery of a constitutionally adequate education.[60]

Whether more than four decades of educational finance litigation has resulted in greater equity or an overall improvement in educational quality remains the subject of research and debate. Given the complexity of producing and assessing educational equity and quality, the educational results of educational finance litigation in individual states and overall may always remain uncertain. Nevertheless, a number of state courts have embraced the following principles:

- The legislature is responsible for funding all the state's public schools.
- If a state constitution mandates a "thorough and efficient" or "suitable" system of education, it means that the education provided by the state must be equitably distributed and at least minimally adequate.
- Even in the absence of such language, an education article may be interpreted to require equitable and adequate provision of education to all children within the jurisdiction of the state.
- The legislature cannot discharge its educational responsibilities simply by creating local school boards with the power to raise money at varying levels based on local wealth and desires.
- It is the role of state courts to ensure that the legislature lives up to its constitutional responsibilities for the provision of education.

Local School Board Authority to Raise and Spend Money

School boards have no inherent constitutional authority to tax, borrow, and spend. Such authority must be expressly granted; it cannot be inferred from general grants of authority to operate

57 801 N.E. 2d 326 (N.Y. 2003).
58 *See* Connecticut Coalition for Justice in Education Funding v. Rell, 176 A.3d 28 (Conn, 2018).
59 Aristy-Farer v. State, 81 N.E.3d 360, 369 (N.Y. 2017).
60 *See* Claremont Sch. Dist. v. Governor, 794 A.2d 744 (N.H. 2002).

schools.[61] Money earmarked by law for specific purposes cannot be spent for any other purpose.[62] State laws and state constitutional provisions sometimes limit year-to-year increases in local taxes and cap the total amount of money that may be raised and borrowed. School authority to tax and spend is also circumscribed by federal and state constitutional limitations that prohibit the establishment of religion, and by state constitutional provisions that limit expenditures to "public" purposes.[63]

A mostly older, but still valid, body of case law explored the limitations on school boards' authority to spend. Expenditures not specifically authorized by law are permitted if reasonably implied by the authority granted to the school board by the legislature or if necessary to carry out the school board's educational mandate. Three early twentieth-century cases in Washington State challenging the authority of school boards to build and operate playgrounds, gymnasiums, and medical clinics illustrate these principles.[64] As the court in *McGilvra v. Seattle School District* explained:

> Playgrounds in connection with public schools have for generations been so common that it must be presumed that the legislature, by giving the general power to maintain public schools, incidentally intended to also give the authority to provide such playgrounds in connection therewith; and while gymnasiums in connection with public schools have not been so common, the work and exercise of the students carried on therein is manifestly so intimately connected with the education of the pupil as to warrant the assumption that the legislature intended the school districts and their officers to possess the power providing the same as a proper public school equipment …
>
> The rendering of medical, surgical and dental services to the pupils, however, is, and always has been, we think, so foreign to the powers to be exercised by a school district or its officers that such power cannot be held to exist in the absence of express legislative language so providing.

School boards must formulate and manage their budgets in accordance with state law. Statutes may limit the board's budgetary authority such as by putting a cap on the annual percentage increase or by prohibiting the annual budget from exceeding the amount of money anticipated to be available from tax levies and state aid.[65]

In some states, local school boards must submit their budgets either to the voters or to a higher government authority for approval. In New York, if the voters fail to approve the proposed budget, the board must adopt an austerity budget that covers only teacher salaries and "ordinary contingent expenses."[66] In Arizona, if a proposed budget exceeds the budget limit for the year, the district must hold an override election and simultaneously prepare an alternative budget in case the override fails.[67] In California, if a local district's proposed budget fails to win approval from the county and state, the county superintendent has authority to adopt a budget for the district and to control the district's expenditures to keep them within that budget.[68] School districts in Georgia are permitted to hold an election seeking a special-purpose local-option sales tax to be used "exclusively for the purpose or purposes specified in the resolution or ordinance calling for

---

61 Manges v. Freer Indep. Sch. Dist., 653 S.W.2d 553 (Tex. App. 1983), *rev'd on other grounds*, 677 S.W.2d 488 (Tex. 1984).
62 Barth v. Bd. of Educ., 322 N.W.2d 694 (Wis. Ct. App. 1982).
63 See North Carolina v. Whittle Communications, 402 S.E.2d 556 (N.C. 1991).
64 State *ex rel.* Sch. Dist. No. 56 v. Superior Court, 124 P. 484 (Wash. 1912) (playground); Sorenson v. Perkins & Co., 129 P. 577 (Wash. 1913) [*gymnasium*]; McGilvra v. Seattle Sch. Dist. No. 1, 194 P. 817 (Wash. 1921) [*medical clinic*].
65 Marsh v. Erhard, 47 A.2d 713 (Pa. 1946).
66 N.Y. EDUC. LAW § 2023.
67 Ariz. Rev. Stat. Ann. § 15–481.
68 CAL. EDUC. CODE § 42127.3(b)(1).

imposition of the tax."[69] In *Johnstone v. Thompson*,[70] plaintiffs successfully claimed the district's use of local-option sales-tax money to purchase laptop computers for all middle school students violated the resolution, which said the money should be used for capital projects such as system-wide technological improvements.

State statutes place specific requirements and limitations on local school board procedures for dealing with financial exigency. Most states authorize districts wishing to initiate large-scale building or remodeling projects to finance them with bonds. Procedures for issuing bonds are often quite specific and may include limits on indebtedness and a requirement of local voter approval. Most states also authorize school boards to secure short-term loans when cash on hand is temporarily insufficient to cover expenses. Statutes may specify procedures for securing short-term loans and impose limitations such as maximum terms, rates of interest, and levels of indebtedness. Some states permit districts to maintain a "contingency fund" to deal with unexpected needs for cash. Some states also permit school boards to deal with unexpected needs by shifting funds from one category of expense to another[71] or to increase their budgets in the middle of a school year to deal with necessary expenses that could not reasonably have been foreseen at the time the budget was adopted.[72] School districts wishing to sell or lease unneeded school facilities must also comply with the requirements of state law.

State statutes generally authorize schools to charge fees for attending school activities such as sports, and some specify how the money is to be used.[73] School districts sometimes wish to impose fees on students for admission to the school or to a particular class, for books and other supplies, for specific services, or for participation in extracurricular activities. The judicial opinions concerning the legality of school fees deal mostly with two questions: Is the fee consistent with the state constitution's guarantee of a free education? Does the fee discriminate against students from lower income households? The resolution of these issues depends on the precise language of the state constitution, the court's conception of what services are essential, and the court's notion of equity.

Because all state constitutions guarantee a free education, public schools may not charge district residents for access to the basic program during the regular school year. However, some rulings permit tuition for summer school[74] and for non-residents of the district.[75] Courts are split on the question of fees for non-required courses: Some allow course fees, some forbid them, and some allow them unless the course can be used for credit toward graduation.[76] Courts are also split on the question of whether fees may be charged for the use of textbooks. Some courts permit the fee provided it is waived for poor children.[77] In general, textbook fees are allowed in states where the constitution requires a system of education "free of" or "without" tuition, but are prohibited where the constitution mandates "free public schools."[78] For example, because West Virginia guarantees "free schools," its highest court held that a school district could not lawfully impose a fee for textbooks and other classroom materials.[79]

69 O.C.G.A. § 48-8-111(a)(1).
70 631 S.E.2d 650 (Ga. 2006).
71 Isley v. Sch. Dist. No. 2, 305 P.2d 432 (Ariz. 1956).
72 Raffone v. Pearsall, 333 N.Y.S. 2d 316 (N.Y. App. Div. 1972).
73 Kan. Stat. Ann. § 72-8208a; Miss. Code Ann. § 37-7-301; Title 70 Okla. Stat. § 5-129.
74 Washington v. Salisbury, 306 S.E.2d 600 (S.C. 1983).
75 Oracle Sch. Dist. No. 2 v. Mammoth High Sch. Dist. No. 88, 633 P.2d 450 (Ariz. Ct. App. 1981).
76 Concerned Parents v. Caruthersville Sch. Dist. 18, 548 S.W.2d 554 (Mo. 1977) (*en banc*); Norton v. Bd. of Educ., 553 P.2d 1277 (N.M. 1976).
77 Vandevender v. Cassell, 208 S.E.2d 436 (W. Va. 1974).
78 Cardiff v. Bismarck Pub. Sch. Dist., 263 N.W.2d 105 (N.D. 1978); Sneed v. Greenboro City Bd. of Educ., 264 S.E.2d 106 (N.C. 1980); *see generally* Kate Barnes, *"Free" Education: The Inclusion of Educational Materials and Supplies as Part of the Right to Free Education*, 40 J.L. & EDUC. 373 (2011).
79 Randolph Cty. Bd. of Educ. v. Adams, 467 S.E.2d 150 (W. Va. 1995).

A majority of courts have upheld reasonable fees for school supplies or activities.[80] In some cases, the acceptability of fees depends on the availability of waivers in cases of economic hardship or whether the activity is required or closely related to the school's educational goals. The Supreme Court of Montana stated the latter principle as follows:

> Is a given course or activity reasonably related to a recognized academic and educational goal of the particular school system? If it is, it constitutes part of the free, public school system commanded by … the Montana Constitution and additional fees or charges cannot be levied, directly or indirectly, against the student or his parents. If it is not, reasonable fees or charges may be imposed.[81]

When money is tight, school districts may resort to cost-cutting measures such as deferred building maintenance or reduction in staff size. In addition to its educational consequences, deferred maintenance may have legal consequences if poorly maintained buildings pose a danger to health and safety (see Chapter 12). Personnel may not be reduced beyond the level needed to satisfy legal mandates (e.g., state statutes specifying maximum class size and federal and state laws mandating services to students with disabilities). In addition, any reduction in certified personnel necessitated by financial exigency must comply with statutory and contractual mandates concerning **reduction in force** (see Chapter 11) and constitutional and statutory antidiscrimination laws.

In a few cases, school boards have decided to bring the school year to a premature conclusion because the school district ran out of funds. However, in *Butt v. State*,[82] the California Supreme Court refused on equal protection grounds to permit a school district that ran out of money to close its doors six weeks ahead of schedule. Finding that the early closing would "cause an extreme and unprecedented disparity in educational service and progress" to the district's students, the court ruled that the state was obliged to lend the school district enough money to keep the schools open until the scheduled end of the year. Similarly, in 2012, a Pennsylvania school district that was in danger of running out of funds argued that the state should come to its aid. The federal court agreed, and said that "[i]f there is one sacred cow in the pasture of public education, it is the concept that public schools should stay open during the school year."[83]

If a school district runs out of money as a result of school board mismanagement, the board may be subject to removal from office by methods established in state law.[84] Furthermore, statutes in 33 states provide for state takeover of school districts. Depending on the state, takeovers can be pursued for academic, administrative, or financial reasons, such as when funds have allegedly been mismanaged by the local school board.[85]

---

80 Hamer v. Bd. of Educ., 367 N.E.2d 739 (Ill. App. Ct. 1977); Paulson v. Minidoka County Sch. Dist. No. 331, 463 P.2d 935 (Idaho 1970); Kelley v. E. Jackson Pub. Sch., 372 N.W.2d 638 (Mich. Ct. App. 1985); *contra*, Hartzell v. Connell, 679 P.2d 35 (Cal. 1984).

81 Granger v. Cascade County Sch. Dist. No. 1, 499 P.2d 780 (Mont. 1972).

82 842 P.2d 1240 (Cal. 1992).

83 Chester Upland Sch. Dist. v. Pennsylvania, 2012 U.S. Dist. LEXIS 66341 (E.D. Pa. May 11, 2012); see Dara Zeehandelaar Shaw, Victoria McDougald, and Alyssa Schwenk, *Who Should Be in Charge When School Districts Go into the Red?* Fordham Institute Policy Brief (August 6, 2015); Online at https://fordhaminstitute.org/national/research/who-should-be-charge-when-school-districts-go-red (last accessed January 16, 2020).

84 Tautenhahn v. State, 334 S.W.2d 574 (Tex. App. 1960).

85 Education Commission of the States (2018) (www.ecs.org/wp-content/uploads/State-Information-Request_Financial-Insolvency.pdf last accessed April 28, 2020); Joseph O. Oluwole and Preston C. Green, III, *State Takeovers of School Districts: Race and the Equal Protection Clause*, 42 Ind. L. Rev. 343 (2009).

Summary

All levels of government play a part in funding public education. Although not obliged by the Constitution, Congress has chosen to provide funding to public schools. Most federal aid is in the form of categorical aid or block grants and is given on condition that certain programs be offered, certain procedures be followed, certain progress be made, and that there be no discrimination against specified groups.

In accordance with the mandates of their own constitutions, state legislatures are responsible for ensuring an adequate level of funding to the state's public schools. With some variation, legislatures have chosen to finance public schools by delegating to local school boards the authority to tax real property within their districts and supplementing local revenue with state funds allocated according to a complex formula. Depending on state and locality, school district funds may be further enhanced by direct transfers of funds from municipal or country governments as authorized and required by the state legislature.

This multi-faceted, complex system has engendered a great variety of litigation. Much of this litigation, especially in the early years of public schooling, involved general issues of taxation and spending authority. It is now well settled that Congress has the authority to use tax money to aid schools, that state legislatures have the power to tax on behalf of schools, and that school boards have only as much taxing and spending authority as specifically delegated to them by the state legislature.

The primary focus of most significant recent litigation in the area of educational finance is on issues involving questions of equity and adequacy in education. In *San Antonio Independent School District v. Rodriguez*, the Supreme Court ruled that state systems of educational finance that result in significantly different levels of per pupil expenditures across districts do not violate the Equal Protection Clause. However, this ruling suggests and subsequent cases confirm that total denial of education to a defined group of students is likely unconstitutional.

Many suits have also been brought in state courts attacking the constitutionality of state educational finance systems, including the systems for funding charter schools. These suits have objected to inter-district funding inequities or to the alleged inadequacy of the educational program offered in some or all of the state's schools. The suits have been based on the particular state's equal protection clause or the education article in the state constitution. Regardless of their specific claims, these lawsuits have produced mixed results.

Some state courts have ratified school funding plans despite wide disparities in school districts' power to raise money and in per pupil expenditures across districts and others have sought to equalize these financial indicators. Still other state courts have interpreted their state constitutions as requiring the state legislature to provide to every child in the state an educational opportunity that is both adequate and equivalent to the opportunity provided to other children. Some courts have even offered a detailed analysis of what constitutes an adequate education.

10 The Rights of Public School Employees

In the next two chapters, we discuss the legal framework of the relationship between public school districts and their employees. The law concerning a district's treatment of its employees emanates from many sources, including state and federal constitutional provisions, state and federal statutes, and the common law. For example, a tenured teacher can only be dismissed for reasons specified in state law, in accordance with procedures required by state law, the teacher's contract, the collective bargaining agreement, and the Due Process Clause. The dismissal may not violate the free speech or other constitutional rights of the teacher or federal or state statutes prohibiting various forms of discrimination in employment. This chapter examines the federal constitutional and statutory rights of teachers and other employees. Chapter 11 deals with employment and personnel matters like hiring, evaluation, and dismissal, as well as labor relations issues such as collective bargaining, contracts, and the role of professional unions.

The Constitution places limitations on the power of the State to control the behavior of individuals. There are certain behaviors that under normal circumstances government may not regulate and certain laws that it cannot make. Viewed from the perspective of the individual, these limitations are the civil rights and liberties enjoyed by every member of society. School officials, as representatives of the government, are bound to respect these rights in their dealings not only with students but also with their subordinate employees. However, as with students, there are times when the special circumstances of the school necessitate a balancing between the constitutional rights of employees and the promotion of important educational goals. In addition, the legal power of the government over its employees is greater than its power over ordinary citizens. Thus, there are circumstances when school boards may impose requirements and restrictions on employees that government in general could not impose on everyday citizens. At times, however, school districts must accommodate the constitutional rights of employees.

In this chapter, we examine the constitutional provisions affecting public school teachers that have engendered the most conflict: freedom of speech, freedom of religion, the right to privacy, protection against unreasonable search and seizure, and the right to equal protection of the law. Our discussion assumes knowledge of the constitutional principles and doctrines presented in earlier chapters affecting public school students. In addition to the Constitution, we examine the application of federal anti-discrimination statutes to employment practices in public education. A significant body of federal statutes regulates the employment practices of public school districts. These statutes supplement and expand the requirements of the Equal Protection Clause by prohibiting discrimination in employment on the basis of race, ethnicity, gender, religion, disability, or age.

Political Activity and Non-Curricular Speech

May a school board insist that employees embrace its political and educational views? May school employees publicly oppose board policies or directly criticize their employer? May public school teachers reveal or advocate their political or personal beliefs to a captive audience of students? May a school board inculcate its values by controlling the speech of its teachers? Do public school officials have a duty to protect students from viewpoints they consider undesirable or dangerous? In addressing these questions, courts have had to strike a balance between the freedom of speech of teachers and the educational mission of public schools. As with students, the balance depends in part on whether the speech occurs on- or off-campus and whether the speech is part of the school curriculum. This section deals with non-curricular speech by teachers and other school employees.

Public school teachers have always occupied a sensitive and a visible role in the community. In the public schools of colonial New England, people could not be teachers unless the town minister certified their religious and moral rectitude. Although states no longer impose a religious qualification on public school teachers, they have in more recent times employed ideological tests. Practices designed to enforce these qualifications have included political background checks, disqualification of members of political groups considered dangerous or subversive, and loyalty oaths. In keeping with the strong anti-communist sentiments of the time, the Supreme Court during the 1950s generally found these practices constitutionally permissible. For example, in *Adler v. Board of Education of New York*,[1] the Supreme Court upheld a New York law disqualifying from employment in civil service or public schools any person who "advocates, advises or teaches" governmental overthrow by force or violence or who organizes or joins any group advocating such doctrine.

By the 1960s, during the Civil Rights Era, however, the Supreme Court viewed the constitutionality of such security measures in a new light. In 1960, in *Shelton v. Tucker*,[2] the Court prohibited school boards from requiring teachers to disclose all their associational ties and memberships. In 1964, in *Baggett v. Bullitt*,[3] the Court forbade the use of vaguely worded loyalty oaths. In 1967, in *Keyishian v. Board of Regents*,[4] the Court prohibited states and school boards from dismissing teachers for membership in disfavored organizations, even those with violent or unlawful goals such as the Communist Party. Such dismissals, reasoned the Court, would violate the First Amendment rights of teachers. It would be permissible to fire a teacher for "specific intent to further the unlawful aims of an organization" but not for "mere membership" or even knowledge of the organization's unlawful goals.

Though *Keyishian*, *Baggett*, and *Shelton* stand against attempts to impose ideological qualifications on teachers, the Supreme Court continues to allow states or school boards to require **affirmative oaths**, such as a pledge to uphold and defend the Constitution or oppose the overthrow of the government by illegal means.[5] **Negative oaths**, such as, "I have never been a member of a subversive organization," are impermissible. The Court has also upheld a state policy denying teacher certification to immigrants who were eligible but refused to apply for US citizenship.[6] Thus, although no one may be excluded from teaching solely because of membership in a disfavored political organization, school districts may require prospective teachers to take a loyalty oath (or apply for citizenship) without violating the First Amendment.

On a related issue, the Supreme Court has made it clear that public employees generally may not be dismissed, punished, or rewarded solely because of their party affiliation or political beliefs. Thus, the Court has sought an end to the traditional practice of political patronage, which in schools often meant the replacement of administrators and even teachers after municipal or school board elections. The major exception to this limitation pertains to those positions for which "party affiliation is an appropriate requirement for the effective performance of the public

---

1 342 U.S. 485 (1952).
2 364 U.S. 479 (1960).
3 377 U.S. 360 (1964).
4 385 U.S. 589 (1967).
5 Cole v. Richardson, 405 U.S. 676 (1972); Connell v. Higginbotham, 403 U.S. 207 (1971).
6 Ambach v. Norwick, 441 U.S. 68 (1979).

office involved."[7] Based on these principles, teachers have been protected from dismissal because they either supported the recall or opposed the reelection of incumbent school board members.[8] One court ruled that the refusal to hire teachers for summer employment because they supported the losing candidates for school board was impermissible.[9] In a 2014 case raising explicit political discrimination claims, an applicant for a school director position in Puerto Rico alleged that she was passed over because she belonged to the Progressive Democratic Party, whereas the favored candidate belonged to the New Progressive Party. Citing Supreme Court precedent, the federal district court refused to dismiss the applicant's claims.[10]

It may be permissible to replace top central office administrators whose politics conflict with those of the board on matters directly related to the operation of its schools. However, in *Castle v. Colonial School District*,[11] a federal district court enjoined a school board policy prohibiting teachers from engaging in political activities on school property at any time. The purpose of the policy was to prevent off-duty teachers from soliciting votes at polling places located in the schools. But there was also evidence that board members were "annoyed about teachers advocating the election of rival board candidates." The court ruled in favor of the teachers, finding that the very essence of free speech was at stake. Teachers had a right to criticize the school board and were in a unique position to provide the public with information on the quality of the board and its schools.

Because of the great potential for **conflict of interest**, public school employees may be prohibited from becoming school board members in the district in which they are employed.[12] However, they may not be prohibited from serving on the school board of another district, or from running for or holding other public office.[13] In overruling an earlier decision, Kentucky's highest court found that school employees who seek public office may be required to take an unpaid leave of absence. The rationale, the court explained, is that mere candidacy for public office does not qualify for First Amendment protection.[14]

Criticism of School Policies or Personnel

In a significant number of cases, school districts have sought to punish teachers for criticizing school policies, the school board or board members, or particular administrators. The district's rationale for punishing the teacher is usually that the communication had the potential to undermine public support for the school or to damage working relationships within the school. Over the years, the Supreme Court has considered whether such punitive actions violate teachers' free speech rights. The outcome of these cases provides a **six-part framework** for dealing with such claims in any public employment context including a public school:

- First, employees objecting to the actions of a public employer on free speech grounds bear the burden of showing that they were subjected to an **adverse employment decision**. Dismissal, demotion, negative job evaluations, and forced unpaid leave qualify as adverse employment decisions, while lateral transfers generally do not.

---

7   Rutan v. Republican Party of Illinois, 497 U.S. 62 (1990); Branti v. Finkel, 445 U.S. 507 (1980); Elrod v. Burns, 427 U.S. 347 (1976).
8   Childers v. Indep. Sch. Dist. No. 1, 676 F.2d 1338 (10th Cir. 1982); Guerra v. Roma Indep. Sch. Dist., 444 F. Supp. 812 (S.D. Tex. 1977).
9   Solis v. Rio Grande City Indep. Sch., 734 F.2d 243 (5th Cir. 1984).
10 Vázquez-Pagán v. Borges-Rodríguez, No. 12-1972 (MEL), 2014 U.S. Dist. LEXIS 148341 (D.P.R. Oct. 16, 2014).
11 933 F. Supp. 458 (E.D. Pa. 1996).
12 Haskins v. State *ex rel.* Harrington, 516 P.2d 1171 (Wyo. 1973); Unified Sch. Dist. No. 501 v. Baker, 269 Kan. 239, 6 P.3d 848 (2000).
13 Minielly v. State, 411 P.2d 69 (Or. 1966).
14 Cook v. Popplewell, 394 S.W.3d 323 (Ky. 2011), *overruling* Allen v. Bd. of Educ., 584 S.W.2d 408 (Ky. Ct. App. 1979).

- The second question is whether the employee spoke **pursuant to his or her official duties or as a citizen**. If the employee spoke pursuant to his or her official duties, the employee does not enjoy First Amendment protection.
- If the employee spoke as a citizen, the third question is whether the subject of the speech was **a matter of public concern**. If the speech was not a matter of public concern, the employee is not afforded First Amendment protection.
- If the speech was a matter of public concern, the fourth question is whether the public interest in what the employee had to say outweighs any interference with the efficient operation of the workplace. If the employer's interest in avoiding the workplace interference outweighs the public interest in the speech, the employee again does not receive First Amendment protection. But if the public interest in the speech outweighs the workplace interference, the employee's speech falls into the category of **protected speech**.
- As the fifth step, the employee must establish that the protected speech was a **substantial factor** in the adverse employment decision.
- If the employee successfully meets this burden of proof, the burden switches to the employer for the sixth and final step. The employer must show that the **same** adverse employment decision would have been made in the absence of the protected speech. Otherwise the employee will win the case.

In the following watershed case, the Supreme Court distinguished between a public employee speaking "pursuant to his [or her] official duties" and a public employee speaking "as a citizen." The case concerned a disagreement between Richard Ceballos, a deputy district attorney, and his superiors over the handling of a criminal prosecution. Ceballos not only expressed doubts about the case in a memo to his superiors but also testified for the defense that a police affidavit that had been used to gather evidence against a defendant was inaccurate. Ceballos was subsequently reassigned to a different position and denied a promotion. After affirming that "the First Amendment protects a public employee's right, in certain circumstances, to speak as a citizen addressing matters of public concern," the Court went on to explain why, in this case, the public employee was not protected.

⚖️

GARCETTI v. CEBALLOS
Supreme Court of the United States
547 U.S. 410 (2006)

JUSTICE KENNEDY delivered the opinion of the Court.

... [For] many years, "the unchallenged dogma was that a public employee had no right to object to conditions placed upon the terms of employment—including those which restricted the exercise of constitutional rights." That dogma has been qualified in important respects. The Court has made clear that public employees do not surrender all their First Amendment rights by reason of their employment. Rather, the First Amendment protects a public employee's right, in certain circumstances, to speak as a citizen addressing matters of public concern.

Pickering provides a useful starting point in explaining the Court's doctrine.[15] There the relevant speech was a teacher's letter to a local newspaper addressing issues including the funding policies of his school board. "The problem in any case," the Court stated,

is to arrive at a balance between the interests of the teacher, as a citizen, in commenting upon matters of

15 Pickering v. Bd. of Educ., 391 U.S. 563 (1968).

public concern and the interest of the State, as an employer, in promoting the efficiency of the public services it performs through its employees.

The Court found the teacher's speech "neither [was] shown nor can be presumed to have in any way either impeded the teacher's proper performance of his daily duties in the classroom or to have interfered with the regular operation of the schools generally." Thus, the Court concluded that "the interest of the school administration in limiting teachers' opportunities to contribute to public debate is not significantly greater than its interest in limiting a similar contribution by any member of the general public."

Pickering and the cases decided in its wake identify two inquiries to guide interpretation of the constitutional protections accorded to public employee speech. The first requires determining whether the employee spoke as a citizen on a matter of public concern. If the answer is no, the employee has no First Amendment cause of action based on his or her employer's reaction to the speech. If the answer is yes, then the possibility of a First Amendment claim arises. The question becomes whether the relevant government entity had an adequate justification for treating the employee differently from any other member of the general public. This consideration reflects the importance of the relationship between the speaker's expressions and employment. A government entity has broader discretion to restrict speech when it acts in its role as employer, but the restrictions it imposes must be directed at speech that has some potential to affect the entity's operations.

To be sure, conducting these inquiries sometimes has proved difficult. This is the necessary product of "the enormous variety of fact situations in which critical statements by teachers and other public employees may be thought by their superiors ... to furnish grounds for dismissal." The Court's overarching objectives, though, are evident.

When a citizen enters government service, the citizen by necessity must accept certain limitations on his or her freedom. Government employers, like private employers, need a significant degree of control over their employees' words and actions; without it, there would be little chance for the efficient provision of public services. Public employees, moreover, often occupy trusted positions in society. When they speak out, they can express views that contravene governmental policies or impair the proper performance of governmental functions. At the same time, the Court has recognized that a citizen who works for the government is nonetheless a citizen. The First

Amendment limits the ability of a public employer to leverage the employment relationship to restrict, incidentally or intentionally, the liberties employees enjoy in their capacities as private citizens. So long as employees are speaking as citizens about matters of public concern, they must face only those speech restrictions that are necessary for their employers to operate efficiently and effectively.

The Court's employee-speech jurisprudence protects, of course, the constitutional rights of public employees. Yet the First Amendment interests at stake extend beyond the individual speaker. The Court has acknowledged the importance of promoting the public's interest in receiving the well-informed views of government employees engaging in civic discussion. *Pickering* again provides an instructive example. The Court characterized its holding as rejecting the attempt of school administrators to "limi[t] teachers' opportunities to contribute to public debate." It also noted that teachers are "the members of a community most likely to have informed and definite opinions" about school expenditures. The Court's approach acknowledged the necessity for informed, vibrant dialogue in a democratic society. It suggested, in addition, that widespread costs may arise when dialogue is repressed. The Court's more recent cases have expressed similar concerns.

The Court's decisions, then, have sought both to promote the individual and societal interests that are served when employees speak as citizens on matters of public concern and to respect the needs of government employers attempting to perform their important public functions. Underlying our cases has been the premise that while the First Amendment invests public employees with certain rights, it does not empower them to "constitutionalize the employee grievance."

III

With these principles in mind we turn to the instant case. Respondent Ceballos believed the affidavit used to obtain a search warrant contained serious misrepresentations. He conveyed his opinion and recommendation in a memo to his supervisor. That Ceballos expressed his views inside his office, rather than publicly, is not dispositive. Employees in some cases may receive First Amendment protection for expressions made at work. Many citizens do much of their talking inside their respective workplaces, and it would not serve the goal of treating public employees like "any member of the general public" to hold that all speech within the office is automatically exposed to restriction.

The memo concerned the subject matter of Ceballos' employment, but this, too, is non-dispositive. The First Amendment protects some expressions related to the speaker's job. As the Court noted in *Pickering*:

Teachers are, as a class, the members of a community most likely to have informed and definite opinions as to how funds allotted to the operation of the schools should be spent. Accordingly, it is essential that they be able to speak out freely on such questions without fear of retaliatory dismissal.

The same is true of many other categories of public employees.

The controlling factor in Ceballos' case is that his expressions were made pursuant to his duties as a calendar deputy. That consideration—the fact that Ceballos spoke as a prosecutor fulfilling a responsibility to advise his supervisor about how best to proceed with a pending case—distinguishes Ceballos' case from those in which the First Amendment provides protection against discipline. We hold that when public employees make statements pursuant to their official duties, the employees are not speaking as citizens for First Amendment purposes, and the Constitution does not insulate their communications from employer discipline.

Ceballos wrote his disposition memo because that is part of what he, as a calendar deputy, was employed to do. It is immaterial whether he experienced some personal gratification from writing the memo; his First Amendment rights do not depend on his job satisfaction. The significant point is that the memo was written pursuant to Ceballos' official duties. Restricting speech that owes its existence to a public employee's professional responsibilities does not infringe any liberties the employee might have enjoyed as a private citizen. It simply reflects the exercise of employer control over what the employer itself has commissioned or created. Contrast, for example, the expressions made by the speaker in *Pickering*,[16] whose letter to the newspaper had no official significance and bore similarities to letters submitted by numerous citizens every day.

Ceballos did not act as a citizen when he went about conducting his daily professional activities, such as supervising attorneys, investigating charges, and preparing filings. In the same way he did not speak as a citizen by writing a memo that addressed the proper disposition of a pending criminal case.

When he went to work and performed the tasks he was paid to perform, Ceballos acted as a government employee. The fact that his duties sometimes required him to speak or write does not mean his supervisors were prohibited from evaluating his performance.

This result is consistent with our precedents' attention to the potential societal value of employee speech. Refusing to recognize First Amendment claims based on government employees' work product does not prevent them from participating in public debate. The employees retain the prospect of constitutional protection for their contributions to the civic discourse. This prospect of protection, however, does not invest them with a right to perform their jobs however they see fit.

Our holding likewise is supported by the emphasis of our precedents on affording government employers sufficient discretion to manage their operations. Employers have heightened interests in controlling speech made by an employee in his or her professional capacity. Official communications have official consequences, creating a need for substantive consistency and clarity. Supervisors must ensure that their employees' official communications are accurate, demonstrate sound judgment, and promote the employer's mission. Ceballos' memo is illustrative. It demanded the attention of his supervisors and led to a heated meeting with employees from the sheriff's department. If Ceballos' superiors thought his memo was inflammatory or misguided, they had the authority to take proper corrective action.

Ceballos' proposed contrary rule, adopted by the Court of Appeals, would commit state and federal courts to a new, permanent, and intrusive role, mandating judicial oversight of communications between and among government employees and their superiors in the course of official business. This displacement of managerial discretion by judicial supervision finds no support in our precedents. When an employee speaks as a citizen addressing a matter of public concern, the First Amendment requires a delicate balancing of the competing interests surrounding the speech and its consequences. When, however, the employee is simply performing his or her job duties, there is no warrant for a similar degree of scrutiny. To hold otherwise would be to demand permanent judicial intervention in the conduct of governmental operations to a degree inconsistent with sound principles of federalism and the separation of powers.

16 391 U.S. 563 (1968).

The Court of Appeals based its holding in part on what it perceived as a doctrinal anomaly. The court suggested it would be inconsistent to compel public employers to tolerate certain employee speech made publicly but not speech made pursuant to an employee's assigned duties. This objection misconceives the theoretical underpinnings of our decisions. Employees who make public statements outside the course of performing their official duties retain some possibility of First Amendment protection because that is the kind of activity engaged in by citizens who do not work for the government … When a public employee speaks pursuant to employment responsibilities, however, there is no relevant analogue to speech by citizens who are not government employees.

The Court of Appeals' concern also is unfounded as a practical matter. The perceived anomaly, it should be noted, is limited in scope: It relates only to the expressions an employee makes pursuant to his or her official responsibilities, not to statements or complaints (such as those at issue in cases like *Pickering* and *Connick*) that are made outside the duties of employment.[17] If, moreover, a government employer is troubled by the perceived anomaly, it has the means at hand to avoid it. A public employer that wishes to encourage its employees to voice concerns privately retains the option of instituting internal policies and procedures that are receptive to employee criticism. Giving employees an internal forum for their speech will discourage them from concluding that the safest avenue of expression is to state their views in public.

Proper application of our precedents thus leads to the conclusion that the First Amendment does not prohibit managerial discipline based on an employee's expressions made pursuant to official responsibilities. Because Ceballos' memo falls into this category, his allegation of unconstitutional retaliation must fail.

Two final points warrant mentioning. First, as indicated above, the parties in this case do not dispute that Ceballos wrote his disposition memo pursuant to his employment duties. We thus have no occasion to articulate a comprehensive framework for defining the scope of an employee's duties in cases where there is room for serious debate. We reject, however, the suggestion that employers can restrict employees' rights by creating excessively broad job descriptions. The proper inquiry is a practical one. Formal job descriptions often bear little resemblance to the duties an employee actually is expected to perform, and the listing of a given task in an employee's written job description is neither necessary nor sufficient to demonstrate that conducting the task is within the scope of the employee's professional duties for First Amendment purposes.

Second, Justice Souter suggests today's decision may have important ramifications for academic freedom, at least as a constitutional value. There is some argument that expression related to academic scholarship or classroom instruction implicates additional constitutional interests that are not fully accounted for by this Court's customary employee-speech jurisprudence. We need not, and for that reason do not, decide whether the analysis we conduct today would apply in the same manner to a case involving speech related to scholarship or teaching.

IV

Exposing governmental inefficiency and misconduct is a matter of considerable significance. As the Court noted in *Connick*, public employers should, "as a matter of good judgment," be "receptive to constructive criticism offered by their employees." The dictates of sound judgment are reinforced by the powerful network of legislative enactments—such as whistle-blower protection laws and labor codes—available to those who seek to expose wrongdoing. Cases involving government attorneys implicate additional safeguards in the form of, for example, rules of conduct and constitutional obligations apart from the First Amendment. These imperatives, as well as obligations arising from any other applicable constitutional provisions and mandates of the criminal and civil laws, protect employees and provide checks on supervisors who would order unlawful or otherwise inappropriate actions.

We reject, however, the notion that the First Amendment shields from discipline the expressions employees make pursuant to their professional duties. Our precedents do not support the existence of a constitutional cause of action behind every statement a public employee makes in the course of doing his or her job. The judgment of the Court of Appeals is reversed, and the case is remanded for proceedings consistent with this opinion.

---

17 Connick v. Myers, 461 U.S. 138 (1982).

Ceballos does not "articulate a comprehensive formula" for determining when public employees may be regarded as having spoken pursuant to their official duties, beyond suggesting that official job descriptions are not the determining factor. Several school-based circuit court cases have addressed this issue. The Tenth Circuit has said that speech is linked to official duties if it is generally consistent with the type of activities the employee was paid to do, even if it dealt with activities the employee was not expressly required to perform. Speech flows from official duties if "the speech reasonably contributes to or facilitates the employee's performance of the official duty." But not all speech that occurs at work pertains to official duties, nor is all speech that concerns the subject matter of an employee's work necessarily linked to official duties. "Instead, we must take a practical view of all the facts and circumstances surrounding the speech and the employment relationship."

In *Brammer-Hoelter v. Twin Peaks Charter Academy*,[18] the Tenth Circuit sorted through a variety of statements made by teachers at a charter school and concluded that some were expressed pursuant to their duties and some were not. Statements found to be made pursuant to their duties as teachers concerned student behavior, curriculum and pedagogy, and expenditures for instructional aids, furniture, and computers. Statements found to be made not pursuant to their duties as teachers concerned the resignation of other teachers, whether the school's code restricted their freedom of speech, staffing levels, spending on teacher salaries, the visibility of the principal at school board meetings and important events, lack of feedback by and poor communication with the principal, treatment of parents by the principal, favoritism by the principal, the renewal of the school's charter, and the upcoming board elections.

In *Williams v. Dallas Independent School District*,[19] the plaintiff was removed from his post as athletic director after writing a letter to the school principal criticizing the handling and disbursements of gate receipts. In ruling in favor of the district, the Fifth Circuit drew a distinction between the kind of speech activity engaged in by citizens and activities undertaken in the course of performing one's job. The plaintiff's statements were job-related, said the court, because he wanted the gate receipts to pay for costs he was responsible for paying; and because his comments were based on special knowledge he had as athletic director.

In *Van Deelen v. Cain*,[20] a teacher dismissed for pushing a student and holding him against a locker alleged the district had fired him in **retaliation** for filing police reports concerning student misbehavior. The court afforded *Garcetti* a broader reach, concluding that the teacher's complaints to the police regarding student misbehavior were job-related.

In *Casey v. West Las Vegas Independent School District*,[21] the Tenth Circuit reached the conclusion that, in effect, there are circumstances when *Ceballos* dictates that whistleblowing (reporting misconduct by a public official) is *not* protected speech. A school superintendent whose job included serving as CEO of the district's Head Start program reported to federal authorities that as many as 50 percent of the children served in the program were not eligible. She previously had raised the same concern with the school board, which told her "not to worry about it, to leave it alone, or not to go there." On a separate matter, the superintendent also reported to the state's attorney general her belief that the school board was violating the state's open meeting law. After she was demoted to assistant superintendent she brought suit claiming the demotion was in retaliation for exercise of her free speech rights. The court ruled that as the CEO of Head Start, the superintendent was the person primarily responsible for administering the program in compliance with federal regulations,

---

18 492 F.3d 1192 (10th Cir. 2007).

19 480 F.3d 689 (5th Cir. 2007); *see also* United States *ex rel.* Battle v. Bd. of Regents for Ga., 468 F.3d 755 (11th Cir. 2006).

20 628 F. App'x 891 (5th Cir. 2015); *see also* Mattix v. Dekalb Cty. Sch. Dist., No. 1:13-CV-2501-RWS, 2014 U.S. Dist. LEXIS 147281 (N.D. Ga. Oct. 16, 2014).

21 473 F.3d 1323 (10th Cir. 2007); *see also* Vercos v. Bd. of Cty. Comm'rs for El Paso, 259 F. Supp. 3d 1169 (D. Colo. 2017).

so she in fact risked civil and criminal liability for remaining silent. Based on *Ceballos*, therefore, the court reached the ironic conclusion that although her speech was clearly on a matter of public concern, it was not protected under the First Amendment.

When whistle-blowers allege fraud concerning federal funds, they may be protected under the federal *False Claims Act*.[22] A number of states have counterpart False Claims Acts protecting whistle-blowers who allege fraud regarding state funds.

The Second Circuit has also made clear that engaging in whistle-blowing does not enable school employees to bypass *Ceballos*. In *Morey v. Somers Central School District*,[23] a school custodian who alerted his superiors to asbestos contamination in the gym could be fired without offending the First Amendment, as checking for hazards in the gym was part of his official duties. Similarly, in *Ross v. Breslin*,[24] a school payroll clerk discovered that another employee was forging signatures to obtain illegal pay. When she alerted her superiors, she was fired. The Court held that her speech was not entitled to First Amendment protection, for discovering and reporting pay irregularities were part of her job duties. Similarly, in a federal case in Oklahoma, a school secretary who reported fabricated invoices by her supervisor was not protected from retaliation, even when the supervisor ultimately pleaded guilty to federal embezzlement charges. The court lamented the apparent injustice: "It seems a bizarre result that [plaintiff]'s speech is denied protection because she followed [district] policy and reported wrongdoing through internal channels rather than going straight to the media or an outside agency. However, this is the result of *Garcetti* …"[25]

In the wake of *Garcetti*, public school employees can only hope to receive First Amendment protection when they speak as private citizens and not pursuant to their official job responsibilities. A special education teacher who complains to her supervisors that her teaching caseload violates the class size parameters imposed by the *Individuals with Disabilities Education Act* (IDEA) would be speaking pursuant to her official duties. Her speech would not be protected.[26] The same teacher making the same point at a meeting of a local advocacy group might be speaking as a private citizen. Her speech would then be protected if its subject was judged to be a matter of public concern and if the importance of what the teacher had to say was judged to outweigh any disruption the speech might cause.

In the following illustrative case, cited extensively in *Garcetti*, the Supreme Court was called upon to determine whether a public school teacher had been dismissed for speaking as a private citizen, in violation of the First Amendment.

⚖️ PICKERING v. BOARD OF EDUCATION
Supreme Court of the United States
391 U.S. 563 (1968)

MR. JUSTICE MARSHALL delivered the opinion of the Court.

Appellant Marvin L. Pickering, a teacher in Township High School District 205, Will County, Illinois, was dismissed from his position by the appellee Board of Education for sending a letter to a local newspaper in connection with a recently proposed tax increase that was critical of the way in which the Board and the district superintendent of schools had handled past proposals to raise new revenue for the schools. Appellant's dismissal resulted from a determination by the Board, after a full hearing, that the

22 31 U.S.C. §§ 3729–3733.
23 410 Fed. Appx. 398 (2d Cir. 2011).
24 693 F.3d 300 (2d Cir. 2012).
25 Murphy v. Spring, 58 F. Supp. 3d 1241, 1259 (N.D. Okla. 2014).
26 Fox v. Traverse City Area Public Schools Bd. of Educ., 605 F.3d 345 (6th Cir. 2010); Evans-Marshall v. Bd. of Educ. of the Tipp City Exempted Vill. Sch. Dist., 624 F.3d 332 (6th Cir. 2010); *but see* Reinhardt v. Albuquerque Public Schools Bd. of Educ., 595 F.3d 1126 (10th Cir. 2010).

publication of the letter was "detrimental to the efficient operation and administration of the schools of the district" and hence, under the relevant Illinois statute, that "interests of the school require[d] [his dismissal]."

Appellant's claim that his writing of the letter was protected by the First and Fourteenth Amendments was rejected. Appellant then sought review of the Board's action in the Circuit Court of Will County, which affirmed his dismissal on the ground that the determination that appellant's letter was detrimental to the interests of the school system was supported by substantial evidence and that the interests of the schools overrode appellant's First Amendment rights. On appeal, the Supreme Court of Illinois, two Justices dissenting, affirmed the judgment of the Circuit Court. ... For the reasons detailed below we agree that appellant's rights to freedom of speech were violated and we reverse.

I.

In February of 1961 the appellee Board of Education asked the voters of the school district to approve a bond issue to raise $4,875,000 to erect two new schools. The proposal was defeated. Then, in December of 1961, the Board submitted another bond proposal to the voters which called for the raising of $5,500,000 to build two new schools. This second proposal passed and the schools were built with the money raised by the bond sales. In May of 1964 a proposed increase in the tax rate to be used for educational purposes was submitted to the voters by the Board and was defeated. Finally, on September 19, 1964, a second proposal to increase the tax rate was submitted by the Board and was likewise defeated. It was in connection with this last proposal of the School Board that appellant wrote the letter to the editor that resulted in his dismissal.

Prior to the vote on the second tax increase proposal a variety of articles attributed to the District 205 Teachers' Organization appeared in the local paper. These articles urged passage of the tax increase and stated that failure to pass the increase would result in a decline in the quality of education afforded children in the district's schools. A letter from the superintendent of schools making the same point was published in the paper two days before the election and submitted to the voters in mimeographed form the following day. It was in response to the foregoing material, together with the failure of the tax increase to pass, that appellant submitted the letter in question to the editor of the local paper. The

letter constituted, basically, an attack on the School Board's handling of the 1961 bond issue proposals and its subsequent allocation of financial resources between the schools' educational and athletic programs. It also charged the superintendent of schools with attempting to prevent teachers in the district from opposing or criticizing the proposed bond issue.

The Board dismissed Pickering for writing and publishing the letter. Pursuant to Illinois law, the Board was then required to hold a hearing on the dismissal. At the hearing the Board charged that numerous statements in the letter were false and that the publication of the statements unjustifiably impugned the "motives, honesty, integrity, truthfulness, responsibility and competence" of both the Board and the school administration. The Board also charged that the false statements damaged the professional reputations of its members and of the school administrators, would be disruptive of faculty discipline, and would tend to foment "controversy, conflict and dissension" among teachers, administrators, the Board of Education, and the residents of the district. Testimony was introduced from a variety of witnesses on the truth or falsity of the particular statements in the letter with which the Board took issue. The Board found the statements to be false as charged. No evidence was introduced at any point in the proceedings as to the effect of the publication of the letter on the community as a whole or on the administration of the school system in particular, and no specific findings along these lines were made.

The Illinois courts reviewed the proceedings solely to determine whether the Board's findings were supported by substantial evidence and whether, on the facts as found, the Board could reasonably conclude that appellant's publication of the letter was "detrimental to the best interests of the schools." Pickering's claim that his letter was protected by the First Amendment was rejected on the ground that his acceptance of a teaching position in the public schools obliged him to refrain from making statements about the operation of the schools "which in the absence of such position he would have an undoubted right to engage in." It is not altogether clear whether the Illinois Supreme Court held that the First Amendment had no applicability to appellant's dismissal for writing the letter in question or whether it determined that the particular statements made in the letter were not entitled to First Amendment protection. In any event, it clearly rejected Pickering's claim that, on the facts of this case, he could not constitutionally be dismissed from his teaching position.

II.

To the extent that the Illinois Supreme Court's opinion may be read to suggest that teachers may constitutionally be compelled to relinquish the First Amendment rights they would otherwise enjoy as citizens to comment on matters of public interest in connection with the operation of the public schools in which they work, it proceeds on a premise that has been unequivocally rejected in numerous prior decisions of this Court … At the same time[,] it cannot be gainsaid that the State has interests as an employer in regulating the speech of its employees that differ significantly from those it possesses in connection with regulation of the speech of the citizenry in general. The problem in any case is to arrive at a balance between the interests of the teacher, as a citizen, in commenting upon matters of public concern and the interest of the State, as an employer, in promoting the efficiency of the public services it performs through its employees.

III.

The Board contends that

the teacher by virtue of his public employment has a duty of loyalty to support his superiors in attaining the generally accepted goals of education and that, if he must speak out publicly, he should do so factually and accurately, commensurate with his education and experience.

Appellant, on the other hand, argues that the test applicable to defamatory statements directed against public officials by persons having no occupational relationship with them, namely, that statements to be legally actionable must be made "with knowledge that [they were] … false or with reckless disregard of whether [they were] … false or not" should also be applied to public statements made by teachers.

Because of the enormous variety of fact situations in which critical statements by teachers and other public employees may be thought by their superiors, against whom the statements are directed, to furnish grounds for dismissal, we do not deem it either appropriate or feasible to attempt to lay down a general standard against which all such statements may be judged. However, in the course of evaluating the conflicting claims of First Amendment protection and the need for orderly school administration in the context of this case, we shall indicate some of the general lines along which an analysis of the controlling interests should run.

An examination of the statements in appellant's letter objected to by the Board reveals that they, like the letter as a whole, consist essentially of criticism of the Board's allocation of school funds between educational and athletic programs, and of both the Board's and the superintendent's methods of informing, or preventing the informing of, the district's taxpayers of the real reasons why additional tax revenues were being sought for the schools. The statements are in no way directed towards any person with whom appellant would normally be in contact in the course of his daily work as a teacher. Thus no question of maintaining either discipline by immediate superiors or harmony among co-workers is presented here. Appellant's employment relationships with the Board and, to a somewhat lesser extent, with the superintendent are not the kind of close working relationships for which it can persuasively be claimed that personal loyalty and confidence are necessary to their proper functioning.

Accordingly, to the extent that the Board's position here can be taken to suggest that even comments on matters of public concern that are substantially correct … may furnish grounds for dismissal if they are sufficiently critical in tone, we unequivocally reject it.

We next consider the statements in appellant's letter which we agree to be false. The Board's original charges included allegations that the publication of the letter damaged the professional reputations of the Board and the superintendent and would foment controversy and conflict among the Board, teachers, administrators, and the residents of the district. However, no evidence to support these allegations was introduced at the hearing. So far as the record reveals, Pickering's letter was greeted by everyone but its main target, the Board, with massive apathy and total disbelief. The Board must, therefore, have decided, perhaps by analogy with the law of libel, that the statements were *per se* harmful to the operation of the schools.

However, the only way in which the Board could conclude, absent any evidence of the actual effect of the letter, that the statements contained therein were per se detrimental to the interest of the schools was to equate the Board members' own interests with that of the schools. Certainly an accusation that too much money is being spent on athletics by the administrators of the school system (which is precisely the import of that portion of appellant's letter containing the statements that we have found to be false) cannot reasonably be regarded as *per se* detrimental to the district's schools. Such an accusation reflects rather a difference of opinion between Pickering and the Board as to the preferable manner of operating the school system, a difference of opinion that clearly concerns an issue of general public interest.

In addition, the fact that particular illustrations of the Board's claimed undesirable emphasis on athletic programs are false would not normally have any necessary impact on the actual operation of the schools, beyond its tendency to anger the Board. For example, Pickering's letter was written after the defeat at the polls of the second proposed tax increase. It could, therefore, have had no effect on the ability of the school district to raise necessary revenue, since there was no showing that there was any proposal to increase taxes pending when the letter was written.

More importantly, the question whether a school system requires additional funds is a matter of legitimate public concern on which the judgment of the school administration, including the School Board, cannot, in a society that leaves such questions to popular vote, be taken as conclusive. On such a question, free and open debate is vital to informed decision-making by the electorate. Teachers are, as a class, the members of a community most likely to have informed and definite opinions as to how funds allotted to the operation of the schools should be spent. Accordingly, it is essential that they be able to speak out freely on such questions without fear of retaliatory dismissal.

In addition, the amounts expended on athletics which Pickering reported erroneously were matters of public record on which his position as a teacher in the district did not qualify him to speak with any greater authority than any other taxpayer. The Board could easily have rebutted appellant's errors by publishing the accurate figures itself, either via a letter to the same newspaper or otherwise. We are thus not presented with a situation in which a teacher has carelessly made false statements about matters so closely related to the day-to-day operations of the schools that any harmful impact on the public would be difficult to counter because of the teacher's

presumed greater access to the real facts. Accordingly, we have no occasion to consider at this time whether under such circumstances a school board could reasonably require that a teacher make substantial efforts to verify the accuracy of his charges before publishing them. ...

What we do have before us is a case in which a teacher has made erroneous public statements upon issues then currently the subject of public attention, which are critical of his ultimate employer but which are neither shown nor can be presumed to have in any way either impeded the teacher's proper performance of his daily duties in the classroom or to have interfered with the regular operation of the schools generally. In these circumstances we conclude that the interest of the school administration in limiting teachers' opportunities to contribute to public debate is not significantly greater than its interest in limiting a similar contribution by any member of the general public.

IV.

The public interest in having free and unhindered debate on matters of public importance—the core value of the Free Speech Clause of the First Amendment—is so great that it has been held that a State cannot authorize the recovery of damages by a public official for defamatory statements directed at him except when such statements are shown to have been made either with knowledge of their falsity or with reckless disregard for their truth or falsity. ...

[A]bsent proof of false statements knowingly or recklessly made by him [sic], a teacher's exercise of his [sic] right to speak on issues of public importance may not furnish the basis for his [sic] dismissal from public employment. Since no such showing has been made in this case regarding appellant's letter, his dismissal for writing it cannot be upheld and the judgment of the Illinois Supreme Court must, accordingly, be reversed and the case remanded for further proceedings not inconsistent with this opinion.

Four other Supreme Court cases help to clarify the issues raised in *Pickering*. In *Givhan v. Western Line Consolidated School District*,[27] the Court held that speech need not be made in a public forum to be considered a matter of public concern. Thus, although a teacher's criticism of the school board's policies on racial issues was privately expressed to the principal, it still received the protection of the First Amendment. In *Connick v. Myers*,[28] an assistant district attorney was

27 439 U.S. 410 (1979).
28 461 U.S. 138 (1983).

dismissed in part for circulating a questionnaire soliciting the support of her co-workers for crit-
icisms of the policies and practices of her superiors in the office. In analyzing the questionnaire,
the Court found one question that was not a purely personal grievance. The Court concluded
nevertheless that the questionnaire was an act of insubordination that could (and did) cause a
"mini-insurrection" within the district attorney's office. Thus, the Court concluded that Myers'
dismissal did not violate her free speech rights.

In *Rankin v. McPherson*,[29] the Court held that a clerical employee in a local constabulary could
not be discharged for saying over the telephone, after hearing of the attempted assassination of
President Reagan, "If they go for him again, I hope they get him." In finding that McPherson's
remark dealt with a matter of public concern, the Court noted it was made in the context of a
conversation addressing the policies of the Reagan administration. In *Waters v. Churchill*,[30] the
Supreme Court again used the *Pickering* and *Connick* doctrines to decide the case of a nurse at a
public hospital dismissed after a private conversation at work with a trainee. The Court ruled that
the nurse's First Amendment rights had not been violated because the hospital had made a "reasonable, good-faith" effort to determine if the speech dealt with matters of public concern before
concluding it did not.

Cases that have been decided to date indicate that courts will view comments by public school
employees on the following topics as matters of public concern: The school curriculum and program, the safety and physical well-being of students, issues raised in collective bargaining, alleged
corruption by school or other public officials, and issues that are already the subject of widespread
public discussion.[31] Indeed, union membership itself, even when an employee has not spoken on
union matters, satisfies the public concern test.[32]

In *McKay v. Dallas Independent School District*,[33] a teacher who criticized a school district for
polices that fostered racial segregation was found to have spoken on a matter of public concern.
In *Fisher v. Wellington Exempted Village School Board of Education*,[34] the allegedly lenient treatment
by a school board of a teacher who had viewed pornography on a school computer was found to be
a matter of public concern. However, the Seventh Circuit has ruled that a teacher who discussed
class size in response to criticism about her performance was not speaking on a matter of public concern.[35] Similarly the Fifth Circuit ruled that a principal did not speak on a matter of public concern
in a memo regarding allegations of the misuse of a student activity fund, because the content, form,
and context of the memo showed it was only an effort by the principal to clear his name.[36]

Purely private communications on issues of no importance to the public may also be unprotected. In one case, the court upheld the dismissal of a teacher who told some of her colleagues at
work that she was bisexual and had a female partner, ruling that private communication of this
kind was not protected speech.[37] Similarly, a high school football coach who wanted to join in
student prayers was not entitled to do so under the First Amendment. The Third Circuit held that
his religious expression was not a matter of public concern.[38]

---

29   483 U.S. 378 (1987).
30   511 U.S. 661 (1994).
31   *See, e.g.*, Morfin v. Albuquerque Pub. Sch., 906 F.2d 1434 (10th Cir. 1990); Jeffries v. Harleston, 52 F.3d 9 (2d
     Cir. 1995); Levin v. Harleston, 770 F. Supp. 895 (S.D.N.Y. 1991); Kelly v. Huntington Union Free Sch. Dist., 675
     F.Supp.2d 283 (E.D.N.Y. 2009).
32   Baloga v. Pittston Area Sch. Dist., 927 F.3d 742 (3d Cir. 2019).
33   2009 U.S. Dist. LEXIS 17590 (N.D. Tex. Mar. 3, 2009).
34   223 F. Supp. 2d 833 (N.D. Ohio 2002).
35   Cliff v. Bd. of Sch. Comm'rs of Indianapolis, 42 F.3d 403 (7th Cir. 1994); *see also* Carey v. Aldine Indep. Sch. Dist.,
     996 F. Supp. 641 (S.D. Tex. 1998).
36   Bradshaw v. Pittsburg Ind. Sch. Dist., 207 F.3d 814 (5th Cir. 2000).
37   Rowland v. Mad River Local Sch. Dist., 730 F.2d 444 (6th Cir. 1984).
38   Borden v. School Dist. of Tp. of East Brunswick, 523 F.3d 153 (3rd Cir. 2008).

The more important the issue and the more significant the information supplied by the public school employee, the more the courts seem willing to insist that some disruption be tolerated. However, the more vituperative or abusive the language used by the public school employee, the less disruption need be tolerated. Speech that urges colleagues to engage in unlawful disruptive activities such as illegal strikes is less likely to receive protection, as is speech that discloses the content of confidential or private files or speech that contains significant errors or deliberate falsehoods. In *Munroe v. Central Bucks School District*,[39] a teacher attracted national attention after she complained about the rudeness and lack of motivation in her students, referring to them as "rat-like" and "frightfully dim" in blog posts. She added that parents were "breeding a disgusting brood of insolent, unappreciative, selfish brats." She also referred to a co-worker by name (and with a vulgar epithet). The teacher was dismissed. The court ruled that the blog posts were too disruptive to be entitled to constitutional protection, reasoning that they contained "gratuitously demeaning and insulting language inextricably intertwined with … occasional discussions of public issues."

On issues relating to their "official responsibilities," school employees deemed to work in policy-making positions (including most administrators) may have less protection of freedom of speech than non-policy-making employees (including teachers). In *Vargas-Harrison v. Racine Unified School District*,[40] the Seventh Circuit permitted the demotion and ultimate dismissal of a principal who, against the orders of her superiors, publicly criticized the district's reformulation of a grant proposal. The court found that as a policy-maker in the district, the principal owed her superiors a "duty of loyalty" on this subject even though it was a matter of public concern. The principal's remarks had in fact created tension between the teacher's union and school board. In *McCullough v. Wyandanch*,[41] the Second Circuit held that "high level employees are entitled to limited *Pickering* protection" because generally "the likelihood of disruption will outweigh the employee's right to speak."

School officials may not seek to stifle open criticism by teachers of school policies by requiring that genuine issues of public concern be pursued exclusively through in-house channels.[42] Nor may regulations of employee speech be unconstitutionally **vague** or **overbroad** (see Chapter 6), such as, for example, prohibitions against "criticism" of colleagues or superiors.[43] School officials should also be aware that most states have enacted whistleblower statutes that protect teachers and other public employees from adverse employment actions if they in good faith report a violation of law, government waste, or specific dangers to public health and safety.

School employees who succeed in establishing that they have suffered an adverse employment decision and that they have engaged in protected speech still bear the burden of showing that the protected speech was a substantial factor in the adverse decision. It is not enough that the protected speech occurred sometime before the adverse decision; the employee must show that the decision was motivated by or in retaliation for the protected speech. In *Deschenie v. Board of Education of Central Consolidated School District No. 22*,[44] a bilingual education coordinator's criticism of supervisors a year prior to her dismissal was judged too remote in time to permit an inference of retaliatory discharge.

If an employee-plaintiff succeeds in establishing that protected speech was a substantial motivating factor in an adverse employment decision, the burden of proof then switches to the school district to establish by clear and convincing evidence that the same decision would have been reached regardless of the teacher's speech. That is, school officials must establish that the administrative action occurred for some other reason, such as because of the teacher's incompetence.

39 34 F. Supp. 3d 532 (E.D. Pa. 2014).
40 Vargas-Harrison v. Racine Unified Sch. Dist., 272 F.3d 964 (7th Cir. 2001).
41 187 F.3d 272 (2d Cir. 1999).
42 Brocknell v. Norton, 732 F.2d 664 (8th Cir. 1984).
43 Westbrook v. Teton County Sch. Dist. No. 1, 918 F. Supp. 1475 (D. Wyo. 1996).
44 473 F.3d 1271 (10th Cir. 2007).

Thus, a teacher cannot be disciplined for engaging in protected speech, but a teacher cannot *avoid* discipline by engaging in protected speech.[45]

Academic Freedom and Curricular Speech

In Chapter 3, we saw that states and school districts retain the power to control the curriculum even in the face of most parental and student objections. Do public school teachers have a right to control what they teach? No court has recognized a constitutional right for public school teachers to control course content or instructional methods. Although university professors customarily enjoy considerable **academic freedom**, the following case shows public school teachers do not.

⚖️

EVANS-MARSHALL v. BOARD OF EDUCATION OF THE TIPP CITY EXEMPTED VILLAGE SCHOOL DISTRICT
US Court of Appeals for the Sixth Circuit
624 F.3d 332 (2010)

JEFFREY S. SUTTON, Circuit Judge

Does a public high school teacher have a First (and Fourteenth) Amendment right "to select books and methods of instruction for use in the classroom without interference from public officials"? Yes, says the teacher, Shelley Evans-Marshall. No, says the Tipp City Board of Education. Because the right to free speech protected by the First Amendment does not extend to the in-class curricular speech of teachers in primary and secondary schools made "pursuant to" their official duties, we affirm the judgment rejecting this claim as a matter of law.

I.

In 2000, the Tipp City Board of Education hired Evans-Marshall to teach English and to supervise Tippecanoe High School's literary magazine, *Birch-Bark*, for the 2000–2001 school year. The Board renewed her contract for the 2001–2002 school year, when Evans-Marshall taught English to 9th and 11th grade students and a creative writing course to 11th and 12th grade students. At the beginning of the fall semester, Evans-Marshall assigned Ray Brad-bury's *Fahrenheit 451* to her 9th graders. To the end of exploring the book's theme of government censorship, she distributed a list compiled by the American Library Association of the "100 Most Frequently Challenged Books." Students divided into groups,

and Evans-Marshall asked each group to pick a book from the list, to investigate the reasons why the book was challenged and to lead an in-class debate about the book. Two groups chose *Heather Has Two Mommies* by Leslea Newman.

A parent complained about *Heather Has Two Mommies*, and the principal, Charles Wray, asked Evans-Marshall to tell the students to choose a different book. She complied, explaining to her class that "they were in a unique position to ... use this experience as source material for their debate because they were in the ... position of having actually experienced censorship in preparing to debate censorship." After the class completed the *Fahrenheit 451* unit, Evans-Marshall assigned *Siddhartha* by Hermann Hesse and used it as the basis for in-class discussions about "spirituality, Buddhism, romantic relationships, personal growth, [and] familial relationships."

At the October 2001 meeting of the school board, twenty-five or so parents complained about the curricular choices in the schools, including *Siddhartha* and the book-censorship assignment. The next day, Principal Wray called a meeting of the English department and told Evans-Marshall that she was "on the hot seat." Nearly 100 parents, as well as the local news media, attended the board's November meeting. For over an hour, parents expressed concerns about books in the curriculum and in the

45 Mt. Healthy City Sch. Dist. Bd. of Educ. v. Doyle, 429 U.S. 274 (1977), superseded in part by 5 U.S.C.A. § 1221(e) 2); *see also* Rivera v. United States, 924 F.2d 948 (9th Cir. 1991).

school libraries. While the parents mentioned many books, they raised particular objections to the materials in Evans-Marshall's classroom and her teaching methods. Superintendent John Zigler explained that the school board had purchased many of the materials, including *Siddhartha*, several years before, making it difficult to criticize Evans-Marshall for teaching a book the school board had bought. "You should be embarrassed," one parent responded, referring to the explicit language and sexual themes in the book. ...

The meeting was not one-sided. A member of the board—a parent himself—warned that the school district's policies about potentially objectionable material "have to be well thought out because what you might find offensive, I might not." Another board member reminded the group that, as elected officials, the board "must walk the middle of the road to some extent," even if the community might "err ... on the conservative side." And a parent who made a formal statement said that he "[did not] condone" the behavior of some of the more vocal parents and trusted that school officials "want what's best for our kids."

The matter did not end there. In teaching creative writing, Evans-Marshall maintained a file of student writing samples that she shared with students who asked for additional guidance on assignments. Running low on copies of some of the samples, she sent three of them to support staff to be copied. A member of the copy room staff, apparently not a friend, showed the writing samples to Wray, saying he "ought to read this." After reading the papers, Wray called Evans-Marshall to his office. When she arrived, he waved two of the writing samples in his hand, one a first-hand account of a rape, the other a story about a young boy who murdered a priest and desecrated a church. "[A]re you going to use these in class after everything that's happened?" he shouted.

Evans-Marshall explained that the writing samples were not intended for in-class distribution and that she would refrain from sharing the papers if he wanted. Wray said that he did not like the materials she was using in her classroom or the themes of her in-class discussions and that he "intended to rei[n] it in."

The two soon had another argument in the school library about Evans-Marshall's plans to give a final exam involving group discussions and student self-evaluations. Evans-Marshall asked Wray to give her a model exam so she could "give [him] back exactly what [he] want[ed]," prompting Wray to

call her a "smart a–." The next day, Evans-Marshall complained to Superintendent Zigler about Wray's behavior. Zigler told her to meet with Wray after the semester break to work things out and offered to speak with Wray in the meantime. He also said that she should feel free to file a formal grievance if things had not been worked out by January.

Things did not work out by January. Wray and Evans-Marshall talked, but they fell back into the same channels of disagreement. Evans-Marshall asked whether there was anything aside from her curricular decisions that bothered Wray. "I'll see what other issues I can come up with," Wray responded, "for your evaluation next week." Wray's evaluations criticized Evans-Marshall's attitude and demeanor as well as her "[u]se of material that is pushing the limits of community standards." Evans-Marshall filed written objections to Wray's evaluations and a grievance with Superintendent Zigler.

At its March 2002 meeting, the school board voted unanimously not to renew Evans-Marshall's contract. She requested an explanation, and the school board sent her a letter on April 9, 2002, saying that her non-renewal was "due to problems with communication and teamwork." At Evans-Marshall's request, the board held a formal hearing about the employment decision. Principal Wray, Superintendent Zigler and Evans-Marshall all testified, and the board again voted unanimously not to renew her contract. ...

In March 2003, Evans-Marshall filed this § 1983 action against the school board, Wray and Zigler. She alleged that the school board and other defendants had retaliated against her "curricular and pedagogical choices," infringing her First Amendment right "to select books and methods of instruction for use in the classroom without interference from public officials." The defendants moved to dismiss the complaint for failure to state a claim under Civil Rule 12(b)(6), but the district court held that Evans-Marshall had sufficiently alleged a First Amendment violation. We affirmed.

After discovery by both sides, the defendants again moved for summary judgment, arguing that the Supreme Court's intervening decision in *Garcetti v. Ceballos* and the unrebutted facts gleaned from discovery foreclosed Evans-Marshall's claim. In the alternative, they sought summary judgment on the ground that the school board should prevail under the balancing test announced in *Pickering v. Board of Education*,[46] or that there was no causal link

---

46 391 U.S. 563 (1968).

between Evans-Marshall's curricular choices and the non-renewal of her contract. The district court granted the defendants' summary judgment motion. It declined to apply *Garcetti* to the dispute and held that Evans-Marshall's teaching methods and curricular choices survived the *Pickering* balancing test. But it concluded that she had not provided sufficient evidence "link[ing] her teaching" methods and curricular choices to "the Board's decision to not renew her contract."

II.

This free-speech-retaliation case implicates two competing intuitions. On the one side, doesn't a teacher have the First Amendment right to choose her own reading assignments, decide how they should be taught and above all be able to teach a unit on censorship without being censored or otherwise retaliated against? On the other side, doesn't a school board have the final say over what is taught, and how, in the public schools for which it is responsible? Who wins depends on which line of legal authority controls.

A.

In free-speech retaliation cases arising in the employment context, we ask three questions: Was the individual involved in "constitutionally protected" activity–here activity protected by the free speech clause of the First Amendment? Would the employer's conduct discourage individuals of "ordinary firmness" from continuing to do what they were doing? Was the employee's exercise of constitutionally protected rights "a motivating factor" behind the employer's conduct? The claimant must win each point to prevail.

The first question requires some elaboration. Three Supreme Court cases define the contours of the free-speech rights of public employees.

The "Matters of Public Concern" Requirement.

The First Amendment protects the speech of employees only when it involves "matters of public concern." In *Connick*,[47] an assistant district attorney, after learning that her supervisor planned to transfer her, solicited information from her colleagues

about the office's transfer policy, about office morale and about whether supervisors had pressured anyone to participate in political campaigning. When the supervisor fired her for refusing to accept the transfer, she sued, alleging retaliation against protected speech, namely her initiation of the survey. In rejecting her claim, the Court explained that not all employee speech is protected, only speech that "fairly [may be] considered as relating to" issues "of political, social, or other concern to the community." When, by contrast, an employee's speech does not relate to a matter of public concern, public officials enjoy "wide latitude" in responding to it without "intrusive oversight by the judiciary in the name of the First Amendment."

The "Balancing" Requirement

If the employee establishes that her speech touches "matters of public concern," a balancing test determines whether the employee or the employer wins. In *Pickering*,[48] the Court considered the claim of a high school teacher whom the principal fired after the teacher wrote a letter to the local newspaper, criticizing the school board's budgetary decisions. In resolving the claim, the Court "balance[d] … the interests of the teacher, as a citizen, in commenting upon matters of public concern" against "the interest of the State, as an employer, in promoting the efficiency of the public services it performs through its employees." Reasoning that there was no relationship between the contents of the letter and the "proper performance of [the teacher's] daily duties in the classroom," the Court ruled for the teacher, concluding that the school board's interests did not outweigh his desire to "contribute to public debate" like any other citizen.

The "Pursuant To" Requirement.

In [*Garcetti*,[49]] the last case in the trilogy, a prosecutor reviewed a private complaint that a police officer's affidavit used to obtain a search warrant contained several misrepresentations. After confirming that the affidavit contained serious falsehoods, the prosecutor wrote a memo to his superiors about his findings, recommended that the office dismiss the case and eventually testified to the same effect at a hearing to suppress the evidence discovered

---

47 Connick v. Myers, 461 U.S. 138 (1983).
48 Pickering v. Board of Education, 391 U.S. 563 (1968).
49 Garcetti v. Ceballos, 547 U.S. 410 (2006).

during the search. In the aftermath of these and other actions, the prosecutor claimed that the office retaliated against him by transferring him to another courthouse and by denying him a promotion.

In rejecting his free-speech claim, the Court did not deny that the prosecutor's speech related to a matter of "public concern" under *Connick*, and it did not take on the lower court's reasoning that *Pickering* balancing favored the employee. It instead concluded that the First Amendment did not apply. "The controlling factor," the Court reasoned, "is that his expressions were made pursuant to his duties as a calendar deputy," making the relevant speaker the government entity, not the individual. "We hold that when public employees make statements pursuant to their official duties, the employees are not speaking as citizens for First Amendment purposes, and the Constitution does not insulate their communications from employer discipline."

B.

A First Amendment claimant must satisfy each of these requirements: the *Connick* "matter of public concern" requirement, the *Pickering* "balancing" requirement and the *Garcetti* "pursuant to" requirement. Evans-Marshall clears the first two of these hurdles but not the third.

The content of Evans-Marshall's speech "relat[ed] to ... matter[s] of political, social, or other concern to the community." A teacher's curricular speech, we have said on several occasions, ordinarily covers these matters. "[T]he essence of a teacher's role is to prepare students for their place in society as responsible citizens," and the teacher that can do that without covering topics of public concern is rare indeed, perhaps non-existent. Look no further than the November 2001 meeting of the school board to confirm the point. Members of the community had a lot to say about the topics discussed in Evans-Marshall's class, and they went to the school board meeting to say it.

That large segments of the community disagreed with Evans-Marshall's speech—her class assignments and teaching methods—is beside the point. The question is whether the topics discussed are "of ... concern" to the community, not whether the community approved of the teacher's position on each topic. On this summary-judgment record, Evans-Marshall's curricular speech passes the *Connick* "matter of public concern" test, as the district court correctly determined.

Evans-Marshall also satisfies *Pickering* "balancing"—that her "interests ... as a citizen, in

commenting upon matters of public concern" through her in-class speech outweighed the school board's "interest ... as an employer, in promoting the efficiency of the public services it performs." As the district court correctly concluded, a legitimate factual dispute exists over whether Evans-Marshall's interest in teaching *Siddhartha* (and in making other curricular choices) overshadowed any interest the school board might claim in disciplining her for doing so. Although the school board has "the ability to select and require adherence to a ... stated curriculum," the court concluded, its interest in enforcing curricular standards is severely undermined if it disciplines a teacher for teaching a book the board "had purchased ... and made ... available to teachers as an optional text[.]" ...

After addressing the *Pickering* point, however, the district court concluded that Evans-Marshall stumbled over causation. The court did not believe that Evans-Marshall could show that her exercise of free speech rights was "a motivating factor" behind the school board's conduct. That is a harder point to sell. And a brief accounting of the evidence and the chronology of events shows why.

Before any parents complained about her reading assignments and classroom discussions, Evans-Marshall had never received a negative performance review. Dozens of parents flooded the school board's November 2001 meeting, and many complained about Evans-Marshall's teaching. One parent told the school board that it "should be embarrassed" about the book she was teaching. Principal Wray thereafter told Evans-Marshall that she would have to clear any potentially controversial material with him. He later told Evans-Marshall that he "intended to rei[n] ... in" her classroom discussions. In December 2001, Evans-Marshall complained to Superintendent Zigler about Wray's behavior. And when the semester resumed in January 2002, Wray told Evans-Marshall that he would "see what ... [he could] come up with for [her] evaluations," after which he gave her negative performance reviews for the first time. Only a short time later, the board voted not to renew her contract. To deny a causal relationship between Evans-Marshall's speech and the Board's actions does not come to grips with this sequence of events or with the imperative at this stage of the litigation that we draw all inferences in favor of the non-moving party: the teacher. Evans-Marshall satisfies *Pickering* balancing and has shown that her teaching choices caused the school board to fire her.

Evans-Marshall, however, cannot overcome *Garcetti*. When government employees speak "pursuant to their official duties," *Garcetti* teaches that they are "not speaking as citizens for First Amendment purposes." Any dispute over the board's motivations, *Pickering* balancing or the "public concerns" of her speech under *Connick* is beside the point if, as Evans-Marshall does not dispute, she made her curricular and pedagogical choices in connection with her official duties as a teacher.

In the light cast by *Garcetti*, it is clear that the First Amendment does not generally "insulate" Evans-Marshall "from employer discipline," even discipline prompted by her curricular and pedagogical choices and even if it otherwise appears (at least on summary judgment) that the school administrators treated her shabbily. When a teacher teaches, "the school system does not 'regulate' [that] speech as much as it hires that speech. Expression is a teacher's stock in trade, the commodity she sells to her employer in exchange for a salary." ... Only the school board has ultimate responsibility for what goes on in the classroom, legitimately giving it a say over what teachers may (or may not) teach in the classroom.

It is true that teachers, like students, do not "shed their constitutional rights to freedom of speech or expression at the schoolhouse gate." But that does not transform them into the employee and employer when it comes to deciding what, when and how English is taught to fifteen-year-old students.

Consider the difference between the speech of Evans-Marshall and Marvin Pickering, teachers both. When Pickering sent a letter to the local newspaper criticizing the school board, he said something that any citizen has a right to say, and he did it on his own time and in his own name, not on the school's time or in its name. Yet when Evans-Marshall taught 9th grade English, she did something she was hired (and paid) to do, something she could not have done but for the Board's decision to hire her as a public school teacher. As with any other individual in the community, she had no more free-speech right to dictate the school's curriculum than she had to obtain a platform—a teaching position—in the first instance for communicating her preferred list of books and teaching methods. "[N]o relevant analogue" exists between her in-class curricular speech and speech by private citizens.

Teachers are not everyday citizens, Evans-Marshall insists, and they have a right "to select books and methods of instruction for use in the classroom without interference from public officials."

But that is not what Ohio law provides or the First Amendment requires. Start with Ohio law.[50] Under it, "[t]he board of education of each city ... shall prescribe a curriculum."

State law gives elected officials—the school board—not teachers, not the chair of a department, not the principal, not even the superintendent, responsibility over the curriculum. This is an accountability measure, pure and simple, one that ensures the citizens of a community have a say over a matter of considerable importance to many of them—their children's education—by giving them control over membership on the board.

The First Amendment does not ban this policy choice or this accountability measure. The Constitution does not prohibit a State from creating elected school boards and from placing responsibility for the curriculum of each school district in the hands of each board. ...

How at any rate would a contrary approach work? If one teacher, Evans-Marshall, has a First Amendment right "to select books and methods of instruction for use in the classroom," so presumably do other teachers. Evans-Marshall may wish to teach *Siddhartha* in the first unit of the school year in a certain way, but the chair of the English department may wish to use the limited time in a school year to teach *A Tale of Two Cities* at that stage of the year. Maybe the head of the upper school has something else in mind. When educators disagree over what should be assigned, as is surely bound to happen if each of them has a First Amendment right to influence the curriculum, whose free-speech rights win? Why indeed doesn't the principal, Wray, have a right to defend the discharge on the ground that he was merely exercising his First Amendment rights in rejecting Evans-Marshall's curricular choices and methods of teaching? Placing the First Amendment's stamp of approval on these kinds of debates not only would "demand permanent judicial intervention in the conduct of governmental operations," but it also would transform run-of-the-mine curricular disputes into constitutional stalemates.

That is not the only problem. What employer discipline arising from an employee's manner of teaching—choices of books and the methods of teaching them—does not implicate speech? Could a teacher respond to a principal's insistence that she discuss certain materials by claiming that it improperly compels speech? Could a teacher continue to assign materials that members of the community perceive as racially

50 O.R.C. § 3313.60(A).

insensitive even after the principal tells her not to? Could a teacher raise a controversial topic (say, the virtues of one theory of government over another or the virtues of intelligent design) after a principal has told her not to? Could a teacher introduce mature sexual themes to fifteen year olds when discussing a work of literature after a principal has told her not to? …

Because "one man's vulgarity is another's lyric," or, as one school board member put the point at the November 2001 meeting, "what you might find offensive, I might not," parents long have demanded that school boards control the curriculum and the ways of teaching it to their impressionable children. Permitting federal courts to distinguish classroom vulgarities from lyrics or to pick sides on how to teach Siddhartha not only is a recipe for disenfranchising the 9,000 or so members of the Tipp City community but also tests judicial competence. …

The key insight of Garcetti is that the First Amendment has nothing to say about these kinds of decisions. An employee does not lose "any liberties the employee might have enjoyed as a private citizen" by signing on to work for the government, but by the same token, the government, just like a private employer, retains "control over what the employer itself has commissioned or created": the employee's job. And that insight has particular resonance in the context of public education. Every child in Ohio must attend school, providing public school teachers with a captive audience for their in-class speech, and providing a compelling reason for putting curricular choices in the hands of "someone [they] can vote out of office," or who is otherwise democratically accountable …

In concluding that the First Amendment does not protect primary and secondary school teachers' in-class curricular speech, we have considerable company. The Seventh Circuit invoked Garcetti in concluding that the curricular and pedagogical choices of primary and secondary school teachers exceed the reach of the First Amendment.

The Fourth Circuit has not applied Garcetti to teachers' in-class speech,[51] and is sometimes cited as creating a division among the circuits.[52] But that is because the Fourth Circuit disposed of the teacher's retaliation claim based on pre-Garcetti precedent, namely Connick, holding that "speech that occurs within a compulsory classroom setting" "does not

constitute speech on a matter of public concern" when it is "curricular in nature." The Fourth Circuit's approach changes nothing here: A teacher's curricular and pedagogical choices are categorically unprotected, whether under Connick or Garcetti.

The Third Circuit also has declined to resolve the applicability of Garcetti to this sort of speech, but that too makes no difference. Its pre-Garcetti cases hold that, "although [a teacher] has a right to advocate outside of the classroom for the use of certain curriculum materials, he does not have a right to use those materials in the classroom."

The Tenth Circuit has applied Garcetti to a school teacher's speech about curriculum and pedagogy, even when made outside the classroom,[53] but has not addressed in-class curricular speech.

The Second Circuit determined, in an unpublished decision, that it need not resolve whether a teacher's in-class speech is governed by Garcetti or by its earlier cases applying the "reasonably related to legitimate pedagogical concerns" standard of Hazelwood School District v. Kuhlmeier.[54]

Other courts of appeals, including this one, have applied Garcetti in rejecting school employees' speech claims, though not in the context of curricular and pedagogical choices. The common thread through all of these cases is that, when it comes to in-class curricular speech at the primary or secondary school level, no other court of appeals has held that such speech is protected by the First Amendment.

Our decision also respects Sixth Circuit authority. In Cockrel and in our initial decision in this case, we held that a school teacher's curricular and pedagogical choices (1) are "speech," (2) touch on "matters of public concern" and (3) may satisfy Pickering balancing depending on the circumstances developed in discovery or at trial. We do not disturb those holdings and indeed have ruled for the plaintiff on each one of these points today.

Not one of these Sixth Circuit cases, however, addressed whether in-class curricular speech survives the threshold inquiry announced in Garcetti: whether the speech was "pursuant to" the claimant's official duties. How could they? Garcetti came down after both decisions and established a new threshold requirement in this area. Evans-Marshall's failure to satisfy this requirement governs us here. "[A] plaintiff may not run home before she reaches first base."

51 See Lee v. York County Sch. Div., 484 F.3d 687 (4th Cir. 2007).
52 See, e.g., Gorum v. Sessoms, 561 F.3d 179, 186 n.6 (3d Cir. 2009).
53 See Brammer-Hoelter v. Twin Peaks Charter Acad., 492 F.3d 1192, 1204 (10th Cir. 2007).
54 484 U.S. 260 (1988).

Nor can Evans-Marshall sidestep this conclusion on the theory that *Garcetti* does not apply. In his dissent in *Garcetti*, as Evans-Marshall points out, Justice Souter raised concerns about the applicability of the decision to "academic freedom in public colleges and universities." The majority disclaimed any intent to resolve the point.

Garcetti's caveat offers no refuge to Evans-Marshall. She is not a teacher at a "public college[]" or "universit[y]" and thus falls outside of the group the dissent wished to protect. The concept of "academic freedom," moreover, does not readily apply to in-class curricular speech at the high school level. As a cultural and a legal principle, academic freedom "was conceived and implemented in the university" out of concern for "teachers who are also researchers or scholars—work not generally expected of elementary and secondary school teachers."[55] ... Even to the extent academic freedom, as a constitutional rule, could somehow apply to primary and secondary schools, that does not insulate a teacher's curricular and pedagogical choices from the school board's oversight, as opposed to the teacher's right to speak and write publicly about academic issues outside of the classroom. "[I]t is the educational institution that has a right to academic freedom, not the individual teacher." ...

In the context of in-class curricular speech, this court has already said in the university arena that a teacher's invocation of academic freedom does not warrant judicial intrusion upon an educational institution's decisions: "The First Amendment concept of academic freedom does not require that a non-tenured professor be made a sovereign unto himself." A school "may constitutionally choose not to renew the contract of a non-tenured professor" when that professor's "pedagogical attitude and teaching methods do not conform to institutional standards." Just so here.

III.

For these reasons, we affirm the judgment of the district court.

In *Demers v. Austin*,[56] a college case, the Ninth Circuit held that "*Garcetti* does not—indeed, consistent with the First Amendment, cannot—apply to teaching and academic writing that are performed 'pursuant to the official duties' of a teacher and professor." The court held that "academic employee speech not covered by *Garcetti* is protected under the First Amendment, using the analysis established in *Pickering*."

Although *Hazelwood v. Kuhlmeier* involved *student* speech (see Chapter 4), a number of courts have relied on its basic doctrine that public school officials may control "school-sponsored expressive activities so long as their actions are reasonably related to legitimate pedagogical concerns"— to reject *teacher* claims of academic freedom.[57] In *Boring v. Buncombe County Board of Education*,[58] a teacher was disciplined for allowing students to perform a play featuring a lesbian and an unmarried woman with an unplanned pregnancy. The Fourth Circuit found for the district, citing *Hazelwood*. In *Kirkland v. Northside Independent School District*,[59] the Fifth Circuit cited *Hazelwood* and *Pickering* in denying a teacher's right to select a class reading list without first obtaining prior approval. In *Kirby v. Yonkers School District*,[60] a health teacher was disciplined for asking seventh- and eighth-graders to draw the male reproductive system on the blackboard. The district court found no First Amendment violation, citing *Hazelwood*. In *Kramer v. New York City Board of Education*,[61] a district court allowed the school board to discipline a junior high school teacher

---

55 *Citing* J. Peter Byrne, *Academic Freedom: A "Special Concern of the First Amendment"*, 99 YALE L.J. 251, 288 n.137 (1989).
56 746 F.3d 402 (9th Cir. 2014).
57 484 U.S. 260 (1988).
58 136 F.3d 364 (4th Cir. 1998).
59 890 F.2d 794 (5th Cir. 1989).
60 767 F.Supp.2d 452 (S.D.N.Y. 2011).
61 715 F. Supp. 2d 335 (E.D.N.Y. 2010).

who had allowed her students to use "vulgar slang" in a sex education class. And in *LeVake v. Independent School District No. 656*,[62] a state court permitted the reassignment of a science teacher who would not teach the theory of evolution without including a criticism of the theory, which was not part of the curriculum.

In-School, Non-Curricular Speech

School districts have broad latitude to determine what and how their teachers will teach. Does this mean districts can control everything their teachers say while at work or in the presence of students? Do teachers have a right to express their personal views to colleagues and students, for example, by wearing an armband or button or distributing religious literature?

In deciding disputes over in-school, non-curricular speech by teachers, many courts have applied the approach first developed for use with in-school, non-curricular speech by students in *Tinker* (see Chapter 4).[63] A teacher's speech is protected as long as it does not materially and substantially disrupt the school and its operations. In *James v. Board of Education of Central District No. 1*,[64] a teacher wore a black armband in school to protest US involvement in the Vietnam War. When James refused his administrator's order to remove the armband, he was suspended and eventually dismissed. The school board justified its action by arguing that all teacher speech occurring during a class is curricular speech over which the school has broad control. While the Second Circuit agreed with the board's claim of control over the curriculum and with the principle that teachers cannot claim the right to substitute political proselytizing or indoctrination for carrying out their assigned duties, it nevertheless found the dismissal unconstitutional. The court noted that there was no hint of disruption caused by James' actions nor any reason to expect disruption. Most importantly, wearing the armband did not in any way interfere with James' ability to carry out his teaching functions. Furthermore, the board had engaged in viewpoint discrimination because it had permitted another teacher to display a slogan supportive of US foreign policy and, in firing James, had cast a "pall of orthodoxy" over the classroom in direct violation of the principles announced by the Supreme Court in *Tinker*.

In *Downs v. Los Angeles Unified School District*,[65] a case with facts similar to *James*, the Ninth Circuit ruled against a teacher who was prohibited from posting materials on his school bulletin board in opposition to Gay and Lesbian Awareness Month. The school had posted materials promoting observance of the event, and it had permitted other teachers to post their own supporting materials. The court ruled that the school had not created a public forum because the principal retained control over the bulletin board (a crucial difference from *James*). In permitting some materials and prohibiting others, the school was deciding what it wished to say and what it wished not to say. Citing *Hazelwood*, the court noted that the school is not required to be content-neutral with regard to speech that bears its "imprimatur." Similarly, in *Lee v. York County School District*,[66] the Fourth Circuit ruled against a Spanish teacher who had posted religious-oriented materials on the bulletin board in his own classroom. Although the teacher claimed that he was expressing his personal views, the Court found that, under *Hazelwood*, students and parents would attribute materials on the bulletin board to the school.

In *Johnson v. Poway Unified School District*,[67] a math teacher had posted banners in his classroom containing Judeo-Christian messages for over 25 years, with no evidence of disruption. The school

62 625 N.W.2d 502 (Minn. Ct. App. 2001).
63 Tinker v. Des Moines Independent Community School District, 393 U.S. 503 (1969).
64 461 F.2d 566 (2d Cir. 1972).
65 228 F.3d 1003 (9th Cir. 2000).
66 484 F.3d 687 (4th Cir. 2007).
67 658 F.3d 954 (9th Cir. 2011), *cert. denied*, 132 S. Ct. 1807 (2012).

district ordered their removal, but allowed other teachers to continue to post materials founded in personal (and religious) expression, including posters of the Dalai Lama and Tibetan prayer flags. In direct contradiction of *James*, the Ninth Circuit found that such viewpoint discrimination was permissible, on the ground that teachers had no right to personal expression in the classroom.

In *Grossman v. South Shore Public School District*,[68] the contract of a guidance counselor who threw out approved literature on the use of birth control and distributed "abstinence-only" literature to students instead was not renewed. The guidance counselor unsuccessfully claimed the district was hostile to her religious beliefs, in violation of her free exercise rights. The Seventh Circuit concluded that the district had legal authority to control the curriculum, but individual staff members did not. "Teachers and other public school employees have no right to make the promotion of religion a part of their job description and by doing so precipitate a possible violation of the [Establishment Clause]," wrote the court. "The First Amendment is 'not a teacher license for uncontrolled expression at variance with established curricular content.'"[69]

In *Kennedy v. Bremerton School District*,[70] a football coach routinely encouraged students and spectators to join him in Christian prayers, attracting considerable media attention. When a Satanist group sought to lead similar prayers, however, the school district cracked down. In ruling against the football coach, the Ninth Circuit reiterated that public school teachers are employees, who have no right to individual expression under the First Amendment.

Investigation, Surveillance, and Searches of School Employees

There are two types of privacy issues that can lead to conflict between a school district and its employees. The first type arises when districts seek to control the personal lifestyle choices and behaviors of employees. The second arises when districts seek to acquire information about employees that the employees do not wish them to have.

Many states have statutes authorizing the dismissal of a teacher for "immorality" or "unprofessional" conduct (see Chapter 11). These somewhat vague categories seem to authorize firing for behavior and lifestyle choices that the community or school board deems wrong or inappropriate for teachers. However, some personal choices, no matter how a community might view them, are protected by the constitutional right to **privacy**.[71] This does not mean that the Constitution provides teachers absolute immunity from discharge for lifestyle choices. It does mean, however, that if the right of privacy is implicated, the school must have an especially good reason for the dismissal.

School districts may have a variety of reasons for seeking information about their employees. In order to protect their students and avoid liability for **negligent hiring** or **negligent retention** (see Chapter 12), they may wish to inquire into the behavior of current and prospective employees, particularly with regard to criminality and sexual or other misconduct involving children. In order to assess their fitness for work, districts may want to learn about the mental or physical health or the use of drugs by current or prospective employees (see Chapter 11).

To make sure that employees are not shirking their duties or engaging in misconduct and to avoid liability for **negligent supervision** (see Chapter 12), school districts may want to use open or hidden electronic surveillance techniques or monitor employee use of email or the Internet on the school's computer system. The need for investigation may be particularly strong with regard to employee behaviors that the school is legally obligated to prevent, such as racial and sexual harassment (see Chapter 7) or copyright infringements (see Chapter 3).

---

68 507 F.3d 1097 (2007).
69 Palmer v. Board of Education, 603 F.2d 1271 (7th Cir. 1979).
70 869 F.3d 813 (9th Cir. 2017).
71 Griswold v. Connecticut, 381 U.S. 479 (1965).

Whatever the motivation, the collection and disclosure by schools of information about their employees raises a variety of legal issues. The Fourteenth Amendment's protection of personal privacy prohibits school districts from inquiring into areas of personal behavior like marriage and sex unless they have a compelling reason to do so. The need to protect students from employee misconduct can provide the necessary rationale. In *Flaskamp v. Dearborn Public Schools*,[72] for example, a federal court allowed a school district to inquire into the post-graduation relationship between a female teacher and a former student. To be constitutional, inquiries such as these must be justified by the legitimate interests of the school district and narrowly tailored to meet those interests.[73]

Medical Records

In cases involving either the collection of information or its disclosure to the public, courts must balance the privacy interests of the employee against the needs of the school and the public.[74] In *O'Connor v. Pierson*,[75] the Second Circuit found that a school board's insistence on receiving a teacher's medical records regarding substance abuse treatment could serve no legitimate purpose because the "board was not competent to independently evaluate those records." The court also noted that revealing private medical information without consent may also violate due process. In *McVetty v. Valley Stream Union Free School District*,[76] a school custodian was accused of threatening his ex-wife (also a school employee). The highest court in New York held that the school district was justified in subjecting him to a psychiatric examination, but found its request for "any and all medical records" to be overly broad. In *Down v. Ann Arbor Public Schools*,[77] a teacher accused of verbally abusing students could be compelled to undergo a psychological examination. Although the exam was a search for purposes of the Fourth Amendment, the court found it was not an unreasonable search given the diminished expectation of privacy of public school teachers.

In addition to the Fourteenth Amendment, the **Rehabilitation Act of 1973** and the **Americans with Disabilities Act**, as discussed later in this chapter, limit the authority of school districts to order applicants and employees to undergo medical and psychiatric examinations, as do some state statutes.[78]

Open Records Laws

All states have **Open Records** laws requiring that the records of public entities be open to public scrutiny, subject to certain exceptions. When a school district receives a request for information under an Open Records law, the district must either comply or assert that a specific exemption prohibits it from disclosing the information. Records regarding an ongoing investigation of employee misconduct may be subject to an exception that covers preliminary drafts and recommendations as opposed to completed documents and decisions. Some personnel files may be covered by a "personal privacy" exception. The Supreme Court of Washington upheld an exception for sexual misconduct investigations of teachers that resulted in no charges against the teachers. The court reasoned that the teachers' privacy interests outweighed the broad policy favoring the public's right to know.[79]

---

72 232 F. Supp. 2d 730 (E.D. Mich. 2002); *see also* Hughes v. N. Olmsted, 93 F.3d 238 (6th Cir. 1996).
73 *See* Thorne v. El Segundo, 726 F.2d 459 (9th Cir. 1983).
74 Sterling v. Minersville, 232 F.3d 190 (3d Cir. 2000); Kallstrom v. Columbus, 136 F.3d 1055 (6th Cir. 1998).
75 426 F.3d 187 (2d Cir. 2005); *but see* Thompson v. City of Arlington, Texas, 838 F. Supp. 1137 (N.D. Texas 1993).
76 63 N.Y.S.3d 388 (N.Y. App. Div. 2d Dept. 2017).
77 29 F. Supp. 3d 1030 (E.D. Mich. 2014).
78 Sch. Dist. No. 1 v. Teachers' Retirement Fund Ass'n, 95 P.2d 720 (Or. 1939); Cude v. State, 377 S.W.2d 816 (Ark. 1964).
79 Bellevue John Does 1-11 v. Bellevue School Dist. #405, 189 P.3d 139 (Wash. 2008).

What about the disclosure of teacher evaluations and "value added scores" (see Chapter 11), which pit the public's interest in discerning teacher effectiveness against claims that such evaluations are potentially misleading? The states are divided as to whether such information should be made public.[80]

Searches and Seizures

The Fourth Amendment protects individuals from unreasonable searches and seizures by agents of the State. *New Jersey v. T.L.O.* established the principle that public school officials may search students only if they have reasonable suspicion that the search will reveal evidence of wrongdoing (see Chapter 5). But does the same principle apply to teachers and other public school employees?

In *O'Connor v. Ortega*,[81] a doctor objected to his employer's search of his office in a public hospital. Although the case produced only a plurality opinion, a majority of the justices agreed that the Fourth Amendment's protection against unreasonable search and seizure extends to public employees. It applies only to areas where an employee has a reasonable expectation of privacy, a determination made on a case-by-case basis. Employees do have reasonable expectations of privacy with regard to personal items such as handbags, luggage, and briefcases as well as lockers, desks, filing cabinets, and computers owned by the employer but used exclusively by the employee. However, an employee's expectation of privacy regarding lockers, desks, filing cabinets, and computers "may be reduced by actual office practices and procedures, or by legitimate regulation." The more other employees and supervisors have access to these areas, the less the expectation of privacy.

Even if a public employee has a reasonable expectation of privacy, said the *Otega* plurality, the employer may still conduct a search if the search is "reasonable":

> Ordinarily, a search of an employee's office by a supervisor will be "justified at its inception" when there are reasonable grounds for suspecting that the search will turn up evidence that the employee is guilty of work-related misconduct, or that the search is necessary for a non-investigatory work-related purpose such as to retrieve a needed file … The search will be permissible in its scope when "the measures adopted are reasonably related to the objectives of the search and not excessively intrusive in light of … the nature of the [misconduct]."

The plurality and concurring opinion in *Ortega* indicate that the majority of the Court would accept reasonable intrusions into a protected area for routine work-related purposes such as to hunt for needed supplies or to uncover evidence of work-related malfeasance. One case found that a state agency had reasonable grounds to search an employee's computer based on an anonymous tip that the employee spent the majority of his time at work on activities unrelated to the agency's work. The search revealed that the employee was carrying on a tax preparation service while at work.[82]

Because *Ortega* occurred in a non-school setting and because the case produced no majority opinion, it does not fully settle the application of the Fourth Amendment to searches involving public school employees. Nevertheless, it does seem clear that school employees have reasonable expectations of privacy in their handbags, briefcases, and other personal packages brought to school. To the extent that desks, filing cabinets, storage areas, and lockers are shared with other employees, no reasonable expectation of privacy would exist. Where an expectation of privacy does exist, the requirements of the Fourth Amendment apply so a search may only be conducted in accordance with the "reasonable grounds."

80 Steven Sawchuck, *Access to Teacher Evaluations Divides Advocates*, Education Week (March 28, 2012).
81 480 U.S. 709 (1987).
82 Leventhal v. Knapek, 266 F.3d 64 (2d Cir. 2001).

Searches of employee email accounts on public school computer systems raise a number of legal issues, most not fully decided. Messages sent to or from a general school account as opposed to a personal, password-protected account may be deemed in "plain view" and therefore not entitled to Fourth Amendment protection, as may messages disseminated to a wide audience or chat room. Messages sent to a supervisor have been voluntarily disclosed, so they receive no Fourth Amendment protection.[83] In *Brown-Criscuolo v. Wolfe*,[84] the court held that a principal retained an expectation of privacy in her personal emails when the district did not have access to her password and when the district's email policy granted employees "a limited privacy expectation in the contents of their personal files on the District system." Indeed, messages between individuals sent from or to an employee's personal account should be treated like telephone messages; districts can examine them only if the *Ortega* criteria are met.[85] It is probably not permissible for a school district to require employees to waive Fourth Amendment rights if they wish to have access to their school's e-mail or computer system.[86]

The federal statute known as the **Electronic Communications Privacy Act of 1986** (ECPA),[87] as modified by the **USA Patriot Act**,[88] generally prohibits the interception of messages sent by telephone or email.[89]

The use of **electronic surveillance** also raises both Fourth Amendment and statutory issues. In *Brannen v. Kings Local School District Board of Education*,[90] school officials placed a hidden camera in a break room to determine if custodians were slacking off. The court ruled there was no Fourth Amendment violation because the custodians did not have a reasonable expectation of privacy in a break room available to all. In *State v. McLellan*,[91] a custodian caught by a hidden camera stealing money from an envelope in a classroom argued unsuccessfully that the camera violated his Fourth Amendment rights. The court ruled he had no reasonable expectancy of privacy in the classroom, even at 5 a.m. Similarly, in *Plock v. Bd. of Educ. of Freeport Sch. Dist. No. 145*,[92] teachers could not enjoin the installation of surveillance cameras. "A classroom in a public school is not the private property of any teacher," write the court. Like students, public school employees have a legitimate expectation of privacy in restrooms and other private areas.[93]

Devices that record sound are covered by the *ECPA*, but when visibly placed in work areas, they are permissible.

Drug Testing

Drug testing of public school employees is a search for Fourth Amendment purposes. If school officials have reasonable grounds to suspect that an employee is intoxicated or possesses drugs or alcohol at school, testing does not violate the Fourth Amendment. Thus, the Eleventh Circuit upheld the testing of a teacher after sniffer dogs detected drugs in the teacher's car and a subsequent search of the car revealed marijuana in the ashtray.[94] Random drug testing of employees in

83 Smyth v. Pillsbury Co., 914 F. Supp. 97 (E.D. Pa. 1996).
84 601 F. Supp. 2d 441 (D. Conn. 2009).
85 United States v. Charbonneau, 979 F. Supp. 1177 (S.D. Ohio 1997); United States v. Maxwell, 45 M.J. 406 (C.A.A.F. 1996).
86 *Compare* Wyman v. James, 400 U.S. 309 (1971).
87 18 U.S.C. § 2510–2522, *amended by* the *Electronics Communication Privacy Act of 1986*, 100 Stat. 1848.
88 115 Stat. 272 (2001).
89 Steve Jackson Games, Inc. v. United States Secret Serv., 36 F.3d 457 (5th Cir. 1994); United States v. Reyes, 922 F. Supp. 818 (S.D.N.Y. 1996).
90 761 N.E.2d 84 (Ohio Ct. App. 2001).
91 744 A.2d 611 (N.H. 1999).
92 545 F. Supp. 2d 755, 758 (N.D. Ill. 2007).
93 People v. Triggs, 506 P.2d 232 (Cal. 1973).
94 Hearn v. Bd. of Pub. Educ., 191 F.3d 1329, *reh'g denied*, 204 F.3d 1124 (11th Cir. 1999) [*unpublished*].

the absence of individualized suspicion raises a much more difficult issue. In *Independent School District No. 1 of Tulsa County v. Logan*,[95] the court found that requiring school bus drivers to undergo annual "toxicological urinalysis" was not

> unreasonable under the [F]ourth [A]mendment ... (T)he school district has a sufficient safety interest in maintaining a pool of bus drivers free from the effects of drug use to require drug screening as part of the annual physical examination without a particularized suspicion of drug use directed at any one individual employee.

The same reasoning might justify random testing of shop or driver education teachers, but do most teachers occupy "safety-sensitive" positions? The highest state court of New York concluded that a school district's mandatory drug testing of all probationary teachers was an impermissible infringement of their Fourth Amendment rights.[96] An appellate court in North Carolina reached a similar conclusion regarding random drug testing of all teachers, staff, and administrators.[97] But after deciding that teaching is a safety-sensitive occupation with a diminished expectation of privacy, the Sixth Circuit upheld a school's program of random drug testing of teachers.[98] This approach was criticized by another federal court, which concluded that the safety risks associated with teaching were not comparable to the risks associated with "police officers carrying firearms [or] nuclear power plant engineers." In its view, safety concerns could not override the teachers' Fourth Amendment rights.[99]

The federal **Drug-Free Schools and Communities Act Amendments of 1989**[100] requires that schools receiving federal assistance establish programs for both employees and students designed to prevent drug and alcohol abuse. Schools must annually distribute written materials specifying that it is unlawful to possess or distribute illicit drugs and alcohol, describing the legal sanctions for violation of the law, explaining the health risks associated with drugs and alcohol, listing available counseling programs, and warning that the school will impose its own sanctions for possession and use. The statute does not require districts to institute drug testing, but it does require enforcement of sanctions against those employees and students who violate drug and alcohol rules.

Race, Ethnicity, Gender and Identity, Sexual Orientation and Identity

Adverse employment decisions may lead to claims of discrimination based on race, ethnicity, alienage, gender, sexual orientation, sexual identity, religion, disability, or age. Plaintiffs may challenge an allegedly inequitable salary or benefit structure or an adverse decision regarding hiring, promotion, transfer, demotion, or dismissal. Most of these legal challenges are based on federal statutes, which are the primary focus of this section.

There are, however, some cases in which employees base their claims on the Equal Protection Clause. In *Chang v. Glynn County School District*,[101] the teacher-plaintiffs successfully relied on the Equal Protection Clause to block a school district from firing them based on a state statute

---

95   789 P.2d 636 (Okla. Ct. App. 1989); *see also* Skinner v. Ry. Labor Executives' Ass'n, 489 U.S. 602 (1989).

96   Patchogue-Medford Congress of Teachers v. Bd. of Educ. of Patchogue-Medford, 510 N.E.2d 325 (N.Y. 1987).

97   Jones v. Graham County Bd. of Educ., 677 S.E.2d 171 (N.C. App. 2009); *see also* Smith County Educ. Ass'n v. Smith County Bd. of Educ., 781 F.Supp.2d 604 (M.D. Tenn. 2011).

98   Knox County Education Association v. Knox County Board of Education, 158 F.3d 361 (6th Cir.1998), *cert. denied*, 528 U.S. 812 (1999).

99   Am. Fed'n of Teachers-W. Va, AFL-CIO v. Kanawha Cty. Bd. of Educ., 592 F. Supp. 2d 883, 903 (S.D.W. Va. 2009).

100 20 U.S.C. § 1145g.

101 457 F. Supp. 2d 1378 (S.D. Ga. 2006).

prohibiting schools from employing "any alien for any purpose until a thorough investigation has been made and it is ascertained that there is no qualified American citizen available to perform the duty desired." In a Montana case, an unmarried same-sex couple successfully argued that denying them fringe benefits provided to unmarried heterosexual couples violated the Equal Protection Clause of the state's constitution.[102] Another court refused to dismiss a transgender man's claim of denial of equal protection after an offer of employment was withdrawn because he was planning to undergo sex reassignment surgery.[103]

Some older cases have rejected claims that firing teachers who underwent gender reassignment surgeries violated due process or privacy rights,[104] but given the Supreme Court's more recent protection of the privacy rights of members of LGBTQ communities,[105] these decisions may no longer be sound precedent: As the Court noted in *Lawrence v. Texas*,[106] "Liberty presumes an autonomy of self that includes freedom of thought, belief, expression, and certain intimate conduct."

In *Schroeder v. Hamilton School District*,[107] a teacher claimed the school district discriminated against him on the basis of his sexual orientation by not taking sufficient steps to stop a campaign of harassment by students, parents, and staff members. For five years the teacher endured taunts, slurs, libelous comments, harassing phone calls, and having his tires slashed, culminating in a mental breakdown and his resignation. The teacher argued the district should have handled his complaints in a manner similar to those based on race or gender. In evaluating this claim, the court relied on the **rational-basis equal-protection** test because differential treatment based on sexual orientation does not trigger strict scrutiny (see Chapter 7). A divided court found that the higher priority placed on stopping other forms of harassment was rational: "[I]t is not irrational for school administrators to devote more time and effort to defusing racial tensions among many students than to preventing harassment of one [LGBTQ] teacher." The court noted that the teacher had not been treated differently from heterosexual teachers and that the district had taken some steps to address the harassment, such as punishing students for using homophobic slurs. This showed that the school had not been "deliberately indifferent" to the harassment, which the court said was all that was necessary to defeat the equal protection claim.

Other courts have ruled differently. For example, in *Weaver v. Nebo School District*,[108] the court held that even though strict scrutiny did not apply, it was irrational and therefore unconstitutional under the Equal Protection Clause for a high school to bar a teacher from coaching volleyball because of her sexual orientation.

Title VII of the *Civil Rights Act of 1964* forbids discrimination in public and private employment on the basis of race, gender, color, religion, or national origin.[109] The ***Civil Rights Act of 1991*** supplements Title VII with additional antidiscrimination requirements.[110] **Title IX of the *Education Amendments of 1972*** also prohibits gender discrimination in employment in schools receiving federal financial assistance.[111] The ***Pregnancy Discrimination Act of 1978***[112] prohibits employers from discriminating on the basis of pregnancy and specifies that Title VII's prohibition

102 Snetsinger v. Montana Univ. System, 104 P.3d 445 (Mont. 2004).
103 Doe v. United States Postal Service, 1985 U.S. Dist. LEXIS 18959.
104 Ashlie v. Chester-Upland Sch. Dist., 1979 U.S. Dist. LEXIS 12516; *see also* Grossman v. Sch. Dist. of Twp. of Bernards, 316 A.2d 39 (N.J. Super. Ct. App. Div. 1974).
105 Obergefell v. Hodges, 135 S. Ct. 2584 (2015).
106 539 U.S. 558 (2003).
107 282 F.3d 946 (7th Cir. 2002).
108 Weaver v. Nebo Sch. Dist., 29 F.Supp.2d 1279 (Utah 1998); *see also* Glover v. Williamsburg Local Sch. Dist. Bd. of Educ., 20 F.Supp.2d 1160, 1174 (S.D. Ohio 1998).
109 42 U.S.C. § 2000(e).
110 42 U.S.C. § 1981.
111 N. Haven Bd. of Educ. v. Bell, 456 U.S. 512 (1982).
112 42 U.S.C. § 2000(e).

of discrimination on the basis of gender includes discrimination on the basis of "pregnancy, child-birth, or related medical conditions."[113]

The federal agency charged with enforcing federal laws prohibiting discrimination in employment is the **Equal Employment Opportunity Commission (EEOC)**. Employment discrimination complaints must be filed first with the EEOC or a related state fair-employment agency. If the EEOC ultimately fails to act or chooses not to take legal action, the employee may then go to court with a private suit.

Title VII states:

> It shall be an unlawful employment practice for an employer—(1) to fail or refuse to hire or to discharge any individual, or otherwise to discriminate against any individual with respect to his compensation, terms, conditions, or privileges of employment, because of such individual's race, color, religion, sex, or national origin ...[114]

There is disagreement as to whether Title VII prohibits discrimination on the basis of sexual orientation; most federal courts that have considered the issue hold that it does not.[115] Thus, in most jurisdictions it is not a Title VII violation to deny employment benefits to unmarried same-sex couples that are provided to unmarried heterosexual couples or, as two courts have said, to provide benefits to unmarried same-sex but not heterosexual couples.[116]

Discrimination based on failure to conform to a sex stereotype, whether in appearance or behavior, is covered by Title VII.[117] Some courts have also ruled that Title VII protects people who are transgender against discrimination either on the basis of gender non-conforming conduct or because of self-identification as transgender.[118] Yet most courts have ruled that Title VII does not prohibit discrimination on these bases.[119] Not surprisingly, these rulings have led to the conclusion that Title VII is not violated when transgender persons are denied the use of their preferred restroom based on gender identity.[120]

But the reasoning in cases denying protection to people who are transgender may be inconsistent with the Supreme Court's decision in *Price Waterhouse v. Hopkins*,[121] which extended Title VII protection to people who do not conform to a sexual stereotype.[122] Influenced by *Price Waterhouse*, a district court ruled that Title VII was violated when a transgender woman was required to use the male restroom. The basis of the discrimination was that she failed to conform to the

---

113 *See* Mitchell v. Bd. of Trustees of Pickens County, 599 F.2d 582 (4th Cir. 1979).
114 42 U.S.C. § 2000e–2(a)(1).
115 *See* Ayala-Sepulveda v. Municipality of San German, 661 F. Supp. 2d 130 (D.P.R. 2009); Simonton v. Runyon, 232 F.3d 33 (2d Cir. 2000); Bibby v. Philadelphia Coca-Cola Bottling Co., 260 F.3d 257 (3d Cir. 2001); Spearman v. Ford Motor Co., 231 F.3d 1080 (7th Cir. 2000); Williamson v. A.G. Edwards & Sons, 876 F.2d 69 (8th Cir. 1989); Desantis v. Pac. Tel. & Tel. Co., 608 F.2d 327 (9th Cir. 1979); United States Dep't of Hous. & Urban Dev. v. Federal Labor Relations Auth., 964 F.2d 1 (D.C. Cir. 1992); *but see* Rene v. MGM Grand Hotel, Inc., 305 F.3d 1061 (9th Cir. 2002) (*en banc*); Nichols v. Azteca Rest. Enterprises, Inc., 256 F.3d 864 (9th Cir. 2001).
116 Foray v. Bell Atlantic, 56 F. Supp. 2d 327 (S.D.N.Y. 1999); Cleaves v. City of Chicago, 21 F. Supp. 2d 858 (N.D. Ill. 1998), *amended on reconsideration*, 68 F. Supp. 2d 963 (N.D. Ill. 1999).
117 Price Waterhouse v. Hopkins, 490 U.S. 228 (1989); Rene v. MGM Grand Hotel, Inc., 305 F.3d 1061 (9th Cir. 2002) (*en banc*); Nichols v. Azteca Rest. Enters., Inc., 256 F.3d 864 (9th Cir. 2001).
118 Equal Employment Opportunity Comm'n v. R.G. &. G.R. Harris Funeral Homes, Inc., 884 F.3d 560, 572 (6th Cir. 2018), *cert. granted in part sub nom.* R.G. & G.R. Harris Funeral Homes, Inc. v. E.E.O.C., 139 S. Ct. 1599 (2019); Schroer v. Billington, 424 F. Supp. 2d 203 (D.D.C. 2006); Lopez v. River Oaks Imaging & Diagnostic Grp., Inc., 542 F. Supp. 2d 653 (S.D. Tex. 2008).
119 Holloway v. Arthur Andersen & Co., 566 F.2d 659 (9th Cir. 1977); James v. Ranch Mart Hardware, 881 F. Supp. 478 (D. Kan. 1995); Dobre v. Nat'l R.R. Passenger Corp. (AMTRAK), 850 F. Supp. 284 (E.D. Pa. 1993); Powell v. Read's, Inc., 436 F. Supp. 369 (D. Md. 1977); Voyles v. Ralph K. Davies Medical Center, 403 F. Supp. 456 (N.D. Cal. 1975).
120 Sommers v. Budget Mktg., Inc., 667 F.2d 748 (8th Cir. 1982).
121 490 U.S. 228 (1989).
122 Schwenk v. Hartford, 204 F.3d 1187 (9th Cir. 2000).

employer's (stereotypical) expectations regarding gender identity. The court also interpreted Title IX to extend the same protection.[123] On a related issue, the Eighth Circuit ruled that a school district's policy of allowing a transgender man to use the women's restroom did not create a hostile work environment. The federal courts are now divided on this issue.[124]

In 2020, the United States Supreme Court is expected to resolve this divide.[125] In addition, California, Minnesota, Rhode Island, New Mexico, and New York have state laws prohibiting gender-identity discrimination,[126] while courts and administrative tribunals in Connecticut, Massachusetts, and New Jersey have interpreted state laws as barring such discrimination.[127]

The outline that follows lists the major categories of cases—whether based on race, color, religion, sex, or national origin—that may be brought under Title VII. The subsections that follow the outline explain each category or case, including how the law allocates the burden of proof between the employee and employer and the kind of evidence each may be asked to produce.

I. Disparate treatment of an individual

  A. overt

    1. bona fide occupational qualification
    2. affirmative action

  B. covert or hidden motive
  C. mixed motive

II. Pattern or practice

    1. disparate treatment
    2. disparate impact

III. Sexual and racial harassment

  A. quid pro quo
  B. hostile environment

Disparate Treatment of an Individual (DTI)

The hallmark of DTI cases is that the employer acted with intent to discriminate on the basis of race or gender.[128] DTI cases may involve either overt or covert discrimination. The *Civil Rights Act of 1991* amends Title VII by allowing DTI plaintiffs to seek not only reversal of the discriminatory decision, costs, and attorney fees but also compensatory damages and a jury trial.[129]

In **overt DTI** cases, the employer openly bases a difference in treatment on race or gender. A school might insist, for example, that a coach for girls' sports be female and thus, refuse to hire an otherwise qualified male. In cases like these, there is no need for the complaining party to establish

123 Kastl v. Maricopa County Cmty. Coll. Dist., 2004 U.S. Dist. LEXIS 29825.
124 *See* Fabian v. Hosp. of Cent. Connecticut, 172 F. Supp. 3d 509, 524 (D. Conn. 2016).
125 See *Equal Emp't Opportunity Comm'n v. R.G. &. G.R. Harris Funeral Homes, Inc.*, 884 F.3d 560 (6th Cir. 2018), *cert. granted*, 139 S.Ct. 1599 (2019).
126 *See, e.g.*, N.Y. Executive Law §§291, 296-a (2019).
127 Rentos v. OCE-Office Systems, 1996 U.S. Dist. LEXIS 19060 (S.D.N.Y. 1996); Enriquez v. West Jersey Health Systems, 2001 N.J. Super. LEXIS 283 (N.J. Super. 2001); Declaratory Ruling on Behalf of John/Jane Doe (Conn. Human Rights Comm'n 2000); Doe v. Yunits, 15 Mass. L. Rep. 278 (2001), *aff'd sub nom*, Doe v. Brockton Sch. Comm.,) 2000 Mass. App. LEXIS 1128 (Mass. App. 2000).
128 Tex. Dep't of Cmty. Affairs v. Burdine, 450 U.S. 248 (1981).
129 42 U.S.C. § 10201.

that gender or race was a criterion in the employment decision because it is admitted. The crucial issue is whether the school has an adequate reason for using the criterion.

Title VII explicitly permits gender to be the basis of a hiring decision when gender is a **bona fide occupational qualification (BFOQ)**. Race can never be a BFOQ. The Supreme Court has said that the BFOQ exception is to be strictly limited to cases where an employee of a specific gender is "reasonably necessary to the normal operation of a particular business or enterprise."[130] In a case rejecting the exclusion of women from telephone line repair, the court said that the central question was whether the employer "had a factual basis for believing that all or substantially all women would be unable to perform safely and efficiently the duties of the job involved."[131] In another case, the court held that gender could be a criterion in the hiring of a night security officer at a university because rape victims would be more comfortable reporting an attack to a female counselor.[132] Analogous reasoning might justify same-sex counselors at a school birth control clinic. A few other school jobs such as positions requiring supervision of a locker room or lavatory might also have gender as a BFOQ.

Another important exception to the prohibition against discrimination on the basis of sex is that Title VII permits employers to impose different appearance and dress standards on men and women.[133] Sex-differentiated appearance regulations like different hair length requirements for men and women must not significantly deprive either sex of employment opportunities, and the employer must evenhandedly apply the policy to employees of both sexes.[134] Any unequal burden on one of the sexes must be justified as a BFOQ.[135] In *Barnes v. City of Cincinnati*,[136] a police officer was denied promotion because of their "feminine" appearance. Under the *Price Waterhouse* doctrine, the Sixth Circuit extended Title VII protection to the officer, a male-to-female transgender person who lived as a male while on duty but often lived as a woman while off-duty. The court found that the employer violated Title VII by denying promotion to the plaintiff based on their failure to conform to a sex stereotype. If a school were to bar a male teacher from wearing make-up or women's clothes, presumably the school would have to establish that the prohibition was a BFOQ.

Another type of overt DTI case challenges the use of an **affirmative action** program. Affirmative action programs seek to remedy past discrimination by giving preference to a particular gender or race. Objections to an affirmative action employment program may be brought under Title VII or the Equal Protection Clause. In *McDonnell Douglas Corp. v. Green*,[137] the Supreme Court fashioned the following three-step framework for dealing with cases brought under Title VII:

1. The complainant … must carry the initial burden under the statute of establishing a *prima facie* case [proof that will suffice unless refuted by other evidence] of racial discrimination. This may be done by showing (i) that he belongs to a racial minority; (ii) that he applied and was qualified for a job for which the employer is seeking applicants; (iii) that, despite his qualifications, he was rejected; and (iv) that, after his rejection, the position remained open and the employer continued to seek applications from persons of complainant's qualifications. …

---

130 Dothard v. Rawlinson, 433 U.S. 321 (1977); UAW v. Johnson Controls, Inc., 499 U.S. 187 (1991).
131 Weeks v. Southern Bell Tel. & Tel. Co., 408 F.2d 228 (5th Cir. 1969); *see also* Hayes v. Shelby Mem'l Hosp., 726 F.2d 1543 (11th Cir. 1984).
132 Moteles v. Univ. of Pennsylvania, 730 F.2d 913 (3d Cir. 1984).
133 Barker v. Taft Broadcasting Co., 549 F.2d 400 (6th Cir. 1977); Earwood v. Cont'l Southeastern Lines, Inc., 539 F.2d 1349, 1351 (4th Cir. 1976); Longo v. Carlisle DeCoppet & Co., 537 F.2d 685 (2d Cir. 1976).
134 Jespersen v. Harrah's Operating Co., 444 F.3d 1104 (9th Cir. 2006).
135 Frank v. United Airlines, Inc., 216 F.3d 845 (9th Cir. 2000).
136 401 F.3d 729 (6th Cir. 2005); *but see* Oiler v. Winn-Dixie Louisiana Inc., 2002 U.S. Dist. LEXIS 17417 (E.D. La., 2002).
137 411 U.S. 792 (1973).

2. The burden then must shift to the employer to articulate some legitimate, nondiscriminatory reason for the employee's rejection.
3. Once the employer has offered its explanation, the employee must show that the defense is a pretext for intentional wrongful discrimination.

In *Johnson v. Transportation Agency, Santa Clara County*,[138] the male plaintiff complained that he was more qualified than the female who was promoted and that he was denied the promotion because he was male. However, the Supreme Court upheld the affirmative action plan adopted by the Transportation Agency in order to increase the number of women employed as "skilled craft workers." The Court agreed that there existed a "manifest imbalance" that reflected underrepresentation of women in a job category that was "traditionally segregated." The Court also noted that gender was but one factor in the hiring decision, that the plan was temporary, and that there were no quotas. Similarly, in *Shea v. Kerry*,[139] the D.C. Circuit rejected a "reverse discrimination" lawsuit brought by a white employee of the federal State Department. The State Department had established a valid affirmative action program to remedy past racial discrimination, which allowed the State Department to install the employee at a lower rank.

Compare this analysis and result to the following affirmative action case brought at about the same time as *Johnson* under the Equal Protection Clause (rather than Title VII).

⚖️

WYGANT v. JACKSON BOARD OF EDUCATION
Supreme Court of the United States
476 U.S. 267 (1986)

JUSTICE POWELL announced the judgment of the Court …

This case presents the question whether a school board, consistent with the Equal Protection Clause, may extend preferential protection against layoffs to some of its employees because of their race or national origin.

I.

In 1972 the Jackson Board of Education, because of racial tension in the community that extended to its schools, considered adding a layoff provision to the Collective Bargaining Agreement (CBA) between the Board and the Jackson Education Association (Union) that would protect employees who were members of certain minority groups against layoffs. The Board and the Union eventually approved a new provision, Article XII of the CBA, covering layoffs. It stated:

In the event that it becomes necessary to reduce the number of teachers through layoff from employment

by the Board, teachers with the most seniority in the district shall be retained, except that at no time will there be a greater percentage of minority personnel laid off than the current percentage of minority personnel employed at the time of the layoff. In no event will the number given notice of possible layoff be greater than the number of positions to be eliminated. Each teacher so affected will be called back in reverse order for positions for which he is certificated maintaining the above minority balance.

When layoffs became necessary in 1974, it was evident that adherence to the CBA would result in the layoff of tenured nonminority teachers while minority teachers on probationary status were retained. Rather than complying with Article XII, the Board retained the tenured teachers and laid off probationary minority teachers, thus failing to maintain the percentage of minority personnel that existed at the time of the layoff. The Union, together with two minority teachers who had been laid off, brought suit in federal court (*Jackson I*), claiming that the Board's failure to adhere to the layoff provision violated the

138 480 U.S. 616 (1987).
139 796 F.3d 42 (D.C. Cir. 2015).

Equal Protection Clause of the Fourteenth Amendment and Title VII of the *Civil Rights Act of 1964*. … Following trial, the District Court concluded that it lacked jurisdiction over the case. …

Rather than taking an appeal, the plaintiffs instituted a suit in state court (*Jackson II*), raising in essence the same claims that had been raised in *Jackson I*. In entering judgment for the plaintiffs, the state court found that the Board had breached its contract with the plaintiffs, and that Article XII did not violate the *Michigan Teacher Tenure Act*. …

After *Jackson II*, the Board adhered to Article XII. As a result, during the 1976–1977 and 1981–1982 school years, nonminority teachers were laid off, while minority teachers with less seniority were retained. The displaced nonminority teachers, petitioners here, brought suit in Federal District Court, alleging violations of the Equal Protection Clause, Title VII, 42 U.S.C. § 1983, and other federal and state statutes. … With respect to the equal protection claim, the District Court held that the racial preferences granted by the Board need not be grounded on a finding of prior discrimination. Instead, the court decided that the racial preferences were permissible under the Equal Protection Clause as an attempt to remedy societal discrimination by providing "role models" for minority school-children, and upheld the constitutionality of the layoff provision. The Court of Appeals for the Sixth Circuit affirmed. We now reverse.

II.

Petitioners' central claim is that they were laid off because of their race in violation of the Equal Protection Clause of the Fourteenth Amendment. …

The Court has recognized that the level of scrutiny does not change merely because the challenged classification operates against a group that historically has not been subject to governmental discrimination. In this case, Article XII of the CBA operates against whites and in favor of certain minorities, and therefore constitutes a classification based on race. "Any preference based on racial or ethnic criteria must necessarily receive a most searching examination to make sure that it does not conflict with constitutional guarantees." There are two prongs to this examination. First, any racial classification "must be justified by a compelling governmental interest." Second, the means chosen by the State to effectuate its purpose must be "narrowly tailored

to the achievement of that goal." We must decide whether the layoff provision is supported by a compelling state purpose and whether the means chosen to accomplish that purpose are narrowly tailored.

III.

A.

The Court of Appeals, relying on the reasoning and language of the District Court's opinion, held that the Board's interest in providing minority role models for its minority students, as an attempt to alleviate the effects of societal discrimination, was sufficiently important to justify the racial classification embodied in the layoff provision. The court discerned a need for more minority faculty role models by finding that the percentage of minority teachers was less than the percentage of minority students.

This Court never has held that societal discrimination alone is sufficient to justify a racial classification. Rather, the Court has insisted upon some showing of prior discrimination by the governmental unit involved before allowing limited use of racial classifications in order to remedy such discrimination. This Court's reasoning in *Hazelwood School District v. United States* illustrates that the relevant analysis in cases involving proof of discrimination by statistical disparity focuses on those disparities that demonstrate such prior governmental discrimination.[140] … Based on that reasoning, the Court in *Hazelwood* held that the proper comparison for determining the existence of actual discrimination by the school board was "between the racial composition of [the school's] teaching staff and the racial composition of the qualified public school teacher population in the relevant labor market." *Hazelwood* demonstrates this Court's focus on prior discrimination as the justification for, and the limitation on, a State's adoption of race-based remedies.

Unlike the analysis in *Hazelwood*, the role model theory employed by the District Court has no logical stopping point. The role model theory allows the Board to engage in discriminatory hiring and layoff practices long past the point required by any legitimate remedial purpose. …

Moreover, because the role model theory does not necessarily bear a relationship to the harm caused by prior discriminatory hiring practices, it actually could be used to escape the obligation to remedy such practices by justifying the small percentage of

---

140   433 U.S. 299 (1977).

black teachers by reference to the small percentage of black students. Carried to its logical extreme, the idea that black students are better off with black teachers could lead to the very system the Court rejected in *Brown v. Board of Education.*[141]

Societal discrimination, without more, is too amorphous a basis for imposing a racially classified remedy. The role model theory announced by the District Court and the resultant holding typify this indefiniteness. There are numerous explanations for a disparity between the percentage of minority students and the percentage of minority faculty, many of them completely unrelated to discrimination of any kind. In fact, there is no apparent connection between the two groups. Nevertheless, the District Court combined irrelevant comparisons between these two groups with an indisputable statement that there has been societal discrimination, and upheld state action predicated upon racial classifications. No one doubts that there has been serious racial discrimination in this country. But as the basis for imposing discriminatory *legal* remedies that work against innocent people, societal discrimination is insufficient and over[ly] expansive. In the absence of particularized findings, a court could uphold remedies that are ageless in their reach into the past, and timeless in their ability to affect the future.

B.

Respondents also now argue that their purpose in adopting the layoff provision was to remedy prior discrimination against minorities by the Jackson School District in hiring teachers. Public schools, like other public employers, operate under two interrelated constitutional duties. They are under a clear command from this Court, starting with *Brown v. Board of Education,*[142] to eliminate every vestige of racial segregation and discrimination in the schools. Pursuant to that goal, race-conscious remedial action may be necessary. On the other hand, public employers, including public schools, also must act in accordance with a "core purpose of the Fourteenth Amendment" which is to "do away with all governmentally imposed discriminations based on race." These related constitutional duties are not always harmonious; reconciling them requires public employers to act with extraordinary care. In particular, a public employer like the Board must ensure that, before it embarks on an affirmative-action

program, it has convincing evidence that remedial action is warranted. That is, it must have sufficient evidence to justify the conclusion that there has been prior discrimination.

Evidentiary support for the conclusion that remedial action is warranted becomes crucial when the remedial program is challenged in court by nonminority employees. In this case, for example, petitioners contended at trial that the remedial program—Article XII—had the purpose and effect of instituting a racial remedial purpose. In such a case, the trial court must make a factual determination that the employer had a strong basis in evidence for its conclusion that remedial action was necessary. The ultimate burden remains with the employees to demonstrate the unconstitutionality of an affirmative-action program. But unless such a determination is made, an appellate court reviewing a challenge by non-minority employees to remedial action cannot determine whether the race-based action is justified as a remedy for prior discrimination.

Despite the fact that Article XII has spawned years of litigation and three separate lawsuits, no such determination ever has been made. ...

IV.

The Court of Appeals examined the means chosen to accomplish the Board's race-conscious purposes under a test of "reasonableness." That standard has no support in the decisions of this Court. As demonstrated in Part II above, our decisions always have employed a more stringent standard—however articulated—to test the validity of the means chosen by a State to accomplish its race-conscious purposes. ...

Here ... the means chosen to achieve the Board's asserted purposes is that of laying off non-minority teachers with greater seniority in order to retain minority teachers with less seniority. We have previously expressed concern over the burden that a preferential-layoffs scheme imposes on innocent parties. In cases involving valid hiring goals, the burden to be borne by innocent individuals is diffused to a considerable extent among society generally. Though hiring goals may burden some innocent individuals, they simply do not impose the same kind of injury that layoffs impose. Denial of a future employment opportunity is not as intrusive as loss of an existing job.

---

141 347 U.S. 483 (1954) (Brown I).
142 349 U.S. 294 (1955).

Many of our cases involve union seniority plans with employees who are typically heavily dependent on wages for their day-to-day living. Even a temporary layoff may have adverse financial as well as psychological effects. A worker may invest many productive years in one job and one city with the expectation of earning the stability and security of seniority. "At that point, the rights and expectations surrounding seniority make up what is probably the most valuable capital asset that the worker 'owns,' worth even more than the current equity in his home." Layoffs disrupt these settled expectations in a way that general hiring goals do not.

While hiring goals impose a diffuse burden, often foreclosing only one of several opportunities, layoffs impose the entire burden of achieving racial equality on particular individuals, often resulting in serious disruption of their lives. That burden is too intrusive. We therefore hold that, as a means of accomplishing purposes that otherwise may be legitimate, the Board's layoff plan is not sufficiently narrowly tailored. Other, less intrusive means of accomplishing similar purposes—such as the adoption of hiring goals—are available. For these reasons, the Board's selection of layoffs as the means to accomplish even a valid purpose cannot satisfy the demands of the Equal Protection Clause.

V.

We accordingly reverse the judgment of the Court of Appeals for the Sixth Circuit.

The reasoning in *Wygant* suggests that if the *Johnson* case had been brought under the Equal Protection Clause instead of Title VII, the result would have been reversed. This makes no legal sense because a statute cannot authorize a government action that is impermissible under the Constitution. The Supreme Court clarified the situation somewhat in *Richmond v. J. A. Croson Co.*[143] by ruling that public employer affirmative action plans are constitutionally permissible only when: (a) undertaken to correct identifiable past racial discrimination by the very employer adopting the plan (not to redress the effects of past societal racial discrimination), (b) necessary to correct the past discrimination because racially neutral policies will not work, and (c) narrowly tailored to correct the past discrimination without aiding people who have not suffered discrimination or unnecessarily harming innocent people.

The Third Circuit applied these criteria to a Title VII case in ruling against a school district that, in response to a financial crisis, used race as the criterion for laying off a white teacher instead of an African-American teacher with equal seniority. The court rejected the district's affirmative action plan on three grounds. First, it was not designed to remedy past discrimination but rather to achieve a desired level of faculty diversity. Second, it was not sufficiently limited in time or scope. Finally, the harm imposed on the innocent white teacher was substantial.[144] Although the case was never heard by the Supreme Court because the parties agreed to settle, we believe that the Court would have agreed with the Third Circuit that public employer affirmative action plans are permissible under Title VII only if they meet the *Richmond* criteria. In any case, public school affirmative action plans must comply with the *Richmond* criteria in order not to violate the Equal Protection Clause.

School affirmative action plans designed to achieve desired diversity in the teaching staff or to rectify a long history of racial discrimination in society in general now appear to be unconstitutional; however, affirmative action plans may be permissible in school districts that have been guilty of racial discrimination in their employment practices in the past. Affirmative action plans that include race-based transfers of teachers among schools may also be used as one element of a court-ordered desegregation plan; however, once desegregation has been achieved and the district

---

143 488 U.S. 469 (1989).
144 Taxman v. Bd. of Educ. of Piscataway, 91 F.3d 1547 (3d Cir. 1996), *cert. granted*, 521 U.S. 1117 (1997), *cert. dismissed*, 522 U.S. 1010 (1997).

declared "unitary" by a court, a school district may not continue to make employment decisions on the basis of race (see Chapter 7).[145]

In affirmative action and other overt DTI cases, plaintiffs do not have to prove that employment decisions were based on race because it is admitted. In **covert or hidden motive DTI** cases, plaintiffs allege that considerations of race or gender affected hiring, firing, promotion, pay, or other employment decisions but there is no direct proof. Plaintiffs bear the burden of convincing the court that the employer intended to discriminate. The determination is made by using the three-part *McDonnell Douglas* framework introduced earlier. Plaintiffs bear the initial burden of making a *prima facie* case of discriminatory intent. Plaintiffs need only show that they suffered **an adverse employment decision**. Adverse employment decisions include rejection for a position for which one is qualified (but not necessarily as qualified as the person hired) or transfer to a position with reduced benefits or privileges.[146] Even an unfavorable letter of reference can be an adverse employment decision.[147]

If the plaintiff succeeds, then the employer may attempt to refute the *prima facie* case by offering a **non-discriminatory reason** for the decision. The employer need not persuade the court that it was actually motivated by the proffered reason but need only raise a genuine question regarding what motivated the action.[148]

If the employer does so, then the plaintiff may attempt to show that the employer's reason was a **pretext** to justify intentional discrimination. In 1993, the Supreme Court explained the application of the framework to covert DTI cases as follows:

> Assuming then that the employer has met its burden of producing a non-discriminatory reason for its actions, the focus of proceedings … will be on whether the jury could infer discrimination from the combination of (1) the plaintiff's *prima facie* case; (2) any evidence the plaintiff presents to attack the employer's proffered explanation for its actions; and (3) any further evidence of discrimination that may be available to the plaintiff (such as independent evidence of discriminatory statements or attitudes on the part of the employer) or any contrary evidence that may be available to the employer (such as evidence of a strong track record in equal opportunity employment).[149]

The most common method of proving pretext is to show that similarly situated persons of a different race or gender than the plaintiff received more favorable treatment (e.g., if a school district dismissed an African-American employee for improperly using sick leave but did not discipline a white employee guilty of similar conduct).[150] Pretext may also be established if the proffered reason is simply false (e.g., if a school district lays off a Latinx teacher, claiming a budget shortfall that does not in fact exist).[151] Similarly, pretext may be established if the proffered reason is wholly implausible (e.g., if an employer claims an employee was laid off for unsatisfactory performance, when the employee never received a negative job evaluation and had recently been awarded a six percent raise).[152] A showing that the employer's reasons are a pretext is usually, but not always, sufficient to support a finding of discrimination depending on the overall strength of the plaintiff's case.[153]

---

145 *See, e.g.*, Parents Involved in Cmty. Sch. v. Seattle Sch. Dist. No. 1, 551 U.S. 701, 721 (2007).
146 Mitchell v. Baldrige, 759 F.2d 80 (D.C. Cir. 1985); Abrams v. Johnson, 534 F.2d 1226 (6th Cir. 1976).
147 Robinson v. Shell Oil Company, 519 U.S. 337 (1997); Smith v. St. Louis Univ., 109 F.3d 1261 (8th Cir. 1997).
148 Texas Dep't of Cmty. Affairs v. Burdine, 450 U.S. 248 (1981).
149 St. Mary's Honor Ctr. v. Hicks, 509 U.S. 502 (1993); *see also* Fisher v. Vassar Coll., 114 F. 3d 1332 (2d Cir. 1997).
150 *See, e.g.*, Abasiekong v. City of Shelby, 744 F.2d 1055 (4th Cir. 1984).
151 *See, e.g.*, Hallquist v. Local 276, Plumbers, 843 F.2d 18 (1st Cir. 1988).
152 Primmer v. CBS Studios, Inc., 667 F. Supp.2d 248 (S.D.N.Y. 2009).
153 Reeves v. Sanderson Plumbing Prods., Inc., 530 U.S. 133 (2000).

In *Ridler v. Olivia Public School System No. 653*,[154] a male applicant turned down for a job as a school cook brought a sex discrimination suit against the school. Ridler made his *prima facie* case by showing that he was a member of a protected class (gender) and that he had sought the job, that he was trained as a cook and had had several jobs as a cook (including related large-scale cooking in the National Guard), that despite his qualifications he was not interviewed for the job (in fact none of the male applicants were interviewed), and that the job was offered to a woman. The woman who was ultimately hired had no formal training in cooking, and her experience was limited to substitute work at the school and volunteer work at her church. The school offered as its non-discriminatory reason that it had chosen the woman based on considerations of previous experience as a cook (especially for a large number of people), previous employment in the school district, and the applicants' work record and dependability. The school claimed that in light of these criteria the male applicants were less qualified.

Ridler, however, was able to establish that this explanation was a pretext for intentional discrimination. The record showed that the district had never hired a male cook and that generally several other job categories in the district were segregated by sex. The head cook referred to a position in the kitchen as "sandwich girl." The requirement that candidates have experience in the district had an illegitimate discriminatory effect because the school had never hired a male cook and, in any case, was an "after-the-fact" rationalization: The application form did not request information regarding this criterion, one interviewed applicant had no substitute cooking experience with the school, and the district did not interview another applicant who did have such experience. Furthermore, the district had acted inconsistently regarding the work-record criterion: Ridler was not interviewed despite his work in the National Guard, but a female candidate with no work record outside the home was interviewed. The district also applied the reliability criterion inconsistently when it interviewed a female applicant with a record of job stability no better than Ridler's. So, the court found that the school had discriminated against Ridler on the basis of gender in violation of Title VII and awarded him damages and attorney fees.

Plaintiffs can cite many factors as evidence of intent to discriminate: (a) inconsistent application of employment criteria (e.g., asking women about family responsibilities but not men), (b) exclusive use of subjective criteria, (c) selective judgments made by evaluators of all one race or sex, (d) lack of objective proof that evidence was collected to support subjective judgments, (e) ad hoc tailoring of criteria in order to predetermine the outcome of a personnel decision, (f) establishment of job criteria that are not truly necessary job requirements, (g) proof that the plaintiff was objectively better qualified than the person selected, and (h) statistical evidence of a pattern in similar decisions.

This does not mean that Title VII requires an employer to hire or promote the objectively most qualified employee. Subjective criteria may enter into the decision-making process as long as they are legitimate, non-discriminatory judgments related to the requirements of the job—such as a perceived deficiency in communication skills.[155] A school board is not restricted to hiring the candidates with the highest grades in college or the highest scores on a teacher's exam.

Title VII specifically forbids discrimination against employees founded in **retaliation**; i.e., adverse action taken because of opposition to practices made unlawful by Title VII, because the employee filed a suit charging the employer with discrimination, or because the employee participated in an investigation or proceeding dealing with employer discrimination. In *Crawford v. Metropolitan Government of Nashville and Davidson County*,[156] the Supreme Court ruled that protection against retaliation extended to an employee who did not speak out against harassment on her own initiative but answered questions posed to her during an employer's internal investigation of

154   432 N.W.2d 777 (Minn. Ct. App. 1988).
155   Saweress v. Ivey, 354 F. Supp. 3d 1288 (M.D. Fla. 2019).
156   129 S. Ct. 846 (2009).

another employee. The Supreme Court has also ruled that the prohibition against retaliation even extends to former employees. In *Robinson v. Shell Oil Company*,[157] after the plaintiff had been fired he filed a charge with the EEOC under Title VII. While those charges were pending he sought another job, and the prospective employer contacted the first employer for a reference. The plaintiff then filed suit claiming he got a negative reference for having filed his original charge with the EEOC. The Supreme Court ruled that even if the alleged retaliation of the negative reference took place after he was no longer an employee, Title VII still protected him.

In **retaliatory discharge** cases, the plaintiff asserts that an adverse employment decision was made because the plaintiff asserted legal claims under Title VII. A modified version of the *McDonnell Douglas* framework is used in these cases. To make the *prima facie* case, plaintiffs must prove that they were engaged in a protected activity such as asserting rights under Title VII, they suffered adversely for it, and there was a causal link between the protected activity and the employment decision.[158] Interestingly, such plaintiffs need not be members of a protected class in order to invoke the protection against retaliation.[159] Plaintiffs may also rely on a federal statute known as **Section 1981** to object to retaliation for asserting race-based non-discrimination rights.[160]

In **mixed motive DTI** cases, the plaintiff establishes that an employment decision was made partially because of a discriminatory reason. For example, a school may have had a preference for a male science teacher, but the female plaintiff may also have been less qualified or experienced than the successful male applicant. According to the **Civil Rights Act of 1991**, "an unlawful employment practice is established when the complaining party demonstrates that race, color, religion, sex, or national origin was a motivating factor for any employment practice, even though other factors also motivated the practice." The demonstration may be by direct or circumstantial evidence,[161] but the evidence (e.g., derogatory racial comments) must be proven to be related to the challenged decision.[162] When the employer is able to demonstrate that the same action would have been taken in the absence of the impermissible motivating factor, the court may not order reversal of the challenged decision, only cessation of the impermissible practice and attorney fees.

Pattern or Practice (PP)

In PP cases, either the federal government brings a civil suit charging an employer with a pattern of discrimination against a particular race or gender or other protected group, or members of a protected group initiate a class action suit based on similar allegations. The alleged discrimination may consist of systematic **disparate treatment** of members of the group or of the use of policies that have a **disparate impact** on the group. PP cases are evaluated using the *McDonnell Douglas* framework. In disparate treatment PP cases, the plaintiff's *prima facie* case is usually based on statistics. For example, in a case alleging discrimination against African-Americans in a school district's hiring policy, the plaintiff had to show "a statistically significant discrepancy between the racial composition of the teaching staff and the racial composition of the qualified public school teacher population in the relevant labor market."[163] In a case charging a pattern of discrimination in promotions and

---

157 519 U.S. 337 (1997).

158 Ruggles v. Cal. Polytechnic State Univ., 797 F.2d 782 (9th Cir. 1986); Murray v. Sapula, 45 F.3d 1417 (10th Cir. 1995).

159 *See, e.g.*, Stephan v. West Irondequoit Central School Dist. 769 F.Supp.2d 104 (W.D.N.Y. 2011), *aff'd*, 2011 U.S. App. LEXIS 24773 (2d Cir. N.Y., 2011).

160 CBOCS West, Inc. v. Humphries, 128 S. Ct. 1951 (2008).

161 Desert Palace, Inc. v. Costa, 539 U.S. 90 (2003).

162 Rayl v. Fort Wayne Cmty. Schs., 87 F. Supp. 2d 870 (N.D. Ind. 2000), *citing* Emmel v. Coca-Cola Bottling Co. of Chicago, 95 F.3d 627 (7th Cir. 1996).

163 Hazelwood Sch. Dist. v. United States, 433 U.S. 299 (1977); *see also* Kelly v. DOL, 2019 MSPB LEXIS 1404 (M.S.P.B. May 1, 2019).

salary, the plaintiff had to show that with all other variables—such as credentials and experience—held constant, the salary differences could only be explained by gender discrimination.[164]

Disparate impact cases "involve employment practices that are facially neutral in their treatment of different groups but that in fact fall more harshly on one group than another and cannot be justified by business necessity."[165] For example, a racial or ethnic group might challenge the use of tests for hiring teachers that exclude a disproportionate number of minority candidates. Foreign-born candidates might challenge a preference for hiring teachers who speak unaccented English or who obtained their credentials in the United States. A woman might object to the practice—still found in some school districts—of seeking superintendents with nonworking spouses. However, rules prohibiting the hiring of spouses of employees are permissible even if they have a disparate impact on one gender.[166] The use of a selection committee disproportionately comprised of one race or gender might also lead to a disparate impact claim especially if the selection criteria are primarily subjective.[167] In disparate impact cases, unlike disparate treatment cases, intent to discriminate need not be proved. Disparate impact cases may not be brought under the Equal Protection Clause because the Supreme Court has said that disparate impact is not *per se* unconstitutional.[168]

According to Title VII, to make a *prima facie* disparate impact case, the plaintiff must establish that the employer uses a particular employment practice that causes a disparate impact on a protected group, for example, a pre-employment test that "selects applicants for hire or promotion in a racial [or gender] pattern significantly different from that of the pool of applicants."[169] What counts as a significant difference is a matter of some controversy, but plaintiffs must demonstrate—often with statistics—a real difference that would have been unlikely to occur by chance. Once the *prima facie* case has been made, the employer may defend itself by showing that the challenged practice is "job related for the position in question and consistent with business necessity."[170]

Although the precise meaning of this phrase is not clear, a plausible interpretation is that the challenged practice must have a significant, not just trivial, relation to the job. For example, an employer might argue for the validity of a strength test in a job requiring the loading of heavy packages by hand even though the test excluded most female candidates.

The third and final stage in disparate impact cases affords the plaintiff the opportunity to prevail by establishing pretext. The plaintiff must convince the court that the challenged practice unnecessarily disadvantages the protected group because it does not in fact aid the employer's business in any significant way. This can be done by showing that the challenged practice does not select the employees best able to serve the employer's legitimate (nondiscriminatory) business purposes, or by demonstrating the availability of other not excessively costly tests or selection devices that would serve the employer's legitimate interests equally well without the disparate impact and that the employer refuses to adopt.[171]

Equal Pay

Gender discrimination in compensation is illegal both under Title VII and under another federal statute, the **Equal Pay Act**.[172] This law is violated when unequal wages are paid to men

---

164 Craik v. Minn. State Univ. Bd., 731 F.2d 465 (8th Cir. 1984).
165 Int'l Bhd. of Teamsters v. United States, 431 U.S. 324 (1977).
166 Sime v. Trustees of California State Univ. & Colleges, 526 F.2d 1112 (9th Cir. 1975).
167 *See, e.g.*, Rowe v. Cleveland Pneumatic Co., 690 F.2d 88 (6th Cir. 1982).
168 Washington v. Davis, 426 U.S. 229 (1976); Personnel Adm'r of Mass. v. Feeney, 442 U.S. 256 (1979).
169 Albemarle Paper Co. v. Moody, 422 U.S. 405 (1975).
170 42 U.S.C. § 2000e–2(k)(1)(B)(ii).
171 Albermarle Paper Co. v. Moody, 422 U.S. 405 (1975).
172 20 U.S.C. § 206(d).

and women for "equal work on jobs the performance of which requires equal skill, effort, and responsibility and which are performed under similar working conditions." A difference in pay, however, can be justified by four defenses: a seniority system, a merit pay system, a system that measures pay by quality and quantity of production, or any other factor not based on sex. The most common equal-pay issue in education is paying male and female coaches different salaries. Resolution depends on actual job content, not job descriptions, regarding such matters as amount of time worked.[173] Fringe benefits such as health and pension plans must also be provided on a non-discriminatory basis.[174]

In *Ledbetter v. Goodyear Tire and Rubber Company*,[175] the Supreme Court ruled that employees have either 180 days or 300 days, depending on the state, to file a complaint of gender wage discrimination with the Equal Employment Opportunity Commission from the time the discriminatory pay-setting decision was made. In 2009, however, Congress overturned this narrow limitation on the window for filing claims. Congress passed the **Lilly Ledbetter Fair Pay Act of 2009**,[176] which allows people who receive a discriminatory paycheck to sue, even if the decision to discriminate was made much earlier in time.[177]

Sexual and Racial Harassment

The regulations implementing Title VII define sexual harassment as follows:[178]

> Unwelcome sexual advances, requests for sexual favors and other verbal or physical conduct of a sexual nature constitute sexual harassment when (1) submission to such conduct is made either explicitly or implicitly a term or condition of an individual's employment, (2) submission to or rejection of such conduct by an individual is used as the basis for employment decisions affecting such individual, or (3) such conduct has the purpose or effect of unreasonably interfering with an individual's work performance or creating an intimidating, hostile, or offensive working environment.

As the regulations indicate, only behaviors of a sexual nature can constitute sexual harassment. The creation of a generally unpleasant or offensive work atmosphere or nonsexual practical jokes played on all faculty members regardless of gender would not violate Title VII.[179] In order for behavior to constitute sexual harassment, it must be unwelcome. The harassed person must not have solicited the behavior and must have communicated to the harasser that the behavior was not desired. Either direct confrontation of the harasser or a persistent failure to respond to advances may be sufficient to communicate the unwelcome nature of the behavior.[180] That a person may have welcomed some sexual advances or conduct does not mean that all such behaviors are welcome. However, some courts do not view a supervisor's retaliation against an employee who terminates a consensual sexual relationship as sexual harassment.[181]

---

173 Brock v. Georgia. Southwestern Coll., 765 F.2d 1026 (11th Cir. 1985); EEOC v. Madison Cmty. Unit Sch. Dist., 818 F.2d 577 (7th Cir. 1987); Perdue v. City Univ. of N.Y., 13 F. Supp. 2d 326 (E.D.N.Y. 1998).

174 Ariz. Governing Comm. for Tax Deferred Annuity & Deferred Compensation Plans v. Norris, 463 U.S. 1073 (1983); Los Angeles v. Manhart, 435 U.S. 702 (1978).

175 550 U.S. 618 (2007).

176 123 Stat. 5 (2009).

177 *See* Davis v. Bombardier Transp. Holdings (USA) Inc., 794 F.3d 266 (2d Cir. 2015).

178 29 C.F.R. § 1604.11(a).

179 *See, e.g.*, Vermett v. Hough, 627 F. Supp. 587 (W.D. Mich. 1986).

180 Lipsett v. Univ. of P.R., 864 F.2d 881 (1st Cir. 1988).

181 Keppler v. Hinsdale Twp. Sch. Dist. 86, 715 F. Supp.862 (N.D.Ill.1989); Succar v. Dade County Sch. Bd., 229 F.3d 1343 (11th Cir. 2000).

Behavior by a member of the same sex is covered by Title VII as long as it fits the definition of harassment.[182] So is harassment that is based on the victim's failure to conform to a sex-stereotype.[183] Yet, as noted earlier, some courts do not view harassment based on sexual orientation as covered by Title VII. Thus, the issue in some cases is whether the harasser actually knew the sexual orientation of the victim. The same act may be impermissible under Title VII if motivated by sex stereotyping but not prohibited if based on sexual orientation.[184]

There are two different forms of sexual harassment. In *quid pro quo* **harassment**, an employee is asked to exchange sex for job benefits, continued employment, or promotion. Most courts require a showing of denial or loss of a tangible employment benefit as part of a *prima facie* case of *quid pro quo* harassment. Thus, in one case, a teacher lost a sexual harassment suit against her principal because she was not discharged or denied promotion or any other job benefit; she was dismissed only after refusing an offer to transfer to another school.[185] Employees who submit to unwelcome sexual advances must show that they were threatened with adverse consequences in order to make their *prima facie* case.[186] To defend against a charge of *quid pro quo* harassment, the employer may either present a legitimate reason for the adverse employment action or show that the person who committed the harassment was not involved in the adverse decision.[187] The employee may then show that the employer's reason is a pretext; for example, by proving that a supervisor rewarded those employees who submitted and punished those who did not.[188]

Hostile-environment harassment, either sexual or racial, entails the claim that an employee was subjected to an intimidating, hostile, or offensive working environment because of the employee's sex or race. Although there have been more lawsuits involving sexual than racial harassment, both generally and in schools, the principles controlling both kinds of cases are similar. Both verbal and nonverbal conduct may create a hostile environment but only if (a) the conduct is "sufficiently severe or pervasive to alter the conditions of the victim's employment and create an abusive working environment,"[189] (b) the conduct is offensive (but not necessarily psychologically harmful) to the victim,[190] and (c) a reasonable person would also have been offended by the conduct.

To determine whether conduct is sufficiently pervasive or severe to constitute harassment, courts consider the nature of the conduct (touching is worse than verbal abuse),[191] the frequency or repetitiveness of the conduct, and the period of time over which the conduct occurred.[192] Thus, isolated jokes, inappropriate remarks, or a single sexual proposition or lewd comment (including in one case, the remark, "My penis stretches from here to District 1") is not usually sufficient to establish a hostile environment.[193] However, repeated generalized sexist jokes or comments or gender- or race-based commentary about a person's appearance or behavior do constitute hostile-environment harassment.[194]

---

182 Oncale v. Sundowner Offshore Servs. Inc., 523 U.S. 75 (1998).
183 Price Waterhouse v. Hopkins, 490 U.S. 228 (1989), superseded on other grounds by the *Civil Rights Act* of 1991, §107; *see* Landgraf v. Usi Film Prods., 511 U.S. 244 (1994); Burrage v. United States, 571 U.S. 204 (2014).
184 *See* Dandan v. Radisson Hotel Lisle, No. 97-C-8342 2000 WL 336528 (N.D. Ill. March 28, 2000); Spearman v. Ford Motor Co., 231 F.3d 1080 (7th Cir. 2000); Carrasco v. Lenox Hill Hosp., No. 99-C-927 2000 WL 520640 (S.D.N.Y. April 28, 2000).
185 Trautvetter v. Quick, 916 F.2d 1140 (7th Cir. 1990).
186 Karibian v. Columbia Univ., 14 F.3d 773 (2d Cir. 1994); Williams v. Joe Lowther Ins. Agency, Inc., 177 P.3d 1018 (Mont. 2008).
187 Anderson v. Univ. Health Center, 623 F. Supp. 795 (W.D. Pa. 1985).
188 Priest v. Rotary, 634 F. Supp. 571 (N.D. Cal. 1986).
189 Meritor Savings Bank v. Vinson, 477 U.S. 57 (1986).
190 Harris v. Forklift Sys., Inc., 510 U.S. 17 (1993).
191 Redman v. Lima City Sch. Dist. Bd. of Educ., 889 F. Supp. 288 (N.D. Ohio 1995).
192 Ross v. Double Diamond, Inc., 672 F. Supp. 261 (N.D. Tex. 1987).
193 Cohen v. Litt, 906 F. Supp. 957 (S.D.N.Y. 1995); *see also* Clark County Sch. Dist. v. Breeden, 532 U.S. 268 (2001).
194 Smith v. St. Louis Univ., 109 F.3d 1261 (8th Cir. 1997); King v. Bd. of Regents of Univ. of Wis. Sys., 898 F.2d 533 (7th Cir. 1990); *but see* Becker v. Churchville-Chili Cent. Sch., 602 N.Y.S.2d 497 (N.Y. Sup. Ct. 1993).

Because the statute is directed at employers, not individuals, educators harassed at work may sue their school district under Title VII but not the harassers themselves. This raises the issue of whether and under what circumstances a school district or other employer will be held responsible for the harassment of an employee by a supervisor, a colleague, or even a student. In *Burlington Industries, Inc. v. Ellerth*,[195] the Supreme Court ruled that:

> An employer is subject to vicarious liability to a victimized employee for an actionable hostile environment created by a supervisor with immediate (or successively higher) authority over the employee … No affirmative defense is available … when the supervisor's harassment culminates in a tangible employment action, such as discharge, demotion, or undesirable reassignment …

> [However,] [w]hen no tangible employment action is taken, a defending employer may raise an affirmative defense to liability or damages, subject to proof by a preponderance of the evidence, … The defense comprises two necessary elements: (a) that the employer exercised reasonable care to prevent and correct promptly any sexually harassing behavior, and (b) that the plaintiff employee unreasonably failed to take advantage of any preventive or corrective opportunities provided by the employer or to avoid harm otherwise. While proof that an employer had promulgated an anti-harassment policy with complaint procedure is not necessary in every instance as a matter of law, the need for a stated policy suitable to the employment circumstances may appropriately be addressed in any case when litigating the first element of the defense. And while proof that an employee failed to fulfill the corresponding obligation of reasonable care to avoid harm is not limited to showing any unreasonable failure to use any complaint procedure provided by the employer, a demonstration of such failure will normally suffice to satisfy the employer's burden under the second element of the defense.

In *Molnar v. Booth*,[196] the Seventh Circuit ruled that a teaching intern had been subjected to a "tangible employment action" when, because she rejected her principal's sexual advances, the principal took back art supplies that he had previously given her and wrote a mixed evaluation that caused her to fail her internship. And in *Pennsylvania State Police v. Suders*,[197] the Supreme Court found that an employee who is constructively discharged (purposely forced by employer-created circumstances to resign) as a result of a supervisor's harassment had suffered a tangible employment action.

In order to minimize the possibility of liability for harassment by their supervisory employees, school districts should create, publicize, and enforce anti-harassment policies with clearly defined complaint procedures and plans for dealing with allegations of harassment. A school should respond to allegations of harassment as quickly as possible, usually within hours or, at most, days. The investigation and any necessary remedial steps should be properly undertaken because a bungled investigation or ineffective remedial steps will not prevent liability.[198] School officials should also carefully document the prompt and appropriate remedial steps they take; not to do so may cause a jury to disbelieve the district's claims that it responded appropriately to a harassment complaint.[199]

The Supreme Court has not yet ruled on whether and when an employer is responsible for sexual or racial harassment of an employee by a colleague. Because one colleague cannot subject another to an adverse employment decision, the Fifth Circuit has ruled that harassment by a

195 524 U.S. 742 (1998); *see also* Faragher v. City of Boca Raton, 524 U.S. 775 (1998).
196 229 F.3d 593 (7th Cir. 2000).
197 542 U.S. 129 (2004).
198 Carr v. Allison Gas Turbine Div., 32 F.3d 1007 (7th Cir. 1994).
199 Hathaway v. Runyon, 132 F.3d 1214 (8th Cir. 1997).

colleague does not fit the Title VII definition of harassment.[200] However, other courts have ruled that employers may be liable under Title VII if supervisors knew about, acquiesced in, or orchestrated the harassment.[201] Indeed, at least one federal court has ruled that school districts may be liable under Title VII for harassment of teachers by *students*, if this same test is met.[202] As student-on-teacher harassment becomes more common, one might expect teachers to rely more frequently on Title VII to address this problem.[203]

Because schools have been held liable for not dealing appropriately with known student-on-student harassment (see Chapter 7), it seems likely that most courts would take the same position regarding employee harassment of colleagues. For this reason, schools should include measures designed to prevent harassment by colleagues in their anti-harassment policies. At the same time, in their investigations and responses to allegations of racial or sexual harassment of employees, whether by supervisors or colleagues, school officials should be careful not to violate the constitutional, statutory, or contractual rights of the accused.[204]

Religious Expression

Teachers who wish to practice their religion, wear religious garb, or otherwise manifest their religious beliefs at school pose a difficult constitutional problem. To permit publicly paid teachers in religious clothing to teach a captive audience of impressionable children runs the risk of violating the Establishment Clause's prohibition against government promotion of religion. Yet, to prohibit teachers from wearing such clothes or taking other actions that are a requirement of their beliefs runs the risk of violating their right to the free exercise of religion.

In *Cooper v. Eugene School District No. 4J*,[205] the court upheld the constitutionality of a state law prohibiting public school teachers from wearing "religious dress while engaged in the performance of duties as a teacher," and the revocation of the teaching certificate of teachers who violate the rule. The rule was challenged by a middle school teacher punished for wearing a white turban as part of her practice of the Sikh religion. The teacher claimed that the rule violated her free exercise rights, but the court felt that the rule was a legitimate way for schools to maintain religious neutrality. The *Cooper* court was careful to point out that it would not be permissible to fire a teacher for wearing an unobtrusive religious symbol such as a cross on a necklace or for occasionally wearing religious clothes. Only when a teacher's overt and repeated display of religious garb or symbols might convey the message of school approval or endorsement does the court authorize dismissal. Nevertheless, one might still question whether the case was correctly decided. Is it true that children will perceive the wearing of a turban or yarmulke by a teacher as endorsement by the school of the religious beliefs of the teacher? In any case, how is Cooper's wearing of a white turban to express a religious belief different from the wearing of an armband to express a political belief? Indeed, the EEOC compliance manual includes as examples of legally protected religious practices the wearing of a head scarf by a Muslim or a turban by a Sikh.[206]

200 Mattern v. Eastman Kodak Co., 104 F.3d 702 (5th Cir. 1997).
201 Knox v. Indiana, 93 F.3d 1327 (7th Cir. 1996); Gunnell v. Utah Valley State Coll., 152 F.3d 1253 (10th Cir. 1998); Whidbee v. Garzarelli Food Specialties, Inc., 223 F.3d 62 (2d Cir. 2000); Caban v. Richline Group, Inc., 2012 WL 2861377 (S.D.N.Y. July 10, 2012).
202 Plaza-Torres v. Rey, 376 F. Supp. 2d 171, 175 (D.P.R. 2005).
203 *See* Richard D. Shane, *Teachers as Sexual Harassment Victims: The Inequitable Protections of Title VII in Public Schools*, 61 FLORIDA L. REV. 355 (2009).
204 *See, e.g.*, Lyons v. Barrett, 851 F.2d 406 (D.C. Cir. 1988).
205 723 P.2d 298 (Ore. 1986); *appeal dismissed*, 480 U.S. 942 (1987); *see also* United States v. Bd. of Educ. for Sch. Dist. of Philadelphia, 911 F.2d 882 (3d Cir. 1990); Webb v. City of Philadelphia, 562 F.3d 256 (3d Cir. 2009).
206 *See* www.eeoc.gov/policy/docs/religion.html (last accessed April 19, 2020).

Related issues arise when teachers seek to distribute religious materials on school grounds or to use school facilities for religious exercises prior to the start of the school day. Although these issues are not fully decided, courts seem likely to allow school districts to prohibit any activity likely to give the appearance of school endorsement of religion. Therefore, a general ban on the distribution of religious literature by teachers might not violate the Free Exercise Clause and would probably be required under the Establishment Clause (see Chapter 3). However, at least one court has suggested that a school that permits teachers to meet informally before school to discuss topics of their own choosing might not be permitted to prohibit teacher prayer meetings, especially if the students and community are unaware of the meetings.[207]

A different problem arises when teachers seek exemption from job requirements on free exercise grounds. In one case, a teacher refused to lead her kindergarten class in the pledge of allegiance, patriotic songs, or celebrations of holidays. Based on the framework developed in *Wisconsin v. Yoder* (see Chapter 2),[208] the Seventh Circuit ruled that although the teacher's refusal was based on a sincere religious belief, it was not her right to reject the board's officially adopted curriculum.[209] In general, a free exercise challenge by a public school teacher to the school's rules or curriculum would be unlikely to succeed unless the rules or curriculum were adopted for the purpose of preventing the teacher from satisfying religious mandates. This principle follows from the Supreme Court's current view that the Free Exercise Clause does not relieve an individual of the obligation to comply with generally applicable valid laws.[210]

The desire to celebrate religious holidays sometimes puts teachers at odds with their employers. In one case, a Jewish teacher claimed that the school infringed upon his free exercise of religion when it required him to take personal leave or unpaid leave in order to observe his religious holidays. In contrast, Christian teachers could take their holidays without penalty because the school was closed. The court rejected the teacher's claim, reasoning that because the loss of a day's pay for time not worked did not constitute substantial pressure to modify behavior, the school's policy did not constitute an infringement of religious liberty.[211] In another case, the California Supreme Court ruled that it was a violation of the state constitution to dismiss a teacher for being absent without permission in order to observe a religious holiday. The court said that the district was required to accommodate the teacher's religious needs by allowing a reasonable amount of unpaid leave, five to ten days a year.[212]

In addition to the Constitution, Title VII of the *Civil Rights Act of 1964* protects teachers against religious discrimination in employment. The term religion is not defined in Title VII, but the courts have given it a sufficiently broad definition to include not only traditional theistic religions but also a sincere and meaningful belief that plays a role analogous to belief in a god. The regulations of the EEOC state that the

> Commission will define religious practices to include moral or ethical beliefs as to what is right and wrong which are sincerely held with the strength of traditional religious views ... The fact that no religious group espouses such beliefs or the fact that the religious group to which the individual professes to belong may not accept such belief will not determine whether the belief is a religious belief of the employee or prospective employee.[213]

---

207 May v. Evansville-Vanderburgh Sch. Corp., 787 F.2d 1105 (7th Cir. 1986).
208 406 U.S. 205 (1972).
209 Palmer v. Bd. of Educ. of Chicago, 603 F.2d 1271 (7th Cir. 1979).
210 Employment Div., Dep't of Human Resources v. Smith, 494 U.S. 872 (1990).
211 Pinsker v. Joint Dist. No. 28J of Adams & Arapahoe Counties, 735 F.2d 388 (10th Cir. 1984).
212 Rankins v. Comm'n on Prof'l Competence, 593 P.2d 852 (Cal.), *appeal dismissed*, 444 U.S. 986 (1979).
213 29 C.F.R. § 1605.1.

One court held that Title VII protected an employee's atheistic beliefs and prohibited requiring her to attend employee meetings that included religious ceremonies.[214] However, employee beliefs will not be protected if they are merely personal lifestyle preferences[215] or if they are not sincerely held. An employee who claimed he should not work on Sundays lost his Title VII claim when it was shown that in the past he had worked on Sundays.[216] Nevertheless, the courts are willing to tolerate a degree of inconsistency, recognizing that a person's commitment to religion can change over time.[217]

Title VII permits religious schools to discriminate in hiring and other employment decisions on the basis of religion (but not on the basis of race or gender).[218] Title VII also recognizes that religion can be a **bona fide occupational qualification**, which conceivably might justify religious discrimination in some private school employment but never in public schools. Cases alleging covert disparate treatment of individuals on the basis of religion are litigated using the *McDonnell Douglas* framework discussed earlier.

Title VII requires accommodation of "all aspects of religious observances and practices as well as belief, unless an employer demonstrates that he is unable to accommodate an employee's or prospective employee's religious observance or practice without undue hardship on the conduct of the employer's business." Furthermore, "an employer may not permit an applicant's need for a religious accommodation to affect in any way its decision whether to hire the applicant unless it can demonstrate that it cannot reasonably accommodate the applicant's religious practices without undue hardship."

The Supreme Court has defined "undue hardship" as "more than *de minimus* costs to the employer."[219] In *Cloutier v. Costco Wholesale Corp.*,[220] the First Circuit ruled that it would have been an undue hardship to accommodate an employee who claimed that her religion required her to display all her facial jewelry. The company, said the court, would lose control of its public image if it went along with the employee's demand. In some cases, a school may be able to reject a requested accommodation such as the display of religious objects in classrooms on the grounds that to grant it would violate the Establishment Clause.[221]

Sectarian Schools

The opposite situation is presented when teachers in sectarian schools wish to invoke their federal statutory rights against discrimination. If the attempt to invoke federal anti-discrimination laws conflicts with the school's religious beliefs or practices, the Constitution usually ensures that the school, not the teacher, will prevail.

For example, in *Hosanna–Tabor Evangelical Lutheran Church and School v. E.E.O.C.*,[222] a teacher at a sectarian school who taught both sectarian and non-sectarian subjects (although her religious teaching duties only amounted to 45 minutes per day) charged that she had been fired because of her disability, in violation of the *ADA*. Because the school recognized her as a "minister," however, the Supreme Court held that the school's constitutional rights under both the Free Exercise

---

214 Young v. Southwestern Savings & Loan Ass'n, 509 F.2d 140 (5th Cir. 1975).
215 Brown v. Pena, 441 F. Supp. 1382 (S.D. Fla. 1977); *aff'd*, 589 F.2d 1113 (5th Cir. 1979).
216 Hansard v. Johns-Manville Prod. Corp., 1973 U.S. Dist. LEXIS 14889 (E.D. Tex. 1973); *see also* Abdelwahab v. Jackson State Univ., 2010 U.S. Dist. LEXIS 7729 (S.D. Miss. Jan. 27, 2010).
217 *See, e.g.*, Cooper v. Oak Rubber Co., 15 F.3d 1375 (6th Cir. 1994).
218 Corp. of Presiding Bishop of Church of Jesus Christ of Latter-Day Saints v. Amos, 483 U.S. 327 (1987); Little v. Wuerl, 929 F.2d 944 (3d Cir. 1991).
219 TWA v. Hardison, 432 U.S. 63 (1977).
220 390 F.3d 126 (1st Cir. 2004).
221 Helland v. South Bend Cmty. Sch. Corp., 93 F.3d 327 (7th Cir. 1996).
222 132 S.Ct. 694 (2012).

Clause and the Establishment Clause afforded the school religious freedom, which included the freedom to fire ministers. The Court implied, however, that if the same teacher had not been recognized as a minister, she might have been entitled to invoke federal anti-discrimination laws.

The question of who is a "minister" will be addressed by the Supreme Court in two cases scheduled for 2020. The first case involves a parochial school teacher who taught only secular subjects. The second case involves a teacher with cancer who was dismissed after requesting leave to receive chemotherapy.[223]

Disability

School employees with disabilities are protected by two of the same federal laws that protect students with disabilities (see Chapter 8). The older of these two laws, the *Rehabilitation Act of 1973* (Section 504),[224] provides that "no otherwise qualified individual with a disability" shall be excluded from participation in a program receiving federal financial assistance "solely by reason of her or his disability." This law applies only to programs receiving federal financial assistance. However, the newer law, the **Americans with Disabilities Act** (ADA) of 1990,[225] is not restricted in this manner. Regardless of whether an entity receives federal aid, the ADA stipulates that no employer

> shall discriminate against a qualified individual with a disability because of the disability of such individual in regard to job applications procedures, the hiring, advancement, or discharge of employees, employee compensation, job training, and other terms, conditions and privileges of employment.

Eligibility

Both of these laws apply to people who have "a physical or mental impairment which substantially limits one or more such person's major life activities," have a record of such an impairment, or are regarded as having such an impairment. As explained in detail in Chapter 8, the ADA Amendments Act (ADAAA), passed in 2008 and effective January 1, 2009, greatly expanded eligibility for both Section 504 and the ADA. For example, a condition that is episodic, in remission, or ameliorated through a "mitigating measure" such as medication or hearing aids would previously not be covered under Section 504 or the ADA, but now would be. Moreover, in implementing the congressional mandate, the EEOC has promulgated a lengthy list of conditions (including, for example, PTSD and OCD) that are presumptively covered under Section 504 and the ADA. Consequently, teachers and other school employees who have a documented disability are very likely to be found to have an "actual disability," triggering coverage.

What about people who, although lacking an "actual disability," have a record of a physical or mental impairment, or are regarded as having such an impairment? Such persons are still eligible under the ADAAA, and, indeed, the ADAAA has also broadened the test for being found "regarded as" disabled. "Under the ADAAA, a regarded-as claim only requires proof that the adverse action was taken because of an actual or perceived impairment; there is no requirement that the impairment be limiting in any way (either actually or as perceived)."[226]

One caveat is that such people are no longer entitled to accommodations. They are protected from discrimination based on their perceived disability, but if they do not actually have a

223 *Cert. granted in* Our Lady of Guadalupe School v. Morrissey-Berru and St. James School v. Biel (December, 2019).
224 29 U.S.C. ss. 701-796.
225 42 U.S.C. ss. 12101–12213.
226 Employee and Union Member Guide to Labor Law § 7:43; see also Cannon v. Jacobs Field Services North America, Inc., 813 F.3d 586 (5th Cir. 2016).

disability, Congress reasoned, they would not need accommodations.[227] In *Weber v. Community Medical Center*,[228] an employee "covered in head-to-toe skin lesions" was dismissed from a medical center. The court refused to dismiss her *ADA* discrimination claim, reasoning that she could have been "regarded as" having a disability.

In addition to prohibiting discrimination against employees who are themselves disabled, the *ADA* also prohibits discrimination against employees "because of the … disability of an individual with whom the [employee] is known to have a relationship or association."[229] This provision is violated if the employer declines to hire someone because the employer believes the applicant would miss work or leave work early to care for a family member with a disability or if the employer provides reduced health insurance benefits because the employee has a dependent with a disability. However, the law does not require reasonable accommodation—for example, a change in work schedule—of an employee without a disability in order to enable the employee to care for a dependent with a disability.

People currently engaged in the illegal use of drugs are not covered by Section 504 and *ADA*, but those participating in a drug rehabilitation program are. And, although alcoholism is a covered disability under the *ADA*, an employer

> may prohibit the illegal use of drugs and the use of alcohol at the workplace by all employees; and may require that employees shall not be under the influence of alcohol or be engaging in the illegal use of drugs at the workplace.[230]

Seemingly random traits are excluded from coverage as well, including transvestitism, compulsive gambling, kleptomania, and pyromania.[231]

Infectious diseases such as tuberculosis are covered under Section 504 and the *ADA*.[232] So is HIV, according to guidance from the EEOC.[233] The *ADA*, however, provides a defense to employers if an employee poses a "direct threat" to the health and safety of others.[234] The term "direct threat" means a significant risk of substantial harm that cannot be eliminated by reasonable accommodation.[235] In deciding whether a teacher with AIDS could be excluded from the classroom and reassigned to an administrative position, the Ninth Circuit looked at four factors: (a) the nature of the risk—how the disease is transmitted, (b) how long the carrier is infectious, (c) the potential harm to third parties, and (d) the probability the disease would be transmitted and cause harm. After examining the scientific evidence, the court found that there was no apparent risk of HIV infection to individuals exposed only through the type of contact that occurs in the course of a teacher's job and so ordered the teacher returned to the classroom.[236]

Of course, the fact that a person has a disability does not mean that the person must be hired. The law only prohibits discrimination against people with disabilities who are **otherwise qualified**; that is, people who have the training, experience, abilities, and skills to perform the

---

227 29 C.F.R. § 1630.2(g)(3); *see also* Alexander v. Washington Metropolitan Area Transit Authority, 826 F.3d 544 (D.C. Cir. 2016).

228 Weber v. Cmty. Med. Ctr., 2017 U.S. Dist. LEXIS 181615 (M.D. Pa. Nov. 2, 2017).

229 42 U.S.C.A. § 1211.

230 42 U.S.C.A. § 12114.

231 42 USCA § 12211.

232 Sch. Bd. of Nassau County v. Arline, 480 U.S. 273 (1987); Chalk v. United States Dist. Court & Orange County Superintendent of Schs., 840 F.2d 701 (9th Cir. 1988).

233 29 C.F.R. 1630.2 (j).

234 42 U.S.C. § 12113(b).

235 42 U.S.C. § 12111(3).

236 Chalk v. United States Dist. Court & Orange County Superintendent of Schs., 840 F.2d 701 (9th Cir. 1988); *see also* Stragapede v. City of Evanston, Illinois, 865 F.3d 861, 866 (7th Cir. 2017) (*as amended*).

essential requirements of the job they seek or hold.[237] When interviewing job applicants, school officials may "inquire into the ability of an applicant to perform job-related functions, and/or may ask an applicant to describe or to demonstrate how, with or without reasonable accommodation, the applicant will be able to perform job-related functions." When interviewing applicants, one may not inquire whether an applicant is an individual with a disability, the nature or severity of an applicant's disability, or ask how often the individual will require leave for treatment or use leave as a result of a disability. Neither may school districts require an applicant to undergo a medical examination prior to making a job offer, but they may require a medical examination after making an offer.

Reasonable Accommodation

If an otherwise qualified job applicant or employee with a disability can perform the essential functions of a job with reasonable accommodation, a failure to provide reasonable accommodation is unlawful unless the school can demonstrate that the accommodation would impose an undue hardship.[238] As noted earlier, the reasonable accommodation requirement does not apply to people who are merely regarded as having an impairment. The essential functions of a job are its fundamental duties as opposed to marginal functions, the elimination of which would not significantly alter the position as the employer has defined it. For example, being able to convey information orally is an essential function of most teaching jobs, but being able to type quickly usually is not. Undue hardship is determined by taking into account the costs and financial resources of the school district as a whole, the effect of the accommodation on other employees, and whether the accommodation would fundamentally alter the nature or operation of the education program. Reasonable accommodation may include modifying facilities, equipment, or work schedules; job restructuring; or the acquisition of special equipment. The Supreme Court has ruled, however, that when an employer has an established seniority system, a request for an accommodation in the form of job reassignment is likely unreasonable if it would install a less senior employee over a more senior one.[239]

When an employee requests reasonable accommodations, the ADA requires the employer to engage in an informal "interactive process" with the employee, which constitutes a good faith effort to design accommodations that will make it possible for the employee to perform the essential functions of the job.[240] In *Stewart v. Snohomish County Public Utility District No. 1*,[241] after a county employee experienced chronic and debilitating migraine headaches that affected her at work, the county pursued disciplinary action, rather than engaging in a dialogue regarding potential accommodations. In an unpublished opinion, the Ninth Circuit found that the county's offer under *Family Medical Leave Act* (FMLA) did not excuse its violation of a state anti-discrimination law mirroring the ADA.

School districts accused of failing to make reasonable accommodations may defend themselves by demonstrating either that they did offer reasonable accommodations that were rejected or that any possible effective accommodations would impose undue hardship on the district. To successfully defend a suit charging retaliation, the school would have to show that the adverse employment decision was taken for legitimate reasons other than retaliation.

---

237 *See* Strathie v. Dep't of Transp., 716 F.2d 227 (3d Cir. 1983).
238 Southeastern Cmty. Coll. v. Davis, 442 U.S. 397 (1979).
239 U.S. Airways, Inc. v. Barnett, 535 U.S. 391 (2002).
240 U.S. E.E.O.C. v. UPS Supply Chain Sols., 620 F.3d 1103, 1110 (9th Cir. 2010).
241 752 F. App'x 444 (9th Cir. 2018) [*unpublished*].

Violations of Section 504 and the ADA

Schools may be accused of violating Section 504 and ADA for engaging in hidden motive **disparate treatment** of an employee with a disability, for adopting policies and practices with a **disparate impact** on such employees, for **failing to make reasonable accommodations** for otherwise qualified employees with disabilities, or for engaging in **retaliation** against employees for asserting rights under the statutes or aiding in investigations to enforce the statutes.

Disparate treatment cases employ the *McDonnell Douglas* framework examined earlier. The plaintiff bears the initial burden of establishing a *prima facie* case of intentional discrimination: That the plaintiff was an otherwise qualified individual with disabilities who suffered an adverse employment decision. The school may then defend itself by showing that the adverse employment decision was taken for legitimate nondiscriminatory reasons. In *Raytheon Co. v. Hernandez*,[242] the Supreme Court explained that "[b]oth disparate-treatment and disparate-impact claims are cognizable under the ADA."[243] However, perhaps because the vast majority of ADA cases focus on the specific accommodations needed by a particular plaintiff, disparate impact cases focusing on systemic barriers have yet to be fleshed out in the courts.[244]

A person with a disability victimized by intentional discrimination may sue a school for compensatory damages, but the Supreme Court has ruled that ADA and Section 504 do not permit plaintiffs to sue entities that receive federal funds (such as public schools) for punitive damages.[245] The Equal Employment Opportunity Commission may pursue an employee's ADA claim even if the employee is personally prohibited by an arbitration agreement from doing so.[246]

Disability Harassment/Hostile Work Environment

Just as disability-related harassment of students may be viewed as analogous to racial or sexual harassment (see Chapter 7), a number of federal circuit courts and district courts have ruled that the ADA protects workers with disabilities (including teachers and other school staff) from harassment or a "hostile work environment" related to their disability.[247] However, as is the case with Title IX, a plaintiff claiming disability harassment cannot prevail unless he or she can show that the harassment is pervasive and severe.

In *Insalaco v. Anne Arundel County Public Schools*,[248] a special education teacher who had a neurological condition and needed a walker as an accommodation asserted that school staff had moved her belongings to a closet and had removed her documents from the school system's server. The court held that such behavior, even if targeted to her disability, was not sufficiently pervasive and severe to enable her case to proceed. By contrast, in *Hines v. Boston Public Schools*,[249] a paraprofessional had "a physical impairment including a weak left leg and stiff knee and a mental impairment including diagnoses of a learning disability and attention deficit disorder." She was

---

242 540 U.S. 44 (2003).
243 See 42 U.S.C. § 12112(b).
244 *See* Jeannette Cox, *Reasonable Accommodations and the ADA Amendments' Overlooked Potential*, 24 Geo. Mason L. Rev. 147, 156 (2016).
245 Barnes v. Gorman, 536 U.S. 181 (2002).
246 EEOC v. Waffle House, 534 U.S. 279 (2002).
247 *See* Ballard-Carter v. Vanguard Grp., 703 F. App'x 149 (3d Cir. 2017) [*unpublished*]; Colon-Fontanez v. Municipality of San Juan, 660 F.3d 17 (1st Cir. 2011); Fox v. General Motors Corp., 247 F.3d 169 (4th Cir. 2001); Flowers v. Southern Reg'l Physician Servs., Inc., 247 F.3d 229(5th Cir. 2001); Shaver v. Indep. Stave Co., 350 F.3d 716 (8th Cir. 2003); Hudson v. Lorotex Corp., 1997 WL 159282 (N.D.N.Y. April 2, 1997); Hendler v. Intelecom USA, Inc., 963 F. Supp. 200 (E.D.N.Y. 1997); Disanto v. McGraw-Hill, Inc., 1998 WL 474136 (S.D.N.Y. Aug. 11, 1998).
248 2012 U.S. Dist. LEXIS 9110 (D. Md. 2012).
249 264 F. Supp. 3d 329 (D. Mass. 2017).

forced to work in a special education classroom where she had to take the stairs. When she was assaulted by several students, she sought a transfer, which was denied. Finally, she was "verbally berated" by the school's teachers. The court refused to dismiss her hostile work environment claim under the ADA, stating that she had plausibly alleged pervasive harm.

Even where the alleged disability-related harassment would appear to be pervasive and severe, plaintiffs have still lost when courts ruled that they did not have a true disability within the meaning of the ADA. In *Stephan v. West Irondequoit Cent. School District*,[250] for example, a school cafeteria worker with a learning disability asserted that "her supervisor … referred to her by derogatory names including 'retard' and 'Special Edna'[.]" The Second Circuit ruled that, nevertheless, she was not covered under the ADA, for the evidence she presented pointed "merely to an unspecified learning disability as opposed to a medically diagnosed impairment." The court noted, however, that the harassment had taken place prior to 2008, and that "Congress [had] amended the ADA in 2008 in order to expand its coverage." Under the expanded definition of ADA eligibility, plaintiffs with disabilities who can demonstrate severe and pervasive disability-related harassment should fare better in the courts.

Age

Intentionally treating employees differently on the basis of age raises both constitutional and statutory issues. The Supreme Court dealt with the constitutionality of mandatory retirement in *Massachusetts Board of Retirement v. Murgia*.[251] Because age classifications do not trigger strict scrutiny, the Court rejected the plaintiffs' claim that a mandatory retirement policy violated the Equal Protection Clause. The policy was rationally related to the goal of assuring a physically fit police force. Applying this approach, the Second Circuit concluded that a mandatory retirement policy was constitutionally permissible in that it served, among other things, to foster employment of young people.[252] However, the Seventh Circuit held that mandatory retirement might be unconstitutional.[253]

The uncertainty regarding the constitutionality of mandatory retirement of teachers is a moot point in light of the **Age Discrimination in Employment Act** of 1978 (ADEA). This federal statute protects people above the age of 40 from discrimination on the basis of age with regard to hiring, firing, and other terms and conditions of employment.[254] Thus, mandatory retirement for teachers is prohibited by law. Disparate treatment litigation brought under the ADEA follows the same framework as other disparate treatment cases.[255] Although the ADEA recognizes that age may sometimes be a **bona fide occupational qualification**, it is unlikely that this narrowly defined exception would ever apply to a teaching position. Thus, a school charged with disparate treatment age discrimination must defend itself by showing that the adverse employment decision was based on legitimate factors other than age.[256]

In *Smith v. City of Jackson*[257] the Supreme Court settled a dispute among the circuit courts by ruling that ADEA permits disparate impact suits. However, the Court also said that the scope of disparate impact liability under ADEA was narrower than under Title VII. The plaintiff bears the burden of identifying the specific practice of the employer that has a disparate impact on older

250 2011 U.S. App. LEXIS 24773 (2d Cir. 2011) [*unpublished*].
251 427 U.S. 307 (1976).
252 Palmer v. Ticcione, 576 F.2d 459 (2d Cir. 1978).
253 Gault v. Garrison, 569 F.2d 993 (7th Cir. 1977).
254 29 U.S.C.A. §§ 623, 631.
255 Western Air Lines v. Criswell, 472 U.S. 400 (1985).
256 *See, e.g.*, Alberty v. Columbus Twp., 730 F. App'x 352, 363 (6th Cir. 2018) [*unpublished*].
257 544 U.S. 228 (2005).

workers. Even if the plaintiff meets this burden, the employer might still prevail by showing that the disparate impact "is based on reasonable factors other than age discrimination."[258]

An employer can also assert a defense by showing that it was implementing a bona fide seniority system or employment benefit plan that was not a pretext to evade the law. Moreover, unlike race or gender discrimination claims under Title VII, claimants asserting age discrimination under the ADEA cannot prevail if the employer had a "mixed motive" (based partly on age discrimination and partly on a legitimate cause). They must be able to show that the employer's action was based *solely* on age discrimination.[259]

In *Aberman v. Board of Education of City of Chicago*,[260] a 58-year-old teacher challenged a board policy that allowed it to conduct layoffs "by first laying off teachers who were not properly certified and then those who were rated unsatisfactory." Although this policy potentially disadvantaged older teachers (i.e., those with more seniority), the court rejected the teacher's claim that it imposed an impermissible disparate impact under the ADEA.

Early retirement plans and **reductions in force** may raise difficult issues under the ADEA. Truly voluntary early retirement plans are permitted.[261] However, when incentives are offered for early retirement, the employer must demonstrate legitimate, non-discriminatory reasons for the plan.[262] Retirement benefits may also be keyed to the age of retirement as long as the differences in benefits are based on non-age-related reasons like cost.[263] Laying off employees in accordance with a legitimate seniority system is permissible, but laying off older workers first in order to save money is not.[264] The Supreme Court has also interpreted ADEA's prohibition against age discrimination to include protection against retaliation for complaining of age discrimination.[265]

Summary

The school has both a right and an obligation to ensure that all of its employees perform their duties. However, the school's power over its teachers and other employees is limited because they retain the same constitutional rights as any citizen. Many cases require balancing an employee's constitutional rights against a school's need to promote its educational goals.

Freedom of speech protects a teacher's right to advocate any political belief, either by symbolic or actual speech or through membership in a political party or organization. When acting as private citizens, teachers may speak freely on any matter of public concern including education issues, if their speech is not excessively disruptive to their school's educational mission, but the airing of private grievances (e.g., about supervisors) may be prohibited even if not disruptive. Even on matters of public concern, speech that materially and substantially disrupts the school may be barred.

Within the classroom, freedom of speech affords only limited protection to teachers. K–12 teachers, unlike university professors, have little academic freedom; they may be required to adhere closely to the curriculum and instructional methods chosen by the school.

The right of privacy affords school employees some protection in matters of lifestyle and morality. Although some issues such as the right to use contraception or to become pregnant are well settled, others are not. Before allowing dismissal for personal lifestyle choices, most courts require a proven connection between the behavior and the ability to do the job. Teachers enjoy

---

258 *See* Meacham v. Knolls Atomic Power Lab., 554 U.S. 84 (2008).
259 Gross v. FBL Financial Services, Inc., 557 U.S. 167 (2009).
260 242 F. Supp. 3d 672, 683 (N.D. Ill. 2017).
261 Henn v. Nat'l Geographic Soc'y, 819 F.2d 824 (7th Cir. 1987).
262 Cipriano v. Bd. of Educ. of North Tonawanda, 785 F.2d 51 (2d Cir. 1986).
263 Karlen v. City Colls. of Chicago, 837 F.2d 314 (7th Cir. 1988).
264 29 C.F.R. § 1625.7(f).
265 Myrna Gomez-Perez v. Potter, 128 S. Ct. 1931 (2008).

Fourth Amendment protection against unreasonable searches and seizures. Mandatory drug testing may be permissible for bus drivers and other employees whose impairment would pose a direct and significant threat to the safety of students; however, random drug testing of all teachers is questionable.

Although schools must make reasonable accommodations for a teacher's religious beliefs, freedom of religion does not provide an exemption from the essential duties of the job. In particular, a teacher may not claim a religion-based right to modify the curriculum, a practice that would violate the Establishment Clause. In accommodating employees' religious beliefs, schools must avoid appearing to endorse them. Thus, the Free Exercise Clause does not give teachers the right to recite prayers openly within the classroom or, at least according to some courts, to dress in religious garb. Free exercise does protect a teacher's right to take a reasonable number of days off for religious observance, not necessarily with pay, or to wear unobtrusive symbols of faith.

Discrimination is a very active and complex area of employment law. The Equal Protection Clause and a number of federal statutes including the *Civil Rights Acts* of 1964 and 1991 protect both school employees and prospective school employees from discrimination based on race, gender, religion, disability, or age. Although summarizing the thrust of these laws is difficult, employment decisions must not be based on any of these characteristics unless there is an extremely compelling rationale. Race must never influence employment decisions, except possibly in certain carefully crafted affirmative action programs designed to remedy past discrimination by a particular employer. Gender may perhaps be a bona fide occupational qualification for a few education jobs, but the justification must be strong. Schools must make reasonable accommodations for employees with disabilities but are not obliged to employ persons with disabilities who are unable to perform the essential functions of the job. Mandatory retirement or gearing salary or benefits directly to age is illegal. Schools must not permit employees to be subjected to racial, sexual, or disability harassment.

11 Teacher Employment

In Chapter 10, we examined the federal constitutional and statutory laws that govern the relationship between public school districts and their employees. In this chapter, we focus on the working conditions of teachers in public schools, including certification, hiring, job assignment, transfer, evaluation, nonrenewal, and dismissal. We also examine aspects of the relationship between teachers and public school districts, including collective bargaining, unions, and employment contracts.

The primary sources of law for the topics we explore in this chapter are the statutes of the 50 states, although federal labor laws and the Constitution are also relevant, particularly the Due Process Clause of the Fourteenth Amendment. In recent years, several states have significantly changed their laws regarding the evaluation of teachers, the length of probation, pay, and tenure, among other things. Because of these interstate differences, it is imperative that instructors and practitioners supplement the material in this chapter with applicable state statutes.

Eligibility for Employment

Certification

Eligibility for employment as a teacher in a public school requires a state-issued certificate or license. State certification requirements may include good moral character, a college degree, specified courses, practice teaching, and in most states, a passing grade on one or more state examinations. Most states have "alternative" certification programs for people with demonstrated expertise in subjects such as science and math. Many states require a background check and fingerprinting and deny certification to anyone with a record of a serious criminal offense or wrongdoing involving a child.[1] In 1971, a California court upheld the denial of certification to an applicant who had been convicted six times for public drunkenness and impaired driving.[2] More recently, however, three DUI convictions did not render a teacher automatically ineligible. In *Broney v. California Commission on Teacher Credentialing*,[3] the same court found a teacher was entitled to a fitness hearing before being suspended.

A teaching certificate grants only eligibility for employment. It does not create an entitlement to employment, nor does it automatically signify **competence**. In the absence of a state-authorized waiver, school districts may not hire a candidate without the proper certificate. Thus, a West Virginia court held that a school district abused its discretion when it hired a person certified in general education and mathematics as a teacher of the gifted instead of someone certified in gifted education.[4]

---

1 *See, e.g.*, IND. CODE ANN. § 20-26-5-11.
2 Watson v. State Bd. of Educ., 99 Cal. Rptr. 468 (Cal. Ct. App. 1971).
3 108 Cal. Rptr. 3d 832 (Cal. Ct. App. 2010).
4 Johnson v. Cassell, 387 S.E.2d 553 (W.Va. 1989); *see also* Bradford Cent. Sch. Dist. v. Ambach, 436 N.E.2d 1256 (N.Y. 1982).

Because teaching certificates have value, the Due Process Clause prohibits arbitrary and capricious denial of a certificate to a candidate meeting all specified requirements.[5] A number of states require that the grounds for revocation be connected to teaching effectiveness. In *Erb v. Iowa State Board of Public Instruction*,[6] the Supreme Court of Iowa prohibited the state board from revoking a high school teacher's certificate on grounds of adultery. The court wrote:

> We emphasize the board's power to revoke teaching certificates is neither punitive nor intended to permit exercise of personal moral judgment by members of the board. Punishment is left to the criminal law, and the personal moral views of board members cannot be relevant ... The sole purpose of the board's power ... is to provide a means of protecting the school community from harm ... [A] certificate can be revoked only upon a showing before the board of a reasonable likelihood that the teacher's retention in the profession will adversely affect the school community.

Teaching certificates do not confer a right of **retention**. Because certificates are not **contracts**, states may change retention requirements without violating constitutional prohibitions against the impairment of contracts.[7] Retention requirements may include ongoing professional education.[8] Such requirements must be consistent with the authority granted to the district by statute and must not be preempted by state law.[9]

Revocation

In addition, teaching certification may be revoked **for cause** in accordance with the procedures spelled out in state law. Teachers have lost their certificates for multiple DUI convictions,[10] for growing 52 marijuana plants in a greenhouse,[11] for the improper sexual touching of students,[12] and for grooming students for sexual relations after graduation.[13] In *Professional Standards Commission v. Adams*,[14] the teaching certificate of a school principal who failed to take action promptly after seeing a video of students engaging in oral sex was revoked on grounds of **callous indifference**.

Citizenship

Some states require citizenship for certification, sometimes with specified exceptions.[15] In *Ambach v. Norwick*,[16] the Supreme Court upheld a New York state regulation denying certification to non-US citizens who had not shown an intention to apply for citizenship. More recently, in *Chang v. Glynn County School District*,[17] a federal court concluded that regulations barring all non-citizens from public employment violated the Equal Protection Clause.

---

5   Commonwealth v. Great Valley Sch. Dist., 352 A.2d 252 (Pa. Commw. Ct. 1976).

6   216 N.W.2d 339 (Iowa 1974).

7   State v. Project Principle, Inc., 724 S.W.2d 387 (Tex. 1987).

8   Harrah Indep. Sch. Dist. v. Martin, 440 U.S. 194 (1979).

9   *See* Governing Bd. of Ripon Unified Sch. Dist. v. Commission on Professional Conduct, 99 Cal. Rptr.3d 903 (Cal. Ct. App. 2009).

10 Broney v. Commission on Teaching Credentialing, 108 Cal. Rptr.3d 832 (Cal. App. 3 Dist. 2010).

11 Adams v. State Professional Practices Council, 406 So.2d 1170 (Fla. Dist. Ct. App. 1981).

12 Boguslawski v. Dept. of Educ. and Professional Standards and Practices Commission, 837 A.2d 614 (Pa. Commw. Ct. 2003).

13 Mudge v. Huxley, 914 N.Y.S.2d 339 (A.D. 3 Dept. 2010).

14 702 S.E.2d 675 (Ga. App. 2010).

15 105 ILCS 5/21–1 (2008); N.J. STAT. § 18A:26–1; NEV. REV. STAT. ANN. § 391.060; 24 P.S. § 11–110.

16 441 U.S. 68 (1979).

17 457 F. Supp. 2d 1378 (S.D. Ga. 2006).

Residency

In *McCarthy v. Philadelphia Civil Service Commission*,[18] the Supreme Court upheld a school board policy requiring its employees to live within the district. The Court reasoned that residency requirements for governmental employees did not violate their constitutional right to interstate travel. In *Crowley v. Board of Education of City of Chicago*,[19] several teachers challenged a Chicago residency requirement on the ground that the school board enforced it selectively and sporadically. The court rejected this argument, finding the board retained the right to enforce its residency requirements.

Hiring Practices

As we saw in the previous chapter, **hiring practices** must comply with all constitutional and statutory anti-discrimination requirements. Even the appearance of illegal discrimination should be avoided, including the questions asked at interviews and composition of selection committees.[20] Once teachers have been hired, the board enjoys considerable discretion in assigning them to specific schools, classes, and extra duties. Like all personnel actions, however, assignments may not be discriminatory, violate state seniority or other statutory requirements, be made in retaliation for the legitimate exercise of a constitutional right, violate the terms of the teaching certificate, or violate either the teacher's contract or any applicable collective bargaining agreement.[21]

Working Conditions

School boards are required to assign teachers primarily to the area(s) in which they are certificated because schools are not permitted to hire unqualified teachers.[22] But assignment to areas in which the teacher is certified does not ensure retention. In *Sekor v. Board of Education of the Town of Ridgefield*,[23] the plaintiff was certified to teach business, and did so from 1981 to 1990. In face of declining enrollments, she subsequently obtained "endorsements" to teach social studies and English. Starting in 1990, the mix of subjects she was assigned to teach changed. In 1991, she taught two business classes and three English classes. Although she was a component business teacher, the district dismissed her because of her inadequate skills as an English teacher. On appeal, the court agreed with the board that a finding of "general incompetence" is warranted when a teacher manifests incompetence in two of the three subject areas in which she holds endorsements.

Furthermore, there are limitations regarding assigning a teacher out of his or her **tenure** area. A New York regulation states that

> No professional educator, whether on tenure or in probationary status, may be assigned to devote a substantial portion of his [sic] time in a tenure area other than that in which he [sic] has acquired tenure or is in probationary status, without his [sic] prior written consent.[24]

---

18 424 U.S. 645 (1976) (*per curiam*); *see also* Newport Indep. Sch. Dist./Newport Bd. of Educ. v. Commonwealth, 300 S.W.3d 216 (Ky. Ct. App. 2009).
19 8 N.E.3d 1101 (Ill. App. 2014).
20 *See, e.g.*, W. Va. Code § 18A-2-7.
21 Gibbons v. New Castle Area Sch. Dist., 543 A.2d 1087 (Pa. 1988); Adelt v. Richmond Sch. Dist., 58 Cal. Rptr. 151 (Cal. Ct. App. 1967); Burnett v. Sch. Dist. of Philadelphia, 166 A.3d 521 (Pa. Commw. Ct. 2017).
22 MCL § 380.1233; NY CLS Educ § 3009.
23 689 A.2d 1112 (Conn. 1997).
24 8 NYCRR § 30-1.9(c).

Assignment, Transfer, Demotion

Refusal to accept an assignment within the teacher's certification area is grounds for dismissal.[25] In *King v. Lodge Pole Public School District*, Montana's highest court upheld the reassignment of a high school principal to an elementary teaching position.[26]

School districts also enjoy broad discretion in transferring teachers. Unless a teacher can establish that a transfer was unlawful, exercised in bad faith, or an abuse of discretion, refusal to accept the transfer constitutes **insubordination**.[27] As noted earlier, transferring a teacher outside his or her tenure area may be prohibited unless the teacher consents. However, tenure does not give a teacher a vested interest in a particular class or school. In *Thomas v. Smith*,[28] the Fifth Circuit ruled against a teacher who claimed he should have been given due process rights before being relieved of his coaching duties and transferred to another school within the district. New York's highest court upheld the authority of a district to assign teachers who were on disciplinary suspension to non-teaching posts such as the board's personnel office or curriculum division.[29] In another case, a New York court ruled that the reassignment of coaches to central office positions that did not entail any diminution of salary or benefits was not a disciplinary action that triggered a right to protective procedures.[30]

Depending on state law, a transfer may constitute a **demotion** if it involves loss of pay, rank, reputation, or prestige. If a transfer amounts to a **demotion**, as evidenced by a change in title or reduction in pay, a court may regard it as a contract violation, allowing the teacher to remain in place.[31] Demotions are permissible when, like dismissals, they are done for reasons specified in state law including **insubordination** or **budget cuts**. A demotion may entail the loss of a constitutionally protected property interest and hence trigger constitutional due process protections. State law may also specify a hearing or other procedures to be followed when demoting a teacher.[32] Demotions must also conform to the requirements of any applicable collective bargaining agreement.

Extra Duty Assignments

Refusal to accept an assignment within the teacher's certification area is grounds for dismissal.[33] Similarly, unless a state statute provides otherwise, refusal to accept lawful extra-duty assignments reasonably related to their job exposes teachers to dismissal for **insubordination**.[34] In judging the reasonableness of an extra-duty assignment, the courts consider such factors as the degree to which the assignment relates to the educational function of the school, the number of hours of the assignment, the relation of the assignment to the teacher's expertise, and the degree of impartiality in the assignment of extra duties.[35] Extra duties may, however, be so removed from the basic responsibilities of a teacher that they cannot be required except by a supplemental contract that provides

---

25 Commonwealth *ex rel.* Wesenberg v. Sch. Dist. of Bethlehem, 24 A.2d 673 (Pa. Super. Ct. 1942); Shiers v. Richland Parish Sch. Bd., 902 So. 2d 1173 (La. App. 2d Cir. 2005).
26 259 P.3d 772 (Mont. 2011).
27 Goodwin v. Bennett County High Sch. Indep. Sch. Dist., 226 N.W.2d 166 (S.D. 1975).
28 897 F.2d 154 (5th Cir. 1989).
29 Matter of Alderstein v. Board of Education of the City of New York, 474 N.E.2d 209 (N.Y. 1984).
30 McElroy v. Bd. of Educ. of Bellmore-Merrick Cent. Sch. Dist., 783 N.Y.S.2d 781 (Sup. Ct. 2004).
31 Reid v. Huron Bd. of Educ., Huron Sch. Dist. No. 2-2, 449 N.W.2d 240 (S.D. 1989).
32 Burnett v. Sch. Dist. of Philadelphia, 166 A.3d 521 (Pa. Commw. Ct. 2017).
33 Commonwealth *ex rel.* Wesenberg v. Sch. Dist. of Bethlehem, 24 A.2d 673 (Pa. Super. Ct. 1942); Shiers v. Richland Parish Sch. Bd., 902 So. 2d 1173 (La. App. 2d Cir. 2005).
34 Harrisburg R-VIII Sch. Dist. v. O'Brian, 540 S.W.2d 945 (Mo. Ct. App. 1976); Dist. 300 Educ. Ass'n v. Bd. of Educ. of Dundee Cmty., 334 N.E.2d 165 (Ill. App. Ct. 1975).
35 Bd. of Educ. of Asbury Park v. Asbury Park Educ. Ass'n, 368 A.2d 396 (N.J. Super. Ct. Ch. Div.), *aff'd* in part and appeal dismissed in part, 382 A.2d 392 (N.J. Super. Ct. App. Div. 1977).

extra pay. Teachers who refuse to take on these extra-pay duties are not subject to dismissal.[36] However, teachers who perform extra duties do not obtain an entitlement to these jobs. Thus districts are generally free to remove teachers from coaching positions, for example.[37]

Probation, Evaluation, and Tenure

States have typically created systems in which teachers are hired on a probationary basis followed by tenure, even though this is not constitutionally required. State laws also specify certain procedures to be followed in renewing these contracts (and granting tenure) or in not renewing these contracts (and dismissing the teacher). While districts have discretion in deciding whether or not a teacher is sufficiently competent to be given tenure, they must base their decisions on valid reasons and follow procedures in accordance with the law. Once a teacher achieves tenure the teacher may still be dismissed, but unlike probationary teachers, the tenured teacher can only be dismissed **for cause** as defined in state statutes, and the teacher must also be afforded due process protection.

The general picture outlined in the previous paragraph is changing as states adopt new processes and requirements regarding probation and tenure. Some of the changes are designed to make the receipt of tenure a more rigorous process, and others change the rules regarding the revocation of tenure. One significant change is the requirement that student performance on standardized tests be taken into account in granting or revoking tenure. Historically, when a state abolished tenure, it had to honor previous tenure commitments.[38] Idaho has abolished tenure retroactively, placing teachers on annual contracts.[39] Florida has effectively eliminated tenure.[40]

Probationary Period

The length of the probationary period is changing in many states. Traditionally, the probationary period was three years, at which point the probationary teacher was either rehired (and automatically granted tenure) or the contract was not renewed. In Louisiana, for example, the probationary period is now five years.[41] In other states, the length of the probationary period can depend on how highly rated a teacher is. Thus a highly rated teacher in Oklahoma may have a three-year probationary period, while others may have a four-year probationary period.[42]

The manner in which probationary teachers are evaluated is also changing. Some states require each school district to design a teacher evaluation plan within the boundaries set by state law and to submit the plan to the state board of education. Other states specify the evaluation system to be used by the district. Iowa requires elaborate "induction" and comprehensive evaluation procedures for beginning teachers and conditions the issue of a permanent teaching license on the results of these evaluations.[43] Alaska requires that probationary teachers be evaluated twice a year and that students, parents, community members, teachers, and administrators be given the opportunity to "provide information on the performance of the teacher."[44]

---

36 Swager v. Bd. of Educ., Unified Sch. Dist. No. 412, 688 P.2d 270 (Kan. Ct. App. 1984).
37 Lexington County Sch. Dist. 1 Bd. of Trustees v. Bost, 316 S.E.2d 677 (S.C. 1984); *but see* Reid v. Huron Bd. of Educ., Huron Sch. Dist. No. 2-2, 449 N.W.2d 240 (S.D. 1989).
38 Indiana *ex rel.* Anderson v. Brand, 303 U.S. 95 (1938).
39 Idaho Code § 33-515.
40 Fla. Stat. § 1012.33.
41 La. R.S. 17: 442.
42 Okla. Stat. Ann. 70, § 6-101.3.
43 IOWA CODE §284.5; ILL. REV. STAT. CH. 105 §5/21A-20.
44 Alaska Stat. Ann. § 14.20.149.

A teacher whose performance does not meet district standards must be provided with a **plan of improvement** unless the teacher's performance warrants immediate dismissal.[45] State laws also provide for support and professional development for new and low performing teachers.[46] The frequency of teacher evaluations during probation is also often specified by state law. Two evaluations per year are not uncommon, but some states require as many as five or six.[47]

Non-Renewal Criteria

Traditionally, states have granted local school districts considerable discretion to terminate a probationary teacher or grant tenure. An Alaska statute explicitly states that non-tenured teachers are subject to non-retention "for any cause that the employer determines to be adequate."[48] The Rhode Island Supreme Court upheld a rule that said that probationary teachers who missed 27 days or more during any one of their three probationary years would not be renewed or granted tenure.[49]

Historically, some states permitted school boards not to renew a probationary teacher's contract if they believed a better teacher could be found. Teachers had recourse only if they could prove that non-renewal in such circumstances violated a constitutional or statutory right (e.g., discrimination on the basis of race, religion, or age). Probationary teachers dismissed during a contract year (as opposed to non-renewal at the end of a contract year) receive the same due process protections as tenured teachers. A number of states now require that for probationary teachers to obtain tenure, they must meet performance criteria based on **value-added evaluations**.[50]

Non-Renewal Procedures

Historically, decisions not to renew a probationary teacher have not been subject to many procedural requirements. All states drew a sharp distinction between the procedures required for the **non-renewal of probationary teachers** and the **dismissal of tenured** teachers. This distinction still exists in many states. In Massachusetts, a court ruled that non-renewal was not the same as dismissal, thus non-renewal did not trigger the procedural protections required when a teacher was dismissed.[51] Older statutes generally required only that the teacher be notified by a specified date of the decision not to renew. In general, no hearing or other due process is required by either state statute or the Constitution. State courts are divided on whether a probationary teacher automatically achieves tenure if the school board fails to notify the teacher by the specified date.[52] However, almost half the states currently require that any teacher, tenured or not, whose contract is not to be renewed be given a statement of reasons as well as other significant procedural protections.[53] Failure to follow these procedures could result in the teacher automatically obtaining tenure by default.[54]

45 ALASKA STAT. §14.20.149; *see also* A.R.S. §15-537.
46 J.D. Zinth, *Teacher Evaluation: New Approaches for a New Decade*, EDUCATION COMMISSION OF THE STATES ISSUE BRIEF (June, 2010).
47 National Council on Teacher Quality, *Trends and Early Lessons on Teacher Evaluation and Effectiveness Policies*, October, 2011, Figure 3, p. 13.
48 Alaska Stat. §14.20.175.
49 Asadoorian v. Warwick Sch. Comm., 691 A.2d 573 (R.I. 1997).
50 National Council on Teacher Quality, *Trends and Early Lessons on Teacher Evaluation and Effectiveness Policies*, October, 2011; *see also* C.R.S. 22-63-103; MCL §38.83b & §380.1249; Tenn. Code Ann. § 49-5-504.
51 Laurano v. Superintendent of Schools of Saugus, 945 N.E.2d 933 (Mass. 2011).
52 Cases granting tenure: Harrodsburg Bd. of Educ. v. Powell, 792 S.W.2d 376 (Ky. Ct. App. 1990); Day v. Prowers County Sch. Dist. RE-1, 725 P.2d 14 (Colo. Ct. App. 1986); Fucinari v. Dearborn Bd. of Educ., 188 N.W.2d 229 (Mich. Ct. App. 1971); *but see* Bessler v. Bd. of Educ. of Chartered Sch. Dist., 356 N.E.2d 1253 (Ill. App. Ct. 1976), *modified*, 370 N.E.2d 1050 (Ill. 1977); Snell v. Brothers, 527 S.W.2d 114 (Tenn. 1975).
53 State v. Bd. of Educ. of South Point, 339 N.E.2d 249 (Ohio 1975); Hedrick v. Pendleton County Bd. of Educ., 332 S.E.2d 109 (W.Va. 1985).
54 Farrington v. Sch. Comm. of Cambridge, 415 N.E.2d 211 (Mass. 1981).

An Ohio statute illustrates the procedural rights probationary teachers now enjoy in many states.[55] In the year prior to non-renewal, a probationary teacher must be evaluated twice. Each evaluation must be based on two 30-minute observations and specific criteria regarding expected job performance in the teacher's field. A required written report on the evaluation must contain recommendations for improvement regarding any deficiencies noted. The board must notify the teacher by April 30 of its intention not to renew. The teacher may demand a hearing. If the hearing affirms the decision not to renew, the decision may be appealed to a court, but the court's review is limited to determining whether the board complied with the statutory procedures. The court may not review the grounds for non-renewal.

Dismissal for Cause

The contract of a post-probationary or tenured teacher must be renewed from year to year unless the teacher is **dismissed for cause**. State statutes protect tenured teachers by limiting the permissible grounds for dismissal. Tenured teachers may not be dismissed for engaging in constitutionally or statutorily protected behavior or because the school board believes that a better teacher could be found (or even if a better teacher is found). When dismissing a tenured teacher, the school board bears the burden of showing by substantial evidence that it has statutory grounds for dismissal. In some states, the grounds for dismissal may be subject to a time limitation. In New York, for example, dismissal may not be imposed for an act that occurred more than three years prior, unless the act constituted a crime.[56] In Arizona and California, the rule is four years.[57]

Many states also require that teachers be given the opportunity to remediate their deficiencies prior to dismissal. Dismissal is allowed only if remediation fails or if there is a finding that deficiencies are **irremediable**.[58] Failures in maintaining classroom discipline or performance of instructional duties are typically viewed as remediable, but serious misconduct that may do permanent harm, such as having sex with students, is not.[59] Indeed, teacher conduct that is criminal or deemed to be "immoral" is irremediable *per se*.[60]

Statutory Grounds

Although the wording varies from state to state, **statutory grounds** for dismissal can be grouped into five general categories. Each category has been given a descriptive label, which may differ from the terms actually used in state statutes. None of these grounds is precisely defined in statute or case law, and each has been disputed in a significant number of cases.

Incompetence or Inefficiency

Although most state statutes do not define the term **incompetence** or the term **inefficiency**, Tennessee has elaborate and specific definitions for both:

> (5) "Incompetence" means being incapable, lacking adequate power, capacity or ability to carry out the
> duties and responsibilities of the position. This may apply to physical, mental, educational, emotional or

---

55 ORC ANN. 3319.11; 14 DEL. C. § 1410.
56 DeMichele v. Greenburgh Cent. Sch. Dist. No. 7, 167 F.3d 784 (2d Cir. 1999).
57 A.R.S. § 15-539; Cal Ed Code § 44944; NY CLS Educ § 3020-a.
58 Gilliland v. Bd. of Educ. of Pleasant View, 365 N.E.2d 322 (Ill. 1977).
59 *See, e.g.,* Lehto v. Bd. of Educ. of Caesar Rodney Sch. Dist., 962 A.2d 222 (Del. 2008).
60 Younge v. Bd. of Educ. of City of Chicago, 788 N.E.2d 1153, 1161 (Ill. App. 2003).

other personal conditions. It may include lack of training or experience, evident unfitness for service, a physical, mental or emotional condition making the teacher unfit to instruct or associate with children or the inability to command respect from subordinates or to secure cooperation of those with whom the teacher must work;

(6) "Inefficiency" means being below the standards of efficiency maintained by others currently employed by the board for similar work, or habitually tardy, inaccurate or wanting in effective performance of duties. The definition of inefficiency includes, but is not limited to, having evaluations demonstrating an overall performance effectiveness level that is "below expectations" or "significantly below expectations" as provided in the evaluation guidelines adopted by the state board of education pursuant to § 49-1-302.[61]

Thus Tennessee has authorized the dismissal of teachers based on **value-added evaluations**. Florida law has grounded teacher dismissal on student test scores. In *Sherrod v. Palm Beach County School Board*,[62] the district court held that "the statute in question requires the school board to base a decision to terminate primarily on student performance on the annual tests." Student performance on standardized tests and other measures of student performance such as grades may play a role in determining a teacher's competence. A Minnesota court upheld the dismissal of a teacher based on lack of student progress, poor rapport with students, insufficient communication with parents, and unwillingness to follow administrative directives.[63]

Because state statutes are generally not specific as to what constitutes **incompetence** or **inefficiency**, one has to turn to judicial decisions for guidance. Factors such as a lack of knowledge of the subject matter; inability or failure to impart the designated curriculum; failure to work effectively with colleagues, supervisors, and parents; and failure to maintain adequate discipline or to supervise students have been recognized as indicative of incompetence. One court upheld the dismissal of a teacher whose students were disruptive, daydreamed, and left class without permission.[64] However, in another case, a teacher who was unable to establish rapport with his students was found not incompetent.[65] The Pennsylvania Supreme Court permitted the dismissal of a teacher whose classroom was filthy and who failed to plan lessons or keep order.[66] The Connecticut Supreme Court allowed the dismissal of a teacher who was competent in one of the two subject areas that she taught but incompetent in the other.[67] In some states, teaching out of certificate is proof of incompetence.[68]

Can a teacher can be found incompetent for a one-off instructional mistake? In *Collins v. Faith School District No. 46-2*,[69] a teacher challenged his dismissal for frankly answering a student's question about gay sexuality. The Supreme Court of South Dakota emphasized that incompetence usually involves a habitual failure to perform work with the degree of skill or accuracy displayed by other persons while acknowledging that "there are times when only one incident may be of such magnitude or of such far reaching consequences that a teacher's ability to perform his or her duties will be permanently impaired and a finding of 'incompetence' would be proper." In this case, however, there was no showing that the teacher's ability to teach had been impaired or that students

61 Tenn. Code Ann. § 49-5-501(4) and (5).
62 963 So. 2d 251 (Fla. Dist. Ct. App. 2006), *rehearing denied*, 2007 Fla. App. Lexis 15667 (2006); *see also* Young v. Palm Beach County Sch. Dist., 968 So. 2d 38 (Fla. 4th Dist. App. 2006).
63 *In Re* Proposed Termination of James E. Johnson, 451 N.W.2d 343 (Minn. 1990).
64 Bd. of Dir. of Sioux City v. Mroz, 295 N.W.2d 447 (Iowa 1980).
65 Powell v. Bd. of Trustees of Crook County Sch. Dist. No. 1, 550 P.2d 1112 (Wyo. 1976).
66 Bd. of Educ. of Philadelphia v. Kushner, 530 A.2d 541 (Pa. 1987).
67 Sekor v. Bd. of Educ. of Ridgefield, 689 A.2d 1112 (Conn. 1997).
68 Chambers v. Bd. of Educ. of Lisbon Cent. Sch. Dist., 391 N.E.2d 1270 (N.Y. 1979).
69 574 N.W.2d 889 (S.D. 1998).

were detrimentally affected. In *Chattooga County Board of Education v. Searels*,[70] a teacher was dismissed after opining, in the presence of a student with cerebral palsy, that the student "would probably be dead before he was two."

Insubordination or Neglect of Duty

Not surprisingly, teachers have been dismissed for filing false sick leave claims, theft of school property, misappropriation of funds, making unjustified reimbursement claims, and even making personal use of bonus points the school had earned for the purchase of materials.[71] Under some state statutes, such behavior may be termed **insubordination** or **neglect of duty**. Insubordination refers usually to willful, but sometimes to inadvertent **disobedience** either to an officially adopted school rule or to the legitimate order of a supervisor. In *Meckley v. Kanawha County Board of Education*,[72] the court upheld the dismissal of a teacher who refused to attend faculty meetings or meetings with parents.

In *Osborne v. Bullitt County Board of Education*,[73] the Kentucky Court of Appeal held that a teacher could not be dismissed for insubordination when merely charged with having failed to "cooperate" with the principal. To prove insubordination, the school had to point to a refusal on the part of the teacher to follow a specific school rule or order. In *Howard v. West Baton Rouge Parish School Board*,[74] a teacher was successful in overturning his dismissal for "willful neglect of duty" for having a wholly concealed handgun in his car parked on school grounds. The court ruled that in the absence of a school policy on the subject and in the absence of any specific directive to the teacher, the school failed to establish that the teacher had "willfully or deliberately neglected his duties or acted in contravention of an order or school policy."

Teachers may not be dismissed for disobedience when a school rule or order violates their constitutional or statutory rights. Thus, in *Pickering v. Board of Education*,[75] the Supreme Court ruled that the dismissal of a competent teacher for publicly criticizing the school board's budgetary policies was an impermissible violation of the teacher's right of free speech.

To find a teacher **insubordinate**, it is not necessary to prove a pattern of misbehavior. A single instance may suffice. For example, a Pennsylvania teacher was dismissed for using sick leave to take a ski vacation.[76] However, when extenuating circumstances exist (such as using sick leave to attend a school function for one's grandchild), dismissal for sick leave violations might not be justified.[77]

A finding of **neglect of duty** may also be based on a single incident. In *Flickinger v. Lebanon School District*,[78] the court upheld the dismissal of a principal who failed immediately to respond to several requests from the assistant principal for assistance in dealing with a report that a specific student possessed a gun. Refusal to take a new teaching assignment is insubordination,[79] as

70 691 S.E.2d 629 (Ga. App. 2010).
71 Katz v. Maple Height City Sch. Dist. Bd. of Educ., 87 Ohio App. 3d 256; 622 N.E.2d 1 (Ct. of App. 8th Dist. 1993); Ahmad v. Bd. of Educ. City of Chicago, 365 Ill. App. 3d 155; 847 N.E.2d 810; 2006 (App. Ct. 1st Dist. (2006); Kimble v. Worth County R-III Bd. of Educ., 669 S.W.2d 949 (Mo. App. W.D. 1984); Cochran v. Bd. of Educ. of Mexico Sch. Dist. No. 59, 815 S.W. 2d 55 (Mo. App. E.D. 1991); Giffels v. Millington Comm. Schools Bd. of Educ., 2010 Mich. App. LEXIS 227 (Ct. App. 2010) [*unpublished*]; Tampani v. Lakeside Sch. Dist., 2011 Ark. App. 668 (Ct. App. 2011).
72 383 S.E.2d 839 (W. Va. 1989).
73 415 S.W.2d 607 (Ky. Ct. App. 1967).
74 793 So. 2d 153 (La. 2001).
75 Pickering v. Bd. of Educ., 391 U.S. 563 (1968).
76 Riverview Sch. Dist. v. Riverview Educ. Ass'n, 639 A.2d 974 (Pa. Commw. Ct. 1994).
77 Gateway Sch. Dist. v. Teamsters Local 205, 181 A.3d 461, Pa. Commw. Ct. 2018).
78 898 A.2d 62 (Pa. Commw. Ct. 2006).
79 Thomas v. Mahan, 886 S.W.2d 199 (Mo. App. 1994).

is violating a rule prohibiting corporal punishment (including hitting a student on the head with a three-foot-long wooden pointer).[80] Insubordination includes using "extreme profanity" when reprimanding students.[81] However, some courts will not permit dismissal for minor acts of disobedience that result in no harm to the school.[82]

Academic Dishonesty

Acts of **academic dishonesty** such as helping students cheat on tests or obtain a diploma under false pretenses are also generally upheld as sufficient cause for dismissal.[83] In *Altsheler v. Board of Education of the Great Neck Union Free School District*,[84] five students reported to their parents that some words on their SAT exams had been the subject of review in class. The students in the plaintiff's sixth-grade class increased their scores over the previous year by an average of 26 percentile points, and her fifth-grade class by over 20 points. The fifth-grade scores dropped significantly the following year. Of 285 "key words" on the test, 41.4 percent appeared on the teacher's vocabulary drill cards, but only two to three percent of the words on the cards appeared on other standardized tests. New York's highest court upheld the teacher's dismissal, finding that the teacher had "improperly disclosed to her pupils words on which they were to be tested on a standard achievement test and thus distort[ed] the comparative value of those tests."

Incapacity

In some instances, **incapacity** may be referred to as **unfitness** or **neglect of duty**. In one case, the dismissal of a teacher with a severe personality disorder was upheld,[85] while in another case, the dismissal of a teacher with a temporary mental illness was overruled.[86] A Connecticut court upheld the dismissal of a teacher for, among other things, an anger management problem. An Arkansas court concluded the district could dismiss a teacher for poor judgment following her arrest while impaired and hiding in a vehicle in the driveway of her former boyfriend with her minor child.[87]

Poor Role Model

In some state statutes, this may be referred to as **immorality** or **conduct unbecoming a teacher**, or **unfitness**. Cases in this category are of three types: Teachers convicted or accused of violating a criminal law, teachers engaging in noncriminal extramarital affairs, and teachers committing other non-criminal acts condemned by the school board such as lying.

In general, any serious criminal behavior is grounds for dismissal, especially if it involves violence or theft.[88] Courts have permitted the dismissal of teachers convicted of theft, welfare fraud, income

80 Fisher v. Fairbanks N. Star Borough Sch. Dist., 704 P.2d 213 (Alaska 1985); Bd. of Educ. of W. Yuma Sch. Dist. RJ-1 v. Flaming, 938 P.2d 151, 159 (Colo. 1997).
81 Ware v. Morgan County Sch. Dist. No. RE-3, 748 P.2d 1295 (Colo. 1988) (*en banc*).
82 Rust v. Clark County Sch. Dist., 683 P.2d 23 (Nev. 1984); Bd. of Educ. of Round Lake Area Sch. v. Cmty. Unit Sch. Dist. No. 116, 685 N.E.2d 412 (Ill. App. 1997).
83 Carangelo v. Ambach, 515 N.Y.S.2d 665 (N.Y. App. Div. 1987).
84 441 N.Y.S.2d 142 (N.Y.A.D.2d 1981); *rev'd* 464 N.E.2d 979 (N.Y. 1984).
85 Fitzpatrick v. Bd. of Educ. of Mamaroneck, 465 N.Y.S.2d 240 (N.Y. App. Div. 1983).
86 Smith v. Bd. of Educ. of Fort Madison, 293 N.W.2d 221 (Iowa 1980).
87 Bonamg v. New Haven Bd. of Educ., 2011 Conn. Super. LEXIS 862 (Supr. Ct. Dist. New Haven 2011) [*unpublished*]; Harter v. Wonderview Sch. Dist., 2007 Ark. App. LEXIS 757 (Ct. of App. Div. 4 2007) [*unpublished*].
88 *In re* Thomas, 926 S.W.2d 163 (Mo. Ct. App. 1996); Skripchuk v. Austin, 379 A.2d 1142 (Del. Super. Ct. 1977).

tax evasion, mail fraud, and sometimes even shoplifting.[89] Other cases have supported teacher dismissals for public intoxication, fighting, battery of a fiancée at a nightclub, negligent homicide arising out of an automobile accident, and driving under the influence of alcohol.[90] In *Moffitt v. Tunkhannock Area School District*,[91] a Pennsylvania court ruled that a principal could be dismissed as a poor role model after two DUI convictions. Teachers caught possessing illegal drugs, growing marijuana, or teaching while under the influence of illegal drugs have also been subject to dismissal.[92]

In *C.F.S. v. Mahan*,[93] a teacher was successfully dismissed following an arrest for masturbating in a public restroom, exposing himself, and making an advance to an undercover police officer. In *Purvis v. Marion County School Board*,[94] a teacher acquitted of charges of domestic violence and resisting arrest in a jury trial was subsequently dismissed from his job because in the course of the proceeding he committed **perjury**. The court wrote:

> Here, Purvis lied under oath and resisted arrest. This is a level of misconduct which would support the inference that Purvis' effectiveness as a teacher has been impaired, even though no parent, student or co-worker was called as a witness to say so. The fact that Purvis was willing to lie under oath is particularly damaging to Purvis' effectiveness as a teacher and coach, since it harms his credibility in his dealings with others. The hearing officer's reliance on his teaching and coaching skills and the lack of public scandal are irrelevant to the trust issues articulated by the School Board.

Despite these cases, many courts do not permit dismissal for nonviolent or relatively minor crimes unless the school board can establish a connection between the behavior and teaching effectiveness. The West Virginia Supreme Court has ruled that in order for a teacher to be fired for any act committed away from the job, either the conduct must have directly affected the teacher's job performance or the notoriety surrounding the teacher's conduct must have significantly affected the teacher's ability to perform his or her teaching duties. In the latter case, the notoriety must have been caused by the act itself, not by the school board's consideration of the act.[95]

Other courts have adopted positions similar to West Virginia's. In *Hoagland v. Mount Vernon School District No. 320*,[96] a Washington court disallowed the dismissal of a teacher convicted of grand larceny for purchasing a stolen motorcycle, stating that "simply labeling an instructor a convicted felon will not justify a discharge." In *Hale v. Board of Education of Lancaster*,[97] an Ohio court protected a teacher from dismissal even though he had been convicted of leaving the scene of a traffic accident. In *Lindgren v. Bd. of Trustees, High Sch. Dist. No. 1*,[98] a Montana court ruled

---

89 Bd. of Dir. of Lawton-Bronson v. Davies, 489 N.W.2d 19 (Iowa 1992); Startzel v. Commonwealth, Dep't of Educ., 562 A.2d 1005 (Pa. Commw. Ct. 1989); *In re* Shelton, 408 N.W.2d 594 (Minn. Ct. App. 1987); Perryman v. Sch. Comm. of Boston, 458 N.E.2d 748 (Mass. App. Ct. 1983); McCullough v. Illinois State Bd. of Educ. by Feuille, 562 N.E.2d 1233, 1237 (Ill. App. 1990).

90 Watson v. State Bd. of Educ., 99 Cal. Rptr. 468 (Cal. Ct. App. 1971); Williams v. Sch. Dist. No. 40 of Gila County, 417 P.2d 376 (Ariz. Ct. App. 1966); Purvis v. Marion County Sch. Bd., 766 So. 2d 492 (Fla. Dist. Ct. App. 2000); Ellis v. Ambach, 124 A.D.2d 854 (N.Y. App. Div. 1986); Scott v. Bd. of Educ. of Alton, 156 N.E.2d 1 (Ill. App. Ct. 1959).

91 192 A.3d 1214 (Pa. Commw. Ct. 2018).

92 Younge v. Bd. of Educ. of City of Chicago, 788 N.E.2d 1153 (Ill. App. 2003); Adams v. State Prof'l Practices Council, 406 So. 2d 1170 (Fla. App. 1981); Dominy v. Mays, 257 S.E.2d 317 (Ga. Ct. App. 1979); Gedney v. Bd. of Educ., 703 A.2d 804 (Conn. App. Ct. 1997).

93 934 S.W.2d 615 (Mo. Ct. App. 1996); *see also* Elsass v. St. Mary's City Sch. Dist. Bd. of Educ., 2011 Ohio 1870 (Ct. of App. Ohio, 3d A.D. 2011).

94 766 So. 2d 492 (Ct. App. Fl. 5th Dist. 2000).

95 Golden v. Bd. of Educ., 285 S.E.2d 665 (W. Va. 1982); *see also* Rogliano v. Fayette County Bd. of Educ., 347 S.E.2d 220 (W.Va. 1986).

96 623 P.2d 1156 (Wash. 1981).

97 234 N.E.2d 583 (Ohio 1968).

98 558 P.2d 468 (Mont. 1976).

that a teacher who had been found guilty three times of driving under the influence could not be dismissed because his crime was not "tantamount to immorality" and there was no proof that the convictions affected his performance as a teacher. A New Mexico court reached the same conclusion in *In Re Termination of Kibbe*,[99] a case involving a driver's education teacher arrested for DUI and charged with resisting arrest and battery. The court found no relationship between the teacher's ability to teach and the circumstances giving rise to his arrest. The court noted that the teacher had used the incident as a lesson with his students.

When a teacher's off-campus sexual behavior comes to the attention of the board, it may lead to efforts to dismiss. In *Lawrence v. Texas*,[100] the Supreme Court struck down as unconstitutional laws criminalizing same-sex intimate relationships, so it is no longer possible to dismiss teachers on this basis. But districts may still seek to dismiss teachers on the general proposition that certain behaviors make them **unfit to teach**. In *Morrison v. State Board of Education*,[101] the California Supreme Court fleshed out the statutory concept of **unfitness to teach** with the following checklist of considerations:

(1) the likelihood that the conduct may have adversely affected students or fellow teachers [and] the degree of such adversity anticipated;
(2) the proximity or remoteness in time of the conduct;
(3) the type of teaching certificate held by the party involved;
(4) the extenuating or aggravating circumstances, if any, surrounding the conduct;
(5) the praiseworthiness or blameworthiness of the motives resulting in the conduct;
(6) the likelihood of the recurrence of the questioned conduct; and
(7) the extent to which disciplinary action may inflict an adverse impact or chilling effect upon the constitutional rights of the teacher involved or other teachers.

Relying on these considerations, the court blocked the revocation of the teaching certificate of a successful teacher who had had a brief same-sex relationship. However, the same court upheld the dismissal of another California teacher who had posted an ad on Craigslist seeking a same-sex relationship featuring graphic language and photos, including an image of his genitalia.[102] No student had actually seen the ad. The teacher testified he had previously posted five or six similar ads and said he would continue to do so. The court upheld the teacher's dismissal based on his inability to serve as a role model at school.

In *Land v. L'Anse Creuse Public School Board of Education*,[103] a teacher was dismissed after pictures of her engaging in a simulated act of fellatio with a male mannequin surfaced on the Internet. Overturning the dismissal, the court found there was no evidence that the teacher had "persistently and publicly violated important and universally shared community values." In *Bertolini v. Whitehall City School District Board of Education*, the court overturned the dismissal of an associate superintendent, finding that his affair with a school employee did not have a serious impact on his professional duties. The court specifically rejected the argument that he was a **poor role model** on the grounds that it "would open the door to allow other teachers to be terminated because of race, religion, political beliefs, and/or sexual orientation simply because the teacher was not 'the type of

---

99 996 P.2d 419 (N.M. 1999).
100 539 U.S. 558 (1976).
101 461 P.2d 375 (Cal. 1969).
102 San Diego Sch. Dist. v. Comm. on Professional Competence, 124 Cal. Rptr. 3d 320 (Ct. of App. Ca. 4th A.D., Div. 1 2011).
103 2010 Mich. App. LEXIS 999, *leave to appeal denied*, 488 Mich. 913, 789 N.W.2d 458 (Ct. Apps. Michigan 2010) [*unpublished*].

role model parents want their children to have.'"[104] Other courts have taken a similar approach, rejecting dismissal and certificate revocation for consensual extramarital affairs,[105] unless they involve sexual activity in public.[106]

Immorality

Lying to school officials might sometimes be the basis for a finding of **immorality**. In *Bethel Park School District v. Krall*,[107] a tenured teacher who had been denied permission to attend a conference went anyway. Upon returning, the teacher submitted a request for an excused absence based on illness. The court upheld the dismissal, finding that immoral behavior was not limited to sexual conduct.

Despite some cases to the contrary, most courts insist that school boards wishing to fire teachers for **immorality** demonstrate a connection between the allegedly immoral conduct and teaching effectiveness. If the teacher has committed a serious crime involving violence or a significant theft, a connection—that the teacher's presence in the school poses a danger to persons or property— may be assumed. For less serious crimes, the connection must be established affirmatively. If the alleged connection is that notoriety surrounding the teacher's conduct has led to a loss of respect from students or community members, the notoriety must have occurred as a result of the conduct itself and not because the board publicized the conduct.

Posing a Threat to Students

In some state statutes, behavior that harms or endangers students may be referred to as **immorality**, **unprofessional conduct**, or **unfitness to teach**. Drinking or using drugs or engaging in illegal, dangerous, or reckless behavior with students is grounds for dismissal, as is the physical or verbal abuse of students.[108] In *Walthart v. Board of Directors of Edgewood-Colesburg Community School District*,[109] the court upheld the dismissal of a teacher who permitted students to camp on her property on a Saturday and later realized that the students were drinking. Her failure to stop the drinking and adequately monitor the students may have contributed to a fatal accident.

Teachers may be dismissed for subjecting students to vulgar or racial invective, as well as threats or intimidation, in or out of class.[110] Inappropriate classroom commentary may also be dangerous enough to justify dismissing a teacher. One twelfth-grade teacher was dismissed for explaining the operation of brothels, including minimum age requirements for admission, for discussing the size of a penis, and for telling stories about intercourse with virgins and a cow.[111] In *School District Board of Directors v. Lundblad*,[112] an Iowa court upheld the dismissal of a ninth-grade English teacher who said to a student who had written a paper on suicide, "For extra credit, why don't you try it?" In

104 744 N.E.2d 1245 (Ohio Ct. App. 2000).
105 Sherburne v. Sch. Bd. of Suwannee County, 455 So. 2d 1057 (Fla. App. 1984); Erb v. Iowa State Bd. of Pub. Instruction, 216 N.W.2d 339 (Iowa 1974).
106 Pettit v. State Bd. of Educ., 513 P.2d 889 (Cal. 1973); *see also* Bd. of Educ. v. Calderon, 110 Cal. Rptr. 916 (Cal. Ct. App. 1973); Stephens v. Bd. of Educ., Sch. Dist. No. 5, 429 N.W.2d 722 (Neb. 1988).
107 Bethel Park Sch. Dist. v. Krall, 445 A.2d 1377 (Pa. Commw. Ct. 1982).
108 Bd. of Educ. of Hopkins County v. Wood, 717 S.W.2d 837 (Ky. 1986).
109 694 N.W.2d 740 (Iowa, 2005).
110 Bd. of Directors of Ames Cmty. Sch. Dist. v. Cullinan, 745 N.W.2d 487 (Iowa 2008); Ware v. Morgan County Sch. Dist., 748 P.2d 1295 (Colo. 1988); Bovino v. Bd. of Sch. Dir. of the Indiana Area Sch. Dist., 377 A.2d 1284 (Pa. 1977); Clarke v. Bd. of Educ. of Omaha, 338 N.W.2d 272 (Neb. 1983).
111 State v. Bd. of Sch. Dir. of Milwaukee, 111 N.W.2d 198 (Wis. 1961), *appeal dismissed*, 370 U.S. 720 (1962).
112 528 N.W.2d 593 (Iowa 1995).

Johnson v. Edgewood City School District,[113] an Ohio court ruled that dismissal was not warranted for a teacher who asked students to make predictions about their classmates' futures.

Not surprisingly, the physical injury of students has been grounds for dismissal. In *Adkins v. Board of Education, City of Chicago*,[114] a teacher with a history of using force, was again charged with violating the rule against corporal punishment after grabbing a student by the shirt and twisting it, pinching the skin on the student's chest. Given her prior record and the specific injury in this instance, the court found her behavior to be **irremediable**. In *Bethany St. Pierre v. Smithfield School Committee*,[115] a teacher performed a "stapler trick" he had executed many times before without mishap, but which resulted on this occasion in a minor puncture wound. Despite a stellar teaching record, the incident led to the teacher's dismissal. The court noted that the teacher had made four mistakes—the trick itself, failure to obtain medical care for the student, lack of candor in failing to report the incident, and involving students in a cover-up.

Dismissal of teachers who have sex with minors is always upheld.[116] It does not matter whether the minor was enrolled in the teacher's school or even in the same school district. Thus, in *Elvin v. City of Waterville*,[117] the court upheld the dismissal of a teacher who had sexual intercourse with a 15-year-old, even though the teenager did not live in the town where she taught. Nor does it matter if the sexual relationship took place prior to the teacher's employment. In *Fisher v. Independent School District No. 622*, a 23-year-old plaintiff established that his former elementary school teacher had sexually abused him many years before. The court upheld the teacher's dismissal.[118] In *Toney v. Fairbanks North Star Borough School District*,[119] an Alaska court upheld the dismissal of a teacher who had had a sexual relationship with a 15-year-old student while employed in another school district 12 years earlier.

There is some question as to whether a consensual relationship with a student who has reached the legal age of consent is cause for dismissal. In *Mudge v. Huxley*,[120] a New York court upheld the dismissal of a teacher who invited students to major league baseball games prior to their graduation. After they graduated, he again took them to a professional baseball game. After the game, he had sex with them in his car. The court described the teacher's behavior as "grooming" the students for a sexual relationship after they turned 18.

The use of sexualized statements and **innuendo** has also been the basis of teacher dismissal. Thus, in *Lackow v. Department of Education*,[121] a New York court upheld the dismissal of a teacher who repeatedly used sexual innuendo in the classroom. Among other things, while showing students a model of female reproductive organs, the teacher said to a male student, "You'll never see one, so enjoy it." In *Taylor v. Clarksville Montgomery County School System*,[122] a teacher in Tennessee was dismissed for writing "I love you" on students' papers and for kissing a student on the cheek.

In *Halter v. Iowa Board of Education Examiners*,[123] the Iowa Court of Appeal found that the abuse of any child can automatically bear upon a person's fitness to teach. School districts that hire or retain teachers with a history of sexual relationships with minors may be vulnerable to lawsuits for **negligent hiring** if such behavior is repeated (see Chapter 12). School districts that fail to

---

113 2009 Ohio 3827 (Ct. of App., 12th A. D. 2009).
114 2012 Ill. App. Unpub. LEXIS 890 (App. Ct. 1st Dist. 2012) [*unpublished*].
115 2009 R.I. Super. LEXIS 121 (R.I. 2009).
116 Lehto v. Bd. of Educ., 962 A.2d 222 (Del. 2008).
117 573 A.2d 381 (Me. 1990).
118 357 N.W.2d 152 (Minn. Ct. App. 1984).
119 881 P.2d 1112 (Alaska 1994).
120 914 N.Y.S.2d 339 (A.D. 3 Dept. 2010).
121 51 A.D.3d 563; 859 N.Y.S.2d 52; 2008 (A.D. NY 2008).
122 2010 Tenn. App. LEXIS 522 (Ct. of App. Ky. 2010).
123 698 N.W.2d 337 (Iowa Ct. App. 2005).

respond to instances of sexual involvement between teachers and students may be vulnerable to lawsuits under Title IX (see Chapter 7). However, districts must be careful to differentiate between sexual abuse or harassment and inoffensive, non-sexual contact.

The case for dismissal becomes stronger when it contains any of the following elements:

- documented observations of the teacher according to a formalized and properly followed evaluation procedure;
- establishment of a connection between the behavior and teaching effectiveness in the classroom;
- evidence of incompetence or other grounds based on more than the subjective evaluation by a single school official (but subjective impressions may be part of a properly executed evaluation);[124]
- proof that formal steps of remediation were undertaken and failed, proof that the teacher's behavior undermined the educational goals of the school;
- evidence of specific harm or disruption of the school's educational mission;
- proof of the violation of a written school rule or policy;
- the establishment of a pattern of offending behavior;
- evidence of notices and warnings provided to the teacher;
- the absence of any sound educational justification for the teacher's behavior;
- evidence of notoriety over the teacher's behavior diminishing the school's or teacher's effectiveness (but not notoriety resulting primarily from the school board's actions);
- the absence of mitigating circumstances explaining or excusing the teacher's behavior; or
- evidence that the continuing presence of the teacher in the school poses an educational or physical risk to the students.

In the following illustrative case involving an elementary school teacher dismissed for a having a sexual relationship with a 17-year-old high school student, a number of these elements were present.

LEHTO v. BOARD OF EDUCATION
Supreme Court of Delaware
962 A.2d 222 (2008)

HENRY D. RIDGELY, Justice

Appellant, Christopher Lehto ... was an art teacher at the Star Hill Elementary School ("Star Hill)" in the Caesar Rodney School District in Camden, Delaware (the "District"), for eight years. In early 2007, Lehto became involved in a sexual relationship with a seventeen-year-old female (the "Student") who attended Polytech Senior High School in Woodside, Delaware. At the time, Lehto was thirty-four years old.

Lehto was previously the Student's teacher when she attended Star Hill. He became reacquainted with his former student in December 2006 when she began to come to the elementary school to pick up her younger sibling, who attended Star Hill at the time. The two soon began to speak on the phone and Lehto provided assistance to the Student with at least one school project.

The relationship became sexual in nature a few months later and Lehto and the Student engaged in several instances of sexual contact. On one occasion, Lehto called in sick and stayed home from work. During school hours, Lehto communicated with the Student and she came to his home during her

---

124 Iverson v. Wall Bd. of Educ., 522 N.W.2d 188 (S.D. 1994).

lunch hour. They watched a movie and began to kiss, eventually moving to the floor where the Student's shirt was removed. The couple then moved to Lehto's bedroom where he fondled and licked the Student's breasts. They also engaged in "grinding," or simulated sexual intercourse, but the episode ended without Lehto and the student engaging in actual sexual intercourse.

Several other occasions of sexual contact occurred in a Wal-Mart parking lot after Lehto and the Student met for lunch. During these trysts, Lehto and the Student kissed and Lehto licked and fondled the Student's breasts. On at least one occasion, Lehto sexually penetrated the Student by putting his hand down her pants and inserting his finger into her vagina.

Eventually, the Student told a friend about her relationship with Lehto and that friend told her parent, who informed the Delaware State Police. Lehto was charged with fourth degree rape based on the Student's age and his position as a person "in a position of trust, authority or supervision" over her. However, a *nolle prosequi* was entered on the charge on June 14, 2007 for lack of prosecutive merit.

On July 2, 2007, the Board notified Lehto of its intention to terminate his services as a teacher because of immorality and/or misconduct in office. At a hearing held on August 15, 2007, the District presented evidence through Detective Kevin McKay of the Delaware State Police, who had conducted the investigation of Lehto. Detective McKay had interviewed Lehto and the Student, both of whom detailed the numerous instances of sexual contact described above. In an effort to show that the relationship had not affected his job performance, Lehto presented evidence of his teaching evaluations, all of which had been positive. Lehto also presented proof that the State dismissed the rape charge initially filed against him.

On August 27, 2007, the Board issued its written decision terminating Lehto. The Board found that there was no factual dispute that the relationship between Lehto and the Student was of a sexual nature. It concluded that Lehto's conduct in initiating and engaging in a sexual relationship with a minor constituted immorality, violated the common mores of society, and provided just cause for his termination. The Board noted: "Such conduct certainly interferes with Mr. Lehto's important function of serving as a role model to the students in his school, and threatens the moral and social orientation of such students." The Board based its finding of immorality on the fact that the relationship "sends the wrong message to students of the District regarding appropriate relationships between teachers and students" and that "the referenced relationship evinces a serious lack of judgment that is far below the standard of such judgment acceptable for teachers employed by the Caesar Rodney School District."

Lehto appealed to the Superior Court, arguing that there was no substantial evidence in the record or any legal basis to support the Board's ruling. Particularly, Lehto focused on the fact that the Student did not attend a school within the District, that he did not engage in criminal activity, and that the affair had no impact on his professional duties. The Superior Court acknowledged that "[t]he definition of immorality does not lend itself to methodical application," and found that the Board's determination that Lehto could no longer serve as an effective role model to the students in his school because of his conduct was supported by substantial evidence. The Superior Court affirmed the Board's decision and this appeal followed.

II.

When reviewing an appeal from a decision of a board of education, we apply the substantial evidence review standard. "Substantial evidence has been defined as 'such relevant evidence as a reasonable mind might accept as adequate to support a conclusion.'" "If there was presented substantial and credible evidence to support the charges and a fair administrative hearing was had, the Superior Court cannot substitute its judgment for the judgment of the school authorities."

Immorality Requires a Nexus with Fitness to Teach

The Board terminated Lehto because of "immorality" pursuant to 14 Del. C. § 1411, which provides:

Termination at the end of the school year shall be for 1 or more of the following reasons: Immorality, misconduct in office, incompetency, disloyalty, neglect of duty, willful [sic] and persistent insubordination, a reduction in the number of teachers required as a result of decreased enrollment or a decrease in education services. The board shall have power to suspend any teacher pending a hearing if the situation warrants such action.

Immorality is not defined in this statute, or anywhere else in 14 Del. C. ch. 14; however, in *Skripchuk v. Austin*,[125] the Superior Court addressed the meaning of "immorality" as follows:

Although there might be disagreement about the meaning of 'immorality' in some cases, by the very nature of the term, which refers to the common mores of society, one would expect broad agreement in most cases. Moreover, the term will be construed in the context in which it appears in this chapter to refer to such immorality as may reasonably be found to impair the teacher's effectiveness by reason of his unfitness or otherwise.

We adopt this definition for purposes of Section 1411.

Consistent with *Skripchuk*, a majority of courts have required that "a nexus exist between the off-duty conduct and a teacher's duties before allowing termination of the teacher based on immorality." An early decision in this area was *Morrison v. State Board of Education*,[126] in which California's State Board of Education, acting pursuant to a state statute, revoked a teacher's "life diplomas" because he had engaged in "immoral conduct." The California Supreme Court ruled that the statute upon which the revocation was based was not unconstitutionally vague, but only to the extent that its terms—including "immoral conduct"—were construed to implicate only conduct that impacts the fitness to teach.

Since *Morrison*, numerous courts have similarly interpreted analogous statutes to require a nexus. That nexus typically focuses "on how the conduct may affect the teacher's ability to teach," which includes "the teacher's ability to maintain discipline in the classroom, the effect the act will have on the teacher's students, and the attitudes of the teacher's [students'] parents." Additionally, "off-campus acts for which a teacher is being disciplined need not be limited to teacher-student interactions, but must relate to his/her fitness as a teacher and must have an adverse effect on or within the school community." We conclude that in cases involving termination for "immorality," this nexus test strikes a proper balance under Section 1411 for school boards to apply.

The Nexus Was Sufficient to Support Lehto's Termination

The record demonstrates a sufficient nexus between the undisputed sexual relationship between Lehto and the Student and Lehto's fitness to teach. Lehto argues to the contrary and cites performance reviews that predate the public disclosure of his relationship. However, this argument discounts the sexual nature of his relationship with the Student that began in the school environment, that involved a minor sibling of another minor student who attended his school, and the public controversy which followed Lehto's arrest and the disclosure of the relationship.

Many decisions have upheld the termination of a teacher because of immorality based on a teacher's affair with a student. Although this case involves a sexual relationship with a minor who is a former, but not current, student, this distinction does not make a difference. Other jurisdictions have also considered the nexus between a teacher's fitness to teach and his sexual conduct outside of the school with a non-student who is a minor. Despite the lack of a direct connection with the classroom, these jurisdictions have found a nexus based on the effect of the conduct on the teacher's position as a role model and the parents' ability to trust the safety of their children to the school.

In *Tomerlin v. Dade County School Board*,[127] the Florida District Court of Appeals upheld the dismissal of an elementary school teacher on grounds of immoral conduct for performing oral sex on his stepdaughter. Although the incident occurred after school hours and in the teacher's own home, the court explained that "[m]others and fathers would question the safety of their children; children would discuss [his] conduct and morals. All of these related to [his] job performance." The court continued:

A school teacher holds a position of great trust. We entrust the custody of our children to the teacher. We look to the teacher to educate and to prepare our children for their adult lives. To fulfill this trust, the teacher must be of good moral character; to require less would jeopardize the future lives of our children.

125 379 A.2d 1142 (Del. Super. Ct. 1977).
126 461 P.2d 375 (Cal. 1969).
127 318 So.2d 159 (Fla. Dist. Ct. App. 1975).

Similarly, in *In re Appeal of Morrill*,[128] a high school teacher was terminated for lack of good moral character after pleading *nolo contendere* to charges of simple assault against a minor female who was not one of his students. The Supreme Court of New Hampshire found that even though the victim was a non-student, there was a sufficient nexus to the teacher's fitness to teach because the "conduct demonstrates serious disregard for students under his supervision and care. Parents and school administrators would reasonably be concerned about the well-being and education of children in such an environment."

Here, part of Lehto's job as a teacher was to serve as a role model for his students. Because a teacher's interpersonal relationships are observed by and reflected in the conduct of students, teacher-student relationships must be kept within the bounds of acceptable conduct. If proven, Lehto's sexual contact with a minor directly related to his fitness to teach other minors and impacted the school community. There was a proper nexus between his alleged off-duty conduct and his fitness to teach.

The Evidence Was Sufficient to Support the Board's Decision.

Our review for substantial evidence looks only for "such relevant evidence as a reasonable mind might accept as adequate" to support the Board's conclusion. Detective McKay's testimony, based on corroborating interviews with both Lehto and the Student, detailed Lehto's sexual relationship with a seventeen-year-old former student—a relationship initiated in the school environment where the Student's younger sibling was enrolled. The community learned of this relationship. The Board could reasonably conclude that the relationship itself threatened Lehto's "important function of serving as a role model to the students in his school ..." Moreover, the public disclosure of that relationship permitted the Board to infer a significant detrimental impact on the school community if Lehto continued to teach, as Lehto's actions and his continuation in his position could reasonably undermine parents' confidence in both Lehto and the District.

The record also provided substantial evidence from which the Board could conclude that Lehto's actions in pursuing and engaging in this relationship "threaten[ed] the moral and social fabric of the school environment, ... sen[t] the wrong message to students of the District regarding appropriate relationships between teachers and students" and "evince[ed] a serious lack of judgment that is far below the standard of such judgment acceptable for teachers employed by the Caesar Rodney School District." We conclude that there was substantial evidence to support the Board's decision that Lehto's relationship with the Student constituted immorality justifying dismissal under 14 Del. C. § 1411. ... The judgment of the Superior Court is AFFIRMED.

The testimony of students may be used in support of dismissal, as may the results of a polygraph test.[129] A California court has ruled that even illegally obtained evidence—evidence that could not be used in a criminal proceeding against the teacher—may be used in a dismissal proceeding.[130] Some courts may exclude hearsay evidence from teacher dismissal hearings or give hearsay less weight.[131]

Few things can diminish a school's effectiveness more than a teacher who does not perform adequately, yet far fewer teachers are actually dismissed than are considered incompetent by their supervisors. Reasons for the discrepancy include reluctance to cause harm to the incompetent person, fear of litigation or other unpleasant repercussions, and the belief that incompetence can more easily be dealt with through other methods such as forced resignation. The latter approach— forcing resignation by making working conditions intolerable—is known as **constructive discharge**. Although it may be tempting to give an unsatisfactory employee the opportunity to resign instead of instituting formal proceedings, courts often view constructive discharge as a violation of

128 765 A.2d 699 (N.H. 2001).
129 Libe v. Bd. of Educ. of Twin Cedars, 350 N.W.2d 748 (Iowa Ct. App. 1984).
130 Governing Bd. of Mountain View Sch. Dist. v. Metcalf, 111 Cal. Rptr. 724 (Cal. Ct. App. 1974).
131 *See* Youngman v. Doerhoff, 890 S.W.2d 330 (Mo. App. 1994).

due process. Employees who voluntarily resign will usually find courts unsympathetic if they try to rescind their action unless they can show a significant degree of coercion.

Whereas failing to dismiss an incompetent teacher rarely results in litigation, dismissals for constitutionally or statutorily impermissible reasons often do lead to lawsuits. Typically, these cases arise when administrators act out of anger or personal animosity toward a teacher, in the face of community pressure, or when the teacher lives an unconventional lifestyle. School officials are far less likely to find themselves on the losing side of a lawsuit when they act on the basis of professional standards and statutory requirements and not out of personal pique or political pressure.

Rules of Evidence and Procedural Due Process

A teacher with tenure may be dismissed only **for cause**, as specified by state statute and case law. Tenure also means that the school district must bear the burden of proof that dismissal is warranted. This burden must be met in accordance with the rules guiding the admissibility of evidence and other due process requirements.

Rules of Evidence

Anybody who follows accounts of criminal trials knows that the state must prove beyond a reasonable doubt that the accused committed the crime with which he or she is charged. Teacher dismissal cases are civil matters, so the burden of proof is lighter than in criminal cases. The charge must be supported by **substantial evidence** or by a **preponderance of the evidence**. These kinds of formulations of the burden can be understood to mean that the proof must be such that a reasonable person can believe the charge as more likely than not to be true.

It is also widely known that criminal trials place important restrictions on the kind of evidence that may be introduced to prove the charge. The rules of evidence in criminal trials are most importantly marked by the requirement that the evidence be relevant. For example, in *Elsass v. St. Mary's City School District Board of Education*,[132] the attorney for the plaintiff attempted to present evidence consisting of performance reviews from another school district. In response, the school district argued that this evidence was not relevant to the sole issue of whether or not the teacher had masturbated in the school parking lot. The court upheld the objection.

In addition to the requirement of relevancy, there are other rules that may result in evidence being blocked in a judicial proceeding—rules such as the privilege against self-incrimination, the exclusion of illegally seized evidence, attorney-client privilege, the rule against character evidence, the exclusion of character evidence, and the exclusion of hearsay evidence, as well as many other rules.

The rules regarding the exclusion of hearsay evidence are very complex. For the purposes of this chapter, the rules can be generally summarized as follows.

First, a court should only make its findings of fact based on statements made by witnesses who testify before the court. Second, when a witness testifies as to what somebody else said outside the court, that witness is offering an out of court declaration that the court may not accept as expressing something true. For example, a central issue in a case may be whether the floor in the cafeteria had spilled oil on it for more than a day. A witness, Consuela, may testify that another person, Barbara, not in the courtroom, told her that the oil had been on the floor for three days. In a court, Consuela's testimony would be inadmissible, since it was only a repeated out-of-court statement

---

132 2011 Ohio 1870 (Ct. App. 3d A.D. 2011).

by Barbara that was offered to prove the truth of the matter in the quoted statement, i.e., that oil was on the floor for more than one day.

The rules of evidence in teacher dismissal cases are, however, less restrictive as to what must be excluded. In fact, the strict rules of evidence that apply to civil proceedings in a *court* do not apply to dismissal hearings before a school board. An Iowa statute reads:

> The board shall not be bound by common law or statutory rules of evidence or by technical or formal rules of procedure, but it shall hold the hearing in such manner as is best suited to ascertain and conserve the substantial rights of the parties.[133]

This means, among other things, that it is possible for a school board to base its finding of fact *in part* on hearsay evidence. Thus, a Tennessee court ruled that a police detective who, while pursuing a criminal investigation of a teacher, had interviewed students about the behavior of the teacher could testify as to what those students told him about the teacher's improper behavior.[134]

Polygraph Tests

Though polygraph tests are not admissible in criminal court proceedings, school boards are permitted to take them into account in dismissal proceedings. In *Waisanen v. Clatskanie School District*,[135] the results of a polygraph test were permitted in the 2005 dismissal of a teacher accused of having sex with a former student two and a half decades earlier. Because school dismissal cases are civil matters, school districts may not be required to exclude evidence used to support the dismissal even if seized in violation of the teacher's Fourth Amendment rights.[136]

Although school districts may consider types of evidence that courts may consider unreliable, they must still base their findings on substantial evidence. Thus dismissing a teacher wholly on the basis of hearsay testimony invites the dismissal to be overturned by a court.[137] When the hearsay testimony is itself supported by other corroborating testimony the reliance on hearsay is not fatal.[138] Similarly, districts need to assess the credibility of the witnesses, e.g., testimony that contains contradictions is clearly not reliable. The mere fact a witness may be a student does not, however, make the testimony unreliable.

School districts must have sufficient evidence to support claims of instructional ineffectiveness, for example, if a dismissal is to be upheld by a court. In *Weston v. Independent School District*,[139] the test scores of the plaintiff's students were better than some teachers and worse than others. The plaintiff had for the three preceding years received strong evaluations, and 18 former students and parents also attested to his effectiveness. Thus, the court overturned the plaintiff's dismissal, noting that the issue was not about his effectiveness but was instead a dispute over teaching methodology.

---

133   Iowa Code § 279.16; *see also* 14 Del. C. § 1413(a)(6).17; Kroll v. Independent Sch. Dist. No. 5, 304 N.W.2d 338 (Minn. 1981).

134   Taylor v. Clarksville Montgomery Cty. Sch. System, 2010 Tenn. App. LEXIS 522 (Ct. of App. Tenn. 2010); *see also* Walhart v. Bd. of Directors of Edgewood-Colesburg Comm. Sch. Dist., 694 N.W.2d 740 (Iowa 2005); Bethel v. Bd. of Educ. Capital Sch. Dist., 985 A.2d 389 (Del. 2009); Bd. of Directors of Ames Cmty. Sch. Dist. v. Cullinan, 745 N.W.2d 487 (Iowa 2008).

135   215 P.3d 882 (Ct. App. Oregon 2009).

136   United States v. Janis, 428 U.S. 433 (1976); Pike v. Gallagher, 829 F. Supp. 1254 (D.N.M. 1993).

137   Waisanen v. Clatskanie Sch. Dist., 215 P.3d 882 (Ct. App. Oregon 2009).

138   Crosby v. Holt, 320 S.W.3d 805 (Ct. of App. Tenn. Knoxville 2009).

139   170 P.3d 539 (Okla. 2007).

As with students, rules that govern the behavior of teachers must meet the basic due process requirement that they not be unconstitutionally **vague** or **overbroad** (see Chapter 6). In *Daily v. Board of Education of Morrill County School District*,[140] a Nebraska teacher argued that the state law banning corporal punishment was impermissibly vague. He had either "tapped" or "slapped" a student on the back of the head in frustration when the student repeatedly ignored his instructions. Although the court agreed that corporal punishment might have been more carefully defined, it nonetheless found the law was not so vague as to violate due process.

Due Process

In making a case for the dismissal of a teacher, the school board must follow certain procedures. The Constitution, as the supreme law of the land, lays down the minimum procedural requirements that all dismissals must satisfy. State statutory law and local policy must at least comply with these minimum requirements, but states and school districts may and often do adopt additional or stronger procedural requirements than the Constitution requires. Local school district procedures regarding teacher firings may be found in individual teacher contracts, collective-bargaining agreements, or the policy statements of local school boards. Whatever their source, school district procedures must be consistent with state requirements.

As we discussed in Chapter 6, the **Due Process Clause** of the Fourteenth Amendment requires that "due process" be provided prior to the deprivation of life, liberty, or property. The Supreme Court in three important cases has laid out the basic constitutional requirements regarding due process when it comes to the dismissal of school personnel, cases that address two major questions: (a) to whom are due process procedures owed; and (b) assuming due process is owed, what process is due?[141] The short answer to the first question is that in order to have a constitutional right to due process that employee must have a property interest in the job; tenure, and an existing contract is the usual grounds for concluding the teacher has a property interest at stake. The legal phrase used in these situations is that the employee has a legal expectation, not merely a personal, subjective, expectation or desire, of continued employment.

Probationary teachers do not have a property interest in their jobs beyond the expiration date of their contract, thus probationary teachers do not have a *constitutional* right to due process when their contracts are not renewed. However, dismissal while the contract is still in force would trigger a right to due process. The Tenth Circuit Court of Appeals even held that a property interest was at stake when a teacher was dismissed mid-contract from an extra-duty coaching position.[142]

Two other circumstances may also trigger a right to due process. First, the Supreme Court has said that due process is triggered when the adverse employment decision is taken in **retaliation** for speech activities, apart from the matter of having a property interest in the position. Second, the Court has suggested that an adverse personnel decision that might seriously damage a teacher's **reputation** or **standing** within the community or impair prospects for future employment may be viewed as a deprivation of a liberty interest requiring due process.

Thus, teachers, whether tenured or not, have occasionally succeeded in claiming that transfers, demotions, failure to provide salary increases, failure to grant tenure, or temporary suspensions should have been accompanied by procedural protections. This is most likely to occur when an

---

140 588 N.W.2d 813 (Neb. 1999).

141 Board of Regents of State Colleges v. Roth, 408 U.S. 564 (1972); Perry v. Sinderman, 408 U.S. 593 (1972), *overruled on other grounds by* Rust v. Sullivan, 500 U.S. 173 (1991); Cleveland Board of Education v. Loudermill, 470 U.S. 532 (1985).

142 Kelly v. Indep. Sch. Dist. No. 12 of Okla. Cty., 80 Fed. Appx. 36 (10th Cir. 2003) [*unpublished*].

adverse decision is based on publicly made charges. Charges of intoxication, racism, and mental instability have been found sufficiently stigmatizing to require due process.[143] In other cases, however, allegations of poor job performance such as incompetence, inadequacy, and insubordination have not been found to require due process.[144]

Once it is decided that a teacher has a right to procedural due process, what process is due? In the following landmark case, the Supreme Court considered whether the Constitution requires specific due process procedures for tenured public employees in addition to the due process rights that may be specified by state law.

⚖

CLEVELAND BOARD OF EDUCATION v. LOUDERMILL
Supreme Court of the United States
470 U.S. 532 (1985)

JUSTICE WHITE delivered the opinion of the Court.

In 1979 the Cleveland Board of Education, petitioner ... hired respondent James Loudermill as a security guard. On his job application, Loudermill stated that he had never been convicted of a felony. Eleven months later, as part of a routine examination of his employment records, the Board discovered that in fact Loudermill had been convicted of grand larceny in 1968. By letter dated November 3, 1980, the Board's Business Manager informed Loudermill that he had been dismissed because of his dishonesty in filling out the employment application. Loudermill was not afforded an opportunity to respond to the charge of dishonesty or to challenge his dismissal. On November 13, the Board adopted a resolution officially approving the discharge.

Under Ohio law, Loudermill was a "classified civil servant." Such employees can be terminated only for cause, and may obtain administrative review if discharged. Pursuant to this provision, Loudermill filed an appeal with the Cleveland Civil Service Commission on November 12. The Commission appointed a referee, who held a hearing on January 29, 1981. Loudermill argued that he had thought that his 1968 larceny conviction was for a misdemeanor rather than a felony. The referee recommended reinstatement. On July 20, 1981, the full Commission heard argument and orally announced that it

would uphold the dismissal. Proposed findings of fact and conclusions of law followed on August 10, and Loudermill's attorneys were advised of the result by mail on August 21.

Although the Commission's decision was subject to judicial review in the state courts, Loudermill instead brought the present suit in the Federal District Court for the Northern District of Ohio. The complaint alleged that § 124.34 was unconstitutional on its face because it did not provide the employee an opportunity to respond to the charges against him prior to removal. As a result, discharged employees were deprived of liberty and property without due process. The complaint also alleged that the provision was unconstitutional as applied because discharged employees were not given sufficiently prompt post-removal hearings.

Before a responsive pleading was filed, the District Court dismissed for failure to state a claim on which relief could be granted. It held that because the very statute that created the property right in continued employment also specified the procedures for discharge, and because those procedures were followed, Loudermill was, by definition, afforded all the process due. The post-termination hearing also adequately protected Loudermill's liberty interests. Finally, the District Court concluded that, in light of the Commission's crowded docket, the delay in processing Loudermill's administrative appeal was constitutionally acceptable. ...

143 McKnight v. Southeastern Pennsylvania Transp. Auth., 583 F.2d 1229 (3d Cir. 1978); Wellner v. Minnesota State Junior Coll. Bd., 487 F.2d 153 (8th Cir. 1973); Bomhoff v. White, 526 F. Supp. 488 (D. Ariz. 1981).
144 Gray v. Union County Intermediate Educ. Dist., 520 F.2d 803 (9th Cir. 1975); Beitzell v. Jeffrey, 643 F.2d 870 (1st Cir. 1981).

A divided panel of the Court of Appeals for the Sixth Circuit reversed in part and remanded. After rejecting arguments that the actions were barred by failure to exhaust administrative remedies and by *res judicata*—arguments that are not renewed here—the Court of Appeals found that [Loudermill] had been deprived of due process. It disagreed with the District Court's original rationale. Instead, it concluded that the compelling private interest in retaining employment, combined with the value of presenting evidence prior to dismissal, outweighed the added administrative burden of a pre-termination hearing. With regard to the alleged deprivation of liberty, and Loudermill's 9-month wait for an administrative decision, the court affirmed the District Court, finding no constitutional violation. ... Loudermill sought review of the rulings adverse to him. We granted all three petitions, and now affirm in all respects.

II

[Loudermill's] federal constitutional claim depends on [his] having had a property right in continued employment. If [so], the State could not deprive [him] of this property without due process. ... The Board stresses that in addition to specifying the grounds for termination, the statute sets out procedures by which termination may take place. The procedures were adhered to in these cases. According to petitioner, "[to] require additional procedures would in effect expand the scope of the property interest itself."

This argument, which was accepted by the District Court, has its genesis in the plurality opinion in *Arnett v. Kennedy*.[145] *Arnett* involved a challenge by a former federal employee to the procedures by which he was dismissed. The plurality reasoned that where the legislation conferring the substantive right also sets out the procedural mechanism for enforcing that right, the two cannot be separated:

The employee's statutorily defined right is not a guarantee against removal without cause in the abstract, but such a guarantee as enforced by the procedures which Congress has designated for the determination of cause. ...

[Where] the grant of a substantive right is inextricably intertwined with the limitations on the procedures which are to be employed in determining that right, a litigant in the position of appellee must take the bitter with the sweet.

This view garnered three votes in *Arnett*, but was specifically rejected by the other six Justices. Since then, this theory has at times seemed to gather some additional support.

More recently, however, the Court has clearly rejected it. In *Vitek v. Jones*,[146] we pointed out that "minimum [procedural] requirements [are] a matter of federal law, they are not diminished by the fact that the State may have specified its own procedures that it may deem adequate for determining the preconditions to adverse official action." This conclusion was reiterated in *Logan v. Zimmerman Brush Co.*,[147] where we reversed the lower court's holding that because the entitlement arose from a state statute, the legislature had the prerogative to define the procedures to be followed to protect that entitlement.

In light of these holdings, it is settled that the "bitter with the sweet" approach misconceives the constitutional guarantee. If a clearer holding is needed, we provide it today. The point is straightforward: The Due Process Clause provides that certain substantive rights—life, liberty, and property—cannot be deprived except pursuant to constitutionally adequate procedures. The categories of substance and procedure are distinct. Were the rule otherwise, the Clause would be reduced to a mere tautology. "Property" cannot be defined by the procedures provided for its deprivation any more than can life or liberty. The right to due process

is conferred, not by legislative grace, but by constitutional guarantee. While the legislature may elect not to confer a property interest in [public] employment, it may not constitutionally authorize the deprivation of such an interest, once conferred, without appropriate procedural safeguards.

In short, once it is determined that the Due Process Clause applies, "the question remains what process is due." The answer to that question is not to be found in the Ohio statute.

145 416 U.S. 134 (1974).
146 445 U.S. 480 (1980).
147 455 U.S. 422 (1982).

An essential principle of due process is that a deprivation of life, liberty, or property "be preceded by notice and opportunity for hearing appropriate to the nature of the case."

We have described "the root requirement" of the Due Process Clause as being "that an individual be given an opportunity for a hearing before he is deprived of any significant property interest."[148] This principle requires "some kind of a hearing" prior to the discharge of an employee who has a constitutionally protected property interest in his employment. ...

The need for some form of pre-termination hearing, recognized in these cases, is evident from a balancing of the competing interests at stake. These are the private interest in retaining employment, the governmental interest in the expeditious removal of unsatisfactory employees and the avoidance of administrative burdens, and the risk of an erroneous termination.

First, the significance of the private interest in retaining employment cannot be gainsaid. We have frequently recognized the severity of depriving a person of the means of livelihood. While a fired worker may find employment elsewhere, doing so will take some time and is likely to be burdened by the questionable circumstances under which he left his previous job.

Second, some opportunity for the employee to present his side of the case is recurringly of obvious value in reaching an accurate decision. Dismissals for cause will often involve factual disputes. Even where the facts are clear, the appropriateness or necessity of the discharge may not be; in such cases, the only meaningful opportunity to invoke the discretion of the decision maker is likely to be before the termination takes effect.

The [case] before us illustrate these considerations. [Loudermill] had plausible arguments to make that might have prevented [his] discharge ... [G]iven the Commission's ruling we cannot say that the discharge was mistaken. Nonetheless, in light of the referee's recommendation, neither can we say that a fully informed decision-maker might not have exercised its discretion and decided not to dismiss him, notwithstanding its authority to do so. In any event, the termination involved arguable issues, and the right to a hearing does not depend on a demonstration of certain success.

The governmental interest in immediate termination does not outweigh these interests. As we

shall explain, affording the employee an opportunity to respond prior to termination would impose neither a significant administrative burden nor intolerable delays. Furthermore, the employer shares the employee's interest in avoiding disruption and erroneous decisions; and until the matter is settled, the employer would continue to receive the benefit of the employee's labors. It is preferable to keep a qualified employee on than to train a new one. A governmental employer also has an interest in keeping citizens usefully employed rather than taking the possibly erroneous and counterproductive step of forcing its employees onto the welfare rolls. Finally, in those situations where the employer perceives a significant hazard in keeping the employee on the job, it can avoid the problem by suspending with pay.

IV

The foregoing considerations indicate that the pre-termination "hearing," though necessary, need not be elaborate. We have pointed out that "[the] formality and procedural requisites for the hearing can vary, depending upon the importance of the interests involved and the nature of the subsequent proceedings." In general, "something less" than a full evidentiary hearing is sufficient prior to adverse administrative action. Under state law, respondents were later entitled to a full administrative hearing and judicial review. The only question is what steps were required before the termination took effect.

In only one case, *Goldberg v. Kelly*,[149] has the Court required a full adversarial evidentiary hearing prior to adverse governmental action. However, as the *Goldberg* Court itself pointed out, that case presented significantly different considerations than are present in the context of public employment. Here, the pre-termination hearing need not definitively resolve the propriety of the discharge. It should be an initial check against mistaken decisions—essentially, a determination of whether there are reasonable grounds to believe that the charges against the employee are true and support the proposed action.

The essential requirements of due process, and all that respondents seek or the Court of Appeals required, are notice and an opportunity to respond. The opportunity to present reasons, either in person or in writing, why proposed action should not

148 Board of Regents v. Roth, 408 U.S. 564 (1972); Perry v. Sindermann, 408 U.S. 593 (1972).
149 397 U.S. 254 (1970).

be taken is a fundamental due process requirement. The tenured public employee is entitled to oral or written notice of the charges against him, an explanation of the employer's evidence, and an opportunity to present his side of the story. To require more than this prior to termination would intrude to an unwarranted extent on the government's interest in quickly removing an unsatisfactory employee.

V

Our holding rests in part on the provisions in Ohio law for a full post-termination hearing. In his cross-petition Loudermill asserts, as a separate constitutional violation, that his administrative proceedings took too long. The Court of Appeals held otherwise, and we agree.

The Due Process Clause requires provision of a hearing "at a meaningful time." At some point, a delay in the post-termination hearing would become a constitutional violation. In the present case, however, the complaint merely recites the course of proceedings and concludes that the denial of a "speedy resolution" violated due process. This reveals nothing about the delay except that it stemmed in part from the thoroughness of the procedures. A 9-month adjudication is not, of course, unconstitutionally lengthy *per se*. Yet Loudermill offers no indication that his wait was unreasonably prolonged other than the fact that it took nine months. The chronology of the proceedings set out in the complaint, coupled with the assertion that nine months is too long to wait, does not state a claim of a constitutional deprivation.

VI

We conclude that all the process that is due is provided by a pre-termination opportunity to respond, coupled with post-termination administrative procedures as provided by the Ohio statute. Because [Loudermill alleges in his complaint that he] had no chance to respond, the District Court erred in dismissing for failure to state a claim. The judgment of the Court of Appeals is affirmed, and the case is remanded for further proceedings consistent with this opinion.

Loudermill makes it clear that the Constitution imposes due process procedures independent of the requirements of state law. Where state law specifies post-termination procedures adequate to "definitively resolve the propriety of the discharge," pre-termination proceedings need not be elaborate. All that is required is some notice of the charges and supporting evidence and an opportunity to refute them. An investigation, no matter how thorough, cannot substitute for a hearing. Thus, a teacher who was suspended for four days and then transferred following an investigation for possible child abuse, but without a hearing, successfully claimed that his due process rights had been violated. The court ruled that the suspension and transfer implicated both property and liberty interests thereby requiring an opportunity to present evidence and cross-examine adverse witnesses.[150]

Loudermill does not fully specify the level of due process required when educational employment contracts are terminated. In teacher dismissal cases, state statutes generally require advanced notice of the charges and a hearing before an impartial tribunal. To satisfy constitutional and statutory requirements, the notice must be given sufficiently in advance of the hearing and be sufficiently precise to allow the preparation of a defense.[151] In one case, a notice informing a teacher being charged with "insubordination based upon the fact you refuse to cooperate with the principal of your school" was found to be inadequate.[152] Similarly, merely charging a teacher with "incompetence" is not adequate notice.[153] To satisfy due process requirements, the notice

---

150   Winegar v. Des Moines Indep. Cmty. Sch. Dist., 20 F.3d 895 (8th Cir. 1994).
151   Staton v. Mayes, 552 F.2d 908 (10th Cir. 1977); Benton v. Bd. of Educ. of Winnebago, 361 N.W.2d 515 (Neb. 1985); Hawkins v. Bd. of Pub. Educ. in Wilmington, 468 F. Supp. 201 (D. Del. 1979).
152   Osborne v. Bullitt County Bd. of Educ., 415 S.W.2d 607 (Ky. Ct. App. 1967).
153   Bd. of Educ. of Clarke County v. Oliver, 116 So. 2d 566 (Ala. 1959).

should delineate the specific unacceptable behaviors and deficiencies. Careful crafting of charges is important also because failing to include notice of an issue may preclude raising the issue in a hearing.

Due process requires that the outcome of the hearing be determined by impartial decision makers. Impartiality may be questioned if the decision maker has a conflict of interest, harbors personal animosity toward the employee, prejudges the case, acts as both judge and "prosecutor," meets with the "prosecutor" or others with interests opposed to the employee outside the hearing, or considers evidence not presented at the hearing.

For the most part the due process requirements districts must adhere to are spelled out by state statute. These statutes vary in their details from state to state. In broad outline the statutes may address some or all of the following elements of the dismissal process:

1. **Written Notice of Charges, Opportunity for Remediation, Pre-termination Hearing**
   a. Content of the notice
   b. Who is to bring the charge (e.g. superintendent or principal)
   c. Remediation requirements
   d. Timing of notice prior to any dismissal hearing
   e. Right of employee to demand a hearing
   f. Suspension, pending final determination, with or without pay
   g. Power of hearing officer at pre-hearing.
2. **Discovery Prior to the Hearing**
   a. Guidelines regarding sharing of information between adverse parties prior to any hearing
   b. Possible requirement that lists of witnesses be shared
   c. Rules regarding depositions.
3. **Impartial Hearing**
   a. Who is to make the findings of fact and decision whether or not to dismiss (*e.g.* hearing officer, hearing panel, school board)
   b. Method of appointment of hearing officer/hearing panel
   c. Powers of hearing officer(s)
   d. Hearing schedule and deadlines to be met
   e. Procedures to be followed at the hearing
   f. Rules of evidence
   g. Issuance of notice re time, place of the hearing
   h. Right to present evidence, right to subpoena witnesses; requirement of an oath, right to question/cross examine witnesses
   i. Right to representation
   j. Right to request public hearing
   k. Right of charged employee not to testify
   l. Right to written transcript
   m. Requirement of majority vote by school board.
4. **Post-Hearing and Appeal**
   a. Deadline for written decision
   b. Required elements of written decision
   c. Right of employee to further proceedings (e.g. arbitration, appeal to a state commissioner of education, appeal to a court)
   d. Power of the reviewing tribunal
   e. Time lines regarding appeals
   f. Right to have record expunged in case of acquittal
   g. Right to attorney's fees if charges are found to be frivolous.

There may of course be legal disagreements regarding the meaning and implementation of these statutory provisions, e.g., whether the employee received notice sufficient in substance and form fairly to inform her of the charges against her thus enabling her to prepare her defense in advance of the hearing.[154]

Reduction in Force

Reduction in force (RIF) refers to the dismissal of personnel because of financial exigency, declining enrollment, or a decision to discontinue a particular program or service. Most states have policies that guide or regulate RIFs. There are important variations among the states regarding what must or may not be considered by executing a reduction in force. It is common for older laws to require that non-tenured teachers be let go first and that seniority be counted so that the least senior are released first. In a few states, including Arizona, Idaho, and Michigan, laws now explicitly forbid making tenure and seniority a factor. Some states, including Colorado, Missouri, Nevada, and New Hampshire, permit tenure to be considered but exclude the consideration of seniority or say that seniority may not be the sole criterion. RIF laws in Colorado, Florida, Illinois, Indiana, Michigan, Oklahoma, Tennessee, Texas, and Utah require that a comparative evaluation of teachers be the basis for reduction in force decisions. The laws in these states, by making evaluation the primary factor, implicitly bar reliance on tenure or seniority in deciding who is to be let go for financial reasons.[155]

State statutes often incorporate, in keeping with constitutional due process requirements, the right of an employee to notice, statement of reasons, and a pre-termination hearing to determine if the statutory grounds for the RIF have been met.[156] A pre-termination hearing may not be constitutionally required, however, as two federal circuit courts have said that a post-termination hearing also satisfies the due process clause.[157] Of course, even to claim a due process violation, having been "riffed," the plaintiff must have a property interest in the job.[158] Collective bargaining agreements may also affect RIF policies and procedures. Legal challenges to RIFs have included claims that:

- Economic circumstances or drops in enrollment did not justify the RIF;[159]
- Abolition of a position did not in fact occur; instead, the same position was retained under a different title;[160]
- The RIF prevented the provision of mandated services or improperly affected the quality of the education program;[161]
- The order of dismissal violated seniority or another statutory mandate;[162]
- A demotion as part of the RIF plan was arbitrary and violated seniority rights;[163]
- The statutorily prescribed order of reinstatement and recall was violated;[164]

---

154 Kelly v. Indep. Sch. Dist. No. 12 of Okla. Cty., 80 Fed. Appx. 36 (10th Cir. 2003) [*unpublished*].
155 Emily Workman, *Reduction in Force Policies*, EDUCATION COMMISSION OF THE STATES, March 2012.
156 Cal Ed Code § 87740; R.R.S. Neb. § 79-847; Rev. Code Wash. (ARCW) § 28A.405.210; Nickel v. Saline County Sch. Dist. No. 163, 559 N.W.2d 480 (Neb. 1997).
157 Strasburger v. Bd. of Educ., 143 F.3d 351 (7th Cir. 1998); Washington Teachers' Union Local #6 v. Bd. of Educ. District of Columbia, 1098 F.3d 774 (Cir. Ct. D.C. 1997).
158 Lacy v. The Dayton Bd. of Educ., 550 F. Supp. 835 (S.D. Ohio 1982).
159 Laird v. Indep. Sch. Dist. No. 317, 346 N.W.2d 153 (Minn. 1984).
160 Baron v. Mackreth, 260 N.E.2d 554 (N.Y. 1970); *see also* Miller v. Sch. Dist. No. 18–0011 of Clay Cty, Nebraska, 278 Neb. 1018, 775 N.W.2d 413 (Neb. 2009).
161 Geduldig v. Bd. of Educ. of N.Y., 351 N.Y.S.2d 167 (N.Y. App. Div. 1974).
162 Peck v. Indep. Sch. Dist. No. 16, 348 N.W.2d 100 (Minn. Ct. App. 1984).
163 Green v. Jenkintown Sch. Dist., 441 A.2d 816 (Pa. Commw. Ct. 1982).
164 Massey v. Argenbright, 683 P.2d 1332 (Mont. 1984).

- RIF procedures violated statutory due process requirements;[165]
- RIF procedures violated contractual requirements;[166] and
- The RIF policy was racially discriminatory.[167]

Leaves of Absence

School boards have the authority to grant leaves of absence for personal reasons (such as illness or bereavement), for professional reasons (such as additional training), and for public service (such as military or jury duty). Boards also have the authority to impose involuntary leave on teachers who are physically or mentally unfit if the teachers' procedural due process rights are satisfied.[168] Boards may not, however, grant a leave that constitutes a gift of public money to a private individual.

Litigation concerning a leave of absence may involve the claim that a school board violated its own policy, the collective bargaining agreement, state statute, federal antidiscrimination law, or the Constitution. In 1974, the Supreme Court ruled that mandatory pregnancy or postpartum leaves of absence violate the teachers' right of privacy.[169] Federal anti-discrimination laws prohibit treating pregnancy differently from other conditions, such as not allowing pregnant teachers to use sick leave.[170] Federal law also prohibits religious discrimination in the administration of a personal leave policy (see Chapter 10).

The *Family and Medical Leave Act*[171] seeks "to balance the demands of the workplace with the needs of families; and to promote national interest in preserving family integrity." The Act "entitles employees to take reasonable leave for medical reasons, for the birth or adoption of a child, and for the care of a child, or parent, who has a serious health condition." The term "child" includes biological, adopted, and foster children, stepchildren, and legal wards. The Act applies to public school districts and private schools with fifty or more employees at any one site. Employees are covered once they have worked for at least a year, provided that they worked at least 1,250 hours during the year prior to the leave. Employees may take up to 12 weeks of unpaid leave within a 12-month period. The employee may take the leave intermittently (e.g., a day or two at a time), or as a reduced work week. The leave arrangement has to be coordinated with the employer unless it is a "medical necessity."

Teachers or others whose absence would disrupt the instructional program of the school are subject to special provisions. When a teacher requests a leave that is "foreseeable based on planned medical treatment" and when the teacher would be on leave for more than 20 percent of the total work days during an instructional period, the school may require that the leave be taken for a particular time period not to exceed the planned medical treatment or require the employee to temporarily transfer to an alternative position.

State statutes dealing with leaves of absence have been the subject of litigation. An Arizona court had to address the meaning of the following statutory provision: "If leave is granted, all rights of tenure, retirement, accrued leave with pay, salary increments and other benefits provided by law shall be preserved and available to the applicant after the termination of the leave of absence."[172] In this case, the teacher who took a leave of absence was given her job back upon return but at

---

165 Palone v. Jefferson Parish Sch. Bd., 306 So. 2d 679 (La. 1975).
166 Law v. Mandan Pub. Sch. Dist., 411 N.W.2d 375 (N.D. 1987).
167 Taxman v. Bd. of Educ. of Piscataway, 91 F.3d 1547 (3d Cir. 1996), *cert. granted*, 521 U.S. 1117 (1997), *cert. dismissed*, 522 U.S. 1010 (1997).
168 Newman v. Bd. of Educ. of N.Y., 594 F.2d 299 (2d Cir. 1979).
169 Cleveland Bd. of Educ. v. LaFleur, 414 U.S. 632 (1974).
170 42 U.S.C. § 2000(e).
171 29 U.S.C. § 2601.
172 McEldowney v. Osborn Dist. No.8 Maricopa Cty., 123 Ariz. 416; 600 P.2d 29 (Ariz. 1979).

the same salary she would have received had she not taken the leave. The plaintiff argued that she "should have been advanced on the salary scale during her two leaves of absence so that, on a percentage basis, she would have received a salary proportionately higher than the one offered to her upon her return." But the court disagreed, saying that "the statute speaks of benefits 'preserved,' not increased. Plaintiff was offered compensation at the same level that she would have received if she had taught in Arizona during the school year in question. All her benefits, consequently, were preserved."

A somewhat different result was reached in a New Jersey case.[173] The issue in the case was whether the time on leave—the plaintiff was on involuntary leave because of a work-related injury—was time that counted toward acquiring tenure. To obtain tenure under New Jersey law a teacher had to have been "employed" for the equivalent of more than three academic years within a period of any four consecutive academic years. The plaintiff argued that "employment" includes periods of sick leave, and the New Jersey court agreed, thus the plaintiff acquired tenure while on leave. And in New Jersey a court agreed that while on leave because of a work-related injury the plaintiff was not entitled to payment for her extra-work assignment as a coach since the term "full salary," as used in the New Jersey statute referred only to the compensation received for the plaintiff's full-time teaching position, and not to the part-time coaching salary.[174]

Workers' Compensation

Teachers injured on the job have two possible paths to compensation from their school district. If the teacher's injury results from careless, reckless, or intentionally wrongful behavior on the part of the district or another of its employees, the teacher may be able to sue the district for negligence or another tort (see Chapter 12). However, such suits may only be brought for injuries that are not eligible for redress under the system known as **workers' compensation**. A teacher who was injured when she voluntarily inserted herself, contrary to school policy, into a fight between two emotionally disturbed students whom the teacher knew were inclined to act violently was required to rely on workers' compensation, and could not directly bring a tort suit against the district.[175]

In most, but not all, states, teachers are covered by workers' compensation statutes. Although workers' compensation laws vary from state to state, all are designed to provide compensation to employees for on-the-job injuries regardless of whether their employers were negligent. The idea is that employers should be responsible for the harm suffered by employees in the course of conducting their employer's business. In most states, an employee's injury resulting from the intentionally wrongful behavior of the employer or a co-worker is not covered by workers' compensation, but workers' compensation is the exclusive remedy for injuries caused by negligence (see Chapter 12) on the part of an employer.

Workers' compensation systems apply to employees, not volunteers. A Wisconsin court ruled that the plaintiff who had signed a contract with the district to serve as a volunteer assistance basketball coach for no compensation was not an employee, thus the injury he sustained while coaching was not covered by workers' compensation.[176]

---

173 Kletzkin v. Bd. of Educ. of the Borough of Spotswood, 136 N.J. 275; 642 A.2d 993 (N.J. 1994).
174 Daganya v. Bd. of Educ. of Twn. of Old Bridge, 2009 N.J. Super. Unpub. LEXIS 2973 (Sup. Ct. A.D. 2009) [*unpublished*].
175 Patrick v. Palm Beach Cty. Sch. Bd., 50 So. 3d 1161 (Ct. App. 4th Dist. 2010).
176 Hall v. Sch. Dist. of St. Croix Falls, 778 N.W.2d 172 (Ct. App. Dist. 3 2009).

To be eligible for compensation, a teacher or any employee must prove the existence of three elements: (a) an injury by accident, (b) arising out of, and (c) in the course of, employment. At one time, the accident requirement meant that the employee had to prove the occurrence of a sudden impact related to something other than routine work. Occupational diseases and back injuries or hernias suffered during routine lifting were excluded from coverage. This narrow notion of an accident has given way to a broader interpretation so that now teachers may also seek compensation for injuries that developed slowly over time or were caused by routine tasks, such as lifting books.

Teachers are also covered if pre-existing conditions are aggravated by their work. Thus, an on-the-job heart attack may be compensable even if it results in part from years of unhealthy living. However, some states will not require workers' compensation to cover heart attacks unless caused by work stress greater than most people experience during normal daily living.

The employee must also establish that the accident was the cause of the injury. Proof of this point turned out to be complex in the case of a teacher with a hemarthrosis—blood in her knee joint—which led to inflammation.[177] The dispute was whether the hemarthrosis was a side effect of an operation on her knee or the result of her having banged her knee following the operation. The court ultimately concluded that the medical testimony supported the conclusion the cause was her banging of her knee on a metal desk.

Once the accident element is proven, a teacher claiming workers' compensation must next show that the injury arose out of the job of teaching. In most states, to satisfy this element, the teacher must show that the act of doing the job increased the probability of the injury. For example, this element can usually be proven in the case of a teacher injured by a student's assault because teaching increases the likelihood of being assaulted.

Under some conditions, job-induced mental illness and even stress may be compensable. Harassment of any kind—sexual, racial, or just personal animosity—is a common source of compensable stress. In one case, a teacher successfully claimed workers' compensation after being falsely accused of sexually harassing a student.[178] However, unless the employer acts unreasonably, claims for compensation for stress arising from overwork, discipline, denial of promotion, layoff, or discharge are usually denied. A California statute is clear that no compensation is to be paid for psychiatric injury "if the injury was substantially caused by a lawful, non-discriminatory, good faith personnel action."[179] In another state one court refused to allow a claim for work-related mental stress because there was no proof that the claimant's particular working conditions were uniquely stressful (she supervised bus routes and other transportation-related matters). The court noted that there was no evidence to suggest that the stress the claimant experienced was the result of anything other than her own mismanagement of the position.[180]

The Supreme Court of South Carolina refused to conclude that the panic attack experienced by a special education teacher was a covered by workers' compensation.[181] The claimant experienced the attack after an argument with her aides with whom she had for a year been in a tense relationship regarding the quality of their work. The court agreed that the claimant had failed to prove that her mental injuries were the result of exposure to unusual and extraordinary conditions and that these conditions were the proximate cause of the mental disorder. Another teacher also

177 Elgin Bd. of Educ. Sch. Dist. U-46 v. Illinois Workers' Compensation Comm., 949 N.E.2d 198 (App. Ct. 1st Dist. 2011).

178 Crochiere v. Bd. of Educ., 630 A.2d 1027 (Conn. 1993).

179 *See, e.g.*, Fields v. Interim Inc., No. H043478, 2019 WL 2083521 (Cal. Ct. App. May 13, 2019), *review denied* (Aug. 14, 2019).

180 King v. Bd. of Educ., 716 A.2d 1077 (Md. Ct. Spec. App. 1998).

181 Tennant v. Beaufort Cty. Sch. Dist., 674 S.E.2d 488 (S.C. 2009).

was denied compensation for post-traumatic stress disorder following an incident in which a student perpetrating a practical joke entered her classroom claiming that people were shooting inside the school.[182] The court upheld the finding that the teacher failed to meet her burden of proof that this distasteful joke—and the students in her class perceived it as a practical joke—was an "extraordinary event" because "people of reasonable sensibilities would and did not find the act [the prank] to be extraordinary in the life of a high school teacher."

North Carolina's highest court denied workers' compensation to a teacher who claimed her general anxiety disorder arose when the students in her class were disrespectful and disobedient and verbally and physically harassed her. To win her case, said the court, the plaintiff had to establish that her anxiety disorder "arose due to stresses and conditions unique to her employment." But the court found that:

> There is substantial evidence … to show that, although the environment in plaintiff's classroom was certainly stressful, such stress was not created by defendant, nor was it characteristic of plaintiff's particular employment. Rather, the evidence showed that the stressful classroom environment was caused by plaintiff's inability to effectively manage her classroom. Other teachers at plaintiff's school who taught the same students did not experience the disciplinary problems encountered by plaintiff. Defendant did not require plaintiff to do anything other than perform her job duties as a teaching professional. Such duties included maintaining control of the classroom learning environment, a task plaintiff unfortunately was unable to perform. Defendant attempted to intervene and assist plaintiff in her endeavors to better manage her classroom, but such attempts were ultimately unsuccessful. We conclude there was substantial evidence to support the … findings that plaintiff was responsible for the stressful work environment, and that such stress was not characteristic of the teaching profession.[183]

The final element of a workers' compensation claim is to show that the injury occurred in the course of employment. This element focuses on where the injury occurred and what the employee was doing at the time. Hence, a teacher who is injured in a car accident while commuting to work would not be covered, but once the teacher crosses the school's property line the commute is over and coverage begins. Teachers injured while driving off-campus on school business would also be covered. A teacher may lose coverage by engaging in willful misconduct, such as being drunk or disobeying the law or school rules.

In most states, the workers' compensation system operates outside the regular court system. Claims must be prosecuted through an administrative agency created specifically for that purpose. Some states have a separate agency for public employees like teachers. In most states, a claim is first decided by a hearing officer, and both sides have the option of appealing to the full agency. The agency's decisions may then be appealed to a court on either procedural or substantive grounds.

Workers' compensation systems in all states require the employee to promptly notify the employer of any injury and establish time limits and procedures for filing claims. Failure to satisfy these requirements will result in a denial of claims. Successful claims may result in compensation for medical expenses, rehabilitation, lost wages, disability or disfigurement, or death benefits to surviving dependents, but there is a limit to the amount that may be awarded, and no punitive damages are allowed. Monetary damages under workers' compensation are usually less than they would have been had a successful tort suit been filed.[184]

---

182 Delrie v. Peabody Magnet H.S., 40 So.3d 1158 (La. App. 3d Cir. 2010).
183 Hassell v. Onslow County Bd. of Educ., 641 S.E.2d 324 (N.C. 2007).
184 Dudley v. Victor Lynn Lines, Inc., 161 A.2d 479 (N.J. 1960).

Collective Bargaining

Many aspects of the relationship between a board of education and its employees are regulated by federal and state statutes, along with the federal Constitution. Within the boundaries of these laws, the terms and conditions of a teacher's employment are outlined in a contractual agreement. For most public school teachers, terms of employment are determined through a process of collective bargaining in which a union represents and negotiates for all teachers within a district simultaneously.[185] Indeed, 79 percent of the nation's teachers are covered by collective bargaining agreements.[186] Ultimately, whether or not collective bargaining takes place, each teacher must sign a contract with the employing board of education.

In the absence of statutory authorization, do public employees have a constitutional right to join a union? In 1968, the Seventh Circuit ruled that free association under the First Amendment includes such a right.[187] Despite legal and and political setbacks for unions over the years, this principle retains some measure of vitality to this day. As a federal court has explained, "Unions are among the quintessential types of associations the First Amendment freedom of association protects."[188]

In previous discussions of the rights of students and teachers, we noted that freedom of association and assembly are corollaries of free speech. By joining with others of like mind, people seek to amplify their voices and to increase their influence. The courts have recognized that insofar as they are expressive acts, forming and joining a union are constitutionally protected. Would not the same reasoning then apply to collective bargaining? After all, collective bargaining is a way for a group of people (employees) to speak as one. The courts that have considered the issue say that it does not: Collective bargaining is not just a form of expression for union members because it also compels the government (the employer) to participate in the process.

Unions and their members are free to exercise their constitutional rights to try to influence their employer, and while some states have enshrined a right to collective bargaining in their state constitutions, there is no free speech or other constitutional provision requiring a governmental employer to engage in collective bargaining with a union under the federal Constitution.

There is also no federal statute giving public sector employees the right to bargain collectively. Thus, states may prohibit collective bargaining by public school teachers, and in states where public sector collective bargaining is not required by statute, school boards are free to refuse to negotiate with unions.[189] Even in states where a statute or the state constitution gives teachers the right to bargain collectively, there is no constitutional right for individuals to select the union that will represent them.[190] Although the absence of a constitutional right to collective bargaining renders the constitutional right to unionize of lesser importance, the right to unionize might retain some independent value.[191] Nevertheless, in *City of Round Rock v. Rodriguez*,[192] the highest court in Texas rejected a claim by teachers, who had no collective bargaining rights, to union representation during disciplinary investigations.

185 Randall W. Eberts, *Teachers Unions and Student Performance: Help or Hindrance?* 17 THE FUTURE OF CHILDREN (Princeton/Brookings) 175, 178 (Spring 2007).

186 National Education Association, State Teacher Salary Benchmark Data for 2017-2018 (April 22, 2019).

187 *McLaughlin v. Tilendis*, 398 F.2d 287 (7th Cir. 1968); *see also* Am. Fed'n of State, County & Mun. Employees v. Woodward, 406 F.2d 137 (8th Cir. 1969).

188 Quinn v. Vill. of Elk Grove Vill. Bd. of Fire & Police Comm'rs, 2002 U.S. Dist. LEXIS 402 (N.D. Ill. Jan. 10, 2002).

189 Winston-Salem/Forsyth County Unit of the N.C. Ass'n of Educators v. Phillips, 381 F. Supp. 644 (M.D.N.C. 1974).

190 Indiana State Teachers Ass'n v. Bd. of Sch. Comm'rs, 918 F.Supp. 266 (D. Ind. 1996), *aff'd*, 101 F.3d 1179 (7th Cir. 1996).

191 *See* Ann C. Hodges, *Southern Solutions for Wisconsin Woes*, 43 U. TOL. L. REV. 633, 654 (2012).

192 399 S.W.3d 130 (Tex. 2013).

Today, most states have statutes authorizing some form of collective negotiations between teachers and school boards. In more than two-thirds of the states, actual collective bargaining is now required in districts where teachers have formed a union.[193] Missouri joined this group as recently as 2007 when its highest court overruled longstanding precedent and said that a clause in the state constitution gave school employees the right to bargain collectively.[194] Other states require only that the board meet and confer with the representative union. Collective bargaining by public employees, including public school teachers, is prohibited by statute in six states, including North Carolina, Virginia, and Texas.[195]

Private and Charter School Teachers

Private school teachers are not covered by state public sector collective bargaining laws but may seek redress under the **National Labor Relations Act** (NLRA).[196] Whether **charter school** teachers are covered by the NLRA or state public sector collective bargaining laws depends on the terms of state law and the specific school's charter. In the following illustrative case, the Fifth Circuit ruled that Louisiana's charter schools were private organizations rather than political subdivisions of the state. Accordingly, the charter schools were not exempt from the collective bargaining provisions of the NLRA.

⚖️

VOICES FOR INTERNATIONAL BUSINESS & EDUCATION v. NLRB
US Court of Appeals for the Fifth Circuit
905 F.3d 770 (2018)

GREGG COSTA, Circuit Judge

The *National Labor Relations Act* does not apply to a "political subdivision" of a state. We decide whether a Louisiana charter school qualifies for that exemption from federal labor law.

I.

Nowhere in the country has the charter school movement garnered a greater foothold than New Orleans. More than 90 percent of public-school students in Orleans Parish now attend charters. The reconstruction of the city after Hurricane Katrina was the impetus for the meteoric growth of charter schools.

But the Louisiana law allowing charter schools predates that disaster. Enacted in 1995, the Louisiana Charter School Demonstration Programs law "authoriz[es] the creation of innovative kinds of independent public schools for pupils."[197] It allows various groups and entities, such as "ten or more citizens" or a "business or corporate entity registered to do business in Louisiana" to form a non-profit corporation for the purpose of forming a charter school. A local school board may enter into a charter with such a corporation if the board finds that the charter is "valid, complete, financially well-structured, and educationally sound." The state board of education may also approve charters. A charter school's governing board, not the state, employs faculty and staff,

---

193 *See* Amicus Brief of the National Education Association in Support or Respondents, Janus v. AFSCME, Council 31 (January 19, 2018).

194 Independence-National Educ. Assoc. v. Independence Sch. Dist., 223 S.W.3d 131 (Mo. 2007).

195 N.C. GEN. STAT. §§ 95–98; Va. Code Ann. § 40.1-57.2; Tex. Gov't Code Ann. § 617.002; Tex. Loc. Gov't Code Ann. §174.023 (West 2010); *see* Amicus Brief of the National Education Association in Support or Respondents, Janus v. AFSCME, Council 31 (January 19, 2018).

196 *In re* Pinkerton Academy, 920 A.2d 1168 (N.H. 2007).

197 La. Rev. Stat. Ann. § 17:3972(A).

and the non-profit operator shall have "exclusive authority over all employment decisions at the charter schools."

A group of citizens incorporated Voices for International Business and Education as a non-profit in 2009. That same year Voices began operating the International High School of New Orleans under a Type 21 charter with the Louisiana Board of Elementary and Secondary Education. The charter provides that Voices will not participate in the Teachers' Retirement System of Louisiana or the Louisiana School Employees' Retirement System; that Voices shall be the "final authority" in all matters affecting the school; and that Voices is "not acting as the agent of, or under the direction and control of" the state education board, except as specifically required by law or the charter.

Voices' corporate bylaws vest its powers in a board of directors. The articles of incorporation name the original directors. The original board has to approve any new directors, officers, and committee chairs. Any board member may be removed with or without cause by a three-fourths vote of the remaining members. The state can remove a board member only if the member violates state ethics rules.

A labor union, the United Teachers of New Orleans, filed a petition with the National Labor Relations Board seeking to represent Voices employees. Voices objected on the ground that the Board lacked jurisdiction because Voices is a political subdivision of Louisiana. A hearing officer rejected that argument. Over a dissent, the NLRB agreed that Voices is not a political subdivision because it "was neither created directly by the state of Louisiana so as to constitute a department or administrative arm of the government nor administered by individuals who are responsible to public officials or the general electorate." The Board also rejected Voices' request that it exercise its discretion to decline jurisdiction under 29 U.S.C. § 164(c)(1).

In the election that followed, the employees voted in favor of union representation. Voices refused to recognize or negotiate with the union, maintaining the view that it is exempt from NLRB jurisdiction. The union then filed a charge against Voices for refusal to bargain. The NLRB found that Voices had committed an unfair labor practice and ordered it to recognize and bargain with the union. This petition for review, which presents only the "political subdivision" question, followed.

II.

The *National Labor Relations Act* applies to most private employers. But its jurisdiction does not extend to the federal government or "any State or political subdivision thereof." The reason it does not regulate the labor relations of government employees is that they "did not usually enjoy the right to strike." That is not the case in Louisiana, but its anomalous state labor law does not affect the question of federal labor law we confront: whether Voices is a political subdivision of Louisiana.

The Act does not define "political subdivision." The NLRB has long defined it to include two situations: when an entity is "(1) created directly by the state, so as to constitute departments or administrative arms of the government, or (2) administered by individuals who are responsible to public officials or to the general electorate." The Supreme Court has said that this agency definition is "entitled to great respect."

But we need not give any deference to the Board on this question. The Board's definition is consistent with the common meaning of "political subdivision" of a state. The Board's first category—entities created by and operated as part of state or local government—fits easily within that ordinary meaning. So does an entity that is controlled by public officials or the polity more generally. The key is that for both of the Board's definitions of political subdivision, ultimate authority over policymaking remains with the public.

Voices lacks that political accountability. That is by design. One of the perceived virtues, if not the virtue, of charter schools is that a lack of political oversight gives them freedom to experiment. Successful innovations, the idea is, will not just benefit the school that tests them but will set an example for reform that even traditional public schools might later adopt.

Louisiana charter school operators like Voices enjoy that greater freedom to innovate because they are not controlled by political actors. The corporation selected the inaugural board of directors. Those privately selected board members are the only ones who can nominate and select additional or replacement members. The self-perpetuating board can also remove a member with or without cause. Unlike traditional public schools, which are typically governed by elected school boards, there is thus no public mechanism for changing the policies in schools Voices operates. Privately selected citizens set those policies and get to decide whether they are altered.

Voices points to one narrow way in which public officials can affect the composition of its board. The charter allows the Louisiana Ethics Adjudicatory Board to remove a Voices director for violations of laws it enforces. But this possibility of for-cause termination when a Voices board member violates state ethics laws does not give public officials policymaking authority over the corporation. In the event of a director's removal for ethics violations (something that has never happened at Voices), the corporation's board of directors would have sole authority to select any replacement. ...

A recent NLRB ruling that a Texas charter school is a "political subdivision" illustrates the importance the Board places on whether the public has a role in selecting an entity's policymakers.[198] What differed in that case is the Texas Education Agency retained "full authority to reconstitute" the charter school's board. The state agency could remove board members for a host of reasons, including violations of the charter; fiscal malfeasance; student health and welfare concerns; violations of applicable laws or rules; failure to satisfy performance standards; and insolvency. Following any such removal, the state had "broad, and practically unreviewable, authority to reconstitute the Board," which led the NLRB to conclude the charter was "administered by individuals who are responsible to public TEA officials."

There is no way for the public to select the board members who set policy for Voices. We thus agree with the Board that Voices is "not administered by individuals who are responsible to public officials or to the general electorate." And we have already said that standard is faithful to the ordinary meaning of "political subdivision." There may be some situations in which it is ambiguous whether an entity is subject to enough public control to make it a political subdivision of the state. This is not such a case. Louisiana does not control Voices.

That brings us to Voices' broader complaint. It argues that the Board ignored factors that demonstrate Voices' political character even if it is not run by people the public selects. It relies on the public features of a utility district the Supreme Court identified in addressing whether it was a political subdivision. In addition to emphasizing that the "commissioners [] are beholden to an elected public official for their appointment, and are subject to removal procedures applicable to

all public officials," Hawkins County cites further indicators of political subdivision status such as the entity's tax-exempt position, eminent domain power, and obligation to comply with open records laws. Voices contends that a number of those same factors demonstrate its political nature, including public funding, tax-exempt status, and being subject to open records laws.

Was it error for the NLRB to look solely at whether the public created Voices or controls its administrators in deciding whether the charter is a political subdivision of Louisiana? At a minimum, case law recognizes that that the direct questions the Board's definition asks—(1) public creation or (2) public control—are the predominant considerations. Our first "political subdivision" case concluded that an electric power association was not exempt because it did not meet either of those NLRB criteria. ...

Our most recent case on this topic, which addressed the same exemption in the *Occupational Safety and Health Act*, discussed those factors only in a "we also note" footnote.[199] More important than that, *StarTran* observed that "[t]here are simply no ... cases" rejecting political subdivision status for "an entity a majority of whose board of directors is selected and removable by public officials and whose principle executive officers are likewise selected and removable by public officials." The clincher is what *StarTran* emphasizes about the opposite situation, which is the one we confront:

if a majority of the board of directors of the claimed political subdivision is not subject to selection or removal by public officials or the general electorate, then the entity for that reason fails the second alternative test for being a[]political subdivision.

We thus cannot fault the Board for basing its decision on the appointment and removal power that has been the decisive factor in every reported judicial decision addressing "political subdivision" status under the *NLRA* or *OSHA*. That is especially so when Voices did not just have a majority of its board members selected without public input; private actors selected all of them. The additional factors Hawkins County noted may provide guidance to the Board and courts in some cases, perhaps those when there is both public and private influence over the policymakers. But in this case they

198 LTTS Charter Sch., Inc. d/b/a Universal Acad., 366 N.L.R.B. No. 38 (2018).
199 StarTran, Inc. v. OSHRC, 608 F.3d 312, 321 n.12 (5th Cir. 2010).

cannot override the significance of the entirely private selection of school policymakers, a feature at odds with the ordinary conception of a political subdivision of a state.

Voices contends that a different result is warranted because of the "unique factual context" in which roughly 90 percent of public school students in New Orleans attend charters. Charters essentially are the public school system in New Orleans, it argues. We do not disagree, but the prevalence of charters does not transform them into politically accountable entities. It would make little sense if a charter located in northern Louisiana but otherwise identical to Voices were subject to federal labor law but Voices were exempt solely because it is in a city with a lot of other charters. Or imagine a scenario in which a legislature decided to privatize an entire state function, prisons for example. If those prisons were not subject to public control, we do not see why they would become political subdivisions just because they held all prisoners in the state. Nothing about the ordinary meaning of political subdivision

turns on the prevalence of charter schools as opposed to their public accountability.

We recognize that charters like Voices are "independent public school[s]" under Louisiana law and are treated as part of the public school system for some purposes. But that is not the same thing as saying they are political subdivisions of the state. The Louisiana Attorney General has recognized this distinction, concluding that "a charter school is not a political subdivision of the state." Indeed, the "independent" part of the state law label reflects their lack of political accountability.

That lack of political influence over Louisiana charters was a choice the legislature made in its enabling legislation. Private control was not a bug of that law; it was a reason for it. Because Louisiana chose to insulate its charters from the political process, Voices like most other privately controlled employers is subject to the *National Labor Relations Act.*

Voices' petition for review is DENIED. The Board's cross-petition for enforcement is GRANTED.

There are important variations from state to state in public sector collective bargaining laws. For example, some states designate a wider range of topics as negotiable than others. Some states permit or require arbitration, while others prohibit it. In short, some state legislatures have been more willing than others to encourage or force local school boards to share power with teacher unions.

Nevertheless, many states' collective bargaining laws have certain key features in common. At the heart of the standard public collective bargaining law are provisions specifically giving public employees the right to join a union and prohibiting public employers such as school boards from transferring or disciplining employees for engaging in union activities. These statutes also impose on the employer a duty to bargain with the union in good faith. This means, among other things, that the employer may not take unilateral action on certain categories of issues if the employee union wants to negotiate them.

Not every employee, however, is allowed to join a collective bargaining unit. State statutes often exclude supervisors, those in managerial positions, and even employees who work for supervisors and managers.[200] Depending on the authority delegated to the faculty, school site management arrangements—such as those found in some charter schools—have the potential to turn a school's entire faculty into managers prohibited from joining a union.[201] In the analogous context of higher education, in 2019 a federal appeals court found that even non-tenure-track faculty could potentially be viewed as managers, precluding their ability to bargain collectively.[202]

200 Michigan Educ. Ass'n v. Clare-Gladwin Intermediate Sch. Dist., 396 N.W.2d 538 (Mich. Ct. App. 1986); Missouri Nat'l Educ. Ass'n v. Missouri State Bd. of Mediation, 695 S.W.2d 894 (Mo. 1986) (*en banc*).
201 N.L.R.B. v. Yeshiva Univ., 444 U.S. 672 (1980).
202 Univ. of S. California v. Nat'l Labor Relations Bd., 918 F.3d 126 (D.C. Cir. 2019).

To get to the point of actually bargaining, several steps need to be taken. First, the bargaining unit must be defined. Different categories of employees have different interests in common, so more than one union may be necessary in one school district. The standard state law provides for a formal process to officially designate and recognize the bargaining units. Although these laws vary regarding the criteria for defining an appropriate bargaining unit, two criteria are generally used: Employees should be divided into as few separate bargaining units as possible and a bargaining unit should include only members who share a "community of interests." Disputes over the makeup of education employee unions sometimes end up in court. For example, a Michigan case decided that non-teaching coaches should not form a separate bargaining unit.[203] A federal court in Connecticut concluded that when a tenured teacher had assumed additional administrative responsibilities but had not obtained administrative certification, she was properly assigned to the teachers' bargaining unit, rather than the more lucrative administrators' bargaining unit.[204]

Once the number and makeup of bargaining units have been decided, employees must be given an opportunity to decide if they want to be collectively represented by a union, and, if so, which union. The school board may not unilaterally select the union.[205] States employ different approaches as to whether employees must be union members. For example, some states have permitted an agency shop arrangement under which, as a condition of continued employment, teachers must either be dues-paying union members or pay a service charge to the union. In contrast, about 28 states have enacted **right-to-work laws** prohibiting employers and unions from compelling employees to become union members or pay any fee.

The relation between agency shop arrangements and **right-to-work laws** was addressed in *North Kingstown v. North Kingstown Teachers Association*.[206] In exchange for the privilege of becoming the exclusive representatives of the employees in the bargaining unit, state law imposes on the union a **duty of fair representation**. It must represent all the employees in the unit, members or not, and may not sacrifice the interests of those who have chosen not to join for the sake of its members.

When bargaining begins, both parties are obligated to bargain in good faith. This difficult-to-define concept imposes on the parties a duty to bargain with a sincere desire to reach an agreement but no obligation to make concessions. Legal mechanisms are established by statute for bringing and resolving charges that a party is not bargaining in good faith. If the negotiators manage to come to an agreement, the contract must be ratified by a majority vote of both the school board and the teachers who will work under it. When negotiations do not produce a contract agreeable to both sides, states designate a variety of procedures designed to break the impasse. Again, depending on the specific provisions of state law, dispute resolution schemes may include mediation, fact-finding, or arbitration (also called **interest arbitration**).

Many states permit school boards to issue **unilateral contracts** if they are unable to come to terms with their teachers. In these states, after all other procedures have failed, the board will issue a contract that the union has no opportunity to ratify or reject as a group. Individual teachers still have the choice of working under the contract as offered, resigning, or, in some states, continuing to work under the previous year's contract. State laws also contain provisions regarding the obligations of the parties when bargaining or impasse resolution continues beyond the termination date of the previous contract. Some courts have ordered employers to meet their obligations under the old contract, such as providing salary step increases, in order to maintain the status quo pending a new agreement.[207] A complete impasse can sometimes lead teachers to strike.

203 Michigan Coaches Ass'n v. Warren Consol. Sch., 326 N.W.2d 432 (Mich. Ct. App. 1982).
204 Belinsky v. Petruny, 562 F. Supp. 2d 235 (D. Conn. 2008).
205 Fayette County Educ. Ass'n v. Hardy, 626 S.W.2d 217 (Ky. Ct. App. 1980).
206 297 A.2d 342 (R.I. 1972).
207 Indiana Educ. Empl. Rel. Bd. v. Mill Creek Classroom Teachers Ass'n, 456 N.E.2d 709 (Ind. 1983).

Work Stoppages

In 2012, a highly publicized teachers' strike in Chicago resulted in a negotiated settlement after seven days. Because teachers risk angering parents and school boards, however, teachers generally strike only as a last resort. There have been fewer than 1,000 teacher strikes in the United States since 1968 (most of them in Pennsylvania), and the Chicago strike was the first teachers' strike in a large urban district since 2006, when Detroit teachers went on strike.[208] Although teachers' strikes remain relatively rare, teachers in Seattle and Los Angeles voted to strike in 2015 and 2019, respectively. In addition, in 2018, teachers mobilized on a statewide basis in West Virginia, Oklahoma, and Arizona.[209]

In *Hortonville Joint School District No. 1 v. Hortonville Education Association*,[210] the Supreme Court ruled that a public school board did not violate the Due Process Clause when it fired teachers who went on strike after contract negotiations had broken down. Courts have denied claims that laws prohibiting teacher strikes are a form of involuntary servitude, violate the right of freedom of speech or assembly, or deny due process.[211] In *School Community of Westerly v. Westerly Teachers Association*,[212] a Rhode Island court rejected the argument that prohibiting public school teacher strikes while permitting private sector strikes violates the Equal Protection Clause, noting:

> The state has a compelling interest that one of its most precious assets—its youth—have the opportunity to drink at the font of knowledge so that they may be nurtured and develop into the responsible citizens of tomorrow. No one has the right to turn off the fountain's spigot and keep it in a closed position. Likewise, the equal protection afforded by the [F]ourteenth [A]mendment does not guarantee perfect equality. There is a difference between a private employee and a public employee, such as a teacher who plays such an important part in enabling the state to discharge its constitutional responsibility. The need of preventing governmental paralysis justifies the "no strike" distinction we have drawn between the public employee and his counterpart who works for the private sector within our labor force.

State statutes vary with regard to the definition of a strike. Kansas defines a strike as any

> action taken for the purpose of coercing a change in the terms and conditions of professional service or the rights, privileges or obligations thereof, through any failure by concerted action with others to report to duty including, but not limited to, any work stoppage, slowdown, or refusal to work.[213]

Where such broad and vague definitions apply, courts may consider organized refusals to perform extracurricular duties or work-to-rule actions as strikes.[214]

Thirty-five states do not permit any organized work stoppages by teachers.[215] In these states, a variety of penalties may be imposed against the union and individual teachers who defy the law.

---

208 Melissa Maynard, *Public Strikes Explained: Why There Aren't More of Them*, STATELINE: THE DAILY NEWS SERVICE OF THE PEW CENTER ON THE STATES (Sept. 25, 2012), found at www.pewstates.org/projects/stateline/headlines/public-strikes-explained-why-there-arent-more-of-them-85899419275.

209 Education Week, *Teacher Strikes: 4 Common Questions* (January 18, 2019), found at www.edweek.org/ew/issues/teacher-strike/index.html (last accessed April 20, 2020).

210 426 U.S. 482 (1976).

211 City of New York v. DeLury, 243 N.E.2d128; *amended*, 244 N.E.2d 472 (N.Y. 1968); United Fed'n of Postal Clerks v. Blount, 325 F. Supp. 879 (D.D.C.), *aff'd*, 404 U.S. 802 (1971).

212 299 A.2d 441 (R.I. 1973).

213 KAN. STAT. ANN. § 72–5413.

214 Bd. of Educ. of Asbury Park v. Asbury Park Educ. Ass'n, 368 A.2d 396 (N.J. Super. Ct. Ch. Div. 1976).

215 Education Week, *Teacher Strikes: 4 Common Questions* (January 18, 2019) found at www.edweek.org/ew/issues/teacher-strike/index.html (last accessed April 20, 2020).

These penalties include loss of pay, fines, and even dismissal of striking employees; fines and jail terms for union leaders who defy a court order to return to work; and union reimbursement of the board for substitute teachers, legal fees, and other expenses incurred in dealing with a strike.[216]

In states where statutes or common law give teachers the right to strike, the board may not retaliate against strikers, provided the strike is conducted according to law. Only about eight states grant teachers a full right to strike equal to that of private sector employees. In the remaining states that allow strikes, the board may still seek a court injunction ordering striking teachers back to work if the board can show that the strike creates a significant threat to public safety or is otherwise seriously detrimental to the public welfare.[217]

Statutes vary regarding the procedures to be followed in obtaining an injunction to end a strike, the penalties faced by striking employees, the extent to which these penalties are mandatory or subject to procedural rights or to modification by mitigating circumstances, the procedural rights of teachers before they may be dismissed or otherwise punished for illegal strike activity, the penalties that can be imposed upon the union itself (such as fines), and the authority of the courts to issue anti-strike injunctions and to impose penalties for disobeying the court's order.

A majority of state courts have held that a hearing prior to dismissal of illegally striking teachers is not constitutionally required. These courts generally view illegally striking teachers as having abandoned their contracts, thus giving up any property rights to their jobs and any claims to procedural due process. A prompt hearing following dismissal to consider a case in which a teacher claims not to have been on strike is required.[218]

Rights of Union and Non-Union Members

In-School Union-Related Speech

Freedom of speech does protect the right of teachers to promote unionization during non-class time. As long as the effort to persuade other faculty members does not materially and substantially disrupt the school, one court said, school officials may not restrict it.[219] Another court said that teachers could not be precluded from using the school mail system and bulletin boards for the same purposes, but upheld school rules restricting the hours that non-school-employee union organizers could visit the school. The court reasoned that school grounds were not a public forum, so school authorities could impose reasonable regulations on the use of the school's property.[220] A California court said that under a provision of the state's collective bargaining law giving employee organizations "the right of access at reasonable times to areas in which employees work," teachers had the right to wear union buttons at school during non-instructional time. But the court also said that, because a state law authorized school districts to prohibit employees from "engaging in political activity during working hours," a school could prohibit the buttons during instructional time.[221]

The First Amendment protects the right of employees publicly to criticize school officials regarding union issues that are a matter of public concern.[222] As with all political speech by teachers, whether such speech is protected will depend on the factors discussed in Chapter 10,

216 Passaic Township Bd. of Educ. v. Passaic Teachers Ass'n, 536 A.2d 1276 (N.J. Super. Ct. App. Div. 1987); Nat'l Educ. Ass'n v. S. Bend Cmty. Sch. Corp., 655 N.E.2d 516 (Ind. App. 1995).
217 Jersey Shore Area Sch. Dist. v. Jersey Shore Educ. Ass'n, 548 A.2d 1202 (Pa. 1988).
218 Sanford v. Rockefeller, 324 N.E.2d 113 (N.Y. 1974); *appeal dismissed*, 421 U.S. 973 (1975); Farrelly v. Timberlane Reg'l Sch. Dist., 324 A.2d 723 (N.H. 1974).
219 Ga. Ass'n of Educators v. Gwinnett County Sch. Dist., 856 F.2d 142 (11th Cir. 1988).
220 Texas State Teachers Ass'n v. Garland Indep. Sch. Dist., 777 F.2d 1046 (5th Cir. 1985).
221 Turlock Joint Elementary Sch. Dist. v. Pub. Employment Relations Bd., 5 Cal. Rptr. 3d 308 (Cal. App. 5 Dist. 2003).
222 Hickman v. Valley Local Sch. Dist. Bd. of Educ., 619 F.2d 606 (6th Cir. 1980).

in particular, whether the speech is made as a private citizen or pursuant to the teacher's official duties. Ironically, teachers who serve as union leaders as part of their official duties might enjoy less protection when they speak out on union issues than teachers who do not. Picketing also enjoys an important degree of free speech protection,[223] but courts are likely to allow prohibition of picketing when accompanied by force, violence, or intimidation or performed for illegal purposes such as to promote an illegal strike.[224]

If a state prohibits unions from funding political activities through employee payroll deductions, is the First Amendment violated? No, the Supreme Court has said, but only if the prohibition is applied in an even-handed manner.[225] When Michigan enacted a law which barred only school district employers from collecting union dues through payroll deductions, a federal appeals court held that singling out the school unions was viewpoint-neutral and therefore likely constitutional. A dissenting judge disagreed, arguing that the law "impermissibly discriminates against school unions because Michigan disagrees with the positions they advocate."[226]

Rights of Non-Union Members

Is it permissible to deny participation in the collective bargaining process to teachers who decline to join the union? May non-union teachers be forced to pay union dues or fees? May schools adopt rules that make it easier for the officially designated union than for rival unions or individuals to communicate with teachers? The central issue raised by these questions is how to protect the rights of non-union members without violating the rights of union members or damaging the effectiveness of the collective bargaining process.

Two Supreme Court cases have considered whether and under what circumstances a school board may give a teachers' union and its members more opportunity to speak to the board than is granted to non-union members. In *Madison Joint School District No. 8 v. Wisconsin Employment Relations Commission*,[227] a school board was accused of an unfair labor practice for allowing a non-union teacher to speak at a public meeting in which the board was considering an issue being negotiated with the union. The president of the union was also permitted to speak and to present a petition signed by union members. The Supreme Court ruled that it would have been impermissible to deny the non-union teacher the right to speak:

> Regardless of the extent to which true contract negotiations between a public body and its employees may be regulated—an issue we need not consider at this time—the participation in public discussion of public business cannot be confined to one category of interested individuals. To permit one side of a debatable public question to have a monopoly in expressing its views to the government is the antithesis of constitutional guarantees. Whatever its duties as an employer, when the board sits in public meetings to conduct public business and hear the views of citizens, it may not be required to discriminate between speakers on the basis of their employment, or the content of their speech.

In *Minnesota State Board for Community Colleges v. Knight*,[228] non-union teachers challenged a Minnesota statute requiring public employers to engage in "meet-and-confer" sessions with their

---

223 Pittsburgh Unified Sch. Dist. v. Cal. Sch. Employees Ass'n, 213 Cal. Rptr. 34 (Cal. Ct. App. 1985).
224 Teamsters Local 695 v. Vogt, 354 U.S. 284 (1957); Bd. of Educ. of Martins Ferry City Sch. Dist. v. Ohio Educ. Ass'n, 235 N.E.2d 538 (Ohio Ct. Common Pleas 1967).
225 Ysursa v. Pocatello Education Association, 555 U.S. 353 (2009).
226 Bailey v. Callaghan, 715 F.3d 956, 966 (6th Cir. 2013); *see also* Wisconsin Educ. Ass'n Council v. Walker, 705 F.3d 640, 667 (7th Cir. 2013).
227 429 U.S. 167 (1976).
228 465 U.S. 271 (1984).

employees to exchange views on policy issues outside the scope of collective bargaining. The statute further specified that if an agency's professional employees were unionized, only representatives of the union could participate in the meet-and-confer sessions with the agency administration.

Non-union teachers argued that permitting unionized teachers to express their views to supervisors while denying non-union members the right to express theirs in the same forum was a violation of their right of free speech. In considering this claim, the Supreme Court was careful to distinguish the *Knight* case from *Madison*. Whereas the school board meeting in *Madison* was a traditional forum for the expression of public views, the meet-and-confer sessions in *Knight* were not. "It is a fundamental principle of First Amendment doctrine that for government property to be a public forum, it must by long tradition or by government designation be open to the public at large for assembly and speech." No one, explained the Court, has a constitutional right to speak in a non-public forum, even people directly affected by the issues under consideration. To hold otherwise would require revision of the procedures of every governmental body from Congress to school boards. Minnesota's law did not restrict employees from speaking or from joining with others of like mind. It simply restricted access to the formal meet-and-confer sessions to the duly elected representatives of the majority of an agency's professional employees. This, concluded the Court, was neither unconstitutional nor unreasonable.

Agency Fees

The school board in the *Madison* case was considering whether to force non-union members to pay a service or "agency shop" fee to the union. Some states do not permit mandatory agency shop fees, while others do. The Supreme Court considered constitutional issues relating to agency shop fees in *Abood v. Detroit Board of Education*.[229] In that case, a state statute authorized charging non-union members a service charge to support union activities. Since such activities included political and ideological advocacy, the Court held that this scheme essentially forced or coerced non-union members to express political views with which they disagreed. Because it compelled speech in this manner, the service charge imposed upon non-union members violated the First Amendment. But *Abood* did not invalidate the agency-shop fee system itself. Although acknowledging that such fees could implicate First Amendment rights, the Court held that these interests were outweighed "by the legislative assessment of the important contribution of the union shop to the system of labor relations established by Congress."

In the following watershed case, a divided Supreme Court overruled *Abood*, holding that agency fees violate the First Amendment rights of non-union members.

⚖

JANUS v. AFSCME, COUNCIL 31
Supreme Court of the United States
138 S. Ct. 2448 (2018)

JUSTICE ALITO delivered the opinion of the Court.

Under the *Illinois Public Labor Relations Act* (*IPLRA*), employees of the State and its political subdivisions are permitted to unionize. If a majority of the employees in a bargaining unit vote to be represented by a union, that union is designated as the exclusive representative of all the employees. Employees in the unit are not obligated to join the union selected by their co-workers, but whether they join or not, that union is deemed to be their sole permitted representative.

---

229 431 U.S. 209 (1977).

Once a union is so designated, it is vested with broad authority. Only the union may negotiate with the employer on matters relating to "pay, wages, hours[,] and other conditions of employment." And this authority extends to the negotiation of what the *IPLRA* calls "policy matters," such as merit pay, the size of the work force, layoffs, privatization, promotion methods, and non-discrimination policies.

Designating a union as the employees' exclusive representative substantially restricts the rights of individual employees. Among other things, this designation means that individual employees may not be represented by any agent other than the designated union; nor may individual employees negotiate directly with their employer. Protection of the employees' interests is placed in the hands of the union, and therefore the union is required by law to provide fair representation for all employees in the unit, members and non-members alike.

Employees who decline to join the union are not assessed full union dues but must instead pay what is generally called an "agency fee," which amounts to a percentage of the union dues. Under *Abood*,[230] non-members may be charged for the portion of union dues attributable to activities that are "germane to [the union's] duties as collective-bargaining representative," but non-members may not be required to fund the union's political and ideological projects. In labor-law parlance, the outlays in the first category are known as "chargeable" expenditures, while those in the latter are labeled "non-chargeable."

Illinois law does not specify in detail which expenditures are chargeable and which are not. The *IPLRA* provides that an agency fee may compensate a union for the costs incurred in "the collective bargaining process, contract administration[,] and pursuing matters affecting wages, hours[,] and conditions of employment." Excluded from the agency-fee calculation are union expenditures "related to the election or support of any candidate for political office."

Applying this standard, a union categorizes its expenditures as chargeable or non-chargeable and thus determines a non-member's "proportionate share." [T]his determination is then audited; the amount of the "proportionate share" is certified to the employer; and the employer automatically deducts that amount from the non-members' wages. Non-members need not be asked, and they are not required to consent before the fees are deducted.

After the amount of the agency fee is fixed each year, the union must send non-members what is known as a *Hudson* notice.[231] This notice is supposed to provide non-members with "an adequate explanation of the basis for the [agency] fee." If non-members "suspect that a union has improperly put certain expenses in the [chargeable] category," they may challenge that determination.

As illustrated by the record in this case, unions charge non-members, not just for the cost of collective bargaining *per se*, but also for many other supposedly connected activities. Here, the non-members were told that they had to pay for "[l]obbying," "[s]ocial and recreational activities," "advertising," "[m]embership meetings and conventions," and "litigation," as well as other unspecified "[s]ervices" that "may ultimately inure to the benefit of the members of the local bargaining unit." The total chargeable amount for non-members was 78.06 percent of full union dues.

B

Petitioner Mark Janus is employed by the Illinois Department of Healthcare and Family Services as a child support specialist. The employees in his unit are among the 35,000 public employees in Illinois who are represented by respondent American Federation of State, County, and Municipal Employees, Council 31 (Union). Janus refused to join the Union because he opposes "many of the public policy positions that [it] advocates," including the positions it takes in collective bargaining. Janus believes that the Union's "behavior in bargaining does not appreciate the current fiscal crises in Illinois and does not reflect his best interests or the interests of Illinois citizens." Therefore, if he had the choice, he "would not pay any fees or otherwise subsidize [the Union]." Under his unit's collective-bargaining agreement, however, he was required to pay an agency fee of $44.58 per month, which would amount to about $535 per year.

Janus's concern about Illinois' current financial situation is shared by the Governor of the State, and it was the Governor who initially challenged the statute authorizing the imposition of agency fees. The Governor commenced an action in federal court, asking that the law be declared unconstitutional, and the Illinois attorney general (a respondent here) intervened to defend the law. Janus and two other

---

230 Abood v. Detroit Board of Education, 431 U.S. 209 (1977).
231 *See* Teachers v. Hudson, 475 U. S. 292 (1986).

state employees also moved to intervene—but on the Governor's side.

Respondents moved to dismiss the Governor's challenge for lack of standing, contending that the agency fees did not cause him any personal injury. The District Court agreed that the Governor could not maintain the lawsuit, but it held that petitioner and the other individuals who had moved to intervene had standing because the agency fees unquestionably injured them. Accordingly, "in the interest of judicial economy," the court dismissed the Governor as a plaintiff, while simultaneously allowing petitioner and the other employees to file their own complaint. They did so, and the case proceeded on the basis of this new complaint.

The amended complaint claims that all "non-member fee deductions are coerced political speech" and that "the First Amendment forbids coercing any money from the non-members." Respondents moved to dismiss the amended complaint, correctly recognizing that the claim it asserted was foreclosed by *Abood*. The District Court granted the motion, and the Court of Appeals for the Seventh Circuit affirmed.

Janus then sought review in this Court, asking us to overrule *Abood* and hold that public-sector agency-fee arrangements are unconstitutional. We granted certiorari to consider this important question. …

III

In *Abood*, the Court upheld the constitutionality of an agency-shop arrangement like the one now before us, but in more recent cases we have recognized that this holding is "something of an anomaly,"[232] and that *Abood*'s "analysis is questionable on several grounds …"[233] … We now address that question. We first consider whether *Abood*'s holding is consistent with standard First Amendment principles.

A

The First Amendment, made applicable to the States by the Fourteenth Amendment, forbids abridgment of the freedom of speech. We have held time and again that freedom of speech "includes both the right to speak freely and the right to refrain from speaking at all." The right to eschew association for expressive purposes is likewise protected. As Justice Jackson memorably put it:

If there is any fixed star in our constitutional constellation, it is that no official, high or petty, can prescribe what shall be orthodox in politics, nationalism, religion, or other matters of opinion or force citizens to confess by word or act their faith therein.[234]

Compelling individuals to mouth support for views they find objectionable violates that cardinal constitutional command, and in most contexts, any such effort would be universally condemned. Suppose, for example, that the State of Illinois required all residents to sign a document expressing support for a particular set of positions on controversial public issues—say, the platform of one of the major political parties. No one, we trust, would seriously argue that the First Amendment permits this.

Perhaps because such compulsion so plainly violates the Constitution, most of our free speech cases have involved restrictions on what can be said, rather than laws compelling speech. But measures compelling speech are at least as threatening.

Free speech serves many ends. It is essential to our democratic form of government, and it furthers the search for truth. Whenever the Federal Government or a State prevents individuals from saying what they think on important matters or compels them to voice ideas with which they disagree, it undermines these ends.

When speech is compelled, however, additional damage is done. In that situation, individuals are coerced into betraying their convictions. Forcing free and independent individuals to endorse ideas they find objectionable is always demeaning, and for this reason, one of our landmark free speech cases said that a law commanding "involuntary affirmation" of objected-to beliefs would require "even more immediate and urgent grounds" than a law demanding silence.

Compelling a person to subsidize the speech of other private speakers raises similar First Amendment concerns. As Jefferson famously put it, "to compel a man to furnish contributions of money for the propagation of opinions which he disbelieves and abhor[s] is sinful and tyrannical." We have therefore recognized that a "significant impingement on First Amendment rights" occurs when public employees are required to provide financial support for a union that "takes many positions during collective

232 Knox v. Service Employees, 567 U. S. 298 (2012).
233 Harris v. Quinn, 573 U.S. 616 (2014).
234 West Virginia Bd. of Ed. v. Barnette, 319 U. S. 624 (1943).

bargaining that have powerful political and civic consequences."

Because the compelled subsidization of private speech seriously impinges on First Amendment rights, it cannot be casually allowed. Our free speech cases have identified "levels of scrutiny" to be applied in different contexts, and in three recent cases, we have considered the standard that should be used in judging the constitutionality of agency fees.[235]

In *Knox*, the first of these cases, we found it sufficient to hold that the conduct in question was unconstitutional under even the test used for the compulsory subsidization of commercial speech. Even though commercial speech has been thought to enjoy a lesser degree of protection, prior precedent in that area, specifically United Foods, supra, had applied what we characterized as "exacting" scrutiny, a less demanding test than the "strict" scrutiny that might be thought to apply outside the commercial sphere. Under "exacting" scrutiny, we noted, a compelled subsidy must "serve a compelling state interest that cannot be achieved through means significantly less restrictive of associational freedoms."

In *Harris*, the second of these cases, we again found that an agency-fee requirement failed "exacting scrutiny." But we questioned whether that test provides sufficient protection for free speech rights, since "it is apparent that the speech compelled" in agency-fee cases "is not commercial speech."

Picking up that cue, petitioner in the present case contends that the Illinois law at issue should be subjected to "strict scrutiny." The dissent, on the other hand, proposes that we apply what amounts to rational-basis review, that is, that we ask only whether a government employer could reasonably believe that the exaction of agency fees serves its interests. This form of minimal scrutiny is foreign to our free-speech jurisprudence, and we reject it here. At the same time, we again find it unnecessary to decide the issue of strict scrutiny because the Illinois scheme cannot survive under even the more permissive standard applied in *Knox* and *Harris*. ...

B

In *Abood*, the main defense of the agency-fee arrangement was that it served the State's interest in "labor peace". By "labor peace," the *Abood* Court meant avoidance of the conflict and disruption that it envisioned would occur if the employees in a unit

were represented by more than one union. In such a situation, the Court predicted, "inter-union rivalries" would foster "dissension within the work force," and the employer could face "conflicting demands from different unions." Confusion would ensue if the employer entered into and attempted to "enforce two or more agreements specifying different terms and conditions of employment." And a settlement with one union would be "subject to attack from [a] rival labor organizatio[n]."

We assume that "labor peace," in this sense of the term, is a compelling state interest, but *Abood* cited no evidence that the pandemonium it imagined would result if agency fees were not allowed, and it is now clear that *Abood*'s fears were unfounded. The *Abood* Court assumed that designation of a union as the exclusive representative of all the employees in a unit and the exaction of agency fees are inextricably linked, but that is simply not true.

The federal employment experience is illustrative. Under federal law, a union chosen by majority vote is designated as the exclusive representative of all the employees, but federal law does not permit agency fees. Nevertheless, nearly a million federal employees—about 27 percent of the federal work force—are union members. The situation in the Postal Service is similar. Although permitted to choose an exclusive representative, Postal Service employees are not required to pay an agency fee, and about 400,000 are union members. Likewise, millions of public employees in the 28 States that have laws generally prohibiting agency fees are represented by unions that serve as the exclusive representatives of all the employees.

Whatever may have been the case 41 years ago when *Abood* was handed down, it is now undeniable that "labor peace" can readily be achieved "through means significantly less restrictive of associational freedoms" than the assessment of agency fees.

C

In addition to the promotion of "labor peace," *Abood* cited "the risk of 'free riders'" as justification for agency fees. Respondents and some of their *amici* endorse this reasoning, contending that agency fees are needed to prevent non-members from enjoying the benefits of union representation without shouldering the costs.

Petitioner strenuously objects to this free-rider label. He argues that he is not a free rider on a bus

235 *See* Friedrichs v. California Teachers Assn., 136 S. Ct. 1083 (2016) (*per curiam*).

headed for a destination that he wishes to reach but is more like a person shanghaied for an unwanted voyage.

Whichever description fits the majority of public employees who would not subsidize a union if given the option, avoiding free riders is not a compelling interest. As we have noted, "free-rider arguments … are generally insufficient to overcome First Amendment objections." To hold otherwise across the board would have startling consequences. Many private groups speak out with the objective of obtaining government action that will have the effect of benefiting non-members. May all those who are thought to benefit from such efforts be compelled to subsidize this speech?

Suppose that a particular group lobbies or speaks out on behalf of what it thinks are the needs of senior citizens or veterans or physicians, to take just a few examples. Could the government require that all seniors, veterans, or doctors pay for that service even if they object? It has never been thought that this is permissible. "[P]rivate speech often furthers the interests of non-speakers," but "that does not alone empower the state to compel the speech to be paid for." In simple terms, the First Amendment does not permit the government to compel a person to pay for another party's speech just because the government thinks that the speech furthers the interests of the person who does not want to pay.

Those supporting agency fees contend that the situation here is different because unions are statutorily required to "represen[t] the interests of all public employees in the unit," whether or not they are union members. Why might this matter?

We can think of two possible arguments. It might be argued that a State has a compelling interest in requiring the payment of agency fees because (1) unions would otherwise be unwilling to represent non-members or (2) it would be fundamentally unfair to require unions to provide fair representation for non-members if non-members were not required to pay. Neither of these arguments is sound.

First, it is simply not true that unions will refuse to serve as the exclusive representative of all employees in the unit if they are not given agency fees. As noted, unions represent millions of public employees in jurisdictions that do not permit agency fees. No union is ever compelled to seek that designation. On the contrary, designation as exclusive representative is avidly sought. Why is this so?

Even without agency fees, designation as the exclusive representative confers many benefits. As noted, that status gives the union a privileged place in negotiations over wages, benefits, and working conditions. Not only is the union given the exclusive right to speak for all the employees in collective bargaining, but the employer is required by state law to listen to and to bargain in good faith with only that union. Designation as exclusive representative thus "results in a tremendous increase in the power" of the union.

In addition, a union designated as exclusive representative is often granted special privileges, such as obtaining information about employees, and having dues and fees deducted directly from employee wages. The collective-bargaining agreement in this case guarantees a long list of additional privileges.

These benefits greatly outweigh any extra burden imposed by the duty of providing fair representation for non-members. What this duty entails, in simple terms, is an obligation not to "act solely in the interests of [the union's] own members."

What does this mean when it comes to the negotiation of a contract? The union may not negotiate a collective-bargaining agreement that discriminates against non-members, but the union's bargaining latitude would be little different if state law simply prohibited public employers from entering into agreements that discriminate in that way. And for that matter, it is questionable whether the Constitution would permit a public-sector employer to adopt a collective-bargaining agreement that discriminates against non-members. To the extent that an employer would be barred from acceding to a discriminatory agreement anyway, the union's duty not to ask for one is superfluous. It is noteworthy that neither respondents nor any of the 39 amicus briefs supporting them—nor the dissent—has explained why the duty of fair representation causes public-sector unions to incur significantly greater expenses than they would otherwise bear in negotiating collective-bargaining agreements.

What about the representation of non-members in grievance proceedings? Unions do not undertake this activity solely for the benefit of non-members—which is why Illinois law gives a public-sector union the right to send a representative to such proceedings even if the employee declines union representation. Representation of non-members furthers the union's interest in keeping control of the administration of the collective-bargaining agreement, since the resolution of one employee's grievance can affect others. And when a union controls the grievance process, it may, as a practical matter, effectively subordinate "the interests of [an] individual employee … to the collective interests of all employees in the bargaining unit."

In any event, whatever unwanted burden is imposed by the representation of non-members in disciplinary matters can be eliminated "through means significantly less restrictive of associational freedoms" than the imposition of agency fees. Individual non-members could be required to pay for that service or could be denied union representation altogether. Thus, agency fees cannot be sustained on the ground that unions would otherwise be unwilling to represent non-members.

Nor can such fees be justified on the ground that it would otherwise be unfair to require a union to bear the duty of fair representation. That duty is a necessary concomitant of the authority that a union seeks when it chooses to serve as the exclusive representative of all the employees in a unit. As explained, designating a union as the exclusive representative of non-members substantially restricts the non-members' rights. Protection of their interests is placed in the hands of the union, and if the union were free to disregard or even work against those interests, these employees would be wholly unprotected. That is why we said many years ago that serious "constitutional questions [would] arise" if the union were not subject to the duty to represent all employees fairly.

In sum, we do not see any reason to treat the free-rider interest any differently in the agency-fee context than in any other First Amendment context. We therefore hold that agency fees cannot be upheld on free-rider grounds.

IV

Implicitly acknowledging the weakness of *Abood*'s own reasoning, proponents of agency fees have come forward with alternative justifications for the decision, and we now address these arguments.

A

The most surprising of these new arguments is the Union respondent's originalist defense of *Abood*. According to this argument, *Abood* was correctly decided because the First Amendment was not originally understood to provide any protection for the free speech rights of public employees.

As an initial matter, we doubt that the Union—or its members—actually want us to hold that public employees have "no [free speech] rights." It is particularly discordant to find this argument in a brief that trumpets the importance of *stare decisis*. Taking away free speech protection for public employees would mean overturning decades of landmark precedent. Under the Union's theory, *Pickering* and its progeny would fall.[236] Yet *Pickering*, as we will discuss, is now the foundation for respondents' chief defense of *Abood*. And indeed, *Abood* itself would have to go if public employees have no free speech rights, since *Abood* holds that the First Amendment prohibits the exaction of agency fees for political or ideological purposes. Our political patronage cases would be doomed. Respondents presumably want none of this, desiring instead that we apply the Constitution's supposed original meaning only when it suits them—to retain the part of *Abood* that they like. We will not engage in this halfway originalism. ...

Ultimately, the Union relies, not on founding-era evidence, but on dictum from a 1983 opinion of this Court stating that, "[f]or most of th[e 20th] century, the unchallenged dogma was that a public employee had no right to object to conditions placed upon the terms of employment—including those which restricted the exercise of constitutional rights." Even on its own terms, this dictum about twentieth-century views does not purport to describe how the First Amendment was understood in 1791. And a careful examination of the decisions by this Court that *Connick* cited to support its dictum[237] reveals that none of them rested on the facile premise that public employees are unprotected by the First Amendment. Instead, they considered (much as we do today) whether particular speech restrictions were "necessary to protect" fundamental government interests.

The Union has also failed to show that, even if public employees enjoyed free speech rights, the First Amendment was nonetheless originally understood to allow forced subsidies like those at issue here. We can safely say that, at the time of the adoption of the First Amendment, no one gave any thought to whether public-sector unions could charge non-members agency fees. Entities resembling labor unions did not exist at the founding, and public-sector unions did not emerge until the mid-twentieth century. The idea of public-sector unionization and agency fees would astound those who framed and ratified the Bill of Rights. Thus, the Union cannot point to any accepted founding-era practice that even remotely resembles the compulsory assessment of agency fees from public-sector

236 Pickering v. Board of Ed. of Township High School Dist. 205, Will Cty., 391 U. S. 563 (1968).
237 Connick v. Myers, 461 U.S. 138 (1983).

employees. We do know, however, that prominent members of the founding generation condemned laws requiring public employees to affirm or support beliefs with which they disagreed. As noted, Jefferson denounced compelled support for such beliefs as "sinful and tyrannical," and others expressed similar views.

In short, the Union has offered no basis for concluding that *Abood* is supported by the original understanding of the First Amendment.

B

The principal defense of *Abood* advanced by respondents and the dissent is based on our decision in *Pickering*, which held that a school district violated the First Amendment by firing a teacher for writing a letter critical of the school administration. Under *Pickering* and later cases in the same line, employee speech is largely unprotected if it is part of what the employee is paid to do, or if it involved a matter of only private concern. On the other hand, when a public employee speaks as a citizen on a matter of public concern, the employee's speech is protected unless "the interest of the state, as an employer, in promoting the efficiency of the public services it performs through its employees' outweighs 'the interests of the [employee], as a citizen, in commenting upon matters of public concern."

Pickering was the centerpiece of the defense of *Abood* in *Harris*, and we found the argument unpersuasive ... The intervening years have not improved its appeal.

1

As we pointed out in *Harris*, *Abood* was not based on *Pickering*. The *Abood* majority cited the case exactly once—in a footnote—and then merely to acknowledge that "there may be limits on the extent to which an employee in a sensitive or policymaking position may freely criticize his superiors and the policies they espouse." That aside has no bearing on the agency-fee issue here.

Respondents' reliance on Pickering is thus "an effort to find a new justification for the decision in *Abood*." And we have previously taken a dim view of similar attempts to recast problematic First Amendment decisions.[238] We see no good reason, at this late date, to try to shoehorn *Abood* into the *Pickering* framework.

2

Even if that were attempted, the shoe would be a painful fit for at least three reasons.

First, the *Pickering* framework was developed for use in a very different context—in cases that involve "one employee's speech and its impact on that employee's public responsibilities." This case, by contrast, involves a blanket requirement that all employees subsidize speech with which they may not agree. While we have sometimes looked to *Pickering* in considering general rules that affect broad categories of employees, we have acknowledged that the standard Pickering analysis requires modification in that situation. A speech-restrictive law with "widespread impact," we have said, "gives rise to far more serious concerns than could any single supervisory decision." Therefore, when such a law is at issue, the government must shoulder a correspondingly "heav[ier]" burden, and is entitled to considerably less deference in its assessment that a predicted harm justifies a particular impingement on First Amendment rights ... The end product of those adjustments is a test that more closely resembles exacting scrutiny than the traditional *Pickering* analysis.

The core collective-bargaining issue of wages and benefits illustrates this point. Suppose that a single employee complains that he or she should have received a 5 percent raise. This individual complaint would likely constitute a matter of only private concern and would therefore be unprotected under *Pickering*. But a public-sector union's demand for a 5 percent raise for the many thousands of employees it represents would be another matter entirely. Granting such a raise could have a serious impact on the budget of the government unit in question, and by the same token, denying a raise might have a significant effect on the performance of government services. When a large number of employees speak through their union, the category of speech that is of public concern is greatly enlarged, and the category of speech that is of only private concern is substantially shrunk. By disputing this, the dissent denies the obvious.

Second, the *Pickering* framework fits much less well where the government compels speech or speech subsidies in support of third parties. Pickering is based on the insight that the speech of a public-sector employee may interfere with the effective operation of a government office. When a public

---

238 *See, e.g.*, Citizens United v. Federal Election Comm'n, 558 U. S. 310 (2010).

employer does not simply restrict potentially disruptive speech but commands that its employees mouth a message on its own behalf, the calculus is very different. Of course, if the speech in question is part of an employee's official duties, the employer may insist that the employee deliver any lawful message.[239] Otherwise, however, it is not easy to imagine a situation in which a public employer has a legitimate need to demand that its employees recite words with which they disagree. And we have never applied *Pickering* in such a case.

Consider our decision in *Connick*. In that case, we held that an assistant district attorney's complaints about the supervisors in her office were, for the most part, matters of only private concern. As a result, we held, the district attorney could fire her for making those comments. Now, suppose that the assistant had not made any critical comments about the supervisors but that the district attorney, out of the blue, demanded that she circulate a memo praising the supervisors. Would her refusal to go along still be a matter of purely private concern? And if not, would the order be justified on the ground that the effective operation of the office demanded that the assistant voice complimentary sentiments with which she disagreed? If Pickering applies at all to compelled speech—a question that we do not decide—it would certainly require adjustment in that context.

Third, although both *Pickering* and *Abood* divided speech into two categories, the cases' categorization schemes do not line up. Superimposing the *Pickering* scheme on *Abood* would significantly change the *Abood* regime.

Let us first look at speech that is not germane to collective bargaining but instead concerns political or ideological issues. Under *Abood*, a public employer is flatly prohibited from permitting non-members to be charged for this speech, but under *Pickering*, the employees' free speech interests could be overcome if a court found that the employer's interests outweighed the employees'.

A similar problem arises with respect to speech that is germane to collective bargaining. The parties dispute how much of this speech is of public concern, but respondents concede that much of it falls squarely into that category. Under *Abood*, non-members may be required to pay for all this speech, but Pickering would permit that practice only if the employer's interests outweighed those of the employees. Thus,

recasting Abood as an application of *Pickering* would substantially alter the Abood scheme.

For all these reasons, *Pickering* is a poor fit indeed.

V

Even if we were to apply some form of *Pickering*, Illinois' agency-fee arrangement would not survive.

A

Respondents begin by suggesting that union speech in collective-bargaining and grievance proceedings should be treated like the employee speech in *Garcetti*, i.e., as speech "pursuant to [an employee's] official duties." ... Many employees, in both the public and private sectors, are paid to write or speak for the purpose of furthering the interests of their employers. There are laws that protect public employees from being compelled to say things that they reasonably believe to be untrue or improper, but in general when public employees are performing their job duties, their speech may be controlled by their employer. Trying to fit union speech into this framework, respondents now suggest that the union speech funded by agency fees forms part of the official duties of the union officers who engage in the speech.

This argument distorts collective bargaining and grievance adjustment beyond recognition. When an employee engages in speech that is part of the employee's job duties, the employee's words are really the words of the employer. The employee is effectively the employer's spokesperson. But when a union negotiates with the employer or represents employees in disciplinary proceedings, the union speaks for the employees, not the employer. Otherwise, the employer would be negotiating with itself and disputing its own actions. That is not what anybody understands to be happening.

What is more, if the union's speech is really the employer's speech, then the employer could dictate what the union says. Unions, we trust, would be appalled by such a suggestion. For these reasons, *Garcetti* is totally inapposite here.

B

Since the union speech paid for by agency fees is not controlled by *Garcetti*, we move on to the next

---

239 *See* Garcetti v. Cebellos, 547 U.S. 410 (2006).

step of the *Pickering* framework and ask whether the speech is on a matter of public or only private concern. In *Harris*, the dissent's central argument in defense of *Abood* was that union speech in collective bargaining, including speech about wages and benefits, is basically a matter of only private interest. We squarely rejected that argument, and the facts of the present case substantiate what we said at that time: "[I]t is impossible to argue that the level of ... state spending for employee benefits ... is not a matter of great public concern."

Illinois, like some other States and a number of counties and cities around the country, suffers from severe budget problems. As of 2013, Illinois had nearly $160 billion in unfunded pension and retiree healthcare liabilities. By 2017, that number had only grown, and the State was grappling with $15 billion in unpaid bills. We are told that a "quarter of the budget is now devoted to paying down" those liabilities. These problems and others led Moody's and S&P to downgrade Illinois' credit rating to "one step above junk"—the "lowest ranking on record for a U. S. state." The Governor, on one side, and public-sector unions, on the other, disagree sharply about what to do about these problems. ...

In addition to affecting how public money is spent, union speech in collective bargaining addresses many other important matters. As the examples offered by respondents' own amici show, unions express views on a wide range of subjects—education, child welfare, healthcare, and minority rights, to name a few. What unions have to say on these matters in the context of collective bargaining is of great public importance.

Take the example of education, which was the focus of briefing and argument in *Friedrichs*. The public importance of subsidized union speech is especially apparent in this field, since educators make up by far the largest category of state and local government employees, and education is typically the largest component of state and local government expenditures.

Speech in this area also touches on fundamental questions of education policy. Should teacher pay be based on seniority, the better to retain experienced teachers? Or should schools adopt merit-pay systems to encourage teachers to get the best results out of their students? Should districts transfer more experienced teachers to the lower performing schools that may have the greatest need for their skills, or should those teachers be allowed to stay where they have put down roots? Should teachers be given tenure protection and, if so, under what conditions? On what grounds and pursuant to what procedures should teachers be subject to discipline or dismissal? How should teacher performance and student progress be measured—by standardized tests or other means?

Unions can also speak out in collective bargaining on controversial subjects such as climate change, the Confederacy, sexual orientation and gender identity, evolution, and minority religions. These are sensitive political topics, and they are undoubtedly matters of profound "value and concern to the public." We have often recognized that such speech "occupies the highest rung of the hierarchy of First Amendment values" and merits "special protection."

What does the dissent say about the prevalence of such issues? The most that it is willing to admit is that "some" issues that arise in collective bargaining "raise important non-budgetary disputes." Here again, the dissent refuses to recognize what actually occurs in public-sector collective bargaining.

Even union speech in the handling of grievances may be of substantial public importance and may be directed at the "public square." For instance, the Union respondent in this case recently filed a grievance seeking to compel Illinois to appropriate $75 million to fund a 2 percent wage increase. In short, the union speech at issue in this case is overwhelmingly of substantial public concern.

C

The only remaining question under *Pickering* is whether the State's proffered interests justify the heavy burden that agency fees inflict on nonmembers' First Amendment interests. We have already addressed the state interests asserted in *Abood*—promoting "labor peace" and avoiding free riders—and we will not repeat that analysis. ...

We readily acknowledge, as *Pickering* did, that "the State has interests as an employer in regulating the speech of its employees that differ significantly from those it possesses in connection with regulation of the speech of the citizenry in general." Our analysis is consistent with that principle. The exacting scrutiny standard we apply in this case was developed in the context of commercial speech, another area where the government has traditionally enjoyed greater-than-usual power to regulate speech.

It is also not disputed that the State may require that a union serve as exclusive bargaining agent for its employees—itself a significant impingement on associational freedoms that would not be tolerated in other contexts. We simply draw the line at allowing the government to go further still and require all employees to support the union irrespective of whether they share its views. Nothing in the *Pickering* line of cases requires us to uphold every speech restriction the government imposes as an employer.

VI

For the reasons given above, we conclude that public-sector agency-shop arrangements violate the First Amendment, and *Abood* erred in concluding otherwise. ...

In light of the Supreme Court's decision in *Janus*, teachers' unions can no longer collect "agency shop" fees from non-members. Although this ruling sent shock waves through the labor movement, the impact might not be as great as initially believed. First, even before *Janus*, 28 states had already prohibited agency shop fees. Second, a state that wished to restore the pre-*Janus* paradigm could simply reimburse unions for the revenue lost from the prohibition on fees.[240]

Some states permit individuals who object on religious grounds to union membership or the activities of a given union to in effect pay the equivalent of union dues to a charity of their choice in lieu of paying the money to the union.[241] Depending on the precise phrasing of such a law, it may be open to challenge as a violation of the Establishment Clause.[242] A California teacher who objected on religious grounds to paying union dues was unsuccessful in arguing that the accommodation provided by state law violates Title VII. Under California statute, a religious objector must pay full union dues, which are donated to a designated charity, but a political objector must pay only a lower "representation" fee. The court also ruled that this arrangement does not violate the Establishment Clause or the Equal Protection Clause.[243]

Incumbent unions have sought protections against the activities of rival unions. Some states permit the incumbent union to be given exclusive access to school facilities. The constitutionality of a union's exclusive access to teacher mailboxes and an internal mail delivery system was addressed by the Supreme Court in *Perry Education Association v. Perry Local Educators' Association*.[244] The Court began its analysis by noting that the school's internal mail system was not a public forum. Rather, it was created and employed for specific purposes relating to the conduct of the school's business. "Implicit in the concept of the non-public forum," said the Court,

> is the right to make distinctions in access on the basis of subject matter and speaker identity. These distinctions may be impermissible in a public forum but are inherent and inescapable in the process of limiting a non-public forum to activities compatible with the intended purpose of the property.

Furthermore, said the Court, the differential access in this case was reasonable:

> The differential access provided PEA [the official union] and PLEA [the rival union] is reasonable because it is wholly consistent with the District's legitimate interest in preserving the property ... for the use to which it is lawfully dedicated. Use of school mail facilities enables PEA to perform effectively its obligations as exclusive representative of all Perry Township teachers. Conversely, PLEA does not have any official responsibility in connection with the School District ... Moreover, exclusion of the

---

240 Aaron Tang, *Life After Janus*, 119 Colum. L. Rev. 677 (April 2019).
241 *See, e.g.*, 115 ILCS 5/11; ALM GL Ch.150E, § 12.
242 Katter v. Ohio Employment Relations Bd., 492 F. Supp. 2d 851 (S.D. Ohio 2007).
243 Madsen v. Associated Chino Teachers, 317 F. Supp. 2d 1175 (C.D. Cal. 2004).
244 460 U.S. 37 (1983).

rival union may reasonably be considered a means of insuring labor peace within the schools. The policy serves to prevent the District's schools from becoming a battlefield for inter-union squabbles.

Finally, the Court noted that the school had made no attempt to prevent the rival union from communicating with teachers by other means, either in or out of school. Thus, the official union's exclusive access to the internal mail system was upheld.

State statutes impose a duty of **fair representation** on unions. A union must not enter into a contract that discriminates against any of its members. A New York court explained the union's obligation as follows:

> The bargaining agent has the duty to serve the interests of all members of a unit without hostility or discrimination toward any, to exercise its discretion with complete good faith and honesty, and to avoid arbitrary conduct ... The deliberate sacrifice of a particular employee as consideration for other objectives must be a concession the union cannot make.[245]

Thus, in another New York case, a court concluded that a union had breached its duty of fair representation when it failed to bargain vigorously on behalf of female coaches. In settling for an unfair salary for these union members because the burden of representing them became onerous, the union discriminated as surely as if it had proposed the inadequate salary.[246]

The Scope of Collective Bargaining

The **scope of bargaining**—which subjects must be negotiated—has implications for the balance of power between teachers and school boards. The typical state statute defines the scope of bargaining to include wages, hours, and, somewhat vaguely, "terms and conditions of employment." The courts have classified these using two general categories: First, **mandatory subjects** must be bargained over at the request of either party. A refusal to negotiate over a mandatory subject of bargaining is a violation of the duty to negotiate in good faith and an improper or unfair labor practice. Second, **permissive subjects** may be bargained over if both parties agree. Sometimes, a state statute specifies a policy that must be used; for example, to carry out a **reduction in force** (RIF), unless the union and school board agree to negotiate a different policy.[247] Refusal to bargain over a permissive subject is not a violation of the duty to negotiate in good faith. Some subjects are beyond the statutory scope of bargaining and hence **non-negotiable** or **illegal subjects**.

State laws regarding which issues are mandatory, permissible, and illegal subjects of negotiation vary significantly, so the law of each state should be consulted. Issues relating to the terms and conditions of employment have historically been mandatory subjects of negotiation. These include hours of employment, length of work year, workload, extra duties, salary, sick leave, dispute resolution, issues of teacher safety and fringe benefits including health insurance and retirement benefits.[248] Several states have now amended their laws regarding the scope of bargaining by simultaneous narrowing of the category of mandatory subjects of bargaining and expanding the

245 Union Free Sch. Dist. No. 6 Babylon v. N.Y. State Div. of Human Rights, 349 N.Y.S.2d 757 (N.Y. App. Div. 1973), *app. dismissed*, 309 N.E.2d 137 (N.Y. 1974).
246 United Teachers of Seaford v. N.Y. State Human Rights Appeal Bd., 414 N.Y.S.2d 207 (N.Y. App. Div. 1979).
247 Bd. of Ed. of Cmty. Sch. Dist. No. 201-U v. Crete-Monee Educ. Ass'n, 497 N.E.2d 1348 (Ill. 1986).
248 Lorain City Sch. Dist. v. State Employment Relations Bd., 533 N.E.2d 264 (Ohio 1988); Local 195 IFPTE, AFL. CIO v. State, 443 A.2d 187 (N.J. 1982).

category of impermissible subjects. Wisconsin law states that school districts are prohibited from bargaining with respect to

> Any factor or condition of employment except wages, which includes only total base wages and excludes any other compensation, which includes, but is not limited to, overtime, premium pay, merit pay, performance pay, supplemental compensation, pay schedules, and automatic pay progressions.[249]

Idaho law authorizes school boards to bargain over "compensation" which is defined to mean only "salary and benefits" and, in turn "benefits" are limited to "employee insurance, leave time and sick leave benefits."[250] Thus these states in effect place such fringe benefits as health insurance and retirement in the category of impermissible subjects of bargaining. Required "collaborative conferencing" in Tennessee specifically excludes pensions and retirement programs.[251] Nevada takes a different approach by narrowing the scope of mandatory bargaining to, among other things, "salary or wage rates or other forms of direct monetary compensation."[252] The other items on the list of mandatory subjects do not include retirement and health insurance. But neither does the section of the law dealing with subjects reserved to the discretion of local government mention retirement and health insurance. Thus it appears that in Nevada these topics are "permissible" subjects of bargaining.

Issues of educational policy and school management such as who shall be hired and fired (sometimes referred to as **managerial prerogatives**) are generally illegal subjects of negotiation.[253] Other subjects ruled non-negotiable by some courts or designated as non-negotiable by some state statutes include promotions, curriculum, length of school year, transfer and assignment, staff size, academic freedom, outsourcing, use of volunteers, and adoption of experimental programs.[254] Also non-negotiable are issues controlled by constitutional or statutory law such as which categories of employees are eligible for tenure.[255] A Wisconsin court ruled that a race-conscious layoff provision was unconstitutional and thus, an illegal subject of negotiation.[256]

The line between **mandatory**, **permissive**, and **illegal** subjects of negotiation is often not clearly drawn. For example, in some states, class size is a mandatory subject of negotiations, but in most it is permissive. In Oregon, this issue resulted in a tug of war between the courts and the legislature: the state supreme court ruled that class size was a mandatory subject of negotiation, but the state legislature overturned this ruling, enacting a statute that restored class size to permissive status.[257]

Even in states where class size is not mandatory, the impact of class size on teacher workload may be.[258] The school calendar may also be mandatory or permissive. Curriculum is at most a permissive subject of negotiations, but the effect of a curriculum adopted by the board on the workload of teachers is a mandatory subject. A Tennessee court ruled that dress code is not a mandatory

---

249 Wis. Stat. §111.70.4.
250 Idaho Code §33-1272.
251 Tenn. Code Ann. §49-5-608.
252 Nev. Rev. Stat. Ann. §288.150.
253 Bd. of Educ. of North Bergen v. North Bergen Fed'n of Teachers, Local 1060, 357 A.2d 302 (N.J. Super. Ct. App. Div. 1976).
254 Boston Teachers Union, Local 66 v. Sch. Comm. of Boston, 434 N.E.2d 1258 (Mass. 1982); Unified Sch. Dist. No. 501 v. Kan. Dep't of Human Resources, 685 P.2d 874 (Kan. 1984); MICH. COMP. LAWS § 423.215.
255 Spiewak v. Bd. of Educ. of Rutherford, 447 A.2d 140 (N.J. 1982).
256 Milwaukee Bd. of Sch. Dir. v. Wis. Employment Relations Comm., 472 N.W.2d 553 (Wis. 1991).
257 See Tualatin Valley Bargaining Council v. Tigard Sch. Dist. 23J, 808 P.2d 101 (Or. Ct. App. 1991), rev'd and remanded, 840 P.2d 657 (Or. 1992); Or. Rev. Stat. § 243.650(7)(e); see Martin H. Malin, The Paradox of Public Sector Labor Law, 84 IND. L.J. 1369 (2009).
258 Decatur Bd. of Educ. No. 61 v. Illinois Educ. Labor Relations Bd., 536 N.E.2d 743 (Ill. App. Ct. 1989); Beloit Educ. Ass'n v. Wisconsin Employment Relations Comm'n, 242 N.W.2d 231 (Wis. 1976).

subject of negotiations, but the enforcement of a dress code is.[259] In most states, the criteria for the evaluation of teachers are non-negotiable, but the procedures for evaluation are mandatory. An Iowa court ruled that not only the procedures of evaluation but also the substantive criteria of evaluation are mandatory subjects of negotiation.[260]

Conversely, a Connecticut court ruled that even the procedures of evaluation are not a mandatory subject of negotiation.[261] In New York, a 2010 statute provided for a "hybrid" scheme, under which portions of both substantive evaluation criteria and evaluation procedures were nonnegotiable, whereas other portions were mandatory subjects of negotiation.[262] When the state issued regulations that set forth a different ratio than found in the statute, litigation ensued, and a state court ruled that the regulations had categorized a smaller portion of the evaluation criteria as mandatory than the statute warranted.

Most states take the position that an initial decision to carry out a RIF is a non-negotiable **management prerogative**, but that RIF procedures and the impact of a RIF on staff are mandatory. An Illinois court, however, ruled that even the initial decision to lay off teachers was a mandatory subject of negotiation.[263] Conversely, a New Jersey court ruled that both the initial RIF decision and the impact of the decision were illegal subjects of negotiation.[264] Another New Jersey court ruled that the decision whether to hold school on recess days to make up for snow days was not a mandatory subject, but the impact of the decision was negotiable unless negotiations would significantly interfere with managerial prerogatives. The court said that only if the impact of the decision could be severed from the basic decision were negotiations over the impact mandatory.[265]

Some states seek to avoid confusion by specifying a list of subjects in each category. Whatever the level of specificity of the statutes, disputes over the negotiability of specific subjects may arise because many educational issues involve both teacher working conditions and questions of policy and school management. A further complication is that the statutory language defining the scope of bargaining must be reconciled with other state statutes such as those addressing the promotion and evaluation of teachers.[266]

Grievance Procedures

Most collective bargaining agreements include grievance procedures for dealing with alleged contract violations and settling differences in contract interpretation. Depending on the terms of the agreement and state law, even alleged violations of anti-discrimination statutes, constitutional rights, and other state and federal laws may be subject to grievance procedures.[267] In about 20 states, the law permits submitting teacher contract disputes to **grievance arbitration**, in which a neutral third party is empowered to make a decision that both sides must accept. Courts have affirmed the legality of grievance arbitration with regard to subjects within the scope of

259 Polk County Bd. of Educ. v. Polk County Educ. Assn., 139 S.W.3d 304 (Tenn. Ct. App. 2004).
260 Aplington Cmty. Sch. Dist. v. Iowa Pub. Employment Relations Bd., 392 N.W.2d 495 (Iowa 1986).
261 Wethersfield Bd. of Educ. v. Conn. State Bd. of Labor Relations, 519 A.2d 41 (Conn. 1986).
262 New York State United Teachers *ex rel.* Iannuzzi v. Bd. of Regents of Univ. of State of New York, 33 Misc. 3d 989, 929 N.Y.S.2d 699 (Sup. Ct. 2011).
263 Cent. City Educ. Ass'n v. Ill. Educ. Labor Relations Bd., 557 N.E.2d 418 (Ill. App. Ct. 1990); *appeal granted*, 561 N.E.2d 687 (Ill. 1990); *modified* 599 N.E.2d 892 (Ill. 1992).
264 Maywood Bd. of Educ. v. Maywood Educ. Ass'n, 401 A.2d 711 (N.J. Super Ct. App. Div.); *appeal denied*, 405 A.2d 836 (N.J. 1979).
265 Piscataway Township Educ. Ass'n v. Piscataway Township Bd. of Educ., 704 A.2d 981 (N.J. Super. Ct. App. Div. 1998).
266 Bethlehem Township Bd. of Educ. v. Bethlehem Township Educ. Ass'n, 449 A.2d 1254 (N.J. 1982).
267 Gray v. Caddo Parish Sch. Bd., 938 So.2d 1212 (La. App. 2 Cir. 2006).

bargaining.[268] The Supreme Court has ruled that contractual agreements to arbitrate disputes over rights granted by employment statutes are legally permissible.[269] As we discussed in the previous chapter, the First Amendment protections afforded to teacher grievances are governed by *Ceballos* and *Pickering* principles.[270]

Usually the law requires exhausting all available grievance procedures before submitting a dispute to a court; however, there may be times when state law and the collective bargaining agreement give teachers two separate options for contesting what they believe to be a contractually impermissible action by their employer. For example, a dismissed teacher might seek review of the decision through the grievance mechanism of the contract or through the procedures spelled out in state law. Courts are in agreement that where these options exist, teachers may choose either of them.[271] Election of one procedure sometimes, but not always, has been held to bar the use of the other.[272] New York permits a teacher to pursue the grievance procedure and statutory procedure simultaneously even if this creates the possibility of inconsistent results.[273] Once a particular procedure has been pursued to its final step and a final decision rendered, the other procedure can no longer be used.[274]

Collective bargaining contracts often give the union the exclusive power to decide whether a grievance will be filed. A teacher whose union refuses to prosecute a grievance could not use this avenue of redress. In deciding whether to prosecute a grievance, private sector unions are under a federal statutory obligation to act fairly.[275] State courts have found a similar duty under state public sector bargaining laws as part of the union's duty of fair representation.[276] On the same basis, when two members of the same union are in conflict regarding which one will be retained and which one let go, the union may not hire an attorney to defend only one of them.[277]

An issue that frequently arises in the context of grievance procedures is whether the school board has the authority to submit a particular issue to arbitration. For example, is it permissible for the board to agree to arbitrate a teacher dismissal or must the board reserve the ultimate decision to itself? The answers to questions like this vary from state to state depending on statute.[278] Assuming the board has the authority to submit a particular issue to arbitration, a school board and teacher can still disagree on whether the contract requires the issue to be arbitrated. In other words, disputes can arise concerning the scope of the negotiated arbitration agreement itself.

State courts have taken divergent approaches to resolving these issues.[279] For example, in *Niles Township High School District 219 v. Illinois Educational Labor Relations Board*,[280] a union grieved the

268 W. Fargo Pub. Sch. Dist. No. 6 of Cass Cty v. W. Fargo Educ. Ass'n, 259 N.W.2d 612 (N.D. 1977).
269 Gilmer v. Interstate/Johnson Lane Corp., 500 U.S. 20 (1991); E.E.O.C. v. Waffle House, 534 U.S. 279 (2001); Wright v. Universal Maritime Service Corp., 525 U.S. 70 (1998).
270 *See* Brammer-Hoelter v. Twin Peaks Charter Academy, 492 F.3d 1192 (10th Cir. 2007).
271 Bd. of Educ. of Huntington v. Associated Teachers, 282 N.E.2d 109 (N.Y. 1972); Pub. Empl. Rel'ns Comm'n. v. Dist. Sch. Bd. of DeSoto County, 374 So. 2d 1005 (Fla. Ct. App. 1979).
272 Pedersen v. S. Williamsport Area Sch. Dist., 677 F.2d 312 (3d Cir. 1982).
273 *In re* Susquehanna Valley Teachers Ass'n, 429 N.Y.S.2d 741 (N.Y. App. Div. 1980), *aff'd*, 420 N.E.2d 400 (N.Y. 1981); *but see* Bd. of Educ. Cattaraugus Cent. Sch. v. Cattaraugus Teachers Ass'n, 447 N.Y.S.2d 51 (N.Y. App. Div. 1981), *aff'd*, 434 N.E.2d 262 (N.Y. 1982).
274 Bd. of Educ. of Huntington v. Associated Teachers, 282 N.E.2d 109 (N.Y. 1972).
275 Vaca v. Sipes, 386 U.S. 171 (1967).
276 Baker v. Bd. of Educ. of W. Irondequoit, 514 N.E.2d 1109 (N.Y. 1987).
277 Jacobs v. Bd. of Educ. of E. Meadow, 405 N.Y.S.2d 159 (N.Y. Sup. Ct. 1977), *rev'd*, 409 N.Y.S.2d 234 (N.Y. App. Div. 1978).
278 Acting Super. of Sch. of Liverpool Cent. Sch. Dist. v. United Liverpool Faculty Ass'n, 369 N.E.2d 746 (N.Y. 1977); Sch. Comm. of Danvers v. Tyman, 360 N.E.2d 877 (Mass. 1977); Bd. of Educ. of Philadelphia v. Philadelphia Fed'n. of Teachers Local No. 3, 346 A.2d 35 (Pa. 1975).
279 Wyandanch Union Free Sch. Dist. v. Wyandanch Teachers Ass'n, 397 N.E.2d 384 (N.Y. 1979); Sch. Dist. of Erie v. Erie Educ. Ass'n, 447 A.2d 686 (Pa. Commw. Ct. 1982).
280 883 N.E. 2d 29 (Ill. App. 1 Dist. 2007).

dismissal of probationary teachers, and alleged that procedural violations by the school board triggered mandatory arbitration under the collective bargaining agreement. A divided state appellate court disagreed, and held that, even if the procedural irregularities alleged by the union were true, these procedural issues were not covered by the collective bargaining agreement and therefore could not violate the agreement. Since the union had failed to even "state a claim" under the collective bargaining agreement, the school board could not be forced to arbitrate the claim and the case was dismissed. State courts are also divided over the related issue of whether the arbitrator or the courts decide whether an issue may be decided by arbitration.

Once a grievance has been settled by arbitration, most courts consider the decision to be valid and binding and will not review or overturn the decision unless it is totally unreasonable[281] or violates state or federal law or policy such as by contradicting a legitimate school board decision concerning a nonnegotiable issue.[282] When an elementary school classroom assistant overdosed on Fentanyl in the school bathroom, an arbitrator overturned her termination. A Pennsylvania court, however, reversed the arbitrator's decision and reinstituted the termination, pointing to "the public policy of educating our children about the dangers of illicit drugs and drug abuse and protecting children from exposure to drugs and drug abuse."[283]

Similarly, the remedy granted by the arbitrator to the winning party such as reinstatement or damages must conform to the contract and not violate state law[284] or contravene public policy.[285]

Individual Teacher Contracts

As we have previously noted, many aspects of the relationship between teachers and their employers are controlled by federal and state constitutional and statutory law. School boards and teachers—either collectively or individually—may not enter into contracts that contradict state law; for example, by allowing teachers to make personnel decisions that the law reserves to school boards.[286] State law may even permit school boards to make decisions that have the effect of modifying the contract between the board and its teachers; for example, by revising the school calendar to make up for days missed because of weather. Teachers may be required to follow the modified calendar, even to attend school on days specifically designated by the contract as vacations.

As discussed earlier in this chapter, in school districts with collective bargaining, many of the terms of employment governing a school district's teachers are set by an agreement between a teacher union and school board. The collective bargaining agreement is a mandatory part of the contract of each individual teacher within a school district, so school boards and teachers may not enter into contracts that contradict the collective bargaining agreement even if both wish to do so.[287] For example, where the collective bargaining agreement specifies a single salary schedule for all teachers, the school board may not agree to a higher than scheduled salary for a teacher it considers particularly valuable.

However, the collective bargaining agreement is not by itself specific enough to constitute an enforceable contract between the school board and any individual teacher. Teachers must still

281 Niagara Wheatfield Adm'r Ass'n v. Niagara Wheatfield Cent. Sch. Dist., 375 N.E.2d 37 (N.Y. 1978).
282 Buffalo Council of Supervisors & Adm'r v. City of Buffalo Sch. Dist., 626 N.Y.S.2d 623 (N.Y. App. Div. 1995).
283 Westmoreland Intermediate Unit #£7 v. Westmoreland Intermediate Unit #£7 Classroom Assistants Educ. Support Pers. Ass'n, 72 A.3d 755 (Pa. Commw. Ct. 2013).
284 Kennewick Educ. Ass'n v. Kennewick Sch. Dist. No. 17, 666 P.2d 928 (Wash. App. Ct. 1983).
285 See In Re Binghamton City School District, 848 N.Y.S.2d 382 (App. Div. 3d Dep't 2007).
286 In re Brighton Cent. Sch. Dist., 505 N.Y.S.2d 522 (N.Y. Sup. Ct. 1986); Bd. of Educ. v. Round Valley Teachers Ass'n, 914 P.2d 193 (Cal. 1996); Oak Harbor Sch. Dist. v. Oak Harbor Educ. Ass'n, 545 P.2d 1197 (Wash. 1976); see also Consedine v. Portville Central Sch. Dist., 907 N.E.2d 684 (N.Y. 2009).
287 See, e.g., Mount Holly Township Bd. of Ed. v. Mount Holly Township Educ. Assoc., 972 A.2d 387 (N.J. 2009).

have individual contracts spelling out, among other things, the specific positions they are to hold, the hours they are to work, and the salary and benefits they are to receive. Teachers may also have separate or supplementary contracts regarding coaching or other extra-duty assignments. The collective bargaining agreement may be viewed as setting the framework of the agreement between a teacher and school board, with the individual contract filling in the details. In school districts without collective bargaining, each teacher is theoretically free to negotiate the entire contract from scratch. In practice, however, the board generally insists on fairly similar general terms for all of its teachers, with the only variations similar to those in collective bargaining districts.

Whether an individual teacher's contract emanates from a collective bargaining agreement or not, an extensive and complex set of statutory and common laws regulates its formation and implementation. Employment contracts in education are usually bilateral, meaning that each party makes promises in advance to the other, and are express rather than implied, meaning that the promises are made in words rather than inferred from actions. Where permitted by law, teaching contracts or, more frequently, supplemental duty contracts, may be oral. Oral contracts are difficult to enforce because it is hard to prove what was said. Even where there is no written contract, an employee is entitled to reasonable compensation for services performed at the request of and for the benefit of an employer.

The five essential elements of a binding employment contract in education are: (a) manifestation of mutual assent; (b) consideration; (c) competence of the parties; (d) legality of subject; and (e) satisfaction of statutory requirements for formation of a contract. Each of these elements must be satisfied to create an enforceable contract.

Questions sometimes arise over whether a teacher's contract may include more than what is written on the document both parties signed. Specifically, cases have addressed the question of whether school rules, a teachers' handbook, or a school publication is part of the contract. The courts have said that such materials may be part of the contract if their terms are sufficiently specific, the employee is aware of them, and the materials are part of the bargained exchange.[288] Courts in several states, however, have ruled that if there is evidence that the employer reserved the right to unilaterally change the handbook, then it is not considered part of the contract.[289] Also, if the handbook specifically contains a statement that it does not constitute a contract, then the courts will not enforce it.[290]

Courts are in general agreement that state law is part of the contract.[291] The power of legislatures to change the terms of the contract by changing the law may be an implied or an express provision of the contract. Some states permit school boards to unilaterally change employment contracts under exigent circumstances. In 1991, in response to a severe budget crisis, the City of Baltimore decided to pay its teachers approximately one percent less than the salary specified in their contracts. The teachers sued the city, claiming that the unilateral contract modification violated Article 1, Section 10 (the Contract Clause) of the Constitution. The Contract Clause prohibits states from passing any law "impairing the obligation of contracts." In rejecting the claim, the Fourth Circuit noted that the Contract Clause is not an absolute bar to modification of a state's own financial obligations. Unilateral contract modifications must be "reasonable and necessary to serve an important public purpose." The salary reduction was permissible because

288 Law v. Mandan Pub. Sch. Dist., 411 N.W.2d 375 (N.D. 1987); Pine River State Bank v. Mettille, 333 N.W.2d 622 (Minn. 1983).

289 Heideck v. Kent Gen. Hosp., Inc., 446 A.2d 1095 (Del. 1982); Jackson v. Action for Boston Cmty. Dev., Inc., 525 N.E.2d 411 (Mass. 1988); Johnson v. McDonnell Douglas Corp., 745 S.W.2d 661 (Mo. 1988).

290 Domenichetti v. Salter Sch., 2013 U.S. Dist. LEXIS 57201 (D. Mass. Apr. 19, 2013).

291 Haverland v. Tempe Elementary Sch. Dist. No. 3, 595 P.2d 1032 (Ariz. Ct. App. 1979); Paczosa v. Cartwright Elementary Sch. Dist. No. 83, 213 P.3d 222, 226 (Ariz. Ct. App. 2009).

Baltimore had made concerted but unsuccessful efforts to find alternative solutions, the reduction was no greater than necessary, and the plan was abandoned at the first opportunity.[292]

Sometimes, the parties to a contract have expressed themselves in both a specific document and other oral or written statements, known as **parol evidence**. The general rule is that when the basic written contract is an integrated agreement, **parol evidence** will not be permitted to modify it in any way.[293] A written contract is an integrated agreement when the parties so intended. To manifest this intention, many contracts contain a clause affirming that the contract constitutes the entire agreement between the parties.[294]

Even when the parties know what words constitute their contract, they may disagree on their meaning. Carefully worded contracts are less likely to engender these disputes. When disagreements do arise, the courts may be asked to interpret the contract. Although there is no procedure that guarantees discovery of the true meaning of a contract, certain rules of interpretation serve as guidelines. Contracts are interpreted in accordance with the purpose and intentions of the parties insofar as these are ascertainable. Ordinary words are given their usual meaning and technical words their technical meaning. Separately negotiated terms are given greater weight than standardized terms and specific terms greater weight than general terms. Interpretations that render the contract and all its provisions reasonable, lawful, meaningful, and consistent are preferred.

When one party fails to live up to the terms of the contract, the disappointed party can sue for **breach of contract**. The law seeks to provide a remedy that places the injured party in the same position as if the contract had been fulfilled. Sometimes, this only requires a court to issue an order prohibiting continued violation of a contractual term or requiring specific execution of a provision of the contract such as the procedures governing teacher dismissal. Most often, the remedy for breach of contract is the awarding of monetary damages to compensate the aggrieved party for what would have been gained had the breach not occurred and for expenses incurred because of the breach. Employees who fail to complete the term of their contracts might have to compensate their employers for expenses incurred in obtaining a replacement. Aggrieved employees may be awarded salary and any other expenses incurred as a result of an employer's breach, such as the cost of seeking and moving to a new job.[295] In fairness to the defaulting party, the law says the injured party cannot recover damages that could have been avoided through the exercise of reasonable diligence and without incurring undue risk, expense, or humiliation. The injured party is expected to take reasonable steps to **mitigate damages** by, for example, seeking another job, but the injured party does not have to take a job inferior to the one lost. In one case, a principal dismissed in violation of his contract was not required to accept a job as a teacher, even though his salary would have remained the same.[296]

In some employment contracts, the parties agree that an employee who breaches the contract will pay a specified amount of money in lieu of damages based on actual loss. These **liquidated damage** clauses are enforceable when it is difficult for the contracting parties to determine the exact monetary value of the contract breach, provided the amount is reasonable and not punitive.[297] State statutory law may require that individual contracts contain a damages provision and specify the kinds and limits of the damages to be awarded. The highest court in Colorado interpreted a statutory provision limiting damages to "ordinary and necessary expenses" not to include salaries paid to employees who would have been paid anyway when those employees helped to search for

292 Baltimore Teachers Union v. Mayor of Baltimore, 6 F.3d 1012 (4th Cir. 1993).
293 *But see* Lillibridge v. Meade School Dist. #46-1, 746 N.W.2d 428 (S.D. 2008).
294 *See* Chandler v. Lamar County Bd. of Educ., 528 So. 2d 309 (Ala. 1988).
295 McBeth v. Bd. of Educ. of DeValls Bluff Sch. Dist. No. 1, 300 F. Supp. 1270 (E.D. Ark. 1969).
296 Williams v. Albemarle City Bd. of Educ., 508 F.2d 1242 (4th Cir. 1974).
297 Bowbells Pub. Sch. Dist. No. 14 v. Walker, 231 N.W.2d 173 (N.D. 1975).

a replacement teacher after the plaintiff resigned without giving sufficient notice.[298] A Montana court upheld as consistent with a state statute a liquidated damage clause that required the plaintiff to pay 20 percent of his salary. The court found the 20 percent requirement not unduly oppressive and not a penalty, as opposed to a true damages provision. And the fact that the district found a replacement teacher at a lower salary than was paid to the plaintiff did not preclude enforcement of the liquidated damage clause.[299]

Unless there is a statute to the contrary, the law permits teachers to work without a contract, but when there is no contract the issue may arise regarding the salary owed to the teachers. When a statute is available to govern the noncontract situation, its terms control the level of payment owed, but when there is no statute, courts resolve such questions in a manner designed "to assure a just and equitable result."[300] In one case, the court ruled that teachers who did agree to a new contract would be paid retroactively under the new salary schedule, whereas teachers who did not agree were to be paid under the terms of the previous year's salary schedule, including the experience increment due to them under that schedule.[301]

Summary

Most of the law relevant to the hiring and firing of professional school employees is found in state statutes. States are free to set whatever teacher certification requirements they wish, except that standards may not be arbitrary, racially discriminatory, or otherwise violative of constitutional rights. Because certification does not amount to a contractual agreement, states may also set new standards for certification retention even by tenured employees.

For their part, schools are free to offer employment to whomever they deem most qualified, provided that the candidate meets state eligibility requirements, including certification, and that the hiring process does not violate statutory provisions or the Constitution. Once hired, teachers may be assigned to any school, grade level, or subject matter for which they are qualified unless their contract says otherwise. They may also be assigned extra duty and tasks reasonably connected to the legitimate educational goals of the school and their job, again subject to contractual constraints.

Schools also have wide latitude in the evaluation and contract renewal decision concerning probationary teachers. In many states, a school may decide not to renew the contract of a teacher in the first three years of employment for any constitutionally permissible reason and without granting a hearing or following any specific procedures. In recent years, some states have changed the probationary period from three to four and even five years.

While tenure is still widely available, a number of states have abolished it. Tenured teachers may be dismissed for cause. Each state's statutes establish a list of the only acceptable bases for termination. Although the wording varies considerably from state to state, acceptable causes for dismissal can be grouped into five categories: incompetence, violation of role model obligations, poor citizenship within the school, posing a threat to students, and incapacity. The law places the burden of proof on the school to show, in many states through a prescribed evaluation process, that the teacher falls into one of these categories.

In addition to the requirement that dismissal be for a specified cause, both the Constitution and state statutes impose significant procedural due process requirements on tenured-teacher firings.

298 Klinger v. Adams County Sch. Distr. No. 50, 130 P.3d 1027 (Colo. 2006).
299 Arrowhead Sch. Dist. No. 75 Park County v. Klyap, 79 P.3d 250 (Mont. 2003).
300 Bradkin v. Leverton, 257 N.E.2d 643 (N.Y. 1970).
301 Davis v. Bd. of Educ. of Aurora Pub. Sch. Dist. No. 131, 312 N.E.2d 335 (Ill. App. Ct. 1974).

In general, the Constitution requires an impartial hearing including a statement of charges and a reasonable opportunity to refute them. Most states' statutes specify additional procedures.

Reduction in force—dismissal of teachers because funds are lacking or programs eliminated—is also primarily controlled by state statute. Most of the litigation challenging a specific RIF is resolved by comparing the specific procedures employed with the requirements of state statutes. A common but not universal feature of these statutes is that more recently hired teachers be let go before those with greater seniority. But some states now prohibit reliance on seniority.

School boards may grant voluntary leaves of absence or impose involuntary leaves consistent with federal and state law and their own policies and contractual agreements. Leave-of-absence policies may not discriminate on the basis of race, religion, or pregnancy. Teachers injured at work may receive payment in accordance with the workers' compensation laws of their state. To be eligible for workers' compensation, a teacher must sustain an injury by accident arising out of and in the course of employment.

Within the boundaries of federal and state law, the terms and conditions of a teacher's employment are set down in a contract. In most school districts, the contract is developed through a process of collective negotiations between a union representing all the district's teachers and the school board. Teachers have a constitutional right to join a union, but collective bargaining is at the discretion of the legislature and courts of each state. Most states do allow some form of collective bargaining for teachers.

The process for selecting the union, the terms of the relationship between the union and its members and between the union and the school board, and the duties and obligations of both sides in collective bargaining are established by state law. The union is required to fairly represent all teachers within the district, even those who choose not to join. Both sides are obliged to bargain in good faith, (i.e., with an intention of reaching a mutually satisfactory agreement) over issues specified or implied by state law as mandatory subjects of negotiation. Generally, these issues relate to the welfare and working conditions of teachers. Certain other issues may be bargained at the discretion of both sides. Collective bargaining agreements often include an agreement to submit certain employment disputes to arbitration by a neutral third party.

12 Torts

A visiting grandparent slips on an ice-covered walkway and breaks a hip. An intruder forces students into a supply closet and assaults them. A high school senior severs a finger in shop class. A football player suffers multiple concussions leading to cognitive impairments. Cheerleaders falsely describe their coach as a pedophile on social media. For victims of these kinds of harm, recourse may be available through the body of law known as **torts**. Like many legal terms, "tort" came into the English language from Medieval Latin and French. In Latin, *tortus* (the root of terms including *torso, torque, contort,* and *distort*) meant "twisted" or "out of line." In modern French, *tort* means "wrong."

Unlike **criminal law**, by which the State punishes wrongdoers for a range of public offenses, **tort law** allows individuals who have suffered wrongful interference with their **person**, their **property**, their **peace of mind**, or their **reputation** to seek compensation from wrongdoers. The usual remedy in tort suits is **monetary damages**, although courts may also issue **injunctions** to prohibit the continuation of harmful activities. A typical tort case involves an individual suing another individual, a corporate body, a government agent or agency, or some level of government for damages.

As we have noted in previous chapters, a federal law known as Section 1983 includes a statutory tort mechanism allowing individuals to sue government agencies and employees, including public school districts and employees, for monetary damages.[1] Public school districts and school officials may be vulnerable to Section 1983 claims if they violate the constitutional or federal statutory rights of students, parents, or employees. School officials may also be sued and required to pay monetary damages if they personally violate the constitutional or federal statutory rights of others or, under certain circumstances, if they permit their subordinates to do so. Although many of the tort suits against school districts and public school officials discussed in this chapter include Section 1983 claims, we will focus on the **common law** tort claims to which private and public school officials are equally vulnerable.

Because most students are legal minors, they lack standing to file lawsuits in their own right and must be represented by a parent or litigation guardian acting on their behalf. Minors may be named as defendants in tort suits, but this is rare. First, it can be difficult to prove the elements of a tort case against a young child, particularly for torts requiring **intent**. Second, it can be difficult to collect monetary damages from children. Few children have assets of their own, and fewer still carry liability insurance.

Based on what is sometimes called the **deep pocket principle**, individuals injured while on school property or while engaging in school-sponsored activities typically seek to hold public and private schools liable. Although public schools and school officials once enjoyed protection from tort suits under principles of **sovereign immunity** or **government officer immunity**, these immunities have been limited or abolished in most states. As a result, tort suits may be brought against individual school officials and even individual school board members.

---

1 42 U.S. Code § 1983.

School officials may be held **personally liable** for their own tortious acts. School officials may also be held **vicariously liable** for the tortious conduct of others. A court may find, for example, that the tortious conduct of a teacher would not have occurred if school officials had provided adequate training and supervision. Under the doctrine of *respondeat superior*, private schools, charter schools, and public school districts may be held **vicariously liable** for the tortious acts of employees acting within the scope of their duties. Thus school officials are frequently named alongside their employers in tort suits.

In both private and public school contexts, most school officials will have to deal with individuals threatening lawsuits. They should seek legal advice from a qualified attorney whenever this occurs. Concern for the safety of others is a paramount consideration. But as a practical matter, school officials must be mindful of the potential for liability in tort should anyone suffer foreseeable harm. Private and public schools carry liability insurance and indemnify school officials for legal costs and monetary damages, but even unsuccessful lawsuits consume enormous amounts of time and energy.

While school officials cannot guarantee that no one will ever be injured on their watch, they have a duty to foresee potential harm and take reasonable steps to minimize risks. This chapter presents an overview of the types of tort suits most common in public and private school contexts.

Intentional Torts

When individuals act intentionally, it is assumed that they wish to bring about the consequences of their actions. The specific harm caused by an intentional act may not always be what the actor anticipated, but **foreseeability** is an element of **negligence**, not of **intentional torts**. It is important to note that some intentional torts also constitute **crimes** or other **statutory offenses**. Hence intentional wrongdoing can lead to liability in civil or criminal proceedings (or both).

Battery

The tort of **battery** is defined in terms of unwanted and offensive **bodily contact** with **intent** to cause harm. Battery can involve direct bodily contact, as when one person punches another in the stomach. It can involve indirect bodily contact, as when one person grabs another by their clothing. Indirect bodily contact also includes the use of an **object** (such as a stick or a vehicle or the ground) or a **projectile** (such as a rock or a glass beaker), or actions which lead to unwanted harmful contact with the ground (such as pulling a chair out from under someone). **Contact** is viewed as offensive if a reasonable person would be unlikely to consent to it. However, consent to some bodily contact is assumed in everyday situations in which physical contact is inevitable (such as crowded elevators or subway cars).

Assault

The tort of **assault** is distinct from the tort of **battery**. An **assault** is defined in terms of an intentional act that causes someone to believe he or she is in danger of imminent bodily harm or offensive contact. The apprehension of harm must be reasonable. Words accompanying an assault can add to this apprehension. Whereas battery protects **bodily integrity**, assault protects **peace of mind**. Thus, a person in danger of imminent bodily harm must be aware of the danger.

Scenario 1   Rob is tossing glass beakers at a target he has drawn on the wall in an empty science lab. One of the beakers ricochets off the wall and through an open window, striking Kristina, who is sitting on the grass two stories below. It is clear that Rob intended to throw the beaker. He enjoyed the sound each beaker made as it shattered. But is not clear that he intended to harm anyone. While it might be argued that Rob intended to damage school property, this intent to harm cannot be transferred to Kristina, because damaging school property does not constitute a battery. Hence Rob will probably not be liable to Kristina for the intentional tort of **battery**. School officials could, however, be liable in **negligence** for leaving Rob unsupervised.

Scenario 2   Rob sees Kristina sitting on the grass two stories below. He leans out the window and shouts, "I'm going to get you, Kristina!" and hurls a beaker at her. The beaker misses Kristina and instead strikes Denise, who is engrossed in watching fluffy cat videos on her smartphone a few yards away. In this case, it is clear that Rob intended both to hurl the beaker and to cause harm to Kristina. Since he intended to commit a battery, his intent to harm Kristina can be transferred to Denise, and Rob will be liable to Denise for **battery**.

An **assault** typically precedes a **battery**. Even if no battery occurs, the assault is still actionable. Thus, in the second scenario above, Rob would be liable to Kristina for **assault**. Because the beaker struck Denise, Rob would be liable to her for **battery**. Because Denise remained engrossed in her smartphone until she was struck by the beaker, Rob will probably not be liable to her for **assault**.

As illustrated in the hypothetical scenarios above, **motive** is distinguishable from **intent** in tort law. Both are states of mind associated with what a person does, but **motive** relates to a person's reasons for engaging in a harmful course of action, while **intent** relates to the harmful consequences of a course of action. Rob had neither motive nor intent to harm Kristina in the first example given above. However, in the second example, **intent** to harm Kristina can be inferred by his words and actions.

What if Rob were a kindergartener? Minors may be liable for their intentional acts, but a child's age, level of maturity, and intelligence are important considerations. In *Garratt v. Dailey*,[2] five-year-old Brian pulled a lawn chair out from under his arthritic aunt Ruth, who fell to the ground and fractured her hip. The court ultimately held that, despite his tender age, Brian "knew, with substantial certainty … that [his aunt] would attempt to sit in the place where the chair had been." Hence intent to harm was established, and Ruth Garrett was awarded $11,000 in damages for **assault** and **battery**. In *Ghassemieh v. Schafer*,[3] an injured teacher sued a 13-year-old student who likewise yanked a chair out from under her. The suit was unsuccessful because the teacher sought a remedy in **negligence** for what was clearly an **intentional tort**.

In *Walker v. Kelly*,[4] in a suit brought under state legislation holding parents jointly and severally liable for the tortious conduct of their minor children,[5] a Connecticut court found the requisite intent to harm could not be imputed to a five-year-old boy who threw a rock at an eight-year-old girl, lacerating her forehead. "Ordinarily, tort liability attaches regardless of age where the nature of the act is such that children of a like age would realize its injurious consequences," wrote the court. "However, where a tort requires a particular state of mind, and [a child] because of his age or mental capacity is incapable of forming such state of mind, he cannot be found guilty of the tort."

False Imprisonment

The tort of false imprisonment involves intentionally confining or restricting the movement of someone without legal authority or justification. To establish a false imprisonment claim, plaintiffs must show (1) that the defendant intended to confine them; (2) that they were aware of their

---

2 279 P.2d 1091 (1955); 304 P. 2d 681 (1956).
3 294 Md. 543 (1982).
4 314 A.2d 785 (1973).
5 Conn. Gen. Stat. § 52-572.

confinement; (3) that they did not consent to their confinement; and (4) that the defendant's conduct was not privileged.[6]

In *Zegarelli-Pecheone v. New Hartford Central School District*,[7] school officials questioned a student about an incident at a football game for an extended period of time, both in the principal's office and in a nurse's office. The court denied the school district's invocation of **privilege**, noting that "[a] confinement such as the one at issue herein is privileged only if it is reasonable under the circumstances, including its duration and manner."

False imprisonment can take various forms, including the use of physical barriers, threats, and false claims of legal authority. False imprisonment suits on their own are rare, in part because of the custodial nature of school authority and the legal privileges of school officials. But false imprisonment claims are frequently levied against school districts in conjunction with other torts and Section 1983 claims,[8] as the following case illustrates.

⚖️

PETERS v. ROME CITY SCHOOL DISTRICT
Supreme Court of New York, Appellate Division (4th Department)
298 A.D.2d 864 (2002)

GREEN, J.P., WISNER, SCUDDER, BURNS, AND GORSKI, JJ.

… Plaintiff commenced this action on behalf of her son, Christopher, asserting causes of action for, *inter alia*, false imprisonment, negligent infliction of emotional distress and a violation of the prohibition against unlawful seizure under the Fourth Amendment of the United States Constitution.

During the 1992–1993 school year, defendant developed an individualized education plan (IEP) for Christopher, who has a learning disability and was then in the second grade. As part of the IEP, to which plaintiff consented, defendant developed a behavior plan that included the use of a "time-out" room as the last resort to correct inappropriate behavior exhibited by Christopher in the classroom.

It is undisputed that Christopher was placed in the time-out room 75 times from October 1992 to March 19, 1993. On March 19, 1993, plaintiff observed that Christopher's hands were reddened and blistered as a result of Christopher's efforts to open the door in order to leave the time-out room. Although the door was not locked, a staff person held the door closed if Christopher attempted to leave the time-out room.

It is also undisputed that the time-out room was "small," although there is no evidence in the record concerning its precise dimensions. It is further undisputed that the time-out room was unfurnished and had padding on the walls, door and floor to ensure a child's safety. Although defendant notified plaintiff each time Christopher was placed in the time-out room, plaintiff did not observe the room until March 22, 1993, and she testified at trial that it lacked ventilation and had an odor of "dirty feet [and] urine," and she described the padding on the floor as ripped and dirty.

Defendant's expert testified at trial that there was nothing inappropriate about the room. It is undisputed that Christopher was not permitted to leave the time-out room until he had remained seated in an upright position without moving for three consecutive minutes; that on at least one occasion Christopher fell asleep in the room; and that there were occasions when Christopher was confined to the room for periods in excess of one hour. …

With respect to the cause of action for false imprisonment, we conclude that there was evidence from which the jury could rationally find that defendant intended to confine Christopher; that Christopher was conscious of the confinement; that in consenting to the IEP plaintiff did not thereby consent to

6 Broughton v. State, 335 N.E.2d 310 (N.Y. App. 1975), *cert. denied*, 423 U.S. 929 (1975).

7 132 A.D.3d 1258 (N.Y. App. Div. 4th 2015).

8 *See, e.g.*, A.G. v. Paradise Valley Unified Sch. Dist. No. 69, 815 F.3d 1195 (9th Cir. 2016); J.M. v. Francis Howell Sch. Dist., 850 F.3d 944 (8th Cir. 2017); Hassan v. Lubbock Indep. Sch. Dist., 55 F.3d 1075 (5th Cir. 1995), *cert. denied*, 516 U.S. 995 (1995).

Christopher's confinement in the time-out room inasmuch as plaintiff was unaware of the conditions of the room or Christopher's reaction to placement in the room; and that the confinement was not otherwise privileged.

With respect to the cause of action for negligent infliction of emotional distress, we conclude that there was evidence from which the jury could rationally find that defendant breached a duty owed to Christopher and thereby endangered Christopher's safety or caused Christopher to fear for his physical safety. With respect to that cause of action, we further conclude that there was evidence from which the jury could rationally find that the frequency, duration and manner of confinement were "so outrageous in character, and so extreme in degree, as to go beyond all possible bounds of decency, and to be regarded as atrocious, and utterly intolerable in a civilized community."

The evidence presented by plaintiff included, *inter alia*, the testimony of Christopher that he was placed face-down on the floor and physically restrained in the time-out room. We further conclude that the jury could rationally find that the seizure of Christopher by defendant was not reasonable under the circumstances and that defendant thereby violated Christopher's rights under the Fourth Amendment of the United States Constitution. ...

Defendant did not object to the court's failure to instruct the jury that defendant had a privilege pursuant to federal and state law to confine a student in the time-out room, and failed to object to the court's charge regarding the reasonableness of the seizure of Christopher. Thus, defendant failed to preserve for our review its contentions that the charge was improper in those respects. Finally, we conclude that the verdict awarding plaintiff damages of $75,000 is not excessive.

Intentional Infliction of Emotional Distress

The tort of intentional infliction of emotional distress allows for the recovery of damages from persons who have intentionally or recklessly interfered with an individual's **peace of mind**. It is very difficult for plaintiffs to succeed in such suits, largely because the conduct of the defendant must be **outrageous** and **conscience-shocking**, much like the standard in **substantive due process** suits (see Chapter 6).

In the *Peters* case excerpted above, the court found a jury could reasonably conclude that Christopher's repeated confinement in a filthy time-out room was "so outrageous in character, and so extreme in degree, as to go beyond all possible bounds of decency, and to be regarded as atrocious, and utterly intolerable in a civilized community."[9] In the following illustrative case from Nebraska, the deplorable conduct of a music teacher did not meet this standard.

COSTELLO v. MITCHELL PUBLIC SCHOOL DISTRICT 79
US Court of Appeals for The Eighth Circuit
266 F.3d 916 (2001)

ROGER LELAND WOLLMAN, Chief Judge

James and Jamie Costello (the Costellos), and their daughter Sadonya Costello (Sadonya) (collectively, the plaintiffs), appeal from the district court's grant of summary judgment in favor of Mitchell Public School District 79, the school board and superintendent of Mitchell Public Schools, the principal of Mitchell High School (Mitchell or the school), and a teacher at Mitchell (collectively, defendants). We affirm. ...

At the end of her first semester at Mitchell, Sadonya was having difficulty with her band teacher,

---

9 *Citing* Dillon v City of New York, 261 A.D.2d 34 (N.Y. App. Div. 1st. 1999).

Roger Kercher. She testified in her deposition that he daily called her "retarded," "stupid," and "dumb," in front of her classmates. In one instance, after belittling her in front of the class for a bad grade on an assignment in her notebook, he threw the notebook at her, hitting her in the face. During a basketball game in either late December or early January at which the band was playing, Sadonya came to her mother and explained that Kercher had just told her that she could no longer play in the band because she was too stupid and that he did not have to teach students like her and that he would not. Jamie Costello asked Kercher about it, who just laughed and said "yeah, something like that."

Jamie Costello subsequently met with Halley, Yauney, Kercher, and Sadonya's therapist about the problems with band, although Kercher became angry and left the meeting. During the meeting, Jamie Costello asked Sadonya's therapist what she thought about Sadonya remaining in band class, and "she said if Mr. Kercher feels that way, [Sadonya's] not going to gain anything by being in one of his classes." Sadonya was then removed from band and placed in a required music appreciation class, which was also taught by Kercher. Sadonya completed the music appreciation class despite Kercher's comments. Several other students and parents mentioned to Jamie Costello that Kercher had also been verbally, and occasionally physically, abusive toward other students in his classes. ...

In May of 1997, Dr. Mark R. Scanlan, a psychiatrist, wrote a letter to Mitchell, concluding that if Sadonya "returns to school at this point her situation would only worsen, both physically and mentally." Sadonya has been home-schooled since that time. She has suffered from depression and suicidal thoughts and receives counseling and treatment. ...

On November 22, 1999, the district court granted partial summary judgment against the Costellos and Sadonya, holding that the individual defendants were entitled to qualified immunity and dismissing on the merits the intentional infliction of emotional distress claim. On September 14, 2000, the court granted summary judgment in favor of the remaining defendants. ...

E. Intentional Infliction of Emotional Distress

With regard to the intentional infliction of emotional distress claim, the district court concluded that the Costellos and Sadonya had failed to present a genuine issue of material fact under Nebraska law on whether Kercher's actions were so outrageous in character and so extreme in degree as to go beyond all possible bounds of decency.

To constitute intentional infliction of emotional distress, a plaintiff must show (1) that there has been intentional or reckless conduct; (2) that the conduct was so outrageous in character and so extreme in degree as to go beyond all possible bounds of decency and is to be regarded as atrocious and utterly intolerable in a civilized community; and (3) that the conduct caused emotional distress so severe that no reasonable person should be expected to endure it.

Assuming that the plaintiffs have raised a genuine issue of material fact on the first and third parts of the test, we agree with the district court that Kercher's words and conduct, however unprofessional, intemperate, and unworthy of one entrusted with the responsibility of educating students, did not rise to the level that would satisfy part two of the test .... Accordingly, the district court did not err in granting summary judgment in favor of all defendants on the merits of this claim. The judgment is affirmed.

Repeated verbal or physical abuse by teachers or students may readily meet a number of statutory definitions of **bullying** (see Chapter 4) or **harassment** (see Chapter 7). But as the *Costello* case excerpted above illustrates, abusive conduct may not be sufficiently **outrageous** and **conscience-shocking** for an intentional infliction of emotional distress claim to succeed. Note that plaintiffs in intentional infliction of emotional distress cases must also show they suffered psychological trauma as a result of the defendant's outrageous and conscience-shocking conduct.

In *Price v. Scranton School District*,[10] a seventh-grade student in Pennsylvania suffering from recurrent yeast infections unsuccessfully filed intentional infliction of emotional distress claims against school officials, teachers, and students for repeatedly calling her a "bitch," a "skank,"

10 2012 U.S. Dist. LEXIS 1651 (M.D. Pa. Jan. 6, 2012).

a "slut," a "tramp," and a "whore." To establish an intentional infliction of emotional distress claim in Pennsylvania, "the conduct must be so outrageous in character, and so extreme in degree, as to go beyond all possible bounds of decency, and to be regarded as atrocious, and utterly intolerable in a civilized society."[11]

In *DiSalvio v. Lower Merion High School District*,[12] a Pennsylvania court allowed an intentional infliction of emotional distress claim to proceed against a football coach colloquially known as "Chester the Molester." The coach had sexually harassed a student for months, causing her to relapse into bulimia and drop out of school. In *Elizabeth S. v. Oklahoma City Public School*,[13] a district court allowed an intentional infliction of emotional distress claim to proceed against a teacher who had forced a student to engage in oral sex during lunch breaks. In *Spears v. Jefferson Parish School Board*,[14] a gym coach's cruel "joke" on a kindergarten student easily met the standard for establishing an intentional infliction of emotional distress claim. After threatening to "kill" several students, the coach asked two of the boys to "play a trick" on the kindergartener by lying on the floor and pretending to be dead. The kindergartener was subsequently diagnosed with PTSD and anxiety.

Common Law and Statutory Privileges

Defendants are not liable for intentional torts if their actions were **privileged**. Hence defendants in tort suits will often invoke a statutory or common law privilege. While plaintiffs carry the burden of persuading the court that a tort has occurred, defendants have the burden of establishing that they are entitled to one of more of the following privileges:

Correction and Control of a Minor

Sometimes called the privilege of **discipline**, parents and teachers may use **reasonable force** for the **correction and control** of the minor children. This is a statutory privilege that may be invoked in both tort and criminal cases. For example, New York penal law provides as follows:[15]

§ 35.10. Justification; use of physical force generally

The use of physical force upon another person which would otherwise constitute an offense is justifiable and not criminal under any of the following circumstances:

1. A parent, guardian or other person entrusted with the care and supervision of a person under the age of twenty-one or an incompetent person, and a teacher or other person entrusted with the care and supervision of a person under the age of twenty-one for a special purpose, may use physical force, but not deadly physical force, upon such person when and to the extent that he reasonably believes it necessary to maintain discipline or to promote the welfare of such person.

The reasonableness of any disciplinary force deployed in school contexts depends on the age, sex, and physical and mental condition of the student, the nature of the wrongdoing, whether the use

---

11 Hoy v. Angelone, 720 A.2d 745, 754 (Pa. 1998); Buczek v. First Nat'l Bank of Mifflintown, 531 A.2d 1122, 1125 (Pa. 1987).
12 158 F. Supp. 2d 553 (E.D. Pa. June 12, 2001); *later proceeding at* 2002 U.S. Dist. LEXIS 6987 (E.D. Pa. Apr. 19, 2002).
13 2008 U.S. Dist. LEXIS 67099 (W.D. Okla. Sept. 3, 2008).
14 646 So. 2d 1104 (La App. 5th Cir. 1994).
15 NY Penal Law § 35.10 (2012).

of force was necessary to compel obedience, whether the force was proportionate to the offense, and whether the use of force caused serious harm. In *Fort Wayne Community Schools v. Haney*,[16] a teacher nudged a first-grader back into her seat by pushing on her backside. The student had ducked under her desk repeatedly to retrieve erasers she had dropped during a test. The Indiana Court of Appeals affirmed that the use of force was reasonable and that the privilege of discipline applied.

Abuse of the disciplinary privilege is most commonly found in cases in which a student suffers serious physical injury and in cases in which a teacher or school official acts out of **malice**. In addition, school discipline must not be **degrading** or **cruel**. In *Rolando v. School Director of District No. 125*,[17] a teacher who used a cattle prod to discipline students was dismissed on grounds of cruelty. In *Fender v. School District No. 59283*,[18] a teacher who repeatedly slapped students in the face with an open hand and bashed one student's head into a desk was likewise dismissed on grounds of cruelty.[19] Under Illinois law,[20] tenured teachers and principals may be dismissed for conduct that is "cruel, immoral, negligent, or criminal or that in any way causes psychological or physical harm or injury to a student."

In *Ingraham v. Wright*,[21] a divided Supreme Court ruled that **corporal punishment** in public schools does not violate the Eighth Amendment, which prohibits **cruel and unusual punishment**. Moreover, because the reasonable use of corporal punishment in public schools is **privileged** and constrained by the common law, the Court held that the Fourteenth Amendment's due process requirements do not require a hearing or prior notice to parents.

Common law and statutory **privileges** may be limited or extinguished by legislation. In *W.E.T. v. Mitchell*,[22] the court found that a teacher who had used tape to stop an asthmatic child from talking in class could not claim any disciplinary privilege because the "tying, taping, or strapping down of a student" had been specifically prohibited by statute.[23]

Public school officials who successfully invoke a statutory or common law privilege may avoid liability in tort suits, but these privileges may not protect them from penalties associated with violating state and district policies, collective bargaining agreements, state and federal laws (including Section 1983), or the Fourth and Fourteenth Amendments. Hence public school officials should *never* use physical force to discipline students, particularly in the 31 states which have banned corporal punishment.[24] In early 2019, Rep. Alcee Hastings of Florida introduced the *Ending Corporal Punishment in Schools Act* in Congress.[25] If enacted, the proposed legislation would deny federal funding to any school that permits corporal punishment.

Both the right to **bodily integrity** and the **substantive due process** provisions of the Fourteenth Amendment (see Chapter 6) may be violated by school discipline that is "arbitrary, egregious and shocking to the conscience."[26] The Eighth Circuit used similar language in the *Costello* case

---

16 94 N.E.3d 325 (Ind. Ct. App. 2018).

17 358 N.E.2d 945 (Ill. App. Ct. 1976).

18 347 N.E.2d 270 (Ill. App. 1976).

19 *See, e.g.* Flores v. Bd. of Educ. of the City of Chicago, 2019 IL App (1st) 180611-U (2019); Bd. of Educ. of Peoria Pub. Sch. Dist. No. 150 v. Davis, 2015 IL App (3d) 130705-U (2015) [*unpublished*].

20 105 ILCS 5/34-85c (2018).

21 430 U.S. 651 (1977).

22 2008 U.S. Dist. LEXIS 2036 (M.D.N.C. 2008).

23 N.C. Gen. Stat. § 115C-391.1(d)(2) (2005).

24 New Jersey, Massachusetts, Hawaii, Maine, New Hampshire, Vermont, California, Nebraska, Wisconsin, Alaska, Connecticut, Iowa, Michigan, Minnesota, North Dakota, Oregon, Virginia, South Dakota, Montana, Utah, Maryland, Nevada, Washington, Illinois, West Virginia, Rhode Island, Delaware, Pennsylvania, Ohio, and New Mexico (along with the District of Columbia) have banned corporal punishment in public schools. New Jersey and Iowa have also prohibited corporal punishment in private schools.

25 H.R. 727, Ending Corporal Punishment in Schools Act of 2019, 116th Congress (2019-20); available at www.congress.gov/bill/116th-congress/house-bill/727/text (last accessed April 27, 2020).

26 Peterson v. Baker, 504 F.3d 1331 (11th Cir. 2007); *reh'g denied*, 284 Fed. Appx. 805 (11th Cir. 2008).

discussed above,[27] noting that school discipline violates the Fourteenth Amendment if it "either shock[s] the conscience or offend[s] judicial notions of fairness or human dignity." In *Johnson v. Newburgh Enlarged School District*,[28] a teacher grabbed a student by the throat, lifted him off the ground by his neck and dragged him across the gymnasium floor, choked and slammed the student's head against some bleachers four times, punched him in the face, and finally rammed his head into a fuse box. The Second Circuit found this behavior crossed the line. "[This] assault … is conscience-shocking because it constitutes conduct (1) maliciously and sadistically employed in the absence of a discernible government interest and (2) of a kind likely to produce substantial injury," wrote the court. Even in states where corporal punishment has not been statutorily prohibited, it must not be used maliciously or recklessly.[29]

In states and districts where corporal punishment in schools has not been prohibited, it may be difficult for parents to opt their children out. In *Setliff v. Rapides Parish School Board*,[30] a school principal in Louisiana successfully invoked the privilege of discipline after paddling a student for biting a classmate. Because the student's parents had specifically requested that corporal punishment not be used, they sued for battery. The court ruled that "in giving the discretion to use corporal punishment to the school systems, the legislature made no requirement that parents had to first consent to such punishment."

Consent

Consent by the plaintiff to the conduct of the defendant generally precludes liability in a tort suit. This privilege extends only to the specific conduct to which the plaintiff has consented. Consent is not effective if the plaintiff was manipulated or coerced by the defendant, if the plaintiff was dependent on or otherwise vulnerable to the defendant, or if the plaintiff lacked capacity to consent.

Capacity to consent to particular forms of conduct varies by age or level of maturity, so the issue of consent must be evaluated on a case-by-case basis. The general rule in tort is called the **Rule of Sevens**.[31] Below age seven, a minor lacks the capacity to consent to harmful conduct. Between the ages of seven and 13, there is a rebuttable presumption of incapacity to consent. From age 14 on, there is a rebuttable presumption of capacity to consent.

In general, the more serious the harm, the less likely a minor plaintiff in a tort suit will be found to have had the requisite capacity to consent. In education law, this is most evident in cases involving sexual relationships between teachers and students. Any adult who has sexual relations with someone below the statutory age of consent may be charged with **statutory rape**, even if the minor consented, because the consent of a minor is invalid.[32]

Some states apply the statutory age of consent in tort cases, making any adult who engages in sexual relations with a minor both **criminally liable** (for statutory rape) and **civilly liable** (for sexual assault and battery), regardless of consent. In other states, however, the consent of a minor will preclude civil liability, even when the defendant has been found criminally liable for statutory

---

27 Costello v. Mitchell Pub. Sch. Dist. 79, 266 F.3d 916 (8th Cir. 2001).

28 239 F.3d 246 (2d Cir. 2001).

29 Corporal punishment has not been statutorily prohibited in Utah, Wyoming, Colorado, Arizona, Texas, Oklahoma, Kansas, Arkansas, Louisiana, Missouri, Indiana, Kentucky, Tennessee, North Carolina, South Carolina, Georgia, Florida, Alabama, and Mississippi.

30 888 So. 2d 1156 (La. App. 3 Cir. 2004); *rehearing denied*, 896 So. 2d 1011 (2005).

31 *See, e.g.*, D.S. Wendler, *Assent in paediatric research: theoretical and practical considerations*, 32(4) JOURNAL OF MEDICAL ETHICS 229–234 (2006).

32 See, *e.g.*, Campbell v. Hollis Indep. Sch. Dist. No. 66, 2017 U.S. Dist. LEXIS 126996 (W.D. Okla. Aug. 10, 2017); H.S. v. Stroudsburg Area Sch., Dist., 2019 U.S. Dist. LEXIS 12722 (M.D. Pa. Jan. 28, 2019).

rape. Thus, in *Romero v. City of New York*,[33] a math teacher who had pleaded guilty to the statutory rape of a 14-year-old student was not liable for the tort of battery because the student had consented.

Self-Defense and Defense of Others

The privilege of self-defense and defense of others allows the use of **reasonable force** to defend oneself or someone else from **imminent bodily harm**. In some cases, a person may reasonably believe there is danger, even if no danger actually exists. The past conduct, reputation, words, and gestures of plaintiffs can be taken into account in determining if their apprehension of danger was reasonable.

If a teacher reasonably believes a student is about to inflict intentional harm on someone, the privilege will apply. But any force deployed by the teacher must be proportionate to the threat. In *Barry v. Cedar Rapids Community School District*,[34] a teacher slapped a student who had cerebral palsy and epilepsy. The teacher unsuccessfully claimed she was defending herself from flying spittle. In *Landry v. Ascension Parish School Board*, a student attacked a teacher and chased him with a two-by-four. The teacher successfully claimed self-defense when he pulled a gun from the glove compartment of his car and brandished it at the student.[35]

A majority of states allow individuals to **stand their ground** and fight when threatened, even if flight is possible. For example, legislation in Florida provides as follows:[36]

(1) A person is justified in using or threatening to use force, except deadly force, against another when and to the extent that the person reasonably believes that such conduct is necessary to defend himself or herself or another against the other's imminent use of unlawful force. A person who uses or threatens to use force in accordance with this subsection does not have a duty to retreat before using or threatening to use such force.

(2) A person is justified in using or threatening to use deadly force if he or she reasonably believes that using or threatening to use such force is necessary to prevent imminent death or great bodily harm to himself or herself or another or to prevent the imminent commission of a forcible felony. A person who uses or threatens to use deadly force in accordance with this subsection does not have a duty to retreat and has the right to stand his or her ground if the person using or threatening to use the deadly force is not engaged in a criminal activity and is in a place where he or she has a right to be.

Revenge and **retaliation** do not qualify as self-defense.[37] The privilege of self-defense ends when an assailant has been disarmed or defeated, withdraws, or surrenders. Students are not privileged to use force to resist teachers physically enforcing lawful orders. For example, if a teacher orders a student to leave the classroom, the student refuses, and the teacher escorts the student out by the arm, the student is not privileged to use self-defense against the teacher. One may invoke the privilege of self-defense only against *unprivileged* uses of force.

With the encouragement of the Trump Administration, school districts across the country have begun allowing teachers to carry guns.[38] Idaho, Kansas, Louisiana, Missouri, South Dakota,

---

33 839 F. Supp. 2d 588 (E.D.N.Y. 2012).
34 2019 U.S. Dist. LEXIS 42151 (N.D. Iowa Mar. 15, 2019).
35 415 So. 2d 473 (La. Ct. App. 1982).
36 FS 776.012 (2018).
37 *See* Reis-Campos v. Biter, 832 F.3d 968 (9th Cir. 2016).
38 E.L. Green and M. Fernandez, *Trump wants to arm teachers. These schools already do*, New York Times (March 1, 2018). Online at www.nytimes.com/2018/03/01/us/armed-teachers-guns-schools.html (last accessed April 27, 2020).

Tennessee, Texas, and Wyoming allow teachers to carry guns on school property, usually with the permission of their school district.[39] Twenty-eight states allow school resource officers to carry guns, and 25 states empower school districts to permit other school personnel to carry guns.[40] Ten states allow for individuals with concealed weapons permits to carry guns in schools,[41] notwithstanding the federal **Gun-Free Schools Act of 1990**.[42] In 2018, Florida created a $67 million program to arm classroom teachers in the wake of the mass shooting in Parkland.[43] Whether an armed teacher can successfully defend students from an armed attacker remains to be seen. In theory, and in the absence of **Good Samaritan laws** or other statutory immunities, an armed teacher who fails to thwart an armed attack could be liable for **negligence** and other torts.

Defamation

When individuals spread gossip about school officials or students, write bogus reference letters or inaccurate performance evaluations, publish false claims in a website or blog, or make malicious comments about school officials at a public meeting, they may be liable for defamation. The tort of **defamation** involves the publication of **false facts** that cause damage to an individual's **reputation** or **standing** in the community. **Libel** is written defamation and **slander** is spoken defamation, though this distinction has fallen out of use in a number of states.

False Facts

To establish a defamation claim, the defendant must have communicated **false facts** concerning the plaintiff. This element requires more than a minor error or technical untruth.[44] A statement by a school principal that a biology teacher missed class at least once a week for a year would satisfy the **false facts** element if the teacher missed only a handful of classes.

 False facts can also be communicated by **implication**. In one case, a former employer told investigators he "couldn't go into" the reasons for the plaintiff's dismissal, falsely implying that the plaintiff had been terminated for serious misconduct.[45] In *Kennedy v. Richland County School District Two*,[46] a school official sent a confidential email directing that a security officer not be given additional room keys, implying that the officer was responsible for recent thefts. In *Parnigoni v. St. Columba's Nursery School*,[47] a district court found a private school liable for defaming the mother of one of its students by disclosing her husband's sex offender status, implying that she was dangerous by association.

39 K. Dwyer, *Guns in school? Here's a list of states that allow armed teachers*, THE [ALLENTOWN, PA] MORNING CALL (February 14, 2019). Online at www.mcall.com/news/education/mc-nws-guns-in-schools-list-20181108-story.html (last accessed April 27, 2020).

40 Alaska, Arizona, Connecticut, Georgia, Idaho, Indiana, Iowa, Kansas, Kentucky, Louisiana, Massachusetts, Michigan, Mississippi, Montana, Nevada, Ohio, Rhode Island, South Carolina, Texas, New Jersey, New York, Utah, Vermont, and West Virginia.

41 Alabama, Alaska, Idaho, Illinois, Michigan, Missouri, New Hampshire, Oregon, Rhode Island, South Dakota, Utah, and Wyoming.

42 18 U.S.C. 44 § 921 *et seq.*

43 V. Strauss, *Florida legislators take steps to arm teachers — despite opposition from school shooting survivors*, WASHINGTON POST (February 28, 2018). Online at www.washingtonpost.com/news/answer-sheet/wp/2018/02/28/florida-legislators-take-steps-to-arm-teachers-despite-opposition-from-school-shooting-survivors/?noredirect=on&utm_term=.bbb8a09a9eef (last accessed April 27, 2020).

44 Masson v. New Yorker Magazine, Inc., 85 F.3d 1394 (9th Cir. 1996).

45 Frank B. Hall & Co. v. Buck, 678 S.W.2d 612 (Tex. Ct. App. 1984), *cert. denied*, 472 U.S. 1009 (1985).

46 2019 S.C. App. LEXIS 66 (S.C. Ct. App. July 24, 2019).

47 681 F. Supp. 2d 1 (D.D.C. 2010).

Statements of **pure opinion** cannot be defamatory because they do not state facts. A statement such as, "I don't like Ms. Serafini" cannot be proved true or false. Subjective judgments based on facts and conclusions from facts assumed to be generally known cannot be defamatory. **Rhetorical hyperbole** such as, "Mr. Sidhu is the worst teacher in the school" cannot be defamatory, even if it is unreasonable or unfair.[48] Nor is testimony based on **pure hearsay** defamatory—a plaintiff's claim that a third party told him or her that the defendant had made untrue statements.[49] **Humor** and **satire** are protected speech and cannot generally be defamatory. Thus, in *Salek v. Passaic Collegiate School*,[50] a New Jersey court found that the caption, "Not tonight Ms. Salek. I have a headache" under the teacher's photo in the funny pages of the school yearbook was not defamatory.

On the other hand, statements of **mixed opinion** may satisfy the first element of defamation. **Mixed opinions** are statements apparently based on facts not expressly stated, implying that the speaker or writer possesses facts that justify their opinion. A statement such as, "In my opinion, Mr. Hwang is an alcoholic" may be defamatory because it implies a set of facts that may be false. In *True v. Lander*,[51] a former teacher successfully sued the district superintendent for statements he had made to a prospective employer implying that True had received unfavorable evaluations, was uninvolved in school extracurricular activities, and had failed to assist students outside the classroom. The court construed these statements to be opinions implying undisclosed facts.

Distinguishing between **statements of fact** and **opinion** can be difficult, particularly in cases involving **epithets** and **rhetorical hyperbole**. In *Stevens v. Tillman*,[52] the Seventh Circuit found that calling a principal "racist" as part of a campaign to oust her from office was a statement of opinion: "In daily life 'racist' is hurled about so indiscriminately that it is no more than a verbal slap in the face," wrote the court. "It is not actionable unless it implies the existence of undisclosed, defamatory facts …" In *I.G. v. Board of Education of the Aztec Municipal School District*,[53] a student alleged, among other things, that an administrative assistant referred to him as a "butt head" in a text message. "[T]his insulting moniker seems no more subject to being proved false or true than are other forms of 'rhetorical hyperbole' and 'vigorous epithets' that defy provability," wrote the court.

Whether the burden of proof regarding the truth or falsity of an allegedly defamatory statement lies with the plaintiff or defendant varies with the type of case. The Supreme Court has ruled that when the statement involves a matter of **public concern**, the plaintiff must prove that it was false.[54] Thus, in *Williams v. Detroit Board of Education*,[55] the Sixth Circuit denied the defamation claims of a school official alleged to have misappropriated public funds on the ground that his actions were "a matter of public concern, triggering a requirement that he prove that the allegedly defamatory statements [were] false." The school official failed to do this.

Reputational Harm

The second element of defamation requires the defendant's statement to have caused harm to the plaintiff's **reputation** or **standing** in the community. In most states, stating that someone has committed a crime, suffers from a "loathsome disease," is professionally incompetent, or has engaged in serious sexual misconduct may be considered **defamatory** *per se*, meaning the statements are

---

48 Moyer v. Amador Valley Joint Union High Sch. Dist., 275 Cal. Rptr. 494 (Cal. Ct. App. 1990); *see also* Morrow v. Los Angeles Unified School Dist., 57 Cal. Rptr. 3d 885 (Cal. App. 2d Dist. 2007).
49 Bosen v. Manatee County Sch. Bd., 2013 U.S. Dist. LEXIS 44610 (M.D. Fla. Mar. 28, 2013); *citing* Fortson v. Colangelo, 434 F.Supp. 2d 1369 (S.D. Fla. 2006).
50 Salek v. Passaic Collegiate Sch., 605 A.2d 276 (N.J. 1992).
51 513 A.2d 257 (Me. 1986).
52 855 F.2d 394 (7th Cir. 1988), *cert. denied*, 489 U.S. 1065 (1989).
53 2018 U.S. Dist. LEXIS 168710 (D.N.M. Sept. 30, 2018).
54 Milkovich v. Lorain Journal Co., 497 U.S. 1 (1990).
55 306 Fed. Appx. 943 (6th Cir. 2009).

inherently harmful.[56] In *McBride v. School District of Greenville*,[57] the South Carolina Supreme Court allowed defamation *per se* claims to proceed after a school principal asserted that a teacher had "cleaned us out" (*viz.*, she had engaged in theft) after her dismissal.

In the past, falsely describing someone as gay or lesbian was considered defamatory *per se*. But as a district court in California noted in *Greenly v. Sara Lee Corporation*,[58] "The majority of the courts that have previously found an accusation of homosexuality to be [defamatory] *per se* emphasized the fact that such a statement imputed criminal conduct." This rationale was extinguished when the Supreme Court decriminalized same-sex activity between consenting adults in *Lawrence v. Texas*,[59] overruling *Bowers v. Hardwick*.[60] The Supreme Court subsequently recognized same-sex marriage as a fundamental right under the Fourteenth Amendment in *Obergefell v. Hodges*.[61]

Many states have eliminated or restricted the availability of defamation *per se* claims, requiring plaintiffs to prove damages in all defamation suits. This effectively makes previously *per se* claims into *per quod* claims. To establish **defamation *per quod***, plaintiffs must explain how statements could be construed as defamatory in the context in which they were made. The plaintiff must also demonstrate **actual harm**. Unlike *per se* claims, reputational harm cannot be assumed.[62]

Publication

The third element of defamation is **publication**. The defendant must have intentionally made an **unprivileged** and **false statement** to a person or persons other than the plaintiff. Employers sometimes seek to avoid defamation suits by informing employees of the reasons for discipline or dismissal in person. Some employers refuse to provide reference letters, or will provide only letters confirming dates of employment.

The doctrine of **compelled self-publication** holds that when defamatory statements are made to terminated employees, publication will be assumed because employees will be forced to repeat the reasons for their dismissal when seeking re-employment.[63] Not all states recognize this doctrine,[64] particularly if plaintiffs have chosen to make public the contents of their employment records.[65] In *Anderson v. Independent School District*,[66] defamation claims against a school district failed because the plaintiff bus driver, not his employer, had communicated the contents of a letter to third parties implying that he had failed or declined to take a drug test.

Clear Reference

The fourth element of defamation, **clear reference**, means that it must be reasonably apparent that the defendant was speaking about the plaintiff. Statements regarding a group of people can satisfy this element if the plaintiffs can show the statements referred to them as part of the group.

---

56 Restatement (Second) of Torts § 570 (2013).
57 698 S.E.2d 845 (S.C. Ct. App. 2010).
58 2008 U.S. Dist. LEXIS 35472 (E.D. Cal. Apr. 30, 2008).
59 539 U.S. 558 (2003).
60 478 U.S. 186 (1986).
61 135 S. Ct. 2584 (2015).
62 *See* Razavi v. Sch. of the Art Inst. of Chicago, 122 N.E.3d 361 (Ill. App. 1st 2018); Paradis v. Charleston Cty. Sch. Dist., 819 S.E.2d 147 (S.C. Ct. App. 2018).
63 Lewis v. Equitable Life Assurance Soc'y, 389 N.W.2d 876 (Minn. 1986).
64 See, *e.g.*, Mis v. Fairfield Coll. Preparatory Sch., 2018 Conn. Super. LEXIS 6228 (Conn. Super. Ct. June 12, 2018) [*unpublished*]; Dougherty v. Sch. Dist., 772 F.3d 979 (3d Cir. 2014); Knelman v. Middlebury College, 570 Fed. Appx. 66 (2d Cir. 2014).
65 *See* Hughes v. City of Garland, 204 F.3d 223 (5th Cir. 2000); Rawlings v. Houston Indep. Sch. Dist., 2013 U.S. Dist. LEXIS 167747 (S.D. Tex. Nov. 26, 2013).
66 357 F.3d 806 (8th Cir. 2004).

Standard of Fault

The **standard of fault** in defamation suits depends on the status of the plaintiff within the community, the topic of the allegedly defamatory communication, and the relevant state law. If the plaintiff is a **public official** and the topic relates to the official's performance of duty or fitness for office, defamation can be found only if the defendant knew of the falsity of the statement or spoke with reckless disregard of the truth.[67] This same standard, known as **actual malice**, also applies in cases involving **public figures**. In general, cases involving public matters employ the actual malice standard, and private matters employ a lesser standard of fault.

Meeting the **actual malice** standard in defamation suits involving **public figures** can be extremely difficult, as the following case illustrates.

⚖️

LEVESQUE v. DOOCY
US Court of Appeals for the First Circuit
560 F.3d 82 (2009)

NORMAN H. STAHL, Circuit Judge.

Rare is there an opportunity to interrupt today's twenty-four-hour news cycle, fueled by cable television's incessant need for content and the explosion of Internet websites that promptly apprise us of events across the world. This appeal offers such a moment as we pause to review plaintiff-appellant Leon Levesque's claim that defendants-appellees Fox News Network, LLC ("Fox"), Steve Doocy, and Brian Kilmeade defamed him during a show on the Fox News Channel ("FNC"). The district court, after considering Levesque's claims, granted the defendants' motion for summary judgment, and upon careful review, we affirm.

I.

... The parties' dispute arises from a FNC morning program's coverage of an incident in Lewiston, Maine, where Levesque is the superintendent of the Lewiston Public Schools.

On April 11, 2007, a student at Lewiston Middle School placed a bag containing leftover ham on the cafeteria table where Somali Muslim students were sitting for lunch. The Somali students reported the incident to Bill Brochu, a Lewiston police officer stationed at the school. After an investigation of the incident, the middle school's assistant principal suspended the offending student for ten school days, a decision in which the principal concurred. The assistant principal classified the incident as "Hate Crime/Bias" in the school's computer system, and Brochu filed a police report under the direction of his superior officer, characterizing the incident as "Crime: Harassment/Hate Bias." Levesque was informed of the suspension and endorsed the decision.

The following week, while the Lewiston schools were closed for April vacation, Bonnie Washuk, a reporter for the Lewiston *Sun Journal*, contacted Superintendent Levesque to discuss an article she intended to write about the incident. Published on April 19, 2007, ... Washuk quoted Levesque as describing the offending student's conduct as "a hate incident" and acknowledging, "We've got some work to do to turn this around and bring the school community back together ... All our students should feel welcome and safe in our schools." ...

On April 23, four days after the *Sun Journal* ran Washuk's article, Nicholas Plagman uploaded a piece he had written about the April 11 incident to Associated Content, a website platform that permits registered users to publish content on topics of their choosing. While the Plagman article purported to describe the incident as a news story, it mischaracterized some facts, such as reporting that the students left a ham sandwich, rather than ham steak, on the cafeteria table. Similarly, where Washuk reported that the Center was working with the school to create a response plan, Plagman described it as "an anti-ham 'response plan.'"

---

67 New York Times Co. v. Sullivan, 376 U.S. 254 (1964); Harte-Hanks Communications, Inc. v. Connaughton, 491 U.S. 657 (1989).

Plagman also included fictitious quotations which generally built upon those accurately used in Washuk's article. For example, according to Plagman, Levesque stated, "We've got work to do to turn this around and bring the school community back together again. These children have got to learn that ham is not a toy." Plagman also quoted Wessler as stating, "It's extraordinarily hurtful and degrading. They probably felt like they were back in Mogadishu starving and being shot at." Finally, Plagman falsely listed the Associated Press ("AP") as a source. Because Plagman indicated that his story should be housed under Associated Content's "humor" and "news" categories, the article was retrievable through Google News, a computer-generated website that aggregates headlines from news sources worldwide.

Around 3:30 a.m. on April 24, a line producer for FNC's morning news talk show "Fox & Friends" discovered the Plagman article. "Fox & Friends" runs each weekday from 6 a.m. until 9 a.m., its hosts discussing current events, interviewing guests, and reporting the weather. Producers for the show search for compelling stories for the hosts to discuss. The line producer sent the Plagman article to the Fox News Research Department for additional research. An information specialist was able to confirm some of the facts presented in the article …

By 4:15 a.m., the Plagman article and research materials were delivered to three of the show's four co-hosts, including Doocy and Kilmeade. Doocy used Google News to conduct additional research and also found the Plagman article, the Washuk article, and a brief article on the Boston Globe's website which both corroborated the general story of the incident and confirmed that the Center was working with the school on a response plan. The defendants agreed to include the story in that morning's show.

During the three-hour cablecast, the defendants repeatedly raised and discussed the April 11 incident, frequently ridiculing Levesque, ascribing the handling of the incident largely to him. They reported as true several of the fabricated quotations that Plagman attributed to Levesque including the "ham is not a toy" statement and also cited Levesque for the phony statement comparing the incident to Mogadishu, a comment that had been falsely attributed to Wessler in the Plagman article. …

Sometime after the cablecast, Levesque contacted FNC to complain about the show's inaccuracies. On May 16, 2007, "Fox & Friends" issued a retraction and apology, agreeing that various statements attributed to Levesque were fictitious and noting that had the show realized the Plagman article

was not legitimate, it would not have repeated the fabricated statements.

The following month, Levesque filed a complaint asserting libel, libel per se, false light invasion of privacy, and punitive damages, claiming that five statements made by the defendants during the cablecast were defamatory.

First, he took issue with the defendants' claim that he classified the incident as a hate crime. He next objected to the defendants' references to an "anti-ham response plan." Third, Levesque asserted that the repeated mentions of "a ham sandwich" were defamatory. Fourth, he challenged the statement "Leon Levesque—he says, 'These children have got to learn that ham is not a toy.'" Finally, Levesque disputed the defendants' assertion that "the superintendent … says it's akin to making these kids feel like they're being shot at back in Mogadishu and being starved to death."

The defendants moved for summary judgment, contending that the statements were not defamatory and alternatively, that Levesque, who stipulated that he was a public official, could not show that the defendants acted with actual malice in making them.

The district court held that the statements were protected on multiple grounds. … It found the reference to a "hate crime" substantially true and the "anti-ham response plan" quip protected rhetorical hyperbole. The court determined that the references to a ham sandwich, the "ham is not a toy" comment, and the Mogadishu statement were materially false, reasonably susceptible of a defamatory meaning, and highly offensive for purposes of the false light claim. Nevertheless, the court granted the defendants' motion, concluding that Levesque failed to produce evidence that the defendants acted with constitutional malice when making the statements.

II.

… Under Maine common law, a plaintiff alleging defamation must show a false and defamatory statement published without privilege to a third party resulting in harm to the plaintiff. … Meanwhile, discussions of public officials like Levesque deserve constitutionally-protected "breathing space" in a democratic society and thus are subject to a conditional privilege that is overcome only by clear and convincing evidence that the defamatory statement was made with actual malice, in other words "with knowledge that [the statement] was false or with reckless disregard of whether it was false or not." …

A. *Defamatory in Nature*

The district court held that a jury could find defamatory the defendants' attribution to Levesque of two false and absurd quotations—"ham is not a toy" and "it's akin to making these kids feel like they're being shot at back in Mogadishu and being starved to death"—along with repeated references to a "ham sandwich" which included a recreation of the incident. The court found that the defendants' statements that Levesque and the Lewiston Middle School considered the incident to be a potential "hate crime" and the use of the term "anti-ham response plan" were not defamatory, concluding that the former was substantially true and the latter was rhetorical hyperbole. ...

We dispense first with those comments which the district court found non-actionable. ...

We also agree that the defendants' references to an "anti-ham response plan" were not defamatory. Statements that contain "imaginative expression" or "rhetorical hyperbole" are protected. Here, the defendants augmented Washuk's accurate reporting—"the [Center] is working with the school to create a response plan"—with Plagman's creative flourish—"the [Center is] working with the school to create an anti-ham 'response plan.'" This loosely rhyming phrase provided the defendants with a succinct, perhaps distasteful, jingle through which to express their derision, but such a device does not qualify as a provably false statement, capable of a defamatory nature. Further, it "cannot reasonably be interpreted as stating actual facts about [Levesque]" ...

We turn next to those statements which the trial court found defamatory in nature, the defendants' repeated references to a ham sandwich and two fabricated statements attributed to Levesque. While the district court found that the defendants' mischaracterization of the ham placed on the Somali students' table presented a jury question as to whether the remarks were defamatory in nature, we think it is a close question whether the references to a ham sandwich would have a different effect on the mind of a listener than an accurate report about a leftover ham steak. ... However, because our ultimate resolution of this case makes such a determination unnecessary, we do not disturb the district court's findings.

We concur with the district court that a jury reasonably could conclude that the two fabricated statements attributed to Levesque were defamatory. The Supreme Court has observed:[68]

[i]n general, quotation marks around a passage indicate to the reader that the passage reproduces the speaker's words verbatim. They inform the reader that he or she is reading the statement of the speaker, not a paraphrase or other indirect interpretation by an author. By providing this information, quotations add authority to the statement and credibility to the author's work. Quotations allow the reader to form his or her own conclusions and to assess the conclusions of the author, instead of relying entirely upon the author's characterization of her subject ... [T]he attribution may result in injury to reputation because the manner of expression or even the fact that the statement was made indicates a negative personal trait or an attitude the speaker does not hold.

During the "Fox and Friends" cablecast, the hosts persistently ridiculed the Lewiston Public Schools and Levesque for the response to the April 11 incident and emphasized several times two false and particularly ridiculous quotations which they attributed to Levesque, "ham is not a toy" and a comparison of the incident to Mogadishu. The attribution of these comments to Levesque coupled with the defendants' "laughter tinged with contempt," ... encouraged viewers to form negative conclusions about Levesque, thus tending to harm his reputation. Therefore, we agree with the district court that a genuine issue of material fact exists as to whether the statements were defamatory.

B. *Actual Malice*

A public official advancing a defamation claim must show "that the [challenged] statement was made with a high degree of awareness of ... probable falsity." In other words, the defendant must act either with actual knowledge of the falsity or with reckless disregard for the truth. Actual malice then is measured neither by reasonably prudent conduct, nor an industry's professional standards ... Levesque does not suggest that the defendants actually knew the Plagman article provided false information. Thus, he must show "sufficient evidence to permit the conclusion that the defendant[s] in fact entertained serious doubts as to the truth of" the Plagman article and the statements it attributed to Levesque.

Because direct evidence of actual malice is rare, it may be proved through inference and circumstantial evidence. Recklessness amounting to actual

---

68 Masson v. New Yorker Magazine, Inc., 501 U.S. 496 (1991).

malice may be found where a publisher fabricates an account, makes inherently improbable allegations, relies on a source where there is an obvious reason to doubt its veracity, or deliberately ignores evidence that calls into question his published statements.

Levesque contends that the defendants' failure to corroborate the fabricated quotes from the Plagman article coupled with incredulous statements during the cablecast (e.g., "I hope we're not being duped," and "I thought this was a joke") establish that the defendants acted with reckless disregard for the truth. He notes that Fox rushed to broadcast the two-week-old story even though it was not breaking news. … It is true that a more deliberate consideration of the Plagman article should have caused reasonable skepticism about the source and that the defendants were careless in relying on it, but this is an indication of negligence, not actual malice, and Superintendent Levesque faces the heavy burden of providing evidence that the defendants recognized the carelessness with which they were proceeding.

In preparing for the cablecast, the defendants authenticated the April 11 incident and various facts reported in the Plagman article through reputable sources. … In the present case, the two actionable statements attributed to Levesque were certainly absurd, but the Plagman article presented them within larger, accurate comments that could be corroborated with the Washuk article. Further, it is true that the Lewiston incident was not "hot news," but Levesque has offered no evidence that the defendants deliberately limited their investigatory inquiry.

During discovery, the defendants and other Fox employees consistently stated that they believed the Plagman article was reliable, both because it cited the AP and because they corroborated many of the article's facts with other sources. To rebut these assertions, Levesque emphasizes Doocy and Kilmeade's statements during the cablecast expressing incredulity as evidence that the defendants harbored doubts about the veracity of the quotes. In certain contexts,

a statement like "I hope we're not being duped" likely would raise a genuine issue of material fact on the question of actual malice. …

Beyond noting the ridiculous quality of the fabricated quotations and Doocy and Kilmeade's statements of incredulity during the cablecast, Levesque offered no additional evidence, let alone any of "convincing clarity" … to show that the defendants disbelieved or entertained serious doubts about the challenged statements in the Plagman article, an evidentiary burden required at the summary judgment stage … The defendants were negligent in their failure to question adequately the reliability of the Plagman article and conduct further research before attributing the outrageous quotations to Levesque, and like the district court, we hope that this conduct was "an extreme departure from professional standards." … That the negligence was accompanied by derisive contempt and ridicule directed at Levesque makes all the more distasteful the defendants' carelessness. But while the defendants reported as true false statements, they did so after verifying the underlying facts of the April 11 incident. Their vetting process was perhaps too cursory and perfunctory, but no facts indicate that the defendants purposefully avoided the truth, and we think the substantial truth of the story which they reported obviates a finding of actual malice.

The actual malice standard, adopted to ensure a vibrant media check on official action, requires more of Levesque to survive summary judgment. Certainly, as we noted above, "it exacts a … high price from the victims of defamatory falsehood. Plainly many deserving plaintiffs, including some intentionally subjected to injury, will be unable to surmount the barrier of the *New York Times* test."

This action reminds us that in a court of law, sympathy does not always to the victor go. We find that Levesque cannot survive the defendants' motion for summary judgment … [and] affirm the district court's grant of summary judgment.

No Privilege

Even when the first five elements of defamation can be proved, some defendants are **immune** from liability for defamation as a matter of **privilege**. This is the sixth and final element of defamation.

An **absolute privilege** protects individuals from liability for defamation, even for false statements made with malice or intent to harm. An absolute privilege of speech obtains concerning statements made in judicial or legislative proceedings; statements made by certain government executive officers (including district superintendents in some states) in the course of their duties;

statements made with the consent of the person spoken about; and statements made between husband and wife when they are alone. Broadcasters are also immune from suit when a candidate for public office makes a defamatory comment on air.

Qualified or conditional privileges can be forfeited if the speaker goes beyond the scope of the privilege, uses it for reasons other than for which it was created, speaks with the intent of causing harm,[69] or otherwise abuses the privilege. A commonly used standard finds the privilege to have been abused when the defendant knew the defamatory statement to be false or had no reasonable grounds for believing it to be true.[70] Thus, a qualified privilege may be lost because of actual malice, or a reckless or callous disregard for the truth.[71] In all cases, the defendant has the burden of invoking a privilege, while the plaintiff must establish that it was abused.

As noted earlier, school officials may invoke a qualified privilege to monitor, discuss, and attempt to improve the performance of teachers and other school staff. Unsatisfactory performance evaluations are well-recognized as a valid, non-discriminatory basis for adverse employment decisions.[72] But this privilege may be void if a plaintiff can demonstrate actual malice on the part of a school official.[73] In *Santora v. Bedford Central School District*,[74] a teacher was dismissed for drawing a cat in washable ink on the arm of a student with special needs in the presence of other staff members and with the approval of the principal. He successfully filed defamation claims after the principal later sent an email indicating, "I am so disappointed that Andrew, a staff [member] I had trusted so much, would touch one of our students inappropriately" and advising recipients to contact the police if the plaintiff were seen on campus.

Most states extend qualified immunity to public school officials, including principals, board members, and district superintendents. In *Peters v. Baldwin Union Free School District*,[75] a guidance counsellor unsuccessfully filed defamation claims against her school principal for deficiencies he had noted in her performance evaluations. The Second Circuit affirmed that the comments fell "within the scope of an employer's qualified privilege to comment on matters affecting the employment." In *Johnson v. Riverhead Central School District*,[76] a teacher subject to disciplinary proceedings unsuccessfully filed defamation claims against school officials who (a) noted that he had lied about his prior criminal record; and (b) expressed safety concerns after a weapon was found in his vehicle. "Defendants argue that any statements made during the course of the § 3020-a proceedings are protected by privilege," noted the district court, adding, "Defendants are correct."

In *Kirsch v. Board of Education of the Williamsville Central School District*,[77] an assistant superintendent unsuccessfully filed defamation claims against the district superintendent after he remarked that she was on "unpaid leave" during an administrative retreat. The district court observed,

> Plaintiff does not appear to challenge Defendants' invocation of qualified privilege. Thus, in order to survive summary judgment, she is required to raise a triable question of fact whether Martzloff "acted out of personal spite or ill will, with reckless disregard for the statements' truth or falsity, or with a high degree of belief that their statements were probably false."

---

69 Karnes v. Milo Beauty & Barber Shop Co., 441 N.W.2d 565 (Minn. Ct. App. 1989); Manguso v. Oceanside Unified Sch. Dist., 200 Cal. Rptr. 535 (Cal. Ct. App. 1984).
70 Gardner v. Hollifield, 549 P.2d 266 (Idaho 1976).
71 Moss v. Stockard, 580 A.2d 1011 (D.C. 1990).
72 *See* Evans v. Techs. Applications & Serv. Co., 80 F.3d 954, 960 (4th Cir. 1996); *cited in* Wakefield-Brace v. Greenwood Sch. Dist. 50, 2017 U.S. Dist. LEXIS 91146 (D.S.C. June 14, 2017).
73 *See* Diorio v. Ossining Union Free School Dist., 139 A.D.3d 790 (N.Y. App. Div. 2d 2016).
74 2019 N.Y. Misc. LEXIS 2290 (N.Y. Sup. Ct. May 6, 2019) [*unpublished*].
75 320 F.3d 164 (2d Cir. 2003).
76 Johnson v. Riverhead Cent. Sch. Dist., 2018 U.S. Dist. LEXIS 154812 (E.D.N.Y. Sep. 11, 2018).
77 2019 U.S. Dist. LEXIS 44151 (W.D.N.Y. Mar. 15, 2019), *summary judgment granted*, 2019 U.S. Dist. LEXIS 112741 (W.D.N.Y. July 8, 2019).

The evidence in the record indicates that the remark most certainly gave the administrators pause, however, it does not "demonstrate with convincing clarity that statements were made with malice," under either the common law or constitutional standard.

In some states, parents enjoy **absolute immunity** when airing complaints about teachers to school boards. Thus, a New York court ruled that parents enjoyed absolute immunity from a libel suit for claiming in a petition to the school board that a teacher had missed classes, struck a student, threatened bodily harm to a student's mother, accused a student of being a liar without justification, and insulted a student with an ethnic slur.[78] Some states extend only **qualified immunity** to parents.[79] Either way, the privilege may be lost for parents who have engaged in wrongful behavior. In *Posner v. Lewis*,[80] for example, a teacher was forced to resign after his in-laws disclosed that he had had an affair with the mother of one of his students. He sued his in-laws, arguing that their statements to school officials were malicious. His in-laws could not avail themselves of an absolute privilege because they had attempted to blackmail the teacher, disclosing the affair only after Posner had refused to accept a sum of money to relinquish his rights to his newborn daughter.

The **fair report privilege** protects fair and accurate reports of governmental proceedings, official actions, and even non-governmental proceedings on matters of **public concern**. As a district court noted in *Adelson v. Harris*,[81]

> Although the fair report privilege is most commonly asserted by media defendants, it "extends to any person who makes a republication of a judicial proceeding from material that is available to the general public." In Nevada, if the privilege applies, it is "absolute," meaning it "precludes liability even where the defamatory statements are published with knowledge of their falsity and personal ill will toward the plaintiff."

> In order to receive the benefit of the fair report privilege, (1) it must be "apparent either from specific attribution or from the overall context that the article is quoting, paraphrasing, or otherwise drawing upon official documents and proceedings;" and (2) the statement must constitute a "fair and accurate" description of the underlying proceeding.

Once the defendant has made a *prima facie* case for the **fair report** privilege, the burden shifts to the plaintiff to establish substantial inaccuracy or unfairness in the report.

Intentional Interference with Prospective Contractual Relations

Reference letters written by school officials to prospective employers frequently give rise to tort suits. As we have seen, plaintiffs filing defamation claims in these kinds of cases cannot succeed unless the defendant acted with **actual malice** or otherwise abused a **qualified privilege**.

In cases when a school official knowingly and maliciously distorts the truth to prevent a former teacher or staff member from securing a new job, damages may be awarded to compensate the employee for harm done to reputation, loss of earnings, and mental anguish. In extreme cases, punitive damages may also be awarded.

False and malicious recommendations that prevent an applicant from securing a job can also lead to liability under the tort of **intentional interference with prospective contractual relations**

---

78 Weissman v. Mogol, 462 N.Y.S.2d 383 (N.Y. Sup. Ct. 1983).
79 Desselle v. Guillory, 407 So. 2d 79 (La. Ct. App. 1981).
80 2012 N.Y. LEXIS 315 (Feb. 21, 2012).
81 973 F. Supp. 2d 467 (S.D.N.Y. 2013), *aff'd*, 876 F.3d 413 (2d Cir. 2017).

and, in most states, criminal liability under anti-blacklisting statutes. In *Posner v. Lewis*,[82] discussed earlier, the plaintiff filed an **interference with prospective contractual relations** claim against his in-laws for disclosing his affair with the mother of a student to the school board and forcing his resignation.

In the following illustrative case, a district court allowed **interference with prospective contractual relations** claims to proceed against a former chair of the board of a charter school in Philadelphia.

⚖️

AFRIKA v. KHEPERA CHARTER SCHOOL
US District Court for the Eastern District of Pennsylvania
2017 U.S. Dist. LEXIS 38520 (2017)

Opinion by: ANITA B. BRODY

For approximately ten years, Mukasa Afrika worked at Khepera Charter School ("KCS"), a Philadelphia charter school. In July 2014, KCS promoted Afrika to the position of Chief Administrative Officer. Afrika was a contract employee, who was contracted to work for a one-year term that could be renewed annually by a board meeting and executive session.

In July 2015, Afrika began contacting Lauren Iannuccilli at the Charter School Office for the School District of Philadelphia ("Charter School Office"). Afrika reported to Iannuccilli that numerous board meetings were being held out of compliance with the *Sunshine Act* and expressed concern that the Trustees were overreaching into the administration of the school and mismanaging the school's finances.

Throughout the remainder of 2015, Afrika continued to report to Iannuccilli about financial and administrative improprieties occurring at KCS. For instance, on November 23, 2015, Afrika emailed Iannuccilli to report potential financial fraud based on the school's failure to produce the 2013–2014 audit. Afrika also sent this email to the Charter School Office, the Pennsylvania Department of Education, the Office of the District Attorney for the City of Philadelphia and the Auditor General's Office.

Throughout 2015 and 2016, Afrika communicated with the Trustees, the attorney for KCS, and the Chief Financial Officer, regarding his concerns about the mishandling of administrative and financial matters. In discussions with the attorney for KCS, Afrika also asserted his protection under the Pennsylvania Whistleblower Law.

On March 17, 2016, the Trustees sent a letter to Afrika in response to the numerous concerns he had raised about the mishandling and mismanagement of KCS. In the letter, the Trustees told Afrika that they found his "continuous reporting agitating." The "Trustees further reprimanded [Afrika] for not only reporting alleged financial deficiencies and calling for transparency for Defendant KCS's finances, but also for invoking his [w]histleblower protections." The letter concluded: "Desist, and adhere to the duties and responsibilities as outlined in your contract, any other course of conduct will be considered insubordination, and dealt with accordingly going forward."

After Afrika received this letter from the Trustees, he continued to voice his concerns to the them. Additionally, Afrika met with Iannuccilli and representatives of the Charter School Office regarding KCS's incorrect financial statements.

On June 29, 2016, Afrika received a letter signed by Defendant Richard Isaac, the President of the Khepera Charter School Board of Trustees. The letter informed Afrika that the Khepera Charter School Board of Trustees (the "Board") had determined that it was not going to renew his contract as Chief Administrative Officer for the 2016–2017 school year, even though the Board had never met to discuss whether to renew Afrika's employment contract. Rather, Isaac "unilaterally made the decision to terminate [Afrika's] employment."

In 2015, prior to Isaac making this decision, the Charter School Office had notified the Board that Isaac should step down because his term had expired. In response, the Board proposed an amendment to the bylaws to extend Isaac's term of service on the

Board. Accordingly, "[a]t all times material, Defendant Richard Isaac ... [was] the President of the Board."

However, when he made the decision not to renew Afrika's contract, he "act[ed] outside the scope of his authority," and in his "individual capacity." "Isaac was not privileged or justified, but rather, acted maliciously in retaliation for [Afrika's] ongoing reporting to appropriate government agencies." ...

B. Intentional Interference with Prospective Contractual Relations

In order to establish a claim for intentional interference with prospective contractual relations, a plaintiff must prove the following: (1) the existence of a contractual, or prospective contractual relation between the complainant and a third party; (2) purposeful action on the part of the defendant, specifically intended to harm the existing relation, or to prevent a prospective relation from occurring; (3) the absence of privilege or justification on the part of the defendant; and (4) the occasioning of actual legal damage as a result of the defendant's conduct.

Afrika contends that his contract with KCS was not renewed because Khepera Defendants interfered with his prospective contractual relations with KCS. Khepera Defendants argue that Afrika cannot succeed on this claim because the first element of a tortious interference claim requires the existence of a prospective contractual relationship between the complainant and a third party and none of the moving Defendants were third parties to the potential contract. Rather, Khepera Defendants—KCS, the Board, and the Trustees—were all parties to the prospective contract.

In response to Khepera Defendants, Afrika contends only that Isaac was a third party to the contract because, after his term as a board member had expired, he maliciously and unilaterally made the decision not to renew Afrika's contract based on his own personal interest.

Fundamental to an intentional interference claim is the existence of a contractual relationship between the plaintiff and a party other than the defendant. Thus, a corporation cannot tortiously interfere with a contract to which it is a party. "Because a corporation acts only through its agents and officers, such agents or officers cannot be regarded as third parties when they are acting in their official capacities."

Likewise, in a school setting where the contract at issue is an employment contract, a school district employee cannot make a tortious interference with contractual relations claim against a school district's employees, agents, or members of the School Board, because, when acting in their official capacity, they are not "third parties."

A school district employee, agent, or board member can be a third party if he or she acts outside the scope of authority, such as when "the individual's 'sole motive in causing the corporation to breach the contract is actual malice toward the plaintiff, or if the officer's conduct is against the corporation's interest.'"

Under the Pennsylvania Charter School Law, the Board has "the authority to employ, discharge and contract with necessary professional and non-professional employees." As the entity possessing the authority to contract with employees, the Board was clearly a party to any potential contract between KCS and Afrika, as were the Trustees who were acting in their official capacity as board members. Accordingly, as Afrika essentially concedes, KCS, the Board, and all of the Trustees, except Isaac, were parties to Afrika's prospective contract. Therefore, Afrika cannot establish a claim for intentional interference with prospective contractual relations against them.

Unlike the other Trustees, Afrika pleads that Isaac unilaterally and maliciously made the decision not to renew Afrika's contract. Afrika alleges that Isaac made this decision after his term as a board member expired, but that Isaac continued to act as President of the Board and the Board had proposed an amendment to the bylaws to extend Isaac's term.

Afrika additionally alleges that Isaac acted outside the scope of his authority and made the decision in his individual capacity not to renew Afrika's contract. It remains an open question whether Isaac was operating within the scope of his authority when he made the non-renewal decision. At this stage in the litigation, Afrika has sufficiently pled that Isaac was a third party to Afrika's prospective contract. ...

IV. Conclusion

For the reasons set forth above ... I will deny the motion to dismiss the ... intentional interference with prospective contractual relations claim against Isaac.

In theory, a school official who either fails to disclose negative information or misrepresents a former employee could also be held liable for **negligent nondisclosure** or **negligent misrepresentation**.[83]

Invasion of Privacy

Closely related to the tort of defamation, **invasion of privacy** involves

"(1) unreasonable intrusion upon the seclusion of another; (2) appropriation of the name or likeness of another; (3) unreasonable publicity given to private facts; and (4) publicity unreasonably placing another in a false light before the public."[84] The invasive behavior must have been highly offensive to a reasonable person and must have caused mental anguish, shame, or humiliation. The plaintiff must have had a reasonable expectation of privacy in the circumstances.[85] The truth of the private facts is not a defense for the defendant in an invasion of privacy suit as it would be in a defamation suit.

Invasion of privacy claims may be filed if school officials disclose information about teachers or students concerning their sexual behavior, medical history, family problems, school performance, substance abuse, socio-economic status, or other private matters without a legitimate educational purpose. In some situations, the law recognizes a privilege to disclose private facts as a defense in invasion of privacy suits. Educators have a **qualified privilege** to disclose private information about students to other educators on a need-to-know basis. For example, school officials should inform only those who have a need to know about the HIV status of a student or staff member. Invasion of privacy claims are often made in conjunction with other tort claims, particularly in Section 1983 suits against public schools and school officials.

Not everything that staff members might wish to keep secret is considered a private matter by law. In *Trout v. Umatilla County School District*,[86] school officials spoke with the media about an alcohol-related accident involving three teachers. An Oregon appellate court reversed a verdict of invasion of privacy against the school officials because both the accident and the school district's campaign to stop drinking were public knowledge. In *Bellevue John Does 1–11 v. Bellevue School District No. 405*,[87] 15 teachers sought to stop their school district from releasing their names to a newspaper for a report on sexual misconduct against students. The Washington Supreme Court held that the names of teachers could be released "only when alleged sexual misconduct was substantiated or when that teacher's conduct resulted in some form of discipline, even if only a reprimand" under the state's public disclosure laws.

Invasion of privacy may also be claimed in connection with unreasonable or unjustified searches, including the drug testing of teachers and prospective teachers. In *Jones v. Graham County Board of Education*,[88] the North Carolina Court of Appeals affirmed that the privacy interests of teachers outweighed the school board's interest in conducting suspicionless drug and alcohol tests. However, in *Friedenberg v. School Board of Palm Beach County*,[89] the Eleventh Circuit reached the opposite conclusion for prospective substitute teachers.

---

83 Randi W. v. Muroc Joint Unified Sch. Dist., 929 P.2d 582 (Cal. 1997); *see also* Davis v. Bd. of County Comm'rs of Dona Ana County, 987 P.2d 1172 (Ct. App. N.M. 1999) and C.A. v. William S. Hart Union High School Dist., 53 Cal. 4th 861, 138 Cal. Rptr. 3d 1 (Cal. 2012).

84 People for Ethical Treatment of Animals v. Bobby Berosini, Ltd., 895 P.2d 1269 (Nev. 1995); Casillas v. Clark County Sch. Dist., 2013 U.S. Dist. LEXIS 70503 (D. Nev. May 17, 2013).

85 *See* Doe v. Boyertown Area Sch. Dist., 276 F. Supp. 3d 324 (E.D. Pa. 2017).

86 712 P.2d 814 (Or. 1985).

87 189 P.3d 139 (Wash. 2008).

88 677 S.E.2d 171 (N.C. App. 2009).

89 911 F.3d 1084 (11th Cir. 2018).

In *Brown-Criscuolo v. Wolfe*,[90] a teacher successfully sued her district superintendent for **invasion of privacy** after he accessed her email account without permission. The superintendent argued he had a right to read the plaintiff's emails because they were school-related. The Court rejected these arguments, noting that "even if the Defendant had a right to 'know about' the communication, [this] does not necessarily mean he has a right to access another's email account so that he could read it." In *Doe v. Dearborn Public Schools*,[91] a district court allowed invasion of privacy claims to proceed against a principal who had placed video cameras in a staff office adjacent to a locker room used by coaches and students. However, in *Doe v. Boyertown Area School District*,[92] the Third Circuit denied invasion of privacy claims by students challenging a district policy permitting transgender students to use the locker rooms and restrooms of their choice.

Student Records

In 1974, Congress enacted the **Family Education Rights and Privacy Act** (FERPA), sometimes called the **Buckley Amendment**.[93] The Act is designed to protect the privacy of students and ensure fairness in the keeping and use of school records. School records include most materials directly related to students and maintained by the school district. However, certain types of records are not included, such as the personal instructional records of teachers kept in their sole possession and shown only to substitute teachers; records of the law enforcement unit of a school district; and the records of physicians, psychiatrists, psychologists, or other recognized healthcare professionals or paraprofessionals, made, maintained, or used only in connection with the treatment of a student. The Supreme Court has ruled that FERPA is not violated by the practice of letting students grade each other's tests.[94]

All rights conferred by the Act belong to parents until the child reaches 18 years of age, after which they belong to the former child and no longer to the parents. The Act requires that parents, including non-custodial natural parents,[95] be granted access to all records maintained by the school concerning their children within a reasonable period of time, in no case more than 45 days after requesting it. After inspecting the records, parents have a right to request the modification of any portion they believe false, misleading, or invasive of the privacy or other rights of their children. If the school refuses to modify the record, parents must be given a full and fair hearing before an impartial hearing officer to decide whether the record will be changed. At the hearing, each side may be represented by counsel, present evidence, call witnesses, and cross-examine the other's witnesses. The hearing officer must render a decision in writing based solely on the evidence and testimony presented at the hearing with nothing outside the record considered. Should the parents prevail, the school must modify the record in accordance with the hearing officer's findings. Even if the school prevails, parents must still be allowed to add a statement to the record presenting their side of the story.

In addition to making school records available to parents, FERPA requires that they be kept confidential from all others, with certain specified exceptions. Records may be shown to educators within the school system who have a legitimate educational interest in them, but a log must be kept of all those viewing the record. Records may be sent to other schools in which the

90 601 F. Supp. 2d 441 (D. Conn. 2009).
91 Doe v. Dearborn Public Schools, 2008 U.S. Dist. LEXIS 25514 (E.D. Mich. Mar. 31, 2008).
92 897 F.3d 518 (3d Cir. 2018), *cert. denied*, 139 S. Ct. 2636 (2019).
93 20 U.S.C. § 1232h; 34 C.F.R. § 99. 1–99.8.
94 Owasso Indep. Sch. Dist. No. I–011 v. Falvo, 534 U.S. 426 (2002).
95 Matter of Unido R., 441 N.Y.S.2d 325 (N.Y. Fam. Ct. 1981).

student seeks to enroll or in response to a subpoena, but in such cases, parents must be notified. Schools may disclose personally identifiable information to appropriate parties in connection with an emergency if the information is necessary to protect the health or safety of the student or other individuals. Records may also be shown to state and federal education agencies for research and statistical purposes. Otherwise, records must not be released without written permission of the parents, except that the school may, if it wishes, provide "directory" information such as names, addresses, fields of study, activities, and awards.

The Supreme Court has ruled that *FERPA* does not create a private right of action, meaning that an individual may not sue a school either directly or under Section 1983 for violations of *FERPA*.[96] However, school districts may have their federal funds withheld by the Secretary of Education, and educators may be liable if statements contained in student records are defamatory or invasive of privacy.

Reporting Child Abuse

Conservative estimates suggest more than a million children are abused each year in this country. The child abuse death rate in the US is higher than anywhere else in the industrialized world.[97] In response, all 50 states have enacted statutes requiring that cases of actual or suspected child abuse be reported to various authorities. Although these laws vary from state to state, they tend to embrace a broad definition of child abuse, including physical and emotional abuse, neglect and abandonment, incest, sexual molestation, and sexual exploitation, including using children for pornographic purposes.

The duty to report suspected child abuse generally extends to health practitioners and teachers, school administrators, and other school personnel. In addition to those required to report suspected child abuse, any person with reasonable cause to suspect that a child was abused may make a report. Reports must be made to a specifically designated state agency responsible for child protective services. In some states, the law also requires that school employees notify the person in charge of the school or a designated agent, who then becomes responsible for making the report. Every school is expected to maintain an internal system for processing child abuse reports.

To allay fears of legal reprisals, the law grants immunity from civil and criminal liability to individuals who report child abuse. In some states, the immunity is **absolute**, meaning there is no liability even for maliciously and knowingly submitting a false report.[98] In other states, immunity is granted only for reports made in good faith. Good faith will be presumed if reporters were "acting in discharge of their duties and within the scope of their employment" without "willful misconduct or gross negligence."[99] In *Wenk v. O'Reilly*,[100] the Sixth Circuit denied qualified immunity to a school official who had filed a false child abuse report to retaliate against a parent seeking to have his daughter's education plan changed.

Despite the availability of legal immunity, educators often hesitate to make child abuse reports. As the 2011 scandal at Penn State made clear, failure to report suspicions of child abuse can have

96 Gonzaga Univ. v. Doe, 536 U.S. 273 (2002).
97 N. Antelava, *US Child Abuse 'worst in developed world,'* BBC News (October 17, 2011). Online at http://news.bbc.co.uk/today/hi/today/newsid_9617000/9617401.stm (last accessed April 27, 2020); N. Antelava, *Child dies in US 'every five hours,'* BBC News (October 17, 2011). Online at www.bbc.co.uk/news/world-us-canada-15331102 (last accessed April 27, 2020).
98 Storch v. Silverman, 186 Cal. App. 3d 671 (Cal. Ct. App. 1986); Stecks v. Young, 45 Cal. Rptr. 2d 475 (Cal. App. 4th Dist. 1995).
99 N.Y. SOC. SERV. LAW § 419.
100 783 F.3d 585 (6th Cir. 2015).

serious consequences,[101] prolonging the suffering of child victims and exposing educators to criminal prosecution, termination, and public disgrace. Civil liability is also possible for child abuse that would not have occurred or continued but for the failure of an educator to report it. Whether or not it is a legal requirement, there is a moral imperative to file a report with the appropriate authorities whenever child abuse is suspected.

Negligence

Negligence suits filed by persons injured on school property constitute the most common type of litigation involving public and private schools. **Negligence** can be defined as the failure to exercise reasonable care resulting in foreseeable harm to another person. Ordinary negligence is not a crime, but some negligent acts can expose a person both to civil liability in tort and separate criminal negligence charges.

To succeed with a **negligence** claim, plaintiffs must establish the following four elements:

1. The defendant must have owed a **duty of care** to the plaintiff;
2. The defendant must have **breached** their duty of care;
3. The defendant's action or inaction must have **caused harm** to the plaintiff; and
4. The harm must have been both **foreseeable** and **compensable**.

Duty and Standard of Care

Despite the fears of many school officials, not all accidents or injuries in schools give rise to liability in negligence. Negligence can be found only in connection with behavior that "falls below the standard established by law for the protection of others against unreasonable risk of harm."[102] The generally applicable standard of behavior established by statute or common law in most situations is that of **a reasonable person acting prudently in the circumstances**. Thus, in order to avoid a finding of negligence, every person has a duty to act as a hypothetical reasonable person would.

If a person fails to live up to this duty and someone suffers compensable harm as a result, there may be liability for negligence. However, the harm must have been foreseeable. **Foreseeability** is central to negligence. Where harm is foreseeable, a reasonable person would take care to avoid or prevent it. Thus, a school bus driver would be liable for injuries caused by her own carelessness behind the wheel, but she would not be liable for an accident resulting from a sudden heart attack (unless she had a history of heart trouble).

Teachers are expected to do a better job of protecting students from injury than ordinary citizens. For example, if visiting grandparents ignored a student throwing beakers from a classroom window, this would not fall below the applicable standard of care. However, if teachers assigned to supervise the playground ignored a student throwing beakers from a classroom window, this would fall below the applicable standard.

Breach of Duty

Determining whether the standard of care has been breached in particular cases generally turns on the **foreseeability** of the injury sustained by the plaintiff. But the mere existence of an injury is

---

101 *See* Freeh, Sporkin & Sullivan, LLP, Report Of The Special Investigative Counsel Regarding The Actions Of The Pennsylvania State University Related To The Child Sexual Abuse Committed By Gerald A. Sandusky (2012); *see also* Paterno v. Pa. State Univ., 688 Fed. Appx. 128 (3d Cir. 2017) [*unpublished*].
102 Rogers v. Christina Sch. Dist., 73 A.3d 1 (Del. 2013).

not proof of a breach of duty. As noted earlier, school officials are not expected to prevent every conceivable injury. They have a duty to take reasonable precautions designed to prevent foreseeable injuries. Nor is the absence of a teacher when an injury occurs in itself proof of breach of duty. School officials are not ordinarily required to supervise every student every minute of the school day, although the longer students are left unsupervised, the more likely it becomes that a court will find a **breach of duty**.

Different school activities pose different sets of known dangers, and appropriate precautions must be taken accordingly. Students must be properly instructed in the performance of potentially dangerous activities in advance. Supervision and precautions must increase if past occurrences indicate an increased likelihood of danger. The age, capacity, and past behavior of students are also relevant to the foreseeability of danger. The likelihood of a finding of breach of duty is increased if a state law, regulation, or a school's own policy is violated. Ultimately, however, the determination of foreseeability and breach of duty occurs on a case-by-case basis.

The following are examples of cases in which school officials were found to have breached their duty of care:

- In *L.E. v. Plainfield Public School District*,[103] the defendant school district was found liable in negligence after a student was sexually assaulted by classmates during an unsupervised gym class.
- In *Fenrich v. Blake School*,[104] the Minnesota Supreme Court allowed negligence claims to proceed against a private school after a student caused a fatal accident while driving a volunteer coach and several teammates to a cross-country skiing event.
- In *Verhel v. Independent School District*,[105] the defendant school district was found liable for negligent supervision after 12 cheerleaders were injured in a car accident while "bannering" the homes of football players early in the morning.
- In *Ackerman v. Franklin Township Board of Education*,[106] a New Jersey appellate court allowed negligent supervision claims to proceed against the defendant school board after a sixth-grade student was injured on a merry-go-round at recess.
- In *District of Columbia v. Doe*,[107] a student was abducted from school by an intruder and raped. The doors of the school were not locked, even though there was a history of sexual assaults and other violent crimes in the neighborhood.
- In *Roberts v. Robertson County Bd. of Education*,[108] a student was injured by a drill press after the teacher, who had neither properly instructed students nor provided safety warnings, left the shop area to buy a drink.
- In *Kush v. Buffalo*,[109] a 15-year-old student stole chemicals from an unlocked chemistry lab and dropped them in bushes outside the school. The chemicals were found by an eight-year-old who was badly burned when he put a match to them.
- In *Dworzanski v. Niagara-Wheatfield Central School District*,[110] a student was injured when another student slid down a "slide pole" and landed on him five minutes into a supervised recess period.

103 194 A.3d 105 (N.J. App. Div. 2018).
104 920 N.W.2d 195 (Minn. 2018).
105 359 N.W.2d 579 (Minn. 1984).
106 2014 N.J. Super. Unpub. LEXIS 2978 (N.J. App. Div. December 30, 2014) [*unpublished*].
107 524 A.2d 30 (D.C. 1987).
108 692 S.W.2d 863 (Tenn. Ct. App.1985).
109 449 N.E.2d 725 (N.Y. 1983).
110 89 A.D.3d 1378 (N.Y. App. 4th Div. 2011).

- In *Cureton v. Philadelphia School District*,[111] negligence claims against the defendant school district were allowed to proceed after a 13-year-old lost part of his index finger while attempting to dislodge his untucked shirttails from the pulleys of a scroll saw in shop class.
- In *Mirand v. City of New York*,[112] a student threatened another student and subsequently attacked her. There were no security personnel in their assigned locations at the relevant times.
- In *T.M. v. Detroit Public Schools*,[113] a district court allowed negligence claims to proceed after a school bus driver allowed students to disembark at an unauthorized stop. The students then assaulted a sixth-grade student.
- In *Bell v. Board of Education of New York*,[114] a student attending a school-sponsored event in a park was given permission to buy lunch at a nearby pizzeria. While the student was in the pizzeria, her class left the park. The student was accosted and raped while walking home alone.
- In *Eisel v. Board of Education of Montgomery County*,[115] two school counselors were informed by a student's friends that the student intended to kill herself, but the counselors did not notify the student's parents. The student subsequently committed suicide.
- In *Tyrrell v. Seaford Union Free School District*,[116] a district court allowed negligence claims to proceed after a student was drugged and made to perform sexual acts with another female student. Images of the assault were later displayed as "wallpaper" on classroom computer screens, despite the district's commitment to keep pornography off its computers.

Public policy does not require that school boards or school officials be insurers against any and all harms that might befall students. Constant supervision is not required. Avoiding liability in negligence requires the care that a reasonable and prudent person would take in the circumstances. When unusual dangers exist, special caution must be employed. This duty extends to principals, teachers, bus drivers, and all other school personnel having care and control of students.

School officials in public and private schools have a common law duty to ensure adequate levels of supervision in light of the age and capacities of the students in their charge. Similarly, they have a duty to provide safe shop, laboratory, and gym equipment and proper instruction and warnings regarding the performance of potentially dangerous tasks. State health and safety regulations must be enforced as well as the school's own rules. Appropriate medical care should be provided in the case of accidents. If supervision is undertaken when not required by law, it must still meet legal standards of adequacy.

Legal Cause

In all states, the law imposes liability only for harms that are closely associated with negligent acts or omissions. Different states interpret the notion of legal causation differently, and it is not always easy to reconcile cases even within the same state. Generally, a finding of **legal cause** requires that two conditions be met:

(1) **Causation in fact**: The injury must be a result of the negligent party's act; and
(2) **Proximate cause**: The act must be sufficiently connected to the injury to be considered its cause.

---

111 798 A.2d 279 (Pa. Commw. Ct. 2002).
112 637 N.E.2d 263 (N.Y. 1994).
113 2016 U.S. Dist. LEXIS 96983 (E.D. Mich. July 26, 2016).
114 687 N.E.2d 1325 (N.Y. 1997).
115 597 A.2d 447 (Md. 1991); *see also* Grant v. Bd. of Trustees of Valley View Sch. Dist., 676 N.E.2d 705 (Ill. App. Ct. 1997); *but see* Carrier v. Lake Pend Oreille Sch. Dist. No. 84, 134 P.3d 655 (Idaho 2006).
116 2010 U.S. Dist. LEXIS 30113 (E.D.N.Y. February 9, 2010).

The term "**proximate cause**" is often also used synonymously with "**legal cause**" to encompass both requirements.

The "**but-for**" **test** is widely used to determine causation in fact: Would the injury have occurred but for the act or omission of the defendant? Or would the injury have occurred regardless? For example, school officials decide not to erect a fence around the playground. A cement truck driver loses control and enters the playground, killing a student. In this example, the lack of a fence is not the proximate cause of the student's death because the cement truck would have hit the student whether there was a fence to crash through or not.

Even when the "**but-for**" **test** is met, courts sometimes decline to find proximate cause for reasons of fairness or public policy, particularly when the cause of an injury is overly remote. **Remoteness** is a function of time, space, or intervening events. For example, Joanne is walking around the chemistry lab with a beaker filled with an explosive liquid. The teacher, Ms. Zafiris, is in the supply closet for a half hour. Ali, a student known for horseplay, pushes Joanne. The beaker falls and sets off an explosion. The impact of the explosion knocks a ceramic vase off a shelf in another room across the hall. The vase hits the floor, breaks, and sends ceramic shards into Kwame's eyes. Kwame then files a negligence suit against Ms. Zafiris and the school board.

Arguably the prolonged absence of Ms. Zafiris is the "but-for" cause of the accident. Had she been present, she might have prevented Joanne from walking around with the dangerous liquid. She might have controlled Ali's horseplay. But should her actions be considered a proximate cause of Kwame's injury? As a matter of public policy and fairness, are people to be held liable for any bizarre chain of events their behavior might set into motion? How proximate does a cause have to be? Generally, courts do not find proximate cause in cases like the one described.[117] However, there is no set rule for determining when an act or omission is sufficiently closely connected to a consequence to be considered its proximate cause.

The above hypothetical also raises the issue of **intervening causes**. Suppose a defendant's carelessness causes an injury but someone else's action or inaction contributes to that harm. Generally, the courts will hold the defendant liable even in the face of an intervening cause if the intervening cause was itself foreseeable. Thus, it would be reasonable for a teacher who leaves a candle burning on her desk to foresee that a student might push another student into the flame or knock the candle over and start a fire. Similarly, it would be reasonable for a teacher who shirks his hall monitoring duties in a school in a high-crime neighborhood to foresee that an intruder might enter the school and harm a student. On the other hand, it would not be reasonable for a teacher who sends her students to the playground without proper supervision to foresee that they might be injured by a truck crashing through the fence.

In *Palella v. Ulmer*,[118] a 14-year-old student left school in the middle of the day to go joyriding. A high-speed police chase and crash resulted in serious injuries. The student's parents unsuccessfully argued that the accident would not have occurred but for the school's failure to notify them of their son's truancy. In *Fagan v. Summers*,[119] a student threw a small rock that hit a larger rock on the ground and ricocheted, striking another student in the eye. The supervising teacher had just walked past this group of boys when the incident occurred. The court ruled that

> [w]here the time between an act of a student and injury to a fellow student is so short that the teacher had no opportunity to prevent injury, it cannot be said that negligence of the teacher is a proximate cause of the injury.

---

117 *See* Palsgraf v. Long Island R.R. Co., 162 N.E. 99 (N.Y. 1928).

118 518 N.Y.S.2d 91 (N.Y. Sup. Ct. 1987); *see also* Kazanjian v. Sch. Bd., 967 So. 2d 259 (Fla. Dist. Ct. App. 4th Dist. 2007).

119 Fagan v. Summers, 498 P.2d 1227 (Wyo. 1972); *but see* Dworzanski v. Niagara-Wheatfield Central School District, 89 A.D.3d 1378 (N.Y. App. 4th Div. 2011).

Compensable Harm

In addition to establishing a **breach of a duty of care** and **legal cause,** the plaintiff must establish both the existence of an injury and the monetary value of that injury. If a previous injury of the plaintiff is aggravated by the defendant, the defendant is liable only for the additional loss. Plaintiffs can receive compensation for property damage, physical injury (including past and future medical expenses), lost earnings, pain and suffering, loss of consortium, and emotional distress. Most courts do not permit recovery for emotional distress unaccompanied by physical injury or illness.

Affirmative Defenses

Even if all four elements of negligence are established, a defendant's liability may be eliminated or reduced by the availability of an **affirmative defense.** While plaintiffs carry the burden of persuading the court that negligence has occurred, defendants have the burden of establishing their entitlement to one of more of the following affirmative defenses.

Contributory Negligence

If an adult plaintiff's own carelessness contributed in part to an injury, the defendant may not be held fully liable. The principles of proximate cause apply to the contributory negligence defense. Historically, contributory negligence was a **complete defense;** no plaintiffs could recover any damages if their injuries could be attributed in part to their own carelessness. However, this is no longer the case in the vast majority of states.

The standard of care expected of a minor depends on the child's age, experience, and capacities. In *Foster v. Nash-Rocky Mount County Board of Education,*[120] a teacher was not liable in negligence for failing to prevent a seven-year-old with special needs from sustaining head injuries after slipping in a toilet stall.

A ten-year-old and a 17-year-old will not necessarily be held to the same standard in terms of avoiding foreseeable risk. In some states, children below the age of seven are presumed incapable of contributory negligence. The **contributory negligence** defense may be effective in cases where older students disobey express instructions from teachers regarding the use of dangerous equipment,[121] or if older students mix chemicals just to see what might happen or with the deliberate intention of building an explosive device.[122] Contributory negligence may not be asserted when a minor student is sexually abused by a teacher, because a minor "lacks the capacity to consent and is under no legal duty to protect herself from the sexual abuse."[123]

Comparative Negligence

The contributory negligence doctrine can produce an unfortunate outcome: Slight negligence on the part of a plaintiff can let a more negligent defendant off the hook. Hence, an increasing majority of states have adopted the **comparative negligence** doctrine. Comparative negligence holds that plaintiffs whose negligence has contributed to their own injuries can recover damages

120 665 S.E.2d 745 (N.C. Ct. App. 2008).
121 Izard v. Hickory City Sch. Bd. of Educ., 315 S.E.2d 756 (N.C. Ct. App. 1984).
122 Wilhelm v. Bd. of Educ. of New York., 227 N.Y.S.2d 791 (N.Y. App. Div. 1962); Hutchinson v. Toews, 476 P.2d 811 (Or. Ct. App. 1970).
123 Christensen v. Royal Sch. Dist., 124 P.3d 283 (Wash. 2005); Hendrickson v. Moses Lake Sch. Dist., 428 P.3d 1197 (Wash. 2018).

only for what can be attributed to the negligence of the defendant. Comparative negligence does not totally bar recovery by the plaintiff, but it reduces the damages in proportion to the plaintiff's fault. Some states have modified comparative negligence rules to bar recovery if the plaintiff's negligence was greater than the defendant's.

In *Marcantel v. Allen Parish School Board*,[124] a seventh-grade student broke his leg playing a pickup game of tackle football in violation of school rules. A teacher was found to be negligent for not stopping the game, but the court also found that the students were old enough to know that tackling could cause injury. The court pegged the percentage of fault attributable to the teacher and school board at five percent. In *T.D. v. Des Moines Independent Community School District*,[125] a jury verdict of $60,000 to a student whose fingers had been severed in shop class, discounted by the student's comparative negligence of 45 percent, was affirmed.

Assumption of Risk

The assumption of risk defense is generally limited to negligence suits arising in the context of athletic activities and sports. It is not available as a defense in other circumstances in which negligence is alleged. Hence in *Trupia v. Lake George Central School District No. 53*,[126] a case involving an 11-year-old student injured while engaging in "horseplay" on a banister, the defendant school board was not allowed to invoke assumption of risk because "horseplay" is not an athletic activity or sport.

Assumption of risk is not available if the plaintiff was coerced or otherwise given no choice but to participate. Hence, in *Stoughtenger v Hannibal Central School District*,[127] the district could not claim assumption of risk when a 125-pound student was injured while wrestling a 220-pound student in a compulsory physical education class.

Students can consent only to the risks normally associated with participation in a particular sport. Assumption of risk is not available where a higher than normal level of risk is present, or where plaintiffs were not advised of higher than normal risks associated with their participation in a sport or athletic activity.[128] For example, athletes cannot assume the risks associated with substandard or improperly maintained equipment. In *Viola v. Carmel Central School District*,[129] a case involving a tenth-grade softball player who injured her foot sliding into an improperly positioned base plate, the defendant board could not invoke assumption of risk. In *Morgan v. State*,[130] a case involving a tennis player who tripped on a torn net, the defendants could not invoke assumption of risk. In *Simmons v. Saugerties Central School District*,[131] a case involving a student who tripped in a pothole while playing touch football during recess, the district could not invoke assumption of risk.

In the following illustrative case, a student unsuccessfully sued her school district for negligence after she was injured in a voluntary teacher-student basketball game. Among other things, this case illustrates both the assumption of risk principle and our earlier assertion that the mere existence of an injury is not proof of a breach of duty.

---

124 Marcantel v. Allen Parish Sch. Bd., 490 So. 2d 1162 (La. Ct. App. 1986).
125 881 N.W.2d 469 (Iowa Ct. App. 2016).
126 927 N.E.2d 547 (N.Y. App. 2010).
127 90 A.D.3d 1696 (N.Y. App. 2011).
128 *See* Benitez v. New York City Bd. of Educ., 541 N.E.2d 29 (N.Y. App. 1989).
129 95 A.D.3d 1206 (N.Y. App. 2012).
130 685 N.E.2d 202 (N.Y. App. 1997).
131 82 A.D.3d 1407 (N.Y. App. 2011).

C.H. v. RAHWAY BOARD OF EDUCATION
Superior Court of New Jersey, Appellate Division
209 A.3d 222 (2018)

ROBERT J. GILSON, J.A.D.

Plaintiff C.H. was injured while playing in a student-teacher fundraising basketball game. She appeals from an August 23, 2017 order granting summary judgment and dismissing her claims against defendants, who were her school, the school board, and a teacher.

We affirm because the undisputed facts establish that defendants did not breach a duty of care to plaintiff.

I

We take the facts from the summary judgment record and view them in the light most favorable to plaintiff. In June 2013, plaintiff was fourteen years old, in eighth grade, and a member of her school basketball team. On June 11, 2013, plaintiff participated in a basketball game in which a team of teachers played against a team of students. The game was an annual fundraising event, and student participation was voluntary. Approximately fifteen teachers and school safety officials and seventeen students participated in the game. The game was officiated by at least one referee. There were also five other teachers who did not play in the game, but attended to provide supervision.

During the game, plaintiff went up for a rebound, and made contact with defendant Garry Martin, who was a teacher. Plaintiff landed awkwardly, fell, and injured her knee. At her deposition, plaintiff described how her injury occurred:

Everyone swarm[ed] in, but the teacher [came] running down, like, I guess, because he wanted to get the ball, and it was offensive rebound I was going for. And he went up, I went up. But he shoved me, like, to get me out of the way so that he could get the rebound. And when I came down I had to stop myself from falling. And I couldn't plant right.

Defense counsel questioned plaintiff further as to the details of the events that preceded her injury. Specifically, counsel asked and plaintiff answered:

[Counsel] [I]f I understood your testimony, when you went up, everybody close to the basket went up also?
[Plaintiff] Yes. ...
[Counsel] So you are going up for the rebound, and contact is made?
[Plaintiff] Yes.
[Counsel] And do you know who made contact with you?
[Plaintiff] Mr. Martin.
[Counsel] And where was Mr. Martin when he made contact with you?
[Plaintiff] On my left side. ...
[Counsel] Mr. Martin is to your left. Is he even with you?
[Plaintiff] No. He's on an angle.
[Counsel] Is he on an angle in front of you or behind you?
[Plaintiff] Yes, in front of me.
[Counsel] So he's closer to the basket?
[Plaintiff] Yes. ...
[Counsel] So as he's in front of you to the left and he's going up for the rebound and you're going up for the rebound, what happens?
[Plaintiff] He shoves back to try to rip through.
[Counsel] When you say "he shoves back," does he push his body backwards to create more space between him and the rim?
[Plaintiff] Yes.

In October 2015, plaintiff, through her guardian ad litem, filed a complaint against Martin, her school, and the school board. Thereafter, she amended her complaint.

In her amended complaint, plaintiff asserted claims for negligence and intentional conduct and she and he guardian ad litem sought damages related to plaintiff's knee injury. The parties engaged in and completed discovery. Thereafter, defendants moved for summary judgment.

The trial court heard oral arguments and, on August 23, 2017, the court issued a written opinion and entered an order granting summary judgment to defendants. The court first determined that plaintiff had failed to present evidence that defendants had engaged in negligent supervision. In that regard, the court found that the game was officiated by a referee and there were approximately five teachers, who did not participate in the game, but who attended to provide supervision. The court went on to reason that there was no showing that plaintiff's injury, which occurred when the players jumped for a rebound, could have been prevented by further supervision.

The court next held that a participant in recreational sport activity cannot assert a claim of negligence against a co-participant who causes her injury. Instead, such a plaintiff must show that the co-participant engaged in reckless or intentional conduct that caused the injury. Accepting plaintiff's description of the incident, the court found that there were no facts showing that Martin had acted recklessly or intentionally. Plaintiff now appeals.

II

On appeal, plaintiff makes two arguments. First, she contends that Martin, as a teacher, and her school and the school board, as Martin's employers, owed her a duty of supervisory care, which they breached. Second, she argues that there was a material fact issue concerning whether Martin acted recklessly during the basketball game. We disagree. There are no facts showing defendants breached their duty to provide supervision to plaintiff as a student participating in a basketball game. Moreover, accepting plaintiff's description of the incident, the material undisputed facts do not show that Martin acted recklessly or intentionally. …

A. The School's Duty to Supervise

School officials have a duty to supervise the children in their care. Accordingly, "[t]eachers must at times be present to oversee students on school playgrounds and in hallways, classrooms, lunchrooms and auditoriums." That duty may be violated by inactions, as well as actions. The supervisory duty extends to "foreseeable dangers … [that] arise from the careless acts or intentional transgressions of others." School officials must exercise "that degree of care which a person of ordinary prudence, charged with comparable duties, would exercise under the same circumstances."

Here, there was no showing of a breach of the duty to supervise plaintiff. The basketball game was officiated by a referee. Moreover, additional supervision was provided by approximately five teachers who did not participate in the game. There were no facts showing that the game was being conducted in a reckless or out-of-control manner before plaintiff was injured. In that regard, plaintiff testified that she had only played for a few minutes in the first half of the game, and her injury occurred within five minutes of the start of the second half of the game. While plaintiff testified that the teachers were beginning to play "aggressively," she also acknowledged that the game was a typical basketball game and the referee was not calling many fouls.

Plaintiff was injured when she jumped for a rebound and came into contact with another player who happened to be a teacher. Those undisputed facts establish that plaintiff's injury did not result from a lack of supervision. Instead, the undisputed facts establish that plaintiff was injured while participating in a recreational sport activity.

B. Injuries in Recreational Sports

"[T]he duty of care applicable to participants in informal recreational sports is to avoid the infliction of injury caused by reckless or intentional conduct." Accordingly, a participant who causes injury to another participant in a recreational sporting activity cannot be found liable for simple negligence. Our Supreme Court has explained that two considerations support this heightened standard: "the promotion of vigorous participation in athletic activities, and the avoidance of a flood of litigation generated by participation in recreational games and sports."

The Supreme Court has reasoned that a recklessness standard is more appropriate because a certain level of risk of harm is a normal part of a recreational game. In that regard, the Court has explained:

Our conclusion that a recklessness standard is the appropriate one to apply in the sports context is founded on more than a concern for a court's ability to discern adequately what constitutes reasonable conduct under the highly varied circumstances of informal sports activity. The heightened standard will more likely result in affixing liability for conduct that is clearly unreasonable and unacceptable from the perspective of those engaged in the sport yet leaving free from the supervision of the law the risk-laden conduct that is inherent in sports and more often than not assumed to be "part of the game."

Here, plaintiff has conceded that Martin "was not intentionally trying to injure [her]." Indeed, the record contains no facts that would support a finding that Martin acted intentionally to injure plaintiff. Consequently, the question here is whether plaintiff has presented facts showing that Martin acted recklessly when he jumped for a rebound. According to plaintiff's own testimony, Martin was on an angle in front of her. Martin then pushed his body backward to create more space between himself and the basketball rim while jumping for the ball. The contact occurred when plaintiff leaned and jumped forward to try to get the ball and her upper body came into contact with Martin's upper body. Such facts, even when viewed in the light most favorable to plaintiff, do not establish reckless conduct in a basketball game. Instead, those facts describe normal activity that occurs when players attempt to make rebounds during a basketball game.

Plaintiff did not describe any conduct by Martin that could be found to be excessively harmful conduct. Moreover, plaintiff's testimony provides no evidence that Martin disregarded a known or obvious risk that was so great as to make it highly probable that harm would follow. Indeed, there was no evidence that Martin was aware that plaintiff was angled behind him and was jumping forward as he was pushing backwards and jumping for the rebound.

To the extent that plaintiff argues that a negligence standard should apply because Martin was a teacher, we find no support for such a change in the law. Martin and plaintiff participated in the game as players. As already pointed out, the school provided appropriate supervision by a referee and other teachers. In her candid testimony, plaintiff described Martin's actions as the actions typical of any basketball player. There are no facts in the record to demonstrate that Martin used his position as a teacher to conduct himself differently than a normal player. Accordingly, there is no basis to impose a greater duty on Martin than any other participant in a recreational sporting activity. Affirmed.

Waivers and Release Forms

School boards often try to protect themselves from negligence suits by asking parents to sign forms releasing the school from liability for any injuries a student might sustain while engaging in athletic activities. The Florida High School Athletic Association has garnered attention for a release form that includes the following language in all caps:[132]

YOU ARE AGREEING TO LET YOUR MINOR CHILD ENGAGE IN A POTENTIALLY DANGEROUS ACTIVITY. YOU ARE AGREEING THAT, EVEN IF MY CHILD'S/WARD'S SCHOOL, THE SCHOOLS AGAINST WHICH IT COMPETES, THE SCHOOL DISTRICT, THE CONTEST OFFICIALS AND FHSAA USES REASONABLE CARE IN PROVIDING THIS ACTIVITY, THERE IS A CHANCE YOUR CHILD MAY BE SERIOUSLY INJURED OR KILLED BY PARTICIPATING IN THIS ACTIVITY BECAUSE THERE ARE CERTAIN DANGERS INHERENT IN THE ACTIVITY WHICH CANNOT BE AVOIDED OR ELIMINATED. BY SIGNING THIS FORM, YOU ARE GIVING UP YOUR CHILD'S RIGHT AND YOUR RIGHT TO RECOVER FROM MY CHILD'S/WARD'S SCHOOL, THE SCHOOLS AGAINST WHICH IT COMPETES, THE SCHOOL DISTRICT, THE CONTEST OFFICIALS AND FHSAA IN A LAWSUIT FOR ANY PERSONAL INJURY, INCLUDING DEATH, TO YOUR CHILD OR ANY PROPERTY DAMAGE THAT RESULTS FROM THE RISKS THAT ARE A NATURAL PART OF THE ACTIVITY. YOU HAVE THE RIGHT TO REFUSE TO SIGN THIS FORM, AND MY CHILD'S/WARD'S SCHOOL, THE SCHOOLS AGAINST WHICH IT COMPETES, THE SCHOOL DISTRICT, THE CONTEST OFFICIALS AND FHSAA HAS THE RIGHT TO REFUSE TO LET YOUR CHILD PARTICIPATE IF YOU DO NOT SIGN THIS FORM.

132 Florida High School Athletic Association, Consent and Release from Liability Certificate (revised 04/16); online at http://www.fhsaa.org/sites/default/files/el03_consent_8_0.pdf (last accessed April 27, 2020).

Are such pre-injury liability waivers legally effective? Courts in a number of states have found that release forms signed by a parent or parents can indeed protect schools and municipalities from liability when students are injured in the course of athletic activities and school-sponsored events and excursions. In *Sharon v. City of Newton*, a case involving a student injured in the course of cheerleading practice, Massachusetts' highest court held that the release form signed by the student's father was legally effective.[133] In *Gonzalez v. City of Coral Gables*,[134] a release form precluded negligence claims against the defendant city after a student slipped and fell while visiting a fire station as part of a school-sponsored training program. In *Hohe v. San Diego Unified School District*,[135] a release form prevented negligence claims against the defendant school district after a 15-year-old was injured at a hypnotism show.

Other courts have held that such releases or waivers are contrary to public policy.[136] Plaintiffs so argued in *Kelly v. United States*,[137] a case involving a cadet in a high school ROTC program who was injured during an orientation visit to a US Marine Corps base. While the plaintiffs had advocated for a public policy exemption based on the public interest, the court found the proper focus "is not whether the release violates public policy but rather that public policy itself justifies the enforcement of this agreement," ultimately deciding in favor of the defendants on principles of contract: "Plaintiff Terry Kelly cannot be allowed to accept the benefits of the Release Form through his daughter's attendance, while at the same time denying the release that was required as a condition of that attendance."

In a significant number of jurisdictions, any ambiguity in a waiver will be interpreted against the school district.[138] Other courts have said that although waivers may be valid as to the parents, they do not block suits by the injured children themselves.[139] At a minimum, release forms help distinguish the risk normally associated with school-sponsored activities (to which parents might reasonably consent) from other kinds of risks not normally associated with school activities (for which consent cannot be assumed).[140]

The following long-running case involving an elite private school student who contracted meningitis on a school-sponsored trip to China illustrates public policy considerations that undergird **duties of care**, **foreseeability**, **assumption of risk**, and other principles of negligence discussed in this section.

⚖️

MUNN v. THE HOTCHKISS SCHOOL
US Court of Appeals for the Second Circuit
795 F.3d 324 (2015), *aff'd*, 724 Fed. Appx. 25 (2d Cir. 2018)

JOHN M. WALKER, JR., Circuit Judge

Cara Munn and her parents brought suit against the Hotchkiss School after Munn contracted tick-borne encephalitis on a school-organized trip to China. At trial, a jury found Hotchkiss negligent and awarded the Munns $41.5 million in damages, $31.5 of which were non-economic damages. On appeal, the school argues that it did not have a legal duty to

133 769 N.E.2d 738 (Mass. 2002).
134 871 So. 2d 1067 (Fla. Dist. Ct. App. 2004).
135 274 Cal. Rptr. 647 (1990).
136 Whittington v. Sowela Technical Inst., 438 So. 2d 236 (La. Ct. App. 1983); Wagenblast v. Odessa Sch. Dist. No. 105–157–166J, 758 P.2d 968 (Wash. 1988) (*en banc*).
137 2014 U.S. Dist. LEXIS 135289 (E.D.N.C. Sept. 25, 2014).
138 Doyle v. Bowdoin Coll., 403 A.2d 1206 (Me. 1979); Sweeney v. City of Bettendorf, 762 N.W.2d 873 (Iowa 2009).
139 Fedor v. Mauwehu Council, Boy Scouts of Am., 143 A.2d 466 (Conn. Super. Ct. 1958); *see also* Scott v. Pacific West Mountain Resort, 834 P.2d 6 (Wash. 1992) and Galloway v. State, 790 N.W.2d 252 (Iowa 2010); *but see* Zivich v. Mentor Soccer Club, Inc., 696 N.E.2d 201 (Ohio 1998).
140 *See* Hohe v. San Diego Unified Sch. Dist., 274 Cal. Rptr. 647 (Cal. Ct. App. 1990).

warn about or protect against tick-borne encephalitis and that the jury award is excessive. Although we agree with the plaintiffs that there was sufficient evidence for a jury to find Munn's illness foreseeable, we are unable to determine whether public policy supports imposing a legal duty on Hotchkiss. This case implicates important and unresolved issues of Connecticut state law and public policy. It is likely to have repercussions on future negligence cases in Connecticut, and existing case law provides insufficient guidance on some of the issues raised. Accordingly, we certify two questions to the Connecticut Supreme Court: (1) Does Connecticut public policy support imposing a duty on a school to warn about or protect against the risk of a serious insect-borne disease when it organizes a trip abroad? (2) If so, does an award of approximately $41.5 million in favor of the plaintiffs, $31.5 million of which are non-economic damages, warrant remittitur?

Background

We recite the facts in the light most favorable to the plaintiffs in light of the jury verdict in their favor.

A. *The Trip to China*

During her freshman year, Cara Munn ("Munn"), then a fifteen-year-old student at the Hotchkiss School ("Hotchkiss"), a private boarding school, decided to participate in a summer program in Tianjin, China, organized by Hotchkiss. The month-long program immersed students in Chinese language classes and included weekend trips to cultural landmarks.

Jean Yu, the school's Chinese Language and Culture Program Director, served as the trip leader. In preparation for the trip, in March 2007, she sent parents a packet outlining activities and a set of legal forms for the participants and parents to waive legal claims against the school. The packet mentioned a visit to Mount Panshan, referred to by the parties as "Mt. Pan." The school also sent medical advice for the trip, including a link to a Centers for Disease Control and Prevention ("CDC") webpage and a note that the school's infirmary could "serve as a travel clinic." The webpage linked to the CDC's Central America site instead of its China site, however, and the infirmary was unable to provide independent medical advice. Finally, the school sent an itinerary, packing list, and a handbook on international travel. The packing list mentioned bug spray in its "miscellaneous" category, but included no warning about insect-borne

diseases in the section where other health risks were mentioned.

On June 23, 2007, while on the trip, the students went for a weekend excursion to the Great Wall and to Mt. Pan. Mt. Pan is a forested mountain. Again, no warnings to wear bug spray were given. Trip leader Yu left her bug spray on the bus. After hiking to the top of the mountain, a group of three or four students, including Munn, decided to hike down, while the others took a cable car. Yu pointed them to the path and said that she would wait for them at the bottom. Munn testified that the students decided to leave the paved path and follow narrow dirt trails instead. The students got lost and walked among trees and through brush.

Munn testified at trial that after the trip to Mt. Pan she had many insect bites and an itchy welt on her left arm. Ten days later, she awoke with a headache, a fever, and wooziness. Her condition deteriorated rapidly and she was taken to a local hospital. Munn was then transferred to a Beijing hospital and her parents came from the United States. Severely ill and partially paralyzed, Munn was soon airlifted back to New York. Munn was diagnosed with tick-borne encephalitis ("TBE"), a viral infectious disease which affects the central nervous system.

Because of her illness, Munn lost the ability to speak. At trial, she testified through a machine into which she typed her answers. She has difficulty controlling her facial muscles, causing her to drool. Her mother testified about Munn's frustration with her inability to speak and stated that Munn experiences "a lot of rejection." Munn has also lost some cognitive function, particularly in terms of reading comprehension and math. Still, Munn has managed to live a functional life. She finished high school and attended Trinity College. She can play sports, still travels, and has held summer internships.

B. *Procedural History*

On June 11, 2009, Munn and her parents filed this diversity action against Hotchkiss alleging that the school's negligent planning and careless supervision of the trip caused her illness.

In their lawsuit, the Munns alleged that Hotchkiss was negligent in 1) failing to warn the Munns about the risks of viral encephalitis; 2) failing to provide for proper protective clothing, insect repellent, or vaccinations; 3) failing to provide medical personnel on the trip; 4) failing to establish procedures for addressing medical emergencies; and 5) failing to advise the Munns on the availability of vaccines against viral encephalitis for children traveling to rural areas of China. At trial, the Munns proceeded only on the first and second theories of liability—failure to warn and failure to protect.

Hotchkiss asserted a number of affirmative defenses, including that the Munns assumed the risk by signing the school's "Agreement, Waiver, and Release of Liability." However, the district court excluded the waiver, finding both that its language was ambiguous and that it was against public policy under Connecticut law.

At trial, the plaintiffs offered two experts, Stuart Rose, an expert on travel medicine, and Peter Tarlow, an expert on tourism-risk management who testified about standards of care. Hotchkiss also offered two experts, David Freedman, a travel-medicine expert, and William Fluharty, profered as an expert on standards of care followed by similarly-situated schools. The district court, however, excluded Fluharty's testimony after it was given, finding that he had fabricated and misrepresented support for his testimony.

At the conclusion of the plaintiffs' case, Hotchkiss sought a directed verdict under Rule 50(a) of the Federal Rules of Civil Procedure, arguing that Munn contributed to her own injuries and that the risk of contracting TBE was unforeseeable. The district court denied that motion.

On March 27, 2013, after a seven-day trial, the jury found Hotchkiss solely liable. Specifically, the jury found that Hotchkiss was negligent in failing to warn Munn of the risk of serious insect-borne illnesses and in failing to ensure that she took protective measures. The jury also found no contributory negligence on the part of Munn. It awarded $10.25 million in past and future economic damages, and $31.5 million in non-economic damages. Hotchkiss renewed its Rule 50 motion and filed a motion for a new trial under Rule 59.

On June 5, 2014, the district court denied both of these motions. Pursuant to the parties' stipulation, it reduced the monetary award by the amount that the Munns had collected from collateral sources. The total award against Hotchkiss is now approximately $41.5 million.

Discussion

Hotchkiss argues on appeal that it did not have a legal duty to warn about or protect against tick-borne encephalitis and that the $41.5 million jury award is excessive. The school asserts that the jury verdict is not supported by sufficient evidence and that it contravenes Connecticut public policy to impose a duty

to warn about or protect against a disease as remote as tick-borne encephalitis. ...

I. Foreseeability

Hotchkiss first argues that there was insufficient evidence to support the jury verdict that it was foreseeable Munn would contract a serious insect-borne illness on the trip to China. We disagree. Upon review of the record, we find that the plaintiffs presented sufficient evidence at trial that Hotchkiss should have known of the risk of serious insect-borne diseases.

We will overturn a jury verdict only if there is such a

complete absence of evidence supporting the verdict that the jury's findings could only have been the result of sheer surmise and conjecture, or such an overwhelming amount of evidence in favor of the appellant that reasonable and fair minded men could not arrive at a verdict against the appellant.

In addition, "assessments of the weight of the evidence or the credibility of witnesses are for the jury and not grounds for reversal on appeal; we defer to the jury's assessments of both of these issues."

Under Connecticut negligence law, a legal duty requires that (1) "an ordinary person in the defendant's position, knowing what the defendant knew or should have known, would anticipate that harm of the general nature of that suffered was likely to result," and (2) a determination by the court "on the basis of a public policy analysis, of whether the defendant's responsibility for its negligent conduct should extend to the particular consequences or particular plaintiff in the case." Recently, the Connecticut Supreme Court reiterated that "as long as harm of the general nature as that which occurred is foreseeable there is a basis for liability even though the manner in which the accident happens is unusual, bizarre or unforeseeable."

Connecticut decisions construe foreseeability broadly. For example, in *Ruiz*, where a ten-year-old child dropped a piece of concrete from the third floor resulting in the injury of a seven-year-old child below, the Connecticut Supreme Court held that it could be foreseeable that backyard debris in an apartment building would lead to injury when children used the area as a playground. In reaching this conclusion, the court emphasized that its "cases have attempted to safeguard children of tender years from their propensity to disregard dangerous conditions." Cara Munn was several years older than the children in *Ruiz*, the decision can be read to indicate that

Connecticut courts construe foreseeability broadly, especially as it relates to children.

Here, the evidence presented at trial was sufficient to support the jury's verdict that Munn's illness was foreseeable. Hotchkiss introduced a CDC China advisory last modified on August 1, 2007 that included a warning that "[t]ickborne encephalitis occurs in forested regions in northeastern China and in South Korea." The evidence also showed that Mt. Pan is a forested mountain in the northeastern Chinese province of Tianjin. In addition, Hotchkiss's expert, David Freedman, testified that the August 1, 2007 advisory would put a school on notice that there was a risk of TBE in northeastern China. Although the August 1, 2007 advisory was dated more than one month after Munn's visit to Mt. Pan, the school's Director of International Programs, David Thompson, testified that he had seen a warning about TBE on the CDC's China page before the trip. ...

Hotchkiss argues on appeal that the jury could not have found the disease foreseeable based on the August 1, 2007 travel advisory because the advisory was released after the trip. Hotchkiss, which introduced the advisory as a defense trial exhibit and from which its own witness testified as to trip preparation awareness, now attempts to discredit its own exhibit. The school instead asks us to consider an earlier advisory dated May 23, 2007, which does not mention TBE. That advisory, however, was not introduced at trial and is not part of the record. We will not consider new evidence "absent extraordinary circumstances" and no such circumstances are present here. Furthermore, while the August 1, 2007 advisory postdates the trip, it is possible that a similar advisory was on the website before, which would explain Thompson's testimony about seeing the advisory. Neither party presented evidence about what was posted on the CDC website when the trip actually occurred, and we will not disturb the jury's assessment of the evidence and its finding of reasonable foreseeability.

II. Public Policy

A. Duty

Hotchkiss also argues on appeal that imposing a legal duty to warn or protect in this case contravenes Connecticut public policy. This argument presents a closer question. However, Connecticut precedent does not offer sufficient guidance on whether public

policy supports imposing a duty on Hotchkiss, and the parties present compelling arguments on both sides. In these circumstances, rather than attempting to discern Connecticut public policy ourselves, we think it preferable to certify the question to the Connecticut Supreme Court. ...

1. The Applicable Law

Under Connecticut law, foreseeability of harm alone is not determinative of duties in tort and the imposition of a duty of care also implicates questions of public policy. The Connecticut Supreme Court has stated:

A simple conclusion that the harm to the plaintiff was foreseeable cannot by itself mandate a determination that a legal duty exists. Many harms are quite literally foreseeable, yet for pragmatic reasons, no recovery is allowed. A further inquiry must be made, for we recognize that duty is not sacrosanct in itself, but is only an expression of the sum total of those considerations of policy which lead the law to say that the plaintiff is entitled to protection ... The final step in the duty inquiry, then, is to make a determination of the fundamental policy of the law, as to whether the defendant's responsibility should extend to such results.

No Connecticut case closely resembles this one, but in at least two cases, the Connecticut Supreme Court has overturned jury verdicts by finding that public policy did not support the imposition of a duty on the tortfeasor. In *Jaworski v. Kiernan*,[141] the Connecticut Supreme Court overturned a jury verdict finding a recreational soccer player responsible for another player's injury based on a theory of negligence. The court reasoned that public policy favors encouraging competitive sports. In reaching this conclusion, it noted that other jurisdictions have required deliberate or reckless conduct, not just negligence. ...

More recently, in *Mercier v. Greenwich Academy, Inc.*,[142] a federal judge applying Connecticut law declined to impose a duty on a coach and school after a player was injured during a basketball game. The court reasoned that Connecticut public policy weighs in favor of encouraging "vigorous participation in recreational sporting activities," even if

141 696 A.2d 332 (Conn. 1997).
142 2013 U.S. Dist. LEXIS 103950 (D. Conn. July 25, 2013).

those activities create safety risks. Holding the coach responsible, the court concluded, would chill the coach's role of encouraging competition in sports.

Cases like *Jaworski* and *Mercier* indicate that courts place a high value on recreational activities for children, even if they sometimes create safety concerns. Although the present case does not involve competitive sports, it also implicates important questions of public policy because of the benefits of educational trips for children.

Connecticut courts addressing public policy questions have considered four factors to determine whether to impose a duty in negligence cases:

(1) the normal expectations of the participants in the activity under review; (2) the public policy of encouraging participation in the activity, while weighing the safety of the participants; (3) the avoidance of increased litigation; and (4) the decisions of other jurisdictions.

The four public policy factors do not point to an obvious answer in this case as both parties present colorable arguments on either side.

First, the expectations of the parties depend on the level of generality applied to describe the events that occurred in this case. Parents and children participating in a school-sponsored international trip might expect a school to warn about or protect against some of the risks of the trip, including potentially the dangers of serious insect-borne diseases. However, as Hotchkiss and several amici point out, it is unreasonable to expect a trip organizer to warn students about or protect them against every danger. Field trips are intended to expose children to situations outside of their comfort zones and of the organizers' control. Such trips thus naturally entail a certain level of risk. Here, the risk of contracting tick-borne encephalitis was undeniably remote. No American had ever before contracted TBE in China. Thus, although travelers may generally expect a school to warn about or protect against dangers, including serious insect-borne diseases, no one could have expected that Munn would contract TBE.

Second, international trips and outdoor activities, while sometimes posing substantial health and safety risks, offer important benefits to their participants. The public benefits of international education

and student exchanges are written into Connecticut statutory law. Connecticut General Statute Section 10–27(a) states:

It shall be the policy of the state to encourage its students, teachers, administrators and educational policy makers to participate in international studies, international exchange programs and other activities that advance cultural awareness and promote mutual understanding and respect for the citizens of other countries.

At the same time, the safety of minors, who in varying degrees are under the care and protection of schools on these trips, is an important concern. Minors on such trips are in the custody of the organizations leading them, and the health and safety of the children must have a bearing on how these trips are conducted.

Third, this case is likely to have repercussions on litigation in the area of child safety, especially in light of the substantial damages awarded to these plaintiffs. If the award stands, it would set an important precedent for negligence cases arising from educational trips. In fact, the effects of this case are already manifest. Munn's attorney recently brought another lawsuit in which the plaintiff seeks the same damage award for contracting Lyme disease at a YMCA camp. This case is likely to encourage future victims of unusual accidents on educational trips to seek compensation, placing a heavy financial burden on trip providers. On the other hand, it is reasonable to suppose that such liability could also cause an increase in diligence on the part of trip providers, potentially avoiding catastrophic injuries such as befell Munn.

Fourth, no case is exactly analogous to this one, but courts in several other jurisdictions have declined to impose a duty in similar cases and have construed the duties of schools more narrowly. In *David v. City of New York*,[143] the court found that a school did not breach a duty of supervision where a child was injured on a hay ride. The court noted that previous hay rides had occurred without incident and that the school had "no knowledge or notice that [the] hay ride would be hazardous." In *Mancha v. Field Museum of Natural History*,[144] the court declined to impose a duty where a child on a field trip was assaulted by unaffiliated students. The court found that "the

---

143 40 A.D.3d 572 (N.Y. App. Div. 2007).
144 283 N.E.2d 899 (Ill. 1972).

risk that a 12-year-old boy would be assaulted in a museum is minimal" and that recognizing a duty would impose a significant burden of supervision on the school. ...

These two cases indicate efforts by other jurisdictions to encourage extracurricular activities by limiting the duties of schools to warn about or protect against unlikely or unusual events. At the same time, there are also instances where courts have found that schools owe a duty in the context of extracurricular activities.

Upon review of these four factors and of Connecticut precedent in negligence cases, we are unable to determine whether Connecticut public policy supports imposing a duty to warn or protect in this case. Although prior Connecticut decisions in the area of recreational sports suggest that public policy may favor placing limits on schools' legal duties in the context of school trips because of their educational benefits, no case has yet addressed this precise question and no case is close to the facts of this case.

2. Certification

Because Connecticut case law does not offer sufficient guidance on the question of public policy in negligence cases, we think it best to let the Supreme Court of Connecticut determine whether Connecticut public policy supports imposing a legal duty on Hotchkiss. ...

Certification is appropriate in this case for at least three reasons. First, as discussed above, Connecticut case law provides limited guidance on this issue and no prior case is authoritative here. Whether Hotchkiss owed a duty of care is determinative in this case. Second, the scope of duty in negligence law is "paradigmatically a state field," typically addressed by state, rather than federal, courts. Third and most

importantly, this case is likely to have repercussions beyond this particular fact pattern as it implicates broad questions of Connecticut public policy.

Defining the scope of a school's duty when it leads an international trip could have significant consequences for negligence litigation in Connecticut, which is home to many private and public schools. Although cost-benefit analysis in most cases assumes that all interested parties are represented in the case, this is not so here. The societal impact of finding a duty here extends far beyond Hotchkiss. To impose a duty on Connecticut schools to warn about or protect against risks as remote as tick-borne encephalitis might discourage field trips that serve important educational roles. If the costs imposed on schools and non-profit organizations become too high, such trips might be curtailed or cease completely, depriving children of valuable opportunities. Public policy may thus require that participants bear the risks of unlikely injuries and illnesses such as the one that occurred in this case so that institutions can continue to offer these activities.

On the other hand, imposing a duty of reasonable care on Hotchkiss may not have the effect of increasing litigation. If schools take steps to protect students from foreseeable harms, legal actions may in fact decrease. Alternatively, those actions premised on an absolute demand to ensure student safety "as opposed to the failure ... to take reasonable precautions, likely will be dismissed in the absence of negligence." Balancing these factors is a task primarily for state decision makers rather than federal courts.

We conclude that certification would allow Connecticut to carefully consider and weigh the policy concerns at play in this case and to shape its own state negligence law as to the responsibilities of schools on field trips. ...

Contact Sports

Are waivers like those of the Florida High School Association cited above legally enforceable when football players suffer concussions and other foreseeable injuries? In *Mullenix v. St. John County School Board*,[145] a federal circuit court reviewed the language in the Florida High School Association waiver excerpted earlier and rejected the defendant school district's claim that the student and his parents had expressly assumed the risk of the injuries he had sustained in deciding to play an "inherently risky contact sport." But in this particular case, the student was injured in the course of a weight training exercise selected by his football coaches, not in the course of a football game.

145 2019 Fla. Cir. LEXIS 1977 (June 24, 2019).

In 2016, former professional football players filed a successful class action suit alleging that the NFL had failed to inform them about and protect them from concussion risks, leading to a billion-dollar settlement.[146] The same year, former collegiate football players alleged the NCAA had failed to inform them about and protect them from concussion risks.[147] Yet a suit a year earlier by a former high school football player seeking the creation of a $70 million in medical monitoring fund to monitor students for post-concussive symptoms failed. In *Piercionek v. High School Association*,[148] the court held, among other things, that Piercionek's execution of an "athletic permit" constituted an assumption of risk:

> Defendant urges that plaintiff's complaint is subject to dismissal because he expressly assumed the risk of injury. Both plaintiff and his parent signed an Athletic Permit which contained language expressly assuming the risk.
>
> The actual language is: "I am also aware of certain risks of physical injury and I agree to assume the full risk of any injuries that may occur." In conjunction with the Athletic Permit, a Concussion Information Sheet was also provided to plaintiff and signed by plaintiff and his parent.
>
> Plaintiff urges that the terms of these documents did not provide that plaintiff had expressly assumed the risk, the documents were not executed by IHSA, and that any waiver contained in the documents cannot be enforced against a minor. Plaintiff also argues that fact questions exist as to whether he actually understood the risk associated with the sport and he has attached his affidavit stating that he did not know of the risks involved at the time he signed the documents relied upon by defendant.
>
> In considering the arguments regarding assumption of the risk, the court finds defendant's argument in reply regarding ratification of a contract by a minor if he fails to disaffirm it within a reasonable time after attaining majority to be compelling.
>
> Plaintiff signed his affidavit, which purports to disaffirm the Athletic Permit he (and his parent) executed which contains an express assumption of the risk, approximately 16 months after he turned 18. The court concludes that plaintiff's conduct operated to ratify the Athletic Permit he executed.

Liability insurance premiums have risen for schools offering football and other contact sports in the wake of the NFL settlement. Meanwhile, declining participation rates across the country suggest that many parents and students have already come to the conclusion that football is not worth the risk of traumatic brain injury. Among elite private schools, the Lawrenceville School in New Jersey dropped its intramural football program in 2013; Princeton Day School, also in New Jersey, dropped its varsity program in 2010. Marshall, Texas, the football-mad town featured in the television show *Friday Night Lights*, dropped entry-level tackle football for seventh-graders in 2014. In 2015, the number of high school football players across the country declined to just over one million as suburban schools from Ridgefield Memorial in New Jersey to Maplewood Richmond Heights in Missouri dropped their varsity football programs.[149]

---

146 *In re* NFL Players Concussion Injury Litig., 821 F.3d 410 (3d Cir. 2016).
147 *In re* NCAA Student-Athlete Concussion Injury Litig., 314 F.R.D. 580 (N.D. Ill. 2016).
148 2015 Ill. Cir. LEXIS 24 (October 27, 2015).
149 R. Curren & J.C. Blokhuis, *Friday Night Lights Out: The End of Football in Schools*, 88(2) Harvard Educational Review 141–162 (2018); citing M. Pilon, *Anger and indifference after a school ends a full-contact tradition*, New York Times (October 12, 2013) D2; K. Belson, *Football's risks sink in, even in the heart of Texas*, New York Times (May 12, 2014) A1; K. Belson, *As worries rise and players flee, football is cut*, New York Times (September 29, 2015) B11.

Respondeat Superior

Under the doctrine of *respondeat superior*, employers may be held vicariously liable for the negligent and, in some states, intentional wrongdoing of employees acting within the scope of their duties. Thus, teachers in private and public schools who negligently supervise their students may expose not only themselves but also their employers to liability. Students and parent volunteers who negligently perform services for the school under the school's direction and control, even if they are not compensated, may also expose the school to **vicarious liability**.

Whether a school will be held liable under the doctrine of *respondeat superior* depends on a number of factors that vary somewhat from state to state. Often, the main issue is whether tortious acts were within the scope of an employee's duties. This is determined on a case by case basis, in light of the time, place, and purpose of the act, its similarity to what was authorized or required of the employee, and a host of other factors. An employer cannot avoid vicarious liability by ordering employees not to be negligent.

In *Alma W. v. Oakland Unified School District*,[150] a case involving an 11-year-old student who was sexually assaulted by a school custodian, the California Court of Appeal found that the defendant's "act of rape was not an integral part of a course of action on behalf of his employer, but rather an independent, self-serving pursuit wholly unrelated to his custodial duties." Accordingly, the school district could not be held vicariously liable under the doctrine of *respondeat superior*. Similarly, in *Doe 175 v. Columbia Heights School District*,[151] the sexual abuse of a ninth-grade student by a football coach could not give rise to vicarious liability for the school district because sexual abuse did not fall with the scope of the coach's "office or employment."

A school district may be held vicariously liable for acts outside the scope of a teacher's employment if it permits the teacher to act with **apparent authority**. Thus, in *Lynch v. Board of Education of Collinsville Community Unit District 10*,[152] a case involving a student injured during a "powder puff" football game, the district was found vicariously liable even though the game was not sponsored by the school. The players had used the school's field and locker room, and the school had helped to publicize the game. Accordingly, the school had a duty to ensure that the players had proper safety equipment.

Negligent Hiring, Retention, and Supervision

An employer may also be held directly liable for having acted negligently in **hiring, retaining, or supervising** an employee who has caused harm to others. To establish that a school should be held responsible for **negligent hiring**, **negligent retention**, or **negligent supervision** an injured plaintiff must establish three points:

1. That the employee whose act or omission caused the injury was unfit for employment and ought not to have been hired or retained;
2. That the injury would not have occurred but for the hiring or retention of the unfit employee; and
3. That the employer knew or ought to have known of the employee's unfitness.

Liability on these grounds typically turns on whether an employer should have known of a particular employee's unfitness, either by more carefully investigating the employee's references and

---

150 176 Cal. Rptr. 287 (Cal. Ct. App. 1981).
151 873 N.W.2d 352 (Minn. Ct. App. 2016).
152 412 N.E.2d 447 (Ill. 1980).

credentials prior to his or her employment, or by more carefully supervising the employee after his or her employment.[153] However, an employer will not be held responsible in cases of misrepresentation. In *Medlin v. Bass*,[154] the Supreme Court of North Carolina ruled that a school district could not be held liable for negligent hiring of a principal who had resigned from his previous position, ostensibly for health reasons. Telephone interviews with former employers did not reveal his history of sexual impropriety and letters of reference referred to him as "one of the most promising men in education" and lamented having "lost a very valuable educator."

In the following illustrative case, the Supreme Court of California found a school district liable for the **negligent hiring, retention, and supervision** of a guidance counselor with an alleged propensity for sexually abusing minors.

⚖️

C.A. v. WILLIAM S. HART UNION HIGH SCHOOL DISTRICT
Supreme Court of California
270 P.3d 699 (2012)

KATHRYN M. WERDEGAR, J.—

C.A., a minor, sued his public high school guidance counselor and the school district for damages arising out of sexual harassment and abuse by the counselor. The trial court sustained the school district's demurrer, and the Court of Appeal affirmed. On review, the question presented is whether the district may be found vicariously liable for the acts of its employees—not for the acts of the counselor, which were outside the scope of her employment, but for the negligence of supervisory or administrative personnel who allegedly knew, or should have known, of the counselor's propensities and nevertheless hired, retained and inadequately supervised her. ...

C.A. alleged that while he was a student at Golden Valley High School in the William S. Hart Union High School District (the District), he was subjected to sexual harassment and abuse by Roselyn Hubbell, the head guidance counselor at his school. Plaintiff was born in July 1992, making him 14 to 15 years old at the time of the harassment and abuse, which is alleged to have begun in or around January 2007 and continued into September 2007.

Plaintiff was assigned to Hubbell for school counseling. Representing that she wished to help him do well at school, Hubbell began to spend many hours with plaintiff both on and off the high school premises and to drive him home from school each day. Exploiting her position of authority and trust, Hubbell engaged in sexual activities with plaintiff and required that he engage in sexual activities, including sensual embraces and massages, masturbation, oral sex and intercourse. As a result of the abuse, plaintiff suffered emotional distress, anxiety, nervousness and fear. ...

In a cause of action for negligent supervision, plaintiff alleges (again on information and belief) that defendants, through their employees, knew or should have known of Hubbell's "dangerous and exploitive propensities" and nevertheless "failed to provide reasonable supervision" over her and "failed to use reasonable care in investigating" her. Specifically, defendants neither had in place nor implemented a system or procedure for investigating and supervising personnel "to prevent pre-sexual grooming and/or sexual harassment, molestation and abuse of children." In a cause of action for negligent hiring and retention, plaintiff alleges defendants were on notice of Hubbell's molestation of students both before and during her employment by the District, but did not reasonably investigate Hubbell and failed to use reasonable care to prevent her abuse of plaintiff.

The District demurred to the complaint, arguing the negligent supervision and negligent hiring and retention causes of action failed to state a claim because of the lack of statutory authority for

---

153 Ponticas v. K.M.S. Inv., 331 N.W.2d 907 (Minn. 1983); *see also* DiCosala v. Key, 450 A.2d 508 (N.J. 1982); Garcia v. Duffy, 492 So. 2d 435 (Fla. Ct. App. 1986).

154 Medlin v. Bass, 398 S.E.2d 460 (N.C. 1990); *see also* Randi W. v. Muroc Joint Unified Sch. Dist., 929 P.2d 582 (Cal. 1997).

holding a public entity liable for negligent supervision, hiring or retention of its employees. The trial court sustained the District's demurrer to the entire complaint without leave to amend and dismissed the action as to the District. ...

The Court of Appeal affirmed in a divided decision. The majority first rejected the viability of a vicarious liability theory under section 815.2, on the ground that ... in this case the alleged sexual misconduct of the guidance counselor cannot be considered "within the scope of her employment." Second, the majority held no theory of direct liability for negligent hiring, supervision or retention could lie because plaintiff had adduced no statutory authority for it.

The Court of Appeal dissenter opined that "[a]lthough the school district cannot be held liable for the intentional misconduct of the guidance counselor, it may be liable through respondeat superior for the negligence of other employees who were responsible for hiring, supervising, training, or retaining her." Because school personnel were in a special relationship with plaintiff, they owed him a duty of taking reasonable care to prevent the abuse by Hubbell. Consequently,

the failure of a school administrator to exercise ordinary care in protecting students from harm should render a school district liable ... where the administrator hires an applicant known to have a history of molesting students or where, after hiring an applicant, the administrator first learns about the employee's sexual misconduct and does not properly supervise, train, or discharge her.

We granted plaintiff's petition for review.

Discussion

... The District maintains its employees owed plaintiff no legal duty to protect him against abuse by another employee; the responsibility for hiring, supervising and dismissing employees belongs exclusively to the District itself, and no statute provides for the District's direct liability in this regard. Plaintiff, in turn, argues the special relationship between public school personnel and students imposes on the District's administrative and supervisory employees a duty of reasonable care to protect a student from foreseeable dangers, including those from other school employees. For the reasons given below, we agree with plaintiff.

While school districts and their employees have never been considered insurers of the physical safety of students, California law has long imposed on school authorities a duty to "supervise at all times the conduct of the children on the school grounds and to enforce those rules and regulations necessary to their protection." The standard of care imposed upon school personnel in carrying out this duty to supervise is identical to that required in the performance of their other duties. This uniform standard to which they are held is that degree of care "which a person of ordinary prudence, charged with [comparable] duties, would exercise under the same circumstances." Either a total lack of supervision or ineffective supervision may constitute a lack of ordinary care on the part of those responsible for student supervision. ...

In addition, a school district and its employees have a special relationship with the district's pupils, a relationship arising from the mandatory character of school attendance and the comprehensive control over students exercised by school personnel, "analogous in many ways to the relationship between parents and their children."

Because of this special relationship ... the duty of care owed by school personnel includes the duty to use reasonable measures to protect students from foreseeable injury at the hands of third parties acting negligently or intentionally. This principle has been applied in cases of employees' alleged negligence resulting in injury to a student by another student, injury to a student by a nonstudent, and—on facts remarkably close to the present case—injuries to a student resulting from a teacher's sexual assault.

In *Virginia G.*,[155] the plaintiff, a junior high school student, alleged the defendant district had performed an inadequate background check before hiring as a teacher Ernest Ferguson, who had been fired from another school for sexual misconduct with students and who had then sexually harassed and assaulted the plaintiff. Analyzing the case within the same statutory framework as applies here, the appellate court held the district could be liable for Virginia G.'s injuries under a theory of vicarious liability for other school personnel's negligent hiring and supervision of the molester ...

The District acknowledges that a special relationship making an employee potentially liable for a

---

155 Virginia G. v. ABC Unified School Dist., 15 Cal. App. 4th 1848 (1993).

student's injury at the hands of a third party "might exist where the individual employee is in direct charge of and supervising the student," but insists that a "principal, school superintendent, or other administrator who oversees the overall functioning" of the school cannot be liable on this theory: "They have no special relationship with any particular student. Their relationship is with the entity." We disagree.

Responsibility for the safety of public school students is not borne solely by instructional personnel. School principals and other supervisory employees, to the extent their duties include overseeing the educational environment and the performance of teachers and counselors, also have the responsibility of taking reasonable measures to guard pupils against harassment and abuse from foreseeable sources, including any teachers or counselors they know or have reason to know are prone to such abuse. ...

We cannot say from the face of the complaint that the District had no supervisory or administrative personnel whose responsibilities included hiring, training, supervising, disciplining or terminating a guidance counselor. ...

More broadly, the District argues that "[i]ndividual co-workers, whether peers or supervisors, have no personal legal relationship with other employees" and therefore cannot be personally liable to third parties for "how they hire, fire, retain, or discipline co-workers." As applied here, the argument is a *non sequitur*. Plaintiff relies not on the supervisory or administrative employees' legal relationship to Hubbell, their coworker, for the duty of care they owed plaintiff, but on their recognized special relationship with plaintiff, a pupil under their control and supervision. ...

This is not the first time we have held public school personnel may be individually liable for their negligent failure to protect students from harm at others' hands. In *Dailey v. Los Angeles Unified School District*,[156] one high school student unintentionally killed another while roughhousing during the lunch recess. The decedent's parents sued not only the district, but also two individual members of the school's physical education staff who were responsible for the area around the gymnasium where the incident took place but had failed to supervise students in the area during the lunch period. ...

Nor does our holding that public school administrators and supervisors may be held legally respon-

sible for their negligence in hiring and retaining as well as supervising school staff subject the great majority of public school personnel, much less other employees, to potential liability for acts committed by their fellow workers. The scope and effect of our holding on individual liability is limited by requirements of causation and duty, elements of liability that must be established in every tort action.

With regard to causation, plaintiff alleges he suffered emotional and physical injuries "[a]s a result of" defendants' negligent hiring and retention of the guidance counselor, and the District does not argue the causation element is inadequately pled. But where an individual defendant did not have final authority over the hiring or firing of the malefactor employee, but was merely in a position to propose or recommend such action, proving causation may present a significant obstacle.

Plaintiff here, and those similarly alleging individual negligence in hiring and firing, must demonstrate that the individual employee's proposal or recommendation, or failure to take such action, was a substantial factor in causing the malefactor to be hired or retained. While it may well be possible to prove that a public school principal's recommendation, particularly as to hiring, effectively determined the governing board's decision, the same could not be said of every individual employee who recommends to management that a particular person be hired into the organization, or who could have, but did not, seek a coworker's discipline or termination. Even if other elements of the tort action were established, then, an employee who did not actually make the hiring or retention decision and whose recommendations were not, in the particular circumstances of the organization, likely to be highly influential to the decision maker would not face the potential for individual liability.

Turning to the duty element, we have explained that the potential legal responsibility of District administrators and supervisors for negligently hiring or retaining Hubbell arises from the special relationship they had with plaintiff, a student under their supervision, which relationship entailed the duty to take reasonable measures to protect plaintiff from injuries at the hands of others in the school environment. Absent such a special relationship, there can be no individual liability to third parties for negligent hiring, retention or supervision of a fellow employee, and hence no vicarious liability ...

156 470 P.2d 360 (1970).

Unless the individual alleged to be negligent in a hiring or retention decision knew or should have known of the dangerous propensities of the employee who injured the plaintiff, there is little or no moral blame attached to the person's action or inaction. And unless the employee's propensities posed a substantial risk of personal injury to the plaintiff or others in the same circumstances, there is again little moral blame to assign, and the undesirable consequences of imposing potential liability—the possible chilling of recommendations and proposals for hiring and retention—will tend to outweigh the policy of preventing harm by imposing costs on negligent conduct.

In *John R. v. Oakland Unified School District*,[157] we noted with concern the undesirable consequences that could flow from imposing vicarious liability on public school districts for sexual misconduct by teachers, including "the diversion of needed funds from the classroom to cover claims" and the likelihood districts would be deterred "from encouraging, or even authorizing, extracurricular and/or one-on-one contacts between teachers and students." To these still valid concerns we should add the possibility that unsubstantiated rumors of sexual misconduct might curtail or destroy the careers of innocent teachers, counselors or other employees.

Against these concerns, we have weighed in this case the value of negligence actions in providing compensation to injured parties and preventing future harm of the same nature, and have followed *John R.*'s suggestion that these remedial goals are best addressed "by holding school districts to the exercise of due care" in their administrators' and supervisors'

"selection of [instructional] employees and the close monitoring of their conduct," rather than by making districts vicariously liable for the intentional sexual misconduct of teachers and other employees.

At the same time, we emphasize that a district's liability must be based on evidence of negligent hiring, supervision or retention, not on assumptions or speculation. That an individual school employee has committed sexual misconduct with a student or students does not of itself establish, or raise any presumption, that the employing district should bear liability for the resulting injuries. We note, as well, that even when negligence by an administrator or supervisor is established, the greater share of fault will ordinarily lie with the individual who intentionally abused or harassed the student than with any other party, and that fact should be reflected in any allocation of comparative fault.

Within these limits, we conclude a public school district may be vicariously liable ... for the negligence of administrators or supervisors in hiring, supervising and retaining a school employee who sexually harasses and abuses a student. Whether plaintiff in this case can prove the District's administrative or supervisory personnel were actually negligent in this respect is not a question we address in this appeal from dismissal on the sustaining of a demurrer.

Disposition

The judgment of the Court of Appeal is reversed, and the matter is remanded to that court for further proceedings consistent with our opinion.

Vicarious Liability of Parents

If school districts can be held vicariously liable for the tortious acts of their employees, can parents be held vicariously liable for the tortious acts of their children? Because, traditionally, parents were not automatically liable for torts committed by their children, the problem has been addressed with legislation. **Parental responsibility laws** hold parents responsible for at least some of the damage caused by their children through intentional torts, as well as vandalism, shoplifting, other types of property damage.[158] For example, legislation in Connecticut provides as follows:

§ 52-572. Parental liability for torts of minors

(a) The parent or parent or guardians ... of any unemancipated minor or minors, which minor or minors willfully or maliciously cause damage to any property or injury to any person, or, having

---

157 769 P.2d 948 (1989).

158 See Matthiesen, Wickert & Lehrer, S.C., Parental Responsibility Laws In All 50 States (2012).

> taken a motor vehicle without the permission of the owner thereof, cause damage to the motor vehicle, shall be jointly and severally liable with the minor or minors for the damage or injury to an amount not exceeding five thousand dollars, if the minor or minors would have been liable for the damage or injury if they had been adults.

Although tort law does not recognize it as a cause of action *per se*, bullying may in some cases include unwanted and harmful or offensive bodily contact. Accordingly, in such cases, bullies may be sued for battery. Although student bullies do not usually have sufficient resources to make such tort suits worthwhile, their parents often do. Hence parental responsibility statutes may be a useful legal tool for victims of schoolyard bullying. In *Albert v. Kelly*,[159] Kevin Albert knocked Christopher Albert into a piece of concrete on the floor of the school locker room. Nine sutures were needed to close the wound, leaving Christopher with a permanent scar on his lower back. Kevin's parents, John and Nancy Kelly, were held liable for almost half of the $10,456 in damages awarded to Christopher.

Parents may also be found liable if they directed or encouraged their child to commit a tortious act, or if they facilitated harm by allowing a weapon to fall into the hands of their child. More broadly, parents who know of their child's dangerous tendencies may be held liable in negligence for failing to exercise reasonable control or for failing to warn others. In *Nieuwendorp v. American Family Insurance Company*,[160] the parents of a nine-year-old student with attention deficit hyperactivity disorder unilaterally stopped giving him his prescribed medication without informing school officials. Several months later, while a teacher was attempting to remove the student from the classroom for misbehavior, he grabbed the teacher by the hair with such force that she fell, herniating a disc in her neck. The court found the parents negligent.

Liability for Dangerous Buildings and Grounds

Owners of land and buildings, including private school boards and public school districts, owe duties to everyone who uses their property. Traditionally and in most states today, the law divides property users into three categories: **trespassers**, **licensees**, and **invitees**. The duty of owners to inspect, repair and maintain their property and to warn entrants of possible hazards varies according to the category of entrant, with the highest duty owed to invitees and the lowest to trespassers.

A number of states have adopted an alternative system which, in effect, extends the standard rules of negligence to property liability cases. This approach imposes a standard of reasonable care on owners with the status of the user as one factor in deciding whether the owner should be held liable for the user's injuries. A few states have systems of property liability that combine elements of both approaches.[161] Property liability cases in schools can involve many kinds of hazards, including jagged edges on equipment, ice and snow on walkways, falling ceiling tiles, slippery floors, potholes on playgrounds, unsafe electrical equipment, inadequate lighting, defective playground and gym equipment, and attacks on visitors attending school events.

Trespassers, Licensees, and Invitees

A **trespasser** is a person who enters the property of another without permission or license to do so. One can also become a trespasser by leaving the part of a property to which one has been admitted

---

159 2005 Conn. Super. LEXIS 2403 (Conn. Super. Ct. Sept. 12, 2005).
160 529 N.W.2d 594 (Wis. 1995).
161 *See, e.g.*, Nelson v. Freeland, 507 S.E.2d 882, 892 (N.C. 1998).

and entering another part without permission. A person who breaks into a school at night to use the gym is a trespasser, but someone who uses an outdoor playing field on school grounds that is readily accessible and regularly used by the public for recreation is not.

Trespassers have a duty to take care of themselves, even in encounters with inherently dangerous conditions, such as an open pit with no railing or warning sign. The property owner is not liable for a trespasser's failure to exercise reasonable care, and there is no obligation to make the property safe for persons using it without permission. However, a property owner is not permitted intentionally to inflict injury on trespassers by setting booby traps. The law protects property interests, but it also recognizes a trespasser's interest in personal safety.

An important exception to the rules regarding trespassers is the **attractive nuisance doctrine**, applicable exclusively to children.[162] The idea is that if a child is likely to be lured onto property by a play structure or a swimming pool, the owner must exercise reasonable care to eliminate the risk. Property owners can minimize the potential for liability under this doctrine by building fences around play structures and swimming pools. Municipalities across the country have enacted bylaws requiring this.

A **licensee** is anyone who has a privilege—tacit or explicit consent—to enter onto property. Licensees include social guests, salespeople calling at private homes, and people who have business dealings with employees of the owner or tenant of a property. Outside groups meeting at a school would generally fall into the category of licensees. Most courts treat trespassers similarly to licensees if the trespasser's presence is known to the owner. The duty owed to licensees is to warn or otherwise protect them from unreasonable risks of which the owner is aware. Licensees generally must assume the risks associated with hazards of which the owner is unaware.

An **invitee** may enter land as a business visitor or as a member of the public. Business visitors include customers and clients of businesses, drivers picking up and delivering goods, people seeking employment, independent contractors and their employees doing work on the premises, and guest speakers. Staff, students, and members of the public using playgrounds or attending lectures or open house events are **public invitees**.[163] Invitees have a legal expectation that the property will be kept safe for them. Owners must protect invitees not only from known hazards, but also from hazards that the owner could have discovered by careful inspection of the property.

The duty owed the invitee does not guarantee absolute safety. Nor is the possessor of land expected to discover all hazards instantly. What is required is reasonable prudence under the circumstances (e.g., taking steps to warn people away from floors made slippery by mopping).

Invitees and licensees are expected to take some care in protecting themselves from obvious hazards. The standard rule has been that the owner has no duty to protect the invitee against hazards that are known or obvious. However, many courts have in recent years found this rule unsatisfactory in cases where invitees are legitimately distracted and thus unable to protect themselves against known or obvious dangers. Thus, an increasing number of jurisdictions now embrace a different rule:

> A possessor of land is not liable to his invitees for physical harm caused to them by any activity or condition on the land whose danger is known or obvious to them, unless the possessor should anticipate the harm despite such knowledge or obviousness.[164]

---

162 Ruiz v. Victory Properties, LLC, 107 A.3d 381 (Conn. 2015); Colon v. Metro-North Commuter R.R. Co., 2017 U.S. Dist. LEXIS 169572 (D. Conn. October 13, 2017).
163 McIntosh v. Omaha Pub. Sch., 544 N.W.2d 502 (Neb. 1996).
164 Ward v. K-Mart Corp., 554 N.E.2d 223 (Ill. 1990).

A hole in a school playground may be obvious, but the school district should anticipate that running students may not pay attention to the hole.[165]

Some states have adopted recreational use statutes that protect landowners from liability when the landowner invites members of the public to use the land for recreational purposes without charging a fee. The landowner will only be held liable for willful or wanton negligence. However, even where such laws exist, they may not apply to schools.[166] In New Jersey, for example, the **attractive nuisance** doctrine does not apply to public entities.[167]

The Negligence Approach to Property Liability

In the more than twenty states that have abolished the traditional categories of property users, property liability cases are decided in a manner similar to other negligence cases. Liability is determined based on the reasonableness of the owners' actions in light of the foreseeability of the injury. When making this determination, the courts look at a variety of factors including the expected use of the premises; the reasonableness of the inspection, repair, and warning; and the burden on the owner to provide adequate protection. Schools in these states may face a heightened risk of premises liability especially with regard to entrants who traditionally would have been classified as licensees. For example, under the traditional approach, a student voluntarily using a school's athletic field for a summer workout would be considered a licensee. The student would therefore be unable to collect damages for injuries sustained as a result of a hazardous condition at the field of which the school was unaware. However, in states that take the new approach, the student could collect damages if the school's inspection and maintenance of the field was not adequate given its foreseeable use.

In *Kurshals v. Connetquot Central School District*,[168] a 15-year-old student was injured when he climbed onto the roof of his school to retrieve a ball, stepped on a plastic skylight, and fell through to the gymnasium floor below. The court found that although the school district had a duty to warn users of its property of potentially dangerous conditions, there was nothing foreseeably dangerous about the skylight. "The skylight was not defective in any way. It was not an observable dangerous condition," wrote the court. "Rather, it is clear that the accident was the result of the injured plaintiff's misuse of the skylight, which was an extraordinary occurrence that need not have been guarded against."

Res Ipsa Loquitur

In the following illustrative case from New York, the plaintiff was unable to demonstrate that the defendant school district had failed to maintain the football field on which he sustained an injury. As in *C.H. v. Rahway Board of Education*,[169] excerpted earlier in this chapter, the mere fact that the plaintiff sustained an injury was not, in itself, proof of negligence. In the following illustrative case, the court explains the doctrine of *res ipsa loquitur*—negligence that "speaks for itself"—and rejects its application.

---

165 *See* Simmons v. Saugerties Central School District, 82 A.D.3d 1407 (N.Y. App. 2011).
166 Rankey v. Arlington Bd. of Educ., 603 N.E.2d 1151 (Ohio Ct. App. 1992); *contra* McIntosh v. Omaha Pub. Sch., 544 N.W.2d 502 (Neb. 1996).
167 Lanin v. Borough of Tenafly, 2014 U.S. Dist. LEXIS 256, 2014 WL 31350 (D.N.J. January 2, 2014).
168 643 N.Y.S.2d 622 (N.Y. App. Div. 1996).
169 209 A.3d 222 (N.J. Super. Ct. App. Div. 2018).

⚖️

FEROLITO v. PLAINVIEW-OLD BETHPAGE CENTRAL SCHOOL DISTRICT
Supreme Court of New York, Nassau County
2009 N.Y. Misc. LEXIS 2543 (July 16, 2009)

Opinion by: UTE WOLFF LALLY

This is an action by plaintiffs to recover money damages for personal injuries and economic loss sustained as a result of defendants alleged negligence in causing infant plaintiff to sustain personal injuries during a middle school football practice.

Plaintiffs allege that the doctrine of *res ipsa loquitur* applies to this situation in which it is claimed that defendants created or permitted a dangerous condition to exist; were negligent in the maintenance, operation, and control of their premises; failed to inspect the premises; and were negligent in the supervision of the football practice.

On October 9, 2007 at approximately 4:00 p.m. during a football practice on a practice field at the Plainview Old Bethpage Middle School located at 121 Central Park Road, Plainview, New York, the infant plaintiff was participating in a tackling drill. Another player of similar height and weight tackled the infant plaintiff to the ground in accordance with drill procedures. Plaintiffs and defendants allege that it was a "clean tackle." While on the ground, the infant plaintiff felt tingling in his right arm and claims that he did not see anything unusual on the ground after he was tackled.

Coach Lucchio in his affidavit stated that he supervised the drill approximately 15 yards from the plaintiff. After the infant plaintiff was tackled, Coach Lucchio immediately went over to the infant plaintiff and observed the injury. Coach Lucchio stated that he had inspected the grassy location of the drill prior to its commencement and found no foreign objects or dangerous conditions and that three coaches reexamined the said location for foreign objects and/or defective conditions. Finally, the coach stated that upon inspection after the occurrence there were no foreign objects and/or defective conditions on the field.

The infant plaintiff was sent to the hospital for medical treatment. Plaintiffs reexamined the field on August 28, 2008 and did not find any foreign objects and/or defective conditions at the location of the accident.

In support of defendants' motion for summary judgment the defendants allege that they maintained their premises in a reasonably safe condition, that the plaintiff cannot establish the existence of a defective condition, that the supervision of the infant plaintiff was proper, that improper supervision, if any, was not the proximate cause of this incident and that the doctrine of *res ipsa loquitur* does not apply.

Landowners have

> a duty to exercise reasonable care in maintaining [their] property in a safe condition under all the circumstances, including the likelihood of injury to others, the seriousness of the potential injuries, the burden of avoiding the risk, and the foreseeability of a potential plaintiff's presence on the property.

> In order for a landowner to be liable in a tort action to a plaintiff injured on the landowner's property, the plaintiff must establish that a dangerous or defective condition actually existed and that the landowner had to have created it or had actual or constructive notice of the allegedly defective condition.

In the instant case plaintiffs have not offered any evidence to show that there was a dangerous and/or defective condition, which actually existed on the field or that defendants had actual or constructive notice of such a condition. They have not met their burden to prove defendants were negligent in their duties as landowners.

The court rejects plaintiffs' argument that even though there was no known dangerous and/or defective condition on the field at the time of the accident, the doctrine of res ipsa loquitur allows for the inference of negligence on the part of defendants. Ordinarily, pleading *res ipsa loquitur* creates a presumption that satisfies plaintiff's duty of producing evidence sufficient to go to jury. However, in the case at bar plaintiff has not met its burden for application of *res ipsa loquitur*.

In order to invoke a *res ipsa loquitur* inference of negligence plaintiffs must establish the following: (1) the injury does not ordinarily occur in the absence of negligence; (2) the instrumentality that caused the injury is within the defendants' exclusive control; and (3) the injury is not the result of any voluntary action by the plaintiff.

The plaintiffs submitted an affidavit from Sports and Recreation Consultant Steve Bernheim, who claimed that there was no way the infant plaintiff's Injury could have been caused by the equipment worn by the players. He alleges that the injury must have been caused by the defendants' negligence in maintaining the field and those defendants were in exclusive control of the field. The expert's allegations are conclusory in nature and are insufficient to establish that this type of injury does not ordinarily occur in the absence of negligence. Said affidavit contains no factual findings upon which these conclusions are based. Therefore, this court finds that *res ipsa loquitur* is not applicable herein.

There is no showing that the supervision of the infant plaintiff was improper. A school is obligated to exercise care over students equivalent to that which a parent of ordinary prudence would exercise under comparable circumstances. There is a failure to establish that supervision to any degree would have prevented this occurrence.

Where an accident occurs in so short a span of time and even the most intense supervision could not have prevented it, any lack of supervision of a student is not the proximate cause of the injury and summary judgment in favor of school defendants is warranted.

Plaintiffs offer no proof that the alleged lack of supervision on the part of Coach Lucchio could or would be deemed a proximate cause of the accident, and more intense supervision would have prevented the injury from occurring. ...

Accordingly, defendants' motion for summary judgment is granted plaintiffs having failed to demonstrate the existence of triable issues of fact and plaintiff's complaint is dismissed.

Educational Malpractice

The basic claim in a malpractice case is that a practitioner has caused harm by failing to provide services in accordance with the standards of the profession. Because malpractice is a category of **negligence**, all four elements of negligence must be proven. Thus, in medicine, the profession whose malpractice litigation has been the most widely publicized, undesirable results or even mistakes in medical treatment do not automatically give rise to liability. A finding of medical malpractice requires proof that a doctor had a professional duty to treat a patient in a certain manner; that the doctor failed to live up to that duty, thus placing the patient at unreasonable risk of injury; and that the failure of performance was the legal cause of actual injury.

In education, two types of malpractice claims have been brought. In the first type, plaintiffs allege that low achievement is evidence of a school's failure to deliver an instructional program, including an individualized education program. Sometimes, plaintiffs also make the related claim that a school was negligent in certifying learning that did not in fact occur, either by assigning passing grades or by granting a diploma.[170] In the second type, plaintiffs allege that low achievement is the result of a failure to properly assess or classify.[171]

---

170 Donohue v. Copiague Union Free Sch Dist., 391 N.E.2d 1352 (N.Y. App. 1979); Suriano v. Hyde Park Cent. Sch. Dist., 203 A.D.2d 553 (N.Y. App. 1994); Sain v. Cedar Rapids Cmty. Sch. Dist., No. 155, 626 N.W.2d 115 (Iowa 2001).
171 Snow v. State, 475 N.E.2d 454 (N.Y. 1984); Doe v. Bd. of Educ. of Montgomery County, 453 A.2d 814 (Md. 1982); Hoffman v. Bd. of Educ. of New York, 400 N.E.2d 317 (N.Y. 1979); B.M. v. State, 649 P.2d 425 (Mont. 1982); Rick v. Kentucky Day, Inc., 793 S.W.2d 832 (Ky. App. 1990).

Courts have rejected educational malpractice claims in both categories on the grounds that educators have no statutory or common law duty to their students to meet a professional standard and that, in any case, considerations of public policy preclude recognition of educational malpractice as a cause of action. In *Torres v. Little Flower Children's Services*,[172] New York's highest court affirmed that "an action grounded in educational malpractice is barred by public policy considerations when brought against a school because the courts will not second-guess the professional judgments of public school educators and administrators in selecting programs for particular students." Similar policy considerations would "bar plaintiff's claim for damages from his legal guardians for his failure to receive an appropriate education."

In the following illustrative case, the Appellate Court of Connecticut echoed these public policy arguments barring judicial cognizance of educational malpractice claims.

⚖️

VOGEL v. MAIMONIDES ACADEMY OF WESTERN CONNECTICUT INC.
Appellate Court of Connecticut
754 A.2d 824 (2000)

PETER T. ZARELLA, J.

... In March, 1992, the plaintiff resided with his wife and two daughters in Newtown. At that time, his three and one-half year old daughter was enrolled in a school operated by the defendant. While enrolled in the defendant's school, the plaintiff's daughter was taught a course titled "Family Life Educational Philosophy." The purpose of the course was to help students to develop skills that would enable them to make sound value judgments and moral decisions regarding interpersonal relationships. Part of the curriculum was designed to teach the difference between proper and improper touching.

On March 27, 1992, while at the defendant's school, the plaintiff's daughter vocalized words about "daddy" and "touching." The personnel of the defendant school reported this statement to the department of children and families (department). The department investigated the plaintiff concerning the possible sexual abuse of his daughter.

The first count of the plaintiff's revised complaint alleges that the defendant's false accusations placed him in a false light and subjected him to unjustified criticism. The plaintiff claims that as a result of the defendant's actions, his reputation was damaged, his family life was disrupted and he required psychiatric counseling, incurred medical expenses and lost wages and employment opportunities.

The second count of the revised complaint incorporates many of the allegations of the first count and alleges that the defendant intentionally inflicted emotional distress on the plaintiff.

In the third count of the revised complaint, the plaintiff alleges that the defendant acted recklessly in modifying the course and teaching it to children his daughter's age and, as a result, the plaintiff sustained the injuries previously discussed. ...

The defendant filed its motion for summary judgment on July 7, 1997, accompanied by a memorandum of law. The plaintiff objected, and filed an opposing memorandum and his affidavit. The key paragraphs of the affidavit state that the conduct of the defendant was reckless in modifying and teaching the program to a three and one-half year old. The affidavit basically reiterated the allegations in the revised complaint. The court, after hearing arguments, granted the motion. Thereafter, the plaintiff filed a motion to reargue and for reconsideration. The court denied the motion, and the plaintiff appealed.

I

The plaintiff claims first that the court improperly granted the defendant's motion for summary judgment on the third count of his revised complaint. We disagree. ...

172 474 N.E.2d 223 (N.Y. Ct. App. 1984).

The plaintiff alleges in the third count of his revised complaint that the defendant recklessly brought about his injuries by improperly instructing his child. The plaintiff's claim for reckless instruction of an improper curriculum is essentially a claim for educational malpractice, a claim our Supreme Court declined to recognize in *Gupta v. New Britain General Hospital*.[173]

In *Gupta*, the court joined the vast majority of states that have rejected educational malpractice claims sounding in tort. The court noted in dictum that a claim for educational malpractice "raises questions … that must be answered by reference to principles of duty, standards of care, and reasonable conduct associated with the law of torts."

Because these tort principles are difficult, if not impossible, to apply in the academic environment, courts have almost universally held that claims of educational malpractice are not cognizable. Among other problems for adjudication, these claims involve the judiciary in the awkward tasks of defining what constitutes a reasonable educational program and of deciding whether that standard has been breached. In entertaining such claims, moreover, courts are required not merely to make judgments as to the validity of broad educational policies … but, more importantly, to sit in review of the day-to-day implementation of these policies. … Our Supreme Court has recently had occasion to address this issue in detail. In *Doe v. Yale University*,[174] the court stated, "If the duty alleged to have been breached is the duty to educate effectively, the claim is not cognizable." … The allegations of the plaintiff's complaint clearly allege a breach of a duty to educate effectively and, thus, the claim is not cognizable.

We conclude, therefore, that under the facts of this case, the plaintiff's claim of educational malpractice properly did not survive the defendant's motion for summary judgment.

II

The plaintiff contends finally that the court improperly denied his motion to reargue and for reconsideration of the court's decision to grant the defendant's motion for summary judgment. We disagree. Our standard of review regarding challenges to a trial court's ruling on a motion for reconsideration is abuse of discretion. Because we conclude that the motion for summary judgment properly was granted, the court did not abuse its discretion in denying the plaintiff's motion to reargue and for reconsideration. The judgment is affirmed.

Immunities

At common law, the doctrine of **sovereign immunity** historically protected state governments from tort suits. The decision by state governments to prohibit their laws and courts from being used against them was descended from a principle of English law that "the King can do no wrong." The doctrine of sovereign tort immunity has been extended from the state itself to agencies of the state such as municipalities and school districts. As agencies of the state, they are said to partake in its sovereignty.

The immunity of local governments from suit is often called "governmental" or "municipal" or "official immunity." But it has never been absolute. One of the most common exceptions permits liability regarding activities deemed **proprietary**, rather than **governmental**. However, the criteria used for distinguishing the proprietary and governmental activities of local governments are not very precise. Some states consider all school district activities governmental, whereas others classify fee-charging activities and services as proprietary.

Another traditional common law distinction is between **discretionary** and **ministerial** acts. Discretionary acts involve planning, goal setting, evaluation, and the exercise of judgment; whereas ministerial acts are to be performed in a prescribed manner and do not require judgment. In some

173 687 A.2d 111 (Conn. 1996).
174 748 A.2d 834 (Conn. 2000).

jurisdictions, governments may be immune from liability for discretionary but not ministerial acts. For example, a school district could not be liable regarding the formulation of its snow removal policy, but it could be liable for the negligent execution of the policy.[175]

Today, there is considerable variation in state law on the question of sovereign immunity. In a few states, it protects school districts from liability for the torts of **negligent hiring, negligent retention, and negligent supervision**. Some states allow suits regarding nondiscretionary functions only. Others limit the dollar amounts that may be collected. Some permit suits for personal injury or death caused by dangerous conditions of property,[176] while others allow official immunity when specific statutory conditions are met.[177]

Government Officer Immunity

In addition to sovereign immunity, a second type of immunity protects certain government officers from tort liability. Judges and legislators enjoy **absolute immunity** from tort suits regarding judicial or legislative acts even if performed in bad faith, with malice, or with corrupt motives. Superintendents, school board presidents and other "high officials" are entitled to absolute official immunity in states such as Pennsylvania.[178]

Under traditional common law, school officials and employees may also enjoy **qualified immunity** for discretionary acts (as opposed to ministerial acts) performed without bad faith or malice. This distinction has been difficult for the courts to apply with any consistency. The Court of Appeals of Georgia has ruled that a principal was engaged in a discretionary function when he ordered maintenance personnel to repair a school gate, and was therefore immune from a negligence suit filed by a parent who sustained injuries after crashing her car into it.[179]

In *Killen v. Independent School District No. 706*,[180] a Minnesota court found a guidance counselor was immunized against a suit brought by the parents of a student who had committed suicide. In a decision overruled two years later,[181] the court held that the decision whether or not to tell parents about the student's contemplation of suicide was a matter of professional discretion and thus subject to immunity. In *Anderson v. Anoka Hennepin Independent School District 11*,[182] the same court ruled the use of a power saw without a blade guard in place for some types of cuts in shop class was a matter of professional discretion and thus subject to immunity. School policies regarding the supervision of students, the hiring and assignment of security guards, and school safety are matters of discretion generally subject to immunity.[183]

Sexual Assault and Abuse

In cases involving the sexual assault and abuse or students, school officials may be liable in negligence if they had "actual knowledge" of the problem. However, this can be extremely difficult to establish.

---

175 Lostumbo v. Bd. of Educ. of Norwalk, 418 A.2d 949 (Conn. Super. Ct. 1980); Fear v. Indep. Sch. Dist. 911, 634 N.W.2d 204 (Minn. App. 2001).
176 See Stahl v. Cocalico Sch. Dist., 534 A.2d 1141 (Pa. Commw. Ct. 1987).
177 Fear v. Independent School District 911, 634 N.W.2d 204 (Minn. App. 2001).
178 *See* Ruder v. Pequea Valley Sch. Dist., 790 F. Supp.2d 377 (E.D. Pa. 2011) and Smith v. School Dist. of Philadelphia, 112 F.Supp.2d 417 (E.D. Pa. 2000).
179 Cooper v. Paulding County School District, 595 S.E.2d 671 (Ga. App. 2004).
180 Killen v. Indep. Sch. Dist. No. 706, 547 N.W.2d 113 (Minn. Ct. App. 1996).
181 S.W. v. Spring Lake Park Sch. Dist. No. 16, 580 N.W.2d 19 (Minn. Sup. Ct. 1998).
182 678 N.W.2d 651 (Minn. Sup. Ct. 2004).
183 Mosley v. Portland Sch. Dist. No. 1J, 843 P.2d 415 (Or. 1992); Coyle v. Harper, 622 So.2d 302 (Ala. 1993).

In *Doe v. Willits Unified School District*,[184] a district court ruled that a charter school principal's knowledge that a teacher had cupped a 15-year-old student's buttocks while severely intoxicated at a party was not sufficient to establish actual knowledge of an ongoing sexual relationship.

In *Jojola v. Chavez*,[185] a school principal knew that a teacher spied on students through a hole in the locker room wall, that he made sexual comments to female students, that he had been removed from a previous position for unhooking students' brassieres. Nonetheless, the Tenth Circuit ruled this knowledge did not constitute actual knowledge by the school administration.

In *Plumeau v. Yamhill County School District*,[186] a case involving a janitor who hugged and held hands with students, the court held such behavior did not plainly point toward the conclusion that school officials needed to launch a sexual abuse investigation.

In *Jane Doe A v. Special School Dist. of St. Louis*,[187] the Eight Circuit Court held that isolated reports of a bus driver kissing, fondling, and snuggling students were not enough to prove actual knowledge.

Statutory Immunity

As noted earlier in this chapter, negligence and some intentional torts may constitute criminal or statutory offenses. Hence intentional wrongdoing can lead to liability in civil or criminal proceedings (or both). A number of states offer **qualified immunity** to educators charged or indicted for violating criminal versions of various torts. In the following illustrative case from Georgia, a special education teacher indicted on **cruelty to children** and **false imprisonment** charges successfully invoked the statutory immunity available to educators in that state.

STATE v. PICKENS
Court of Appeals of Georgia
769 S.E.2d 594 (2015)

ANNE ELIZABETH BARNES, Presiding Judge.

Melanie Pickens was a special education teacher who was indicted on six counts of cruelty to children and five counts of false imprisonment for actions involving five of her students. Pickens moved to dismiss the indictment based on her immunity as an educator under OCGA § 20-2-1001, and after a three-day hearing, the trial court granted her motion. The State appeals, arguing that the trial court erred because Pickens' actions did not constitute "discipline" and she did not act in good faith, both of which the statute requires for immunity from criminal prosecution. For the reasons that follow, we affirm.

OCGA § 20-2-1001 was enacted in 1997 as part of the "*School Safety Act*" and provides that:

(a) As used in this Code section, the term educator means any principal, school administrator, teacher, school counselor, paraprofessional, school bus driver, volunteer assisting teachers in the classroom, tribunal members, or certificated professional personnel.

(b) An educator shall be immune from criminal liability for any act or omission concerning, relating to, or resulting from the discipline of any student or the reporting of any student for misconduct, provided that the educator acted in good faith.

Thus, to be entitled to immunity from prosecution under OCGA § 20-2-1001, a defendant must establish three things: (1) she is an educator; (2) the acts

184 2010 U.S. Dist. LEXIS 125816 (N.D. Cal. Nov. 29, 2010), *aff'd*, 2012 U.S. App. LEXIS 11640 (9th Cir. Cal. 2012).
185 55 F.3d 488 (10th Cir. 1995).
186 907 F. Supp. 1423, 1440 (D. Ore. 1995).
187 901 F.2d 642 (8th Cir. 1990).

or omissions in questions were related to or resulting from disciplining a student or reporting a student for misconduct; and (3) the educator acted in good faith. ... The burden of proving entitlement to immunity by a preponderance of the evidence falls on the defendant. ...

Pickens' indicted charges involved five different special education students and were based on three types of conduct: confining students in a restrictive chair in the classroom or confining them and leaving them alone (six counts), recording a child's screams and playing them back to the child or imitating a child's screams or cries to the child (three counts), and "slamming" a child against school walls and lockers (two counts). She filed a motion to dismiss the indictment for immunity from prosecution under OCGA § 20-2-1001, contending that she acted to maintain discipline and order and that she acted in good faith.

The trial court held a three-day evidentiary hearing during which Pickens called five witnesses and the State called six. One of the State's witnesses was qualified as an expert in behavior management strategies for students with moderate and severe developmental disabilities, and one witness investigated the claims against Pickens for the Georgia Professional Standards Commission (GPSC). The other eight witnesses had worked with or alongside Pickens in the special education hall of the middle school in question during the 2006–2007 school year, which is the underlying actions allegedly occurred.

At the end of the hearing, the trial court orally granted Pickens' motion for immunity from criminal prosecution under OCGA § 20-2-1001, and subsequently issued a lengthy written order summarizing the testimony and concluding that Pickens met her "burden of showing by a preponderance of the evidence that all actions were done to maintain discipline and order and the actions were done in good faith." The court thus dismissed the indictment.

On appeal, the State does not dispute that Pickens was an "educator" under the statute, but argues that the record does not support the trial court's conclusions that Pickens' actions were "used to discipline the misbehaving student and maintain order and safety in the classroom," or that Pickens acted in good faith.

1. The State argues first that the record does not support the trial court's conclusion that Pickens' actions were "used to discipline the misbehaving student and maintain order and safety in the classroom," but instead showed that

Pickens acted "from an inability to control her anger and frustration with the job."

As the State points out, our Supreme Court has defined "discipline" as "control obtained by enforcing compliance or order." While the State submitted evidence in this case that Pickens acted in frustration at times, other evidence revealed that in a classroom like Pickens', with five to seven developmentally disabled children, a single child's actions could disrupt the entire classroom. Thus, actions taken to address the source of the disruption could constitute disciplinary actions, whether or not a teacher was frustrated when she took them.

For example, while the State argues that "crying was not a basis for disciplining a child," evidence presented at the hearing showed that a child's loud, continuous screams and cries prevented the other children from attending to their own work. A child who grabbed at other students, pushed their work onto the floor, turned over his desk, and performed other disruptive actions became the focus of the class and prevented the other children from learning. A child who "plopped" onto the floor and refused to get up blocked the path of other students and had to be attended while the other children were deprived of the attendee's time.

The five false imprisonment counts and one of the cruelty to children counts against Pickens were based on allegations that at some point during the 2006–2007 school year, she confined and isolated without supervision three different students, either across the hall from her classroom or in the bathroom, and also confined one of those students within her class. When the children were placed across the hall, they were secured in physically supportive seating designed for special needs students, and the child who was placed in the bathroom was secured in a version of the chair that could be rolled over a toilet.

One child was placed alone across the hall to quell his loud disruptive crying. Either Pickens or her paraprofessional would check on him, and when he stopped crying she would bring him back into the classroom. The longest he remained across the hall was 15 minutes, and she placed him there so he could become quiet again, not to be malicious or hurt him.

Another child was placed across the hall when he became aggressive toward other students, tripping, pushing, and hitting them, pulling their hair, throwing their work on the floor, knocking things over, and screaming. He seemed calmer in the chair sometimes, but at other times he would just moved the chair around the room even when secured within it. When other methods failed, Pickens or her paraprofessional would move him across the hall by himself for some period of time. There was no evidence about the length of time the student remained across the hall, other than that the testimony of Pickens' paraprofessional that he was only once left there "for a good while," on the day that precipitated the investigation and charges against Pickens. That day the student was placed across the hall both before and after lunch because he would not stop hitting and pulling at the other students. He was calmer when seated in the supportive chair and when placed alone because he got no attention from other students.

Other educators knew that Pickens was placing disruptive children across the hall and understood that its purpose was to maintain discipline and order in the classroom. If a child behaved, he stayed in the classroom with the other students.

Pickens was charged with false imprisonment for leaving the third student confined alone in a handicapped bathroom. This student had "bathrooming" issues, and sometimes would remain unattended in the supportive chair in a private toilet space for "a little while" when he was trying to have a bowel movement. While Pickens was also charged with false imprisonment for confining the child within the classroom, the only testimony regarding that count was from a teacher who once saw him in class reclining in the supportive chair at an angle from which it would have been difficult for him to get out.

Pickens was also charged with three counts of cruelty to three different children for recording them while they were screaming and playing it back to them or for imitating their screams or cries. One of the children would scream at a very high pitch when asked to do something he did not want to do. As noted earlier, these episodes of screaming and crying disrupted the class, and Pickens tried playing back or imitating their screams in an effort to make them stop

by showing them that the noise they were making was disruptive and upsetting to the other students. When the children heard themselves, sometimes they stopped screaming and crying and sometimes they did not.

Finally, Pickens was charged with two counts of cruelty to children for "slamming" them "face-first into lockers and walls." Evidence was adduced at the hearing that Pickens developed a technique to prop one of the students up against the wall with her body to prevent him from "plopping" onto the floor or to get him up after he did so.

The trial court concluded that this evidence was sufficient to show by a preponderance of the evidence that Pickens' actions were undertaken to maintain discipline and restore order in her classroom. Based on our review of the evidence presented, we cannot conclude that the trial court erred in its findings of fact that Pickens acted to maintain discipline and order in her classroom.

2. The State also contends that the record does not support the trial court's conclusion that Pickens acted in good faith. "'Good faith' is a subjective standard: a state of mind indicating honesty and lawfulness of purpose; belief that one's conduct is not unconscionable or that known circumstances do not require further investigation."

The State notes that this Court in *Cohen* clarified that the determination of good faith under OCGA § 20-2-1001 does not rest solely upon whether the educator was complying with school policy.[188] We agree with the State, however, that violations of school policy are relevant to whether an educator acted in good faith, if not determinative. But here, although the State elicited testimony that there were no county policies permitting the use of restraint and isolation of developmentally disabled students during this time period, the evidence also established that there were also no county- or state-wide policies prohibiting the practice then, as there are now. The county offered little training in methods of handling children with more difficult behavior problems, and only later made available training in the prevention and management of aggressive behavior in developmentally disabled students. As Pickens

188 State v. Cohen, 711 S.E.2d 418 (2011).

observes, the school's policy about touching and discipline in *Cohen* was unclear, while in this case the county had no policy at all. Pickens was therefore left to develop her own coping strategies to manage "a rough group of kids," including one 13-year-old who was larger than she and who grew progressively more aggressive as the year passed.

Pickens gathered data documenting this child's aggression and attempted unsuccessfully to have him moved to a different program that dealt with more aggressive developmentally disabled children. In fact, two months after entering high school the following year, the student was placed into the other program. The investigator for the Georgia Professional Standards Commission testified that Pickens thought it was necessary for her to physically restrain or remove this student because his behavior could endanger the other children in her care, and she believed that it was okay for her to place disruptive children across the hall. She did so either to have them calm down or to remove the source of the disruption for the benefit of the other students.

The county behavioral therapist testified that "time-out" is an effective intervention for children seeking attention inappropriately, and the facility for more aggressive students had a "time-out" room where out-of-control students were placed by themselves, although they were observed. The State's expert psychologist testified that restraint was appropriate to avoid allowing a student to injure himself or to protect other children, although he also thought children who were restrained should be supervised. Further, he testified that putting a child into "time-out" was an appropriate response to certain behaviors, such as aggression. The county had no specific rules regarding "time-outs" until after a civil lawsuit related to these acts was filed.

Other educators were aware that Pickens placed students across the hall from her main classroom, and while some of them testified that they would never have left any student alone at any time, none of them made any attempts to stop it. Pickens' paraprofessional also placed the children across the hall when directed to do so. The only teacher who reported Pickens to her superiors did so only after one of the children smeared feces all over himself and his surroundings in the short time between when Pickens' para-professional checked on him before attending the other teacher's classroom and a few minutes later when the educator was returning to her class. That teacher also admitted there were times when she had no choice but to leave a child unattended in the bathroom when she went to retrieve her para-professional to change places with her.

As to Pickens' attempts to come up with methods to stop her students from screaming, shouting, or crying so loudly that classroom activities were effectively halted, she admitted that she came up with what she called "scream therapy" on her own, to mirror the screaming child's actions and help him or her see how the loud noise disrupted class and upset the others. Although the method was effective sometimes, she stopped using it when another educator told her to stop and she realized its use was inappropriate.

Further, the evidence showed that Pickens developed the technique of propping students against the wall to keep them from plopping onto the floor or to get them up after they did so. In fact, when one of her students plopped on the floor in gym class, Pickens was summoned to get him back on his feet. While the behavioral psychologist testified that when a student plopped on the floor and refused to get up, the best course was to leave him there, or at least obtain assistance in moving him, at times Pickens was unable to "get people from the front to help" deal with a recalcitrant student. If a student plopped down and no one was around to help, Pickens was on her own.

Pickens told the investigator that her actions were never malicious, that she never tried to hurt any of her students, and that whatever she did with her students was aimed at helping them. One of the paraprofessionals testified that the more aggressive child loved Pickens, and another educator testified that Pickens seemed fond of the child, who remained in Pickens' classroom for three years.

Considering the evidence presented at the hearing, we conclude that the trial court was authorized to find that a preponderance of evidence showed that Pickens acted in good faith and was entitled to the benefits of the immunity statute. Judgment affirmed.

Summary

Tort law allows individuals to sue for compensation for injuries caused by the wrongful acts or carelessness of others. The injury can be to the individual's body, property, reputation, or emotional well-being. Depending on the circumstances, school districts, individual school boards and board members, administrators, and teachers may all be held liable for tortious conduct. However, a variety of common law and statutory immunities and other limitations on tort suits against governmental bodies and their employees may apply. Like many aspects of tort law, these immunities and limitations vary considerably from state to state.

Intentional torts are either acts designed to produce harm or acts likely to cause harm to another. In education law, these include the torts of **battery, assault, false imprisonment, intentional interference with prospective contractual relations, invasion of privacy, and intentional infliction of mental distress**. Educators may use reasonable force in self-defense or to enforce legitimate orders or school rules. Also, except where prohibited by statute, educators may claim a common law privilege to discipline students using corporal punishment. Students may sue successfully for assault and battery if corporal punishment is excessive or otherwise unreasonable.

Defamation refers to false communications that harm an individual's reputation. Libel is written defamation, and slander is oral defamation. The law of defamation varies depending on whether the communication deals with a matter of public concern and whether the person defamed was a public official, public figure, or private individual. School officials and school boards may be held liable for defamatory statements that meet the publication requirement. School officials may be liable if they knowingly write false and damaging letters of recommendation.

Negligence is careless or reckless behavior that causes injury. It is by far the most common type of lawsuit for public and private schools. School boards and individual educators can be found negligent for injuries to students, employees, or visitors to the school if they had a duty to live up to a standard of care recognized in law, they failed to live up to the duty, and someone suffered compensable harm as a result. Teachers have a general duty to behave as would a reasonable and prudent parent. The exact level of supervision and care depends on the circumstances, but school officials are not expected to guarantee that accidents will never occur.

Table of Cases

Excerpts of court reports of cases listed in **bold** face are set out on the pages indicated in bold face. Cases listed in light face are discussed or referenced on the pages indicated.

Chapter 4

Chapter 5

Chapter 6

Chapter 7

Chapter 8

Chapter 9

Chapter 10

Chapter 11

Chapter 12

Index

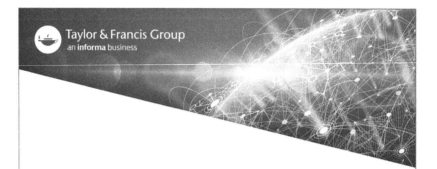

Lightning Source UK Ltd.
Milton Keynes UK
UKHW031813280822
407750UK00016B/331

9 780367 195250